LAW: ITS NATURE, FUNCTIONS, AND LIMITS

LAW: ITS NATURE, FUNCTIONS, AND LIMITS

Third Edition

Robert S. Summers
McRoberts Research Professor of Law
Cornell University

Kevin M. Clermont
Professor of Law
Cornell University

Robert A. Hillman
Professor of Law
Cornell University

Sheri Lynn Johnson
Associate Professor of Law
Cornell University

John J. Barceló III
Noll Professor of Law
Cornell University

Doris Marie Provine
Associate Professor, Political Science
Syracuse University

West Publishing
Paul   New York   Los Angeles   San Francisco

Library of Congress Cataloging-in-Publication Data

Law: its nature, functions, and limits.

  Rev. ed. of: Law: its nature, functions, and
limits/Robert S. Summers.
  Bibliography: p.
  Includes index.
  1. Jurisprudence. 2. Law—United States.
I. Summers, Robert S. II. Summers, Robert S. Law:
its nature, functions, and limits.
KF386.L38 1986   349.73   86–1639
ISBN 0–314–93519–3   347.3

Preface

Looking at the list of authors of this book should suggest that a number of law teachers share a firm conviction that law is an unjustly neglected part of general education—and that these new teaching materials fill a felt need.

We have long found it striking that most of even the best-educated students leave college in unblemished ignorance of the concept of law and with little idea of the legal system under which they will live. The would-be educated citizen, and surely the graduate beginning any of many specialized disciplines, cannot justify such ignorance. A survey course on introduction to law provides a ready cure, and also usually provides a lot of fascinating fun. But we are getting ahead of ourselves by addressing this question of why even a generalist should pursue a survey course on law. Section 3 of the General Introduction makes what turns out to be the easy case for including law in the program of general education.

The harder question is how to introduce law. Certainly a survey of only the contents of law, studying contracts in a nutshell and then torts and so on, makes no educational sense. Leaping instead to the abstract level of legal philosophy, without first providing students with sufficient concrete information, results in conveying little. Worse yet and perhaps even dangerous is the popular approach of reprinting selected readings that deliver strong attitudes about law to an audience that knows little about the subject. In brief, the shortcomings of all three approaches reflect the often-noted difficulty of trying to teach anything about law without somehow managing to teach all of law.

The correct approach must be more analytic, breaking law down into a manageable number of comprehensible units that students can reassemble into a coherent concept of law. This approach would put natural bounds on and give a sense of direction to an introductory book and course, affording students a sense of concrete but significant learning. However, the usual analytic approach divides law into the legal institutions of the judiciary, legislature, executive, and administrative agency. This parochial division distorts the operation of law. Law actually performs its social tasks by collaborative effort, with roles for private persons as well as for players such as courts, legislators, and other official actors.

v

A sounder and more comprehensive breakdown would look at the means and ends of social ordering through law. We therefore try to get at what law is by examining, first, how law does what it does and, second, what it can and cannot do. We present law as a set of five basic techniques for addressing many problems of any society. We believe this approach is an accurate and productive way to learn and think about law. But again we are getting ahead of ourselves. Section 4 of the General Introduction, along with the Prefatory Notes to Parts 1 and 2, further outlines this instrumentalist conception of law.

Our approach is not untried. In 1965 Charles G. Howard and Robert S. Summers wrote the first edition of Law: Its Nature, Functions, and Limits. In 1972 Professor Summers revamped the book into its successful second edition. Years of teaching experience with it only heightened our admiration for the book and our resolve to sustain it. We therefore produced this thoroughly updated third edition. Our aim was to turn out an even more provocative, readable, and teachable book.

Robert S. Summers is a distinguished senior professor at Cornell Law School. Among his areas of great strength is jurisprudence, where he has carefully developed the framework of his ideas by a prodigious flow of books and articles. We owe the conceptual structure of this book to him. Unfortunately, his heavy research commitments precluded active participation in the third edition. The traditional acknowledgment accordingly is particularly appropriate here: he deserves much of the credit for this book but absolutely none of the blame for those passages where we wandered from the path.

I acted as coordinating author. I also prepared the General Introduction, revised Chapter 1, and composed the book's connective materials. Furthermore, I admit to the wisdom of turning to experts to revise the other chapters falling within their respective fields of expertise. We collaborated on much of the work, but the following paragraphs describe the allocation of ultimate responsibility.

Sheri Lynn Johnson has a B.A. from the University of Minnesota and a J.D. from Yale Law School. After a practice in criminal law, she turned to teaching and writing in both criminal and constitutional law. She revised Chapter 2 and wrote Chapter 7.

Robert A. Hillman, with a B.A. from the University of Rochester and a J.D. from Cornell Law School, followed a federal clerkship with a New York City practice and then a teaching career. He specializes in contracts and commercial law, and he has written extensively in those fields. He revised Chapter 5 and wrote Chapter 6.

Doris Marie Provine brings a different dimension to our team. After graduating from the University of Chicago, she obtained both a law degree and a Ph.D. in government from Cornell University, and she now teaches political science at Syracuse University. She revised Chapter 4.

John J. Barceló III combined a B.A. and a J.D. from Tulane University with an S.J.D. from Harvard Law School. Now a chaired professor, he includes administrative law among his areas of specialization. He revised Chapter 3.

Finally, as to conventions in preparing this new edition, I should note that we used the original numbers for footnotes by judges in judicial opinions and by authors in quoted materials, when we retained their footnotes. We omitted other such footnotes without any indication. We lettered rather than numbered our own footnotes. We also omitted many case and statutory citations by courts and commentators without so indicating. On those mundane notes I close, but with the hope that students and teachers will come to agree that this book usefully fills a gap in general education.

Kevin M. Clermont

January 1986

Summary of Contents

	Page
PREFACE	v
TABLE OF CASES	xxvii

General Introduction 1

Section
1. Introductory Case 1
2. Sample Brief with Annotations 7
3. General Education and the Law 17
4. Pedagogic Notes 24
5. Bibliography 25

PART ONE: THE MEANS OF LAW

PREFATORY NOTE TO PART ONE 28

Chapter 1. Law as a Grievance-Remedial Instrument 30

Section
1. Introduction 30
2. Grievance-Remedial Techniques 31
3. Authorized Makers of Grievance-Remedial Law and Their Appropriate Collaborative Roles 33
4. Structures and Processes for Applying Grievance-Remedial Law and Techniques 71
5. Necessity for and Nature of Coercive Power 129
6. Roles of Private Citizens and Their Lawyers 138
7. Process Values 147
8. Improving the Grievance-Remedial Instrument 156
9. Limitations of Law as a Grievance-Remedial Instrument 169
10. Bibliography 178

Chapter 2. Law as a Penal-Corrective Instrument 180

Section
1. Introduction 180
2. Penal-Corrective Techniques 185
3. Authorized Makers of Penal-Corrective Law and Their Appropriate Collaborative Roles 201
4. Structures and Processes for Applying Penal-Corrective Law and Techniques 209
5. Necessity for and Nature of Coercive Power 224
6. Roles of Private Citizens and Their Lawyers 230
7. Process Values 244

Section		Page
8.	Improving the Penal-Corrective Instrument	260
9.	Limitations of Law as a Penal-Corrective Instrument	280
10.	Bibliography	297

Chapter 3. Law as an Administrative-Regulatory Instrument 299
Section
1.	Introduction	299
2.	Administrative-Regulatory Techniques	305
3.	Authorized Makers of Administrative-Regulatory Law and Their Appropriate Collaborative Roles	320
4.	Structures and Processes for Applying Administrative-Regulatory Law and Techniques	352
5.	Necessity for and Nature of Coercive Power	378
6.	Roles of Private Citizens and Their Lawyers	382
7.	Process Values	386
8.	Improving the Administrative-Regulatory Instrument	390
9.	Limitations of Law as an Administrative-Regulatory Instrument	393
10.	Bibliography	405

Chapter 4. Law as an Instrument for Organizing Conferral of Public Benefits 406
Section
1.	Introduction	406
2.	Public-Benefit Techniques	407
3.	Authorized Makers of Public-Benefit Law and Their Appropriate Collaborative Roles	417
4.	Structures and Processes for Applying Public-Benefit Law and Techniques	436
5.	Necessity for and Nature of Coercive Power	487
6.	Roles of Private Citizens and Their Lawyers	494
7.	Process Values	510
8.	Improving the Public-Benefit Instrument	522
9.	Limitations of Law as a Public-Benefit Instrument	529
10.	Bibliography	532

Chapter 5. Law as an Instrument for Facilitating Private Arrangements 533
Section
1.	Introduction	533
2.	Private-Arrangement Techniques	534
3.	Authorized Makers of Private-Arrangement Law and Their Appropriate Collaborative Roles	579
4.	Structures and Processes for Applying Private-Arrangement Law and Techniques	595
5.	Necessity for and Nature of Coercive Power	598
6.	Roles of Private Citizens and Their Lawyers	603
7.	Process Values	612
8.	Improving the Private-Arrangement Instrument	630

Section   Page
  9. Limitations of Law as a Private-Arrangement Instrument 631
 10. Bibliography 632

PART TWO: THE ENDS OF LAW

PREFATORY NOTE TO PART TWO 636

Chapter 6. Law Can Help Promote Safety 639
Section
  1. Introduction 639
  2. Product Safety and the Private-Arrangement Instrument 645
  3. Product Safety and the Grievance-Remedial Instrument 648
  4. Product Safety and the Administrative-Regulatory Instrument 657
  5. Product Safety and the Penal-Corrective Instrument 678
  6. Product Safety and the Public-Benefit Instrument 698
  7. Bibliography 702

Chapter 7. Law Can Help Promote Equality 703
Section
  1. Introduction 703
  2. Racial Equality and the Penal-Corrective Instrument 704
  3. Racial Equality and the Grievance-Remedial Instrument 713
  4. Racial Equality and the Private-Arrangement Instrument 723
  5. Racial Equality and the Administrative-Regulatory Instrument 742
  6. Racial Equality and the Public-Benefit Instrument 757
  7. Bibliography 774

APPENDICES 775
Appendix
  A. The Constitution of the United States of America 775
  B. Bibliography on Law and Literature 793

INDEX 795

Table of Contents

		Page
PREFACE		v
TABLE OF CASES		xxvii

General Introduction 1

Section

1. Introductory Case 1
   Village of Skokie v. *National Socialist Party of America* 1
2. Sample Brief with Annotations 7
3. General Education and the Law 17
   Kalven & Zeisel, Law, Science, and Humanism 17
   H. Berman, On the Teaching of Law in the Liberal Arts Curriculum 18
   Appel, Law as a Social Science in the Undergraduate Curriculum 19
   Giamatti, The Law and the Public 21
   Comments and Questions 23
4. Pedagogic Notes 24
   A. Themes This Book Seeks to Develop 24
   B. Methods This Book Seeks to Employ 24
5. Bibliography 25

PART ONE: THE MEANS OF LAW

PREFATORY NOTE TO PART ONE	28
GENERAL BIBLIOGRAPHY FOR PART ONE	29

Chapter 1. Law as a Grievance-Remedial Instrument 30

Section

1. Introduction 30
2. Grievance-Remedial Techniques 31
   C. McCormick, Handbook on the Law of Damages 31
   Comments and Questions 33
3. Authorized Makers of Grievance-Remedial Law and Their Appropriate Collaborative Roles 33
   A. Origin of a Doctrine 33
   Butterfield v. *Forrester* 33
   Comments and Questions 34
   Davies v. *Mann* 35
   Comments and Questions 37

Section   Page
3. Authorized Makers of Grievance-Remedial Law and Their Ap-
       propriate Collaborative Roles—Continued
           The English Common Law and Its Reception in the United
              States 38
           A. Goldberg, Equal Justice 39
           K. Llewellyn, The Bramble Bush 40
           British Columbia Electric Railway v. *Loach* *43*
              Comments and Questions 46
           Prosser, Comparative Negligence 46
       B. Reform of the Doctrine 49
           Peck, The Role of the Courts and Legislatures in the Re-
              form of Tort Law 51
           Maki v. *Frelk* *52*
              Comments and Questions 54
           Williams, The Law Reform (Contributory Negligence) Act,
              1945 54
           Judicial Reaction to Legislative Intervention 55
           Alvis v. *Ribar* *58*
              Comments and Questions 69
           R. Posner, Economic Analysis of Law 69
4. Structures and Processes for Applying Grievance-Remedial Law
       and Techniques 71
       A. The Injury Occurs 72
       B. Retaining a Lawyer 73
       C. The Lawyer's Preliminary Determinations of Relevant
              Facts and Law 74
       D. Efforts at Private Settlement 76
       E. Commencing Legal Proceedings in a Proper Court 76
       F. Getting Any Disputed Issues of Fact and Law Defined and
              Separated So They Can Be Adjudicated 77
           Complaint 78
           Demurrer 82
              Comments and Questions 82
           Answer 83
           Reply 84
       G. Preparing for Trial (and Seeking Settlement or Other Dispo-
              sition Without Trial) 85
           D. Karlen, Civil Litigation 85
           F. James & G. Hazard, Civil Procedure 88
           M. Kane, Civil Procedure in a Nutshell 90
       H. Trial of the Case 91
           The Trial Begins 92
           Plaintiff's Case 93
           Defendant's Case 102
           Rebuttal 103
           Instructions 104
           The Trial Ends 107
              Comments and Questions 107
           Summers, Law, Adjudicative Processes, and Civil Justice 108

Section   Page

4. Structures and Processes for Applying Grievance-Remedial Law
    and Techniques—Continued

        R. Field, B. Kaplan & K. Clermont, Materials for a Basic
        Course in Civil Procedure 111

        Procedural Justice 112

        Pursuit of Truth 113

        Trial by Jury 115

    I. Post-Trial Procedures: Enforcement of Judgments and Ap-
        pellate Review 116

        Extracts from Defendant's Brief 119

        Extracts from Plaintiff's Reply Brief 121

            Comments and Questions 123

        "White v. *Island Amusement Co."* *124*

            Comments and Questions 126

        Fact and Law 126

            Comments and Questions 128

        Three Common End Uses of Law as a Grievance-Remedial
        Instrument 128

5. Necessity for and Nature of Coercive Power 129

    H. Kelsen, General Theory of Law and State 129

        Comments and Questions 131

    Reizakis v. *Loy* *131*

        Comments and Questions 137

6. Roles of Private Citizens and Their Lawyers 138

    Joint Conference on Professional Responsibility, Report 139

        Comments and Questions 141

    J. Frank, Courts on Trial 142

        Comments and Questions 144

    Adverse Fact and Law 146

7. Process Values 147

    Parrish v. *Board of Commissioners of the Alabama State Bar* ... *149*

        Comments and Questions 155

8. Improving the Grievance-Remedial Instrument 156

    A. General 156

        H. Zeisel, H. Kalven & B. Buchholz, Delay in the Court 157

        Posner, An Economic Approach to Legal Procedure and
        Judicial Administration 158

    B. Abandonment of Adversarial Adjudication 160

        Kaplan, Civil Procedure—Reflections on the Comparison of
        Systems 161

            Comments and Questions 165

    C. Abandonment of Adjudication Altogether 166

        W. Keeton, D. Dobbs, R. Keeton & D. Owen, Prosser and
        Keeton on the Law of Torts 167

            Comments and Questions 168

Section	Page
9. Limitations of Law as a Grievance-Remedial Instrument	169
Pound, The Limits of Effective Legal Action	169
Hurley v. *Eddingfield*	*171*
Comments and Questions	172
Cockrum v. *Baumgartner*	*173*
10. Bibliography	178

Chapter 2. Law as a Penal-Corrective Instrument | **180**

Section

1. Introduction	180
I. Kant, The Metaphysical Elements of Justice	181
J. Bentham, An Introduction to the Principles of Morals and Legislation	182
A. Goodhart, English Law and the Moral Law	182
Murphy, Marxism and Retribution	183
Comments and Questions	185
2. Penal-Corrective Techniques	185
Regina v. *Dudley & Stephens*	*186*
Comments and Questions	189
M'Naghten's Case	*190*
Durham v. *United States*	*192*
Dershowitz, Psychiatry in the Legal Process: "A Knife That Cuts Both Ways"	197
Comments and Questions	199
C. Cerf & V. Navasky, The Experts Speak	200
Rex v. *Esop*	*201*
Comments and Questions	201
3. Authorized Makers of Penal-Corrective Law and Their Appropriate Collaborative Roles	201
Keeler v. *Superior Court*	*202*
United States v. *Wiltberger*	*207*
Preuss, Punishment by Analogy in National Socialist Penal Law	208
Comments and Questions	208
4. Structures and Processes for Applying Penal-Corrective Law and Techniques	209
A. The Police	212
C. Silberman, Criminal Violence, Criminal Justice	212
B. The Prosecutor	215
B. Forst, J. Lucianovic & S. Cox, What Happens After Arrest?	215
J. Sirica, To Set the Record Straight	215
C. The Jury	216
D. The Judge	217
Proceedings of the 1971 Sentencing Institute for Superior Court Judges	217
Browder v. *United States*	*222*

Section   **Page**

  5. Necessity for and Nature of Coercive Power 224

    A. Camus, Resistance, Rebellion, and Death 226

    E. van den Haag, Punishing Criminals 226

    To Abolish the Death Penalty 227

    van den Haag, The Death Penalty Vindicates the Law 229

        Comments and Questions 230

  6. Roles of Private Citizens and Their Lawyers 230

    A. Ethical Issues Concerning Defense Counsel's Role 231

        American Bar Association, Model Rules of Professional Conduct 231

        Freedman, Professional Responsibility of the Criminal Defense Lawyer: The Three Hardest Questions 232

        Noonan, The Purposes of Advocacy and the Limits of Confidentiality 238

            Comments and Questions 242

    B. Effect of Counsel's Advice on Criminal Liability 242

        Hopkins v. *State* 242

            Comments and Questions 243

  7. Process Values 244

    A. Confessions 244

        Brown v. *Mississippi* 244

            Comments and Questions 247

        Miranda v. *Arizona* 248

            Comments and Questions 252

    B. Guilty Pleas 253

        Henderson v. *Morgan* 253

            Comments and Questions 256

        Bordenkircher v. *Hayes* 256

            Comments and Questions 260

  8. Improving the Penal-Corrective Instrument 260

    J. Mills, On the Edge 260

        Comments and Questions 280

  9. Limitations of Law as a Penal-Corrective Instrument 280

    J. Mill, On Liberty 281

    P. Devlin, The Enforcement of Morals 281

    People v. *Onofre* 284

    Kadish, The Crisis of Overcriminalization 291

    D. Richards, Sex, Drugs, Death, and the Law 294

        Comments and Questions 297

 10. Bibliography 297

Page

Chapter 3. Law as an Administrative-Regulatory Instrument 299
Section
1. Introduction ___ 299
  A. Reasons for Government Intervention ___ 300
  B. Reasons for Resort to the Administrative-Regulatory Instrument ___ 303
    Attorney General's Committee on Administrative Procedure, Administrative Procedure in Government Agencies ___ 303
      Problem 1 ___ 304
      Problem 2 ___ 305
2. Administrative-Regulatory Techniques ___ 305
  A. Setting and Publishing Substantive Regulatory Standards ___ 306
  B. Horack, Cases and Materials on Legislation ___ 306
  B. Encouraging Self-Regulation in Light of Published Standards ___ 306
  C. Licensing ___ 306
    Warp, Licensing as a Device for Federal Regulation ___ 307
  D. Investigating; Requiring Periodic Reports ___ 308
  E. Using or Threatening to Use Publicity ___ 309
    Rourke, Law Enforcement Through Publicity ___ 309
  F. Threatening Formal Administrative Proceedings; Other Informal Methods of Securing Compliance ___ 310
    Comments and Questions ___ 311
  G. Resort to Full-Scale Administrative Proceedings to Procure Formal Cease and Desist Orders ___ 311
  H. Administrative Resort to Courts for Appropriate Enforcement ___ 312
    Comments and Questions ___ 312
  I. Private Resort to Courts to Secure Appropriate Regulatory Action ___ 312
    Office of Communication of the United Church of Christ v. FCC ___ *313*
    Comments and Questions ___ 318
3. Authorized Makers of Administrative-Regulatory Law and Their Appropriate Collaborative Roles ___ 320
  A. The Legislature's Role: Delegation of Power to Administrative Agencies ___ 320
    Parker, Why Do Administrative Agencies Exist? ___ 321
    Dodd, Administrative Agencies as Legislators and Judges ___ 322
    Comments and Questions ___ 323
    United States Code, Title 47 ___ 323
    Comments and Questions ___ 326
    Stewart, The Reformation of American Administrative Law ___ 327
    Comments and Questions ___ 328
  B. The Agency's Role: Adjudication and Rulemaking ___ 329
    In re Application of Great Lakes Broadcasting Co. ___ *330*
    Comments and Questions ___ 331
    Evolution of Fairness Doctrine ___ 331

Section   Page
3. Authorized Makers of Administrative-Regulatory Law and Their
   Appropriate Collaborative Roles—Continued
     Trinity Methodist Church, South v. *FRC* _____ 332
         Comments and Questions _____ 332
     FCC, Editorializing by Broadcast Licensees _____ 333
     FCC, Applicability of the Fairness Doctrine in the Handling
         of Controversial Issues of Public Importance _____ 334
         Comments and Questions _____ 335
     Baker, Policy by Rule or Ad Hoc Approach—Which Should
         It Be? _____ 336
     FCC, The Handling of Public Issues Under the Fairness
         Doctrine and the Public Interest Standards of the Com-
         munications Act _____ 340
         Comments and Questions _____ 340
     C. The Court's Role: Judicial Review of Agency Action _____ 342
         J. Landis, The Administrative Process_____ 342
         Comments and Questions _____ 344
     Columbia Broadcasting System v. *FCC* _____ 345
         Comments and Questions _____ 349
     National Broadcasting Co. v. *FCC*_____ 349
         Comments and Questions _____ 352
4. Structures and Processes for Applying Administrative-Regulato-
   ry Law and Techniques _____ 352
   United States Code, Title 47 _____ 353
         Comments and Questions _____ 356
   Background of *Red Lion* _____ 356
   FCC Letter _____ 358
         Comments and Questions _____ 361
   Red Lion Broadcasting Co. v. *FCC* _____ 362
         Comments and Questions _____ 374
   Another View of *Red Lion* and the Fairness Doctrine _____ 376
         Comments and Questions _____ 377
   The Crucial Importance of Facts, Fact-Finders, and Fact-Finding_ 377
         Comments and Questions _____ 378
5. Necessity for and Nature of Coercive Power _____ 378
   Sayre, Public Welfare Offenses _____ 379
   Schwenk, The Administrative Crime, Its Creation and Punish-
         ment by Administrative Agencies _____ 381
         Comments and Questions _____ 381
6. Roles of Private Citizens and Their Lawyers_____ 382
   Panel II: Standing, Participation, and Who Pays? _____ 384
         Comments and Questions _____ 385
7. Process Values_____ 386
   United States Code, Title 5 _____ 387
         Comments and Questions _____ 387
   Lovett, Ex Parte and the FCC: The New Regulations_____ 388
         Comments and Questions _____ 388
   United States Code, Title 5 _____ 389
         Comments and Questions _____ 389

Section   **Page**
  8. Improving the Administrative-Regulatory Instrument 390
      Jaffe, Book Review 390
          Comments and Questions 392
  9. Limitations of Law as an Administrative-Regulatory Instrument. 393
      FCC, General Fairness Doctrine Obligations of Broadcast Licensees 394
          Comments and Questions 402
10. Bibliography 405

Chapter 4. Law as an Instrument for Organizing Conferral of Public Benefits **406**
Section
  1. Introduction 406
  2. Public-Benefit Techniques 407
      Salamon, Rethinking Public Management: Third-Party Government and the Changing Forms of Government Action 409
          Comments and Questions 414
      Stalker & Glymour, The Malignant Object: Thoughts on Public Sculpture 415
  3. Authorized Makers of Public-Benefit Law and Their Appropriate Collaborative Roles 417
      United States Code, Title 42 418
      Grove City College v. *Bell* *426*
          Comments and Questions 433
      M. Lipsky, Street-Level Bureaucracy 434
  4. Structures and Processes for Applying Public-Benefit Law and Techniques 436
      A. Setting Up the Basic Distributive Structure 437
          Project, Education and the Law: State Interests and Individual Rights 439
          Peterson, The Politics of American Education 441
          J. Coons & S. Sugarman, Education by Choice 444
          Levin, Educational Vouchers and Social Policy 448
             Comments and Questions 451
      B. Recruiting and Retaining the Personnel 452
          C. Summers, Public Sector Bargaining: Problems of Governmental Decisionmaking 452
          R. Summers, Collective Bargaining and Public Benefit Conferral: A Jurisprudential Critique 454
             Comments and Questions 457
          L. McDonnell & A. Pascal, Organized Teachers in American Schools 457
      C. Specifying the Detailed Form of the Benefit 460
          In re the Appeal of Donna Percosky and Others from Action of the Board of Education, Central School District No. 3 ..... *460*
          Board of Education, Island Trees Union Free School District No. 26 v. *Pico* *461*
             Comments and Questions 473

Section   Page
  4. Structures and Processes for Applying Public-Benefit Law and
      Techniques—Continued
      D. Securing the Necessary Funding 473
          M. Yudof, D. Kirp, T. van Geel & B. Levin, Kirp & Yudof's
          Educational Policy and the Law 474
          Thomas, Equalizing Educational Opportunity Through
          School Finance Reform: A Review Assessment 482
          Equal Protection Analysis 485
          Comments and Questions 486
  5. Necessity for and Nature of Coercive Power 487
      Brown v. Board of Education 488
          Comments and Questions 492
      D. Kirp, Just Schools: The Idea of Racial Equality in American
      Education 492
          Comments and Questions 494
  6. Roles of Private Citizens and Their Lawyers 494
      Board of Education v. Rowley 496
          Comments and Questions 507
      Hanson v. Cushman 508
  7. Process Values 510
      Goss v. Lopez 512
      Rose v. Nashua Board of Education 519
          Comments and Questions 522
  8. Improving the Public-Benefit Instrument 522
      T. Lowi, The End of Liberalism 522
      J. Pressman & A. Wildavsky, Implementation 525
          Comments and Questions 529
  9. Limitations of Law as a Public-Benefit Instrument 529
      H. Spencer, Over-Legislation 531
          Comments and Questions 532
 10. Bibliography 532

Chapter 5. Law as an Instrument for Facilitating Private
            Arrangements 533
Section
  1. Introduction 533
  2. Private-Arrangement Techniques 534
      A. Types of Private Arrangements 535
          i.   Marriages 535
               H. Clark, The Law of Domestic Relations in the United
               States 535
          ii. Private Associations 536
               2 A. de Tocqueville, Democracy in America 536
               Developments in the Law—Judicial Control of Actions
               of Private Associations 537
               Note, Judicial Intervention in the Conduct of Private
               Associations: Bases for the Emerging Trend of Judi-
               cial Activism 538

Section   Page

2. Private-Arrangement Techniques—Continued

    iii. Contracts _____ 538

        R. Pound, An Introduction to the Philosophy of Law ___ 538

        Jones, The Jurisprudence of Contracts _____ 539

        Llewellyn, What Price Contract?—An Essay in Perspective _____ 541

        Division of Labor and the Origins of Exchange _____ 541

            Comments and Questions_____ 543

    iv. Corporations_____ 543

        C. Stone, Where the Law Ends_____ 543

        A. Conard, R. Krauss & S. Siegel, Corporations_____ 544

        Epstein, Societal, Managerial, and Legal Perspectives on Corporate Social Responsibility—Product and Process _____ 544

    v. Wills _____ 544

        T. Atkinson, Handbook of the Law of Wills _____ 544

        Friedman, The Law of the Living, The Law of the Dead: Property, Succession, and Society_____ 545

        M. Rheinstein & M. Glendon, The Law of Decedents' Estates _____ 545

  B. Rules of Validation _____ 547

    i. Contracts _____ 547

        Lucy v. *Zehmer* _____ 547

        Lefkowitz v. *Great Minneapolis Surplus Store, Inc.* ____ 552

        Hamer v. *Sidway* _____ 554

        1 S. Williston, A Treatise on the Law of Contracts ___ 556

        Fuller, Consideration and Form _____ 557

        Gratuitous Promises _____ 558

        James Baird Co. v. *Gimbel Bros.* _____ 558

        Shattuck, Gratuitous Promises—A New Writ? _____ 558

        Boyer, Promissory Estoppel: Requirements and Limitations of the Doctrine _____ 558

        Ricketts v. *Scothorn*_____ 559

        The Proliferation of Promissory Estoppel _____ 561

    ii. Corporations_____ 561

        Oregon Revised Statutes _____ 561

        North Dakota Century Code _____ 562

        Weiss v. *Anderson* _____ 562

  C. Legal Consequences _____ 563

    Note, Judicial Intervention in the Conduct of Private Associations: Bases for the Emerging Trend of Judicial Activism _____ 563

    i. Contracts _____ 564

        Cooper v. *Clute*_____ 564

        Hadley v. *Baxendale*_____ 565

        Specific Performance _____ 567

        Pierce-Odom, Inc. v. *Evenson*_____ 568

        3 R. Pound, Jurisprudence_____ 569

            Comments and Questions_____ 569

Section   Page

2. Private-Arrangement Techniques—Continued

        Adler, Barish, Daniels, Levin & Creskoff v. *Epstein* ___ 570

        Comments and Questions _____ 575

    ii. Corporations _____ 576

        Cranson v. *IBM* _____ 576

        A. Conard, Corporations in Perspective _____ 578

        Secondary Techniques for Facilitating Private Arrangements _____ 579

3. Authorized Makers of Private-Arrangement Law and Their Appropriate Collaborative Roles _____ 579

    A. Private Persons _____ 579

        Articles of Incorporation _____ 580

        Bylaws _____ 582

        Minutes of Organization Meeting _____ 583

        Letter _____ 585

        Agreement for Construction and Purchase of Track _____ 586

        The Kiwi and Kid _____ 587

    B. Legislatures _____ 588

    C. Courts _____ 588

        Riggs v. *Palmer* _____ 589

        Ermolieff v. *RKO Radio Pictures, Inc.* _____ 591

        H. Jones, E. Farnsworth & W. Young, Cases and Materials on Contracts _____ 592

        Pennyrile Tours, Inc. v. *Country Inns, USA, Inc.* _____ 593

4. Structures and Processes for Applying Private-Arrangement Law and Techniques _____ 595

    Adler, Child Abuse Victims: Are They Also Victims of an Adversarial and Hierarchial Court System? _____ 597

    Dyson & Dyson, Family Courts in the United States _____ 597

5. Necessity for and Nature of Coercive Power _____ 598

    Wilson v. *Sandstrom* _____ 599

    Hale, Coercion and Distribution in a Supposedly Non-Coercive State _____ 601

6. Roles of Private Citizens and Their Lawyers_____ 603

    Agreement as to Supply of Water _____ 603

    White v. *Benkowski* _____ 605

    H. Edwards & J. White, The Lawyer as a Negotiator _____ 609

        Comments and Questions _____ 610

    Letter _____ 610

        Comments and Questions _____ 612

7. Process Values_____ 612

    Kessler, Contracts of Adhesion—Some Thoughts About Freedom of Contract _____ 612

    Uniform Commercial Code _____ 613

    Williams v. *Walker-Thomas Furniture Co.* _____ 613

        Comments and Questions _____ 617

    Hillman, Debunking Some Myths About Unconscionability: A New Framework for U.C.C. Section 2–302_____ 617

    Alaska Packers' Ass'n v. *Domenico* _____ 618

Section	Page
7. Process Values—Continued	
Weintraub v. *Krobatsch*	*621*
Estate of Baker	*624*
8. Improving the Private-Arrangement Instrument	630
9. Limitations of Law as a Private-Arrangement Instrument	631
10. Bibliography	632

PART TWO: THE ENDS OF LAW

	Page
PREFATORY NOTE TO PART TWO	636
GENERAL BIBLIOGRAPHY FOR PART TWO	638

	Page
Chapter 6. Law Can Help Promote Safety	**639**
Section	
1. Introduction	639
R. Epstein, Modern Products Liability Law	640
M. Shapo, A Nation of Guinea Pigs	642
Comments and Questions	644
2. Product Safety and the Private-Arrangement Instrument	645
Comments and Questions	646
Magnuson-Moss Warranty Act	647
Priest, A Theory of the Consumer Product Warranty	647
3. Product Safety and the Grievance-Remedial Instrument	648
Greenman v. *Yuba Power Products, Inc.*	*649*
T. Dalrymple, Brief Opposing Strict Liability in Tort	651
Prosser, The Assault upon the Citadel (Strict Liability to the Consumer)	652
R. Hillman, J. McDonnell & S. Nickles, Common Law and Equity Under the UCC	653
Williams, Mass Tort Class Actions: Going, Going, Gone?	655
Comments and Questions	657
4. Product Safety and the Administrative-Regulatory Instrument	657
Henderson, Judicial Review of Manufacturers' Conscious Design Choices: The Limits of Adjudication	658
Consumer Product Safety Act	659
Southland Mower Co. v. *Consumer Product Safety Commission*	*660*
Comments and Questions	671
Wilson v. *Piper Aircraft Corp.*	*672*
Comments and Questions	677
5. Product Safety and the Penal-Corrective Instrument	678
Developments in the Law—Corporate Crime: Regulating Corporate Behavior Through Criminal Sanctions	678
Wheeler, Manufacturers' Criminal Liability	682
Comments and Questions	683
Wheeler, Manufacturers' Criminal Liability	684
Note, Corporate Homicide: A New Assault on Corporate Decision-making	692

Section   Page

5. Product Safety and the Penal-Corrective Instrument—Continued
    Maakestad, *State* v. *Ford Motor Co.*: Constitutional, Utilitarian,
        and Moral Perspectives _____ 693
            Comments and Questions _____ 696
    Epilogue _____ 696
    Prod. Safety & Liab. Rep. (BNA) _____ 696
    Prod. Safety & Liab. Rep. (BNA) _____ 697
    Specific Criminal Statutes _____ 698
6. Product Safety and the Public-Benefit Instrument _____ 698
    Preclinical and Clinical Testing by the Pharmaceutical Industry,
        1977 _____ 700
            Comments and Questions _____ 702
7. Bibliography _____ 702

Chapter 7. Law Can Help Promote Equality _____ 703
Section
1. Introduction _____ 703
2. Racial Equality and the Penal-Corrective Instrument _____ 704
    A. Racial Equality as a Limit on the Penal-Corrective Mode ___ 704
        Korematsu v. *United States* _____ 705
            Comments and Questions _____ 709
    B. Racial Equality as the Goal of the Penal-Corrective Mode __ 709
        Beauharnais v. *Illinois* _____ 709
            Comments and Questions _____ 713
3. Racial Equality and the Grievance-Remedial Instrument _____ 713
    A. Racial Equality as a Limit on the Grievance-Remedial Mode_ 713
        Blake v. *Cich* _____ 714
            Comments and Questions _____ 716
    B. Racial Equality as the Goal of the Grievance-Remedial
        Mode _____ 716
        United States Code, Title 42 _____ 717
            Comments and Questions _____ 720
        Pornography as Discrimination _____ 720
            Comments and Questions _____ 723
4. Racial Equality and the Private-Arrangement Instrument _____ 723
    A. Racial Equality as a Limit on the Private-Arrangement
        Mode _____ 723
        Palmore v. *Sidoti* _____ 724
            Comments and Questions _____ 727
        Shelley v. *Kraemer* _____ 727
            Comments and Questions _____ 730
    B. Racial Equality as the Goal of the Private-Arrangement
        Mode _____ 730
        Runyon v. *McCrary* _____ 731
            Comments and Questions _____ 739
        Note, The Expanding Scope of Section 1981: Assault on
            Private Discrimination and a Cloud on Affirmative Ac-
            tion _____ 739

Section   **Page**

5. Racial Equality and the Administrative-Regulatory Instrument .. 742

   A. Racial Equality as a Limit on the Administrative-Regulatory Mode 742

      Yick Wo v. *Hopkins* 742

         Comments and Questions 745

      Moose Lodge No. 107 v. *Irvis* 745

         Comments and Questions 751

   B. Racial Equality as the Goal of the Administrative-Regulatory Mode 751

         Comments and Questions 757

6. Racial Equality and the Public-Benefit Instrument 757

   A. Racial Equality as a Limit on the Public-Benefit Mode 757

      Fullilove v. *Klutznick* 758

         Comments and Questions 766

   B. Racial Equality as the Goal of the Public-Benefit Mode 767

      Bob Jones University v. *United States* 767

         Comments and Questions 773

7. Bibliography 774

APPENDICES 775

Appendix

A. The Constitution of the United States of America 775

B. Bibliography on Law and Literature 793

INDEX 795

Table of Cases

The principal cases are in italic type. Cases cited or discussed within the authors' text are in roman type. References are to pages.

Adler, Barish, Daniels, Levin & Creskoff v. Epstein, 570, 575
A.L.A. Schechter Poultry Corp. v. United States, 327
Alaska Packers' Ass'n v. Domenico, 618, 630
Alvis v. Ribar, 58, 69
Alyeska Pipeline Service Co. v. Wilderness Society, 384, 385, 386
American Booksellers Association v. Hudnut, 16
Arlington Heights v. Metropolitan Housing Development Corp., 745

Baird Co., James v. Gimbel Bros., 558
Baker, Estate of, 624, 630
Banzhaf v. FCC, 335
Beauharnais v. Illinois, 709, 713, 723
Black Citizens For a Fair Media v. FCC, 390, 394
Blake v. Cich, 714
Board of Education v. Rowley, 496, 507
Board of Education, Island Trees Union Free School District No. 26 v. Pico, 461
Bob Jones University v. United States, 767
Bordenkircher v. Hayes, 256
British Columbia Electric Railway v. Loach, 43, 46, 69, 138
Browder v. United States, 222
Brown v. Board of Education, 488, 492, 507, 757
Brown v. Mississippi, 244, 248
Burlington School Committee v. Department of Education, 507
Butterfield v. Forrester, 33, 34, 35, 37, 38, 46, 69, 138

Chaplinsky v. New Hampshire, 14
Cigarette Advertising & Antismoking Presentations, In re, 335
Cockrum v. Baumgartner, 173
Cohen v. California, 14
Columbia Broadcasting System v. FCC, 345

Cooper v. Clute, 564, 567
Cranson v. IBM, 576

Davies v. Mann, 35, 37, 38, 46, 56, 69, 138
Democratic National Committee v. FCC, 349
Dred Scott v. Sandford, 713
Dudley & Stephens, Regina v., 186
Durham v. United States, 192, 199

Ermolieff v. RKO Radio Pictures, Inc., 591
Esop, Rex v., 201, 243
Estate of (see name of party)

FCC v. League of Women Voters, 403
Ford Motor Co. v. Stubblefield, 677
Ford Motor Co., State v., 678, 684, 696
Friends of the Earth v. FCC, 336
Fudickar v. Guardian Mutual Life Insurance Co., 596
Fuller v. Illinois Central R.R., 38
Fullilove v. Klutznick, 758

Goss v. Lopez, 512
Great Lakes Broadcasting Co., In re Application of, 330, 331
Greater Boston Television Corp. v. FCC, 389
Greenman v. Yuba Power Products, Inc., 649
Grove City College v. Bell, 426, 433
Gryc v. Dayton-Hudson Corp., 672

Hadley v. Baxendale, 565, 567
Hamer v. Sidway, 554, 632
Hanson v. Cushman, 508
Henderson v. Morgan, 253
Henley v. Cameron, 57
Holmes, United States v., 190
Hopkins v. State, 242
Hurley v. Eddingfield, 171

In re (see name of party)
INS v. Chadha, 433

James Baird Co. v. Gimbel Bros., 558
Johnson v. Hot Springs Land & Improvement Co., 120, 121, 122, 123

Keeler v. Superior Court, 202
Kitchen v. Herring, 567
Korematsu v. United States, 705, 709

Larus & Brother Co. v. FCC, 336
Lee v. Washington, 727
Lefkowitz v. Great Minneapolis Surplus Store, Inc., 552, 631
Lucy v. Zehmer, 547

McNabb v. United States, 244
Maki v. Frelk, 52, 54, 56
Mayflower Broadcasting Corp., In re, 333
Miami Herald Publishing Co. v. Tornillo, 374, 375
Miranda v. Arizona, 248, 252, 253
M'Naghten's Case, 190, 199
Moose Lodge No. 107 v. Irvis, 745

National Broadcasting Co. v. FCC, 349
New York v. Ferber, 16
New York v. Quarles, 253

Office of Communication of the United Church of Christ v. FCC, 313, 319, 320, 344, 383, 384, 385
Onofre, People v., 284

Palmore v. Sidoti, 724, 727
Parrish v. Board of Commissioners of the Alabama State Bar, 149, 156
Pennyrile Tours, Inc. v. Country Inns, USA, Inc., 593, 631
People v. _____ (see opposing party)
Pierce-Odom, Inc. v. Evenson, 568, 588

Red Lion Broadcasting Co. v. FCC, 362, 374, 375, 376, 377, 378, 383, 389
Regina v. _____ (see opposing party)
Reizakis v. Loy, 131
Rex v. _____ (see opposing party)
Reynolds v. Nichols, 172
Ricketts v. Scothorn, 559
Riggs v. Palmer, 589

Roberts v. United States Jaycees, 739
Rose v. Nashua Board of Education, 519, 522
Runyon v. McCrary, 731

SEC v. Chenery Corp., 389
Schechter Poultry Corp., A.L.A. v. United States, 327
Shelley v. Kraemer, 727, 730
Skokie, Village of v. National Socialist Party of America, 1, 7, 9, 14, 15, 16, 713
Smith v. Collin, 12, 16
Southland Mower Co. v. Consumer Product Safety Commission, 660, 671
State v. _____ (see opposing party)
Strauder v. West Virginia, 714
Syracuse Peace Council v. WTVH, 404

Thiel v. Southern Pacific Co., 714
Trinity Methodist Church, South v. FRC, 332, 344
Turner v. FCC, 384

United States v. _____ (see opposing party)

Village of (see name of village)

Wahba v. H & N Prescription Center, Inc., 659
Weintraub v. Krobatsch, 621, 630
Weiss v. Anderson, 562
White v. Benkowski, 605, 631
White v. Island Amusement Co., 71, 124, 128, 129, 138
Wilderness Society v. Morton, 385
Williams v. Walker-Thomas Furniture Co., 613, 630
Wilson v. Piper Aircraft Corp., 672
Wilson v. Sandstrom, 599
Wiltberger, United States v., 207
Wisconsin v. Constantineau, 244

Yick Wo v. Hopkins, 742, 745
Young Peoples' Association for the Propagation of the Gospel, In re, 333

LAW: ITS NATURE, FUNCTIONS, AND LIMITS

General Introduction

Law is probably the most neglected phase of our culture in the liberal arts curriculum.

PAUL A. FREUND

This book derives from the conviction that law is a valuable and even necessary part of an education in the liberal arts. Unfortunately, law is often misconceived as a vast collection of unconnected rules to be memorized by law students. The study of law is too frequently confined to vocational preparation. Nevertheless, we propose to demonstrate that law has a potentially vital role to play in liberal education.

Study of law at this general level should include not only legal philosophy but also a more descriptive foray into our legal system. What is law, and what can it do and not do? This book presents law as a set of varied techniques for resolving conflicts and addressing many other social problems. Our method will expose students to many original legal sources. The constant intention, however, is to enhance students' general education, not directly to serve a prelaw program of study.

This introduction is divided into five sections. Partly because one skill this book intends to foster is the careful and insightful reading of judicial opinions, the first section of these introductory materials contains an actual case. The second section consists of a sample brief of the case accompanied by comments and questions. The third section of the introductory materials comprises secondary sources discussing why law is indeed an appropriate subject for the generalist's study. The fourth section provides commentary on how best to approach and use this book. The fifth section is a general bibliography.

Section One. Introductory Case

VILLAGE OF SKOKIE v. NATIONAL SOCIALIST PARTY OF AMERICA

Supreme Court of Illinois, January 27, 1978.
69 Ill.2d 605, 373 N.E.2d 21.

David Goldberger and Barbara O'Toole, of Roger Baldwin Foundation of ACLU, Inc., Chicago, for appellants.

1

Harvey Schwartz, Corp. Counsel, Skokie (Gilbert Gordon, Chicago, of counsel), for appellee.

Per Curiam:

Plaintiff, the village of Skokie, filed a complaint in the circuit court of Cook County seeking to enjoin defendants, the National Socialist Party of America (the American Nazi Party) and 10 individuals as "officers and members" of the party, from engaging in certain activities while conducting a demonstration within the village. The circuit court issued an order enjoining certain conduct during the planned demonstration. The appellate court modified the injunction order, and, as modified, defendants are enjoined from "[i]ntentionally displaying the swastika on or off their persons, in the course of a demonstration, march, or parade." (51 Ill.App. 3d 279, 295, 366 N.E.2d 347, 357.) We allowed defendants' petition for leave to appeal.

The pleadings and the facts adduced at the hearing are fully set forth in the appellate court opinion, and only those matters necessary to the discussion of the issues will be repeated here. The facts are not disputed.

It is alleged in plaintiff's complaint that the "uniform of the National Socialist Party of America consists of the storm trooper uniform of the German Nazi Party embellished with the Nazi swastika"; that the plaintiff village has a population of about 70,000 persons of which approximately 40,500 persons are of "Jewish religion or Jewish ancestry" and of this latter number 5,000 to 7,000 are survivors of German concentration camps; that the defendant organization is "dedicated to the incitation of racial and religious hatred directed principally against individuals of Jewish faith or ancestry and non-Caucasians"; and that its members "have patterned their conduct, their uniform, their slogan and their tactics along the pattern of the German Nazi Party . . . . "

. . . In an affidavit . . . , defendant Frank Collin, who testified that he was "party leader," stated that on or about March 20, 1977, he sent officials of the plaintiff village a letter stating that the party members and supporters would hold a peaceable, public assembly in the village on May 1, 1977, to protest the Skokie Park District's requirement that the party procure $350,000 of insurance prior to the party's use of the Skokie public parks for public assemblies. The demonstration was to begin at 3 p.m., last 20 to 30 minutes, and consist of 30 to 50 demonstrators marching in single file, back and forth, in front of the village hall. The marchers were to wear uniforms which include a swastika emblem or armband. They were to carry a party banner containing a swastika emblem and signs containing such statements as "White Free Speech," "Free Speech for the White Man," and "Free Speech for White America." The demonstrators would not distribute handbills, make any derogatory statements directed to any ethnic or religious group, or obstruct traffic. They would cooperate with any reasonable police instructions or requests.

At the hearing on plaintiff's motion for an "emergency injunction" a resident of Skokie testified that he was a survivor of the Nazi holocaust. He further testified that the Jewish community in and around Skokie feels the purpose of the march in the "heart of the Jewish population" is to remind the two million survivors "that we are not through with you" and to show "that the Nazi threat is not over, it can happen again." Another resident of Skokie testified that as the result of defendants' announced intention to march in Skokie, 15 to 18 Jewish organizations, within the village and surrounding area, were called and a counterdemonstration of an estimated 12,000 to 15,000 people was scheduled for the same day. There was opinion evidence that defendants' planned demonstration in Skokie would result in violence.

The circuit court entered an order enjoining defendants from "marching, walking or parading in the uniform of the National Socialist Party of America; marching, walking or parading or otherwise displaying the swastika on or off their person; distributing pamphlets or displaying any materials which incite or promote hatred against persons of Jewish faith or ancestry or hatred against persons of any faith or ancestry, race or religion" within the village of Skokie. The appellate court, as earlier noted, modified the order so that defendants were enjoined only from intentional display of the swastika during the Skokie demonstration.

The appellate court opinion adequately discussed and properly decided those issues arising from the portions of the injunction order which enjoined defendants from marching, walking, or parading, from distributing pamphlets or displaying materials, and from wearing the uniform of the National Socialist Party of America. The only issue remaining before this court is whether the circuit court order enjoining defendants from displaying the swastika violates the first amendment rights of those defendants.

In defining the constitutional rights of the parties who come before this court, we are, of course, bound by the pronouncements of the United States Supreme Court in its interpretation of the United States Constitution. The decisions of that court, particularly Cohen v. California (1971), 403 U.S. 15, 91 S.Ct. 1780, in our opinion compel us to permit the demonstration as proposed, including display of the swastika.

"It is firmly settled that under our Constitution the public expression of ideas may not be prohibited merely because the ideas are themselves offensive to some of their hearers" (Bachellar v. Maryland (1970), 397 U.S. 564, 567, 90 S.Ct. 1312, 1315), and it is entirely clear that the wearing of distinctive clothing can be symbolic expression of a thought or philosophy. The symbolic expression of thought falls within the free speech clause of the first amendment (Tinker v. Des Moines Independent Community School District (1969), 393 U.S. 503, 89 S.Ct. 733), and the plaintiff village has the heavy burden of justifying the imposition of a prior restraint upon defendants' right to freedom of speech (Carroll v. President of Princess Anne County (1968), 393 U.S. 175, 89 S.Ct. 347; Organization for a Better Austin v. Keefe (1971), 402 U.S. 415, 91 S.Ct. 1575).

The village of Skokie seeks to meet this burden by application of the "fighting words" doctrine first enunciated in Chaplinsky v. New Hampshire (1942), 315 U.S. 568, 62 S.Ct. 766. That doctrine was designed to permit punishment of extremely hostile personal communication likely to cause immediate physical response, "no words being 'forbidden except such as have a direct tendency to cause acts of violence by the persons to whom, individually, the remark is addressed.'" In *Cohen* the Supreme

Court restated the description of fighting words as "those personally abusive epithets which, when addressed to the ordinary citizen, are, as a matter of common knowledge, inherently likely to provoke violent reaction." Plaintiff urges, and the appellate court has held, that the exhibition of the Nazi symbol, the swastika, addresses to ordinary citizens a message which is tantamount to fighting words. Plaintiff further asks this court to extend *Chaplinsky,* which upheld a statute punishing the use of such words, and hold that the fighting-words doctrine permits a prior restraint on defendants' symbolic speech. In our judgment we are precluded from doing so.

In *Cohen,* defendant's conviction stemmed from wearing a jacket bearing the words "Fuck the Draft" in a Los Angeles County courthouse corridor. The Supreme Court for reasons we believe applicable here refused to find that the jacket inscription constituted fighting words. That court stated:

> The constitutional right of free expression is powerful medicine in a society as diverse and populous as ours. It is designed and intended to remove governmental restraints from the arena of public discussion, putting the decision as to what views shall be voiced largely into the hands of each of us, in the hope that use of such freedom will ultimately produce a more capable citizenry and more perfect polity and in the belief that no other approach would comport with the premise of individual dignity and choice upon which our political system rests. See Whitney v. California, 274 U.S. 357, 375–377, 47 S.Ct. 641 (1927) (Brandeis, J., concurring).
>
> To many, the immediate consequence of this freedom may often appear to be only verbal tumult, discord, and even offensive utterance. These are, however, within established limits, in truth necessary side effects of the broader enduring values which the process of open debate permits us to achieve. That the air may at times seem filled with verbal cacophony is, in this sense not a sign of weakness but of strength. We cannot lose sight of the fact that, in what otherwise might seem a trifling and annoying instance of individual distasteful abuse of a privilege, these fundamental societal values are truly implicated. . . . "so long as the means are peaceful, the communication need not meet standards of acceptability," Organization for a Better Austin v. Keefe, 402 U.S. 415, 419, 91 S.Ct. 1575 (1971).
>
> Against this perception of the constitutional policies involved, we discern certain more particularized considerations that peculiarly call for reversal of this conviction. First, the principle contended for by the State seems inherently boundless. How is one to distinguish this from any other offensive word [emblem]? Surely the State has no right to cleanse public debate to the point where it is grammatically palatable to the most squeamish among us. Yet no readily ascertainable general principle exists for stopping short of that result were we to affirm the judgment below. For, while the particular four-letter word [emblem] being litigated here is perhaps more distasteful than most others of its genre, it is nevertheless

often true that one man's vulgarity is another's lyric. Indeed, we think it is largely because governmental officials cannot make principled distinctions in this area that the Constitution leaves matters of taste and style so largely to the individual. . . .

Finally, and in the same vein, we cannot indulge the facile assumption that one can forbid particular words without also running a substantial risk of suppressing ideas in the process. Indeed, governments might soon seize upon the censorship of particular words [emblems] as a convenient guise for banning the expression of unpopular views. We have been able, as noted above, to discern little social benefit that might result from running the risk of opening the door to such grave results.

The display of the swastika, as offensive to the principles of a free nation as the memories it recalls may be, is symbolic political speech intended to convey to the public the beliefs of those who display it. It does not, in our opinion, fall within the definition of "fighting words," and that doctrine cannot be used here to overcome the heavy presumption against the constitutional validity of a prior restraint.

Nor can we find that the swastika, while not representing fighting words, is nevertheless so offensive and peace threatening to the public that its display can be enjoined. We do not doubt that the sight of this symbol is abhorrent to the Jewish citizens of Skokie, and that the survivors of the Nazi persecutions, tormented by their recollections, may have strong feelings regarding its display. Yet it is entirely clear that this factor does not justify enjoining defendants' speech. The *Cohen* court spoke to this subject:

Finally, in arguments before this Court much has been made of the claim that Cohen's distasteful mode of expression was thrust upon unwilling or unsuspecting viewers, and that the State might therefore legitimately act as it did in order to protect the sensitive from otherwise unavoidable exposure to appellant's crude form of protest. Of course, the mere presumed presence of unwitting listeners or viewers does not serve automatically to justify curtailing all speech capable of giving offense. See, e.g., Organization for a Better Austin v. Keefe, 402 U.S. 415, 91 S.Ct. 1575 (1971). While this Court has recognized that government may properly act in many situations to prohibit intrusion into the privacy of the home of unwelcome views and ideas which cannot be totally banned from the public dialogue, e.g., Rowan v. Post Office Dept., 397 U.S. 728, 90 S.Ct. 1484 (1970), we have at the same time consistently stressed that "we are often 'captives' outside the sanctuary of the home and subject to objectionable speech." Id., at 738, 90 S.Ct. at 1491. The ability of government, consonant with the Constitution, to shut off discourse solely to protect others from hearing it is, in other words, dependent upon a showing that substantial privacy interests are being invaded in an essentially intolerable manner. Any broader view of this authority would effectively empower a majority to silence dissidents simply as a matter of personal predilections.

See also Kunz v. New York (1951), 340 U.S. 290, 71 S.Ct. 312; Street v. New York (1969), 394 U.S. 576, 89 S.Ct. 1354.

Similarly, the Court of Appeals for the Seventh Circuit, in reversing the denial of defendant Collin's application for a permit to speak in Chicago's Marquette Park, noted that courts have consistently refused to ban speech because of the possibility of unlawful conduct by those opposed to the speaker's philosophy.

> Starting with Terminiello v. City of Chicago, 337 U.S. 1, 69 S.Ct. 894 (1949), and continuing to Gregory v. City of Chicago, 394 U.S. 111, 89 S.Ct. 946 (1969), it has become patent that a hostile audience is not a basis for restraining otherwise legal First Amendment activity. As with many of the cases cited herein, if the actual behavior is not sufficient to sustain a conviction under a statute, then certainly the anticipation of such events cannot sustain the burden necessary to justify a prior restraint.

Collin v. Chicago Park District (7th Cir.1972), 460 F.2d 746, 754.

Rockwell v. Morris (1961), 12 A.D.2d 272, 211 N.Y.S.2d 25, aff'd mem. (1961), 10 N.Y.2d 721, 749, 219 N.Y.S.2d 268, 605, 176 N.E.2d 836, 177 N.E.2d 48, cert. denied (1961), 368 U.S. 913, 82 S.Ct. 194, also involved an American Nazi leader, George Lincoln Rockwell, who challenged a bar to his use of a New York City park to hold a public demonstration where anti-Semitic speeches would be made. Although approximately 2½ million Jewish New Yorkers were hostile to Rockwell's message, the court ordered that a permit to speak be granted, stating:

> A community need not wait to be subverted by street riots and storm troopers; but, also, it cannot, by its policemen or commissioners, suppress a speaker, in prior restraint, on the basis of news reports, hysteria, or inference that what he did yesterday, he will do today. Thus, too, if the speaker incites others to immediate unlawful action he may be punished—in a proper case, stopped when disorder actually impends; but this is not to be confused with unlawful action from others who seek unlawfully to suppress or punish the speaker.
>
> So, the unpopularity of views, their shocking quality, their obnoxiousness, and even their alarming impact is not enough. Otherwise, the preacher of any strange doctrine could be stopped; the anti-racist himself could be suppressed, if he undertakes to speak in "restricted" areas; and one who asks that public schools be open indiscriminately to all ethnic groups could be lawfully suppressed, if only he choose to speak where persuasion is needed most.

In summary, as we read the controlling Supreme Court opinions, use of the swastika is a symbolic form of free speech entitled to first amendment protections. Its display on uniforms or banners by those engaged in peaceful demonstrations cannot be totally precluded solely because that display may provoke a violent reaction by those who view it. Particularly is this true where, as here, there has been advance notice by the demonstrators of their plans so that they have become, as the complaint alleges, "common knowledge" and those to whom sight of the swastika banner or uniforms would be offensive are forewarned and need not view them. A speaker who gives prior notice of his message has not compelled a confrontation with those who voluntarily listen.

As to those who happen to be in a position to be involuntarily confronted with the swastika, the following observations from Erznoznik v. City of Jacksonville (1975), 422 U.S. 205, 95 S.Ct. 2268, are appropriate:

> The plain, if at all times disquieting, truth is that in our pluralistic society, constantly proliferating new and ingenious forms of expression, "we are inescapably captive audiences for many purposes." Rowan v. Post Office Dept., [397 U.S. 728,] 736, 90 S.Ct. 1484. Much that we encounter offends our esthetic, if not our political and moral, sensibilities. Nevertheless, the Constitution does not permit government to decide which types of otherwise protected speech are sufficiently offensive to require protection for the unwilling listener or viewer. Rather, absent the narrow circumstances described above [home intrusion or captive audience], the burden normally falls upon the viewer to "avoid further bombardment of [his] sensibilities simply by averting [his] eyes." Cohen v. California [403 U.S. 15,] 21, 91 S.Ct. 1780.

Thus by placing the burden upon the viewer to avoid further bombardment, the Supreme Court has permitted speakers to justify the initial intrusion into the citizen's sensibilities.

We accordingly, albeit reluctantly, conclude that the display of the swastika cannot be enjoined under the fighting-words exception to free speech, nor can anticipation of a hostile audience justify the prior restraint. Furthermore, *Cohen* and *Erznoznik* direct the citizens of Skokie that it is their burden to avoid the offensive symbol if they can do so without unreasonable inconvenience. Accordingly, we are constrained to reverse that part of the appellate court judgment enjoining the display of the swastika. That judgment is in all other respects affirmed.

Affirmed in part and reversed in part.

CLARK, JUSTICE, dissenting.

Section Two. Sample Brief with Annotations

The following is a sample brief of the *Skokie* case, accompanied by comments and questions. A brief is a summary of a case that presents the essence of a judicial opinion in a set format. Our brief serves as a sample of the written notes you should usually bring to class. Although the comments and questions are much longer than any written material you will probably prepare, this should give you a good idea of the kind of queries you should pose to yourself in tackling a case.

———

Sample Brief	Comments and Questions
Facts:	(1) In this part of your brief, you should state who
The American Nazi party wanted to conduct a demonstration, peacefully but in uniform and with swas-	the parties are and what happened to them before reaching the courthouse. Limit yourself to the legally relevant facts. For example, the Nazi party had its headquarters in Chicago, and Skokie is a suburb

tika, to protest a local requirement that insurance be procured prior to public assemblies in the public parks. The village of Skokie, which has a large Jewish population including many survivors of Nazi concentration camps, wanted to restrict the demonstration that the Nazis planned for May 1, 1977, in front of the village hall.

of Chicago. These facts are not relevant and so should be omitted from your brief, just as they were omitted from the court's opinion itself. In our case, the Supreme Court of Illinois expressly limited the facts it presented to the narrow issue being considered on review. To get a fuller version of the events in suit, as we have done for some of our comments and questions, you would have to consult the appellate opinion in the court below or even the documents that constitute the record in the case. Sometimes, however, judicial opinions will include a great many irrelevant facts, and you will have to sift through them for the essence in order to write this part of your brief.

Write the "Facts" (and the other entries) in your own words. Nothing is gained by merely transcribing the opinion. By recording the case in your own language, you will be less likely to assume mistakenly that you understand what some judge has written.

(2) In briefing a case, you should follow a logical and set format. As to choice of format, many possibilities are defensible. We choose to begin with the out-of-court facts in the interest of chronology and as an indication of their enormous importance in shaping the decision.

However, under "Facts" we do not record the fruits of some abstract historical inquiry. Instead, we record the facts as they are accepted by the court for the purpose of decision. The court's set of facts depends on the procedural posture of the case at the time of decision. Fixing this version of the facts will sometimes prove difficult for you. You will be unable to write this first part of your brief until you determine how the facts fit into the entire case or, in other words, until you have thought about the rest of your brief. This warning reveals that briefing should serve not only as a record of completed reading and study but also as a stimulus to further investigation and analysis.

Prior Proceedings:
Plaintiff, the village of Skokie, sued the defendants, the American Nazi party and ten individuals as officers and members, in order to keep the peace and prevent offensive conduct.

(3) This very important portion of your brief should be detailed, covering everything that happens from crossing the threshold of the trial court to the moment as of which the opinion before you speaks. Often impossible is knowing precisely what or why a court is deciding without knowing the procedural background in the case. Put a better way, "Now a case never reaches a court of review until it has first been through a tribunal of trial—else there would be nothing to review. But the cases, so-called, in your case-books are almost exclusively chosen from courts of review. To understand them, therefore, you must get at least some quick picture of what has gone on

before they got there." K. Llewellyn, The Bramble Bush 20 (7th printing 1981).

Brought in the Circuit Court of Cook County, this civil suit sought an injunction against certain activities by the defendants while demonstrating in the village.

(4) To initiate the lawsuit, the village filed a complaint on April 28, 1977, in a circuit court. This first court is a trial court. It is in this forum that pleadings are filed and evidence taken. Although the parties will have an opportunity to renew their legal arguments in courts of appeal, usually through both oral arguments and written briefs, the nature of the claims and defenses and the factual record are determined at this initial trial-court stage. Crucial, therefore, is that a party raise all potential grounds and present its facts fully at the trial level.

(5) One question you must ask in considering a case is whether it is within state or federal jurisdiction. Unlike state courts of general jurisdiction, federal courts are courts of limited jurisdiction. This means that federal courts normally have the power to hear only those kinds of cases that are within the constitutional grant of federal judicial power (see article III, section 2 of the United States Constitution, which appears in Appendix A of this book) and that have also been entrusted by congressional enactment to the federal courts. State courts generally have wider jurisdiction. They will often hear cases that federal courts cannot.

The plaintiff brought this case in a trial court of the state of Illinois. This meant that Illinois law would govern the lawsuit, although any applicable federal laws including the Constitution would be binding on the state.

(6) A second question you should address is whether the case is civil or criminal. The answer is not always obvious. The *Skokie* case is potentially confusing because a governmental body, the village, was a party. Although the government is always a party in criminal proceedings, not every case involving the government is a criminal one.

This case was civil in nature because the village did not function as a prosecutor, it alleged no specific criminal violation by the Nazis, and the village was not attempting to punish the Nazis. Instead, the plaintiff alleged a threatened civil wrong and sought civil relief from the court.

(7) A third question to consider is the particular type of relief that the plaintiff requests. Most forms of civil relief fall into two major categories: money damages and injunctions. Here, the village was not suing for money damages as compensation, but rather it requested the court to order the defendants not to do something. The village wanted to invoke this injunctive power to restrain the Nazis' march.

The courts' exercise of their power to grant injunctions is sometimes highly controversial. Some scholars argue that courts abuse this power, and infringe on the function and power of the legislature, by making policy decisions best left to representative bodies. Other scholars hail the courts' use of this power as the only practical way to safeguard constitutional rights. Indisputably, injunctive remedies have formed the core of the most far-reaching decisions of our day, such as mandatory school busing to achieve integration.

Plaintiff moved for a preliminary injunction, in connection with which the circuit court considered the plaintiff's complaint, a defendant's affidavit, and oral testimony.

(8) A motion is an application to the court for an order. A preliminary injunction is a provisional order intended to preserve the status quo until the trial court can decide on permanent relief. Before issuing a preliminary injunction, the trial court will conduct a hearing but not a full trial.

The circuit court preliminarily enjoined the defendants from demonstrating in Nazi uniform, displaying the swastika, and distributing or displaying materials that promoted racial or religious hatred.

(9) The circuit judge, sitting alone, issued the preliminary injunction on April 29, 1977. Any injunction is a powerful remedy, with the court ready to enforce its order with its drastic contempt powers. The defendants here obeyed.

Defendants appealed the circuit court's decision to the Appellate Court of Illinois.

(10) The defendants now had a right to appeal to the next highest court, here the First District, First Division, of the Appellate Court of Illinois. By taking an appeal the defendants became the so-called appellants, while the plaintiff became the so-called appellee.

On an appeal, the appellant asserts that the trial court, over the appellant's objection, committed some prejudicial error in rendering decision. The appellee defends that decision. Courts of appeal give great deference to the facts found by the trial court below. In questions of legal interpretation, however, courts of appeal feel free to reexamine the lower court's legal conclusions.

The appellate court modified the circuit court's injunction to prohibit only intentional display of the swastika.

(11) In reality, a good deal of procedural jockeying occurred at this stage of the case. Its outcome was the appellate court's decision, under an expedited schedule, on July 12, 1977. This court acts by decision of a three-judge panel.

Although the appellate court agreed with the circuit court that some limitation on the Nazi protest was appropriate, the appellate court obviously felt that the circuit court had gone too far in restricting the Nazis' activity. The opinion before you does not explicitly present the reasoning behind the appellate court's decision. To find out exactly why the appellate court permitted the Nazis to demonstrate in uniform, for instance, you would have to read the appellate court's opinion. Courts of appeal normally act by written decision and opinion, and most of these are printed. This one appears officially in volume 51 of the Illinois Appellate Reports, Third Series, at page 279. It also appears in volume 366 of the parallel, unofficial regional reporter called North Eastern Reporter, Second Series, at page 347. The citation is therefore 51 Ill.App.3d 279, 366 N.E.2d 347 (1977).

Defendants petitioned for leave to appeal the appellate court's decision to the Supreme Court of Illinois.

(12) Neither party had fully attained its stated goal. Either party, or both, could have sought further review. The defendants were still sufficiently unhappy with the swastika ban to desire an appeal to the Supreme Court of Illinois.

The Illinois Supreme Court is mainly a court of discretionary review. No party normally has an automatic right to this second tier of review. Like the United States Supreme Court when it considers petitions for certiorari, the Illinois Supreme Court decides which cases it wants to hear. It chooses in accordance with Illinois Supreme Court Rule 315(a): "The following, while neither controlling nor fully measuring the court's discretion, indicate the character of reasons which will be considered: the general importance of the question presented; the existence of a conflict between the decision sought to be reviewed and a decision of the Supreme Court, or of another division of the Appellate Court; the need for the exercise of the Supreme Court's supervisory authority; and the final or interlocutory character of the judgment sought to be reviewed."

The supreme court granted leave to appeal.

(13) The Supreme Court of Illinois is the highest court of the state. It comprises seven justices, who sit together on each case.

Why do you think the Illinois Supreme Court agreed to hear this case?

Issue:
Did the court order enjoining the Nazis from displaying the swastika during their planned demonstration in Skokie violate their First Amendment rights?

(14) In this part of the brief, you should list the precise question or questions the court is to decide. In our case, the court focused the question explicitly. Often, however, the issues are far from obvious, and this entry in the brief may require much digging on your part.

Decision:
Yes.

(15) Here you should give the decision on each one of the prior-listed issues.

The supreme court therefore reversed on this point.

Also indicate the disposition of the case. Although the supreme court agreed with most of the appellate court's decision, it rejected the remaining ban on the swastika. Thus, the supreme court affirmed the appellate court's decision in part and reversed in part.

The supreme court's opinion was by the whole court, or per curiam, which means that all the justices except the one dissenter agreed but no individual justice was credited with authoring the opinion. Justice Clark did not write an opinion, so his reasons for dissenting are unknown.

(16) The plaintiff chose not to pursue this particular lawsuit any further, either in the United States Supreme Court or in the lower courts. However, the Skokie controversy had not ended.

On May 2, 1977, the village had enacted a series of three ordinances intended to prohibit the Nazis' planned demonstration and specifying *criminal* penalties for violation. In other words, the village had begun to invoke a different instrumentality of the law to help in achieving its ends. But now the Nazis sued civilly to enjoin enforcement of the ordinances, suing this time in federal court and alleging unconstitutional infringement of their civil rights. The United States District Court for the Northern District of Illinois struck down the ordinances, the United States Court of Appeals for the Seventh Circuit affirmed, and the Supreme Court of the United States eventually declined to review the case. Smith v. Collin, 439 U.S. 916, 99 S.Ct. 291 (1978).

Ironically, with all legal obstacles to a Skokie demonstration removed, Collin canceled that demonstration three days before its rescheduled date of June 25, 1978. Relying on the Skokie rulings, the Nazis had obtained a federal court order overcoming Chicago's attempt to block Nazi demonstrations. "Collin explained that the aim of the Nazis' Skokie efforts had been 'pure agitation to restore our right to free speech.' He stated that 'he had used the threat of the Skokie march to win the right to rally in [Chicago].' No serious violence occurred when about 25 Nazis held a rally in a Chicago park on July 9, 1978." G. Gunther, Constitutional Law 1240 (11th ed. 1985). The resulting mob scene was, however, the occasion for seriously offensive conduct. See S. Stamberg, Every Night at Five 32–38 (1982) (transcript of National Public Radio's report on the Nazi rally).

Reasons:
The court began with the premise that the First Amendment, which applies to the states through the Fourteenth Amendment, protects *speech* from most governmental *re-*

(17) In this part of your brief, you should state the gist of the court's reasoning. Sometimes a great deal of work is necessary to perceive the court's reasoning, especially because some opinions are expressed in the form of free association. Moreover, even though clearly reasoned and crisply written, an opinion may not be easy to follow if it assumes a basic knowledge that the reader does not possess. This

strictions. This freedom of speech extends to the expression of even repugnant messages; and, according to prior case law, it also extends to so-called symbolic speech, which is nonverbal conduct intended to be communicative. The forms of possible governmental restrictions are (1) prior restraints, or censorship, and (2) subsequent sanctions, which could be civil or criminal in nature. Prior restraints are particularly suspect, and so are treated as presumptively unconstitutional. This means that the government bears the considerable burden of justifying its action, as by showing that a content-based prior restraint falls clearly within one of the limiting exceptions to the First Amendment, such as obscenity.

Accordingly, in this case the village tried to justify a prior restraint on certain speech by getting within the previously established exception for fighting words or perhaps an exception for a hostile audience.

First, the court ruled that the swastika ban did not fit within the fighting-words exception (1) because prior cases had narrowly defined fighting words, and indeed had seemingly used this exception to permit only subsequent sanctions, and (2) because an analysis of the benefits and harms of both the speech and its restriction argued against an exception to the First

particular case is not a model of clarity, and it requires careful attention to First Amendment principles and case law with which you may be somewhat unfamiliar.

When you trace the court's reasoning, another difficult task is separating, as well as possible, that reasoning directly involved in and necessary to the decision (holding) from asides unnecessary to the decision (dicta).

(18) In this course, the "Reasons" part of your brief represents the key component of your study. Unlike the law student, who may be misled by a compulsion to memorize the "black letter" or bottom-line rule (e.g., in our case, the swastika may be displayed), you should feel freer to concentrate on the process of legal reasoning. The justifications of a court's decision are even more crucial to understanding the role of law in our society than is the actual legal rule itself.

We do not intend this sample brief to be complete or definitive. Although it contains more background than you would ordinarily include, our otherwise short entry under "Reasons" conveys merely one way of analyzing and distilling the holding. Try your hand at composing your own version of the court's reasoning.

(19) In doing so, you should attempt to identify the types of reasons that the court finds persuasive.

This might lead you to consider the fundamental question of *who* really shapes the law. If, for example, you believe that judges act on their own behalf or for a socioeconomic elite, you may dismiss most legal reasoning as mere rhetoric. If you take a more sophisticated view of the tensions among the competitors for this role, you will give careful attention to legal reasoning for the light it sheds on who wields ultimate power.

Analysis of legal reasoning should lead you to consider the critical questions of *why* we have law. Why is law necessary? Why do we have the law that we have? Here the judges' different types of reasons should be directly instructive.

To analyze the reasoning of a judicial opinion, it is useful to identify four basic, albeit overlapping, types of reasons: authoritative, institutional, goal, and rightness reasons. These kinds of reasons have counterparts in daily-life decision making, but considering them systematically in a legal context is desirable here.

(20) Authoritative reasons relate to a court's obligation to follow any applicable law previously established by a competent lawmaker. For instance, a

Amendment here, especially where the audience was not truly captive. Second, the court ruled that the ban did not fit within any exception for speech that provokes a hostile audience to unlawful action, with the court using those same two supporting arguments to avoid this supposed exception that looks more to the public risks deriving from the subjective reaction of the particular crowd. Third, the court refused to recognize any First Amendment exception for offensive speech or any other exception arguably applicable to this case's facts.

Hence, the court struck down the swastika ban.

court might deny an injunction because of some provision in the federal Constitution forbidding judicial action. Other such formal reasons include those based on applicable and valid federal statutes, state constitutions, and state statutes.

An important example of an authoritative reason lies in a court's reference to precedent. The Anglo-American legal system has traditionally relied heavily on judge-made law, as opposed to statutory codes like the modern Internal Revenue Code. An important corollary of that system is the doctrine of *stare decisis.* This doctrine dictates that a court normally must follow relevant holdings of its own prior decisions and those of higher courts. *Stare decisis* tends to restrain the judges' exercise of power and also to enhance the efficiency and fairness of the legal system.

What role did precedent play in our *Skokie* case? How did the court distinguish the *Chaplinsky* case, which upheld the criminal conviction of a street proselytizer who had called the city marshal "a damned Fascist" and said other fighting words to him? Were authoritative reasons dispositive, or did other kinds of reasons influence this court's decision?

(21) Institutional reasons relate to a court's concerns with observing the bounds on its proper governmental role and following proper processes. For instance, a court might deny an injunction because of the impracticality of supervising and enforcing it. Other institutional reasons include those based on the proper division of legal labor among institutions, the efficient operation of the judicial machinery, values inherent in fair processes, and limitations of law's efficacy.

An actual example of an institutional reason appears in the *Skokie* court's reference to the difficulties of line drawing that issuing an injunction would impose. That is, distinguishing impermissible from permissible speech in future cases would be impractical; also, such distinctions would offend a generally accepted notion that courts should draw only principled and not arbitrary distinctions.

From where does the *Skokie* court derive this institutional reason? Does the court treat the quoted *Cohen* case as formally binding precedent on this point, or does the court here look to *Cohen* because of the persuasiveness of the substantive reasons underlying that earlier decision? How persuasive are they?

(22) The third type of reason is the goal reason. Such a reason derives its justificatory force from the prediction that the decision it supports will have future effects that serve a good social goal. For

example, a court might deny an injunction because enjoining the defendant would impede the free flow of information and hence debilitate democracy. Other goal reasons include those based on social equality, general safety, public health, and family harmony.

Goal reasons are often difficult to work with. They are sometimes difficult to construct, exposing judges to various errors such as mispredicting effects or misjudging the goodness of a social goal. There is sometimes more than one applicable goal reason, and they may point toward opposite decisions. The goal reasons sometimes conflict with apparent fairness in the present case, as where a fear that "hard cases make bad law" prompts a court to render a harsh decision in order to create a precedent that will more justly handle the stream of future cases.

What did you think of the *Skokie* court's use of goal reasons? Were there competing goal reasons, mentioned or unmentioned? What other kinds of reasons should have influenced the court's decision?

(23) Rightness reasons, the last type of reason, derive their force from the decision's accord with sociomoral norms of rightness as applied to the parties' past actions. For example, a court might deny an injunction because the plaintiff was more to blame for creating the present situation than was the defendant. Other such reasons include those based on imposing punitive desert, requiring compensation for lack of due care, and protecting justified reliance.

Of the four types of reasons, rightness reasons may seem the most intuitively obvious. However, in similar ways these, too, prove complex and so require careful analysis. See generally Summers, Two Types of Substantive Reasons: The Core of a Theory of Common-Law Justification, 63 Cornell L.Rev. 707 (1978).

Did the *Skokie* court invoke any rightness reasons to support its decision? Did the court seem happy with its decision, so that it was simply packaging a result that it wanted? What rightness reasons can you construct to support the denial or grant of a swastika ban?

(24) Ultimately, by the process of legal reasoning, the court must combine its reasons into a decision, yielding what will henceforth be the law.

The court here held that the swastika ban came within no exception to the First Amendment and so had to fall. But is this technical pigeonholing the ideal approach for First Amendment cases, or should courts more freely balance benefits, harms, and other equities in the particular case to decide whether to restrict speech?

More specifically, the court held inapplicable the fighting-words exception. When the court has finished narrowing that exception, does its continued existence make any sense? Indeed, does it still exist—if *Skokie* does not come within that exception, what case would?

Remarks:

(25) Here you should jot down your comments on and criticisms of the case. You might make a preliminary attempt before class, but this should be supplemented during and after class.

Emphasize the validity of the reasoning. What kind of job do you think the court did overall? Do you find its reasoning compelling? This is, after all, a tough case. As Justice Blackmun said in dissenting from the United States Supreme Court's denial of certiorari in *Smith* v. *Collin*: "On the one hand, we have precious First Amendment rights vigorously asserted and an obvious concern that, if those asserted rights are not recognized, the precedent of a 'hard' case might offer a justification for repression in the future. On the other hand, we are presented with evidence of a potentially explosive and dangerous situation, enflamed by unforgettable recollections of traumatic experiences in the second world conflict. . . . I also feel that the present case affords the Court an opportunity to consider whether, in the context of the facts that this record appears to present, there is no limit whatsoever to the exercise of free speech. There indeed may be no such limit, but when citizens assert, not casually but with deep conviction, that the proposed demonstration is scheduled at a place and in a manner that is taunting and overwhelmingly offensive to the citizens of that place, that assertion, uncomfortable though it may be for judges, deserves to be examined." See also Rabinowitz, Nazis in Skokie: Fighting Words or Heckler's Veto?, 28 DePaul L.Rev. 259 (1979).

Try to think beyond the confines of the case, too. For example, what would you think of a city ordinance that outlaws, as a form of sex discrimination, the dissemination of "pornography," which it defines not in narrow terms of obscenity but as "the graphic sexually explicit subordination of women, whether in pictures or in words"? Compare American Booksellers Association v. Hudnut, 598 F.Supp. 1316 (S.D.Ind. 1984), aff'd, 771 F.2d 323 (7th Cir.1985) (striking down such an Indianapolis ordinance), with New York v. Ferber, 458 U.S. 747, 102 S.Ct. 3348 (1982) (upholding legislation outlawing dissemination of child pornography). See also Note, Anti-Pornography Laws and First Amendment Values, 98 Harv.L. Rev. 460 (1984).

Section Three. General Education and the Law

General education is to be distinguished from special education. General education is broad, humanistic, and liberal. Special education is technical, preparing the student for a specific vocation or profession.

In American law schools, law is studied as a specialist's subject—as preparation for a professional pursuit. But from this it does not follow that law cannot also be a subject for general education. A fallacious argument is that any subject studied vocationally is automatically disqualified as a subject for general education. As Alfred North Whitehead pointed out: "Again, there is not one course of study which merely gives general culture, and another which gives special knowledge. The subjects pursued for the sake of a general education are special subjects specially studied . . . . " A. Whitehead, The Aims of Education and Other Essays 18 (1929).

Nevertheless, not all subjects that specialists pursue necessarily qualify for a place in general education. To qualify, they must have a core of humanistic and liberal content.

Does law have a core of humanistic and liberal content?

KALVEN & ZEISEL, LAW, SCIENCE, AND HUMANISM

in The Humanist Frame 329, 331–33 (J. Huxley ed. 1961).*

Humanism appears to involve at least two related notions: respect for human values, notably those of dignity and individuality, and a concern with the aesthetic side of life, as reflected in art and literature. In both these senses the law is deeply humanistic. It is not an accident that the most revered American legal heroes such as Justice Holmes or Judge Learned Hand have been cultural heroes also. They have not only been distinguished as judges but have style as men and in particular as writers. If one wanted to locate the best image law has of itself he might well study the values implicit in the law's extraordinary admiration for Justice Holmes. For the American lawyer he is the beau ideal, and the lawyer quotes his aphorisms as the literate layman quotes Hamlet. This fascination with wit, style, felicity of phrase suggests that for those who have made it their lifework, law has a strong aesthetic appeal, and is at its best a kind of literature.

Further, law deals with the full range of human problems which with all their variety and colour have been the domain of the novel and the drama. As Justice Holmes once put it: "Law is as good a window as any through which to look at life." . . .

Law is also sensitive to history, because in one way law is history. The English and American system of precedent requires the careful preservation and carrying forward of the history of prior adjudications. And although the great multiplicity of modern precedents has blunted the

---

practice, it is routine for the lawyer, judge, or law student to cite a case which may date from the early eighteenth century.

Finally and foremost law is always engaged in translating the values of society into legal norms. All laws involve the resolution of issues of policy, and under the American system of a written constitution and judicial review, adjudication of constitutional issues brings the larger issues of the day into dramatic focus. The law is thus a remarkable repository of dramatic debate over values. At its best, this debate will be as good as anything written on these themes.

————

H. BERMAN, ON THE TEACHING OF LAW IN THE LIBERAL ARTS CURRICULUM
9–12 (1956).*

Is law a proper subject of study in the liberal arts curriculum?

An imposing array of distinguished men—most of them, to be sure, lawyers—have said that it is not only proper but very important that "every gentleman and scholar," as Blackstone put it in 1758, should have "a competent knowledge of the laws of that society in which we live." Such a knowledge, Blackstone added, is "an highly useful, I had said almost essential, part of liberal and polite education."

The famous Commentaries on the Laws of England comprise Blackstone's lectures given at Oxford University not primarily to prospective lawyers but to students of the liberal arts. Their influence upon the thinking of generations of Englishmen and Americans, laymen as well as lawyers, is well known. Edmund Burke referred to their impact on the American colonists in a well-known passage in his Speech on Conciliation with America.

> "In no country perhaps in the world," Burke said, "is the law so general a study. The profession itself is numerous and powerful, and in most provinces it takes the lead. The greater number of the deputies sent to the congress were lawyers. But all who read, and most do read, endeavour to obtain some smattering in that science. I have been told by an eminent bookseller, that in no branch of his business, after tracts of popular devotion, were so many books as those on the law exported to the plantations. The colonists have now fallen into the way of printing them for their own use. I hear that they have sold nearly as many of 'Blackstone's Commentaries' in America as in England . . . . "

The colonists' zeal for the study of law, Burke added, gave them a capacity to "snuff the approach of tyranny in every tainted breeze."

. . .

Among the many reasons given in more recent years for introducing courses in law in the liberal arts curriculum are—

1. that an understanding of the nature of the legal order and of legal reasoning is of significant cultural value in itself;

* Copyright © 1956 by The Foundation Press, Inc. Reprinted by permission.

2. that an understanding of law is essential to an understanding of the political values of American society and of the international community; and that it illuminates not only political science but also other disciplines such as philosophy, history, economics, sociology, and anthropology;

3. that the diffusion of an understanding of law to wider segments of the scholarly community will result in a greater illumination of legal science, as scholars of other disciplines come to give more attention to legal data;

4. that the study of law is an important means of developing the student's sense of justice and his capacity for responsible judgment;

5. that the study of law is an important foundation in the training of students for the responsibilities of social, economic and political activity.

Assuming there is some merit in these reasons for teaching law as part of general education, how are we to explain the fact that such teaching is more or less a rarity in this country, and that legal education is for the most part confined to the professional law schools?　.　.　.

Unquestionably the professional law school as it has developed in the United States has been an extremely important instrument for improving not only the character of the Bar but also the quality of the legal system itself.　Yet a price has been paid for this gain, in that by and large general education in law for non-lawyers has been sacrificed.　With the emergence of professional graduate schools of law it seems simply to have been taken for granted by most people that the nature of our legal system is a subject beyond the ken or the interest of the undergraduate and the non-specialist.

To the historical factors which have removed law from the undergraduate curriculum there must be added the factor of professional academic mistrust which has developed between legal scholars and social scientists.

APPEL, LAW AS A SOCIAL SCIENCE IN THE UNDERGRADUATE CURRICULUM

10 J.Legal Educ. 485, 485–87 (1958).*

To be sure, law is, at present, the partial or total subject matter of many college courses.　Some of these can only with difficulty be termed general liberal arts courses, but rather are technical, and primarily devised as necessary adjuncts to a specialized vocational program.　Examples, which might be multiplied, are courses in law of the press (and other communications media) for journalism students, and law of business organization and finance for students of accounting or business administration.　Other law courses on the college level are less obviously vocational in purpose and content, and these include labor law, jurisprudence, and constitutional law—commonly found in the undergraduate (or graduate) departments of economics, philosophy, and history or political science. Although this latter group might properly be considered part of a liberal arts curriculum, the courses are nevertheless, specialized in approach, and their value is considered to lie in the light they may shed on a particular field of study.

A third group are those courses, few in number, which treat law as an independent social science, deserving of its own place in liberal education. . . .

. . . Conceding that a man cannot aspire to be his own lawyer, he can, at the least, learn when to seek professional help. This line of reasoning is the justification for the first type of law course in the undergraduate curriculum, the vocationally-oriented course in law of business, engineering, the press, or agriculture. Good clients need to be developed—clients well enough informed to see a lawyer before they are in trouble, and also to have a minimum amount of both confidence in the conduct of their own affairs and ability to avoid dangerous situations. But for the student in a nonvocational area of liberal arts study, such courses are both too much and too little. They all omit some basic areas, and they all contain overly-intensive coverage of others from the standpoint of the person outside the vocation.

There is, however, practically no area of study in a present-day liberal arts curriculum that does not touch upon, and is not touched by, law. Understanding of the social sciences, particularly, cannot possibly be divorced from an understanding of legal systems, past and present, American and foreign. The students of history, economics, political science, psychology, sociology, and allied fields must consider the legal order, and particularly legal institutions, and often the nature of legal analysis, in order to see their special fields in the perspective essential to a true liberal education.

For this reason, law courses which are not vocationally-constructed, but which are, nevertheless, oriented to the content of a specific field of social science, have a proper place in the liberal arts college. Furthermore, such courses are partially, because of the very nature of legal study, interdisciplinary in character. For the student of political science who studies constitutional law is enabled (or perhaps forced) to consider the historical, economic, social, and philosophical aspects of his own discipline—and the same holds true for a student in any department of the liberal arts curriculum. But in such a course, often taught by members of that one department, the broad view may be more theoretical than actual. Perhaps the student would derive a greater benefit from a law course not oriented to a particular social science. Perhaps each student might contribute something of his own to those outside his field of specialization, and, in turn, benefit from the ideas of other disciplines.

At this point, it is reasonable to suggest that the truly educated man, whatever his intended vocation or area of study at the college level, must have a basic conception of legal institutions and reasoning—to suggest, in other words, that law is an essential part of a liberal education. But this statement is too broad to be of much value. It is not one reason, but several, all justifying, in different ways, the inclusion in the liberal arts curriculum of a basic course or courses in law

oriented neither to vocational advantage nor to the scope of an individual liberal arts discipline.

————

GIAMATTI, THE LAW AND THE PUBLIC

97 F.R.D. 545, 608–11 (1982), reprinted in 38 Rec.A.B.City N.Y. 34,
35–40 (1983).*

The question is: Why do the American people know and understand so
little about the law?

Consider the circumstances of the question. We Americans care
deeply about the law. The Constitution has a sacred place in our culture
and its framers constitute a shadowy pantheon, the Olympians at the
beginning. From the perception of a revealed text whose interpretation is
entrusted to the least understood and most mystified branch of our
government comes the American reverence for the law, a reverence
bordering on obsession, revealed in innumerable ways.

Some of these ways paradoxically entail criticisms or what we may call
negative tributes. The courts are too slow or too soft; the Constitution is
incomplete: we need an amendment to produce fiscal balance or equal
rights for women or a proper regard for the sacredness of life. Other
ways are simply part of daily speech. We hear every day on all sides:
someone's "rights" are assured or abridged; the law is too weak or too
strong; there are too many lawyers; they are too powerful; they are
clearly indispensable. (Americans go to lawyers as in other times and
places humankind went to shamans or wise elders, constantly and cautiously.) The fact remains that the lay public is endlessly concerned with
the law. From the level of that most American of catch phrases—"there
oughta be a law"—to the insight that, in legal processes consented to by a
free people, a people may guard its several freedoms and thus insure a
free Republic in diversity, Americans chafe under and kick against, but
finally worship every day at, the law.

Whatever the law means. And that is how my question arises. Why
the ignorance? The beginnings of an answer to that question may reside
in the fact that the institutions and people best fitted to tell them do not
tell them. By institutions and people, I mean us. I believe a large share
of the responsibility for educating the public in the nature and purposes of
the law resides with your [legal] profession and with the press. I think,
however, the first responsibility to educate about the law obviously lies
with the centers of education.

It is remarkable how small a role the law plays in our undergraduate
curricula or in our view of a liberal education. We have various theories
and practices regarding general education, areas of concentration, required courses, "core" curricula and so forth to insure breadth and depth
in undergraduate education. We construct a general grounding in values
and skills with specific foci, all meant to instill a love of learning for its
own sake and intended to fashion the intensely practical capacities to

think clearly and to express oneself cogently. But learning about the law is almost completely absent.

The study of the law is a complex, technical and professional discipline, not appropriate to a liberal education for undergraduates, one is told. I agree. But the study of economics or mathematics or Greek in college is also complex and must be pursued in postgraduate school in order to become professionally adept. We teach mathematics, economics and Greek, yet we do not believe that the law has a place, and I do not understand such an omission. . . .

In our success in encouraging the necessary specialities we have forgotten two things: the lesser being, that specialists can only communicate with other specialists; the greater being, that if no one communicates the principles and purposes upon which the specialists depend to the larger society, the larger society will continue to be dependent but, without any understanding of broad principles or purposes, will only grow resentful and suspicious. It will increasingly come to distrust the specialist. What is far worse, the lay public will deepen in ignorance and indifference regarding the essential goals of the law about which no one has deigned to speak publicly and clearly. The cynicism about lawyers, the suspicions about courts, the lust to supplant law with decree that one hears on all sides worries me a great deal and it should worry you. While one may, as I have, argue that such reactions are often negative tributes by the American people to law and legal process, the force of the reactions begins to pass into a sentiment corrosive of those values and processes you are sworn to uphold and I, like you, cherish.

I look, therefore, to the academy, as part of a liberal education, to educate the society of the future about the law. Were such courses to be created, they should not be for those who plan to devote themselves professionally to the law. They should be for the future lay people without which your profession cannot exist—not in the easy sense that the layman is the client pool but in the larger sense that uninformed consent is no consent at all but simply the subscription to myth. And that is no basis for a just society.

After the academy, I look to your profession to educate the public. You must at least be perceived to be thinking about the public's need better to understand the principles and purposes you uphold. Otherwise you are laboring in a vacuum. At the present, the lay American of almost any social or economic condition knows the names of three or four gorgeously notorious lawyers; has a negative view of "palimony" and the insanity defense; thinks well of Associate Justice O'Connor; cannot name more than two other Justices and believes the First and Fifth Amendments do most of the work—for good or ill. The "law" in everyday thought means the police and the court system—both viewed as either overreacting or overworked. Books by members of the bar about famous cases they have won do not bring the full light of the profession to bear on the stresses, responsibilities, intricacies, decisions or deep pleasures that practice engages. Between Perry Mason, "The Paper Chase," and idealized public defenders the entertainment industry continues to do what it always does, sell stereotypes created by itself to advertisers. The American people's instinctive respect for the law is there but it remains uninformed. And untutored instincts do not grow unaided into wisdom or rational awareness. It is not enough to be seen "doing" the law if no one really knows what you are doing or why you do it or what, in the long term, it is for.

Your profession cannot ignore the need to educate the public. You hold the society's processes and accumulated wisdom about our civic and secular means to resolution (if not satisfaction or justice) in public trust. And your trust is not fulfilled if the public is ignorant of their obligations. Lawyers and judges on their lay, community rounds, teachers of law in their popular writings, the associations of the Bar, the various members of the profession in public forums of many kinds, all must do an immense amount, now not done and necessary to do, to foster an understanding of the principles and purposes of the law. Even more to the point, you must educate us in the limits of the law. This last is especially important.

Someone is obliged to convince the American people that if they ask everything of legal process, it will not be able to do much of anything; someone is obliged to say, clearly and persuasively, that if the means for the resolution of conflict is asked only to legitimize every form of contention, paralysis will result; someone is obliged to say what the law *cannot do*; and what lawyers are not good for; what courts ought neither to consider nor to control. It is the obligation of your profession to say these things because you alone have standing sufficient to increase the public's understanding.

Finally, some among you ought to be seized of the need to shape self-criticism of a responsible and knowledgeable sort. Otherwise the position of privileged trusteeship you now rightly enjoy will be increasingly viewed as an interest only in private prerogatives unaware of public obligations. You must believe it is worth educating the public or your profession will lose the respect without which neither the profession nor the law can function. I ask you not to be publicists in some narrow sense. I ask you to clarify and to communicate the broad limits of your profession in the interest of furthering the effectiveness of your essential efforts.

———

Comments and Questions

1. Professors Kalven and Zeisel identify two respects in which law can qualify curricularly as a humanistic discipline. Consider, too, this argument: "We use law as an instrument to serve human purposes. Legal resources are means to social ends. The faith that we can affect our destiny is one of the most enduring tenets of humanism. From this it follows that law is fundamentally humanistic in character." Do you accept that argument?

2. Can you add to Professor Berman's catalog of reasons for the generalist's studying law? To his reasons that law is usually not so studied nowadays?

3. Educators commonly view as general subjects not only the humanities but also the social sciences. Do you agree with Professor Appel that a course in law, properly conceived and taught, could qualify as the study of a kind of social science?

4. President Giamatti scores the American ignorance of the nature and functions of law. But he especially censures ignorance of the limits of law. Why?

To be more specific for purposes of illustration, of what importance is a study of the limits of law to a student of policy, specializing perhaps in economics or political science? Isolating policies for study, without regard to the methods of their implementation, is not possible. In social ordering, the means through which we pursue ends define the very character of our realization of those ends. Limits on the means impose limits on the ends. Now, means to social ends—that comprises the law, does it not?

Section Four.   Pedagogic Notes

A.   Themes This Book Seeks to Develop

This book embraces the purposes of general education. Thus, it seeks to convey a general understanding of law in society. Its themes are broad. Some of its main themes may usefully be listed as follows:

1.   Law is essentially instrumental in character, serving as one of the tools that any organized society may use to deal with social problems.

2.   The available resources of law break down into five basic instruments, or modes of legal activity by the government, with possible variants of each and possible combinations of several: the grievance-remedial instrument, the penal-corrective instrument, the administrative-regulatory instrument, the public-benefit instrument, and the private-arrangement instrument. For some social problems, only one of these means may prove appropriate, but for others more than one or all five may contribute, each in its own way, toward solving the problem.

3.   Societies typically apply legal resources to a wide variety of important end uses that range from ensuring general safety to redressing social inequality, although legal resources are more effective at some tasks than at others. Even where law is useful, certain of its instruments that have been applied to the particular social end may be inappropriate for the task, and certain others may not have been applied in their most effective form.

4.   This way of looking at the nature of law naturally highlights the functions of law, but one must not overlook the limits of law. Law is not omnicompetent.

B.   Methods This Book Seeks to Employ

This book proceeds on the theory that showing is better than merely telling. Therefore, it includes many primary legal source materials.

Moreover, this book reflects the belief that insight and perspective most effectively develop from close examination of particulars, rather than from reading generalized text. Thus, we intend the primary sources not only to show by way of illustration but also to serve as vehicles for developing general insights and perspectives. For example, the materials on negligence law in Chapter 1 aim not at providing instruction on negligence law as such, but instead serve to teach about process values, improving the law, limitations of law, and more. Students must have an inside view of something before they can think profitably about it.

Surprisingly, this approach does not require much technical orientation. We warn students that if they find themselves preoccupied with unexplained legal technicality in any of the pages ahead, they may not be approaching the materials in the proper spirit. We also observe that if in the years to come these materials no longer fully reflect the current state of the law, their utility should remain largely intact because their mission does not involve conveying the precise state of the law at any given time. The shared object of student and teacher is general insight and perspective.

What this approach does require is careful, critical, and active thinking about the subject matter. Students cannot stand ready as mere passive recipients of information but instead must read and reread with word-by-word care and must analyze with critical faculties in high gear. Students should be constantly asking themselves significant questions and trying to answer them, always thinking beyond the confines of the instant case or illustration, and continually summarizing and synthesizing the materials. Active students engage not in the process of receiving information but instead in the process of creating understanding. The materials reflect this approach in their dialectic emphasis, the juxtaposition of conflicting views, the court cases full of argument, and the authors' frequent questions.

In sum, hard work lies ahead. Although the sole aspiration is the big picture, students will not get there by passive and uncritical skimming. Such skimming may work to give the gist in some courses. But since a casebook is no ordinary textbook, skimming a casebook will yield nothing more than a collection of meaningless fact patterns from unrelated cases and perhaps a few legal rules that by themselves have little or no importance. Instead, under the so-called case method, only a long series of painstaking microscopic views will reveal the big picture. The work is hard but exciting.

We close this introduction with two pedagogic notes that are more specific.

First, this book is highly structured. The parts, chapters, and sections fall into a strict pattern. They need not be read in the order they appear, but an awareness of the pattern will remove much of the confusion from whatever route is taken through the book. Readers should examine the whole book at the outset to perceive that pattern.

Second, numerous bibliographies appear throughout this book. They are meant to be suggestive, not comprehensive. They should help students in pursuing special projects and teachers in preparing classes. In particular, the bibliographies should help lead the way into the rich literature of legal periodicals. Typically, the bibliographies do not repeat all the references that appear in the text.

Section Five.   Bibliography

1. *General Education and the Law.* H. Berman, On the Teaching of Law in the Liberal Arts Curriculum (1956); Law and the Liberal Arts (A. Broderick ed. 1967); Barkman, Law-in-the-Liberal Arts: An Appraisal and a Proposal for Experimentation, 19 J.Legal Educ. 1 (1966); Beaney, Teaching of Law Courses in the Liberal Arts College: A View from the College, 13 J.Legal Educ. 55 (1960); Boorstin, The Humane Study of Law, 57 Yale L.J. 960 (1948); Eliot, Law in the Liberal Arts Curriculum, 9 J.Legal Educ. 1 (1956); Freund, The Law and the Schools, 36 Harv.Educ.Rev. 470 (1966); Freund, Law and the Universities, 1953

Wash.U.L.Q. 367; Lader, Experiments in Undergraduate Legal Education: The Teaching of Law in the Liberal Arts Curriculum of American Colleges and Universities, 25 J.Legal Educ. 125 (1973); Symposium: Humanistic Perspectives on Legal Education, 32 J.Legal Educ. 1 (1982); Symposium: Undergraduate Legal Education, 28 J.Legal Educ. 1 (1976).

2. *Introduction to Law.* K. Hegland, Introduction to the Study and Practice of Law in a Nutshell (1983); E. Levi, An Introduction to Legal Reasoning (1948); K. Llewellyn, The Bramble Bush (1960); S. Mermin, Law and the Legal System (2d ed. 1982); B. Schwartz, The Law in America: A History (1974).

Part One

THE MEANS OF LAW

Chapter One

LAW AS A GRIEVANCE–REMEDIAL INSTRUMENT
*Recognition of Claims to Enforceable Remedies for Grievances,
Actual or Threatened*

Chapter Two

LAW AS A PENAL–CORRECTIVE INSTRUMENT
Prohibition, Prosecution, and Punishment of Bad Conduct

Chapter Three

LAW AS AN ADMINISTRATIVE–REGULATORY INSTRUMENT
Generally Prospective Regulation of Wholesome Activity, Business and Otherwise

Chapter Four

LAW AS AN INSTRUMENT FOR ORGANIZING CONFERRAL OF PUBLIC BENEFITS
*Governmental Conferral of Substantive Benefits Such as Education,
Welfare, and Highways*

Chapter Five

LAW AS AN INSTRUMENT FOR FACILITATING PRIVATE ARRANGEMENTS
Facilitation of Voluntary Arrangements, Economic and Otherwise

Each of the foregoing chapters breaks down into ten sections: (1) introduction, (2) techniques, (3) lawmakers, (4) structures and processes for applying law and techniques, (5) coercive power, (6) roles of private citizens and their lawyers, (7) process values, (8) improvements, (9) limitations, and (10) bibliography.

PREFATORY NOTE TO PART ONE

What is the nature of law? In an account of the nature of a complex form of social organization such as law, it is possible and fruitful to consider a variety of questions, including: (1) What are its basic structural features? (2) What are its characteristic minimal substantive contents? (3) What are its characteristic normative dimensions? (4) What are its relationships to cognate phenomena, for example, morality, politics, and other social forces? (5) What are the range and limits of its methodology? (See especially Part 1.) (6) What are the basic social functions on which this methodology is commonly put to work? (See especially Part 2.)

In this book, all the foregoing questions are considered. Obviously, considering each in depth is not possible. Of all these questions, the one selected for most intensive treatment concerns law's methodology or, as Roscoe Pound might have called it, the "technique element" in law. Thus, the emphasis here is on an instrumentalist conception of law. From this it should not be thought, however, that law has value only insofar as it serves as means to substantive social ends. As Section 7 of each of Chapters 1–5 demonstrates, law may have value, too, insofar as it incorporates and protects basic "process values."

As that last observation implies, both of the major parts of the book subdivide into chapters. Part 1 comprises Chapters 1–5. These chapters respectively treat the five basic legal instruments by study of how law acts through remedying grievances, imposing punishment, regulating administratively, conferring public benefits, and facilitating private arrangements. Together these five chapters offer an overview of the means at law's disposal.

Each of these chapters contains ten sections that flesh out the particular instrument in a logical and comprehensive manner. For example, using negligence law to illustrate the grievance-remedial instrument, Chapter 1 introduces the subject, examines the technique of money damages for negligently inflicted injuries, explores the roles of courts and legislatures in making negligence law, demonstrates the application of that technique and law by tracing an actual case from accident to appeal, and so on through the list of ten sections. We repeat those same ten sections in each of the first five chapters to encourage comparative analysis of those partially differentiating characteristics. By comparing, say, the instruments' reliance on coercive power or the varying roles of private citizens and their lawyers, and by observing that as to each such characteristic some instruments conform and others differ, students can acquire a deeper understanding of the five distinct instruments.

After Part 1 so treats the instruments of law, Part 2 applies them to a few selected social tasks. Sketching the law in action there elaborates what the law can do and cannot do. Thus, although we divide the book into Part 1 on the means of law and Part 2 on the ends of law, our hope throughout is to convey a sense of the nature, functions, and limits of law.

GENERAL BIBLIOGRAPHY FOR PART ONE

1. *Methods of Characterizing the Nature of Law.* H.L.A. Hart, The Concept of Law ch. 1 (1961); R. Pound, Jurisprudence (1959); Wollheim, The Nature of Law, 2 Pol.Stud. 128 (1954).

2. *An Instrumentalist Conception of Law.* K. Popper, The Open Society and Its Enemies (5th ed. 1966); R. Pound, Social Control Through Law (1942); R. Summers, Instrumentalism and American Legal Theory (1982); R. von Jhering, Law as a Means to an End (1913); Hocking, Conference on the Relation of Law to Social Ends, 10 J.Phil. 512 (1913); Kelsen, The Law as a Specific Social Technique, 9 U.Chi.L.Rev. 75 (1941); Radin, The Permanent Problems of the Law, 15 Cornell L.Q. 1 (1929); Rooney, Law as an Instrument of Social Policy—The Brandeis Theory, 22 St. John's L.Rev. 1 (1947); Summers, The Technique Element in Law, 59 Calif.L.Rev. 733 (1971).

3. *Variety of Legal Instrumentalities (Resources).* H. Berman & W. Griener, The Nature and Functions of Law (4th ed. 1980); H.M. Hart & A. Sacks, The Legal Process (tent. ed. 1958).

Law as a Grievance-Remedial Instrument

*[T]he method . . . by which an end
was obtained was of more consequence
than the nature of the end itself.*

SIR HENRY SUMNER MAINE

*If a plaintiff has a right, he must
of necessity have a . . . remedy
. . . .*

LORD CHIEF JUSTICE HOLT

*Such words as "right" are a constant
solicitation to fallacy.*

JUSTICE OLIVER WENDELL HOLMES

Section One. Introduction
(Pedagogic Vehicles Drawn Mainly from Negligence Law)

Jones hits Smith. Brown carelessly crashes his car into Olson's, killing him. Carlson overirrigates his land and floods Bright's property. Gye entices a highly valued employee away from his competitor, Brooks. Harper defames Joseph. Thomas infringes Cooper's trademark.

Events of this kind, which might be enumerated endlessly, occur daily in any society. Should anything be done about them or about the threat of their occurrence?

One possible modus operandi of law is the provision of remedies for grievances, threatened as well as actual. Our law so acts in many circumstances. The pedagogic vehicles chosen here to show law operating as a grievance-remedial instrument consist mainly of primary source materials from the law of negligence. In studying these materials, students should bear in mind three things.

First, the general grievance-remedial mode leaves room for much variety of legal technique and process and the like. We shall be focusing on a particular scheme. The general combination of legal resources reflected in these materials is not the only one possible. This combination, however, is not mere happenstance either. Moreover, these materials reflect the basic grievance-remedial methodology of Anglo-American legal systems.

Second, law as used here has significance beyond that of providing remedies for grievances, actual or threatened. For example, its mere availability can and does influence the Joneses of the world not to hit the Smiths in the first place, or the Browns of the world not to drive carelessly in the first place. And, as we shall show, its availability allows for the possibility of rational dispute settlement of a private kind vitally significant to society.

Third, the grievance-remedial instrument may or may not be put into use alone, so to speak. People may or may not use it together with any or all of the four other basic legal instruments considered respectively in Chapters 2 through 5. Take the social problem of slaughter on the highways as an example. People might content themselves with using the law merely to provide monetary compensation for those injured or bereaved. But then the law, too, might punish reckless drivers (Chapter 2), test drivers for proficiency and license only those qualified (Chapter 3), build safe highways (Chapter 4), or encourage and facilitate some forms of private transportation instead of others (Chapter 5).

Section Two. Grievance-Remedial Techniques

Of grievance-remedial techniques, what lawyers call money damages is the most common. Damages are a form of substitutional redress. Because the law cannot replace a victim's lost hand, lost time at work as such, or lost reputation, some substitute is necessary. The idea of requiring the loss causer to pay money has ancient and interesting antecedents in Anglo-American law. But the idea is not always easy to implement.

––––––––

C. McCORMICK, HANDBOOK ON THE LAW OF DAMAGES
21–24, 64–65 (1935).*

The practice of assessing damages, that is, of finding rationally a measure in money for a loss or injury not directly connected with money, is so familiar to us, that it seems an inherent and necessary part of our procedure. Nevertheless, this practice, in anything like its present form, came as a fairly late development in English remedial law.

It is true that long before the Norman Conquest we find among the Anglo-Saxon peoples a system of money compensation for wrongs of violence. This was a step in the gradual substitution of judicial redress for the vengeance of the blood feud. To make it easier for the parties to reach a compromise or settlement of the feud, the state published a schedule of payments, fixing the prices at which the wrongdoer should make *bot*, or compensation for various kinds of injuries. The following items are selected from a long list contained in the Laws of Ethelbert, of about 600 A.D.

34. If there be an exposure of the bone, let bot be made with III shillings.

39.   If an ear be struck off, let bot be made with XII shillings.

40.   If the other ear hear not, let bot be made with XXV shillings.

43.   If an eye be (struck) out, let bot be made with L shillings.

.   .   .

51.   For each of the four front teeth, VI shillings; for the tooth which stands next to them, IV shillings; for that which stands next to that, III shillings; and then afterwards, for each a shilling.   .   .   .

The particularity of the classification and the rigid tariff of payments are evidently designed to lessen possibility of dispute over the amount to be paid.   While compensation for loss is one of the ends in view, the payments thus fixed in advance are not closely comparable to awards of damages made by a tribunal which is allowed to use its judgment in assessing an equivalent in money for an injury brought to its attention.

This system of compromise, compelled by custom and the courts, or by the threat of clan vengeance in the offing, and aided by the published tariffs of standardized prices for wrongdoing, seems to have remained through the Saxon era the everyday method of redress and to have made unnecessary the development of a practice of awarding damages until more than a hundred years after the Norman Conquest.   The scarcity of coined money in England in the period before the Conquest must likewise have operated to delay the emergence of a flexible remedy of money damages.   .   .   .

It seems, then, a substantial probability that the remedy of damages came first into English practice at about the same time that English courts began to use juries [in the late twelfth century] .   .   .   .   At all events, from the beginnings of the *practice* of giving damages in the King's Court, the jurors are normally called upon to assess the damages.   As long as the jurors are left free to fix the amount by their own lights, no *law* of damages is needed.   The development of that law is the by-product of the widening control by the judges over the action of the jurors.   .   .   .

In cases where the claim is for unliquidated damages, where the law furnishes no rule for precise measurement in money of the loss or injury, it will often be a difficult process for twelve men to reach an agreement upon the sum to be awarded.   Nevertheless, they must somehow agree if a verdict is to be reached, and this can only be done through individual concessions, and a final adoption by all of a figure mutually satisfactory. While this is recognized in the opinions, the courts have made certain pronouncements disapproving the use by the jurors of certain expedients for reaching agreement.   Drawing lots, tossing a coin, or other resort to chance is, of course, forbidden.   The courts go further and announce the doctrine that the jurors must not make a compromise which entails the abandonment by one group of their convictions as to one vital point, in return for a similar sacrifice of the convictions held by another group upon a different issue.   An illustration is an award which represents a compromise of the issues of liability and amount.   In a leading case, a young man under 21 was injured through the negligence, as he claimed, of the defendant, so that it was necessary to remove one of his eyes by an operation.   The injury was conceded, but the negligence was hotly contested at the trial.   The jury returned a verdict for the plaintiff for $200.

It was held that the verdict, in view of these circumstances, must have been the result of an improper compromise, and that a new trial should be ordered.

Comments and Questions

1. Injunctions against the occurrence of threatened grievances are another form of remedy. Other remedies are introduced throughout this book.

2. "The idea of allowing money damages for grievances seems easy enough to implement, but the procedural means chosen to implement the idea may significantly limit the character of what is achieved in particular cases." Would Dean McCormick have agreed with this assertion? Do you?

3. Note again the example given at the end of the passage from McCormick. The example distinguishes between the issues of liability and of damages. The remedy of money damages is not available for just any grievance, however great. The remedy is available only when the law says it is. For one thing, the substantive law must recognize the particular grievance by creating liability for it. This we now take up, using the first of our selections from negligence law as a vehicle for developing relevant understandings.

Section Three.   Authorized Makers of Grievance-Remedial Law and Their Appropriate Collaborative Roles

A. Origin of a Doctrine

Remedies, then, must be premised on substantive law. For example, the general rule that one who negligently harms another must compensate the victim serves as a premise for countless claims to money damages in the Anglo-American law of today. More specifically, if the defendant owed the plaintiff a *duty* to use reasonable care and if the defendant *breached* that duty so as to *cause* the plaintiff *injury*, then the plaintiff is entitled to a court judgment that plaintiff recover money damages from defendant. This general rule slowly evolved from ancient origins; and as we shall illustrate, it has been modified by counter, or qualifying, rules.

BUTTERFIELD v. FORRESTER

King's Bench, 1809.
103 Eng.Rep. 926.

This was an action . . . . for obstructing a highway, by means of which obstruction the plaintiff, who was riding along the road, was thrown down with his horse, and injured, etc. At the trial before Bayley, J., at Derby, it appeared that the defendant, for the purpose of making some repairs to his house, which was close by the roadside at one end of the town, had put up a pole across part of the road, a free passage being left by another branch or street in the same direction. That the plaintiff left a public house not far distant from the place in question at 8 o'clock in the evening in August, when they were just beginning to light candles, but while there was light enough left to discern the obstruction at one hundred yards distance; and the witness who proved this, said that if the plaintiff had not been riding very hard he might have observed and avoided it; the plaintiff, however, who was riding violently, did not observe it, but rode against it, and fell with his horse and was much hurt in consequence of the accident; and there was no evidence of his being intoxicated at the time. On this evidence, Bayley, J., directed the jury, that if a person riding with reasonable and ordinary care could have seen and avoided the obstruction; and if they were satisfied that the plaintiff was riding along the street extremely hard, and without ordinary care, they should find a verdict for the defendant, which they accordingly did.

[The plaintiff's attorney moved for a new trial.]

BAYLEY, J. The plaintiff was proved to be riding as fast as his horse could go, and this was through the streets of Derby. If he had used ordinary care he must have seen the obstruction; so that the accident appeared to happen entirely from his own fault.

LORD ELLENBOROUGH, C.J. A party is not to cast himself upon an obstruction which has been made by the fault of another, and avail himself of it, if he do not himself use common and ordinary caution to be in the right. In cases of persons riding upon what is considered to be the wrong side of the road, that would not authorize another purposely to ride up against them. One person being in fault will not dispense with another's using ordinary care for himself. Two things must concur to support this action: an obstruction in the road by the fault of the defendant, and no want of ordinary care to avoid it on the part of the plaintiff.

[The court as a whole refused a new trial.]

———————

Comments and Questions

1. The foregoing is a court decision by an important English *trial* court, not an *appellate* court. A trial court resolves disputes over issues of fact and law. An appellate court reviews trial-court decisions for prejudicial errors. But at the end of a trial, a trial court may undertake to correct its own errors as by granting a new trial. In the *Butterfield* case, the trial court consisted of four judges. One had been sent to the locality as the court's delegate to try the facts with a jury. The plaintiff's lawyer thought that this judge, Justice Bayley, had erred in stating the applicable law to the jury. Afterward, upon a motion for a new trial, this legal issue was sent back to Westminster for the whole trial court to consider. The judges then rendered the foregoing opinions orally.

2. A common fallacy about law is that courts, especially trial courts, do not make any law. Here the court plainly made law. Try to formulate the new exception to the general negligence rule. What kinds of considerations do you think influenced the court? Were the general rule and its exception, when put together, fair? Were they efficient?

3. From what source does a court derive its authority to make law?

4. What different kinds of people participated in the lawmaking process in *Butterfield*? Begin thinking about the different roles they might have played.

5. What appear to be some of the other characteristics of the lawmaking process here? Consider that court-made law is announced in the course of

resolving a disputed grievance. One meaning of the old maxim *ex facto jus oritur* is that "law grows out of fact." Does the *Butterfield* case show this?

6. Professor Lon Fuller, in The Morality of Law 48 (rev. ed. 1969), has argued that the nature of law requires general rules. Fuller suggests that it is characteristic of legal systems to function largely through general rules rather than through specific orders. Law is not, in his words, merely "a series of patternless exercises of political power." In *Butterfield* the court might simply have denied the new trial without announcing any generalities. Consider the disadvantages this practice would involve, especially if all courts adopted it.

———

DAVIES v. MANN

Exchequer, 1842.
152 Eng.Rep. 588.

Case for negligence. The declaration stated that the plaintiff theretofore, and at the time of the committing of the grievance thereinafter mentioned, to-wit, on, &c., was lawfully possessed of a certain donkey, which said donkey of the plaintiff was then lawfully in a certain highway, and the defendant was then possessed of a certain wagon and of certain horses drawing the same, which said wagon and horses of the defendant were then under the care, government, and direction of a certain then servant of the defendant, in and along the said highway; nevertheless the defendant, by his said servant, so carelessly, negligently, unskilfully, and improperly governed and directed his said wagon and horses, that by and through the carelessness, negligence, unskilfulness, and improper conduct of the defendant, by his said servant, the said wagon and horses of the defendant then ran and struck with great violence against the said donkey of the plaintiff, and thereby then wounded, crushed, and killed the same, &c.

The defendant pleaded not guilty.

At the trial, before Erskine, J., at the last Summer Assizes for the county of Worcester, it appeared that the plaintiff, having fettered the fore feet of an ass belonging to him, turned it into a public highway, and at the time in question the ass was grazing on the off side of a road about eight yards wide, when the defendant's wagon, with a team of three horses, coming down a slight descent, at what the witness termed a smartish pace, ran against the ass, knocked it down, and the wheels passing over it, it died soon after. The ass was fettered at the time, and it was proved that the driver of the wagon was some little distance behind the horses. The learned Judge told the jury, that though the act of the plaintiff, in leaving the donkey on the highway so fettered as to prevent his getting out of the way of carriages travelling along it, might be illegal, still, if the proximate cause of the injury was attributable to the want of proper conduct on the part of the driver of the wagon, the action was maintainable against the defendant; and his Lordship directed them, if they thought that the accident might have been avoided by the exercise of ordinary care on the part of the driver, to find for the plaintiff. The jury found their verdict for the plaintiff, damages 40s.

[The defendant's attorney] now moved for a new trial, on the ground of misdirection. The act of the plaintiff in turning the donkey into the public highway was an illegal one, and, as the injury arose principally from that act, the plaintiff was not entitled to compensation for that injury which, but for his own unlawful act, would never have occurred. [Parke, B. The declaration states that the ass was lawfully on the highway, and the defendant has not traversed that allegation; therefore it must be taken to be admitted.] The principle of law, as deducible from the cases, is, that where an accident is the result of faults on both sides, neither party can maintain an action. Thus, in Butterfield v. Forrester, 11 East, 60, it was held that one who is injured by an obstruction on a highway, against which he fell, cannot maintain an action, if it appear that he was riding with great violence and want of ordinary care, without which he might have seen and avoided the obstruction. So, in Vennall v. Garner, 1 C. & M. 21 [(Exch.1832)], in case for running down a ship, it was held, that neither party can recover when both are in the wrong; and Bayley, B., there says, "I quite agree that if the mischief be the result of the combined negligence of the two, they must both remain in statu quo, and neither party can recover against the other." Here the plaintiff, by fettering the donkey, had prevented him from removing himself out of the way of accident; had his fore feet been free, no accident would probably have happened. [The defendant's attorney here cited a few other cases.]

LORD ABINGER, C.B. I am of opinion that there ought to be no [new trial] in this case. The defendant has not denied that the ass was lawfully in the highway, and therefore we must assume it to have been lawfully there; but even were it otherwise, it would have made no difference, for as the defendant might, by proper care, have avoided injuring the animal, and did not, he is liable for the consequences of his negligence, though the animal may have been improperly there.

PARKE, B. This subject was fully considered by this Court in the case of Bridge v. The Grand Junction Railway Company, 3 M. & W. 246 [(Exch. 1838)], where, as appears to me, the correct rule is laid down concerning negligence, namely, that the negligence which is to preclude a plaintiff from recovering in an action of this nature, must be such as that he could, by ordinary care, have avoided the consequences of the defendant's negligence. I am reported to have said in that case, and I believe quite correctly, that "the rule of law is laid down with perfect correctness in the case of *Butterfield* v. *Forrester*, that, although there might have been negligence on the part of the plaintiff, yet unless he might, by the exercise of ordinary care, have avoided the consequences of the defendant's negligence, he is entitled to recover; if by ordinary care he might have avoided them, he is the author of his own wrong." In that case of *Bridge* v. *Grand Junction Railway Company*, there was a plea imputing negligence on both sides; here it is otherwise; and the Judge simply told the jury, that the mere fact of negligence on the part of the plaintiff in leaving his donkey on the public highway, was no answer to the action, unless the donkey's being there was the immediate cause of the injury; and that, if they were of opinion that it was caused by the fault of the defendant's servant in driving too fast or, which is the same thing, at a smartish pace, the mere fact of putting the ass upon the road would not bar the plaintiff of his action. All that is perfectly correct; for although the ass may have been wrongfully there, still the defendant was bound to go along the road at such a pace as would be likely to prevent mischief. Were this not so, a man might justify the driving over goods left on a public highway, or even over a man lying asleep there, or the purposely running against a carriage going on the wrong side of the road.

[The other judges concurred in denying a new trial.]

Comments and Questions

1. The prior decision came from another English trial court, the Exchequer, which was staffed by judges entitled barons. Did this court lay down any new law beyond that laid down in *Butterfield*?

2. In *Butterfield,* the plaintiff lost; here, the plaintiff won. Is the *Davies* case decided consistently with the law of the *Butterfield* case? If you think so, identify the factor or factors present in this case but not in *Butterfield,* or absent in this case but present in *Butterfield,* that justify a different view of the merits of the two cases.

3. Should judges be concerned about whether their present decisions are consistent with decisions previously made on similar facts? Why?

4. For one reason or another, the *Davies* case has received lots of attention, as exemplified by The Case of Mr. Davies' Donkey, 9 Can.L.Times 95, 95–96 (1889):

LORD ABINGER, C.B. loq.

DAVIES possessed an ass: no doubt
　　Trained to the horticultural load;
One day he turned his donkey out,
　　Its fore-feet fettered, on the road.
Here one remark seems necessary—
　　'Twas very wrong of DAVIES—very!

CHORUS OF BARONS.

Oh fair judicial harmony!
In this great truth we all agree.

LORD ABINGER, C.B.

While thus the ingenuous creature fed,
　　MANN's man came driving, all too fast.
O'er the mild brute the roadsters sped,
　　And DAVIES' donkey breathed its last.
We dwell not on the owner's sense
　　Of loss—it's not in evidence.

CHORUS OF BARONS.

DAVIES, thy grief, thy bosom's rents,
Thy groans—are not in evidence!

LORD ABINGER, C.B.

Who caused this crisis asinine?
　　MANN's man—and MANN must foot the bill:

Had his man passed the road's decline
   With ordinary caution, still,
Still might the rich unstinted strain
   Of DAVIES' donkey shake the plain.

CHORUS OF BARONS.

Wisdom hath given sentence! though
   The donkey was not rightly there,
Was MANN's rude man excused? Oh, no!
   He ought to drive with proper care.
Wherefore we do adjudge and say,
   For DAVIES' donkey MANN must pay!

ALL, STERNLY.

For DAVIES' donkey MANN must pay!

(He pays)

5. Was the decision just? Was it well reasoned? For example, do you think that from the evidence reasonable jurors could conclude that the accident was *solely* "caused by the fault of the defendant's servant in driving too fast"?

6. The case of *Davies* v. *Mann* is often said to be the origin of the so-called last opportunity, or last clear chance, rule, according to which a negligent plaintiff may recover if the defendant negligently failed to take advantage of a "last clear chance to avoid the accident." This rule is sometimes said to modify the *Butterfield* rule, which is said to be that a contributorily negligent plaintiff cannot recover. Do these cases truly represent these rules?

The English Common Law and Its Reception in the United States

Law of the kind laid down in *Butterfield* and in *Davies* is called common law. This name originally implied a uniform or common law for the entire country on the legal points involved, in place cf diverse local customs. The name then came to distinguish the characteristic Anglo-American legal system from other legal systems, such as the civil-law regimes of France and Germany with their comprehensive codes. But today common law frequently means judge-made law, as opposed to statutory law.

The last opportunity, or last clear chance, rule favors negligent plaintiffs when applicable. The rule was widely adopted throughout the Anglo-American legal world, including the United States, as explained by Judge McLain in Fuller v. Illinois Central R.R., 100 Miss. 705, 717–18, 56 So. 783, 786 (1911):

The groans, ineffably and mournfully sad, of Davies' dying donkey, have resounded around the earth. The last lingering gaze from the soft, mild eyes of this docile animal, like the last parting sunbeams of the softest day in spring, has appealed to and touched the hearts of men. There has girdled the globe a band of sympathy for Davies' immortal "critter." Its ghost, like Banquo's ghost, will not down at the behests of the people who are charged with inflicting injuries, nor can its groanings be silenced by the rantings and excoriations of carping critics. The law as enunciated in that case has come to stay.

Adoption of such English common-law rules in this way has been a familiar feature of American legal experience. Indeed, many states, in their beginnings, passed so-called reception statutes. The one enacted by Colorado in 1861 is illustrative: "The common law of England so far as the same is applicable and of a general nature . . . shall be the rule of decision, and shall be considered as of full force until repealed by legislative authority." One scholar has commented on such statutes as follows:

> One aspect of the constitutional and statutory provisions by which the common law was continued in effect deserves particular emphasis. Because of the terms in which such provisions were written, the American courts exercised powers far more extensive than those possessed by judges in England administering the common law. For under the constitutions [and statutes] which gave them their authority the American judges were bound to enforce the common law of England only if it was applicable to American circumstances. As a consequence, they were quick to discard an English doctrine if, in the language of our own time, it seemed "un-American."

Howe, The Migration of the Common Law: The United States of America, 76 L.Q.Rev. 49, 51 (1960); see also Ford, The Common Law: An Account of Its Reception in the United States, 4 Vand.L.Rev. 791 (1951).

———

A. GOLDBERG, EQUAL JUSTICE
75–76 (1971).*

The doctrine of stare decisis has been called "a natural evolution from the very nature of our institutions." Lacking a comprehensive statement of legal rules, the common law system relied instead upon the courts to rationally develop preexisting, general principles. The aim was uniformity of decision over time and throughout the judicial system. Realization of the aim necessitated narrowing of the judges' discretion to modify the preexisting principles, and this came to be accomplished by the strong presumption against overruling prior decisions that we call stare decisis.

The desire for uniformity was not based solely or even primarily on theoretical grounds; it was sought for some very practical reasons, of which I offer you five familiar ones. First, stare decisis fostered public confidence in the judiciary and public acceptance of individual decisions by giving the appearance of impersonal, consistent, and reasoned opinions. Second, while the respect shown old decisions thus buttressed courts against the world, such respect also induced in fact a greater impersonality of decision and thereby buttressed the judges against their own natural tendencies and prejudices. This pushed us a giant step away from a government of men toward a government of laws. Third, a rule against overruling facilitates private ordering, since settled law encourages reliance at the stage of primary private activity and also helps lawyers in the counseling of that activity. Fourth, stare decisis eases the judicial burden by discouraging suits—potential litigants cannot expect to get a different view from a different judge—and also by facilitating decision once suits are brought. As Justice Cardozo put it:

> The labor of judges would be increased almost to the breaking point if every past decision could be reopened in every case, and one could not lay one's own course of bricks on the secure foundation of . . . [those] laid by others.

Fifth and last, justice in the case at hand is served by eliminating the injustices of unfair surprise and unequal treatment.

K. LLEWELLYN, THE BRAMBLE BUSH

72–76 (7th printing 1981).*

But it will have occurred to you that despite all that I have said in favor of precedent, there are objections. It may be the ignorance or folly, or idleness, or bias of the predecessor which chains a new strong judge. It may be, too, that conditions have changed, and that the precedent, good when it was made, has since become outworn. The rule laid down the first time that a case came up may have been badly phrased, may have failed to foresee the types of dispute which later came to plague the court. Our society is changing, and law, if it is to fit society, must also change. Our society is stable, else it would not be a society, and law which is to fit it must stay fixed. Both truths are true at once. Perhaps some reconciliation lies along this line; that the stability is needed most greatly in large things, that the change is needed most in matters of detail. At any rate, it now becomes our task to inquire into how the system of precedent which we actually have works out in fact, accomplishing at once stability and change.

We turn first to what I may call the orthodox doctrine of precedent . . . . Every case lays down a rule, the rule of the case. The express ratio decidendi is prima facie the rule of the case, since it is the ground upon which the court chose to rest its decision. But a later court can reexamine the case and can invoke the canon that no judge has power to decide what is not before him, can, through examination of the facts or of the procedural issue, narrow the picture of what was actually before the court and can hold that the ruling made requires to be understood as thus restricted. In the extreme form this results in what is known as expressly "confining the case to its particular facts." This rule holds only of redheaded Walpoles in pale magenta Buick cars. And when you find this said of a past case you know that in effect it has been overruled. Only a convention, a somewhat absurd convention, prevents flat overruling in such instances. It seems to be felt as definitely improper to state that the court in a prior case was wrong, peculiarly so if that case was in the same court which is speaking now. It seems to be felt that this would undermine the dogma of the infallibility of courts. So lip service is done to that dogma, while the rule which the prior court laid down is disembowelled. The execution proceeds with due respect, with mandarin courtesy.

Now this orthodox view of the authority of precedent—which I shall call the *strict* view—is but *one of two views* which seem to me wholly contradictory to each other. It is in practice the dogma which is applied to *unwelcome* precedents. It is the recognized, legitimate, honorable technique for whittling precedents away, for making the lawyer, in his argument, and the court, in its decision, free of them. It is a surgeon's knife.

It is orthodox, I think, because it has been more discussed than is the other. Consider the situation. It is not easy thus to carve a case to pieces. It takes thought, it takes conscious thought, it takes analysis. There is no great art and no great difficulty in merely looking at a case, reading its language, and then applying some sentence which is there expressly stated. But there is difficulty in going underneath what is said, in making a keen reexamination of the case that stood before the court, in showing that the language used was quite beside the point, as the point is revealed under the lens of leisured microscopic refinement. . . . The strict doctrine, then, is the technique to be learned. *But not to be mistaken for the whole.*

For when you turn to the actual operations of the courts, or, indeed, to the arguments of lawyers, you will find a totally different view of precedent at work beside this first one. That I shall call, to give it a name, the *loose view* of precedent. That is the view that a court has decided, and decided authoritatively, *any* points or all points on which it chose to rest a case, or on which it chose, after due argument, to pass. No matter how broad the statement, no matter how unnecessary on the facts or the procedural issues, if that was the rule the court laid down, then that the court has held. Indeed, this view carries over often into dicta, and even into dicta which are grandly obiter. In its extreme form this results in thinking and arguing exclusively from *language* that is found in past opinions, and in citing and working with that language wholly without reference to the facts of the case which called the language forth.

Now it is obvious that this is a device not for cutting past opinions away from judges' feet, but for using them as a springboard when they are found convenient. This is a device for *capitalizing welcome precedents.* And both the lawyers and the judges use it so. And judged by the *practice* of the most respected courts, as of the courts of ordinary stature, this doctrine of precedent is like the other, recognized, legitimate, honorable.

What I wish to sink deep into your minds about the doctrine of precedent, therefore, is that it is two-headed. It is Janus-faced. That it is not one doctrine, nor one line of doctrine, but two, and two which, *applied at the same time to the same precedent, are contradictory of each other.* That there is one doctrine for getting rid of precedents deemed troublesome and one doctrine for making use of precedents that seem helpful. That these two doctrines exist side by side. That the same lawyer in the same brief, the same judge in the same opinion, may be using the one doctrine, the technically strict one, to cut down half the older cases that he deals with, and using the other doctrine, the loose one, for building with the other half. Until you realize this you do not see how it is possible for law to change and to develop, and yet to stand on the past. You do not see how it is possible to avoid the past mistakes of courts, and yet to make use of every happy insight for which a judge in writing may have found expression. Indeed it seems to me that here we may have part of the answer to the problem as to whether precedent is not as bad as good—supporting a weak judge with the labors of strong predecessors, but binding a strong judge by the errors of the weak. For look again at this matter of the *difficulty* of the doctrine. The strict view—that view that cuts the past away—is *hard* to use. An ignorant, an unskilful judge will find it hard to use: the past will bind him. But the skilful judge—he whom we would make free—*is* thus made free. He has the knife in hand; and he can free himself.

Nor, until you see this double aspect of the doctrine-in-action, do you appreciate how little, in detail, you can predict *out of the rules alone*; how much you must turn, for purposes of prediction, to the reactions of the judges to the facts and to the life around them. Think again in this connection of an English court, all the judges unanimous upon the conclusion, all the judges in disagreement as to what rule the outcome should be rested on.

Applying this two-faced doctrine of precedent to your work in a case class you get, it seems to me, some such result as this: You read each case from the angle of its *maximum* value as a precedent . . . . Contrariwise, you will also read each case for its *minimum* value as a precedent, to set against the maximum. In doing this you have your eyes out for the narrow issue in the case, the narrower the better. The first question is, how much can this case fairly be made to stand for by a later court to whom the precedent is welcome? You may well add—though this will be slightly flawed authority—the dicta which appear to have been well considered. The second question is, how much is there in this case that cannot be got around, even by a later court that wishes to avoid it?

You have now the tools for arguing from that case as counsel on *either* side of a new case. You turn them to the problem of prediction. Which view will this . . . court, on a later case on slightly different facts, take: will it choose the narrow or the loose? . . . Here you will call to your aid the matter of attitude that I have been discussing. Here you will use all that you know of individual judges, or of the trends in specific courts, or, indeed, of the trend in the line of business, or in the situation, or in the times at large—in anything which you may expect to become apparent and important to the court in later cases. But always and always, you will bear in mind that each precedent has not one value, but two, and that the two are wide apart, and that whichever value a later court assigns to it, such assignment will be respectable, traditionally sound, dogmatically correct. Above all, as you turn this information to your own training you will, I hope, come to see that in most doubtful cases the precedents *must* speak ambiguously until the court has made up its mind whether each one of them is welcome or unwelcome. And that the job of persuasion which falls upon you will call, therefore, not only for providing a technical ladder to reach on authority the result that you contend for, but even more, if you are to have *your* use of the precedents made as *you* propose it, the job calls for you, on the facts, to persuade the court your case is sound.

People—and they are curiously many—who think that precedent produces or ever did produce a certainty that did not involve matters of judgment and of persuasion, or who think that what I have described involves improper equivocation by the courts or departure from the court-ways of some golden age—such people simply do not know our system of precedent in which they live.

————

BRITISH COLUMBIA ELECTRIC RAILWAY v. LOACH

Privy Council, 1915.
[1916] 1 A.C. 719 (B.C.).

LORD SUMNER. This is an appeal from a judgment of the Court of Appeal of British Columbia in favor of the administrator of the estate of Benjamin Sands, who was run down at a level crossing by a car of the appellant railway company and was killed. One Hall took Sands with him in a cart, and they drove together on to the level crossing, and neither heard nor saw the approaching car till they were close to the rails and the car was nearly on them. There was plenty of light and there was no other traffic about. The [special] verdict, though rather curiously expressed, clearly finds Sands guilty of negligence in not looking out to see that the road was clear. It was not suggested in argument that he was not under a duty to exercise reasonable care, or that there was not evidence for the jury that he had disregarded it. Hall, who escaped, said that they went "right on to the track," when he heard Sands, who was sitting on his left say "Oh," and looking up saw the car about fifty yards off. He says he could then do nothing, and with a loaded wagon and horses going two or three miles an hour he probably could not. It does not seem to have been suggested that Sands could have done any good by trying to jump off the cart and clear the rails. The car knocked cart, horses, and men over, and ran some distance beyond the crossing before it could be stopped. It approached the crossing at from thirty-five to forty-five miles an hour. The driver saw the horses as they came into view from behind a shed at the crossing of the road and the railway, when they would be ten or twelve feet from the nearest rail, and he at once applied his brake. He was then 400 feet from the crossing. If the brake had been in good order it should have stopped the car in 300 feet. Apart from the fact that the car did not stop in time, but overran the crossing, there was evidence for the jury that the brake was defective and inefficient and that the car had come out in the morning with the brake in that condition. The jury found that the car was approaching at an excessive speed and should have been brought under complete control, and although they gave as their reason for saying so the presence of possible passengers at the station by the crossing, and not the possibility of vehicles being on the road, there can be no mistake in the matter, and their finding stands. It cannot be restricted, as the trial judge and the [defendant] sought to restrict it, to a finding that the speed was excessive for an ill-braked car, but not for a properly-braked car, or to a finding that there was no negligence except the "original" negligence of sending the car out ill-equipped in the morning.

Clearly if the deceased had not got on to the line he would have suffered no harm, in spite of the excessive speed and the defective brake, and if he had kept his eyes about him he would have perceived the approach of the car and would have kept out of mischief. If the matter stopped there, his administrator's action must have failed, for he would certainly have been guilty of contributory negligence. He would have owed his death to his own fault, and whether his negligence was the sole cause or the cause jointly with the railway company's negligence would not have mattered.

It was for the jury to decide which portions of the evidence were true, and, under proper direction, to draw their own inferences of fact from such evidence as they accepted. No complaint was made against the summing-up, and there has been no attempt to argue before their Lordships that there was no evidence for the jury on all points. If the jury accepted the facts above stated, as certainly they well might do, there was no further negligence on the part of Sands after he looked up and saw the car, and then there was nothing that he could do. There he was, in a position of extreme peril and by his own fault, but after that he was guilty of no fresh fault. The driver of the car, however, had seen the horses some perceptible time earlier, had duly applied his brakes, and if they had been effective he could, as the jury found, have pulled up in time. Indeed, he would have had 100 feet to spare. If the car was 150 feet off when Sands looked up and said "Oh," then each had the other in view for fifty feet before the car reached the point at which it should have stopped. It was the motorman's duty, on seeing the peril of Sands, to make a reasonable use of his brakes in order to avoid injuring him, although it was by his own negligence that Sands was in danger. Apparently he did his best as things then were, but partly the bad brake and partly the excessive speed, for both of which the [defendant was] responsible, prevented him from stopping, as he could otherwise have done. On these facts, which the jury were entitled to accept and appear to have accepted, only one conclusion is possible. What actually killed Sands was the negligence of the railway company, and not his own, though it was a close thing.

Some of the judges in the Courts below appear to have thought that because the equipment of the car with a defective brake was the original cause of the collision, and could not have been remedied after Sands got on the line, no account should be taken of it in considering the motorman's failure to avoid the collision after he knew that Sands was in danger. . . .

These considerations were again urged at their Lordships' bar under somewhat different forms. It was said . . . that the negligence relied on as an answer to contributory negligence must be a new negligence, the initial negligence which founded the cause of action being spent and disposed of by the contributory negligence. . . .

This matter was much discussed in Brenner v. Toronto Ry. Co., 13 Ont. L.R. 423, when Anglin J. delivered a valuable judgment in the Divisional Court. . . .

The facts of that case were closely similar to those in the present appeal, and it was much relied on in argument in the Court below. Anglin J., following the decision in Scott v. Dublin and Wicklow Ry. Co., 1861, 11 Ir.C.L.Rep. 377, 394, observed as follows: ". . . If, notwithstanding the difficulties of the situation, efforts to avoid injury duly made would have been successful, but for some self-created incapacity which rendered such efforts inefficacious, the negligence that produced such a state of disability is not merely part of the inducing causes—a remote cause or a cause merely sine qua non—it is, in very truth, the efficient, the proximate, the decisive cause of the incapacity, and therefore of the mischief. . . . Negligence of a defendant incapacitating him from taking due care to avoid the consequences of the plaintiff's negligence, may, in some cases, though anterior in point of time to the plaintiff's negligence, constitute 'ultimate' negligence, rendering the defendant liable notwithstanding a finding of contributory negligence of the plaintiff. . . . "

Their Lordships are of opinion that, on the facts of the present case, the above observations apply and are correct. Were it otherwise the defendant company would be in a better position, when they had supplied a bad brake but a good motorman, than when the motorman was careless but the brake efficient. If the superintendent engineer sent out the car in the morning with a defective brake, which, on seeing Sands, the motorman strove to apply, they would not be liable, but if the motorman failed to apply the brake, which, if applied, would have averted the accident, they would be liable.

. . . Many persons are apt to think that, in a case of contributory negligence like the present, the injured man deserved to be hurt, but the question is not one of desert or the lack of it, but of the cause legally responsible for the injury. . . . The inquiry is a judicial inquiry. . . . The object of the inquiry is to fix upon some wrong-doer the responsibility for the wrongful act which has caused the damage. It is in search not merely of a causal agency but of the responsible agent. . . .

In the present case their Lordships are clearly of opinion that, under proper direction, it was for the jury to find the facts and to determine the responsibility, and that upon the answers which they returned, reasonably construed, the responsibility for the accident was upon the [defendant] solely, because, whether Sands got in the way of the car with or without negligence on his part, the [defendant] could and ought to have avoided the consequences of that negligence, and failed to do so, not by any combination of negligence on the part of Sands with [its] own, but solely by the negligence of [its] servants in sending out the car with a brake whose inefficiency operated to cause the collision at the last moment, and in running the car at an excessive speed, which required a perfectly efficient brake to arrest it. Their Lordships will accordingly humbly advise His Majesty that the appeal should be dismissed with costs.

Comments and Questions

1. Unlike *Butterfield* and *Davies,* the *Loach* case is an appellate case. (The English Privy Council then had some power to review Canadian court decisions.) Loach, as administrator of Sands's estate, had sued the railway in the trial court for wrongful death. He lost, and then he appealed on error of law. The court of appeal reversed. The railway then appealed. (As appellant, the railway company's name appears first in the caption of the case.) The Privy Council affirmed. Was that decision just?

2. A persuasive argument can be made that the decision here is inconsistent with the last opportunity rule. Among other things, note that the railway had no *last* opportunity to avoid the result. Any contrary description would be a fiction. Note that the court instead says that the fault was "solely" that of the railway. This might be construed as an effort to square the result with the dictates of the last opportunity rule.

3. Should we now say the court has changed the law? In the *Butterfield, Davies,* and *Loach* cases, courts developed a body of common-law rules that serve as premises for the remedy of money damages. Prior to *Loach,* this law might have been stated thus: A defendant who negligently harmed another is liable, unless the victim had been contributorily negligent, except where the defendant negligently failed to take advantage of the last opportunity to avoid the accident. How did *Loach* modify or add to this law? Note that in the United States today, one or another variant of this cluster of doctrine is still the governing law in a number of states.

4. Over the centuries, Anglo-American courts have, in the fashion illustrated here, developed a great mass of grievance-remedial common law. In evaluating this important work of courts, distinguishing several different kinds of criticism is useful. Thus, of a given decision, or series of decisions, it may or may not be possible to say: (a) "These results are unsound," or (b) "These results are inconsistent," or (c) "The courts' rationales are inconsistent," or (d) "The courts' rationales are otherwise unsatisfactory," or (e) "It is inappropriate for courts to make law of this kind at all," or (f) "Though it is not inappropriate for courts to make such law, it is, relatively speaking, more appropriate for legislatures to make it."

5. When all is said and done, is the foregoing cluster of negligence doctrine satisfactory? Is further change called for? If the court's search for the more blameworthy party is what led to the doctrinal refinement in *Loach,* can you imagine other factual settings that would require still further refinements? Is the real problem, however, that in an all-or-nothing system of money damages, one party must lose and the other win, even though both were at fault?

PROSSER, COMPARATIVE NEGLIGENCE

51 Mich.L.Rev. 465, 467–74 (1953).*

The defense of contributory negligence originated in 1809 with the case of *Butterfield* v. *Forrester.* The defendant, who was repairing his house, had left a pole projecting across part of the highway; and the plaintiff, riding home from a public house in the dusk, did not see the pole, rode into it, and was thrown from his horse and injured. Lord Ellenborough disposed of the matter very briefly with the statement that "A party is not to cast himself upon an obstruction which has been made by the fault of another, and avail himself of it, if he did not himself use common and ordinary caution to be in the right."

There has been much speculation as to why the rule thus declared found such ready acceptance in later decisions, both in England and in the United States. The explanations given by the courts themselves never have carried much conviction. . . . It has been said that the defense has a penal basis, and is intended to punish the plaintiff for his own misconduct; or that the court will not aid one who is himself at fault, and he must come into court with clean hands. But this is no explanation of the many cases, particularly those of the last clear chance, in which a plaintiff clearly at fault is permitted to recover. It has been said that the rule is intended to discourage accidents, by denying recovery to those who fail to use proper care for their own safety; but the assumption that the speeding motorist is, or should be, meditating on the possible failure of a lawsuit for his possible injuries lacks all reality, and it is quite as reasonable to say that the rule promotes accidents by encouraging the negligent defendant. Probably the true explanation lies merely in the highly individualistic attitude of the common law of the early nineteenth century. The period of development of contributory negligence was that of the industrial revolution, and there is reason to think that the courts found in this defense, along with the concepts of duty and proximate cause, a convenient instrument of control over the jury, by which the liabilities of rapidly growing industry were curbed and kept within bounds.

Criticism of the denial of all recovery was not slow in coming, and it has been with us for more than a century. The attack upon contributory negligence has been founded upon the obvious injustice of a rule which visits the entire loss caused by the fault of two parties on one of them alone, and that one the injured plaintiff, least able to bear it, and quite possibly much less at fault than the defendant who goes scot free. No one ever has succeeded in justifying that as a policy, and no one ever will. Its outrageousness became especially apparent in the cases of injuries to employees, where a momentary lapse of caution after a lifetime of care in the face of the employer's negligence might wreck a man's life and leave him uncompensated as a charge upon society; and the demand for some modification of the rule became an integral part of the movement which finally led to the workmen's compensation acts. . . .

Although the courts almost from the beginning have displayed an uneasy consciousness that something is wrong, they have been slow to move. . . . The defense was one to a negligence action only, and it never applied to intentional torts such as assault and battery; and from this there developed the first exception, that mere contributory negligence is no defense where the defendant's conduct is so aggravated that it approaches intent, and can be characterized as "wilful," "wanton," or "reckless." In such a case the plaintiff is barred from recovery only when his own conduct is similarly aggravated, and can be described in the same terms. There is here, of course, a rough balancing of one fault against the other, but the difference is declared to be one of kind rather than of degree. . . .

The most important common law modification is that which bears the name of the last clear chance. It originated in 1842 in the case of *Davies* v. *Mann,* where the plaintiff left his ass fettered in the highway and the defendant drove into it. The doctrine found ready acceptance in the United States; but from its origin it has acquired forever the name of the "jackass doctrine," with whatever implications that may carry. In its original form, it was stated to be that where the defendant had the last, and therefore the better, opportunity to avoid the accident, his negligence superseded that of the plaintiff, and contributory negligence was no defense. As in the case of contributory negligence itself, the explanations given are not at all convincing. It is sometimes said that the later negligence of the defendant must necessarily be the greater negligence, and that it is a rule of comparative fault which is being applied. This may be true in some instances where the defendant discovers the plaintiff's helpless situation and his conduct displays reckless disregard of it; but it can scarcely account for many others in which the negligence consists merely of failure to discover the situation at all, or of slowness, clumsiness, inadvertence or an error in judgment in dealing with it. . . .

The real explanation would appear to be nothing more than a dislike for the defense of contributory negligence, and a rebellion against its application in a group of cases where its hardship is most apparent. The last clear chance has been called a "transitional doctrine," a way station on the road to apportionment of damages; but its effect has been to freeze the transition rather than to speed it. Actually the last clear chance cases present one of the worst tangles known to the law. In some jurisdictions the application of the rule has been limited to cases where the plaintiff is helpless and the defendant has in fact discovered the situation; in others it is extended to cases where the defendant might have discovered it by the exercise of reasonable care. In still others it is applied to situations where the plaintiff is not helpless at all and continues to be negligent, but is unaware of his danger, while the defendant has discovered it. In still others it is applied to cases where the defendant's antecedent negligence, as in driving a car with defective brakes, has rendered him unable to take advantage of the "last clear chance" he would otherwise have had.[41] . . .

Quite apart from all this confusion, the real objection to the last clear chance is that it seeks to alleviate the hardships of contributory negligence by shifting the entire loss due to the fault of both parties from the plaintiff to the defendant. It is still no more reasonable to charge the defendant with the plaintiff's share of the consequences of his fault than to charge the plaintiff with the defendant's; and it is no better policy to relieve the negligent plaintiff of all responsibility for his injury than it is

---

41. British Columbia Elec. R. Co. v. Loach . . . . .

to relieve the negligent defendant. The whole floundering, haphazard, makeshift device operates in favor of some plaintiffs by inflicting obvious injustice upon some defendants; but it leaves untouched the greater number of contributory negligence cases in which the necessary time interval or element of discovery does not appear and the last clear chance cannot apply.

———

B. Reform of the Doctrine

Assuming the desirability of reform, and assuming that some kind of comparative negligence formula apportioning damages in accordance with the respective fault of the parties is the best overall solution, still further questions arise: Would it be inappropriate for a court to make this change, leaving the legislature as the only appropriate body to do so? If it would not be inappropriate for a court so to act, still, would it be more appropriate for the legislature to act? Contrary to a common fallacy about law, courts and legislatures are not fungible as lawmakers. What factors are relevant in deciding which institution or body ought to have primary responsibility for originating or evolving the governing precepts? Relevant factors of appropriateness and comparative appropriateness will now be canvassed.

Legislatures are generally thought of as lawmakers par excellence in modern societies. They embody the voice of the demos, constituting the supreme lawmaker within constitutional limits but answering to the people. And they are well equipped to make certain kinds of law.

First, unlike courts as we traditionally know them, a legislature can set up committees and commissions to investigate social problems in depth and in breadth preparatory to making law. Such an apparatus for "legislative" fact-finding is unavailable to a court, which normally must rely on what the contending parties want to put before it, some of which may not even be admissible under rules of evidence.

Second, a legislature can act on its own initiative, and it can deal with more aspects of a social problem at one time than can a court. A court cannot take the initiative but must wait until two parties present a case to it for decision before it can make law at all. Even when a case is presented to a court, the decision will always address only part of the underlying social problem. Often not until a number of cases have arisen will a court even be able to see what the whole problem entails, and sometimes this sporadic approach masks the general pattern altogether. For these reasons, it will at best take a court longer to work out a comprehensive and sound solution.

Third, when a court does act definitively, this will usually have a retroactive effect, whereas a legislature may better secure fairness by acting prospectively.

Fourth, in general a court's decision coercively binds only the parties, whereas a legislature can speak directly to the populace as a whole.

Fifth, what a court decides to do about a social problem might be buried in a mass of arcane law reports, whereas a legislature can adopt methods of promulgation and publicity better designed to get the word around and thus to allow the citizenry to conform their primary conduct.

Sixth, courts do not have all the techniques for dealing with a social problem that legislatures have. A court cannot allocate more funds to prosecutors. A court cannot set up a licensing system. A court cannot impose a tax. A court cannot start giving weather reports. Some things remain beyond the innovative powers of courts.

Seventh, legislatures can act without the restrictions of the theoretical expectations we impose on courts. As a society we feel, for example, that courts should draw only principled distinctions and that courts should not work obviously major social changes—at least as we traditionally conceive of the courts' role.

Yet, as makers of certain other kinds of law, courts have important advantages over legislatures:

1. For example, in dissecting and elaborating statutory pronouncements in particular cases, courts make a kind of interpretational law that legislators are distinctly unsuited to make. Specific questions of legal right arising under statutory law ought not to be subject to the influence of political pressures and considerations extrinsic to the statutorily defined merits. If legislatures were to decide such questions, keeping such pressures and considerations out of the picture would be far more difficult. Legislatures are not set up to deal with such questions anyway. Many of their personnel do not have the requisite training. And their procedures are not appropriate for careful definition of issues of fact between particular opponents, nor for the requisite dispassionate "adjudicative" fact-finding in particular cases, and so on. Also, legislatures simply could not take on such work. They would not have time.

2. Moreover, statutes do not and indeed cannot foresee and provide for all eventualities. Gaps abound in the statutory law. To do justice, courts should sometimes generate law on such interstitial matters rather than await the possibility of the legislature returning to the subject.

3. Even as a wholly original matter, if neither legislature nor court has had much prior experience with a social problem, letting the courts wrestle with the problem on a case-by-case basis may be best. Courts operate on a level that enables them to test general propositions against the reality of concrete situations. And courts can more readily modify basic law of their own making as necessity arises than bend statutory language supposedly applicable.

4. Even when legislatures do not lack relevant knowledge of the field, courts may still be better suited to originate the basic governing law. The factors relevant to sound solution may vary so much from case to case within the field as to defy statutory formulation. Or the issues arising within the field may call for commonsense solutions in terms of familiar everyday moral concepts such as "blame." Judges have more relevant experience in formulating law of this kind than have legislators. This has not gone unrecognized. Our law of negligence, for example, is largely judge-made.

5. When the issue is not one on which political parties divide, there is less reason for insisting that it be resolved in the first instance by a

legislative body. Consider questions such as what the measure of damages should be for breach of contract. Generally speaking, these are relatively apolitical matters. Courts can thrash them out in the context of relevant particulars under enhanced conditions of institutional impartiality.

6. Or the issue may be one that has become a political football within the legislative body but clearly ought not to be left that way. Again, the matter might be best left to courts, but a third possibility is the more-or-less independent administrative body empowered to make governing regulations within a basic framework hewn out by the legislature. The desire to remove a matter from politics has often prompted the establishment of such bodies. On this, more later.

7. Finally, if the courts have done much of the original work in developing an area of the law, allowing them to continue the evolutionary task of clarifying and reshaping that law may be preferable. Legislatures might lack either the aptitude or the time for this task, which has traditionally been performed by the courts. Indeed, legislative enactments overriding the common law might prove quite disruptive in the law's development.

————

PECK, THE ROLE OF THE COURTS AND LEGISLATURES IN THE REFORM OF TORT LAW

48 Minn.L.Rev. 265, 304–07 (1963).*

The doctrine of comparative negligence should replace the absolute bar imposed by the contributory negligence rule, and this substitution should be made by the judiciary. . . . In Illinois, a limited form of comparative negligence, based on a distinction between gross and slight negligence, was judicially adopted in 1858 and ultimately abandoned, also by judicial decision, in 1894. The significance of the abandonment is not that comparative negligence is unsound . . . but that such changes were made by courts, rather than legislatures, at a time when the creative role of the judiciary was not as well understood as at the present time.

It is unlikely that sufficient support for a comparative negligence rule could be organized to obtain its passage through a state legislature. As in other areas appropriate for judicial reform, lobby and pressure groups are active and successful in preventing bills incorporating comparative negligence principles from obtaining full legislative consideration. Judicial experience with jury verdicts provides the courts with ample proof that the contributory negligence rule is not compatible with the values of our society, and it has been abandoned in most common-law jurisdictions outside the United States. Moreover, scholars almost unanimously agree that a comparative negligence standard is a workable and more just scheme than the contributory negligence rule. For these reasons a number of important voices have recently and quite properly urged that courts make the change to comparative negligence without waiting for legislative action.

Moreover, empirical data bearing upon the subject is as available to courts as it is to legislatures and their committees. Probably the most important consideration is the effect that such a change would have upon the operations of insurance companies. Few others could justifiably claim to have made commitments and taken action in reliance upon the existence of a rule by which contributory negligence bars recovery. What evidence there is indicates that a change in the rule would have a minimal and perhaps undiscernible effect on the total operations of insurers. The apparent explanation of this fact is that comparative negligence is in fact the standard by which parties negotiate settlements. The proportion of cases controlled by a judgment, which may involve as little as two percent of all claims, is too small to affect the overall result even if juries did conscientiously follow the instructions given them. Other concerns, such as the extent to which a contributory negligence rule deters risk-creating conduct, is something that probably cannot be tested empirically because appropriate laboratory experiments cannot be practiced on human beings and the variables affecting the accident rate are so numerous that no effect can be attributed to the presence of a comparative negligence rule.

Finally, the involved and convoluted features of the last clear chance doctrine seem to ameliorate what would otherwise appear to be the harsh consequences of a rule barring recovery on the basis of contributory negligence. They provide for the layman the appearances of a system carefully designed to work justice between the parties to accident litigation. To judges and members of the legal profession, of course, the doctrine represents nothing more than an illogical scheme, difficult to apply, and frequently impossible to justify, the existence of which is tolerated only because it permits courts to escape the harsh consequences of the contributory negligence rule. As elsewhere, such doctrinal complications not only establish the need for reform; they also establish the propriety of judicial action.

MAKI v. FRELK

Supreme Court of Illinois, 1968.
40 Ill.2d 193, 239 N.E.2d 445.

KLINGBIEL, JUSTICE.

On this appeal we are presented with a question arising solely on the pleadings. In 1965 Minnie Maki, as administrator of the estate of her deceased husband, filed a complaint under the Wrongful Death Act against Calvin Frelk in the circuit court of Kane County.[a] The complaint is in three counts. Defendant answered as to the allegations of counts I and II, and moved to strike count III. The court granted the motion, striking count III for failing to state a cause of action. In its order the

---

a. A wrongful-death act, such as that of Illinois, simply allows a representative of the decedent to sue for negligence or tort resulting in death. Such a statute was necessary to change the old common-law rule that the cause of action died with the victim.

court recited that there was no just reason for delaying enforcement or appeal.

The plaintiff thereupon sought review . . . . The appellate court reversed and remanded (Maki v. Frelk, 85 Ill.App.2d 439, 229 N.E.2d 284), and we granted petitions by both the plaintiff and the defendant for leave to appeal from the appellate court judgment. The National Association of Independent Insurers and a group of trial lawyers called "Illinois Defense Counsel" have appeared as *amici curiae*.

The complaint alleges that on October 16, 1964, at about 9 P.M. the plaintiff's decedent was driving his car in a westerly direction on Plato Road near the intersection with Illinois Route 47, in Kane County, and the defendant was driving a car in a northerly direction along Illinois Route 47 near the intersection, that defendant was guilty of driving too fast, failing to yield the right of way, failing to keep a proper lookout for other cars, failing to keep his own car under control, failing to stop so as to avoid a collision, otherwise improperly operating the vehicle, and operating it without sufficient brakes, and that as a direct and proximate result of one or more of such acts his car collided with the car operated by plaintiff's decedent, causing the latter's death. The third count, stricken for failure to state a cause of action, did not allege due care on the part of the plaintiff and the decedent. Instead it alleged that "if there was any negligence on the part of plaintiff or plaintiff's decedent it was less than the negligence of the defendant, Calvin Frelk, when compared."

There is no dispute that under the rule as it now exists a plaintiff must be free from contributory fault in order to recover, and that contributory negligence of the deceased is a bar to recovery under the Wrongful Death Act. (Howlett v. Doglio, 402 Ill. 311, 83 N.E.2d 708.) In contending the third count nevertheless states a cause of action, plaintiff urges that the rule ought now be changed in favor of a form of comparative negligence. The appellate court agreed. It reviewed the history of contributory negligence, considered arguments generally advanced for and against the adoption of a comparative negligence rule, and concluded that contributory negligence shall no longer bar recovery if it is not as great as the negligence of the person against whom recovery is sought but that any damages allowed shall be diminished in proportion to the amount of negligence attributable to the person recovering. . . .

After full consideration we think, however, that such a far-reaching change, if desirable, should be made by the legislature rather than by the court. The General Assembly is the department of government to which the constitution has entrusted the power of changing the laws.

Where it is clear that the court has made a mistake it will not decline to correct it, even though the rule may have been re-asserted and acquiesced in for a long number of years. No person has a vested right in any rule of law entitling him to insist that it shall remain unchanged for his benefit. But when a rule of law has once been settled, contravening no statute or constitutional principle, such rule ought to be followed unless it can be shown that serious detriment is thereby likely to arise prejudicial to public interests. The rule of *stare decisis* is founded upon sound principles in the administration of justice, and rules long recognized as the law should not be departed from merely because the court is of the opinion that it might decide otherwise were the question a new one.

Counsel on both sides have argued this case at length, supplying the court with a comprehensive review of many authorities. But we believe that on the whole the considerations advanced in support of a change in the rule might better be addressed to the legislature. As *amici* have pointed out, the General Assembly has incorporated the present doctrine of contributory negligence as an integral part of statutes dealing with a number of particular subjects (see, e.g., provisions imposing liability for injuries caused by the negligence of firemen "without the contributory negligence of the injured person . . ." . . .), and the legislative branch is manifestly in a better position than is this court to consider the numerous problems involved. We recently observed, with regard to a contention that exculpatory clauses in residential leases ought to be declared void, that "In our opinion the subject is one that is appropriate for legislative rather than judicial action." (O'Callaghan v. Waller & Beckwith Realty Co., 15 Ill.2d 436, 441, 155 N.E.2d 545, 547.) We think the same must be said with respect to the change urged in the case at bar.

The circuit court was correct in striking count III of the complaint in the case at bar, and the appellate court erred in reversing its order. The judgment of the appellate court will therefore be reversed, the order of the circuit court affirmed, and the cause remanded to the circuit court for further proceedings not inconsistent with the views herein expressed.

[Of the seven justices, Justice Ward, joined by Justice Schaefer, dissented. His dissenting opinion is omitted.]

Comments and Questions

1. Can you better articulate reasons for the *Maki* court's rejecting the arguments of Professor Peck?

2. In England, in 1945, Parliament adopted the Law Reform (Contributory Negligence) Act, 8 & 9 Geo. 6, ch. 28, which is explained next.

WILLIAMS, THE LAW REFORM (CONTRIBUTORY NEGLIGENCE) ACT, 1945
9 Mod.L.Rev. 105, 105–06 (1946).*

Thus

Was justice ever ridiculed in Rome:
Such be the double verdicts favoured here
Which send away both parties to a suit
Nor puffed up nor cast down—for each a crumb
Of right, for neither of them the whole loaf.

(The Ring and the Book, ii, 747–752.)

Thus Robert Browning: and from his lines we may perhaps gather what he would have thought of the Law Reform (Contributory Negligence)

Act, 1945. But then, Browning was not a lawyer, or he could not have supposed that one party to a suit must necessarily be wholly in the right and the other wholly in the wrong. The new Act endeavors to reflect in terms of legal result the fact that in the world as we know it damage may be caused by the fault of both parties. It thus relieves the hardship caused by the common-law rule under which one of two negligent parties might emerge from the accident penniless while the other went unscathed. Even if nature left the loss equally distributed between the parties, the result of the last-opportunity rule at common law might be to pile the whole upon one of them; and perhaps the Act remedies this too. The advantage of the Act is not only that it enables the loss to be apportioned in accordance with ordinary ideas of fairness, but also that, by rendering possible the division of loss between two pairs of shoulders, it makes the loss in appropriate cases easier to be borne. . . .

In general terms the object of the Act is to enable the Judge in cases of contributory negligence to apportion the damages between the parties according to the respective degrees of responsibility for the damage. Thus if either sues the other he will get such damages as are attributable to the other party's portion of the responsibility.

A simple illustration will make this clear. Suppose that A and B are involved in an accident, through the negligence of both, and A suffers £500 damage while B suffers £100 worth of damage. It is held that A's responsibility for the damage amounts to four-fifths and B's to one-fifth of the total, that is to say, that A's responsibility is four times that of B's. Then A will recover from B one-fifth of his damages, amounting to £100, and B will recover from A four-fifths of his damages, amounting to £80. Thus on balance B will owe A £20 in respect of damages. Reviewing the situation, and leaving costs out of account, it will be seen that A suffers his original £500 damage less the £20 received from B, = £480 while B suffers his original £100 damage plus the sum of £20 paid to A, = £120. Thus A's loss is four times that of B, which reflects the Court's assessment of the responsibility for the situation.

In cases where the Court cannot assess the degrees of responsibility—cases of "inscrutable fault"—there will probably be equal apportionment.

The operative provision of the Act is in the first part of section 1(1), which runs as follows:—

> Where any person suffers damage as the result partly of his own fault and partly of the fault of any other person or persons, a claim in respect of that damage shall not be defeated by reason of the fault of the person suffering the damage, but the damages recoverable in respect thereof shall be reduced to such extent as the Court thinks just and equitable having regard to the claimant's share in the responsibility for the damage.

Judicial Reaction to Legislative Intervention

Legislative contributions to the growth of common law are not without risks, and some of these risks can be compounded by judicial attitudes toward the interpretation of legislative enactments.

One kind of risk is that the legislature may become preoccupied with only one context in which the problem arises and as a result come up with a statute that incorporates terms referring only to the particular context, when in fact the statute ought to apply to other contexts as well. The effect of such an enactment may be to stunt the growth of the law, for the legislature may be slow to return to the problem, and the courts may insist on reading the statute narrowly rather than extending it by analogy.

For example, suppose that the English apportionment statute expressly applied only "in all actions brought for personal injuries, or where such injuries have resulted in death," as some such statutes did. Further suppose that a case like *Davies* v. *Mann* then arises under this statute, and the plaintiff sues for damage to his *property*. By the literal language of the statute, would the court be empowered to apportion damages? Should the court extend the statute by analogy? Unfortunately, Anglo-American courts have not always been so bold. Indeed, they have frequently read statutes of the kind here under consideration quite restrictively. This phenomenon has been described by Justice Schaefer (who dissented in *Maki*) in his article, Precedent and Policy, 34 U.Chi.L. Rev. 3, 19–20 (1966):[b]

> The contrast between the impact of a statute and that of a common law decision upon the body of the law is graphically shown in Dean Landis' description of the effect of *Rylands* v. *Fletcher* upon Anglo-American law. There the House of Lords decided that one who artifically accumulated water upon his land was absolutely liable for damage caused by its escape. The decision was based upon the analogy drawn from earlier cases which had dealt with the liability of the man who kept wild animals upon his land. The doctrine of *Rylands* v. *Fletcher* has been important in our law since 1868, and the rule there announced has been applied in many situations. Dean Landis says:
>
> > Had Parliament in 1868 adopted a similar rule, no such permeating results to the general body of Anglo-American law would have ensued. And this would be true, though the act had been preceded by a thorough and patient inquiry by a Royal Commission into the business of storing large volumes of water and its concomitant risks, and even though the same Lords who approved Mr. Fletcher's claim had in voting "aye" upon the measure given reasons identical with those contained in their judgments. Such a statute would have caused no ripple in the processes of adjudication either in England or on the other side of the Atlantic, and the judicial mind would have failed to discern the essential similarity between water stored in reservoirs, crude petroleum stored in tanks, and gas and electricity confined and maintained upon the premises.

Whether to extend a statute by analogy is one kind of question judges must face once legislators have made their own imprint on the common law. However, there is a more fundamental question: How should judges determine the meaning of such a statute in the first place?

Observe, for example, that the English Law Reform (Contributory Negligence) Act, 1945, begins: "Where any person suffers damage as the result partly of his own fault and partly of the fault of any other person . . . . " The clearest kind of case to which this language applies is one where plaintiff and defendant are simultaneously negligent thus causing the injury, as for example where plaintiff and defendant both enter a diagonal intersection against a red light and run into each other. But again consider a case like *Davies* v. *Mann.* Does the English act apply? By the literal language just quoted, one can strongly argue that it does not. Lord Justice Asquith made the following argument in Henley v. Cameron, 118 L.J.K.B. (n.s.) 989, 996 (C.A.1948) (dissenting opinion):

> The rule of "last clear opportunity" is based on causation and assumes that where the last opportunity resided definitely with X (who failed to use it), the damage was suffered *not* partly as the result of X's fault and partly as the result of some other person's, but wholly and solely as the result of that of X.

On this view, what words of the statute would not be satisfied in such a case as *Davies*? Yet, should the literal meaning of words alone be decisive? What is the desirable result? How then should the statute be interpreted?

Nevertheless, there are limits on how far a court should run with the "spirit" of a statute like the English act. If the defendant acted intentionally in inflicting injury, should the statute still work to reduce the damages for a contributorily negligent plaintiff? Most courts have said no. But what of willful, wanton, or reckless behavior by the defendant, rather than intentional infliction of harm? The courts have split on this issue. And what of other issues on which the "letter" of the statute seems at odds with good policy? At some point, the unambiguous words of a statute should come to control decision.

This difficult task of statutory interpretation is summarized in these terms by W. Reynolds, Judicial Process in a Nutshell 236–37 (1980):

> The legislature has the primary voice when it acts within the Constitution. The court's job, then, is to give effect to what the legislature has passed. In doing so, the most important factor is the language of the statute, the manner in which the legislature expressed its desires. The touchstone of this process is purpose: the aim or goal of the statute. In understanding purpose the court must set the statute in context; context is found by looking at the circumstances that surrounded its passage. Useful in this process is legislative history, especially committee and conference reports.

———

ALVIS v. RIBAR

Supreme Court of Illinois, 1981.
85 Ill.2d 1, 421 N.E.2d 886.

MORAN, JUSTICE:

These two cases, consolidated for appeal, present a question which arises solely from the pleadings. In each, plaintiff's complaint included a count based on the doctrine of comparative negligence, which count was dismissed by the trial court on motion by the defendants. In *Alvis* v. *Ribar,* the appellate court affirmed summarily, stating, ". . . it is not for this court to attempt to reverse the many cases and opinions of the Illinois Supreme Court in this area." (78 Ill.App.3d 1117, 1119, 398 N.E.2d 124.) This court allowed leave to appeal. [A description of the other case, which was brought under the Wrongful Death Act, is omitted.]

Plaintiffs ask this court to abolish the doctrine of contributory negligence and to adopt in its place the doctrine of comparative negligence as the law in Illinois.

In *Alvis* v. *Ribar,* a motor vehicle operated by defendant Ribar skidded out of control and collided with a metal barrel which anchored an official intersection stop sign. The sign had been temporarily placed at the intersection while construction work on the intersecting road was being done by the defendant contractor, Milburn Brothers, Inc., under the supervision of defendant Cook County. Plaintiff Alvis, who was a passenger in defendant Ribar's vehicle, sustained injuries as a result of the collision. He filed a multicount personal injury complaint seeking damages from all three defendants. . . .

I

THE HISTORY OF CONTRIBUTORY NEGLIGENCE

. . . .

Case law developed the doctrine of contributory negligence in Illinois. In Aurora Branch R.R. Co. v. Grimes (1852), 13 Ill. 585, 587–88, this court followed the *Butterfield* case and added the requirement that the burden of proof is upon the plaintiff to show not only negligence on the part of the defendant, but also that plaintiff himself exercised proper care and circumspection. In the next few years the decisions involving "last clear chance" (Moore v. Moss (1852), 14 Ill. 106, 110 . . .), degrees of negligence (Chicago & Mississippi R.R. Co. v. Patchin (1854), 16 Ill. 198, 203), and proximate cause (Joliet & Northern Indiana R.R. Co. v. Jones (1858), 20 Ill. 221, 227) created confusion. Mr. Justice Breese reviewed these decisions in Galena & Chicago Union R.R. Co. v. Jacobs (1858), 20 Ill. 478, a case which involved a 4½-year-old boy who had been run over by a railroad locomotive. There the court ultimately disagreed with the *Butterfield* holding and adopted a form of comparative negligence in its place.

This, and all the cases subsequent, to which we have referred, have one common basis, and that is found in the old law maxim that "no man shall take advantage of his own wrong or negligence" in his prosecution or defense against another.

The court concluded that liability does not depend absolutely on the absence of all negligence on the part of the plaintiff but upon the relative degrees of care or want of care manifested by both parties.

> [A]ll care or negligence is at best but relative, the absence of the highest possible degree of care showing the presence of some negligence, slight as it may be. The true doctrine, therefore, we think is, that in proportion to the negligence of the defendant, should be measured the degree of care required of the plaintiff—that is to say, the more gross the negligence manifested by the defendant, the less degree of care will be required of the plaintiff to enable him to recover. Although these cases do not distinctly avow this doctrine in terms, there is a vein of it very perceptible, running through very many of them, as, where there are faults on both sides, the plaintiff shall recover, his fault being to be measured by the defendant's negligence, the plaintiff need not be wholly without fault . . . .
>
> We say, then, that in this, as in all like cases, the degrees of negligence must be measured and considered, and wherever it shall appear that the plaintiff's negligence is comparatively slight, and that of the defendant gross, he shall not be deprived of his action.

Thus, in 1858, Illinois became a State which followed the doctrine of comparative negligence. . . .

. . . . No attempt was made to divide the damages under this "comparative negligence" rule, and where it was applied the effect was full recovery by the plaintiff. The injured person was required to show not only that his negligence was slight and that the defendant's negligence was gross, but also that they were so when compared with each other, since the element of comparison was the essence of the doctrine.

During the next 27 years, the rule stated in *Jacobs* was followed and then abandoned by this court in Calumet Iron & Steel Co. v. Martin (1885), 115 Ill. 358, 368–69, 3 N.E. 456, and City of Lanark v. Dougherty (1894), 153 Ill. 163, 165–66, 38 N.E. 892, where it unequivocally made any contributory negligence on the part of the plaintiff a complete bar to recovery. Dean Green summarized the reasons for abandonment: the formula was not complete in that the "degrees of negligence" did not mitigate the damages which the plaintiff could recover; the "degrees of negligence" resulted in doctrinal conflict and confusion; and the *Jacobs* case had not overruled the *Grimes* case . . . . Green, Illinois Negligence Law, 39 Ill.L.Rev. 36, 47–51 (1944).

Other jurisdictions found problems in the doctrine of contributory negligence. Criticism of the harshness of the doctrine came as swiftly as did its acceptance into the law, and courts found exceptions [such as the "last clear chance" rule] to soften that harshness. . . .

Comparative negligence made its first permanent entry into American law in 1908 in the form of the Federal Employers' Liability Act (45 U.S.C. sec. 53). The Act applied to all negligence cases for injuries sustained by railroad employees engaged in interstate commerce, whether such cases were brought in a State or a Federal court. The concept of comparative negligence provided that the contributory negligence of the employee would not act as a bar to recovery, but that recovery would be diminished

in proportion to the amount of negligence attributable to him. The introduction of the Federal Employers' Liability Act was the catalyst for a flood of State statutes which established a comparative negligence standard for injuries to laborers, and, especially, for railroad employees.
. . .

In 1910, Mississippi became the first State to adopt a comparative negligence statute applicable to negligence cases generally. (Miss.Code Ann. sec. 11-7-15 (1972).) The statute adopted the "pure" form of comparative negligence under which each responsible party would pay for the injuries sustained according to the relative percentage of his fault. Another form of comparative negligence was enacted by Wisconsin in 1931. (Wis.Stat.Ann. sec. 895.045 (West 1966).) This "modified" form allowed a negligent plaintiff to recover for his injuries [in proportion to the defendant's share of negligence, but only if the plaintiff's] negligence was "not as great as that of the defendant."

Today, a total of 36 States have adopted comparative negligence.
. . .

Twenty-three States have adopted the Wisconsin "modified" approach. Ten States have adopted the Mississippi "pure" comparative negligence approach. Two States, Nebraska and South Dakota, have a system which allows the plaintiff to recover only if his negligence is "slight" and that of defendant's is "gross." Georgia has its own unique system. It is important to note that 29 of these 36 States have adopted comparative negligence in the last 12 years.

In England, the birthplace of *Butterfield* v. *Forrester,* the concept of contributory negligence was long ago abandoned and replaced by a system of comparative negligence. Similarly, in many jurisdictions outside the United States the rule of contributory negligence has been abandoned in favor of comparative negligence. (Canada, the Canal Zone, Switzerland, Spain, Portugal, Austria, Germany, France, the Philippines, Japan, Russia, New Zealand, West Australia, Poland, and Turkey. See H. Woods, The Negligence Case: Comparative Fault 17 (1978).) In light of these changes the Supreme Court of Michigan, in Placek v. City of Sterling Heights (1979), 405 Mich. 638, 653, 275 N.W.2d 511, 515, stated:

> This precedent is so compelling that the question before remaining courts and legislatures is not whether but when, how and in what form to follow this lead.

II

CONTRIBUTORY NEGLIGENCE v. COMPARATIVE NEGLIGENCE

The contributory negligence defense has been subject to attack because of its failure to apportion damages according to the fault of the parties. Under a comparative negligence standard, the parties are allowed to recover the proportion of damages not attributable to their own fault. The basic logic and fairness of such apportionment is difficult to dispute.

The defendants herein claim that no change of circumstances has been shown which would call for a change from the established doctrine of contributory negligence. The Illinois Defense Counsel, in its *amicus curiae* brief, relies on the words of Mr. Justice Powell for the proposition that change is not demanded by the public.

> [T]here is little evidence that the public generally is concerned. If indeed the present rule is as "archaic" and "unjust" as is contended, one would normally expect much greater support for the organized efforts being made to abolish it. (Powell, Contributory Negligence: A Necessary Check on the American Jury, 43 A.B.A.J. 1005, 1008 (1957).)

It must be noted, however, that at the time of Mr. Justice Powell's quoted assessment, only six States had adopted the doctrine of comparative negligence. That 30 additional States have since adopted the doctrine evidences that the basis for the assessment has changed and that today there is, indeed, a compelling public demand to abolish the old rule. Certainly, the concern which prompted the adoption of the rule can no longer support its retention. There is no longer any justification for providing the protective barrier of the contributory negligence rule for industries of the nation at the expense of deserving litigants. It must be pointed out that today most cases against industrial defendants are brought under the Worker's Compensation Act, under which plaintiff's negligence is not an issue. (Ill.Rev.Stat.1979, ch. 48, par. 138.1 et seq.) . . . We believe that the concept of comparative negligence which produces a more just and socially desirable distribution of loss is demanded by today's society.

Defendants contend that the apportionment of relative fault by a jury cannot be scientifically done, as such precise measurement is impossible. The simple and obvious answer to this contention is that in 36 jurisdictions of the United States such apportionment is being accomplished by juries. The Supreme Court of California, in responding to a similar contention, stated:

> These inherent difficulties are not, however, insurmountable. Guidelines might be provided the jury which will assist it in keeping focussed upon the true inquiry [citation], and the utilization of special verdicts or jury interrogatories can be of invaluable assistance in assuring that the jury has approached its sensitive and often complex task with proper standards and appropriate reverence. (Li v. Yellow Cab Co. (1975), 13 Cal.3d 804, 824, 119 Cal.Rptr. 858, 872, 532 P.2d 1226, 1240.)

We agree that such guidelines can assist a jury in making apportionment decisions and view the necessary subtle calculations no more difficult or sophisticated for jury determination than others in a jury's purview, such as compensation for pain and suffering. Although it is admitted that percentage allocations of fault are only approximations, the results are far superior to the "all or nothing" results of the contributory negligence rule. "Small imperfections can be disregarded, small inequities tolerated, if the final result is generally satisfactory." Turk, Comparative Negligence on the March, 28 Chi.-Kent L.Rev. 189, 341–42 (1950).

Defendants assert that the contributory negligence rule should be retained in that the comparative negligence doctrine rewards carelessness and ignores the value of requiring prudent behavior. . . . Contrary to defendants' assertion, we believe that the need to deter negligent parties supports the adoption of the comparative negligence doctrine in which each party would be liable for damages in direct proportion to his degree of carelessness.

Defendants claim that the change to comparative negligence will cause administrative difficulties due to an increase in claims, a decrease in settlements, and a resulting overcrowded docket. An Arkansas study showed that, there, the adoption of comparative negligence prompted no drastic change in court burden; that the change increased potential litigation but promoted more pretrial settlements. The report concluded that concern over court congestion should not be a factor in a State's decision to adopt comparative negligence. Rosenberg, Comparative Negligence in Arkansas: A "Before and After" Survey, 13 Ark.L.Rev. 89, 108 (1959).

. . . We believe that the defendants' fears concerning the judicial administrative problems attendant upon the adoption of comparative negligence are exaggerated. But were defendants' fears well founded, we could nevertheless not allow the contributory negligence rule to remain the law of this State in the face of overwhelming evidence of its harsh and unjust results.

Defendants claim that the adoption of comparative negligence would escalate insurance rates to an unbearable level. This has not been found to be the case. Effects, in fact, have been found to be minimal. Rosenberg, Comparative Negligence in Arkansas: A "Before and After" Survey, 13 Ark.L.Rev. 89, 108 (1959).

The *amicus curiae* brief submitted by the Illinois Defense Counsel suggests that, under the contributory negligence rule, the jury has sufficient flexibility to do substantial justice and that this flexibility negates the necessity for the adoption of comparative negligence. In essence, the Illinois Defense Counsel alludes to the oft-observed phenomenon that, once inside the jury room, juries often ignore the harshness of the contributory negligence rule and, instead, dole out justice by a common sense approach according to the relative culpability of the litigants. We agree that such may be the case and, in fact, find the proclivity of juries to ignore the law to be a compelling reason for the abolition of that law. The Supreme Court of Florida addressed this concern.

> [T]here is something basically wrong with a rule of law that is so contrary to the settled convictions of the lay community that laymen will almost always refuse to enforce it, even when solemnly told to do so by a judge whose instructions they have sworn to follow. . . .
>
> The disrespect for law engendered by putting our citizens in a position in which they feel it is necessary to deliberately violate the law is not something to be lightly brushed aside; and it comes ill from the mouths of lawyers, who as officers of the courts have sworn to uphold the law, to defend the present system by arguing that it works because jurors can be trusted to disregard that very law. (Hoffman v. Jones (Fla.1973), 280 So.2d 431, 437.)

There is something inherently wrong with a rule of law so repulsive to a jury's common sense of justice that veniremen feel compelled to ignore the law.

III

JUDICIAL v. LEGISLATIVE CHANGE

It is urged by defendants that the decision to replace the doctrine of contributory negligence with the doctrine of comparative negligence must be made by the legislature, not by this court. In each of the States that have judicially adopted comparative negligence, the court addressed the propriety of judicial versus legislative adoption. In each, the court found that contributory negligence is a judicially created doctrine which can be altered or totally replaced by the court which created it. (Claymore v. City of Albuquerque (N.M.Ct.App., Dec. 8, 1980), Nos. 4804, 4805, slip op. at 77–78; Placek v. City of Sterling Heights (1979), 405 Mich. 638, 657, 275 N.W.2d 511, 517; Bradley v. Appalachian Power Co. (W.Va.1979), 256 S.E. 2d 879, 881; Li v. Yellow Cab Co. (1975), 13 Cal.3d 804, 813–14, 119 Cal. Rptr. 858, 864–65, 532 P.2d 1226, 1232–33; Kaatz v. State (Alaska 1975), 40 P.2d 1037, 1049; Hoffman v. Jones (Fla.1973), 280 So.2d 431, 434.) . . .

The Illinois Defense Counsel has, in its brief, urged that the legislature is better equipped to enact comparative negligence, asserting that "the legislative process . . . involves a broad examination of the entire problem without emphasis on a particular fact situation." The Defense Counsel and defendants claim that judicial adoption of comparative negligence would result in a piecemeal approach that would leave for future cases many ancillary questions. They claim that the law would be left in confusion and turmoil.

An examination of the States from which comparative negligence statutes have emerged reveals that such statutes are very general and brief and do not address collateral issues. Rather, the legislators apparently deemed it wise to leave the solution of collateral issues to the courts.

Defendants point out that, since 1976, six bills were introduced in the Illinois legislature to abolish the doctrine of contributory negligence. They interpret the failure of each bill to pass as a sign of the General Assembly's desire to retain the present status of the rule. Another conclusion may be drawn, however, as pointed out by Mr. Justice Ward in his dissenting opinion in Maki v. Frelk (1968), 40 Ill.2d 193, 203, 239 N.E.2d 445:

> It can be argued that the legislature's inaction in this area is attributable to its feeling that it is more appropriate, considering the history of the question in Illinois, for the judiciary to act.

In support of their view that the legislature intends to retain the rule, defendants point to various statutes which have incorporated the contributory negligence defense. They claim that these statutes act as a legislative ratification of the doctrine of contributory negligence. We do not agree. We believe that in enacting such statutes the legislature did not focus on the merits of the contributory negligence rule, but, rather, conformed the statutes to the then-existing law as announced by the court.

We believe that the proper relationship between the legislature and the court is one of cooperation and assistance in examining and changing the common law to conform with the ever-changing demands of the community. There are, however, times when there exists a mutual state of inaction in which the court awaits action by the legislature and the legislature awaits guidance from the court. Such a stalemate is a manifest injustice to the public. When such a stalemate exists and the legislature has, for whatever reason, failed to act to remedy a gap in the common law that results in injustice, it is the imperative duty of the court to repair that injustice and reform the law to be responsive to the demands of society.

IV

STARE DECISIS

Defendants urge us to abide by the doctrine of *stare decisis* and follow the holding in Maki v. Frelk (1968), 40 Ill.2d 193, 239 N.E.2d 445. They contend that it is crucial to the due administration of justice, especially in a court of last resort, that a question once deliberately examined and decided be closed to further scrutiny. It must first be pointed out that the *Maki* decision, filed 13 years ago, did not, as claimed by defendants, address the merits of the case. On the contrary, the court avoided the merits by holding that the problem was one for the legislature.

It is interesting to observe that if Illinois courts had, in fact, rigidly adhered to the *stare decisis* rule throughout this State's legal history, the comparative standard could not have been adopted in Galena & Chicago Union R.R. Co. v. Jacobs (1858), 20 Ill. 478. Similarly, the comparative rule could not have been later discarded in Calumet Iron & Steel Co. v. Martin (1885), 115 Ill. 358, 3 N.E. 456, and City of Lanark v. Dougherty (1894), 153 Ill. 163, 38 N.E. 892.

The tenets of *stare decisis* cannot be so rigid as to incapacitate a court in its duty to develop the law. Clearly, the need for stability in law must not be allowed to obscure the changing needs of society or to veil the injustice resulting from a doctrine in need of reevaluation. This court can no longer ignore the fact that Illinois is currently out of step with the majority of States and with the common law countries of the world. We cannot continue to ignore the plight of plaintiffs who, because of some negligence on their part, are forced to bear the entire burden of their injuries. Neither can we condone the policy of allowing defendants to totally escape liability for injuries arising from their own negligence on the pretext that another party's negligence has contributed to such injuries. We therefore hold that in cases involving negligence the common law doctrine of contributory negligence is no longer the law in the State of Illinois, and in those instances where applicable it is replaced by the doctrine of comparative negligence.

V

THE "PURE" VERSUS THE "MODIFIED" FORM OF COMPARATIVE NEGLIGENCE

There remains the question of the form of comparative negligence to be adopted. Under a "pure" form, the plaintiff's damages are simply reduced by the percentage of fault attributable to him. Under a "modified" form, a negligent plaintiff may recover so long as the percentage of his fault does not exceed 50% of the total.

Defendants argue that should this court decide to adopt comparative negligence, the modified approach should be selected. They point to the basic unfairness of the "pure" system by example: A plaintiff who is 90% negligent has suffered $100,000 in damages. A defendant who is only 10% negligent has suffered only $10,000 in damages. Defendants here point out the basic unfairness of requiring the 10% negligent defendant to pay $10,000 to a plaintiff who was 90% at fault. . . . In a suit under a "pure" form of comparative negligence in which the defendant counterclaims for his own damages, each party must bear the burden of the percentage of damages of all parties in direct proportion to his fault. In the example above, the 90% negligent plaintiff will bear 90% of his own damages as well as 90% of defendant's. On the other hand, the 10% negligent defendant will be made to bear 10% of his own damages as well as 10% of plaintiff's. Neither party is unjustly enriched. Neither party escapes liability resulting from his negligent acts or omissions. It is difficult to see unfairness in such a distribution of liability.

Opponents of the "pure" form of comparative negligence claim that the "modified" form is superior in that it will increase the likelihood of settlement and will keep down insurance costs. However, studies done comparing the effects of the "pure" versus the "modified" forms show the differences in insurance rates to be inconsequential. (V. Schwartz, Comparative Negligence 346 (1974).) Fears as to the likelihood of settlement are not supported in fact or logic. It is argued that the negligent plaintiff will refuse to settle knowing that, under the "pure" system he will be able to recover "something" in court. The converse can as easily apply: the defendant may be encouraged to settle knowing that he cannot rely on the "modified" 50% cut-off point to relieve him of liability. . . .

Wisconsin's "modified" system has been criticized because a large number of cases appealed focused on the narrow question of whether plaintiff's negligence amounted to 50% or less of the aggregate. (Prosser, Comparative Negligence, 41 Cal.L.Rev. 1, 23 (1953).) This, in fact, caused the Wisconsin Supreme Court to examine the question of whether the "modified" system should be replaced with the "pure" form of comparative negligence. (Vincent v. Pabst Brewing Co. (1970), 47 Wis.2d 120, 177 N.W.2d 513.) There, as in Maki v. Frelk (1968), 40 Ill.2d 193, 239 N.E. 445, the merits of the case were not addressed, for the majority of the court ruled that the determination should be left to the legislature, which had originally adopted the "modified" form by statute. One dissenting and three concurring justices, however, expressed their intent to judicially adopt the "pure" form if the legislature failed to do so.

The "pure" form of comparative negligence is the only system which truly apportions damages according to the relative fault of the parties and, thus, achieves total justice. We agree with the *Li* court that "the '50 percent' system simply shifts the lottery aspect of the contributory negligence rule to a different ground." (Li v. Yellow Cab Co. (1975), 13 Cal.3d 804, 827, 119 Cal.Rptr. 858, 874, 532 P.2d 1226, 1242.) There is no better justification for allowing a defendant who is 49% at fault to completely escape liability than there is to allow a defendant who is 99% at fault under the old rule to escape liability.

Mindful of the facts stated and that the vast majority of legal scholars who have studied the area recommend the "pure" approach, we are persuaded that the "pure" form of comparative negligence is preferable, and we therefore adopt it as the law of Illinois.

. . . We have already noted that the doctrine of "last clear chance" was created to escape the harshness of the contributory negligence rule. As the need for it disappears in the face of this decision, the vestiges of the doctrine of "last clear chance" are hereby abolished.

We believe that the use of special verdicts and special interrogatories will serve as a guide to assist the jury in its deliberations. We leave the resolution of other collateral issues to future cases.

VI

APPLICATION

Finally, we address the question of the applicability of the rule here announced. We hold that this opinion shall be applied to the parties before us on appeal, and to all cases in which trial commences on or after June 8, 1981, the date on which the mandate in this case shall issue. This opinion shall not be applicable to any case in which trial commenced before that date—except that if any judgment be reversed on appeal for other reasons, this opinion shall be applicable to any retrial.

For the reasons stated, we hereby abolish the common law doctrine of contributory negligence and adopt in its place the doctrine of comparative negligence in its pure form. The judgments of the appellate court and circuit courts are reversed and the causes are remanded to the respective circuit courts for further proceedings in accordance with the views expressed herein.

UNDERWOOD, JUSTICE, dissenting:

While I acknowledge the court's power to radically change a rule of law which has existed in this State for nearly a century, I still believe, as I did when Maki v. Frelk (1968), 40 Ill.2d 193, 239 N.E.2d 445, was decided, that the decision to change is best left to the General Assembly.

. . . One of the major problems with a judicially decreed change of this magnitude is its effect upon a great many other, related areas of law. What modifications, for example, are now to be made in the doctrines of . . . wilful and wanton misconduct . . . and many others? While the newly decreed rule of comparative negligence may ultimately affect all of these situations to a now unknown degree, the court can consider only one case at a time. Unless the legislature acts, it will in all probability be years before these questions can be judicially answered. Meanwhile, litigants and the trial courts must attempt to predict the manner in which this court will eventually resolve these now unresolved questions. The fact that the General Assembly could, if it considered a change desirable, adopt one of the comprehensively drafted bills with which it has been presented and resolve these related questions simultaneously is, to me, a persuasive reason for this court to exercise a greater degree of judicial restraint.

There are other reasons to prefer legislative action. If a change is to be made, what should the new rule be? . . .

While I do not totally disagree with the proposition that modification of our heretofore existing contributory negligence rule is desirable, I am not at all certain that the pure form of comparative negligence is the preferred substitute. If it is, it seems odd that of the 36 States which have adopted some form of comparative negligence approximately two thirds have chosen a modified form. And, while the majority says the pure form "achieves total justice," the fact that this form permits a grossly negligent but severely injured plaintiff to recover substantial damages from a slightly negligent defendant with only minor injuries certainly represents a radical departure from the concept of individual responsibility which has heretofore underlain our system of tort law. Despite the assertion by the majority that the pure form produces a utopian form of justice, most of the States adopting a comparative negligence rule have preferred to deny recovery to one whose own negligence was the principal cause of his injuries.

Whether a change is desirable, and, if so, what that change should be, are major policy questions. Their resolution will have a substantial effect upon the people of this State. Recovery will henceforth be possible for conduct of a significantly less reprehensible nature than heretofore. Litigation will surely increase, thus augmenting the burden upon our already overburdened courts, and insurance rates will likely rise in unknown amounts. Policy choices such as those involved here are, it seems to me, best left to the judgment of a General Assembly staffed and equipped to explore, consider, and resolve simultaneously these many-faceted questions.

The majority emphasizes as justification for its action the cliche that courts which created a rule can modify it, and cites cases from some six States which have adopted comparative negligence. There are a greater number, including *Maki,* to the contrary. . . .

It is to me anomalous for the majority to cite the introduction, consideration, and rejection of six bills in the legislature in less than five years as support for the proposition that there has been legislative "inaction" on the subject. Rather, it seems to me, the introduction of so many bills indicates a considerable amount of activity, and an additional bill, House Bill 0142, providing a system of comparative negligence, is presently pending. The General Assembly has been well aware from our annual reports to it that the large majority of the judges of Illinois were in favor of legislative adoption of some form of comparative negligence. There is no reason to believe, as the majority suggests, that the absence of legislation doing so should now be viewed as indicating the legislature is awaiting action by this court. Rather, I would have thought the substantial volume of proposed legislation on the subject which had failed to pass indicated the General Assembly's considered judgment that no change should be made. If that assumption is correct, my colleagues are simply overruling the judgment of the members of our General Assembly on a major question of public policy because they "believe that the concept of comparative negligence which produces a more just and socially desirable distribution of loss is demanded by today's society" and "it is the imperative duty of the court to repair that injustice [contributory negligence] and reform the law to be responsive to the demands of society." I would respectfully suggest that the 236 members of the General Assembly are far better situated than the members of this court to determine what is "socially desirable" and to gauge the "demands of society." In a republic in which law-making power is vested, at least theoretically, in our elected representatives, I would have thought a greater degree of judicial self-restraint desirable. The willingness of the judiciary to invade the legislative realm simply encourages additional resort to the courts for resolution of difficult questions of public policy better left to the legislative branch.

. . .

RYAN, JUSTICE, dissenting:

I join in the dissent of Mr. Justice Underwood. . . .

For the sake of stability, if for no other reason, it would appear preferable to have such a radical change as this made by the legislature. . . . Now, just 12 years later, with only two members of the *Maki* court still serving [Justices Underwood and Ward], this court has reversed itself and has held that this court and not the legislature should reject contributory negligence in favor of comparative negligence. Conceivably in a few years, when the present members of this court will no longer be serving and when their replacements may be less enthusiastic about comparative negligence, this court could reject the judge-made law of this case. If we were to adhere to the holding of *Maki* and accept the action or inaction of the legislature, as the case may be, as the policy of this State, the law would be free from this possible uncertainty and we would either follow the doctrine of contributory negligence or comparative negligence free from judicial tinkering. . . .

Contributory negligence is, of course, based upon the fault concept of tort law. Comparative negligence, while ostensibly involving the fault concept, is, in reality, a product of that school of tort law which has held that it was unjust for one who is injured not to be compensated for his loss. This is particularly true of "pure," as compared with "modified," comparative negligence. Thus the focus of pure comparative negligence is on compensation and the distribution of the loss and retains only a semblance of the fault basis as a means of accomplishing its main purpose. In other words, in my opinion, pure comparative negligence is another fiction in the law which those who refuse to accept the no-fault theory of recovery have promoted to accomplish essentially no-fault recovery.

. . .

To say that a jury will discount a plaintiff's recovery by his degree of negligence is not realistic. Just as sympathetic juries operating under limitations of contributory negligence apply a form of comparative negligence, juries operating under pure comparative negligence will, in effect, compensate a plaintiff for his injuries, regardless of the degree of his fault.

.   .   .

Comments and Questions

1. The preceding is a sharply edited version of a much longer report of the case, which also included many citations. Worth noting is that American judicial opinions are written, in contrast to the oral tradition of the English.

2. Another common fallacy about law is that "law is nothing but politics." But what is meant by "politics"? Generally true is that law rests on political power. Generally true is that questions for lawmakers such as courts and legislatures are questions of policy and in that sense political. Also generally true is that the content of even judge-made law is, over the long run, influenced to some extent by political considerations: the specific wants of political pressure groups, the specific wants of political parties, the specific wants of political creditors and constituents. But making too much of these general truths is easy. For instance, is it wholly appropriate to say that the courts in the *Butterfield, Davies,* and *Loach* cases were responding to political wants? Consider, too, the proper interpretation of grievance-remedial statutes. When courts interpret these, are they responding merely to such wants? And what of the usual judicial deference to *stare decisis*? Whether or not one case is decided consistently with another is a political question only in a special sense. Nevertheless, the *Alvis* case destroys the opposing fallacious view of the court as an ivory tower, does it not?

3. Up to here in our materials, all the modern authorities have seemed almost to *assume* that the old all-or-nothing doctrine of contributory negligence and its exceptions was bad and that the new doctrine of comparative negligence, which apportions damages in some manner, is good—the main dispute being who should effect the reform. In your view, how sound is that assumption? Does the difficulty of this question tend to make you rethink the issue of "judicial v. legislative change"?

4. As a first step in reanalyzing the desirability of this reform, consider the following excerpt from the growing body of literature on law and economics. Note, incidentally, that Judge Posner's view has been rebutted, primarily by taking a broader view, in Schwartz, Contributory and Comparative Negligence: A Reappraisal, 87 Yale L.J. 697 (1978).

R. POSNER, ECONOMIC ANALYSIS OF LAW

122–24 (2d ed. 1977).*

The legal standard applicable to most unintentional tort cases is that of negligence, defined by Judge Learned Hand as follows: the defendant is guilty of negligence if the loss caused by the accident, multiplied by the probability of the accident's occurring, exceeds the burden of the precau-

* Copyright © 1972, 1973, 1977 by Richard A. Posner. Reprinted by permission of Little, Brown and Company.

tions that the defendant might have taken to avert it.[1] This is an economic test. The burden of precautions is the cost of avoiding the accident. The loss multiplied by the probability of the accident is the expected accident cost, i.e., the cost that the precautions would have averted. If a larger cost could have been avoided by incurring a smaller cost, efficiency requires that the smaller cost be incurred.

Although the Hand formula is of relatively recent origin, the method that it capsulizes has been the basic one used to determine negligence ever since negligence was first adopted as the standard to govern accident cases. For example, in the old case of *Blyth* v. *Birmingham Water Works,*[5] the question was whether a water company had been negligent in failing to bury its water pipes deeply enough to prevent them from bursting because of frost and inflicting damage on the plaintiff's home. In holding that the water company had not been negligent, the court emphasized that the frost which burst the pipe in question had been of unprecedented severity—i.e., the probability of the loss in question had been low. Nor was the loss caused by the bursting pipe so great as to have justified the heavy expense of burying the pipes deeper, in light of the improbability that the loss would occur. The discounted loss, or expected cost, of the accident was less than the cost of prevention. . . .

Applied only to the defendant, the Hand formula would not always produce the efficient solution. Suppose that an accident cost (after discounting) of $1000 could be prevented by the defendant at a cost of $100, but by the plaintiff at a cost of only $50. The efficient solution is to make the plaintiff liable by refusing to allow him to recover damages from the defendant. If the defendant is liable, the plaintiff will have no incentive to take preventive measures (unless the damages to which he would be entitled would not fully compensate him for his injury), and the value-maximizing solution to the accident problem will not be obtained.

The doctrine of contributory negligence is the law's answer to this problem. If the plaintiff could have prevented the accident at a cost lower than the discounted accident cost, he cannot recover. This takes care of the previous example. But suppose it is the plaintiff who can prevent the $1000 accident at a cost of $100, and the defendant at a cost of $50. If the plaintiff is barred from recovery by the doctrine of contributory negligence, as the Hand formula, applied literally to the plaintiff, would require, the defendant will have no incentive to take what turns out to be the more efficient preventive measure.

Several states have replaced contributory negligence with a comparative negligence standard, whereby the plaintiff's damages are reduced by the percentage by which his own negligence contributed to the accident. This is not the correct economic standard either; in a case like the last one, it would result in the parties' spending more than the efficient amount on accident prevention. If the defendant in that case was fully liable for the accident, he would spend $50 to prevent it and the plaintiff nothing, so the accident would be prevented at a cost of only $50. But

1. United States v. Carroll Towing Co., 159 F.2d 169 (2d Cir.1947). . . .
5. 11 Exch. 781, 156 Eng.Rep. 1047 (1856).

suppose he were liable for only two thirds, say, of the accident cost, because the plaintiff was also negligent (i.e., could also have prevented the accident at a cost, $100, that was less than the accident cost). Being liable for a judgment of $666.67, the defendant would still have an incentive to spend $50 on accident prevention, while the plaintiff, since he must bear a cost of $333.33 if an accident occurs, would have an incentive to spend $100 to prevent the accident. The parties might therefore invest a total of $150 in accident prevention, resulting in a $100 increase in the cost of preventing the same accident; or they might invest nothing (either party, knowing that the other party had an incentive to prevent the accident, might, in reliance thereon, make no attempt to prevent it himself), resulting in an avoidable cost of $950.

Section Four.　Structures and Processes for Applying Grievance-Remedial Law and Techniques

Grievance-remedial techniques and the general rules specifying the conditions for their availability would not alone be sufficient to constitute an effective grievance-remedial instrument. We have yet to show why and how this is so. Indeed, we have not yet even shown the origins of the felt need for courts, because grievance-remedial premises might after all be formulated solely by legislatures. Therefore, here we shall turn to the need for authoritatively applying the law and techniques to particular facts.

Before considering authoritative structures and processes for applying law and techniques to facts of particular cases, however, we must stress that such law is often applied by private parties on their own, without resort to authoritative schemes set up by the legal system. A common fallacy about law is that occasions to apply it arise only after a dispute arises and that law is something only authorized officials can and do apply. Yet, in advance of disputed grievances, many private persons seek legal advice from lawyers about how to avoid such grievances in the first place. And when disputed grievances do occur, many private persons are able to settle these disputes on their own in light of what they are told by their lawyers about the relevant law and techniques. Moreover, most private persons similarly act without the aid of lawyers.

In the materials that follow, an actual contested case, *White* v. *Island Amusement Co.,* will be used as the vehicle for presenting an inside view of structures and processes widely used in Anglo-American countries for authoritatively applying law and techniques to facts. The *White* case is also a negligence case, arising in a jurisdiction that had not yet adopted an apportionment approach to contributory negligence. The real case has been only slightly altered for pedagogic purposes.

Before plunging into the case at hand, several caveats are called for. First, there are other uses of the grievance-remedial mode of legal action besides its use to redress personal injuries negligently caused by others. Such a use, however, is nicely representative. Some of those other uses will be encountered in later chapters of this book. Second, there are other processes for resolving disputed issues of fact and law besides a compulsory adjudicative process adversarially initiated and informed. Such a process has, however, been so dominant in Anglo-American legal evolution that it is commonly thought to be intrinsic to the grievance-remedial mode. In a later section of this chapter, some possible alternatives will be explored. Third, the assumption should not be made that the particular version of the general adjudicative-adversarial process reflected in the upcoming case is the only version in use in Anglo-American jurisdictions. Thus, for example, important differences exist between it and the version in federal courts governed by the so-called Federal Rules of Civil Procedure, but systematically taking account of such differences lies beyond the purposes of this book. Fourth, in what follows the emphasis will be on the process through which the grievance-remedial mode has traditionally functioned rather than on the outcome of whether the legal system does or does not provide a remedy. This process-oriented emphasis is deliberate, for the main aim of this chapter is to show the law in action in one of its most important operational modes. Fifth, we repeat that the assumption should not be made that in Anglo-American law, when one party seeks a remedy against another for a grievance, the parties always choose to "have it out in court." On the contrary, far more such cases are settled by the parties themselves than by judicial intervention.

Why trace an actual case through from beginning to end? If students are truly to understand the basic elements of the grievance-remedial mode, they must be able to visualize the relevant occurrences. This students can do satisfactorily only if exposed to these events as they occur in the concrete. Moreover, the adjudicative-adversarial process itself breaks down into stages, but these can be adequately grasped only in relation to each other. This being so, the whole interdependent process can be adequately grasped only through an overview of what occurs at sequential stages and why these stages are as they are. Finally, what follows will serve as useful background for understanding the many appellate decisions that appear later in this book, for such decisions are always concerned with something that happened "below" at the trial level.

A. The Injury Occurs

The city of Eyre, in the state of New Fetter, had a population of 350,000. It also had nineteen public swimming areas. On the evening of June 7, 1958, Sharon Ann White, a fifteen-year-old high school student, bought a ticket to swim at a public swimming area located at Hansen Beach Park on the outskirts of the city of Eyre. The swimming area included four pools: two for wading, one "shallow pool," and one "deep pool." The area was owned by the Island Amusement Company. Miss White was admitted to the pool area. After changing into her swimsuit, she walked to the edge of the shallow pool and dove in, striking her head on the bottom. As a result, she was hospitalized for thirty-one days with a broken neck and thereafter suffered from other ailments, which she traced to the accident.

B. Retaining a Lawyer

Today, the United States has a fast-growing body of well over 600,000 lawyers. Of these, over 400,000 are in private practice, or about 2 per 1,000 population in this country. Most such lawyers now work as partners or associates in law firms, although many still work as solo practitioners. Arrangements for the retention of a private-practice lawyer by a client vary considerably.

In cases where the plaintiff retains a lawyer to assert a claim for damages for personal injuries, lawyer and client frequently sign a so-called contingent fee agreement whereby the lawyer receives nothing if he recovers nothing but receives a percentage (fixed or variable) of whatever he does recover. In many states, contingent fees of one-third are not uncommon.

On the other hand, a lawyer defending against a personal injury claim would, in many cases, be retained on an hourly basis by an insurance company that had insured the defendant against such liability. Stating a meaningful average fee is difficult, but fees in the range of $40 to $100 per hour are most common.

In America, each party usually ends up paying her own lawyer the agreed fee. At the conclusion of litigation, the court normally awards *costs*, to be paid by the losing party to the prevailing party. Costs include relatively small, direct expenses of litigation, such as filing fees, but they ordinarily do not include the large item of counsel fees. Note that in most of the rest of the Western world, including England, the losing party also pays the attorneys' fees of the prevailing party.

In a fairly large city like Eyre, how is the typical citizen to locate a good lawyer when he has a need for one? It is not particularly easy. The citizen may know or learn of an attorney through informal contacts or a legal directory or sometimes through the lawyer's advertising or a lawyer referral program sponsored by a bar association.

In the Swimming Pool case, Paul R. White, Miss White's father and a worker in a manufacturing plant, considered seeing a lawyer about his daughter's case but put the idea of a lawsuit out of his mind after mulling over "all the difficulties of getting involved with the courts and with lawyers." Over two years later, however, he changed his mind when he became acquainted at a church picnic with a young lawyer named Al Stone. Stone, an associate in a firm of fifteen lawyers, had been in practice only a year and a half and had never "tried a case" entirely on his own. The senior members of the firm were reluctant to turn over such responsibility to a new associate. But Stone was eager to try a case all alone and knew his chances would be better with his seniors if he "brought in a client."

On December 18, 1960, the Whites went to Stone's office where, among other things, they signed a contingent fee agreement, calling for the lawyer to receive 30 percent of whatever recovery he secured from the Island Amusement Company, whether via settlement or via litigation.

C. The Lawyer's Preliminary Determinations of Relevant Facts and Law

As we indicated earlier, facts, for purposes of litigation, are not facts as such. Someone has to decide them, on the basis of what lawyers put before the adjudicative body. Much time has been wasted because of inadequate factual investigations—and many cases lost. The good lawyer will seldom make up her own mind about the probable facts merely on the basis of an interview with her own client. But in that interview, she will try to be thorough about the facts.

On December 18, 1960, the day the White family went to Stone's office, Stone interviewed mother, father, and daughter thoroughly, and then they all visited the pool area where the accident had occurred. That evening before going home, Stone dictated detailed memoranda on the interview and visit.

Here is a puzzle: On the one hand, can a lawyer know what facts are relevant to the legal validity of a claim before he researches the relevant law? (He cannot be expected to carry all such law in his head.) On the other hand, can the lawyer know what law to research before he has determined all the relevant facts? At any rate, will all questions divide neatly into either questions of pure fact or questions of pure law? In the Swimming Pool case, we shall encounter an important example of a mixed question of fact and law, viz., the question whether, in a given case, a party's conduct was negligent conduct.

It is sometimes said that many claimants' lawyers commence legal proceedings without first investigating the facts or the law very thoroughly. In so doing, they are sometimes motivated to state their clients' claims generally and in several versions so as not to foreclose the possibility that at least some facts will turn up before or at trial on which the clients can recover. We shall have occasion to evaluate this kind of practice at a later point. It may not be all bad.

Other claimants' lawyers at the outset try to be specific in thinking about the facts and about the substantive rules of liability and defense with which they will have to contend. We shall assume that Stone is of this ilk.

The first thing such a lawyer will have to concern himself with is whether he can, with some expectation of being able to prove them, allege facts that, if proved, would constitute a *cause of action*. What is a cause of action? It may be viewed as a prima facie right to a remedy. To ascertain this right, the claimant's lawyer must consult the substantive law. That law will lay down the *elements* of the relevant cause of action—the minimal facts the claimant must establish to prevail lawfully.

But a good cause of action will not, in many cases, be enough, for it is only a prima facie right to a remedy. The defendant may have a good defense. The plaintiff's counsel will do well to check into the facts and the law on this, too. Counsel is bound by the rules of professional conduct not to stir up baseless litigation. Also, he could not afford to waste his time.

Let us assume that Stone has turned up probable facts that lead him to consider (1) whether he can justifiably allege facts constituting a cause of action against the Island Amusement Company for negligence in operating its pool and (2) whether he can justifiably meet a possible defense by the Island Amusement Company that Miss White was contributorily negligent and therefore not entitled to recover anything. We may assume, then, that Stone has dug up two general rules of substantive law of potential relevance. Can you state what they are, in rough-and-ready terms?

Students should not assume that Stone will end his research on facts and law at this point. To now we have spoken of preliminary determinations. Through discovery devices and other means to be explained later, he will inform himself further, provided he has decided on the basis of his preliminary determinations that his client appears to have a good case.

D. Efforts at Private Settlement

On January 20, 1961, Miss White, on the advice of her parents, agreed to authorize Stone to settle the case for anything at or over two thousand dollars (which would cover medical bills and other related expenses). Stone then got in touch with the Island Amusement Company and learned for the first time that Henry Story was the company's lawyer. After Stone discussed the case with Story on two occasions, it emerged that no settlement could be had, at least none at the two-thousand-dollar figure. Thus, litigation loomed.

The assumption should not be made that settlement efforts always precede steps in litigation. Often the two proceed concurrently. Often no effort at settlement is made until many steps toward trial have been taken. This is not hard to explain. A claimant who starts formal proceedings may lead a doubting potential defendant to take her seriously for the first time. At least the defendant will be put to the expense of having to respond. Furthermore, by starting formal proceedings, the claimant can gain access to compulsory discovery devices for learning more facts about the case, should she be in the dark.

E. Commencing Legal Proceedings in a Proper Court

A distinction has already been drawn between trial courts and appellate courts. In a federal system such as the American one, each state has both kinds of courts, and the federal government itself has both trial and appellate courts as well.

Miss White's case had to be commenced in a state court because there was no basis for federal jurisdiction. In a typical state judicial system, one finds trial courts of limited jurisdiction (for example, courts handling the probate of wills), trial courts of general jurisdiction, possibly one or more intermediate appellate courts, and certainly one ultimate appellate court (usually called the supreme court of the state).

Miss White's lawyer had to determine in which state court he should bring Miss White's case. We shall assume that he decided upon a proper adjudicative body, namely, the trial court of general jurisdiction named the Circuit Court of the State of New Fetter for the County of Temple.

How would Miss White's lawyer, Mr. Stone, actually start proceedings against the Island Amusement Company in the foregoing court? He did so on January 26, 1961, by filing with the clerk of the court a *complaint* — a document that states his client's grievance and asks for an appropriate remedy.

On February 2, 1961, Stone had a copy of the complaint and a *summons* he had prepared served by the Temple County sheriff on Mr. J.F. Thomas, who was manager of Hansen Beach Park and an officer of the Island Amusement Company.   The actual summons read in part as follows:

> You are hereby required to appear and answer the Complaint filed against you .   .   . within ten days from the date of service of this Summons upon you .   .   . ; and if you fail so to answer, for want thereof, the plaintiff will take judgment against the defendant in the amount of $1116.35 special damages and $10,000.00 general damages and for costs .   .   . incurred herein.

F.   Getting Any Disputed Issues of Fact and Law Defined and Separated So They Can Be Adjudicated

After the plaintiff has properly haled the proper defendant before the proper adjudicative body, the next step has traditionally been for the lawyers to go to work defining and separating the issues of fact and law to be adjudicated.   And this would seem the natural next step.   If the issues are defined at this stage, the lawyers will not waste time and money preparing for presentation of evidence or argument on matters they really agree on.   Also, they will know what they do have to prepare for and can go right to work.

Or so it has seemed to the many devisers of adjudicative procedure who have provided that the next stage in the process would be one of defining issues, largely through *pleadings*.   Because this approach has been so influential, and because the Swimming Pool case was litigated via this approach, we shall here take up, as the next stage in the process, getting the basic issues of fact and law defined and separated.   But note that the Federal Rules take a different approach.   They reflect a belief that expecting the pleadings to define the issues, rather than merely give general notice of positions, is expecting too much and opens the door to abusive practice and inefficient squabbling.   So they rely heavily on the use of devices such as discovery, rather than on pleadings, to get the issues defined.   Among other things, this means that under the Federal Rules, the two stages of issue definition and preparation for hearings on certain issues of law or for trial of certain issues of fact are not so clear-cut and tend to merge.

Students may wonder why we also speak of *separating* issues of fact from issues of law.   For now, suffice it to say that in our system, a jury is frequently called upon to resolve issues of fact, whereas a judge resolves issues of law.   In the Swimming Pool case, a jury was to sit.

Getting back to *defining* the issues, we have already seen that the plaintiff's lawyer, Stone, filed a complaint to which the defendant had to respond within ten days from the date of service.   This complaint was drafted by Stone to read basically as follows (students should not assume that any of the pleadings in this case are offered as models of perfection).

———

IN THE CIRCUIT COURT OF THE STATE OF NEW
FETTER FOR THE COUNTY OF
TEMPLE

Sharon Ann White by Paul R.
White, her Guardian ad litem,
                                Plaintiff,
                                                    COMPLAINT
            vs.
Island Amusement Co.,
                                Defendant.

COMES NOW Sharon Ann White by her Guardian ad litem, Paul R.
White, and for complaint against the defendant alleges:

I

That Sharon Ann White was at all times mentioned herein and is at
the present time a minor child born April 10, 1943.

II

That Paul R. White is her father and the duly appointed Guardian ad
litem.

III

That on June 7, 1958, plaintiff was a paying guest at the swimming
pool operated by defendant at Hansen Beach Park, Temple County, New
Fetter.

IV

That on the above date she, upon arrival at the pool and after
changing into her swimming suit, attempted to join her friends in the pool
and dived into the pool at the end gauging the depth of the water at the
point where she dived in by the position of the top of the water on the
bodies of her friends standing together in the pool at a point near the
center of the pool and approximately even with the point on the end of the
pool from which she dived.

V

That plaintiff reasonably assumed that the depth of the water in the
pool was in accordance with the type of construction used generally in the
construction of swimming pools; that is, deep at her end and shallow at
the other, with a uniform depth from side to side.

VI

That unknown to plaintiff the depth of the water was not in accordance with said type of construction but was much shallower near the
edge from which she dived than at the point even therefrom where her
friends were standing.

VII

That when plaintiff dived into the water her head struck the bottom of
the pool resulting in injuries as hereinafter described.

VIII

That the sole and proximate cause of said injuries was the negligence
of the defendant in the following particulars, to-wit:

(a) In misleading the plaintiff as to the depth of the swimming pool at the place where she dived.

(b) In failing to warn the plaintiff that the bottom of this pool was not constructed in the same manner as other swimming pools in the vicinity of the City of Eyre, New Fetter, in regard to depth of water near the end of the pool.

(c) In failing to properly care for the plaintiff by calling a doctor and ambulance after the defendant knew of the accident and injury and the nature thereof.

IX

That as a direct and proximate result of the defendant's negligence, the plaintiff's neck was crushed, broken and dislocated; the ligaments, muscles and soft tissues were torn and stretched; her head was cut to a length necessarily requiring approximately fourteen stitches. That on account of such injuries she was necessarily required to have medical attention and on account of her broken neck she was necessarily required to be hospitalized for a period of approximately 31 days; all of which she became obligated to pay in the amount of $1116.35 special damages, the same being a reasonable amount for the services rendered. That plaintiff's injuries are permanent and she has had considerable pain and suffering all to her general damages of $10,000.00.

X

That the above medical attention and hospitalization were reasonable necessities furnished to said minor plaintiff in treatment of the aforesaid injuries.

WHEREFORE, plaintiff prays judgment against defendant in the amount of $1116.35 special damages and $10,000.00 general damages and for costs incurred herein.

[signature]

[The diagram Annex *A* was attached to the foregoing complaint.]

ANNEX *A:* Pool Layout

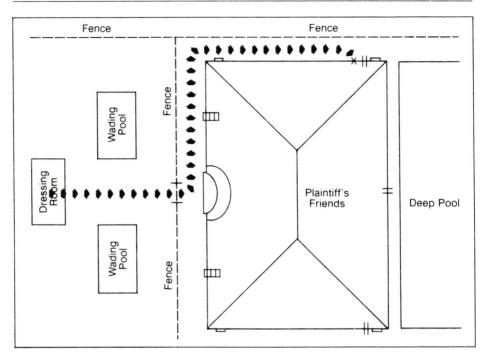

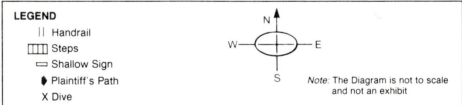

Observe that the foregoing complaint does not purport to constitute proof of any facts. Instead it alleges that certain facts occurred on which Miss White bases her claim. If the defendant should deny any of these allegations of fact, then and only then would it be necessary to determine what the facts were, and this might be done in a trial at a later stage of the proceedings. Incidentally, does Miss White merely allege raw facts, or does she also allege some conclusions?

Observe also that the foregoing complaint includes no explicit references to any rules of law that might support Miss White's claim. In drafting her complaint, it was necessary for Miss White's lawyer only to allege facts that, if proved, would constitute a valid claim under the relevant law—a good cause of action. But to do this, he had to know the principle of law that entitled a person to compensation for negligently caused harm, and he had to know how this principle had been applied in similar cases.

If the complaint does not prove facts, and if it does not set forth the law on which it is based, then what does it do? For one thing, it informs the defending party that a claim based on allegations of fact is being asserted against him. A fundamental principle of procedural justice is that a person should not be required to satisfy the claim of another if he has not received notice of that claim and had an opportunity to defend against it. When the complaint and summons are delivered to the defendant, he has a certain number of days in which to respond to the complaint.

Suppose the defendant, when the complaint and summons are delivered, simply ignores them? In Anglo-American law, a plaintiff generally has the power, by starting a legal action, to require the defendant to choose between (1) responding to the complaint and (2) having a judgment entered against him. That is, if the defendant should choose not to respond, the plaintiff would become entitled to a *default* judgment in her favor. And the effect of having a default judgment entered against the defendant for a sum of money would be that the sheriff, pursuant to an appropriate writ, could lawfully sell enough of the defendant's property to satisfy the judgment. Why should a plaintiff have power to impose such a choice on the defendant? Why should one be entitled to summon another into court at any time?

Normally the defendant, through his lawyer, responds in some way, but in timely fashion, to the plaintiff's complaint. On the one hand, his response might conceivably take the form of an *admission* of his liability for the relief requested. Upon the payment of the compensation demanded, the proceedings would end. On the other hand, he might choose to *defend.* In so doing, he might take one or more of the following three courses of action.

First, he might say to the plaintiff: "So what? The facts you allege— even if proved—would not constitute a valid legal cause of action." Second, he might say: "I deny the facts you allege. Your side of the story is quite different from mine." Third, he might say: "The facts you allege do not tell the whole story. Other facts afford me a good defense to your cause of action." We shall now take up each of these three basic types of defenses in order.

Consider the first basic defense. Under many systems of adjudicative procedure, including the procedure applicable in the Swimming Pool case, the appropriate pleading for the defendant to use to contest the legal validity of the plaintiff's stated cause of action is called a *demurrer.* In other systems of adjudicative procedure, the issue here is raised by other means, for example, a "motion to dismiss for failure to state a claim upon which relief can be granted" as provided by Federal Rule 12(b)(6).

After arranging for a small delay, Story, the lawyer for the Island Amusement Company, filed a demurrer to Miss White's complaint on February 27, 1961. The demurrer read in effect as follows:

DEMURRER

Defendant demurs to the complaint on the ground that it fails to state a cause of action on which relief can be granted.

March 17, 1961, was set by the court as the date for the hearing on this demurrer. Commonly, the opposing lawyers will support their respective positions by filing *memoranda of law* with the court around the time for oral argument on the demurrer.

After the hearing on the demurrer, Judge Hart struck paragraph VIII(c) of Miss White's complaint, but he otherwise overruled the demurrer. He did so on April 28, 1961.

Comments and Questions

1. Why do you think the judge eliminated the plaintiff's cause of action based on the defendant's alleged failure to care properly for the injured plaintiff? Had the defendant breached a legal duty to act?

2. Would any rational adjudicative process for resolution of disputed claims in accordance with preexisting general substantive rules provide some means to test the validity of such a claim against these rules in advance of trial? Does it make any sense to determine disputed facts if upon their determination favorably to the claimant she would still not, under the relevant general rules, be entitled to a remedy? But does it necessarily make sense to allow the parties to present for determination a disputed legal issue that arises from bare factual allegations in the complaint, which may prove obviously untrue or incomplete?

3. In common-law systems, the rendering of preliminary trial-court rulings on the validity of claims is an important avenue for the growth of the law. A common fallacy about law is that only appellate judges have a hand in lawmaking. Another common fallacy is that general rules already exist by which to test the legal validity of all claims to remedies. At any given time, various as yet unrecognized claims lie just around the corner. By refusing to sustain a demurrer, a trial judge may recognize the validity of a wholly new kind of claim. If his action survives on appeal, he will have had a hand in making significant new law. This is generally the way much of negligence law developed and, for another example, how students obtained some due process rights when faced with disciplinary suspensions by educational institutions.

4. A student sues for breach of contract, alleging that this introductory law course does not live up to its catalog description. As lawyer for the defendant university, what would your response be? What should the judge do? See Time, Mar. 3, 1975, at 73.

The lawyer for Miss White later amended the complaint primarily to conform to the ruling of the judge, and this attempt withstood a new demurrer. Presumably, if at a trial the remaining allegations of Miss White's complaint could be proved, she would be entitled to compensation. But must there necessarily be a trial? No, a trial is not necessary unless some facts are in dispute between the parties.

Thus, the second basic defense that a defendant may raise against the plaintiff's complaint is not that it fails to allege facts constituting a valid legal claim but that the facts alleged are not true. The defendant denies the plaintiff's allegations in a pleading called an *answer*. When a defendant so denies some or all of the allegations of the complaint, factual issues arise.

The third basic defense that the defendant may interpose can also give rise to issues of fact. When defending in this third manner, the defendant says in effect: "The facts you allege do not tell the whole story. Even if you proved them, other facts afford me a good defense to your cause of action." Such a defense is called an affirmative defense. The defendant alleges such defenses also in the pleading called the answer. If the plaintiff chooses to deny that there are such additional facts, further factual issues arise. Such a denial may be set forth by the plaintiff in yet another pleading, which is called a *reply*.

In Miss White's case, the defendant company, through its lawyer, not only denied most of the allegations in Miss White's complaint but also alleged other facts that, if proved, would constitute a good defense. These denials and also the allegations supporting the affirmative defense were embodied in the defendant's answer. The answer, filed with the court by the lawyer for the defendant company on June 30, 1961, read basically as follows.

––––––––––

[caption]　　　　　　　　　　　　　　　　　　　　　　　　ANSWER

In answer to plaintiff's amended complaint, defendant admits, denies and alleges as follows:

I

Denies the allegations thereof generally and specifically and the whole thereof, except admits the allegations of paragraphs I and II thereof.

FOR AN AFFIRMATIVE DEFENSE, defendant alleges:

I

Any injuries or damages suffered by the plaintiff at the time and place referred to in her amended complaint and herein were proximately caused by her own carelessness and negligence in diving into a swimming pool without ascertaining the depth of the water at the place where she was diving and in failing to take heed of the "shallow" signs at said pool and in making an improper type of dive into the pool in view of the depth of the water at the place where plaintiff dived.

WHEREFORE, defendant prays judgment herein.

[signature]

––––––––––

The defendant's affirmative defense thus was contributory negligence. In response to the foregoing pleading, and after yet a little more procedural maneuvering, the lawyer for Miss White filed a reply on August 21, 1961. The reply read in part as follows:

REPLY

Comes now plaintiff and for reply to defendant's answer denies each and every allegation and the whole thereof.

There were no further pleadings in the case. The pleadings that were used are typical of those used in many cases. Looking back, what are the functions of these written documents called pleadings? The complaint tells the defendant why she is sued. The defendant's demurrer is used to challenge the complaint's sufficiency in law. The defendant's answer is used to deny facts alleged in the complaint and to set forth affirmative defenses. The reply of the plaintiff is used to deny the allegations constituting any affirmative defenses. A demurrer may also be used by the plaintiff to challenge the legal sufficiency of any affirmative defenses.

At the conclusion of the pleading stage, what has been accomplished? In some cases, the court may have decided that the plaintiff had no valid legal cause of action, or the defendant may have admitted all alleged facts and may have lost on the legal sufficiency of claim and defense, or the plaintiff may have admitted all alleged facts of an affirmative defense and may have unsuccessfully challenged its legal sufficiency. Most disputed claims, however, are not so decided on the pleadings. Ordinarily, a trial of the facts will appear necessary and will indeed occur unless the parties themselves reach some settlement before trial (which often happens).

What, in theory, are these pleadings supposed to accomplish as far as a prospective trial is concerned? The pleadings usually do not go to the jury. But they do serve a number of purposes with respect to trial. First, they disclose whether any facts are in dispute, thus enabling the parties to determine whether a trial is appropriate. Second, when facts are in dispute, they disclose what those facts are. As a result, the parties know how to prepare for the trial. Presumably, the parties will not, therefore, waste time and money on unnecessary preparation. Third, because a party generally cannot introduce evidence at the trial to prove facts he has not alleged in his pleadings, the pleadings help protect against surprise attacks. Fourth, because the party who alleges facts normally has the burden of proving them, at the end of the pleading stage each party will know what her burden of proof is. Fifth, these pleadings separate disputes over fact from disputes over the applicable law.

Cutting against the pleadings' accomplishing a great deal is the parties' power to amend their pleadings. During the pleading stage or later, even at trial, a party can move to amend a pleading that has proved confining or otherwise troublesome. The judge will allow such an amendment when justice so requires—meaning that the judge will discretionarily balance (1) the fault of the movant for the delay in finally stating his position, as well as the prejudice to him that would unavoidably be caused by denying the amendment, against (2) any fault of the opponent in inducing the delay and the prejudice to her reliance interests that would unavoidably be caused by allowing the amendment, with the judge also throwing onto the balance (3) any considerations of public interest. The judge may allow the amendment subject to conditions, such as a postponement, or *continuance,* of proceedings to give the opponent time to prepare anew.

The pleading stage has been the subject of this subsection. Any rational system of procedure for resolving claims must provide for pleadings of some kind. Much controversy has arisen in Anglo-American law over the kind of pleadings that should be required and how much they should be expected to accomplish. Further discussion of this controversy is, however, beyond the scope of an introductory book.

G. Preparing for Trial (and Seeking Settlement or Other Disposition Without Trial)

After the pleading stage, normally a considerable lapse of time occurs before the trial takes place. During this period, the lawyers for plaintiff and defendant will prepare for the trial. They will also usually try to work out a compromise settlement. This was attempted in Miss White's case, but without success.

The principal problem for the lawyer preparing for trial is to find out how he can best prove his case. This will require an investigation to determine possible witnesses and other sources of evidence that may be presented at the trial. The lawyer who prepares well not only will investigate his own side of the case but also will try to learn as much as he can about the way the opposing lawyer proposes to prove her side of the case.

In preparing for trial, much of this investigation is done by private means. But since no one is bound to talk with or display papers to an investigator, the law provides a machinery for compulsory disclosure called discovery. New Fetter law then relied primarily on the two discovery devices called deposition and inspection. The following passage describes how these devices work in general use today.

————

D. KARLEN, CIVIL LITIGATION
49–52, 54 (1978).*

The main purpose of discovery is to enable either party, backed by judicial sanctions but under minimal judicial supervision, to explore in advance of trial the evidence needed to sustain his own contentions and to rebut those of the other side. The goal is to make the lawsuit less of a "sporting contest" than it would be if the parties went to trial with no more information than is furnished by the pleadings and their own private, unofficial inquiries. An additional important purpose is to preserve evidence which otherwise might be lost before trial through the death or disappearance of key witnesses. . . .

The most commonly used discovery procedure is an oral deposition. Here is how it works. Any person believed to possess information relevant to the lawsuit—whether a party to the action or a third person—can be questioned under oath by either or both sides. The questioning takes place outside of court, usually in the office of the lawyer initiating the procedure, and without securing advance permission from any judge. That lawyer secures the attendance of the "deponent" (the person to be examined) by "subpoena," which is a command to the deponent to appear for examination, issued routinely by the clerk of court upon proof that the lawyer has served notice on the other side that the deposition is to be taken at a certain time and place.[2] At the time and place fixed, the deponent is sworn to tell "the truth, the whole truth and nothing but the truth" by a person authorized to administer oaths. Normally this is a notary public, and not infrequently the same person who stenographically records the proceeding. The lawyer who initiated the procedure questions the deponent just as if he were on the witness stand in court. After this "direct examination" is completed, the lawyer for the other side "cross-examines" the deponent, again as if the proceeding were taking place in court. . . . The scope of questioning is broad, limited only by the requirements that (1) the information sought must be relevant, (2) not privileged, and (3) not the "work product" of opposing counsel. Information is considered relevant if it throws light upon any issue framed by the pleadings or if it might lead to relevant evidence, as by disclosing the names and addresses of other persons who were present at the incident involved in the lawsuit. Information is privileged only if the rules of evidence in effect in the state protect it from disclosure because of some extrinsic consideration of social policy, such as the belief that no person should be compelled to incriminate himself or that certain confidential relationships, as between lawyer and client, doctor and patient, or husband and wife would be imperiled by the forced disclosure of communications between them. The lawyer's work product consists of material prepared by him or for him in anticipation of trial—notes of private interviews with potential witnesses, mental impressions, memoranda concerning tests made by experts and the like.

If the deponent should fail to appear for examination or refuse to testify or balk at answering a particular question, the lawyer seeking his testimony can schedule a hearing before a judge of the court where the action is pending. If the judge finds that deponent was not justified in failing to cooperate, he orders the witness to respond. If the witness refuses, the judge can hold him in contempt of court and imprison him until he complies. Should the deponent be a party to the lawsuit, additional sanctions can be imposed—striking out his pleading, precluding him from offering proof at the trial or accepting without proof the other side's version of the facts.

The questions posed by the lawyers and the answers given by the deponent are taken down in shorthand. After the conclusion of the examination, the stenographer makes a written transcript . . . .

Whether the deposition can be used at the trial, and if so how, depends upon whether or not the deponent is a party to the action. If a party, the other side can introduce his deposition into evidence regardless of whether he is available to testify. If the deponent is not a party, his deposition can

---

2. [A subpoena can also command the deponent to bring with him and produce documents and other things.—Ed.] If the person to be examined is an adverse party, no subpoena is necessary. Notice is enough. . . .

be introduced only if at the time of trial he is dead, out of the jurisdiction or otherwise unavailable to testify. If he is available, he must be put on the witness stand and examined and cross-examined in the presence of the judge and jury, so that they can appraise his credibility in the light of his demeanor—his tone of voice, facial expressions, etc. If the deponent, whether a party or an ordinary witness, does testify, his deposition may be used to "impeach" (contradict) him by showing that his testimony in court is inconsistent with prior statements made by him. . . .

Written as well as oral depositions are possible. Taking a deposition in written form is less expensive because it does not require the presence of lawyers. But it is also less satisfactory because each question they ask must be formulated in advance, without knowledge of how the deponent will have responded to previous questions. . . . The questions are then sent to an official authorized to administer oaths. He calls in the person to be examined, reads the questions to him and takes down the answers in writing. The scope of examination is the same as on an oral deposition, so are the sanctions available for one who is unwilling to cooperate, and so are the rules regulating the use of the deposition at trial. . . .

When the information sought is not in the minds of individuals but in the form of documents or physical things, another type of discovery is available: inspection of those things or documents with the right to make copies, tests, etc. A request for inspection can be directed only to a party to the lawsuit, who is obliged to make the documents or things available, unless upon application to the court he is relieved of that necessity. Again the procedure is designed to work without prior judicial permission; a judge's ruling becomes necessary only if objection is made to the procedure invoked.[19]. . .

Generally speaking, discovery procedures are operated by the lawyers without judicial help or supervision. The judge's role is relatively passive: only to rule on disputes arising during the course of discovery. If neither lawyer initiates discovery, none will take place. If discovery takes place and no dispute arises, no judge will be aware of it unless and until an attempt is made to use the information gained thereby at trial.

————

Observe that a lawyer can use the foregoing procedures to "force" information from people who may otherwise refuse to cooperate. This is a vital power given a lawyer preparing for trial. Should the lawyer have such power? Should parties and witnesses be permitted to remain silent? Students should consider whether the administration of justice would suffer if lawyers could not compel the disclosure of testimony prior to trial.

In Miss White's case, the lawyers had approximately two months after the end of the pleading stage in which to prepare for trial. During this time, they made various investigations, and both visited the scene of Miss White's accident. On August 25, 1961, at the instance of the lawyer for

19. Courts have broad power to enter protective orders to prevent discovery procedures from being used to annoy, embarrass, oppress or unduly burden any party or other person. . . .

the defendant, Miss White's oral deposition was taken before an officer
who transcribed the entire proceeding. Although lawyers for both sides
were present, the defendant's lawyer asked nearly all of the questions.
These related to Miss White's background, the way in which the swimming pool accident happened, and the consequences of this accident. The
transcript numbered thirty-seven pages.

After the lawyers have completed preparation for trial, and one of
them has concluded that the other has insufficient evidence to prove his
side of the case, should there be some method of avoiding a trial? Some
legal systems have recognized that a rational system of procedure not only
should provide some means of testing the legal basis of a claim or defense
in advance of trial but also should provide a means of testing its factual
basis. Such a procedure is described in the following passage.

F. JAMES & G. HAZARD, CIVIL
PROCEDURE
206, 271–74 (3d ed. 1985).*

The motion for summary judgment combines certain features of the
general demurrer with certain features of the answer. Its aim is suggested by the standard form of the motion: "Defendant moves for judgment in
his favor on the ground that there is no genuine issue as to the facts
established in the affidavits attached hereto and, on those facts, defendant
is entitled to judgment as a matter of law." A comparable motion can be
made by the plaintiff after defendant has had opportunity to answer. . . .

The weakness of the old demurrer and [similar devices such as a]
motion for judgment on the pleadings was that they could not go behind
the pleadings. They had to take the adversary's pleading at full face
value. They provided no way to test whether the pleader could support
the allegations by proof or whether there was anything of substance
behind a denial. And since there was no very strong sanction against
either pleading or denying groundlessly, it has been traditionally easy for
either a plaintiff or defendant to run successfully the gauntlet of demur-
rers and motions by tendering paper issues in the pleadings, which would
evaporate when proof is made at trial.

A natural question is why anyone should want to plead groundlessly
when he or she should know that it will not be possible to make the
pleading good when proof is called for. Unfortunately there are reasons.
A defendant from whom payment is sought (e.g., for services rendered or
goods sold and delivered) often wants delay. Indeed, that may well be the
very reason why suit had to be brought. And defendant can have delay
by the simple device of denying the debt, and perhaps gilding the lily by
adding pleas of payment and breach of warranty—a trilogy that was
known in the trade as the last refuge of the deadbeat. It is a little less

obvious what plaintiffs can gain by pleading falsely, but they, too, may have a reason. Even groundless suits cost money to defend and therefore may have a nuisance value in settlement if they cannot be disposed of by a speedy and inexpensive pretrial device. In addition to the downright dishonest pleader there is the incurable optimist who pleads without presently known grounds in the hope that something may turn up.

The summary judgment motion is an attempt to meet the problem of the paper or sham issue in a way that is speedier and less expensive to all concerned than a full-dress trial. The motion is typically supported by affidavits of witnesses who would be competent to testify at trial—affidavits containing statements of fact which would be admissible at trial if made by these witnesses. The movant's opponent then has the chance to submit counter-affidavits of similarly competent witnesses. Both sides may also use the products of discovery . . . .

If the opponent does not controvert the proofs offered in support of the motion, and the movant's affidavits show without contradiction facts which would entitle movant to judgment as a matter of law, then summary judgment may be granted. If, on the other hand, the proofs fail to exclude all bases on which judgment might be rendered in favor of the person against whom the motion is made, summary judgment must be denied. And this would be true whether the issue is one of disputed fact or a question of how the trier would characterize admitted facts (e.g., as constituting negligence or the reverse). The device is not intended to resolve issues that are within the traditional province of the trier of fact, but rather to see whether there are such issues. . . .

Partial summary judgment may be granted when it appears that some aspects of a claim are not genuinely controvertible. Thus, a plaintiff may be granted a summary determination of the question of liability, leaving for trial the issue of damages. Either party may be granted summary determination of a part of a claim when it is shown to be incontrovertibly valid or invalid but where genuine issues remain regarding the rest of the claim.

The concept and purpose of the summary judgment motion is clear enough. In practice, the motion is put to little use except in cases that depend on documentary evidence or on determination of a question of law in a case involving undisputed facts that have been brought into sharper focus than is possible with generalized pleadings. The reason is that the interpretive decisions have not permitted the motion to be granted if there is any possibility that the factual aspects of the case will look different at trial from the evidence tendered in support of and against the motion.

Some legal systems have also recognized that a rational system of procedure should provide a means to propel the case through the pretrial process or to refocus the case just before trial. Such a procedure is described in the following passage.

M. KANE, CIVIL PROCEDURE IN A NUTSHELL

149–54 (2d ed. 1985).*

Because of the increased liberalization of pleading requirements, the pretrial conference has become the point in time at which the case becomes crystallized. The conference typically occurs after discovery, when counsel, talking informally with the judge, are able to agree as to what issues are in dispute. They can plan the course of the trial since they know what evidence and witnesses they intend to introduce. In complex litigation, a series of conferences may be used to schedule discovery and to structure the trial.

The judge has discretion to schedule a pretrial conference in both state and federal systems, although some courts have provided by local rules that conferences are mandatory in all cases. The question whether pretrial conferences should be mandatory or discretionary is tied to the perennial debate on their ultimate usefulness. In simple cases, is more time wasted in the conference, than is saved at trial or is it really a means of coercing settlement? In complicated cases, are the trials actually simplified and better organized and therefore speedier or does the pretrial conference merely add another hurdle and more time to the case? . . .

It is truly the judge who controls the effectiveness of the pretrial conference. The judge's interest, familiarity with the case, and belief as to the need to reach some agreement between the parties generally determines whether the parties actually will work toward some accord. The judge must tread a careful line between coercing the parties and helping them to reach reasonable conclusions. . . .

[For example, consider] the propriety of the judge urging the parties to settle the case out of court. Courts and commentators are split on this issue. Most judges seem to feel that it is proper to suggest that a settlement may be appropriate once the actual issues are revealed, and that one of the purposes of the conference is to see if an agreement can be reached and trial avoided. However, it is improper to coerce the parties into the settlement. The problem is one of degree. . . .

[Another] question involving the pretrial judge's power concerns what sanctions may be applied if the parties fail to appear at the conference or refuse or fail to reveal certain information requested by the court, such as the witnesses who will be called or the evidence that will be introduced at trial. It generally is recognized that the court may enter a default judgment or, in the case of a delinquent plaintiff, an involuntary dismissal with prejudice against parties whose counsel fail to appear at a scheduled conference. However, this sanction is so powerful that, as a practical matter, its use is strictly limited to situations in which the party has been exceptionally dilatory. This usually means that the counsel not only has failed to appear at the conference, but also generally has delayed the course of the litigation. A more common sanction is to limit the evidence to be used at the trial to only that which was revealed at the conference pursuant to the court's request. . . . .

At the end of the pretrial conference, the judge enters a pretrial order incorporating all the parties' stipulations, the list of witnesses and evidence agreed upon, and any other matters that were decided at the conference. The order supersedes the pleadings and controls the remainder of the proceedings in that action. If the attorneys wish to introduce a new issue or additional evidence at trial, they must petition the court for relief. Relief will be allowed to prevent manifest injustice, but it is within the discretion of the court to require adherence to the original order. Thus, the trial judge will weigh carefully the possible prejudice to the opposing party (who may have relied on the order when preparing for trial), the importance of the proposed change, and whether the moving party was dilatory in not introducing the proposed matter at the conference. If the movant succeeds, the relief typically will take the form of an amendment to the pretrial order.

––––––

In summary, in a modern procedural system, pleadings do not do all the work of getting a case into shape for trial or disposing of the case short of trial. Three other mechanisms share the burden: discovery, motion for summary judgment, and pretrial conference. Note that the three are not used in all cases or in any fixed order.

In Miss White's case, however, New Fetter law provided neither for a motion for summary judgment nor for a routine pretrial conference. Accordingly, on September 7, 1961, the date of October 25, 1961, was officially set as the date for the trial.

H. Trial of the Case

Much of what the nonlawyer knows of the law she learns from watching trials or from reading descriptions of trials. For her the trial is the heart of the law. But this view is distorted. First, relatively few cases in which factual disputes arise are ever tried. In the vast majority of cases, the parties, often through their lawyers, are able to negotiate a satisfactory compromise settlement. Perhaps, then, negotiation should be thought of as the heart of the law. Second, the courtroom is only one of the many places where the law is to be seen in action.

Yet, the law of the courtroom—the law governing the way in which the facts of a case are determined—is a critical part of that important body of law called civil procedure. An adjudicative process that did not provide a means of resolving factual as well as legal disputes would be unsatisfactory because often there is no dispute as to the applicable law but there is a vigorous dispute as to the facts. Moreover, the law of the courtroom influences the application of law in many other formal and informal contexts. Let us therefore look in some detail at what transpires in the courtroom.

In many Anglo-American jurisdictions, the factual basis of a money claim may be tried—at the choice of either party's lawyer—before a jury of six to twelve persons, who will listen to the evidence and at the close of the trial render their verdict. A judge will preside throughout the proceedings. (If the parties do not desire a jury, then the judge will decide the facts.) What are the steps in a jury trial of an ordinary case in which one party is asserting a claim against another?

After the jury has been selected, the lawyers will each present a sort of introductory road map of the case entitled an *opening statement,* with which they help the jury follow the proceedings by outlining their respective sides of the case and explaining how they propose to prove their allegations of fact. The plaintiff will then introduce his *evidence.* (The way in which evidence is introduced is illustrated at a later point in this subsection.) After the plaintiff has finished, or *rested,* the defendant's lawyer may think that the plaintiff's lawyer has not introduced sufficient evidence for a jury to reasonably find that the plaintiff's allegations have been proved. The defendant's lawyer may then move that the judge dismiss the case by granting a *judgment of involuntary nonsuit.*

If this motion is denied, the defendant will then introduce her evidence, either trying to meet the plaintiff's allegations or trying to prove new matter on which the defendant has the burden of proof. To meet new facts put in evidence by the defendant, the plaintiff can next offer rebuttal evidence. Conceivably, the defendant could then introduce rebutting evidence, too, and so on.

After all of the evidence has been introduced, if either lawyer thinks that the thrust of the entire evidence of both parties is so strong in his client's favor that no reasonable jury could rule against his client, he may then move that the judge direct a verdict. When the judge directs a verdict, she in effect decides the facts herself, for she renders a judgment in favor of the moving party. Is this an invasion of the province of the jury? No, jurors are only supposed to decide genuine issues of fact, issues over which reasonable persons could differ. If the overwhelming weight of the evidence is on one side, then reasonable jurors could not differ, and the judge should withdraw the case from the jury. However, this standard is stringent, so that a *directed verdict* is proper only in very lopsided cases.

If the motion or motions for a directed verdict are denied, each lawyer will then, in turn, make a *closing argument* to the jury, in which he will review the evidence and advance reasons why the jury should return a verdict in favor of his client. The trial judge will then give *instructions* to the jury, in which she will state the applicable law and tell the jury what findings they would have to make in order to render a verdict for the plaintiff and what findings they would have to make in order to render a verdict for the defendant. Thereafter, the jury, after retiring to deliberate in the jury room, will return a *verdict.*

The judge will then entertain motions to render *judgment notwithstanding the verdict* (for example, on the ground that the judge should have granted a motion for a directed verdict) or to grant a *new trial* (for example, on the ground that the judge committed some error of law during the trial) and will rule thereon. Eventually, the clerk of the court will enter a *judgment.* An *appeal* will then be possible.

The Trial Begins

Miss White's case was tried before a twelve-person jury on October 25, 26, and 27, 1961. After the jury was selected, the lawyers, Mr. Stone for the plaintiff and Mr. Story for the defendant, made their opening statements. The presiding judge, Judge Hart, then told the jury that they would take a bus to the scene of the accident. This visit to the swimming pool was designed to provide the jurors with background for understanding the testimony to follow.

Plaintiff's Case

Upon returning from the scene, the presiding judge asked Mr. Stone to call his first witness to the witness stand. This witness, a Dr. Sole, who had treated Miss White, testified as to the nature and the extent of the injuries she had suffered as a result of diving into the defendant's pool. The questions by Mr. Stone, and the answers by Dr. Sole, follow in part.

Q. What did you find in your examination? Did you find any fractures?

A. Yes. On the physical examination, the patient had marked spasm and guarding of the neck against all motion. She also had a laceration on the scalp, which is about two inches long and which had been sutured. The X rays showed that she had a fracture of the first cervical vertebra and another fracture of the fifth cervical vertebra. The fracture of the first one, which is the first vertebra in the neck directly under the head, was comminuted or compressed. And the fifth vertebra had a fracture out of it, out of the body of the vertebra, and was dislocated forward on the vertebra below it.

Q. I assume they are the X rays that were taken?

A. Yes.

MR. STONE: May I have these marked for identification, your Honor?

THE COURT: I believe they are already marked.

MR. STORY: There will be no objection to admitting them into evidence.

THE COURT: One through seven are received.

(Whereupon Plaintiff's Exhibits Nos. 1 to 7 inclusive were received in evidence. X rays.)

Q. (By Mr. Stone) At this time, doctor, I would like to hand you Plaintiff's Exhibits 1 through 7 so you may use those and explain the injuries that the plaintiff sustained.

.   .   .   .

Q. Doctor, did you feel the injuries that Sharon had sustained were of a permanent nature?

A. Yes, definitely. These X-ray findings will never change. I think that it is reasonable that the things that she complains of now, such as fatigue, tiring, aching with the fatigue, are due to the accident. She certainly disclaimed having them before. And, very reasonably, this degree of injury would be the cause of these symptoms.

Q. In other words, the dislocation is something of a permanent nature; the bone that you showed dislocated—

A. The dislocation is not there. That has been reduced. But the defect in the bone is there.

The next witness called to the stand by Mr. Stone was the plaintiff, Sharon White. Part of her testimony given in response to questions by Mr. Stone is hereafter presented, followed by part of her testimony given in response to cross-examination by Mr. Story. Then follows further testimony in response to questions by Mr. Stone, and so on.

Note that all this testimony is still part of the plaintiff's case in chief. In other words, as the plaintiff's lawyer presents his case, the defendant's lawyer is not totally passive but instead participates in the presentation of evidence, primarily by cross-examination.

Direct Examination

By MR. STONE:

Q. Would you state your name and address for the record?

A. Sharon White, 11525 Southeast Powell, Eyre, New Fetter.

Q. That's your home address. What is your temporary address at the present time?

A. At the present time I am living at Lausanne Hall, which is at the campus at Willamette University.

Q. Where did you live in June of 1958?

A. In June, 1958, I lived on 71st and Harold in Southeast Eyre.

Q. And where did you go to school? Let's start with grade school.

A. I went to two grade schools: I went to Buckman Grade School for the first and second grades and then I transferred to Arleta Grade School where I completed grade school.

Q. Where did you go to high school?

A. I went two years to Franklin High and then my junior and senior years I went to David Douglas High School.

. . . .

Q. Do you want to tell us a little bit about your swimming, what experience you have had, when you started swimming, and so forth?

A. Well, we lived at—when we lived at 71st and Harold we lived right across from the Mount Scott Pool and so for about six years I was swimming almost every day of the summer and I hadn't swum before that time. But as soon as we moved there I began swimming and I swam for six years steadily.

. . . .

Q. . . . Were you an average swimmer or better than average swimmer?

A. I was a better than average swimmer. I had had quite a bit of experience.

Q. Had you ever done any diving?

A. Yes.

Q. Would you tell us about your diving?

A. Well, I had done diving off of a board and the side and was doing some kinds of trick diving that you just fool around with.

Q. So, in other words, you did all types of diving?

A. Yes.

Q. When did you start your diving . . . ?

A. Oh, I started diving about a year after I first started to swim, about the fourth grade.

Q. Can you explain to us briefly what the Mount Scott Pool is like?

A. The Mount Scott Pool is only composed of two pools—a shallow pool and a deeper pool. The shallow pool was towards the dressing rooms as you come out of the dressing room. The shallow pool is before you and beyond that is the deeper pool. Facing in this direction the diving board is in the left-hand side of the deeper pool, and so the deepest side of the deep pool is in the left and so it gets shallower towards the right. . . .

. . . .

Q. . . . Now, you say, Sharon, you had been accustomed of diving in the shallow pool at Mount Scott. Was that a common practice?

A. Yes, it was.

Q. For both yourself and other people?

A. Yes.

Q. In other words, your friends would dive in that pool?

A. That's right. And I have a brother who's two years younger than I am and who is also a swimmer and did that diving.

Q. And I assume there are other people besides you and your brother?

A. Oh, yes, definitely.

Q. What type of diving did you do?

A. Oh, from the side, shallow diving.

   MR. STORY: You are now talking about the Mount Scott Pool, aren't you?

   MR. STONE: Yes.

.   .   .   .

Q. And you mentioned the depth of the Mount Scott shallow pool was what?

A. At that spot in the pool it's approximately four to five feet deep.

Q. Was it deeper in any other parts?

A. In any other or than any—

Q. No, no, in any other parts what was the depth?

A. That was the deepest part of the shallow pool.

Q. Four to five feet?

A. Yes.

Q. And people commonly dived in this pool?

A. Yes.

Q. And now, on June 7th did you go to Hansen Beach to go swimming?

A. Yes, I did.

.   .   .   .

Q. Now, when you came around the pool what did you see, other than what you described so far, let's say when you came around the corner there?

A. Well, I saw what I thought was the same kind of arrangement as the Mount Scott Pool, a shallow pool and a deep pool; and I took it for granted that this spot where I dove in would be deeper, as it was at the Mount Scott Pool.

Q. Did you see your friends in the pool?

A. Yes, I did.

Q. How deep was the water where they were?

A. Approximately chest deep.

Q. About how tall were your friends?

A. They varied in height from about, oh, five-eleven to six, six-three.

Q. In other words, they were fairly tall?

A. Yes.

Q. When you saw the water on your friends did you draw any conclusions as to the depth of the water in the pool where you were to dive?

A. Yes, I did. I figured if it was that deep on them, then it must be even deeper towards this end, since I figured that was a gradual deepening of the water towards where I was standing so I assumed it would be deep enough for a dive.

Q. Did you see any signs at all indicating the depth of the pool?

A. No, I didn't.

Q. Did you look for them?

A. I glanced around before I dove in but there were no signs that I could see.

Q. Did you see any other signs of any nature indicating that you should not dive in this pool?

A. No, I didn't.

Q. When you came upon the pool was there any question in your mind that this was not what is termed the shallow pool?

A. No, I knew that it was a shallow pool. . . .

Q. What type of a dive did you do? Would you describe that to us?
A. I did a shallow dive.
Q. Well, would you describe what is a shallow dive?
A. It's rather hard to describe; at an angle, at—about a forty-five degree angle to the pool.

Q. Did you stop stationary at the pool before you dove in or was it a running dive, or what kind of a dive?
A. I paused just before I came to the edge and I took about two steps before I dove.
Q. Well, would you term that a running dive?
A. It's kind of in-between.

Q. Would you describe what happened, now, when you dove into the pool?
A. Well, I dove into the pool and my hands hit the bottom and jerked back and my head hit and I realized I had obviously hit the bottom of the pool and I stood up and I was pretty dizzy, although I wasn't unconscious, and the kids around me asked me if I was all right and I said yes, I was. The only thing that was abnormal about me at that time was that I couldn't turn my head from side to side in that direction like that (indicating). And they suggested that I go back into the warmer water of the deep pool because the warmer water might make my neck feel better. They kind of assumed that I just wrenched it. No one had thought that I had broken my neck, none of us did, so I got into the deeper pool, which had warmer water, thinking that it might help a little bit.
Q. What did you do then?
A. I breast stroked across the pool, up to the middle wall between the deep and shallow pool, to that point, where a few of my friends were standing and the girls started massaging my neck hoping that it would help, which of course it didn't, and since that didn't help one of the girls told me I had blood on my lip so I went into the dressing room and took off my bathing cap; and when I took off my bathing cap that blood came cascading down and I realized I had cut my head and the bathing cap had not split but it had been holding the blood up there all this time and I was pretty shocked. . . .

Q. . . . . I want to ask you when you stood up in the water after you dove in and hit your head, how deep was the water upon you then?
A. My recollection is rather hazy. I think it was about waist deep, as I can remember, on me.

Q. How deep would that be in terms of feet?
A. About three feet deep.

Q. . . . . I want to go back and ask you one more question about the Hansen Beach Pool. Had you ever been to the Hansen Beach Pool before this time?
A. No, I hadn't.
Q. Had you ever heard of anybody talking about it with regard to the construction of the pool?
A. No, I had never heard anybody talk about it in regards to construction.
Q. How had you heard people talk about it?

A. Well, I knew there was a pool at Hansen Beach and that's where we were going. That's all I heard about it.

Q. Before you went did you have knowledge of how pools are built, in other words, the shallow pool and a deep pool, this two-pool setup?

A. Well, my knowledge as to how swimming pools in general were built was based on my previous experiences with the Mount Scott Pool and pools around that area where I had gone swimming.

. . . .

Q. When you went out to the Hansen Beach Pool—now, back to the 7th of June—was there anything to indicate to you that you should not dive into this pool?

MR. STORY: We object to that question, your Honor, as calling for a conclusion.

THE COURT: Objection sustained.

Q. (By Mr. Stone) Were there any signs indicating you should not dive into the pool?

A. No.

Q. Did anyone tell you or indicate to you that you should not dive into the pool?

MR. STORY: Your Honor, I object to the question as leading and—

THE COURT: Objection overruled. Go ahead.

Q. (By Mr. Stone) Was anything said to you? Do you want to answer that last question?

A. No, there was nothing said to me.

Q. Did you see anything indicating that you should not dive into the pool?

MR. STORY: I object to that question again, your Honor, as calling for a conclusion.

THE COURT: You may ask her if she saw any signs, or anything of that kind, but you are getting pretty general.

MR. STONE: I have no further questions, your Honor.

Cross-Examination

By MR. STORY:

Q. You say you arrived out there at Hansen Beach between six and seven?

A. Approximately between six and seven.

Q. And in June that's broad daylight, isn't it?

A. I'd say it's dusk.

. . . .

Q. Well, could you see, for instance, to read outdoors there where you were by the pool? Was it that light?

A. I guess I probably could read. We didn't have to have headlights coming down to Hansen Beach.

Q. Now, I understand you had been doing some substantial swimming and diving for, what, ten years or—no, seven or eight years before this?

A. Six or seven years.

Q. You mentioned that you did some trick diving. What kinds of trick diving have you done?

A. Well, things like diving backwards and doing sailor dives and—

Q. What is the sailor dive?

A. Oh, that's diving with your hands down at your side, just diving in. You don't do this sort of dive in a shallow pool.

. . . .

Q. Now, when you went there to that pool, you say you knew before you went in that it was a shallow pool?

A. I knew when I saw the way the pools were arranged that it was a shallow pool.

Q. And that's before you went in the water?

A. Before I went in the water, yes, sir.

Q. And then you said you looked around, or you said you glanced around before you dove. What were you glancing around for?

A. Well, any indication that it might be dangerous to dive.

Q. Well, you already knew that the water was shallow?

A. Yes, sir.

Q. And there were a lot of other people in that shallow pool besides your friends, were there not?

A. I really don't remember.

Q. Don't you remember on your deposition that you took you told us about other people being there?

A. I said there could have been and there more than likely would have been. It was on a weekend and—

Q. Well, when you glanced around to see if there was any indication of anything, did you look around to see how far the water came up on people in various parts of that pool?

A. No, I just looked at my friends.

Q. Oh? Well, on your deposition, with reference to other people around there, was this your testimony? This is page fourteen:

Q. Was there anybody else in the shallow pool at the time you dove in?
A. Yes, sir.
Q. And were they all over the pool or in any particular spot?
A. They were scattered throughout the pool. There were a few in this place and a few in this other place. They weren't all grouped together.
Q. So people generally scattered around throughout the pool?
A. Yes, sir.

Was that your testimony on your deposition?

A. Yes, sir, it was.

Q. And does that refresh your memory now with reference to people being scattered all around the pool?

A. What I meant by that, I knew that there weren't any grouped around my friends.

Q. That you what?

A. That there weren't any people grouped around my friends. My friends were in a general group around the pool. If there were any other people around in the pool they weren't in a central group, they were scattered around.

Q. That's what you meant here, that there were people scattered all around but you weren't paying any particular attention to them?

A. I wasn't paying attention to them, yes.

Q. The Mount Scott Pool you had swum in hundreds of times, probably?

A. Yes, sir.

Q. And so the thing that the difficulty arose over, you assumed that this—pool out here was constructed the same as the Mount Scott Pool?

A. Yes, sir.

Q. And that is, would have a deep place in the same corner as the Mount Scott Pool had a deep place?

A. Yes, sir.

. . . .

Q. Now, have you on occasion ever scraped the bottom when you dove at Mount Scott?

A. By "scraped the bottom" do you mean brush your nose against the bottom?

Q. No, anything.

A. Yes, I have done that. I have skinned my nose a few times.

. . . .

Q. . . . Now, the water was clear out there at Hansen Beach so that you could see the bottom, wasn't it?

A. Yes, sir.

. . . .

Q. And you knew, I take it from your testimony, that all pools would have different depths at different parts of the pool?

A. I don't quite understand your question.

Q. Well, like you knew at the Mount Scott shallow pool that it was deeper in some places than it was at others.

A. Yes, sir.

Q. And you knew that all pools have places in them that are deeper than other places in the pools?

A. Yes, sir.

Q. You say you had no information about where it was deeper or where it was shallower at Hansen Beach excepting that you supposed it was like Mount Scott?

A. That's right.

Q. Now, you say that at the place where you dove, your best estimate is that the water was about three feet deep there?

A. Yes, and that's a rough estimate.

Q. I understand that, doing the best you can as in your condition after you were hurt?

A. That's right.

Q. And about how many feet of water would you say would be required to safely make the type of dive that you did make?

A. I would say that I had been used to doing this type of a dive in four feet of water.

MR. STORY: I think that's all.

THE COURT: Anything further?

MR. STONE: I have a few, your Honor. . . .

. . . .

Redirect Examination

By MR. STONE:

. . . .

Q. With reference to your deposition and the number of people in the pool, in the area where you dived, in the immediate area, were there any other people?

A. No.

Q. Was anybody standing along the wall?

A. No.

Q. That would be the north wall.

A. No, sir.

.   .   .   .

Q. . . . Is there any indication of the depth of the water where you dove in?

A. Not that I could see.

Q. You saw the boys in the middle of the pool?

A. Yes, sir.

Q. Where was the water upon them?

A. About chest deep.

Q. Did you notice the railing there before you dove in?

MR. STORY: What's that?

MR. STONE: The rail before you get out of the pool at the north end.

Q. (By Mr. Stone) I assume, then, before you dove into the pool there was something more than just your knowledge of the Mount Scott Pool regarding the depth here, is that right?

A. Yes, sir.

Q. And what was that?

A. Well, I assumed that it must be deep enough to require one of those handrailing things to get out of the water.

Q. Anything else?

A. Other than the fact that I assumed it must be at least as deep as approximately chest deep on my friends.

MR. STONE: I have no further questions, your Honor.

Recross-Examination

By MR. STORY:

Q. You mean when you went around there and walked over towards the place where you took two steps and a partial running dive you considered all those things, that they would not construct a handrail and a ladder unless it was chest deep on you? You considered—

A. In considering these things I didn't stand there and say, "Now, it's chest deep on my friends and there's a handrail there so it must be at least as deep on me." I just kind of generally took in the whole situation and drew a conclusion, I guess.

Q. You looked at the bottom? You could see the bottom through the water?

A. Yes.

Q. You saw some steps that went down, didn't you, into the shallow pool, steps that you'd walk into the pool as distinguished from how it is over here where you dive in (indicating)?

A. Yes, sir.

Q. What did you think they meant, though, when you were considering these things before you dove?

A. That it must be pretty shallow in that part.

MR. STORY: That's all.

MR. STONE: Two more questions, then.

Redirect Examination

By MR. STONE:

Q. Can you tell how deep the pool is by looking at the bottom?

A. No.

Q. Where were the steps that counsel is referring to?

A. On the right-hand side and the left-hand side of the circular steps in the front of the pool.

.   .   .   .

MR. STONE: No further questions.

THE COURT: You may step down.

In completing his case, Mr. Stone called three additional witnesses to testify, each of whom Mr. Story cross-examined. These were Mr. and Mrs. Paul White (Miss White's parents) and Mr. Harold Mullins (assistant chief sanitary engineer for the state board of health). Mr. White testified, in part, that he had viewed the pool several times, but the first time, sometime probably in July 1958, he saw only faintly imprinted "shallow" signs. Mrs. White supported that testimony. Mr. Mullins testified, in part, that he knew of no pools other than the 165′ × 100′ Hansen Beach pool that were shallow all around and sloped toward the middle, and that no purpose other than drainage was served by having a pool deep at one end and shallow at the other.

At the close of the plaintiff's case, the following events occurred:

MR. STONE: Plaintiff will rest, your Honor.

THE COURT: Defendant may proceed.

MR. STORY: I have a matter we ought to take up in chambers, I suppose.

THE COURT: Very well. We will have a recess. The court reporter and counsel in chambers.

(Whereupon the Court and counsel for the respective parties retired to the Court's chambers out of the presence of the jury and the following proceedings were had, to-wit:)

MR. STORY: The defendant moves to the Court for a judgment of involuntary nonsuit in favor of the defendant and against the plaintiff for the reason that there is no evidence in the case to show any negligence on the part of the defendant that was the proximate cause of the injury to the plaintiff; and for the further reason that the evidence affirmatively shows that plaintiff was negligent as a matter of law proximately contributing to her injury . . . . I am not going to argue unless you want me to.

.   .   .   .

THE COURT: . . . . I will deny defendant's motion for involuntary nonsuit. Exception allowed.[c]

.   .   .   .

MR. STONE: Comes now the plaintiff and moves this Court to amend Paragraph VIII, Subsection (a) to read in the place of that portion stricken the following: "In failing to provide adequate markings showing the depth of the water in the pool." And this motion is made so as to conform with the evidence.

THE COURT: Do you have any objection, Mr. Story?

MR. STORY: Yes, we object to it. In the first place, it doesn't conform to the evidence and it brings in a new element in the case without adequate notice to the defendant so the defendant can properly prepare for trial. It is not sufficiently definite and certain as to what we have failed to provide in the way of markings, and it takes us by surprise.

THE COURT: The motion will be allowed and exception allowed to the defendant.

c. An "exception" is a party's formal objection to a legal decision, recorded at trial and intended to preserve the point for possible appeal.

MR. STORY: Will we be permitted a time to reinvestigate our case?

THE COURT: How much time do you want, Mr. Story?

MR. STORY: Probably one day.

THE COURT: You mean until tomorrow morning. That will give you all afternoon now being a quarter to three.

MR. STORY: I just can't tell how long it would take me, but I would hope that I can do it by tomorrow afternoon.

THE COURT: Off the record.

(Whereupon an off-the-record discussion was had.)

MR. STORY: I have announced that I am unable to find anybody to go get my witness and I am willing to go ahead.

THE COURT: All right. I want the record to show that I am willing to give you additional time if you desire.

MR. STORY: Yes, you told me that and I said that I am willing to go ahead.

THE COURT: All right, let's go.

Defendant's Case

The only witness called by Mr. Story to testify on behalf of the defendant company was Mr. J.F. Thomas, manager of Hansen Beach Park. Mr. Thomas testified in part as follows:

Q. . . . Mr. Thomas, are there markings around that pool showing the various depths of the water?

A. You are talking about the shallow pool?

Q. Yes, the shallow pool?

.   .   .   .

A. Yes, there are figures that show the depth of the pool.

Q. How long have they been there?

A. Well, they have been there for six years that I know of.

Q. And you say six years because that's the length of time you have been manager?

A. That's right, that's right.

Q. Well, just describe where those markings are and what they say.

A. Well, they are a set of steps on either side of the fountain as you come out of the dressing room and on either side there are markings of the depth of the water.

Q. And what does it say?

A. Two feet.

Q. And then what about on the north end of the shallow pool?

A. When the pools were built on the north side, on either side, more or less about twenty-five per cent of the end in from either side, they are embedded in tile and it says "Shallow." They are embedded, as I remember, in white tile with red markings signifying shallow.

.   .   .   .

Q. . . . What time of the year do you repaint these markings?

A. Well, we opened the pool the 15th of May this year and they were painted previous to our opening.

Q. Well, that's this year. How about '58?

A. The same. I can't remember what date we opened in '58, to be very frank with you, but they were painted before we opened the pool.

Q. And what color of paint?

A. Red.

Q. Red?

A. Red.

.   .   .   .

Q. . . . Now, has there ever been any complaint about your pool from any authority?

MR. STONE: Objection to it, your Honor.

THE COURT: Objection sustained. It doesn't make any difference whether there was or not.

MR. STORY: I think that's all. . . .

Rebuttal

Mr. Stone called Mr. Paul White to the stand and asked more about the signs seen at the pool in July 1958. Then Mr. Story cross-examined, concluding:

Q. You didn't particularly look all around, did you?

A. We walked all along the wire there.

Q. But you never got inside the pool?

A. No, there was the wires.

Q. And you didn't ask to get inside?

A. No, there was nobody around there, sir.

Q. Nobody around there in July?

A. Well, I don't know. There wasn't anybody at the fence.

MR. STONE: Object to the question. It's improper cross-examination.

THE COURT: Objection overruled.

Q. (By Mr. Story) You say there was nobody by the fence?

A. There was nobody there, that's right, by the fence. We parked the car outside there and went to the gate out by the parking lot.

Q. And you didn't go in the office to see if you could get a view right there?

A. No, we didn't.

Q. And you didn't do that either on the second occasion you were there?

A. No, we didn't, sir.

Q. And that fence is quite a high fence there that's several feet from the edge of the pool?

A. As near as I could estimate I'd say about eight, nine feet, sir.

MR. STORY: I think that's all.

THE COURT: You may step down.

(Witness excused.)

MR. STONE: Plaintiff will rest, your Honor.

THE COURT: We will have a short recess prior to argument, gentlemen. The jury can retire.

(Whereupon the midafternoon recess was taken.)

MR. STORY: At this time the defendant moves for a directed verdict in favor of defendant and against plaintiff for the same reasons and upon the grounds as stated with reference to the motion for involuntary nonsuit.

THE COURT: Motion denied, exception allowed.

MR. STORY: Very well.

THE COURT: You may proceed with your argument, Mr. Stone.

(Whereupon counsel for the respective parties presented their closing arguments to the jury.)

THE COURT: Ladies and gentlemen of the jury, we are going to recess now until tomorrow morning when I will instruct you. It is not proper that you discuss this case with anybody, not even among yourselves, and until such time as you have been instructed and have retired to the jury room to deliberate. When you are back in the jury room deliberating, you can discuss it to your heart's content, but prior to that time with no one.

Now we are switching courtrooms tomorrow, and tomorrow morning we will be in Courtroom 540 down on the fifth floor. . . .

Instructions

THE COURT: Ladies and gentlemen of the jury, it is now my duty to instruct you upon the law of this case and it is your duty to follow my instructions. Your determination of the facts and as to what actually happened and what the circumstances were is final and I can't interfere with that. But those facts, before they can be interpreted in the form of a judgment, must first have the law applied to them as I give it to you and you have to take that as I say it is.

.   .   .   .

Now to start out with, the slate is clear. The presumption is that persons are not negligent and are not careless; therefore, the presumption is in this case that neither the plaintiff nor the defendant was negligent or at fault in any way. So, when plaintiff charges in her complaint that the defendant was guilty of negligence, the burden of proof is upon her to prove such claims by a preponderance of the evidence and in the absence of such proof she cannot recover; likewise, when defendant in its answer claims the plaintiff was guilty of negligence, the burden of proof is upon it to prove such claims by a preponderance of the evidence.

By preponderance of the evidence is meant the outweighing of the evidence. It doesn't necessarily mean the greater number of witnesses nor the greater volume of evidence; it is that evidence which is more convincing, more worthy of belief, and which makes out the better case. It means that the facts asserted must have been proved more probably true than false.

If after consideration you cannot make up your minds who has made the better case upon a particular point, the burden of proof has not been carried as regards this point.

Now, the defendant has charged negligence against the plaintiff in three particulars. It isn't necessary for the defendant to prove all three of the acts of negligence charged to prove that the plaintiff was negligent, but it is necessary that one or more be proved before the burden of proof is sustained in this regard.

Now, what is negligence? Negligence is the doing of that or the failure to do that which a reasonably careful person would or would not have done under the same or similar circumstances. It's just a common-sense rule. In other words, in this case the law requires that the plaintiff take due care to keep from injuring herself and that is such care as a reasonably prudent person of her age and her experience would have taken under the same and similar circumstances to prevent injury to herself.

Now, what is the duty of the landowner in this particular case? In this particular case, the plaintiff being a paying customer at defendant's place of business, the plaintiff is known at law what we call an invitee. And what I am going to read to you now is the responsibility which the invitor has to his invitee in the conduct of his premises and his business. The possessor, and when I say possessor in this particular case, I mean the defendant in this particular case, is required to exercise reasonable care and to warn the invitee, that is, the plaintiff in this case, or to make the premises safe for her as to conditions of which the possessor knows or those which he could discover with reasonable care.

Now, when you decide whether or not this defendant has complied with that duty which the law lays upon it, you should consider that in considering whether the defendant has complied with this standard of care, that the rules should be applied to them: What would have a reasonably prudent person done under the same and similar circumstances? In other words, that standard of care is the standard of care which is put up to the defendant in deciding whether or not it has complied with this duty which the law lays upon it.

Now, should you find from the evidence that the defendant was negligent . . . . Before plaintiff may recover, such negligence must be the proximate cause of the accident and her injuries.

What do we mean by proximate cause? By proximate cause is meant the thing which actually caused the injury. It need not be the only cause but it must be one of them and such as might have been reasonably foreseen as leading to injury. A person may do a negligent act but unless that negligence directly causes an injury it is not the proximate cause and such person is not responsible; likewise, if you should find from the evidence that plaintiff was guilty of negligence in one or more of the particulars claimed in defendant's answer, before such negligence will prevent a recovery by plaintiff it must be the proximate cause of the accident and her injuries under the rule of proximate cause which I have just given.

A party asserting that certain claimed negligence was the proximate cause of the accident has the burden of proving it by a preponderance of the evidence the same as any other claim that they make. Now, the defendant in charging the plaintiff's negligence caused or contributed to the accident and her injuries has thereby raised the defense of contributory negligence. Contributory negligence consists of acts or omissions charged by the defendant amounting to negligence on the part of the person injured which were a proximate cause of her injuries. If you find from all the evidence in this case that plaintiff was guilty of such negligence, even though the defendant might be negligent also, there could be no recovery. Now, that's just a nice way of saying that if they were both at fault in this matter and that fault contributed to the happening of the accident, then there could be no recovery.

Now, if you find from the evidence that defendant was guilty of negligence in one or more of the particulars set out in plaintiff's complaint which was the proximate cause of the injuries to plaintiff, and that plaintiff was free from negligence which was the proximate cause of the accident and her injuries, then and only then would you have a right to go to the question of damages. . . .

You ladies and gentlemen can just remain seated while I retire into chambers with counsel so they may take an opportunity to take exceptions to the instructions I may or may not have given.

(Whereupon the Court and counsel for the respective parties retired to the Court's chambers out of the presence of the jury and the following proceedings were had, to-wit:)

THE COURT: Are there any exceptions on instructions as given, by the plaintiff?

MR. STONE: The only other exception I have is that the Court referred to the question of coming down to negligence and contributory negligence as determining if parties were at fault.

THE COURT: And that fault contributed to the accident, I added.

MR. STONE: And I believe this is misleading as it does not distinguish between the duties of the parties regarding the defendant's part to a business invitee.

THE COURT: You don't contend that I didn't in another part of my instruction, and just previous to this, state what their duties were and apply the rules to it?

MR. STONE: Yes, but I did not hear it stated that the girl was to be considered in the light of a reasonably prudent fourteen-year-old girl.

THE COURT: I am sure that I did say that. I—

MR. STORY: Of her age and experience.

THE COURT: A person of her age and experience, but you are allowed an exception. Anything else?

MR. STONE: Nothing further, your Honor.

THE COURT: I presume the defendant has no exceptions at all. Normally the defendant has none.

.   .   .   .

MR. STORY: With reference to the third instruction on contributory negligence, that contributory negligence is nothing more nor less than if both parties were at fault; then the defense of contributory negligence would be available. That amounts to a statement that by setting forth contributory negligence, defendant admits that it was negligent. The defendant is entitled to rely on contributory negligence and does not thereby necessarily admit negligence.

And, in connection with that, we take exception to the Court's failure to give the Defendant's Requested Instruction No. 11 which states the rule— which I believe is the rule in New Fetter that by setting up the defense of contributory negligence in its answer in this case, the defendant is not deemed to admit that it was negligent in the matter under consideration.

THE COURT: You've got me. You've got me in that I did exclude from that a statement to that effect. What I should have said and, of course, that is what I get for ad-libbing and trying to make it plain for those people. Whenever you make it plain that's understandable to them it's always a mistake. And when I ad-libbed I made a mistake. What I should have said, "What this means is that it means if the plaintiff was solely at fault, or they were both at fault, and that contributed to the happening of the accident then she is not entitled." That's what I should have said. I will go back and say it because I did exclude the possibility that she could be solely at fault. So I will go back and tell the jury if she's solely at fault she can't recover.

.   .   .   .

MR. STORY: The defendant excepts to the refusal of the Court to give Defendant's Requested Instruction No. 7 which has to do with the duties of the plaintiff where she knew, as she admitted as she did, that this was a shallow pool; that she has a duty to do something to ascertain the depth of the water before making the type of dive that she did and I don't think the jury was properly instructed on that subject.

THE COURT: I think the thing that you stated now is a complete defense to your lawsuit, in all probability, and is the reason I contemplate I will set this plaintiff's judgment aside.

MR. STORY: In other words, that you couldn't have given that without giving me a directed verdict?

.   .   .   .

THE COURT: .   .   . I just happened to think that as a matter of law she was guilty of contributory negligence and not doing other things for her own safety.   And, as I say, that's why I contemplated setting aside the judgment if and when it is returned.

.   .   .   .

The Trial Ends

After Judge Hart gave additional instructions to the jury, the jury retired, elected a foreman, deliberated, and returned a unanimous verdict in favor of the plaintiff for $10,000 on October 27, 1961.

On November 3, 1961, Mr. Story moved that the court set this verdict aside and render judgment for the defendant notwithstanding the verdict, in effect renewing his directed verdict motion.   The date of November 17 was set for argument on the merits of this motion, and it was argued on that day.   On November 27, Judge Hart granted the defendant's motion. The clerk of the court then entered judgment for the defendant, including $48 in costs.   On December 18, Mr. Stone filed notice that the plaintiff would appeal.

Judge Hart set aside the plaintiff's verdict.   Yet, at the trial, he was unwilling to direct a verdict for the defendant on the same grounds.   Are these positions consistent?   First, observe that if the trial judge had not allowed the jury to return a verdict—that is, if he had directed a verdict for the defendant—and later the appellate court determined that this was an error, a whole new trial would be necessary.   However, if entering judgment notwithstanding the verdict should be deemed error on appeal, it would only be necessary to reinstate the jury verdict for the plaintiff. The latter route may be an economical way to proceed.   Second, if the case is so lopsided as to warrant a directed verdict for the defendant, it is perhaps likely that the jury will find for the defendant.   And if the jury does so find, then there will be no need to deal further with the legal question posed by the motion for a directed verdict, and also the judge will have avoided any appearance of intruding into the jury's sphere.   Again, denying the directed verdict motion, but possibly later granting the same party's motion for judgment notwithstanding the verdict, may be a sound course for the judge to follow.

––––––––

Comments and Questions

1.   The remedy the plaintiff sought here was monetary compensation.   What were her losses?   Were they reasonably measurable in money?

2.   The plaintiff based her claim on the principle that one who negligently causes harm to another must compensate therefor.   The defendant defended in part on the basis of the principle that a contributorily negligent plaintiff loses. Courts rather than legislatures first laid down these principles, and courts continue to play a role in laying down such principles today.   Compare a law requiring all swimming pool owners to mark their pools in certain ways.   Would a legisla-

ture be better qualified than a court to make such a law? Would an administrative board be best? Why?

3. The grievance-remedial mode comes retrospectively into play in two kinds of cases: (a) where the loss causer voluntarily pays and (b) where the loss causer disputes the legal or factual premises of the plaintiff's claim, as in the Swimming Pool case. In the latter type of case, Anglo-American legal systems have traditionally offered an adjudicative process adversarially informed to resolve the disputed issues of law and fact, and this process has even come to be commonly thought of as intrinsic to the grievance-remedial mode. In this mode and process, who takes the original *initiative* to put the law in motion: the aggrieved or some public official? (The Swimming Pool case is typical.) What is the importance of this?

4. Except for the appeal, we have now seen the grievance-remedial mode operate from beginning to end in a representative case in which the defendant disputed the legal and factual premises of the plaintiff's claim. The judge resolved some of the disputed issues, and the jury others. Were judge and jurors alike *adjudicators*? Notice that one of the features of adjudication is impartiality. Does the required impartiality extend to issues of law as well as to issues of fact? Would it be acceptable for a judge who openly favored a change in the rule that contributory negligence completely barred recovery to hear and rule on a plaintiff's demurrer challenging the legal sufficiency of a contributory negligence defense?

5. In the Swimming Pool case, the adjudicators were *adversarially informed.* What does this mean? Did the judge go out and look up the law on the legal issues raised? Did the jury go out and dig up the evidence on the factual issues involved? Or was nearly all this informing done through the efforts of the opposing lawyers? How did the legal issues arise in the first place? The factual issues? Through the initiative of judge and jury, or through the initiative of lawyers and parties?

6. Notice how the plaintiff, the defendant, the lawyers, the jury, and the judge all shared in administering (albeit in differing ways) the grievance-remedial mode in the Swimming Pool case, a case in which the legal and factual premises of the plaintiff's claim were disputed. From this case it can be seen that, in general, legal issues are presented to the judge by the lawyers and are resolved on the basis of argument as a matter of judgment as to which has the stronger side. By contrast, here the factual issues are resolved by the jury on the basis of the parties' evidence and in accord with the preponderance of the evidence. This is not to say that the judge has no power to control the jury. On the contrary, one of the beauties of the Swimming Pool case is that it also illustrates so-called judicial controls on so-called jury irrationality.

SUMMERS, LAW, ADJUDICATIVE PROCESSES, AND CIVIL JUSTICE

in Law, Reason, and Justice 169, 176–79 (G. Hughes ed. 1969).*

Some students of adjudicative processes focus on their human component, for example, behavior of adjudicators, parties, witnesses, lawyers, and other participants in the process. But it is possible also to focus on the rules and principles—procedural in nature—that, in some sense, define the process itself. An ancient and disputed view has it that in adjudication, Man is far more important than Rule.[9] To debate this view is fruitless.

However, the procedural "rule and principle" component of adjudicative processes in many legal systems is probably far more substantial and complex than most laymen, some "legal realists," and at least a few social scientists think necessary. Some sense of the potential scope and complexity of this component can be grasped from the following outline of legal needs that "procedural" rules and principles may be introduced to help meet. These needs are for some means of providing for:

1. Identifying authorized adjudicators;
2. opening the process up to all potential claimants and defenders on a fair and reasonable basis;
3. affording lawyers an opportunity to represent and advise claimants and defenders who resort to the process or are drawn into it without, so far as feasible, visiting responsibility for any mistakes of lawyers upon the claimants and defenders whom they represent;
4. setting the adjudicative process in motion in a particular case;
5. notifying the defender that the claimant has set the process in motion, that he will have an opportunity to defend, and that he will be bound by the outcome of the process even if he chooses not to defend at all;
6. binding both parties to the outcome once the process has been properly set in motion;
7. disqualifying an adjudicator as unqualified on grounds of partiality, incompetence, or the like;
8. allowing the defender as early as feasible in the proceedings to terminate or postpone them because:
   (a) the claimant has haled the defender before the wrong adjudicator; or
   (b) the defender is not the right, or not the only proper, defender; or
   (c) the claimant's claim is baseless in law (no substantive principle or rule of law allows or should allow relief on the facts alleged, even assuming their truth); or
   (d) the claimant's claim is baseless in fact (he has no evidence to prove his allegations of fact); or
   (e) the claimant's claim, while *prima facie* good in law and *prima facie* factual, is wholly defeasible (because defender has a valid defense, for example, statute of limitations, whose factual basis the claimant cannot deny);
9. defining what *genuine* issues of fact the adjudicator is to resolve;

9. This dispute is but one aspect of a more general one. Compare, for example, Pope and Hume, in order:
- For forms of government let fools contest,
  Whate'er is best administered is best.
- So great is the force of laws and of particular forms of government, and so little dependence have they on the humors and tempers of men, that consequences almost as general and certain may sometimes be deduced from them as any which the mathematical sciences afford us.

10. identifying and defining such further issues of law as might arise in the course of resolving the genuine issues of fact put before the adjudicator;

11. maximizing the likelihood that the adjudicator will suspend judgment on genuine issues of fact or of law until such time as both sides have been heard and decision is called for;

12. allocating responsibility for proving facts in issue, and responsibility for pre-hearing preparations;

13. determining the nature and quantum of required proof on factual issues, and appropriateness and weight of argument on legal issues;

14. obtaining adequate pre-hearing preparations for presentations of all relevant and admissible evidence or argument;

15. holding orderly hearings with fair opportunity for claimant and defender alike to present their cases and offer rebuttals;

16. deciding impartially, deliberately, and rationally all factual and legal issues presented, in terms of
    (a) relevance and weight of proof, and
    (b) appropriateness and force of argument;

17. deciding solely on the basis of evidence and arguments that are presented
    (a) by the parties or others, and
    (b) before the adjudicator, and
    (c) with both sides present;

18. articulating publicly the reasons on which resolutions of issues of fact and of law are based;

19. appealing from harmful errors of the adjudicator in administering the adjudicative process itself;

20. securing that errorless decisions are final with neither claimant nor defender being entitled to reopen them;

21. extending, restricting, or otherwise modifying the substantive legal principles and rules invoked by the parties to the proceeding at its various stages;

22. expediting the entire process so that justice is not delayed and therefore denied.

It is not claimed that any existing adjudicative process includes rules and principles that satisfy all of the foregoing needs. Nor is it claimed that the foregoing are the only relevant needs to be met. However, their enumeration is at least sufficient to indicate that the problems involved are many, substantial, and complex—more so than is commonly assumed.

An adjudicative process could be set up with a bare minimum of rules and principles—far fewer than those indicated here. The probable advantages of a more extensive and sophisticated procedural law, however, are several. The adjudicator who follows sound general rules and principles of procedure seems likely to do more justice to the merits of claims in the mine-run of cases than the adjudicator who follows a policy of determining, *ad hoc* as he goes along, the appropriate adjudicative steps to be taken in each case. Moreover, if an adjudicator follows general rules and principles made known to participants in advance, they and their lawyers can know better what to expect and can therefore prepare better for appearances.

In addition, an adjudicator's compliance with just procedural rule or principle guarantees procedural justice. Here, the rule or principle is a sure guide, whereas *ad hoc*-ism is not.

Further, to adopt an extensive and sophisticated procedural law is to provide a better foundation for appeals based on charges of procedural irregularity. The concept of "procedural error" is given more precision, review, as such, is given more focus, and determinations of deviation can be more objective.

Finally, when the relevant procedural rules and principles are appropriately designed, compliance therewith guarantees the overtness essential if justice is to be seen to be done.

But it cannot be denied that a price is paid for the introduction of extensive and sophisticated procedural rules and principles, for they bring problems of their own, including the problem of devising ways to enforce them and the problem of devising ways to assure that they will be interpreted and administered in enlightened fashion. The enlightened adjudicator will strike a proper balance between the interest in giving parties a reliable and efficient procedural basis on which to proceed and the interest in preserving sufficient flexibility to allow cases to be resolved according to substantive law in those instances in which rigid adherence to procedural rule and principle might get in the way.

He will also, when necessary, strike a proper balance between the interest in procedural fairness and the interest in doing justice according to substantive law.

––––––––

R. FIELD, B. KAPLAN & K. CLERMONT, MATERIALS FOR A BASIC COURSE IN CIVIL PROCEDURE
3–4 (5th ed. 1984).*

Some [procedural] rules look principally to preserving a settled order of proceeding; they could be radically altered without important consequence. In respect to other rules, there are powerful reasons of policy why they should be as they are or should not be as they are. . . .

It may be argued that procedural rules ought to be so definite and clear-cut as always to furnish a sure guide for the behavior of the parties in court proceedings. Whether or not this would be the ideal situation, it can be said at the outset that it has not been attained, and it may be doubted whether it ever could be attained. We must approach the study of procedure with full awareness that we shall be bedeviled by many of the same doubts and difficulties about what the rule is or ought to be that characterize the study of substantive law.

Therefore, although the rules of procedure are designed to isolate and sharpen the issues in dispute and thus to simplify the controversy, the uncertainties in the procedural rules may serve to inject a further disputatious ingredient into a lawsuit. Procedural problems are more obtrusive in our law than a beginner is likely to suppose, and perhaps more obtrusive than they ought to be.

————

Procedural Justice

Consider the following excerpt from Sir Frederick Pollock's Essays in the Law 275 (1922):

> Perhaps the greatest of all the fallacies entertained by lay people about the law is one which, though seldom expressed in terms, an observant lawyer may quite commonly find lurking not far below the surface. This is that the business of a court of justice is to discover the truth. Its real business is to pronounce upon the justice of particular claims, and incidentally to test the truth of the assertions of fact made in support of the claim in law, provided that those assertions are relevant in law to the establishment of the desired conclusion; and this is by no means the same thing.

Surely readers will ask, "How can there be any inconsistency between justice and truth? Indeed, justice can only be done on the basis of the facts. Justice cannot be done in the dark." So? A distinction between procedural justice and substantive justice may help here. Pollock may have been considering procedural justice. For example, giving each side an equal chance to present his case may, in a particular case, lead to substantive injustice—one side, the weaker side factually, may nonetheless be able to demonstrate a better case factually than can the other side. Yet, recognition of this risk has not induced us to deny each side an equal opportunity to be heard.

Pollock's remark can be generalized: The pursuit of truth may, in an adjudicative process, be subordinated to still other social aims. One of these is that of offering the parties a day in court, a forum in which to "have it out." In the end, we may lose sight of the truth, but the parties will have had their say against each other, and this will have served as a substitute for disorderly forms of self-help. Furthermore, evidentiary privileges may frustrate the pursuit of truth. Thus the adjudicator may be forced to apply rules of evidence that limit or close off relevant lines of factual inquiry altogether. A rule that, say, privileges a witness not to testify because her testimony would violate a confidential relation may operate to keep an adjudicator in the dark in the particular case. When this happens, substantive justice (insofar as it is necessarily premised on truth) is sacrificed to the social policy of inducing and protecting confidential relations.

A way to summarize is to say that the grievance-remedial mode, with its elaborate procedures for resolving disputes over the factual premises of particular remedies, is a multipurpose institutional scheme, only one of the purposes of which is the pursuit of truth, with other purposes thereof either cooperatively or antagonistically involving themselves in this pursuit of truth.

————

Pursuit of Truth

In some cases, the actual facts are found. And striving to find the truth is usually laudable. But even where truth is the proper aim, how much certainty is possible anyway?

Consider, for example, what the sources of proof are in a court of law. Testimony of witnesses predominates. Is such testimony somewhat unreliable? Students who think not should consider (1) that witnesses do not always perceive events accurately in the first place, (2) that they do not always remember well, (3) that they do not always communicate what they experienced, (4) that they sometimes, even in good faith, distort their experience, and (5) that they may lie. Do you think any of these things could have occurred in the Swimming Pool case? Illustrate.

So fact-finding is a very human endeavor, and additionally the humans who undertake it do so subject to significant institutional limitations on their efforts. For example, the court does not have a subpoena power broad enough to bring in witnesses from anywhere in the world.

But even if all this were not so, how much certainty is optimal? Time and money are not unlimited resources.

Yet, surely, improved truth-finding deserves consideration. After all, some of the antecedents of the modern trial appear to present-day eyes to be far less rational than what we now have. Consider this account from T. Plucknett, A Concise History of the Common Law 114–17 (5th ed. 1956): [d]

> The most ancient of these was the ordeal, which took a variety of different forms. Its origin must date from before the introduction of Christianity, but the practice was so deep-rooted that the Church, in this as in other cases, felt bound to adopt it. In consequence we find the ordeal surrounded by Christian ceremonies which must, no doubt, have added considerably to its moral effectiveness—and perhaps even to its practical value as a psychological test of truth-telling. Of the several forms of ordeal in use the ordeal of hot iron was that most common for freemen. It was administered at the most solemn moment of the Mass; a special ritual was prescribed in the old service books telling us how the heated iron was to be carried by the accused over a distance of nine feet; then—
>
>> the hand was sealed and kept under seal for three nights and afterwards the bandages removed. If it is clean, God be praised; but if unhealthy matter is found where the iron was held he shall be deemed guilty and unclean.
>
> Another variant was the ordeal of boiling water, where the accused had to plunge his hand into a bowl of boiling water and take out a stone; his guilt or innocence was ascertained by inspecting his hand after three days. The ordeal of cold water was more often applied to the unfree. The accused was solemnly exhorted by the priest during Mass to confess his guilt if he were guilty; if he persisted in maintaining his innocence then—

d. Copyright © 1929, 1936 by Theodore F.T. Plucknett. Reprinted by permission of Little, Brown and Company.

let the hands of the accused be bound together under the bent knees after the manner of a man who is playing the game of *Champ-estroit.* Then he shall be bound around the loins with a rope strong enough to hold him; and in the rope will be made a knot at the distance of the length of his hair; and so he shall be let down gently into the water so as not to make a splash. If he sinks down to the knot he shall be drawn up saved; otherwise let him be adjudged a guilty man by the spectators.

Still another variety of ordeal was that of the cursed morsel, which was used only for the trial of clergy. This consisted in making the accused swallow a piece of food in which was concealed a feather or such like; if he was successful, he was innocent, but if he choked he was guilty. Although the Church adopted the ordeals which it found in use among the populace, some of the more critical clergy had misgivings. Then also there was obviously the possibility of the priest manipulating the ordeal, and Peter the Chanter, a celebrated theologian of the university of Paris (*ob.* 1197), suggests that he had some sort of moral responsibility for the rightness of the result. Its abolition was rendered all the more difficult by the system of fees which grew up around it—always a powerful obstruction in the way of reform. A particular church, like St. Peter's, Northampton, might have a monopoly of the proceedings; elsewhere, the archdeacon might be entitled to dues—as at Coventry where he received thirty pence for each ordeal. . . .

The "wager of law" . . . , although still essentially an ordeal, contained features which give the impression that its principle was rather more rational. The party who was called upon to make his law had to find a number of people, twelve or some other number fixed by the court according to circumstances, and then take a solemn oath that he was innocent. His companions, or "compurgators" as they were called, then swore that the oath which he had taken was clean. In other words, the court calls upon the accused to produce a specified number of people (occasionally from a particular class or even from the names on a given list) who are prepared to swear that in their opinion his oath is trustworthy. They do not swear to the facts of the case, but merely to their judgment that the accused is a credible person. Wager of law, therefore, reduces itself to a character test; in the earlier period when there were strong religious sanctions surrounding the oath it is clear that a disreputable person would have difficulty in finding compurgators. Cases of failure to make one's law do occur from time to time in the records. . . . Opinion as to its value seems always to have been divided. . . .

In civil matters, however, there are signs that it had a place; contemporaries seem to have regarded it as superior in some cases to witness proof. The citizens of London as late as 1364 obtained a statute preserving their right to wage law as a defence to debts which were claimed on the evidence of a merchant's books—it is significant that a mercantile community should consider compurgation successfully performed as more weighty evidence than a merchant's accounts. In the actions of debt and detinue wager of law as a defence lasted until the nineteenth century. The courts in such cases endeavoured to substitute jury trial as far as possible, both by developing alternative actions and by strictly defining those few cases in which it lay. It was not finally abolished until 1833.

.   .   .

The Normans introduced trial by battle—unless, indeed, "trial by battle may well have been known in the Danelaw throughout the tenth century". In civil cases it was not fought between the parties themselves, but between their respective champions. The ancient formula suggests that the champion was originally a witness who was also a tenant bound by homage to defend his lord's title, and that a judicial duel between contradictory witnesses was allowed to decide the rights of the parties. The champion's regular oath (which soon became a matter of mere form) stated that his father on his deathbed had informed him that the plaintiff had the right which was then in dispute, and charged him to maintain that right with all his power.   .   .   . We very soon find from the rolls that there was a professional band of champions who undertook business all over the country; courts would arrange the dates of battle so that the champions could fit in their engagements conveniently. Some very great landowners, such as the larger monasteries, were so constantly involved in litigation that they maintained their own full-time champions. The names of these champions constantly appear on the rolls, and we sometimes hear of a champion's "master" or manager, and of a champion who abandoned his client because the other side offered him a premium.

"The rational element of law must, it would seem, have asserted itself in the judgment which decided how and by whom the proof should be given .   .   .   . " F. Maitland, The Forms of Action at Common Law 16 (1936). Nevertheless, it was the limitations and uncertainties of the ancient methods of proof that led to the development of the modern trial by jury.

––––––––

Trial by Jury

It is well to note some of the details of the jury's functioning in the Swimming Pool case, given the current prominence of lay finders of fact in our system. Review or think through the following questions: How did the jury learn of the episode at the swimming pool? Was it the jury's job merely to find facts or was it also, in the first instance, the jury's job to apply the law to the facts it found? Does applying the law presuppose understanding the law—understanding, for example, that contributory negligence is a complete bar? It would have been possible, as in the Loach case, to have the jury find detailed facts by a special verdict, leaving the judge to apply the law to the facts as found. But here, as in most cases, the verdict was a general verdict, which just finds for the plaintiff in a certain amount or for the defendant and which thus involves the jury in applying the law.

Observe that the jury merely rendered a verdict in the form of a conclusion without reasons. Observe, too, that the court reporter did not go into the jury room and transcribe what occurred there. There was no way of knowing whether the jury decided on the basis of some utter irrelevancy. Contrast the other aspects of the trial. Reflect on the following comment of Lord Devlin, a noted British jurist, in Trial by Jury 13–14 (1956):

> Judges give their reasons, either so as to satisfy the parties or because they themselves want to justify their judgments. . . . The jury just says yes or no. Indeed, it is not allowed to expand upon that and its reasons may not be inquired into. It is the oracle deprived of the right of being ambiguous. The jury was in its origin as oracular as the ordeal: neither was conceived in reason: the verdict, no more than the result of the ordeal, was open to rational criticism. This immunity has been largely retained and is still an essential characteristic of the system.

Today, judges have various devices by which they may, often on motion of one of the parties, exercise control over certain kinds of jury unreasonableness. In the Swimming Pool case, we saw one of these devices put to work when Judge Hart set aside the jury's verdict. But the assumption must not be made that the jury's work is fully and effectively reviewable by the trial judge (or appellate judges). Suppose, for example, that in the jury room, the jury in the Swimming Pool case decided to make some law of its own. That is, suppose it (as have some legislatures) rejected the law that proof of contributory negligence constitutes a complete bar and substituted a comparative negligence principle, giving the plaintiff a general verdict for $5,000. Even though the jury actually found the plaintiff to have been contributorily negligent, it decided that the defendant should bear half of the plaintiff's $10,000 loss because the defendant had been in good part negligent, too. When the jury returned such a verdict, the verdict would not be vulnerable as lawless, would it? Such a verdict is consistent, is it not, with underlying findings that the defendant was negligent, the plaintiff was not contributorily negligent, and the damages were only $5,000 and not $10,000?

Why is the jury allowed so to operate? Does it merely represent a historical throwback? Another aspect of the unknowability of the truth? The predominance of other social aims? Or is the jury an effective route to either procedural or substantive justice? These questions are worth thinking about, even though firmer answers would require delving into the literature on such disputed matters as how competent and equitable jurors are as decision makers.

I. Post-Trial Procedures: Enforcement of Judgments and Appellate Review

In Anglo-American law, after a jury returns a verdict in favor of the plaintiff in a civil action, and the court enters judgment for the plaintiff, the defendant must satisfy the judgment unless he appeals. If the judgment calls for money, and the defendant does not voluntarily pay, the plaintiff can obtain a *writ of execution* from the clerk of the court. This writ is addressed to the local sheriff and orders him to seize property owned by the defendant, sell it, and pay the plaintiff the amount of her judgment. By obtaining a judgment in her favor, the plaintiff thus becomes entitled to invoke the strong arm of the law in her behalf. However, if the defendant appeals from the entry of judgment against him, he can normally *stay* satisfaction of this judgment until the outcome of the appeal has been determined.

In Miss White's case, although the jury returned a verdict in her favor, the trial judge refused to permit a judgment for her. Instead, he set aside the verdict and rendered judgment for the defendant. In circumstances such as these, the plaintiff may appeal to an appellate court, and this is what Miss White, through her lawyer, did.

The appeal idea is firmly entrenched in modern systems of law. Nearly all such systems have appellate as well as trial courts. Unlike trial courts, which now seldom consist of more than one judge, appellate courts normally consist of several judges. The chief business of Anglo-American appellate judges is to decide appeals from rulings made by trial-court judges, and in so doing appellate judges perform two distinct functions. First, they correct, or provide for the correction of, prejudicial errors made by trial judges in particular cases. Second, they keep the law uniform and sound. Without appellate judges to perform this institutional function, the law applied by trial judges might vary from trial judge to trial judge throughout the territory in which the appellate court has jurisdiction. Appellate judges also have primary responsibility for the development of the common law and for sound interpretational law. Their decisions, unlike most decisions of trial judges, are published and bound in volumes accessible to lawyers and, theoretically, to the public. These decisions constitute case law binding in all similar cases that later arise in the same court or in lower courts.

To return to the first of the two functions performed by appellate judges in deciding appeals, we said that appellate judges correct, or provide for the correction of, prejudicial errors made by trial judges. Of all officials who make decisions in our legal system, trial judges in their rulings are subject to the closest scrutiny. The whole of civil procedure provides at every step of the way for the merciless exposure of the errors made by trial judges.

Should the rulings of trial judges be subject to such intensive scrutiny? The decisions of other officials in the legal system are not similarly subjected to scrutiny. Why single out trial judges in this way? The merciless exposure and correction of trial judges' errors might lead people to disrespect these judges. Further, appeals are costly and time-consuming. The justification for them should therefore be clear. Is it clear? These are questions on which students should reflect. Students will probably conclude that the system of appellate review of a trial judge's rulings is sound. Students should then consider whether they would extend the appeal idea. Should the statutory enactments of a legislature be subject to appeal to a higher legislature? Should the policy decisions of an administrator be subject to appeal? Should nonpolicy decisions of the administrator be subject to appeal? Should appellate courts themselves review not only the trial judge's rulings on legal questions but also the findings of fact of the jury? Should the appellate court itself hear witnesses and, in effect, conduct a second full trial of a case? The appeal idea has limits, and students who reflect on the foregoing questions should understand more fully what these limits are.

Observe that mistakes only of the trial judge are subject to correction on appeal, and these are usually mistakes of law. The nature of the questions on which a trial judge may be required to rule before, during, and after a trial is highly varied. For example, he may have to rule whether the plaintiff has alleged facts constituting a valid legal claim; whether the defendant has alleged facts constituting a valid affirmative defense to the plaintiff's claim; whether one of the parties or some witness should be compelled to make various disclosures prior to trial; whether evidence offered at trial is legally admissible; whether a party has introduced sufficient evidence to justify a verdict in her favor; whether particular instructions should be given to the jury; whether a verdict for one of the parties should be set aside and judgment rendered notwithstanding the verdict; whether a new trial should be granted; or whether essential facts have been established in a nonjury trial. The trial judge's rulings on all such questions are subject to appeal. On questions of law, the appellate court will substitute its view for the trial judge's; but on factual rulings, the appellate court will defer to the trial judge's view and will overturn only when it rather strongly disagrees with him.

In Anglo-American law, a lawyer in proceedings before a trial court is normally required to object to any and all judicial rulings that she thinks erroneous in order to appeal successfully from such rulings at a later time. This requirement is imposed to ensure that the trial judge will have every opportunity to correct his own errors when they are made. But an effect of imposing the requirement is that the client is the one who suffers if her lawyer fails to object to an erroneous ruling.

In Anglo-American law, appellate courts normally do not correct errors on their own but instead wait for lawyers to appeal them. Again, students should consider why this should be. If a trial judge has made an error, should it be corrected even though the lawyer whose client is affected does not appeal the particular error?

Appeal is usually allowed only from the final judgment in the trial court, after which time the losing party asserts a list of prejudicial errors appearing in the record and duly objected to. However, an immediate appeal may lie from certain important orders issued during the course of trial-court proceedings.

How do our appellate courts operate? The losing party may appeal within a prescribed period of time after the entry of a judgment. The law requires the losing party to file a notice of appeal, as well as to serve it on the opposing party so that he, too, can make necessary preparations. The appealing party is called the appellant or petitioner, and the other party the appellee or respondent. With the help of counsel, the clerk of the trial court will assemble and transmit to the clerk of the appellate court all papers necessary for the appellate judges to understand what the appeal is about. In some cases, a transcript of the entire trial will be transmitted.

In most courts, the parties to an appeal must file *briefs* on the law relating to the questions to be considered in the appeal. The briefs are almost always prepared by lawyers. The appellant's brief will state the facts of the case, list the alleged errors to be corrected, present arguments that these are truly errors deserving correction, and discuss cases or statutes that presumably support these arguments. The appellee will then prepare and file a similar brief presenting her side of the case. The appellant might submit a reply brief.

Ordinarily, lawyers for both sides will also be given an opportunity to appear together before the appellate court and orally argue their respective sides of the case.

After the appellate court has heard these arguments, deliberated on the case, and decided by majority vote, it will typically prepare an opinion stating its decision and the reasoning on which the decision is based. If the appellate court decides that the trial judge erred, the appellate court will, unless the error was not prejudicial, require that it be corrected. This may involve a new trial with its expenditures of time and money, or it may involve much less.

Recall that on November 27, 1961, the trial judge who presided in Miss White's case set aside her verdict and rendered judgment for the Island Amusement Company notwithstanding the verdict, chiefly because he thought that as a matter of law she had been contributorily negligent. On December 18, 1961, Miss White's lawyer filed notice of appeal to the appropriate appellate court, which was the supreme court of the state. Thereafter, the lawyers for both sides prepared and filed briefs. On October 5, 1962, the lawyers presented their oral arguments before the supreme court. On February 20, 1963, the court handed down its decision.

The following excerpts are from the eighty-seven pages of briefs filed by the lawyers for both sides. Several different issues of law were considered in these briefs. However, the following excerpts are addressed to only one issue of law: whether the evidence showed overwhelmingly that Miss White's own actions constituted contributory negligence so that she could not prevail. If the only reasonable view was that her actions constituted contributory negligence, then, even though a jury had decided that her actions were not contributory negligence, the defendant should prevail—"as a matter of law."

Extracts from Defendant's Brief

Defendant of course concedes the well-known general rules pointed out by plaintiff for determination of the question of contributory negligence as a matter of law. In other words, it is defendant's position that under the facts conceded by plaintiff's own evidence reasonable men could not differ in this case.

What were the circumstances?

Plaintiff was an intelligent, athletically inclined young lady. She was a "better than average swimmer," an experienced swimmer with years of experience in performing "all types of diving" . . . . She was experienced in diving in a shallow pool . . . and knew what the dangers thereof were if not done properly, as she had hit bottom before when diving in a shallow pool . . . . She knew the pool was shallow before she dove into it . . . . However, before she dove she could not see "any indication of the depth of the water where you dove in" . . . . It was daylight . . . and there was no problem in seeing . . . . She knew how to dive in a shallow pool . . . . Although there were numerous other people standing in various parts of the pool (other than her friends in one place) she made no attempt to measure the water on them . . . . The water was clear . . . . She could plainly see the bottom of the pool . . . .

Taking plaintiff at her word, as we must, that, although she could plainly see the bottom of the pool, still she could not see "any indication of the depth of the water where you dove in" . . . , we submit that no reasonable man could possibly differ that she was not exercising the degree of care and prudence to be expected of a reasonably prudent, intelligent, fifteen-year-old, experienced swimmer and diver when she dove into this water onto the top of her head . . . under those circumstances, that is, without having "any indication of the depth" . . . , except her knowledge that it was shallow.

This case is basically the same as Johnson v. Hot Springs Land & Improvement Co., [76 Or. 333, 148 P. 1137 (1915)], excepting in *Johnson* defendant provided a diving board at the place where plaintiff dove and such diving board was an invitation to use it for diving. In *Johnson* plaintiff was told upon entering the pool that the water was shallow, and was 3 to 3½ feet deep, but was coming in fast, and it would not be long until the tank was full. "They were neither told that the pool was safe for diving nor warned that it was unsafe." Plaintiff thereupon waited "about twenty minutes" and then apparently made his own assumptions as to the depth of the water at that time. Plaintiff was nineteen years old, of ordinary intelligence, and was a good swimmer and diver. Apparently, without having any precise information as to how much deeper the water had gotten, he dove off the diving board and sustained injury, for which he sued, making a similar allegation as that upon which plaintiff relies in this case, that "defendant failed to warn (him) that on account of the shallowness it was dangerous to dive into the water." He claimed that he was unfamiliar with the premises and did not know the risk of diving, and that he had a right to rely upon the assurances of the defendant arising from the fact that defendant had rented him a bathing suit and charged him an admission. The Supreme Court stated as follows:

One of the objects of the rule requiring the owner of a place of amusement like the one maintained by defendant to warn patrons of danger is to acquaint the patron with the hazard so that he may avoid injury. If the deceased had knowledge of the shallowness of the water and the danger incident to diving from the spring-board, then he knew all and no less than he could have known had defendant expressly warned him of the risk. If the defendant had, in fact, cautioned Johnson against the peril, and, notwithstanding such warning, the latter dived off the spring-board, then, on the facts of the instant case, the defendant would not be liable because of the knowledge imparted to Johnson; and so, too, the same result follows if Johnson did, in fact, know of the danger, even though not told by the defendant. *If with knowledge of the danger, Johnson placed himself in peril, and, on account thereof, was injured, he was chargeable with contributory negligence.* (Emphasis supplied)

We submit that this holding in *Johnson* is apropos to our case because in our case plaintiff knew that the water was shallow, although there is evidence that she did not know the precise depth. She appreciated the consequences of diving into a shallow pool and she dove anyway. . . .

. . . By the exercise of the slightest care, such as [merely] jumping into the [water] feet first, or simply looking at the bottom, or by looking "around to see how far the water came up on people in various parts of that pool" . . . where "they were scattered around," . . . to whom she "wasn't paying any attention" . . . she would have been accurately advised of the precise depth of the pool.

Extracts from Plaintiff's Reply Brief

Defendant concedes that in determining if the plaintiff was contributorily negligent or not, reasonable men must all conclude she failed to use reasonable care. However, the defendant has apparently overlooked the well established rule of law that in order to reach this conclusion all evidence must be considered in the light most favorable to the plaintiff.

The defendant states "she had hit bottom before when diving into a shallow pool" when in fact the plaintiff testified she had brushed her nose against the bottom . . . . Also, it is stated the plaintiff made no attempt to measure the water on other people in the pool when in fact the transcript states she wasn't paying any particular attention to them . . . and nobody was near the north wall . . . . Defendant takes the plaintiff's statement that she looked at the bottom of the pool, leaving out the fact she could not tell the depth by looking at the bottom, seizes upon a statement by the plaintiff relating to depth markings and argues all reasonable men would agree she was contributorily negligent as a matter of law "when she dove into this water on top of her head" . . . .

. . . Also, the defendant omitted the plaintiff's testimony that she "generally took in the whole situation and drew a conclusion" . . . . The defendant must have necessarily overlooked . . . the evidence that prior to making a 45° angle dive the plaintiff noted a handrail to her immediate left, the depth of the water on her friends in the pool . . . , the steps going into shallow water across the pool . . . , and she looked but did not see anything indicating she should not dive into the pool . . . or that it would be dangerous to dive into the pool . . . .

In Johnson v. Hot Springs Land Co., 76 Or. 333, 338, 148 P. 1137 (1915), the decedent knew exactly how deep the water was or at least reasonable men would all agree he should have known. He and his friends had been swimming and diving into a half filled pool for fifteen minutes. In reviewing the evidence, the court said:

> Arthur Johnson was a good diver; he had been in the plunge at least on two prior occasions when the water was at its usual depth of about seven feet; he and his friends were told, upon making inquiry, that the water was between 3 and 3½ feet deep, and that it was shallow, but that the water was coming in fast; he and his companions sat around and waited "for the water to fill up" because the shallowness was apparent; he could not well have avoided seeing his friends standing up in the water; and consequently he must have known the depth of the water. It is also clear that he realized the danger of diving off the spring-board into the water at the same time because, as Halvorsen said, Johnson was going "to make a long dive to make it shallow in the water," and his feet slipped, or he lost his balance in the air, and he came down straight.
>
> The evidence has been narrated, and considered in a light most favorable to the plaintiff, and the conclusion is inevitable not only that Johnson knew the depth of the water, but that he also appreciated the danger. The fact that he attempted "to make a long dive to make it shallow in the water" reflects the knowledge then had by the deceased.

Defendant argues since the case at bar involves a shallow pool and the plaintiff failed to measure the "precise depth," she was contributorily negligent as a matter of law based upon the holding of *Johnson*. Counsel ignores the fact the defendant did nothing to warn the plaintiff of the depth of the water in the case at bar and argues everything the plaintiff did to ascertain the depth of the water short of "merely jumping into the water feet first" was unreasonable or did not fulfill her "duty."

The plaintiff was entitled to rely upon what she observed to indicate the depth of the water. Unlike the *Johnson* case, this was the plaintiff's first visit to defendant's pool. Unlike the *Johnson* case, there was no warning given regarding the depth of the water, nor was there any warning she should not dive into the defendant's shallow pool or that she did so at her own risk. In the *Johnson* case, the court reviewed the decedent's knowledge with respect to the depth of the water as follows:

> Murphy, Peck and Halvorsen each testified that after entering the water and by standing up in it the depth was found to be between 3 and 3½ feet, but no one remembered having seen Johnson standing up in the water, although they were together in plain view of each other all the time. They had been swimming and diving about 15

minutes. Peck and Halvorsen each had dived off the bank three or four times, *and Johnson had done the same thing twice.* (Emphasis added)

The plaintiff did not have any knowledge of the actual depth as the decedent must have had in the *Johnson* case, since she had not been in the water. She did everything possible to ascertain the depth of the water but actually measure the "precise depth" with a yardstick which the defendant didn't even bother to do and mark on the side of the pool. It is hard to see how defendant can argue that all men would agree the plaintiff failed to act in a reasonable manner to ascertain the depth of the water. Plaintiff submits she certainly acted in a reasonable manner which, of course, is what twelve reasonable persons concluded in this case. . . .

Defendant argues if the plaintiff had looked around "she would have been accurately advised of the precise depth of the pool" . . . . However, she did look around and there were no markings to indicate the precise depth of the pool and there were no people in the water along the north wall or in the area where she dove.

Comments and Questions

1. The chief reason why Judge Hart set aside the plaintiff's verdict was that he believed the plaintiff had been contributorily negligent as a matter of law. The plaintiff's lawyer challenged as error the grant of judgment notwithstanding the verdict, and both lawyers naturally devoted a large part of their briefs to this contributory negligence issue. Another issue was whether, as a matter of law, the defendant had been negligent at all, and each brief included several pages on this issue. How did this issue arise from the trial-court proceedings?

2. Observe that the lawyers, through the pleading process, defined the issues of fact to be resolved at the trial. Likewise, the lawyers, through the entire pretrial, trial, and post-trial process, defined issues of law, which they might possibly present later to appellate judges for decision on appeal. Students should understand how issues are defined for decision by an appellate court. The foregoing excerpts from the briefs of both lawyers reveal not only the relevant arguments but also the precise question to be decided. Thus, lawyers are very much in control. The appellate court does not control what questions it will decide—it generally must decide one or more of the questions posed by the lawyers. Does this leave too much control in the hands of the lawyers? Is there any feasible alternative?

3. Observe that in the foregoing briefs, the lawyers argued over whether a prior decision was "in point." What is meant by saying a decision is in point? Do you think that the decision cited was in point or that it was "distinguishable," as lawyers say? Why should prior decisions be relevant at all?

4. The plaintiff's reply brief said, "Plaintiff submits she certainly acted in a reasonable manner which, of course, is what twelve reasonable persons concluded in this case." Was the jury verdict relevant at all in deciding the question before the appellate court?

5. How would you expect the appellate court to decide the appeal? The appellate court's decision now follows.

"WHITE v. ISLAND AMUSEMENT CO."

Supreme Court of Oregon (a.k.a. New Fetter), 1963.
233 Or. 416, 378 P.2d 953.

LUSK, J.

The plaintiff, a girl fifteen years of age, brought this action to recover damages for personal injuries sustained by her when she dived into a swimming pool owned and maintained by the defendant and struck her head on the bottom of the pool. She alleged that the defendant was negligent (a) in failing to provide adequate markings showing the depth of the water in the pool and (b) in failing to warn the plaintiff that the bottom of this pool was not constructed in the same manner as other swimming pools in the vicinity of Portland, Oregon, in regard to depth of water near the sides of the pool. There was a jury trial and at the conclusion of the testimony the court denied a motion for a directed verdict made by the defendant. . . . The jury returned a verdict for the plaintiff. Thereafter the court, on motion of the defendant, entered judgment for the defendant notwithstanding the verdict and the plaintiff has appealed.

[The supreme court's recital of the trial-court evidence is omitted.]

In Johnson v. Hot Springs Land & Imp. Co., 76 Or. 333, 337–338, 148 P. 1137, 1139, where the plaintiff, who was injured in diving from a springboard into a pool maintained by the defendant, was denied recovery because of contributory negligence, Mr. Justice Harris, speaking for the court, stated the rule applicable to a case of this kind as follows:

> Stating the law with reference to, and as limited by, the facts in the instant case, it may be said that the defendant was not an insurer of the safety of Arthur Johnson. . . . Where a person, however, provides accommodations of a public nature, that person is required to use reasonable care and diligence in furnishing and maintaining such accommodations in a reasonably safe condition for the purpose for which they are apparently designed and to which they are adapted. If for any reason the accommodations are not reasonably safe and suitable for the purposes for which they are ordinarily used in a customary way, then the public should be excluded entirely, or appropriate notice of the unsafe and unsuitable condition should be given, and persons warned of the dangers in using them. The springboard and the water beneath it constituted the accommodations which the defendant furnished to the deceased, who was a patron for hire, and, as such, was using them for diving purposes, to which they were adapted, and in the way in which they were customarily used. Persons patronizing the natatorium have a right to assume that the defendant has performed its duty, and that reasonably safe and suitable accommodations have been furnished. 38 Cyc. 268; Barrett v. Lake Ontario Beach Imp. Co., 174 N.Y. 310, 66 N.E. 968.

This language has been cited and quoted with approval by many courts throughout the country.

In applying it to the present case, it is to be borne in mind that, as the plaintiff knew, the defendant maintained for the use of its patrons two pools, one, the shallow pool in which she received her injury and which was not equipped with a diving board, and the other the deep pool which was so equipped. There is no evidence that the shallow pool was "ordinarily used in a customary way" for diving or indeed that anyone had ever dived into it before. The plaintiff did not allege in her complaint that the defendant was negligent in failing to warn her by signs or otherwise against diving into this pool, but she did allege that it was negligent in failing to mark the depth of the water. What this actually comes to is a claim that the defendant should have given notice not only that the pool was shallow, but how shallow it was. We think that no such duty rested upon the defendant and that notice to its patrons that the pool was shallow was sufficient notice to a reasonably prudent person that it was a pool of a particular character maintained for certain limited uses, one of which was not diving. The deep pool with its diving board was an invitation to dive. The shallow pool by contrast carried a warning that it was intended to serve a different purpose.

In this connection it is worthy of note, since the case of the plaintiff is largely built on her experience at the Mount Scott pool, where she had swum hundreds of times, that there is no evidence that the depth of the water at that pool was marked, and that in testifying to its depth the plaintiff resorted to approximations.

The defendant was not charged with knowledge that the plaintiff would assume that the water at the place where she dived was of sufficient depth for diving with safety to herself. She was not warranted in assuming that the pool was deeper at one end than another or, if this were the case, that she was at the deep end; for in going to the spot from which she dived she passed one marker indicating that the water was shallow at the north end of the pool and she decided to dive from a spot only a few feet from a similar marker. She did not testify that she saw the markers, but neither did she deny that she saw them. They were there to be seen and the defendant could rightly assume that they would be seen. The defendant was entitled to assume "that patrons would act as reasonable men act" and that they "would possess such perception of the surrounding circumstances as a reasonable man would have, that they would possess such knowledge of other pertinent matters as a reasonable man would have, and that they would correlate such perception and knowledge with reasonable intelligence and judgment . . . . " Glaze v. Benson, 205 Md. 26, 33, 106 A.2d 124, 128. See, also, Restatement, Torts § 289.

The evidence on behalf of the plaintiff as to the faded appearance of one of the markers at some undetermined time is not sufficiently substantial to show that this was the condition of the marker on the day of the accident. . . .

The plaintiff seems to have assumed that because people dive from a particular spot in the Mount Scott pool it would be safe for her to dive at a correspondingly located spot at the Hansen Beach pool. The defendant was not charged with knowledge of the construction of the Mount Scott pool, nor of the manner in which it was used by the plaintiff and others. The defendant was under no duty to maintain a pool constructed as are other pools in the Portland area so long as its pool, as constructed and maintained, was reasonably safe, considering the purpose for which it was built and its customary use. . . .

The mere fact that a pool of the kind in question is not deep at one end and shallow at the other is no evidence of negligence. There must be something in addition which might mislead a reasonable person as to the depth of the water. It is necessary that a pool be deeper at some point than at others for drainage, but beyond this no purpose is served by having a "shallow" pool deep at one end and shallow at the other. The plaintiff's witness Mullins so testified.

The plaintiff testified that she judged the depth of the water by the fact that it was breast high on her friends in the pool some seventy feet distant from her. She thought that it must be even deeper where she dived, but here again she indulged the unwarranted assumption that the Hansen Beach pool was built like the Mount Scott pool. Moreover, if, as she testified, she "took in the whole situation" and saw people "scattered throughout the pool" (though not in "the immediate area" where she dived) it must have occurred to her as a reasonably prudent person that this was not a pool the floor of which sloped gradually from the south end to the north end. . . .

We have examined the cases cited by the plaintiff involving diving accidents in public swimming pools or at bathing beaches in which the courts have held that the questions of negligence and contributory negligence were for the jury, and others collected in the Annotation, 48 A.L.R.2d 104, but we see no occasion to discuss these cases in this opinion. Of necessity, the decision in each case must depend on its own particular facts and circumstances. The governing principles, as stated in Johnson v. Hot Springs Land & Imp. Co., supra, are clear and well established. The task of the court is simply to apply those principles to the evidence. The plaintiff sustained serious injuries in this unfortunate accident which befell her, but the defendant was not an insurer of her safety, and, since there is no evidence of a departure from the standard of care which the law imposes upon the defendant, the court rightly allowed the motion for judgment [notwithstanding the verdict]. The judgment is affirmed.

SLOAN, J., dissenting.

Defendant solicits people of all ages and experience to use its pools. Some are acquainted with the peculiar design of the pools, others, like plaintiff, are not. It seems to me that we are not justified in judging plaintiff's actions from the caution of mature years blessed with a measurable degree of hindsight.

The jury should decide if defendant had given adequate warning to unwary patrons of the hazards inherent in this pool.

Comments and Questions

1. What was the supposed error of law that the plaintiff, through her lawyer, said the trial judge made? Does the appellate court here decide the defendant was, as a matter of law, not negligent, or did it decide the plaintiff was, as a matter of law, contributorily negligent, or both?

2. In discharging its surveillance function—that of helping to ensure that prejudicially erroneous rulings of law made by the trial judge and appealed by one of the parties do not go uncorrected—must the appellate court go behind the fact-findings by the trial court? Did this appellate court take new evidence?

————

Fact and Law

Is the distinction between fact and law a clear one? Consider this from R. Field, B. Kaplan & K. Clermont, Materials for a Basic Course in Civil Procedure 594–95 (5th ed. 1984):

> Among the "issues of fact" assigned to the jury, there may be two types of questions: (1) determining what happened, that is, what the parties did and what the circumstances were; and (2) evaluating those facts in terms of their legal consequences, for instance, whether the conduct of the defendant in the circumstances was not that of a reasonable person. But the court always sets the outside limits within which the jury may perform its function. For example, with respect to the latter type of question the Court, in Railroad Co. v. Stout, 84 U.S. (17 Wall.) 657, 663 (1874), said: "So if a coach-driver intentionally drives within a few inches of a precipice, and an accident happens, negligence may be ruled as a question of law. On the other hand, if he had placed a suitable distance between his coach and the precipice, but by the breaking of a rein or an axle, which could not have been anticipated, an injury occurred, it might be ruled as a question of law that there was no negligence and no liability."

This point is pursued in F. James & G. Hazard, Civil Procedure 337–38 (3d ed. 1985):

> It is clear that rules of law could be so formulated and so administered as to exclude the jury altogether from making these evaluations. A court could decide, for instance, that under a given set of circumstances motorists must blow their horns, that under a different set of circumstances they need not do so. Under such a pair of rules, the theoretical function of the jury would be only to decide whether the circumstances existed and whether the horn was blown, the question whether it should have been blown being decided by the court. On the other hand, it would be perfectly possible so to formulate the rule that the jury is to decide not only whether the horn was blown but also whether the horn should have been blown.
>
> Whether rules of law shall be administered in one or the other of these two ways is of great importance in many cases; where the facts are not disputed it is, of course, decisive. It is not surprising therefore that considerations of policy have played a part in dictating whether an issue is regarded as one of law or of fact. By and large the measure of "reasonableness," which recurs at so many points in our law, is construed as invoking the community standard of what the reasonably prudent person would do in the circum-

stances, and the application of this standard is committed to the community's representatives on the jury. This is the prevailing rule today in negligence cases. . . .

The policy considerations underlying the characterization of an issue as one of "fact" or "law" go beyond the roles of jury and trial judge in a given case. They also involve the role of the appellate courts. If an issue is treated as one of "law," the decision of the issue is finally determinable by the appellate courts, whereas a "fact" issue as determined in the trial court is conclusive unless the appellate court can say there was insufficient evidence to sustain the finding. Furthermore, if an issue is one of law, appeal can be taken in every case where that issue is presented in a context that is slightly different from those in the precedents as to that issue. On the other hand, if an issue is one of fact, the trial court determination terminates the litigation—again unless the appellate court can say that it was not sustained by the evidence. One reason for calling the matter of negligence . . . an issue of fact is to bar appellate review of determination of such issues; one reason for calling obscenity an issue of law is to make the appellate courts the final arbiters of what kinds of literature can be suppressed.

Comments and Questions

1. Was justice done in the *White* case? Did you agree with the appellate-court decision?

2. The appellate-court opinion here is of a kind ordinarily published and bound in reports available to the legal profession if not also to the citizenry. This being so, are appellate decisions likely to have more influence on persons not immediate parties than outcomes of trial-court proceedings, which are usually not so published?

3. Appellate judges typically give reasons for their decisions. How many different reasons did Justice Lusk give? How good were his reasons? Why should reasons be given?

4. Students sometimes read appellate opinions as if they were short essays on some branch of the law. This is not the best approach. It is best to read such opinions as efforts to resolve particular issues—as problems to be solved in a specific context.

Three Common End Uses of Law as a Grievance-Remedial Instrument

In many societies, law as a grievance-remedial instrument functions (1) to influence behavior *before the fact* so that harms and losses do not occur in the first place, (2) to settle disputes between private parties, and (3) to provide for the redress of such harms and losses when they do occur. Each of these has its own independent value. Part 2 of this book is concerned with such end uses of legal instruments, and including a separate chapter on each would have been possible there.

Law as an influencer of behavior before the fact can be driven home with reference to the *White* case and the process reflected therein. Consider the role of this process as a determinant of behavior beyond that of the immediate parties. In the *White* case, the defendant was insured by an independent insurer against liability to the Miss Whites of the world. Had the insured company lost on the ground that its warning signs were not adequate, the insurer could be expected to instruct other pool owners whom it insures on how to provide adequate warning signs. Absent an insurer in the picture, who might act as above? Are there any other ways the grievance-remedial mode can influence others besides the immediate parties to particular cases?

Section Five. Necessity for and Nature of Coercive Power

Remedies, substantive general rules defining their availability, structures and processes for applying remedial law to facts of particular cases—all these are integral features of the anatomy and physiology of law as a grievance-remedial instrument. But what value would this instrument have if it lacked power to coerce? What if the defendant in the *White* case had refused to be haled into court at all? What if a default judgment were then entered, but when the sheriff came to confiscate some of the defendant's property to pay the judgment, the defendant's agent met him at the entrance with a shotgun? What if subpoenaed witnesses refused to show up at the actual trial? What if jurors declined to serve? Or what if someone staged a demonstration in the courtroom while the Island Amusement Company official was testifying? Plainly, law could not operate as a grievance-remedial instrument without power to apply coercive force.

Some legal philosophers, in analyzing the nature of law, stress the power to coerce. The most famous of these is Hans Kelsen.

H. KELSEN, GENERAL THEORY OF LAW AND STATE
18–21 (1945).*

The evil applied to the violator of the order when the sanction is socially organized consists in a deprivation of possessions—life, health, freedom, or property. As the possessions are taken from him against his will, this sanction has the character of a measure of coercion. This does not mean that in carrying out the sanction physical force must be applied. This is necessary only if resistance is encountered in applying the sanction. This is only exceptionally the case, where the authority applying the sanction possesses adequate power. A social order that seeks to bring about the desired behavior of individuals by the enactment of such measures of coercion is called a coercive order. Such it is because it threatens socially harmful deeds with measures of coercion, decrees such measures of coercion. As such it presents a contrast to all other possible social orders—those that provide reward rather than punishment as sanctions, and especially those that enact no sanctions at all, relying on the technique of direct motivation. In contrast to the orders that enact coercive measures as sanctions, the efficacy of the others rests not on coercion but on voluntary obedience. Yet this contrast is not so distinct as it might at first sight appear. This follows from the fact that the technique of reward, as a technique of indirect motivation, has its place between the technique of indirect motivation through punishment, as a technique of coercion, and the technique of direct motivation, the technique of voluntary obedience. Voluntary obedience is itself a form of motivation, that is, of coercion, and hence is not freedom, but it is coercion in the psychological sense. If coercive orders are contrasted with those that have no coercive character, that rest on voluntary obedience, this is possible only in the sense that one provides measures of coercion as sanctions whereas the other does not. And these sanctions are only coercive measures in the sense that certain possessions are taken from the individuals in question against their will, if necessary by the employment of physical force.

In this sense, the law is a coercive order.

If the social orders, so extraordinarily different in their tenors, which have prevailed at different times and among the most different peoples, are all called legal orders, it might be supposed that one is using an expression almost devoid of meaning. What could the so-called law of ancient Babylonians have in common with the law that prevails today in the United States? What could the social order of a Negro tribe under the leadership of a despotic chieftain—an order likewise called "law"— have in common with the constitution of the Swiss Republic? Yet there is a common element, that fully justifies this terminology, and enables the word "law" to appear as the expression of a concept with a socially highly significant meaning. For the word refers to that specific social technique of a coercive order which, despite the vast differences existing between the law of ancient Babylon and that of the United States of today, between the law of the Ashantis in West Africa and that of the Swiss in Europe, is yet essentially the same for all these peoples differing so much in time, in place, and in culture: the social technique which consists in bringing about the desired social conduct of men through the threat of a measure of coercion which is to be applied in case of contrary conduct. What the social conditions are that necessitate this technique, is an important sociological question. I do not know whether we can answer it satisfactorily. Neither do I know whether it is possible for mankind to emancipate itself totally from this social technique. But if the social order should in the future no longer have the character of a coercive order, if society should exist without "law," then the difference between this society of the future and that of the present day would be immeasurably greater than the difference between the United States and ancient Babylon, or Switzerland and the Ashanti tribe. . . .

Among the paradoxes of the social technique here characterized as a coercive order is the fact that its specific instrument, the coercive act of the sanction, is of exactly the same sort as the act which it seeks to prevent in the relations of individuals, the delict; that the sanction against socially injurious behavior is itself such behavior. For that which is to be accomplished by the threat of forcible deprivation of life, health, freedom, or property is precisely that men in their mutual conduct shall refrain from forcibly depriving one another of life, health, freedom, or property. Force is employed to prevent the employment of force in society. This seems to be an antinomy; and the effort to avoid this social antinomy leads to the doctrine of absolute anarchism which proscribes force even as sanction. Anarchism tends to establish the social order solely upon voluntary obedience of the individuals. It rejects the technique of a coercive order and hence rejects the law as a form of organization.

The antinomy, however, is only apparent. The law is, to be sure, an ordering for the promotion of peace, in that it forbids the use of force in relations among the members of the community. Yet it does not absolutely preclude the use of force. Law and force must not be understood as absolutely at variance with one another. Law is an organization of force. For the law attaches certain conditions to the use of force in relations among men, authorizing the employment of force only by certain individuals and only under certain circumstances. The law allows conduct which, under all other circumstances, is to be considered as "forbidden"; to be legally forbidden means to be the very condition for such a coercive act as a sanction. The individual who, authorized by the legal order, applies the coercive measure (the sanction), acts as an agent of this order, or—what amounts to the same—as an organ of the community constituted thereby. Only this individual, only the organ of the community, is authorized to employ force. And hence one may say that law makes the use of force a monopoly of the community. And precisely by so doing, law pacifies the community.

Comments and Questions

1. Sharply distinguish the question whether the law requires the power to coerce from the question whether a legal system can preserve itself solely through force and the threat of force.

2. Distinguish both of those questions from the question whether the law can act only through force and the threat of force and from the question whether the law acts only to prevent the improper employment of private coercion.

REIZAKIS v. LOY

United States Court of Appeals, Fourth Circuit, 1974.
490 F.2d 1132.

Thomas J. Harrigan, Arlington, Va. (Harrigan, Morris & Artz, Arlington, Va., on brief), for appellant.

Richard H. Lewis, Fairfax, Va. (Brault, Lewis, Geschickter & Palmer, Fairfax, Va., on brief), for appellee.

Before BOREMAN, SENIOR CIRCUIT JUDGE, and BUTZNER and RUSSELL, CIRCUIT JUDGES.

BUTZNER, CIRCUIT JUDGE:

Paris Reizakis appeals from an order dismissing his action against Albert E. Loy with prejudice.[1] Because the circumstances disclosed by this record do not justify the sanction imposed by the district court, we reverse.

[This personal injury action arose from an automobile accident on April 13, 1970, in Fairfax County, Virginia. The Canadian plaintiff-pedestrian sued the American defendant-driver on April 16, 1971, in the United States District Court for the Eastern District of Virginia. During the discovery phase, the plaintiff's counsel engaged in some minor foot-dragging.]

During these proceedings, Reizakis was represented by Peter A. Chaconas, of Washington, D.C., and Rudolph N. D'Agaris, of Maryland. Because neither were residents of Virginia with offices in the state, they were prohibited by a local rule of the district court from representing Reizakis without being associated with a Virginia attorney who had been admitted to practice in the court. Reizakis' Virginia attorney was Robert C. Watson. In the latter part of May [1972], Watson, with Reizakis' consent, prepared an order to permit D'Agaris and him to withdraw. At the June [15th] pretrial conference, the court denied withdrawal until Watson was replaced by another Virginia lawyer and set the case for trial on Tuesday, September 12, 1972. Notwithstanding the denial of his motion to withdraw, Watson took the position that Reizakis had released him in May. He notified Reizakis of the trial date, but apparently neither he nor D'Agaris did anything further to prepare for trial.

Sometime after the middle of August, Chaconas satisfied himself that the doctors who were to be Reizakis' witnesses would be available for the September trial. However, he did not obtain subpoenas for them. In the meantime, acting on behalf of Reizakis, he made several unsuccessful attempts to engage local counsel to replace Watson, but not until the first week of September did he succeed in obtaining a new Virginia associate.

On Thursday, September 7, five days before the scheduled trial, Thomas J. Harrigan, the replacement for Watson, and Richard H. Lewis, attorney for Loy appeared before the district court. They were accompanied by Watson who moved for a continuance of the trial so that Harrigan could have a reasonable time to prepare the case. The record does not indicate that Lewis offered any objection at this time. The court, however, denied the continuance, and Harrigan declined to enter a formal appearance because he believed he could not prepare adequately in the short time remaining. Harrigan promptly told Chaconas of the court's

1. The court acted under Fed.R.Civ.P. 41(b), which provides in part:
For failure of the plaintiff to prosecute or to comply with these rules or any order of court, a defendant may move for dismissal of an action or of any claim against him. . . . Unless the court in its order for dismissal otherwise specifies, a dismissal under this subdivision . . . operates as an adjudication upon the merits.
The statute of limitations also bars reassertion of Reizakis' claim.

ruling, and although he had not entered a formal appearance, he nevertheless said that if the witnesses were available he would attempt to prepare the case. The next day, Friday, Chaconas told Harrigan that the doctors were available and that the case was ready. Harrigan studied the file over the week end, but when he telephoned the doctors on Monday, September 11, he learned that none of them could be present. By this time it was too late to subpoena them.

On the day of trial, Tuesday, September 12, Reizakis, Chaconas, Watson, D'Agaris, and Harrigan appeared in the district court. Chaconas, citing the absence of the doctors, moved for a continuance. Lewis, noting the inconvenience to Loy's witnesses, objected, and the court denied the motion. Chaconas then stated that the witnesses who were to testify on the issue of liability were present, and he moved to have the trial proceed on this issue and for a continuance of the damage issue only. Again, Lewis objected, and the court denied the motion. Chaconas then conceded that in view of the court's rulings it was impossible to proceed, and Lewis moved to dismiss the case for lack of prosecution. The court granted the motion and assessed the costs, including jury fees, mileage, and per diem against Reizakis. It then granted Watson's and D'Agaris' motion to withdraw.

A district court unquestionably has authority to grant a motion to dismiss for want of prosecution. Fed.R.Civ.P. 41(b). Indeed, as the Supreme Court held in Link v. Wabash R.R., 370 U.S. 626, 82 S.Ct. 1386 (1962), the trial court can take such action on its own motion. But courts interpreting the rule uniformly hold that it cannot be automatically or mechanically applied. Against the power to prevent delays must be weighed the sound public policy of deciding cases on their merits. Consequently, dismissal "must be tempered by a careful exercise of judicial discretion." Durgin v. Graham, 372 F.2d 130, 131 (5th Cir.1967). While the propriety of dismissal ultimately turns on the facts of each case, criteria for judging whether the discretion of the trial court has been soundly exercised have been stated frequently. Rightfully, courts are reluctant to punish a client for the behavior of his lawyer. Therefore, in situations where a party is not responsible for the fault of his attorney, dismissal may be invoked only in extreme circumstances. Indeed, it has been observed that "[t]he decided cases, while noting that dismissal is a discretionary matter, have generally permitted it only in the face of a clear record of delay or contumacious conduct by the plaintiff." Durham v. Florida East Coast Ry. Co., 385 F.2d 366, 368 (5th Cir.1967). Appellate courts frequently have found abuse of discretion when trial courts failed to apply sanctions less severe than dismissal. And generally lack of prejudice to the defendant, though not a bar to dismissal, is a factor that must be considered in determining whether the trial court exercised sound discretion.

It is in the light of the foregoing interpretation of Rule 41(b) that we must consider the circumstances of this case. The facts do not depict "a drawn out history" of "deliberately proceeding in dilatory fashion," as in Link v. Wabash R.R., 370 U.S. 626, 633, 82 S.Ct. 1386, 1390 (1962). Moreover, Reizakis was not shown to be personally responsible for any of the incidents that delayed the case. While he knew that Watson wished to withdraw, he not unreasonably expected his principal counsel, Chaconas, to arrange for a local associate to comply with the rules. Furthermore, he apparently knew nothing about the failure to subpoena the doctors. To the contrary, it appears that he advanced money for witness fees and expected the case to be tried as scheduled. His attorneys were unable to proceed either because they failed to give the doctors adequate notice, or because Chaconas relied on his understanding that the doctors would be available without taking the precaution of subpoenaing them. In selecting an appropriate sanction for this dereliction, the district court did not consider measures less drastic than dismissal, such as imposing a fine or costs against Reizakis' attorneys. Finally, it does not appear that a continuance would have prejudiced Loy's defense. Of course, Loy, his witnesses, and his attorney would have been subjected to extra expenses and inconvenience if the case had been rescheduled, but monetary sanctions were available to rectify this harm as well. Moreover, inconvenience to some of the witnesses could have been prevented by trying the issue of liability as suggested by Reizakis' counsel.

The District Court for the Eastern District of Virginia is exceptionally busy, and the demands on the time of its judges and its jurors are great. Its judges properly are diligent in bringing litigation to trial without delay. But the interpretation of Rule 41(b) found in the well reasoned cases cited above bars dismissal for the circumstances disclosed by this record. Available to the district court were lesser sanctions sufficient to assure prompt disposition of this case and to discourage similar conduct in the future. Additionally, the liability issue could have been tried, and if Reizakis lost, the case would have ended without further delay.

The judgment is reversed, and this case is remanded with directions that it be reinstated.

BOREMAN, SENIOR CIRCUIT JUDGE (dissenting):

With all due regard and respect for the opinion of my brothers, somewhat reluctantly I state this note of disagreement. Naturally, our sympathies are with any litigant who suddenly discovers that the results of his counsel's inattention, indifference, lack of diligence, or negligence, are visited upon him in terms of the dismissal of his case and the loss of an opportunity to be compensated in damages for personal injuries; but sympathy can have no place in the decision process. Each case properly is to be considered on its own peculiar facts and circumstances. . . .

[The following] excerpt [is] from the transcript of the proceedings before the court when the case was called for trial.

MR. CHACONAS: At this moment, Your Honor, I would like to make a motion.

THE COURT: All right, sir.

MR. CHACONAS: I would like to make an oral motion to ask for a continuance in this case due to the fact that our expert witnesses are not available at this moment. We do not know when they will be, and if your Honor does not grant us the motion, therefore, I ask that the case will not be submitted to this Court at this time.

THE COURT: The case has been set for trial since June 15. Ample time has been had to prepare the case. If there was a question of the unavailability of any witnesses, that should have been ascertained from depositions taken. There was ample time for those depositions.

MR. CHACONAS: For the record, I would like also to state that these Doctors are not available because they are performing their duties in the medical profession as we are attempting here to perform our duties in the legal profession.

I do respect the Court's opinion in denying me the motion for a continuance, but I want the record to clearly show that there was an attempt by the Attorneys for the Plaintiff to obtain and retain these Doctors to appear here today, and I want the record to clearly state that.

THE COURT: Were subpoenas issued?

MR. CHACONAS: There were not subpoenas issued. There were telephone conversations and telegrams to ascertain the presence of these Doctors, but unfortunately, apparently, their emergencies were above their presentation here for the purposes of their patients, I suppose.

THE COURT: Can you tell me when you first ascertained that they would not be available?

MR. CHACONAS: Well, we began three and four weeks ago and as of Friday we ascertained that one of the Doctors would be available today, but he is out of town, and through secretaries or answering service or whatever it may be, but the point is that they were contacted through their agencies or agents or through the answering bureau or the Medical Bureau, and they were put on notice and we have taken our position that they were put on notice.

THE COURT: Three or four weeks ago when you ascertained that some of them might be unavailable was any effort made—

MR. CHACONAS: No, your Honor, we were not put on that notice. We were put on notice that they would be in contact and be available, and that is where we stand. I don't think that a legal profession should be running around on a horse looking for Tonto or something like that. These people are owed money. They have for two years been taking care of Mr. Reizakis. I don't know what it is. It is just a situation that is difficult for our profession, and I do hope you sympathize with our position that we just cannot put these people in line to just come in sometimes, and it is not a question that they are being denied their fee because the fees are available; they are income, and I do believe that the client—and the client is not a citizen of this country. This is the unfortunate part about it.

Your Honor, the client has a right to be represented and he has a right to be represented in the sense that we do have available people to testify for him, and the surety of the situation is with professionism, whatever it may be.

I am not trying to put on a speech. They are just not here, and we did our duty as officers of the court, and that is all we can do. . . .

No citation of authority is needed to support the premise that district courts must have control of their dockets without disruption or interference in order to assure the orderly conduct of the court's business. I take judicial notice of the fact that the Eastern District of Virginia is an extremely busy district; the dockets . . . are overburdened with cases involving litigants who are often anxiously and impatiently awaiting the opportunity to have their "turn at bat"—to have their day in court. The rapidly developing policy of the judicial system looks with disfavor upon counsel's lack of diligence or negligence in preparing cases for trial. The court is in position to get the "feel" of the case and to appraise the attitude of counsel toward the diligent prosecution of the litigation. . . .

The court, in States Steamship Company v. Philippine Air Lines, 426 F.2d 803, 804 (9 Cir.1970), had this to say:

> Whether the judge misused or abused his discretion, of necessity, depends upon the facts of each case. This court has never attempted to fix guidelines, although a good rule of thumb might be to follow Judge Magruder's oft-quoted phrase in In Re Josephson, 218 F.2d 174, 182 (1st Cir.1954), that the exercise of discretion of the trial judge should not be disturbed unless there is "a definite and firm conviction that the court below committed a clear error of judgment in the conclusion it reached upon a weighing of the relevant factors." . . .

In an action for damages for personal injuries, Link v. Wabash Railroad Co., 370 U.S. 626, 82 S.Ct. 1386 (1962), it appears that after extended pretrial proceedings which delayed the maturing of the case the trial court, on September 29, 1960, scheduled a pretrial conference for one o'clock on October 12, 1960, and notified counsel for both sides. Late in the morning of October 12 plaintiff's counsel telephoned the judge's secretary that he was otherwise engaged in another city, that he could not attend the conference at the appointed hour but that he would be there on the afternoon of October 13 or anytime on October 14 if the pretrial conference could be reset. When plaintiff's counsel failed to appear on October 12 the court, *sua sponte*, dismissed the action for failure of counsel to appear and for failure to prosecute. The Court upheld the action of the trial court, even in the absence of a motion to dismiss, and at pages 633 and 634, 82 S.Ct. at page 1390 stated:

> On this record we are unable to say that the District Court's dismissal of this action for failure to prosecute, as evidenced only partly by the failure of petitioner's counsel to appear at a duly scheduled pretrial conference, amounted to an abuse of discretion. It was certainly within the bounds of permissible discretion for the court to conclude that the telephone excuse offered by petitioner's counsel was inadequate to explain his failure to attend. And it could reasonably be inferred from his absence, as well as from the drawn-out history of the litigation, . . . that petitioner had been deliberately proceeding in dilatory fashion.
>
> There is certainly no merit to the contention that dismissal of petitioner's claim because of his counsel's unexcused conduct imposes an unjust penalty on the client. Petitioner voluntarily chose this attorney as his representative in the action, and he cannot now avoid the consequences of the acts or omissions of this freely selected agent. Any other notion would be wholly inconsistent with our system of

representative litigation, in which each party is deemed bound by the acts of his lawyer-agent and is considered to have "notice of all facts, notice of which can be charged upon the attorney." Smith v. Ayer, 101 U.S. 320, 326.

Lack of diligence of plaintiff and his counsel in the preparation of the instant case and in complying with the court's orders and directions is evident. We have no satisfactory information as to the problems confronting the court with respect to granting a continuance, but I venture the statement that if every plaintiff-litigant requested a continuance on the date fixed for the trial of his case and refused to proceed any attempt by the court to maintain the orderly control of its business would be an exercise in futility. No court can succeed if it permits the lawyers, officers of the court, to control the dockets and the court's business.

In the case at bar it is argued, and the majority holds, that the negligent conduct of plaintiff's counsel should not operate to the disadvantage and prejudice of their client. However, the district court noted that the plaintiff himself was not blameless:

> THE COURT: In June when I set this case for trial Mr. Watson then said that he was then requesting to withdraw. I wouldn't let him withdraw. I told him he would have to tell his client that the case was definitely going to be tried on September 12, and that if he had to get another counsel that there were two months left for him to get counsel at least, three months, and so the Plaintiff, insofar as counsel is concerned, is not blameless in this matter.
>
> He has known for some time that the case was going to be tried today with or without Mr. Watson, and there was no reason that he could not have notified his Doctors as early as June and ascertained then their availability.

As the late Judge Sobeloff . . . wrote in Universal Film Exchanges, Inc. v. Lust, 479 F.2d 573, 577:

> Our decision does not leave a client without remedy against the negligent attorney. Lawyers are not a breed apart. Where damages are inflicted upon innocent clients by other professionals, such as doctors or dentists, the remedy is a suit for malpractice. The same is true where damage is inflicted upon a client through an attorney's professional negligence. Indeed, the Supreme Court explicitly pointed out in *Link*, supra, 370 U.S. 626, 82 S.Ct. 1386 at n. 10, that if the attorney's conduct was substantially below what was reasonable under the circumstances, the client's remedy was a suit for malpractice.

Upon this record I am not convinced that there was a clear abuse of the court's discretion in granting the defendant's motion to dismiss under Rule 41(b).

Comments and Questions

1. Dismissal for failure to prosecute is within the discretion of the trial judge. However, the appellate court can specify the procedures for exercising that

discretion. Also, even if the trial court acts in accordance with all procedural requirements, the appellate court can review the outcome for abuse of discretion. As the dissent explains, reversal for abuse of discretion means that the appellate court quite strongly disagrees with the trial court's outcome, not merely that as an original matter the appellate judges would have decided otherwise. What exactly, then, did the majority in this case hold?

2. What coercive sanction did this case entail? Why does the law authorize that sanction? What conditions does the law attach to its use?

Section Six. Roles of Private Citizens and Their Lawyers

Now is an appropriate time to start exploring another common fallacy about law: the top-and-bottom fallacy. In this view, the law divides people in a society into the public officials (judicial, legislative, administrative) and the private citizens; the officials are on the top, and the citizens are at the bottom; and the officials dictate in various ways to the citizens below. This picture of law operating as a grievance-remedial instrument is dramatically false. And its falsity does not depend on any distinction between dictatorships and democracies. One can imagine a dictatorship making use of law as a grievance-remedial instrument in ways that call upon private citizens and their lawyers to perform important roles. Certainly in our system, these actors perform important roles.

First, in standard instances of the operation of the grievance-remedial mode, the decision whether to put the law in motion is in private hands. As a rule, we have no public prosecutor of private claims to money damages, injunctions, and the like.

Second, the private litigant also functions as a lawmaker. Who was Butterfield? Davies? Loach? Appropriately, their names appear on cases, each of which made some new law. Private parties typically assert remedial claims and defenses and then advance arguments in support of their legality, all through lawyers who are professionally trained for such purposes. Thus, private citizens and their lawyers work together to help make law. Courts declare the law, yes, but they do not do so in a vacuum. They do not do so in the absence of a specific "case or controversy." Without actual private litigants, there would be no occasion for courts to declare any law. Further, when courts do declare law, this is on the basis of contentions and arguments put before them by the opposite sides in the case. Students might profitably review the *Butterfield, Davies, Loach,* and *White* cases with the thought of identifying some of the very contentions and arguments in those cases that the courts were either rejecting or accepting. These contentions and arguments did not spring solely from the judges themselves. Most of them were urged upon the courts by the lawyers for the parties.

Third, as for determining the facts of particular grievance-remedial disputes and applying law thereto, private citizens and their lawyers are thoroughly active from beginning to end, as we demonstrated in depth in the Swimming Pool case. Students might profitably reflect anew on some of the respects in which this is so.

Fourth, once the plaintiff secures judgment, this is by no means equivalent to satisfaction of judgment. We saw that in the grievance-remedial mode as we know it, the citizen, through his lawyer, again must often take further steps to bring the strong arm of the law into play. In short, the whole process is in large part privately propelled.

Fifth, private persons dissatisfied with the basic grievance-remedial techniques, law, structures, or processes can always turn to legislators to seek reforms. The initiative for legislative action commonly comes from outside the legislature—from private citizens and their lawyers. For example, in getting the law changed from a contributory negligence approach to an apportionment approach, private citizens have played significant roles.

Let us now look more closely at the roles of the lawyer. At this stage of the book, an appropriate step is to narrow the focus to the lawyer's role as advocate in court, but we shall eventually consider the lawyer's other roles such as adviser and negotiator. The best general statement on the advocate's role, as ideally conceived, is probably that adopted by a joint conference of the American Bar Association and the Association of American Law Schools. That statement, which follows, also offers a rationale for the so-called adversary system.

JOINT CONFERENCE ON PROFESSIONAL RESPONSIBILITY, REPORT
44 A.B.A.J. 1159, 1160–61 (1958).*

The lawyer appearing as an advocate before a tribunal presents, as persuasively as he can, the facts and the law of the case as seen from the standpoint of his client's interest. It is essential that both the lawyer and the public understand clearly the nature of the role thus discharged. Such an understanding is required not only to appreciate the need for an adversary presentation of issues, but also in order to perceive truly the limits partisan advocacy must impose on itself if it is to remain wholesome and useful.

In a very real sense it may be said that the integrity of the adjudicative process itself depends upon the participation of the advocate. This becomes apparent when we contemplate the nature of the task assumed by any arbiter who attempts to decide a dispute without the aid of partisan advocacy.

Such an arbiter must undertake, not only the role of judge, but that of representative for both of the litigants. Each of these roles must be played to the full without being muted by qualifications derived from the others. When he is developing for each side the most effective statement of its case, the arbiter must put aside his neutrality and permit himself to be moved by a sympathetic identification sufficiently intense to draw from his mind all that it is capable of giving—in analysis, patience and creative power. When he resumes his neutral position, he must be able to view with distrust the fruits of this identification and be ready to reject the products of his own best mental efforts. The difficulties of this undertaking are obvious. If it is true that a man in his time must play many parts, it is scarcely given to him to play them all at once.

It is small wonder, then, that failure generally attends the attempt to dispense with the distinct roles traditionally implied in adjudication. What generally occurs in practice is that at some early point a familiar pattern will seem to emerge from the evidence; an accustomed label is waiting for the case and, without awaiting further proofs, this label is promptly assigned to it. It is a mistake to suppose that this premature cataloguing must necessarily result from impatience, prejudice or mental sloth. Often it proceeds from a very understandable desire to bring the hearing into some order and coherence, for without some tentative theory of the case there is no standard of relevance by which testimony may be measured. But what starts as a preliminary diagnosis designed to direct the inquiry tends, quickly and imperceptibly, to become a fixed conclusion, as all that confirms the diagnosis makes a strong imprint on the mind, while all that runs counter to it is received with diverted attention.

An adversary presentation seems the only effective means for combatting this natural human tendency to judge too swiftly in terms of the familiar that which is not yet fully known. The arguments of counsel hold the case, as it were, in suspension between two opposing interpretations of it. While the proper classification of the case is thus kept unresolved, there is time to explore all of its peculiarities and nuances.

These are the contributions made by partisan advocacy during the public hearing of the cause. When we take into account the preparations that must precede the hearing, the essential quality of the advocate's contribution becomes even more apparent. Preceding the hearing, inquiries must be instituted to determine what facts can be proved or seem sufficiently established to warrant a formal test of their truth during the hearing. There must also be a preliminary analysis of the issues, so that the hearing may have form and direction. These preparatory measures are indispensable whether or not the parties involved in the controversy are represented by advocates.

Where that representation is present there is an obvious advantage in the fact that the area of dispute may be greatly reduced by an exchange of written pleadings or by stipulations of counsel. Without the participation of someone who can act responsibly for each of the parties, this essential narrowing of the issues becomes impossible. But here again the true significance of partisan advocacy lies deeper, touching once more the integrity of the adjudicative process itself. It is only through the advocate's participation that the hearing may remain in fact what it purports to be in theory: a public trial of the facts and issues. Each advocate comes to the hearing prepared to present his proofs and arguments, knowing at the same time that his arguments may fail to persuade and that his proofs may be rejected as inadequate. It is a part of his role to absorb these possible disappointments. The deciding tribunal, on the other hand, comes to the hearing uncommitted. It has not represented to the public that any fact can be proved, that any argument is sound, or that any particular way of stating a litigant's case is the most effective expression of its merits.

The matter assumes a very different aspect when the deciding tribunal is compelled to take into its own hands the preparations that must precede the public hearing. In such a case the tribunal cannot truly be said to come to the hearing uncommitted, for it has itself appointed the channels along which the public inquiry is to run. If an unexpected turn in the testimony reveals a miscalculation in the design of these channels, there is no advocate to absorb the blame. The deciding tribunal is under a strong temptation to keep the hearing moving within the boundaries originally set for it. The result may be that the hearing loses its character as an open trial of the facts and issues, and becomes instead a ritual designed to provide public confirmation for what the tribunal considers it has already established in private. When this occurs adjudication acquires the taint affecting all institutions that become subject to manipulation, presenting one aspect to the public, another to knowing participants.

These, then, are the reasons for believing that partisan advocacy plays a vital and essential role in one of the most fundamental procedures of a democratic society. But if we were to put all of these detailed considerations to one side, we should still be confronted by the fact that, in whatever form adjudication may appear, the experienced judge or arbitrator desires and actively seeks to obtain an adversary presentation of the issues. Only when he has had the benefit of intelligent and vigorous advocacy on both sides can he feel fully confident of his decision.

Viewed in this light, the role of the lawyer as a partisan advocate appears not as a regrettable necessity, but as an indispensable part of a larger ordering of affairs. The institution of advocacy is not a concession to the frailties of human nature, but an expression of human insight in the design of a social framework within which man's capacity for impartial judgment can attain its fullest realization.

When advocacy is thus viewed, it becomes clear by what principle limits must be set to partisanship. The advocate plays his role well when zeal for his client's cause promotes a wise and informed decision of the case. He plays his role badly, and trespasses against the obligations of professional responsibility, when his desire to win leads him to muddy the headwaters of decision, when, instead of lending a needed perspective to the controversy, he distorts and obscures its true nature.

———

Comments and Questions

1. Consider this argument concerning the Swimming Pool case: "Miss White's lawyer actually lost the case by his own mishandling of it. He should have emphasized from the outset the failure of the defendant to post adequate warning signs against diving rather than the fact that the pool was oddly constructed. With the evidence structured in accordance with this theory, the jury would have properly found the defendant negligent. And, equally important, Miss White's own negligent failure to look around carefully would not, on this view, have constituted contributory negligence, because the defendant blew the last clear chance to avoid the accident by failing to give adequate warning. Miss White's lawyer mishandled her case in other ways as well. This was his first trial all

alone, whereas defense counsel was a seasoned professional." Do you agree with the foregoing argument?

2. What are the sources of lawyer mismatches in our system?

3. What might our system do about lawyer mismatches?

J. FRANK, COURTS ON TRIAL
80–85 (1949).*

When we say that present-day trial methods are "rational," presumably we mean this: The men who compose our trial courts, judges and juries, in each law-suit conduct an intelligent inquiry into all the practically available evidence, in order to ascertain, as near as may be, the truth about the facts of that suit. That might be called the "investigatory" or "truth" method of trying cases. Such a method can yield no more than a guess, nevertheless an educated guess. . . .

. . . Our mode of trials is commonly known as "contentious" or "adversary." It is based on what I would call the "fight" theory, a theory which derives from the origin of trials as substitutes for private out-of-court brawls.

Many lawyers maintain that the "fight" theory and the "truth" theory coincide. They think that the best way for a court to discover the facts in a suit is to have each side strive as hard as it can, in a keenly partisan spirit, to bring to the court's attention the evidence favorable to that side. Macaulay said that we obtain the fairest decision "when two men argue, as unfairly as possible, on opposite sides," for then "it is certain that no important consideration will altogether escape notice."

Unquestionably that view contains a core of good sense. The zealously partisan lawyers sometimes do bring into court evidence which, in a dispassionate inquiry, might be overlooked. Apart from the fact element of the case, the opposed lawyers also illuminate for the court niceties of the legal rules which the judge might otherwise not perceive. The "fight" theory, therefore, has invaluable qualities with which we cannot afford to dispense.

But frequently the partisanship of the opposing lawyers blocks the uncovering of vital evidence or leads to a presentation of vital testimony in a way that distorts it. . . .

What is the role of the lawyers in bringing the evidence before the trial court? As you may learn by reading any one of a dozen or more handbooks on how to try a law-suit, an experienced lawyer uses all sorts of stratagems to minimize the effect on the judge or jury of testimony disadvantageous to his client, even when the lawyer has no doubt of the accuracy and honesty of that testimony. The lawyer considers it his duty to create a false impression, if he can, of any witness who gives such testimony. If such a witness happens to be timid, frightened by the unfamiliarity of court-room ways, the lawyer, in his cross-examination, plays on that weakness, in order to confuse the witness and make it appear that he is concealing significant facts. Longenecker, in his book Hints on the Trial of a Law Suit (a book endorsed by the great Wigmore), in writing of the "truthful, honest, over-cautious" witness, tells how "a skilful advocate by a rapid cross-examination may ruin the testimony of such a witness." The author does not even hint any disapproval of that accomplishment. Longenecker's and other similar books recommend that a lawyer try to prod an irritable but honest "adverse" witness into displaying his undesirable characteristics in their most unpleasant form, in order to discredit him with the judge or jury. "You may," writes Harris, "sometimes destroy the effect of an adverse witness by making him appear more hostile than he really is. . . . " Taft says that a clever cross-examiner, dealing with an honest but egotistic witness, will "deftly tempt the witness to indulge in his propensity for exaggeration, so as to make him 'hang himself.' And thus," adds Taft, "it may happen that not only is the value of his testimony lost, but the side which produces him suffers for seeking aid from such a source"—although, I would add, that may be the only source of evidence of a fact on which the decision will turn.

. . . Anthony Trollope, in one of his novels, indignantly reacted to these methods. "One would naturally imagine," he said, "that an undisturbed thread of clear evidence would be best obtained from a man whose position was made easy and whose mind was not harassed; but this is not the fact; to turn a witness to good account, he must be badgered this way and that till he is nearly mad; he must be made a laughing-stock for the court; his very truths must be turned into falsehoods, so that he may be falsely shamed; he must be accused of all manner of villainy, threatened with all manner of punishment; he must be made to feel that he has no friend near him, that the world is all against him; he must be confounded till he forget his right hand from his left, till his mind be turned into chaos, and his heart into water; and then let him give his evidence. What will fall from his lips when in this wretched collapse must be of special value, for the best talents of practiced forensic heroes are daily used to bring it about; and no member of the Humane Society interferes to protect the wretch. Some sorts of torture are as it were tacitly allowed even among humane people. Eels are skinned alive, and witnesses are sacrificed, and no one's blood curdles at the sight, no soft heart is sickened at the cruelty." This may be a somewhat overdrawn picture. Yet, referring to this manner of handling witnesses, Sir Frederic Eggleston recently said that it prevents lawyers from inducing persons who know important facts from disclosing them to lawyers for litigants. He notes, too, that "the terrors of cross-examination are such that a party can often force a settlement by letting it be known that a certain . . . counsel has been retained."

The lawyer not only seeks to discredit adverse witnesses but also to hide the defects of witnesses who testify favorably to his client. If, when interviewing such a witness before trial, the lawyer notes that the witness has mannerisms, demeanor-traits, which might discredit him, the lawyer teaches him how to cover up those traits when testifying: He educates the irritable witness to conceal his irritability, the cocksure witness to subdue his cocksureness. In that way, the trial court is denied the benefit of observing the witness's actual normal demeanor, and thus prevented from sizing up the witness accurately.

Lawyers freely boast of their success with these tactics. They boast also of such devices as these: If an "adverse," honest witness, on cross-examination, makes seemingly inconsistent statements, the cross-examiner tries to keep the witness from explaining away the apparent inconsistencies. "When," writes Tracy, counseling trial lawyers, in a much-praised book, "by your cross-examination, you have caught the witness in an inconsistency, the next question that will immediately come to your lips is, 'Now, let's hear you explain.' Don't ask it, for he may explain and, if he does, your point will have been lost. If you have conducted your cross-examination properly (which includes interestingly), the jury will have seen the inconsistency and it will have made the proper impression on their minds. If, on re-direct examination the witness does explain, the explanation will have come later in the case and at the request of the counsel who originally called the witness and the jury will be much more likely to look askance at the explanation than if it were made during your cross-examination." Tracy adds, "Be careful in your questions on cross-examination not to open a door that you have every reason to wish kept closed." That is, don't let in any reliable evidence, hurtful to your side, which would help the trial court to arrive at the truth. . . .

In short, the lawyer aims at victory, at winning in the fight, not at aiding the court to discover the facts. He does not want the trial court to reach a sound educated guess, if it is likely to be contrary to his client's interests. Our present trial method is thus the equivalent of throwing pepper in the eyes of a surgeon when he is performing an operation. . . .

However unpleasant all this may appear, do not blame trial lawyers for using the techniques I have described. If there is to be criticism, it should be directed at the system that virtually compels their use, a system which treats a law-suit as a battle of wits and wiles. As a distinguished lawyer has said, these stratagems are "part of the maneuvering . . . to which [lawyers] are obliged to resort to win their cases. Some of them may appear to be tricky; they may seem to be taking undue advantage; but under the present system it is part of a lawyer's duty to employ them because his opponent is doing the same thing, and if he refrains from doing so, he is violating his duty to his client and giving his opponent an unquestionable advantage. . . . " These tricks of the trade are today the legitimate and accepted corollary of our fight theory.

Comments and Questions

1. Try your hand at formulating appropriate limits on cross-examination.
2. Are any problems revealed in the following "war story" from Lebar, Shadows in the Courtroom, Case & Com., Nov.-Dec. 1975, at 49, 51–53? [e]

Louis J, at 38 years of age was such a physical specimen that after meeting him, you would go home and start doing push-ups. A college tennis champ and all around "comer", he had married well and things had been on the rise ever since. His wife, Adeline, "my Addie" as Lou liked to say, was a svelt campus queen from a high placed social family and a fine sportswoman herself. She was also a straightforward and likeable person.

Although it's been many years, I cannot think of the old Monterey Hotel in Asbury Park without seeing Lou and Addie. In 1949 the Monterey was the "in" spot at Asbury. A huge, bluish tinted cement building with white ornamental woodwork, the place dominated the maze of hotels pressed against the colorful boardwalk. The Monterey, like all such grand ladies was to fall on hard times but it was then a place of grace and luxury. Lou was part owner of a heavy equipment company in New York and on the verge of closing an important business deal in South Jersey. To be certain of the details, he decided to come out and finalize the transaction. He arranged to stay at the Monterey. On a Friday evening in August he drove a shiny white Cadillac up to the entrance of the Hotel. The car was less than a week old. After signing the register, he turned the keys of the car over to the bellhop to park. In those days, many of the bellhops were farm boys from surrounding rural Monmouth County with an inordinate interest in motor cars. In any event, the bellhop took the car for a joy ride, instead of the parking lot, and late that evening—smashed it into a utility pole. The Caddie was a total wreck as was the bellhop, although the boy survived to tell the tale. A cash purchase, for some reason the comprehensive insurance on the car was not operative at the time of the accident. The company denied coverage.

I had known Lou only slightly, meeting him as a co-member of an interstate charity board but he was really out of my league. At the time we filed suit against the hotel for the value of the car (having failed to collect from the insurance company) he was a fast rising political star and prime candidate for a major appointment in New York. Our suit alleged that the Hotel Monterey was responsible for the negligence of its employee, the badly battered bellhop. A simple matter . . . only the value of the car was in issue. The answering pleadings admitted that Lou was a guest at the hotel and had paid his bill. In response to my client's pointed inquiries over the ensuing months, I stated that the case had been narrowed to the matter of auto damages.

The trial was scheduled for a hot July morning in the old County Courthouse on Main Street in Freehold, New Jersey. A special summer date was assigned the hearing so that Lou might attend a business convention in Brussels. Outside the dusty parking lot, the temperature seemed cool compared to the heat of the courtroom. The air hung heavy, sliced quietly by the circling overhead ceiling fan. Other than the judge and jury, the only persons in attendance were a little knot of principals who sat close to the counsels' bench during the trial. Just before opening, we tried to settle the case for a bit under book value but to no avail. By the time we broke for lunch at 1 P.M., we had proved the accident through the local police; the employment relationship between hotel and bellhop, and other details.

Lou had driven to Freehold with his wife, Addie and both were in high spirits during our lunch at the American Restaurant and Bar across the street. We were having such a good time, that it was downright unpleasant returning to the sweltering courtroom. In the afternoon, our first witness was Lou himself. We whizzed through the direct examination, Lou proving a sharp, articulate and impressive witness. Under cross-examination, the defendant's counsel spoke quietly . . . barely audible. Lou fenced the opening questions nicely and then it happened. Opening his briefcase, the lawyer produced the hotel registry book and, with voice rising, asked that it be marked for identification. I objected, noting lightly that registration had *already* been admitted in the hotel's answering pleading but the lawyer persisted in placing the book in evidence anyway. He was allowed to pursue the matter. At this point I should have noticed that Lou's perennial tan was turning chalky white well before the crucial question by counsel: "Is this your signature in the registry for Mr. and *Mrs.* Louis J?" *MRS.* LOUIS J? Mrs. J, Addie, that is, shot up straight and stared at her husband. She told me at lunch she had never been to Asbury Park . . . certainly not that night, anyway. In the meantime, before I could object further, Lou was turning increasingly pallid, his solid confidence fading fast. Words weren't coming out . . . just sounds. I started to mumble something about the Fifth Amendment and self-incrimination but Lou wasn't listening. He was busy just cracking up. We asked for and received a halt in the trial so that my client might regain his composure but by 4 P.M. he was still unable to return to the witness stand forcing us to settle the case for less than half its worth. I still regret it. The question of possible adultery, while it might bear on credibility, was really irrelevant to the issue. I doubt if it would have made any difference even before a rural jury of that day. But it was no longer of consequence.

I watched Lou and Addie spin away from the parking lot in yet another new Cadillac heading towards Route # 9 and New York City. She was sitting in the back. They would never be the same.

It was more than a year later that I read of their marital separation and property settlement. *This* story was widely covered by the New York press. I doubt if any of the reporters ever heard of the Monterey Hotel. Lou wished he hadn't either.

––––––––

Adverse Fact and Law

Although a lawyer is under a general duty of truthfulness that proscribes outright lying, it is accepted that a lawyer need not volunteer facts known to her but adverse to her client's interests, except in certain special circumstances. Indeed, in her proper role as a zealous representative, a lawyer is under a *duty* not to reveal voluntarily any adverse facts, unless her client consents. Thus, an ethics committee approved the conduct of the defendant's attorney in the following circumstances:

> In an action on behalf of an infant three years of age, for injuries sustained by falling off a porch owned by the defendant, due to the alleged negligence of the defendant, where there is no eyewitness known to the plaintiff's attorney, and thereafter when the case came to trial, the infant's case was dismissed on motion of the defendant's attorney on the ground that the infant plaintiff was unable to make out a sufficient case of circumstantial evidence. During the presentation of the plaintiff's case, said attorney for the defendant had an eyewitness to said accident actually present in court, and did not mention said fact, either to the plaintiff's attorney or to the Court and kept the Court in ignorance of the fact

that a person did exist who actually saw said accident, and was present in court.

New York County Lawyers' Association Comm. on Professional Ethics, Op. 309 (1933).

Strangely enough, the prevailing ethical rules, which are adopted by the American Bar Association as a model for binding rules within the several states, provide that a lawyer shall not knowingly "fail to disclose to the tribunal legal authority in the controlling jurisdiction known to the lawyer to be directly adverse to the position of the client and not disclosed by opposing counsel." Model Rules of Professional Conduct Rule 3.3(a)(3) (1983).

These contrasting commands present many problems of interpretation and application. But let us cut to the heart of the matter: Why do you think that there is a duty to disclose adverse law but not fact?

On the one hand, perhaps the need for disclosure is greater for law than for fact. Which is the court more likely to learn on its own: law or fact? But which, if nondisclosed, holds a greater potential for eventually embarrassing the judge? Which would lawyers more likely disclose, if obligated to? Which is more important to society, as opposed to the parties, to resolve accurately? But is law always readily distinguishable from fact in this context?

On the other hand, perhaps the seeming inconsistency does imply that either the disclosure rule for law or the nondisclosure rule for fact is wrong. Which, then, should be reformed? Disclosure of adverse law appears to be both a beneficial exception to adversary behavior and an exception that the system can sustain. "A common-law tradition where individual decisions strongly affect the development of legal doctrine for future cases almost necessarily implies a reasoning together of bench and bar and a candid and thorough exploration of the legal issues and precedents." Weinstein, Judicial Notice and the Duty to Disclose Adverse Information, 51 Iowa L.Rev. 807, 810 (1966). This suggests more broadly that there may be structural reforms (e.g., alleviating lawyer mismatches) or new limits on the advocate's behavior (e.g., tempering cross-examination) that could be implemented with beneficial effect but without endangering or abandoning the system itself. Other changes, however, may be basically at odds with the system. Could disclosure of adverse fact, then, be instituted without undermining the spirit of partisan advocacy essential to the adversary system? At any rate, would such a disclosure rule discourage private factual investigation, give unethical lawyers a big advantage, or damage the attorney-client relationship? In the long run and in a practical sense, would truth, procedural justice, and party satisfaction be served thereby?

Section Seven. Process Values

Besides basic substantive law governing the availability of remedies, legal actors (i.e., private citizens, their lawyers, and public officials) must also take account of much law of a process-oriented character. This law, if well designed, will reflect important values. These values generate standards or criteria for judging the goodness or badness of processes such as adjudication, legislation, and administration.

The total significance of such values is not exhaustively accounted for merely by stressing their relationship to quality of outcome. Some values have significance quite apart from impact on outcome, and some indeed lead to a negative impact on outcome. This fact is overlooked by some contemporary reformers who have their tunnel vision focused on result and result alone. There is independent worth, for example, in having processes in which those most vitally affected can be meaningfully heard and in having processes free of the taint of undue influence. The kinds of values reflected thereby, which are independent of outcome values, we shall call process values. One conclusive test of the independent importance of process values is that we know from experience that we would condemn public processes that did not reflect such values even if the processes' decisional output were invariably good. For independent reasons, we want processes in which affected parties are heard and in which decision makers are free of undue influence.

We shall use the phrase *process values* to refer to values by which we can judge a legal process to be good as a process, apart from any good outcomes it may yield. Readers may use *process-value efficacy* to refer to the capacity of a legal process to serve process values, as distinguished from its capacity to yield good outcomes.

Now we want to look at the grievance-remedial instrument from this angle. However, there is no such thing as a unitary "grievance-remedial process." Rather, the grievance-remedial mode breaks down into many different processes, including the various processes for creating the basic substantive rules on which private remedies are premised; processes of negotiation and settlement of disputed claims that avoid the necessity of formal adjudication; processes of adjudication of both law and fact; processes of surveillance of adjudication, including appellate review; and various processes for enforcement of adjudicative outcomes against unwilling parties. Most of these processes reflect many of the same process values, though not always in the same form. At any rate, here it is possible only to look at parts of some of these processes and to introduce a few key process values.

We previously referred to the illustrative principle that a person should not be required to satisfy the claim of another if he has not received notice of that claim at the outset. This procedural principle surely serves outcome values, it being a generally efficacious means to proper results in lawsuits. But this fundamental principle also serves process values, such as participatory governance and procedural fairness. Accordingly, a huge body of law has grown up to ensure adequacy of notice to the defendant, and it applies even where society is otherwise assured of the "justice" of the plaintiff's claim.

Few process values are as important as those reflected in the rules of notice. Yet, the following case grapples with ways of fostering other process values of at least equal importance, as well as some of the same process values in different forms. Incidentally, the case should also help to flesh out the role of the adjudicator in our adversary system, thus complementing the attention given in Section 6 to the advocate's role.

PARRISH v. BOARD OF COMMISSIONERS OF THE ALABAMA STATE BAR

United States Court of Appeals, Fifth Circuit, 1975.
524 F.2d 98, cert. denied, 425 U.S. 944, 96 S.Ct. 1685 (1976).

Before Brown, Chief Judge, Tuttle, Wisdom, Gewin, Bell, Thornberry, Coleman, Goldberg, Ainsworth, Godbold, Dyer, . . . Morgan, Clark, Roney and Gee, Circuit Judges.

Bell, Circuit Judge:

This appeal involves one assignment of error directed to the denial of a motion . . . to disqualify the district judge who decided the matter. There are other assignments of error arising from the merits of the [unsuccessful] suit which claimed discrimination in the administration of the Alabama bar examination. We consider en banc only the assignment of error having to do with disqualification. As will be seen, we find no error in the denial of the motion to disqualify, and thus the cause will be remanded to the original hearing panel for disposition of the other questions presented.

I.

The threshold requirement under the [28 U.S.C.] § 144 disqualification procedure is that a party file an affidavit demonstrating personal bias or prejudice on the part of the district judge against that party or in favor of an adverse party.[3] Once the affidavit is filed, further activity of the judge against whom it is filed is circumscribed except as allowed by the statute. In terms of the statute, there are three issues to be determined: (1) was the affidavit timely filed; (2) was it accompanied by the necessary certificate of counsel of record; and (3) is the affidavit sufficient in statutory terms? See generally 13 Wright, Miller & Cooper, Federal Practice and Procedure §§ 3541–53 (1975).

We are concerned only with the third issue. As we said in Davis v. Board of School Commissioners of Mobile County, 5 Cir., 1975, 517 F.2d 1044:

> Once the motion is filed under § 144, the judge must pass on the legal sufficiency of the affidavit, but may not pass on the truth of the matters alleged. See Berger v. United States, 1921, 255 U.S. 22, 41 S.Ct. 230.

Legal sufficiency is determined as a question of law on the basis whether the affidavit sets out facts and reasons for the party's belief that the judge has a personal bias and prejudice against the party or in favor of the adverse party. The facts and reasons set out in the affidavit "must

---

3. § 144:

Whenever a party to any proceeding in a district court makes and files a timely and sufficient affidavit that the judge before whom the matter is pending has a personal bias or prejudice either against him or in favor of any adverse party, such judge shall proceed no further therein, but another judge shall be assigned to hear such proceeding.

The affidavit shall state the facts and the reasons for the belief that bias or prejudice exists, and shall be filed not less than ten days before the beginning of the term at which the proceeding is to be heard, or good cause shall be shown for failure to file it within such time. A party may file only one such affidavit in any case. It shall be accompanied by a certificate of counsel of record stating that it is made in good faith.

give fair support to the charge of a bent of mind that may prevent or impede impartiality of judgment." Berger v. United States, supra, 255 U.S. at 33, 41 S.Ct. at 233.

The legal question presented is determined by applying the reasonable man standard to the facts and reasons stated in the affidavit. See United States v. Thompson, 3 Cir., 1973, 483 F.2d 527, which states the standard as requiring that the facts be such, their truth being assumed, as would "convince a reasonable man that a bias exists". The tripartite test of the Third Circuit is as follows:

> In an affidavit of bias, the affiant has the burden of making a three-fold showing:
>
> 1. The facts must be material and stated with particularity;
>
> 2. The facts must be such that, if true they would convince a reasonable man that a bias exists.
>
> 3. The facts must show the bias is personal, as opposed to judicial, in nature.

The pertinent part of the affidavit filed against Judge Varner is set out in [a footnote].[5] We consider it in light of the transcript developed in an examination of the district judge some weeks before the affidavit was filed. . . .

II.

With these facts and the recited legal principles in mind, we proceed to a consideration of the sufficiency of the affidavit. Personal bias or

5. 2. Plaintiff believes and avers that the judge before whom this action is pending, the Honorable Robert E. Varner, has a personal bias and prejudice against him, the other named plaintiffs, and the class represented by plaintiffs in this action.

3. The facts and reasons for the belief that such personal bias and prejudice exist are as follows:

a. The instant action complains, *inter alia*, that the defendants maintain a policy of excluding blacks from the practice of law in the State of Alabama. The Honorable Robert E. Varner is presently a member of the Montgomery County (Alabama) Bar Association; and when he served as President of that association two years ago, black lawyers were excluded from membership in the said association under the terms of its by-laws. The Honorable Judge Varner was then acquainted with the five or six black lawyers who then practiced in Montgomery; but never made an effort to invite them to join the association. It was only after the aforesaid judge became interested in a federal judgeship that he, as president of the Montgomery County Bar Association, appointed a committee to revise the said by-laws; and the record is unclear as to whether the "white only" membership clause of the Montgomery County Bar Association was removed during his tenure as president of the aforesaid association.

b. None of the plaintiffs in this case are personally acquainted with the Honorable Robert E. Varner. The said judge considers the defendant Commissioner Hill as a personal friend; he is a friend of Reginald Hamner, one of the chief defendants in the case; he is a friend of John Scott, defendant Hamner's predecessor in office and proposed to be called by the plaintiffs as an adverse witness; he is also a friend of counsel for all of the defendants. Further the said judge is personally acquainted with many of the other defendants in this cause. Although the testimony of the witnesses at the trial of this cause is expected to be conflicting in nature, the aforesaid Judge Varner has indicated that he does not believe that any of the defendants with whom he is acquainted would intentionally misrepresent any of the matters related to this lawsuit. Thus, plaintiffs sincerely believe that where the judge is called upon to make credibility choices throughout the trial, as he will be, he will attach undue weight to the testimony of his friends and acquaintances, all to the detriment of the plaintiffs and the class they represent.

prejudice is required under § 144. Neither of the factual bases alleged for recusal here raises an inference of personal bias or prejudice.

The first ground asserted, Judge Varner's past activities in the Montgomery Bar Association, is essentially an allegation based on the judge's background and states no specific facts that would suggest he would be anything but impartial in deciding the case before him. The claim of bias is general or impersonal at best.

The second ground, regarding Judge Varner's acquaintance with some of the defendants and counsel, has been rejected as a basis for requiring the disqualification of a trial judge. [Citations omitted.] The argument is that Judge Varner would be biased when it came to making credibility choices among witnesses. His statements made when being examined by counsel as to his possible disqualification were no more than an acknowledgement of friendship or acquaintanceship, and a refusal to condemn these persons as unworthy of belief in advance of whatever their testimony might prove to be. A statement by Judge Varner that he would believe, without question, any testimony of such persons would require a different result. Here, however, Judge Varner's answers did not reflect a lack of impartiality. The additional ground of the friendship between the judge and counsel for appellees, without more, is so lacking in merit as to warrant no discussion.

In short, the affidavit, including the facts on which it was based, was legally insufficient under § 144 to require disqualification. Judge Varner did not err in so ruling.

III.

[The court went on to consider the application of the recently amended 28 U.S.C. § 455, an alternative standard for disqualification of a federal judge. The statute speaks directly to the judge, although as in this case the statute's application can be suggested by a party.]

There are now several standards in § 455.[9] Some go to specific conduct, but one, set out in § 455(a), is general and does not rest on the personal bias and prejudice stricture of §§ 144 and 455(b)(1). As we noted in *Davis,* supra, the language of § 455(a) was intended to displace the subjective "in the opinion of the judge" test for recusal under the old

---

9. 28 U.S.C.A. § 455, reads in pertinent part:

(a) Any justice, judge, magistrate, or referee in bankruptcy of the United States shall disqualify himself in any proceeding in which his impartiality might reasonably be questioned.

(b) He shall also disqualify himself in the following circumstances:

(1) Where he has a personal bias or prejudice concerning a party, or personal knowledge of disputed evidentiary facts concerning the proceedings; . . .

(4) He knows that he, individually or as a fiduciary, or his spouse or minor child residing in his household, has a financial interest in the subject matter in controversy or in a party to the proceeding, or any other interest that could be substantially affected by the outcome of the proceeding; . . . .

(d) For the purposes of this section the following words or phrases shall have the meaning indicated: . . .

(4) "financial interest" means ownership of a legal or equitable interest, however small, or a relationship as director, adviser, or other active participant in the affairs of a party, ...

[§ 455], and the so-called "duty to sit decisions". We also noted that § 455(a) was intended to substitute a "reasonable factual basis—reasonable man test" in determining whether the judge should disqualify himself.

Considering first the § 455(a) claim, and the relevant facts and circumstances, we are of the view that a reasonable man would not infer that Judge Varner's "impartiality might reasonably be questioned". The facts have been stated in our discussion of the § 144 issue.

Judge Varner was president of a local bar association in which black lawyers were denied membership. This policy was changed during or shortly after his administration as president. As the affidavit makes clear, he, at the least, set the change in policy in motion by appointing a committee to revise the by-laws. He is faulted for not making an effort to obtain membership for black lawyers through inviting them to join, yet he, in effect, did just this in having the by-law changed. Appellants' logic would catch saint and sinner alike. There is hardly any judge in this circuit who was not a member of a segregated bar association at one time, and many have held a high office in the bar associations. The way of life which included segregated bar associations has been eliminated but only a new generation of judges will be free from such a charge. In any event, this circumstance will not support a claim of lack of impartiality. Such a claim must be supported by facts which would raise a reasonable inference of a lack of impartiality on the part of a judge in the context of the issues presented in a particular law suit. There are no such facts here. The stated conduct of Judge Varner does not support such an inference.

The allegation of lack of impartiality stemming from Judge Varner's acquaintanceship or friendship with witnesses and defense counsel is likewise tenuous. It does not exceed what might be expected as background or associational activities with respect to the usual district judge. As a factual basis, the allegations fall short of supporting an inference of lack of impartiality under § 455(a).

The factual basis also falls short under § 455(b)(1), in that there is no particularized allegation that Judge Varner had "personal knowledge of disputed evidentiary facts concerning the proceeding". Credibility choices are not disputed facts.

There are two additional claims of disqualification under amended § 455. They are based on the membership of Judge Varner in the Alabama State Bar, an organization in which membership has long been compulsory . . . . Title 46, §§ 30, 42, Code of Alabama. Each claim is attenuated in the extreme.

First, it is suggested that Judge Varner has a substantial interest in the success of defendants in the suit because of his identification with the bar association. Appellants rely on § 455(b)(4) for this proposition. No interest exceeding mere membership is asserted. This is not a ground for disqualification.

The second ground based on the judge's bar association membership is that he has a financial interest in the outcome of this case because the bar association may be compelled [under a provision of the federal civil rights statutes] to pay attorneys' fees should plaintiffs succeed. Although the amended § 455 states that any "financial interest" in the subject matter in controversy or any party to the proceeding requires recusal, the spectre of the potential obligation of the Board of Commissioners, a judicial organ of the state, Title 46, § 21 et seq., Code of Alabama, for attorneys' fees does not fall within the statutory definition of "financial interest".

We affirm as to the denial of the motion to disqualify. Except as to that issue, the appeal is remanded to the original panel for disposition.

[A majority of the circuit judges composing a federal court of appeals can order that the whole court will hear an important appeal en banc, rather than by the usual three-judge panel. Here, fifteen judges decided this portion of the appeal. Of them, some disagreed with the foregoing opinion. Four judges specially concurred, agreeing with the result but disagreeing with some of the reasoning. Three other judges dissented. One of the concurrences and one of the dissents follow, illuminating how process values and the reading of § 144 interrelate.]

GEE, CIRCUIT JUDGE (specially concurring):

The proper interpretation of Section 144 is a vexed matter with which I have long struggled. The belief of the parties that they are receiving even-handed justice, the apparency of justice to those not parties, the importance of both perceptions in maintaining the legitimacy of the judicial institution, the difficult decisions faced by a judge called upon to stand recused, and the practical implications of § 144 for the continued efficient functioning of the district courts in our circuit are some of the competing considerations. They are not easily harmonized, and, indeed, there may be no entirely satisfactory manner of implementing Section 144. And though I concur fully in the opinion of the court on the assumption that Berger v. United States, 255 U.S. 22, 41 S.Ct. 230 (1921), remains good law, I feel obliged to express my doubt that it does or should. For, in my respectful view, *Berger* represents an outdated rule which has been made tolerable in present circumstances only by engraftment of dubious exceptions.

The majority opinion reaffirms *Berger*'s antique rule that whatever "facts" the recusal affidavit may assert cannot be questioned but must be accepted as gospel. Such an approach gives free play to the unscrupulous or reckless affiant, willing to run his chance of a ponderous and unlikely prosecution for perjury—and perhaps in little danger, since *Berger* seems to say that "affidavit" assertions made on mere information and belief will suffice for § 144 purposes. Perjury charges have traditionally been based on falsely stated physical facts, and are rarely extended to representation of opinions. Suffice to say, establishing beyond reasonable doubt bad faith in assertion of a belief purportedly held at the time of an affidavit's filing is no light task. For similar reasons, counsel will not likely fear disciplinary proceedings initiated by the local bar. I am reluctant to join in mandating a procedure which envisions, for example, that a judge must take as true an affidavit asserting, perhaps on "information and belief," that he has recently engaged in an acrimonious personal dispute with a defendant—complete with particulars—and is therefore disqualified to sit in his case, when the judge well knows that the affidavit has misidentified him and is mistaken. We go far enough when we read § 144 as withdrawing from the judge decision of the final fact, his own actual bias. We should not require him to conduct such a curious and hypothetical proceeding as deciding whether an apprehension or bias is reasonably supported by whatever suppositious state of facts a daring and unscrupulous, or perhaps merely misadvised and agitated, party may be willing to swear to.

Factual matters necessary to decision of preliminary questions, of which recusal is a prickly example, are routinely resolved by weighing and evaluating affidavits. Only three workable modes of deciding this particular question occur: (1) peremptory disqualification upon the mere filing of an affidavit; (2) decision of the issue by another magistrate than the one accused; or (3) decision either of actual bias or the reasonable appearance of it by the magistrate sought to be disqualified.

There are indications in the legislative history that peremptory disqualification was the legislative intent; but this construction has never been adopted by any court. Reference to another magistrate is utterly foreign to the statutory scheme and raises its own problems of administrative inconvenience and delay. The statute's language gives fair support to the construction that the judge is not to determine bias-in-fact, and common sense supports the view that few if any humans can fairly decide whether they themselves are or are not biased in any given matter. But it is not too much to ask that a conscientious magistrate determine whether a given affidavit contains enough truth to fairly support a reasonable apprehension that he may be biased, or that an appellate court review that decision effectively. There is, therefore, no need to discern in § 144 a rule by which a party who really wants to do so and has the nerve can at pleasure disqualify any federal judge in a given proceeding by presenting to him a spurious set of ex parte "facts" which he cannot question—and by which his opponent can disqualify his first replacement by the same means.

I freely admit that *Berger* appears on its face to foreclose my reading of § 144. The *Berger* decision, however, has not gone unscathed—even by its authors—in the many years since 1921. It is notorious that, faced with its quixotism, courts on the firing line have, addressing other issues, limited its scope in ways perhaps dubious. . . . I am all but convinced that if faced with the facts of *Berger* today the Supreme Court would decide it otherwise. Being so persuaded, I would not lightly expose our circuit to such risks of wholesale disruption as an untimely resurrection of *Berger* in its pristine and literal form threatens, to be endured until the Supreme Court—grappling with the mighty concerns which face it—is able to reconsider these questions. . . .

TUTTLE, CIRCUIT JUDGE, with whom GOLDBERG, CIRCUIT JUDGE, joins, dissenting.

With deference I disagree with the opinion of the Court as to the standard that is to be used by the Court in determining whether an affidavit for bias filed under § 144 is "sufficient." I agree with the statement quoted in the opinion from *Davis* . . . . I cannot agree, however, that the standard of determining the "legal sufficiency of the affidavit" is one that requires that the facts be such, their truth being assumed, as would "convince a reasonable man that a bias exists." . . .

I am of the view that the standard is one that merely requires that the facts be such, their truth being assumed, as would convince a reasonable man that the affiant reasonably *believed* that bias exists. . . .

    . . . This view has been expressed in the following language:

> A formulation . . . in keeping with the purpose of the statute would require only that the facts alleged must justify a reasonable apprehension on the part of the affiant that the judge may be biased [footnote omitted]. This formulation shifts the emphasis from the judge's *actual state of mind* to the reasonableness of the *litigant's fear*, an emphasis at least supported, and possibly required, by the statutory language . . . . [Emphasis added.]

Disqualification of Judges for Bias in the Federal Courts, 79 Harv.L.Rev. 1435, 1446–47 (1966).

The approach which I would take to the construction of this statute seems to me much more consistent with the expression of this Court in United States v. Columbia Broadcasting System, Inc., 497 F.2d 107 (5th Cir.1974) dealing with the basic right of a party to a fair and impartial tribunal:

> . . . The guarantee to the defendant of a totally fair and impartial tribunal, and the protection of the integrity and dignity of the judicial process from *any hint or appearance* of bias is the palladium of our judicial system. [Emphasis supplied.]

I would conclude that a trial court cannot be free from "any hint or appearance of bias" unless a party's sworn *belief* of the existence of bias, supported by substantial facts, and tested by a standard of reasonableness, is of primary concern. . . .

Under this test, therefore, I would have no doubt but that the affidavit in this case, considered in connection with the transcript of the hearing, which is proper in that it was attached as an exhibit to the affidavit, meets the test. We must bear in mind when we consider the facts alleged that what the whole case is about was the allegations that the defendants had intentionally discriminated in the conducting of bar examinations, the only means by which black applicants could become members of the Alabama Bar. Thus, the significance of each of the several facts, and the effect of their accumulation is what we should bear in mind. . . .

Comments and Questions

1. Our legal system could handle judicial disqualification for bias in any of a variety of ways. For example, the presiding judge herself could decide on disqualification, or some other judge could intercede just to decide that issue. Although various states differ in their approach, the federal scheme directs the suspect judge to decide the question herself.

2. The standard of decision by the trial judge could conceivably fall anywhere on, or even beyond, a range extending from disqualification only upon his finding actual bias by a preponderance of the evidence down to disqualification automatically upon challenge by a party. The federal scheme rejects these two extremes in reading § 144 and instead applies some standard in the middle. For the applica-

ble standard, there are three leading possibilities, in order of decreasing stringency:

a. Judge Gee suggests that the trial judge decide "whether a given affidavit contains enough truth to fairly support a reasonable apprehension that he may be biased." This standard would not require that bias be established by a preponderance, but it would have the judge consider the truthfulness of the party's allegations of bias. This seems to amount to some sort of "fairly possible" standard.

b. Judge Griffin Bell rules that under § 144 the judge must accept the factual allegations as true and then decide whether those facts "would convince a reasonable man that a bias exists." This reference to the reasonable man seems to call for applying a preponderance-of-the-evidence test, but merely to an unquestioned set of allegations.

c. Judge Tuttle argues that the judge should accept the factual allegations as true and then decide whether they "would convince a reasonable man that the affiant reasonably believed that bias exists." This standard seems to combine the more lenient aspects of the two preceding approaches, asking whether bias is fairly possible to exist given an unquestioned set of allegations.

3. If you are experiencing a growing sensation that all this is hairsplitting and that these distinct standards make no difference, recall that under his standard, Judge Tuttle would have decided the *Parrish* case differently from Judges Bell and Gee. Also, observe that the *Parrish* case did face the societally critical issue of how we should ensure the suitability of the adjudicator (i.e., when we should disqualify a judge). Which of the five contenders would be the most desirable standard of decision, putting aside considerations of statutory directives and binding precedent? Outcome values are largely irrelevant to the answer, which turns instead on process values such as efficiency, legitimacy, procedural fairness, and participatory governance.

4. Now apply your standard to the *Parrish* facts. For what were the plaintiffs suing? Why did they challenge the trial judge's impartiality? Should he be disqualified?

Section Eight. Improving the Grievance-Remedial Instrument

The resources or means of law are not static. They, like the end uses of law, change. When we think of law reform, we normally think of changes in the substantive uses of law. But the improvement of law's own resources is itself a vitally important field for reform. Accordingly, this and the next four chapters include a separate section stressing this point.

A. General

In our exploration of the grievance-remedial instrument, many reform proposals have surfaced regarding its techniques, law, structures, processes, and use of coercive power. For example, we have considered the proper role of the jury and also possible excesses of the adversary system. We could have formulated many other proposals for reform. A prerequisite to any serious proposal is careful study. But undoubtedly, room exists for significant reform of the basic grievance-remedial instrument exemplified by the Swimming Pool case.

Let us consider a representative reform proposal. You have probably heard a criticism that sounds like this: "Our system involves appalling delay. In some cities the civil calendar is several years behind. Courts are clogged with cases, principally those arising from accidents. Something must be done. Justice delayed is justice denied." Do you agree? What might be done?

————

H. ZEISEL, H. KALVEN & B. BUCHHOLZ, DELAY IN THE COURT

xxii–xxvi (2d ed. 1978).*

Delay in the courts is unqualifiedly bad. It is bad because it deprives citizens of a basic public service; it is bad because the lapse of time frequently causes deterioration of evidence and makes it less likely that justice be done when the case is finally tried; it is bad because delay may cause severe hardship to some parties and may in general affect litigants differentially; and it is bad because it brings to the entire court system a loss of public confidence, respect, and pride. It invites in brief the wisecrack made a few years ago in a magazine editorial: "Okay, blind, but why so slow?"

These are obvious evils and scarcely require a statement. But in addition, a delayed court system brings in its wake many not so obvious secondary evils. It produces an unhealthy emphasis on the desirability of settlement and on the impropriety of litigation. It creates a stimulus for major changes in substantive law and procedure, such as the abolition of jury trial in civil cases, or shifting large areas of tort law to compensation schemes analogous to workmen's compensation, or changing the rules as to contributory negligence as defense or payment of interest on tort damages. These proposals, whatever their merits, should not be adopted or rejected simply because of extrinsic pressures from a delayed court system. Again, extended delay may result in, indeed almost compel, departure from legal ethics, as lawyers find it necessary to provide financial support for indigent clients over the long interval between accident and trial. And a delayed calendar creates totally new issues for a court, as it seeks to determine what if any cases should be given preference and tried ahead of the others. As Judge Ulysses S. Schwartz of the Illinois Appellate Court eloquently pointed out in a recent opinion, delay in the law is an old, old evil:

The law's delay in many lands and throughout history has been the theme of tragedy and comedy. Hamlet summarized the seven burdens of man and put the law's delay fifth on his list. If the meter of his verse had permitted, he would perhaps have put it first. Dickens memorialized it in Bleak House, Chekhov, the Russian, and Molière, the Frenchman, have written tragedies based on it. Gilbert and Sullivan have satirized it in song. Thus it is no new problem for the profession, although we doubt that it has ever assumed the proportions which now confront us. "Justice delayed is justice denied," and regardless of the antiquity of the problem and the difficulties it presents the courts and the bar must do everything possible to solve it.[6] . . .

In any study of court congestion questions of tone are important. Concern with the elimination of delay must not blind us to the distinctive nature of the judicial enterprise. The administration of a court is not simply the administration of a business, judges are not simply employees, and the values of the efficiency expert are not the only ones involved. . . .

And yet deference to the subtle values involved should not make it inadmissible to recognize that the administration of justice too involves problems of management and efficiency.

———

POSNER, AN ECONOMIC APPROACH TO LEGAL PROCEDURE AND JUDICIAL ADMINISTRATION

2 J.Legal Stud. 399, 400–01, 445–48 (1973).*

An important purpose of substantive legal rules (such as the rules of tort and criminal law) is to increase economic efficiency. It follows . . . that mistaken imposition of legal liability, or mistaken failure to impose liability, will reduce efficiency. Judicial error is therefore a source of social costs and the reduction of error is a goal of the procedural system. . . .

Even when the legal process works flawlessly, it involves costs—the time of lawyers, litigants, witnesses, jurors, judges, and other people, plus paper and ink, law office and court house maintenance, telephone service, etc. These costs are just as real as the costs resulting from error: in general we would not want to increase the direct costs of the legal process by one dollar in order to reduce error costs by 50 (or 99) cents. The economic goal is thus to minimize the sum of error and direct costs.

Despite its generality, this formulation provides a useful framework in which to analyze the problems and objectives of legal procedure. It is

6. Gray v. Gray, 6 Ill.App.2d 571, 578–579, 128 N.E.2d 602, 606 (1955). We might add to Judge Schwartz's roster the report of the law's most distinguished poet laureate on what must have been easily the world's most delayed court. Goethe, after having received his doctor juris degree, practiced law for a while before the Reichskammer Court in Wetzlar, about which he writes in the twelfth chapter of his autobiography: "An immense mountain of swollen files lay there growing every year, since the seventeen assessors were not even able to handle the current workload. Twenty thousand cases had piled up, sixty could be disposed of every year, while twice as many were added." It was not unusual for a case to remain on the docket for more than a hundred years. One, for instance, involving the city of Gelnhausen, began in 1459 and was in 1734 still waiting for the court's decision. A dispute between the city of Nuremberg and the electorate of Brandenburg had begun in 1526 and remained for ever undecided when in 1806 the court was dissolved. The piteous state of the court created the unique profession of "solicitants" whose sole job it was to secure preferments for their clients. This custom resulted eventually in the jailing of its leading practitioner and in the removal of three judges from the court because of bribery.

The effects of this delayed court on Goethe were profound and in the end salutary. It made him lose whatever taste he had for the law, gave him sufficient leisure (the court had 174 holidays annually) to fall into desperate love with Charlotte Buff, the heroine of Werther, the novel which was to catapult him firmly into world fame.

usable even when the purpose of the substantive law is to transfer wealth or to bring about some other noneconomic goal, rather than to improve efficiency. All that is necessary is that it be possible, in principle, to place a price tag on the consequences of failing to apply the substantive law in all cases in which it was intended to apply, so that our two variables, error cost and direct cost, remain commensurable.   .   .   .

.   .   . To most experts in judicial administration, delay between the filing and final disposition of a legal claim is an unmitigated evil and the proper focus of judicial reform. This is an odd way to look at the matter. Delay is an omnipresent feature of social and economic life. It is only excessive delay that is undesirable, and what is excessive can be determined only by comparing the costs and benefits of different amounts of delay.

A major cost associated with queuing as a method of rationing goods is the opportunity cost of the time people spend in the queue. Where the parties' time is their own while they wait (as when a theatergoer is forced to "wait" for six months to see a popular musical), the queue is merely a "figurative" queue. The court queue is a literal queue for defendants incarcerated awaiting trial and for some owners of property "tied up" in litigation. Otherwise it is a figurative queue, but this does not mean that it is costless. Court delay increases error costs because the adaptation of legal rules to altered circumstances is retarded and because evidence decays over time, increasing the probability of an erroneous decision. Clearly, at some level of delay error costs would become prohibitive. Delay also increases error costs by widening the gap between damages and judgments that is created by the fact that the legal interest rate is lower than the market rate and interest is usually allowed not from the date of the event giving rise to the suit but only from the date of judgment. This particular source of error cost from delay could be eliminated simply by increasing the interest rate and computing interest from the date of violation.

Delay is also a source of benefits. Presumably it enables a reduction in the number of judges and other court personnel, court houses, etc. It may increase the settlement rate.   .   .   .

Whether existing levels of delay are optimum is very difficult to judge, in part because the usual statistics of delay do not measure the court queue—the waiting period—accurately. Delay is generally measured from the filing of the defendant's answer to the complaint to the final disposition of the case. This interval is too long because it includes time during which the parties are not waiting at all, but litigating or preparing to litigate or attempting to negotiate a settlement. It is too short because it excludes the period between the event giving rise to the legal dispute (or the earliest time when a settlement might have been made) and the filing of the answer.

In 1972, the average interval between answer and final disposition, in personal-injury cases tried before juries in state courts, was 21.7 months, an increase of only three months since 1963. Delays in other kinds of cases, and in the federal courts, appear to be substantially shorter. The situation in a few major cities, however, is a good deal worse. Statistics that actually measure either the court queue or the costs and benefits of court queues of different length are unavailable.

The marked difference in waiting times between jury and nonjury trials is interesting because it suggests that courts are encouraging the choice of the cheaper method of trial by subjecting the more expensive to a much longer queue. A more straightforward method of accomplishing this end would be to charge a substantial fee for plaintiffs demanding a jury trial. The use of price as a method of rationing access to the courts would have the additional advantage, compared to queuing, of providing the court system with information on whether there is in fact a strong demand for prompt trials. But the use of the price system is not among the commonly proposed methods of reducing court delay, and the methods commonly proposed—such as procedural reform to simplify the trial of cases and thereby increase the effective litigation capacity of the courts, and the appointment of additional judges—have, in comparison to the use of price, some serious drawbacks. . . .

The proposal to reduce delay by adding judges—usually considered the sovereign remedy—ignores several realistic possibilities that might undermine the effectiveness of the measure. The reduction in delay brought about by the addition of judges might be offset by the lower settlement rate in the personal-injury area, and perhaps in other areas, that can be foreseen if delay is reduced; the additional litigation would create a new source of delay. Moreover, with litigation a speedier method of dispute resolution, disputants who under existing conditions of delay substitute other methods of dispute resolution (such as arbitration) because they value prompt resolution would be attracted back to the courts, and again a new source of delay would be created. An analogy may be drawn to building a new freeway: by improving road transportation the freeway induces some people who previously used other modes of transportation to switch to driving, and this leads to new congestion.

The essential point is that minimization of delay is not an appropriate formulation of the goal of judicial reform. The goal, it has been argued in this article, is to minimize the sum of the error costs and of the direct costs of legal dispute resolution. The problem of delay must be placed within that larger framework of inquiry. Indeed, unless that is done, delay cannot even be defined in a meaningful fashion.

B. Abandonment of Adversarial Adjudication

Some criticisms may require consideration of more drastic alternatives. For example, we have seen how the grievance-remedial mode demands structures and processes for applying law and techniques to facts of particular cases, and how adversarial and adjudicative processes are used for this purpose in Anglo-American systems. Are there vices of the adversarial form of adjudication that cannot be eliminated? Are there alternatives to *adversarial* adjudication?

First, we shall present a summary account of a set of structures and processes that is far less adversarial than our own, though still adjudicative. Second, we shall consider whether adoption of such a setup would be likely to eliminate or minimize certain specific objections to adversarial adjudication.

KAPLAN, CIVIL PROCEDURE—REFLECTIONS ON THE COMPARISON OF SYSTEMS

9 Buffalo L.Rev. 409, 409–14 (1960).*

To begin, the rules governing civil procedure in Germany today are laid down by legislative enactment stemming from the famous code of 1877; judicial rule-making plays virtually no part. There is no jury. The courts, at least those concerned in the regular proceedings for cases of consequence, are collegial in structure, acting through benches of three or—in the court of final review—five judges. To some extent, however, the plural bench may use a single judge as a representative or helper.

One of the leitmotifs of the German process is sounded by the Siegfried horn of the summons in the action. This invites appearance at a *Termin zur mündlichen Verhandlung,* a court-session for oral-argument, or rather for conference, since the ideal style of proceeding is less that of a contentious confrontation than a cooperative discussion. The conference is set perhaps three to four weeks after initial service of the papers— which by the way is usually accomplished by mail—and it is commonly attended by the parties as well as counsel. Now the point to be made is that the whole procedure up to judgment may be viewed as being essentially a series of such conferences, the rest of the process having a sort of dependent status. Prooftaking occurs to the extent necessary in the spaces, as it were, between conferences. Intermediate decisions are made along the way. But the conferences are the heart of the matter. Very promptly, then, the litigants are brought under the eye of the court and the case begins to be shaped; and this treatment is applied to the action at intervals until it is fully opened and finally broken. "Conference" betokens informality and this characterizes the entire German procedure. "Conference" also suggests what is the fact, that possibilities of settlement are openly, vigorously, and continually exploited.

I must relate German pleadings to the conference method—I shall use the word "pleadings" although these writings are quite different from the American variety. The action starts with a complaint served together with the summons, but beyond this there is no prescribed number or sequence of pleadings. Pleadings are to be put in in such numbers and at such times as to prepare for, strengthen, and expedite the conferences and thereby the general movement of the case. They have no position independent of the conferences. Indeed the framers of the code of 1877 looked to a free, oral restatement of the pleadings at conference. Such oral recapitulation no longer occurs: the court reads the pleadings in advance and the lawyers are assumed to adopt the pleadings except as they speak up to the contrary. Still no question arises as to the sufficiency of the pleadings as such, nor is there any motion practice directed to the pleadings themselves. In short, pleadings merge into, are an ingredient of the conferences. What is wanted from the pleadings as adopted and perhaps revised at conference is a narrative of the facts as the parties see them at the time, with offers of proof—mainly designated witnesses and documents—and demands for relief. There is no insistence on niceties of form, and legal argumentation, though strictly out of place, is common in today's pleadings. Amendments, even drastic amendments, of the statements can be made until the end of the case, normally without any penalty for late change. This malleability of the pleadings flows from the realization and expectation that a case may change its content and color as it is repeatedly discussed and as proof is from time to time adduced.

Returning to the conduct of the conferences, we find the presiding judge highly vocal and dominant, the parties themselves often voluble, the lawyers relatively subdued. To understand the judicial attitude and contribution at conference, we must take account of two related concepts. First, there is the principle jura novit curia, the court knows and applies the law without relying on the parties to bring it forward. Second, article 139 of the code, as strengthened in recent years, imposes a duty on all courts to clarify the cause and lead the parties toward full development of their respective positions. Thus with awareness of the law implicit in the case, the court is obliged to discuss it freely with the litigants, and in that light to indicate what will be material to decision. By discussion with counsel and the parties the court completes the picture of the controversy as presented by the litigants, throwing light upon obscurities, correcting misunderstandings, marking out areas of agreement and disagreement. It spurs and guides the parties to any necessary further exploration of facts and theories, and may suggest appropriate allegations, proof offers, and demands. The court, however, is not bound to take over and commandeer the litigation, nor does it have the power to do so in an ultimate sense. To some degree—the power is greater in "family" matters than in ordinary cases—the court may call up evidence and background information. The calling of experts is basically a matter for the court. But, in general, allegations, proof offers, and demands can be made only by the parties and so in the last analysis major control of the cause-materials remains with them. Nevertheless, as the parties are likely to follow the court's suggestions, we have here a significant potential in the court which imparts a special quality to the procedure; and this is so despite the fact that clarification and leading are hardly noticeable in simpler cases where the lawyers seem to be providing competent representation. The role of the court not only at conference but throughout the proceedings is envisioned as being both directive and protective. The court as vigorous chairman is to move the case along at a good pace, stirring the parties to action on their own behalf, exercising its limited sua sponte powers where necessary, conscious of a duty to strive for the right solution of the controversy regardless of faults of advocacy.

Conferences propel the lawsuit. Most dates are set by the court in open session. It acts in discretion with due regard to the convenience of the parties: few "iron" time provisions are laid down in the code, and the parties cannot control the pace by stipulation. When discussions disclose ripe questions of law, a time will be set for decision. If they show up disputed issues of fact, there will be an order and a time set for prooftaking.

To understand German prooftaking, we have first to ask what investigation of the facts a German lawyer customarily makes. He consults his client and his client's papers. But he has substantially no coercive means of "discovering" material for the purpose of preparing his proof offers or readying himself for prooftaking. Moreover he is by no means at liberty to go out and talk informally with prospective witnesses. He is hobbled by the principle that he is to avoid all suspicion of influencing those who may be later called to give evidence in court. I shall not attempt to mark the exact boundaries of this inhibition or to dredge up the possible evasive contrivances. I shall simply say that German lawyers are not prime movers with respect to the facts. The régime just described does make for unrehearsed witnesses. It begins to explain why a party in German litigation is not charged with any "proprietorship" over the witnesses whom he has nominated and neither "vouches" for them nor is "bound" by their testimony.

The court draws up the order for prooftaking, the *Beweisbeschluss,* from the nominations set out in the pleadings as they may have been revised at conference. Prooftaking need not be concentrated at a single session, and is in fact not often so concentrated. Accordingly the court may pick and choose what it wants to hear at particular sessions. It can take proof in any order—evidence on a defense ahead of evidence on the main case, even evidence on the negative of an issue ahead of the affirmative.

Witnesses are sequestered, kept out of the courtroom until called. The court asks the witness to state what he knows about the proof theme on which he has been summoned. When the witness has done that in narrative without undue interruption, the court interrogates him, and this is the principal interrogation. Counsel put supplemental questions. Lawyers' participation is likely to be meager. If a lawyer puts too many questions he is implying that the court does not know its business, and that is a dubious tactic. A full stenographic transcript is not kept. Instead the court dictates a summary of the witness' testimony for the minutes which is then read back and perhaps corrected.

German law has few rules excluding relevant evidence. In general relevant evidence is admissible and when admitted is freely evaluated: thus there is no bar to the admission of hearsay. But a few qualifications must be made. German law recognizes a series of privileges. It is somewhat irresolute in compelling production in court of various kinds of documentary proof. Testimony will be received from the parties themselves only in particular circumstances defined by law, and in no event may a party be compelled to testify. Party-testimony is viewed as a kind of last resort. This raises a quiddity, for parties are regularly heard in conference, nominally for purposes of clarification, not proof. I say "nominally" because German law tends to blur the line between evidence stricto sensu and other happenings in the courtroom.

Prooftaking is succeeded by conference, conference by prooftaking, and so on to the end of the regular proceedings in the first-instance court; and now we naturally ask, are there any shortcuts, any special devices for closing a case out promptly when it appears that there is overwhelming strength on one side and corresponding weakness on the other? The answer is no. The German system relies on the succession of conferences and prooftakings to show up strength or weakness with reasonable dispatch. Nor is there much in the way of stage-preclusion, that is, rules intended to discourage delaying afterthoughts by requiring that particular offers or objections be made at fixed points in the proceeding on pain of being otherwise lost to the party. The German action is not segmented into clear-cut stages—recall how pleadings may be thrown in late in the day—and it has in general a quality of "wholeness" or unity. But we do need to say here that the German system makes interestingly brisk provision for handling defaults; and we should also call attention to certain special speed-up devices: "dunning" proceedings, *Mahnverfahren,* available for "collection" cases and carried on regardless of amount in the inferior one-judge court; and "documentary-process," *Urkundenprozess,* used chiefly in suits on commercial paper, with proof initially limited to documents and party-testimony.

We come now to appellate review. The most notable fact about it is that on appeal to the court of second instance from final judgment, or from the important type of intermediate judgment which determines liability but leaves damages to be ascertained, the parties are entitled to a redoing of the case. The record made below, so far as it is thought to be free of error, stands as part of the proceedings, but the parties may add new proofs and invoke new legal theories, and the conduct of the cause is quite similar to that in the court below. Remember that article 139 on clarification and leading, with related duties and powers, continues to apply. The final court of review hears "revisions" on questions of law. As to matters of substance as distinguished from procedure, the court is not confined to the grounds urged by counsel. It seems a mark of the reality of the principle jura novit curia that this national court, dealing with a very large number of revisions coming up from the lower courts administered by the states, the *Länder,* is served by a bar limited by law to less than a score of lawyers.

The German court system is manned by a quite sizeable number of judges. They are career men, appointed on the basis of government examinations, modestly paid, of good but not exalted social prestige, looking primarily to ministerial departments of justice for advancement. In normal times men customarily enter into judicial service at an early age, generally without substantial experience in practice. Judges have traditionally been chided for *Lebensfremdheit,* undue detachment from the rough-and-tumble of life. We have caught a hint of their paternalistic role in the court procedure. This is not far distant from, indeed it comprises, an element of the bureaucratic. Working, many of them, in collegial courts whose judgments, stiffly authoritative in style, disclose neither individual authorship nor individual dissent, German judges live rather anonymous lives. And they are desk-bound through a large part of their working time, for files must be read in preparation for court sessions, and most decisions in actions large and small must be compendiously written up.

As to the German lawyers, I must avoid leaving the impression that their contribution to litigation is unimportant, or that their attitude is flaccid. Despite the court's capacity for active interposition, the frame of the case is made by the lawyers and there is room for contentious striving. Still the procedural system we have outlined does not make for notably vigorous performance by counsel. Moreover the education of lawyers tends against their full identification with clients as combatants: a significant part of their post-University required training is as apprentice-judges. Most important, we must notice some economic facts. Lawyers' fees for litigation, generally corresponding with statutory scales fixed in relation to the amount in controversy, are low.

Court costs are also fixed by statute in relation to the amount in suit, so that a litigant is on the one hand prompted to moderate his demand for judgment, and can on the other hand make a reasonably accurate advance estimate of the expense of litigation. Taking all elements of expense into consideration, German litigation is cheap by comparison with the American brand. But on the threshold a German litigant must conjure with the fact that if as plaintiff or defendant he turns out loser in the lawsuit, he will have to reimburse his opponent's expenses—counsel fees and court costs at the statutory rates together with ordinary disbursements. Let us note here that contingent-fee arrangements—agreements for quota litis— are proscribed in German practice. A comprehensive system of state-provided legal aid aims to enable not only downright paupers but any citizens of insufficient means to prosecute or defend civil cases upon a plausible showing of a prospect of success.

Lastly I must respond to the nervous question which any American lawyer would surely want to ask: Does the German system get over its court business without undue delay? German court statistics—at least those publicly available and not held in subterranean tunnels by the ministries—are curiously sparse; but these figures combine with the opinion of German lawyers familiar with the scene to indicate that the courts, although handling a very considerable volume of cases, are disposing of their calendars with fair speed. However, the court of final review—the *Bundesgerichtshof* sitting in Karlsruhe, successor to the famous *Reichsgericht* which used to reside in Leipzig—has had a hard time in recent years overcoming a serious backlog.

Comments and Questions

1. What are the major differences between the system outlined by Justice Kaplan and that in the *White* case?

2. Which of the following objections to Anglo-American adversarial adjudication would adoption of such a system as the foregoing obviate?

a. "In an ideal grievance-remedial mode, outcomes would not be influenced by extraneous factors but only by factors relevant to the legal and factual merits of the claimant's claim. To the extent that we cannot devise adequate means of coping with unjust influences such as disparity in abilities of lawyers, then we are forced to consider more fundamental alterations in our processes. Therefore, for example, we should seek out alternatives that do not rely so heavily on efforts of *opposing* lawyers to inform decision makers." But is there any way of substantially playing down the role of lawyers? And would there be any significant costs of doing this?

b. "The adversarial atmosphere scares off witnesses and naturally repels evidence, especially testimony and things under the control of disinterested persons, so that the litigants have available for use only the partisan and coerced residue after people with ingenuity have made themselves anonymous." To the extent this is so, does it call for radical modification of adversarial adjudication?

c. "Adversarial-adjudicative processes of the kind under consideration inherently tend to become complicated and sophisticated. Thus, they invite a multitude of procedural rules and principles of a constitutive and regulative character. These rules and principles in turn invite litigation concerning their own meaning and applicability with the consequence that the whole system tends to become litigiously incestuous. Worse yet, these rules can and sometimes do frustrate the quest for substantive justice."

d. "We must not forget the hidden social costs in adversarial adjudication. Recalling how it all got started in Anglo-American law is sobering. Many early 'trials' were really trials by battle in which the disputants' champions actually fought each other physically. Modern procedure is partly an outgrowth of this system. Today, we continue to pit two parties against each other. The abrasive character of this confrontation atmosphere cannot be denied. The resulting trauma to participants, particularly to the parties themselves as opposed to their lawyers, may not be measurable, but it is nonetheless real and damaging."

e. "Then there is simply the direct cost of all this in economic terms. The processes involved are highly formal and closely regimented, they call for considerable professional expertise, and they consume time voraciously. All this costs money, and lots of it. Finally, when it is recalled that many courts are way behind on their dockets, one wonders whether the whole system should not be radically revised."

C. Abandonment of Adjudication Altogether

In the preceding passages, a variety of criticisms of adversarial adjudication were offered. It may be, though, that if a social thinker really wanted to justify abandonment of adversarial adjudication, she ought to urge abandonment of adjudication. *Adjudication* —referral of two-sided disputes to impartial third parties for decision—begets adversarial adjudication, does it not? But how could the need for adjudication itself be eliminated and aggrieved citizens still be left with something resembling a grievance-remedial mode? This is not impossible, at least for some types of claims.

In the Swimming Pool case, the relevant rule of law might have provided that "any person suffering personal injuries caused by another in the course of leisure activity shall be entitled to compensation therefor from public funds upon application to the appropriate public official. Satisfactory proof of such injuries, of causation by another, and of nature of activity must be submitted."

Observe that an arrangement of this kind would not, in the first instance, call for adjudication at all. It would not even require the loss causer to be present at the official determination of loss and causation and activity, let alone pay out of his own pocket (or that of his insurer). Indeed, there would be no reason to permit the loss causer himself to demand an elaborate day in court, for he does not risk bearing the loss and he is not being branded a wrongdoer. He would be involved only indirectly.

In short, here we do not have a two-sided dispute for reference to a third party. A dispute could arise between the aggrieved and the relevant public official over facts of loss and causation and activity or over law, and *this* dispute would be of a two-sided kind that might then be referred to a third-party adjudicative body for resolution. But absent this, no need for adjudication would arise.

Would you recommend a system of the foregoing kind to handle personal injury claims arising from automobile accidents?

————

W. KEETON, D. DOBBS, R. KEETON & D. OWEN, PROSSER AND KEETON ON THE LAW OF TORTS

606–08 (5th ed. 1984).*

In 1965, Professors Robert E. Keeton and Jeffrey O'Connell proposed a plan of "Basic Protection" for the traffic victim. The plan was accompanied by a proposed statute, which became the basis for bills introduced before many state legislatures. A great deal of discussion and debate immediately followed, during which plans generally based on the Keeton-O'Connell proposal came to be known as "No-Fault Plans."

Rather than traditional liability insurance with its three-party claims procedure, the Keeton-O'Connell plan relied primarily on loss insurance, analogous to medical payments coverage, under which the victim ordinarily claims directly against the insurance company covering the insured's own car, or, if a guest, the host's car, or, if a pedestrian, the car striking the pedestrian. The coverage applies regardless of fault.

The plan calls for compulsory insurance providing "basic protection" for bodily injuries up to $10,000 for reasonable expenses incurred and loss of income from work, less a small deductible amount, and less any losses covered by benefits from other sources.

The most distinctive feature of the Keeton-O'Connell Plan is its partial tort exemption. Under this provision, unless damages for pain and suffering exceed $5,000, or other personal damages exceed $10,000, the basic protection coverage replaces any tort action for damages. If the damages do exceed these figures, the negligence action is preserved but recovery is reduced by these amounts. . . .

The first state to adopt an automobile accident reparations statute was Massachusetts in 1970, to become effective January 1, 1971. The Massachusetts Compulsory Personal Injuries Protection Act took many of its features from the Keeton-O'Connell Plan, which had passed one house of the legislature a few years before; but it is obviously an independent piece of legislation.

The Massachusetts statute is based on the existing compulsory bodily injury liability insurance provisions (the limits of $5,000 per person and $10,000 per accident being retained). Strict liability is required as a part of the liability insurance policy, in favor of the named insured, members of the household, any authorized operator or passenger of the vehicle, or any pedestrian it strikes. There is also coverage for the insured and members of the household if they are hit by an uninsured motorist.

The benefits run up to $2000. Within a period of two years after the accident they cover reasonable medical and hospital expenses; net loss of wages, or for unemployed persons, net loss of earning power, up to 75%; costs of substitute services, such as hiring individuals for family services which would have been rendered by the injured person. Some collateral benefits are not deducted, but others are, such as wages paid under a wage continuation program.

Although the Massachusetts statute adopted the distinctive feature of the partial tort exemption, the form of that exemption differs substantially from that proposed by Keeton and O'Connell. Under this act, the benefits are in lieu of tort damages; and any person covered by the compulsory insurance is exempted from liability to the extent of the coverage. An injured person can recover in tort for pain and suffering only if reasonable medical expenses exceed $500, or the injury results in death, loss of a body member or sight or hearing, a fracture, or "permanent and serious disfigurement." Property damage is not covered, and is left to the common law. The policy may provide for exclusion of benefits to a person injured while driving under the influence of alcohol or drugs, committing a felony, or intending to cause injury to himself or others.

During the 1970's, sixteen states enacted statutes that are "no-fault" legislation in the sense of providing for a partial tort exemption from claims for bodily injury arising out of the operation of a motor vehicle. Eight additional states enacted statutes that, though not providing for any tort exemption, are nevertheless sometimes referred to as "no-fault" statutes. Critics of the type of legislation enacted in these eight states have referred to such a statute as an "add-on" statute—one that simply adds no-fault coverage without the trade-off of a partial tort exemption.

With the enactment of no-fault laws, controversy over needs for reform was transformed into controversy over performance, together with continued debate over validity of the claims of deficiencies in the tort and liability insurance system. The controversy remains unresolved.

Comments and Questions

1. Could and should a *court*, say, the Supreme Court of Illinois, adopt a scheme like that of Massachusetts?

2. Proponents of no-fault argued that reducing lawsuits would give us a more efficient automobile insurance system, and more victims would be compensated more quickly. But the no-fault movement of the 1970s has now stalled. Why?

3. Consider this explanation from What Ever Happened to No-Fault, 49 Consumer Rep. 511, 512, 546 (1984):

In the early 1970's, a movement toward some type of no-fault system swept through state legislatures. But state trial lawyers' associations and individual trial lawyers lobbied hard to prevent no-fault laws. They were largely successful either in blocking no-fault laws or in so watering them down as to make the new system barely less litigious . . . . than the old.

. . . . In states where lawyers managed to preserve most of their business, no-fault hasn't kept its promises. . . .

. . . . The no-fault movement has been stalled primarily by trial lawyers, who have fought vigorously to obstruct passage of good no-fault laws and to weaken or repeal existing laws.

Section Nine.   Limitations of Law as a Grievance-Remedial Instrument

Under what circumstances is law most effective as a grievance-remedial instrument? Here is only the beginning of a list of those circumstances: the grievance is readily definable; the loss sustained (or threatened) thereby can readily be determined and remedied; the law itself that defines the availability of the remedy has already been formulated in readily understandable terms; the aggrieved who sustained such a loss will be motivated to seek such a remedy; in event of disputes between the parties over the rightfulness of the claim to a remedy under the law and the facts, a well-designed set of structures and processes exists for authoritative resolution thereof; and proof of the facts in particular cases can typically be made on the basis of reliable kinds of evidence.

These, then, are some of the conditions for the maximal effectiveness of law as a grievance-remedial instrument. It should be obvious, too, that this instrument is not without its correlative limitations.

————

POUND, THE LIMITS OF EFFECTIVE LEGAL ACTION
27 Int'l J.Ethics 150, 161–66 (1917).*

One set of limitations grows out of the difficulties involved in ascertainment of the facts to which legal rules are to be applied. This is one of the oldest and most stubborn problems of the administration of justice. . . . For example, the law is often criticised because it does not protect against purely subjective mental suffering except as it accompanies or is incident to some other form of injury and within disputed limits even then. There are obvious difficulties of proof in such cases. False testimony as to mental suffering may be adduced easily and is very hard to detect. Hence the courts, constrained by the practical problem of proof to fall short of the requirements of the logical system of rights of personality, have looked to see whether there has been some bodily impact or some wrong infringing some other interest which is objectively demonstrable, and have put nervous injuries which leave no bodily record and purely mental injuries in the same category.

Another set of limitations grows out of the intangibleness of duties which morally are of great moment but legally defy enforcement. I have spoken already of futile attempts of equity at Rome and in England to make moral duties of gratitude or disinterestedness into duties enforceable by courts. In modern law not only duties of care for the health, morals and education of children, but even truancy and incorrigibility are coming under the supervision of juvenile courts or courts of domestic relations. But note that the moment these things are committed to courts, administrative agencies have to be invoked to make the legal treatment effective. Probation officers, boards of children's guardians and like institutions at once develop. Moreover one may venture to doubt whether such institutions or any that may grow out of them will ever take the place of the old-time interview between father and son in the family woodshed by means of which the intangible duties involved in that relation were formerly enforced.

A third set of limitations grows out of the subtlety of modes of seriously infringing important interests which the law would be glad to secure effectively if it might. Thus grave infringements of individual interests in the domestic relations by tale-bearing or intrigue are often too intangible to be reached by legal machinery. Our law has struggled hard with this difficulty. But the results of our action on the case for criminal conversation and alienation of affections, which long ago excited the ridicule of Thackeray, do not inspire confidence nor does the sole American precedent for enjoining a defendant from flirting with the plaintiff's wife assure a better remedy. So also with the so-called right of privacy. The difficulties involved in tracing injuries to their source and in fitting cause to effect compels some sacrifice of the interests of the retiring and the sensitive.

A fourth set of limitations grows out of the inapplicability of the legal machinery of rule and remedy to many phases of human conduct, to many important human relations and to some serious wrongs. One example may be seen in the duty of husband and wife to live together and the claim of each to the society and affection of the other. . . . To-day this interest has no sanction beyond morals and the opinion of the community. . . .

. . . The scope of preventive relief is necessarily narrow. In the case of injuries to reputation, injuries to the feelings and sensibilities—to the "peace and comfort of one's thoughts and emotions"—the wrong is ordinarily complete before any preventive remedy may be invoked, even if other difficulties were not involved. Specific redress is only possible in case of possessory rights and of certain acts involving purely economic advantages. A court can repossess a plaintiff of Blackacre, but it cannot repossess him of his reputation. It can make a defendant restore a unique chattel, but it cannot compel him to restore the alienated affections of a wife. It can constrain a defendant to perform a contract to convey land, but it cannot constrain him to restore the peace of mind of one whose privacy has been grossly invaded. Hence in the great majority of cases substitutional redress by way of money damages is the only resource and this has been the staple remedy of the law at all times. But this remedy is palpably inadequate except where interests of substance are involved. The value of a chattel, the value of a commercial contract, the value of use and occupation of land—such things may be measured in money. On the other hand attempt to reach a definite measure of actual money compensation for a broken limb is at least difficult; and valuation of the feelings, the honor, the dignity of an injured person is downright impossible. We try to hide the difficulty by treating the individual honor, dignity, character and reputation, for purposes of the law of defamation, as assets, and Kipling has told us what the Oriental thinks of the result. "Is a man sad? Give him money, say the Sahibs. Is he dishonored? Give him money, say the Sahibs. Hath he a wrong upon his head? Give him money, say the Sahibs." It is obvious that the Oriental's point is well taken. But it is not so obvious what else the law may do. If, therefore, the law secures property and contract more elaborately and more adequately than it secures personality, it is not because the law rates the latter less highly than the former, but because legal machinery is intrinsically well adapted to securing the one and intrinsically ill adapted to securing the other.

Finally, a fifth set of limitations grows out of the necessity of appealing to individuals to set the law in motion. All legal systems labor under this necessity. But it puts a special burden upon legal administration of justice in an Anglo-American democracy. For our whole traditional polity depends on individual initiative to secure legal redress and enforce legal rules. It is true, the ultra individualism of the common law in this connection has broken down. We no longer rely wholly upon individual prosecutors to bring criminals to justice. We no longer rely upon private actions for damages to hold public service companies to their duties or to save us from adulterated food. Yet the possibilities of administrative enforcement of law are limited also, even if there were not grave objections to a general regime of administrative enforcement. For laws will not enforce themselves. Human beings must execute them, and there must be some motive setting the individual in motion to do this above and beyond the abstract content of the rule and its conformity to an ideal justice or an ideal of social interest.

HURLEY v. EDDINGFIELD

Supreme Court of Indiana, 1901.
156 Ind. 416, 59 N.E. 1058.

BAKER, J. The appellant sued appellee for $10,000 damages for wrongfully causing the death of his intestate. The court sustained appellee's demurrer to the complaint, and this ruling is assigned as error.

The material facts alleged may be summarized thus: At and for years before decedent's death appellee was a practicing physician at Mace, in Montgomery county, duly licensed under the laws of the state. He held himself out to the public as a general practitioner of medicine. He had been decedent's family physician. Decedent became dangerously ill, and sent for appellee. The messenger informed appellee of decedent's violent sickness, tendered him his fee for his services, and stated to him that no other physician was procurable in time, and that decedent relied on him for attention. No other physician was procurable in time to be of any use, and decedent did rely on appellee for medical assistance. Without any reason whatever, appellee refused to render aid to decedent. No other patients were requiring appellee's immediate service, and he could have gone to the relief of decedent if he had been willing to do so. Death ensued, without decedent's fault, and wholly from appellee's wrongful act. The alleged wrongful act was appellee's refusal to enter into a contract of employment. Counsel do not contend that, before the enactment of the law regulating the practice of medicine, physicians were bound to render professional service to every one who applied. Whart.Neg. § 731. The act regulating the practice of medicine provides for a board of examiners, standards of qualification, examinations, licenses to those found qualified, and penalties for practicing without license. Acts 1897, p. 255; Acts 1899, p. 247. The act is a preventive, not a compulsive, measure. In obtaining the state's license (permission) to practice medicine, the state does not require, and the licensee does not engage, that he will practice at all or on other terms than he may choose to accept. Counsel's analogies, drawn from the obligations to the public on the part of innkeepers, common carriers, and the like, are beside the mark. Judgment affirmed.

Comments and Questions

1. In a more recent Oregon case, Reynolds v. Nichols, 276 Or. 597, 556 P.2d 102 (1976), plaintiff, who was visiting defendants' next-door neighbors, was stabbed by Simmons, who was a social guest of defendants. Plaintiff sued to recover damages for his personal injuries, alleging that defendants failed to discourage or otherwise restrain Simmons when they knew or should have known of Simmons' intent and that they failed to warn plaintiff when Simmons' intent became known to them. The lower court granted defendants' motion for judgment on the pleadings. The appellate court affirmed, explaining:

> The allegations that defendants failed to give warning of Simmons' intent to assault plaintiff and to restrain Simmons do not state a cause of action. As we said in Cramer v. Mengerhausen, 275 Or. 223, 227, 550 P.2d 740, 743 (1976), "[t]here is no duty to aid one in peril in the absence of some special relation between the parties which affords a justification for the creation of a duty."

Why does the law generally not impose a duty to aid someone in peril?

2. A Vermont criminal statute imposes a fine of not more than $100 for willful failure to aid, but only a few states have followed suit. Vt.Stat.Ann. tit. 12, § 519(a):

> A person who knows that another is exposed to grave physical harm shall, to the extent that the same can be rendered without danger or peril to himself or without interference with important duties owed to others, give reasonable assistance to the exposed person unless that assistance or care is being provided by others.

Do you think this represents a desirable approach? See Shotland, When Bystanders Just Stand By, Psychology Today, June 1985, at 50.

3. California has a program for compensating volunteers injured during a rescue. Cal.Gov't Code §§ 13970–13974.

4. If a person, say a doctor, chooses to act, then she will be liable for her negligent conduct in the course of the rescue. "The result of all this is that the good Samaritan who tries to help may find himself mulcted in damages, while the priest and the Levite who pass by on the other side go on their cheerful way

rejoicing." W. Keeton, D. Dobbs, R. Keeton & D. Owen, Prosser and Keeton on the Law of Torts 378 (5th ed. 1984). This has led most states to enact a "Good Samaritan Act" that absolves from liability for negligence any doctor who gratuitously helps in an emergency.

———

COCKRUM v. BAUMGARTNER

Supreme Court of Illinois, 1983.
95 Ill.2d 193, 447 N.E.2d 385, cert. denied, 464 U.S. 846, 104 S.Ct. 149 (1983).

WARD, JUSTICE:

This appeal concerns the extent of the damages that may be recovered in a malpractice action based on a so-called "wrongful pregnancy" or "wrongful birth." The issue was raised in two medical malpractice suits that were consolidated on appeal from the circuit court of Cook County to the appellate court. In both cases, the plaintiffs had alleged that but for the negligence of the defendants each of the female plaintiffs would not have borne a child. In both actions, the plaintiffs sought to recover for the pain of childbirth, the time lost in having the child, and the medical expenses involved. The plaintiffs sought also to recover as damages the future expenses of raising the children, who, it would appear, are healthy and normal. The circuit court dismissed the counts that set out the claims for the expenses of rearing the children. The plaintiffs appealed, and the appellate court reversed those judgments. We granted the defendants leave to appeal . . . .

. . . *Cockrum* v. *Baumgartner* was brought by Donna and Leon Cockrum against Dr. George Baumgartner and a laboratory that performed tests according to Dr. Baumgartner's instructions. The Cockrums alleged that Dr. Baumgartner negligently performed a vasectomy upon Leon Cockrum. Also, they claimed that he was negligent in telling them that a sperm test conducted by the laboratory showed no live sperm when he should have known that the laboratory report showed that the vasectomy had been medically unsuccessful. The Cockrums also alleged that after the attempted vasectomy Donna Cockrum became pregnant and gave birth to a child, and they claimed that she would not have become pregnant if the physician had not been negligent.

In *Raja* v. *Tulsky*, Edna and Afzal Raja brought an action against Dr. A. Tulsky and Michael Reese Hospital and Medical Center. The Rajas alleged that Dr. Tulsky negligently performed a bilateral tubal cauterization upon Edna Raja, which operation was designed to make her sterile. They alleged that about five years after the operation Edna Raja began to experience signs of pregnancy. She was examined at Michael Reese's gynecology clinic and advised, however, that she was not pregnant. Later, after the time in which the plaintiffs say it was medically safe to have an abortion, she learned that she was in fact pregnant. Edna Raja alleged that she suffers from hypertensive cardiac disease, and that she had been informed that it would be medically dangerous for her to have a child. The Rajas claim that Michael Reese was negligent in failing to determine that she was pregnant. They say that if Michael Reese had told her that she was pregnant, she would have elected to terminate the pregnancy.

Those counts in which Dr. Tulsky was named as a defendant were dismissed as barred by the statute of limitations and are not at issue here.
 . . . The only issue is whether the trial court erred in dismissing the counts in which the plaintiffs sought to recover as damages the future expenses of rearing the child. . . .

The courts in the majority of States that have considered "wrongful pregnancy" or "wrongful birth" actions have recognized a cause of action against a physician where it is alleged that because of the doctor's negligence the plaintiff conceived or gave birth. (See Annot., Tort Liability for Wrongfully Causing One to be Born, 83 A.L.R.3d 15, 29 (1978).) These courts have generally held that in such actions the infant's parents may recover for the expenses of the unsuccessful operation, the pain and suffering involved, any medical complications caused by the pregnancy, the costs of delivery, lost wages, and loss of consortium. There is sharp disagreement, however, on the question involved here: whether plaintiffs may recover as damages the costs of rearing a healthy child.

There are courts which have allowed the recovery of the cost of rearing a child on the ground that such expense is a foreseeable consequence of the negligence. Those courts also have held that this recovery may be offset, however, by an amount representing the benefits received by the parents from the parent-child relationship.

In a substantially greater number of jurisdictions, however, courts have denied recovery in suits for costs of rearing a child.

Some of these courts have pointed to the speculative nature of the damages. Others have expressed concern for the child who will learn that his existence was unwanted and that his parents sued to have the person who made his existence possible provide for his support. . . . Courts have also stated that allowing such damages would open the door to various false claims and fraud.

Too, many courts have declared an unwillingness to hold that the birth of a normal healthy child can be judged to be an injury to the parents. That a child can be considered an injury offends fundamental values attached to human life. . . .

Beardsley v. Wierdsma (Wyo.1982), 650 P.2d 288, is another decision in which the court refused to permit the recovery of rearing costs. In rejecting the notion that would allow the recovery of rearing costs with an offset for the benefits of parenthood, it was observed:

> We believe that the benefits of the birth of a healthy, normal child outweigh the expense of rearing a child. The bond of affection between child and parent, the pride in a child's achievement, and the comfort, counsel and society of a child are incalculable benefits, which should not be measured by some misplaced attempt to put a specific dollar value on a child's life.
>
> The benefit or offset concept smacks of condemnation law, where the trier of fact determines the value of the land taken by the condemnor. The trier of fact then determines the benefit that results to the land owner, which benefit is deducted from the original value to determine the proper award. If the concept of benefit or offset was applied to "wrongful birth" actions, we can conceive of the ridiculous

result that benefits could be greater than damages, in which event someone could argue that the parents would owe something to the tortfeasors. We think that a child should not be viewed as a piece of property, with fact finders first assessing the expense and damage incurred because of a child's life, then deducting the value of that child's life.

Similarly, in Terrell v. Garcia (Tex.Civ.App.1973), 496 S.W.2d 124, 128, cert. denied (1974), 415 U.S. 927, 94 S.Ct. 1434, the court, not without emotion, reasoned:

> [A] strong case can be made that, at least in an urban society, the rearing of a child would not be a profitable undertaking if considered from the economics alone. Nevertheless, . . . the satisfaction, joy and companionship which normal parents have in rearing a child make such economic loss worthwhile. These intangible benefits, while impossible to value in dollars and cents are undoubtedly the things that make life worthwhile. Who can place a price tag on a child's smile or the parental pride in a child's achievement? Even if we consider only the economic point of view, a child is some security for the parents' old age. Rather than attempt to value these intangible benefits, our courts have simply determined that public sentiment recognizes that these benefits to the parents outweigh their economic loss in rearing and educating a healthy, normal child. We see no compelling reason to change such rule at this time.

We consider that on the grounds described the holding of a majority of jurisdictions that the costs of rearing a normal and healthy child cannot be recovered as damages to the parents is to be preferred. One can, of course, in mechanical logic reach a different conclusion, but only on the ground that human life and the state of parenthood are compensable losses. In a proper hierarchy of values the benefit of life should not be outweighed by the expense of supporting it. Respect for life and the rights proceeding from it are at the heart of our legal system and, broader still, our civilization. . . .

We would observe, too, that it is clear that public policy commands the development and the preservation of family relations. Exemplary of that policy in the tort context is the rule prohibiting suits by children against their parents for negligence. (Thomas v. Chicago Board of Education (1979), 77 Ill.2d 165, 171, 395 N.E.2d 538.) To permit parents in effect to transfer the costs of rearing a child would run counter to that policy. As stated earlier, those jurisdictions that permit a recovery for rearing costs have recognized that the recovery should be offset by the measure by which the plaintiffs have been benefited by becoming parents. . . . It can be seen that permitting recovery then requires that the parents demonstrate not only that they did not want the child but that the child has been of minimal value or benefit to them. They will have to show that the child remains an uncherished, unwanted burden so as to minimize the offset to which the defendant is entitled. . . .

We cannot on balance accept the plaintiffs' contention too that we should rigidly and unemotionally, as they put it, apply the tort concept that a tortfeasor should be liable for all of the costs he has brought upon the plaintiffs. It has been perceptively observed, by distinguished authority, that the life of the law is not logic but experience. Reasonableness is an indispensable quality in the administration of justice. The New York Court of Appeals, in rejecting a claim made in very different context, used language, however, that is not without appropriateness here:

> While it may seem that there should be a remedy for every wrong, this is an ideal limited perforce by the realities of this world. Every injury has ramifying consequences, like the ripplings of the waters, without end. The problem for the law is to limit the legal consequences of wrongs to a controllable degree. (Tobin v. Grossman (1969), 24 N.Y.2d 609, 619, 249 N.E.2d 419, 424, 301 N.Y.S.2d 554, 561.)

The reasons given for denying so-called rearing costs are more convincing than the reasons for abstractly applying a rule not suited for the circumstances in this character of case.

As we have noted, the plaintiffs themselves also rely upon considerations of public policy to temper the harshness of a proposed mechanical application of a principle of damages. In general, under the law of damages a plaintiff cannot recover for elements of damage he could reasonably have avoided. It has been said that this avoidable consequences rule might prevent recovery for rearing costs where the parents had an opportunity to avoid parenthood through abortion or adoption. In contending that the avoidable-consequences rule should not be applied, it was argued for the plaintiffs in oral argument that applying the rule here would violate a policy based on natural appreciation and affection, which favors the rearing of children by their natural parents.

The area of law we consider here is new, but there is reason to believe this question and related issues will be presented with increasing frequency. As the decisions we have cited show, courts regard the questions as matters of high social importance, transcending the individual controversies involved.

Dean Prosser recognized that considerations of public policy are of great importance in the law of torts. He commented:

> Perhaps more than any other branch of the law, the law of torts is a battleground of social theory. Its primary purpose, of course, is to make a fair adjustment of the conflicting claims of the litigating parties. But the twentieth century has brought an increasing realization of the fact that the interests of society in general may be involved in disputes in which the parties are private litigants. The notion of "public policy" involved in private cases is not by any means new to tort law, and doubtless has been with us ever since the troops of the sovereign first intervened in a brawl to keep the peace; but it is only in recent decades that it has played a predominant part. Society has some concern even with the single dispute involved in a particular case; but far more important than this is the system of precedent on which the entire common law is based, under which a rule once laid down is to be followed until the courts find good reason to depart from it, so that others now living and even those yet unborn may be affected by a decision made today. There is good reason, therefore, to make a conscious effort to direct the law along lines which will achieve a

desirable social result, both for the present and for the future. (Prosser, Torts sec. 3, at 14–15 (4th ed. 1971).)

For the reasons given, the judgment of the appellate court is reversed and the judgments of the circuit court are affirmed.

CLARK, JUSTICE, dissenting:

This court today has come to the conclusion that child-rearing costs are not recoverable in a wrongful birth action in Illinois. The court relies primarily on what it sees as a necessary public policy posture in reaching the conclusion it does. However, I believe the court's opinion is internally inconsistent, and I feel that, upon a careful examination, it mischaracterizes the issues without any substantive legal foundation upon which to build. The court inconsistently has said that the birth of a normal child cannot be judged to be an injury to parents and yet, at the beginning of the opinion, the court recognizes that a cause of action exists for wrongful birth in this State, and that plaintiffs can recover for the pain of childbirth, the time lost in having the child, and the medical expenses incurred. The court in effect has found that the birth of a normal child is recognized as an injury in "wrongful birth actions" in Illinois; the issue is what damages are recoverable as a result of that injury to the parents. If, as the court hypothesizes, the birth of a normal child cannot be construed as an injury, how then can the plaintiff recover for the "pain" of childbirth? Should, then, the court characterize the time "lost in having the child" as "lost" time (which in effect is found to be compensable)? Why then allow for the medical costs of childbirth if they represent the first installment in an investment in the preservation and development of family relations? The opinion of the court contradicts itself. Once the court has agreed that the cause of action for wrongful birth can be brought in Illinois, the policy questions that the opinion grapples with are moot.

The court determines that while other jurisdictions have applied "mechanical logic" in reaching a different conclusion than this court does, such a result can only be reached "on the ground that human life and the state of parenthood are compensable losses." .   .   . I believe the court has mischaracterized the issue in a most unfortunate and hyperbolic way. It is not at all that human life or the state of parenthood are inherently injurious; rather it is an unplanned parenthood and an unwanted birth, the cause of which is directly attributable to a physician's negligence, for which the plaintiffs seek compensation. .   .   .

I would also follow those other jurisdictions where child-rearing costs, while recoverable, are offset to a certain degree by the benefits of parenthood. Potential benefits, including companionship, that the parents may derive from that parent-child relationship should be considered by the trier of fact in determining the ultimate amount of damages. I do not believe that the many benefits of having a child should be excluded as a matter of law; nor do I feel that such benefits can be held to automatically offset all expenses. Plaintiffs who choose to rear this unplanned child should be allowed to recover for damages according to the degree of the injury. That will inevitably vary. .   .   .

While such a computation in offsetting the benefits that accrue to the parents against the expenses to be incurred is difficult, it is no more formidable a task than determining the amount of damages to be awarded for loss of consortium in a wrongful death action.

In reaching the result arrived at today, I believe the court has taken a myopic view of prospective parents' considerations. A couple privileged to be bringing home the combined income of a dual professional household may well be able to sustain and cherish an unexpected child. But I am not sure the child's smile would be the most memorable characteristic to an indigent couple, where the husband underwent a vasectomy or the wife underwent a sterilization procedure, not because they did not desire a child, but rather because they faced the stark realization that they could not afford to feed an additional person, much less clothe, educate and support a child when that couple had trouble supporting one another. The choice is not always giving up personal amenities in order to buy a gift for the baby; the choice may only be to stretch necessities beyond the breaking point to provide for a child that the couple had purposely set out to avoid having. The court today expresses concern about putting a negative imprimatur on a child's life and yet, in denying damages for child rearing, the court may well be accomplishing the very result it seems so intent on avoiding—making a child of an unwanted birth a victim of a very real continuing financial struggle and thus a painful reminder of the obligations of parenthood to a couple who had no appetite for a parental lifestyle. Does that child then become more wanted because this court has seen fit to deny foreseeable expenses in a case where a physician's negligence is undisputed?

SIMON, J., joins in this dissent.

Section Ten. Bibliography

1. *General.* O. Holmes, The Common Law (1881); Williams, The Aims of the Law of Tort, 4 Current Legal Probs. 137 (1951).

2. *Grievance-Remedial Techniques.* D. Dobbs, Handbook on the Law of Remedies (1973).

3. *Authorized Makers of Grievance-Remedial Law and Their Appropriate Collaborative Roles.* W. Keeton, D. Dobbs, R. Keeton & D. Owen, Prosser and Keeton on the Law of Torts (5th ed. 1984); S. Mermin, Law and the Legal System (2d ed. 1982); R. Rabin, Perspectives on Tort Law (2d ed. 1983); Comments on *Maki* v. *Frelk*—Comparative v. Contributory Negligence: Should the Court or Legislature Decide?, 21 Vand.L.Rev. 889 (1968); Keeton, Creative Continuity in the Law of Torts, 75 Harv.L.Rev. 463 (1962).

4. *Structures and Processes for Applying Grievance-Remedial Law and Techniques.* R. Cover & O. Fiss, The Structure of Procedure (1979); D. Crump & J. Berman, The Story of a Civil Case (2d ed. 1985); M. Franklin, The Biography of a Legal Dispute (1968); P. Simon, The Anatomy of a Lawsuit (1984); W. Zelermyer, The Legal System in Operation (1977).

5. *Necessity for and Nature of Coercive Power.* F. James & G. Hazard, Civil Procedure 281–85 (3d ed. 1985); 9 C. Wright & A. Miller, Federal Practice and Procedure 191–242 (1971); Hale, Force and the State: A Comparison of "Political" and "Economic" Compulsion, 35 Colum.L.Rev. 149 (1935).

6. *Roles of Private Citizens and Their Lawyers.* R. Field, B. Kaplan & K. Clermont, Materials for a Basic Course in Civil Procedure 253–91 (5th ed. 1984).

7. *Process Values.* T. Franck, The Structure of Impartiality (1968); Summers, Evaluating and Improving Legal Processes—A Plea for "Process Values," 60 Cornell L.Rev. 1 (1974).

8. *Improving the Grievance-Remedial Instrument.* Council on the Role of Courts, The Role of Courts in American Society (J. Lieberman ed. 1984); D. Saari, American Court Management (1982); Special Comm. on the Tort Liability System, ABA, Towards a Jurisprudence of Injury: The Continuing Creation of a System of Substantive Justice in American Tort Law (1984); Kaplan, An American Lawyer in the Queen's Courts: Impressions of English Civil Procedure, 69 Mich.L.Rev. 821 (1971).

9. *Limitations of Law as a Grievance-Remedial Instrument.* Hazard, Social Justice Through Civil Justice, 36 U.Chi.L.Rev. 699 (1969); Henderson, Process Constraints in Tort, 67 Cornell L.Rev. 901 (1982); Silver, The Duty to Rescue: A Reexamination and Proposal, 26 Wm. & Mary L.Rev. 423 (1985).

CHAPTER TWO

Law as a Penal-Corrective Instrument

Whatever views one holds about the penal law, no one will question its importance in society. This is the law on which men place their ultimate reliance for protection against all the deepest injuries that human conduct can inflict on individuals and institutions. By the same token, penal law governs the strongest force that we permit official agencies to bring to bear on individuals.

HERBERT WECHSLER

Section One. Introduction
(Pedagogic Vehicles Drawn Mainly from Substantive Criminal Law)

Conduct that offends public morals and social mores is extremely common. Maybe you like to gamble or use drugs; more likely you speed on the highway; possibly you will intentionally injure someone; and certainly you occasionally say something rude. Society will obviously be interested in these antisocial behaviors and will respond to them in some way. Not so obvious is whether that response should include punishment. The penal-corrective, or criminal, law is distinguished by its reliance on punishment. Punishment may be defined as the deliberate infliction of pain (or other unpleasant consequences) for the violation of a legal rule. Because the infliction of pain appears to be a bad thing, asking what justifies punishment is natural.

One answer to this question is *retribution.* A retributivist believes that punishment is inherently good and morally required when it is deserved. A second possible justification is *deterrence.* Deterrence may be either specific or general: punishment may deter the person upon whom it is inflicted from committing a second crime, or it may deter by example someone who has not yet committed a crime. A third justification for punishment is *rehabilitation,* or the reform of the rule breaker. Punishment is sometimes more modestly justified as providing *incapacita-*

tion, or the physical restraint of the would-be offender. Are there other justifications for punishment?

The question of what justifies punishment is not a purely theoretical one, for it leads to asking what the purposes or goals of the criminal law should be. This in turn has important implications for determining who should be punished and how severe the punishment should be.

The criminal law shares the justifications (and hence the goals) of deterrence, rehabilitation, and incapacitation with other instruments of the law, but the rationale of retribution is uniquely important in the penal-corrective mode. Perhaps this uniqueness contributes to the strong feelings that permeate discussions of retribution. Should we ignore such feelings in determining the proper role of retribution in the criminal justice system? Consider the legitimacy of retribution as the justification and goal for the imposition of punishment in light of the following excerpts.

I. KANT, THE METAPHYSICAL ELEMENTS
OF JUSTICE

100–01 (J. Ladd trans. 1965) (1st ed. Konigsberg 1797).

Judicial punishment (*poena forensis*) is entirely distinct from natural punishment (*poena naturalis*). In natural punishment, vice punishes itself, and this fact is not taken into consideration by the legislator. Judicial punishment can never be used merely as a means to promote some other good for the criminal himself or for civil society, but instead it must in all cases be imposed on him only on the ground that he has committed a crime; for a human being can never be manipulated merely as a means to the purposes of someone else . . . . His innate personality [that is, his right as a person] protects him against such treatment, even though he may indeed be condemned to lose his civil personality. He must first be found to be deserving of punishment before any consideration is given to the utility of this punishment for himself or for his fellow citizens. The law concerning punishment is a categorical imperative, and woe to him who rummages around in the winding paths of a theory of happiness looking for some advantage to be gained by releasing the criminal from punishment or by reducing the amount of it—in keeping with the Pharisaic motto: "It is better that one man should die than that the whole people should perish." If legal justice perishes, then it is no longer worth while for men to remain alive on this earth. If this is so, what should one think of the proposal to permit a criminal who has been condemned to death to remain alive, if, after consenting to allow dangerous experiments to be made on him, he happily survives such experiments and if doctors thereby obtain new information that benefits the community? Any court of justice would repudiate such a proposal with scorn if it were suggested by a medical college, for [legal] justice ceases to be justice if it can be bought for a price.

What kind and what degree of punishment does public legal justice adopt as its principle and standard? None other than the principle of equality (illustrated by the pointer on the scales of justice), that is, the principle of not treating one side more favorably than the other. Accordingly, any undeserved evil that you inflict on someone else among the people is one that you do to yourself. If you vilify him, you vilify yourself; if you steal from him, you steal from yourself; if you kill him, you kill yourself. Only the Law of retribution (*jus talionis*) can determine exactly the kind and degree of punishment; it must be well understood, however, that this determination [must be made] in the chambers of a court of justice (and not in your private judgment). All other standards fluctuate back and forth and, because extraneous considerations are mixed with them, they cannot be compatible with the principle of pure and strict legal justice.

J. BENTHAM, AN INTRODUCTION TO THE PRINCIPLES OF MORALS AND LEGISLATION

170–71 (rev. ed. 1907) (1st ed. London 1789).

I. The general object which all laws have, or ought to have, in common, is to augment the total happiness of the community; and therefore, in the first place, to exclude, as far as may be, every thing that tends to subtract from that happiness; in other words, to exclude mischief.

II. But all punishment is mischief: all punishment in itself is evil. Upon the principle of utility, if it ought at all to be admitted, it ought only to be admitted in as far as it promises to exclude some greater evil.

III. It is plain, therefore, that in the following cases, punishment ought not to be inflicted.

1. Where it is *groundless*: where there is no mischief for it to prevent; the act not being mischievous upon the whole.

2. Where it must be *inefficacious*: where it cannot act so to prevent the mischief.

3. Where it is *unprofitable,* or too *expensive*: where the mischief it would produce would be greater than what it prevented.

4. Where it is *needless*: where the mischief may be prevented, or cease of itself, without it: that is, at a cheaper rate.

A. GOODHART, ENGLISH LAW AND THE MORAL LAW

92–93 (1953).*

It is when we turn to retributive punishment that we find our most difficult moral problem. On this subject the greatest of German philosophers, Immanuel Kant, has said: "The penal law is a categorical imperative; and woe to him who creeps through the serpentine windings of utilitarianism to discover some consideration which, by its promise or advantage, should free the criminal from the penalty, or even from any degree thereof." This "categorical imperative" has never made much impression upon the English law. Nor has the view that the essential equality of crime and punishment must always be established. Unfortunately, these exaggerated doctrinaire statements have led to a reaction, with the result that it has become the generally accepted view that retributive punishment can never be justified. Retribution and revenge are regarded as synonymous. It must be remembered, however, that criminal law does not function in a vacuum, and that it cannot ignore the human beings with whom it has to deal. There seems to be an instinctive feeling in most ordinary men that a person who has done an injury to others should be punished for it. As civilisation develops this feeling is limited to intentional or negligent injuries, but the principle remains the same. It has, therefore, been pointed out that if the criminal law refuses to recognise retributive punishment then there is a danger that people will take the law into their own hands. A far greater danger, to my mind, is that without a sense of retribution we may lose our sense of wrong. Retribution in punishment is an expression of the community's disapproval of crime, and if this retribution is not given recognition then the disapproval may also disappear. A community which is too ready to forgive the wrongdoer may end by condoning the crime.

———

MURPHY, MARXISM AND RETRIBUTION

2 Phil. & Pub.Aff. 217, 233–43 (1973).*

In outline, then, I want to argue the following: that when Marx challenges the material adequacy of the retributive theory of punishment, he is suggesting (a) that it presupposes a certain view of man and society that is false and (b) that key concepts involved in the support of the theory (e.g., the concept of "rationality" in Social Contract theory) are given analyses which, though they purport to be necessary truths, are in fact mere reflections of certain historical circumstances.

In trying to develop this case, I shall draw primarily upon Willem Bonger's Criminality and Economic Conditions (1916), one of the few sustained Marxist analyses of crime and punishment. . . .

. . . Put bluntly, his theory is as follows. Criminality has two primary sources: (1) need and deprivation on the part of disadvantaged members of society, and (2) motives of greed and selfishness that are generated and reinforced in competitive capitalistic societies. Thus criminality is economically based—either directly in the case of crimes from need, or indirectly in the case of crimes growing out of motives or psychological states that are encouraged and developed in capitalistic society. In Marx's own language, such an economic system alienates men from themselves and from each other. It alienates men from themselves

* Jeffrie G. Murphy, "Marxism and Retribution," *Philosophy & Public Affairs* 2, no. 3 (Spring 1973). Copyright © 1973 by Princeton University Press. Excerpts from pp. 233–41 reprinted with permission of Princeton University Press.

by creating motives and needs that are not "truly human." It alienates men from their fellows by encouraging a kind of competitiveness that forms an obstacle to the development of genuine communities to replace mere social aggregates. And in Bonger's thought, the concept of community is central. He argues that moral relations and moral restraint are possible only in genuine communities characterized by bonds of sympathetic identification and mutual aid resting upon a perception of common humanity. All this he includes under the general rubric of reciprocity. In the absence of reciprocity in this rich sense, moral relations among men will break down and criminality will increase. Within bourgeois society, then, crimes are to be regarded as normal, and not psychopathological, acts. That is, they grow out of need, greed, indifference to others, and sometimes even a sense of indignation—all, alas, perfectly typical human motives. . . .

. . . The essence of this theory has been summed up by Austin J. Turk. "Criminal behavior," he says, "is almost entirely attributable to the combination of egoism and an environment in which opportunities are not equitably distributed."

No doubt this claim will strike many as extreme and intemperate—a sample of the old-fashioned Marxist rhetoric that sophisticated intellectuals have outgrown. Those who are inclined to react in this way might consider just one sobering fact: of the 1.3 million criminal offenders handled each day by some agency of the United States correctional system, the vast majority (80 percent on some estimates) are members of the lowest 15-percent income level—that percent which is below the "poverty level" as defined by the Social Security Administration. Unless one wants to embrace the belief that all these people are poor because they are bad, it might be well to reconsider Bonger's suggestion that many of them are "bad" because they are poor. . . .

. . . The retributive theory claims to be grounded on justice; but is it just to punish people who act out of those very motives that society encourages and reinforces? If Bonger is correct, much criminality is motivated by greed, selfishness, and indifference to one's fellows; but does not the whole society encourage motives of greed and selfishness ("making it," "getting ahead"), and does not the competitive nature of the society alienate men from each other and thereby encourage indifference—even, perhaps, what psychiatrists call psychopathy? The moral problem here is similar to one that arises with respect to some war crimes. When you have trained a man to believe that the enemy is not a genuine human person (but only a gook, or a chink), it does not seem quite fair to punish the man if, in a war situation, he kills indiscriminately. For the psychological trait you have conditioned him to have, like greed, is not one that invites fine moral and legal distinctions. There is something perverse in applying principles that presuppose a sense of community in a society which is structured to destroy genuine community.

Related to this is the whole allocation of benefits in contemporary society. The retributive theory really presupposes what might be called a "gentlemen's club" picture of the relation between man and society—i.e., men are viewed as being part of a community of shared values and rules.

The rules benefit all concerned and, as a kind of debt for the benefits derived, each man owes obedience to the rules. In the absence of such obedience, he deserves punishment in the sense that he owes payment for the benefits. For, as rational man, he can see that the rules benefit everyone (himself included) and that he would have selected them in the original position of choice.

Now this may not be too far off for certain kinds of criminals—e.g., business executives guilty of tax fraud. (Though even here we might regard their motives of greed to be a function of societal reinforcement.) But to think that it applies to the typical criminal, from the poorer classes, is to live in a world of social and political fantasy. Criminals typically are not members of a shared community of values with their jailers; they suffer from what Marx calls alienation. And they certainly would be hard-pressed to name the benefits for which they are supposed to owe obedience. If justice, as both Kant and Rawls suggest, is based on reciprocity, it is hard to see what these persons are supposed to reciprocate for. .   .   .

It does, then, seem as if there may be some truth in Marx's claim that the retributive theory, though formally correct, is materially inadequate. At root, the retributive theory fails to acknowledge that criminality is, to a large extent, a phenomenon of economic class. To acknowledge this is to challenge the empirical presupposition of the retributive theory—the presupposition that all men, including criminals, are voluntary participants in a reciprocal system of benefits and that the justice of this arrangement can be derived from some eternal and ahistorical concept of rationality.

Comments and Questions

1. Do you find Professor Murphy's arguments against retribution convincing? If his view of society is correct, would that also invalidate punishment based upon a deterrence or rehabilitation model of the penal-corrective instrument?

2. If you think retribution is a legitimate goal of the penal-corrective instrument, would you support a code based on the popular interpretation of "an eye for an eye and a tooth for a tooth"? If retribution departs from this literal interpretation of just deserts, how can we know what amount of punishment is deserved?

Section Two. Penal-Corrective Techniques

When the state invokes the penal-corrective instrument, individuals may lose their property, their liberty, or even their lives. Against which individuals should the government wield such powerful techniques? Punishing all who are discovered to have violated a legal rule is possible, and early English criminal law opted for this simple but harsh method of selection. As the criminal law became more sophisticated, however, its awesome reach was limited by *excuses*. A defendant may admit he violated a criminal prohibition, but may claim that the court should recognize some mitigating circumstances as precluding his punishment. He will try to persuade the court that the presence of the circumstances renders punishment ineffective or unfair or both. If the court accepts the new excuse, the defendant will escape punishment, although he may still be subject to civil legal action for his conduct.

Many different excuses have been argued to exonerate the defendant. The following cases address only three: necessity, insanity, and mistake of law.

REGINA v. DUDLEY & STEPHENS

Queen's Bench Division, 1884.
14 Q.B.D. 273.

Indictment for the murder of Richard Parker on the high seas within the jurisdiction of the Admiralty.

At the trial before Huddleston, B., at the Devon and Cornwall Winter Assizes, November 7, 1884, the jury, at the suggestion of the learned judge, found the facts of the case in a special verdict which stated "that on July 5, 1884, the prisoners, Thomas Dudley and Edward [*sic*] Stephens, with one Brooks, all able-bodied English seamen, and the deceased also an English boy, between seventeen and eighteen years of age, the crew of an English yacht, a registered English vessel, were cast away in a storm on the high seas 1600 miles from the Cape of Good Hope, and were compelled to put into an open boat belonging to the said yacht. That in this boat they had no supply of water and no supply of food, except two 1 lb. tins of turnips, and for three days they had nothing else to subsist upon. That on the fourth day they caught a small turtle, upon which they subsisted for a few days, and this was the only food they had up to the twentieth day when the act now in question was committed. That on the twelfth day the remains of the turtle were entirely consumed, and for the next eight days they had nothing to eat. That they had no fresh water, except such rain as they from time to time caught in their oilskin capes. That the boat was drifting on the ocean, and was probably more than 1000 miles away from land. That on the eighteenth day, when they had been seven days without food and five without water, the prisoners spoke to Brooks as to what should be done if no succour came, and suggested that some one should be sacrificed to save the rest, but Brooks dissented, and the boy, to whom they were understood to refer, was not consulted. That on the 24th of July, the day before the act now in question, the prisoner Dudley proposed to Stephens and Brooks that lots should be cast who should be put to death to save the rest, but Brooks refused to consent, and it was not put to the boy, and in point of fact there was no drawing of lots. That on that day the prisoners spoke of their having families, and suggested it would be better to kill the boy that their lives should be saved, and Dudley proposed that if there was no vessel in sight by the morrow morning the boy should be killed. That next day, the 25th of July, no vessel appearing, Dudley told Brooks that he had better go and have a sleep, and made signs to Stephens and Brooks that the boy had better be killed. The prisoner Stephens agreed to the act, but Brooks dissented from it. That the boy was then lying at the bottom of the boat quite helpless, and extremely weakened by famine and by drinking sea water, and unable to make any resistance, nor did he ever assent to his being killed. The prisoner Dudley offered a prayer asking forgiveness for them all if either of them should be tempted to commit a rash act, and that their souls might be saved. That Dudley, with the assent of Stephens, went to the boy, and telling him that his time was come, put a knife into his throat and killed him then and there; that the three men fed upon the body and blood of the boy for four days; that on the fourth day after the act had been committed the boat was picked up by a passing vessel, and the prisoners were rescued, still alive, but in the lowest state of prostration. That they were carried to the port of Falmouth, and committed for trial at Exeter. That if the men had not fed upon the body of the boy they would probably not have survived to be so picked up and rescued, but would within the four days have died of famine. That the boy, being in a much weaker condition, was likely to have died before them. That at the time of the act in question there was no sail in sight, nor any reasonable prospect of relief. That under these circumstances there appeared to the prisoners every probability that unless they then fed or very soon fed upon the boy or one of themselves they would die of starvation. That there was no appreciable chance of saving life except by killing some one for the others to eat. That assuming any necessity to kill anybody, there was no greater necessity for killing the boy than any of the other three men. But whether upon the whole matter by the jurors found the killing of Richard Parker by Dudley and Stephens be felony and murder the jurors are ignorant, and pray the advice of the Court thereupon, and if upon the whole matter the Court shall be of opinion that the killing of Richard Parker be felony and murder, then the jurors say that Dudley and Stephens were each guilty of felony and murder as alleged in the indictment."

LORD COLERIDGE, C.J.

. . . [T]he real question in the case [is] whether killing under the circumstances set forth in the verdict be or be not murder. The contention that it could be anything else was, to the minds of us all, both new and strange, and we stopped the Attorney General in his negative argument in order that we might hear what could be said in support of a proposition which appeared to us to be at once dangerous, immoral, and opposed to all legal principle and analogy. All, no doubt, that can be said has been urged before us, and we are now to consider and determine what it amounts to. First it is said that it follows from various definitions of murder in books of authority, which definitions imply, if they do not state, the doctrine, that in order to save your own life you may lawfully take away the life of another, when that other is neither attempting nor threatening yours, nor is guilty of any illegal act whatever towards you or any one else. But if these definitions be looked at they will not be found to sustain this contention. . . .

The one real authority of former time is Lord Bacon, who, in his commentary on the maxim, "necessitas inducit privilegium quoad jura privata," lays down the law as follows:—"Necessity carrieth a privilege in itself. . . . [I]f a man steal viands to satisfy his present hunger, this is no felony nor larceny. So if divers be in danger of drowning by the casting away of some boat or barge, and one of them get to some plank, or

on the boat's side to keep himself above water, and another to save his life
thrust him from it, whereby he is drowned, this is neither se defendendo
nor by misadventure, but justifiable." . . . Lord Bacon was great even
as a lawyer; but it is permissible to much smaller men, relying upon
principle and on the authority of others, the equals and even the superiors
of Lord Bacon as lawyers, to question the soundness of his dictum. There
are many conceivable states of things in which it might possibly be true,
but if Lord Bacon meant to lay down the broad proposition that a man
may save his life by killing, if necessary, an innocent and unoffending
neighbour, it certainly is not law at the present day. . . .

    . . . Now it is admitted that the deliberate killing of this unoffending
and unresisting boy was clearly murder, unless the killing can be justified
by some well-recognized excuse admitted by the law. It is further admitted
that there was in this case no such excuse, unless the killing was justified
by what has been called "necessity." But the temptation to the act which
existed here was not what the law has ever called necessity. Nor is this to
be regretted. Though law and morality are not the same, and many things
may be immoral which are not necessarily illegal, yet the absolute divorce
of law from morality would be of fatal consequence; and such divorce
would follow if the temptation to murder in this case were to be held by law
an absolute defence of it. It is not so. To preserve one's life is generally
speaking a duty, but it may be the plainest and the highest duty to sacrifice
it. War is full of instances in which it is a man's duty not to live, but to
die. The duty, in case of shipwreck, of a captain to his crew, of the crew to
the passengers, of soldiers to women and children, as in the noble case of
the *Birkenhead*; these duties impose on men the moral necessity, not of the
preservation, but of the sacrifice of their lives for others, from which in no
country, least of all, it is to be hoped, in England, will men ever shrink, as
indeed, they have not shrunk. It is not correct, therefore, to say that there
is any absolute or unqualified necessity to preserve one's life. "Necesse est
ut eam, non ut vivam," is a saying of a Roman officer quoted by Lord Bacon
himself with high eulogy in the very chapter on necessity to which so much
reference has been made. It would be a very easy and cheap display of
commonplace learning to quote from Greek and Latin authors, from
Horace, from Juvenal, from Cicero, from Euripides, passage after passage,
in which the duty of dying for others has been laid down in glowing and
emphatic language as resulting from the principles of heathen ethics; it is
enough in a Christian country to remind ourselves of the Great Example
whom we profess to follow. It is not needful to point out the awful danger
of admitting the principle which has been contended for. Who is to be the
judge of this sort of necessity? By what measure is the comparative value
of lives to be measured? Is it to be strength, or intellect, or what? It is
plain that the principle leaves to him who is to profit by it to determine the
necessity which will justify him in deliberately taking another's life to save
his own. In this case the weakest, the youngest, the most unresisting, was
chosen. Was it more necessary to kill him than one of the grown men?
The answer must be "No"—

    So spake the Fiend, and with necessity,
    The tyrant's plea, excused his devilish deeds.

It is not suggested that in this particular case the deeds were "devilish," but it is quite plain that such a principle once admitted might be made the legal cloak for unbridled passion and atrocious crime. There is no safe path for judges to tread but to ascertain the law to the best of their ability and to declare it according to their judgment; and if in any case the law appears to be too severe on individuals, to leave it to the Sovereign to exercise that prerogative of mercy which the Constitution has intrusted to the hands fittest to dispense it.

It must not be supposed that in refusing to admit temptation to be an excuse for crime it is forgotten how terrible the temptation was; how awful the suffering; how hard in such trials to keep the judgment straight and the conduct pure. We are often compelled to set up standards we cannot reach ourselves, and to lay down rules which we could not ourselves satisfy. But a man has no right to declare temptation to be an excuse, though he might himself have yielded to it, nor allow compassion for the criminal to change or weaken in any manner the legal definition of the crime. It is therefore our duty to declare that the prisoners' act in this case was wilful murder, that the facts as stated in the verdict are no legal justification of the homicide; and to say that in our unanimous opinion the prisoners are upon this special verdict guilty of murder.[1]

The Court then proceeded to pass sentence of death upon the prisoners.[2]

Comments and Questions

1. Why did the court think it better for the Crown to exercise clemency than to recognize the excuse of necessity? Are there any disadvantages to leaving the defendants' deaths within the Crown's discretion?

2. Suppose Dudley and Stephens had killed the cabin boy because another person threatened to kill them if they refused to do so. Would this court be more sympathetic to that excuse of duress? Should it be?

3. When Dudley, Stephens, and Brooks were rescued, they willingly told of the events that led to Parker's death. If they had remained silent, no prosecution would have been possible. Their statements to their rescuers and later to law enforcement officials made it clear that they did not expect to be punished. When all three were charged with murder, they expressed great surprise. (Eventually, charges against Brooks were dropped so that he could be a witness for the prosecution; in England, as in this country, no person may be compelled to be a witness against him- or herself.) To the modern reader, their attitudes seem strange, but it appears that their expectations were entirely reasonable given the custom of the time. After a detailed review of earlier instances of shipwreck and survival cannibalism, A.W. Brian Simpson concluded:

> [I]t is quite clear that the situation confronting the survivors of the yacht *Mignonette* was one for which they were well prepared and that in a general

---

1. My brother Grove has furnished me with the following suggestion, too late to be embodied in the judgment but well worth preserving: "If the two accused men were justified in killing Parker, then if not rescued in time, two of the three survivors would be justified in killing the third, and of the two who remained the stronger would be justified in killing the weaker, so that three men might be justifiably killed to give the fourth a chance of surviving."—C.

2. This sentence was afterwards commuted by the Crown to six months' imprisonment.

sense, Dudley and his companions knew the proper thing to do; someone must be killed that the others might live. They also knew that to obtain blood to drink, a living victim was preferable; to wait until death occurred was unwise. They knew too the appropriate preliminary course of action, which was to draw lots, a practice viewed as legitimating killing and cannibalism, particularly if agreed upon by a council of sailors. . . . What sailors did when they ran out of food was to draw lots and eat someone.

A. Simpson, Cannibalism and the Common Law 140 (1984). Should the fact that the defendants clearly thought their actions proper—and that most seamen of the time would have thought them proper—exonerate them?

4. The other famous criminal case arising from a shipwreck is United States v. Holmes, 26 F.Cas. 360 (C.C.E.D.Pa.1843) (No. 15,383). Several members of the crew threw fourteen male passengers overboard in order to lighten the leaking lifeboat. One of the crew members, Holmes, was tried for manslaughter. In that case, the judge charged the jury that necessity could be a complete defense to the charges, but only if a case of necessity did exist, the slayer was faultless, he owed no duty to the victim, and he was under no obligation to make his own safety a secondary concern. The jury had to consider whether it was the duty of the sailors to prefer the passengers, whether all on board should have drawn lots, or whether, in order to work the boat, it was necessary to prefer the sailors to the passengers. The jury convicted Holmes, recommending mercy. Holmes was sentenced to six months' imprisonment at hard labor and fined twenty dollars; his conviction was upheld on appeal. Do you think the rule given by the judge in the *Holmes* case is preferable to the *Dudley & Stephens* rule? Would the *Holmes* rule have acquitted Dudley and Stephens?

M'NAGHTEN'S CASE

House of Lords, 1843.
8 Eng.Rep. 718.

The prisoner had been indicted for [the murder of Edward Drummond, secretary to the prime minister, Sir Robert Peel].

The prisoner pleaded Not guilty.

Evidence having been given of the fact of the shooting of Mr. Drummond, and of his death in consequence thereof, witnesses were called on the part of the prisoner, to prove that he was not, at the time of committing the act, in a sound state of mind. The medical evidence was in substance this: That persons of otherwise sound mind, might be affected by morbid delusions: that the prisoner was in that condition: that a person so labouring under a morbid delusion, might have a moral perception of right and wrong, but that in the case of the prisoner it was a delusion which carried him away beyond the power of his own control, and left him no such perception; and that he was not capable of exercising any control over acts which had connexion with his delusion: that it was of the nature of the disease with which the prisoner was affected, to go on gradually until it had reached a climax, when it burst forth with irresistible intensity: that a man might go on for years quietly, though at the same time under its influence, but would all at once break out into the most extravagant and violent paroxysms. . . .

Verdict, Not guilty, on the ground of insanity.

This verdict, and the question of the nature and extent of the unsoundness of mind which would excuse the commission of a felony of this sort, having been made the subject of debate in the House of Lords (the 6th and 13th March 1843; see Hansard's Debates, vol. 67, pp. 288, 714), it was determined to take the opinion of the Judges on the law governing such cases.　.　.　.[a]

LORD CHIEF JUSTICE TINDAL:

.　　　.　　　.　　　.　　　.　　　.　　　.　　　.　　　.　　　.

The first question proposed by your Lordships is this: "What is the law respecting alleged crimes committed by persons afflicted with insane delusion in respect of one or more particular subjects or persons: as, for instance, where at the time of the commission of the alleged crime the accused knew he was acting contrary to law, but did the act complained of with a view, under the influence of insane delusion, of redressing or revenging some supposed grievance or injury, or of producing some supposed public benefit?"

In answer to which question, assuming that your Lordships' inquiries are confined to those persons who labour under such partial delusions only, and are not in other respects insane, we are of opinion that, notwithstanding the party accused did the act complained of with a view, under the influence of insane delusion, of redressing or revenging some supposed grievance or injury, or of producing some public benefit, he is nevertheless punishable according to the nature of the crime committed, if he knew at the time of committing such crime that he was acting contrary to law; by which expression we understand your Lordships to mean the law of the land.

Your Lordships are pleased to inquire of us, secondly, "What are the proper questions to be submitted to the jury, where a person alleged to be afflicted with insane delusion respecting one or more particular subjects or persons, is charged with the commission of a crime (murder, for example), and insanity is set up as a defence?" And, thirdly, "In what terms ought the question to be left to the jury as to the prisoner's state of mind at the time when the act was committed?" And as these two questions appear to us to be more conveniently answered together, we have to submit our opinion to be, that the jurors ought to be told in all cases that every man is to be presumed to be sane, and to possess a sufficient degree of reason to be responsible for his crimes, until the contrary be proved to their satisfaction; and that to establish a defence on the ground of insanity, it must be clearly proved that, at the time of the committing of the act, the party accused was labouring under such a defect of reason, from disease of the mind, as not to know the nature and quality of the act he was doing; or, if he did know it, that he did not know he was doing what was wrong. The mode of putting the latter part of the question to the jury on these occasions has generally been, whether the accused at the time of doing the act knew the difference between right and wrong: which mode, though rarely, if ever, leading to

***

a. This is not an appeal from an acquittal. The lords asked the judges to give their opinions on the proper rule to be applied in such cases. The most famous of the seven responses follows.

any mistake with the jury, is not, as we conceive, so accurate when put generally and in the abstract, as when put with reference to the party's knowledge of right and wrong in respect to the very act with which he is charged. If the question were to be put as to the knowledge of the accused solely and exclusively with reference to the law of the land, it might tend to confound the jury, by inducing them to believe that an actual knowledge of the law of the land was essential in order to lead to a conviction; whereas the law is administered upon the principle that every one must be taken conclusively to know it, without proof that he does know it. If the accused was conscious that the act was one which he ought not to do, and if that act was at the same time contrary to the law of the land, he is punishable; and the usual course therefore has been to leave the question to the jury, whether the party accused had a sufficient degree of reason to know that he was doing an act that was wrong: and this course we think is correct, accompanied with such observations and explanations as the circumstances of each particular case may require.

The fourth question which your Lordships have proposed to us is this:—"If a person under an insane delusion as to existing facts, commits an offence in consequence thereof, is he thereby excused?" To which question the answer must of course depend on the nature of the delusion: but, making the same assumption as we did before, namely, that he labours under such partial delusion only, and is not in other respects insane, we think he must be considered in the same situation as to responsibility as if the facts with respect to which the delusion exists were real. For example, if under the influence of his delusion he supposes another man to be in the act of attempting to take away his life, and he kills that man, as he supposes, in self-defence, he would be exempt from punishment. If his delusion was that the deceased had inflicted a serious injury to his character and fortune, and he killed him in revenge for such supposed injury, he would be liable to punishment. . . .

DURHAM v. UNITED STATES

United States Court of Appeals, District of Columbia Circuit, 1954.
214 F.2d 862.

Before EDGERTON, BAZELON and WASHINGTON, CIRCUIT JUDGES.
BAZELON, CIRCUIT JUDGE.

Monte Durham was convicted of housebreaking, by the District Court sitting without a jury. The only defense asserted at the trial was that Durham was of unsound mind at the time of the offense. We are now urged to reverse the conviction (1) because the trial court did not correctly apply existing rules governing the burden of proof on the defense of insanity, and (2) because existing tests of criminal responsibility are obsolete and should be superseded.

I.

Durham has a long history of imprisonment and hospitalization. In 1945, at the age of 17, he was discharged from the Navy after a psychiatric examination had shown that he suffered "from a profound personality disorder which renders him unfit for Naval service." In 1947 he pleaded guilty to violating the National Motor Theft Act and was placed on probation for one to three years. He attempted suicide, was taken to Gallinger Hospital for observation, and was transferred to St. Elizabeths Hospital, from which he was discharged after two months. In January of 1948, as a result of a conviction in the District of Columbia Municipal Court for passing bad checks, the District Court revoked his probation and he commenced service of his Motor Theft sentence. His conduct within the first few days in jail led to a lunacy inquiry in the Municipal Court where a jury found him to be of unsound mind. Upon commitment to St. Elizabeths, he was diagnosed as suffering from "psychosis with psychopathic personality." After 15 months of treatment, he was discharged in July 1949 as "recovered" and was returned to jail to serve the balance of his sentence. In June 1950 he was conditionally released. He violated the conditions by leaving the District. When he learned of a warrant for his arrest as a parole violator, he fled to the "South and Midwest obtaining money by passing a number of bad checks." After he was found and returned to the District, the Parole Board referred him to the District Court for a lunacy inquisition, wherein a jury again found him to be of unsound mind. He was readmitted to St. Elizabeths in February 1951. This time the diagnosis was "without mental disorder, psychopathic personality." He was discharged for the third time in May 1951. The housebreaking which is the subject of the present appeal took place two months later, on July 13, 1951.

According to his mother and the psychiatrist who examined him in September 1951, he suffered from hallucinations immediately after his May 1951 discharge from St. Elizabeths. Following the present indictment, in October 1951, he was adjudged of unsound mind in proceedings under § 4244 of Title 18 U.S.C., upon the affidavits of two psychiatrists that he suffered from "psychosis with psychopathic personality." He was committed to St. Elizabeths for the fourth time and given subshock insulin therapy. This commitment lasted 16 months—until February 1953—when he was released to the custody of the District Jail on the certificate of Dr. Silk, Acting Superintendent of St. Elizabeths, that he was "mentally competent to stand trial and . . . able to consult with counsel to properly assist in his own defense."

He was thereupon brought before the court on the charge involved here. . . .

[The appellate court reversed because the trial court had mishandled the burden of proof on insanity.]

II.

It has been ably argued by counsel for Durham that the existing tests in the District of Columbia for determining criminal responsibility, i.e., the so-called right-wrong test supplemented by the irresistible impulse test, are not satisfactory criteria for determining criminal responsibility. We are urged to adopt a different test to be applied on the retrial of this case. This contention has behind it nearly a century of agitation for reform.

A. The right-wrong test, approved in this jurisdiction in 1882, was the exclusive test of criminal responsibility in the District of Columbia until 1929 when we approved the irresistible impulse test as a supplementary test in *Smith* v. *United States.* The right-wrong test has its roots in England. There, by the first quarter of the eighteenth century, an accused escaped punishment if he could not distinguish "good and evil," i.e., if he "doth not know what he is doing, no more than . . . a wild beast." Later in the same century, the "wild beast" test was abandoned and "right and wrong" was substituted for "good and evil." And toward the middle of the nineteenth century, the House of Lords in the famous M'Naghten case restated what had become the accepted "right-wrong" test in a form which has since been followed, not only in England but in most American jurisdictions as an exclusive test of criminal responsibility:

> . . . the jurors ought to be told in all cases that every man is to be presumed to be sane, and to possess a sufficient degree of reason to be responsible for his crimes, until the contrary be proved to their satisfaction; and that, to establish a defence on the ground of insanity, it must be clearly proved that, at the time of the committing of the act, the party accused was labouring under such a defect of reason, from disease of the mind, as not to know the nature and quality of the act he was doing, or, if he did know it, that he did not know he was doing what was wrong.

As early as 1838, Isaac Ray, one of the founders of the American Psychiatric Association, in his now classic Medical Jurisprudence of Insanity, called knowledge of right and wrong a "fallacious" test of criminal responsibility. This view has long since been substantiated by enormous developments in knowledge of mental life. In 1928 Mr. Justice Cardozo said to the New York Academy of Medicine: "Everyone concedes that the present [legal] definition of insanity has little relation to the truths of mental life."

Medico-legal writers in large number, The Report of the Royal Commission on Capital Punishment 1949–1953, and The Preliminary Report by the Committee on Forensic Psychiatry of the Group for the Advancement of Psychiatry present convincing evidence that the right-and-wrong test is "based on an entirely obsolete and misleading conception of the nature of insanity." The science of psychiatry now recognizes that a man is an integrated personality and that reason, which is only one element in that personality, is not the sole determinant of his conduct. The right-wrong test, which considers knowledge or reason alone, is therefore an inadequate guide to mental responsibility for criminal behavior. . . .

The fundamental objection to the right-wrong test, however, is not that criminal irresponsibility is made to rest upon an inadequate, invalid or indeterminable symptom or manifestation, but that it is made to rest upon *any* particular symptom. In attempting to define insanity in terms of a symptom, the courts have assumed an impossible role, not merely one for which they have no special competence. As the Royal Commission emphasizes, it is dangerous "to abstract particular mental faculties, and to lay it down that unless these particular faculties are destroyed or gravely impaired, an accused person, whatever the nature of his mental disease, must be held to be criminally responsible . . . . ” In this field of law as in others, the fact finder should be free to consider all information advanced by relevant scientific disciplines.

Despite demands in the name of scientific advances, this court refused to alter the right-wrong test at the turn of the century. But in 1929, we reconsidered in response to “the cry of scientific experts” and added the irresistible impulse test as a supplementary test for determining criminal responsibility. Without “hesitation” we declared, in *Smith* v. *United States,* “it to be the law of this District that, in cases where insanity is interposed as a defense, and the facts are sufficient to call for the application of the rule of irresistible impulse, the jury should be so charged.” We said:

> . . . The modern doctrine is that the degree of insanity which will relieve the accused of the consequences of a criminal act must be such as to create in his mind an uncontrollable impulse to commit the offense charged. This impulse must be such as to override the reason and judgment and obliterate the sense of right and wrong to the extent that the accused is deprived of the power to choose between right and wrong. The mere ability to distinguish right from wrong is no longer the correct test either in civil or criminal cases, where the defense of insanity is interposed. The accepted rule in this day and age, with the great advancement in medical science as an enlightening influence on this subject, is that the accused must be capable, not only of distinguishing between right and wrong, but that he was not impelled to do the act by an irresistible impulse, which means before it will justify a verdict of acquittal that his reasoning powers were so far dethroned by his diseased mental condition as to deprive him of the will power to resist the insane impulse to perpetrate the deed, though knowing it to be wrong.

As we have already indicated, this has since been the test in the District.

Although the *Smith* case did not abandon the right-wrong test, it did liberate the fact finder from exclusive reliance upon that discredited criterion by allowing the jury to inquire also whether the accused suffered from an undefined “diseased mental condition [which] deprive[d] him of the will power to resist the insane impulse . . . . ” The term “irresistible impulse,” however, carries the misleading implication that “diseased mental condition[s]” produce only sudden, momentary or spontaneous inclinations to commit unlawful acts. As the Royal Commission found:

> . . . In many cases . . . this is not true at all. The sufferer from [melancholia, for example] experiences a change of mood which alters the whole of his existence. He may believe, for instance, that a future of such degradation and misery awaits both him and his family that death for all is a less dreadful alternative. Even the thought that the acts he contemplates are murder and suicide pales into insignificance in contrast with what he otherwise expects. The criminal act, in such circumstances, may be the

reverse of impulsive. It may be coolly and carefully prepared; yet it is still the act of a madman. This is merely an illustration; similar states of mind are likely to lie behind the criminal act when murders are committed by persons suffering from schizophrenia or paranoid psychoses due to disease of the brain.

We find that as an exclusive criterion the right-wrong test is inadequate in that (a) it does not take sufficient account of psychic realities and scientific knowledge, and (b) it is based upon one symptom and so cannot validly be applied in all circumstances. We find that the "irresistible impulse" test is also inadequate in that it gives no recognition to mental illness characterized by brooding and reflection and so relegates acts caused by such illness to the application of the inadequate right-wrong test. We conclude that a broader test should be adopted.

B. In the District of Columbia, the formulation of tests of criminal responsibility is entrusted to the courts and, in adopting a new test, we invoke our inherent power to make the change prospectively.

The rule we now hold must be applied on the retrial of this case and in future cases is not unlike that followed by the New Hampshire court since 1870. It is simply that an accused is not criminally responsible if his unlawful act was the product of mental disease or mental defect.

We use "disease" in the sense of a condition which is considered capable of either improving or deteriorating. We use "defect" in the sense of a condition which is not considered capable of either improving or deteriorating and which may be either congenital, or the result of injury, or the residual effect of a physical or mental disease.

Whenever there is "some evidence" that the accused suffered from a diseased or defective mental condition at the time the unlawful act was committed, the trial court must provide the jury with guides for determining whether the accused can be held criminally responsible. We do not, and indeed could not, formulate an instruction which would be either appropriate or binding in all cases. But under the rule now announced, any instruction should in some way convey to the jury the sense and substance of the following: If you the jury believe beyond a reasonable doubt that the accused was not suffering from a diseased or defective mental condition at the time he committed the criminal act charged, you may find him guilty. If you believe he was suffering from a diseased or defective mental condition when he committed the act, but believe beyond a reasonable doubt that the act was not the product of such mental abnormality, you may find him guilty. Unless you believe beyond a reasonable doubt either that he was not suffering from a diseased or defective mental condition, or that the act was not the product of such abnormality, you must find the accused not guilty by reason of insanity. Thus your task would not be completed upon finding, if you did find, that the accused suffered from a mental disease or defect. He would still be responsible for his unlawful act if there was no causal connection between such mental abnormality and the act. These questions must be determined by you from the facts which you find to be fairly deducible from the testimony and the evidence in this case. . . .

Finally, in leaving the determination of the ultimate question of fact to the jury, we permit it to perform its traditional function which, as we said in *Holloway,* is to apply "our inherited ideas of moral responsibility to individuals prosecuted for crime . . . . " Juries will continue to make moral judgments, still operating under the fundamental precept that "Our collective conscience does not allow punishment where it cannot impose blame." But in making such judgments, they will be guided by wider horizons of knowledge concerning mental life. The question will be simply whether the accused acted because of a mental disorder, and not whether he displayed particular symptoms which medical science has long recognized do not necessarily, or even typically, accompany even the most serious mental disorder. . . .

Reversed and remanded for a new trial.

————

DERSHOWITZ, PSYCHIATRY IN THE LEGAL PROCESS: "A KNIFE THAT CUTS BOTH WAYS"

51 Judicature 370, 370–71 (1968).*

In the trial scene from Brothers Karamozov, Dostoyevsky, speaking through the lips of the defense attorney, issued a stern warning to the legal profession:

Profound as psychology is, it's a knife that cuts both ways. . . . You can prove anything by it. I am speaking of the abuse of psychology, gentlemen.

I will speak today about another knife that cuts two ways: psychiatry in the legal process. Much has been written about one cutting edge: the contributions made by psychiatry. I will focus on the other side of the blade: the social costs incurred by the increasing involvement of the psychiatrist in the administration of justice. An important—if subtle—consequence of psychiatric involvement has been the gradual introduction of a medical model in place of the laws' efforts to articulate legally relevant criteria. The cost of this substitution has been confusion of purpose, and in some instances, needless deprivation of liberty.

A brief look at the history of the insanity defense will serve to illustrate this process. The law had, for centuries, been groping for a rule which would express the deeply felt conviction that some people who commit condemnable acts are not themselves deserving of condemnation. In the 17th century, a person was held irresponsible if he "doth not know what he was doing, no more than an infant or a wild beast." There was an obvious relationship between this "wild beast" test and the rest of the criminal law: neither an infant nor a wild beast was held responsible; so why, it was asked, should an adult who was functionally similar. In the much villified *McNaghten* case, the House of Lords also analogized irresponsibility to a deeply rooted principle of the criminal law. It held that a man who suffers from delusions "must be considered in the same situation as to responsibility as if the facts with respect to which the delusion exists were real." This was a simple extension of the traditional mistake of fact defense to certain unreasonable mistakes. The Lords' attempt to generalize this principle under the rubric "know the nature and quality of the act," and know that it was "wrong," was surely not the clearest way of saying what they meant. But it *was* clear that they—like the framers of the "wild beast" test—were setting down a *legal* rule designed to further *legal* policies; they were not attempting to identify and exculpate a particular psychiatric category of persons—the mentally ill, the insane or the psychotic. Indeed, the ruling explicitly recognized the rather limited role of the psychiatrist in administering the insanity defense. Nevertheless, much of the criticism of *McNaghten* has been premised on the erroneous assumption that the purpose of that test *was* to describe a psychiatric entity. Thus, Dr. Isaac Ray, an early psychiatric critic, called the *McNaghten* rule a "fallacious" test of criminal responsibility, arguing that: "Insanity is a disease, and, as in the case with all other diseases, the fact of its existence is never established by a single diagnostic symptom"—such as inability to distinguish right from wrong. But the Lords had not focused on inability to distinguish right from wrong because they thought it was a scientifically valid symptom of disease; they focused on it because they deemed it a just and useful legal criterion for distinguishing those who should be held responsible and punished from those who should be held irresponsible and hospitalized. Now this criterion may be criticized as unjust or unworkable, but to say it is "fallacious" is to misunderstand the nature of legal rules. Ray was attempting to substitute a medical model of responsibility for the legal one; and the law was not engaging in a fallacy by insisting on asking its own questions and establishing criteria relevant to its own purposes.

This attempt to impose a medical model on the legal process of distinguishing the responsible from the irresponsible continued through the 19th century and into the 20th. It culminated in the case of *Durham* v. *United States* decided in 1954. The argument for the *Durham* rule was simple—if one accepted Ray's erroneous premise. For if *McNaghten* was simply an attempt to identify those persons considered mentally ill by psychiatrists, then why bother to go through the indirection of listing symptoms? Why not make the test the existence of mental illness itself? Abe Fortas, counsel for Durham and now Justice Fortas, argued that substitution of a new rule for *McNaghten* would permit psychiatrists to testify in "the terms of their own discipline, and not in the terminology of an irrelevant formula." Why the "right-wrong" formula was irrelevant for legal purposes the court was never told, except that it did not permit psychiatrists to testify in terms of their own discipline. The possibility that the terms of their own discipline are not particularly relevant to a perfectly rational legal rule was never considered. The court was simply urged to adopt the psychiatrists' medical model of "insanity" and abandon any efforts of its own to articulate legally functional rules. The United States Court of Appeals for the District of Columbia accepted Fortas' arguments and adopted a rule framed in medical terms: "an accused is not responsible if his unlawful act was the product of a mental disease or defect." Although the author of *Durham*, Judge Bazelon, has always regarded that case as merely an opening wedge in a continuing search for just and workable criteria of responsibility, many psychiatrists interpreted *Durham* as an invitation for them to decide who should and who should not be held criminally responsible. Indeed, in one famous episode, the staff of a large mental hospital apparently took a vote to determine whether or not sociopathic personality was to be regarded as a mental disease. The issue of criminal responsibility was finally where Isaac Ray thought it belonged: in the therapeutic hands of the psychiatrist.

This then is a capsule history of one encounter between law and psychiatry. It is not a complete history. There have been judicial adumbrations of disillusionment with the medical model. But it is a discouraging history of usurpation and abdication: of an expert being summoned for a limited purpose, assuming his own indispensibility, and then persuading the law to ask the critical questions in terms which make him more comfortable and his testimony more relevant. The upshot has been to make the psychiatrist's testimony more relevant to the questions posed, but to make the questions themselves less relevant to the purpose of the law.

Comments and Questions

1. When people are acquitted by reason of insanity, they do not walk away from the courthouse free from restraints. Instead, they will become subjects of civil commitment hearings; in almost every case, they will be involuntarily committed to a mental hospital until they are no longer dangerous to themselves or to others. Studies done on insanity acquittees show that on the average, they spend as much time in a mental hospital as they would spend in prison if they had been convicted of the crime with which they were charged. Moreover, some convicted defendants will be evaluated by prison psychiatrists and sent to mental hospitals to serve their sentences. Why, then, is the insanity defense so controversial?

2. Is the *Durham* rule an improvement over the *M'Naghten* rule? The *Durham* court repeatedly tinkered with the formulation of its insanity test until Congress passed the Insanity Defense Reform Act of 1984, which provides:

> (a) Affirmative defense. It is an affirmative defense to a prosecution under any Federal statute that, at the time of the commission of the acts constituting the offense, the defendant, as a result of a severe mental disease or defect, was unable to appreciate the nature and quality or the wrongfulness of his acts. Mental disease or defect does not otherwise constitute a defense.

> (b) Burden of proof. The defendant has the burden of proving the defense of insanity by clear and convincing evidence.

18 U.S.C. § 20. Is this a step backward?

3. How do you think the *Durham* court would view a proposed defense of alcoholism or drug addiction?

4. Poverty is probably a more direct "cause" of crime than is insanity. Should we recognize poverty as a defense to economic crimes? Should we recognize having been the victim of child abuse as a defense to crimes of violence?

C. CERF & V. NAVASKY, THE EXPERTS SPEAK
69–70 (1984).*

In the late spring of 1982, John Hinckley, Jr., was tried for attempting to assassinate U.S. President Ronald Reagan. Qualified "expert witnesses" were summoned to testify about the state of the defendant's mind at the time he committed the crime.

"[Hinckley suffers from] process schizophrenia."
> — Dr. William T. Carpenter
> (psychiatrist who interviewed Hinckley at length after the assassination attempt),
> June 7, 1982

"Hinckley does not suffer from schizophrenia."
> — Dr. Park E. Dietz
> (specialist in forensic psychiatry),
> June 7, 1982

"[Hinckley was suffering from] a very severe depressive disorder."
> — Dr. Ernst Prelinger
> (psychologist at Yale University),
> May 20, 1982

"There is little to suggest he was seriously depressed [the day of the shootings]."
> — Dr. Park E. Dietz
> (specialist in forensic psychiatry),
> June 4, 1982

"[CAT scans] were absolutely essential [to my diagnosis of schizophrenia]."
> — Dr. David M. Bear
> (Assistant Professor of Psychiatry at Harvard Medical School),
> May 19, 1982

"[CAT scans revealed] no evidence of any significant abnormality whatsoever."
> — Dr. Marjorie LeMay
> (Associate Professor of Radiology at Harvard Medical School),
> May 21, 1982

"There's no possible way that you can predict people's behavior, or whether they're schizophrenic or not schizophrenic, from a CAT scan, period."
> — Dr. David Davis
> (Head of Radiology Department at George Washington University Medical Center),
> June 3, 1982

"[I]t is a psychiatric fact that Mr. Hinckley was psychotic."
> — Dr. David M. Bear
> (Assistant Professor of Psychiatry at Harvard Medical School),
> May 18, 1982

"Mr. Hinckey has not been psychotic at any time."
— Dr. Park E. Dietz
    (specialist in forensic psychiatry),
    June 7, 1982

REX v. ESOP

Central Criminal Court, 1836.
173 Eng.Rep. 203.

The prisoner was indicted for an unnatural offence, committed on board of an East India ship, lying in St. Katherine's Docks. It appeared that he was a native of Bagdad.

[Attorney] for the prisoner.—In the country from which the prisoner comes, it is not considered an offence; and a person who comes into this country and does an act, believing that it is a perfectly innocent one, cannot be convicted according to the law of England. A party must know that what he does is a crime. This is the principle upon which infants, idiots, and lunatics are held not to be answerable. If a person is unconscious that he is doing a wrong act, or believes that it is a right or innocent act, he is exonerated. Where one man kills another under the persuasion that he is doing a good action, he is not liable to punishment, for he knows not the distinction between right and wrong, and upon that point is insane.

Bosanquet, J.—I am clearly of opinion that this is no legal defence.

Vaughan, J.—Where is the evidence that it is not a crime in the prisoner's own country? But if it is not a crime there, that does not amount to a defence here. Numbers have been most improperly executed if it is a defence.

The prisoner, after the examination of some witnesses on his behalf, from whose statements it appeared that the witnesses for the prosecution acted under the influence of spite and ill will, was found

Not guilty.

Comments and Questions

1. If the prospective offender does not know that an act is proscribed, or even wrong in some sense, is punishing her for her ignorance useful or fair? Why should it matter that her lack of awareness that an act is wrong results from ignorance rather than from insanity?

2. Mistake of fact can be an excuse. For example, if a classmate picks up your casebook, thinking it is his, he is not guilty of larceny. How and why is this different from the rule in *Esop*?

Section Three. Authorized Makers of Penal-Corrective Law and Their Appropriate Collaborative Roles

In this section, we consider the appropriate roles of legislative bodies and courts in the creation and interpretation of criminal prohibitions. In

Anglo-American legal systems, legislative bodies have generally superseded courts as the primary source of these prohibitions. The earlier tradition of common-law or judge-made crimes is now widely disapproved. Nevertheless, often in dispute is whether a court is merely *applying* a statute to a new fact situation, thus properly assuming the role of interpreting the prohibition, or whether it is *extending* the statute, thus improperly usurping the legislature's role of creating crimes.

———

KEELER v. SUPERIOR COURT

Supreme Court of California, 1970.
2 Cal.3d 619, 470 P.2d 617, 87 Cal.Rptr. 481.

MOSK, JUSTICE.

In this proceeding for writ of prohibition we are called upon to decide whether an unborn but viable fetus is a "human being" within the meaning of the California statute defining murder (Pen.Code, § 187). We conclude that the Legislature did not intend such a meaning, and that for us to construe the statute to the contrary and apply it to this petitioner would exceed our judicial power and deny petitioner due process of law.

The evidence received at the preliminary examination may be summarized as follows: Petitioner and Teresa Keeler obtained an interlocutory decree of divorce on September 27, 1968. They had been married for 16 years. Unknown to petitioner, Mrs. Keeler was then pregnant by one Ernest Vogt, whom she had met earlier that summer. She subsequently began living with Vogt in Stockton, but concealed the fact from petitioner. Petitioner was given custody of their two daughters, aged 12 and 13 years, and under the decree Mrs. Keeler had the right to take the girls on alternate weekends.

On February 23, 1969, Mrs. Keeler was driving on a narrow mountain road in Amador County after delivering the girls to their home. She met petitioner driving in the opposite direction; he blocked the road with his car, and she pulled over to the side. He walked to her vehicle and began speaking to her. He seemed calm, and she rolled down her window to hear him. He said, "I hear you're pregnant. If you are you had better stay away from the girls and from here." She did not reply, and he opened the car door; as she later testified, "He assisted me out of the car. . . . [I]t wasn't roughly at this time." Petitioner then looked at her abdomen and became "extremely upset." He said, "You sure are. I'm going to stomp it out of you." He pushed her against the car, shoved his knee into her abdomen, and struck her in the face with several blows. She fainted, and when she regained consciousness petitioner had departed.

Mrs. Keeler drove back to Stockton, and the police and medical assistance were summoned. She had suffered substantial facial injuries, as well as extensive bruising of the abdominal wall. A Caesarian section was performed and the fetus was examined *in utero*. Its head was found to be severely fractured, and it was delivered stillborn. The pathologist gave as his opinion that the cause of death was skull fracture with consequent cerebral hemorrhaging, that death would have been immediate, and that the injury could have been the result of force applied to the mother's abdomen. There was no air in the fetus' lungs, and the umbilical cord was intact.

Upon delivery the fetus weighed five pounds and was 18 inches in length. Both Mrs. Keeler and her obstetrician testified that fetal movements had been observed prior to February 23, 1969. The evidence was in conflict as to the estimated age of the fetus; the expert testimony on the point, however, concluded "with reasonable medical certainty" that the fetus had developed to the stage of viability, i.e., that in the event of premature birth on the date in question it would have had a 75 percent to 96 percent chance of survival.

An information was filed charging petitioner, in Count I, with committing the crime of murder (Pen.Code, § 187) in that he did "unlawfully kill a human being, to wit Baby Girl VOGT, with malice aforethought." . . .

Penal Code section 187 provides: "Murder is the unlawful killing of a human being, with malice aforethought." The dispositive question is whether the fetus which petitioner is accused of killing was, on February 23, 1969, a "human being" within the meaning of this statute. If it was not, petitioner cannot be charged with its "murder" and prohibition will lie. . . .

We conclude that in declaring murder to be the unlawful and malicious killing of a "human being" the Legislature of 1850 intended that term to have the settled common law meaning of a person who had been born alive, and did not intend the act of feticide—as distinguished from abortion—to be an offense under the laws of California.

Nothing occurred between the years 1850 and 1872 to suggest that in adopting the new Penal Code on the latter date the Legislature entertained any different intent. . . .

The People urge, however, that the sciences of obstetrics and pediatrics have greatly progressed since 1872, to the point where with proper medical care a normally developed fetus prematurely born at 28 weeks or more has an excellent chance of survival, i.e., is "viable"; that the common law requirement of live birth to prove the fetus had become a "human being" who may be the victim of murder is no longer in accord with scientific fact, since an unborn but viable fetus is now fully capable of independent life; and that one who unlawfully and maliciously terminates such a life should therefore be liable to prosecution for murder under section 187. We may grant the premises of this argument; indeed, we neither deny nor denigrate the vast progress of medicine in the century since the enactment of the Penal Code. But we cannot join in the conclusion sought to be deduced: we cannot hold this petitioner to answer for murder by reason of his alleged act of killing an unborn—even though viable—fetus. To such a charge there are two insuperable obstacles, one "jurisdictional" and the other constitutional.

[The court then held that in California the creation of crimes is a task for the legislature and that judicial enlargement of § 187 would violate the separation of powers.]

The second obstacle to the proposed judicial enlargement of section 187 is the guarantee of due process of law. Assuming *arguendo* that we have the power to adopt the new construction of this statute as the law of California, such a ruling, by constitutional command, could operate only prospectively, and thus could not in any event reach the conduct of petitioner on February 23, 1969.

The first essential of due process is fair warning of the act which is made punishable as a crime. "That the terms of a penal statute creating a new offense must be sufficiently explicit to inform those who are subject to it what conduct on their part will render them liable to its penalties, is a well-recognized requirement, consonant alike with ordinary notions of fair play and the settled rules of law." (Connally v. General Constr. Co. (1926) 269 U.S. 385, 391, 46 S.Ct. 126, 127.)   .   .   .

.   .   . When a new penal statute is applied retrospectively to make punishable an act which was not criminal at the time it was performed, the defendant has been given no advance notice consistent with due process. And precisely the same effect occurs when such an act is made punishable under a preexisting statute but by means of an unforeseeable *judicial* enlargement thereof. (Bouie v. City of Columbia (1964) 378 U.S. 347, 84 S.Ct. 1697.)

In *Bouie* two Negroes took seats in the restaurant section of a South Carolina drugstore; no notices were posted restricting the area to whites only. When the defendants refused to leave upon demand, they were arrested and convicted of violating a criminal trespass statute which prohibited entry on the property of another "after notice" forbidding such conduct. Prior South Carolina decisions had emphasized the necessity of proving such notice to support a conviction under the statute. The South Carolina Supreme Court nevertheless affirmed the convictions, construing the statute to prohibit not only the act of entering after notice not to do so but also the wholly different act of remaining on the property after receiving notice to leave.

The United States Supreme Court reversed the convictions, holding that the South Carolina court's ruling was "unforeseeable" and when an "unforeseeable state-court construction of a criminal statute is applied retroactively to subject a person to criminal liability for past conduct, the effect is to deprive him of due process of law in the sense of fair warning that his contemplated conduct constitutes a crime." Analogizing to the prohibition against retrospective penal legislation, the high court reasoned "Indeed, an unforeseeable judicial enlargement of a criminal statute, applied retroactively, operates precisely like an ex post facto law, such as Art. I, § 10, of the Constitution forbids. An ex post facto law has been defined by this Court as one 'that makes an action done before the passing of the law, and which was *innocent* when done, criminal; and punishes such action,' or 'that *aggravates a crime,* or makes it *greater* than it was, when committed.' Calder v. Bull, 3 Dall. 386, 390. If a state legislature is barred by the Ex Post Facto Clause from passing such a law, it must follow that a State Supreme Court is barred by the Due Process Clause from achieving precisely the same result by judicial construction. Cf. Smith v. Cahoon, 283 U.S. 553, 565, 51 S.Ct. 582, 586. The fundamental principle that 'the required criminal law must have existed when the conduct in issue occurred,' Hall, General Principles of Criminal Law (2d ed. 1960), at 58–59, must apply to bar retroactive criminal prohibitions emanating from courts as well as from legislatures. If a judicial construction of a criminal statute is 'unexpected and indefensible by reference to the law which had been expressed prior to the conduct in issue,' it must not be given retroactive effect. Id., at 61."

The court remarked in conclusion that "Application of this rule is particularly compelling where, as here, the petitioners' conduct cannot be deemed improper or immoral." In the case at bar the conduct with which petitioner is charged is certainly "improper" and "immoral," and it is not contended he was exercising a constitutionally favored right. But the matter is simply one of degree, and it cannot be denied that the guarantee of due process extends to violent as well as peaceful men. The issue remains, would the judicial enlargement of section 187 now proposed have been foreseeable to this petitioner? . . .

Turning to the case law, we find no reported decision of the California courts which should have given petitioner notice that the killing of an unborn but viable fetus was prohibited by section 187. . . .

We conclude that the judicial enlargement of section 187 now urged upon us by the People would not have been foreseeable to this petitioner, and hence that its adoption at this time would deny him due process of law.

Let a peremptory writ of prohibition issue restraining respondent court from taking any further proceedings on Count I of the information, charging petitioner with the crime of murder.

BURKE, ACTING CHIEF JUSTICE (dissenting).

The majority hold that "Baby Girl" Vogt, who, according to medical testimony, had reached the 35th week of development, had a 96 percent chance of survival, and was "definitely" alive and viable at the time of her death, nevertheless was not a "human being" under California's homicide statutes. In my view, in so holding, the majority . . . frustrate the express intent of the Legislature, and defy reason, logic and common sense. . . .

The majority opinion suggests that we are confined to common law concepts, and to the common law definition of murder or manslaughter. However, the Legislature, in Penal Code sections 187 and 192, has defined those offenses for us: homicide is the unlawful killing of a "human being." Those words need not be frozen in place as of any particular time, but must be fairly and reasonably interpreted by this court to promote justice and to carry out the evident purposes of the Legislature in adopting a homicide statute. Thus, Penal Code section 4, which was enacted in 1872 along with sections 187 and 192, provides: "The rule of the common law, that penal statutes are to be strictly construed, has no application to this Code. All its provisions are to be construed according to the fair import of their terms, with a view to effect its objects and to promote justice." . . .

We commonly conceive of human existence as a spectrum stretching from birth to death. However, if this court properly might expand the definition of "human being" at one end of that spectrum, we may do so at the other end. Consider the following example: All would agree that "Shooting or otherwise damaging a corpse is not homicide. . . . " (Perkins, Criminal Law (2d ed. 1969) ch. 2, § 1, p. 31.) In other words, a corpse is not considered to be a "human being" and thus cannot be the subject of a "killing" as those terms are used in homicide statutes. However, it is readily apparent that our concepts of what constitutes a "corpse" have been and are being continually modified by advances in the field of medicine, including new techniques for life revival, restoration and resuscitation such as artificial respiration, open heart massage, transfusions, transplants and a variety of life-restoring stimulants, drugs and new surgical methods. Would this court ignore these developments and exonerate the killer of an apparently "drowned" child merely because that child would have been pronounced dead in 1648 or 1850? Obviously not. Whether a homicide occurred in that case would be determined by medical testimony regarding the capability of the child to have survived prior to the defendant's act. And that is precisely the test which this court should adopt in the instant case.

The common law reluctance to characterize the killing of a quickened fetus as a homicide was based solely upon a presumption that the fetus would have been born dead. . . . Based upon the state of the medical art in the 17th, 18th and 19th centuries, that presumption may have been well-founded. However, as we approach the 21st century, it has become apparent that "This presumption is not only contrary to common experience and the ordinary course of nature, but it is contrary to the usual rule with respect to presumptions followed in this state." [People v. Chavez, 77 Cal.App.2d 621, 626, 176 P.2d 92, 95 (1947).]

There are no accurate statistics disclosing fetal death rates in "common law England," although the foregoing presumption of death indicates a significantly high death experience. On the other hand, in California the fetal death rate in 1968 is estimated to be 12 deaths in 1,000, a ratio which would have given Baby Girl Vogt a 98.8 percent chance of survival. (California Statistical Abstract (1969) Table E–3, p. 65.) If, as I have contended, the term "human being" in our homicide statutes is a fluid concept to be defined in accordance with present conditions, then there can be no question that the term should include the fully viable fetus.

The majority suggest that to do so would improperly create some new offense. However, the offense of murder is no new offense. Contrary to the majority opinion, the Legislature has not "defined the crime of murder in California to apply only to the unlawful and malicious killing one who has been born alive." Instead, the Legislature simply used the broad term "human being" and directed the courts to construe that term according to its "fair import" with a view to effect the objects of the homicide statutes and promote justice. (Pen.Code, § 4.) What justice will be promoted, what objects effectuated, by construing "human being" as excluding Baby Girl Vogt and her unfortunate successors? Was defendant's brutal act of stomping her to death any less an act of homicide than the murder of a newly born baby? No one doubts that the term "human being" would include the elderly or dying persons whose potential for life has nearly lapsed; their proximity to death is deemed immaterial. There is no sound reason for denying the viable fetus, with its unbounded potential for life, the same status.

The majority also suggest that such an interpretation of our homicide statutes would deny defendant "fair warning" that his act was punishable as a crime. Aside from the absurdity of the underlying premise that defendant consulted Coke, Blackstone or Hale before kicking Baby Girl Vogt to death, it is clear that defendant had adequate notice that his act could constitute homicide. Due process only precludes prosecution under a new statute insufficiently explicit regarding the specific conduct proscribed, or under a preexisting statute "by means of an unforeseeable *judicial* enlargement thereof."

Our homicide statutes have been in effect in this state since 1850. The fact that the California courts have not been called upon to determine the precise question before us does not render "unforeseeable" a decision which determines that a viable fetus is a "human being" under those statutes. Can defendant really claim surprise that a 5-pound, 18-inch, 34-week-old, living, viable child is considered to be a human being? . . .

SULLIVAN, J., concurs [in dissent].

UNITED STATES v. WILTBERGER

Supreme Court of the United States, 1820.
18 U.S. (5 Wheat.) 76.

MR. CHIEF JUSTICE MARSHALL delivered the opinion of the Court. . . .

The rule that penal laws are to be construed strictly, is perhaps not much less old than construction itself. It is founded on the tenderness of the law for the rights of individuals; and on the plain principle that the power of punishment is vested in the legislative, not in the judicial department. It is the legislature, not the Court, which is to define a crime, and ordain its punishment.

It is said, that notwithstanding this rule, the intention of the law maker must govern in the construction of penal, as well as other statutes. This is true. But this is not a new independent rule which subverts the old. It is a modification of the ancient maxim, and amounts to this, that though penal laws are to be construed strictly, they are not to be construed so strictly as to defeat the obvious intention of the legislature. The maxim is not to be so applied as to narrow the words of the statute to the exclusion of cases which those words, in their ordinary acceptation, or in that sense in which the legislature has obviously used them, would comprehend. The intention of the legislature is to be collected from the words they employ. Where there is no ambiguity in the words, there is no room for construction. The case must be a strong one indeed, which would justify a Court in departing from the plain meaning of words, especially in a penal act, in search of an intention which the words themselves did not suggest. To determine that a case is within the intention of a statute, its language must authorize us to say so. It would be dangerous, indeed, to carry the principle, that a case which is within the reason or mischief of a statute, is within its provisions, so far as to punish a crime not enumerated in the statute, because it is of equal atrocity, or of kindred character, with those which are enumerated. If this principle has ever been recognized in expounding criminal law, it has been in cases of considerable irritation, which it would be unsafe to consider as precedents forming a general rule for other cases. . . .

PREUSS, PUNISHMENT BY ANALOGY IN NATIONAL SOCIALIST PENAL LAW

26 J.Am.Inst.Crim.L. & Criminology 847, 847–48 (1936).

By an act of June 28, 1935, which has been hailed as "a milestone on the road to a National Socialist penal law," the Government of the Reich has provided that:

> Whoever commits an action which the law declares to be punishable or which is deserving of punishment according to the fundamental idea of a penal law and the sound perception of the people, shall be punished. If no determinate penal law is directly applicable to the action, it shall be punished according to the law, the basic idea of which fits it best.

Thus the principle *nullum crimen, nulla poena sine lege,* which stood at the very head of the Penal Code of 1871 and was included among the fundamental rights of Germans guaranteed by the Weimar Constitution, has been abolished. The new law permits the judge to impose a penalty for acts which, although not expressly made criminal by the written law, are analogous to acts which are declared to be punishable, provided that they are condemned by the popular sense of right and by the fundamental legal conception upon which the statutory prohibition is based. Originally intended as a protection to the individual against judicial arbitrariness, the principle *nulla poena sine lege* had, it is claimed, become "the Magna Charta of the criminal." With the law of June 28, Dr. Hans Frank declares, "a development is closed which, on the one hand, forced the judge to formal-juristic decisions unrelated to real life, and, on the other, gave to the criminal the opportunity to slip through the meshes of the law by crafty manoeuvers, and to avoid just punishment."

Comments and Questions

1. Recall that when law is used as a grievance-remedial instrument, courts have served as a substantial source of governing law. Why is this judicial role acceptable in the grievance-remedial mode but not in the penal-corrective mode?

2. Although courts no longer create crimes, they frequently modify the criminal law by creating excuses. One notable example is the insanity defense. Is the creation of excuses an appropriate activity for courts?

Section Four. Structures and Processes for Applying Penal-Corrective Law and Techniques

If the penal-corrective instrument consisted only of prohibitions, excuses, and prescribed penalties, it would be fundamentally deficient. The penal law is not self-executing. Rather, it requires the participation of many individuals as police, prosecutors, magistrates, grand jurors, judges, petit jurors, and prison officials. An individual in one of these public positions is obviously important for the role she plays in processing an offender through the criminal justice system. Equally important, however, is her decision that a particular suspect should not proceed further in the criminal justice system. Police, prosecutors, juries, and judges all perform a *screening function*. Decisions will often be based upon the suspect's apparent guilt or innocence, but they may be based on other factors as well. Some of the discretion possessed by police, prosecutors, juries, and judges is probably necessary, but ensuring that that discretion is prudently and fairly exercised is difficult. The readings in this section examine the exercise of discretion, but before we turn to them, summarizing the steps in a typical state criminal proceeding may be useful.

The following page provides an overview of the criminal justice system. Cases generally enter the criminal justice system through the police. A crime may be observed by the police or reported to the police. Perhaps further investigation is needed, but perhaps not. At some point, an *arrest* is made, and the adjudicative process begins. Shortly after the arrest, the suspect will be taken before a judicial officer for a *preliminary hearing*, the purpose of which is to determine whether there is probable cause to believe the arrestee has committed an offense. If the judicial officer does not find probable cause to believe an offense has been committed, he will order the release of the person arrested. If, on the other hand, the prosecutor has shown probable cause, the judicial officer will decide whether the defendant should be held in jail, released on bail, or released "on her own recognizance," which means released upon her promise to appear when next summoned.

If the crime is a serious one (i.e., a felony as opposed to a misdemeanor), in many states the prosecution cannot proceed further until the defendant has been indicted by a grand jury. The grand jury will be a body of twelve to twenty-three laypeople who will decide whether enough evidence has been gathered to justify putting the defendant on trial. Usually, only the prosecution's evidence is heard by the grand jury, and if the grand jury is satisfied by the evidence, it will return an *indictment* (also called a true bill), which formally charges the defendant with one or more offenses.

After indictment, or after the prosecutor prepares an *information* if the charge is only a misdemeanor, the defendant will appear to plead to the charges. At this proceeding, usually called an *arraignment*, the defendant may move to quash the indictment (or information). Like the defendant's demurrer in a civil case, this motion challenges the legal sufficiency of the charges. If the motion is denied, the defendant will plead either guilty or not guilty. If she pleads guilty, she will be held for sentencing. If she pleads not guilty, she will be held for trial.

A GENERAL VIEW OF THE CRIMINAL JUSTICE SYSTEM

This chart seeks to present a simple yet comprehensive view of the movement of cases through the criminal justice system. Procedures in individual jurisdictions may vary from the pattern shown here. The differing weights of the line indicate the relative volumes of cases disposed of at various points in the system, but this is only suggestive since no nationwide data of this sort exists.

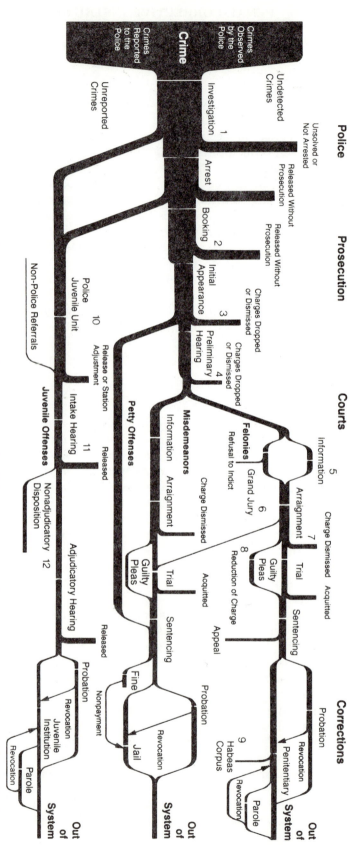

Crime

- Crimes Observed by the Police
- Crimes Reported to the Police
- Undetected Crimes
- Unreported Crimes

Police

- Investigation 1
- Arrest
- Booking 2
- Unsolved or Not Arrested
- Released Without Prosecution
- Released Without Prosecution

Prosecution

- Initial Appearance 3
- Preliminary Hearing 4
- Charges Dropped or Dismissed
- Charges Dropped or Dismissed
- Non-Police Referrals
- Police Juvenile Unit 10
- Release or Station Adjustment

Courts

- Information 5
- Grand Jury 6
- Refusal to Indict
- Information
- Arraignment 7
- Arraignment
- Charge Dismissed Acquitted
- Charge Dismissed
- Charge Dismissed Acquitted
- Felonies
- Misdemeanors
- Petty Offenses
- Intake Hearing 11
- Released
- Juvenile Offenses
- Nonadjudicatory Disposition 12
- Reduction of Charge 8
- Guilty Pleas
- Guilty Pleas
- Trial
- Trial
- Acquitted
- Sentencing
- Sentencing
- Appeal
- Adjudicatory Hearing

Corrections

- Probation
- Penitentiary 9
- Habeas Corpus
- Parole
- Revocation
- Revocation
- Probation
- Nonpayment
- Fine
- Jail
- Revocation
- Juvenile Institution
- Revocation
- Parole
- Revocation

Out of System

1 May continue until trial.

2 Administrative record of arrest. First step at which temporary release on bail may be available.

3 Before magistrate, commissioner, or justice of peace. Formal notice of charge, advice of rights. Bail set. Summary trials for petty offenses usually conducted here without further processing.

4 Preliminary testing of evidence against defendant. Charge may be reduced. No separate preliminary hearing for misdemeanors in some systems.

5 Charge filed by prosecutor on basis of information submitted by police or citizens. Alternative to grand jury indictment; often used in felonies, almost always in misdemeanors.

6 Reviews whether Government evidence sufficient to justify trial. Some States have no grand jury system; others seldom use it.

7 Appearance for plea; defendant elects trial by judge or jury (if available); counsel for indigent usually appointed here in felonies. Often not at all in other cases.

8 Charge may be reduced at any time prior to trial in return for plea of guilty or for other reasons.

9 Challenge on constitutional grounds to legality of detention. May be sought at any point in process.

10 Police often hold informal hearings, dismiss or adjust many cases without further processing.

11 Probation officer decides desirability of further court action.

12 Welfare agency, social services, counseling, medical care, etc., for cases where adjudicatory handling not needed.

At trial, the defendant may represent herself or may be represented by an attorney. If she cannot afford an attorney, the court will appoint one for her or assign the case to the public defender's office. *Opening statements*, first by the prosecutor and then by the defense attorney, begin the trial. The prosecutor then presents his evidence, attempting to prove the defendant's guilt beyond a reasonable doubt. When the prosecutor has finished his presentation, the defendant's lawyer can move to have the case dismissed because of the insufficiency of the evidence. If the court grants this motion, the trial will be over and the defendant will be released.

If the defendant's motion is not granted, the defendant's lawyer will then present the defendant's evidence, if any. The defendant need not testify, and no adverse inference may be drawn from her decision not to testify. After all the evidence has been presented, the defendant's lawyer can move for a directed verdict of not guilty. If the motion is not granted, the prosecution and defense will make *closing arguments*. The judge will then *instruct* the jury on the law relevant to the case. The judge will explain the elements of the crime charged and tell the jurors that to convict the defendant, they must find that every element of the crime has been proved beyond a reasonable doubt.

If the jury returns a *verdict* of guilty, the defendant will be sentenced. Unless the case is one in which a death sentence might be imposed, the judge rather than the jury will usually sentence the defendant. Usually, he is guided by a *presentence report* written by a probation officer who has interviewed the defendant, the defendant's family and employer, if any, the victim, and sometimes other people who have information concerning the offense or the defendant.

After the defendant is convicted and sentenced, her lawyer may *appeal* to a higher court. If the appellate court finds prejudicial error in the conduct of the defendant's trial, it will reverse and remand; if the appellate court finds the evidence insufficient, it will reverse and dismiss the indictment. Otherwise, it will affirm the defendant's conviction.

The decision of the highest court of the state is usually final. If, however, the defendant claims that her federal constitutional rights have been violated, she can ask the United States Supreme Court to review her case and reverse her conviction. It is unlikely that the United States Supreme Court will decide to review the defendant's case, but she has one last chance at a reversal: she may file a *habeas corpus petition* in a federal district court, again alleging a violation of her federal constitutional rights. Upon the finding of such a violation, the federal court may order the state to either retry the defendant or release her.

We turn now to the role that discretion plays in some of these stages of the criminal process.

A. The Police

C. SILBERMAN, CRIMINAL VIOLENCE,
CRIMINAL JUSTICE
229–37 (1978).*

If they are to be effective, policemen need more than the random information they obtain from the people they arrest; they require more regular, and more reliable, sources. Bartenders, cabbies, pawnbrokers, and other "respectable" types represent one kind of source; professional criminals represent another. In New York police circles, "information" is a technical term meaning "a deliberate, sub rosa identification of a crime or perpetrator by some individual who himself is involved or on the borderline of criminal activity."

The relationship always is reciprocal, although the quid pro quo given the criminal in exchange for information varies from officer to officer, and from criminal to criminal. Frequently, information is given the police in return for some past favor or favors—reducing a charge to some lesser offense or dropping it altogether, recommending probation, finding a job for a youthful offender or suggesting that he be placed in a drug rehabilitation program. . . .

ITEM: We stopped a well-known prostitute and, during a long and basically friendly conversation, asked her about a boyfriend who reportedly was selling pills from the hospital where he worked; would she arrange for him to sell some drugs to an undercover policeman? Too risky, she thought, but she would see if she could find anything out. As we left, one of the patrolmen turned to me and said, "She owes me a year in the workhouse; I've busted her three times for prostitution, and she's only drawn eighteen days." . . .

Police relationships with the underworld have always been shrouded in secrecy, and their management always has been a source of concern to conscientious police administrators because of the enormous temptation to corruption that such relationships entail. Police officers often pay off their informants in liquor or drugs; to do so, they hold back some of the heroin or cocaine they seize when they make an arrest.

It is a small step from violating departmental regulations in that manner and holding back larger amounts of heroin to sell on one's own account. In the notorious "French connection" case, New York City narcotics detectives diverted 188 pounds of heroin and 31 pounds of cocaine to their own use, making the Narcotics Bureau's Special Investigating Unit (SIU) perhaps the largest heroin and cocaine dealer in the city. (Some students of law enforcement would assign that honor to the New York office of the old Federal Bureau of Narcotics.)

Most law enforcement officials continue to believe in the value of criminal informants, relying on a variety of administrative devices to hold corruption to a minimum. "Of course it would be nice to have priests, nuns, and rabbis provide information, but they're not involved in crime," one official says. "The people who can tell you about crime are those involved in it. It's an unpleasant business." But because of the secrecy surrounding the use of criminal informants, no one—*no one*—knows whether the gains are worth the cost. . . .

Although police derive their self-image from playing cops and robbers, their other functions are every bit as important and actually predate their role in crime control. Initially, the police were more concerned with maintaining order than with catching criminals, which was the responsibility of the individual citizen. Before police departments as we know them began to take shape in the second quarter of the nineteenth century, cities of any size drafted citizens to serve on the nightly watch. Their responsibility, as an old Boston ordinance put it, was to "walk the rounds in and about the streets, wharves, lanes, and principal inhabited parts, within each town, to prevent any danger by fire, and to see that good order is kept."

Maintaining order remains a major police responsibility; the great majority of the calls patrol officers receive involve breaches of the peace or requests for help, rather than reports of crimes in the usual sense of the term. In poor neighborhoods, in particular, police spend large amounts of time responding to "family (or domestic) disputes"—arguments and fights between relatives, lovers, friends, and acquaintances.
. . .

In dealing with a domestic dispute, a tavern or street-corner brawl, an incipient riot, or any other disturbance, enforcing the law usually is not the police's main concern. Their job is to restore order—to "deal with the situation" and return it to some semblance of normality. Since they have almost unlimited discretion in how they handle breaches of the peace, police vary enormously in the techniques they use and the skill with which they use them. When he was commanding a precinct house, a retired New York City police official told me, he knew that if he sent one particular patrol car to the scene of a barroom brawl, the result would be at least one injured cop and two civilians in the hospital; if he sent a different team, they would manage to settle the brawl without any injuries, and without any arrests. . . .

ITEM (from report of a night on patrol): At 7:50 P.M., we were signaled to stop by the driver of a city transit authority bus. The driver (white) told us that a passenger (black), seated in the rear, had been playing his tape recorder very loudly and had refused to lower it or turn it off despite the driver's repeated requests, and despite the fact that the bus had a sign prohibiting such noisemaking. We got on the bus and went to the back. The man in question, a big and tough-looking twenty-year-old, had turned off the machine before we came aboard. S. came on mild: "What's this all about?" he asked. "I can play this if I want to," the young man answered. When S. pointed to the sign, the man argued, not very convincingly, that it referred to radios and phonographs, not tape recorders. Besides, he added, lots of people in the bus were smoking, and that was forbidden, too. S. turned around and told everyone who was smoking to put out their cigarettes; half a dozen butts hit the floor. The driver came back to tell us again that the passenger had refused his requests to turn the thing off; S. gently suggested that the driver go back to his seat and let him handle it. "Come on," S. told the guy in a low tone, "be reasonable. You don't have to play that thing just to make a point; you're embarrassing your girl friend over nothing." (She did look a *little* embarrassed.) After some more fuming, the passenger agreed not to play the machine and not to "mess" with the driver; "I'm not petty," he said. S. went back to the driver and asked him not to talk to the passenger again unless he started acting up. We got off the bus and it went on its way. "Five or six years ago I'd probably have arrested him," S said; he was pleased that he had been able to settle the situation without an arrest, which would have meant a noisy argument at best and quite possibly a fight. Basically, he explained, he had appealed to the guy's pride—he was making a fool of himself in front of his girl and all those passengers for nothing—and by keeping the driver away and ordering smokers to put out their cigarettes, he had made it possible for the man to back down without losing face.

"Bullshitting"—the police term for the ability to use language as an instrument of persuasion—does not always suffice. When a domestic dispute is violent or noisy and neither party will succumb to police blandishments, one solution is to bring both parties to the station house under the threat of arrest. "They listen better when they're in front of the desk," a veteran officer told me with a smile. Understandably so: the jail cells are visible from the desk in his station house. Bringing combatants there under the threat of arrest forces them to stop fighting each other and to concentrate instead on how to get out of the police station. Most of the time, therefore, bringing them in is all that has to be done; the parties calm down and agree to settle their dispute amicably, and they are released without any charges being filed.

There are times, of course, when police *do* arrest someone. Usually, they regard the arrest as a way of restoring order—of "dealing with the situation"—rather than as a means of enforcing the law as such. The formal charge that is lodged may *justify* the arrest, but it rarely is the *reason* for the arrest. The real reason is to stop a fight; to get a dangerous person off the street or out of the house before he follows through on a threat of violence; to remove a drunk who is standing at a busy intersection, shouting obscenities at and otherwise harassing and frightening female motorists; to prevent a tavern or street-corner brawl from escalating into a riot; to get a drunk off the street before he freezes to death; or any number of equally urgent considerations. The police are expected to dissolve problems, not solve them, and arresting someone can be a useful tool in that process.

ITEM (from notes of a night on patrol): Another call came, to check out a woman with a gun. This was a potential crime in progress, and M. used his siren and lights as we went to the address. Four young black men were standing in the driveway and one of them came up to our car. "I was in a fight with this dude, see, and he went to get his mother, and she came back with this gun and started waving it around." The "dude" was his cousin, and the woman his aunt; she had left in her car just as we turned into the block. We went the way the complainant pointed, after learning that the woman had a small revolver; we found her driving slowly down the block behind the one we had come up. M. pulled her over and went quickly to the car's front door, asking, "Where's the gun?" "In the purse," she said, and got out of the car at M.'s request. He looked inside the purse and found it, loaded with six .22 bullets. After taking some more information from the woman, he made a call for a wagon to pick her up.

Over dinner, M. explained that he had arrested the woman just to get her off the street for the night; he was afraid that if she were not locked up for a few hours, she would return and renew her dispute with the complainant. M. had no interest in seeing her convicted; he felt certain that her anger would have cooled by morning, when she would be released on bail. (M. had made certain that she would be able to post bail before arresting her, and had explained the procedure to her.)

Police arrest people, in short, not only when they have probable cause to believe that the offender has committed a crime, but also when an arrest appears to be the best way to handle a situation that will not brook delay. Given the here-and-now urgency of police work, a certain lack of concern for the niceties of legal procedure is almost inevitable. If arresting one party to a fight and sending the other one home will stop a fracas he fears may turn into a large-scale brawl or small riot, an officer could not care less which of the two combatants is at fault; his job is to restore order. To the district attorney or defense counsel or judge, on the other hand, not to mention the defendant, it makes all the difference in the world whether the officer arrested the "right" individual or the "wrong" one. Much of the tension and misunderstanding between police and lawyers and judges stems from the latter group's failure to understand the degree to which police actions are rooted in exigencies of the moment, in which reflection not only is impossible but may be terribly dangerous as well—to the officer or to the parties involved.

B. The Prosecutor

B. FORST, J. LUCIANOVIC & S. COX, WHAT HAPPENS AFTER ARREST?
89 (1977).

We set out to learn about police operations by posing the question: What happens after arrest? What happens after arrest, most often, is that the prosecutor drops the case.

J. SIRICA, TO SET THE RECORD STRAIGHT
41–42 (1979).*

The case involved a former employee of the federal government, a white man, who had schemed to have his wife raped and murdered by an accomplice, a black man, in order to gain control of her money. The two men first agreed that she would be killed after a shopping trip. But the husband called that off, apparently because his son was to come along. He didn't want the boy to witness his mother's murder.

Instead, a second plan was put into effect. The man and his wife had dinner at a waterfront restaurant, and as they were leaving the parking lot, the accomplice held them up at gun point. He instructed them to drive to the East Capitol Street Bridge. While they drove, the wife reassured her husband, who of course already knew the scenario, that they would be unharmed if they co-operated with what she assumed was simply a robbery attempt. At the lonely bridge site near the Potomac River, the accomplice took the wife out of the car, raped her, shot her twice in the head, and then fled the scene. The husband drove to a nearby gas station to report the crime.

Brilliant work by the Metropolitan Police Department and the U.S. attorney's office broke the case and produced separate first-degree-murder and conspiracy indictments against the two men. Prior to his trial, the husband claimed that the accomplice had been blackmailing him by threatening to disclose his extramarital affair and that the murder was then planned to get the money to buy off the accomplice. In his own defense, the accomplice said that he did know the husband but had not conspired to murder the wife. The prosecutors wanted to let the husband plead guilty to a reduced charge in exchange for his testimony against the accomplice, who would then likely be convicted of premeditated murder and, at a minimum, spend the rest of his life in jail. I rejected the plea bargain, however, relying upon the legal axiom of "equal justice under law." The law states that conspirators are culpable in like degree even if one goes further in carrying out the conspiracy than the other. The two men were equally responsible for this brutal killing, in my view. And another problem was also on my mind. The husband was white; the accomplice was black. I shuddered to think what might be the reaction of Washington's large black community if the white man who planned his own wife's death was let off with a fifteen-year-to-life term while the black man might have to pay with his life. In separate trials each was convicted of first-degree murder. On appeal, my rejection of the husband's guilty plea was overturned and the case was remanded to me to accept a second-degree plea. [The appellate court held that the prosecutor had not abused his discretion in offering a reduced charge to the husband.]

———

C. The Jury

In Chapter 1 we saw how a trial judge instructs the jury on the applicable law. If the jury obviously fails to follow these instructions, the verdict may be set aside and a new trial held. Similarly, if the jury finds facts "contrary to the weight of the evidence," its verdict may be set aside and a new trial held. When the law is used as a penal-corrective instrument, however, judicial control is more limited.

The judge at trial will instruct the jury that it may convict the defendant only if the evidence proves her guilt "beyond a reasonable doubt." If the jury convicts the defendant even though the evidence of guilt was weak, the judge (or an appellate court) will overturn the conviction and dismiss the charges. But if the jury acquits the defendant, even in the face of overwhelming evidence of guilt, the court cannot touch the verdict. An acquittal in a criminal case is final.

Jurors may acquit an obviously guilty defendant for a number of reasons. They may be confused about the law. They may feel sympathy or affection for the defendant. They may dislike the statute the accused is being tried under—or even the prosecutor trying the case. What values are threatened by the jury's unqualified power to acquit in a criminal case? Are other values protected by that power?

D. The Judge

The following case synopses are similar to the probation reports available to judges at sentencing. Do you think all of the information presented is relevant to the sentencing decision? How would you sentence these defendants?

PROCEEDINGS OF THE 1971 SENTENCING INSTITUTE FOR SUPERIOR COURT JUDGES

100 Cal.Rptr. app. 16–17, 25–27, 32–34.

CASE # 1

OFFENSE: POSSESSION OF NARCOTICS (H. & S. § 11500). Defendant was arrested for assault with a deadly weapon and possession of heroin. He was found guilty by a jury for possession of heroin. The victim, who lived next door, stated that defendant entered his residence, pointed a gun at him and his family, fired it once and fled. The defendant claimed that the victim had stolen one of his guns and that he threatened the victim in order to have it returned. The defendant told the arresting officers that he kept his guns in a small overnight case in his bedroom and led the officers to it. It was open and inside was a blank starter pistol and 12 balloons containing 51 grams of heroin. The officers also found a plastic box containing syringes, needles, spoons and razor blades. Defendant was observed to have numerous fresh puncture wounds on his right arm.

PRIOR CRIMINAL HISTORY:

2/53	County Y	Burglary	Ward juvenile ct., 3 mos. camp and probation
6/56	County X	Suspicion of robbery	Released
12/56	County X	Petty theft	2 mos. county jail, 1 yr. probation
1959–65	County Z	Several drunk arrests	Fined
3/66	County Z	Assault	30 days, county jail
4/67	County Z	Possession, dangerous drugs	3 mos. county jail, 2 yrs. probation
2/71	County Z	PRESENT OFFENSE	

CASE HISTORY INFORMATION: Defendant, now age 35, is the youngest of seven children born to a Caucasian laboring class, urban family whose parents separated shortly after his birth. His mother never remarried and the family largely was supported by public welfare. He says he had a very close relationship with his mother, being the youngest child. He dropped out of school in the tenth grade to go to work as an unskilled factory worker.

He was married at the age of 20 and now has two children. The marriage was dissolved five years later in 1961. In recent years he has drifted into a homosexual mode of life, and his mannerisms, gestures and speech are now feminine. He has supported himself during the past four years working steadily as a female impersonator in night clubs. He has not maintained close contact with his mother or with his siblings, one of whom served a prison term, and reveals that there has been open conflict with them because of his homosexuality. He says that he occasionally hears from his former wife on the progress of his children, and that when he is able he sends money for their support, but that his contact has been irregular. He doesn't visit them because he feels it might be adverse for them to see him in his present homosexual status.

He has had a series of arrests and short sentences over the years beginning at the age of 17. He was made a juvenile court ward in 1953 for stealing, and placed in a boys' camp for three months. Later, as an adult, he was arrested for a variety of offenses, including assault (a fight with a homosexual in which the victim was knifed), suspicion of robbery, petty theft, and for furnishing dangerous drugs (amphetamine) to a minor. The latter offense was subsequently reduced to possession of dangerous drugs. He completed his probation successfully on the latter charge and for the past 3½ years he has had no arrest or known law violations.

He denies that he uses or is addicted to heroin and asserts that the drugs belonged to his friend. He maintains the needle marks are from the injection of vitamin supplements to give him additional energy for his performances as a female impersonator.

CASE EVALUATION: Defendant is an admitted homosexual with a long history of social maladjustment, intermixed with periods of superficial social conformity, and abstinence from crime. By embracing homosexuality, he has come to grips with his underlying problem of sexual identification, and that source of conflict seems to have been reduced in part. Coming from a broken family, the youngest of seven children, his delinquent behavior began at age 17, following partly in the footsteps of an older brother. Since then he has had several arrests and brief periods of confinement and intermittent periods of abstinence from criminal behavior. It should be noted, however, that during the past 3½ years he has had no arrests and, in fact, successfully completed probation.

Defendant obviously needs help, and the question is in what form it should take. Since he seems to do well under probationary supervision, several of those who participated in his P.C. § 1203.03 study suggested that he be placed in a specialized probationary caseload, including a testing program to determine whether he is reverting to narcotics use. Others feel that his pattern of aggressive behavior is potentially dangerous and believe that commitment to the California Rehabilitation Program would be inappropriate. They favor confinement either in the Department of Corrections or in a county penal institution.

CASE # 2

OFFENSE: FORCIBLE RAPE. Defendant picked up a 16-year-old girl and drove her to a friend's apartment where he compelled her to submit to acts of sexual intercourse and oral copulation. The victim stated that these acts were accomplished under duress by means of a switchblade knife placed at her throat. The defendant denied the circumstances of the offense and was convicted by a jury.

PRIOR CRIMINAL HISTORY:

8/66	County X	Possession of marijuana	No charges filed
5/67	County X	Burglary 2nd	Fined and placed on 2 yrs. probation
8/68	County X	Drunk driving	Fined
8/70	County X	Attempted rape	Dismissed
2/71	County X	PRESENT OFFENSE	

CASE HISTORY INFORMATION: Defendant is the second of three children from an intact Mexican-American family, who resided in Los Angeles. His parents reportedly had a good relationship and experienced no serious conflict. Defendant says that his father was not a severe disciplinarian, but that he had trouble communicating with him. He regards his mother as somewhat overprotective resulting from the fact that he was the only boy in the family. He is insecure and regards his relationship with his mother as somewhat threatening. He believes her overindulgence and protection hampered his ability to achieve independence. There is no record of overt behavioral problems either at school or at home, despite the fact the family resided in a neighborhood with a relatively high delinquency rate.

He is a high school graduate, and married his wife, who was pregnant at the time, shortly after graduation. They now have four children. Observers describe his wife as rather cold and self-centered. Defendant describes his marriage as being in a constant state of turmoil, and being unable to cope with his wife's rejection. While he describes her as emotionally and sexually cold to him, he feels she is an excellent mother.

Defendant began drinking about a year after his marriage. Unable to handle his wife's rejection, he began to find excuses to be away from home. During this period he became involved with another woman who bore him a child. He says he has contributed to that youngster's support although that is not verified. His wife became aware of this situation, and while she resented his infidelity, no effort was made to resolve the source of their conflicts. Despite their turbulent marital history, the probation officer feels that there are elements within the marriage upon which to build future stability. However, they will need professional help and family counseling to do so.

He has been steadily employed in a skilled job with the same company for the past five years. His employer values his work very highly and rates him as a very reliable employee.

His criminal history is limited. He participated in a burglary of a liquor store in 1967 with several other codefendants while under the influence of alcohol. Probation records indicate that he was not the principal instigator of the offense and he later completed his probationary term successfully. It is noted that he has had increasing problems with drinking, as reflected in part by his drunk driving arrest.

His arrest in August 1970 for attempted rape resulted in dismissal of the charges when the alleged victim, an acquaintance of his, refused to press charges. This alleged offense occurred as the aftermath of a drinking party.

With respect to this offense, he maintains that he never threatened the victim and that she willing participated in the sexual relationship. He says she wanted some money from him and when he refused, she indicated that she would "get even with him." She denies this. The probation officer's report indicates that the victim has been known to juvenile authorities for her association with "gang" activities.

CASE EVALUATION: The consulting psychologist regards defendant as a somewhat immature, sensitive young man, overwhelmed with feelings of inadequacy. His lack of emotional response, and unfulfilled satisfaction from his marriage, has led him to seek other means of finding expression for his hostility through drinking. Despite being raised in a highly delinquent area he did manage to avoid such activities. The burglary 2nd offense and others were committed while he was drinking. He did successfully complete probation despite the fact that he had the one drunk driving arrest in 1968.

The girl's questionable reputation is somewhat mitigating but the defendant's use of a knife and coercion are causes for concern. He was sent to the Department of Corrections for a P.C. § 1203.03 study and their recommendation was not unanimous. Slightly more than half of the Department of Corrections' professionals recommended that he be retained in the community, while a minority felt that prison commitment was appropriate because of the use of physical force.

> CASE # 3

OFFENSE: BURGLARY 2ND. During the night a woman noticed that a strange man was in her neighbors' house while they were away on vacation. She called the police and they apprehended defendant as he was leaving the house. Arresting officers found in his possession jewelry and coins, valued at $500, belonging to the homeowners.

PRIOR CRIMINAL HISTORY:

6/61	County Z	Petty theft/truancy	Informal probation
3/62	County Z	Petty theft/mal. mischief	Ward, juvenile ct., placed with aunt
5/64	County Z	Burglary	Boys camp-probation, released 12/64

4/66	County Y	Drunk/disorderly conduct	Fined and released
10/66	County Z	Petty theft/susp. of burg.	Co. jail 3 mos., 1 yr. probation
2/68	County Y	Petty theft	Co. jail 10 days
4/69	County Z	Burglary	Co. jail 6 mos., 2 yrs. probation
2/70	County Z	Drunk/disorderly conduct	Fined
3/71	County Z	PRESENT OFFENSE	

CASE HISTORY INFORMATION: Defendant, age 23, is the youngest of five children born to a rural Louisiana Negro family. His natural father was unknown to him but when the defendant began getting into trouble, his aunts often suggested to him that he took after his "jailbird" father. An older brother also has an extensive criminal record. His mother remarried (common-law relationship) when the defendant was four years old, and he says his stepfather was a very severe disciplinarian who was a churchgoing, devoutly religious fanatic. Defendant admits he frequently exploited existing conflict between his mother and stepfather, playing one against the other, to divert attention from his own misbehavior. The family moved in 1952 to central California where they settled in an area housing predominantly agricultural laborers. His education is limited, having dropped out of school at the age of 16 while in the ninth grade. Verified reports from school indicate that he was never a disciplinary problem, but he was a poor student and was often truant.

His record as a juvenile delinquent includes arrests for petty theft, malicious mischief, truancy, and running away from home.

He was made a juvenile court ward in 1962 at age 14, and was placed with an aunt and uncle because the court felt that his parents were unable to control him; however, he kept running away from these placements to return home. At the age of 16 he was sent to a boys' camp for violating probation, as a result of a burglary.

More recently, as an adult, he has had a number of arrests for burglary, petty theft, and drunk and disorderly conduct. While he has had several arrests, he has only served two terms in county jails, one a six-month county jail sentence for burglarizing a grocery store, and the other a three-month sentence for petty theft.

His employment record is quite spotty and largely includes short, seasonal unskilled jobs as a farm laborer and as a winery worker. He says he preferred working in the winery, but his employer dismissed him for stealing bottles of wine and for being drunk. He has had several drunk arrests and shows signs of a drinking problem, despite his youth.

He has been legally married once and blames his in-laws for the failure of the marriage. One child was born of that union and on one occasion defendant was prosecuted for failure to provide for his child. He responds that he refused to pay child support because his wife would not allow him to visit the child and therefore he took matters in his own hands. His wife and child are supported by public assistance. About six months prior to the present offense, defendant was living in a common-law relationship but declines to discuss it except to say that it terminated when he was arrested.

He says that although his mother is quite disconcerted at his repeated antisocial behavior, he nevertheless feels that she would offer him assistance if he was placed on probation. He also says he has a job offer and that he realizes his offense was foolish. He tends to blame the present offense on feeling sorry for himself, drinking and being out of work. He asserts this an isolated offense and denies any other burglaries.

CASE EVALUATION: The examining psychologist observed that defendant makes an ineffectual and inadequate response to emotional, social, intellectual and vocational demands placed upon him. While he is not mentally deficient, he does exhibit considerable ineptness, poor judgment and inadaptability. Coupled with his inadequate orientation and antisocial traits, he appears irresponsible, impulsive and hedonistic and finds it difficult to learn either from life, experience or punishment. His frustration tolerance appears low.

While he confesses to misuse of alcohol, there is no evidence that he has used drugs despite arresting officers' suspicions that his burglaries were connected with efforts to get money for drug use.

The prognosis for this individual is that of a marginal social adjustment. His criminal history has largely revolved around crimes against property rather than crimes against persons. He adjusted well to institutional life in past occasions as a juvenile and during his two county jail sentences. He also has had reasonably long intervals in which he does not get involved in serious crimes. The district attorney urges his commitment to the Department of Corrections because of his criminal record, while his mother and the public defender who represented him urge that he be given a jail term, continued on probation and placed in a specialized, close supervision caseload in order that he can be given vocational and social guidance. He was referred to the Department of Corrections for a P.C. § 1203.03 study and they recommended that he be handled on the local level.

BROWDER v. UNITED STATES

United States District Court, District of Oregon, 1975.
398 F.Supp. 1042.

SKOPIL, DISTRICT JUDGE:

Petitioner seeks habeas corpus relief under 28 U.S.C. § 2255.

Petitioner, Edward Browder, alias James Chisum-Burns, was charged by federal indictments in Oregon, Florida, and California and by federal information in Georgia with pledging stolen securities transported in interstate commerce. 18 U.S.C. § 2315. He agreed to transfer the pending out-of-district cases into Oregon for consolidated sentencing under Fed.R.Crim.P. 20. He was arraigned on all four cases before The Honorable Alfred T. Goodwin on November 4, 1970. He was represented by attorney John Flynn, who is now deceased. His pleas of guilty to all charges were accepted by the Court. On January 6, 1971, he was sentenced by The Honorable Gus J. Solomon, who imposed four ten-year terms and one five-year term, twenty-five years of which were to run consecutively.   Petitioner's motions for modification of sentence were denied.   Fed.R.Crim.P. 35.   He is presently incarcerated at the U.S. Penitentiary at McNeil Island in Washington.

Petitioner challenges the validity of his conviction and sentence on the following grounds: .   .   .

(5) The sentence imposed constituted cruel and unusual punishment and denied petitioner equal protection of the law.

Edward Browder is a 53 year old man with extensive business experience in promotion and sales.   He has a college background in aeronautical engineering.   His testimony on the witness stand revealed a degree of intelligence and a facility with the English language that would be the pride of most attorneys.   The quality of his in forma pauperis brief enhances that observation.

In 1958 Mr. Browder somehow became involved with organized crime. A crime syndicate apparently stole the bonds which he was indicted for transporting and pledging.   Browder alleges that in 1967 or 1968 he attempted to sever his connections with the syndicate.   He moved to Ashland, Oregon, from Florida and assumed the name of James Chisum-Burns.

He engaged John Flynn as his legal counsel to represent him regarding purchase of some ranch property.   Flynn is described as a "gruff, very precise, professional man" with a CPA and tax law background.   Browder was impressed with the precision and general competence with which Flynn seemed to be handling his property transaction.   So when Browder was arrested on the securities charges, he immediately contacted Flynn.
.   .   .   .

.   .   . Browder testified that Flynn told him he should avoid trial and reduce his exposure to a ten-year term by pleading guilty.   He testified that Flynn told him he could expect substantially less than ten years— probably three years.   .   .   .

Petitioner's .   .   . argument is that imposition of a twenty-five year sentence for his "white collar" property crimes constituted cruel and unusual punishment and violated equal protection of the law.

The basis for petitioner's claim is a study he conducted of 100 cases involving similar white collar crimes.   If accurate, his study contains startling statistics.   Of the 100 defendants studied, 20% received fines, probation, or suspended sentences only for acts involving $350,000,000 or more.   The others studied received light sentences for a variety of swindles in which the public became victim to members of the Mafia, labor union officials, mayors, attorneys, stock brokers, business executives, bankers, a former state Attorney General, a governor, a federal judge, and others.

I can only speculate on the motivations for sentences rendered in the individual cases listed.   As Mr. Browder observes, "wherein the greater the offense against capital, the lesser the punishment imposed by the sentencing court".   If Mr. Browder's study is accurate, the pattern of sentencing revealed is deplorable.

If there is a logic to this paradox, it eludes me.   I cannot reconcile a policy of sending poorly educated burglars from the ghetto to jail when men in the highest positions of public trust and authority receive judicial coddling when they are caught fleecing their constituencies. Penology's recent enchantment with rehabilitation as a wholesale justification for imprisonment has dissolved in the face of numerous studies proving that rehabilitation rarely occurs. A minority of the prison population are rightfully locked up because they are too dangerous to release. If we are to justify imprisonment for the rest, it must be on the grounds of punishment or deterrence. And if this is our premise, the white collar criminal must come to expect equal or greater treatment than the common, non-violent thief. The consequences of a white collar property crime tend to reach a higher magnitude in direct proportion to the level of status and power held by the criminal involved. The men Browder studied abused their influence to defraud thousands of people throughout the country out of millions of dollars. Apparently this has been tolerated through light sentencing because of the staggering proportions of the crime.

The defect in Browder's reasoning is his conclusion that because other white collar criminals have been receiving disparate treatment, he should too. As a matter of law, I cannot review the propriety of the sentence he received. The sentence was within statutory limits. 18 U.S.C. § 2315. Therefore it was a constitutional product of the trial court's discretion. United States v. Floyd, 477 F.2d 217 (10th Cir.1973); Gurleski v. United States, 405 F.2d 253 (5th Cir.1968). As a matter of jurisprudence, I will comment on his sentence in the context of his study. The sentencing judge may have shared my dismay, and Browder's, at the pattern of white collar crime sentences. White collar crime pays. It will continue to do so as long as judges endorse it through their sentencing policy.

Imprisonment is hardly a panacea. Well-crafted parole and probation programs and requirements of restitution are usually better solutions. I doubt that deterrence will be very effective until the "executive" becomes convinced that if he embarks on a criminal adventure, he will be severely—though proportionately—punished. Certainty is the key.

Edward Browder was convicted of pledging over $500,000 worth of stolen securities. He concedes his guilt for those crimes. The fact that they were accomplished by means of wit and charm rather than a burglar's tool does not minimize the damage done to the public. The judge who sentenced Browder obviously shared that view. It is a tragedy, if Browder's study is accurate, that fewer judges—and not more of them—subscribe to it also.

Petitioner's petition is denied.

Section Five. Necessity for and Nature of Coercive Power

Authority and capacity to use force are obviously integral to the use of law as a penal-corrective instrument. The criminal law is designed to coerce individuals, at least those individuals it fails to persuade. The issue, then, is not whether force should be used but how much force should be used. In earlier times, torture and mutilation were generally accepted as appropriate punishment. Most societies now condemn these practices, which is not to say that they no longer exist.

In the United States, the Eighth Amendment's prohibition of "cruel and unusual punishment" is interpreted to bar most forms of corporal punishment. The notable exception is the death penalty. The Supreme Court has struck down mandatory death penalty statutes; it has also struck down statutes that fail to provide the jury with any guidelines for the imposition of the death penalty. Death penalty statutes between these two extremes (usually setting out aggravating and mitigating circumstances for the jury to consider) have been upheld by the Supreme Court.

These decisions permit each state to make its own determination of whether the death penalty furthers the goals of the criminal law. Advocates of the death penalty, who are sometimes called retentionists, argue that it increases *deterrence* of crime. Although comparative statistical studies have not proved the existence of a deterrent effect, advocates contend that common sense tells us that some people who would not be deterred by a life sentence would be deterred by the death penalty. In particular, they say that someone who has already committed a crime for which a life sentence will be imposed has no reason to refrain from further crimes if there is no death penalty. Opponents of the death penalty, or abolitionists, counter that (1) people who have already committed crimes for which life sentences will be imposed are not very susceptible to deterrence, either because they are acting irrationally or because they do not believe they will get caught, and (2) for some people, the death penalty may act as an incentive to commit crime, either because the prospect of life imprisonment seems worse than death or because they desire the publicity attendant to an execution.

Death penalty advocates also argue that *incapacitation* is more complete with the death penalty than with life imprisonment—and certainly cheaper. Opponents point out that the increased cost of death penalty cases actually exceeds the cost of life imprisonment. (This is a somewhat disingenuous response, because most of the increased cost stems from the exhaustive litigation pursued by opponents of the death penalty.)

Opponents object that the death penalty is contrary to the goal of *rehabilitation*. Advocates would agree but contend that some people have shown themselves to be incapable or undeserving of reform.

The stalemate on these issues leaves us with the rationale of *retribution*. Advocates claim that retribution requires the death penalty. Some opponents believe that retribution is not a legitimate justification of the penal-corrective law. All opponents would argue that the death penalty is too inhumane to be just retribution and that this injustice is increased by the arbitrary selection of its victims and the possibility of error. The following excerpts detail these positions. As you read them, consider whether a logical resolution of this issue will ever be reached. Why was it possible to gain a consensus about mutilation (which might be viewed as a partial death penalty) but not about the death penalty?

A. CAMUS, RESISTANCE, REBELLION, AND DEATH
175–76 (1960).*

Shortly before the war of 1914, an assassin whose crime was particularly repulsive (he had slaughtered a family of farmers, including the children) was condemned to death in Algiers. He was a farm worker who had killed in a sort of bloodthirsty frenzy but had aggravated his case by robbing his victims. The affair created a great stir. It was generally thought that decapitation was too mild a punishment for such a monster. This was the opinion, I have been told, of my father, who was especially aroused by the murder of the children. One of the few things I know about him, in any case, is that he wanted to witness the execution, for the first time in his life. He got up in the dark to go to the place of execution at the other end of town amid a great crowd of people. What he saw that morning he never told anyone. My mother relates merely that he came rushing home, his face distorted, refused to talk, lay down for a moment on the bed, and suddenly began to vomit. He had just discovered the reality hidden under the noble phrases with which it was masked. Instead of thinking of the slaughtered children, he could think of nothing but that quivering body that had just been dropped onto a board to have its head cut off.

Presumably that ritual act is horrible indeed if it manages to overcome the indignation of a simple, straightforward man and if a punishment he considered richly deserved had no other effect in the end than to nauseate him. When the extreme penalty simply causes vomiting on the part of the respectable citizen it is supposed to protect, how can anyone maintain that it is likely, as it ought to be, to bring more peace and order into the community? Rather, it is obviously no less repulsive than the crime, and this new murder, far from making amends for the harm done to the social body, adds a new blot to the first one.

E. VAN DEN HAAG, PUNISHING CRIMINALS
213 (1975).

No matter what can be said for abolition of the death penalty, it will be perceived symbolically as a loss of nerve; social authority no longer is one. Murder is no longer thought grave enough to take the murderer's life, no longer horrendous enough to deserve so fearfully irrevocable a punishment. When murder no longer forfeits the murderer's life (though it will interfere with his freedom), respect for life itself is diminished, as the price for taking it is. Life becomes cheaper as we become kinder to those who wantonly take it. The responsibility we avoid is indeed hard to bear. Can we sit in judgment and find that anyone is so irredeemably wicked that he does not deserve to live? Many of us no longer believe in evil, only in error or accident. How can one execute a murderer if one believes that he became one only by error or accident and is not to blame? Yet if life is to be valued and secured, it must be known that anyone who takes the life of another forfeits his own.

———

TO ABOLISH THE DEATH PENALTY

Hearings on S. 1760 Before the Subcomm. on Criminal Laws and Procedures of the Senate Comm. on the Judiciary, 90th Cong., 2d Sess. 91, 91–94 (July 2, 1968) (statement of Ramsey Clark, Attorney General).

I appreciate this opportunity to appear before you on a matter that should concern all Americans at this very difficult time in our history. We live in days of turbulence. Violence is commonplace: murders occur nearly every hour.

In the midst of anxiety and fear, complexity and doubt, perhaps our greatest need is reverence for life—mere life: our lives, the lives of others, all life. Life is, as Justice Holmes said, after all an end in itself. A humane and generous concern for every individual, for his safety, his health and his fulfillment, will do more to soothe the savage heart than the fear of State-inflicted death which chiefly serves to remind us how close we remain to the jungle.

"Murder and capital punishment are not opposites that cancel one another, but similars that breed their kind," Shaw advises. When the State itself kills, the mandate "thou shalt not kill" loses the force of the absolute.

Surely the abolition of the death penalty is a major milestone in the long road up from barbarism. There was a time when self-preservation necessitated its imposition. Later inordinate sacrifices by the innocent would have been required to isolate dangerous persons from the public. Our civilization has no such excuse.

Today more than 70 nations and 13 of our States have generally abolished the death penalty. While most States and the Federal system reserve the ultimate sanction, it has been rarely used in recent years. There were 199 executions in the United States in 1935. There was only one in 1966; two in 1967. Only one person has been executed under any of the 29 Federal statutes authorizing death in the past 10 years. He can be the last.

Our history shows the death penalty has been unjustly imposed, innocents have been killed by the State, effective rehabilitation has been impaired, judicial administration has suffered, crime has not been deterred. Society pays a heavy price for the penalty of death it imposes.

Our emotions may cry vengeance in the wake of a horrible crime. But reason and experience tell us that killing the criminal will not undo the crime, prevent other crimes, or bring justice to the victim, the criminal, or society. Executions cheapen life. We must cherish life. . . .

The death penalty's impact on the administration of justice has been malign. Mr. Justice Frankfurter strongly opposed it for this reason. "When life is at hazard in a trial," he said, "it sensationalizes the whole thing almost unwittingly." He regarded as "very bad" the effect on juries, the bar, the public, and the judiciary. President Johnson's Crime Commission found that the sensationalism "destroys the factfinding process." In a capital case, realization of the consequences of error permeates the entire proceedings. A jury might acquit because of its fear of the death penalty rather than the weight of the evidence. Mr. Justice Jackson observed that appellate courts in capital cases "are tempted to strain the evidence and even, in close cases, the law, in order to give a doubtfully condemned man another chance."

Fear of mistake produces excruciating delays in executions. Of the 435 men now on death row, who range in age from 16 to 68, half have been waiting death more than 29 months since they were sentenced. Such delays add immeasurably to the inhumanity of capital punishment. Combined with the infrequency of actual imposition, delay eliminates a deterrent effect the penalty might otherwise be thought to have. Moreover, as the American Bar Foundation found in a 1961 study, it weakens public confidence in the law. The President's Crime Commission noted:

> The spectacle of men living on death row for years while their lawyers pursue appellate and collateral remedies tarnishes our image of humane and expeditious justice.

The death penalty is irrevocable. For this reason, LaFayette vowed to oppose capital punishment until "the infallibility of human judgment" was demonstrated to him. Innocent persons have been executed. Mental defectives and incompetents have been executed. A judicial determination that a person is legally responsible for his act is not yet precise.

A small and capricious selection of offenders have been put to death. Most persons convicted of the same crimes have been imprisoned only. Experienced wardens know many prisoners serving life or less whose crimes were equally, or more atrocious, than those of the men on death row.

Death has been visited in a discriminatory fashion. Clarence Darrow observed that, "from the beginning, a procession of the poor, the weak, the unfit, have gone through our jails and prisons to their deaths. They have been the victims." It is the poor, the weak, the ignorant, the hated who are executed. Racial discrimination occurs in the administration of capital punishment. Since we began keeping records in 1930, there have been 2,066 Negroes and 1,751 white persons put to death, although Negroes made up only one-eighth of our population. Of the 455 men executed for rape, 405 were during all of these years Negroes.

As a people, we are committed to the rule of law. We obey the law, not because we are forced to or fear not to, but because we want to. The law, therefore, must be just. It must offer hope to all of our people. When it suggests vengeance or inhumanity, it loses the respect that is necessary if a free people are to fix it in their hearts. . . .

Our difficult days call for rare courage: the willingness to disenthral ourselves, to think anew and to act anew. There is no justification for the death penalty. It cheapens life. Its injustices and inhumanity raise basic questions about our institutions and purpose as a people. Why must we kill? What do we fear? What do we accomplish besides our own embitterment? Why cannot we preserve life and in so doing create in the hearts of our people a love for mankind that will finally still violence?

The death penalty should be abolished.

––––––––––

VAN DEN HAAG, THE DEATH PENALTY VINDICATES THE LAW

A.B.A.J., Apr. 1985, at 38, 40, 42.*

It is often said that poor and black Mr. Jones, guilty of murder, is more likely to be executed than the equally guilty rich and white Mr. Smith. But no injustice is done to the guilty Mr. Jones by executing him, although justice is not done to the guilty Mr. Smith. *Mutatis mutandis* ("change what needs to be changed") applies as well to discrimination based on the color of the victim. Mr. Jones's guilt is not diminished by Mr. Smith's escape. And guilt is personal. Legally, one may question why a discriminatory or capricious distribution of a punishment among the guilty should argue against the punishment rather than against its distribution. Discrimination hardly can be inherent in any penalty per se.

Perhaps the death penalty is capriciously distributed among the guilty as though by lottery. If it were so, the guilt of those selected by the lottery is not diminished because others were not selected. The alleged fact that one person or group escapes deserved punishment is no reason for letting another get away with murder. Indeed, it is well known that most offenders escape punishment most of the time, and only a few, selected by rather accidental circumstances, are punished.

Capital punishment is irrevocable. This makes it impossible to correct miscarriages of justice, which lead to the unintended death of some innocents in the long run. But in the long run nearly all human activities are likely to lead to the unintended death of innocents. Truck driving does. So does golf playing or trying capital cases. We do not give up truck driving (or even golf) because we feel that its usefulness more than offsets the death of innocents unavoidably connected with it. Justice, including the distribution of the death penalty where deserved, seems no less useful, or morally justified, than truck driving, and this outweighs the harm done by miscarriages.

The death penalty has not been shown to deter murder more than alternative punishments. At least, the statistics, as distinguished from common sense, are inconclusive. But abolitionists who argue from the point of non-deterrence would oppose the death penalty anyway, even if each execution would deter a hundred murders, sparing a hundred prospective victims of murder. Abolitionists such as Ramsey Clark, Hugo Adam Bedau or Henry Schwarzschild have confirmed as much to me. The alleged non-deterrence therefore is hardly decisive for them. It is not for me either. Justice is. (However, I do not understand the preference of abolitionists for any convicted murderer over a hundred innocent victims.)

The French writer Albert Camus contended that the convict awaiting death at a certain date suffers more than his victim did. Suffering is hard to measure and compare. But the alleged excess suffering of murderers does not argue against the death penalty. A burglar, rapist or murderer may suffer more, or less, from the penalty than the victim did from the crime. The penalty is meant to vindicate the social order and not just the suffering of the victim. A murderer makes life insecure by defying the law. Society denounces his crime and vindicates its law by executing the murderer regardless of whether the victim did or did not suffer any pain whatever.

Justice Brennan in Furman v. Georgia, 408 U.S. 238 (1972), has insisted that capital punishment is "degrading to human dignity" and inconsistent with "the sanctity of life." Is prison less degrading than death? Perhaps, but Justice Brennan did not say why. Philosophers such as Immanuel Kant and G.W.F. Hegel have insisted that only the death penalty can restore the human dignity of a murderer and vindicate that of his victim. Justice Brennan has not suggested why they were wrong or why the tradition that the death penalty vindicates the sanctity of the life of innocents is wrong.

Those who oppose the death penalty must believe that no crime likely to be committed is heinous enough to deserve death. I wish they were right. But I know, unfortunately, that they are not.

———

Comments and Questions

1. Our emphasis on fines, imprisonment, and execution does not necessarily mean that such sanctions are the principal mechanisms of the penal-corrective instrument. That instrument relies heavily on presanction control devices, such as the deterrent effect of police patrols, the fear of conviction and its associated opprobrium, and the threat rather than the actuality of punishment.

2. A common fallacy about law is that it is essentially restrictive and basically coercive. Criminal law consists mainly of prohibitions, backed up by the official use of force. But it does not follow that even criminal law is restrictive and coercive in fundamental thrust and aim. Rather, the penal-corrective instrumental also keeps malefactors from interfering with the everyday wholesome activities of other citizens and thereby facilitates those activities, does it not?

Section Six. Roles of Private Citizens and Their Lawyers

Private citizens who are the victims of crime play less of a role in the penal-corrective system than do victims of wrong seeking remedies in the grievance-remedial mode. Seekers of private remedies typically must shoulder the entire burden of litigation, whereas crime victims may—indeed must—rely upon public prosecutors to enforce the criminal law. This does not mean that the private citizen's cooperation is unimportant. If he fails to report a crime, neglects to appear for a scheduled court proceeding, refuses to testify truthfully, or testifies apathetically, the case will probably be dropped or lost.

Private citizens are also involved in shaping the penal-corrective instrument. Reform in the criminal law often results from public pressure. For example, in many states increased penalties for drunk driving were the culmination of lobbying efforts by citizen groups.

Finally, private persons are involved in the penal-corrective instrument as the alleged wrongdoer and the wrongdoer's lawyer. The proper role of defense lawyers is a subject of some complexity. It encompasses questions concerning when lawyers should first be provided for the accused, how lawyers for the poor should be selected and compensated, what the ethical limits on defense lawyers' conduct are, and whether erroneous advice from a lawyer should constitute an excuse for criminal conduct. The following readings address these last two questions.

A. Ethical Issues Concerning Defense Counsel's Role

AMERICAN BAR ASSOCIATION, MODEL RULES OF PROFESSIONAL CONDUCT
(1983).

RULE 1.2 Scope of representation

(a) A lawyer shall abide by a client's decision concerning the objectives of representation, subject to paragraphs (c), (d) and (e), and shall consult with the client as to the means by which they are to be pursued. A lawyer shall abide by a client's decision whether to accept an offer of settlement of a matter. In a criminal case, the lawyer shall abide by the client's decision, after consultation with the lawyer, as to a plea to be entered, whether to waive jury trial and whether the client will testify.

(b) A lawyer's representation of a client, including representation by appointment, does not constitute an endorsement of the client's political, economic, social or moral views or activities.

(c) A lawyer may limit the objectives of the representation if the client consents after consultation.

(d) A lawyer shall not counsel a client to engage, or assist a client, in conduct that the lawyer knows is criminal or fraudulent, but a lawyer may discuss the legal consequences of any proposed course of conduct with a client and may counsel or assist a client to make a good faith effort to determine the validity, scope, meaning or application of the law.

(e) When a lawyer knows that a client expects assistance not permitted by the rules of professional conduct or other laws, the lawyer shall consult with the client regarding the relevant limitations on the lawyer's conduct.

RULE 1.6 Confidentiality of Information

(a) A lawyer shall not reveal information relating to representation of a client unless the client consents after consultation, except for disclosures that are impliedly authorized in order to carry out the representation, and except as stated in paragraph (b).

(b) A lawyer may reveal such information to the extent the lawyer reasonably believes necessary:

(1) to prevent the client from committing a criminal act that the lawyer believes is likely to result in imminent death or substantial bodily harm; or

(2) to establish a claim or defense on behalf of the lawyer in a controversy between the lawyer and the client, to establish a defense to a criminal charge or civil claim against the lawyer based upon conduct in which the client was involved, or to respond to allegations in any proceeding concerning the lawyer's representation of the client.

RULE 3.1 Meritorious claims and contentions

A lawyer shall not bring or defend a proceeding, or assert or controvert an issue therein, unless there is a basis for doing so that is not frivolous, which includes a good faith argument for an extension, modification or reversal of existing law. A lawyer for the defendant in a criminal proceeding, or the respondent in a proceeding that could result in incarceration, may nevertheless so defend the proceeding as to require that every element of the case be established.

RULE 3.3 Candor toward the tribunal

(a) A lawyer shall not knowingly:

(1) make a false statement of material fact or law to a tribunal;

(2) fail to disclose a material fact to a tribunal when disclosure is necessary to avoid assisting a criminal or fraudulent act by the client;

(3) fail to disclose to the tribunal legal authority in the controlling jurisdiction known to the lawyer to be directly adverse to the position of the client and not disclosed by opposing counsel; or

(4) offer evidence that the lawyer knows to be false. If a lawyer has offered material evidence and comes to know of its falsity, the lawyer shall take reasonable remedial measures.

(b) The duties stated in paragraph (a) continue to the conclusion of the proceeding, and apply even if compliance requires disclosure of information otherwise protected by Rule 1.6.

(c) A lawyer may refuse to offer evidence that the lawyer reasonably believes is false. .   .   .

FREEDMAN, PROFESSIONAL RESPONSIBILITY OF THE CRIMINAL DEFENSE LAWYER: THE THREE HARDEST QUESTIONS

64 Mich.L.Rev. 1469, 1469, 1474–82 (1966).*

In almost any area of legal counseling and advocacy, the lawyer may be faced with the dilemma of either betraying the confidential communi-

* Copyright © 1966 by the Michigan Law Review Association. Reprinted by permission. Professor Freedman has expanded on the views in this article, and modified them somewhat, in his book, *Lawyers' Ethics in an Adversary System* (1975), and in subsequent law review articles.

cations of his client or participating to some extent in the purposeful deception of the court. This problem is nowhere more acute than in the practice of criminal law, particularly in the representation of the indigent accused. The purpose of this article is to analyze and attempt to resolve three of the most difficult issues in this general area:

1. Is it proper to cross-examine for the purpose of discrediting the reliability or credibility of an adverse witness whom you know to be telling the truth?

2. Is it proper to put a witness on the stand when you know he will commit perjury?

3. Is it proper to give your client legal advice when you have reason to believe that the knowledge you give him will tempt him to commit perjury? . . .

The first of the difficult problems posed above will now be considered: Is it proper to cross-examine for the purpose of discrediting the reliability or the credibility of a witness whom you know to be telling the truth? Assume the following situation. Your client has been falsely accused of a robbery committed at 16th and P Streets at 11:00 p.m. He tells you at first that at no time on the evening of the crime was he within six blocks of that location. However, you are able to persuade him that he must tell you the truth and that doing so will in no way prejudice him. He then reveals to you that he was at 15th and P Streets at 10:55 that evening, but that he was walking east, away from the scene of the crime, and that, by 11:00 p.m., he was six blocks away. At the trial, there are two prosecution witnesses. The first mistakenly, but with some degree of persuasion, identifies your client as the criminal. At that point, the prosecution's case depends on this single witness, who might or might not be believed. Since your client has a prior record, you do not want to put him on the stand, but you feel that there is at least a chance for acquittal. The second prosecution witness is an elderly woman who is somewhat nervous and who wears glasses. She testifies truthfully and accurately that she saw your client at 15th and P Streets at 10:55 p.m. She has corroborated the erroneous testimony of the first witness and made conviction virtually certain. However, if you destroy her reliability through cross-examination designed to show that she is easily confused and has poor eyesight, you may not only eliminate the corroboration, but also cast doubt in the jury's mind on the prosecution's entire case. On the other hand, if you should refuse to cross-examine her because she is telling the truth, your client may well feel betrayed, since you knew of the witness's veracity only because your client confided in you, under your assurance that his truthfulness would not prejudice him.

The client would be right. Viewed strictly, the attorney's failure to cross-examine would not be violative of the client's confidence because it would not constitute a disclosure. However, the same policy that supports the obligation of confidentiality precludes the attorney from prejudicing his client's interest in any other way because of knowledge gained in his professional capacity. When a lawyer fails to cross-examine only because his client, placing confidence in the lawyer, has been candid with him, the basis for such confidence and candor collapses. Our legal system cannot tolerate such a result.

> The purposes and necessities of the relation between a client and his attorney require, in many cases, on the part of the client, the fullest and freest disclosures to the attorney of the client's objects, motives and acts . . . . To permit the attorney to reveal to others what is so disclosed, would be not only a gross violation of a sacred trust upon his part, but it would utterly destroy and prevent the usefulness and benefits to be derived from professional assistance.

The client's confidences must "upon all occasions be inviolable," to avoid the "greater mischiefs" that would probably result if a client could not feel free "to repose [confidence] in the attorney to whom he resorts for legal advice and assistance." Destroy that confidence, and "a man would not venture to consult any skillful person, or would only dare to tell his counsellor half his case."

Therefore, one must conclude that the attorney is obligated to attack, if he can, the reliability or credibility of an opposing witness whom he knows to be truthful. The contrary result would inevitably impair the "perfect freedom of consultation by client with attorney," which is "essential to the administration of justice."

The second question is generally considered to be the hardest of all: Is it proper to put a witness on the stand when you know he will commit perjury? Assume, for example, that the witness in question is the accused himself, and that he has admitted to you, in response to your assurances of confidentiality, that he is guilty. However, he insists upon taking the stand to protest his innocence. There is a clear consensus among prosecutors and defense attorneys that the likelihood of conviction is increased enormously when the defendant does not take the stand. Consequently, the attorney who prevents his client from testifying only because the client has confided his guilt to him is violating that confidence by acting upon the information in a way that will seriously prejudice his client's interests.

Perhaps the most common method for avoiding the ethical problem just posed is for the lawyer to withdraw from the case, at least if there is sufficient time before trial for the client to retain another attorney. The client will then go to the nearest law office, realizing that the obligation of confidentiality is not what it has been represented to be, and withhold incriminating information or the fact of his guilt from his new attorney. On ethical grounds, the practice of withdrawing from a case under such circumstances is indefensible, since the identical perjured testimony will ultimately be presented. More important, perhaps, is the practical consideration that the new attorney will be ignorant of the perjury and therefore will be in no position to attempt to discourage the client from presenting it. Only the original attorney, who knows the truth, has that opportunity, but he loses it in the very act of evading the ethical problem.

The problem is all the more difficult when the client is indigent. He cannot retain other counsel, and in many jurisdictions, including the District of Columbia, it is impossible for appointed counsel to withdraw from a case except for extraordinary reasons. Thus, appointed counsel, unless he lies to the judge, can successfully withdraw only by revealing to the judge that the attorney has received knowledge of his client's guilt. Such a revelation in itself would seem to be a sufficiently serious violation of the obligation of confidentiality to merit severe condemnation. In fact, however, the situation is far worse, since it is entirely possible that the same judge who permits the attorney to withdraw will subsequently hear the case and sentence the defendant. When he does so, of course, he will have had personal knowledge of the defendant's guilt before the trial began. Moreover, this will be knowledge of which the newly appointed counsel for the defendant will probably be ignorant.

The difficulty is further aggravated when the client informs the lawyer for the first time during trial that he intends to take the stand and commit perjury. The perjury in question may not necessarily be a protestation of innocence by a guilty man. Referring to the earlier hypothetical of the defendant wrongly accused of a robbery at 16th and P, the only perjury may be his denial of the truthful, but highly damaging, testimony of the corroborating witness who placed him one block away from the intersection five minutes prior to the crime. Of course, if he tells the truth and thus verifies the corroborating witness, the jury will be far more inclined to accept the inaccurate testimony of the principal witness, who specifically identified him as the criminal.

If a lawyer has discovered his client's intent to perjure himself, one possible solution to this problem is for the lawyer to approach the bench, explain his ethical difficulty to the judge, and ask to be relieved, thereby causing a mistrial. This request is certain to be denied, if only because it would empower the defendant to cause a series of mistrials in the same fashion. At this point, some feel that the lawyer has avoided the ethical problem and can put the defendant on the stand. However, one objection to this solution, apart from the violation of confidentiality, is that the lawyer's ethical problem has not been solved, but has only been transferred to the judge. Moreover, the client in such a case might well have grounds for appeal on the basis of deprivation of due process and denial of the right to counsel, since he will have been tried before, and sentenced by, a judge who has been informed of the client's guilt by his own attorney.

A solution even less satisfactory than informing the judge of the defendant's guilt would be to let the client take the stand without the attorney's participation and to omit reference to the client's testimony in closing argument. The latter solution, of course, would be as damaging as to fail entirely to argue the case to the jury, and failing to argue the case is "as improper as though the attorney had told the jury that his client had uttered a falsehood in making the statement."

Therefore, the obligation of confidentiality, in the context of our adversary system, apparently allows the attorney no alternative to putting a perjurious witness on the stand without explicit or implicit disclosure of the attorney's knowledge to either the judge or the jury. .   .   .

Of course, before the client testifies perjuriously, the lawyer has a duty to attempt to dissuade him on grounds of both law and morality. In addition, the client should be impressed with the fact that his untruthful alibi is tactically dangerous. There is always a strong possibility that the prosecutor will expose the perjury on cross-examination. However, for the reasons already given, the final decision must necessarily be the client's. The lawyer's best course thereafter would be to avoid any further professional relationship with a client whom he knew to have perjured himself.

The third question is whether it is proper to give your client legal advice when you have reason to believe that the knowledge you give him will tempt him to commit perjury. This may indeed be the most difficult problem of all, because giving such advice creates the appearance that the attorney is encouraging and condoning perjury.

If the lawyer is not certain what the facts are when he gives the advice, the problem is substantially minimized, if not eliminated. It is not the lawyer's function to prejudge his client as a perjurer. He cannot presume that the client will make unlawful use of his advice. Apart from this, there is a natural predisposition in most people to recollect facts, entirely honestly, in a way most favorable to their own interest. As Randolph Paul has observed, some witnesses are nervous, some are confused about their own interests, some try to be too smart for their own good, and some subconsciously do not want to understand what has happened to them. Before he begins to remember essential facts, the client is entitled to know what his own interests are. . . .

Assume that your client, on trial for his life in a first-degree murder case, has killed another man with a penknife but insists that the killing was in self-defense. You ask him, "Do you customarily carry the penknife in your pocket, do you carry it frequently or infrequently, or did you take it with you only on this occasion?" He replies, "Why do you ask me a question like that?" It is entirely appropriate to inform him that his carrying the knife only on this occasion, or infrequently, supports an inference of premeditation, while if he carried the knife constantly, or frequently, the inference of premeditation would be negated. Thus, your client's life may depend upon his recollection as to whether he carried the knife frequently or infrequently. Despite the possibility that the client or a third party might infer that the lawyer was prompting the client to lie, the lawyer must apprise the defendant of the significance of his answer. There is no conceivable ethical requirement that the lawyer trap his client into a hasty and ill-considered answer before telling him the significance of the question.

A similar problem is created if the client has given the lawyer incriminating information before being fully aware of its significance. For example, assume that a man consults a tax lawyer and says, "I am fifty years old. Nobody in my immediate family has lived past fifty. Therefore, I would like to put my affairs in order. Specifically, I under-stand that I can avoid substantial estate taxes by setting up a trust. Can I do it?" The lawyer informs the client that he can successfully avoid the estate taxes only if he lives at least three years after establishing the trust or, should he die within three years, if the trust is found not to have been created in contemplation of death. The client then might ask who decides whether the trust is in contemplation of death. After learning that the determination is made by the court, the client might inquire about the factors on which such a decision would be based.

At this point, the lawyer can do one of two things. He can refuse to answer the question, or he can inform the client that the court will consider the wording of the trust instrument and will hear evidence about any conversations which he may have or any letters he may write expressing motives other than avoidance of estate taxes. It is likely that virtually every tax attorney in the country would answer the client's question, and that no one would consider the answer unethical. However, the lawyer might well appear to have prompted his client to deceive the Internal Revenue Service and the courts, and this appearance would remain regardless of the lawyer's explicit disclaimer to the client of any intent so to prompt him. Nevertheless, it should not be unethical for the lawyer to give the advice.

In a criminal case, a lawyer may be representing a client who protests his innocence, and whom the lawyer believes to be innocent. Assume, for example, that the charge is assault with intent to kill, that the prosecution has erroneous but credible eyewitness testimony against the defendant, and that the defendant's truthful alibi witness is impeachable on the basis of several felony convictions. The prosecutor, perhaps having doubts about the case, offers to permit the defendant to plead guilty to simple assault. If the defendant should go to trial and be convicted, he might well be sent to jail for fifteen years; on a plea of simple assault, the maximum penalty would be one year, and sentence might well be suspended.

The common practice of conveying the prosecutor's offer to the defendant should not be considered unethical, even if the defense lawyer is convinced of his client's innocence. Yet the lawyer is clearly in the position of prompting his client to lie, since the defendant cannot make the plea without saying to the judge that he is pleading guilty because he is guilty. Furthermore, if the client does decide to plead guilty, it would be improper for the lawyer to inform the court that his client is innocent, thereby compelling the defendant to stand trial and take the substantial risk of fifteen years' imprisonment.

Essentially no different from the problem discussed above, but apparently more difficult, is the so-called Anatomy of a Murder situation. The lawyer, who has received from his client an incriminating story of murder in the first degree, says, "If the facts are as you have stated them so far, you have no defense, and you will probably be electrocuted. On the other hand, if you acted in a blind rage, there is a possibility of saving your life. Think it over, and we will talk about it tomorrow." As in the tax case, and as in the case of the plea of guilty to a lesser offense, the lawyer has given his client a legal opinion that might induce the client to lie. This is information which the lawyer himself would have, without advice, were he in the client's position. It is submitted that the client is entitled to have this information about the law and to make his own decision as to whether to act upon it. To decide otherwise would not only penalize the less well-educated defendant, but would also prejudice the client because

of his initial truthfulness in telling his story in confidence to the attorney.
. . .

The lawyer is an officer of the court, participating in a search for truth. Yet no lawyer would consider that he had acted unethically in pleading the statute of frauds or the statute of limitations as a bar to a just claim. Similarly, no lawyer would consider it unethical to prevent the introduction of evidence such as a murder weapon seized in violation of the fourth amendment or a truthful but involuntary confession, or to defend a guilty man on grounds of denial of a speedy trial. Such actions are permissible because there are policy considerations that at times justify frustrating the search for truth and the prosecution of a just claim. Similarly, there are policies that justify an affirmative answer to the three questions that have been posed in this article. These policies include the maintenance of an adversary system, the presumption of innocence, the prosecution's burden to prove guilt beyond a reasonable doubt, the right to counsel, and the obligation of confidentiality between lawyer and client.

NOONAN, THE PURPOSES OF ADVOCACY AND THE LIMITS OF CONFIDENTIALITY

64 Mich.L.Rev. 1485, 1485–89, 1491–92 (1966).*

The privilege of confidentiality between lawyer and client is a significant barrier to the search for truth and the attainment of justice. Since bankers, accountants, psychiatrists, and confessors are not entitled at common law to confidentiality in their relationships with those with whom they deal, one may well inquire why lawyers possess such an extraordinary privilege. In the early English case which established the lawyer-client privilege, counsel offered several justifications: (1) A "gentleman of character" does not disclose his client's secrets. (2) An attorney identifies himself with his client, and it would be "contrary to the rules of natural justice and equity" for an individual to betray himself. (3) Attorneys are necessary for the conduct of business, and business would be destroyed if attorneys were to disclose their communications with their clients.

None of the above justifications seems very persuasive today. Gentlemen of character have no legally recognized immunity from testifying about their friends' secrets. The identification of lawyer and client is, at best, only a metaphor, indicating an underlying policy justification for the privilege. Finally, attorneys are no more essential to the conduct of general business than are accountants, bankers, and secretaries, who do not enjoy the privilege. The suspicion arises that the legal profession has carved out for itself a privilege which it is reluctant to grant to other equally necessary and honorable men merely because the privilege is good for the legal business.

However, the secrecy of information communicated by a client to a lawyer may have a more rational justification than those discussed above when the information is divulged in preparation for a trial. The purpose of employing a trial lawyer is to assert one's rights in a lawsuit; this purpose might be defeated if a relevant secret were available to one side merely by calling the opposing counsel to testify. Therefore, if the essential function of lawyers is to conduct trials, they must be able to receive relevant information and keep it confidential.

To say that a lawyer's function is to conduct a trial, however, does not suffice, for one must inquire into the purposes of a trial and of trial advocacy. If one agrees with Charles Curtis that a trial is an irrational process—a substitute for trial by battle which gives the litigant the satisfaction of having "his day in court"—one may conclude that the function of the advocate is to be a friendly champion who, by his wholehearted devotion to the cause, is able to satisfy his client's desire for a day in court. It is hard to deny that many trials of the past, and some of the present, suggest the appropriateness of such an analysis. If this theory of the purposes of a trial and of advocacy is accepted, there is no reason why the solutions proposed by Professor Monroe Freedman to his three hypothetical cases should be rejected. Since many trial lawyers believe, perhaps subconsciously, that the Curtis view is an accurate reflection of what actually happens in a trial, it is easy to understand why Professor Freedman's solutions seem plausible, if not mandatory; he has merely expressed as a norm what is, in fact, current practice for some practitioners. Indeed, the merit of Professor Freedman's exposition is that he candidly exposes the working principles of many lawyers at the same time that he makes those principles vital by showing how they would govern particular cases. This scholarly explication of what is often taken for granted serves a very useful function.

Professor Freedman's analysis, however, presupposes that the Curtis theory, or something approximating it, is a correct description of the trial process. Yet, Curtis' description of the system obscures three important points. First, although a trial may be a battle, not only is physical violence excluded, but some purely peaceful tactics such as the subornation of perjury and the introduction of faked documents are discouraged; the system gives each litigant his day in court, but it also excludes obviously false information. Second, the satisfaction the client receives depends not on his sense of the friendly atmosphere of the court, but rather on his feeling that justice is being done, insofar as he is being heard, for the client will usually believe that once he is heard, truth will prevail. Third, the truth-discovering techniques of Anglo-American law have developed from such crude devices as trial by battle to more refined and more ample procedures such as detailed interrogatories and discovery procedures under the Federal Rules; this evolution must be taken into consideration in any analysis of purposes of the system.

A second, perhaps more appropriate view of a trial and of the adversary system is the view endorsed in 1958 by the Joint Conference on Professional Responsibility of the Association of American Law Schools and the American Bar Association. It is a modern view in that it looks less at the way in which trials have been conducted in the past than at the way in which they may be conducted in the future. A trial is seen as a process "within which man's capacity for impartial judgment can attain its fullest realization," and the function of the advocate is to assist the trier of fact in making this impartial judgment. In a non-adversary system, the tribunal would do its own investigating, have its own theory of the case, and possibly decide the issues too quickly. On the other hand, the adversary system permits the tribunal to remain uncommitted while a case is explored from opposing viewpoints, thus requiring the liability or guilt to be demonstrated publicly to a neutral tribunal. In this view of the system, "the advocate plays his role well when zeal for his client's cause promotes a wise and informed decision of the case."

Evidently, if the Joint Conference's approach is taken, distinctions must be made in answering Professor Freedman's three hypotheticals. As to the first problem, it could be argued that the sole function of an advocate is to produce a wise and informed *ultimate* judgment. In the process of assisting the trier in attaining this final result, counsel therefore may properly obscure or impugn testimony which, while true, would not be relevant to the determination of guilt but rather would merely create an erroneous impression. For example, a defense lawyer could attempt to impair the credibility of a witness who testified truthfully before a jury of Negroes that the defendant was a member of the Ku Klux Klan. By destroying the true but irrelevant testimony, it is argued, the advocate would, in fact, contribute to a wise ultimate result. This reasoning, however, does not seem persuasive. Rather, it resembles the paternalism which is so often invoked as an excuse for not trusting others with the truth. Instead of attempting to destroy the testimony it would be better to refrain from impeaching the truthful witness and to trust the trier of fact to draw the right conclusions. The law itself provides mechanisms for excluding irrelevant and prejudicial evidence; where evidence is not clearly irrelevant, a lawyer should not attempt to exclude it at the cost of attacking a truthful witness. Repeated acts of confidence in the rationality of the trial system are necessary if the decision-making process is to approach rationality.

The second hypothetical is easier than the first to solve in terms of the Joint Conference's theory. To permit a client who will commit perjury to take the stand does not contribute to a wise and informed decision. It is difficult to differentiate among forging documents, suborning another witness, and calling one's own client with the knowledge that he will lie. An impartial, informed, and wise decision presupposes that the person deciding a case has been given the truth. To furnish him with a lie is to mock impartiality, to mislead rather than to inform, and to stultify the decisional process rather than to make it an exploration leading to mature judgment.

The third hypothetical would seem to be answerable, in part, the same way under both Professor Freedman's analysis and that of the Joint Conference. A lawyer should not be paternalistic toward his client, and cannot assume that his client will perjure himself. Furthermore, a lawyer has an obligation to furnish his client with all the legal information relevant to his case; in fulfilling this duty to inform his client, a lawyer would normally not violate ethical standards. Motives may properly be given their weight after the legal consequences of an act are known by the client, for a human being rarely acts with a completely undivided heart. Although the courts have made a generous allowance for this multiplicity of human motivations, there is a point, however, at which it becomes brute rationalization to claim that the legal advice tendered to a client is meant to contribute to wise and informed decision-making. For example, a lawyer may, in substance, be suggesting perjury rather than giving legal advice when the lawyer knows that the facts are completely contrary to the defense which he outlines to his client. In Anatomy of a Murder, Paul Biegler won his case, but lost his fee. Possibly this result reflects the author's own conception of a just reward for Biegler's manipulative use of the system. Professor Freedman seems to feel that to refuse to tell a client of a defense which is not supported by the facts would penalize truth-telling clients; the answer is that truth sometimes has unfortunate consequences.

Thus, if one considers that the function of the advocate is to assist in the formulation of wise and informed decisions, there is a limit to the confidentiality of communication between client and trial counsel. The partisanship involved in keeping a communication confidential must be restricted when it leads to conduct which destroys the truth or presents perjury to the fact-finder. Indeed, in some instances, courts may even compel a lawyer to testify about confidential information revealed to him by a client. The communication of an intention to commit a crime is not privileged; neither does the privilege exist if a lawyer has a pre-existing duty which precludes him from acting for a client. Some courts have held that only relevant information is privileged and that information may not remain confidential after the client's death. All of these qualifications present difficult questions which a naïve client, believing his communications were truly free from disclosure by his lawyer, would not anticipate. Thus, it appears that neither confidentiality nor the adversary system is an absolute; each is justified pragmatically by its ability to serve certain social needs. Professor Freedman repeatedly treats a privileged communication as an absolute which takes precedence over all other values. He justifies this by asserting that complete lawyer-client confidentiality is necessary to the adversary system. Yet such confidentiality is necessary to the adversary system only if the system exists as Professor Freedman views it. Asserted as a standard by which to measure the lawyer's conduct in all situations, absolute confidentiality is inimical to a system which has as its end rational decision-making. . . .

Extensive subordination of the lawyer's interests to those of his client also has an effect on the lawyer himself. Professor Freedman is concerned about the rights of the client; but what of the rights of the lawyer? . . .

A lawyer should not impose his conscience on his client; neither can he accept his client's decision and remain entirely free from all moral responsibility, subject only to the restraints of the criminal law. The framework of the adversary system provides only the first set of guidelines for a lawyer's conduct. He is also a human being and cannot submerge his humanity by playing a technician's role. Although the obligation to be candid is not so absolute that it cannot be affected by context, both the seeking and stating of truth are so necessary to the human personality and so demanded by broad social values that the systematic presentation of falsehood is both personally demeaning and socially frustrating. Moreover, the adversary system itself does not demand active suppression of truth. As a free person, cooperating with another free person—his client—to prove the client's innocence in a way which will also lead to the revelation of truth, the lawyer must act with regard for the requirements of the adversary system and with concern for his own standards as a human person, as well as with regard for the requirements of the society which the system serves.

Comments and Questions

1. The lawyers of many defendants are not private operators—they are public defenders, paid by the state to represent accused indigents. These lawyers do not have the option of rejecting a client, and their clients do not have the option of selecting another attorney. Should the ethical obligations of public defenders be the same as those of private attorneys?

2. How do the ethical obligations of defense counsel compare and contrast with the special responsibilities of the prosecutor?

B. Effect of Counsel's Advice on Criminal Liability

HOPKINS v. STATE

Court of Appeals of Maryland, 1949.
193 Md. 489, 69 A.2d 456.

DELAPLAINE, JUDGE.

This appeal was taken by the Rev. William F. Hopkins, of Elkton, from the judgment of conviction entered upon the verdict of a jury in the Circuit Court for Cecil County for violation of the statute making it unlawful to erect or maintain any sign intended to aid in the solicitation or performance of marriages. Laws of 1943, ch. 532, Code Supp.1947, art. 27, sec. 444A.

The State charged that on September 1, 1947, defendant maintained a sign at the entrance to his home at 148 East Main Street in Elkton, and also a sign along a highway leading into the town, to aid in the solicitation and performance of marriages. Four photographs were admitted in evidence. One photograph, taken on an afternoon in September, 1947, shows the sign in Elkton containing [only] the name "Rev. W.F. Hopkins." Another, taken at night shows the same sign illuminated at night by electricity. The third shows the other sign along the highway containing [only] the words, "W.F. Hopkins, Notary Public, Information." The fourth shows this sign illuminated at night.

The State showed that during the month of August, 1947, thirty ministers performed 1,267 marriages in Cecil County, and of this number defendant performed 286, only three of which were ceremonies in which the parties were residents of Cecil County.

Defendant did not testify. Several witnesses, however, testified that, though he has been residing in Elkton, he has been serving as the pastor of a church with about 40 members in Middletown, Delaware, known as the First Home Missionary Church. . . .

. . . . Defendant contended that the judge erred in excluding testimony offered to show that the State's Attorney advised him in 1944 before he erected the signs, that they would not violate the law. It is generally held that the advice of counsel, even though followed in good faith, furnishes no excuse to a person for violating the law and cannot be relied upon as a defense in a criminal action. Forwood v. State, 49 Md. 531, 538; Miller v. United States, 4 Cir., 277 F. 721. Moreover, advice given by a public official, even a State's Attorney, that a contemplated act is not criminal will not excuse an offender if, as a matter of law, the act performed did amount to a violation of the law. State v. Foster, 22 R.I. 163, 46 A. 833, 50 L.R.A. 339; Staley v. State, 89 Neb. 701, 131 N.W. 1028, 34 L.R.A., N.S., 613; State v. Whiteaker, 118 Or. 656, 247 P. 1077. These rules are founded upon the maxim that ignorance of the law will not excuse its violation. If an accused could be exempted from punishment for crime by reason of the advice of counsel, such advice would become paramount to the law.

While ignorance of fact may sometimes be admitted as evidence of lack of criminal intent, ignorance of the law ordinarily does not give immunity from punishment for crime, for every man is presumed to intend the necessary and legitimate consequences of what he knowingly does. In the case at bar defendant did not claim that the State's Attorney misled him regarding any facts of the case, but only that the State's Attorney advised him as to the law based upon the facts. Defendant was aware of the penal statute enacted by the Legislature. He knew what he wanted to do, and he did the thing he intended to do. He claims merely that he was given advice regarding his legal rights. If there was any mistake, it was a mistake of law and not of fact. If the right of a person to erect a sign of a certain type and size depends upon the construction and application of a penal statute, and the right is somewhat doubtful, he erects the sign at his peril. In other words, a person who commits an act which the law declares to be criminal cannot be excused from punishment upon the theory that he misconstrued or misapplied the law. Levar v. State, 103 Ga. 42, 29 S.E. 467, 470; Lewis v. State, 124 Tex.Cr.R. 582, 64 S.W.2d 972, 975. For these reasons the exclusion of the testimony offered to show that defendant had sought and received advice from the State's Attorney was not prejudicial error. . . .

Judgment affirmed, with costs.

Comments and Questions

1. Compare this case with *Rex* v. *Esop*. Do the reasons in favor of punishing Esop justify punishing Hopkins? Are there other reasons to punish Hopkins?

2. If you think Hopkins should not have been punished, what would you do with the defendant who claims that she would have consulted the state's attorney but did not know him, and instead consulted her own attorney, who told her that

her conduct would be legal? What about the defendant who could not afford to consult any attorney?

Section Seven. Process Values

Justice Douglas once declared: "It is significant that most of the provisions of the Bill of Rights are procedural, for it is procedure that spells much of the difference between rule by law and rule by fiat. Steadfast adherence to strict procedural safeguards is our main assurance that there will be equal justice under law." Wisconsin v. Constantineau, 400 U.S. 433, 436, 91 S.Ct. 507, 509 (1970). Justice Frankfurter, whose political philosophy in other respects was quite different, expressed a similar idea: "The history of liberty has largely been the history of observance of procedural safeguards." McNabb v. United States, 318 U.S. 332, 347, 63 S.Ct. 608, 616 (1943). This agreement over the importance of process values—particularly in criminal proceedings—should not be taken to signal agreement over precisely how and when those values should be fostered. Indeed, disagreement, even within the Supreme Court, has often been heated, in part because the competing interest of society in apprehending and convicting dangerous individuals is so high.

Even a cursory examination of the Bill of Rights suggests the range of process values specially protected in criminal proceedings through features such as the immunity against repeated prosecutions for a single crime, the privilege against compelled self-incrimination, the right to be confronted by adverse witnesses, the availability of compulsory process to obtain witnesses at trial, the assistance of counsel, and the right to reasonable bail pending trial. In addition to such enumerated protections, the Fifth Amendment provides a catchall assurance that no person shall "be deprived of life, liberty, or property, without due process of law."

These provisions have sparked much controversy and spawned many great cases—more than we can review here. The cases that follow focus on the process values implicated when the government asks the defendant to admit his guilt. As you read these cases, keep in mind that only the first decision was unanimous and that the others are still hotly disputed. It would be wrong to assume that the issues they raise have been permanently resolved.

A. Confessions

BROWN v. MISSISSIPPI

Supreme Court of the United States, 1936.
297 U.S. 278, 56 S.Ct. 461.

MR. CHIEF JUSTICE HUGHES delivered the opinion of the Court.

The question in this case is whether convictions, which rest solely upon confessions shown to have been extorted by officers of the state by brutality and violence, are consistent with the due process of law required by the Fourteenth Amendment of the Constitution of the United States.

Petitioners were indicted for the murder of one Raymond Stewart, whose death occurred on March 30, 1934. They were indicted on April 4, 1934, and were then arraigned and pleaded not guilty. Counsel were appointed by the court to defend them. Trial was begun the next morning and was concluded on the following day, when they were found guilty and sentenced to death.

Aside from the confessions, there was no evidence sufficient to warrant the submission of the case to the jury. After a preliminary inquiry, testimony as to the confessions was received over the objection of defendants' counsel. Defendants then testified that the confessions were false and had been procured by physical torture. The case went to the jury with instructions, upon the request of defendants' counsel, that if the jury had reasonable doubt as to the confessions having resulted from coercion, and that they were not true, they were not to be considered as evidence. On their appeal to the Supreme Court of the State, defendants assigned as error the inadmissibility of the confessions. The judgment was affirmed.

. . .

. . . There is no dispute as to the facts upon this point, and as they are clearly and adequately stated in the dissenting opinion of Judge Griffith (with whom Judge Anderson concurred), showing both the extreme brutality of the measures to extort the confessions and the participation of the state authorities, we quote this part of his opinion in full, as follows:

> The crime with which these defendants, all ignorant negroes, are charged, was discovered about 1 o'clock p.m. on Friday, March 30, 1934. On that night one Dial, a deputy sheriff, accompanied by others, came to the home of Ellington, one of the defendants, and requested him to accompany them to the house of the deceased, and there a number of white men were gathered, who began to accuse the defendant of the crime. Upon his denial they seized him, and with the participation of the deputy they hanged him by a rope to the limb of a tree, and, having let him down, they hung him again, and when he was let down the second time, and he still protested his innocence, he was tied to a tree and whipped, and, still declining to accede to the demands that he confess, he was finally released, and he returned with some difficulty to his home, suffering intense pain and agony. The record of the testimony shows that the signs of the rope on his neck were plainly visible during the so-called trial. A day or two thereafter the said deputy, accompanied by another, returned to the home of the said defendant and arrested him, and departed with the prisoner towards the jail in an adjoining county, but went by a route which led into the state of Alabama; and while on the way, in that state, the deputy stopped and again severely whipped the defendant, declaring that he would continue the whipping until he confessed, and the defendant then agreed to confess to such a statement as the deputy would dictate, and he did so, after which he was delivered to jail.

> The other two defendants, Ed Brown and Henry Shields, were also arrested and taken to the same jail. On Sunday night, April 1, 1934, the same deputy, accompanied by a number of white men, one of whom was also an officer, and by the jailer, came to the jail, and the two last named defendants were made to strip and they were laid over chairs and their backs were cut to pieces with a leather strap with buckles on

it, and they were likewise made by the said deputy definitely to understand that the whipping would be continued unless and until they confessed, and not only confessed, but confessed in every matter of detail as demanded by those present; and in this manner the defendants confessed the crime, and, as the whippings progressed and were repeated, they changed or adjusted their confession in all particulars of detail so as to conform to the demands of their torturers. When the confessions had been obtained in the exact form and contents as desired by the mob, they left with the parting admonition and warning that, if the defendants changed their story at any time in any respect from that last stated, the perpetrators of the outrage would administer the same or equally effective treatment.

Further details of the brutal treatment to which these helpless prisoners were subjected need not be pursued. It is sufficient to say that in pertinent respects the transcript reads more like pages torn from some medieval account than a record made within the confines of a modern civilization which aspires to an enlightened constitutional government.

All this having been accomplished, on the next day, that is, on Monday, April 2, when the defendants had been given time to recuperate somewhat from the tortures to which they had been subjected, the two sheriffs, one of the county where the crime was committed, and the other of the county of the jail in which the prisoners were confined, came to the jail, accompanied by eight other persons, some of them deputies, there to hear the free and voluntary confession of these miserable and abject defendants. The sheriff of the county of the crime admitted that he had heard of the whipping, but averred that he had no personal knowledge of it. He admitted that one of the defendants, when brought before him to confess, was limping and did not sit down, and that this particular defendant then and there stated that he had been strapped so severely that he could not sit down, and, as already stated, the signs of the rope on the neck of another of the defendants were plainly visible to all. Nevertheless the solemn farce of hearing the free and voluntary confessions was gone through with, and these two sheriffs and one other person then present were the three witnesses used in court to establish the so-called confessions, which were received by the court and admitted in evidence over the objections of the defendants duly entered of record as each of the said three witnesses delivered their alleged testimony. . . .

. . . The evidence upon which the conviction was obtained was the so-called confessions. Without this evidence, a peremptory instruction to find for the defendants would have been inescapable. The defendants were put on the stand, and by their testimony the facts and the details thereof as to the manner by which the confessions were extorted from them were fully developed, and it is further disclosed by the record that the same deputy, Dial, under whose guiding hand and active participation the tortures to coerce the confessions were administered, was actively in the performance of the supposed duties of a court deputy in the courthouse and in the presence of the prisoners during what is denominated, in complimentary terms, the trial of these defendants. This deputy was put on the stand by the state in rebuttal, and admitted the whippings. It is interesting to note that in his testimony with reference to the whipping of the defendant Ellington, and in response to the inquiry as to how severely he was whipped, the deputy stated, "Not too much for a negro; not as much as I would have done if it were left to me." Two others who had participated in these whippings were introduced and admitted it—not a single witness was introduced who denied it. . . .

The state is free to regulate the procedure of its courts in accordance with its own conceptions of policy, unless in so doing it "offends some principle of justice so rooted in the traditions and conscience of our people as to be ranked as fundamental." Snyder v. Massachusetts, [291 U.S. 97, 105, 54 S.Ct. 330, 332 (1934)]. . . . [The state] may dispense with indictment by a grand jury and substitute complaint or information. Walker v. Sauvinet, 92 U.S. 90; Hurtado v. California, 110 U.S. 516, 4 S.Ct. 111, 292; Snyder v. Massachusetts, supra. But the freedom of the state in establishing its policy is the freedom of constitutional government and is limited by the requirement of due process of law. . . . The rack and torture chamber may not be substituted for the witness stand. The state may not permit an accused to be hurried to conviction under mob domination—where the whole proceeding is but a mask—without supplying corrective process. Moore v. Dempsey, 261 U.S. 86, 91, 43 S.Ct. 265. The state may not deny to the accused the aid of counsel. Powell v. Alabama, 287 U.S. 45, 53 S.Ct. 55. Nor may a state, through the action of its officers, contrive a conviction through the pretense of a trial which in truth is "but used as a means of depriving a defendant of liberty through a deliberate deception of court and jury by the presentation of testimony known to be perjured." Mooney v. Holohan, 294 U.S. 103, 112, 55 S.Ct. 340, 342. And the trial equally is a mere pretense where the state authorities have contrived a conviction resting solely upon confessions obtained by violence. The due process clause requires "that state action, whether through one agency or another, shall be consistent with the fundamental principles of liberty and justice which lie at the base of all our civil and political institutions." Hebert v. Louisiana, 272 U.S. 312, 316, 47 S.Ct. 103, 104. It would be difficult to conceive of methods more revolting to the sense of justice than those taken to procure the confessions of these petitioners, and the use of the confessions thus obtained as the basis for conviction and sentence was a clear denial of due process. . . .

. . . The court thus denied a federal right fully established and specially set up and claimed, and the judgment must be reversed.

———

Comments and Questions

1. Although both cases involved an allegedly involuntary confession, in the preceding case the Court relied upon the Fourteenth Amendment, and in the following case the Court relied upon the Fifth Amendment. The language of the Fifth Amendment, which provides that no one shall be compelled to be a witness

against him- or herself, sounds applicable to involuntary confessions, but early confession cases did not rely on it, because then unclear was whether the Fifth Amendment privilege against self-incrimination was available outside the court-room.

2. The coercion involved in the *Brown* case was extreme. What should happen if the pressure on the defendant is much milder? For example, should a confession be admissible if it is elicited by falsely promising the defendant that charges will be dropped if she will confess?

MIRANDA v. ARIZONA

Supreme Court of the United States, 1966.
384 U.S. 436, 86 S.Ct. 1602.

MR. CHIEF JUSTICE WARREN delivered the opinion of the Court. . . .

The constitutional issue we decide in each of these cases is the admissibility of statements obtained from a defendant questioned while in custody or otherwise deprived of his freedom of action in any significant way. In each, the defendant was questioned by police officers, detectives, or a prosecuting attorney in a room in which he was cut off from the outside world. In none of these cases was the defendant given a full and effective warning of his rights at the outset of the interrogation process. In all the cases, the questioning elicited oral admissions, and in three of them, signed statements as well which were admitted at their trials. They all thus share salient features—incommunicado interrogation of individuals in a police-dominated atmosphere, resulting in self-incriminating statements without full warnings of constitutional rights.

An understanding of the nature and setting of this in-custody interrogation is essential to our decisions today. The difficulty in depicting what transpires at such interrogations stems from the fact that in this country they have largely taken place incommunicado. From extensive factual studies undertaken in the early 1930's, including the famous Wickersham Report to Congress by a Presidential Commission, it is clear that police violence and the "third degree" flourished at that time. In a series of cases decided by this Court long after these studies, the police resorted to physical brutality—beatings, hanging, whipping—and to sustained and protracted questioning incommunicado in order to extort confessions. The Commission on Civil Rights in 1961 found much evidence to indicate that "some policemen still resort to physical force to obtain confessions," 1961 Comm'n on Civil Rights Rep., Justice, pt. 5, 17. The use of physical brutality and violence is not, unfortunately, relegated to the past or to any part of the country. Only recently in Kings County, New York, the police brutally beat, kicked and placed lighted cigarette butts on the back of a potential witness under interrogation for the purpose of securing a statement incriminating a third party. People v. Portelli, 15 N.Y.2d 235, 257 N.Y.S.2d 931, 205 N.E.2d 857 (1965).

The examples given above are undoubtedly the exception now, but they are sufficiently widespread to be the object of concern. Unless a proper limitation upon custodial interrogation is achieved—such as these decisions will advance—there can be no assurance that practices of this nature will be eradicated in the foreseeable future. . . .

Again we stress that the modern practice of in-custody interrogation is psychologically rather than physically oriented.   As we have stated before, "Since Chambers v. State of Florida, 309 U.S. 227, 60 S.Ct. 472, this Court has recognized that coercion can be mental as well as physical, and that the blood of the accused is not the only hallmark of an unconstitutional inquisition."   Blackburn v. State of Alabama, 361 U.S. 199, 206, 80 S.Ct. 274, 279 (1960).   Interrogation still takes place in privacy.   Privacy results in secrecy and this in turn results in a gap in our knowledge as to what in fact goes on in the interrogation rooms.   A valuable source of information about present police practices, however, may be found in various police manuals and texts which document procedures employed with success in the past, and which recommend various other effective tactics.   These texts are used by law enforcement agencies themselves as guides.   It should be noted that these texts professedly present the most enlightened and effective means presently used to obtain statements through custodial interrogation.   By considering these texts and other data, it is possible to describe procedures observed and noted around the country.

The officers are told by the manuals that the "principal psychological factor contributing to a successful interrogation is privacy—being alone with the person under interrogation."   The efficacy of this tactic has been explained as follows:

> If at all practicable, the interrogation should take place in the investigator's office or at least in a room of his own choice.   The subject should be deprived of every psychological advantage.   In his own home he may be confident, indignant, or recalcitrant.   He is more keenly aware of his rights and more reluctant to tell of his indiscretions or criminal behavior within the walls of his home.   Moreover his family and other friends are nearby, their presence lending moral support.   In his office, the investigator possesses all the advantages.   The atmosphere suggests the invincibility of the forces of the law.

To highlight the isolation and unfamiliar surroundings, the manuals instruct the police to display an air of confidence in the suspect's guilt and from outward appearance to maintain only an interest in confirming certain details.   The guilt of the subject is to be posited as a fact.   The interrogator should direct his comments toward the reasons why the subject committed the act, rather than court failure by asking the subject whether he did it.   Like other men, perhaps the subject has had a bad family life, had an unhappy childhood, had too much to drink, had an unrequited desire for women.   The officers are instructed to minimize the moral seriousness of the offense, to cast blame on the victim or on society.   These tactics are designed to put the subject in a psychological state where his story is but an elaboration of what the police purport to know already—that he is guilty.   Explanations to the contrary are dismissed and discouraged. . . .

When the techniques described above prove unavailing, the texts recommend they be alternated with a show of some hostility.   One ploy often used has been termed the "friendly-unfriendly" or the "Mutt and Jeff" act:

> . . . In this technique, two agents are employed. Mutt, the relentless investigator, who knows the subject is guilty and is not going to waste any time. He's sent a dozen men away for this crime and he's going to send the subject away for the full term. Jeff, on the other hand, is obviously a kindhearted man. He has a family himself. He has a brother who was involved in a little scrape like this. He disapproves of Mutt and his tactics and will arrange to get him off the case if the subject will cooperate. He can't hold Mutt off for very long. The subject would be wise to make a quick decision. The technique is applied by having both investigators present while Mutt acts out his role. Jeff may stand by quietly and demur at some of Mutt's tactics. When Jeff makes his plea for cooperation, Mutt is not present in the room.

The interrogators sometimes are instructed to induce a confession out of trickery. The technique here is quite effective in crimes which require identification or which run in series. In the identification situation, the interrogator may take a break in his questioning to place the subject among a group of men in a line-up. "The witness or complainant (previously coached, if necessary) studies the line-up and confidently points out the subject as the guilty party." Then the questioning resumes "as though there were now no doubt about the guilt of the subject." A variation on this technique is called the "reverse line-up":

> The accused is placed in a line-up, but this time he is identified by several fictitious witnesses or victims who associated him with different offenses. It is expected that the subject will become desperate and confess to the offense under investigation in order to escape from the false accusations. . . .

Even without employing brutality, the "third degree" or the specific stratagems described above, the very fact of custodial interrogation exacts a heavy toll on individual liberty and trades on the weakness of individuals. . . .

Today, then, there can be no doubt that the Fifth Amendment privilege is available outside of criminal court proceedings and serves to protect persons in all settings in which their freedom of action is curtailed in any significant way from being compelled to incriminate themselves. We have concluded that without proper safeguards the process of in-custody interrogation of persons suspected or accused of crime contains inherently compelling pressures which work to undermine the individual's will to resist and to compel him to speak where he would not otherwise do so freely. In order to combat these pressures and to permit a full opportunity to exercise the privilege against self-incrimination, the accused must be adequately and effectively apprised of his rights and the exercise of those rights must be fully honored.

It is impossible for us to foresee the potential alternatives for protecting the privilege which might be devised by Congress or the States in the exercise of their creative rule-making capacities. Therefore we cannot say that the Constitution necessarily requires adherence to any particular solution for the inherent compulsions of the interrogation process as it is presently conducted. Our decision in no way creates a constitutional straitjacket which will handicap sound efforts at reform, nor is it intended to have this effect. We encourage Congress and the States to continue their laudable search for increasingly effective ways of protecting the rights of the individual while promoting efficient enforcement of our criminal laws. However, unless we are shown other procedures which are at least as effective in apprising accused persons of their right of silence and in assuring a continuous opportunity to exercise it, the following safeguards must be observed. . . .

. . . [The defendant] must be warned prior to any questioning that he has the right to remain silent, that anything he says can be used against him in a court of law, that he has the right to the presence of an attorney, and that if he cannot afford an attorney one will be appointed for him prior to any questioning if he so desires. Opportunity to exercise these rights must be afforded to him throughout the interrogation. After such warnings have been given, and such opportunity afforded him, the individual may knowingly and intelligently waive these rights and agree to answer questions or make a statement. But unless and until such warnings and waiver are demonstrated by the prosecution at trial, no evidence obtained as a result of interrogation can be used against him.

A recurrent argument made in these cases is that society's need for interrogation outweighs the privilege. This argument is not unfamiliar to this Court. See, e.g., Chambers v. State of Florida, 309 U.S. 227, 240–241, 60 S.Ct. 472, 478–479 (1940). The whole thrust of our foregoing discussion demonstrates that the Constitution has prescribed the rights of the individual when confronted with the power of government when it provided in the Fifth Amendment that an individual cannot be compelled to be a witness against himself. That right cannot be abridged. As Mr. Justice Brandeis once observed:

> Decency, security, and liberty alike demand that government officials shall be subjected to the same rules of conduct that are commands to the citizen. In a government of laws, existence of the government will be imperilled if it fails to observe the law scrupulously. Our government is the potent, the omnipresent teacher. For good or for ill, it teaches the whole people by its example. Crime is contagious. If the government becomes a lawbreaker, it breeds contempt for law; it invites every man to become a law unto himself; it invites anarchy. To declare that in the administration of the criminal law the end justifies the means . . . would bring terrible retribution. Against that pernicious doctrine this court should resolutely set its face. (Olmstead v. United States, 277 U.S. 438, 485, 48 S.Ct. 564, 575 (1928) (dissenting opinion).) . . .

Because of the nature of the problem and because of its recurrent significance in numerous cases, we have to this point discussed the relationship of the Fifth Amendment privilege to police interrogation without specific concentration on the facts of the cases before us. We turn now to these facts to consider the application to these cases of the constitutional principles discussed above. In each instance, we have concluded that statements were obtained from the defendant under circumstances that did not meet constitutional standards for protection of the privilege.

No. 759. *Miranda* v. *Arizona.*

On March 13, 1963, petitioner, Ernesto Miranda, was arrested at his home and taken in custody to a Phoenix police station. He was there identified by the complaining witness. The police then took him to "Interrogation Room No. 2" of the detective bureau. There he was questioned by two police officers. The officers admitted at trial that Miranda was not advised that he had a right to have an attorney present. Two hours later, the officers emerged from the interrogation room with a written confession signed by Miranda. At the top of the statement was a typed paragraph stating that the confession was made voluntarily, without threats or promises of immunity and "with full knowledge of my legal rights, understanding any statement I make may be used against me."

At his trial before a jury, the written confession was admitted into evidence over the objection of defense counsel, and the officers testified to the prior oral confession made by Miranda during the interrogation. Miranda was found guilty of kidnapping and rape. He was sentenced to 20 to 30 years' imprisonment on each count, the sentences to run concurrently. On appeal, the Supreme Court of Arizona held that Miranda's constitutional rights were not violated in obtaining the confession and affirmed the conviction. In reaching its decision, the court emphasized heavily the fact that Miranda did not specifically request counsel.

We reverse. From the testimony of the officers and by the admission of respondent, it is clear that Miranda was not in any way apprised of his right to consult with an attorney and to have one present during the interrogation, nor was his right not to be compelled to incriminate himself effectively protected in any other manner. Without these warnings the statements were inadmissible. The mere fact that he signed a statement which contained a typed-in clause stating that he had "full knowledge" of his "legal rights" does not approach the knowing and intelligent waiver required to relinquish constitutional rights.

[The Court discussed the facts of the other cases.] . . .

[Justices Clark, Harlan, Stewart, and White dissented. The dissenting opinions are omitted.]

Comments and Questions

1. Studies comparing the rate of confessions prior to the *Miranda* decision with the rate of confessions after the *Miranda* rules were in effect show little change. Do these findings suggest that the *Miranda* rules should be abandoned? That different measures should be instituted to protect the privilege against self-incrimination?

2. In 1984 the Court adopted a "public safety" exception to the *Miranda* rules: when imminent danger to the public (such as a loaded weapon that has not been recovered) is present, police may question a suspect without giving him the *Miranda* warnings and yet not forfeit the right to use his statements against him

in court. Is such an exception consistent with the rationale of the *Miranda* decision? See New York v. Quarles, 467 U.S. 649, 104 S.Ct. 2626 (1984).

———

B. Guilty Pleas

HENDERSON v. MORGAN

Supreme Court of the United States, 1976.
426 U.S. 637, 96 S.Ct. 2253.

Mr. Justice Stevens delivered the opinion of the Court.

The question presented is whether a defendant may enter a voluntary plea of guilty to a charge of second-degree murder without being informed that intent to cause the death of his victim was an element of the offense.

The case arises out of a collateral attack on a judgment entered by a state trial court in Fulton County, N.Y., in 1965. Respondent, having been indicted on a charge of first-degree murder, pleaded guilty to second-degree murder and was sentenced to an indeterminate term of imprisonment of 25 years to life. He did not appeal.

. . . [I]n 1973, respondent filed a petition for writ of habeas corpus in the United States District Court for the Northern District of New York. He alleged that his guilty plea was involuntary because he was not aware . . . that intent to cause death was an element of the offense. . . .

. . . [The district court] found that respondent "was not advised by counsel or court, at any time, that an intent to cause the death or a design to effect the death of the victim was an essential element of Murder 2nd degree." On the basis of [this] finding, the District Court held "as a matter of law" that the plea of guilty was involuntary and had to be set aside. This holding was affirmed, without opinion, by the Court of Appeals.

Before addressing the question whether the District Court correctly held the plea invalid as a matter of law, we review some of the facts developed at the evidentiary hearing.

On April 6, 1965, respondent[b] killed Mrs. Ada Francisco in her home.

When he was in seventh grade, respondent was committed to the Rome State School for Mental Defectives where he was classified as "retarded." He was released to become a farm laborer and ultimately went to work on Mrs. Francisco's farm. Following an argument, she threatened to return him to state custody. He then decided to abscond. During the night he entered Mrs. Francisco's bedroom with a knife, intending to collect his earned wages before leaving; she awoke, began to scream, and he stabbed her. He took a small amount of money, fled in her car, and became involved in an accident about 80 miles away. The knife was found in the glove compartment of her car. He was promptly arrested and made a statement to the police. He was then 19 years old and substantially below average intelligence.

b. When the Supreme Court considers a petition for certiorari, which is a request for review usually by the party who lost in the lower court, the party who requests review is called the petitioner, and the other party is called the respondent. Thus, in this case, the petitioner was the warden, and the respondent was the defendant, Morgan.

Respondent was indicted for first-degree murder and arraigned on April 15, 1965. Two concededly competent attorneys were appointed to represent him. The indictment, which charged that he "willfully" stabbed his victim, was read in open court. His lawyers requested, and were granted, access to his written statement and to earlier psychiatric reports. A new psychiatric examination was requested and ordered.

Respondent was found competent to stand trial. Defense counsel held a series of conferences with the prosecutors, with the respondent, and with members of his family. The lawyers "thought manslaughter first would satisfy the needs of justice." They therefore endeavored to have the charge reduced to manslaughter, but the prosecution would agree to nothing less than second-degree murder and a minimum sentence of 25 years. The lawyers gave respondent advice about the different sentences which could be imposed for the different offenses, but, as the District Court found, did not explain the required element of intent.

On June 8, 1965, respondent appeared in court with his attorneys and entered a plea of guilty to murder in the second degree in full satisfaction of the first-degree murder charge made in the indictment. In direct colloquy with the trial judge respondent stated that his plea was based on the advice of his attorneys, that he understood he was accused of killing Mrs. Francisco in Fulton County, that he was waiving his right to a jury trial, and that he would be sent to prison. There was no discussion of the elements of the offense of second-degree murder, no indication that the nature of the offense had ever been discussed with respondent, and no reference of any kind to the requirement of intent to cause the death of the victim.

At the sentencing hearing a week later his lawyers made a statement explaining his version of the offense, particularly noting that respondent "meant no harm to that lady" when he entered her room with the knife. The prosecutor disputed defense counsel's version of the matter, but did not discuss it in detail. After studying the probation officer's report, the trial judge pronounced sentence.

At the evidentiary hearing in the Federal District Court, respondent testified that he would not have pleaded guilty if he had known that an intent to cause the death of his victim was an element of the offense of second-degree murder. The District Judge did not indicate whether or not he credited this testimony.

Petitioner contends that the District Court applied an unrealistically rigid rule of law. Instead of testing the voluntariness of a plea by determining whether a ritualistic litany of the formal legal elements of an offense was read to the defendant, petitioner argues that the court should examine the totality of the circumstances and determine whether the substance of the charge, as opposed to its technical elements, was conveyed to the accused. We do not disagree with the thrust of petitioner's argument, but we are persuaded that even under the test which he espouses, this judgment finding respondent guilty of second-degree murder was defective.

We assume, as petitioner argues, that the prosecutor had overwhelming evidence of guilt available. We also accept petitioner's characterization of the competence of respondent's counsel and of the wisdom of their advice to plead guilty to a charge of second-degree murder. Nevertheless, such a plea cannot support a judgment of guilt unless it was voluntary in a constitutional sense.[13] And clearly the plea could not be voluntary in the sense that it constituted an intelligent admission that he committed the offense unless the defendant received "real notice of the true nature of the charge against him, the first and most universally recognized requirement of due process." Smith v. O'Grady, 312 U.S. 329, 334, 61 S.Ct. 572, 574.

The charge of second-degree murder was never formally made. Had it been made, it necessarily would have included a charge that respondent's assault was "committed with a design to effect the death of the person killed." That element of the offense might have been proved by the objective evidence even if respondent's actual state of mind was consistent with innocence or manslaughter. But even if such a design to effect death would almost inevitably have been inferred from evidence that respondent repeatedly stabbed Mrs. Francisco, it is nevertheless also true that a jury would not have been required to draw that inference. The jury would have been entitled to accept defense counsel's appraisal of the incident as involving only manslaughter in the first degree. Therefore, an admission by respondent that he killed Mrs. Francisco does not necessarily also admit that he was guilty of second-degree murder.

There is nothing in this record that can serve as a substitute for either a finding after trial, or a voluntary admission, that respondent had the requisite intent. Defense counsel did not purport to stipulate to that fact; they did not explain to him that his plea would be an admission of that fact; and he made no factual statement or admission necessarily implying that he had such intent. In these circumstances it is impossible to conclude that his plea to the unexplained charge of second-degree murder was voluntary.

Petitioner argues that affirmance of the Court of Appeals will invite countless collateral attacks on judgments entered on pleas of guilty, since frequently the record will not contain a complete enumeration of the elements of the offense to which an accused person pleads guilty.[18] We think petitioner's fears are exaggerated.

Normally the record contains either an explanation of the charge by the trial judge, or at least a representation by defense counsel that the nature of the offense has been explained to the accused. Moreover, even without such an express representation, it may be appropriate to presume that in most cases defense counsel routinely explain the nature of the offense in sufficient detail to give the accused notice of what he is being

13. A plea may be involuntary either because the accused does not understand the nature of the constitutional protections that he is waiving, see, e.g., Johnson v. Zerbst, 304 U.S. 458, 464–465, 58 S.Ct. 1019, 1023, or because he has such an incomplete understanding of the charge that his plea cannot stand as an intelligent admission of guilt. Without adequate notice of the nature of the charge against him, or proof that he in fact understood the charge, the plea cannot be voluntary in this latter sense. Smith v. O'Grady, 312 U.S. 329, 61 S.Ct. 572.

18. There is no need in this case to decide whether notice of the true nature, or substance, of a charge always requires a description of every element of the offense; we assume it does not. Nevertheless, intent is such a critical element of the offense of second-degree murder that notice of that element is required.

asked to admit. This case is unique because the trial judge found as a fact that the element of intent was not explained to respondent. Moreover, respondent's unusually low mental capacity provides a reasonable explanation for counsel's oversight; it also forecloses the conclusion that the error was harmless beyond a reasonable doubt, for it lends at least a modicum of credibility to defense counsel's appraisal of the homicide as a manslaughter rather than a murder.

Since respondent did not receive adequate notice of the offense to which he pleaded guilty, his plea was involuntary and the judgment of conviction was entered without due process of law.

Affirmed. . . .

[Justice Rehnquist, joined by Chief Justice Burger, dissented. His opinion is omitted.]

Comments and Questions

1. The defendant knew the possible penalties for the offense to which he was pleading guilty and knew that he was charged with killing Mrs. Francisco. How likely do you think it is that he would not have pleaded guilty if he had been informed that the crime to which he was pleading guilty included the element of intent to kill? If he had testified that he did not know whether that information would have changed his decision to plead guilty, do you think the Court would have affirmed?

2. Suppose that the defendant is fully informed of the elements of second-degree murder, denies that he intended to kill the victim, and nevertheless wishes to plead guilty. The Supreme Court has held that he should be allowed to do so. Do you agree? What values are compromised by allowing a person to plead guilty while protesting his innocence? Are other goals of the criminal justice system furthered?

BORDENKIRCHER v. HAYES

Supreme Court of the United States, 1978.
434 U.S. 357, 98 S.Ct. 663.

MR. JUSTICE STEWART delivered the opinion of the Court.

The question in this case is whether the Due Process Clause of the Fourteenth Amendment is violated when a state prosecutor carries out a threat made during plea negotiations to reindict the accused on more serious charges if he does not plead guilty to the offense with which he was originally charged.

I

The respondent, Paul Lewis Hayes, was indicted by a Fayette County, Ky., grand jury on a charge of uttering a forged instrument in the amount of $88.30, an offense then punishable by a term of 2 to 10 years in prison. Ky.Rev.Stat. § 434.130 (1973) (repealed 1975). After arraignment, Hayes, his retained counsel, and the Commonwealth's Attorney met in the presence of the Clerk of the Court to discuss a possible plea agreement.

During these conferences the prosecutor offered to recommend a sentence of five years in prison if Hayes would plead guilty to the indictment. He also said that if Hayes did not plead guilty and "save[d] the court the inconvenience and necessity of a trial," he would return to the grand jury to seek an indictment under the Kentucky Habitual Criminal Act, then Ky.Rev.Stat. § 431.190 (1973) (repealed 1975), which would subject Hayes to a mandatory sentence of life imprisonment by reason of his two prior felony convictions. Hayes chose not to plead guilty, and the prosecutor did obtain an indictment charging him under the Habitual Criminal Act. It is not disputed that the recidivist charge was fully justified by the evidence, that the prosecutor was in possession of this evidence at the time of the original indictment, and that Hayes' refusal to plead guilty to the original charge was what led to his indictment under the habitual criminal statute.

A jury found Hayes guilty on the principal charge of uttering a forged instrument and, in a separate proceeding, further found that he had twice before been convicted of felonies. As required by the habitual offender statute, he was sentenced to a life term in the penitentiary. The Kentucky Court of Appeals rejected Hayes' constitutional objections to the enhanced sentence, holding in an unpublished opinion that imprisonment for life with the possibility of parole was constitutionally permissible in light of the previous felonies of which Hayes had been convicted, and that the prosecutor's decision to indict him as a habitual offender was a legitimate use of available leverage in the plea-bargaining process.

On Hayes' petition for a federal writ of habeas corpus, the United States District Court for the Eastern District of Kentucky agreed that there had been no constitutional violation in the sentence or the indictment procedure, and denied the writ. The Court of Appeals for the Sixth Circuit reversed the District Court's judgment. Hayes v. Cowan, 547 F.2d 42. While recognizing "that plea bargaining now plays an important role in our criminal justice system," id., at 43, the appellate court thought that the prosecutor's conduct during the bargaining negotiations had violated the principles of Blackledge v. Perry, 417 U.S. 21, 94 S.Ct. 2098, which "protect[ed] defendants from the vindictive exercise of a prosecutor's discretion." 547 F.2d, at 44. Accordingly, the court ordered that Hayes be discharged "except for his confinement under a lawful sentence imposed solely for the crime of uttering a forged instrument." Id., at 45. We granted certiorari to consider a constitutional question of importance in the administration of criminal justice. 431 U.S. 953, 97 S.Ct. 2672.

II

It may be helpful to clarify at the outset the nature of the issue in this case. While the prosecutor did not actually obtain the recidivist indictment until after the plea conferences had ended, his intention to do so was clearly expressed at the outset of the plea negotiations. Hayes was thus fully informed of the true terms of the offer when he made his decision to plead not guilty. This is not a situation, therefore, where the prosecutor without notice brought an additional and more serious charge after plea negotiations relating only to the original indictment had ended with the defendant's insistence on pleading not guilty. As a practical matter, in short, this case would be no different if the grand jury had indicted Hayes as a recidivist from the outset, and the prosecutor had offered to drop that charge as part of the plea bargain.

The Court of Appeals nonetheless drew a distinction between "concessions relating to prosecution under an existing indictment," and threats to bring more severe charges not contained in the original indictment—a line it thought necessary in order to establish a prophylactic rule to guard against the evil of prosecutorial vindictiveness. Quite apart from this chronological distinction, however, the Court of Appeals found that the prosecutor had acted vindictively in the present case since he had conceded that the indictment was influenced by his desire to induce a guilty plea. The ultimate conclusion of the Court of Appeals thus seems to have been that a prosecutor acts vindictively and in violation of due process of law whenever his charging decision is influenced by what he hopes to gain in the course of plea bargaining negotiations.

III

We have recently had occasion to observe: "[W]hatever might be the situation in an ideal world, the fact is that the guilty plea and the often concomitant plea bargain are important components of this country's criminal justice system. Properly administered, they can benefit all concerned." Blackledge v. Allison, 431 U.S. 63, 71, 97 S.Ct. 1621, 1627. The open acknowledgment of this previously clandestine practice has led this Court to recognize the importance of counsel during plea negotiations, Brady v. United States, 397 U.S. 742, 758, 90 S.Ct. 1463, 1474, the need for a public record indicating that a plea was knowingly and voluntarily made, Boykin v. Alabama, 395 U.S. 238, 242, 89 S.Ct. 1709, 1711, and the requirement that a prosecutor's plea-bargaining promise must be kept, Santobello v. New York, 404 U.S. 257, 262, 92 S.Ct. 495, 498. The decision of the Court of Appeals in the present case, however, did not deal with considerations such as these, but held that the substance of the plea offer itself violated the limitations imposed by the Due Process Clause of the Fourteenth Amendment. Cf. Brady v. United States, supra, 397 U.S., at 751 n. 8, 90 S.Ct., at 1470. For the reasons that follow, we have concluded that the Court of Appeals was mistaken in so ruling.

IV

Plea bargaining flows from "the mutuality of advantage" to defendants and prosecutors, each with his own reasons for wanting to avoid trial. Brady v. United States, supra, 397 U.S., at 752, 90 S.Ct., at 1471. Defendants advised by competent counsel and protected by other procedural safeguards are presumptively capable of intelligent choice in response to prosecutorial persuasion, and unlikely to be driven to false self-condemnation. 397 U.S., at 758, 90 S.Ct., at 1474. Indeed, acceptance of the basic legitimacy of plea bargaining necessarily implies rejection of any notion that a guilty plea is involuntary in a constitutional sense simply because it is the end result of the bargaining process. By hypothesis, the plea may have been induced by promises of a recommendation of a lenient sentence or a reduction of charges, and thus by fear of the possibility of a greater penalty upon conviction after a trial. See ABA Project on Standards for Criminal Justice, Pleas of Guilty § 3.1 (App.Draft 1968); Note, Plea Bargaining and the Transformation of the Criminal Process, 90 Harv.L. Rev. 564 (1977). Cf. Brady v. United States, supra, at 751, 90 S.Ct., at 1470; North Carolina v. Alford, 400 U.S. 25, 91 S.Ct. 160.

While confronting a defendant with the risk of more severe punishment clearly may have a "discouraging effect on the defendant's assertion of his trial rights, the imposition of these difficult choices [is] an inevitable"—and permissible—"attribute of any legitimate system which tolerates and encourages the negotiation of pleas." Chaffin v. Stynchcombe, [412 U.S. 17, 31, 93 S.Ct. 1977, 1985 (1973)]. It follows that, by tolerating and encouraging the negotiation of pleas, this Court has necessarily accepted as constitutionally legitimate the simple reality that the prosecutor's interest at the bargaining table is to persuade the defendant to forgo his right to plead not guilty.

It is not disputed here that Hayes was properly chargeable under the recidivist statute, since he had in fact been convicted of two previous felonies. In our system, so long as the prosecutor has probable cause to believe that the accused committed an offense defined by statute, the decision whether or not to prosecute, and what charge to file or bring before a grand jury, generally rests entirely in his discretion. Within the limits set by the legislature's constitutionally valid definition of chargeable offenses, "the conscious exercise of some selectivity in enforcement is not in itself a federal constitutional violation" so long as "the selection was [not] deliberately based upon an unjustifiable standard such as race, religion, or other arbitrary classification." Oyler v. Boles, 368 U.S. 448, 456, 82 S.Ct. 501, 506. To hold that the prosecutor's desire to induce a guilty plea is an "unjustifiable standard," which, like race or religion, may play no part in his charging decision, would contradict the very premises that underlie the concept of plea bargaining itself. Moreover, a rigid constitutional rule that would prohibit a prosecutor from acting forthrightly in his dealings with the defense could only invite unhealthy subterfuge that would drive the practice of plea bargaining back into the shadows from which it has so recently emerged. See Blackledge v. Allison, 431 U.S., at 76, 97 S.Ct., at 1630.

There is no doubt that the breadth of discretion that our country's legal system vests in prosecuting attorneys carries with it the potential for both individual and institutional abuse. And broad though that discretion may be, there are undoubtedly constitutional limits upon its exercise. We hold only that the course of conduct engaged in by the prosecutor in this case, which no more than openly presented the defendant with the unpleasant alternatives of forgoing trial or facing charges on which he was plainly subject to prosecution, did not violate the Due Process Clause of the Fourteenth Amendment.

Accordingly, the judgment of the Court of Appeals is
Reversed.

[Justice Blackmun, joined by Justices Brennan and Marshall, dissented, as did Justice Powell. Their opinions are omitted.]

Comments and Questions

1. If a prosecutor obtained a confession by threatening to indict the defendant on more serious charges if she did not confess, the confession would be deemed involuntary and its use at trial would be said to violate due process. Why is it permissible to obtain a guilty plea in this way?

2. Do you think threats such as the one at issue in this case cause some innocent defendants to plead guilty? If so, how can permitting these threats be justified?

Section Eight. Improving the Penal-Corrective Instrument

Possible "improvements" in the penal-corrective system are almost infinite in number. They can range from making prisons more humane to increasing the penalties for drunk driving to legalizing marijuana. We do not all agree on what would be an improvement. In part, differences of opinion here are the inevitable result of different views of what the proper purposes of the criminal law are.

Many books and articles depict various narrow problems in the penal-corrective instrument and propose specific solutions. The following excerpt attempts something different: it presents evidence of the erosion and corruption of an entire portion of the criminal justice system. As you read it, consider who is to blame for present conditions as well as how the conditions might be remedied.

J. MILLS, ON THE EDGE
120–48 (1975).*

Martin Erdmann thinks he might be antisocial. When he was six he liked to sneak across his family's red-carpeted, spiral-staircased entrance hall to the potted palm, and spit in it. At Yankee Stadium, he rooted for the Red Sox. When he went to Dartmouth, he cheered for Yale. He didn't make a lot of friends. He says he doesn't need them. Today he's fifty-seven years old, an unmarried millionaire lawyer, and he has defended more criminals than anyone else in the world. Because he is one of the five or ten best defense lawyers in New York, he gets those criminals turned back into the streets months or years earlier than they have any right to hope for. His clients are not Mafia bosses or bank embezzlers or suburban executives who've shot their wives. He defends killers, burglars, rapists, robbers—the men people mean when they talk about crime in the streets. Martin Erdmann's clients *are* crime in the streets.

---

* Excerpts from ON THE EDGE by James Mills. Copyright © 1971, 1972, 1975 by James Mills. Reprinted by permission of Doubleday & Company, Inc.

In twenty-five years Martin Erdmann has defended more than 100,000 criminals. He has saved them tens of thousands of years in prison and in those years they have robbed, raped, burglarized and murdered tens upon tens of thousands of people. The idea of having had a very personal and direct hand in all that mayhem strikes him as boring and irrelevant. "I have nothing to do with justice," he says. "Justice is not even part of the equation. If you say I have no moral reaction to what I do, you are right."

And *he* is right. As right as our adversary judicial system, as right as jury trials, as right as the presumption of innocence and the Fifth Amendment. If there is a fault in Erdmann's eagerness to free defendants, it is not with Erdmann himself, but with the system. Criminal law to the defense lawyer does not mean equity or fairness or proper punishment or vengeance. It means getting everything he can for his client. And in perhaps 98 per cent of his cases, the clients are guilty. Justice is a luxury enjoyed by the district attorney. He alone is sworn "to see that justice is done." The defense lawyer does not bask in the grandeur of any such noble oath. He finds himself most often working for the guilty and for a judicial system based upon the sound but paradoxical principle that the guilty must be freed to protect the innocent.

And Erdmann does free them, as many as he possibly can. He works for the Legal Aid Society, a private organization with a city contract to represent the 179,000 indigent defendants who flood each year into New York City courtrooms. He heads the society's supreme court branch, has fifty-five lawyers working under him, makes $23,500 a year. Next to the millions left him by his father, a Wall Street bond broker, the money means nothing. Twenty-five years ago, until the accounting office told him he was messing up their books, he kept his paychecks stuffed in a desk drawer. In private practice he could have a six-figure income and, probably, the fame of Edward Bennett Williams, or F. Lee Bailey, or Percy Foreman. He is disgusted when people accuse him of dedication. "That's just plain nonsense. The one word that does *not* describe me is dedicated. I reserve that word for people who do something that requires sacrifice. I don't sacrifice anything. The only reason I'm any good is because I have an ego. I like to win."

Martin Erdmann does not look like a winner. He is slight, unimposing, with balding hair cut short every Monday on his way to work, custom-made suits that come out baggy anyway and a slightly stooped, forward-leaning walk that makes him look, in motion, like Groucho Marx. His face is lean, bony, taut-skinned, with thin lips and bulging eyes. He lives in a one-bedroom co-op on Manhattan's East Side, has no television set and rarely answers his phone ("I learned that from my father—he could sit in a room for hours with a ringing phone"). He plays chess by postcard, buys Christmas presents from catalogues and seldom goes out except to work and eat. Defendants who ask him for loans get them. He finances black student scholarships and is listed as a patron of New York's City Center. His only self-indulgences are a seventy-five-acre weekend Connecticut retreat and a one-month-a-year fishing trip, alone, to the Adirondacks. "I discovered a long time ago," he says, "that I am a very self-contained person."

Like most men who are alone without loneliness, Martin Erdmann is emotionally compact: self-centered, stubborn, at times perverse. He is also a failed idealist. "I had an English professor in college," he says, "who read an essay I wrote and told me, 'Martin, you are looking for better bread than is made of wheat.' I've never forgotten that."

Martin Erdmann gets up at 4:45, reads till 6:30, then subways three miles downtown to the Criminal Court Building. He moves through the dark, empty hallway to his office and unlocks the door. He is there at 7:30, two and a half hours before the courts open, and he is alone. In another ten or fifteen minutes Milton Adler will arrive, his boss, chief attorney in the criminal branch. Then, one or two at a time, come the phone operator and clerks, the other lawyers, the defendants on bail, mothers of men in jail, sick-looking junkies with vomit-stained shirts, frightened people who sit quietly on the seven wooden chairs along the wall, angry people mumbling viciously, insane people dressed in costumes with feathers in their hair.

Before the rush begins, Martin Erdmann sits at his desk in a side office and goes over the folders of the day's cases. Anthony Howard, a twenty-one-year-old Negro, is accused of using a stick and knife to rob a man of his wallet. Howard's mother visits him in jail, brings clean clothes and takes out his laundry. She doesn't know that the greatest danger to her son is not the robbery charge, but the man who sleeps above him in the eight-by-six-foot cell. Robert Phillips, Howard's cellmate, escaped from a state mental hospital seven years ago, was recaptured, released, then arrested for the murder of a twenty-two-year-old girl and an infant boy. After three more years in a mental hospital, he has been declared legally sane and is now awaiting trial for the murders. Erdmann looks over the file. "Prisoners who've been in mental hospitals," he says, "tell me they keep them there until they admit the charges against them. Then they mark them sane and send them down for pleading." He decides to give the Anthony Howard case to Alice Schlesinger, a young lawyer who can still believe her clients are innocent. She's good at what Erdmann calls "hand-holding," giving a defendant and his family more time than the case might need.

Adler walks in, starts to say something, and the phone rings. Erdmann answers it. The call is from a woman out on bail on a charge of throwing lye on her husband. Now she wants Erdmann to help her get a shotgun license. She says she needs it for protection.

"Okay, Mable," he says, "but don't shoot too many people." He hangs up smiling and says to Adler, "Mable's switched from lye to shotguns."

Adler says something about a meeting he went to yesterday with DAs and judges to discuss ways of getting more prisoners out on bail. Erdmann listens and says nothing. What's left of his idealism, the wreckage, he defends against the day's events by affecting an air of playful cynicism. He smiles and laughs and pricks the pretty little bubbles of naiveté that rise around him from other lawyers. Listening to Adler, his face flashes now with the playful-cynic smile. "If they do reduce bail," he says, "it'll be the last they see of the defendants."

Alice Schlesinger appears in the doorway, a small young woman, about thirty, with long black hair. She wants to know what she can do to pressure the DA to start the trial of a bailed defendant charged with robbery. "Can't we put the screws to them a little? My client is very nervous and upset. He wants to get the trial over with."

"Well," says Erdmann, "of course you can always make a motion to dismiss for lack of prosecution. Say your client is suffering great emotional stress at having this dreadfully unjust accusation hanging over his head."

"Don't *smile* like that," she says. "He *is* innocent, this time."

Erdmann gets rid of the smile. "Well, you know," he says, "maybe the DA is having a little trouble locating the complainant, and your defendant's on bail anyway, so why urge them to go right out and track him down? Because if they find the complainant and go to trial and if from some extremely unfortunate occurrence your client should be convicted, then he's going to jail and he'll be a lot worse off than just nervous."

She agrees reluctantly and leaves. Erdmann sits silently at his desk, staring into the piles of papers. Then he says, "She has a lot to learn. She'll learn. With some tears, but she'll learn."

Erdmann gathers up the folders and takes the elevator to a courtroom on the thirteenth floor. He sits in one of the soft upholstered chairs in the jury box and takes another look at the thirty folders of the day's cases: a forgery, robberies (mostly muggings), burglaries, drug sales, assault with a gun, arson, sodomy, an attempted murder. He arranges them on the shelf in front of the jury box and sits back to await the DAs and the judge. He is alone in the courtroom, a dimly lighted, solemn place—meant to be imposing, it is only oppressive. Brown walls, brown tables, brown church-pew seats soak up what little light the low-watt overhead bulbs surrender.

A few spectators walk in and Erdmann calls the names of his bail cases. No one answers. "That's not surprising," he says, "they couldn't possibly get up this early."

A DA comes in and Erdmann asks him about a kidnapping case that's approaching trial. "The DA on that one's on trial on another case, Marty. He won't be finished for a month at least."

"Wonderful." Erdmann laughs. "I hope he stays on trial until the complainant's thirty. Then it won't look so bad. She was eight when it happened and she's already eleven." The DA shakes his head and walks away. Two more DAs arrive and Erdmann talks to them, joking with them, making gentle fun of them, establishing his presence: twice their age, more experienced, more knowledgeable, more cunning. "There's no question that my reputation is much too high," he says. "It's been carefully cultivated. Myths are very important in this business."

The judge enters: Mitchell Schweitzer, tall, thin, gray-haired, on the bench twenty-six years, sixteen of them working closely with Erdmann. He flashes a look around the room, greeting private lawyers, Erdmann and the two assistant DAs.

The clerk calls a name: "José Santiago!"

Erdmann fumbles through his folders and pulls one out. "He's mine," he says. An assistant DA looks at the rows of folders on his table and picks one up. Erdmann and the DA walk slowly toward the judge's bench, pulling out papers as they go. Erdmann has, among other things,

a copy of the complaint and a handwritten interview another Legal Aid
lawyer had earlier with the defendant. The DA has a synopsis of the
grand jury testimony and a copy of the defendant's record. With these
documents, in the next three or four minutes, while the defendant himself
sits unaware in a detention pen beneath the courtroom, the judge, DA and
Erdmann will determine the likelihood of guilt and the amount of time
the man will serve.

Trials are obsolete. In New York City only one arrest in thousands
ends in trial. The government no longer has time and money to afford
the luxury of presuming innocence, nor the belief that the truest way of
determining guilt is by jury trial. Today, in effect, the government says
to each defendant, "If you will abandon your unsupportable claim of
innocence, we will compensate you with a light sentence." The defendant
says, "How light?"—and the DA, defense lawyer and judge are drawn
together at the bench. The conference there is called "plea bargaining,"
and it proceeds as the playing of a game, with moves and countermoves,
protocol, rules and ritual. Power is in the hands of the prisoners. For as
increasing crime has pushed our judicial system to the crumbling edge of
chaos and collapse, the defendant himself has emerged as the only man
with a helping hand. The government needs guilty pleas to move the
cases out of court, and the defendants are selling their guilty pleas for the
only currency the government can offer—time. But no matter what
sentence is finally agreed upon, the real outcome of this bargaining
contest is never truly in doubt. The guilty always win. The innocent
always lose.

To play the game well, a lawyer must be ruthless. He is working
within, but *against,* a system that has been battered to its knees. He
must not hesitate to kick it when it's down, and to take every advantage
of its weakness. No one is better at the game than Martin Erdmann.

Judge Schweitzer glances through the grand jury extract handed him
by the DA, a young bespectacled man named Jack Litman. Then the
judge looks up over his glasses. "What are you looking for, Marty?"

Erdmann isn't sure yet. His client is accused of robbing a man on the
street after stabbing him in the face, neck, chest, stomach and back. The
victim was held from behind by an accomplice. "They have a big
identification problem," Erdmann says. He is looking at a copy of a police
report. "The DD–5 says the complaining witness refused to look at
pictures in the hospital the next day because he said he wouldn't be able
to identify the assailants from photographs."

"Your honor," Litman says, "they put sixty-five stitches in him."

"Just a minute," says the judge, and proceeds to read quickly to
Erdmann from the grand jury extract: "They fled into an apartment
house, the cop asked the super if he'd seen them, the super said they went
into apartment 3–A, the cop went in, placed them under arrest and took
them to the hospital where they were identified by the victim." He looks
up. Erdmann has never heard the grand jury testimony before, and it
hasn't exactly made his day. "So, you see, Marty, it's not such a bad
case." He leans back. "I'll tell you what. A year with credit for time
served." Santiago already has been in jail for ten months. With time off

for good behavior, that sentence will let him out today. Erdmann agrees. The DA nods and starts stuffing papers back into the folder. "Bring him up," he says.

Santiago's accomplice is brought in with him. Both men are twenty-one, short and defiant-looking. The accomplice, Jesus Rodriguez, has his own lawyer, who now joins Erdmann in agreeing to the sentence. The lawyers explain the offer to the defendants. They tell them that the offer can be made only if they are in fact guilty. Neither the judge nor the DA nor the lawyers themselves would permit an innocent man to plead guilty. Santiago and Rodriguez look bewildered. They say they are innocent, they did nothing. Much mumbling and consternation at the counsel table. Then Schweitzer says, "Would you like a second call?"

"Yes, your honor," says Erdmann. "A second call." The defendants are led out and downstairs to a detention pen. Erdmann looks at Santiago's interview sheet, a mimeographed form with blanks for name, age, address, education, employer, and then at the bottom, space for his version of what happened. Santiago's statement begins, "I am not guilty. I did nothing wrong." He has never been arrested before. He says he and Rodriguez were asleep in their apartment when the police charged in and grabbed them. At his arraignment some weeks ago, he pleaded not guilty.

"Talk to them," Judge Schweitzer suggests. Erdmann and his co-counsel walk over to the door of the pen. A court officer opens it and they step from the court's dark, quiet brownness into a bright, noisy, butt-littered hallway. The door slams shut behind them. From somewhere below come voices shouting, and the clang of cell doors closing. A guard yells, "On the gate!" and precedes them down a dark stairway to a barred steel door. An inside guard unlocks the door and they walk into a yellow, men's-room-tiled corridor with windows on the left and a large bench-lined cell on the right. Twenty men are in the cell, almost all of them dirty and bearded, some young and frightened sitting alone on the benches, others older, talking, standing, as at home here as on a Harlem street corner. Suddenly the voices stop and the prisoners, like animals expecting to be fed, turn their heads toward Erdmann and his co-counsel. Three other lawyers walk in, too, and in a moment the voices begin again—prisoners and lawyers arguing with each other, explaining, cajoling, conning in the jailhouse jargon of pleas and sentences: "I can get you one and one running wild [two years consecutive]. . . . I know a guy got an E and a flat [a Class E felony with a year]. . . . So you want a bullet [a year]? You'll take a bullet?"

Erdmann walks to the far end of the cell and Santiago meets him at the bars. Erdmann puts his toe on a cross strip between the bars and balances Santiago's folder and papers on his knee. He takes out a Lucky Strike, lights it and inhales. Santiago watches, and then a sudden rush of words starts violently from his mouth. Erdmann silences him. "First let me find out what I have to know," he says calmly, "and then you can talk as much as you want." Santiago is standing next to a chest-high, steel-plate partition. On the other side of it, a toilet flushes. A few steps away, Rodriguez is talking through the bars to his lawyer.

"If you didn't do anything wrong," Erdmann says to Santiago, "then there's no point even discussing this. You'll go to trial."

Santiago nods desperately. "I ain't done nothing! I was asleep! I *never* been in trouble before." This is the first time since his initial interview seven months ago that he has had a chance to tell his story to a lawyer, and he is frantic to get it all out. Erdmann cannot stop the torrent, and now he does not try. "I never been arrested," Santiago shouts, "never been to jail, never been in *no* trouble, *nothing*. We just asleep in the apartment and the police break in and grab us out of bed and take us, we ain't done nothing, I *never* been in trouble, I never saw this man before, and he says we did it. I don't even know what we did, and I been here ten months, I don't see no lawyer or nothing, I ain't had a shower in two months, we locked up twenty-four hours a day, I got no shave, no hot food, I ain't *never* been like this before, I can't stand it, I'm going to kill myself, I got to get out, I ain't—"

Now Erdmann interrupts, icily calm, speaking very slowly, foot on the cross strip, drawing on his cigarette. "Well, it's very simple. Either you are guilty or you're not. If you're guilty of anything you can take the plea and they'll give you a year, and under the circumstances that's a very good plea and you ought to take it. If you're not guilty, you have to go to trial."

"I'm not guilty." He says it fast, nodding, sure of that.

"Then you should go to trial. But the jury is going to hear that the cop followed you into the building, the super sent him to apartment 3–A, he arrested you there and the man identified you in the hospital. If they find you guilty, you might get fifteen years."

Santiago is unimpressed with all of that. "I'm innocent. I didn't do nothing. But I got to get out of here. I got to—"

"Well, if you *did* do anything and you are a little guilty, they'll give you time served and you'll walk."

That's more like it.

"Today? I walk today?"

"If you are guilty of something and you take the plea."

"I'll take the plea. But I didn't do nothing."

"You can't take the plea unless you are guilty of something."

"I want the year. I'm innocent, but I'll take the year. I walk today if I take the year?"

The papers start to fall from Erdmann's knee and he grabs them and settles them back. "You walk if you take the plea, but no one's going to let you take the plea if you aren't guilty."

"But I didn't *do* nothing."

"Then you'll have to stay in and go to trial."

"When will that be?"

"In a couple of months. Maybe longer."

Santiago has a grip on the bars. "You mean if I'm guilty I get out today?"

"Yes." Someone is urinating on the other side of the partition.

"But if I'm innocent, I got to stay in?" The toilet flushes.

"That's right."

It's too much for Santiago. He lets go of the bars, takes a step back, shakes his head, turns around and comes quickly back to the bars. "But, *man—*"

Back upstairs at the bench, Erdmann says to Schweitzer, "He's got no record, your honor, and I've had no admission of guilt. You know I'm very careful with people who have no records—"

"And I am, too, Marty, you know that."

"He says he hasn't had a shower in two months, he's in a twenty-four-hour-a-day lockup and he wants to get out, and I don't blame him."

"Marty, I'm not taking a guilty plea just because he wants a shower."

"Of course not."

"Do you want me to talk to them?"

"I think it might be a good idea, your honor."

Santiago and Rodriguez are brought up again and led into a small jury room adjoining the courtroom. Schweitzer reads the grand jury extract to the defendants, making sure they know the case against them.

Now Rodriguez says he'll take the plea. Schweitzer asks him to tell what happened the night of the robbery. Rodriguez says he and Santiago were on the street and they ran into the complainant and spoke with him and the complainant had a knife in his pocket and ended up getting cut, "but I didn't do nothing."

This departure from the original story, the admission that they had been with the victim and that there was indeed a knife, is enough for Erdmann. He looks at Schweitzer. "Now I'm convinced he's guilty." Schweitzer and Litman go back to court. Erdmann says to Santiago, "Do you want the plea?"

"Yes, man, I *told* you that, I got to get out—"

"Then the judge will ask you certain questions and you have to give the appropriate answers." He nods towards Rodriguez. "He held him and you stabbed him. Let's go."

They return to the courtroom and stand before the bench. Schweitzer asks Santiago if he wants to change his plea. Santiago is still not buying. What if this whole routine is just a trick to extract a confession from him? "One year," he says.

Schweitzer is patient. "That's not what I asked you. Do you want to change your plea?"

"One year."

Erdmann talks with him, explains that he will get the year but first he has to answer certain questions. Santiago starts off again with just wanting to get out. Erdmann quiets him down, and they try again.

Schweitzer: "Do you now wish to change your plea?"

"I want one year."

Schweitzer is exasperated. Erdmann is angry. Santiago leans over to Erdmann and again starts talking. Erdmann says strongly, "Look, do you want the plea or not? Just yes or no. Answer him. Don't make speeches. You'll *get* the year. Just answer him."

Schweitzer asks again. Santiago turns to Erdmann and starts to talk. Erdmann grimaces and covers his ear with the folder. "I don't *want* any more speeches. I'm losing my patience. You'll *get* the year, but *first* you have to plead."

Schweitzer gives up and moves on to Rodriguez. Rodriguez quickly pleads guilty. Schweitzer asks him to tell the truth about what really happened. Rodriguez says he held the man from behind while Santiago stabbed him. Schweitzer immediately sentences him to a year. Erdmann is leaning against the clerk's desk, his arms crossed over his chest, his eyes burning into Santiago. This ignorant, stupid, vicious kid has been offered a huge, heaping helping of the Erdmann talent, the experience, the knowledge, the myth—and has shoved it away. Erdmann's face is covered with disgust. Through his eyes, way beyond them, is fury, and unclouded, clear contempt.

The defendants are led from the courtroom. Erdmann walks to his seat in the jury box. As he passes the bench, Schweitzer looks down helplessly. "He wants me to sentence him before he pleads. How can I do that?"

The clerk calls a case for a private lawyer, and Erdmann takes advantage of the break to get a cigarette. He goes into a small side room the court officers use for a lounge. The room has lockers, a desk, a refrigerator, toaster and hot plate—all of them old and beaten and scarred. Cops' jackets hang from the chair backs. Erdmann has forgotten Santiago. He stands by the window with his foot up on a radiator and looks across at the Tombs, one of the worst jails in the country, home of many of his clients, a desperate place of rats and rapes, beatings, murders and, so far this year, six suicides. Eighty per cent of the 1,800 men locked up in the Tombs are clients of the Legal Aid Society. One of them, a twenty-five-year-old homosexual named Raymond Lavon Moore, will eventually come to the fleeting attention of Martin Erdmann. At this moment, however, he sits in a small iron box whose only openings are a barred window at the back and a four-inch-wide glass slit in the door. He is doing twenty days in solitary for hitting a guard. Charged with shooting a policeman in a bar, Moore has been in the Tombs ten months, made twenty-four appearances in court and steadfastly refuses to plead guilty to anything more serious than a misdemeanor. He came in weighing 205 pounds, and is now down to 155. He has never been in jail before. He has never been physically examined in the Tombs, but is nevertheless getting frequent heavy doses of tranquilizers. The Tombs doctor, a graduate of the Eclectic Medical College of Cincinnati, is seventy-seven years old (jail records say he's sixty-nine). Moore has been removed to hospitals for mental observation five times, and each time he has been returned to the Tombs. He has twice tried to kill himself. Not long ago some Tombs prisoners, angry at the overcrowding, vermin and lack of official attention, decided to find out what could be accomplished by rioting. The riots were followed by avalanches of studies, committees, investigations and reports—some helpful, some hysterical. None did anything to help Raymond Lavon Moore, the man in the iron box.

Erdmann is looking at workmen on a Tombs setback clearing away shattered glass and broken furniture from beneath burned-out windows. "It will never be the same," he says. "Once they've found out they can riot and take hostages, it will never be the same. Today defendants are telling the judges what sentences they'll take. They say to me, 'Go back and tell him I'll take six months.' I had a guy the other day who told me he knew the system was congested and that they needed guilty pleas, and he was willing to help by pleading guilty for eight months. The judge would only come down to eleven. He wouldn't take it. He was willing to help out for eight months, but not for eleven. The leniency feeds upon itself. They start out settling for a year, then others want six months, then three months, then parole. The guilty are getting great breaks. But the innocent are put under tremendous pressure to take a plea and get out. The innocent suffer, and the community suffers. It's all just get the cases out of court—move the calendar, move the calendar, move the calendar. That's all they're interested in—everyone."

He unwraps another pack of Luckies, forgetting the opened one in his pocket.

"If the defendants *really* get together, they've got the system by the balls. If they all decide to plead not guilty, and keep on pleading not guilty, then what will happen? The offered pleas will get lower and lower—six months, three months. If that doesn't work, and they still plead not guilty, maybe the court will take fifteen or twenty and try them and give them the maximum sentences. And if *that* doesn't work—I don't know. I don't know. They have the power, and when they find out, you're in trouble."

Two workmen standing on a plank are lowering themselves on ropes down the side of the Tombs. "Fixing windows," Erdmann says. Then he smiles. "Or escaping."

Forty minutes have been wasted with the stubborn Santiago, and now comes another problem. An Erdmann client named Richard Henderson says he was asleep in a Welfare Department flophouse when another man "pounced" on him with a stick. The other man says he was trying to wake Henderson when Henderson "jumped up like a jack rabbit" and stabbed him in the chest. Henderson is charged with attempted murder.

Erdmann talks to him in the pen hallway just outside the courtroom door. It has started to rain. A casement window, opaque, with chicken wire between the plates, has been cranked open and cold air and rain are blowing in and making things miserable for Henderson. He's a twenty-one-year-old junkie—wire-thin, with deep, lost, wandering eyes, and a face sad and dead, as if all the muscles that could make it laugh or frown or show fear or anger had been cut. He stands there shivering in a dirty white shirt, no socks, no shoelaces, the backs of his shoes pushed in like slippers, hands stiff-armed down into the pockets of beltless khaki pants. Quietly, he tells Erdmann he wants to go to trial.

"Well you certainly have that right. But if you're guilty, I've spoken to the judge, and he'll give you a year with credit for time served. How long have you been in?" Erdmann turns the folder and looks at a date. "Six months. So with good behavior you'll have four left. It simply depends on whether you're guilty of anything or not."

Henderson nods. "Yes, that's why I want a jury trial."

"Why?"

"To find out if I'm innocent or not."

"Don't you know?" Erdmann takes another look in the folder. Henderson was psychiatrically examined at Bellevue Hospital and returned as legally sane.

"No. I don't know. But I have an opinion." His eyes leave Erdmann and begin to examine the hallway. He has withdrawn from the conversation. Erdmann watches him a moment, then brings him back.

"What is your opinion?"

"That I am."

"Well if you go to trial, it may be four months anyway before you *get* a trial, and then you'll be gambling zero against five or ten years. And even if you are acquitted, you'll still have done the four months."

Henderson moves his feet and shivers. "I understand," he says meekly. "So I think I'd better do that."

"What?"

"Go to trial."

Erdmann just looks at him and walks back into court. "Ready for trial," he announces. "Don't even bother bringing him out." Litman makes a note on his file and they move on to another case.

Erdmann sits down in the jury box. The next few defendants have private lawyers, so he just waits there: watching, smiling, his bulging eyes gently ridiculing those around him who have failed to see as clearly as he into the depths of this charade, and to have found the joke there.

The judge is asking a defendant where he got the loaded gun. "He found it," Erdmann whispers before the man answers.

"I found it," the man says.

"Where?" asks the judge.

"Someone just gave it to him," Erdmann says.

"Someone walked by and handed it to me," says the defendant.

Erdmann smiles. "It's amazing," he says, "how often people rush by defendants and thrust things into their hands—guns, watches, wallets, things like that."

One of the two DAs is Richie Lowe, a black man—young, tall, slender, double-breasted, mod, Afro haircut. Black defendants coming into court glance quickly around, and they see a white judge, white defense lawyers, white clerk, white stenographer, white guards and then, over there, at that table over there, a black, the only black in the room, and he's—the *enemy*.

Now Lowe, the black kid with a law degree from St. John's, sits down next to Erdmann, the millionaire with a Wall Street father and Dartmouth and Yale law, and no one can help but notice the ironic reversal of their roles. Prosecutor and defender. But the irony is superficial—inside, Erdmann's character belies his background. He says he was "far to the left" of his parents, and he spent much of his youth trying to radicalize them. His father was quiet, shy, conservative, "difficult to get close to." His mother he remembers fondly as "a very determined lady, a person of strong likes and dislikes." But not so strong that her son could not attack them. When he was twenty-two, he decided to bring a friend home to dinner. The friend was a black assistant DA.

He smiles as he recalls her reaction. "It was very difficult for her. She told the elevator man and all the maids what was going to happen. She behaved admirably even though I'm sure she hated every minute of it." He reminisces silently for a moment, and then adds, "I read about him years later. I think he ended up marrying the daughter of the Yale registrar and then shooting someone in Detroit."

After law school Erdmann went to work in "a stuffy Wall Street law firm" where his first assignment was discovering whether or not a Florida gambling casino had acted legally in denying admittance to a female client's poodle. He quit, spent World War II in the Army and then joined the Legal Aid Society. "When I run into someone I can't place, I just say, 'Good to see you again, when did you get out?' That covers college, the Army and prison."

A guard leads a black defendant toward the pen door. He's wearing a black headband, a gold earring and a wad of white paper is stuffed up his left nostril. "Can I ask you one thing?" he whispers to the guard as they head for the door.

"Yeah, ask me anything."

"What'd I get?"

"You got a year, a year in jail." The door slams behind him.

In the seats next to Erdmann, a prisoner is being allowed a visit with his wife and small son. "I heard about your commotion in school," the father whispers. "Now you better be good or I'm gonna get you when I get out."

Guards bring in an old, toothless black man with wild white hair and an endless record of rapes, assaults, sodomy and armed robbery. He's accused of trying to rape a four-year-old Puerto Rican girl. Some people driving in a car saw the man sitting on a wall with the girl struggling in his lap and rescued her. Erdmann, Lowe and Judge Schweitzer talk it over. Schweitzer suggests a year. Lowe runs his eyes again over the grand jury extract. He usually goes along with Schweitzer, but this time he balks. "I can't see it, your honor. I can't see it."

Erdmann speaks a few urging words, but Lowe won't budge. "No," he says, "I just can't see it, your honor. If these people hadn't come by in the car and seen the girl, this could have been—it could have been anything."

Schweitzer, himself under great appellate division pressure to dispose of cases, now pressures Lowe, politely, gently. He points out that the girl was not injured.

"I just can't, your honor," Lowe says. "I just can't. This is abhorrent, this—"

Schweitzer breaks in. "It's abhorrent to *me*, too, and it's being discussed *only* in the light of the calendar."

"Your honor, we've been giving away the courthouse for the sake of the calendar. I can't do it. I won't do it." He stuffs his papers back in the folder. "Ready for trial, your honor."

He moves back to the prosecution table and announces for the record, "The people are ready for trial."

Erdmann has been saying nothing. As he passes Lowe's table on his way to the jury box, Lowe says, "Am I being unreasonable, Marty?"

Erdmann stops for a moment, very serious, and then shakes his head. "No, I don't think you are."

Lowe is upset. The next case has not yet been called. He moves around the table, fumbling folders. Then loudly he says, "Your honor, if he takes it *right now* I'll give him a year."

The judge fires Lowe a look. "You'll *recommend* a year. *I'll* give him a year."

Erdmann talks to the defendant at the counsel table. Lowe keeps shaking his head. He is suffering. He takes a step toward the bench. "Your honor," he says desperately, "he should get zip to three, at least."

"I *know* he should," Schweitzer says.

Erdmann now stands and for the record makes the customary speech. "Your honor, the defendant at this time wishes to withdraw his plea of not guilty, previously entered, and plead guilty to the second count of the indictment, attempted assault in the second degree, a Class E felony, that plea to cover the entire indictment."

Now it's Lowe's turn to make the speech of acceptance for the people, to accept the Class E felony, the least serious type of felony in the penal code. He stands. "Your honor, the people respectfully recommend acceptance of this plea, feeling that it will provide the court with adequate scope for punishment—" He stops. The next words should be "in the interest of justice." He sits down and pretends to write something on a folder. Then softly, as if hoping he might not be heard, he speaks down into the table, ". . . in the interest of justice."

He walks over to a visitor. "What do you think about *that*?" he demands. "That took a little *piece* out of me. He got a *year* for trying to *rape* a four-year-old girl."

Schweitzer recesses for lunch, and Lowe and Erdmann ride down in the elevator. Lowe is still upset. "What do I tell that girl's mother when she calls me and wants to know what happened to the man who tried to rape her daughter?"

Erdmann smiles, the playful cynic. *Better bread than is made of wheat.* "Tell her, 'No speeka English, no speeka English, no speeka English.'"

Because Manhattan's Criminal Court Building is on the Lower East Side, in the ethnic no man's land where Little Italy collides with Chinatown, it is surrounded by some of the city's best Italian and Chinese restaurants. But every lunchtime Erdmann ignores these and walks two blocks north to Canal Street, a truck-choked crosstown conduit littered with derelicts overflowing from the Bowery, and eats in the sprawling, Formica-filled, tray-crashing chaos of the foulest cafeteria east of Newark. No number of threats, insults or arguments can persuade him into any other eating place. He has, every day, one scoop of cottage cheese, a slice of melon and one slice of rye bread, buttered. (They give you two slices, want them or not, but he never succumbs.) Today he is at a table with a friend, not a lawyer, who asks how he feels when he goes to trial with a man he knows is guilty and gets the man freed.

"Lovely! Perfectly beautiful! You're dancing on air and you say to yourself, 'How could that have happened? I must have done a wonderful job!' It's a euphoric feeling. Just to see the look of shock on the judge's face when the jury foreman says 'not guilty' is worth something. It's the same sense of greed you get if a horse you bet on comes in at fifteen to one. You've beaten the odds, the knowledgeable opinion, the wise people." He laughs. "The exultation of winning dampens any moral feelings you have."

"But what," he is asked, "if you defended a man who had raped and murdered a five-year-old girl, and he was acquitted and went free and a year later was arrested for raping and murdering another five-year-old girl? Would you defend him again with the same vigor?"

"I'm afraid so."

"Why afraid?"

"Because I think most people would disapprove of that."

"Do you care?"

"No."

"It doesn't concern you?"

"I'm not concerned with the crime committed or the consequences of his going free. If I were, I couldn't practice. I'm concerned with seeing that every client gets as good representation as he could if he had $200,000. I don't want him to get screwed because there wasn't anyone around to see that he not get screwed. If you're a doctor and Hitler comes to you and says you're the one man in the world who can cure him, you do it."

"How much of that is ego?"

"Ninety-nine per cent."

Erdmann eats his cottage cheese. An old derelict—bearded, toothless, with swollen lips—puts his tray down next to Erdmann and sits slurping soup and eying the untouched slice of rye.

In the courthouse lobby after lunch, Erdmann stops to buy a candy bar. Someone says he saw a story in the Times that five thousand of that brand had been recalled after rodent hair was found in some of them. Erdmann smiles and buys two more.

A court officer sees Erdmann coming down the hall. "Hey, Marty," he yells, "he's on the bench, he's starting to call your cases."

"So what do you want me to do," Erdmann says, "break into a run?"

A defendant's name is called and Erdmann and Lowe approach the bench. Erdmann looks at Lowe. "Your move." He smiles.

"Your honor," Lowe says, looking over his file, "this is a robbery, no weapon, two victims. It's a woman who beats up old people in the subway and robs them. One of the complainants is eighty-one years old." He hands Schweitzer her three-page record of drugs, prostitution and assaults.

"Injuries?" Schweitzer asks.

"Just light, your honor. Nothing serious."

"In these times," Erdmann says, "people ought to be grateful when they're not injured while being robbed."

Schweitzer looks up. "What about a year and a year consecutive?" Erdmann and Lowe agree. The defendant comes in—short, fat, built like a cannonball. She starts right in on Erdmann. "I ain't takin' no plea. I didn't do nothin'. I'm innocent and I ain't takin' no plea."

Erdmann is not going to waste his time. He writes on the folder: "NG—ready for trial." He looks back at the woman. "Don't you even want to know what the offer is?"

She's been around. "I know what the offer is. One and one consec."

Erdmann turns away, and they take her out.

Guards bring in a twenty-year-old girl charged with robbery with a knife. Erdmann is talking to her at the counsel table when Lowe strolls over and says, "Marty, an E and a flat?"

The girl looks at Lowe. "What's he saying, who's he?"

Lowe starts away. "Don't listen to me, I'm the enemy."

She wants to know why she has to go to jail. "Well, rightly or wrongly," Erdmann tells her, "people think they shouldn't be robbed. So when they get robbed, they give a little time." She asks if the year can run concurrent with another sentence pending against her. Erdmann asks Lowe and he agrees. She still hesitates, and finally refuses the offer.

"What's wrong?" Lowe says. "She wanted a year, I gave her a year. She wanted it concurrent, I made it concurrent. It's unreal. They tell us what they want and we're supposed to genuflect."

"José Sanchez!" the clerk calls. A drug-sale case.

"Your honor, he hasn't been seen yet," Erdmann says.

"Let me see the file," Schweitzer says to Lowe.

"Your honor," Erdmann protests, "he hasn't even been interviewed. I haven't seen him."

"Well, just let's look at it, Marty," the judge says. He goes over to Lowe's file. "It's one sale, Marty. He doesn't have any robberies. Burglaries, petty larceny. Mostly drugs. I'll tell you what, Marty. I'll give him an E and a flat." Lowe agrees.

Erdmann walks into the pen hallway, and they bring up a defendant. "They're offering an E and a flat," Erdmann says to him. "For a single sale, that's about the—"

The defendant looks mystified. He says nothing. The guard interrupts. "This isn't Sanchez, Marty, it's Fernandez."

Erdmann drops his arms in disgust, and without a word he turns and goes back into court and sits down in the jury box. A defendant has in effect been tried, convicted and sentenced before his lawyer even knew what he looked like.

After court, Alice Schlesinger comes into Erdmann's office to brief him on a client of hers, a woman, who will be in Schweitzer's court tomorrow. "She's absolutely not guilty," Alice says. When she leaves, Erdmann's smile turns wistful and nostalgic. "It must be wonderful," he says, "to have an *absolute* sense of who's guilty and who isn't. I wish I had it."

Adler walks into the office. "What can I tell them?" he asks Erdmann. "Jack says he's leaving because the job's making a cynic of him. He says he thought he was going to defend the downtrodden and he finds out they're hostile and they lie to him. So he's leaving. Alice comes to me and says, 'The system's wonderful for the guilty, but for the innocent it's awful. Some of them *must* be innocent.' What do you *say* to that?"

"You say nothing," Erdmann answers, "because it's true."

"No. You say that in a good system of government the vast majority get fair treatment, but there are bound to be a few who don't." He looks at Erdmann. "You think that's sentimental."

"I think you're a Pollyanna."

Adler turns to another man in the office. "He's called me sentimental, and he's called me a Pollyanna. And you know what? It's *true.*"

Erdmann laughs. "What difference does *that* make?"

That night Erdmann goes home, has three scotches on the rocks, meets a former judge for dinner, has a double scotch and thus fortified appears before the judge's evening seminar at the New York University Law School. Ten students are sitting in upholstered, stainless-steel swivel chairs in a red-carpeted conference room—all very new and rich and modern. Erdmann is supposed to tell them about jury selection and trial tactics, subjects on which he is a recognized master.

He unwraps a pack of cigarettes, lights up and leans close over the table. Two of the students are girls. Most of the men are in jeans and have long hair. Erdmann knows the look in their eyes. They think they will have innocent clients, they think they'll be serving their fellow man, the community, justice. They don't know that what they'll be serving is the system. He wants to give them some of the facts of life. "You are salesmen," he begins, "and you are selling a product that no one particularly wants to buy. You are selling a defendant who in all likelihood is guilty." They give him looks. "So you are going to disguise the product, wrap it in the folds of justice and make it a symbol of justice. You have to convince the jurors that you're sincere, and that the product you are selling is not really this defendant, but justice. You must convince them that your defendant is not on trial. Justice is on trial."

He takes a long drag on the cigarette, inhales and then blows it out toward the ceiling. The students are cautious. No one has taken any notes. "Your job is at the beginning and the end of the trial—the jury picking and the summation. In between comes that ugly mess of evidence. In examining prospective jurors you have to sell your product before they get a look at him, before they hear the evidence. You want also to plant the seeds of your defense, and soften the blow of the prosecution's case. If you know that a cop is going to testify that the defendant stabbed the old lady eighty-nine times, you can't hide from it. You might just as well bring it out yourself, tell them they're going to hear a police officer testify that the defendant stabbed the old lady eighty-nine times and then when the testimony comes you will be spared the sudden indrawing of breath. And maybe you can even leave the impression that the cop is lying."

A girl mentions the Tombs riots and asks Erdmann what could be done to give the prisoners speedy trials. During the riots, inmates' demands for less crowding, better food, extermination of rats and vermin were supported even by the hostage guards. But their demands for speedy trials, though they found strong support in the press, were less sincere.

Virtually every prisoner in the Tombs is guilty, either of the crime charged or of some lesser but connected crime. He knows that he will either plead guilty or be convicted in a trial, and that he will serve time. He knows, too, that delays will help his case. Witnesses disappear, cops' memories fade, complainants lose their desire for vengeance. As prosecutors see their cases decaying, they lower and lower the pleas. Meanwhile, time served in the Tombs before sentencing counts as part of the sentence. Erdmann wants to explain that to the students, but he knows he will not find many believers.

"Let me disabuse you," he says, "of the idea that the prisoners in the Tombs want speedy trials. Most of them are guilty of something, and the *last* thing they want is a trial. They know that if every case could be tried within sixty days, the pleas of one-to-three for armed robbery would be back up to fifteen-to-twenty-five."

"What about the defendants out on bail?" a student asks.

"People out on bail almost *never* have to go to trial. If you can get your client out on bail, he won't be tried for at least three years, if at all. The case will go from one DA's back drawer to another's until it either dissolves into dust or the DA agrees to a plea of time served."

A student asks about the defense lawyer's responsibility to be honest. That triggers Erdmann's smile. "My *only* responsibility," he says, "is to my client. And not to suborn perjury, and not to lie personally. My client may lie as much as he wants."

Since the case of Richard Henderson, the junkie who didn't know if he was guilty, was marked ready for trial, he has been returned each day to the detention pen beneath Schweitzer's courtroom—on the almost nonexistent chance that his lawyer, and the DA assigned to the case, and a judge and courtroom might all become simultaneously available for trial. Each day he sits there in the pen while upstairs in court his case is called and passed, with no more certain consequence than that he will be back again the next day, so that it can be called and passed once more. After several days of this, Erdmann speaks to him again to see if he has changed his mind. He is the same—same clothes, same dead expression, same mad insistence on trial. Erdmann tries to encourage him to take the plea, "if you're guilty of anything."

Henderson still wants a trial.

"What will happen today?" he asks.

"Nothing. They'll set another date for trial, and that date will mean about as much as any date they set, which is nothing. You'll just have to wait in line."

Henderson picks at some mosquito-bite-size scars on his arm. "The other prisoners intimidate me," he says. "They keep asking me about my case, what I did, what I'm in for."

"What do you say?"

"I don't answer them. I don't want to talk about it."

Erdmann leaves him and goes back to court.

Erdmann's disrespect for judges (Schweitzer is a rare exception) is so strong and all-inclusive that it amounts at times to class hatred. When one of his young lawyers was held in contempt and fined $200, Erdmann left Schweitzer's court and rushed to the rescue. He argued with the judge and conned him into withdrawing the penalty. Then, outside the courtroom in the corridor, Erdmann's composure cracked. "He's a bully," he said angrily. "I'll put Tucker [one of his senior lawyers] in there a couple of days and tell him, 'No pleas.' That'll fix *that* wagon." He makes a note, then crumples it up. "No. I'll take it myself—and it'll be on the record this time." Erdmann remembers that two days earlier the judge's car was stolen in front of the courthouse. "I should have told him not to let the theft of his Cadillac upset him so much."

"There are so few trial judges who just judge," Erdmann says, "who rule on questions of law, and leave guilt or innocence to the jury. And appellate division judges aren't any better. They're the whores who became madams."

Would he like to be a judge?

"I would like to—just to see if I could be the kind of judge I think a judge should be. But the only way you can get it is to be in politics or buy it—and I don't even know the going price."

Erdmann is still in the hallway fuming over the contempt citation when a lawyer rushes up and says a defendant who has been in the Tombs five months for homicide has been offered time served and probation—and won't take it. Erdmann hurries to the courtroom. The defendant and his girl friend had been playing "hit and run," a ghetto game in which contestants take turns hitting each other with lead pipes. He said he was drunk when he played it and didn't know how hard he was hitting the girl. They both passed out and when he awoke the next morning she was dead. He had no previous record, and the judge is considering the extraordinarily light sentence agreed upon by the lawyer and DA. Neither the judge nor the DA is in a mood for any further haggling from the defendant. Erdmann talks with the defendant and gets the plea accepted. Five months for homicide. As he leaves the courtroom, a DA says, "Marty, you got away with murder."

Erdmann is gleeful. "I always get away with murder."

He goes down to his office. Alice Schlesinger walks by his desk and Erdmann remembers something he saw in the Times that morning about Anthony Howard, the man with an insane cellmate whose case he assigned to her three weeks ago.

"Hey, Alice," he calls to her, "congratulations on winning your first case."

She shrugs. A lawyer named James Vinci walks in and Erdmann says to him, "Don't forget to congratulate Alice. She just won her first case."

"Really?" says Vinci. "That's great."

"Yeah," Erdmann laughs. "Anthony Howard. His cellmate strangled him to death last night."

Every evening Martin Erdmann walks crosstown to a small French restaurant in the theater district. He sits always at the same table in a rear corner, with his back to whatever other customers there are, and he is happiest when there are none. The owner and his wife are always pleased to see him, and when he does not come they call his apartment to see if everything is all right.

Not long ago he reluctantly agreed to allow a reporter to join him for dinner. When they sat down, the reporter asked if Erdmann could be positive, after twenty-five years, that he had ever defended an innocent man.

"No. That you never know. It is much easier to know guilt than innocence. And anyway, it's much easier to defend a man if you know he's guilty. You don't have the responsibility of saving him from unjust punishment."

"What do you think about the courts today, the judicial system?"

"I think it's time people were told what's really going on. Everyone's so cowardly. Nobody wants to tell the public that the mini-measures proposed to clear up the mess *won't* do it. If you only had two roads going in and out of New York and someone said, 'What can we do about the traffic problem?' the answer would be, 'Nothing—until we get more roads.' You couldn't help it by tinkering around with the lights. Well, tinkering with the courts isn't going to help. We need more courts, more DAs, more Legal Aids, more judges—and it's going to cost a massive amount of money. I wonder how much money you could raise if you could guarantee safety from mugging and burglary and rape for $50 per person. Eight million people in New York? Could you get $20 million? And if you asked for $20 million to provide a workable system of criminal justice, how much would you get? People are more interested in their safety than in justice. They can pay for law and order, or they can be mugged."

"So what's the solution?"

"I've never really felt it was my problem. Everything up to now has benefited the defendant, and he's a member of the community, too. When you say, 'The people versus John Smith'—well, John Smith is part of the people, too. As a Legal Aid lawyer, I don't think it's my problem to make things run smoothly so my clients will get longer sentences. That's the courts' problem."

He stops talking and thinks for a minute. Something is burning inside. "That's the wrong attitude, I suppose, but then the appellate division has never approached me and asked me what can be done to improve justice for the *accused.* They *never* ask *that* question. It's just how can we clear the calendars. It's how can we get these bastards in jail faster for longer. Not in those words—*certainly* not. They *never* in all the years asked, how can we have more justice for the defendants. That's why I'm not too concerned about the system."

He has become angry and impassioned and now draws back. He concentrates on a lamb chop. "I'm loquacious when I'm tired," he says.

After several minutes he begins again. "You know, I really don't think there *is* any solution to the problem, any more than there is to the traffic problem. You do what you can within the problem."

"Is the day coming when the traffic won't move at all?"

"Yes. If every defendant refused to plead and demanded a trial, within a year the system would collapse. There would be three-year delays in reaching trial, prison riots, defendants would be paroled into the streets."

"What's Martin Erdmann going to do when that happens?"

"That's an interesting question. It would be too late by then to do anything. It's going to be too late very soon."

Every Friday, Erdmann assigns himself to a courtroom with a half-day calendar and catches the 1:35 bus for Danbury, Connecticut. From there he drives to his estate in Roxbury and spends the weekend walking, gardening "and talking to myself." He has a three-story house with a junk-jammed attic, a cellar filled with jarred fruit he preserved years ago and never ate and a library cluttered with unread books and magazines. A brook runs down from the acres of Scotch pine, past his garden and under a small bridge to the country below. He walks along the brook, and stops on the bridge to stare down at the trout. He never fishes here. "These are my friends," he says, "and you don't catch your friends."

Most of the weekend he spends coaxing co-operation from the flowers and vegetables. "I worry most about the tomatoes because I like to eat them. The most difficult is what I don't grow any more, roses. They demand constant care and that's why I don't have them." Tulips he likes. He spent a recent four-day weekend putting in four hundred bulbs sent by a friend from Holland. "They're not difficult. You just dig four hundred holes and put them in and they come up in the spring. The only problem is moles. The moles make runs to eat insects and then the mice use the mole runs to eat the tulip bulbs. Years ago I used to be out with spray guns. And then I figured, what the hell, this is nature, the mice don't know they're not supposed to eat tulip bulbs. So I gave up the spraying. I can't be hostile to something that's just doing what comes naturally."

The tulips are all in, it's 9 A.M. Monday morning and Erdmann is back in his office going through the Times. He is stopped by an item about a Legal Aid client, a twenty-five-year-old named Raymond Lavon Moore, the man in the iron box. Last weekend, while Erdmann was on his hands and knees digging the four hundred tulip holes, Moore stripped the white ticking from his mattress, knotted it into a noose and hanged himself from the barred window.

Erdmann slowly folds the paper around the clipping and without expression hands it across his desk to another lawyer. He says nothing.

That noon Erdmann is back talking through the bars of the detention pen beneath Schweitzer's courtroom. He's asking a drug pusher if there's someone who will make bail for him.

"I can't get in touch with no one from in here, man."

"Can I?"

"Yeah. My mamma in Cincinnati." He is about to give Erdmann the phone number when Erdmann moves aside to allow a guard to open the door and insert more prisoners. One of the prisoners is Richard Henderson, the junkie who wants to go to trial. He walks in, foggy and listless, and his momentum carries him to the center of the cell. He stops there, staring straight ahead. For three minutes he does not move or look around. Then he takes two steps to the bench, sits down and puts his hands between his knees. He sits there, rubbing his palms together.

Five hours later, Judge Schweitzer is almost at the end of the day's calendar. The spectators have all left, and no one remains but court personnel. Everyone is tired. To speed things up, Schweitzer has told the guards to bring up everyone left in the pen and keep them in the hall by the door. Five come up. Their cases already have been adjourned and what's happening now is more or less a body count to make sure no one is missed.

The last is Henderson. A guard walks him in, holding his arm, and someone says, "That's Henderson. He's been adjourned."

The guard, just four steps into the courtroom when he hears this news, quickly wheels Henderson around and heads him back out the door. Something in the wide, crack-the-whip arc of Henderson's swift passage through the court, something in his dead, unaware, zombie-eyed stare as he banks around the pivoting guard, strikes everyone who sees it as enormously funny. It's strange and it's pathetic, and no one can keep from laughing.

Comments and Questions

1. This excerpt describes a system of *horizontal representation*, which means that one lawyer works in a given courtroom on a given day—and that defendants are represented by a different lawyer at each appearance. Legal Aid attorneys, who are unionized, went on strike in protest against this system. They won, and a system of *vertical representation*, in which each lawyer is assigned to certain clients and represents them at every appearance, was instated. Do you think the strike was justified?

2. Many of the problems that Mr. Mills describes stem from too many cases and too little money. Problems are also created by too much money. In cases where the defense has large financial resources (either because the defendant is rich or because the case is highly political and funds have been raised on behalf of the defendant), the defendant's money may substantially decrease the likelihood of conviction. For example, social scientists are sometimes employed by the defense team to supervise jury selection so as to maximize the jury's predisposition to acquit. Or, the defense may hire three expert witnesses for every one hired by the prosecution. Is this fair to the prosecution? To other defendants? Does it undermine the public's confidence in the criminal justice system? Must we accept such inequities between rich and poor in the criminal justice system?

3. Is the criminal justice system necessarily chaotic and unjust in a large city? Do you think there are other kinds of problems in smaller cities and rural areas?

Section Nine.   Limitations of Law as a Penal-Corrective Instrument

We began this chapter by noting that conduct offending public morals and social mores is extremely common. Not all of this offensive conduct is best handled by the criminal law. Some of it is better managed by social disapproval or private institutions. In particular, "morals legislation" frequently raises questions about limits on the legitimate and effective use of the penal-corrective instrument.

J. MILL, ON LIBERTY
68–69 (1974) (1st ed. London 1859).

The object of this essay is to assert one very simple principle, as entitled to govern absolutely the dealings of society with the individual in the way of compulsion and control, whether the means used be physical force in the form of legal penalties or the moral coercion of public opinion. That principle is that the sole end for which mankind are warranted, individually or collectively, in interfering with the liberty of action of any of their number is self-protection. That the only purpose for which power can be rightfully exercised over any member of a civilized community, against his will, is to prevent harm to others. His own good, either physical or moral, is not a sufficient warrant. He cannot rightfully be compelled to do or forbear because it will be better for him to do so, because it will make him happier, because, in the opinions of others, to do so would be wise or even right. These are good reasons for remonstrating with him, or reasoning with him, or persuading him, or entreating him, but not for compelling him or visiting him with any evil in case he do otherwise. To justify that, the conduct from which it is desired to deter him must be calculated to produce evil to someone else. The only part of the conduct of anyone for which he is amenable to society is that which concerns others. In the part which merely concerns himself, his independence is, of right, absolute. Over himself, over his own body and mind, the individual is sovereign.

It is, perhaps, hardly necessary to say that this doctrine is meant to apply only to human beings in the maturity of their faculties. We are not speaking of children or of young persons below the age which the law may fix as that of manhood or womanhood. Those who are still in a state to require being taken care of by others must be protected against their own actions as well as against external injury.

———

P. DEVLIN, THE ENFORCEMENT OF MORALS
6–7, 16–18, 22–23 (1965).*

It is true that for many centuries the criminal law was much concerned with keeping the peace and little, if at all, with sexual morals. But it would be wrong to infer from that that it had no moral content or that it would ever have tolerated the idea of a man being left to judge for himself in matters of morals. The criminal law of England has from the very first concerned itself with moral principles. A simple way of testing this point is to consider the attitude which the criminal law adopts towards consent.

Subject to certain exceptions inherent in the nature of particular crimes, the criminal law has never permitted consent of the victim to be used as a defence. In rape, for example, consent negatives an essential element. But consent of the victim is no defence to a charge of murder.

It is not a defence to any form of assault that the victim thought his punishment well deserved and submitted to it; to make a good defence the accused must prove that the law gave him the right to chastise and that he exercised it reasonably. Likewise, the victim may not forgive the aggressor and require the prosecution to desist; the right to enter a *nolle prosequi* belongs to the Attorney-General alone.

Now, if the law existed for the protection of the individual, there would be no reason why he should avail himself of it if he did not want it. The reason why a man may not consent to the commission of an offence against himself beforehand or forgive it afterwards is because it is an offence against society. It is not that society is physically injured; that would be impossible. Nor need any individual be shocked, corrupted, or exploited; everything may be done in private. Nor can it be explained on the practical ground that a violent man is a potential danger to others in the community who have therefore a direct interest in his apprehension and punishment as being necessary to their own protection. That would be true of a man whom the victim is prepared to forgive but not of one who gets his consent first; a murderer who acts only upon the consent, and maybe the request, of his victim is no menace to others, but he does threaten one of the great moral principles upon which society is based, that is, the sanctity of human life. There is only one explanation of what has hitherto been accepted as the basis of the criminal law and that is that there are certain standards of behaviour or moral principles which society requires to be observed; and the breach of them is an offence not merely against the person who is injured but against society as a whole.

Thus, if the criminal law were to be reformed so as to eliminate from it everything that was not designed to preserve order and decency or to protect citizens (including the protection of youth from corruption), it would overturn a fundamental principle. It would also end a number of specific crimes. Euthanasia or the killing of another at his own request, suicide, attempted suicide and suicide pacts, duelling, abortion, incest between brother and sister, are all acts which can be done in private and without offence to others and need not involve the corruption or exploitation of others. Many people think that the law on some of these subjects is in need of reform, but no one hitherto has gone so far as to suggest that they should all be left outside the criminal law as matters of private morality. They can be brought within it only as a matter of moral principle. . . .

I do not think that one can talk sensibly of a public and private morality any more than one can of a public or private highway. Morality is a sphere in which there is a public interest and a private interest, often in conflict, and the problem is to reconcile the two. This does not mean that it is impossible to put forward any general statements about how in our society the balance ought to be struck. Such statements cannot of their nature be rigid or precise; they would not be designed to circumscribe the operation of the law-making power but to guide those who have to apply it. While every decision which a court of law makes when it balances the public against the private interest is an *ad hoc* decision, the cases contain statements of principle to which the court should have regard when it reaches its decision. In the same way it is possible to make general statements of principle which it may be thought the legislature should bear in mind when it is considering the enactment of laws enforcing morals.

I believe that most people would agree upon the chief of these elastic principles. There must be toleration of the maximum individual freedom that is consistent with the integrity of society. It cannot be said that this is a principle that runs all through the criminal law. Much of the criminal law that is regulatory in character—the part of it that deals with *malum prohibitum* rather than *malum in se*—is based upon the opposite principle, that is, that the choice of the individual must give way to the convenience of the many. But in all matters of conscience the principle I have stated is generally held to prevail. It is not confined to thought and speech; it extends to action, as is shown by the recognition of the right to conscientious objection in war-time; this example shows also that conscience will be respected even in times of national danger. The principle appears to me to be peculiarly appropriate to all questions of morals. Nothing should be punished by the law that does not lie beyond the limits of tolerance. It is not nearly enough to say that a majority dislike a practice; there must be a real feeling of reprobation. Those who are dissatisfied with the present law on homosexuality often say that the opponents of reform are swayed simply by disgust. If that were so it would be wrong, but I do not think one can ignore disgust if it is deeply felt and not manufactured. Its presence is a good indication that the bounds of toleration are being reached. Not everything is to be tolerated. No society can do without intolerance, indignation, and disgust; they are the forces behind the moral law, and indeed it can be argued that if they or something like them are not present, the feelings of society cannot be weighty enough to deprive the individual of freedom of choice. I suppose that there is hardly anyone nowadays who would not be disgusted by the thought of deliberate cruelty to animals. No one proposes to relegate that or any other form of sadism to the realm of private morality or to allow it to be practised in public or in private. It would be possible no doubt to point out that until a comparatively short while ago nobody thought very much of cruelty to animals and also that pity and kindliness and the unwillingness to inflict pain are virtues more generally esteemed now than they have ever been in the past. But matters of this sort are not determined by rational argument. Every moral judgment, unless it claims a divine source, is simply a feeling that no right-minded man could behave in any other way without admitting that he was doing wrong. It is the power of a common sense and not the power of reason that is behind the judgments of society. But before a society can put a practice beyond the limits of tolerance there must be a deliberate judgement that the practice is injurious to society. There is, for example, a general abhorrence of homosexuality. We should ask ourselves in the first instance whether, looking at it calmly and dispassionately, we regard it as a vice so abominable that its mere presence is an offence. If that is the genuine feeling of the society in which we live, I do not see how society can be denied the right to eradicate it. Our feeling may not be so intense as that. We may feel about it that, if confined, it is tolerable, but that if it spread it might be gravely injurious; it is in this way that most societies look upon fornication, seeing it as a natural weakness which must be kept within bounds but which cannot be rooted out. It becomes then a question of balance, the danger to society in one scale and the extent of the restriction in the other. . . .

. . . . The boundary between the criminal law and the moral law is fixed by balancing in the case of each particular crime the pros and cons of legal enforcement in accordance with the sort of considerations I have been outlining. . . . But the true principle is that the law exists for the protection of society. It does not discharge its function by protecting the individual from injury, annoyance, corruption, and exploitation; the law must protect also the institutions and the community of ideas, political and moral, without which people cannot live together. Society cannot ignore the morality of the individual any more than it can his loyalty; it flourishes on both and without either it dies.

PEOPLE v. ONOFRE

Court of Appeals of New York, 1980.
51 N.Y.2d 476, 415 N.E.2d 936, 434 N.Y.S.2d 947, cert. denied, 451 U.S. 987, 101 S.Ct. 2323 (1981).

JONES, JUDGE.

These appeals, argued together, present a common question—viz., whether the provision of our State's Penal Law that makes consensual sodomy a crime is violative of rights protected by the United States Constitution. We hold that it is. . . .

The statutes under which these defendants were charged and convicted provide as follows:

§ 130.38 Consensual sodomy.

A person is guilty of consensual sodomy when he engaged in deviate sexual intercourse with another person.

§ 130.00 Sex offenses; definitions of terms.

The following definitions are applicable to this article: . . .

2. Deviate sexual intercourse means sexual conduct between persons not married to each other consisting of contact between the penis and the anus, the mouth and penis, or the mouth and the vulva.

Because the statutes are broad enough to reach noncommercial, cloistered personal sexual conduct of consenting adults and because it permits the same conduct between persons married to each other without sanction, we agree with defendants' contentions that it violates both their right of privacy and the right to equal protection of the laws guaranteed them by the United States Constitution.

As to the right of privacy. At the outset it should be noted that the right addressed in the present context is not, as a literal reading of the phrase might suggest, the right to maintain secrecy with respect to one's affairs or personal behavior; rather, it is a right of independence in making certain kinds of important decisions, with a concomitant right to conduct oneself in accordance with those decisions, undeterred by governmental restraint . . . .

The People are in no disagreement that a fundamental right of personal decision exists; the divergence of the parties focuses on what subjects fall within its protection, the People contending that it extends to only two aspects of sexual behavior—marital intimacy (by virtue of the Supreme Court's decision in Griswold v. Connecticut, 381 U.S. 479, 85 S.Ct. 1678 [striking down a ban on the use of contraceptives as interfering with the right of marital intimacy]) and procreative choice (by reason of Eisenstadt v. Baird, 405 U.S. 438, 92 S.Ct. 1029 [striking down a ban on the distribution of contraceptives to unmarrieds only as having no rational relationship to any legitimate government interest], and Roe v. Wade, 410 U.S. 113, 93 S.Ct. 705 [striking down a ban on abortions as interfering with the fundamental right to procreative choice]). Such a stance fails however adequately to take into account the decision in Stanley v. Georgia, 394 U.S. 557, 89 S.Ct. 1243, and the explication of the right of privacy contained in the court's opinion in *Eisenstadt*. In *Stanley* the court found violative of the individual's right to be free from governmental interference in making important, protected decisions a statute which made criminal the possession of obscene matter within the privacy of the defendant's home. Although the material itself was entitled to no protection against government proscription (Roth v. United States, 354 U.S. 476, 77 S.Ct. 1304) the defendant's choice to seek sexual gratification by viewing it and the effectuation of that choice within the bastion of his home, removed from the public eye, was held to be blanketed by the constitutional right of privacy. That the right enunciated in Griswold v. Connecticut, 381 U.S. 479, 85 S.Ct. 1678, to make decisions with respect to the consequence of sexual encounters and necessarily, to have such encounters, was not limited to married couples was made clear by the language of the court in Eisenstadt v. Baird, 405 U.S. 438, 453, 92 S.Ct. 1029, 1038: "It is true that in *Griswold* the right of privacy in question inhered in the marital relationship. Yet the marital couple is not an independent entity with a mind and heart of its own, but an association of two individuals each with a separate intellectual and emotional makeup. If the right of privacy means anything, it is the right of the *individual*, married or single, to be free from unwarranted governmental intrusion into matters so fundamentally affecting a person as the decision whether to bear or beget a child. See Stanley v. Georgia, 394 U.S. 557, 89 S.Ct. 1243 (1969)." In a footnote appended to the *Stanley* citation the court set out the following quotation from that decision:

> [A]lso fundamental is the right to be free, except in very limited circumstances, from unwanted governmental intrusions into one's privacy.
>
> "The makers of our Constitution undertook to secure conditions favorable to the pursuit of happiness. They recognized the significance of man's spiritual nature, of his feelings and of his intellect. They knew that only a part of the pain, pleasure and satisfactions of life are to be found in material things. They sought to protect Americans in their beliefs, their thoughts, their emotions and their sensations. They

conferred, as against the Government, the right to be let alone—the most comprehensive of rights and the right most valued by civilized man." Olmstead v. United States, 277 U.S. 438, 478, 48 S.Ct. 564, 572 (1928) (Brandeis, J., dissenting).

In light of these decisions, protecting under the cloak of the right of privacy individual decisions as to indulgence in acts of sexual intimacy by unmarried persons and as to satisfaction of sexual desires by resort to material condemned as obscene by community standards when done in a cloistered setting, no rational basis appears for excluding from the same protection decisions—such as those made by defendants before us—to seek sexual gratification from what at least once was commonly regarded as "deviant" conduct, so long as the decisions are voluntarily made by adults in a noncommercial, private setting. Nor is any such basis supplied by the claims advanced by the prosecution—that a prohibition against consensual sodomy will prevent physical harm which might otherwise befall the participants, will uphold public morality and will protect the institution of marriage. Commendable though these objectives clearly are, there is nothing on which to base a conclusion that they are achieved by section 130.38 of the Penal Law. No showing has been made, even in references tendered in the briefs that physical injury is a common or even occasional consequence of the prohibited conduct, and there has been no demonstration either that this is a danger presently addressed by the statute or was one apprehended at the time the statutory section was enacted contemporaneously with the adoption of the new Penal Law in 1965. . . .

Any purported justification for the consensual sodomy statute in terms of upholding public morality is belied by the position reflected in the *Eisenstadt* decision in which the court carefully distinguished between public dissemination of what might have been considered inimical to public morality and individual recourse to the same material out of the public arena and in the sanctum of the private home. There is a distinction between public and private morality and the private morality of an individual is not synonymous with nor necessarily will have effect on what is known as public morality (see State v. Saunders, 75 N.J. 200, 218–220, 381 A.2d 333). So here, the People have failed to demonstrate how government interference with the practice of personal choice in matters of intimate sexual behavior out of view of the public and with no commercial component will serve to advance the cause of public morality or do anything other than restrict individual conduct and impose a concept of private morality chosen by the State.

Finally, the records and the written and oral arguments of the District Attorneys as well are devoid of any support for the statement that a prohibition against consensual sodomy will promote or protect the institution of marriage, venerable and worthy as is that estate. Certainly there is no suggestion that the one is a substitute or alternative for the other nor is any empirical data submitted which demonstrates that marriage is nothing more than a refuge for persons deprived by legislative fiat of the option of consensual sodomy outside the marital bond.

In sum, there has been no showing of any threat, either to participants or the public in general, in consequence of the voluntary engagement by adults in private, discreet, sodomous conduct. Absent is the factor of commercialization with the attendant evils commonly attached to the retailing of sexual pleasures; absent the elements of force or of involvement of minors which might constitute compulsion of unwilling participants or of those too young to make an informed choice, and absent too intrusion on the sensibilities of members of the public, many of whom would be offended by being exposed to the intimacies of others. Personal feelings of distaste for the conduct sought to be proscribed by section 130.38 of the Penal Law and even disapproval by a majority of the populace, if that disapproval were to be assumed, may not substitute for the required demonstration of a valid basis for intrusion by the State in an area of important personal decision protected under the right of privacy drawn from the United States Constitution—areas, the number and definition of which have steadily grown but, as the Supreme Court has observed, the outer limits of which it has not yet marked.

The assertion in the dissent that validation of the consensual sodomy statute is mandated by our recent decision in People v. Shepard, 50 N.Y.2d 640, 431 N.Y.S.2d 363, 409 N.E.2d 840 proceeds from a misconception of our holding in *Shepard*. In that case we upheld the constitutionality of the statutory proscription against the possession of marihuana as applied to possession by an individual in the privacy of his home, noting the existence of a legitimate controversy with respect to whether marihuana is a dangerous substance. The concurring opinion assembled the impressive evidence of the harmfulness which attends the use of marihuana. On such a record we sustained the right of the Legislature to reach the substantive conclusion that the use of marihuana was indeed harmful and accordingly to impose a criminal proscription based on that predicate. . . . It surely does not follow that, because it is constitutionally permissible to enter the privacy of an individual's home to regulate conduct justifiably found to be harmful to him, the Legislature may also intrude on such privacy to regulate individual conduct where no basis has been shown for concluding that the conduct is harmful.

As to the denial of defendants' right to equal protection. Section 130.38 of the Penal Law on its face discriminates between married and unmarried persons, making criminal when done by the latter what is innocent when done by the former. With that distinction drawn, we look to see whether there is, as a minimum, "some ground of difference that rationally explains the different treatment accorded married and unmarried persons" under the statute (Eisenstadt v. Baird, 405 U.S. 438, 447, 92 S.Ct. 1029, 1035). In our view, none has been demonstrated or identified by the People in any of the cases before us. In fact, the only justifications suggested are a societal interest in protecting and nurturing the institution of marriage and what are termed "rights accorded married persons". As has been indicated, however, no showing has been made as to how, or even that, the statute banning consensual sodomy between persons not married to each other preserves or fosters marriage. Nor is there any suggestion how consensual sodomy relates to rights accorded married persons; certainly it is not evident how it adversely affects any such rights. Thus, even if it be assumed that the objectives tendered by the prosecution are legitimate matters of public concern, no relationship—much less rational relationship—between those objectives and the proscription of section 130.38 of the Penal Law is manifested. The statute therefore must fall as violative of the right to equal protection enjoyed by persons not married to each other. . . .

. . . . For the reasons given above, we conclude that the imposition of criminal sanctions such as those contained in section 130.38 of the Penal Law is proscribed by the Constitution of the United States. . . .

GABRIELLI, JUDGE (dissenting).

Without making any effort to define its boundaries or limitations, a majority of my colleagues has recognized for the first time a constitutional right of personal autonomy broad enough to encompass at least the freedom to indulge in those sexual practices which have long been proscribed by our criminal law. Although the majority has attempted to associate this "fundamental right" with the recent Supreme Court decisions creating a "zone of privacy" to protect certain familial decisions, it is apparent that the connection between this case and those decisions exists only on the most superficial level and that the right of sexual choice established today is really a wholly new legal concept bearing little resemblance to the familiar principles enunciated in Griswold v. Connecticut, 381 U.S. 479, 85 S.Ct. 1678, and its progeny. Because I cannot concur in the substance of the majority's conclusion and because I am concerned with the majority's failure to articulate an analytical framework for resolving future claims under this amorphous concept of personal autonomy, I am compelled to cast my vote in dissent. . . .

Under the analysis utilized by the majority, *all* private, consensual conduct would necessarily involve the exercise of a constitutionally protected "fundamental right" unless the conduct in question jeopardizes the physical health of the participant. In effect, the majority has held that a State statute regulating private conduct will not pass constitutional muster if it is not designed to prevent physical harm to the individual. Such an analysis, however, can only be based upon an unnecessarily restrictive view of the scope of the State's power to regulate the conduct of its citizens. In my view, the so-called "police powers" of the State must include the right of the State to regulate the moral conduct of its citizens and "to maintain a decent society." . . .

We [should] utilize a two-tiered approach, taking care to ascertain at the outset whether a "fundamental right" is actually implicated without regard to the nature of the governmental interest involved in the challenged statute. If no such right is found to exist, we must refrain from interfering with the choice made by the Legislature and rest content upon the assurance that when the challenged statute is no longer palatable to the moral sensibilities of a majority of our State's citizens, it will simply be repealed.

. . . . [T]he majority . . . has placed the claim of personal autonomy asserted by defendants in the category of those ill-defined fundamental rights which are protected by the "penumbras" emanating from the Bill of Rights (Griswold v. Connecticut, supra, 381 U.S. at pp. 484–485, 85 S.Ct. at pp. 1681–1682) and by the concept of ordered liberty implicit in the due process clause of the Fourteenth Amendment (Roe v. Wade, supra, 410 U.S. at pp. 152–153, 93 S.Ct. at p. 726). I cannot agree, however, that the right of an individual to select his own form of sexual gratification should stand on any better footing than does the right of an individual to choose his own brand of intoxicant without governmental interference. Admittedly, the issue in this case is superficially distinguishable from the issue in *Shepard,* in that here we are concerned with a claim involving freedom of sexual expression, and it is therefore tempting to equate the "right" asserted by defendants with other well-established sexually related rights such as the right of an individual to obtain contraceptives (Griswold v. Connecticut, supra), the right of a woman to terminate an unwanted pregnancy (Roe v. Wade, supra) and the right of a citizen to consume printed pornographic material in the privacy of his own home (Stanley v. Georgia, 394 U.S. 557, 89 S.Ct. 1243). But the decisions in *Griswold, Roe* and *Stanley* cannot fairly be interpreted as collectively establishing an undifferentiated right to unfettered sexual expression. . . .

This is not to suggest that the Federal Constitution protects only those sexually related decisions that are made within the context of the marital relationship. As the majority notes, such a conclusion was effectively foreclosed when the Supreme Court stated in Eisenstadt v. Baird, 405 U.S. 438, 453, 92 S.Ct. 1029, 1038: "It is true that in *Griswold* the right of privacy in question inhered in the marital relationship. Yet the marital couple is not an independent entity with a mind and heart of its own, but an association of two individuals each with a separate intellectual and emotional makeup. If the right of privacy means anything, it is the right of the *individual,* married or single, to be free from unwarranted governmental intrusion into matters so fundamentally affecting a person as the decision whether to bear or beget a child" (emphasis in original).

Nevertheless, contrary to the position taken by the majority, I cannot agree that this language foreshadows a recognition by the Supreme Court of a generalized right to complete sexual freedom for all adults, whether married or single. Instead, as is suggested by the careful wording of the quoted paragraph, I would conclude that *Eisenstadt* stands only for the narrower proposition that the ancient and "fundamental" right of an individual to decide "whether to bear or beget a child" cannot be limited to married adults (accord Hindes, Morality Enforcement Through The Criminal Law and the Modern Doctrine of Substantive Due Process, 126 U. of Pa.L.Rev. 344, 361–362). Under this view, *Eisenstadt* may be regarded as a simple extension of a long line of cases protecting "freedom of personal choice in matters of marriage *and family life.*" . . .

The majority impliedly recognizes that the Supreme Court has to date limited the protection of the Constitution to decisions relating to the traditionally protected areas of family life, marital intimacy and procreation. Yet the majority has also concluded that there exists "no rational basis . . . for excluding from the same protection decisions . . . to seek sexual gratification from what at least once was commonly regarded as 'deviant' conduct." I must disagree, however, because my reading of the recent Supreme Court cases leads me to the conclusion that the distinction repeatedly drawn in those cases between freedom of choice in

the historically insulated areas of procreation, family life and marital relationships on the one hand and the general freedom of unfettered sexual choice on the other is more than just a temporary or artificial one.[2]
. . . .

In contrast to decisions relating to family life, matrimony and procreation, decisions involving pure sexual gratification have been subject to State intervention throughout the history of western civilization. . . . Indeed, as early as 1553 during the reign of Henry VIII, England enacted statutes prohibiting sodomy which became part of the American common law at the time of the American Revolution and were later embodied in the penal codes of the various States. Thus, although some may take offense at the persistence of the proscriptions against consensual sodomy in our modern law, the fact remains that western man has never been free to pursue his own choice of sexual gratification without fear of State interference. Consequently, it simply cannot be said that such freedom is an integral part of our concept of ordered liberty as embodied in the due process clauses of the Fifth and Fourteenth Amendments.

In view of the continuous and unbroken history of antisodomy laws in the United States, the majority's decision to strike down New York's statute prohibiting consensual sodomy can only be regarded as an act of judicial legislation creating a "fundamental right" where none has heretofore existed. As such, today's decision represents a radical departure from cases such as *Griswold* and *Roe,* in which the Supreme Court merely swept aside State laws which impaired or prohibited entirely the free exercise of rights that traditionally had been recognized in western thought as being beyond the reach of government. I cannot concur in the majority's conclusion.[3] As Justice Black once observed, "I like my privacy

---

2. While the majority has placed great reliance upon the decision of the Supreme Court in Stanley v. Georgia, 394 U.S. 557, 89 S.Ct. 1243, as support for the proposition that the Bill of Rights encompasses a general right of privacy and personal autonomy, that decision, in my view, is not susceptible of such an expansive reading (compare Paris Adult Theatre I v. Slaton, 413 U.S. 49, 93 S.Ct. 2628). In *Stanley,* the court struck down a State statute that penalized the private possession of printed pornographic material in the home. Although the *Stanley* court acknowledged that the obscene materials themselves would not ordinarily be covered by the protections of the First Amendment (see Roth v. United States, 354 U.S. 476, 77 S.Ct. 1304), it made clear that its decision to invalidate the challenged legislation was based in large measure upon the individual's First Amendment "right to receive information and ideas, regardless of their social worth" (394 U.S. at p. 564, 89 S.Ct. at p. 1247). Indeed, in a significant passage of its opinion, the *Stanley* court stated: "If the First Amendment means anything, it means that a State has no business telling a man, sitting alone in his own house, what books he may read or what films he may watch" (id., at p. 565, 77 S.Ct. at p. 1248). The so-called "privacy right" recognized in *Stanley* may thus be regarded as a simple extension of the First Amendment guarantee against governmental interference with the transmission of ideas. That the "privacy right" articulated in *Stanley* does not extend beyond the "right to receive information" and into the claimed right to receive "sensations," whether sexually or chemically induced, was reaffirmed in our recent decision in People v. Shepard, 50 N.Y.2d 640, 43 N.Y.S.2d 363, 409 N.E.2d 840.

3. Without intending to sound a general alarm, I cannot help but wonder what the limits of the majority's new doctrine of "personal autonomy" might be. If, for example, the freedom of an individual to engage in acts of consensual sodomy is truly a "fundamental right," it would seem fairly clear that, absent a "compelling state interest," the State cannot impose a burden upon the free exercise of that right by limiting the individual's access to government jobs (cf. Shapiro v. Thompson, 394 U.S. 618, 89 S.Ct. 1322). Moreover, if the only criterion for determining when particular conduct should be deemed to be constitutionally protected is whether the conduct affects society in a direct and tangible way, then it is difficult to perceive how a State may lawfully interfere with such consensual practices as

as well as the next one, but I am nevertheless compelled to admit that government has a right to invade it unless prohibited by some specific constitutional provision" (Griswold v. Connecticut, 381 U.S. 479, 510, 85 S.Ct. 1678, 1695 [Black, J., dissenting]).[4]   . . .

[Judges Wachtler, Fuchsberg, and Meyer concurred in Judge Jones's opinion; Judge Jasen concurred in the result in an omitted separate opinion, which disagreed with the majority on privacy but agreed on equal protection; and Judge Gabrielli, joined by Chief Judge Cooke, dissented.]

KADISH, THE CRISIS OF OVERCRIMINALIZATION
374 Annals 157, 159–62 (1967).*

The classic instance of the use of the criminal law purely to enforce a moral code is the laws prohibiting extra-marital and abnormal sexual intercourse between a man and a woman. Whether or not Kinsey's judgment is accurate that 95 per cent of the population are made potential criminals by these laws, no one doubts that their standard of sexual conduct is not adhered to by vast numbers in the community, including the otherwise most respectable (and, most especially, the police themselves); nor is it disputed that there is no effort to enforce these laws. The traditional function of the criminal law, therefore—to curtail socially threatening behavior through the threat of punishment and the incapacitation and rehabilitation of offenders—is quite beside the point. Thurman Arnold surely had it right when he observed that these laws "are unenforced because we want to continue our conduct, and unrepealed because we want to preserve our morals."

But law enforcement pays a price for using the criminal law in this way. First, the moral message communicated by the law is contradicted by the total absence of enforcement; for while the public sees the conduct condemned in words, it also sees in the dramatic absence of prosecutions

---

euthanasia, marihuana smoking, prostitution and homosexual marriage. I very much regret that the majority has failed in its discussion of the "fundamental right" to personal autonomy to set forth some analytical framework for resolving difficult questions such as these.

4.   Inasmuch as I conclude that there is no "fundamental right" to sexual gratification, I must also consider whether section 130.38 of the Penal Law represents an irrational classification on the basis of marital status in violation of the equal protection clause of the Fourteenth Amendment. Since marital status has never been recognized as a "suspect classification" (compare Executive Law, § 296), the legislative distinction between marrieds and unmarrieds may stand if it bears some rational relation to a legitimate governmental interest.

Unlike my colleagues in the majority, I have no trouble concluding that the legislative decision to permit married individuals to engage in conduct that is forbidden to the unmarried is rationally based. While the State may prefer that none of its citizens engage in the proscribed forms of sexual gratification, it may properly limit its statutory prohibition to those that are unmarried on the theory that the institution of marriage is so important to our society that even offensive intimacies between married individuals should be tolerated. The statute at issue in this case is thus distinguishable from the statute at issue in Eisenstadt v. Baird, 405 U.S. 438, 92 S.Ct. 1029, where the Supreme Court concluded that a ban on the sale of contraceptives to unmarrieds only had no relation to any legitimate government interest.

that it is not condemned in deed. Moral adjurations vulnerable to a charge of hypocrisy are self-defeating no less in law than elsewhere. Second, the spectacle of nullification of the legislature's solemn commands is an unhealthy influence on law enforcement generally. It tends to breed a cynicism and an indifference to the criminal-law processes which augment tendencies toward disrespect for those who make and enforce the law, a disrespect which is already widely in evidence. In addition:

> Dead letter laws, far from promoting a sense of security, which is the main function of the penal law, actually impair that security by holding the threat of prosecution over the heads of people whom we have no intention to punish.

Finally, these laws invite discriminatory enforcement against persons selected for prosecution on grounds unrelated to the evil against which these laws are purportedly addressed, whether those grounds be "the prodding of some reform group, a newspaper-generated hysteria over some local sex crime, a vice drive which is put on by the local authorities to distract attention from defects in their administration of the city government."

The criminalization of consensual adult homosexuality represents another attempt to legislate private morality. It raises somewhat different problems from heterosexual offenses, in that there are some attempts at enforcement. The central questions are whether the criminal law is an effective way of discouraging this conduct and how wasteful or costly it is.

Despite the fact that homosexual practices are condemned as criminal in virtually all states, usually as a felony with substantial punishment, and despite sporadic efforts at enforcement in certain situations, there is little evidence that the criminal law has discouraged the practice to any substantial degree. The Kinsey Report as well as other studies suggest a wide incidence of homosexuality throughout the country. One major reason for the ineffectiveness of these laws is that the private and consensual nature of the conduct precludes the attainment of any substantial deterrent efficacy through law enforcement. There are no complainants, and only the indiscreet have reasons for fear. Another reason is the irrelevance of the threat of punishment. Homosexuality involves not so much a choice to act wickedly as the seeking of normal sexual fulfillment in abnormal ways (though not abnormal to the individual) preferred by the individual for reasons deeply rooted in his development as a personality. Moreover, in view of the character of prison environments, putting the homosexual defendant into the prison system is, as observed recently by a United States District Court Judge, "a little like throwing Bre'r Rabbit into the briarpatch."

On the other hand, the use of the criminal law has been attended by grave consequences. A commonly noted consequence is the enhanced opportunities created for extortionary threats of exposure and prosecution. Certainly, incidents of this kind have been reported often enough to raise genuine concern. But, of more significance for the administration of justice, enforcement efforts by police have created problems both for them and for the community. Opportunities for enforcement are limited by the private and consensual character of the behavior. Only a small and insignificant manifestation of homosexuality is amenable to enforcement. This is that which takes place, either in the solicitation or the act, in public places. Even in these circumstances, it is not usual for persons to act openly. To obtain evidence, police are obliged to resort to behavior which tends to degrade and demean both themselves personally and law enforcement as an institution. However one may deplore homosexual conduct, no one can lightly accept a criminal law which requires for its enforcement that officers of the law sit concealed in ceilings, their eyes fixed to "peepholes," searching for criminal sexuality in the lavatories below; or that they loiter suggestively around public toilets or in corridors hopefully awaiting a sexual advance. Such conduct corrupts both citizenry and police and reduces the moral authority of the criminal law, especially among those portions of the citizenry—the poor and subcultural—who are particularly liable to be treated in an arbitrary fashion. The complaint of the critical that the police have more important things to do with their time is amply attested by the several volumes of the National Crime Commission's reports.

The offense of prostitution creates similar problems. Although there are social harms beyond private immorality in commercialized sex— spread of venereal disease, exploitation of the young, and the affront of public solicitation, for example—the blunt use of the criminal prohibition has proven ineffective and costly. Prostitution has perdured in all civilizations; indeed, few institutions have proven as hardy. The inevitable conditions of social life unfailingly produce the supply to meet the ever-present demand. As the Wolfenden Report observed: "There are limits to the degree of discouragement which the criminal law can properly exercise towards a woman who has deliberately decided to live her life in this way, or a man who has deliberately chosen to use her services." The more so, one may add, in a country where it has been estimated that over two-thirds of white males alone will have experience with prostitutes during their lives. The costs, on the other hand, of making the effort are similar to those entailed in enforcing the homosexual laws—diversion of police resources; encouragement of use of illegal means of police control (which, in the case of prostitution, take the form of knowingly unlawful harassment arrests to remove suspected prostitutes from the streets; and various entrapment devices, usually the only means of obtaining convictions); degradation of the image of law enforcement; discriminatory enforcement against the poor; and official corruption.

To the extent that spread of venereal disease, corruption of the young, and public affront are the objects of prostitution controls, it would require little ingenuity to devise modes of social control short of the blanket criminalization of prostitution which would at the same time prove more effective and less costly for law enforcement. Apparently, the driving force behind prostitution laws is principally the conviction that prostitution is immoral. Only the judgment that the use of the criminal law for verbal vindication of our morals is more important than its use to protect life and property can support the preservation of these laws as they are.

D. RICHARDS, SEX, DRUGS, DEATH, AND THE LAW

2–7 (1982).*

The utilitarian argument against the Anglo-American conception of criminal justice began with the publication in 1859 of John Stuart Mill's On Liberty. Mill proposed a general doctrine that may be termed the "harm principle." This principle limits the scope of the criminal law in the following ways:

    1. Acts may properly be made criminal only if they inflict concrete harms on assignable persons.

    2. Except to protect children, incompetents, and "backward" peoples, it is never proper to criminalize an act *solely* on the ground of preventing harm to the agent.

    3. It is never proper to criminalize conduct solely because the mere thought of it gives offense to others.

Although Mill's harm principle places a constraint on the criminal law comparable to the one embodied in the French Declaration of Rights, Mill did not justify the constraint on the basis of the human rights paradigm, as did the French Declaration. Rather, Mill appealed to a general utilitarian argument, derived from Jeremy Bentham, that failing to follow the harm principle reduces the aggregate surplus of pleasure over pain. Mill was less doctrinaire in his opposition to the language and thought of rights than Bentham, and some find in On Liberty rights-based arguments of personal autonomy. But although Mill did give great weight to preserving the capacity of persons to frame their own life plans independently, he appears—in accordance with his argument in Utilitarianism—to have incorporated this factor into the utilitarian framework of preferring "higher" to "lower" pleasures. Thus, the argument of On Liberty is utilitarian: the greatest aggregate sum by which pleasure exceeds pain, taking into account the greater weight accorded by utilitarianism to higher pleasures, is secured by granting free speech and observing the harm principle.

The Anglo-American tradition of opposition to overcriminalization, initiated by Mill, has—following Mill—conceived of the issue in utilitarian terms. This tradition relies, when seeking the decriminalization of "victimless crimes," on efficiency-based arguments deploring the pointless or counterproductive use of valuable and scarce police resources in the enforcement of these laws. The pattern of argument and litany of evils are familiar. H.L.A. Hart, for example, in his defense of the recommendation of Great Britain's Wolfenden Committee to decriminalize consensual adult homosexuality and prostitution, conceded that some "victimless crimes" are immoral, and then discussed in detail the countervailing and excessive costs of preventing them. In the United States, commentators have emphasized pragmatic arguments that are implicitly utilitarian, identifying tangible evils that enforcement of intangible moralism appears quixotically to cause. Victimless crimes typically are consensual and

* David A.J. Richards, SEX, DRUGS, DEATH, AND THE LAW (Totowa, N.J.: Rowman and Littlefield, 1982), pp. 2–7.

private, and as a result, there is rarely either a complaining victim or a witness. In such cases, police must resort to enforcement techniques, such as entrapment, that are often unconstitutional or unethical and that tend to corrupt police morals. Enforcement costs also include the cost of forgoing opportunities to enforce more "serious" crimes. When the special difficulty of securing sufficient evidence for conviction and the ineffectiveness of punishment in deterring these acts are considered, the utilitarian balance sheet condemns criminalization as simply too costly.

The utilitarian cast of these arguments is understandable in a nation like Great Britain, where they must be made to a parliament that enjoys constitutional supremacy. In the United States, however, arguments of this kind are made not only to legislatures but also to countermajoritarian courts empowered with judicial supremacy in the elaboration of a charter of human rights. Since 1965, the United States Supreme Court has invoked a constitutional right of privacy to invalidate the use of criminal sanctions against the purchase or use of contraceptives by adults, married and unmarried, and, more recently, minors; the use of pornography in the home; and the use of abortion services by adults and, more recently, minors. In addition, state courts have elaborated a similar right under state constitutions to permit the withdrawal of life support systems from irreversibly comatose, terminally ill patients. One state court has interpreted the privacy right in its state constitution to permit the use of marijuana in the home, and another court has held that the use of peyote by Native Americans in religious ceremonies is a constitutionally protected form of free exercise of religion.

It is difficult, if not impossible, to reconcile the notion of privacy rights that these cases embody with the utilitarian policy arguments that decriminalization proponents generally use. Indeed, the status and rationale of the constitutional right of privacy are at the center of contemporary controversy over constitutional theory and practice. It is argued that the right of privacy is policy-based, legislative in character, and unneutral, and therefore may not properly be adopted by courts, whose decisions must be governed by neutral principles of justification. If the deployment in these cases of the constitutional privacy right or other rights must be construed in utilitarian terms, such objections may be conclusive, and decriminalization arguments would be properly directed only to legislatures, not to courts.

It is quite natural to interpret the harm principle as derivative from some more general utilitarian argument. Harm appears to be a quasi-utilitarian concept at least insofar as utilitarianism seeks to avoid pain. There are several powerful objections to this interpretation, however.

First, utilitarian arguments for decriminalization proselytize the already converted and do not seriously challenge the justifications that defenders of criminalization traditionally offer. For these defenders, the consensual and private character of prohibited acts, even when coupled with the consequent higher enforcement costs, is not sufficient to justify decriminalization. They point out that many consensual acts, such as dueling, are properly made criminal and that many nonconsensual acts are also properly criminal despite comparably high enforcement costs.

The prosecution of intrafamilial homicide, for example, requires intrusion into intimate family relations, and yet intrafamilial homicide is not therefore legalized. Certainly, if there is a good moral reason for criminalizing certain conduct, quite extraordinary enforcement costs will justly be borne. Accordingly, efficiency-based arguments for decriminalization appear to beg the question. They have weight only if the conduct in question is not independently shown to be immoral. But the decriminalization literature concedes the immorality of such conduct, and then elaborates arguments, based on efficiency and costs, that can have no decisive weight.

The absence of critical discussion of the focal issues that divide proponents and opponents of criminalization has made decriminalization arguments much less powerful than they can and should be. In practice, efficiency-based arguments have not been very successful in reducing the scope of "victimless crimes," whether by legislative penal code revision or by judicial invocation of the constitutional right to privacy. The wholesale or gradual decriminalization of contraception, abortion, consensual noncommercial sexual relations between or among adults, and decisions by the terminally ill to decline further treatment has resulted from a shift in moral judgments: these acts are no longer believed to be morally wrong. In contrast, where existing moral judgments have remained unchallenged—as, for example, with commercial sex and many forms of drug use—movement toward decriminalization has been either negligible or haphazard. Yet the decriminalization literature has failed to address these moral questions, perhaps because utilitarianism is presumed to be the only enlightened critical morality. In order to give decriminalization arguments the full force they should have, it is necessary to supply the missing moral analysis. The absence of such analysis has prevented us from seeing the moral needs and interests that decriminalization in fact serves. To this extent, legal theory has not responsibly brought to critical self-consciousness the nature of an important and humane legal development.

A second objection may be made to the utilitarian interpretation of the harm principle. The harm principle is not a necessary corollary of utilitarian tenets. The basic desideratum of utilitarianism is to maximize the surplus of pleasure over pain. If certain plausible assumptions about human nature are made, however, utilitarianism would require the criminalization of certain conduct in violation of the harm principle. Assume, for example, that an overwhelming majority of people in a community take personal satisfaction in their way of life and that their pleasure is appreciably increased by the knowledge that conflicting ways of life are forbidden by the criminal law. Suppose, indeed, that hatred of the nonconforming minority, legitimated by the application of criminal penalties, reinforces the pleasurable feelings of social solidarity, peace of mind, self-worth, and achievement in a way that tolerance, with its invitation to self-doubt, ambivalence, and insecurity, could not. In such circumstances, the greater pleasure thus secured to the majority may not only outweigh the pain to the minority but, as compared to the toleration required by the harm principle, may result in a greater aggregate of pleasure; accordingly, utilitarianism would call for criminalization in violation of the harm principle.

Utilitarians defend the harm principle against such a plausible interpretation of utilitarianism by excluding the offense taken at the mere thought of certain conduct as a ground for criminalization. Yet, how, on utilitarian grounds, can *any* form of pleasure or pain be thus disavowed as morally irrelevant? Mill appears to have argued that this exclusion follows from the greater weight accorded to autonomy by utilitarianism, both in and of itself (as a higher pleasure) and instrumentally as a means of encouraging innovations and experiments that may enable people to realize more pleasure in their lives. Mill did not, however, explain why autonomy should be given such decisive weight, either as a pleasure in and of itself or as an instrument whose value is so great that other pleasures should be wholly excluded from the utilitarian calculus in order to preserve it. Certainly, the exercise of the competences that accompany rational autonomy often gives pleasure, but it also yields the pain of self-doubt, ambivalence, and insecurity. In any event, why should these pleasures and pains be considered more important within the utilitarian scheme than the pleasures of security, peace of mind, and solidarity, which Mill appears to have disavowed? Although the claims for autonomy on instrumental grounds introduce consequentialist arguments to which utilitarians must give weight, it is difficult to see how these arguments can be regarded as decisive. As an empirical matter, autonomy may lead to creative innovation and experiment, but it also may lead to empty distractions, idle fantasies, and wasted lives. The potential effects weigh on both sides of the utilitarian scales, with perhaps some tilt toward protecting autonomy, but not to the degree that Mill's argument requires.

―――――

Comments and Questions

1. How would Professor Kadish respond to Professor Richards's criticism of the pragmatic arguments against punishing victimless crimes?

2. Richards does not conclude that the harm principle must be abandoned. He goes on to argue that although utilitarianism cannot adequately defend it, the harm principle may be defended as the consequence of an ethical conception of human rights, in which autonomy is an ultimate goal. Can you see what the disadvantage of this argument is?

Section Ten.   Bibliography

1. *General.* C. Silberman, Criminal Violence, Criminal Justice (1978); J. Wilson, Thinking About Crime (1975).

2. *Penal-Corrective Techniques.* G. Fletcher, Rethinking Criminal Law (1978); N. Morris, Madness and the Criminal Law (1982); A. Simpson, Cannibalism and the Common Law (1984).

3. *Authorized Makers of Penal-Corrective Law and Their Appropriate Collaborative Roles.* Hall, Strict or Liberal Construction of Penal Statutes, 48 Harv.L. Rev. 748 (1935); Comment, The Role of the Law of Homicide in Fetal Destruction, 56 Iowa L.Rev. 658 (1971).

4. *Structures and Processes for Applying Penal-Corrective Law and Techniques.* H. Kalven & H. Zeisel, The American Jury (1966); J. Skolnick, Justice Without Trial (2d ed. 1975).

5. *Necessity for and Nature of Coercive Power.* W. Berns, For Capital Punishment (1979); C. Black, Capital Punishment: The Inevitability of Caprice and Mistake (1981).

6. *Roles of Private Citizens and Their Lawyers.* J. Casper, American Criminal Justice: The Defendant's Perspective (1972); J. Kunen, How Can You Defend Those People? (1983); D. Mellinkoff, The Conscience of a Lawyer (1973); Alschuler, The Defense Attorney's Role in Plea Bargaining, 84 Yale L.J. 1179 (1975).

7. *Process Values.* L. Baker, Crime, Law, and Politics (1983); A. Lewis, Gideon's Trumpet (1964); Griffiths, Ideology in Criminal Procedure or a Third "Model" of the Criminal Process, 79 Yale L.J. 359 (1970); Packer, Two Models of the Criminal Process, 113 U.Pa.L.Rev. 1 (1964).

8. *Improving the Penal-Corrective Instrument.* E. Borchard, Convicting the Innocent (1932); N. Morris & G. Hawkins, The Honest Politician's Guide to Crime Control (1970).

9. *Limitations of Law as a Penal-Corrective Instrument.* P. Devlin, The Enforcement of Morals (1965); H.L.A. Hart, Law, Liberty, and Morality (1963); D. Richards, Sex, Drugs, Death, and the Law (1982); Finnis, The Rights and Wrongs of Abortion: A Reply to Judith Thomson, 2 Phil. & Pub.Aff. 117 (1972); Thomson, A Defense of Abortion, 1 Phil. & Pub.Aff. 47 (1971).

Law as an Administrative-Regulatory Instrument

*The rise of administrative bodies prob-
ably has been the most significant legal trend of the last century and perhaps more values today are affected by
their decisions than by those of all the
courts . . . .*

JUSTICE ROBERT H. JACKSON

Section One. Introduction
(Pedagogic Vehicles Drawn Mainly from FCC Law)

A common fallacy about law is that it consists almost entirely of criminal
law, with its apparatus of police, prosecutors, juries, judges, and prisons.
A cognate fallacy is that the whole of law is divisible into criminal law
and civil law. But the resources of legal systems are far richer and more
extensive than either of these views implies, as the present and the
following two chapters will demonstrate. The present chapter is addressed to the distinctive ways legal resources may be marshaled to
regulate private primary activity.

Let us begin with a caveat. This chapter is not concerned with
administrative law as that phrase is ordinarily used. It is concerned not
with legal ways of controlling regulatory officials, as such, but with the
use of law by such officials to carry on regulatory tasks in the first place.

The phrase *private primary activity* as used here includes such varied
pursuits as production and marketing of electricity and natural gas;
provision and operation of railroad, air, and other transport facilities;
radio and television broadcasting; commercial fishing and lobstering;
processing and distribution of meat, poultry, and other foodstuffs; manufacturing; and construction of buildings, bridges, and other public facilities. The assumption should not be made that in all legal systems the
foregoing activities are privately owned and conducted. Nor should the
assumption be made that these activities are confined to large-scale affairs
such as electrical production, provision of railroad transport, and the like.
The list can be extended to include purchase and sale of stocks and bonds
by individuals, provision of medical services by doctors, construction of

residences by local builders, ownership and operation of motor vehicles by ordinary citizens, and so forth.

Unlike the antisocial behavior with which the penal-corrective mode deals, and unlike the wrongs of the grievance-remedial mode, the foregoing forms of activity are in themselves positively desirable. How, then, does a legal system become at all concerned with such activities? Particularly, how can such activities generate legal needs that are best met neither through the use of law as a grievance-remedial instrument nor through the penal-corrective mode, but rather through administrative-regulatory activity?

A. Reasons for Government Intervention

We need doctors, transport, and electricity. We want manufactured goods, fish and lobsters on the table, and so on. But these activities are not always carried on properly. An unqualified commercial airline pilot might smash up an airliner and kill everyone on board. An incompetent doctor might extract the pancreas instead of the appendix. A meat processor who does not have an adequate quality control system might poison half a town. Overzealous lobstermen might harvest lobsters to the point of extinction. Improper or excessive waste discharge into air and water from manufacturing and transport activities might destroy parklands and injure health. Apart from incompetence or carelessness, conscious abuses are possible, too. A person might lose his entire savings in buying corporate stock from a fraudulent fly-by-nighter. An electricity supplier might abuse her monopoly position and charge exorbitant rates. An owner of a television station might pander to the public by showing obscene movies. Private primary activity can thus cause harm—avoidable harm.

Such activities can also have great potential for good. High-quality radio and television programming is possible. Airplanes could almost always be safe and on schedule. Medical service could be of first-rate quality. A wide variety of healthy seafood could be regularly supplied to the market.

Legal intervention might then be justifiable on two distinct grounds: the prevention of harm and the promotion of good. The prevention of harm is sometimes considered too limited a goal. For example, in dealing with radio and television, the legal system might concern itself not only with the problem of obscenity but also with the problem of balanced, high-quality programming—covering public affairs as well as sports and entertainment.

Can the affected citizen do something about these things on his own through self-help without any legal intervention at all? As far as harms are concerned, the potentially affected citizen always prefers to prevent them before they occur. But often he will not even be able to identify the risks in advance. For example, he cannot normally tell a competent surgeon from an incompetent one. He cannot normally tell an adulterated can of fish from an unadulterated one. He cannot normally tell a safely constructed airliner from one that is not safe. Even when the affected citizen does know something is wrong, he may be unable, alone, to do anything about it in advance. Thus, consider the natural monopolist that charges exorbitantly for its electricity. Or take the plight of the radio or television viewer whose stations are jammed by competitors in a free-for-all over frequencies or channels. The affected citizen is often powerless to prevent such occurrences.

One way of explaining why we cannot rely on the private consumer's exercise of self-help in the marketplace to obtain the degree of safety he wants in airliners, food, and physician's services or to buy electricity at an unregulated price is the theory of market failure. A perfectly competitive economy with no market failures would theoretically produce the optimal amount of goods and services with the inherent risk characteristics (at a reduced price) desired by consumers. But under market failure conditions, this ideal is not reached, and government intervention is justified to correct the failure.

Inadequate Information

A commonly cited example of market failure is the problem of inadequate information. Producers sometimes supply inadequate or misleading information to consumers, and sometimes the product or service (airliners or medical treatment) is so complex that consumers would need an expert's opinion for proper evaluation. But consumers as a group are not willing to pay the cost of an expert to police misinformation or to evaluate complex products and services. The market in information fails in part because consumers in the first place are unaware of the importance of further information (they lack the information needed to evaluate their need for further information) and in part because of what economists call the free-rider problem. A limited amount of information circulates freely from person to person and from newspapers or other media. Under the free-rider theory, each consumer is unwilling to pay for expert opinions that to some extent will be freely available once someone else has paid for them. To correct this problem, the government intervenes to supply the information, either directly or indirectly. It may do so directly by labeling food (the Agriculture Department's food labeling program) or by requiring producers to supply information (the Securities and Exchange Commission's financial reporting requirements for the sale of securities). Or it may do so indirectly through rules against misinformation (the Federal Trade Commission's control of deceptive advertising), by licensing pilots and inspecting airliners (Federal Aviation Administration), by testing and approval of food additives and drugs (Food and Drug Administration), or by licensing physicians (state boards of medical examiners).

Natural Monopoly

Another example of market failure is the existence of a natural monopoly, such as the supply of gas and electricity. According to economic theory, perfect competition assures that suppliers will produce that quantity of a good at which the incremental cost of producing the last unit equals the price consumers are willing to pay for it. Under monopoly conditions, however, producers restrict output, raise the price, and earn supernormal profits. The antitrust laws attempt to preserve competition in markets generally, but in some industries monopoly conditions are natural. For example, it would be foolishly wasteful for several companies, each operating its own pipe or power lines, to compete with one another in supplying gas and electricity. But to prevent the natural single supplier from charging monopoly prices, the government intervenes to regulate the price at which gas and electricity can be sold.

Common Pool (scarcity)

The common-pool problem arises when a resource, such as whales or fish, is available in limited supply and no individual harvester has an incentive to restrict harvesting so that natural reproduction can generate an optimal supply of the resource. Each harvester knows that individual conservation efforts would simply give some other harvester a larger harvest. Thus, whales and fish could be harvested to extinction if government did not intervene to restrict the size of the catch through game or fishing commissions.

External Costs

The problem of air or water pollution is a good example of external costs or spillover effects—another kind of market failure. The manufacturer who burns sulfur-laden fuel contributes to the damage suffered in distant park and recreation areas through the effects of acid rain, formed from the sulfur dioxide particles spewed into the air combining with natural rain. Manufacturing plants may also discharge chemical and other toxic wastes into local rivers and lakes, causing health hazards to humans, fish, and waterfowl. But the cost of this damage is generally not borne by the many manufacturers who cause it. Hence, manufacturers have no market incentive to limit the damage; they would gain nothing from incurring costly changes in production processes to reduce toxic discharges. Government regulation deals with these problems by setting air and water quality standards that manufacturers must meet, an example being rules promulgated by the Environmental Protection Agency.

External Benefits

External benefits arise when the supplier of a good or service is unable to prevent the general public from benefiting, directly or indirectly, from the service or good supplied. Thus, national defense is a service that could not be supplied to one citizen without benefiting all. Because a private supplier could not collect from each citizen a reasonable fee in any desirable manner, no one would supply appropriate defense. The national government, then, undertakes to defend the country and taxes the general citizenry to finance the undertaking. Government-financed public education can be somewhat similarly explained, because the public at large benefits from an educated populace. Government interventions like national defense and public education, however, are more accurately described not as regulation but as government conferral of public benefits, the topic of Chapter 4.

B. Reasons for Resort to the Administrative-Regulatory Instrument

The theory of market failure helps explain the need for government intervention but not the form that intervention should take. If legal intervention is needed, why is law as a grievance-remedial instrument or as a penal-corrective instrument not adequate to the task? The following excerpt offers insights into some of the factors that explain the need for the administrative-regulatory instrument.

————

ATTORNEY GENERAL'S COMMITTEE ON ADMINISTRATIVE PROCEDURE, ADMINISTRATIVE PROCEDURE IN GOVERNMENT AGENCIES

S.Doc. No. 8, 77th Cong., 1st Sess. 13–14 (1941).

If administrative agencies did not exist in the Federal Government, Congress would be limited to a technique of legislation primarily designed to correct evils after they have arisen rather than to prevent them from arising. The criminal law, of course, operates in this after-the-event fashion. Congress declares a given act to be a crime. The mere declaration may act as a deterrent. But if it fails to do so the courts can only punish the wrongdoer; they cannot wipe out or make good the wrong. Traditional noncriminal, private law operates for the most part in the same after-the-event fashion. A statute or the common law gives one individual a right to go into court and sue another. This procedure is likely to be expensive. It is uncertain. At best, in the ordinary action for money damages, it leads only to compensation for the injury, which is seldom as satisfactory as not having been injured at all. To be sure, courts of equity administer a substantial measure of preventive justice by giving injunctions against threatened injuries. But it is necessary to prove the threat, and other limitations confine the scope of this mode of relief. The desire to work out a more effective and more flexible method of preventing unwanted things from happening accounts for the formation of many (although by no means all) Federal administrative agencies.

The rate-making powers of the Interstate Commerce Commission afford an apt illustration. The common law, from time immemorial recognized a right of action against a common carrier on account of an unreasonable rate. The shipper or the passenger could pay the charge and then sue to recover the unreasonable excess. Preference for a mechanism whereby reasonable rates could be established in advance was a principal factor leading to the Commission's establishment. A more recent example is the Securities and Exchange Commission. Within rather severe limits, the common law recognized a right in a purchaser of securities to recover damages from the seller resulting from false statements made in effecting the sale. The importance of truth in securities led to a demand that honest statements, as well as fuller and more informative statements, be assured so far as possible in advance. If this end were to be accomplished, it could only be done by creating an administrative agency. A similar purpose, effected in a great variety of ways, underlies the formation of many other agencies. Thus, licensing is one of the most significant of all preventive agencies. It would be possible to permit anyone to act as the pilot of a ship or a plane and then to punish those whose incompetence led to accidents or to prohibit them from acting as pilots again. People have preferred, however, to attempt by a licensing method to assure competence in advance; and administrative agencies have had to be created to carry out the licensing system. Licensing of radio broadcasters has, among other purposes, a comparable object of securing advance assurance of conformity to certain standards of broadcasting, as well as the object of security [sic] a ready means of dealing with departures from the standards. Licensing of any activity may be one of the most burdensome forms of regulation, since all who engage in the activity must be licensed in order that the persons who would probably act improperly may be controlled. But it is also one of the most effective, and it is particularly likely to be resorted to where the effort to effectuate policies is made with conviction.

————

Problem 1

1. Consider the problem of controlling air pollution. Assume that a manufacturer burns sulfur-laden fuel and through the acid rain thereby produced causes $10 in property damage to each of 100 people in a tri-state area. Assume that the added cost to the manufacturer of burning sulfur-free fuel, which would eliminate the acid rain problem, is $500. Assume that the cost of a lawsuit against the manufacturer seeking either damages or an injunction is $300. The manufacturer's switching to sulfur-free coal would seem to be in society's interest. Why? (a) Would the grievance-remedial mode or private consensual arrangements be appropriate instruments for reaching the socially desirable outcome? If not, why not? (b) Would the penal-corrective mode be an appropriate instrument for reaching the socially desirable outcome? If not, why not? (c) Would the administrative-regulatory mode be the preferable instrument for legal intervention? If so, why?

2. Assume that Maine lobsters have just become a popular food and demand is growing. But the supply is limited, and it takes time for lobsters to reproduce. As more and more lobstermen put down lobster pots, there is the danger of overexploitation leading to extinction of the Maine lobster. (a) Can this problem be handled adequately through use of the grievance-remedial instrument? (b) The penal-corrective instrument? (c) What features of the administrative-regulatory instrument make it especially appropriate for this task?

Beef is also in high demand as a table food and commands a high price in the market. Why is there not a similar threat of overexploitation of cattle? Could we say that the grievance-remedial and penal-corrective instruments are effective in assuring an orderly market in beef but not in lobsters? If so, what explains the difference?

3. Consider the problem of natural monopoly in the supply of gas and electricity. The social goal is to prevent restricted supply and monopoly

prices.   (a) Is the grievance-remedial mode inappropriate?   (b) Is the penal-corrective mode inappropriate?   (c) What makes the administrative-regulatory instrument effective for this purpose?

————

Problem 2

1.   It came to be recognized, during the first three decades of the twentieth century in the United States, that radio broadcasting as such had to be subjected to some form of regulation.   Neither grievance-remedial nor penal-corrective techniques were thought adequate to cope with the problems that arose.   One problem was that different individuals took it upon themselves to set up transmitters and stations and to broadcast at will.   Consequently, many listeners were treated to incomprehensible jabber, for more than one individual broadcasted at the same time on the same or a closely neighboring frequency.   Consider whether grievance-remedial or penal-corrective techniques would be adequate to deal with this problem.   Which of the three cases in Problem 1 does broadcast regulation most closely resemble?   Is there any resemblance to the other cases?

2.   What should be the goal of broadcast regulation?   Should the regulatory function be solely that of a traffic controller preventing broadcast interference?   How could that goal be best accomplished?   Should government go further and regulate the characteristics of individuals or companies allowed to broadcast?   Should limits be placed on the citizenship of broadcasters or on the number of stations servicing a locality that a given broadcaster would be allowed to own?   Should the government regulate program content (the amount and quality of news, entertainment, advertising, educational programs, and so on) or should that be within the broadcast station's sole discretion?   Could the government regulate program content consistent with the First Amendment's guarantee of free speech?

3.   Can you imagine any other related problems that might have arisen because of technological advances in use of the electromagnetic spectrum, of which broadcasting was one—problems that similarly required use of administrative-regulatory techniques?   The first major regulatory programs in this field were launched via the Radio Act of 1912 and the Radio Act of 1927.[a]

Section Two.   Administrative-Regulatory Techniques

A common fallacy about law is that it achieves control only through the threat or actuality of sanctions such as fines and prison sentences. Concededly, law could not effectively be used as an administrative-regulatory instrument without the authority and capacity to impose sanctions (see Section 5 of this chapter).   But this is not to say that the weaponry of regulators consists merely of the power to set standards and then punish

a. The story of these acts is told in M. Edelman, Licensing of Radio Services in the United States, 1927 to 1947, at 1–6 (1950).

those who fail to comply. The regulatory and the penal differ far more radically than this.

A. Setting and Publishing Substantive Regulatory Standards

F. HORACK, CASES AND MATERIALS ON LEGISLATION
85 (2d ed. 1954).*

The belief that law enforcement is better achieved by prevention than by prosecution has contributed to the emergence of administrative regulation as a primary means of government control. Although administrative rule-making is more accurately classified as a legislative function, the process of formulating administrative rules contributes substantially to the control of activities within the agency's jurisdiction. Prior to the adoption of a new regulation, public hearings must be held and it is customary with good administrators to precede these formal hearings with informal conferences and consultations. In these conferences administrators and group representatives can acquire a better understanding of the problems involved and a mutual respect for each other's positions. As an educational device it provides a basis for making administrative control effective and enforcement by conventional means unnecessary.

B. Encouraging Self-Regulation in Light of Published Standards

Although administrators are seldom explicitly given power to maximize self-regulation by those subject to regulation, this power is frequently exercised and may be classified as a distinctive regulatory technique that takes a variety of forms. Thus, responsible administrators may seek not only to elicit full participation of the industry to be regulated in formulating the governing regulations but also to disseminate relevant information on a continuing basis, offer positive inducements to cooperation, allow opportunities for voluntary compliance once departures from standards are discovered, and so on. These techniques encourage healthy attitudes toward self-regulation, and relying heavily on self-regulation is sometimes necessary. Consider, for example, the role of self-regulation in the broadcasting industry. Administrators must rely heavily on the ability and willingness of broadcasters to comply on their own with relevant minimal standards proscribing indecent and obscene broadcasting. The relevant administrative bodies simply do not have the resources for across-the-board advance policing of program content.

C. Licensing

The power to require licenses is a classic regulatory device. It may be invoked for different kinds of regulatory purposes. For example, it may be used to limit entrance into a field in the interest of assuring economic and efficient service. As suggested in Section 1, having several electricity suppliers string lines side by side and serve customers in the same area is neither economical nor efficient. Or licensing may be utilized to restrict entry because of the physio-technological characteristics of the industry. For example, broadcasters cannot be free simply to broadcast on any frequency they choose at any time. Nor can just anyone engage in commercial fishing or lobstering. Or licensing may be used to set and enforce basic qualifying standards. Doctors and lawyers, for example, must first demonstrate some capability before they can qualify for licenses to practice. Common to all regulatory licensing is denial of a right to engage in the contemplated activity without a license. Licensing must be distinguished from prohibition. We prohibit murder, theft, and rape. These are not, in themselves, even potentially beneficial practices. But licensing is concerned with essentially beneficial activities that in some way need to be regulated.

WARP, LICENSING AS A DEVICE FOR FEDERAL REGULATION

16 Tul.L.Rev. 111, 111–13, 118–19 (1941).*

It has been said that a license, in its broad sense, is "a permit or privilege granted by competent authority to do that which by law would otherwise be unlawful." Licensing, in turn, might be defined as "the administrative lifting of a legislative prohibition." The legislature prohibits in order to make its regulations effective. It denies the right to do a particular thing but permits individual exceptions to be made by an administrative act. The exception constitutes the license and represents an official permit to engage in certain activities otherwise forbidden. In other words, licensing means that citizens stand before their government, one saying, "I wish to operate a securities exchange," another saying, "I desire to set up a radio station," and still another saying, "I want to be an aeroplane pilot." To each of these people and to others the government replies: "What you propose to do is of such public importance that it must be regulated in the interests of the common good. If you cannot or will not meet the standards which we prescribe, you may not go ahead with your plans."

The licensing device has been employed effectively in the field of federal administration only during recent years. Perhaps this is due somewhat to the fact that the licensing power has been associated customarily with some phase of the police power. The police power, of course, has been considered as one of the reserved powers of the states. Until the concept of a federal police power developed, few people thought of using licensing as a federal device. At any rate, the effective use of licensing as an instrument for law enforcement in this country is very largely a development of the twentieth century. Prior to 1900 examples of federal licensing were almost non-existent. One instance, however, occurred in 1789, when the first Congress made provision for the licensing of ships and seamen. Indeed, practically all of the nineteenth century licenses involved the subject of navigation. Finally, in 1902, more than a century after the first licensing act was passed, licenses were required for the preparation of viruses and toxins when these were to be moved in interstate commerce. Ten years later licenses were required for the importation of nursery stock. The first of the great federal licensing acts, however, was the Warehouses Act of 1916. It was followed in rapid succession by other important acts: the Federal Water Power Act of 1920, the Packers and Stockyards Act of 1921, the Grain Futures Act of 1922, the Radio . . . Act of 1927, the National Industrial Recovery Act of 1933, the Agricultural Adjustment Act of 1933, and the Securities Act of 1933. Thus the newness of licensing as a means of federal control is readily apparent. . . .

The terminology of the various license laws varies considerably. The typical law, however, sets forth (1) the conditions under which a license becomes necessary; (2) the requirements which must be met by applicants; (3) the fees charged; (4) the duties imposed upon the licensees; (5) the agency authorized to issue such licenses; (6) the powers enjoyed by this agency; (7) the procedure in revoking licenses; (8) the grounds which constitute cause for revocation; and (9) the penalties for violations. Of course, most federal license laws state these matters in very general terms, leaving broad rule-making powers in the hands of the licensing agent or agency.

D. Investigating; Requiring Periodic Reports

A given regulatory program may or may not be implemented through a licensing scheme. In any event, the administrative officials charged with bringing the relevant regulatory standards and requirements to bear on the individuals or organizations to be regulated will need basic investigatory powers to determine facts of compliance and noncompliance. Not surprising, then, is that the typical regulatory program explicitly and implicitly grants broad investigatory powers to the relevant officials. When investigation is undertaken, it may be more or less continuous. On the one hand, an official may investigate buildings to determine compliance with building codes only occasionally. On the other hand, officials may inspect foodstuffs, such as meat, continuously. Either form of investigative activity serves not only to identify actual noncompliance but also to exert steady pressure for self-regulation, especially when facts of violation, if and when they exist and are discovered, are such that exculpatory error in regard to them cannot be convincingly asserted. As we have already noted, such investigative activity also provides information and data upon which recommendations for changes in governing regulatory standards and requirements can be based.

These programs also frequently impose specific duties of disclosure and reporting on the parties subject to regulation. With such reports in hand, the relevant administrative officials may be able to take appropriate action without investigating on their own. Reports on income realized by regulated electric utilities, for example, may alone offer substantial basis for administrative action.

Sometimes those from whom essential information must be obtained will refuse to give it. In these circumstances, administrators may have the power to compel disclosure. Many statutes provide such power, but they also commonly require that this power be exercised only with judicial approval.

The facts sought by an administrative official may actually be disputed. Under the applicable law, the administrator may be empowered to make definitive findings of fact for administrative purposes (as opposed to, say, the purpose of premising a judicial remedy or penalty such as a fine) without giving the potentially adverse party an administrative (nonjudicial) hearing. But for anything significant, the administrative official will usually be required under applicable law to give the potentially adverse party an opportunity for an administrative hearing on the facts before any action is taken.

Similarly, although the party subject to regulation may agree on the facts, he may differ with the administrative official over whether the facts show a failure of compliance with governing regulatory law. He may, for example, concede that the foodstuffs he processes have certain ingredients but deny that such ingredients make his produce "injurious to health." In such circumstances, the administrator may be empowered to proceed without a formal administrative hearing. When anything significant is at stake, she will commonly be required by law to give the party subject to regulation an opportunity for an administrative hearing at which he may present his arguments on the meaning of the law as applied to his case.

E. Using or Threatening to Use Publicity

ROURKE, LAW ENFORCEMENT THROUGH PUBLICITY

24 U.Chi.L.Rev. 225, 231–35 (1957).*

Traditionally, the employment of publicity by administrative agencies has been looked upon not as a direct instrument of law enforcement but rather as an avenue through which the public may be acquainted—or more than acquainted—with the objectives and achievements of executive agencies. . . .

[A] problem . . . was the authority vested in regulatory agencies to issue a press release at the time judicial action was first initiated against persons suspected of violating the law. This press release, detailing the character of a suspected offense and the culprit involved, inflicted immediate damage upon the reputation of a defendant even before a formal finding of guilt or innocence had been made. . . .

The problem of administrative use of the publicity sanction prior to a formal determination of the culpability of a defendant is complicated by the fact that in some areas such publicity serves a useful if not indispensable control function. In, for example, the enforcement of legislation protecting the consumer against the manufacture and sale of impure food and drugs, the capacity of administrative agencies to inform the public that a product is suspected of containing harmful ingredients may play an invaluable role in preventing consumption of the product under investigation until the accuracy of this administrative suspicion can be determined. It was with this consideration in mind that the Food and Drug Administration was authorized by statute to issue press releases warning the public against the use of products suspected of involving "imminent danger to health or gross deception of the consumer." [Citing 21 U.S.C. § 375(b).] A recent illustration of the use and utility of a similar kind of power was the action of the Public Health Service in giving immediate and national publicity to its withdrawal of approval from the polio vaccine manufactured by the Cutter laboratories in California. In this case, as in others, both the value and the punitive effect of the publicity sanction— possibly unwarranted in the Cutter case—are simultaneously clear.

Whether or not it is applied beforehand, the penalty of adverse publicity has an obvious impact as part of the total punishment received by persons found guilty of violating statutes enforced by regulatory agencies. Indeed this unfavorable publicity may be the most important part of the punishment received on such occasions. This factor needs to be taken into account in any assessment of the total weight of sanction attached to violations of regulatory legislation. These laws are frequently criticized on the grounds that the formal penalties they provide for violations are too trivial to deter potential offenders. This criticism, however reasonable on its face, tends to overlook entirely the deterrent effect of fear of adverse publicity. Certainly, in contemplating behavior likely to be held in violation of a regulatory statute, a business firm risks, in the possible loss of public esteem, a highly vital economic asset—beside which the possibility of a minor fine may pale in significance. . . .

Perhaps the best evidence of the deterrent effect of fear of publicity may be found in the success achieved by regulatory agencies in using the mere threat of adverse public attention to bring about the settlement of complaints by defendants without the necessity of formal hearings. Obviously, fear of adverse publicity is not the sole factor involved in the successful employment by regulatory agencies of this informal adjudication—the so-called "lifeblood of the administrative process."

F. Threatening Formal Administrative Proceedings; Other Informal Methods of Securing Compliance

As Professor Rourke indicated, some publicity techniques are of an informal kind. As such, they are one species of informal methods of enforcing regulatory law, methods that also include fact-finding with the facts speaking for themselves, threats of agency prosecution, issuance of informal advisory opinions and declarations of policy, informal efforts at negotiations and compromise, and so on. So-called informal adjudication sometimes originates with a formal complaint but is followed by informal disposition without conventional reception of testimony, cross-examination, and the like. The great bulk of regulatory law is enforced through informal methods.

When informal methods are successful, they frequently result in a signed settlement agreement or a consent decree by the terms of which the party subject to regulation agrees to comply as required by the administrators and may even agree to stated penalties. The administrative agency is careful to see that any consent decree is published, for it serves as a legal precedent.[b]

Comments and Questions

1. What does informal settlement have in common with (a) private, nonjudicial compromise of grievance-remedial claims and (b) plea bargaining?

2. How do these differ?

G. Resort to Full-Scale Administrative Proceedings to Procure Formal Cease and Desist Orders

Sometimes administrators will not be required to hold a hearing before acting. Sometimes they will be empowered to take so-called direct action against the allegedly offending regulatee; the quarantine is an ancient example, and seizure of contaminated food is another. So-called self-executing negative orders are cognate—for example, refusal to deliver obscene mail and refusal to clear vessels for docking at a port. But such direct action is authorized only exceptionally, and few orders are self-executing in the relevant sense.

Suppose, for example, that a radio station owner permits a private party to use his station to broadcast a public attack on a private person, whom we shall call Mr. Cook. Assume that Mr. Cook requests free use of the facility to broadcast a rebuttal. Assume further that the Federal Communications Commission has promulgated rules that Mr. Cook says require the station owner to comply with his request. Further, the FCC informally orders the station owner to allow such free time, but the owner disobeys, claiming either that the FCC rules do not apply or that the commission had no authority to issue such rules. Here, the commission might choose to prosecute the station owner in an administrative proceeding, the upshot of which could be the issuance of an order by the administrative body to cease and desist from withholding the free time. Pleadings somewhat like those in the Swimming Pool case in Chapter 1 would be used to define the issues. An evidentiary hearing, with cross-examination and the like, would be held before an administrative law judge or, as those officials used to be called, a hearing examiner. Officials higher in the agency would then either adopt the provisional decision of the administrative law judge or make a different final decision.

---

b. For a discussion of the role of an administrative consent decree as a legal precedent, see Davison, Exports of Technical Data and the Export Control Act: Hearing Examiners and Consent Decrees, 33 Geo.Wash.L.Rev. 209, 235–39 (1964).

The foregoing is but one basic pattern of formal administrative adjudication. A result adverse to the regulatee may itself be sufficient to secure compliance. But then, it may not. What course do administrators follow when they have procured a formal order via formal proceedings and the regulatee refuses to comply? Consider the next subsection.

H. Administrative Resort to Courts for Appropriate Enforcement

The law might allow administrative bodies to enforce their own orders. But this has not been the general pattern in Anglo-American law. Rather, the agencies have had to resort to courts to enforce their own orders, including license revocations. (What reasons might there be for this?)

The agency may undertake to prosecute, through the courts, a violation of its order. Such a proceeding would be much like that characteristic of the penal-corrective mode considered earlier in Chapter 2. Or, as a basic alternative, by the procedures of Chapter 1 the agency may apply for a judicial enforcing order, violation of which constitutes *contempt of court* and subjects the defendant to fine or imprisonment. As once noted with respect to licensing cases, "The machinery sometimes runs: statute, regulation, grant of license, [administrative] adjudication of violation, revocation of license, operation without license, [court] injunction, violation of injunction, [court] adjudication of contempt, imprisonment, purgation." L. Jaffe & N. Nathanson, Administrative Law 18 (3d ed. 1968).

Comments and Questions

1. Review the different regulatory techniques of administrative agencies catalogued previously. Are they analogous to the techniques used by the threefold branches of a government: legislative, executive, and judicial?

2. Why is having separate administrative agencies for these purposes necessary or desirable? Why do we not simply utilize the existing governmental branches?

3. Is there something improper or unfair about a single agency acting as lawgiver, police officer and prosecutor, and judge and jury, all at the same time? Can you think of a way of avoiding the actual or seeming impropriety?

I. Private Resort to Courts to Secure Appropriate Regulatory Action

In a variety of ways, private parties—even ordinary citizens—may act to help effectuate a general regulatory program, and such action must be included within any general catalog of regulatory techniques. One form of private action consists in resort to courts by private parties to secure appropriate regulatory action when it appears that the officials or agencies charged with basic regulatory responsibilities are acting or have acted contrary to applicable law.

For example, in the field of broadcast regulation (on which this chapter focuses for illustrative purposes), the agency charged with primary regulatory responsibility is the Federal Communications Commission. The origins and raison d'être of this body will be considered at a later point. For now, we shall consider a case in which private parties sought through court action to force the FCC to take appropriate regulatory action. The case to be considered here is especially fitting for, in addition to showing an important regulatory role for private parties, it also concerns the award of licenses to broadcast. Over the years, Congress and the FCC have utilized the full gamut of regulatory techniques, inventoried in this section, to regulate broadcasting. But the basic legislation—the Radio Act of 1912, the Radio Act of 1927, and the Federal Communications Act of 1934—relies chiefly on the licensing technique.

———

OFFICE OF COMMUNICATION OF THE UNITED CHURCH OF CHRIST v. FCC

United States Court of Appeals, District of Columbia Circuit, 1966.
359 F.2d 994.

Before BURGER, McGOWAN and TAMM, CIRCUIT JUDGES.

BURGER, CIRCUIT JUDGE:

This is an appeal from a decision of the Federal Communications Commission granting to the [licensee] a one-year renewal of its license to operate television station WLBT in Jackson, Mississippi. Appellants filed with the Commission a timely petition to intervene to present evidence and arguments opposing the renewal application. The Commission dismissed Appellants' petition and, without a hearing, took the unusual step of granting a restricted and conditional renewal of the license. Instead of granting the usual three-year renewal, it limited the license to one year from June 1, 1965, and imposed what it characterizes here as "strict conditions" on WLBT's operations in that one-year probationary period.

The questions presented are (a) whether Appellants, or any or them, have standing before the Federal Communications Commission as parties in interest under Section 309(d) of the Federal Communications Act to contest the renewal of a broadcast license; and (b) whether the Commission was required by Section 309(e) to conduct an evidentiary hearing on the claims of the Appellants prior to acting on renewal of the license.

Because the question whether representatives of the listening public have standing to intervene in a license renewal proceeding is one of first impression, we have given particularly close attention to the background of these issues and to the Commission's reasons for denying standing to Appellants.

BACKGROUND

The complaints against [the licensee] embrace charges of discrimination on racial and religious grounds and of excessive commercials. As the Commission's order indicates, the first complaints go back to 1955 when it was claimed that WLBT had deliberately cut off a network program about race relations problems on which the General Counsel of the NAACP was appearing and had flashed on the viewers' screens a "Sorry, Cable

Trouble" sign. In 1957 another complaint was made to the Commission that WLBT had presented a program urging the maintenance of racial segregation and had refused requests for time to present the opposing viewpoint. Since then numerous other complaints have been made.

When WLBT sought a renewal of its license in 1958, the Commission at first deferred action because of complaints of this character but eventually granted the usual three-year renewal because it found that, while there had been failures to comply with the Fairness Doctrine, the failures were isolated instances of improper behavior and did not warrant denial of WLBT's renewal application.

Shortly after the outbreak of prolonged civil disturbances centering in large part around the University of Mississippi in September 1962, the Commission again received complaints that various Mississippi radio and television stations, including WLBT, had presented programs concerning racial integration in which only one viewpoint was aired. In 1963 the Commission investigated and requested the stations to submit detailed factual reports on their programs dealing with racial issues. On March 3, 1964, while the Commission was considering WLBT's responses, WLBT filed the license renewal application presently under review.

To block license renewal, Appellants filed a petition in the Commission urging denial of WLBT's application and asking to intervene in their own behalf and as representatives of "all other television viewers in the State of Mississippi." The petition stated that the Office of Communication of the United Church of Christ is an instrumentality of the United Church of Christ, a national denomination with substantial membership within WLBT's prime service area. It listed Appellants Henry and Smith as individual residents of Mississippi, and asserted that both owned television sets and that one lived within the prime service area of WLBT; both are described as leaders in Mississippi civic and civil rights groups. Dr. Henry is president of the Mississippi NAACP; both have been politically active. Each has had a number of controversies with WLBT over allotment of time to present views in opposition to those expressed by WLBT editorials and programs. Appellant United Church of Christ at Tougaloo is a congregation of the United Church of Christ within WLBT's area.

The petition claimed that WLBT failed to serve the general public because it provided a disproportionate amount of commercials and entertainment and did not give a fair and balanced presentation of controversial issues, especially those concerning Negroes, who comprise almost forty-five per cent of the total population within its prime service area; it also claimed discrimination against local activities of the Catholic Church.

Appellants claim standing before the Commission on the grounds that:

(1) They are individuals and organizations who were denied a reasonable opportunity to answer their critics, a violation of the Fairness Doctrine.

(2) These individuals and organizations represent the nearly one half of WLBT's potential listening audience who were denied an opportunity to have their side of controversial issues presented, equally a violation of the Fairness Doctrine, and who were more generally ignored and discriminated against in WLBT's programs.

(3) These individuals and organizations represent the total audience, not merely one part of it, and they assert the right of all listeners, regardless of race or religion, to hear and see balanced programming on significant public questions as required by the Fairness Doctrine [5] and also their broad interest that the station be operated in the public interest in all respects.

The Commission denied the petition to intervene on the ground that standing is predicated upon the invasion of a legally protected interest or an injury which is direct and substantial and that "petitioners . . . can assert no greater interest or claim of injury than members of the general public." The Commission stated in its denial, however, that as a general practice it "does consider the contentions advanced in circumstances such as these, irrespective of any questions of standing or related matters," and argues that it did so in this proceeding.

Upon considering Petitioners' claims and WLBT's answers to them on this basis, the Commission concluded that

> serious issues are presented whether the licensee's operations have fully met the public interest standard. Indeed, it is a close question whether to designate for hearing these applications for renewal of license.

Nevertheless, the Commission conducted no hearing but granted a license renewal, asserting a belief that renewal would be in the public interest since broadcast stations were in a position to make worthwhile contributions to the resolution of pressing racial problems, this contribution was "needed immediately" in the Jackson area, and WLBT, if operated properly, could make such a contribution. Indeed the renewal period was explicitly made a test of WLBT's qualifications in this respect.

> We are granting a renewal of license, so that the licensee can demonstrate and carry out its stated willingness to serve fully and fairly the needs and interests of its entire area—so that it can, in short, meet and resolve the questions raised.

The one-year renewal was on conditions which plainly put WLBT on notice that the renewal was in the nature of a probationary grant; the conditions were stated as follows:

(a) "That the licensee comply strictly with the established requirements of the fairness doctrine."

(b) ". . . [T]hat the licensee observe strictly its representations to the Commission in this [fairness] area . . . . "

(c) "That, in the light of the substantial questions raised by the United Church petition, the licensee immediately have discussions with communi-

5. In promulgating the Fairness Doctrine in 1949 the Commission emphasized the "right of the public to be informed, rather than any right on the part of the Government, any broadcast licensee or any individual member of the public to broadcast his own particular views on any matter . . . . " The Commission characterized this as "the foundation stone of the American system of broadcasting." Editorializing by Broadcast Licensees, 13 F.C.C. 1246, 1249 (1949). This policy received Congressional approval in the 1959 amendment of Section 315 which speaks in terms of "the obligation imposed upon [licensees] under this Act to operate in the public interest and to afford reasonable opportunity for the discussion of conflicting views on issues of public importance." 73 Stat. 557 (1959), 47 U.S.C. § 315(a) (1964).

ty leaders, including those active in the civil rights movement (such as petitioners), as to whether its programming is fully meeting the needs and interests of its area."

(d) "That the licensee immediately cease discriminatory programming patterns."

(e) That "the licensee will be required to make a detailed report as to its efforts in the above four respects . . . . "

Appellants contend that, against the background of complaints since 1955 and the Commission's conclusion that WLBT was in fact guilty of "discriminatory programming," the Commission could not properly renew the license even for one year without a hearing to resolve factual issues raised by their petition and vitally important to the public. The Commission argues, however, that it in effect accepted Petitioners' view of the facts, took all necessary steps to insure that the practices complained of would cease, and for this reason granted a short-term renewal as an exercise by the Commission of what it describes as a " 'political' decision, 'in the higher sense of that abused term,' which is peculiarly entrusted to the agency." The Commission seems to have based its "political decision" on a blend of what the Appellants alleged, what its own investigation revealed, its hope that WLBT would improve, and its view that the station was needed.

STANDING OF APPELLANTS

The Commission's denial of standing to Appellants was based on the theory that, absent a potential direct, substantial injury or adverse effect from the administrative action under consideration, a petitioner has no standing before the Commission and that the only types of effects sufficient to support standing are economic injury and electrical interference. It asserted its traditional position that members of the listening public do not suffer any injury peculiar to them and that allowing them standing would pose great administrative burdens.

Up to this time, the courts have granted standing to intervene only to those alleging electrical interference, NBC v. FCC (KOA), 132 F.2d 545 (1942), aff'd, 319 U.S. 239, 63 S.Ct. 1035 (1943), or alleging some economic injury, e.g., FCC v. Sanders Bros. Radio Station, 309 U.S. 470, 60 S.Ct. 693 (1940). . . .

The Commission's rigid adherence to a requirement of direct economic injury in the commercial sense operates to give standing to an electronics manufacturer who competes with the owner of a radio-television station only in the sale of appliances, while it denies standing to spokesmen for the listeners, who are most directly concerned with and intimately affected by the performance of a licensee. Since the concept of standing is a practical and functional one designed to insure that only those with a genuine and legitimate interest can participate in a proceeding, we can see no reason to exclude those with such an obvious and acute concern as the listening audience. This much seems essential to insure that the holders of broadcasting licenses be responsive to the needs of the audience, without which the broadcaster could not exist. . . .

We cannot believe that the Congressional mandate of public participation which the Commission says it seeks to fulfill was meant to be limited to writing letters to the Commission, to inspection of records, to the Commission's grace in considering listener claims, or to mere non-participating appearance at hearings. We cannot fail to note that the long history of complaints against WLBT beginning in 1955 had left the Commission virtually unmoved in the subsequent renewal proceedings, and it seems not unlikely that the 1964 renewal application might well have been routinely granted except for the determined and sustained efforts of Appellants at no small expense to themselves. Such beneficial contribution as these Appellants, or some of them, can make must not be left to the grace of the Commission.

Public participation is especially important in a renewal proceeding, since the public will have been exposed for at least three years to the licensee's performance, as cannot be the case when the Commission considers an initial grant, unless the applicant has a prior record as a licensee. In a renewal proceeding, furthermore, public spokesmen, such as Appellants here, may be the only objectors. In a community served by only one outlet, the public interest focus is perhaps sharper and the need for airing complaints often greater than where, for example, several channels exist. Yet if there is only one outlet, there are no rivals at hand to assert the public interest, and reliance on opposing applicants to challenge the existing licensee for the channel would be fortuitous at best. Even when there are multiple competing stations in a locality, various factors may operate to inhibit the other broadcasters from opposing a renewal application. An imperfect rival may be thought a desirable rival, or there may be a "gentleman's agreement" of deference to a fellow broadcaster in the hope he will reciprocate on a propitious occasion.

. . . .

In line with this analysis, we do not now hold that all of the Appellants have standing to challenge WLBT's renewal. We do not reach that question. As to these Appellants we limit ourselves to holding that the Commission must allow standing to one or more of them as responsible representatives to assert and prove the claims they have urged in their petition.

It is difficult to anticipate the range of claims which may be raised or sought to be raised by future petitioners asserting representation of the public interest. It is neither possible nor desirable for us to try to chart the precise scope or patterns for the future. The need sought to be met is to provide a means for reflection of listener appraisal of a licensee's performance as the performance meets or fails to meet the licensee's statutory obligation to operate the facility in the public interest. The matter now before us is one in which the alleged conduct adverse to the public interest rests primarily on claims of racial discrimination, some elements of religious discrimination, oppressive overcommercialization by advertising announcements, and violation of the Fairness Doctrine. Future cases may involve other areas of conduct and programming adverse to the public interest; at this point we can only emphasize that intervention on behalf of the public is not allowed to press private interests but

only to vindicate the broad public interest relating to a licensee's performance of the public trust inherent in every license.

HEARING

We hold further that in the circumstances shown by this record an
evidentiary hearing was required in order to resolve the public interest
issue. Under Section 309(e) the Commission must set a renewal application for hearing where "a substantial and material question of fact is
presented *or* the Commission for any reason is unable to make the
finding" that the public interest, convenience, and necessity will be served
by the license renewal. (Emphasis supplied.)

The Commission argues in this Court that it accepted all Appellants'
allegations of WLBT's misconduct and that for this reason no hearing was
necessary. Yet the Commission recognized that WLBT's past behavior, as
described by Appellants, would preclude the statutory finding of public
interest necessary for license renewal; hence its grant of the one-year
license on the policy ground that there was an urgent need at the time for
a properly run station in Jackson must have been predicated on a belief
that the need was so great as to warrant the risk that WLBT might
continue its improper conduct.

We agree that a history of programming misconduct of the kind
alleged would preclude, as a matter of law, the required finding that
renewal of the license would serve the public interest. It is important to
bear in mind, moreover, that although in granting an initial license the
Commission must of necessity engage in some degree of forecasting future
performance, in a renewal proceeding past performance is its best criterion. When past performance is in conflict with the public interest, a very
heavy burden rests on the renewal applicant to show how a renewal can
be reconciled with the public interest. Like public officials charged with a
public trust, a renewal applicant, as we noted in our discussion of
standing, must literally "run on his record." . . .

Reversed and remanded.

Comments and Questions

1. Evaluate the roles of private citizens in this case.

2. Would the FCC have allowed anyone to enter the proceeding to challenge
WLBT's license renewal application? What could be said in favor of the FCC's
position? Are its fears realistic?

3. How does the court take account of the FCC's concerns? Could a private
citizen with a love of westerns have entered the proceeding to oppose license
renewal on the ground that WLBT did not show enough western movies?

4. The FCC said it accepted as true all the allegations of the citizens' group
opposing renewal. Why, then, did the court send the case back to the FCC for a
hearing instead of just denying WLBT's license renewal petition?

5. After the case was returned to the FCC, a hearing was held before a
hearing examiner, or administrative law judge. The examiner, placing a strict
burden of proof on the citizens' group, discounted virtually all the evidence
presented by the group, labeling it "mere allegations," and decided in favor of

renewing WLBT's license. The FCC adopted this decision, and the citizens' group appealed. In an opinion again written by then Circuit Judge Burger, the court castigated the FCC and the examiner for placing the burden of proof on the citizens' group instead of on WLBT, for the examiner's consistent pattern of discounting the citizens' group's evidence by characterizing it as "mere allegations," and for ignoring the earlier 1965 FCC decision that found WLBT's performance sufficiently questionable to justify only a one-year probationary renewal. Office of Communication of the United Church of Christ v. FCC (II), 425 F.2d 543 (D.C.Cir.1969):

> The Examiner seems to have regarded Appellants as "plaintiffs" and the licensee as "defendant," with burdens of proof allocated accordingly. This tack . . . was a grave misreading of our [earlier] holding on this question. We did not intend that intervenors representing a public interest be treated as interlopers. Rather, if analogues can be useful, a "Public Intervenor" who is seeking no license or private right is, in this context, more nearly like a complaining witness who presents evidence to police or a prosecutor whose duty it is to conduct an affirmative and objective investigation of all the facts and to pursue his prosecutorial or regulatory function if there is probable cause to believe a violation has occurred.
>
> This was all the more true here because prior to the efforts of the actively participating intervenors, the Commission itself had long since found the licensee wanting. It was not the correct role of the Examiner or the Commission to sit back and simply provide a forum for the intervenors; the Commission's duties did not end by allowing Appellants to intervene; its duties began at that stage.
>
> A curious neutrality-in-favor-of-the-licensee seems to have guided the Examiner in his conduct of the evidentiary hearing. [The court proceeded to catalog examples of evidence presented by the public group that the examiner discounted.] . . .
>
> The infinite potential of broadcasting to influence American life renders somewhat irrelevant the semantics of whether broadcasting is or is not to be described as a public utility. By whatever name or classification, broadcasters are temporary permittees—fiduciaries—of a great public resource and they must meet the highest standards which are embraced in the public interest concept. The Fairness Doctrine plays a very large role in assuring that the public resource granted to licensees at no cost will be used in the public interest. . . .
>
> The record now before us leaves us with a profound concern over the entire handling of this case following the remand to the Commission. The impatience with the Public Intervenors, the hostility toward their efforts to satisfy a surprisingly strict standard of proof, plain errors in rulings and findings lead us, albeit reluctantly, to the conclusion that it will serve no useful purpose to ask the Commission to reconsider the Examiner's actions and its own Decision and Order under a correct allocation of the burden of proof. The administrative conduct reflected in this record is beyond repair.
>
> . . .
>
> We are compelled to hold, on the whole record, that the Commission's conclusion is not supported by substantial evidence. For this reason the grant of a license must be vacated forthwith and the Commission is directed to invite applications to be filed for the license.

6. Who are the FCC's clients?

7. "An agency is captured when it favors the concerns of the industry it regulates, which is well-represented by its trade groups and lawyers, over the

interests of the general public, which is often unrepresented. Private groups participate more than public groups in the formulation of policy because most regulatory decisions have a much greater impact on manufacturers and producers than they do on consumers. . . . [For example, t]he benefits of cleaner air are spread over the entire population of an area, but the costs will be borne by electrical utilities and other manufacturers who pollute." R. Pierce, S. Shapiro & P. Verkuil, Administrative Law and Process 19–20 (1985). Does this theory apply to broadcast regulation? Can you think of any legal devices that may be used to combat industry domination?

8. In 1969, after the decision in *United Church of Christ (II)*, the commission stripped the license for WLBT from its former owner and awarded it to a new biracial church and community group. N.Y. Times, May 29, 1984, at A12, col. 1.

Section Three.   Authorized Makers of Administrative-Regulatory Law and Their Appropriate Collaborative Roles

This section is mainly concerned with the creation of substantive regulatory standards, and with those laws that allocate authority to make and to specify the procedures for making substantive regulatory law. First, we consider why legislatures delegate lawmaking and law-applying power to agencies and whether such delegations are proper. Next, we study the development by the Federal Communications Commission of a particular regulatory standard, the so-called fairness doctrine. Finally, we turn to the role of courts in reviewing agency action.

A.   The Legislature's Role: Delegation of Power to Administrative Agencies

The principal potential regulatory lawmakers are legislatures, administrative agencies constituted partly for the purpose, and courts. Observe that a legislative body, not a court, originated the regulatory program in the broadcasting field. (Why are courts distinctively unsuited to originate such regulatory programs?)

If a legislature originates a regulatory program, should it also go further and articulate all the relevant regulatory standards? Or should it create an administrative body and delegate vast lawmaking power to it? Legislatures in the United States have taken this latter course. In 1927, then Professor Felix Frankfurter stated that "[t]he widening area of what in effect is law-making authority, exercised by officials whose actions are not subject to ordinary court review, constitutes perhaps the most striking contemporary tendency of the Anglo-American legal order." Frankfurter, The Task of Administrative Law, 75 U.Pa.L.Rev. 614, 614 (1927). But why this development? And what, generally speaking, are the appropriate collaborative roles of legislative and administrative bodies in making regulatory law?

PARKER, WHY DO ADMINISTRATIVE
AGENCIES EXIST?

45 Geo.L.J. 331, 361–62 (1957).*

"Government by Decree" is an indisputable necessity in the 20th century in a country of 170 million. If we were of the size of the Principality of Liechtenstein, most laws could be enacted by the people themselves and even regulations could be made, if not by the people, then by their elected representatives. This not being the case, we must have a division of legislative labor.

In other words, there are legislative tasks of an enormous variety that are too complex for Congress to perform. Today it is not doubted any longer that to "write a self-executing law prohibiting the issuance of sub-standard utility securities would not only be ineffectual—it would be likely also to paralyze utility financing and cause endless private controversy over whether a proposed security conformed to statutory standards or not." The same can be said of railroad safety standards, the regulation of which must be left to flexible expert agencies, or of pure food and drug standards, or of the hundreds of other fields with which the average member of Congress is but vaguely acquainted. If the legal development had been different, if the courts had insisted that delegated lawmaking is unconstitutional, the end of our legislative branch as we know it would have occurred long ago. Congress would have bogged down under a mass of legislative tasks, which of necessity would have been assigned to committees, with Congress itself a mere rubber-stamp. The committee staffs would have been just as large as the present administrative agencies, while their products, under the shield of congressional laws, would have been more remote from the control of the people and public opinion than the output of agencies are now.

Actually, a certain amount of independence of the rulemaker from his legislative father, the legislator, can be regarded as beneficent. The experience of the French Revolution, when every power was concentrated in the National Convention and its Committee of Public Safety, has taught us that a degree of remoteness from Congress gives the law-applying, regulation-making agency time to reflect, to get out of politics, so to speak.

Against these considerations—that some general "laws" must be made by agencies rather than Congress—no valid argument has been raised. Some critics say that administrative regulations are subject to too many changes or are enacted without prior hearing of interested parties. This does not go to the heart of the matter. Rather, it touches upon the advisability of adjusting rulemaking procedure in order to impose procedural safeguards in favor of those affected by regulation.

––––––––

DODD, ADMINISTRATIVE AGENCIES AS LEGISLATORS AND JUDGES

25 A.B.A.J. 923, 925–26 (1939).*

But the primary system (if it may be called a system) in this country in the past, and the one which is likely to remain for the future, is that of broad delegation with little or no further legislative consideration unless there is grave abuse of the delegated power. Legislative bodies may often conclude and properly conclude that regulatory legislation is necessary, but they may have neither the time nor the capacity to formulate details of regulation. No legislative body can be expert in all the subjects with which it must deal, and the legislative function here is not one of expertness in particular fields but rather one of popular representation in determining matters of general policy. The legislature is no more able to establish specific and more or less permanent standards for drugs and cosmetics than it is to establish labor safety standards in the various types of factories. In the fixing of specific railroad rates, as in most of the present fields of social and economic regulation, the needs of flexibility and expertness in detail make it clear that proper results "can be much more readily secured through the constant thought and ruling of an administrative commission than through the necessarily sporadic acts of a legislative assembly." [21]

Modern regulatory statutes can provide no more than the skeleton, and must leave to administrative bodies the addition of flesh and blood necessary for a living body. But to what extent is an arbitrary discretion to be placed in the hands of administrative bodies? Our statutes are full of indefinite terms which must be given force and meaning by administrative action. In fixing railroad and utility rates, the Interstate Commerce Commission and state utility commissions are restricted to rates that are "just and reasonable"; the Federal Trade Commission is empowered and directed to prevent "unfair methods of competition"; the Federal Communications Commission is authorized to make regulations conducive to the "public convenience, interest or necessity"; in a number of states commissions are authorized to make "reasonable rules" for the safety of employees; the National Labor Relations Board determines "the unit appropriate for the purposes of collective bargaining"; and the Administrator of the Fair Labor Standards Act of 1938 may order minimum wage rates, not in excess of 40 cents an hour, if the rate "will not substantially curtail employment" and "will not give a competitive advantage to any group in the industry." These are but examples. Every relation of life is materially affected by state and federal regulatory legislation. Price-fixing and minimum wage regulation have become important rate activities since the decisions in *Nebbia* v. *New York* and *West Coast Hotel* v. *Parrish*.

In the application of these broad powers, some discretion must be exercised in individual cases, and the process of administrative adjudication must be employed. But even where administrative adjudication is necessary, standards may be established for the guidance of those gov-

* Copyright © 1939 by the American Bar Association Journal. Reprinted by permission.
  21. Ernst Freund, Standards of American Legislation, page 302.

erned by the act and equally for the guidance of those administering the act. Where standards are possible they should be established.

"Standards, if adequately drafted, afford great protection to administration. By limiting the area of the exercise of discretion they tend to routinize administration and to that degree relieve it from the play of political and economic pressures which otherwise might be harmful." [25]

And by amendment or replacement standards can be altered if found erroneous or if changed conditions make alteration necessary.

Where standardization is possible, the alternative to specific administrative regulations is the "trial-and-error" method of developing a rule which may upon its development, be found in the successive decisions of the administrative body in individual cases. The case method of developing law has its place, but not in the development of administrative standards in any case where it is possible to state such standards before the individual is punished for violation of standards which he could not have known. Not only is the "trial-and-error" method unfair to the public but it leads to inefficient administration.

Comments and Questions

1. What distinct reasons do Professor Parker and Mr. Dodd give for legislative delegation of lawmaking power to administrators? Can you think of any other reasons?

2. Note that Dodd speaks of two distinct ways that administrative bodies might make law: by regulations and by adjudication.

3. In 1934 Congress set up the Federal Communications Commission to supersede earlier agencies regulating communications. Congress not only conferred regulatory and adjudicative power on the FCC but also gave it express power to make basic regulatory law.

UNITED STATES CODE, TITLE 47

§ 151. Purposes; Federal Communications Commission created

For the purpose of regulating interstate and foreign commerce in communication by wire and radio so as to make available, so far as possible, to all the people of the United States a rapid, efficient, Nation-wide, and world-wide wire and radio communication service with adequate facilities at reasonable charges, for the purpose of the national defense, for the purpose of promoting safety of life and property through the use of wire and radio communications, and for the purpose of securing a more effective execution of this policy by centralizing authority heretofore granted by law to several agencies and by granting additional authority with respect to interstate and foreign commerce in wire and radio communication, there is hereby created a commission to be known as the "Federal Communications Commission", which shall be constituted as hereinafter provided, and which shall execute and enforce the provisions of this Act.

---

25. Landis, The Administrative Process, page 75.

FEDERAL COMMUNICATIONS COMMISSION ORGANIZATION CHART APRIL 1985

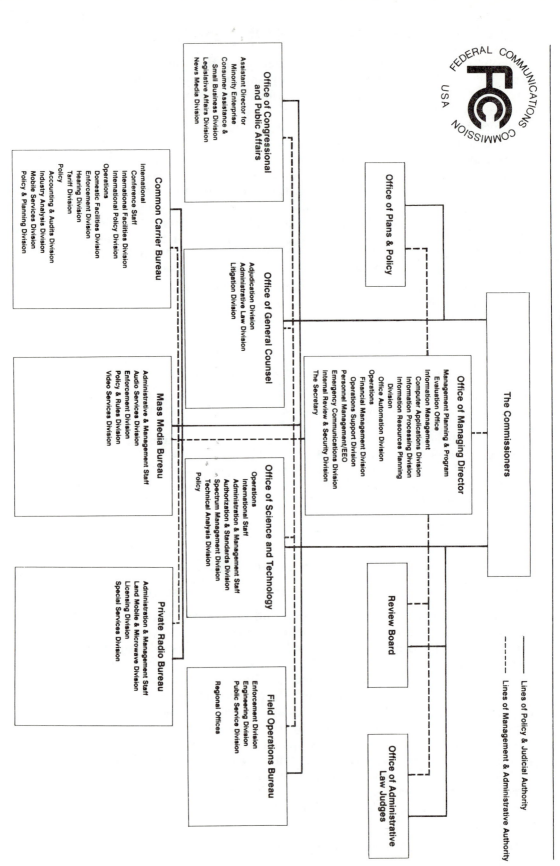

FEDERAL COMMUNICATIONS COMMISSION
USA

The Commissioners

Office of Plans & Policy

Review Board

Office of Administrative Law Judges

Office of Congressional and Public Affairs

Assistant Director for
Minority Enterprise
Consumer Assistance &
Small Business Division
Legislative Affairs Division
News Media Division

Office of General Counsel

Adjudication Division
Administrative Law Division
Litigation Division

Office of Managing Director

Management Planning & Program
Evaluation Office
Information Management
Computer Applications Division
Information Processing Division
Information Resources Planning
Division
Office Automation Division
Operations
Financial Management Division
Operations Support Division
Personnel Management/EEO
Emergency Communications Division
Internal Review & Security Division
The Secretary

Common Carrier Bureau

International
Conference Staff
International Facilities Division
International Policy Division
Operations
Domestic Facilities Division
Enforcement Division
Hearing Division
Tariff Division
Policy
Accounting & Audits Division
Industry Analysis Division
Mobile Services Division
Policy & Planning Division

Mass Media Bureau

Administrative & Management Staff
Audio Services Division
Enforcement Division
Policy & Rules Division
Video Services Division

Office of Science and Technology

Operations
International Staff
Administration & Management Staff
Authorization & Standards Division
Spectrum Management Division
Technical Analysis Division
Policy

Private Radio Bureau

Administration & Management Staff
Land Mobile & Microwave Division
Licensing Division
Special Services Division

Field Operations Bureau

Enforcement Division
Engineering Division
Public Service Division
Regional Offices

——— Lines of Policy & Judicial Authority
- - - - - Lines of Management & Administrative Authority

§ 154.   Federal Communications Commission

(a) Number of commissioners; appointment.   The Federal Communications Commission (in this Act referred to as the "Commission") shall be composed of five commissioners appointed by the President, by and with the advice and consent of the Senate, one of whom the President shall designate as chairman.   .   .   .

(c) Terms of office; vacancies.   Commissioners shall be appointed for terms of seven years and until their successors are appointed and have been confirmed and taken the oath of office, except that they shall not continue to serve beyond the expiration of the next session of Congress subsequent to the expiration of said fixed term of office; except that any person chosen to fill a vacancy shall be appointed only for the unexpired term of the Commissioner whom he succeeds.   No vacancy in the Commission shall impair the right of the remaining commissioners to exercise all the powers of the Commission.   .   .   .

(i) Duties and powers.   The Commission may perform any and all acts, make such rules and regulations, and issue such orders, not inconsistent with this Act, as may be necessary in the execution of its functions. .   .   .

§ 301.   License for radio communication or transmission of energy

.   .   . No person shall use or operate any apparatus for the transmission of energy or communications or signals by radio [which term includes TV] .   .   . except under and in accordance with this Act and with a license in that behalf granted under the provisions of this Act.

§ 303.   Powers and duties of Commission

Except as otherwise provided in this Act, the Commission from time to time, as public convenience, interest, or necessity requires, shall—

.   .   .   .

(r) Make such rules and regulations .   .   . , not inconsistent with law, as may be necessary to carry out the provisions of this Act .   .   .   .

§ 307.   Licenses

(a) Grant.   The Commission, if public convenience, interest, or necessity will be served thereby, subject to the limitations of this Act, shall grant to any applicant therefor a station license provided for by this Act.   .   .   .

(c) Terms.   [This subsection limits the license period to five years for a TV license and seven years for a radio license.   Prior to 1981, the period was three years for all broadcasting licenses.]   Upon the expiration of any license, upon application therefor, a renewal of such license may be granted [for a like period] if the Commission finds that public interest, convenience, and necessity would be served thereby.   .   .   .

———

Comments and Questions

1. What kinds of substantive regulatory laws were needed to regulate broadcasting? Among other things, it was essential to have laws setting standards for the award of broadcast licenses to applicants, laws setting standards that licensees must abide by in the course of their actual operations, and laws providing means of securing compliance with such standards. What should be the collaborative roles of legislature, agency, and court in making such law? In structuring a regulatory program for broadcasting, Congress had essentially three choices. It could have enacted (a) a detailed statute setting down regulatory standards (principles and rules), to be administered by the ordinary courts; (b) a statute with considerable policy detail and rule specificity, to be administered by an agency (thus delegating regulatory power—for example, a licensing function—to the agency, but not legislative power); or (c) a broad and general statute with few guidelines, to be administered by an agency (thus delegating legislative as well as regulatory power to the agency). What allocations of lawmaking roles are reflected in the Federal Communications Act of 1934, excerpted previously? That is, what choice among the three options just listed did Congress make? Why do you think it so chose?

2. Dodd and many others stress that although the legislature may provide only a "skeleton," with administrative bodies providing the "flesh and blood," the legislature should still provide basic policy direction. The foregoing statutory scheme clearly provides a skeleton, but does it fail to provide basic policy guidance? Observe that § 303 says that the FCC is to make law "as public convenience, interest, or necessity requires." This is also the standard given in § 307(a) and (c) to guide the FCC's award and renewal of broadcast licenses. Does this language offer much policy direction? Consider, for example, the all-important question of licensing: Can a license be awarded solely on the basis that the station's technical devices will not interfere with other stations already licensed? Or what if two or more applicants apply for use of the same part of the airwaves? What standards should the commission then apply in awarding the license (or renewing or revoking it)? Comparative financial resources of applicants? Demonstrated efficiency in operation? Quality of proposed programming? Nature of ownership—for example, local versus chain system? Surely the legislative skeleton is too skeletal if it fails to lay down any such standards whatsoever. To this day, Congress has not legislated to give greater policy direction to the FCC in awarding licenses. Why? Is it that Congress itself cannot reach agreement? If so, what kinds of standards should the FCC adopt? Uncontroversial ones?

3. The Radio Act of 1927 contained the same "public convenience, interest, and necessity" standard for granting and renewing licenses that was incorporated into the Federal Communications Act of 1934. Assume that you were one of the early commissioners planning the future of licensing policy. Assume that the commission had already decided upon a nationwide distribution scheme for stations, frequencies, hours of operation, and power. It has also established the minimum engineering and technical skills required of licensees. The remaining task is to decide how to choose among several applicants for the same station license. You have at least the following choices: (a) use a lottery system; (b) auction the license to the highest bidder; and (c) evaluate the applicants under a system of substantive criteria, such as proposed programming (quality, diversity, balance, degree of local programming), number of other stations or other media owned, past experience in broadcasting, financial strength, and so forth. Which approach would you choose and why? If you opt for the third approach, which criteria would you choose and why? Are you free under the statute to choose any

of these approaches [c] and, if the third, any criteria? Are you free to regulate program content through the licensing process? Should Congress have made these choices in the Federal Communications Act of 1934?

4. The legislative body can err by specifying too much. Indeed, in the Radio Act of 1912, Congress did not even give the relevant administrative body power to make regulations, and it enacted a long list of "regulations," two of which read as follows:

> First. Every station shall be required to designate a certain definite wave length as the normal sending and receiving wave length of the station. This wave length shall not exceed six hundred meters or it shall exceed one thousand six hundred meters. . . .
>
> Fourth. At all stations the logarithmic decrement per complete oscillation in the wave trains emitted by the transmitter shall not exceed two-tenths, except when sending distress signals or signals and messages relating thereto.

Congress might have left such matters to the regulatory body to develop in the form of regulations. Congress actually considered this alternative but declined to do so partly on the ground that this would be a "surrendering by Congress of its powers and a bestowal of legislative power . . . upon administrative officers." Was this a sound reason?

5. The Constitution in article I, § 1, provides: "All legislative Powers herein granted shall be vested in a Congress of the United States . . . . " In the famous case of A.L.A. Schechter Poultry Corp. v. United States, 295 U.S. 495, 55 S.Ct. 837 (1935), the Supreme Court struck down a broad congressional delegation of power to trade associations to create codes of fair competition. The delegating statute had contained virtually no standards or policy guidelines; it had said to the trade associations in effect, "Here is the problem—you deal with it." Since that time, however, the Court has largely ignored the nondelegation doctrine, having upheld sweeping delegations in several cases. Should the doctrine be revived? Consider the following view.

STEWART, THE REFORMATION OF AMERICAN ADMINISTRATIVE LAW

88 Harv.L.Rev. 1669, 1695–97 (1975).*

[A]ny large-scale enforcement of the nondelegation doctrine would clearly be unwise. Detailed legislative specification of policies under contemporary conditions would be neither feasible nor desirable in many cases, and the judges are ill-equipped to distinguish contrary cases.

In many government endeavors it may be impossible in the nature of the subject matter to specify with particularity the course to be followed. This is most obvious when a new field of regulation is undertaken. Administration is an exercise in experiment. If the subject is politically and economically volatile—such as wage and price regulation—constant changes in the basic parameters of the problem may preclude the development of a detailed policy that can consistently be pursued for any length

---

c. In 1981 Congress amended the statute expressly to authorize the FCC to award licenses on a random selection basis. Omnibus Budget Reconciliation Act of 1981, Pub.L. No. 97–35, § 1242, 95 Stat. 357, 736 (codified as amended at 47 U.S.C. § 309(i)). Which way does this cut on the question of the FCC's original authority to use a lottery system?

* Copyright © 1975 by the Harvard Law Review Association. Reprinted by permission.

of time. These limitations are likely to be encountered with increasing frequency as the federal government assumes greater responsibility for managing the economy.

In addition, there appear to be serious institutional constraints on Congress' ability to specify regulatory policy in meaningful detail. Legislative majorities typically represent coalitions of interests that must not only compromise among themselves but also with opponents. Individual politicians often find far more to be lost than gained in taking a readily identifiable stand on a controversial issue of social or economic policy. Detailed legislative specification of policy would require intensive and continuous investigation, decision, and revision of specialized and complex issues. Such a task would require resources that Congress has, in most instances, been unable to muster.[127] An across-the-board effort to legislate in detail would also require a degree of decentralized responsibility that might further erode an already weak political accountability for congressional decisions. These circumstances tend powerfully to promote broad delegations of authority to administrative agencies. Moreover, quite apart from these factors, one may question whether a legislature is likely in many instances to generate more responsible decisions on questions of policy than agencies.

Finally, there are serious problems in relying upon the judiciary to enforce the nondelegation doctrine. A court may not properly insist on a greater legislative specification of policy than the subject matter admits of. But how is the judge to decide the degree of policy specification that is possible, for example, in wage and price regulation when it is initially undertaken? How does he decide when knowledge has accumulated to the point where additional legislative specification of policy is now possible? What if the political situation is such that the legislative process cannot be made to yield any more detailed policy resolution? How does the judge differentiate such cases from those where the legislature is avoiding its "proper" responsibilities? Such judgments are necessarily quite subjective, and a doctrine that made them determinative of an administrative program's legitimacy could cripple the program by exposing it to continuing threats of invalidation and encouraging the utmost recalcitrance by those opposed to its effectuation. Given such subjective standards, and the controversial character of decisions on whether to invalidate legislative delegations, such decisions will almost inevitably appear partisan, and might often be so.

Comments and Questions

1. Professor John Hart Ely, a proponent of reviving the nondelegation doctrine, has found unconvincing Professor Stewart's argument that "[i]ndividual politicians often find far more to be lost than gained in taking a readily identifiable stand on a controversial issue of social or economic policy." He has written: "It's an argument, all right, but for which side? That legislators often find it

127. Although the example of taxation shows that Congress is capable of gearing up for detailed legislation (and frequent revision) if there are strong political incentives to do so, such incentives are lacking in many areas.

convenient to escape accountability is precisely the reason *for* a nondelegation doctrine. Were it to turn out that legislators forced to govern wouldn't have the courage to do so energetically, that would be too bad . . . but at least it would be our system. . . . As Judge Wright put it in 1972: 'An argument for letting the experts decide when the people's representatives are uncertain or cannot agree is an argument for paternalism and against democracy.' " J. Ely, Democracy and Distrust: A Theory of Judicial Review 133–34 (1980). With whom do you agree: Stewart or Ely?

2. Do you think the delegation of authority to the FCC in the 1934 act previously quoted is constitutional? Would it be constitutional under a revived nondelegation doctrine?

3. Would a revived nondelegation doctrine lead to better, more carefully drafted statutes or to less legislation? Does your answer affect whether you favor reviving the nondelegation doctrine?

4. Is it a satisfactory answer to the nondelegation proponents that Congress is always free to enact legislation altering any features of agency-developed regulatory law with which it disagrees? A legislative body can also monitor a regulatory program without continuously reentering the arena by way of actual legislation. It can hold hearings to which it "invites" administrators to defend their policies. It can propose legislation without actually enacting it and thereby induce agency action. It can reduce or increase appropriations of funds to the regulatory body. Still other interesting possibilities are considered in W. Gellhorn, C. Byse & P. Strauss, Administrative Law 103–26 (7th ed. 1979).

B. The Agency's Role: Adjudication and Rulemaking

To provide students with a more concrete basis for understanding the general character of regulatory lawmaking, an illustrative context should be considered in some depth. For this purpose, the evolution of laws governing a particular facet of the content of programs that broadcasters are required to present will be considered.

The FCC has undertaken certain forms of regulation to uplift program quality, indirectly and directly. Examples of indirect efforts to secure higher-quality programs include (1) favoring single-interest station applicants for licenses over corporate conglomerates, which might use the station primarily to serve the interests of other members of the corporate family or otherwise abuse their license; (2) awarding licenses to those who promise, in their applications, better program balance; and (3) encouraging competitive educational television.

Two examples of more direct FCC program content regulation involve (1) the so-called equal time doctrine and (2) the so-called fairness doctrine. These doctrines are closely related but distinct. The equal time doctrine is sanctioned by § 315 of the Federal Communications Act of 1934 as amended, and it requires a licensee who permits one political candidate to broadcast to "afford equal opportunities to all other such candidates for that office." The fairness doctrine, in contrast, was not originally sanctioned in so many words in the 1934 act. Instead, the FCC itself originated it. In essence, this doctrine requires that broadcasters give fair treatment of controversial issues without utilizing their facilities to peddle their own pet ideologies. The doctrine was considered necessary partly because broadcast facilities were not sufficiently numerous to provide a separate outlet for every significant point of view.

Some scholars have traced the origin of the fairness doctrine to the case that follows.

IN RE APPLICATION OF GREAT LAKES BROADCASTING CO.

Federal Radio Commission, 1929.
3 FRC Ann.Rep. 32, modified, 37 F.2d 993 (D.C.Cir.), cert. dismissed,
281 U.S. 706, 50 S.Ct. 467 (1930).

[Three stations applied for modified licenses to use the same radio frequency, and the Federal Radio Commission articulated criteria for deciding such cases. Among other things, it set forth these principles:]

Broadcasting stations are licensed to serve the public and not for the purpose of furthering the private or selfish interests of individuals or groups of individuals. The standard of public interest, convenience, or necessity means nothing if it does not mean this. . . .

It may be said that the law has already [provided in] section 18 of the Radio Act of 1927 [that] a broadcasting station is required to afford equal opportunities for use of the station to all candidates for a public office if it permits any of the candidates to use the station. . . . Again the emphasis is on the listening public, not on the sender of the message. It would not be fair, indeed it would not be good service, to the public to allow a one-sided presentation of the political issues of a campaign. In so far as a program consists of discussion of public questions, public interest requires ample play for the free and fair competition of opposing views, and the commission believes that the principle applies not only to addresses by political candidates but to all discussions of issues of importance to the public. The great majority of broadcasting stations are, the commission is glad to say, already tacitly recognizing a broader duty than the law imposes upon them. . . .

Furthermore, the service rendered by broadcasting stations must be without discrimination as between its listeners. . . .

. . . . If, therefore, all the programs transmitted are intended for, and interesting or valuable to, only a small portion of that public, the rest of the listeners are being discriminated against. . . .

In such a scheme there is no room for the operation of broadcasting stations exclusively by or in the private interests of individuals or groups so far as the nature of the programs is concerned. There is not room in the broadcast band for every school of thought, religious, political, social, and economic, each to have its separate broadcasting station, its mouthpiece in the ether. If franchises are extended to some it gives them an unfair advantage over others . . . . Propaganda stations (a term which is here used for the sake of convenience and not in a derogatory sense) are not consistent with the most beneficial sort of discussion of public questions. As a general rule, postulated on the laws of nature as well as on the standard of public interest, convenience, or necessity, particular doctrines, creeds, and beliefs must find their way into the market of ideas by the existing public-service stations [as opposed to "propaganda stations"], and if they are of sufficient importance to the listening public the microphone will undoubtedly be available. If it is not, a well-founded complaint will receive the careful consideration of the commission in its future action with reference to the station complained of. . . .

Comments and Questions

1. Why do you suppose this issue arose in a licensing proceeding? How might the licensing technique be utilized to enforce a fairness doctrine?

2. Note that the agency uses adjudicative methods to allocate licenses, as between competing applicants. For vigorous criticism of this technique, see L. Fuller, The Morality of Law 170–77 (rev. ed. 1969).

3. This case arose under the Radio Act of 1927 and was resolved initially by the Federal Radio Commission, predecessor of the FCC. The Radio Act of 1927 imposed the standard of "public convenience, interest, and necessity." This language does not explicitly authorize the agency to originate and evolve a fairness doctrine, does it? (Distinguish the political candidates context.) Was the FRC action ultra vires?

4. In *Great Lakes Broadcasting,* the FRC struggled over whether broadcast stations were public utilities. It concluded they were not—at least in the sense of telephone or telegraph companies that were required to accept and transmit messages for all comers at nondiscriminatory rates. But they *were* like other public utilities, namely water, gas, and electric companies, that were required to supply a commodity or service to the community. Is there a nondiscrimination obligation imposed on water, gas, and electric companies? Does the analogy help buttress the fairness doctrine for broadcasters?

Evolution of Fairness Doctrine

If there was to be a fairness doctrine, then, to be effective it would have to be given specific content so that station operators could apply it—so they could know in advance what they must do to comply. Such is an obvious sine qua non of self-regulation. But what is needed to give the fairness doctrine more specific content? Consider the following questions that a station operator would want answered: (1) Which kinds of public issues trigger the doctrine? Personal attacks on people who advocate just anything? Religious proposals? Scientific issues? Any issue on which opposing views can be found? (2) Does the doctrine apply to all kinds of programming, including presidential addresses, news, advertising, entertainment, comedy, and documentaries? (3) What constitutes the representation of a point of view? Can this be done indirectly by slanting or editorializing? (4) What constitutes an opposing point of view? (5) How much time should be allocated to the opposing point of view, how should it be placed (in prime time or just anywhere), and with how many exposures? (6) What should be the qualifications of the opposing spokesperson, and so on? Then, too, a need would exist for basic law on whether the doctrine should come into play at all if the area is already served by diverse media reflecting opposing points of view. Can you think of other questions requiring clarification?

Which lawmakers might make such law? The leading possibilities are (1) Congress, (2) the agency, and (3) the courts. Does Congress have time for such matters? Is it any better qualified than the agency? Is there need for agency experimentation in this area? As early as 1930, Congress considered whether it should reenter and speak to the fairness doctrine, but it was not until 1959 that it formally did so; and then it did not seek to answer any of the questions we have raised about the doctrine but only endorsed it in principle by adding to § 315(a) of the Federal Communications Act of 1934 the words "[n]othing . . . shall be construed as relieving broadcasters . . . from the obligation . . . to afford reasonable opportunity for the discussion of conflicting views on issues of public importance."

Meanwhile, the agency undertook to give content to the fairness doctrine. The agency itself had a basic choice: to promulgate regulations or to proceed on a case-by-case basis. What might be the advantages and disadvantages of each? Observe that the difference between the two is not necessarily that, on the one hand, rules are produced and, on the other hand, they are not. The ad hoc approach can yield rules, too, in effect.

Between 1929 and 1967, the relevant agency evolved the fairness doctrine without resorting to formal rulemaking procedures. The materials that follow are more than illustrative; they reflect major developments.

TRINITY METHODIST CHURCH, SOUTH v. FRC

United States Circuit Court of Appeals, District of Columbia Circuit, 1932.
62 F.2d 850, cert. denied, 284 U.S. 685, 52 S.Ct. 204 (1932),
288 U.S. 599, 53 S.Ct. 317 (1933).

[In this license renewal proceeding, the Federal Radio Commission refused to renew the station's license. Dr. Shuler, the minister of the Trinity Methodist Church, had been in charge of the station's operations. The federal court of appeals in upholding the commission's action summarized the commission's reasons as follows:]

. . . [T]he station had been used to attack a religious organization, meaning the Roman Catholic Church; . . . the broadcasts by Dr. Shuler were sensational rather than instructive; and . . . in two instances Shuler had been convicted of attempting in his radio talks to obstruct the orderly administration of public justice.

Comments and Questions

1. Which of the foregoing reasons in *Trinity Methodist Church, South* v. *FRC* is related to the fairness doctrine? Do you think it would have made any difference if the station had allowed equal time? In other similar licensing cases, the commission took the "fairness record" of the applicant into account.

2. In In re Young Peoples' Association for the Propagation of the Gospel, 6 F.C.C. 178 (1938), the Federal Communications Commission, which had replaced the Federal Radio Commission, denied a license to a religious group that proposed to broadcast only its own religious doctrines. How is this related to the fairness doctrine?

3. In In re Mayflower Broadcasting Corp., 8 F.C.C. 333 (1940), the commission granted renewal to a station but roundly condemned its past practice of editorializing, observing: "The record shows . . . it was the policy of Station WAAB to broadcast so-called editorials from time to time urging the election of various candidates for political office or supporting one side or another of various questions in public controversy. . . . [T]his licensee . . . has revealed a serious misconception of its duties and functions under the law." This case generated a controversy that prompted the commission, after hearing forty-nine witnesses and receiving comments from twenty-one other persons or groups, to promulgate in 1949 its famous Editorializing Report. Part of this report, which was sent to all broadcasters, is set forth next. (Has the commission shifted its position in this report? Is it concerned about a different problem now?) The Editorializing Report is followed by parts of the FCC's Fairness Primer, promulgated in 1964 in the form of a digest of the commission's fairness rulings.

FCC, EDITORIALIZING BY BROADCAST LICENSEES [EDITORIALIZING REPORT]

13 F.C.C. 1246, 1254–55 (1949).

The Commission is not persuaded that a station's willingness to stand up and be counted on these particular issues upon which the licensee has a definite position may not be actually helpful in providing and maintaining a climate of fairness and equal opportunity for the expression of contrary views. Certainly the public has less to fear from the open partisan than from the covert propagandist. . . . In the absence of a duty to present all sides of controversial issues, overt editorialization by station licensees could conceivably result in serious abuse. But where, as we believe to be the case under the Communications Act, such a responsibility for a fair and balanced presentation of controversial public issues exists, we cannot see how the open espousal of one point of view by the licensee should necessarily prevent him from affording a fair opportunity for the presentation of contrary positions or make more difficult the enforcement of the statutory standard of fairness upon any licensee.

. . . [T]he licensee's opportunity to express his own views as part of a general presentation of varying opinions on particular controversial issues, does not justify or empower any licensee to exercise his authority over the selection of program material to distort or suppress the basic factual information upon which any truly fair and free discussion of public issues must necessarily depend. The basis for any fair consideration of public issues, and particularly those of a controversial nature, is the presentation of news and information concerning the basic facts of the controversy in as complete and impartial a manner as possible. A licensee would be abusing his position as public trustee of these important means of mass communication were he to withhold from expression over his facilities relevant news or facts concerning a controversy or to slant or distort the presentation of such news. No discussion of the issues involved in any controversy can be fair or in the public interest where such discussion must take place in a climate of false or misleading information concerning the basic facts of the controversy.

FCC, APPLICABILITY OF THE FAIRNESS DOCTRINE IN THE HANDLING OF CONTROVERSIAL ISSUES OF PUBLIC IMPORTANCE [FAIRNESS PRIMER]

29 Fed.Reg. 10,416, 10,416, 10,421 (1964).

The fairness doctrine deals with the . . . question of affording reasonable opportunity for the presentation of contrasting viewpoints on controversial issues of public importance. Generally speaking, it does not apply with the precision of the "equal opportunities" requirement. Rather, the licensee, in applying the fairness doctrine, is called upon to make reasonable judgments in good faith on the facts of each situation—as to whether a controversial issue of public importance is involved, as to what viewpoints have been or should be presented, as to the format and spokesmen to present the viewpoints, and all the other facets of such programming. In passing on any complaint in this area, the Commission's role is not to substitute its judgment for that of the licensee as to any of the above programming decisions, but rather to determine whether the licensee can be said to have acted reasonably and in good faith. There is thus room for considerably more discretion on the part of the licensee under the fairness doctrine than under the "equal opportunities" requirement. . . .

25. *Personal attacks on, and criticism of, candidate; partisan position on campaign issues.* In more than 20 broadcasts, two station commentators presented their views on the issues in the 1962 California gubernatorial campaign between Governor Brown and Mr. Nixon. The views expressed on the issues were critical of the Governor and favored Mr. Nixon, and at times involved personal attacks on individuals and groups in the gubernatorial campaign, and specifically on Governor Brown. The licensee responded that it had presented opposing viewpoints but upon examination there were two instances of broadcasts featuring Governor Brown (both of which were counterbalanced by appearances of Mr. Nixon) and two instances of broadcasts presenting viewpoints opposed to two of the issues raised by the above-noted broadcasts by the commentators. It did not appear that any of the other broadcasts cited by the station dealt with the issues raised as to the gubernatorial campaign.

Ruling. Since there were only two instances which involved the presentation of viewpoints concerning the gubernatorial campaign, opposed to the more than twenty programs of the commentators presenting their views on many different issues of the campaign for which no opportunity was afforded for the presentation of opposing viewpoints, there was not a fair opportunity for presentation of opposing viewpoints with respect to many of the issues discussed in the commentators' programs. The continuous, respective opportunity afforded for the expression of the commentators' viewpoints on the gubernatorial campaign, in contrast to the minimal opportunity afforded to opposing viewpoints, violated that right of the public to a fair presentation of views. Further, with respect to the personal attacks by the one commentator on individuals and groups involved in the gubernatorial campaign, the principle in *Mapoles* and *Billings* [two earlier FCC proceedings] should have been followed. In the circumstances, the station should have sent a transcript of the pertinent continuity on the above programs to Governor Brown and should have offered a comparable opportunity for an appropriate spokesman to answer the broadcasts. (Times-Mirror, FCC 62–1130, 24 R.R. 404, Oct. 26, 1962; FCC 62–1109, 24 R.R. 407, Oct. 19, 1962.)

26. *Personal attacks on, and criticism of, candidates; partisan position on campaign issues—appropriate spokesman.* See facts above. The question was raised whether the candidate has the right to insist upon his own appearance, to respond to the broadcasts in question.

Ruling. Since a response by a candidate would, in turn, require that equal opportunities under Section 315 be afforded to the other legally-qualified candidates for the same office, the fairness doctrine requires only that the licensee afford the attacked candidate an opportunity to respond through an appropriate spokesman. The candidate should, of course, be given a substantial voice in the selection of the spokesman to respond to the attack or to the statement of support. (Times-Mirror Bctg. Co., FCC 62–1130, 24 R.R. 404, 406, Oct. 19, 1962, Oct. 26, 1962.)

Comments and Questions

1. Review our earlier listing of the questions a station operator would want answered about the fairness doctrine. Does the "law" laid down by the agency in the selections so far adequately provide the answers? Or are many large questions left open, thus inhibiting the chances for self-regulation by station owners?

2. In the 1964 Fairness Primer, the FCC used the phrase "controversial issues of public importance" to describe the issues that trigger the fairness doctrine. Is that one test or two? How does a station operator decide which issues these are? See FCC, Fairness Doctrine and Public Interest Standards [Fairness Report], 39 Fed.Reg. 26,372, 26,376 (1974).

3. Suppose in 1968 a TV station broadcasts a commercial for cigarettes, portraying youthful, attractive, sophisticated people enjoying cigarettes in interesting and exciting situations and thus conveying the impression that smoking is socially acceptable and desirable for a rich, full life. Would the station be required to include programs pointing out that smoking is or may be harmful to one's health? What effect would such a ruling have on a station's revenue potential? See Banzhaf v. FCC, 405 F.2d 1082 (D.C.Cir.1968), cert. denied, 396 U.S. 842, 90 S.Ct. 50 (1969). In 1970 Congress passed a statute prohibiting cigarette advertising on radio and television and changing the labeling requirement on cigarette packages from the phrasing "Caution: Cigarette Smoking May Be Hazardous to Your Health" to "Warning: The Surgeon General Has Determined That Cigarette Smoking Is Dangerous to Your Health." 15 U.S.C. §§ 1333, 1335. Suppose after 1971 a station runs an antismoking message. Must it allow time for cigarette manufacturers to present the opposing view that cigarettes may not be harmful to one's health? What would be the precise "controversial issue of public importance"? See In re Cigarette Advertising & Antismoking Presentations, 27

F.C.C.2d 453 (1970), aff'd sub nom. Larus & Brother Co. v. FCC, 447 F.2d 876 (4th Cir.1971). Would the outcome be different if the station runs an editorial in favor of banning all smoking on airplanes?

4. Suppose the product advertised were high-powered, fuel-guzzling automobiles. Would the station be required to balance such commercials with programs presenting the antipollution case? See Friends of the Earth v. FCC, 449 F.2d 1164 (D.C.Cir.1971). What about commercials for butter, eggs, ice cream, or other high-cholesterol products; for soft drinks; or for imported television sets? Would it matter whether the commercials merely stressed the product's desirability, or also commented upon its health benefits or the benefits of importing? See FCC, Fairness Doctrine and Public Interest Standards, 39 Fed.Reg. 26,372, 26,381–82 (1974).

5. Up to 1967, the FCC did not make any formal rules on the fairness doctrine. Instead, the FCC proceeded by an ad hoc approach. How would you attack and defend the FCC's preference for an ad hoc approach in developing the governing law? Should it instead have promulgated a series of rules answering in advance the kinds of questions just posed?

BAKER, POLICY BY RULE OR AD HOC APPROACH— WHICH SHOULD IT BE?

22 Law & Contemp.Probs. 658, 660–65 (1957).*

While agency discretion to choose between proceeding by general rule-making or individual ad hoc decisions is thus clear, the criteria or bases upon which that discretion should be exercised are more obscure. One central proposition does stand out: The agency should set out, as fully and precisely and as soon as possible, "the guiding principles of administrative behavior." For the administrative agency is not in the narrowly confined position of the courts who can develop law in, for example, the antitrust field only when a suitable case is presented to them. The agency has available to it a whole arsenal of administrative devices by which it can develop and announce new policies for the edification of the regulated persons or groups. It is, therefore, almost axiomatic that, wherever feasible or appropriate, such policy should not be "sprung" upon the surprised party in a particular adjudicatory decision, but rather should be made clear through prior rule-making proceedings. As aptly stated by the Court in the second *Chenery* case:

> Since the Commission, unlike a court, does have the ability to make new law prospectively through the exercise of its rule-making powers, it has less reason to rely upon ad hoc adjudication to formulate new standards of conduct within the framework of the Holding Company Act. The function of filling in the interstices of the Act should be performed, as much as possible, through this quasi-legislative promulgation of rules to be applied in the future.

* Reprinted, with permission, from a symposium, Radio and Television (Part I), appearing in *Law and Contemporary Problems* (Vol. 22, No. 4, Winter 1957), published by the Duke University School of Law, Durham, North Carolina. Copyright, 1957, by Duke University.

The question, however, is when is it feasible or appropriate to employ rule-making, and when not. Viewed generally, the considerations or criteria favoring the ad hoc approach are believed to be threefold.

1. *The complex or varying factual nature of the problem*

Where the particular problem is "so specialized" or so dependent for solution on the various complex factual situations presented as to render it "impossible of capture within the boundaries of a general rule," the ad hoc approach is necessary as indicated by the Court in *Chenery*. While . . . this criterion does have validity in many situations, it should not be promiscuously applied. There is a tendency, I think, to decide against rule-making solely because a rule cannot be drawn which will clearly delineate or predict the agency's action on a given problem involving a complex factual situation. But a broad rule can be drawn in many such situations which, although not foretelling the outcome of agency action, does serve the fundamental purpose of unmistakably informing the public of the agency's basis or stake in the particular problem. It is this latter consideration, and not precise predictability of agency action, that is the touchstone of administrative rule-making.

To illustrate, the SEC in the *Chenery* situation could easily have promulgated a very broad rule which simply indicated its concern and future scrutiny of all trading by insiders during reorganization to determine whether such trading met the "fair and equitable" standards of section 11 of the Holding Company Act. While such a rule would not necessarily inform parties of the Commission's ultimate holding as to their particular transaction, it would put them on notice as to the necessity for meeting a general standard of fairness; and it might have led to informal negotiations or consultation with the agency to avoid later controversy. In this way, the harshness of retroactive ad hoc adjudication, which so disturbed the dissenters in *Chenery,* could have been avoided.

2. *Need for accumulating expertise*

The agency may not know enough about the particular problem to warrant issuance of rule-making. This may be due to either the newness of the agency or the problem before it. It may, therefore, be necessary to proceed on a case-by-case basis until the necessary experience to draft an appropriate rule has been accumulated. This method of proceeding slowly and developing the agency rule as the needed expertise is built up has a great deal to recommend it. The first impression or reaction to a matter often turns out to be quite erroneous, after development of all the facts and considerations. In a sense, this question of "ripeness" for rule-making is similar to that dealt with by the Supreme Court in deciding whether some difficult issue is "ripe" for its review. But here again, I believe that this consideration should not be used as an excuse to avoid promulgation of a broad rule, *wherever* appropriate, in order to advise interested parties of the agency's general direction or attitude. Such a broad rule can later be made more specific, when insight on the problem has been obtained through numerous ad hoc adjudications involving application of the rule to factual situations.

3. *Inability to foresee problem*

It is a misnomer to label this factor as one favoring an ad hoc approach. It is, however, a fact of administrative life that no agency can anticipate by rule all the problems, whether general or specific, that may confront it. When such an unforeseen problem arises, the agency has the choice of making a policy determination in the particular case or of withholding action until the conclusion of general rule-making proceedings to establish a governing rule. The latter course may, however, be precluded by the delay entailed. In short, the problem is before the agency, and the fact that it has not been anticipated does not excuse the agency from acting.

On the other side of the coin, the following considerations strongly indicate the use of rule-making:

1. *Desirability of definitive guides to agency action*

This point has already been made and needs no elaboration. To the extent that the agency knows the policy it desires to follow, to that same extent it should inform those coming within its regulation of that policy.

2. *Avoidance of retroactivity*

As a corollary to 1., it is obviously desirable to avoid, if possible, the harsh effect of *retroactive* application of agency policy inherent in the case-by-case method. While, as shown by the second *Chenery* decision, the factor of retroactivity does not render the ad hoc adjudication invalid, it certainly goes against elemental notions of fair play when it is considered that the agency, unlike the courts, is not restricted to this one method of dealing with those regulated.

The FCC, to a large extent, does not engage in retroactive procedures because of the statutory scheme, which requires prior Commission consent to construction of facilities, modification of licenses or permits, transfer of license, etc. Furthermore licenses are for limited periods, must be renewed regularly, and licensees do not obtain property rights on any frequency beyond the term of the license. But there have been occasions where after a grant of the application, the Commission's policy has changed, and after that change, retroactive ad hoc action has been taken. Thus, the Commission's "duopoly policy" was sharply reversed in 1944 and, as a consequence, hearings were held in about 45 cases which resulted in the multiple owner being required to divest himself of one of the two stations which he had previously owned in the same community.

Another example of retroactive Commission ad hoc adjudication reached the courts, and its treatment here is indicative of the distaste and hostility that such a procedure can arouse in given circumstances. In *Churchill Tabernacle* v. *FCC,* the Commission in 1943 had refused to renew a radio station's license until the licensee repudiated a long-term contract between itself and the Tabernacle. The latter had owned the radio station in question, and had sold it in 1931 to the present licensee, upon the contractual provision, inter alia, that it would be allowed to use a substantial portion of the station's broadcast time over a 100-year period. The Commission approved the arrangement and granted the licensee renewals of license until its action in 1943. Upon review, the court of appeals, stressing the importance of exhausting "all possible avenues of compliance with the congressional purpose before requiring complete destruction of the private interest," reversed,

> . . . for the reasons we have stated, we think the case should be remanded to the Commission to determine, on sufficient findings, whether a contract, modified as to the length of its existence, but allowing a reservation for a reasonable broadcast time, would be contrary to public interest. *And we find nothing in the present rules or practice of the Commission to forbid some such arrangement on these lines.*

Upon remand, the Commission promulgated rules defining the length of contract and hours of time which could be legally reserved. Upon appeal, the validity of these rules was sustained. The matter of reserved time contracts thus points up the desirability of avoiding the harsh retroactive situation and of proceeding, wherever possible, by more reasonable rule-making efforts.

3. *Sound administration*

The case-by-case method, involving a lengthy hearing, examining initial decision, exceptions, oral argument, etc., is more time-consuming than the usual rule-making proceeding of comments filed in response to a notice of proposed rule-making. Further, the ad hoc method is likely to involve litigation in a multiplicity of cases, whereas the rule-making, except for the occasional hearing required on a waiver request or difficult factual situation, often settles the matter without any need for future litigation. But what is more important, sound administration demands that an agency which has reached a fixed policy on some matter not require an applicant to go through a burdensome and *useless* hearing. Such a time-consuming procedure is unfair to the applicant and dissipates the agency's resources, which are undoubtedly taxed to the fullest. And it does not promote compliance with agency policy, perhaps without litigation, as a rule can do.

4. *Appropriateness of rule-making techniques*

The development of a quasi-legislative policy on an ad hoc basis suffers from the fact that in individual cases, there are ordinarily a very limited number of participants and a variety of issues. On the other hand, by utilizing the rule-making procedure, the agency is able to afford all interested parties an opportunity to participate and present their views on a single question of basic policy affecting both the public at large and individual licensees or prospective licensees of the agency. In short, broad policy should be shaped by the agency members relying heavily on their expert staffs, with the views of as great a portion of the people likely to be affected taken into account. And here it should be noted that with the congressional tendency to provide for stricter separation of function in adjudicatory cases, the agency is often, to a considerable degree, cut off from its staff when it chooses the adjudicatory route.

5. *Reviewability*

In statutory schemes like the Communications Act, where, to a great extent, the agency regulates by specifying that a license will not be issued on the establishment of certain facts, the fixing of agency policy by rule rather than adjudication makes the seeking of review in the courts more feasible. For, it takes considerable courage for a licensee, whose application for renewal has been denied because of some policy established in an ad hoc case, to challenge that policy in the courts; for the most part, such licensees would simply modify their operation in a way to meet the policy. When the policy has been formulated in a rule, however, that rule can immediately be challenged either by the licensee (without endangering its permit) or by some interested party who is adversely affected. Thus, in the case of the Chain Broadcasting Rules, it was uncertain, as the Supreme Court noted, that any licensee would endanger its license by refusing to comply with regulations. But the networks affected had standing to immediately seek review of the rules and did so. The desirability of having the courts pass on the legality of basic agency policies at the earliest opportunity needs no discussion.

FCC, THE HANDLING OF PUBLIC ISSUES UNDER THE FAIRNESS DOCTRINE AND THE PUBLIC INTEREST STANDARDS OF THE COMMUNICATIONS ACT

36 F.C.C.2d 40, 48 (1972).

From the time of the Editorializing Report [of 1949] to the present, we have been urged to adopt ever more precise rules—always in the cause of insuring robust debate (e.g., the argument, advanced in 1949 and now repeated by the ACLU, that fairness requires the contrasting viewpoint to follow immediately the presentation of the first viewpoint). However well intentioned these arguments are, we believe that increasingly detailed Commission regulation militates against robust, wide-open debate. The genius of the fairness doctrine has been precisely the leeway and discretion it affords the licensee to discharge his obligation to contribute to an informed electorate.

Comments and Questions

1. Traditionally, agencies have favored an adjudicative approach to policymaking, although under persistent prodding from scholars and others, in recent years rulemaking has markedly increased. Consider these comments from a leading scholar:

The typical tendency of agencies to hold back from resort to the rule-making power is understandable and often it is justifiable. Waiting for a case to arise, then clarifying only to the extent necessary to decide the case, and then waiting for the next case is one way to build cautiously. In some circumstances, the slow process of making law only through adjudication is a necessity, for administrators may be truly unable to do more than to decide one case at a time. And sometimes, even when they can do more, they properly refrain from early rule-making. Building law through adjudication is a sound and necessary process; the great bulk of American law is the product of that process.

Even so, I think that American administrators, by and large, have fallen into habits of unnecessarily delaying the use of their rule-making power. They too often hold back even when their understanding suffices for useful clarification through rule-making.

K. Davis, Discretionary Justice: A Preliminary Inquiry 57 (1969). An agency unsure or less than fully committed to a new policy is likely to prefer case-by-case adjudication, because rulemaking has traditionally been viewed as committing an agency more specifically and permanently to the policy in question. One scholar has suggested that an agency may favor case-by-case adjudication over rulemaking for three reasons: (1) an agency's obligation—imposed by courts—to explain any departure in a given case from prior policy has traditionally been more relaxed and flexible where the departure is from a prior adjudicative decision; (2) courts will accept a change in policy with retroactive effect more readily if the prior policy was created by an ad hoc decision, because the reliance interest of regulatees is weaker than when they rely on a formally promulgated rule (is retroactive effect an important consideration with respect to the fairness doctrine?); and (3) a doctrine established by adjudication may more readily survive judicial challenge, because a reviewing court is less likely to focus as sharply on the acceptability of the policy implicit in an ad hoc decision. Shapiro, The Choice of Rulemaking or Adjudication in the Development of Administrative Policy, 78 Harv.L.Rev. 921, 942–58 (1965).

2. Does the FCC's argument in the 1972 report previously excerpted favor an ad hoc approach, or is it an argument concerning the content of the doctrine desirable under either approach?

3. In 1967 the FCC promulgated rules, which now appear as amended in 47 Code of Federal Regulations:

§ 73.1910 Fairness Doctrine.

The Fairness Doctrine is contained in section 315(a) of the Communications Act of 1934, as amended, which provides that broadcasters have certain obligations to afford reasonable opportunity for the discussion of conflicting views on issues of public importance. . . .

§ 73.1920 Personal attacks.

(a) When, during the presentation of views on a controversial issue of public importance, an attack is made upon the honesty, character, integrity or like personal qualities of an identified person or group, the licensee shall, within a reasonable time and in no event later than one week after the attack, transmit to the persons or group attacked [the date and time of the broadcast, the script, and an offer of time for a reply].

(b) The provisions of paragraph (a) of this section shall not apply to broadcast material which falls within one or more of the following categories:

(1) Personal attacks on foreign groups or foreign public figures;

(2) Personal attacks occurring during uses by legally qualified candidates; . . .

(4) Bona fide newscast, bona fide news interviews, and on-the-spot coverage of bona fide news events, including commentary or analysis contained in the foregoing programs. . . .

§ 73.1930 Political editorials.

(a) Where a licensee, in an editorial,

(1) Endorses or

(2) Opposes a legally qualified candidate or candidates, the licensee shall, within 24 hours after the editorial, transmit to [the opposed candidate(s) the date and time of the editorial, the script, and an offer of time for a reply]. . . .

How much do these rules add to the 1964 Fairness Primer? Should the FCC by now have issued more detailed rules? Why has the FCC issued detailed rules only for personal attacks and political editorials?

4. Focusing on only published rules is perhaps misleading, because the commission since 1967 has issued several reports and policy statements concerning the fairness doctrine, some of which have already been cited in the text. These reports often add content to the fairness doctrine. For example, in its Fairness Report, 39 Fed.Reg. 26,372 (1974), the commission announced it would no longer apply the doctrine to standard product commercials. Why does the commission issue reports and policy statements instead of regulations?

C. The Court's Role: Judicial Review of Agency Action

Observe that the courts played no significant role in developing the content of the fairness doctrine, although the courts inevitably got into the act when parties adversely affected by agency decisions appealed those decisions or when agencies turned to them to get enforcement of their orders. But was having an agency evolve the law really necessary? Could the legislature have set up the basic regulatory program with the courts then putting the flesh and blood on the skeleton and with the administrative agency merely administering to the growing beast? Or, compared with the courts, was the agency in some way a better lawmaking body?

J. LANDIS, THE ADMINISTRATIVE PROCESS
30–31, 33–38, 46 (1938).*

Admittedly, the judicial process suffers from several basic and more or less unchangeable characteristics. One of these is its inability to maintain a longtime, uninterrupted interest in a relatively narrow and carefully defined area of economic and social activity. As Ulpian remarked, the science of law embraces the knowledge of things human and divine. A general jurisdiction leaves the resolution of an infinite variety of matters

* Copyright © 1938 by Yale University Press. Reprinted by permission.

within the hands of courts. In the disposition of these claims judges are uninhibited in their discretion except for legislative rules of guidance or such other rules as they themselves may distill out of that vast reserve of materials that we call the common law. This breadth of jurisdiction and freedom of disposition tends somewhat to make judges jacks-of-all-trades and masters of none.

Modern jurisprudence with its pragmatic approach is only too conscious of this problem. To its solution it brings little more than a method of analysis, a method that calls upon the other sciences to provide the norms. It thus expands rather than contracts areas of inquiry. If the issues for decision are sociological in nature, the answers must be on that plane. If the problem is a business problem, the answer must be derived from that source. But incredible areas of fact may be involved in the disposition of a business problem that calls not only for legal intelligence but also for wisdom in the ways of industrial operation. This difficulty is intrinsic to the judicial process. . . .

To these considerations must be added two others. The first is the recognition that there are certain fields where the making of law springs less from generalizations and principles drawn from the majestic authority of textbooks and cases, than from a "practical" judgment which is based upon all the available considerations and which has in mind the most desirable and pragmatic method of solving that particular problem. . . .

The second consideration is, perhaps, even more important. It is the fact that the common-law system left too much in the way of the enforcement of claims and interests to private initiative. Jhering's analysis of the "struggle for law"—the famous essay in which he indicated that the process of carving out new rights had resulted from the willingness of individuals as litigants or as criminal defendants to become martyrs to their convictions—pointed only to a slow and costly method of making law. To hope for an adequate handling of the problem of allowable trade practices by the sudden emergence of a host of Pyms and Hampdens was too delightfully visionary to be of much practical value. The retaliatory powers of business associates or competitors is today such an immensely powerful force that few persons care to run the risk of its offensive vengeance in the effort to secure what they might deem to be their legal rights. . . .

The [administrative] power to initiate action exists because it fulfils a longfelt need in our law. To restrict governmental intervention, in the determination of claims, to the position of an umpire deciding the merits upon the basis of the record as established by the parties, presumes the existence of an equality in the way of the respective power of the litigants to get at the facts. . . .

One other significant distinction between the administrative and the judicial processes is the power of "independent" investigation possessed by the former. The test of the judicial process, traditionally, is not the fair disposition of the controversy; it is the fair disposition of the controversy *upon the record as made by the parties.* True, there are collateral sources of information which often affect judicial determinations. There is the more or less limited discretion under the doctrine of judicial notice; and there is the inarticulated but nonetheless substantial power to choose between competing premises based upon off-the-record considerations. But, in strictness, the judge must not know of the events of the controversy except as these may have been presented to him, in due form, by the parties. Although the power to summon witnesses upon his own initiative in certain cases may theoretically be possessed by him, yet as a matter of fact it is not exercised. The very organization of his office prevents him from doing so. Except in a few cases where the costs of such an investigation can be charged against the res that is the subject matter of the litigation, no funds are available for the purpose; no subordinates are at his beck and call competent to perform the function. Nor is he permitted to conduct an investigation to determine what policy is best adapted to the demands of time and place, even though he is aware that sooner or later he will be confronted with the necessity, through the processes of judicial decision, of shaping policy in that particular field. . . .

It is in the light of these broad considerations that the place of the administrative tribunal must be found. The administrative process is, in essence, our generation's answer to the inadequacy of the judicial and the legislative processes.

Comments and Questions

1. In light of the foregoing, does it seem wise that courts have generally refrained from interfering with agency development of the fairness doctrine?

2. In several of the cases in which the agency was developing the fairness doctrine, the party adversely affected appealed the agency decision, claiming that the agency erred in, say, denying a license, or refusing to renew one, or in issuing an order to make free time available. Appeals from FCC decisions and orders must generally be taken to the United States Court of Appeals for the District of Columbia Circuit. See 47 U.S.C. § 402. Thus, the *Great Lakes Broadcasting* and the *Trinity Methodist* cases were appealed to that court. Yet, in these cases the court in large part let the commission's actions stand. But in other cognate fields, courts have sometimes tended to frustrate the regulatory scheme by substituting their judgment for the agency's judgment. Can you imagine illustrative examples of how a reviewing court might have, had it so chosen, sabotaged the fairness doctrine? Sometimes the agency itself may get completely off the track or not go far enough. The importance of an enlightened judicial role can then be seen clearly. In this regard, our earlier cases of *Office of Communication of the United Church of Christ* v. *FCC (I and II)* are instructive, as are the two cases that follow.

3. Can the legislature have anything to say about the lawmaking role that courts are to play when appeals are taken from the agency? An amendment to the Federal Communications Act of 1934 adopted the Administrative Procedure Act's standards for judicial review of agency action: "The reviewing court shall . . . hold unlawful and set aside agency action . . . found to be . . . arbitrary, capricious, an abuse of discretion, or otherwise not in accordance with law . . . . " See 47 U.S.C. § 402(g). Can an agency simply be wrong in its judgment without being arbitrary or capricious? In such a case, would language of the foregoing nature permit a lawyer to appeal to a court and secure a reversal

of the agency's decision? The two following cases illustrate the "arbitrary and capricious" standard in a fairness doctrine context.

COLUMBIA BROADCASTING SYSTEM v. FCC

United States Court of Appeals, District of Columbia Circuit, 1971.
454 F.2d 1018.

[The FCC order appealed in this case ruled on five fairness doctrine complaints. On four of the complaints, the commission ruled that a programming imbalance occurred when the three television networks between November 3, 1969, and June 3, 1970, carried five prime-time speeches (fifteen to thirty minutes each) by President Nixon, setting out his views on the Vietnam War. These five speeches aside, the commission found a general balance of views in other Vietnam War programming (newscasts, documentaries, interview shows, and the like). To balance the five speeches, the commission ordered the networks to present an uninterrupted program, offering opposing views on the Vietnam War but not necessarily on an equal time basis nor by the complainants in this proceeding (fourteen senators and others).

[On the fifth complaint—brought by the Republican National Committee (RNC) and the subject of this appeal—the commission ruled that a fairness doctrine violation occurred when CBS gave Lawrence O'Brien, chairman of the Democratic National Committee (DNC), twenty-five minutes of prime time for a "loyal opposition" broadcast to counterbalance past appearances by President Nixon and presidential spokesmen. Mr. O'Brien's program was aired July 7, 1970, and "involved presentation of excerpts of previously broadcast presidential statements on various issues, followed by a critical commentary or rebuttal by Mr. O'Brien as to each presidential statement. Topics covered included: (1) the state of the economy; (2) the nation's crime problem; (3) civil rights for blacks and other minorities; (4) federal expenditures for defense versus public domestic issues; (5) air and water pollution; (6) dissent and national unity; and (7) the war in Indochina." The commission found the O'Brien "loyal opposition" broadcast "unresponsive" to the five Nixon speeches on Vietnam, even though CBS had not offered the air time for a response specifically to those speeches, and ordered CBS to offer time to the Republican National Committee to respond to the O'Brien program. Both CBS and the Democratic National Committee appealed the FCC order.

[The first part of the court's opinion deals with the conflict between this O'Brien broadcast ruling and a prior FCC decision, referred to in the following as the *Hays* case. In *Hays* the shoe was on the other foot, in that it was the Democrats who wanted an opportunity to reply to a Republican response to President Johnson's 1968 state of the union address. CBS refused, and the FCC turned down the Democrats' fairness doctrine complaint.]

Before WRIGHT, TAMM and ROBINSON, CIRCUIT JUDGES.

J. SKELLY WRIGHT, CIRCUIT JUDGE:

·   ·   ·   ·   ·   ·   ·   ·   ·   ·

We do not challenge the Commission's well established right to modify or even overrule an established precedent or approach, for an administrative agency concerned with furtherance of the public interest is not bound to rigid adherence to its prior rulings. Lodged deep within the bureaucratic heart of administrative procedure, however, is the equally essential proposition that, when an agency decides to reverse its course, it must provide an opinion or analysis indicating that the standard is being changed and not ignored, and assuring that it is faithful and not indifferent to the rule of law. Moreover, as this court has emphasized, the Commission "must explain its reasons and do more than enumerate factual differences, if any, between . . . [similar] cases; it must explain the relevance of those differences to the purposes of the Federal Communications Act." In our view, the Commission's treatment of the *Hays* case in the proceedings below was clearly violative of these basic tenets of administrative law.

The *Hays* ruling arose in the context of President Johnson's 1968 State of the Union address. As it had done in the preceding two years, CBS invited Republican congressional leaders to respond to the President's address. CBS did not specify which of the many issues discussed by the President should be discussed on the program, require that those issues be discussed at all, or allocate time for presentation of any particular issue. The resulting one-hour broadcast covered a full panoply of issues, devoting a considerable amount of time to some issues treated only briefly by the President, while ignoring others he had examined at length. Indeed, the 1968 Republican broadcast covered a range of issues at least as broad as, if not broader than, the range of issues discussed in the O'Brien broadcast.

The Commission, however, sustained CBS' refusal to provide time to Democratic congressional leaders to reply to the 1968 Republican broadcast. In so doing, the Commission relied upon traditional fairness doctrine principles, stating that its role was not to substitute its own judgment for that of the broadcaster, but rather to determine whether the licensee could be said to have acted in good faith in discharging its obligation to provide a balanced presentation of opposing viewpoints. The Commission concluded that CBS had acted within the wide discretion afforded it under the fairness doctrine, and therefore held that the Republican broadcast did not give rise to any reply-to-reply rights in favor of Democratic spokesmen. . . .

Although *Hays'* relevance to the instant controversy is readily apparent, the Commission failed even to mention it in its initial order of August 18. In an effort to rectify this situation and to compel the Commission to face up to *Hays,* the CBS petition for reconsideration dealt at length with the *Hays* question, asserting vigorously that *Hays* was a controlling precedent which must be squarely confronted by the Commission. RNC's opposition to the CBS petition implicitly acknowledged the relevance of *Hays,* but suggested that it simply be overruled. Undaunted, the Commission persisted in its attempt to sidestep the issue entirely. Rather than face up to the apparent conflict, the Commission's opinion of September 24 [issued in response to CBS's rehearing petition] relegated its "discussion" of *Hays* to a mere citation in a footnote. In so doing, the Commission sought to reaffirm its earlier ruling, in the apparent belief that *Hays* was reconcilable with the decision here under review. The Commission made no attempt, however, to articulate the basis for reconciliation.

Faced with two facially conflicting decisions, the Commission was duty bound to justify their coexistence. The Commission's utter failure to come to grips with this problem constitutes an inexcusable departure from the essential requirement of reasoned decision making. . . .

Our reversal of the decision below, however, is not premised solely upon the Commission's mistreatment of *Hays,* for we find serious fault with other aspects of the opinion as well. In an apparent effort to avoid a direct confrontation with its earlier ruling in *Hays,* the Commission adopted a wholly unreasonable view of the factual setting of this controversy. By selecting rigid and arbitrary blinders, the Commission failed to see beyond Mr. Nixon's five speeches on Vietnam in evaluating the "responsiveness" of the O'Brien broadcast. The result, of course, was an arbitrary and therefore impermissible application of the Commission's own "responsiveness" doctrine.

Congress has delegated to the Commission the responsibility to ensure that broadcast licensees "operate in the public interest and . . . afford reasonable opportunity for the discussion of conflicting views on issues of public importance." As a result, a court reviewing agency action is not at liberty simply to substitute its own judgment for that of administrative officers who have kept within the bounds of their delegated powers. However, these powers are not boundless, and unless administrative action is tempered by judicial supervision, "expertise, the strength of modern government, can become a monster which rules with no practical limits on its discretion."

Cognizant of the potential hazards of unbridled administrative discretion, Congress has wisely devised a scheme whereby "agencies and courts together constitute a 'partnership' in furtherance of the public interest." Thus in the Administrative Procedure Act, 5 U.S.C. § 706 (1970), Congress chose to codify the long-standing rule that courts must "hold unlawful and set aside agency action . . . found to be . . . arbitrary, capricious, an abuse of discretion, or otherwise not in accordance with law." Our task here, then, is simply to determine whether the facts confronting the Commission rationally support its ultimate conclusion that the O'Brien broadcast was "unresponsive" to prior presidential addresses. . . .

[The court here recounted that the O'Brien telecast covered seven separate topics—the Indochina war, economic policy, crime, civil rights, dissent, defense spending, and the environment—each raised in previously aired presidential statements. The commission nevertheless concluded that the O'Brien broadcast was "unresponsive" to prior presidential appearances.] In reaching this conclusion, the Commission considered only those speeches of the President which were televised in the period from November 3, 1969 to June 3, 1970.[73] During this period, the

---

73. It is evident throughout both opinions below that the Commission considered only those speeches broadcast during this time period in reaching its determination of "unresponsiveness." The Commission's decision to limit its consideration to this particular time period may be traced to its initial decision to dispose of the RNC complaint in conjunction with several other complaints which were in fact addressed specifically to the President's recent

President made six televised speeches, five of which dealt exclusively with Indochina.

As a result, the Commission held that, since Mr. Nixon's televised speeches "had by far concentrated on the Indochina war issue," the DNC broadcast should "first and foremost" have been geared to a discussion of that issue. Mr. O'Brien's remarks as to the other six issues were deemed "unresponsive," thereby giving rise to a right to reply in favor of RNC. The Commission's analysis, however, grossly oversimplifies a problem of considerable complexity. That the President's speeches during a limited period of time "largely concentrated" on one issue does not negate the indisputable fact that the President, personally and through his spokesmen, had extensively expounded the administration's views in numerous televised presentations which the Commission arbitrarily ignored.

We fail to see the logic underlying the Commission's decision to limit its consideration solely to presidential speeches televised between November 3, 1969 and June 3, 1970. Indeed, the only discernible purpose served by such a decision is the creation of an illusion that Mr. Nixon had not previously addressed himself to the other six issues discussed in the O'Brien broadcast. Thus the Commission never even attempted to justify its choice of June 3, 1970 as the cutoff date. The O'Brien broadcast was aired on July 7, 1970, and CBS offered the time for the broadcast on June 22. This being so, we see no sense whatever in the Commission's refusal to consider a 22-minute appearance by Mr. Nixon on June 17, 1970, which dealt, not with Indochina, but with the economy generally and with inflation and unemployment specifically—topics covered by Mr. O'Brien in the "Loyal Opposition" broadcast.

Similarly, the Commission offered no explanation for its choice of November 3, 1969 as the starting date for its analysis. The July 7 presentation was, after all, the first "Loyal Opposition" type program to be carried by CBS during the Nixon administration other than the traditional response by Democratic congressional leaders to Mr. Nixon's 1970 State of the Union address. Indeed, on several occasions prior to the July 7 broadcast CBS had rejected Democratic pleas for air time to reply to previously telecast presidential statements. By selecting November 3 as a starting date, however, the Commission excluded consideration of

speeches on the Indochina war issue. Thus in the August 18 opinion the Commission stated that it had "grouped all these complaints because . . . they all involve a common problem—the discharge by broadcast licensees of their responsibilities under the fairness doctrine in dealing with the Indochina war issue."

In the other complaints, the Committee for Fair Broadcasting, Fourteen United States Senators, and Business Executives' Move for Vietnam Peace all urged that network coverage of the presidential addresses on Vietnam (referring specifically to those speeches occurring between November 3, 1969 and June 3, 1970) required that they be given comparable time and format to present their opposing views. The Commission refused to order the networks to grant time to these complainants or to apply an equal opportunities requirement to presidential or other official appearances. The Commission did hold, however, that format should be considered in determining whether a licensee had achieved overall fairness. Accordingly, in light of the imbalance created by the large number of presidential addresses on Vietnam, the Commission required the networks to make additional uninterrupted time available to spokesmen selected by the networks for discussion of the Indochina war issue. Thus consideration of the RNC complaint in this context may well have led the Commission to mischaracterize that complaint as one dealing particularly with the President's recent speeches on Vietnam.

numerous pre-November 3 presidential appearances, many of which dealt in whole or in part with issues other than the Vietnam war.

[The court also considered irrational the commission's exclusion from its responsiveness analysis nonspeech appearances by the president—such as televised news conferences—and televised presentations by presidential spokesmen on other than news-type programs. Many of these appearances and presentations, the court noted, dealt with issues discussed in the O'Brien broadcast.

[The court went on to reverse the FCC order. The concurring opinion of Judge Tamm is omitted.]

Comments and Questions

1. How would you compare the common-law notion of *stare decisis* with the court's reaction to the commission's treatment of its prior *Hays* decision? Is the court saying the FCC may not depart from its prior decision? Recall that for making regulatory law, an agency may prefer adjudication to rulemaking because it may be able to depart more freely from prior ad hoc decisions. This case demonstrates that such departures are not completely unconstrained.

2. If the commission wishes to change its policy in a manner inconsistent with one of its prior ad hoc decisions, how should it go about doing so: through a new decision in a factually analogous case or through rulemaking? What should determine the commission's choice between these two alternatives? See S. Breyer & R. Stewart, Administrative Law and Regulatory Policy 421–25, 531–33 (2d ed. 1985).

3. How would you compare a court's role in reviewing whether a question was appropriately submitted to a jury in a grievance-remedial proceeding with its role in reviewing an agency decision in an administrative-regulatory proceeding? What is the standard of review in each case?

4. Consider the commission's ruling, discussed in the *CBS* case, that the three networks would be required to broadcast a program of views opposed to those of President Nixon on the Vietnam War. Suppose the FCC had ordered the networks to present two such programs airing opposing views, instead of just one. Would a reviewing court have held that decision "arbitrary and capricious"? If not, was the FCC's actual decision to order only one responsive program "arbitrary and capricious"? Suppose, in a subsequent case involving generally balanced programming plus two presidential speeches over a one-year period on a controversial issue, the FCC refused to order the networks to present additional programming of opposing views, explaining that the total programming was still essentially balanced. Would a court reverse this decision as "arbitrary and capricious"? Cf. Democratic National Committee v. FCC, 481 F.2d 543 (D.C.Cir. 1973).

NATIONAL BROADCASTING CO. v. FCC

United States Court of Appeals, District of Columbia Circuit, 1974.
516 F.2d 1101, vacated as moot, 516 F.2d 1180 (D.C.Cir.1975), cert. denied,
424 U.S. 910, 96 S.Ct. 1105 (1976).

[On September 12, 1972, NBC broadcast a television documentary entitled "Pensions: The Broken Promise," narrated by Edwin Newman.

In his closing comments, Newman noted that not all private pension plans
were bad. The bulk of the program, however, studied the conditions
under which a worker covered by a private pension plan might nevertheless not realize any pension rights. The focus was on aging workers left
with no pension rights and no time to develop new pension rights. The
program gave examples of employees who had lost pension rights because
they were discharged, the plant closed, or the employer went bankrupt, all
occurring before pension rights vested. It also highlighted abuses in the
literature explaining the pension plans to employees.

[Accuracy in Media (AIM), a "nonprofit, educational organization acting in the public interest" and devoted to aggressive enforcement of the
fairness doctrine, filed a complaint with the FCC, charging that the
program violated the doctrine because of its antipension slant. NBC
argued that the broadcast had not concerned a "controversial issue of
public importance" because it focused essentially on "some of the problems that have come to light in some pension plans" (about which NBC
asserted there was no controversy), was not aimed at all pension plans,
and did not advocate any specific legislative remedy. The FCC found that
the program had in fact presented views on the overall performance of the
private pension system because of several statements by interviewed
public officials and workers seemingly critical of the entire private pension system and calling for government regulation of private pension
plans. The commission concluded that the few pro-pension statements in
the program were not an adequate counterweight and in effect ordered
NBC to present further pro-pension programming. NBC appealed to the
United States Court of Appeals for the District of Columbia Circuit, which
reversed the FCC.]

Before FAHY, SENIOR CIRCUIT JUDGE, and TAMM and LEVENTHAL, CIRCUIT
JUDGES.

LEVENTHAL, CIRCUIT JUDGE:

.   .   .   .

A. THE FUNCTION OF THE FCC

.   .   .   .

[After concluding that the commission's basic error was in finding for
itself that the principal controversial issue in the "Pensions" program was
the overall performance of the private pension system, instead of deciding
whether NBC was acting reasonably and in good faith in reaching an
opposite conclusion, the court continued as follows:]

Where the Commission has relatively specific rules under the fairness
doctrine, as in the personal attack and political editorializing rules, it has
a more ample role in determining whether the licensee was in compliance
with his obligations. But when the claim is put in terms of the general
obligations concerning controversial issues of public importance, there is
primary reliance on the journalistic discretion of the licensee, subject to
supervision by the government agency only in case he exceeds the bounds
of his discretion. This yields as a corollary that if the broadcast licensee
was reasonable in his premise, and his projection of the subject matter of

the program, he cannot be said by the supervising agency to have abused or exceeded his sound discretion.

The FCC's function becomes that of correcting the licensee for *abuse* of discretion, as our function on judicial review is that of correcting the agency for *abuse* of discretion.

. . . In this case we think it plain that the licensee has not been guilty of an unreasonable exercise of discretion. Where the Commission may have started on the wrong path in its approach is the place where the Commission undertook to determine for itself as a fact whether "the program did in fact present viewpoints on one side of the issue of the overall performance and proposed regulation of the private pension system." This is not a sufficient basis for overturning the licensee. It is not clear from the Commission's opinion that it also appreciated the need for a finding of abuse of discretion by the licensee in concluding that no controversial issue had been presented. . . .

A substantial burden must be overcome before the FCC can say there has been an unreasonable exercise of journalistic discretion in a licensee's determination as to the scope of issues presented in the program. Where, as here, the underlying problem is the thrust of the program and the nature of its message, whether a controversial issue of public importance is involved presents not a question of simple physical fact, like temperature, but rather a composite editorial and communications judgment concerning the nature of the program and its perception by viewers. In the absence of extrinsic evidence that the licensee's characterization to the Commission was not made in good faith, the burden of demonstrating that the licensee's judgment was unreasonable to the point of abuse of discretion requires a determination that reasonable men viewing the program would not have concluded that its subject was as described by the licensee. . . .

B. THE FUNCTION OF THE REVIEWING COURT

When an agency purports to exercise regulatory discretion conferred by Congress, a court reviewing its order generally accords wide latitude to the agency. The court has responsibilities and restraints. Its responsibility is to assure that the agency has not abused or exceeded its authority, that every essential element of the order is supported by substantial evidence, and that the agency has given reasoned consideration to the pertinent factors. The restraint arises out of the consideration that industry regulation has been entrusted by Congress "to the informed judgment of the Commission, and not to the preferences of reviewing courts." If an agency has "genuinely engaged in reasoned decision-making . . . the court exercises restraint and affirms the agency's action even though the court would on its own account have made different findings or adopted different standards."

In the case of the fairness doctrine, a reviewing court is under the same injunction against injecting its own preferences as the rule of decision. And so when the Commission, in the exercise of its discretion, affirms the licensee's exercise of its discretion, the role of the court is most restricted. But the court has a greater responsibility than is normally the case, when it reviews an agency's fairness rulings that upset the licensee's exercise of journalistic discretion, both because the area is suffused with First Amendment freedoms and because Congress has determined that the interest of the public, and its right to know, is furthered by giving primary discretion not to the government agency but instead to the regulated licensee. Congress has sharply narrowed the scope of agency discretion—which the court must see is not exceeded—to a government intervention permissible only for abuse of the licensee's journalistic judgment.[d] . . .

[The court went on to reverse the FCC order. The concurring opinion of Judge Fahy and the dissenting opinion of Judge Tamm are omitted.]

Comments and Questions

1. In this case, did the FCC properly apply the principles it had articulated in the 1964 Fairness Primer? Suppose the FCC in its opinion had simply said that NBC was unreasonable in concluding that the "Pensions" program addressed only some problems in some private pension plans. Would the court have decided the case differently? Who decides whether the broadcaster's judgment is within the bounds of reasonableness: the FCC or the court?

2. Did the court in this case alter the normal standard by which a court should review agency decisions? Is this an example of a judicial attempt to sabotage the fairness doctrine, or does it provide a useful rule for marking the line between the dictates of the fairness doctrine and those of the First Amendment?

3. Should the rule in the "Pensions" case be limited to cases of investigative journalism, like the NBC "Pensions" program, or is it appropriate for the fairness doctrine generally? Would a limited application of the "Pensions" case rule encourage broadcasters to editorialize through investigative journalism?

4. Note that the opinion in the "Pensions" case was ultimately vacated as moot, because the commission withdrew its order to NBC for further pensions programs after Congress passed legislation regulating private pension plans.

5. Compare lawmaking when the law is to be used as a premise for a private remedy with lawmaking for regulatory purposes (Section 3 of Chapter 1 with Section 3 of Chapter 3). Compare lawmaking when the law is to serve as the basis for a criminal penalty with lawmaking for regulatory purposes (Section 3 of Chapter 2 with Section 3 of Chapter 3). Do you see any significant contrasts?

Section Four. Structures and Processes for Applying Administrative-Regulatory Law and Techniques

Regulatory standards are not enough, even if we assume that regulatees are generally disposed to apply the law to themselves without being forced

---

d. The court was presumably referring to § 326 of the Federal Communications Act of 1934:

> Nothing in this Act shall be understood or construed to give the Commission the power of censorship over the radio communications or signals transmitted by any radio station, and no regulation or condition shall be promulgated or fixed by the Commission which shall interfere with the right of free speech by means of radio communication.

The Supreme Court in a prior case quoted this section as supporting the conclusion that "Congress intended to permit private broadcasting to develop with the widest journalistic freedom consistent with its public obligations. . . . The broadcaster, therefore, is allowed significant journalistic discretion in deciding how best to fulfill the Fairness Doctrine obligations . . . . " Columbia Broadcasting System v. Democratic National Committee, 412 U.S. 94, 110–11, 93 S.Ct. 2080, 2090–91 (1973).

to do so by authorized officials.   Some provision must be made for authoritative application of regulatory standards.

In the field of broadcast regulation, we have already seen how Congress set up a special agency—the FCC—to help make basic regulatory law.   Congress has also empowered the FCC, like many other agencies (the SEC, the FTC, the EPA, and so on), to enforce the very regulatory law it helps make, and to perform certain adjudicative functions in the course of that enforcement.   The FCC uses both formal and informal enforcement procedures.   Some of its formal enforcement authority is set forth in the following legislation.   In some cases, as you will see, the FCC must resort to the ordinary courts and the ordinary prosecutors for full enforcement of its orders and regulatory program.

_____

UNITED STATES CODE, TITLE 47

§ 303. Powers and duties of Commission

Except as otherwise provided in this Act, the Commission from time to time, as public convenience, interest, or necessity requires, shall—

(a) Classify radio stations; . . .

(c) Assign bands of frequencies to the various classes of stations, and assign frequencies for each individual station and determine the power which each station shall use and the time during which it may operate;

(d) Determine the location of classes of stations or individual stations;

. . .

(h) Have authority to establish areas or zones to be served by any station;

. . .

(m)(1) Have authority to suspend the license of any operator upon proof sufficient to satisfy the Commission that the licensee—

(A) has violated . . . any provision of any Act, treaty, or convention binding on the United States, which the Commission is authorized to administer, or any regulation made by the Commission under any such Act, treaty, or convention . . .

(n) Have authority to inspect all radio installations associated with stations required to be licensed by any Act . . . or which are subject to the provisions of any Act [or] treaty . . . binding on the United States, to ascertain whether in construction, installation, and operation they conform to the requirements of the rules and regulations of the Commission, the provisions of any Act, the terms of any treaty . . . binding on the United States, and the conditions of the license . . . under which they are constructed, installed, or operated. . . .

§ 312. Administrative sanctions

(a) Revocation of station license or construction permit. The Commission may revoke any station license or construction permit—

(1) for false statements knowingly made either in the application or [in a subsequent application for renewal or modification of the license or permit];

(2) because of conditions coming to the attention of the Commission which would warrant it in refusing to grant a license or permit on an original application;

(3) for willful or repeated failure to operate substantially as set forth in the license;

(4) for willful or repeated violation of, or willful or repeated failure to observe any provision of this Act or any rule or regulation of the Commission authorized by this Act or by a treaty ratified by the United States;

(5) for violation of or failure to observe any final cease and desist order issued by the Commission under this section; . . ..

(b) Cease and desist orders. Where any person (1) has failed to operate substantially as set forth in a license, (2) has violated or failed to observe any of the provisions of this Act . . . , or (3) has violated or failed to observe any rule or regulation of the Commission authorized by this Act or by a treaty ratified by the United States, the Commission may order such person to cease and desist from such action.

(c) Order to show cause. Before revoking a license or permit pursuant to subsection (a), or issuing a cease and desist order pursuant to subsection (b), the Commission shall serve upon the licensee, permittee, or person involved an order to show cause why an order of revocation or a cease and desist order should not be issued. . . . If after hearing, or a waiver thereof, the Commission determines that an order of revocation or a cease and desist order should issue, it shall issue such order, which shall include a statement of the findings of the Commission and the grounds and reasons therefor and specify the effective date of the order, and shall cause the same to be served on said licensee, permittee, or person. . . .

§ 401. Enforcement provisions

.   .   .   .

(b) Orders of Commission. If any person fails or neglects to obey any order of the Commission [other than one for the payment of money, which the commission can order on a complaint by any person against a "common carrier," such as a telephone or telegraph company, and for which there is a separate enforcement procedure], while the same is in effect, the Commission or any party injured thereby, or the United States, by its Attorney General, may apply to the appropriate district court of the United States for the enforcement of such order. If, after hearing, that court determines that the order was regularly made and duly served, and that the person is in disobedience of the same, the court shall enforce obedience to such order by a writ of injunction or other proper process, mandatory or otherwise, to restrain such person or the officers, agents, or representatives of such person, from further disobedience of such order, or to enjoin upon it or them obedience to the same.

(c) Duty to prosecute. Upon the request of the Commission it shall be the duty of any United States attorney to whom the Commission may apply to institute in the proper court and to prosecute under the direction of the Attorney General of the United States all necessary proceedings for the enforcement of the provisions of this Act and for the punishment of all violations thereof . . . .

§ 402. Judicial review of Commission's orders and decisions

(a) Procedure. Any proceeding to enjoin, set aside, annul, or suspend any order of the Commission under this Act (except those appealable under subsection (b) of this section) shall be brought as provided by and in the manner prescribed in chapter 158 of Title 28 [which contains the ordinary rules of procedure for federal courts, including provisions allowing an appeal from an FCC "final order" to be taken to the United States court of appeals for the circuit where the plaintiff resides].

(b) Right to appeal. Appeals may be taken from decisions and orders of the Commission to the United States Court of Appeals for the District of Columbia in any of the following cases:

(1) By any applicant for a construction permit or station license, whose application is denied by the Commission.

(2) By any applicant for the renewal or modification of any such instrument of authorization whose application is denied by the Commission.

(3) By any party to an application for authority to transfer, assign, or dispose of any such instrument of authorization, or any rights thereunder, whose application is denied by the Commission. . . .

(5) By the holder of any construction permit or station license which has been modified or revoked by the Commission.

(6) By any person who is aggrieved or whose interests are adversely affected by any order of the Commission granting or denying any application described in paragraphs (1), (2), [and] (3) . . . hereof.

(7) By any person upon whom an order to cease and desist has been served under section 312 of this title.

(8) By any radio operator whose license has been suspended by the Commission. . . .

§ 501. General penalty

Any person who willfully and knowingly does or causes or suffers to be done any act, matter, or thing, in this Act prohibited or declared to be unlawful, or who willfully and knowingly omits or fails to do any act, matter, or thing in this Act required to be done, or willfully and knowingly causes or suffers such omission or failure, shall, upon conviction thereof, be punished for such offense, for which no penalty (other than a forfeiture) is provided in this Act, by a fine of not more than $10,000 or by imprisonment for a term not exceeding one year, or both; except that any person, having been once convicted of an offense punishable under this section, who is subsequently convicted of violating any provision of this Act punishable under this section, shall be punished by a fine of not more than $10,000 or by imprisonment for a term not exceeding two years, or both.

§ 502. Violation of rules, regulations, etc.

Any person who willfully and knowingly violates any rule, regulation, restriction, or condition made or imposed by the Commission under authority of this Act, or any rule, regulation, restriction, or condition made or imposed by any international radio or wire communications treaty or convention, or regulations annexed thereto, to which the United States is or may hereafter become a party, shall, in addition to any other penalties provided by law, be punished, upon conviction thereof, by a fine of not more than $500 for each and every day during which such offense occurs.

Comments and Questions

1. What are the main methods the FCC can use to formally enforce its regulations?

2. The following is a description by John Dickinson of the role of the government in the grievance-remedial mode examined in Chapter 1. Compare this role with the administrative roles treated in this section.

> [Its] distinctive feature . . . is to postpone the action of the executive branch of government to the last stage in the settlement of a private controversy between individuals. Under such a system the action of government is conditioned upon the existence of a controversy between individuals in the first place. A has a legal right. He thinks B has violated that right. He brings an action against B in a law court, and if a violation is found to have occurred, judgment is given that A recover compensation. The function of the executive begins only at this point, and is simply to step in, in the person of the sheriff, and enforce the judgment against B. Government is thus limited to the role of arbitrating differences between individuals through the courts after the difference has arisen, and then enforcing the court's award through the executive. The only regulating force operating on individuals prior to action by them is their own knowledge, or presumed knowledge, of the law applying to their contemplated act.

J. Dickinson, Administrative Justice and the Supremacy of Law in the United States 7–8 (1927).

Background of *Red Lion*

Generally, the sanction provisions of a regulatory scheme do not have to be formally invoked to secure compliance with applicable regulatory law in particular cases. In the broadcasting field, as elsewhere, compliance is generally secured through either (1) voluntary self-regulation by regulatees in light of published standards or (2) informal administrative action as described in Subsections D, E, and F of Section 2 of this chapter.

Nonetheless, it is essential to consider in some depth one illustrative episode in which officials charged with administering a regulatory standard were forced to rely on such formal means as specific judicial authorization for the enforcement efforts that these officials had undertaken. In the episode that follows, voluntary self-regulation did not suffice. The regulatory agency then sought by informal means to secure compliance. When this failed, it issued an order directing compliance. This, too, failed, for the regulatee appealed to a court challenging the validity of the official order.

The episode to be considered concerns an aspect of the fairness doctrine. Recall that as of late 1964, when the episode here arose, the FCC's fairness doctrine had not been drawn together and formulated in a systematized body of regulations pursuant to the FCC's formal rulemaking power. At this time, the FCC's fairness doctrine was articulated in such diverse sources as its own adjudicative decisions, its famous Editorializing Report, and its Fairness Primer, all of which were discussed in Section 3.

The broadcasters licensed by the FCC are required to comply with valid law made by the agency. Each licensee retains one or more lawyers to advise it of such law. Moreover, some forms of this law—for example, the Editorializing Report and the Fairness Primer—were sent by the FCC to each licensee.

On November 27, 1964, the Red Lion Broadcasting Company, the licensee of radio station WGCB–AM–FM, Red Lion, Pennsylvania, broadcast a fifteen-minute program by a Reverend Billy James Hargis as part of a program series entitled "The Christian Crusade." In the November 27 version of the program, Mr. Hargis commented on the 1964 presidential election and among other things said:

> Who is Cook? Cook was fired from the New York World-Telegram after he made a false charge publicly on television against an unnamed official of the New York City government. New York publishers and Newsweek magazine for December 7, 1959, showed that Fred Cook and his pal Eugene Gleason had made up the whole story and this confession was made to New York District Attorney Frank Hogan. After losing his job, Cook went to work for the left-wing publication The Nation . . . . Now, among other things Fred Cook wrote for The Nation was an article absolving Alger Hiss of any wrongdoing . . . there was a 208-page attack on the FBI and J. Edgar Hoover; another attack by Mr. Cook was on the Central Intelligence Agency . . . now this is the man who wrote the book to smear and destroy Barry Goldwater called "Barry Goldwater—Extremist of the Right."

Mr. Fred J. Cook learned of the foregoing and demanded that the Red Lion Broadcasting Company give him free time for a reply. (Mr. Cook had evidently seen a lawyer.) Red Lion refused. Cook then filed a complaint with the FCC, alleging the foregoing facts and, in effect, demanding free time. At this point, the FCC did not know the actual facts of the controversy. Before acting, the FCC would have to determine the facts. This might be done formally or more or less informally. If Cook's version of the facts stood up, he seemingly would be entitled to an order requiring Red Lion to give him free time for a reply.

Observe that Red Lion might want to dispute Cook's version of the facts or dispute Cook's version of the applicable substantive principles governing Cook's claim to free time. In either event, Red Lion could have insisted on a formal hearing before an FCC hearing examiner. At such a hearing, both Cook and FCC prosecutorial officials would have been entitled to introduce evidence and present legal argument. And Red Lion would have been entitled to respond. At the conclusion of such an administrative adjudication, the FCC hearing examiner would have found the facts, reached conclusions of law, and prepared a proposed order disposing of the case. The FCC, after reviewing the hearing examiner's findings and conclusions, would have decided whether to issue the proposed order or to substitute a different one.

In the actual *Red Lion* case, no formal adjudicative hearing was held. Rather, the FCC adjudicated informally. All this was done with Red Lion's consent. Thus, Red Lion waived any objections it might have had for FCC failure to follow more formal procedures.

In a letter dated October 6, 1965, the FCC ordered Red Lion to "advise the Commission of your plans to comply with the fairness doctrine applicable to the situation." The letter containing this order also recited that Cook had been the victim of a personal attack within the meaning of the fairness doctrine and that Cook was entitled to free use of Red Lion facilities for a response. On November 8, Red Lion sent a letter to the FCC requesting reconsideration of the FCC order. On December 9, the FCC sent another letter to Red Lion, which follows.

FEDERAL COMMUNICATIONS COMMISSION
Washington, D.C. 20554

December 9, 1965

In Reply Refer To: 8427–A 11–186

John H. Norris, Vice President
Red Lion Broadcasting Company, Inc.
Radio Station WGCB
Box 88
Red Lion, Pennsylvania 17356

Dear Sir:

This is in reference to your request that the Commission reconsider its ruling of October [6], 1965 on the complaint of Mr. Fred J. Cook. We have considered the contentions and adhere to our prior ruling for the reasons given below.

1. Your letter states that Mr. Cook in an article in The Nation, entitled "Radio Right: Hate Clubs of the Air", attacked "Billy James Hargis, his program, and his organization . . . "; that your station gave the Democratic National Committee 30 minutes of free time on the Twentieth Century Reformation Hour to broadcast a discussion entitled "Hate Clubs of the Air"; and that you advised Mr. Cook that you would give him free time to reply to the personal attack upon him "if he states that he is unable to pay for the time." In the circumstances, you state that fairness does not require the station to "give Mr. Cook free time to answer an alleged attack upon him made in a paid broadcast by one who had previously been the subject of a nationwide attack by Mr. Cook. . . . "

We have held that "the requirement of fairness, as set forth in the Editorializing Report, applies to a broadcast licensee irrespective of the position which may be taken by other media on the issue involved; and that the licensee's own performance in this respect, in and of itself, must demonstrate compliance with the fairness doctrine." Letter to WSOC Broadcast Co., FCC 58–686, Ruling No. 11, "Applicability of the Fairness Doctrine in the Handling of Controversial Issues of Public Importance" (herein called Fairness Primer) 29 F.R. 10415, 10418–19. Thus, the requirement of the statute is that the *licensee* "afford reasonable opportunity for the discussion of conflicting views on issues of public importance" (Section 315(a)). This requirement is not satisfied by reference to what other media, such as newspapers or magazines, or indeed other stations have presented on a particular issue. It deals solely with the particular station and what it has broadcast on the controversial issue of public importance. It follows that Mr. Cook's article in The Nation does not constitute a ground for absolving the licensee of its responsibility to allow Mr. Cook comparable use of Station WGCB's facilities to reply to the personal attack which had been broadcast.

Nor does the reference to the Democratic National Committee program constitute such a ground. Except for the use of its facilities by legally qualified candidates, the licensee is fully responsible for all matter which is broadcast over its station. Here the licensee, in its presentation of programming dealing with a controversial issue of public importance, has permitted its facilities to be used for a personal attack upon Mr. Cook. Elemental fairness requires that Mr. Cook be notified of the attack and be given a comparable opportunity to reply. You do not claim that the Democratic National Committee program contained such a reply by Mr. Cook to the personal attack made upon him, and therefore that program does not constitute compliance with the fairness doctrine's requirements in the case of Mr. Cook.

As to the contention that you will permit Mr. Cook to air a free response only if he is financially unable to pay, such a position is, we think, inconsistent with the public interest. The licensee has decided that it served the needs and interests of its area to have a personal attack aired over its station; the public interest requires that the public be given the opportunity to hear the other side. The licensee cannot properly make that opportunity contingent upon the payment of money by the person attacked (or the circumstance that he is financially unable to pay). The licensee may, of course, inquire whether the person attacked is willing to pay for airing his response, or take other appropriate steps to obtain sponsorship. See our prior ruling. But if these efforts fail, the person attacked must be presented on a sustaining basis. We believe that this is a matter of both elemental fairness to the person involved and, more important, of affording the public the opportunity to hear the other side of an issue which the licensee has adjudged to be of importance to his listeners. See Cullman Broadcasting Co., FCC 63–849, Ruling No. 17, Fairness Primer.

There are other policy considerations supporting the foregoing conclusion. A contrary position would mean that in the case of a network or widely syndicated program containing a personal attack in discussion of a controversial issue of public importance, the person attacked might be required to deplete or substantially cut into his assets, if he wished to inform the public of his side of the matter; in such circumstances, reasonable opportunity to present conflicting views would not, practically speaking, be afforded. Indeed, it has been argued that under such a construction, personal attacks might even be resorted to as an opportunity to obtain additional revenues.

For all the above considerations, we hold that the licensee may inquire about payment, but cannot insist upon either such payment or a showing of financial inability to pay in this personal attack situation. Here Mr. Cook, in his letters of December 19 and 21, 1964, stated that he was not willing to pay to appear.

2. You have raised the question of a continuing chain of personal attacks. This matter is discussed in the enclosed Letter to the Honorable Oren Harris, FCC 63–851, p. 5, pointing out that the licensee "has discretion (except in the case of an appearance of candidates) to review a proposed program, including the script, to insure that it does not go unreasonably far afield as to the issues." In any event, there is no indication of such a hypothetical chain in the circumstances of this case, nor indeed have you raised any question concerning Mr. Cook's proposed reply except on the ground of payment.

3. [The commission here noted that the Red Lion request to the FCC for reconsideration also asked whether the commission's letter of October 6, 1965, constituted a "final order," from which an appeal could be taken, and also asked for] clarification as to the scope of the directive in that letter, and particularly "by what date Station WGCB is required to put on the broadcast." The ruling is a "final order" . . . . The licensee thus has the choice of complying with the ruling or seeking review thereof. As to the time of compliance, this varies with the factual situation and is a matter to be worked out in good faith end on a reasonable basis by the licensee and the person involved.

4. Finally, you have requested a ruling by the Commission as to the constitutionality of the fairness doctrine, as applied to this situation. We discussed the constitutionality of the fairness doctrine generally in the Report on Editorializing, 13 F.C.C. 1246–1270. We adhere fully to that discussion, and particularly the considerations set out in paragraphs 19 and 20 of the Report.

We believe that the discussion in those paragraphs is equally applicable to our ruling in this case. The ruling does not involve any prior restraint. The licensee is free to select what controversial issue should be covered, and whether coverage of that issue should include a personal attack. The ruling simply requires that if the licensee does choose to present a personal attack, the person attacked must be notified and given the opportunity for comparable response.

The ruling provides that if sponsorship is not forthcoming (see p. 2), the person attacked must be presented on a sustaining basis, because, in line with the above cited discussion in the Editorializing Report the paramount public interest is that the public have the opportunity of hearing the other side of the controversy, and elemental fairness establishes that the person attacked is the appropriate spokesman to present that other side.   Since this personal attack situation is the only area under the fairness doctrine where the licensee does not have discretion as to the choice of spokesmen, the Commission has carefully limited the applicability of the personal attack principle to those situations where there is an attack upon a person's "honesty, character, integrity or like personal qualities."   See Part E, Personal Attack Principle, Fairness Primer, 29 F.R. 10415, 10420–21.   The principle is not applicable simply because an individual is named or referred to, or because vigorous exception is taken to the views held by an individual or group.   Ibid; see also letter to Pennsylvania Community Antenna Association enclosed.

A broadcaster has sought the license to a valuable public frequency, and has taken it, subject to the obligation to operate in the public interest. Valuable frequency space has been allocated to broadcasting in considerable part, so that it may contribute to an informed electorate.   Report on Editorializing, 13 F.C.C. 1246–1270, par. 6.   Viewed against these fundamental precepts, our ruling is, we believe, reasonably related to the public interest "in the larger and more effective use of radio" (Section 303(g) of the Communications Act).   Since that is so, it is a requirement fully consistent with the Constitution.   NBC v. United States, 319 U.S. [190], 227.

> BY DIRECTION OF THE
> COMMISSION
> BEN F. WAPLE
> Secretary

Comments and Questions

1.   Self-regulation by Red Lion, at least in the commission's view, here failed. But this still did not mean that commission administrative efforts would be required, for here there was a further possibility that private regulatory efforts by Cook himself might succeed.   Had Red Lion at the outset granted Cook's request, that would have ended the matter.   Many such cases are disposed of in this fashion.   What are the advantages of this?   Should the importance of the regulatory process be judged solely in terms of the instances in which regulatory power is coercively brought to bear upon those subject to it through the specific acts of administrative officials, or should instances of self-regulation and private regulation, in light of previously articulated standards, also be taken into account?

2.   How did the FCC learn in the first place of the alleged Red Lion violation of the personal-attack aspect of the fairness doctrine?   Do you think the FCC would have been likely to learn of it otherwise?   Does this illustrate the importance of private initiative in setting the administrative-regulatory mode in motion?   Notice that once in motion, Cook himself did not thereafter have to carry the ball alone.   Does this differ from the situation in the grievance-remedial mode?

3.   From the Red Lion episode, do you see any possible advantages of the informal FCC efforts at resolution over more formal ones?   The vast majority of such cases are disposed of informally (though nonetheless authoritatively).

4.   Why did Red Lion not insist on formal adjudication before the FCC?   Were there any factual disputes?   Legal disputes?

5. Observe that after Red Lion had failed to comply with the FCC's October 6 order, the FCC did not, even then, have power on its own to impose any sanction on Red Lion that would stand up without judicial review. Certainly, the FCC could not have fined or imprisoned Red Lion or its officers. And although the FCC could have, after a further proceeding, suspended or revoked Red Lion's license, this, too, would have been subject to judicial review. Do you approve of this setup? Why?

6. Faced with the choice of either complying with the FCC order or seeking review thereof, Red Lion sought review in the United States Court of Appeals for the District of Columbia Circuit, and through briefs and oral argument urged that the FCC order was unauthorized and unconstitutional. Pending this review, Red Lion was not required to comply with the FCC order.

7. On June 13, 1967, the United States Court of Appeals for the District of Columbia Circuit decided Red Lion's appeal in favor of the FCC and thus upheld the FCC's order requiring Red Lion to give Cook free time for a reply. Red Lion then appealed this decision, in turn, to the Supreme Court of the United States. This case was argued before the Court on April 2–3, 1969, by several lawyers, including Archibald Cox, professor at the Harvard Law School, and Solicitor General Erwin Griswold, former dean of the Harvard Law School. On June 9, 1969, the Supreme Court handed down its decision.

RED LION BROADCASTING CO. v. FCC

Supreme Court of the United States, 1969.
395 U.S. 367, 89 S.Ct. 1794.

MR. JUSTICE WHITE delivered the opinion of the Court.

The Federal Communications Commission has for many years imposed on radio and television broadcasters the requirement that discussion of public issues be presented on broadcast stations, and that each side of those issues must be given fair coverage. This is known as the fairness doctrine, which originated very early in the history of broadcasting and has maintained its present outlines for some time. It is an obligation whose content has been defined in a long series of FCC rulings in particular cases, and which is distinct from the statutory requirement of § 315 of the Communications Act that equal time be allotted all qualified candidates for public office. Two aspects of the fairness doctrine, relating to personal attacks in the context of controversial public issues and to political editorializing, were codified more precisely in the form of FCC regulations in 1967. The two cases before us now, which were decided separately below, challenge the constitutional and statutory bases of the doctrine and component rules. *Red Lion* involves the application of the fairness doctrine to a particular broadcast, and *RTNDA* arises as an action to review the FCC's 1967 promulgation of the personal attack and political editorializing regulations, which were laid down after the *Red Lion* litigation had begun.

I.

A.

The Red Lion Broadcasting Company is licensed to operate a Pennsylvania radio station, WGCB. On November 27, 1964, WGCB carried a

15-minute broadcast by Reverend Billy James Hargis as part of a "Christian Crusade" series. A book by Fred J. Cook entitled "Goldwater—Extremist on the Right" was discussed by Hargis, who said that Cook had been fired by a newspaper for making false charges against city officials; that Cook had then worked for a Communist-affiliated publication; that he had defended Alger Hiss and attacked J. Edgar Hoover and the Central Intelligence Agency; and that he had now written a "book to smear and destroy Barry Goldwater." When Cook heard of the broadcast he concluded that he had been personally attacked and demanded free reply time, which the station refused. After an exchange of letters among Cook, Red Lion, and the FCC, the FCC declared that the Hargis broadcast constituted a personal attack on Cook; that Red Lion had failed to meet its obligation under the fairness doctrine as expressed in Times-Mirror Broadcasting Co., 24 P & F Radio Reg. 404 (1962), to send a tape, transcript, or summary of the broadcast to Cook and offer him reply time; and that the station must provide reply time whether or not Cook would pay for it. On review in the Court of Appeals for the District of Columbia Circuit, the FCC's position was upheld as constitutional and otherwise proper. 381 F.2d 908 (1967).

B.

Not long after the *Red Lion* litigation was begun, the FCC issued a Notice of Proposed Rule Making, 31 Fed.Reg. 5710, with an eye to making the personal attack aspect of the fairness doctrine more precise and more readily enforceable, and also to specify its rules relating to political editorials. After considering written comments supporting and opposing the rules, the FCC adopted them substantially as proposed, 32 Fed.Reg. 10303. Twice amended, 32 Fed.Reg. 11531, 33 Fed.Reg. 5362, the rules were held unconstitutional in the *RTNDA* litigation by the Court of Appeals for the Seventh Circuit, on review of the rule-making proceeding, as abridging the freedoms of speech and press. 400 F.2d 1002 (1968).

As they now stand amended, the regulations read as follows:

Personal attacks; political editorials.

(a) When, during the presentation of views on a controversial issue of public importance, an attack is made upon the honesty, character, integrity or like personal qualities of an identified person or group, the licensee shall, within a reasonable time and in no event later than 1 week after the attack, transmit to the person or group attacked (1) notification of the date, time and identification of the broadcast; (2) a script or tape (or an accurate summary if a script or tape is not available) of the attack; and (3) an offer of a reasonable opportunity to respond over the licensee's facilities.

(b) The provisions of paragraph (a) of this section shall not be applicable (1) to attacks on foreign groups or foreign public figures; (2) to personal attacks which are made by legally qualified candidates, their authorized spokesmen, or those associated with them in the campaign, on other such candidates, their authorized spokesmen, or persons associated with the candidates in the campaign; and (3) to bona fide newscasts, bona fide news interviews, and on-the-spot cover-

age of a bona fide news event (including commentary or analysis
contained in the foregoing programs, but the provisions of paragraph
(a) of this section shall be applicable to editorials of the licensee).

NOTE: The fairness doctrine is applicable to situations coming
within [(3)], above, and, in a specific factual situation, may be applicable in the general area of political broadcasts [(2)], above. See, section
315(a) of the Act, 47 U.S.C. 315(a); Public Notice: Applicability of the
Fairness Doctrine in the Handling of Controversial Issues of Public
Importance. 29 F.R. 10415. The categories listed in [(3)] are the
same as those specified in section 315(a) of the Act.

(c) Where a licensee, in an editorial, (i) endorses or (ii) opposes a
legally qualified candidate or candidates, the licensee shall, within 24
hours after the editorial, transmit to respectively (i) the other qualified
candidate or candidates for the same office or (ii) the candidate opposed
in the editorial (1) notification of the date and the time of the editorial;
(2) a script or tape of the editorial; and (3) an offer of a reasonable
opportunity for a candidate or a spokesman of the candidate to respond
over the licensee's facilities: *Provided, however,* That where such
editorials are broadcast within 72 hours prior to the day of the
election, the licensee shall comply with the provisions of this paragraph sufficiently far in advance of the broadcast to enable the
candidate or candidates to have a reasonable opportunity to prepare a
response and to present it in a timely fashion. (47 CFR §§ 73.123,
73.300, 73.598, 73.679 (all identical).)

C.

Believing that the specific application of the fairness doctrine in *Red
Lion*, and the promulgation of the regulations in *RTNDA*, are both
authorized by Congress and enhance rather than abridge the freedoms of
speech and press protected by the First Amendment, we hold them valid
and constitutional, reversing the judgment below in *RTNDA* and affirming the judgment below in *Red Lion*.

II.

The history of the emergence of the fairness doctrine and of the related
legislation shows that the Commission's action in the *Red Lion* case did
not exceed its authority, and that in adopting the new regulations the
Commission was implementing congressional policy rather than embark-
ing on a frolic of its own.

A.

Before 1927, the allocation of frequencies was left entirely to the
private sector, and the result was chaos. It quickly became apparent that
broadcast frequencies constituted a scarce resource whose use could be
regulated and rationalized only by the Government. Without government
control, the medium would be of little use because of the cacophony of
competing voices, none of which could be clearly and predictably heard.
Consequently, the Federal Radio Commission was established to allocate

frequencies among competing applicants in a manner responsive to the public "convenience, interest, or necessity."

Very shortly thereafter the Commission expressed its view that the "public interest requires ample play for the free and fair competition of opposing views, and the commission believes that the principle applies . . . to all discussions of issues of importance to the public." Great Lakes Broadcasting Co., 3 F.R.C.Ann.Rep. 32, 33 (1929), rev'd on other grounds, 37 F.2d 993, cert. dismissed, 281 U.S. 706, 50 S.Ct. 467 (1930). This doctrine was applied through denial of licensee renewals or construction permits, both by the FRC, Trinity Methodist Church, South v. FRC, 62 F.2d 850 (1932), cert. denied, 288 U.S. 599, 53 S.Ct. 317 (1933), and its successor FCC, Young People's Association for the Propagation of the Gospel, 6 F.C.C. 178 (1938). After an extended period during which the licensee was obliged not only to cover and to cover fairly the views of others, but also to refrain from expressing his own personal views, Mayflower Broadcasting Corp., 8 F.C.C. 333 (1940), the latter limitation on the licensee was abandoned and the doctrine developed into its present form.

There is a twofold duty laid down by the FCC's decisions and described by the 1949 Report on Editorializing by Broadcast Licensees, 13 F.C.C. 1246 (1949). The broadcaster must give adequate coverage to public issues, United Broadcasting Co., 10 F.C.C. 515 (1945), and coverage must be fair in that it accurately reflects the opposing views. New Broadcasting Co., 6 P & F Radio Reg. 258 (1950). This must be done at the broadcaster's own expense if sponsorship is unavailable. Cullman Broadcasting Co., 25 P & F Radio Reg. 895 (1963). Moreover, the duty must be met by programming obtained at the licensee's own initiative if available from no other source. . . .

When a personal attack has been made on a figure involved in a public issue, both the doctrine of cases such as *Red Lion* and Times-Mirror Broadcasting Co., 24 P & F Radio Reg. 404 (1962), and also the 1967 regulations at issue in *RTNDA* require that the individual attacked himself be offered an opportunity to respond. Likewise, where one candidate is endorsed in a political editorial, the other candidates must themselves be offered reply time to use personally or through a spokesman. These obligations differ from the general fairness requirement that issues be presented, and presented with coverage of competing views, in that the broadcaster does not have the option of presenting the attacked party's side himself or choosing a third party to represent that side. But insofar as there is an obligation of the broadcaster to see that both sides are presented, and insofar as that is an affirmative obligation, the personal attack doctrine and regulations do not differ from preceding fairness doctrine. The simple fact that the attacked men or unendorsed candidates may respond themselves or through agents is not a critical distinction, and indeed, it is not unreasonable for the FCC to conclude that the objective of adequate presentation of all sides may best be served by allowing those most closely affected to make the response, rather than leaving the response in the hands of the station which has attacked their candidacies, endorsed their opponents, or carried a personal attack upon them.

B.

The statutory authority of the FCC to promulgate these regulations derives from the mandate to the "Commission from time to time, as public convenience, interest, or necessity requires" to promulgate "such rules and regulations and prescribe such restrictions and conditions . . . as may be necessary to carry out the provisions of this chapter . . . . " 47 U.S.C. § 303 and § 303(r). The Commission is specifically directed to consider the demands of the public interest in the course of granting licenses, 47 U.S.C. §§ 307(a), 309(a); renewing them, 47 U.S.C. § 307; and modifying them. Ibid. Moreover, the FCC has included among the conditions of the Red Lion license itself the requirement that operation of the station be carried out in the public interest, 47 U.S.C. § 309(h). This mandate to the FCC to assure that broadcasters operate in the public interest is a broad one, a power "not niggardly but expansive," National Broadcasting Co. v. United States, 319 U.S. 190, 219, 63 S.Ct. 997, 1010 (1943), whose validity we have long upheld. It is broad enough to encompass these regulations.

The fairness doctrine finds specific recognition in statutory form, is in part modeled on explicit statutory provisions relating to political candidates, and is approvingly reflected in legislative history.

In 1959 the Congress amended the statutory requirement of § 315 that equal time be accorded each political candidate to except certain appearances on news programs, but added that this constituted no exception "*from the obligation imposed upon them under this Act to operate in the public interest and to afford reasonable opportunity for the discussion of conflicting views on issues of public importance.*" Act of September 14, 1959, § 1, 73 Stat. 557, amending 47 U.S.C. § 315(a) (emphasis added). This language makes it very plain that Congress, in 1959, announced that the phrase "public interest," which had been in the Act since 1927, imposed a duty on broadcasters to discuss both sides of controversial public issues. In other words, the amendment vindicated the FCC's general view that the fairness doctrine inhered in the public interest standard. Subsequent legislation declaring the intent of an earlier statute is entitled to great weight in statutory construction. And here this principle is given special force by the equally venerable principle that the construction of a statute by those charged with its execution should be followed unless there are compelling indications that it is wrong, especially when Congress has refused to alter the administrative construction. Here, the Congress has not just kept its silence by refusing to overturn the administrative construction, but has ratified it with positive legislation. Thirty years of consistent administrative construction left undisturbed by Congress until 1959, when that construction was expressly accepted, reinforce the natural conclusion that the public interest language of the Act authorized the Commission to require licensees to use their stations for discussion of public issues, and that the FCC is free to implement this requirement by reasonable rules and regulations which fall short of abridgment of the freedom of speech and press, and of the censorship proscribed by § 326 of the Act.

The objectives of § 315 themselves could readily be circumvented but for the complementary fairness doctrine ratified by § 315. The section applies only to campaign appearances by candidates, and not by family, friends, campaign managers, or other supporters. Without the fairness doctrine, then, a licensee could ban all campaign appearances by candidates themselves from the air and proceed to deliver over his station entirely to the supporters of one slate of candidates, to the exclusion of all others. In this way the broadcaster could have a far greater impact on the favored candidacy than he could by simply allowing a spot appearance by the candidate himself. It is the fairness doctrine as an aspect of the obligation to operate in the public interest, rather than § 315, which prohibits the broadcaster from taking such a step.

The legislative history reinforces this view of the effect of the 1959 amendment. Even before the language relevant here was added, the Senate report on amending § 315 noted that "broadcast frequencies are limited and, therefore, they have been necessarily considered a public trust. Every licensee who is fortunate in obtaining a license is mandated to operate in the public interest and has assumed the obligation of presenting important public questions fairly and without bias." S.Rep. No. 562, 86th Cong., 1st Sess., 8–9 (1959). See also, specifically adverting to Federal Communications Commission doctrine, id., at 13.

Rather than leave this approval solely in the legislative history, Senator Proxmire suggested an amendment to make it part of the Act. 105 Cong.Rec. 14457. This amendment, which Senator Pastore, a manager of the bill and Chairman of the Senate Committee, considered "rather surplusage," 105 Cong.Rec. 14462, constituted a positive statement of doctrine and was altered to the present merely approving language in the conference committee. In explaining the language to the Senate after the committee changes, Senator Pastore said: "We insisted that that provision remain in the bill, to be a continuing reminder and admonition to the Federal Communications Commission and to the broadcasters alike, that we were not abandoning the philosophy that gave birth to section 315, in giving the people the right to have a full and complete disclosure of conflicting views on news of interest to the people of the country." 105 Cong.Rec. 17830. Senator Scott, another Senate manager, added that: "It is intended to encompass all legitimate areas of public importance which are controversial," not just politics. 105 Cong.Rec. 17831.

It is true that the personal attack aspect of the fairness doctrine was not actually adjudicated until after 1959, so that Congress then did not have those rules specifically before it. However, the obligation to offer time to reply to a personal attack was presaged by the FCC's 1949 Report on Editorializing, which the FCC views as the principal summary of its *ratio decidendi* in cases in this area:

> In determining whether to honor specific requests for time, the station will inevitably be confronted with such questions as . . . whether there may not be other available groups or individuals who might be more appropriate spokesmen for the particular point of view than the person making the request. The latter's personal involvement in the controversy may also be a factor which must be considered, for elemen-

tary considerations of fairness may dictate that time be allocated to a person or group which has been specifically attacked over the station, where otherwise no such obligation would exist. (13 F.C.C., at 1251–1252.)

When the Congress ratified the FCC's implication of a fairness doctrine in 1959 it did not, of course, approve every past decision or pronouncement by the Commission on this subject, or give it a completely free hand for the future. The statutory authority does not go so far. But we cannot say that when a station publishes personal attacks or endorses a political candidate, it is a misconstruction of the public interest standard to require the station to offer time for a response rather than to leave the response entirely within the control of the station which has attacked either the candidacies or the men who wish to reply in their own defense. When a broadcaster grants time to a political candidate, Congress itself requires that equal time be offered to his opponents. It would exceed our competence to hold that the Commission is unauthorized by the statute to employ a similar device where personal attacks or political editorials are broadcast by a radio or television station.

In light of the fact that the "public interest" in broadcasting clearly encompasses the presentation of vigorous debate of controversial issues of importance and concern to the public; the fact that the FCC has rested upon that language from its very inception a doctrine that these issues must be discussed, and fairly; and the fact that Congress has acknowledged that the analogous provisions of § 315 are not preclusive in this area, and knowingly preserved the FCC's complementary efforts, we think the fairness doctrine and its component personal attack and political editorializing regulations are a legitimate exercise of congressionally delegated authority. The Communications Act is not notable for the precision of its substantive standards and in this respect the explicit provisions of § 315, and the doctrine and rules at issue here which are closely modeled upon that section, are far more explicit than the generalized "public interest" standard in which the Commission ordinarily finds its sole guidance, and which we have held a broad but adequate standard before. We cannot say that the FCC's declaratory ruling in *Red Lion*, or the regulations at issue in *RTNDA*, are beyond the scope of the congressionally conferred power to assure that stations are operated by those whose possession of a license serves "the public interest."

III.

The broadcasters challenge the fairness doctrine and its specific manifestations in the personal attack and political editorial rules on conventional First Amendment grounds, alleging that the rules abridge their freedom of speech and press. Their contention is that the First Amendment protects their desire to use their allotted frequencies continuously to broadcast whatever they choose, and to exclude whomever they choose from ever using that frequency. No man may be prevented from saying or publishing what he thinks, or from refusing in his speech or other utterances to give equal weight to the views of his opponents. This right, they say, applies equally to broadcasters.

A.

Although broadcasting is clearly a medium affected by a First Amendment interest, United States v. Paramount Pictures, Inc., 334 U.S. 131, 166, 68 S.Ct. 915, 933 (1948), differences in the characteristics of news media justify differences in the First Amendment standards applied to them. Joseph Burstyn, Inc. v. Wilson, 343 U.S. 495, 503, 72 S.Ct. 777, 781 (1952). For example, the ability of new technology to produce sounds more raucous than those of the human voice justifies restrictions on the sound level, and on the hours and places of use, of sound trucks so long as the restrictions are reasonable and applied without discrimination. Kovacs v. Cooper, 336 U.S. 77, 69 S.Ct. 448 (1949).

Just as the Government may limit the use of sound amplifying equipment potentially so noisy that it drowns out civilized private speech, so may the Government limit the use of broadcast equipment. The right of free speech of a broadcaster, the user of a sound truck, or any other individual does not embrace a right to snuff out the free speech of others. Associated Press v. United States, 326 U.S. 1, 20, 65 S.Ct. 1416, 1424 (1945).

When two people converse face to face, both should not speak at once if either is to be clearly understood. But the range of the human voice is so limited that there could be meaningful communications if half the people in the United States were talking and the other half listening. Just as clearly, half the people might publish and the other half read. But the reach of radio signals is incomparably greater than the range of the human voice and the problem of interference is a massive reality. The lack of know-how and equipment may keep many from the air, but only a tiny fraction of those with resources and intelligence can hope to communicate by radio at the same time if intelligible communication is to be had, even if the entire radio spectrum is utilized in the present state of commercially acceptable technology.

It was this fact, and the chaos which ensued from permitting anyone to use any frequency at whatever power level he wished, which made necessary the enactment of the Radio Act of 1927 and the Communications Act of 1934, as the Court has noted at length before. National Broadcasting Co. v. United States, 319 U.S. 190, 210–214, 63 S.Ct. 997, 1006–1009 (1943). It was this reality which at the very least necessitated first the division of the radio spectrum into portions reserved respectively for public broadcasting and for other important radio uses such as amateur operation, aircraft, police, defense, and navigation; and then the subdivision of each portion, and assignment of specific frequencies to individual users or groups of users. Beyond this, however, because the frequencies reserved for public broadcasting were limited in number, it was essential for the Government to tell some applicants that they could not broadcast at all because there was room for only a few.

Where there are substantially more individuals who want to broadcast than there are frequencies to allocate, it is idle to posit an unabridgeable First Amendment right to broadcast comparable to the right of every individual to speak, write, or publish. If 100 persons want broadcast licenses but there are only 10 frequencies to allocate, all of them may have the same "right" to a license; but if there is to be any effective communication by radio, only a few can be licensed and the rest must be barred from the airwaves. It would be strange if the First Amendment, aimed at protecting and furthering communications, prevented the Government from making radio communication possible by requiring licenses to broadcast and by limiting the number of licenses so as not to overcrowd the spectrum.

This has been the consistent view of the Court. Congress unquestionably has the power to grant and deny licenses and to delete existing stations. FRC v. Nelson Bros. Bond & Mortgage Co., 289 U.S. 266, 53 S.Ct. 627 (1933). No one has a First Amendment right to a license or to monopolize a radio frequency; to deny a station license because "the public interest" requires it "is not a denial of free speech." National Broadcasting Co. v. United States, 319 U.S. 190, 227, 63 S.Ct. 997, 1014 (1943).

By the same token, as far as the First Amendment is concerned those who are licensed stand no better than those to whom licenses are refused. A license permits broadcasting, but the licensee has no constitutional right to be the one who holds the license or to monopolize a radio frequency to the exclusion of his fellow citizens. There is nothing in the First Amendment which prevents the Government from requiring a licensee to share his frequency with others and to conduct himself as a proxy or fiduciary with obligations to present those views and voices which are representative of his community and which would otherwise, by necessity, be barred from the airwaves.

This is not to say that the First Amendment is irrelevant to public broadcasting. On the contrary, it has a major role to play as the Congress itself recognized in § 326, which forbids FCC interference with "the right of free speech by means of radio communication." Because of the scarcity of radio frequencies, the Government is permitted to put restraints on licensees in favor of others whose views should be expressed on this unique medium. But the people as a whole retain their interest in free speech by radio and their collective right to have the medium function consistently with the ends and purposes of the First Amendment. It is the right of the viewers and listeners, not the right of the broadcasters, which is paramount. It is the purpose of the First Amendment to preserve an uninhibited marketplace of ideas in which truth will ultimately prevail, rather than to countenance monopolization of that market, whether it be by the Government itself or a private licensee. . . .
It is the right of the public to receive suitable access to social, political, esthetic, moral, and other ideas and experiences which is crucial here. That right may not constitutionally be abridged either by Congress or by the FCC.

B.

Rather than confer frequency monopolies on a relatively small number of licensees, in a Nation of 200,000,000, the Government could surely have decreed that each frequency should be shared among all or some of those who wish to use it, each being assigned a portion of the broadcast day or the broadcast week. The ruling and regulations at issue here do not go quite so far. They assert that under specified circumstances, a licensee must offer to make available a reasonable amount of broadcast time to those who have a view different from that which has already been expressed on his station. The expression of a political endorsement, or of a personal attack while dealing with a controversial public issue, simply triggers this time sharing. As we have said, the First Amendment confers no right on licensees to prevent others from broadcasting on "their" frequencies and no right to an unconditional monopoly of a scarce resource which the Government has denied others the right to use.

In terms of constitutional principle, and as enforced sharing of a scarce resource, the personal attack and political editorial rules are indistinguishable from the equal-time provision of § 315, a specific enactment of Congress requiring stations to set aside reply time under specified circumstances and to which the fairness doctrine and these constituent regulations are important complements. That provision, which has been part of the law since 1927, Radio Act of 1927, § 18, 44 Stat. 1170, has been held valid by this Court as an obligation of the licensee relieving him of any power in any way to prevent or censor the broadcast, and thus insulating him from liability for defamation. The constitutionality of the statute under the First Amendment was unquestioned. Farmers Educ. & Coop. Union v. WDAY, 360 U.S. 525, 79 S.Ct. 1302 (1959).

Nor can we say that it is inconsistent with the First Amendment goal of producing an informed public capable of conducting its own affairs to require a broadcaster to permit answers to personal attacks occurring in the course of discussing controversial issues, or to require that the political opponents of those endorsed by the station be given a chance to communicate with the public. Otherwise, station owners and a few networks would have unfettered power to make time available only to the highest bidders, to communicate only their own views on public issues, people and candidates, and to permit on the air only those with whom they agreed. There is no sanctuary in the First Amendment for unlimited private censorship operating in a medium not open to all. "Freedom of the press from governmental interference under the First Amendment does not sanction repression of that freedom by private interests." Associated Press v. United States, 326 U.S. 1, 20, 65 S.Ct. 1416, 1425 (1945) [(deciding that under the antitrust laws the Associated Press, a private news-gathering association, was required to supply news to competitors of its members on a nondiscriminatory basis)].

C.

It is strenuously argued, however, that if political editorials or personal attacks will trigger an obligation in broadcasters to afford the opportunity for expression to speakers who need not pay for time and whose views are unpalatable to the licensees, then broadcasters will be irresistibly forced to self-censorship and their coverage of controversial public issues will be eliminated or at least rendered wholly ineffective. Such a result would indeed be a serious matter, for should licensees actually eliminate their coverage of controversial issues, the purposes of the doctrine would be stifled.

At this point, however, as the Federal Communications Commission has indicated, that possibility is at best speculative. The communications industry, and in particular the networks, have taken pains to present controversial issues in the past, and even now they do not assert that they intend to abandon their efforts in this regard. It would be better if the FCC's encouragement were never necessary to induce the broadcasters to meet their responsibility. And if experience with the administration of these doctrines indicates that they have the net effect of reducing rather than enhancing the volume and quality of coverage, there will be time enough to reconsider the constitutional implications. The fairness doctrine in the past has had no such overall effect.

That this will occur now seems unlikely, however, since if present licensees should suddenly prove timorous, the Commission is not powerless to insist that they give adequate and fair attention to public issues. It does not violate the First Amendment to treat licensees given the privilege of using scarce radio frequencies as proxies for the entire community, obligated to give suitable time and attention to matters of great public concern. To condition the granting or renewal of licenses on a willingness to present representative community views on controversial issues is consistent with the ends and purposes of those constitutional provisions forbidding the abridgment of freedom of speech and freedom of the press. Congress need not stand idly by and permit those with licenses to ignore the problems which beset the people or to exclude from the airways anything but their own views on fundamental questions. The statute, long administrative practice, and cases are to this effect.

Licenses to broadcast do not confer ownership of designated frequencies, but only the temporary privilege of using them. 47 U.S.C. § 301. Unless renewed, they expire within three years. 47 U.S.C. § 307(d). The statute mandates the issuance of licenses if the "public convenience, interest, or necessity will be served thereby." 47 U.S.C. § 307(a). In applying this standard the Commission for 40 years has been choosing licensees based in part on their program proposals. . . .

D.

The litigants embellish their First Amendment arguments with the contention that the regulations are so vague that their duties are impossible to discern. Of this point it is enough to say that, judging the validity of the regulations on their face as they are presented here, we cannot conclude that the FCC has been left a free hand to vindicate its own idiosyncratic conception of the public interest or of the requirements of free speech. Past adjudications by the FCC give added precision to the regulations; there was nothing vague about the FCC's specific ruling in *Red Lion* that Fred Cook should be provided an opportunity to reply. The regulations at issue in *RTNDA* could be employed in precisely the same way as the fairness doctrine was in *Red Lion*. Moreover, the FCC itself has recognized that the applicability of its regulations to situations beyond the scope of past cases may be questionable, 32 Fed.Reg. 10303, 10304 and

n. 6, and will not impose sanctions in such cases without warning. We need not approve every aspect of the fairness doctrine to decide these cases, and we will not now pass upon the constitutionality of these regulations by envisioning the most extreme applications conceivable, United States v. Sullivan, 332 U.S. 689, 694, 68 S.Ct. 331, 334 (1948), but will deal with those problems if and when they arise.

We need not and do not now ratify every past and future decision by the FCC with regard to programming. There is no question here of the Commission's refusal to permit the broadcaster to carry a particular program or to publish his own views; of a discriminatory refusal to require the licensee to broadcast certain views which have been denied access to the airways; of government censorship of a particular program contrary to § 326; or of the official government view dominating public broadcasting. Such questions would raise more serious First Amendment issues. But we do hold that the Congress and the Commission do not violate the First Amendment when they require a radio or television station to give reply time to answer personal attacks and political editorials.

E.

It is argued that even if at one time the lack of available frequencies for all who wished to use them justified the Government's choice of those who would best serve the public interest by acting as proxy for those who would present differing views, or by giving the latter access directly to broadcast facilities, this condition no longer prevails so that continuing control is not justified. To this there are several answers.

Scarcity is not entirely a thing of the past. Advances in technology, such as microwave transmission, have led to more efficient utilization of the frequency spectrum, but uses for that spectrum have also grown apace. [The Court here canvassed such uses as marine and air navigation aids and communication systems for police, ambulance, fire department, public utility, amateur, military, and common carrier users.] . . .

The rapidity with which technological advances succeed one another to create more efficient use of spectrum space on the one hand, and to create new uses for that space by ever growing numbers of people on the other, makes it unwise to speculate on the future allocation of that space. It is enough to say that the resource is one of considerable and growing importance whose scarcity impelled its regulation by an agency authorized by Congress. Nothing in this record, or in our own researches, convinces us that the resource is no longer one for which there are more immediate and potential uses than can be accommodated, and for which wise planning is essential. . . .

. . . The judgment of the Court of Appeals in *Red Lion* is affirmed and that in *RTNDA* reversed and the causes remanded for proceedings consistent with this opinion.

It is so ordered.

Not having heard oral argument in these cases, MR. JUSTICE DOUGLAS took no part in the Court's decision.

Comments and Questions

1. Counsel for Red Lion argued that Congress had never delegated power to the FCC to act as it did here. What did the Court say to this, and are you persuaded? Counsel for Red Lion argued that the Constitution did not allow Congress to grant such power to the FCC, for Congress did not itself have such power in view of the First Amendment. What did the Court say to this, and are you persuaded?

2. Counsel for Red Lion argued that the FCC's "law" on the personal-attack aspect of the fairness doctrine was unduly vague. Part of this law consisted of past FCC cases and official pronouncements, and part of it consisted of regulations. What is the importance of having clear and nonvague regulatory law? How did the Court respond to counsel's argument? Do you agree?

3. Observe that the regulations to which the Court addressed itself were not, as such, in force when the Red Lion episode occurred. Does this mean that the Court here applied the regulations ex post facto? Would ex post facto applications of regulatory law be as bad as ex post facto applications of criminal law? Notice, too, that the FCC itself said that it questioned the retroactive applicability of its own regulations beyond the scope of past cases it had decided. May this help explain why the FCC had been reluctant to promulgate regulations in the first place?

4. The Cook–Hargis–Red Lion affair occurred on radio. If it had occurred on television, would the foregoing opinion of Justice White have been equally applicable?

5. Would the outcome here have been the same if it were demonstrated that airwaves were no longer a scarce technological resource? If it were demonstrated that the fairness doctrine substantially chilled the willingness of broadcasters to allow controversial matters to be treated on their programs? If it could also be established that Congress and therefore the FCC has no power to require stations to carry some publicly controversial programming?

6. The argument has sometimes been made that newspapers and magazines cannot be legally subjected to government-enforced fairness requirements and that Congress is, therefore, without power to treat radio and television media any differently. Did the Court address itself to this argument, and are you persuaded that radio and television are relevantly different from newspapers and magazines? In Miami Herald Publishing Co. v. Tornillo, 418 U.S. 241, 94 S.Ct. 2831 (1974), a case decided after *Red Lion*, the Supreme Court held violative of the First Amendment a Florida statute requiring a newspaper to give equivalent space to a political candidate whom the newspaper had previously attacked in a political editorial. The opinion contained the following discussion:

> The appellee [the political candidate] and supporting advocates of an enforceable right of access to the press vigorously argue that government has an obligation to ensure that a wide variety of views reach the public. . . .

> Access advocates submit that although newspapers of the present are superficially similar to those of 1791 [when the First Amendment was adopted] the press of today is in reality very different from that known in the early years of our national existence. In the past half century a communications revolution has seen the introduction of radio and television into our lives, the promise of a global community through the use of communications satellites, and the spectre of a "wired" nation by means of an expanding cable television network with two-way capabilities. The printed press, it is said, has not escaped the effects of this revolution. Newspapers have become big business and there are far fewer of them to

serve a large literate population. Chains of newspapers, national wire and news services, and one-newspaper towns, are the dominant features of a press that has become noncompetitive and enormously powerful and influential in its capacity to manipulate popular opinion and change the course of events. Major metropolitan newspapers have collaborated to establish news services national in scope. Such national news organizations provide syndicated features and commentary, all of which serve as part of the new school of "advocacy journalism."

The elimination of competing newspapers in most of our large cities, and the concentration of control of media that results from the only newspaper being owned by the same interests which own a television station and a radio station, are important components of this trend toward concentration of control of outlets to inform the public.

The result of these vast changes has been to place in a few hands the power to inform the American people and shape public opinion. Much of the editorial opinion and commentary that is printed is that of syndicated columnists distributed nationwide and, as a result, we are told, on national and world issues there tends to be a homogeneity of editorial opinion, commentary, and interpretative analysis. The abuses of bias and manipulative reportage are, likewise, said to be the result of vast accumulations of unreviewable power in the modern media empires. In effect, it is claimed, the public has lost any ability to respond or to contribute in a meaningful way to the debate on issues. . . . .

The obvious solution, which was available to dissidents at an earlier time when entry into publishing was relatively inexpensive, today would be to have additional newspapers. But the same economic factors which have caused the disappearance of vast numbers of metropolitan newspapers, have made entry into the marketplace of ideas served by the print media almost impossible. It is urged that the claim of newspapers to be "surrogates for the public" carries with it a concomitant fiduciary obligation to account for that stewardship. From this premise it is reasoned that the only effective way to insure fairness and accuracy and to provide for some accountability is for government to take affirmative action. The First Amendment interest of the public in being informed is said to be in peril because the "marketplace of ideas" is today a monopoly controlled by the owners of the market. . . . .

However much validity may be found in these arguments, at each point the implementation of a remedy such as an enforceable right of access necessarily calls for some mechanism, either governmental or consensual. If it is governmental coercion, this at once brings about a confrontation with the express provisions of the First Amendment . . . . .

. . . . A newspaper is more than a passive receptacle or conduit for news, comment, and advertising. The choice of material to go into a newspaper, and the decisions made as to limitations on the size of the paper, and content, and treatment of public issues and public officials—whether fair or unfair—constitutes the exercise of editorial control and judgment. It has yet to be demonstrated how governmental regulation of this crucial process can be exercised consistent with First Amendment guarantees of a free press as they have evolved to this time.

The Court did not mention or cite the *Red Lion* case. Has *Red Lion* been overruled? If printer's ink were suddenly in drastically short supply and the government set up a commission to ration ink, could the commission do what Florida was not permitted to do in *Tornillo*?

7. Observe that in our system, the courts are given a substantial role in the regulatory process. Notice the kinds of questions the Court was called on to decide in *Red Lion*. Several of these questions had to do with whether the FCC was acting within lawful outer boundaries, substantive and procedural. In deciding such questions, the Court may be thought of as exercising a surveillance function. Would it be defensible for the Court to go beyond this and, after deciding that the FCC acted within the relevant outer boundaries, substitute its own judgment for that of the FCC as to whether Cook should get free time from Red Lion in this particular case? Did the court in the "Pensions" case, discussed earlier, exercise an appropriate surveillance function? Was the "Pensions" case consistent with *Red Lion*?

8. As for Cook, he said he was weary of it all and declined to reply when, following the Supreme Court's decision, the station offered him free time.

Another View of *Red Lion* and the Fairness Doctrine

Fred Friendly, then professor of journalism at Columbia University, shed new light on the *Red Lion* case and the fairness doctrine in an article, What's Fair on the Air?, N.Y. Times, Mar. 30, 1975, § 6 (Magazine), at 11, and in a subsequent book, The Good Guys, the Bad Guys, and the First Amendment (1976). Friendly reported that in the early 1960s, Kennedy, Johnson, and the Democratic National Committee (DNC) had actively sought to utilize the fairness doctrine to obtain free air time to reply to far-right political opponents and to intimidate radio stations so that they would cancel far-right programs. According to Friendly, in 1963–64 the DNC launched an effort to monitor extreme right-wing broadcasts and to get individuals and organizations that had been attacked in these broadcasts to request reply time. Under this campaign, the DNC apparently encouraged and helped Mr. Cook prepare his fairness doctrine demand, which was sent to over 200 stations, and counseled him on how to petition the FCC for free time if any station refused to broadcast his reply statement. According to Friendly, the DNC had earlier subsidized Mr. Cook's anti-Goldwater book by guaranteeing in advance the purchase of 50,000 copies, and a DNC staff member had supplied information for, and perhaps inspired, Mr. Cook's "Hate Clubs of the Air" piece in The Nation. Friendly reported, moreover, that some of this anti-right-wing activity was financed by a DNC-created organization with tax-exempt status to which the DNC gave some of its own funds and to which it encouraged Democratic party supporters to contribute.

Friendly cited DNC reports claiming the fairness doctrine effort netted 1,035 letters to stations and 1,678 hours of free time from stations that carried right-wing broadcasts. Friendly quoted one DNC staff member as writing in a report to the DNC that "[e]ven more important than the free radio time was the effectiveness of this operation in inhibiting the political activity of these right-wing broadcasts" and another as writing in another report that the campaign "may have inhibited the stations in their broadcast of more radical and politically partisan programs."

Friendly concluded his article in the New York Times Magazine with the following observations: "[T]he assumption that the problem in the *Red Lion* case was access for Fred Cook's views is, in light of what we know today, demonstrably false. Fred Cook with his Nation magazine attack on Hargis and other 'Hate Clubs of the Air,' and his subsidized book against Goldwater, was hardly a classical case of a man in need of access. And though the Court did not know it when it heard the case, his motivation for taking action against the Red Lion station was not just to gain access to the public air-waves in order to defend himself against an attack so much as it was the product of a carefully orchestrated program initiated by politicians to inhibit views they believed to be harmful to the country, as well as to their own political fortunes."

————

Comments and Questions

1. Does this new information about the role of the Democratic National Committee and Cook's possible motive for his fairness doctrine complaint cause you to have a different attitude toward the *Red Lion* case?

2. Do you think the case was wrongly decided? Should the fairness doctrine be abolished?

————

The Crucial Importance of Facts, Fact-Finders, and Fact-Finding

A common fallacy about law is that facts and fact-finding are somehow of subordinate importance to law. This is also an incoherent fallacy, for on a philosophical level, law cannot be divorced from facts. That is, every law contemplates a state of facts. Law inherently looks to fact. On a pragmatic and policy level, facts are crucial too, as the information about the *Red Lion* case uncovered by Fred Friendly demonstrates. We look to facts, such as those asserted by Friendly, to predict the consequences for society that will flow from alternative legal rules.

Facts in these senses are different, however, from facts of particular situations to which law already made is to be applied. Modern legal systems typically provide elaborate compulsory means of investigating the facts of particular episodes. Some of the relevant techniques were discussed in Chapter 1 with respect to the grievance-remedial mode. Such techniques are available, too, in the penal-corrective and the administrative-regulatory modes.

But investigations are one thing, authoritative fact-finding quite another. Legal cynics have been known to say, "Let me have the power to find the facts, and I'll care not who makes the law or what the law's content is." This cynicism trades on the truth that facts are crucial. Indeed, perhaps 90 percent of litigated disputes are not over legal questions at all but over facts.

Methods of authoritative fact-finding can differ a lot. For example, a lay jury in our system plays a large role in the use of law as a grievance-remedial instrument and in its use as a penal-corrective instrument, but much less of a role in law's use as an administrative-regulatory instrument. Can you think of reasons that might justify this? Because of its importance, fact-finding is commonly subject to some form of review. Trial judges have significant controls over juries. Appellate courts, on request of the parties, will review the authoritative fact-findings of judges and of administrators. But just as trial judges may not upset the fact-findings of juries that are within the bounds of reasonableness, appellate courts may not upset the fact-findings of administrators that are supported by substantial evidence (again a reasonableness test).

Facts bear on the limits of law, too. Possible alternative rules of law contemplate different factual inquiries. Some inquiries are much more susceptible to use of the methods we have for finding facts than are others. Thus, the possibility of reliably determining the relevant facts can have a bearing on the basic choice of governing legal rule. As Sir Frederick Pollock stated: "The law cannot be more finely graduated than the means of ascertaining facts . . . ." F. Pollock, A First Book of Jurisprudence 45 (5th ed. 1923). In ordinary auto accident cases, for example, does it make sense to apply a rule of law that requires ascertaining facts relevant to fault? Are such facts discoverable in ordinary cases? Compare determinations of subjective "guilty mind" in the criminal law.

Comments and Questions

1. Professor Kenneth Culp Davis has divided facts into two groups: "[F]acts are of two kinds—adjudicative and legislative. Adjudicative facts are the facts about the parties and their activities, businesses, and properties. Adjudicative facts usually answer the questions of who did what, where, when, how, why, with what motive or intent; adjudicative facts are roughly the kind of facts that go to a jury in a jury case. Legislative facts do not usually concern the immediate parties but are general facts which help the tribunal decide questions of law and policy and discretion." 1 K. Davis, Administrative Law Treatise 413 (1958). Return to the *Red Lion* case. What facts in the case might be called adjudicative facts? Are there legislative facts in the case as well? How did the fact-finders decide the relevant facts? Which kind of facts—adjudicative or legislative—can generally be determined with greater accuracy?

2. Can you think of basic procedural differences that might apply to deciding adjudicative facts, on one hand, and legislative facts, on the other? How are facts found in an adjudication (with a judge or an agency presiding)? How do legislatures or rulemakers find facts?

3. How would you classify the facts discussed by Professor Friendly? Are they adjudicative or legislative? Would knowledge of them have influenced the Supreme Court's decision in *Red Lion*? Does this distinction between adjudicative and legislative facts—and the difference in procedures for determining them—influence your view of whether the Supreme Court should be relatively more activist or more deferential to Congress in constitutional litigation?

Section Five. Necessity for and Nature of Coercive Power

Ultimate sanctions and the means for applying them are just as necessary in the administrative-regulatory mode as in the grievance-remedial and the penal-corrective modes, and largely for the same reasons. And the threat of their use radically cuts down the necessity for their actual use in particular instances. Moreover, as we saw in Section 2 of this chapter,

the administrative-regulatory mode relies most heavily on a variety of nonsanction and presanction control devices.

But there are important differences between the three modes with respect to sanctions. One of these, a basic difference between the penal and the regulative, will now be considered. Unfortunately, this difference is not always understood by the laity or officials. Consider the soundness of the following analyses.

SAYRE, PUBLIC WELFARE OFFENSES

33 Colum.L.Rev. 55, 68–70, 72, 79–80 (1933).*

[T]he growing complexities of twentieth century life have demanded an increasing social regulation; and for this purpose the existing machinery of the criminal law has been seized upon and utilized. The original objective of the criminal law was to keep the peace; and under the strong church influence of the Middle Ages its function was extended to curb moral delinquencies of one kind or another. For these purposes it developed a suitable procedure, requiring proof of moral blameworthiness or a criminal intent. But today the crowded conditions of life require social regulation to a degree never before attempted. The invention and extensive use of high-powered automobiles require new forms of traffic regulation; the increased social evils from drink due to the more crowded and complex conditions of modern life require new forms of liquor regulation; the development of modern medical science and the congested living accommodations of modern cities require new forms of sanitary and health regulation; the growth of modern factories requires new forms of labor regulation; the development of modern building construction and the growth of skyscrapers require new forms of building regulation. The old cumbrous machinery of the criminal law, designed to try the subjective blameworthiness of individual offenders, is not adapted for exercising petty regulation on a wholesale scale; and consequently a considerable amount of this developing regulation has been placed under administrative control. But unfortunately the criminal law, which from early times had been used to punish those obstructing or endangering the King's highway, threatening the public health or disturbing the peace by reason of intoxication, was seized upon as a convenient instrument for enforcing a substantial part of this petty regulation. . . .

The ready enforcement which is vital for effective petty regulation on an extended scale can be gained only by a total disregard of the state of mind. Thus, there has grown up within comparatively recent times a group of public welfare offenses, consisting of violations of police regulations which are punishable without proof of any individual blameworthiness and which form an exception to the general established doctrines of the criminal law.

The group of offenses punishable without proof of any criminal intent must be sharply limited. The sense of justice of the community will not tolerate the infliction of punishment which is substantial upon those innocent of intentional or negligent wrongdoing; and law in the last analysis must reflect the general community sense of justice. The problem is how to draw the line between those offenses which do and those which do not require mens rea. . . .

How then can one determine practically which offenses do and which do not require mens rea, where the statute creating the offense is entirely silent as to requisite knowledge? Although no hard and fast lines can be drawn, two cardinal principles stand out upon which the determination must turn.

The first relates to the character of the offense. All criminal enactments in a sense serve the double purpose of singling out wrongdoers for the purpose of punishment or correction and of regulating the social order. But often the importance of the one far outweighs the other. Crimes created primarily for the purpose of singling out individual wrongdoers for punishment or correction are the ones commonly requiring mens rea; police offenses of a merely regulatory nature are frequently enforceable irrespective of any guilty intent.

The second criterion depends upon the possible penalty. If this be serious, particularly if the offense be punishable by imprisonment, the individual interest of the defendant weighs too heavily to allow conviction without proof of a guilty mind. To subject defendants entirely free from moral blameworthiness to the possibility of prison sentences is revolting to the community sense of justice; and no law which violates this fundamental instinct can long endure. Crimes punishable with prison sentences, therefore, ordinarily require proof of a guilty intent. . . .

The modern rapid growth of a large body of offenses punishable without proof of a guilty intent is marked with real danger. Courts are familiarized with the pathway to easy convictions by relaxing the orthodox requirement of a mens rea. The danger is that in the case of true crimes where the penalty is severe and the need for ordinary criminal law safeguards is strong, courts following the false analogy of the public welfare offenses may now and again similarly relax the mens rea requirement, particularly in the case of unpopular crimes, as the easiest way to secure desired convictions.

The moral obloquy and the social disgrace incident to criminal conviction are whips which lend effective power to the administration of criminal law. When the law begins to permit convictions for serious offenses of men who are morally innocent and free from fault, who may even be respected and useful members of the community, its restraining power becomes undermined. Once it becomes respectable to be convicted, the vitality of the criminal law has been sapped. It is no answer that judges convinced of the actual moral innocence of the defendant, may impose only a nominal punishment. The harm is wrought through the conviction itself and through the subjection of innocent men to the possibility of having imposed upon them by some ignorant or prejudiced judge the substantial punishment which the crime allows. For true crimes it is imperative that courts should not relax the classic requirement of the mens rea or guilty intent.

SCHWENK, THE ADMINISTRATIVE CRIME, ITS CREATION AND PUNISHMENT BY ADMINISTRATIVE AGENCIES

42 Mich.L.Rev. 51, 85–86 (1943).*

In addition, it seems that the device of punishment for the violation of administrative duties is distinguishable from the type of ordinary crime. In the first place, this "administrative crime" is not the outbirth of a particular unmoral conduct, but is characterized by disobedience to administrative duties. In the second place, the function of this "administrative crime" is deterrence rather than retribution. The mere existence of the penal sanction should make the individual comply with his administrative duties.

To what extent should the legislators use the device of the administrative crime? Since the chief interest of government in the field of administrative law is directed toward compliance with administrative duties, specific performance of administrative duties rather than punishment for their violation must be the primary objective, as the distinguished Swiss professor of administrative law, Fritz Fleiner has urged. Consequently, direct compulsion should be exercised for the purpose of enforcing administrative duties, wherever it is possible. For instance, where a person carries on an enterprise without a license, the enterprise should be closed (direct compulsion). Where a person is bound to perform an administrative duty which can be carried out by a third person, it should be done by the third person at the expense of the individual who is subject to the administrative duty (substituted performance). Only in those cases in which neither direct compulsion nor substituted action is possible, should the concept of the "administrative crime" be used, not as a means of punishment, but as a means of indirect compulsion. This punishment is not to vindicate past conduct, but to enforce future conduct. Consequently, it has nothing to do with the ordinary concept of crime. Therefore, a penalty can be imposed as often as necessary to make the individual comply with the administrative order, and the prohibition of double jeopardy does not apply. On the other hand, once the order is complied with, the penalty can no longer be imposed or exacted. Of course, under this concept, the penal sanction becomes an administrative sanction and the problems which result from the use of the penal sanction in administrative law no longer exist. Even though punishment as an administrative sanction should be employed, there always would remain a proper field for the use of the administrative crime as a penal sanction.

———

Comments and Questions

1. Mr. Schwenk says "the function of . . . 'administrative crime' is deterrence rather than retribution," and Professor Sayre says much the same thing in stressing regulation of the social order rather than "singling out wrongdoers" for punishment or correction as the purpose of what he calls "welfare offenses" (e.g.,

traffic violations or selling adulterated milk). If deterrence is the goal, is it inconsistent to do away with mens rea? If the defendant had no knowledge his milk was adulterated, did not intentionally sell adulterated milk, and was not negligent in allowing his milk to become adulterated, could he have avoided selling adulterated milk? If not, how does removing mens rea as an element of the crime accomplish deterrence? Would the milk seller take additional precautions against adulterated milk once the requirement of mens rea was removed?

2. In the field of broadcast regulation, the ultimate sanction is refusal to renew a license, known in the industry as "the death penalty." The FCC, however, almost never uses this sanction. Nothing in the Federal Communications Act expressly provides a preference at renewal time for the existing licensee, but as a practical matter, the FCC distinctly favors incumbents. Some observers would see this as a sign of "industry capture" of the FCC by broadcasters. Can you think of any other reasons why the FCC might adopt such a policy?

3. Mr. Schwenk argues that direct compulsion (e.g., ordering a broadcaster to allow free time to the target of a personal attack) and substituted performance (e.g., immunizing a pet and charging the owner) should always be used, whenever possible, in place of administrative penalties. Can an argument be made for administrative penalties even when direct compulsion or substituted performance is possible?

Section Six. Roles of Private Citizens and Their Lawyers

The importance of action by administrators in carrying on a regulatory program is obviously great. But private citizens may also play an important role in two ways: (1) by bringing a private claim that in effect enforces an agency standard and (2) by intervening directly in agency adjudicative or rulemaking proceedings.

We saw in Section 1 of this chapter that the grievance-remedial instrument, by itself, is often inadequate for regulatory purposes. Still, private claims can supplement and assist an agency's regulatory program. The violation of an agency's rule or regulation, for example, may serve as the basis, or part of the basis, in an ordinary private action in a court. Can you visualize how this can happen?

Perhaps an illustrative problem would help. Suppose the National Highway Traffic Safety Administration (NHTSA) establishes a safety standard requiring a certain kind of safety spring in the accelerator assembly of cars to prevent the accelerator from sticking. Fast-Buck Auto Manufacturing Company omits the spring in its cars. Smith buys one of Fast-Buck's cars, the accelerator sticks, and Smith is injured in the ensuing accident, which would have been prevented by the spring. How might the NHTSA safety standard be relevant in a suit by Smith against Fast-Buck? What if the accelerator sticks even though Fast-Buck used the NHTSA-required spring, but Smith can prove that a more expensive and better-designed spring would have prevented the accident? How would the NHTSA standard affect this case?

Private citizens may participate directly in agency proceedings either through complaints based on individual interest or as members of public-interest groups that seek to influence agency actions when broad principles are at stake.

An example of the first pattern can be found in an individual's complaint to the FCC against a telephone or telegraph company for excessive or improper charges. Mr. Cook's fairness doctrine complaint in the *Red Lion* case is another example. Note that in these cases, the private complainant is an important source of information about regulatory problems and violations.

The two *United Church of Christ* cases, discussed in Section 2, are examples of public-interest group participation in the regulatory process. These were path-breaking cases greatly expanding the role of private citizens in agency proceedings. In these and in cases concerning other agencies, the courts opened the agency doors wider in part to counterbalance what Dean Landis, writing in 1960, called the "daily machine-gun like impact on both [an] agency and its staff" of lawyers representing industry interests (such as those of broadcasters). J. Landis, Report on Regulatory Agencies to the President-Elect 71 (1960). Consider the following from Staff of Senate Comm. on Governmental Affairs, 95th Cong., 1st Sess., 3 Study on Federal Regulation: Public Participation in Regulatory Agency Proceedings, at VII (Comm.Print 1977):

(3) At agency after agency, participation by the regulated industry predominates—often overwhelmingly. Organized public interest representation accounts for a very small percentage of participation before Federal regulatory agencies. In more than half of the formal proceedings, there appears to be no such participation whatsoever, and virtually none at informal agency proceedings. In those proceedings where participation by public groups does take place, typically it is a small fraction of the participation by the regulated industry. One-tenth is not uncommon; sometimes it is even less than that. This pattern prevails in both rulemaking proceedings and adjudicatory proceedings, with an even greater imbalance occurring in adjudications than in rulemaking.

(4) The single greatest obstacle to active public participation in regulatory proceedings is the lack of financial resources by potential participants to meet the great costs of formal participation.

. . . .

(5) The regulated industry consistently outspends public participants by a wide margin in regulatory agency proceedings. . . . In some instances, industry committed as much as 50 to 100 times the resources budgeted by the public interest participants.

The theory of government regulation, which we explored in Section 1, is consistent with these observations. In general, the interest of private citizens in the services delivered by broadcasters, for example, is too diffuse and unorganized to have much effect. No one family is willing to invest the large resources needed to influence broadcasters' programming policies. This is especially true because other families would benefit without paying any of the cost (the free-rider problem). The FCC was created to look after the broad public interest in broadcasting. But direct citizen participation in the FCC's forging of broadcast regulatory policies, including the fairness doctrine, has been minimal because of the same diffuseness of interest, transactions costs, and free-rider problems that helped explain the creation of the FCC in the first place. This rule has exceptions. Some private groups have been organized and financed, often through charitable contributions from individuals and foundations, to pursue public-interest causes. These include groups like the Office of Communication of the United Church of Christ, the American Civil Liberties Union, the Sierra Club, Ralph Nader's Public Citizen, the Environmental Defense Fund, Action for Children's Television, and so forth. But as the prior Senate committee excerpt notes, the activity level and financial resources of these groups fall well below those of the regulated industry itself.

Should the agencies, the courts, or Congress try to right the balance through some form of financial assistance to public-interest groups? This could be done (1) through agency payments to public-interest groups for participation in agency rulemaking or adjudicative proceedings or (2) through the award of legal expenses and attorneys' fees to public-interest groups successful in litigation before agencies or courts.

In the *United Church of Christ* cases, for example, the appellants must have incurred substantial legal expenses in their ultimately successful action. Assessing those expenses against a losing private litigant or against the government (which in the person of the agency is often a party in judicial review of agency action) would be a way of financing public-interest group participation in the regulatory process. But the general American rule is that each party must bear its own legal expenses and attorneys' fees. And in Alyeska Pipeline Service Co. v. Wilderness Society, 421 U.S. 240, 95 S.Ct. 1612 (1975), the Supreme Court required specific congressional authorization for a court to award legal expenses and attorneys' fees to public-interest group litigants. Some specific statutes, such as the civil rights acts, 42 U.S.C. § 1988, expressly authorize attorney-fee awards. Even the Federal Communications Act does so for actions by private claimants against "common carriers" (telephone and telegraph companies) for improper service or charges, 47 U.S.C. § 206, but not in fairness doctrine or related cases.[e]

A federal statute could thus authorize fee shifting in favor of public-interest groups and against private litigants, the government, or both. As noted previously, the statute could also provide for government payments to such groups for their participation in agency rulemaking proceedings. Consider the following view.

PANEL II: STANDING, PARTICIPATION, AND WHO PAYS?

26 Ad.L.Rev. 423, 449–50 (1974) (H. Russell).

[T]hose who have advocated the expenditure of taxpayers' money to support the intervention of public interest representatives in agency

---

e. For example, in Turner v. FCC, 514 F.2d 1354 (D.C.Cir.1975), the court refused to award legal expenses and attorneys' fees to plaintiffs, Richard Turner, the Black Youth Club, and the Southern Christian Leadership Conference, who had opposed renewal of a radio station's license because of alleged racial discrimination. (The plaintiffs ultimately reached a settlement agreement with the radio station, which presumably agreed to alter its practices.) The *Turner* court based its decision on the *Alyeska Pipeline* rule and the absence of express statutory authorization.

proceedings have generally taken a one-sided view of the problem. Usually, I have heard that such funds would be devoted to fostering the causes of consumers and users and the like, whereas it is undoubtedly true that the public interest also extends to the welfare of the investors and of the employees whose money and labor are expended in the production of the service consumed by the user. All have a right to the proper consideration of their interest, and each is as much entitled to the expenditure of public funds for the protection of his interest as any of the others.

Further, if there were a tax money fund to support public interest participation in agency proceedings, I am confident that we would not lack for allegedly genuine public interests to exhaust that fund, even if it were greater in amount than the combined budgets of the federal agencies. I believe that funding public intervention with tax money would lead to the assertion of spurious interests . . . .

Comments and Questions

1. Would you favor enactment of a federal statute authorizing attorney-fee awards to citizen groups serving as "private attorneys general" in cases like *United Church of Christ (I and II)?* If so, what conditions or qualifications would you include in the statute? Should fees be shifted to private litigants, like WLBT in *United Church of Christ,* or the government only, or both? Would the shifting flow in only one direction, in favor of the winning public-interest group but not against it if it loses?

2. Should the expense of public-interest group participation in rulemaking also be shifted to the government? Is there more or less justification for such shifting than in the case of litigation before agencies and courts?

3. If you favor fee shifting to the government, how do you respond to Mr. Russell's argument in the previous excerpt?

4. How should a public-interest group be defined for fee-shifting purposes? Is it enough that the group represents a broad class of people? Suppose the group is an association of business firms or broadcasters? What about a union or a state or local government? Suppose the group consists of television viewers who favor an increase of westerns in programming or more explicit sex on TV?

5. For an award of attorneys' fees to a public-interest group in connection with litigation, should we require the group to be successful? How would success be defined? In the *Alyeska* case, the Wilderness Society, the Environmental Defense Fund, and Friends of the Earth sued the secretary of the interior to prevent issuance of permits to oil companies who wanted to build an oil pipeline across Alaska. The plaintiffs argued (1) that the permits would violate the Mineral Leasing Act of 1920, 30 U.S.C. § 185, which limits rights-of-way across public lands to a fifty-foot width, and (2) that the environmental impact statement prepared by the Interior Department was inadequate. The court of appeals ruled for the plaintiffs on the width of right-of-way question, without reaching the environmental issue. Thereafter, Congress mooted the merits of the case by passing the Trans-Alaska Pipeline Authorization Act, 43 U.S.C. § 1651, specifically authorizing construction of the pipeline, with certain conditions (including a fund financed by the oil companies to cover pipeline-caused damage), and barring further consideration of environmental issues. On these facts, would the plaintiffs be entitled to attorneys' fees? The court of appeals thought so—before being reversed on other grounds by the Supreme Court, as described earlier. Wilderness

Society v. Morton, 495 F.2d 1026 (D.C.Cir.1974) (en banc), rev'd sub nom. Alyeska Pipeline Service Co. v. Wilderness Society, 421 U.S. 240, 95 S.Ct. 1612 (1975). If the goal is to have public-interest groups raise important issues, why require success at all?

6. Should we require the issue on which the public-interest group is successful to be important? How would importance be defined? In *Alyeska* the court of appeals dealt with the issue as follows:

> It is argued that the width limitation in Section 28 of the Mineral Leasing Act of 1920 does not amount to a congressional policy of preeminent importance. But the dispute in this case was more than a debate over interpretation of that Act. [The Interior Department's] primary argument was that, whatever the width restrictions in the Act originally meant, a settled administrative practice to evade those restrictions took precedence. In the final analysis, this case involved the duty of the Executive Branch to observe the restrictions imposed by the Legislative . . . and the primary responsibility of the Congress under the Constitution to regulate the use of public lands.

Is any successfully raised issue likely to be unimportant under this analysis?

7. Shortly after the Supreme Court decision in *Alyeska*, Senator Kennedy introduced legislation, S. 2715, 94th Cong., 2d Sess. (1975), that would have authorized awards of fees, litigation expenses, and participation expenses to public-interest groups appearing in agency proceedings (adjudication and rulemaking) or judicial review of agency action. The government was to be the principal payor, but in some circumstances the costs could be assessed against opposing private parties. The bill was not enacted. In 1980 Congress did pass the Equal Access to Justice Act, 28 U.S.C. § 2412, which provides for one-way fee shifting in many civil cases (but not just those involving public-interest groups) brought by or against the federal government (including federal agencies).

8. Compare the general roles of private citizens and their lawyers in the grievance-remedial, the penal-corrective, and the administrative-regulatory modes. Are these roles substantially similar in each?

Section Seven. Process Values

In the administrative-regulatory mode, too, one encounters a wide variety of processes: legislative processes originating relevant regulatory programs, processes for formulating and disseminating specific policies, processes of self-regulation in light of these regulatory standards, informal processes of enforcement by agency personnel, prosecutory and adjudicative processes within agencies, judicial processes in courts, and so on.

Here we shall introduce some materials reflecting certain process values that take special form in administrative regulation. The following statutory excerpt is taken from the Administrative Procedure Act (APA) passed by Congress in 1946 to standardize procedure before all federal agencies. The APA provides procedure for rulemaking and administrative adjudication. The excerpt is taken from the APA's provisions for informal rulemaking. Note that § 553 refers to other sections of the APA (§§ 556 and 557) that contain provisions for formal rulemaking. Note also when the formal procedure must be used.

UNITED STATES CODE, TITLE 5

§ 553. Rule making

. . . .

(b) General notice of proposed rule making shall be published in the Federal Register, unless persons subject thereto are named and either personally served or otherwise have actual notice thereof in accordance with law. The notice shall include—

> (1) a statement of the time, place, and nature of public rule making proceedings;
>
> (2) reference to the legal authority under which the rule is proposed; and
>
> (3) either the terms or substance of the proposed rule or a description of the subjects and issues involved.

Except when notice or hearing is required by statute, this subsection does not apply—

> (A) to interpretative rules, general statements of policy, or rules of agency organization, procedure, or practice; or
>
> (B) when the agency for good cause finds (and incorporates the finding and a brief statement of reasons therefor in the rules issued) that notice and public procedure thereon are impracticable, unnecessary, or contrary to the public interest.

(c) After notice required by this section, the agency shall give interested persons an opportunity to participate in the rule making through submission of written data, views, or arguments with or without opportunity for oral presentation. After consideration of the relevant matter presented, the agency shall incorporate in the rules adopted a concise general statement of their basis and purpose. When rules are required by statute to be made on the record after opportunity for an agency hearing, sections 556 and 557 of this title [requiring a formal trial-type hearing, a record of all evidence submitted, and findings and conclusions based upon and supported by the record] apply instead of this subsection.

(d) The required publication or service of a substantive rule shall be made not less than 30 days before its effective date, except—

> (1) a substantive rule which grants or recognizes an exemption or relieves a restriction;
>
> (2) interpretative rules and statements of policy; or
>
> (3) as otherwise provided by the agency for good cause found and published with the rule.

(e) Each agency shall give an interested person the right to petition for the issuance, amendment, or repeal of a rule.

———

Comments and Questions

1. The FCC makes many rules pursuant to its rulemaking powers. Rulemaking is a kind of legislative function. What are the basic procedural elements in § 553?

2. In the Swimming Pool case in Chapter 1, other swimming pool owners besides the defendant would not have been entitled to notice and an opportunity to participate. This is also true in virtually all cases in the penal-corrective mode. Can you rationalize this consistently with the foregoing statute? What other differences do you note between trial-type procedure (that applicable in the Swimming Pool case, for example) and the provisions of § 553?

3. Recall the discussion of adjudicative and legislative facts in Section 4. Is § 553 concerned with adjudicative facts or legislative facts? Can you articulate the process values that explain the major differences between trial-type procedure and the "notice and comment" rulemaking procedure of § 553?

4. Professor Roger Cramton has stressed the factors of accuracy, efficiency, and acceptability in assessing different procedural systems: "Beyond the fundamental principle of meaningful party participation, any evaluation of administrative procedures must rest on a judgment which balances the advantages and disadvantages of each procedural system. In striking this balance, I believe that the following formulation of competing considerations is more helpful than 'fairness' or 'due process': the extent to which the procedure furthers the accurate selection and determination of relevant facts and issues, the efficient disposition of business, and, when viewed in the light of the statutory objectives, its acceptability to the agency, the participants, and the general public." Cramton, A Comment on Trial-Type Hearings in Nuclear Power Plant Siting, 58 Va.L.Rev. 585, 592 (1972). Applying the Cramton analysis, how would you evaluate § 553, by comparison with a trial-type hearing, for the purpose of agency rulemaking?

5. What are the similarities between the informal rulemaking procedure of § 553 and the procedure followed by Congress in enacting statutes? What are the differences?

LOVETT, EX PARTE AND THE FCC: THE NEW REGULATIONS
21 Fed.Com.B.J. 54, 54 (1967).

One of the cornerstones of our judicial system is . . . the fundamental right to a decision based on the merits . . . . [Sometimes] this right . . . has been subverted as a result of "ex parte communications." In judicial proceedings, the phrase generally refers to oral or written statements by any party to an adversary proceeding to one in a decision-making position for the purpose of influencing the outcome of the proceeding, without notice to the other parties. . . .

The same prohibition against ex parte communications has been traditionally applied . . . to matters of adjudication before administrative agencies generally.

Comments and Questions

1. The problem Mr. Lovett is concerned with sometimes arises in competitive adjudicative proceedings before the FCC when two or more parties are seeking one broadcast license. For example, one party might, without notice to the others and off the record, tell the fact-finder of certain alleged facts favorable to her case, such as that she is financially stable but her competitor is not, or that she is in a better position to assure good program balance. In the famous "Boston Channel 5" case, a station ultimately lost its license as a result of ex parte contact with the

chairman of the FCC during comparative license proceedings. See Greater Boston Television Corp. v. FCC, 444 F.2d 841 (D.C.Cir.1970), cert. denied, 403 U.S. 923, 91 S.Ct. 2233 (1971).

2.　What, if anything, is wrong with such ex parte contacts? Try to articulate the process values reflected in prohibitions against such contacts.

3.　Are ex parte communications allowed under § 553 rulemaking? Are they allowed in congressional lawmaking? If so, why the difference?

4.　As mentioned earlier, the Administrative Procedure Act provides for a formal rulemaking procedure in addition to the "notice and comment" informal procedure of § 553. In the case of administrative adjudication, the APA provides in express terms only for formal adjudication, although informal adjudication— such as occurred in the FCC's treatment of the *Red Lion* case—is common and has never been considered prohibited under the APA. The formal procedures, which apply for the most part equally to formal rulemaking and formal adjudication, resemble those of a trial. All information and facts that form the basis of the decision are formally admitted before a presiding agency official and are made a part of the "record" of the proceeding. The decision must then be made "on the record" and must be supported by it. The APA defines the record as follows: "The transcript of testimony and exhibits, together with all papers and requests filed in the proceeding, constitutes the exclusive record for decision . . . . ." 5 U.S.C. § 556(e). The following APA provision reflects the importance in formal rulemaking and adjudication of the record and a reasoned decision based upon it.

UNITED STATES CODE, TITLE 5

§ 557.　Initial decisions; conclusiveness; review by agency; submissions by parties; contents of decisions; record

. . . .

(c) . . . The record shall show the ruling on each finding, conclusion, or exception presented. All decisions, including initial, recommended, and tentative decisions, are a part of the record and shall include a statement of—

(A) findings and conclusions, and the reasons or basis therefor, on all the material issues of fact, law, or discretion presented on the record; and
(B) the appropriate rule, order, sanction, relief, or denial thereof.

. . .

Comments and Questions

1.　Although for informal adjudication, the APA contains no express reason-giving requirement, general concepts of due process and prior case law could be found to supply one. For example, in a famous case decided before the APA was passed and involving an SEC administrative adjudication, the Supreme Court remanded the case to the SEC for a clearer explanation of the basis for the agency's decision. The Court said that "the orderly functioning of the process of review requires that the grounds upon which the administrative agency acted be clearly disclosed and adequately sustained." SEC v. Chenery Corp., 318 U.S. 80, 94, 63 S.Ct. 454, 462 (1943). What process values does a requirement of this sort reflect?

2.　As mentioned earlier, the FCC used informal adjudication in *Red Lion*. Did the FCC comply with the *Chenery* requirement?

3. Ordinary trial judges are generally not required to write opinions setting forth the reasons for their rulings of law. Is their work somehow distinguishable so that it is rationally exempt from the reason-giving requirement?

4. Compare the reason-giving requirement of § 557 with that of "notice and comment" rulemaking under § 553. Would the FCC be required to give reasons to support regulations it adopted by § 553 informal rulemaking procedure?

5. Unless a statute expressly requires formal rulemaking, agencies overwhelmingly prefer to use informal "notice and comment" rulemaking. Why? Why did Congress provide for two different rulemaking procedures?

6. Would judicial review of agency rulemaking be more effective under formal or informal rulemaking? Why? Suppose the FCC proposes to issue new rules allowing broadcasters to submit a postcard application for license renewal instead of the prior long form requiring a detailed report of the station's programming. Black Citizens for a Fair Media, a public-interest group, submits written studies and reasoned arguments demonstrating that the postcard form will make it much more difficult for public-interest groups like itself to monitor whether radio and TV stations are living up to their fairness doctrine obligations in programming. Could the FCC adopt the proposed rule under informal rulemaking without directly addressing the issues raised by the Black Citizens for a Fair Media? Could it do so under formal rulemaking? Cf. Black Citizens For a Fair Media v. FCC, 719 F.2d 407 (D.C.Cir.1983), cert. denied, 104 S.Ct. 3545 (1984). Could a court motivated to scrutinize agency rulemaking closely find a significant requirement of reasoned decision making in the § 553 procedure?

Section Eight. Improving the Administrative-Regulatory Instrument

Scope for improvement always exists, for example, by way of securing better regulatory standards or better personnel, securing more money for better regulatory enforcement or for broader participation of public-interest groups, improving agency procedures (the purpose of the Administrative Procedure Act), and so on. Only one issue will be considered here, and briefly at that.

For good or for ill, many regulatory agencies in the United States are "independent," at least in the following senses: their authority comes from congressional, not presidential, delegation (making them commissions rather than executive departments); their governing officials are not subject to removal by the executive except for malfeasance; and those officials usually serve longer terms of office than the executive. Independence was thought necessary (1) to allow for impartiality of officials when performing adjudicative functions and (2) "to take regulation out of politics." But such independence has not gone unattacked.

JAFFE, BOOK REVIEW

65 Yale L.J. 1068, 1070–74 (1956)

(reviewing M. Bernstein, Regulating Business by Independent Commission (1955)).*

The campaign by the political scientists against the independent agency has proceeded on both constitutional and political grounds. The

Constitution, it is argued, requires that all executive functions be subject to presidential control.   .   .   .

The political argument is based on an attempt to document the charge that the independent agency, having no duly constituted master, is falling under the domination of private interests, characteristically the interests whose activities it is supposed to regulate.   This is the so-called phenomenon of the industry-oriented agency.   .   .   .   First, industry representation is not peculiar to the agencies.   It is to my mind not a little curious that the critics limit their examination of this phenomenon to the independent agency.   I would suppose that it was necessary first to establish the executive agencies as the norm and then to show how the independent agencies tend to depart from that norm. Yet anyone who follows the activities of the Department of Agriculture, for example, comes to feel (though this too is no doubt an exaggeration) that the Department is a glorified farmer's lobby.   An examination of the milk licensing activities suggests the enormous power of the farm cooperatives.   It is certainly not my thesis that all departments, nor for that matter all independent agencies, are industry-oriented; but the current demonstration with respect to the independent agency is neither scientific nor scrupulous.

The distortion in the attack goes much deeper.   As I see it the critics' real quarrel, if they would but recognize and admit it, is with Congress.
.   .   .

The greatest weakness of the critics, to my mind, is that they have failed to face honestly and wholeheartedly the most serious difficulty facing regulation today.   That difficulty is the radical lack of a meaningful statutory policy in many of the areas where the independent agencies function.   In some cases the policy has become obsolete.   .   .   .

In radio the situation is somewhat different, for there never has been a statutory policy.   The FCC was simply told to go ahead and regulate in "the public interest."   I have studied for some years the attempts of the Commission to deal, in the absence of a congressional or popular mandate, with the baffling and manifold complexities in that field.   The Commission has lacked foresight, has often been timid and has sometimes been subservient, but to my mind this is the result of the absence of congressional guidance.   I conclude that it is much easier to criticize than to come up with an administrative program that could command support.   It was long ago pointed out by Herbert Croly, as Professor Bernstein reminds us, that regulation creates a basic problem because it divides the responsibility for management.   The gist of the difficulty, as I see it, is that the regulator accepts no responsibility for the ultimate success of the enterprise, yet his interference discourages entrepreneurial initiative and diminishes the sense of responsibility.   If the regulator is given a clear mandate to remove a perceived evil, he has an adequate and limited basis for validating his interference with management, and management has a basis for calculating the effects of the interference.   But in the absence of a clear mandate, it is not only inevitable, but appropriate that regulation take the form of an accommodation in which industry is the senior partner.   This is the essence of "industry-orientation."

There is very little in our history, I think, to indicate that an executive agency will be much different from an independent agency in periods when public opinion or statutory policy is slack, indeterminate, or lacking in conviction. The odds are that it will respond in much the same way to the climate of opinion. The history of the antitrust division of the Department of Justice, for example, is one of alternation between strict and loose enforcement of the antitrust laws. The Federal Trade Commission, an independent agency, goes through similar oscillations. The Civil Aeronautics Board in the course of its very short history has shown an almost incredible flexibility in moving toward and away from competition. It is, I think, demonstrable that when a new reform is to be undertaken, an independent agency may provide a hard hitting, single-minded authority, oblivious to the immediate partisan requirements of the Administration. The Labor Board proved this up to the hilt. In time, the immediate problem solved, the agency loses its zest and settles into routine. What institution does not? It may be a shade easier at this later stage to infuse the executive agency with a new spirit, for in the absence of an adequate congressional mandate, there is perhaps a better chance that the executive will be able to evolve and gain support for a fresh approach. But if one has a "set" in favor of vigorous regulation, it is pretty much a matter of chance whether he will find it in executive or independent agencies. My arguments, of course, do not make a case *for* the independent agency. As I have already indicated, it seems to me sounder on balance that these policy-making agencies should be subject to presidential control. Rather, these arguments are intended to show that the critics of the agencies have attributed to the factor of agency independence all sorts of political ills and disappointments for which it bears no responsibility whatever.

Comments and Questions

1. Lloyd Cutler, Washington lawyer and former adviser to President Carter, has proposed that Congress pass a statute with the following principal feature: "The President would be authorized to direct any regulatory agency (a) to take up and decide a regulatory issue within a specified period of time, or (b) to modify or reverse an agency policy, rule, regulation or decision [except for the grant or renewal of licenses or privileges to competing applicants]. Such action could be taken only by Executive Order published in the Federal Register, setting forth presidential findings that the action or inaction of an agency on a regulatory issue (or a conflict in the actions or policies of various agencies) threatened to interfere with or delay the achievement of an important national objective, and stating reasons for such findings." Cutler & Johnson, Regulation and the Political Process, 84 Yale L.J. 1395, 1414–15 (1975).

2. Would you favor enactment of such a statute? Would it be likely to curb the problem of agency capture by industry or actually enhance the power of special-interest groups by allowing them a second chance (in the White House) to defeat adverse agency policy? Is the president's policy likely to be more sensible than the agency's? Why? Would the president have better-quality advice available, for example, from the Council of Economic Advisers or the Office of Management and Budget? Do other factors cut in favor of independence of the agency?

Section Nine. Limitations of Law as an Administrative-Regulatory Instrument

Limitations are always relative to aims. The major aim of FCC regulation of radio and TV broadcasting, stated generally, is to enhance the overall quality of what listeners and viewers may hear and see. No one doubts that FCC regulation of the electromagnetic spectrum by assigning frequencies to individual radio and TV stations advances that aim. But does FCC regulation of program content equally advance it—and is that regulation consistent with other social and constitutional values?

One enduring limitation of the administrative-regulatory mode is that pursuit of one regulatory end may undesirably interfere with fulfillment of other, more fundamental social ends. Thus, FCC regulation of program content, through license granting and renewal and through the fairness doctrine, may chill freedom of expression by broadcasters. What is the proper balance between the goals of regulation and potential infringement of First Amendment values?

A related problem of all regulation is that it involves centralized decision making. Through regulation the government determines social values (e.g., desirable program content) and pronounces them to the citizenry. Reliance on the market, if it could be made to work, involves decentralized decision making and arguably results in choices more closely approximating the true desires of the citizenry.

Finally, an administrative-regulatory program, once in place, is not easy to dismantle or curtail—even if technological, political, or other changes remove or modify its original raison d'être. Why?

These three limitations of the administrative-regulatory process—unwanted side effects, the costliness of giving up the market, and the inertia of entrenched regulatory programs—have fueled the deregulation movement. The deregulators, who come from both political parties, want to dismantle major parts of the administrative-regulatory structure that grew up in the 1930s and continued to expand thereafter. Airline deregulation has been perhaps the most visible example. Until its demise early in 1985, the Civil Aeronautics Board (CAB) was deeply enmeshed in regulating rates charged and routes flown by all commercial airlines in the country. In the Airline Deregulation Act of 1978, Pub.L. No. 95–504, 92 Stat. 1705, Congress enacted sweeping reforms that abolished the CAB and left airline rates and routes to be determined largely by competition in the marketplace.

Since 1981 the FCC itself has spearheaded deregulation in the communications field. It first deregulated radio. In 1976, after following "notice and comment" procedures, the FCC issued a policy statement announcing that in radio license renewal and transfer proceedings, it would no longer review past and proposed changes in entertainment format (e.g., a change from classical to rock music). It would rely instead upon the market to ensure entertainment diversity, because the market had already produced bewildering diversity in entertainment formats, would produce variety within a given format as well as variety in kinds of formats, and would respond more flexibly and quickly to changing tastes than could the government.[f] The Supreme Court upheld the change in FCC v. WNCN Listeners Guild, 450 U.S. 582, 101 S.Ct. 1266 (1981). In 1981 the FCC adopted even more sweeping changes by dropping its previous guidelines that had (1) required stations to carry a certain percentage of nonentertainment programs; (2) limited stations in the number of commercial minutes per hour; and (3) required stations to determine community interests through polls, interviews, demographic data, and so on.[g] The court of appeals overturned only the FCC's effort, in this set of changes, to eliminate the program log requirement, under which a station must list the name, category, source, and time of each program broadcast. Office of Communication of the United Church of Christ v. FCC, 707 F.2d 1413 (D.C.Cir.1983), on remand, In re Deregulation of Radio, 96 F.C.C.2d 930 (1984).

Later in 1981, the commission included television in its deregulatory program. For both radio and TV, it changed its license renewal process by substituting a postcard application for the prior lengthy form that had inquired elaborately into the station's programming. A station must still, however, maintain a public file with information about its assessment of community needs, its promises to meet those needs, and its actual broadcasting performance.[h] In 1984 the commission extended to commercial television its earlier deregulation of radio (e.g., abolition of programming and commercial guidelines).[i]

What, then, should be the fate of the fairness doctrine? In August 1985 the five-member FCC unanimously adopted a report favoring abolition of the fairness doctrine but stopping short of actually ordering its abolition. The following excerpts begin with a summary of the report's conclusions, followed by portions of the report that support those conclusions.

FCC, GENERAL FAIRNESS DOCTRINE OBLIGATIONS OF BROADCAST LICENSEES [FAIRNESS DOCTRINE REPORT]

50 Fed.Reg. 35,418 (1985).

Summary

137. We believe the fairness doctrine is an unnecessary and detrimental regulatory mechanism. While we recognize that the fairness doctrine has been a central tenet of broadcast regulation for more than fifty years, we believe that we have a statutorily mandated duty to reassess the

---

f. In re Development of Policy re: Changes in the Entertainment Formats of Broadcast Stations, 60 F.C.C.2d 858 (1976), reconsideration denied, 66 F.C.C.2d 78 (1977).

g. In re Deregulation of Radio, 84 F.C.C.2d 968, clarified, 87 F.C.C.2d 797 (1981).

h. In re Revision of Applications for Renewal of License of Commercial and Noncommercial AM, FM, and Television Licensees, 87 F.C.C.2d 1127 (1981). This action was upheld in Black Citizens For a Fair Media v. FCC, 719 F.2d 407 (D.C.Cir.1983), cert. denied, 104 S.Ct. 3545 (1984).

i. In re Revision of Programming and Commercialization Policies, Ascertainment Requirements, and Program Log Requirements for Commercial Television Stations, 98 F.C.C.2d 1076 (1984).

propriety of even long standing policies in light of changes in the broadcast marketplace and evidence that the policy may not further the public interest.   After careful evaluation of the evidence of record, our experience in enforcing the fairness doctrine, and fundamental constitutional principles, we find that the fairness doctrine disserves the public interest.

138.   Three factors form the basis for this determination.   First, in recent years there has been a significant increase in the number and types of information sources.   As a consequence, we believe that the public has access to a multitude of viewpoints without the need or danger of regulatory intervention.

139.   Second, the evidence in this proceeding demonstrates that the fairness doctrine in operation thwarts the laudatory purpose it is designed to promote.   Instead of furthering the discussion of public issues, the fairness doctrine inhibits broadcasters from presenting controversial issues of public importance.   As a consequence, broadcasters are burdened with counterproductive regulatory restraints and the public is deprived of a marketplace of ideas unencumbered by the hand of government.

140.   Third, the restrictions on the journalistic freedoms of broadcasters resulting from enforcement of the fairness doctrine contravene fundamental constitutional principles, accord a dangerous opportunity for governmental abuse and impose unnecessary economic costs on both the broadcasters and the Commission.   Finally, we believe the record in this proceeding raises significant issues regarding the constitutionality of the fairness doctrine in light of First Amendment concerns.

[The excerpts that follow appear earlier in the report than the summary just quoted and are part of the basis for the FCC's conclusions stated in the summary.   The FCC's discussion of the constitutionality of the fairness doctrine has been omitted.]

The Record Demonstrates that the Fairness Doctrine Causes Broadcasters to Restrict Their Coverage of Controversial Issues

42.   The record reflects that, in operation, the fairness doctrine—in stark contravention of its purpose—operates as a pervasive and significant impediment to the broadcasting of controversial issues of public importance. . . . We recognize that the first prong of the fairness doctrine requires licensees to present controversial issues of public importance to their viewers and listeners; as a consequence, we do not believe that the fear of fairness doctrine obligations typically results in a systematic avoidance of all controversial issues by broadcasters.   The record reflects, however, that the intrusion by government into the editorial decisions of broadcast journalists occasioned by fairness doctrine requirements overall lessens the flow of diverse viewpoints to the public to the detriment of the broadcasters and the public alike.

43.   Journalists who have worked in both the broadcast and print media have testified that the very existence of the fairness doctrine creates a climate of timidity and fear, unexperienced by print journalists, that is antithetical to journalistic freedom.   The inhibitions resulting from

the interjection of a ubiquitous and brooding governmental presence into the editorial decisionmaking process is vividly described by Mr. Dan Rather, Managing Editor and Anchor of CBS News, as follows:

> When I was a young reporter, I worked briefly for wire services, small radio stations, and newspapers, and I finally settled into a job at a large radio station owned by the Houston Chronicle. Almost immediately on starting work in that station's newsroom, I became aware of a concern which I had previously barely known existed—the FCC. The journalists at the Chronicle did not worry about it; those at the radio station did. Not only the station manager but the newspeople as well were very much aware of this Government presence looking over their shoulders. I can recall newsroom conversations about what the FCC implications of broadcasting a particular report would be. Once a newsperson has to stop and consider what a Government agency will think of something he or she wants to put on the air, an invaluable element of freedom has been lost.

44. The record reflects that broadcasters from television network anchors to small radio station journalists perceive the fairness doctrine to operate as a demonstrable deterrent in the coverage of controversial issues. Indeed, the record is replete with descriptions from broadcasters who have candidly recounted specific instances in which they decided not to air controversial matters of public importance because such broadcasts might trigger fairness doctrine obligations. . . .

45. [For example,] after work had begun in the preparation of a series on religious cults, the manager of a Southern California radio station decided that the series would not be broadcast. The decision to cancel this series was not based upon the editorial judgment of the broadcaster but rather upon an assessment of the legal and personnel costs associated with defending a possible fairness doctrine complaint. . . . Another example in the record is the cancellation of a series on the B'nai B'rith by a Pennsylvania radio station. The series was not broadcast because the licensee felt that it could not afford the personnel time to respond to the complaints, the broadcast time to provide responsive programming or the potential legal fees resulting from complaints by perceived extremist groups. . . .

46. Equally or perhaps even more disturbing than the self-censorship of individual broadcasts is the fact that the avoidance of fairness doctrine burdens has precipitated specific "policies" on the part of broadcast stations which have the direct effect of diminishing, on a routine basis, the amount of controversial material presented to the public on broadcast stations. For example, the owner of a broadcast station and two newspapers regularly prints editorials in his newspapers but, inhibited by regulatory restrictions, is reluctant to repeat the same editorials on his radio station. Similarly, the Meredith Corporation acknowledges that one of its television stations has chosen "not to editorialize on matters of public importance, because of its concern that it does not have the resources necessary to seek out and provide exposure to opposing viewpoints in all instances." Unfortunately, the policies of these stations are not atypical.

In fact, a survey conducted by NAB [National Association of Broadcasters] in 1982 found that only 45 percent of responding stations had presented editorials in the preceding two years.   .   .   .

47.   Policies of stations that restrict public issue programming are not limited to editorials; they extend to the airing of political advertisements. For example, as a direct result of fairness doctrine obligations, CBS acknowledges that its owned and operated stations, as a general matter, limit the amount of time they will sell both to persons seeking to place advertisements relating to ballot propositions and to political parties attempting to purchase broadcast time outside of campaign periods.   CBS states that many of the television stations in four of the five markets in which those stations operate also either refuse or severely limit the sale of time for ballot proposition advertising.   .   .   .

49.   The most compelling evidence of the existence of a "chilling effect" with respect to ballot advertising is presented in the Comments of the Public Media Center ("PMC"), an organization which .   .   . is actively involved in prosecuting complaints under the fairness doctrine.   .   .   .

50.   .   .   . For example, PMC describes the successful invocation of the fairness doctrine by [an] anti-smoking group in order to pressure broadcasters into refusing to sell advertising time to their opponents. PMC recounts that the anti-smoking group:

> .   .   . mailed "pre-emptive" letters to every local broadcast station, remarking on the upcoming vote and asking to be notified as soon as the tobacco industry bought airtime.   .   .   . *[T]en Miami stations, seeking to avoid [the group's] predictable demands, simply refused to sell time to the industry front.*

As a consequence, the public was denied information on a matter of important local concern.   .   .   .

60.   Some parties assert that any inhibiting effect of the fairness doctrine is not attributable to the actual requirements of the doctrine itself but rather to the misperception of broadcasters as to their precise obligations under the doctrine.   These commenters contend that broadcasters are not inhibited by the fear of incurring fairness doctrine obligations unless regulatory requirements in fact attach to their programming. However, broadcasters are not lawyers.   A broadcaster may be uncertain as to the precise boundaries of our detailed and complex regulatory scheme or may be uncertain as to whether he or she will be able to convince us, in the course of fairness doctrine litigation, that the station's overall programming complies with our regulatory requirements.   As a consequence, a broadcaster, in order to avoid even the possibility of litigation, may be deterred from airing material even though the Commission, after hearing all the evidence, would have concluded that the program did not trigger fairness doctrine obligations.   Indeed, the uncertainty as to whether or not a broadcast contains information which rises to the level of a controversial issue of public importance may itself have an inhibiting effect.   In any event, it is the fact of deterrence—not whether or not the Commission, in making an adjudicatory determination

on the substantive law would in fact find a fairness doctrine obligation—which is relevant in ascertaining the existence of a chilling effect. . . .

The Administration of the Fairness Doctrine Operates to Inhibit the Expression of Unorthodox Opinions

.   .   .   .

71. . . . [O]ur own administative enforcement of the doctrine provides some support for the contention that some "controversial viewpoint[s] [are] being screened out in favor of the dreary blandness of a more acceptable opinion." [167]   Broadcasters who have been denied or threatened with a denial of the renewal of their licenses due to fairness doctrine violations have generally not been those which have provided only minimal coverage of controversial and important public issues.   Indeed, some licensees that we have not renewed or threatened with non-renewal have presented controversial issue programming far in excess of that aired by the typical licensee.   In a number of situations it was the licenses of broadcasters who aired opinions which many in society found to be abhorrent or extreme which were placed in jeopardy due to allegations of fairness doctrine violations. . . . [W]e are extremely concerned over the potential of the fairness doctrine, in operation, to interject the government, even unintentionally, into the position of favoring one type of opinion over another. . . .

Need for the Fairness Doctrine in Light of the Increase in the Amount and Type of Information Sources in the Marketplace

81. . . . The Commission's last assessment of the information marketplace, and its necessary relationship to the legal and policy underpinnings of the fairness doctrine, occurred in 1974.   At that time the Commission concluded:

> The effective development of an electronic medium with an abundance of channels through the use of cable or otherwise is still very much a thing of the future. *For the present,* we do not believe that it would be appropriate—or even permissible—for a government agency charged with the allocation of the *channels now available* to ignore the legitimate First Amendment interests of the public.   (*emphasis added*)

82.   More than a decade has passed since this examination.   During this time, we have witnessed explosive growth in various communications technologies.   We find the information marketplace of today different from that which existed in 1974, as many of the "future" electronic technologies have now become contributors to the marketplace of ideas.   As will be discussed below, the growth of traditional broadcast facilities, as well as the development of new electronic information technologies, provides the public with suitable access to the marketplace of ideas so as to render the fairness doctrine unnecessary. . . .

167.   Brandywine-Main Line Radio, Inc. v. FCC, 473 F.2d [16, 78 (D.C.Cir.1972) (Bazelon, C.J., dissenting), cert. denied, 412 U.S. 922, 93 S.Ct. 2731 (1973)].

Broadcasting

94. The growth and development of radio broadcasting since the inception of the fairness doctrine has been dramatic. The total number of radio stations has increased by 280 percent since the 1949 [Editorializing] Report. Moreover, there has been a 48 percent increase in the number of radio stations since the Supreme Court's decision in *Red Lion* and a 30 percent increase since the Commission's 1974 Fairness Report. During this period the most significant growth occurred in the FM service where there has been a 113 percent increase since *Red Lion* and a 60 percent increase since our 1974 Fairness Report.

Number of Radio Stations

	1949	1969	1974	1985
AM	1877	4265	4407	4787
FM	687	2330	3094	4979
Total	2564	6595	7501	9766

95. Of particular significance is the fact that the number of radio voices available in each local market has grown. In this regard, we note that competition resulting from an increase in the number of radio outlets was the primary factor in our decision to deregulate the program guidelines, commercial limitations and formal ascertainment requirements for commercial radio. . . .

97. Equally significant has been the dynamic growth of over-the-air television broadcasting. The statistics presented below show the development of this medium.

Number of Television Stations

	1949	1969	1974	1985
VFH (Total)	51	577	605	654
Commercial	—	499	513	541
Educational	—	78	92	113
UHF (Total)	0	`260	333	554
Commerical	0	163	184	369
Educational	0	97	149	185
Total	51	837	938	1208

98. As the above data demonstrate, there has been a 44.3 percent increase in the overall number of television stations since the Supreme Court's decision in *Red Lion Broadcasting*. This represents a 13.3 percent increase in VHF stations and a dramatic 113 percent increase in UHF stations. Television growth since the Commission's 1974 Fairness Report has also been significant, amounting to a 28 percent increase in the overall number of television stations with a 66.4 percent increase in UHF stations.

99. The continued growth in television broadcasting has led directly to an increase in signal availability in local markets.

Stations Receivable per TV Household

Number of Stations Receivable

	1–4	5–6	7–8	9–10	11–14	15–19	20+
1984	4%	11%	21%	22%	24%	15%	3%
1972	17%	22%	30%	31%	—	—	—
1964	41%	33%	18%	8%	—	—	—

As of 1984, 96 percent of the television households received five or more television signals. This figure represents a significant increase in actual signal availability since 1972, where only 83 percent of the television households received five or more signals. The increase is even more dramatic compared to 1964 when only 59 percent of television households were capable of receiving 5 or more stations. Today, only 4 percent of the television households receive fewer than five signals. These statistics demonstrate a significant growth in signal availability throughout the country. . . .

Substitute Electronic Technologies

105. In addition to traditional over-the-air television and radio broadcasting, we find that there exist numerous alternative electronic technologies making a significant contribution to the marketplace of ideas. . . . We believe that in the context of this proceeding consideration should be given to the contributions of cable television, low power television (LPTV), multichannel multipoint distribution service (MMDS), video cassette recorder (VCR), satellite master antenna systems (SMATV) and other electronic media including recent advancements in satellite technology.

106. Universally recognized as a significant non-over-the-air electronic medium, cable television has developed from a means of improving reception into a major industry providing video programming. . . . As of 1985 there are 6,600 operating cable systems in 18,500 communities with approximately 1,600 franchises that have been approved but not built. According to recent A.C. Neilson estimates, U.S. cable households now number 38,673,270 placing national cable penetration at 43.3% of all television households. In comparative terms, the number of cable systems in operation has increased 195 percent since *Red Lion* and 111 percent since the Commission's 1974 Fairness Report. Growth in subscribership amounts to an astronomical 975 percent since the *Red Lion* decision and 345 percent increase since the 1974 Fairness Report. Moreover, cable television will continue to expand in the future. . . .

110. Another developing voice in the information services market is Low Power Television (LPTV). These stations are over-the-air television broadcast facilities, generally limited to 10 watts for VHF and 1,000 watts for UHF stations. [As such, the broadcasts have very limited range and do not interfere with standard high-power television signals.] These facilities were nonexistent at the time of the *Red Lion* decision and our 1974 Fairness Report. Stations of this power were translators, limited to the rebroadcast of signals from full service stations. In 1982, the Commission authorized these stations to originate programming. There are currently 126 licensed low power UHF stations and 215 low power VHF

stations. It is predicted that this source will eventually add an additional 4000 television stations to the marketplace. . . .

112. At the time of the 1974 Fairness Report, multipoint distribution service (MDS) was just beginning to develop as a communications service. Used primarily to provide subscription programming via microwave transmissions, there were approximately 438,578 MDS subscribers out of a potential audience of 13.1 million at the end of 1984. . . .

113. . . . The advantage of this service is that construction costs and time delays are greatly reduced, relative to cable, since wiring to a headend is not necessary. Estimates of subscribership growth by 1990 range between 6 to 12 million subscribers.

114. Satellite Master Antenna Systems (SMATV) are similar to cable systems except that they are built in individual apartment complexes, condominiums, hotels and trailer parks. These "private" cable systems did not exist at the time of the *Red Lion* decision or our 1974 Fairness Report. . . . According to the National Satellite Cable Association about 600,000 to 800,000 homes have been wired with this service. Because of lower capital and construction costs, SMATV systems have become increasingly popular in both rural and urban areas that are currently unserved by cable television.

115. Sales of video cassette recorders continue to have a major impact on the information marketplace. As with many other new technologies, VCR's were not available at the time of the 1974 Fairness Report. The impact of this technology on other electronic video technologies has been significant. By the end of 1985 it is estimated that there will be 23.3 million VCR homes representing 27.4 percent of all TV households. A more recent study of VCR penetration reported that sales are running about one million a month and will reach . . . penetration of one third of all homes by early 1986. . . . Further estimates place VCR usage at 67.9 million homes representing 68 percent of all television households by 1990.

116. We take particular note of the development of video recordings as a means of disseminating issue related video programming. We find this to be a significant development in the information marketplace. To the extent VCR's do not utilize spectrum, anyone who desires to communicate by television may do so by means of a VCR. In this regard, we agree with NBC that VCR's have the potential to become the "electronic handbills" or indeed even the electronic newspaper of the future. Moreover, our own empirical analysis of the relationship between VCR's and television reveals that a VCR is both a substitute and a complement to over-the-air and cable television. In other words, VCR's act not only as a means of time shifting programming, but also as an independent source of programming. Moreover, the ability to reschedule video programming gives viewers the opportunity to acquire additional information from other sources. By time shifting, viewers are able to reallocate their time so as to increase the number of potential viewing options. We believe that the flexibility afforded the public by VCR's represents an important qualitative development in the information services marketplace. . . .

Print Media

123. . . . [T]he overall number of broadcast facilities exceeds the total number of daily newspapers in the United States. This does not mean, however, that the print media is not a significant contributor to the information marketplace. As of 1984, there were 1,701 daily newspapers in the country. [The commission also noted the total number of weekly and monthly newspapers and magazines increased from 6,960 in 1950 to 10,688 in 1982.] . . .

CONCLUSION

[In omitted passages the FCC repeated its conclusion that the fairness doctrine was unnecessary and detrimental.]

176. Notwithstanding these conclusions, we have decided not to eliminate the fairness doctrine at this time. The doctrine has been a long-standing administrative policy and a central tenet of broadcast regulation in which Congress has shown a strong although often ambivalent interest. Indeed, while Congress has not yet chosen to eliminate the doctrine legislatively, several members of Congress have recently sponsored bills seeking to abolish the fairness doctrine and its related policies. Congress also has held hearings to determine whether or not it should enact legislation to eliminate the doctrine. In addition, we recognize that the United States Supreme Court in FCC v. League of Women Voters of California [, 104 S.Ct. 3106 (1984),] has similarly demonstrated an interest in our examination of the constitutional and policy implications underlying the fairness doctrine. Because of the intense Congressional interest in the fairness doctrine and the pendency of legislative proposals, we have determined that it would be inappropriate at this time to eliminate the fairness doctrine. Given our decision to defer to Congress on this matter, we also believe that it would be inappropriate for us to act on the various proposals to modify or restrict the scope of the fairness doctrine. It is also important to emphasize that we will continue to administer and enforce the fairness doctrine obligations of broadcasters and to underscore our expectation that broadcast licensees will continue to satisfy these requirements.

––––––––

Comments and Questions

1. In the case mentioned by the FCC in its ultimate conclusion, the Supreme Court said in a footnote:

The prevailing rationale for broadcast regulation based on spectrum scarcity has come under increasing criticism in recent years. Critics, including the incumbent Chairman of the FCC, charge that with the advent of cable and satellite television technology, communities now have access to such a wide variety of stations that the scarcity doctrine is obsolete. See, e.g., Fowler & Brenner, A Marketplace Approach to Broadcast Regulation, 60 Tex.L.Rev. 207, 221–226 (1982). We are not prepared, however, to reconsider our long-standing approach without some signal from Congress or the

FCC that technological developments have advanced so far that some revision of the system of broadcast regulation may be required.

FCC v. League of Women Voters, 104 S.Ct. 3106, 3116 n.11 (1984). Has the signal been given?

2. Why did the FCC not simply order the fairness doctrine abolished? Recall that Congress amended § 315 of the Federal Communications Act in 1959 to include reference to the fairness doctrine in the act for the first time. The reference was added at the end of a provision excluding bona fide news coverage from the equal time requirements (to be distinguished from the fairness doctrine) as follows:

Appearance by a legally qualified candidate on any—

    (1) bona fide newscast,

    (2) bona fide news interview,

    (3) bona fide news documentary (if the appearance of the candidate is incidental to the presentation of the subject or subjects covered by the news documentary), or

    (4) on-the-spot coverage of bona fide news events (including but not limited to political conventions and activities incidental thereto),

shall not be deemed to be use of a broadcasting station within the meaning of this subsection. Nothing in the foregoing sentence shall be construed as relieving broadcasters, in connection with the presentation of newscasts, news interviews, news documentaries, and on-the-spot coverage of news events, from the obligation imposed upon them under this Act to operate in the public interest and to afford reasonable opportunity for the discussion of conflicting views on issues of public importance.

47 U.S.C. § 315(a). How does this affect your answer?

3. Is it appropriate for an agency entrusted with enforcement of the fairness doctrine to issue a report castigating the doctrine as "an unnecessary and detrimental regulatory mechanism"?

4. For a view opposed to that of the FCC concerning the fairness doctrine, consider Mitchell, Book Review, 37 Fed.Com.L.J. 377 (1985) (reviewing F. Rowan, Broadcast Fairness: Doctrine, Practice, Prospects (1984)). Mr. Mitchell argues that the fairness doctrine has functioned essentially as a "fail safe" mechanism, affecting only the most egregious situations: "If there is to be anything left after [deregulation] runs its course, it would seem it should be this last resort protection for the public against stations which consistently exclude from the air views with which their owners disagree, exult in racial or religious bigotry or blatantly use their facilities to obtain the election of a favored candidate." Id. at 383. Mr. Mitchell, unpersuaded by the argument that we now have a plentitude of broadcast outlets, gives an example of a case for which he thinks the fairness doctrine is needed: "[I]n Dodge City, Kansas, population 18,001, there are 3 FM radio stations, one of which, KTTL, has broadcast hour upon hour of programs described as being 'devoted to the stimulation of racial and religious bias, prejudice and bigotry, using the most crude, derogatory, defamatory and incendiary rhetoric.' [Citing papers filed by petitioners seeking to have the FCC deny a license renewal application.]ʲ As long as there are persons in Dodge City who would use the KTTL frequency for other purposes were it available, there seems good reason why KTTL should at least be required to air some contrasting views on the controversial issues raised by its programming and to provide time for a response by those it

---

    j. Another source says that KTTL broadcast such statements as "If a Jew comes near you, run a sword through him" and "Blacks and brown[s] are the enemy. Jesus Christ is a white man's God." Minow, Being Fair to the Fairness Doctrine, N.Y. Times, Aug. 27, 1985, at A23, col. 3.

has attacked." Id. at 384. To support his point about the mild nature of the fairness doctrine as generally enforced, Mr. Mitchell notes that when the FCC in October 1984 found a Syracuse, New York, TV station in violation of the fairness doctrine (by unbalanced broadcast of advertisements in favor of constructing a particular nuclear plant for New York, see Syracuse Peace Council v. WTVH, 99 F.C.C.2d 1389 (1984)), it was the first time it had made such a finding in more than five years. Furthermore, the only action the FCC took was to ask the station how it proposed to rectify the situation in its future programming.[k] Mitchell concludes: "The public no more wishes to give totally unfettered power over the airwaves to ABC, CBS, Metromedia, or KTTL than it does to the President of the United States or the Chairman of the FCC. While it is far from perfect, the fairness doctrine does provide a fulcrum for . . . balancing [the First Amendment interests of the public and of broadcasters]." Id. at 385–86. Do you agree with Mr. Mitchell or the FCC?

5. Consider also the following response, from a former FCC chairman, to the FCC's argument that broadcast channels and other information sources are no longer so scarce as to require the fairness doctrine:

> The argument is disingenuous. In the last few years, [t]he Washington Star, [t]he Chicago Daily News and [t]he Philadelphia Bulletin all went out of business. No new newspapers took their place. By contrast, when the F.C.C. made RKO's channels available for competitive application, it quickly got 172 applications, each applicant arguing, "Give the license to me, and turn down the other 171." And when the communications commission decided to permit new low-power television stations, it was inundated by almost 14,000 applications.
>
> The test of scarcity cannot be measured by the number of newspapers. The proper test is the number of citizens who want a broadcast license and are unable to obtain one. At that point, a decision must be made as to who is to be allowed, and who denied, the exclusive license to use the channels. Scarcity still exists when channels are not available to all. And as long as scarcity exists, the need for some measure of regulation will exist.

Minow, Being Fair to the Fairness Doctrine, N.Y. Times, Aug. 27, 1985, at A23, col. 3.

6. In its 1974 Fairness Report, the FCC expressly relied upon the First Amendment interests of the public to hear contrasting viewpoints on important issues as a valid reason for the fairness doctrine. Has the FCC in its August 1985 report elevated the broadcasters' First Amendment rights over those of the public? Is this another example of industry capture of an agency?

7. If you favor retention of the fairness doctrine, would you alter it? If so, would you extend it to the print media?

8. If you favor abolition of the fairness doctrine, would you go further and limit the role of the FCC to that of traffic controller regulating only signal interference, leaving all program content to be decided by competition in the marketplace? If so, how would you accomplish that: by action of agency, legislature, or court? How would you decide who gets a license to broadcast, and what would you do about renewals?

---

k. The fairness doctrine is not as insignificant on the FCC agenda, however, as this fact might imply. In its August 1985 report, the FCC states that in 1984 its staff received 6,787 inquiries and complaints regarding the fairness doctrine. Fairness Doctrine Report, 50 Fed. Reg. 35,418, at para. 78 n.188 (1985). Of these, however, typically only very few would be forwarded to a station for comment.

Section Ten.   Bibliography

1. *General.* S. Breyer, Regulation and Its Reform (1982); R. Pierce, S. Shapiro & P. Verkuil, Administrative Law and Process (1985).

2. *Administrative-Regulatory Techniques.* S. Breyer & R. Stewart, Administrative Law and Regulatory Policy 3–6, 20–22 (2d ed. 1985).

3. *Authorized Makers of Administrative-Regulatory Law and Their Appropriate Collaborative Roles.* K. Davis, Discretionary Justice: A Preliminary Inquiry (1969); T. Lowi, The End of Liberalism: Ideology, Policy, and the Crisis of Public Authority (2d ed. 1979); Aronson, Gellhorn & Robinson, A Theory of Legislative Delegation, 68 Cornell L.Rev. 1 (1982); Shapiro, The Choice of Rulemaking or Adjudication in the Development of Administrative Policy, 78 Harv.L.Rev. 921 (1965); Stewart, The Reformation of American Administrative Law, 88 Harv.L. Rev. 1669 (1975).

4. *Structures and Processes for Applying Administrative-Regulatory Law and Techniques.* S. Besen, T. Krattenmaker, A. Metzger & J. Woodbury, Misregulating Television: Network Dominance and the FCC (1985); F. Friendly, The Good Guys, The Bad Guys, and the First Amendment: Free Speech vs. Fairness in Broadcasting (1976); D. Gillmor & J. Barron, Mass Communication Law (4th ed. 1984); D. Ginsburg, Regulation of Broadcasting (1979).

5. *Necessity for and Nature of Coercive Power.* B. Schwartz, Administrative Law 91–141 (1984); Ball & Friedman, Use of Criminal Sanctions in the Enforcement of Economic Legislation—A Sociological View, 17 Stan.L.Rev. 197 (1965); Jaffe, The Judicial Enforcement of Administrative Orders, 76 Harv.L.Rev. 865 (1963); Kovel, A Case for Civil Penalties: Air Pollution Control, 46 J.Urb.L. 153 (1969).

6. *Roles of Private Citizens and Their Lawyers.* Public Participation in Federal Agency Proceedings: Hearings on S. 2715 Before the Subcomm. on Administrative Practice and Procedure of the Senate Comm. on the Judiciary, 94th Cong., 2d Sess. (1976); Bardach & Kagan, Law and Social Regulation, in Social Regulation: Strategies for Reform 237–66 (E. Bardach & R. Kagan eds. 1982); Stewart, The Reformation of American Administrative Law, 88 Harv.L. Rev. 1669 (1975); Tobias, Of Public Funds and Public Participation: Resolving the Issue of Agency Authority to Reimburse Public Participants in Administrative Proceedings, 82 Colum.L.Rev. 906 (1982); Note, Federal Agency Assistance to Impecunious Intervenors, 88 Harv.L.Rev. 1815 (1975).

7. *Process Values.* W. Gellhorn, C. Byse & P. Strauss, Administrative Law 147–419 (7th ed. 1979); Cramton, A Comment on Trial-Type Hearings in Nuclear Power Plant Siting, 58 Va.L.Rev. 585 (1972).

8. *Improving the Administrative-Regulatory Instrument.* S. Breyer, Regulation and Its Reform (1982); Social Regulation: Strategies for Reform (E. Bardach & R. Kagan eds. 1982); Symposium: Presidential Intervention in Administrative Rulemaking, 56 Tul. L. Rev. 811 (1982).

9. *Limitations of Law as an Administrative-Regulatory Instrument.* E. Bardach & R. Kagan, Going by the Book: The Problem of Regulatory Unreasonableness (1982); S. Breyer & R. Stewart, Administrative Law and Regulatory Policy 453–66 (2d ed. 1985); S. Tolchin & M. Tolchin, Dismantling America: The Rush to Deregulate (1983).

CHAPTER FOUR

Law as an Instrument for Organizing Conferral of Public Benefits

Yet in those great state services which increase every day—educational, the poor law, public works, lighting, the postal, telegraph, and telephone systems, the railways—the state intervenes . . . in a manner that has to be . . . ordered by a system of public law.

LÉON DUGUIT

Section One. Introduction
(Pedagogic Vehicles Drawn Mainly from Public Education Law)

Taxation and government spending in the name of the public are the very stuff of modern government in large, highly industrialized nations. At every level, government has authority to raise money through taxes and other charges, and to appropriate that money for various public purposes. Government spends money to build roads, airports, hospitals, dams, courtrooms, and other public structures, to restore waterfronts, historic buildings, and decaying urban mass transit systems, to make health care and other forms of assistance available to those who need help, to provide for public education, parks, museums, police protection, mail delivery, and national defense, and to promote the arts, scientific research, family farms, home ownership, and other purposes deemed in the public interest. Controversy rages over some of these objects of government spending, where the money should come from, how much should be spent, what level of government should spend it, and what forms the benefits should take. Debate over the form and substance of benefit conferral is particularly lively now, for we have entered an era of retrenchment and skepticism about the capacity of government to satisfy some social goals through public spending. Nevertheless, the United States remains firmly committed to an enormous number of programs of public-benefit conferral. We have grown comfortable with the idea of big government, big taxes, and big spending—the so-called welfare state.

Government decisions about benefit conferral involve political actors responding to political pressures from voters, lobbyists, and others concerned with tax and spending decisions. So fundamental is politics to the process of setting spending priorities and allocating tax burdens, that legal ordering—which involves the development of impersonal rules of broad applicability to guide program development and administration—appears insignificant to this form of governmental activity. Does public-benefit conferral have a significant legal dimension, as the administrative-regulatory, the penal-corrective, and the grievance-remedial modes clearly do? Or should benefit conferral be analyzed solely or primarily in terms of pressure groups, political alignments, and political influences affecting legislators and government officials?

To answer this question, consider the kinds of questions that must be resolved if a system of benefit conferral is to be effective and efficient. Assume, for example, that a county legislature decides to feed the poor within its borders. Who qualifies as poor? What type of food will be provided? Where will this food come from? Who will administer the program? Who will bear the cost? Without rules that respond to these issues, a program cannot even get under way.

Rules are also bound to play an important role in the day-to-day administration of a program of public-benefit conferral. Think about the disputes that are sure to arise over both the imposition of burdens and the availability of benefits—disputes that would be much harder to resolve without rules as a point of reference and established processes for deciding what those rules mean. Rules also serve a prophylactic function, offering guidance to officials charged with implementing programs. Equity and fairness in the allocation of burdens and benefits, widely regarded as important goals in any governmental activity in our society, will be much easier to achieve if rules exist to limit ad hoc decision making and to discourage official whim and caprice.

Legal ordering also plays an important role in maintaining the very political process that sets programs for benefit conferral in motion. Electoral laws, rules that differentiate and define legislative and executive functions, and the constitutional guarantees that limit the reach of governmental power—all help connect public wants and public spending, and thus maintain ours as a democratic nation.

Section Two. Public-Benefit Techniques

The benefits that governments confer take a variety of forms. Simple payment of money is one form, and it has been thought appropriate for welfare assistance, farm subsidies, disability benefits, and old-age pensions. Construction of a public facility is another type of benefit; examples are highways, bridges, stadiums, public auditoriums, and marinas. Continuing rendition of a service, such as provision of electricity or public-school instruction, is still another form of public-benefit conferral. All of these are direct forms of government spending. Benefit conferral can be indirect, too, as when government gives tax breaks for home ownership or capital investment or wetlands preservation. Government also benefits groups and individuals indirectly when it guarantees, subsidizes, or underwrites loans, bank deposits, and insurance. Exemptions from what would otherwise be a legal duty, say, military service, are indirect benefits. So are restrictions on competitors, such as tariffs and import quotas. The fact that a benefit is indirect does not reduce its significance to those who receive it.

The way government distributes goods depends to a certain extent on what is to be conferred and to whom. Property tax deductions, for example, can do little to help destitute people get adequate medical care, for the very poor seldom own taxable property. Government is also limited by its own prior decisions regarding benefit conferral. For one thing, the current beneficiaries of government spending programs, whether tobacco growers or defense contractors, can be expected to fight changes in the form of benefit conferral if they perceive new standards as detrimental to their interests. Change can be difficult to effect even when the beneficiaries remain the same, because prior capital commitments limit government's flexibility. In 1971, for example, Congress passed legislation designed to make mail delivery more efficient and cost-effective. The new legislation created a government corporation for this purpose, on the theory that this form of organization would allow the service to be managed in a more businesslike way than it had been as a federal department under direct congressional control. The efforts of the postal system's new managers to modernize mail delivery were stymied at first, however, by the antiquated, labor-intensive, patronage-oriented system they had inherited:

> Clerks still stood before the familiar pigeonhole cases, sorting letters by hand at the rate of about thirty a minute. Antiquated facilities hindered mechanization; weak floors would not support heavy machinery, low ceilings ruled out overhead conveyor systems, and vertical buildings layouts defied any attempt at instituting more efficient horizontal mail-flow systems.

Tierney, Government Corporations and Managing the Public's Business, 99 Pol.Sci.Q. 73, 89 (1984).

Despite such difficulties, experimentation and tinkering with techniques for benefit conferral are common in America. Sometimes the soaring costs of a program create pressure to adjust the means by which benefits are distributed. Proposed adjustments will reflect beliefs about the proper balance between government and market incentives that are dominant at the time. Consider, for example, the current popularity of market-oriented proposals for containing health-care costs, such as increased cost sharing and fixed dollar subsidies for specific health-care services. Sometimes even the success of a program can bring forth calls for changing benefit-conferral techniques. The success of the national park system in attracting visitors is a case in point. In 1983, 244 million people visited the national parks—enough to jam traffic, create long lines for campsites, disrupt wildlife, and eliminate the possibility of solitude at the height of the season in the more popular parks. If they are to achieve one of their primary purposes—relief from urban hassles—park officials must find some way to limit usage, whether by reducing campsites, turning away "excess" visitors, or closing certain sites to automobiles.

Even when the need for adjustment or change is not so obvious, the question of how benefits should be distributed is bound to be a salient political issue. Efficiency is a perennial concern whenever government spends money, even if costs are relatively stable. Economic analysis, a strong and growing field in policy studies, can help determine which distribution is most efficient, or optimal, given the goals of the program. Concerning the goals themselves, this type of analysis is more limited, according to economist Thomas Schelling:

> [E]conomic reasoning is better at helping to choose among ways to accomplish a distributional objective than at helping to choose objectives. It can help in minimizing the cost to the rich of doing something for the poor. And in case that doesn't interest you, economic reasoning can help to point out that it ought to!

Schelling, Economic Reasoning and the Ethics of Policy, 63 Pub.Interest 37, 53 (1981).

Questions about efficiency, important as they are, should not be our only concern when we consider distributive alternatives, however. The means government uses to confer benefits can foster equality among recipients or restrict it; techniques can be more or less intrusive; programs can delegate much or little to experts or other elites; they can discourage or encourage citizen participation; a program can foster the exercise of local or central authority. The same can be said of the financial burdens benefit conferral requires. Taxpayers, residents in the path of public-work projects, military recruits, and other cost bearers have reason to be concerned about the locus and direction of governmental authority to impose burdens. The fact that so many of us are cost bearers for government programs ensures that interest in the comparative advantages of various benefit-conferral techniques will be widespread.

Their significance suggests that we study distributive alternatives systematically, technique by technique. In the excerpt that follows, Lester Salamon suggests some dimensions along which such analysis should proceed. (Though he focuses on the federal level, most of his arguments apply across the board.)

———

SALAMON, RETHINKING PUBLIC MANAGEMENT: THIRD–PARTY GOVERNMENT AND THE CHANGING FORMS OF GOVERNMENT ACTION

29 Pub.Pol'y 255, 257–58, 260–62, 264–72 (1981).*

The need for greater attention to the tools and techniques of public action should be apparent to anyone who has looked closely at recent trends in Federal government activity and operations. While political rhetoric and a considerable body of academic research continue to picture the Federal government as a rapidly expanding behemoth growing disproportionally in both scope and size relative to the rest of the society in order to handle a steadily growing range of responsibilities, in fact something considerably more complex has been underway. For, while the range of Federal responsibilities has indeed increased dramatically, the relative size of the Federal enterprise, in terms of both budget and employment, has paradoxically remained relatively stable. Between 1954 and 1979, for example, the rate of growth of the Federal budget just barely exceeded that of the Gross National Product (GNP), so that the budget's share of the GNP increased only from 19.4 to 20.9%. Even more important, the rate of growth of Federal civilian employment lagged far behind the real growth of the budget, so that the number of Federal employees per 1000 people in the population registered a decline during this 25-year period of more than 10%.

What accounts for this paradox of relatively stable budgets and declining employment despite substantial growth in responsibilities is the dramatic change that has occurred in the forms of Federal action. For one thing, a major proliferation has taken place in the tools of government action, as the Federal government has turned increasingly to a wide range of new, or newly expanded, devices, e.g., loans, loan guarantees, insurance, social regulation, government corporations, many of which do not appear in the budget. In the process, moreover, a significant transformation has taken place in the way the Federal government goes about its business—a shift from direct to indirect or "third-party" government, from a situation in which the Federal government ran its own programs to one in which it increasingly relies on a wide variety of "third parties"—states, cities, special districts, banks, hospitals, manufacturers, and others—to carry out its purposes. . . .

This set of changes has profound implications for the character of democratic government and the management of public programs. In the first place, it raises serious questions of *accountability* because those who exercise public authority in these programs are only tangentially accountable to the elected officials who enact and oversee the programs. This is all the more troublesome, moreover, because many of the "third-party" implementers are especially touchy about the exercise of Federal oversight, creating pressures to restrict accountability to narrow, technical questions of fiscal control and administrative procedure and sidestep more value-laden issues of program results.

Closely related to these questions of accountability, moreover, are serious *issues of management.* . . .

Finally, these changes in the forms of government action have important implications for the *coordination* of government activities. . . .

What these comments suggest is that the failures of public action about which so much has been written may result less from the incompetence or malfeasance of government managers than from the tools we have required them to use and the curious ways we have required them to act. Under these circumstances, the improvement of government performance requires not simply better management, but a clearer understanding of the tools through which the government's business is performed. . . .

The central premise . . . suggested here is that different tools of government action have their own distinctive dynamics, their own "political economies," that affect the content of government action. This is so for much the same reasons that particular agencies and bureaus are now considered to have their own personalities and styles—because each instrument carries with it a substantial amount of "baggage" in the form of its own characteristic implementing institutions, standard operating procedures, types of expertise and professional cadre, products, degree of visibility, enactment and review processes, and relationships with other societal forces. . . .

In short, each tool involves a finely balanced complex of institutional, procedural, political, and economic relationships that substantially shape the character of the government action that results. By the same token, however, these features affect the likelihood that different tools will be enacted. In other words, the choice of program tool is a political, and not just an economic, issue: it involves important questions of power and purpose as well as of equity and efficiency.

Two questions thus form the core of the analysis of tools of government action that is suggested here:

(1) What consequences does the choice of tool of government action have for the effectiveness and operation of a government program?

(2) What factors influence the choice of program tools? In particular, to what extent are political or other administrative or symbolic reasons involved? Why are some tools chosen over others for particular purposes?

Basic Analytics

To answer these questions, it is necessary to begin with a clearer understanding of the major types of program tools, and the central differences among them. At a minimum, this requires a basic descriptive typology of program tools. . . .

Even more important than a descriptive framework, however, is the formulation of a more cross-cutting set of analytical categories in terms of which the various tools can be measured and assessed, and on the basis of which reasonable hypotheses, geared to the two questions above, can be generated and tested. Since this is the more difficult task, it may be useful to sketch out here in a purely suggestive way some of the major dimensions such an analytical framework might entail and some of the hypotheses it might support. Although the discussion here draws on literature where available, it should be clear that the intent is to stimulate further thinking rather than advance a definitive framework for the field. In this spirit, five dimensions of the tools of government action seem worthy of attention:

(1) The Directness/Indirectness Dimension: The first such dimension concerns the extent of reliance on nonfederal actors that a particular tool entails. Direct federal activities have long been suspect in American government, as much out of a philosophical hostility to concentrated governmental power as out of a concern about the rigidity and unresponsiveness supposed to accompany centralized operations. Recent research

on the implementation of public programs suggests, however, that indirect forms of action have their own substantial drawbacks. Pressman and Wildavsky [, Implementation] (1973) demonstrate convincingly, for example, that federal efforts to encourage economic development and employment in Oakland were frustrated by a form of action that vested critical responsibilities in a large number of federal and nonfederal actors, each of whom had his own priorities and perspectives that had to be reconciled anew at each of several dozen decision points that stood between program conception and completion. . . .

What is important about the use of indirect forms of action is not simply the administrative complexity of the resulting program structure, however. Of equal or greater importance is the incongruence that can arise between the goals of the federal government—as articulated, however imperfectly, in legislation, report language, or regulations—and the goals of the nonfederal implementing agents. This is clearly the case when the agent is a for-profit corporation. But it is equally true of state and local governments since different interests, different priorities, and different concerns find effective expression at different levels of government. Proposals to turn more decision-making power over to the states and localities thus involve more than questions of administrative efficiency; they also involve questions of program purpose and substance. . . .

(2) The Automatic/Administered Dimension: A second key dimension of different instruments of government action concerns the extent to which they rely on automatic, as opposed to administered, processes. An automatic process is one that utilizes existing structures and relationships (e.g., the tax structure or the price system) and requires a minimum of administrative decision-making. A tax credit automatically available to all firms investing in new plant or equipment, for example, would represent a largely automatic tool. A similar sum made available through grants on the basis of separately reviewed applications would represent a more highly administered tool.

Generally speaking, automatic tools are operationally more efficient since they involve less administrative oversight and transaction cost. They are also less disruptive of ongoing social processes, such as the price system and the market. . . .

Despite these hypothesized advantages, however, instruments that rely upon essentially automatic processes have significant drawbacks. For one thing, there is far less certainty that they will have the results intended, especially when they are attached to processes with far different purposes. A program that seeks to promote worker safety by levying higher disability insurance charges on companies with poor safety records rather than by imposing detailed safety regulations, for example, may continuously be in the position of doing too little too late. In addition, while promoting administrative efficiency, such tools sacrifice "target efficiency," the effective targeting of program benefits. . . .

(3) The Cash versus In-Kind Dimension: In assistance-type programs in particular, important differences exist between programs that deliver their benefits in the form of cash and those that deliver them in kind. Cash-type programs reserve far more flexibility to recipients and are

typically easier to administer. In-kind programs (e.g., food stamps, housing assistance), by tying benefits to a particular service or good, constrain recipient choices, often providing more of a particular good than a recipient would freely choose and thereby reducing the marginal value of the benefit to the recipient. . . .

While cash forms of assistance have attractions from the point of view of recipients, however, they have drawbacks from the point of view of building political support. In the first place, in-kind programs, by committing resources to the purchase of a particular good or service, can stimulate support from the producers of that good or service that would otherwise not exist. The food stamp program, for example, enjoys support from agricultural and farm interests that would not be forthcoming for a general, cash income-assistance program. Similarly, builder support for aid to the poor is much stronger for programs that tie such aid to the production of housing than for programs that make such assistance available in the form of cash. In the second place, in-kind assistance is more likely to go for the purpose intended than is outright cash. Those who make a case for assistance in terms of a particular need may therefore feel obliged to champion the delivery mechanism most certain to apply that assistance to that particular need. . . .

(4) The Visibility-Invisibility Dimension: Because of the structure of the budget and legislative processes, certain tools of government action are far less visible than others. Tax incentives, for example, are far less open to regular scrutiny than outright grants. "Entitlement" programs, which establish legal rights to program benefits independent of the budget, are far less closely scrutinized than programs that are subject to yearly control. In some cases, the costs of federal action are not even known. This is the case, for example, with regulatory actions, the true impact of which appears not in the federal budget, but in the balance sheets of the regulated industries. . . .

(5) Design Standards versus Performance Standards for Program Control: Attention to the instruments of government action has implications not only for basic choices among different tools, but also for decisions about how different tools, once chosen, are managed. One of the central issues in this regard is the extent to which reliance is placed on performance standards as opposed to design standards in program operations. Design standards involve controls over detailed aspects of program operations: accounting procedures, fund transfers among different program accounts, personnel recruitment procedures, specific technological processes to adopt to reduce air pollution at particular types of sites. Performance standards, by contrast, specify desired outputs but leave to the discretion of program managers or their third-party agents the decisions about how to design activities to achieve these outputs. Students of social regulation have faulted much of the federal government's recent regulatory effort in precisely these terms, arguing that by placing too much stress on design specifications (e.g., the location and numbers of fire extinguishers in industrial plants) rather than on performance standards (the days lost through fires), these activities end up being far less efficient economically and far more cumbersome administratively than is necessary. . . .

Attractive as performance standards are, however, they are not without their problems. For one thing, program purposes are frequently kept
deliberately vague in order to hold together the political coalition often
required for passage. Moreover, programs often serve multiple purposes,
and opinions can differ over the priorities to attach to each. In addition,
the measurement of success and failure in terms of particular performance criteria can often be quite subjective, creating added possibilities for
conflict and confusion, especially where responsibility for program decisions is split between federal authorities and their "third-party" agents.
Finally, the use of performance standards involves greater uncertainty
since results are not apparent for a considerable time and great opportunity exists for mistakes along the way. Those responsible for program
oversight can therefore be expected to find such uncertainty exceedingly
unattractive. . . .

(6) Summary—The Public Management Paradox: Taken together, the
hypotheses identified above suggest an important paradox that may lie at
the heart of much of the recent disappointment with federal program
performance. *Simply put, this paradox is that the types of instruments
that are the easiest to implement may be the hardest to enact; conversely,
the forms that are most likely to be enacted are also the most difficult to
carry out.*

Comments and Questions

1. What role, if any, is there in government for those who take Lester
Salamon's advice and become experts on the "baggage" that various benefit-
conferral techniques bring with them? Salamon believes such experts could
reduce the influence of interest groups in policy formation. Do you agree?

2. How do you explain the relationship that Salamon suggests at the end of
his article between policy effectiveness and policy implementation?

3. Evaluate a distributive policy with which you have some familiarity (possibly public schooling or military recruitment) in light of the five dimensions that
Salamon outlines in the previous excerpt. How well does your specific example fit
with the general concerns he raises?

4. Try to come up with an example of a broad policy goal we commonly
associate with benefit conferral that might be satisfied as well or nearly as well
with some combination of the legal instruments discussed in earlier chapters on
grievance-remedial, penal-corrective, and administrative-regulatory law.

5. Political scientist John Tierney suggests that disappointment with one
benefit-conferral technique, government corporations, is attributable to the "multiple, competing, and irreconcilable" expectations proponents foster in building
political support for the organization's creation. Tierney, Government Corporations and Managing the Public's Business, 99 Pol.Sci.Q. 73, 91 (1984). Sensitivity
to expensive political demands that decrease efficiency, Tierney argues, remains
even after new government corporations are in operation. Can you supply
examples of such demands from your knowledge about these familiar government
corporations: the postal service, Amtrak, and the Tennessee Valley Authority
(TVA)? Can you devise a program for benefit conferral that does not leave
program managers sensitive to some political demands? Would you favor such a
program?

6. Federal aid to the arts has increased dramatically since 1970. It grew from $8 million in 1970 to $60 million in 1974 and has increased steadily since. With the availability of increased public support has come debate over whether federal arts policy should encourage the widest possible dissemination of the arts or the highest levels of artistic achievement. See Wyszomirski, Controversies in Arts Policymaking, in Public Policy and the Arts 11 (K. Mulcahy & C. Swaim eds. 1982). Consider what interests are likely to benefit most from each alternative, and outline a program of benefit conferral in keeping with each of these contrasting objectives. Which approach would the requirement that state arts funds be allocated to each county on a per capita basis promote? What position do the authors of the following excerpt take on arts spending? Do you agree with them?

———

STALKER & GLYMOUR, THE MALIGNANT OBJECT: THOUGHTS ON PUBLIC SCULPTURE
66 Pub.Interest 3, 3–4, 6–7, 10, 12, 20 (1982).*

Millions of dollars are spent in this country on public sculpture—on sculpture that is created for the explicit purpose of public viewing, placed in public settings, and constructed generally by contemporary artists without any intention of commemorating or representing people or events associated with the site. The objects in question may be clothespins, boulders, or tortuous steel shapes. The money may sometimes come from private sources, but much of it comes from public treasuries.

One of the clearest and most general attempts to provide a justification for financing and placing these objects in public spaces is given by Janet Kardon, who is the Director of Philadelphia's Institute of Contemporary Art. "Public art," Ms. Kardon writes, "is not a style or a movement, but a compound social service based on the premise that public well-being is enhanced by the presence of large scale art works in public spaces." Large scale art works executed, to be sure, not to public taste but to the taste of the avant-garde art community. Elsewhere, she writes: "Public art is not a style, art movement or public service, but a compound event, based on the premise that our lives are enhanced by good art and that good art means work by advanced artists thrust into the public domain." The justification here is moral rather than aesthetic, phrased in terms of well-being rather than those of beauty. Public art is good for us. Her thesis is put simply and with clarity; it is perhaps the same thesis as that put forward by many writers who claim that public art "enhances the quality of life" or "humanizes the urban environment," even "speaks to the spirit."

Our view is that much public sculpture, and public art generally as it is created nowadays in the United States, provides at best trivial benefits to the public, but does provide substantial and identifiable harm. This is so for a variety of reasons having to do with the character of contemporary artistic enterprises and with prevalent features of our society as well. We will discuss these issues in due course, but for now we want to make our view as clear as we can.

* Reprinted with permission of the authors from: THE PUBLIC INTEREST, No. 66 (Winter, 1982), pp. 3–21. © 1982 by National Affairs, Inc.

There is abundant evidence, albeit circumstantial, pointing directly to the conclusion that many pieces of contemporary public sculpture, perhaps the majority, are not much enjoyed by the public at large—even though the public firmly believes in a general way that art is a very good thing. . . .

The public distaste for today's public sculpture often goes well beyond mere words. The common responses include petitions, assemblies, litigation, and, occasionally, direct action. Enraged by what is thrust at them, the public often takes up a kind of vigilantism against contemporary public sculpture, and in community after community spontaneous bands of Aesthetic Avengers form, armed with hammers, chisels, and spray-paint cans. Jody Pinto's "Heart Chambers for Gertrude and Angelo," erected on the University of Pennsylvania campus for Ms. Kardon's own Institute of Contemporary Art, was turned into rubble overnight. Barnett Newman's "Broken Obelisk" was rapidly defaced when it was put on display in 1967. Removed to Houston, Texas, it is now placed in a pool away from errant paint. Claes Oldenburg's "Lipstick" was so thoroughly defaced at Yale that the sculptor retrieved it. Of course, for any object there is some thug or madman willing or eager to destroy what he can of it, but the defacement of some pieces of public sculpture seems to enjoy a measure of community support or at least tolerance. . . .

Impressionistic evidence is rightfully mistrusted, and those who advocate public sculpture might well demand more precise evidence as to the extent and intensity of public dislike or indifference for contemporary public sculpture. But the plain fact is that there is little non-impressionistic evidence to be had, one way or the other. Remarkably, although considerable sums are spent on public sculpture in this country by government and by corporations, virtually nothing is spent to find out whether or not the public likes particular objects or dislikes them, how intense such feelings are, or, most importantly, what proportion of the affected public would prefer that the space be put to some other use. . . .

Inevitably, today's public sculpture is justified in a kind of circular way: The very fact that the public dislikes it, or even violently abhors it, is taken to warrant its presentation. . . .

. . . It is not for government to promote new conceptions or realizations of art. In short, the ultimate aesthetic quality of the works is not in question; their public display is.

If today's public sculpture is not much enjoyed for its aesthetic qualities, and if it carries no effective and important message which will enlighten the public, how does it improve the quality of life? How are citizens made better off by its presence? Advocates may dig in their heels and claim that those exposed to such pieces just *are* better off, whether they know it or not, for seeing and living with the things. But an inarticulable and unidentifiable benefit is no benefit at all, only special pleading. . . .

Artists, critics, and art administrators may find this argument to be simply an endorsement of philistinism, but that is a grievous confusion.

Philistines are people too, and, whether or not one shares their tastes, the moral point of view requires that their interests be considered.

Section Three. Authorized Makers of Public–Benefit Law and Their Appropriate Collaborative Roles

Legislators are key actors in benefit conferral. They design and vote upon distributive policy, they authorize funding for particular programs, and they arrange to raise the revenues necessary to make benefit conferral possible. These should be considered three separate types of decisions. The decision to authorize a program, for example, does not necessarily mean the legislature will fund it. Nor do votes to create and fund programs necessarily mean the legislature has solved the problems associated with generating revenues to pay for them, as critics of Congress's tendency toward deficit spending often point out.

Though legislators are essential for getting programs under way, they are by no means the only authorized law makers in benefit conferral. Legislators routinely delegate much of the control they could, in theory, exercise over the implementation of the programs they create. They give officials authority to make binding rules for the distribution of benefits, and to resolve disputes over how those rules should apply. Whether legislators thereby improperly avoid their legislative responsibilities and violate the principle of the separation of powers is a matter of dispute among scholars. The courts, at least, have given their imprimatur to statutes delegating broad authority to administrative officials, as we saw in the previous chapter.

Delegation by legislators proceeds in several directions. Congress delegates authority to state agencies and local governments as well as to federal agencies. On occasion, Congress has even delegated power over benefit conferral to groups of private individuals, as when it provided that marketing restrictions would apply only upon a majority vote of affected farmers.[a] State legislators, who enjoy considerable independent power to design and fund benefit-conferral programs, also delegate much to state officials and to local units of government like cities and school districts, which themselves may delegate authority over benefit conferral to still smaller units, such as individual school boards and neighborhood groups.

Those who design and implement benefit-conferral law usually attach a number of strings to benefits—red tape in the eyes of those who must satisfy these conditions if they are to receive funds or services. Ask a university administrator about the requirements your school must satisfy as a recipient of federal or state aid, or inquire at a local social services agency about qualifications for welfare or other forms of personal assistance. The qualifications, mandates, prohibitions, and incentives that guide and limit the availability of benefits often look even more complex when one tries to read the legislation that authorizes a program, for here legislators are writing primarily for administrative lawmakers. The

---

a. See Currin v. Wallace, 306 U.S. 1, 59 S.Ct. 379 (1939), for a description of the program and the Supreme Court's favorable reaction to it. See also United States v. Rock Royal Co-operative, 307 U.S. 533, 59 S.Ct. 993 (1939), for a similar statute, which was also upheld.

benefit-conferral legislation that follows is an exception to this general rule of complexity, and it has been edited to make it even easier to follow. As you read the Legal Services Corporation Act, decide (1) who the authorized lawmakers are, (2) where the policy fits in terms of the five dimensions Salamon discussed in the previous section, (3) what conditions Congress has imposed upon the availability of funds and why it has imposed these conditions, and (4) which conditions are most likely to give rise to disputes over their applicability.

———

UNITED STATES CODE, TITLE 42

§ 2996. Statement of findings and declaration of purpose

The Congress finds and declares that—

(1) there is a need to provide equal access to the system of justice in our Nation for individuals who seek redress of grievances;

(2) there is a need to provide high quality legal assistance to those who would be otherwise unable to afford adequate legal counsel and to continue the present vital legal services program;

(3) providing legal assistance to those who face an economic barrier to adequate legal counsel will serve best the ends of justice and assist in improving opportunities for low-income persons consistent with the purposes of this Act;

(4) for many of our citizens, the availability of legal services has reaffirmed faith in our government of laws;

(5) to preserve its strength, the legal services program must be kept free from the influence of or use by it of political pressures; and

(6) attorneys providing legal assistance must have full freedom to protect the best interests of their clients in keeping with the Code of Professional Responsibility, the Canons of Ethics, and the high standards of the legal profession. . . .

§ 2996b. Legal Services Corporation

(a) Establishment; purpose. There is established in the District of Columbia a private nonmembership nonprofit corporation, which shall be known as the Legal Services Corporation, for the purpose of providing financial support for legal assistance in noncriminal proceedings or matters to persons financially unable to afford legal assistance. . . .

§ 2996c. Board of Directors

(a) Establishment; membership. The Corporation shall have a Board of Directors consisting of eleven voting members appointed by the President, by and with the advice and consent of the Senate, no more than six of whom shall be of the same political party. A majority shall be members of the bar of the highest court of any State, and none shall be a full-time employee of the United States. Effective with respect to appointments made after the date of enactment of the Legal Services Corporation Act Amendments of 1977 [enacted Dec. 28, 1977] but not later than July 31, 1978, the membership of the Board shall be appointed so as to include eligible clients, and to be generally representative of the organized bar, attorneys providing legal assistance to eligible clients, and the general public. . . .

§ 2996d. Officers and employees

(a) Appointment of president; outside compensation of officers prohibited; terms. The Board shall appoint the president of the Corporation, who shall be a member of the bar of the highest court of a State and shall be a non-voting ex officio member of the Board, and such other officers as the Board determines to be necessary. . . .

§ 2996e. Powers, duties, and limitations

(a) Powers of nonprofit corporation; additional powers. . . . . [T]he Corporation is authorized—

   (1)(A) to provide financial assistance to qualified programs furnishing legal assistance to eligible clients, and to make grants to and contracts with—

      (i) individuals, partnerships, firms, corporations, and nonprofit organizations, and

      (ii) State and local governments . . .

for the purpose of providing legal assistance to eligible clients under this title, and (B) to make such other grants and contracts as are necessary to carry out the purposes and provisions of this title;

   (2) to accept in the name of the Corporation, and employ or dispose of in furtherance of the purposes of this title, any money or property, real, personal, or mixed, tangible or intangible, received by gift, devise, bequest, or otherwise; and

   (3) to undertake directly, or by grant or contract, the following activities relating to the delivery of legal assistance—

      (A) research, except that broad general legal or policy research unrelated to representation of eligible clients may not be undertaken by grant or contract,

      (B) training and technical assistance, and

      (C) to serve as a clearinghouse for information.

(b) Disciplinary powers; representational questions; interference with professional responsibilities of attorneys; bar membership; restrictions; languages other than English. . . . .

   (5) The Corporation shall insure that (A) no employee of the Corporation or of any recipient (except as permitted by law in connection with such employee's own employment situation), while carrying out legal assistance activities under this title, engage in, or encourage others to engage in, any public demonstration or picketing, boycott, or strike; and (B) no such employee shall, at any time, engage in, or encourage others to engage in, any of the following activities: (i) any rioting or civil disturbance, (ii) any activity which is in violation of an outstanding injunction of any court of competent jurisdiction, (iii) any other illegal activity, or (iv) any intentional identification of the Corporation or any recipient with any political activity prohibited by section

1007(a)(6) [42 USC § 2996f(a)(6)]. The Board, within ninety days after its first meeting, shall issue rules and regulations to provide for the enforcement of this paragraph and section 1007(a)(5) [42 USC § 2996f(a)(5)], which rules shall include, among available remedies, provisions, in accordance with the types of procedures prescribed in the provisions of section 1011 [42 USC § 2996j], for suspension of legal assistance supported under this title, suspension of an employee of the Corporation or of any employee of any recipient by such recipient, and, after consideration of other remedial measures and after a hearing in accordance with section 1011 [42 USC § 2996j], the termination of such assistance or employment, as deemed appropriate for the violation in question.

(6) In areas where significant numbers of eligible clients speak a language other than English as their principal language, the Corporation shall, to the extent feasible, provide that their principal language is used in the provision of legal assistance to such clients under this title.

(c) Participation in litigation; lobbying activities. The Corporation shall not itself—

(1) participate in litigation unless the Corporation or a recipient of the Corporation is a party, or a recipient is representing an eligible client in litigation in which the interpretation of this title or a regulation promulgated under this title is an issue, and shall not participate on behalf of any client other than itself; or

(2) undertake to influence the passage or defeat of any legislation by the Congress of the United States or by any State or local legislative bodies, except that personnel of the Corporation may testify or make other appropriate communication (A) when formally requested to do so by a legislative body, a committee, or a member thereof, or (B) in connection with legislation or appropriations directly affecting the activities of the Corporation.

(d) Miscellaneous prohibitions. . . .

(5) No class action suit, class action appeal, or amicus curiae class action may be undertaken, directly or through others, by a staff attorney, except with the express approval of a project director of a recipient in accordance with policies established by the governing body of such recipient. . . .

(e) Political activities of Corporation employees and staff attorneys.

(1) Employees of the Corporation or of recipients shall not at any time intentionally identify the Corporation or the recipient with any partisan or nonpartisan political activity associated with a political party or association, or the campaign of any candidate for public or party office.

. . .

§ 2996f. Grants and contracts

(a) Requisites. With respect to grants or contracts in connection with the provision of legal assistance to eligible clients under this title, the Corporation shall—

(1) insure the maintenance of the highest quality of service and professional standards, the preservation of attorney-client relationships, and the protection of the integrity of the adversary process from any impairment in furnishing legal assistance to eligible clients;

(2) (A) establish, in consultation with the Director of the Office of Management and Budget and with the Governors of the several States, maximum income levels (taking into account family size, urban and rural differences, and substantial cost-of-living variations) for individuals eligible for legal assistance under this title;

(B) establish guidelines to insure that eligibility of clients will be determined by recipients on the basis of factors which include—

(i) the liquid assets and income level of the client,

(ii) the fixed debts, medical expenses, and other factors which affect the client's ability to pay,

(iii) the cost of living in the locality, and

(iv) such other factors as relate to financial inability to afford legal assistance, which may include evidence of a prior determination that such individual's lack of income results from refusal or unwillingness, without good cause, to seek or accept an employment situation; and

(C) insure that (i) recipients, consistent with goals established by the Corporation, adopt procedures for determining and implementing priorities for the provision of such assistance, taking into account the relative needs of eligible clients for such assistance (including such outreach, training, and support services as may be necessary), including particularly the needs for service on the part of significant segments of the population of eligible clients with special difficulties of access to legal services or special legal problems (including elderly and handicapped individuals); and (ii) appropriate training and support services are provided in order to provide such assistance to such significant segments of the population of eligible clients;

(3) insure that grants and contracts are made so as to provide the most economical and effective delivery of legal assistance to persons in both urban and rural areas; . . .

(5) insure that no funds made available to recipients by the Corporation shall be used at any time, directly or indirectly, to influence the issuance, amendment, or revocation of any executive order or similar promulgation by any Federal, State, or local agency, or to undertake to influence the passage or defeat of any legislation by the Congress of the United States, or by any State or local legislative bodies, or State proposals by initiative petition, except where—

(A) representation by an employee of a recipient for any eligible client is necessary to the provision of legal advice and representation with respect to such client's legal rights and responsibilities (which shall not be construed to permit an attorney or a recipient employee to solicit a client, in violation of professional responsibilities, for the purpose of making such representation possible); or

(B) a governmental agency, legislative body, a committee, or a member thereof—

(i) requests personnel of the recipient to testify, draft, or review measures or to make representations to such agency, body, committee, or member, or

(ii) is considering a measure directly affecting the activities under this title of the recipient or the Corporation.

(6) insure that all attorneys engaged in legal assistance activities supported in whole or in part by the Corporation refrain, while so engaged, from—

(A) any political activity, or

(B) any activity to provide voters or prospective voters with transportation to the polls or provide similar assistance in connection with an election (other than legal advice and representation), or

(C) any voter registration activity (other than legal advice and representation);

(7) require recipients to establish guidelines, consistent with regulations promulgated by the Corporation, for a system for review of appeals to insure the efficient utilization of resources and to avoid frivolous appeals (except that such guidelines or regulations shall in no way interfere with attorneys' professional responsibilities);

(8) insure that recipients solicit the recommendations of the organized bar in the community being served before filling staff attorney positions in any project funded pursuant to this title and give preference in filing such positions to qualified persons who reside in the community to be served; . . .

(10) insure that all attorneys, while engaged in legal assistance activities supported in whole or in part by the Corporation, refrain from the persistent incitement of litigation and any other activity prohibited by the Canons of Ethics and Code of Professional Responsibility of the American Bar Association, and insure that such attorneys refrain from personal representation for a private fee in any cases in which they were involved while engaged in such legal assistance activities.

(b) Limitations on uses. No funds made available by the Corporation under this title, either by grant or contract, may be used—

(1) to provide legal assistance (except in accordance with guidelines promulgated by the Corporation) with respect to any fee-generating case (which guidelines shall not preclude the provision of legal assistance in cases in which a client seeks only statutory benefits and appropriate private representation is not available);

(2) to provide legal assistance with respect to any criminal proceeding, except to provide assistance to a person charged with a misdemeanor or lesser offense or its equivalent in an Indian tribal court;

(3) to provide legal assistance in civil actions to persons who have been convicted of a criminal charge where the civil action arises out of alleged acts or failures to act and the action is brought against an officer of the court or against a law enforcement official for the purpose of challenging the validity of the criminal conviction;

(4) for any of the political activities prohibited in paragraph (6) of subsection (a) of this section;

(5) to make grants to or enter into contracts with any private law firm which expends 50 percent or more of its resources and time litigating issues in the broad interests of a majority of the public;

(6) to support or conduct training programs for the purpose of advocating particular public policies or encouraging political activities, labor or antilabor activities, boycotts, picketing, strikes, and demonstrations, as distinguished from the dissemination of information about such policies or activities, except that this provision shall not be construed to prohibit the training of attorneys or paralegal personnel necessary to prepare them to provide adequate legal assistance to eligible clients;

(7) to initiate the formation, or act as an organizer, of any association, federation, or similar entity, except that this paragraph shall not be construed to prohibit the provision of legal assistance to eligible clients;

(8) to provide legal assistance with respect to any proceeding or litigation which seeks to procure a nontherapeutic abortion or to compel any individual or institution to perform an abortion, or assist in the performance of an abortion, or provide facilities for the performance of an abortion, contrary to the religious beliefs or moral convictions of such individual or institution;

(9) to provide legal assistance with respect to any proceeding or litigation relating to the desegregation of any elementary or secondary school or school system, except that nothing in this paragraph shall prohibit the provision of legal advice to an eligible client with respect to such client's legal rights and responsibilities; or

(10) to provide legal assistance with respect to any proceeding or litigation arising out of a violation of the Military Selective Service Act or of desertion from the Armed Forces of the United States, except that legal assistance may be provided to an eligible client in a civil action in which such client alleges that he was improperly classified prior to July 1, 1973, under the Military Selective Service Act or prior corresponding law. . . .

(d) **Program evaluation.** The Corporation shall monitor and evaluate and provide for independent evaluations of programs supported in whole or in part under this title to insure that the provisions of this title and the bylaws of the Corporation and applicable rules, regulations, and guidelines promulgated pursuant to this title are carried out. . . .

§ 2996g. Records and reports

(a) **Authority to require reports.** The Corporation is authorized to require such reports as it deems necessary from any grantee, contractor, or person or entity receiving financial assistance under this title regarding activities carried out pursuant to this title.

(b) **Authority to require recordkeeping; access to records.** The Corporation is authorized to prescribe the keeping of records with respect to funds provided by grant or contract and shall have access to such records at all reasonable times for the purpose of insuring compliance with the grant or contract or the terms and conditions upon which financial assistance was provided.

(c) Annual report to President and Congress. The Corporation shall publish an annual report which shall be filed by the Corporation with the President and the Congress. Such report shall include a description of services provided pursuant to section 1007(a)(2)(C)(i) and (ii) [42 USC § 2996f(a)(2)(C)(i), (ii)].

(d) Copies and retention of reports. Copies of all reports pertinent to the evaluation, inspection, or monitoring of any grantee, contractor, or person or entity receiving financial assistance under this title shall be submitted on a timely basis to such grantee, contractor, or person or entity, and shall be maintained in the principal office of the Corporation for a period of at least five years subsequent to such evaluation, inspection, or monitoring. Such reports shall be available for public inspection during regular business hours, and copies shall be furnished, upon request, to interested parties upon payment of such reasonable fees as the Corporation may establish.

(e) Publication in Federal Register of rules, regulations, guidelines, and instructions. The Corporation shall afford notice and reasonable opportunity for comment to interested parties prior to issuing rules, regulations, and guidelines, and it shall publish in the Federal Register at least 30 days prior to their effective date all its rules, regulations, guidelines, and instructions.

§ 2996h. Audits

(a) Annual audit; availability of records; filing and inspection of report. . . . The accounts of the Corporation shall be audited annually. Such audits shall be conducted in accordance with generally accepted auditing standards by independent certified public accountants who are certified by a regulatory authority of the jurisdiction in which the audit is undertaken. . . .

§ 2996i. Financing

(a) Authorization of appropriations. There are authorized to be appropriated for the purpose of carrying out the activities of the Corporation, $90,000,000 for fiscal year 1975, $100,000,000 for fiscal year 1976, and such sums as may be necessary for fiscal year 1977. There are authorized to be appropriated for the purpose of carrying out the activities of the Corporation $205,000,000 for the fiscal year 1978, and such sums as may be necessary for each of the two succeeding fiscal years. The first appropriation may be made available to the Corporation at any time after six or more members of the Board have been appointed and qualified. Appropriations for that purpose shall be made for not more than two fiscal years, and shall be paid to the Corporation in annual installments at the beginning of each fiscal year in such amounts as may be specified in Acts of Congress making appropriations.

(b) Availability of funds. Funds appropriated pursuant to this section shall remain available until expended. . . .

§ 2996j.   Special limitations

The Corporation shall prescribe procedures to insure that—

(1) financial assistance under this title shall not be suspended unless the grantee, contractor, or person or entity receiving financial assistance under this title has been given reasonable notice and opportunity to show cause why such action should not be taken; and

(2) financial assistance under this title shall not be terminated, an application for refunding shall not be denied, and a suspension of financial assistance shall not be continued for longer than thirty days, unless the grantee, contractor, or person or entity receiving financial assistance under this title has been afforded reasonable notice and opportunity for a timely, full, and fair hearing, and, when requested, such hearing shall be conducted by an independent hearing examiner. Such hearing shall be held prior to any final decision by the Corporation to terminate financial assistance or suspend or deny funding. Hearing examiners shall be appointed by the Corporation in accordance with procedures established in regulations promulgated by the Corporation.   .   .   .

———

The limitations upon subsidized legal services you noted in the Legal Services Corporation Act have not protected the program from controversy. The unpopularity of the act in some quarters arises from the fact that many Legal Services Corporation attorneys have dedicated themselves to ensuring that the bureaucracy delivers the benefits promised by state and federal governments. Sometimes this means bringing a lawsuit, often a class action, against a welfare department or other government agency. Such suits put government in the peculiar position of suing itself and paying lawyers on both sides. The Reagan administration would like to eliminate the Legal Services Corporation, charging that many of the suits it brings are counterproductive and that corporation attorneys have gone beyond their authority to represent the poor in court and have acted politically, as lobbyists for the poor. The administration has succeeded in reducing, but not eliminating, funding for the program, which has brought about the closing of over 300 of the nation's 1,475 local branches. See Caplan, Understanding the Controversy over the Legal Services Corporation, 28 N.Y.L.Sch.L.Rev. 586 (1983).

The relationship between funding, program objectives, and rules limiting eligibility for benefits is not always straightforward. Congress uses its power over benefits to foster policies that have little to do with distribution per se. Congress has, for example, made the availability of federal highway funds dependent upon the willingness of the states to impose fifty-five mile per hour speed limits, and it has used the same tool to require the states to increase the drinking age to twenty-one. Corporate recipients of federal aid are forbidden to discriminate against their employees, and individuals who receive federal financial assistance and are eligible for the draft are required to register. Sometimes Congress simply bars certain uses for its funds, as in its ban on Medicaid assistance for abortion, or its denial of research support to projects involving uninformed human subjects. The large and growing number of activities that receive some form of federal financial support makes the imposition of conditions a powerful tool for regulating behavior that would otherwise lie outside the congressional domain.

The case that follows involves an effort by Congress to combat sex discrimination by limiting the availability of federal aid to education. Does the majority decision deal persuasively with the ambiguity inherent in Title IX of the Education Amendments of 1972?

GROVE CITY COLLEGE v. BELL

Supreme Court of the United States, 1984.
465 U.S. 555, 104 S.Ct. 1211.

JUSTICE WHITE delivered the opinion of the Court.

Section 901(a) of Title IX of the Education Amendments of 1972, Pub.L. 92-318, 86 Stat. 373, 20 U.S.C. § 1681(a), prohibits sex discrimination in "any education program or activity receiving Federal financial assistance," and § 902 directs agencies awarding most types of assistance to promulgate regulations to ensure that recipients adhere to that prohibition. Compliance with departmental regulations may be secured by termination of assistance "to the particular program, or part thereof, in which . . . noncompliance has been . . . found" or by "any other means authorized by law." § 902, 20 U.S.C. § 1682.

This case presents several questions concerning the scope and operation of these provisions and the regulations established by the Department of Education. We must decide, first, whether Title IX applies at all to Grove City College, which accepts no direct assistance but enrolls students who receive federal grants that must be used for educational purposes. If so, we must identify the "education program or activity" at Grove City that is "receiving Federal financial assistance" and determine whether federal assistance to that program may be terminated solely because the College violates the Department's regulations by refusing to execute an Assurance of Compliance with Title IX. Finally, we must consider whether the application of Title IX to Grove City infringes the First Amendment rights of the College or its students.

I

Petitioner Grove City College is a private, coeducational, liberal arts college that has sought to preserve its institutional autonomy by consistently refusing state and federal financial assistance. Grove City's desire to avoid federal oversight has led it to decline to participate, not only in direct institutional aid programs, but also in federal student assistance programs under which the College would be required to assess students' eligibility and to determine the amounts of loans, work-study funds, or grants they should receive. Grove City has, however, enrolled a large number of students who receive Basic Educational Opportunity Grants (BEOGs), 20 U.S.C. § 1070a, under the Department of Education's Alternate Disbursement System (ADS).

The Department concluded that Grove City was a "recipient" of "Federal financial assistance" as those terms are defined in the regulations implementing Title IX, 34 CFR §§ 106.2(g)(1), (h) (1982), and, in July 1977, it requested that the College execute the Assurance of Compliance required by 34 CFR § 106.4 (1982). If Grove City had signed the Assurance, it would have agreed to

> [c]omply, to the extent applicable to it, with Title IX . . . and all applicable requirements imposed by or pursuant to the Department's regulation . . . to the end that . . . no person shall, on the basis of sex, be . . . subjected to discrimination under any education program or activity for which [it] receives or benefits from Federal financial assistance from the Department.

When Grove City persisted in refusing to execute an Assurance, the Department initiated proceedings to declare the College and its students ineligible to receive BEOGs. The Administrative Law Judge held that the federal financial assistance received by Grove City obligated it to execute an Assurance of Compliance and entered an order terminating assistance until Grove City "corrects its noncompliance with Title IX and satisfies the Department that it is in compliance" with the applicable regulations.

Grove City and four of its students then commenced this action in the District Court for the Western District of Pennsylvania, which concluded that the students' BEOGs constituted "Federal financial assistance" to Grove City but held, on several grounds, that the Department could not terminate the students' aid because of the College's refusal to execute an Assurance of Compliance. Grove City College v. Harris, 500 F.Supp. 253 (1980). The Court of Appeals reversed. 687 F.2d 684 (CA3 1982). . . .

We granted certiorari, 459 U.S. 1199, 103 S.Ct. 1181 (1983), and we now affirm the Court of Appeals' judgment that the Department could terminate BEOGs received by Grove City's students to force the College to execute an Assurance of Compliance.

II

In defending its refusal to execute the Assurance of Compliance required by the Department's regulations, Grove City first contends that neither it nor any "education program or activity" of the College receives any federal financial assistance within the meaning of Title IX by virtue of the fact that some of its students receive BEOGs and use them to pay for their education. We disagree.

Grove City provides a well-rounded liberal arts education and a variety of educational programs and student services. The question is whether any of those programs or activities "receiv[es] Federal financial assistance" within the meaning of Title IX when students finance their education with BEOGs. The structure of the Education Amendments of 1972, in which Congress both created the BEOG program and imposed Title IX's nondiscrimination requirement, strongly suggests an affirmative conclusion. BEOGs were aptly characterized as a "centerpiece of the bill," 118 Cong.Rec. 20297 (1972) (Rep. Pucinski), and Title IX "relate[d] directly to [its] central purpose." 117 Cong.Rec. 30412 (1971) (Sen. Bayh).

In view of this connection and Congress' express recognition of discrimination in the administration of student financial aid programs, it would indeed be anomalous to discover that one of the primary components of Congress' comprehensive "package of federal aid," id., at 2007 (Sen. Pell), was not intended to trigger coverage under Title IX.

It is not surprising to find, therefore, that the language of § 901(a) contains no hint that Congress perceived a substantive difference between direct institutional assistance and aid received by a school through its students. The linchpin of Grove City's argument that none of its programs receives any federal assistance is a perceived distinction between direct and indirect aid, a distinction that finds no support in the text of § 901(a). . . .

With the benefit of clear statutory language, powerful evidence of Congress' intent, and a longstanding and coherent administrative construction of the phrase "receiving Federal financial assistance," we have little trouble concluding that Title IX coverage is not foreclosed because federal funds are granted to Grove City's students rather than directly to one of the College's educational programs. There remains the question, however, of identifying the "education program or activity" of the College that can properly be characterized as "receiving" federal assistance through grants to some of the students attending the College.

III

An analysis of Title IX's language and legislative history led us to conclude in North Haven Board of Education v. Bell, [456 U.S. 512, 538, 102 S.Ct. 1912, 1926 (1982)], that "an agency's authority under Title IX both to promulgate regulations and to terminate funds is subject to the program-specific limitations of §§ 901 and 902." Although the legislative history contains isolated suggestions that entire institutions are subject to the nondiscrimination provision whenever one of their programs receives federal assistance, see 1975 Hearings 178 (Sen. Bayh), we cannot accept the Court of Appeals' conclusion that in the circumstances present here Grove City itself is a "program or activity" that may be regulated in its entirety. Nevertheless, we find no merit in Grove City's contention that a decision treating BEOGs as "Federal financial assistance" cannot be reconciled with Title IX's program-specific language since BEOGs are not tied to any specific "education program or activity."

If Grove City participated in the BEOG program through the RDS,[b] we would have no doubt that the "education program or activity receiving Federal financial assistance" would not be the entire College; rather, it would be its student financial aid program. RDS institutions receive federal funds directly, but can use them only to subsidize or expand their financial aid programs and to recruit students who might otherwise be unable to enroll. In short, the assistance is earmarked for the recipient's financial aid program. Only by ignoring Title IX's program-specific

b. Regular Disbursement System, by which the Secretary estimates the total amount the school will need for grants and the school selects eligible students, calculates awards, and distributes the grants. Schools that want to minimize their involvement in the program can use ADS (Alternate Disbursement System), by which the Secretary calculates individual awards and makes disbursements directly to eligible students.

language could we conclude that funds received under the RDS, awarded to eligible students, and paid back to the school when tuition comes due represent federal aid to the entire institution.

We see no reason to reach a different conclusion merely because Grove City has elected to participate in the ADS. Although Grove City does not itself disburse students' awards, BEOGs clearly augment the resources that the College itself devotes to financial aid. As is true of the RDS, however, the fact that federal funds eventually reach the College's general operating budget cannot subject Grove City to institution-wide coverage. Grove City's choice of administrative mechanisms, we hold, neither expands nor contracts the breadth of the "program or activity"—the financial aid program—that receives federal assistance and that may be regulated under Title IX.

To the extent that the Court of Appeals' holding that BEOGs received by Grove City's students constitute aid to the entire institution rests on the possibility that federal funds received by one program or activity free up the College's own resources for use elsewhere, the Court of Appeals' reasoning is doubly flawed. First, there is no evidence that the federal aid received by Grove City's students results in the diversion of funds from the College's own financial aid program to other areas within the institution. Second, and more important, the Court of Appeals' assumption that Title IX applies to programs receiving a larger share of a school's own limited resources as a result of federal assistance earmarked for use elsewhere within the institution is inconsistent with the program-specific nature of the statute. Most federal educational assistance has economic ripple effects throughout the aided institution, and it would be difficult, if not impossible, to determine which programs or activities derive such indirect benefits. Under the Court of Appeals' theory, an entire school would be subject to Title IX merely because one of its students received a small BEOG or because one of its departments received an earmarked federal grant. This result cannot be squared with Congress' intent.

. . . .

We conclude that the receipt of BEOGs by some of Grove City's students does not trigger institution-wide coverage under Title IX. In purpose and effect, BEOGs represent federal financial assistance to the College's own financial aid program, and it is that program that may properly be regulated under Title IX.

IV

[The Court concluded that the federal assistance could be terminated solely for refusal to execute an Assurance of Compliance.]

V

Grove City's final challenge to the Court of Appeals' decision—that conditioning federal assistance on compliance with Title IX infringes First Amendment rights of the College and its students—warrants only brief consideration. Congress is free to attach reasonable and unambiguous conditions to federal financial assistance that educational institutions are not obligated to accept. E.g., Pennhurst State School & Hospital v. Halderman, 451 U.S. 1, 17, 101 S.Ct. 1531, 1539 (1981). Grove City may terminate its participation in the BEOG program and thus avoid the requirements of § 901(a). Students affected by the Department's action may either take their BEOGs elsewhere or attend Grove City without federal financial assistance. Requiring Grove City to comply with Title IX's prohibition of discrimination as a condition for its continued eligibility to participate in the BEOG program infringes no First Amendment rights of the College or its students.

Accordingly, the judgment of the Court of Appeals is

Affirmed.

JUSTICE POWELL, with whom CHIEF JUSTICE BURGER and JUSTICE O'CONNOR join, concurring.

As I agree that the holding in this case is dictated by the language and legislative history of Title IX, and the Regulations of the Department of Education, I join the Court's decision. I do so reluctantly and write briefly to record my view that the case is an unedifying example of overzealousness on the part of the Federal Government.

Grove City College (Grove City) may be unique among colleges in our country; certainly there are few others like it. Founded more than a century ago in 1876, Grove City is an independent, coeducational liberal arts college. It describes itself as having "both a Christian world view and a freedom philosophy," perceiving these as "interrelated." At the time of this suit, it had about 2,200 students and tuition was surprisingly low for a private college. Some 140 of the College's students were receiving Basic Educational Opportunity Grants (BEOGs), and 342 had obtained Guaranteed Student Loans (GSLs). The grants were made directly to the students through the Department of Education, and the student loans were guaranteed by the federal government. Apart from this indirect assistance, Grove City has followed an unbending policy of refusing all forms of government assistance, whether federal, state or local. It was and is the policy of this small college to remain wholly independent of government assistance, recognizing—as this case well illustrates—that with acceptance of such assistance one surrenders a certain measure of the freedom that Americans always have cherished.

This case involves a Regulation adopted by the Department to implement § 901(a) of Title IX (20 U.S.C. § 1681(a)). It is well to bear in mind what § 901(a) provides:

> No person in the United States shall, on the basis of sex, be excluded from participation in, be denied the benefits of, or be subjected to discrimination under any education program or activity receiving federal financial assistance . . . .

The sole purpose of the statute is to make unlawful *"discrimination"* by recipients of federal financial assistance on the "basis of sex." The undisputed fact is that Grove City does not discriminate—and so far as the record in this case shows—never has discriminated against anyone on account of sex, race, or national origin. This case has nothing whatever to do with discrimination past or present. The College therefore has complied to the letter with the sole purpose of § 901(a).

As the Court describes, the case arises pursuant to a Regulation adopted under Title IX that authorizes the Secretary to obtain from recipients of federal aid an "Assurance of Compliance" with Title IX and regulations issued thereunder. At the outset of this litigation, the Department insisted that by accepting students who received BEOG awards, Grove City's entire institution was subject to regulation under Title IX. The College, in view of its policies and principles of independence and its record of non-discrimination, objected to executing this Assurance. One would have thought that the Department, confronted as it is with cases of national importance that involve actual discrimination, would have respected the independence and admirable record of this college. But common sense and good judgment failed to prevail. The Department chose to litigate, and instituted an administrative proceeding to compel Grove City to execute an agreement to operate all of its programs and activities in full compliance with all of the regulations promulgated under Title IX—despite the College's record as an institution that had operated to date in full accordance with the letter and spirit of Title IX. The Administrative Law Judge who heard the case on September 15, 1978, did not relish his task.

On the basis of the evidence, which included the formal published statement of Grove City's strong "non-discrimination policy," he stated:

> It should also be noted that there is *not the slightest hint of any failure to comply with Title IX*, save the refusal to submit an executed Assurance of Compliance with Title IX. This refusal is obviously a matter of conscience and belief. (emphasis added)

The Administrative Law Judge further evidenced his reluctance by emphasizing that the Regulations were "binding" upon him. He concluded that the scholarship grants and student loans to Grove City constituted indirect "federal financial assistance," and in view of the failure of Grove City to execute the Assurance, the Regulation required that the grants and loans to its students must be "terminated." The College and four of its students then instituted this suit in 1978 challenging the validity of the Regulations and seeking a declaratory judgment.

The effect of the Department's termination of the student grants and loans would not have been limited to the College itself. Indeed, the most direct effect would have been upon the students themselves. Absent the availability of other scholarship funds, many of them would have had to abandon their college education or choose another school. It was to avoid these serious consequences that this suit was instituted. The College prevailed in the District Court but lost in the Court of Appeals. Only after Grove City had brought its case before this Court, did the Department retreat to its present position that Title IX applies only to Grove City's financial aid office. On this narrow theory, the Department has prevailed, having taken this small independent college, which it acknowledges has engaged in no discrimination whatever, through six years of litigation with the full weight of the federal government opposing it. I cannot believe that the Department will rejoice in its "victory."

[A concurring opinion by Justice Stevens is omitted.]

JUSTICE BRENNAN, with whom JUSTICE MARSHALL joins, concurring in part and dissenting in part.

The Court today concludes that Grove City College is "receiving Federal financial assistance" within the meaning of Title IX of the Education Amendments of 1972, 20 U.S.C. § 1681(a), because a number of its students receive federal education grants. As the Court persuasively demonstrates in Part II of its opinion, that conclusion is dictated by "the need to accord [Title IX] a sweep as broad as its language," . . . by reliance on the unique postenactment history of Title IX, and by recognition of the strong congressional intent that there is no "substantive difference between direct institutional assistance and aid received by a school through its students." For these same reasons, however, I cannot join Part III of the Court's opinion, in which the Court interprets the language in Title IX that limits application of the statute to "any education program or activity" receiving federal monies. By conveniently ignoring these controlling indicia of congressional intent, the Court also ignores the primary purposes for which Congress enacted Title IX. The result—allowing Title IX coverage for the College's financial aid program, but rejecting institution-wide coverage even though federal monies benefit the entire College—may be superficially pleasing to those who are uncomfortable with federal intrusion into private educational institutions, but it has no relationship to the statutory scheme enacted by Congress. . . .

A proper application of Title IX to the circumstances of this case demonstrates beyond peradventure that the Court has unjustifiably limited the statute's reach. Grove City College enrolls approximately 140 students who utilize Basic Educational Opportunity Grants (BEOGs) to pay for their education at the College. Although the grant monies are paid directly to the students, the Court properly concludes that the use of these federal monies at the College means that the College "receives Federal financial assistance" within the meaning of Title IX. The Court also correctly notes that a principal purpose underlying congressional enactment of the BEOG program is to provide funds that will benefit colleges and universities as a whole. It necessarily follows, in my view, that the entire undergraduate institution operated by Grove City College is subject to the antidiscrimination provisions included in Title IX.

In determining the scope of Title IX coverage, the primary focus should be on the purposes meant to be served by the particular federal funds received by the institution. In this case, Congress has clearly indicated that BEOG monies are intended to benefit any college or university that enrolls students receiving such grants. As the Court repeatedly recognizes, "[t]he legislative history of the [Education Amendments of 1972] is replete with statements evincing Congress' awareness that the student assistance programs established by the amendments would significantly aid colleges and universities. In fact, one of the stated purposes of the student aid provisions was to 'provid[e] assistance to institutions of higher education.' 20 U.S.C. § 1070(a)(5)." . . .

In many respects, therefore, Congress views financial aid to students, and in particular BEOGs, as the functional equivalent of general aid to institutions. Given this undeniable and clearly stated congressional purpose, it would seem to be self-evident that Congress intended colleges or universities enrolling students who receive BEOGs to be covered, in their entirety, by the antidiscrimination provisions of Title IX. That statute's primary purpose, after all, is to ensure that federal monies are not used to support discriminatory practices.

Under the Court's holding, in contrast, Grove City College is prohibited from discriminating on the basis of sex in its own "financial aid program," but is free to discriminate in other "programs or activities" operated by the institution. Underlying this result is the unstated and unsupportable assumption that monies received through BEOGs are meant only to be utilized by the College's financial aid program. But it is undisputed that BEOG monies, paid to the institution as tuition and fees and used in the general operating budget, are utilized to support most, and perhaps all, of the facilities and services that together comprise Grove City College.

The absurdity of the Court's decision is further demonstrated by examining its practical effect. According to the Court, the "financial aid program" at Grove City College may not discriminate on the basis of sex because it is covered by Title IX, but the College is not prohibited from discriminating in its admissions, its athletic programs, or even its various academic departments. The Court thus sanctions practices that Congress clearly could not have intended: for example, after today's decision, Grove City College would be free to segregate male and female students in classes run by its mathematics department. This would be so even though the affected students are attending the College with the financial assistance provided by federal funds. If anything about Title IX were ever certain, it is that discriminatory practices like the one just described were meant to be prohibited by the statute. . . .

Comments and Questions

1. Does this litigation proceed on the premise that Grove City College actually discriminated against anyone on account of sex? If not, why did the government pursue this suit?

2. What if the record had shown that all of the student aid involved here went to athletes (without differentiation on the basis of sex), but that the school's athletic program, which is supported by student tuition, discriminated on the basis of sex? Would the outcome have been the same, given the majority's reasoning?

3. As the *Grove City College* litigation makes clear, courts, too, are authorized distributive lawmakers (though only when justiciable controversies come their way). In *Grove City College*, the issues involved statutory interpretation and the First Amendment rights of beneficiaries. Judges may also become distributive lawmakers when they adjudicate conflicts between other authorized lawmakers. Recall, for example, the Supreme Court's recent decision outlawing the one-house veto, which had been a favorite legislative tool for maintaining control over agency decisions. See INS v. Chadha, 462 U.S. 919, 103 S.Ct. 2764 (1983).

4. Up until this point, we have taken a top-down view of the lawmaking that occurs when government confers benefits. From the perspective of public-benefit consumers, however, the most important lawmakers may be the officials who work directly with the public on a day-to-day basis. These front-line service providers, or "street-level bureaucrats," exercise considerable discretion over the availability

of benefits and their substance, as the excerpt that follows indicates. As you read the following excerpt, consider what kinds of benefit-conferral programs depend most on street-level bureaucrats, and how policies can be designed to encourage intelligent and compassionate decision making at this level.

M. LIPSKY, STREET–LEVEL BUREAUCRACY
3–6 (1980).*

Typical street-level bureaucrats are teachers, police officers and other law enforcement personnel, social workers, judges, public lawyers and other court officers, health workers, and many other public employees who grant access to government programs and provide services within them. People who work in these jobs tend to have much in common because they experience analytically similar work conditions.

The ways in which street-level bureaucrats deliver benefits and sanctions structure and delimit people's lives and opportunities. These ways orient and provide the social (and political) contexts in which people act. Thus every extension of service benefits is accompanied by an extension of state influence and control. As providers of public benefits and keepers of public order, street-level bureaucrats are the focus of political controversy. They are constantly torn by the demands of service recipients to improve effectiveness and responsiveness and by the demands of citizen groups to improve the efficacy and efficiency of government services. Since the salaries of street-level bureaucrats comprise a significant proportion of nondefense governmental expenditures, any doubts about the size of government budgets quickly translate into concerns for the scope and content of these public services. Moreover, public service workers have expanded and increasingly consolidated their collective strength so that in disputes over the scope of public services they have become a substantial independent force in the resolution of controversy affecting their status and position.

Street-level bureaucrats dominate political controversies over public services for two general reasons. First, debates about the proper scope and focus of governmental services are essentially debates over the scope and function of these public employees. Second, street-level bureaucrats have considerable impact on peoples' lives. This impact may be of several kinds. They socialize citizens to expectations of government services and a place in the political community. They determine the eligibility of citizens for government benefits and sanctions. They oversee the treatment (the service) citizens receive in those programs. Thus, in a sense street-level bureaucrats implicitly mediate aspects of the constitutional relationship of citizens to the state. In short, they hold the keys to a dimension of citizenship.

. . . . They comprise a great portion of all public employees working in domestic affairs. State and local governments employ approximately 3.7 million people in local schools, more than 500,000 people in police

---

* From STREET–LEVEL BUREAUCRACY by Michael Lipsky. © 1980 by Russell Sage Foundation. Reprinted by permission of Basic Books, Inc., Publishers.

operations, and over 300,000 people in public welfare. Public school employees represent more than half of all workers employed in local governments. Instructional jobs represent about two-thirds of the educational personnel, and many of the rest are former teachers engaged in administration, or social workers, psychologists, and librarians who provide direct services in the schools. Of the 3.2 million local government public employees not engaged in education, approximately 14 percent work as police officers. One of every sixteen jobs in state and local government outside of education is held by a public welfare worker. In this and other areas the majority of jobs are held by people with responsibility for involvement with citizens.

Other street-level bureaucrats comprise an important part of the remainder of local government personnel rolls. Although the U.S. Census Bureau does not provide breakdowns of other job classifications suitable for our purposes, we can assume that many of the 1.1 million health workers, most of the 5,000 public service lawyers, many of the employees of the various court systems, and other public employees also perform as street-level bureaucrats. Some of the nation's larger cities employ a staggering number of street-level bureaucrats. For example, the 26,680 school teachers in Chicago are more numerous than the populations of many of the Chicago suburbs.

Another measure of the significance of street-level bureaucrats in public sector employment is the amount of public funds allocated to pay them. Of all local government salaries, more than half went to public education in 1973. Almost 80 percent of these monies was used to pay instructional personnel. Police salaries comprised approximately one-sixth of local public salaries not assigned to education.

Much of the growth in public employment in the past 25 years has occurred in the ranks of street-level bureaucrats. From 1955 to 1975 government employment more than doubled, largely because of the baby boom of the postwar years and the growing number of elderly, dependent citizens increased state and local activity in education, health, and public welfare.

Street-level bureaucracies are labor-intensive in the extreme. Their business is providing service through people, and the operating costs of such agencies reflect their dependence upon salaried workers. Thus most of whatever is spent by government on education, police, or other social services (aside, of course, from income maintenance, or in the case of jails and prisons, inmate upkeep) goes directly to pay street-level bureaucrats. For example, in large cities over 90 percent of police expenditures is used to pay for salaries.

Not only do the salaries of street-level bureaucrats constitute a major portion of the cost of public services, but also the scope of public services employing street-level bureaucrats has increased over time. Charity was once the responsibility of private agencies. The federal government now provides for the income needs of the poor. The public sector has absorbed responsibilities previously discharged by private organizations in such diverse and critical areas as policing, education, and health. Moreover, in all these fields government not only has supplanted private organizations but also has expanded the scope of responsibility of public ones. This is evident in increased public expectations for security and public safety, the extension of responsibilities in the schools to concerns with infant as well as post-adolescent development, and public demands for affordable health care services.

Public safety, public health, and public education *may* still be elusive social objectives, but in the past century they have been transformed into areas for which there is active governmental responsibility. The transformation of public responsibility in the area of social welfare has led some to recognize that what people "have" in modern American society often may consist primarily of their claims on government "largesse," and that claims to this "new property" should be protected as a right of citizens. Street-level bureaucrats play a critical role in these citizen entitlements. Either they directly provide public benefits through services, or they mediate between citizens and their new but by no means secure estates.

The poorer people are, the greater the influence street-level bureaucrats tend to have over them. Indeed, these public workers are so situated that they may well be taken to be part of the problem of being poor. Consider the welfare recipient who lives in public housing and seeks the assistance of a legal services lawyer in order to reinstate her son in school. He has been suspended because of frequent encounters with the police. She is caught in a net of street-level bureaucrats with conflicting orientations toward her, all acting in what they call her "interest" and "the public interest."

People who are not able to purchase services in the private sector must seek them from government if they are to receive them at all. Indeed, it is taken as a sign of social progress that poor people are granted access to services if they are too poor to pay for them.

Section Four. Structures and Processes for Applying Public–Benefit Law and Techniques

A common fallacy about law is that it exists solely for purposes of immediate control over the behavior of citizens and, therefore, that all its structures and processes are set up with the idea of securing compliance and resolving disputes over whether requirements are binding in particular cases. Securing compliance *is* a fundamental issue in designing tax legislation and other burden-imposing laws that support public-benefit conferral. But compliance is not the primary purpose of policies that provide for the distribution of benefits. These policies do not usually meet the resistance that administrative regulation or the outright prohibitions of the criminal law do. People are normally more than willing to be recipients of public benefits. As we have seen, however, lawmakers do put conditions on the availability of public money, goods, and services. These conditions are intended to channel the flow of benefits in certain directions, but the primary purpose in welfare assistance, disaster relief, Medicaid, and other benefit-conferral programs still remains distributing goods to people. Given the general willingness of people to accept benefits, even those with conditions attached, it should not be surprising that most distributive law is oriented toward originating and operating programs, not toward resolving controversies over the applicability of the program to specific cases. Usually, "getting organized" to confer benefits is no simple matter, legally speaking. Unless the benefit is simply an exemption from what would otherwise be a burden (a tax break, for example), "getting organized" involves, at a minimum, setting up an agency structure or grafting the program onto an existing structure, specifying the scope of authority at each administrative level, and providing for routine agency operations. For an illustration, reread the Legal Services Corporation legislation and locate these features.

The best way to grasp the role that law plays in ordering the conferral of public benefits may be to analyze a single policy in some depth. A good candidate for such analysis is the policy that government will provide free primary and secondary education. The immensity of the undertaking is impressive: nearly 45 million students attend public primary and secondary schools in over 16,000 school districts, with approximately 3 million teachers; and as a nation we spend over $76 billion annually to support these schools. The goal of educating such numbers requires a complex mixture of legal ordering devices, and the design and operation of some of them create controversy. These attributes make public education an excellent vehicle for learning more about the range of legal structures and processes that can be involved in implementing distributive programs.

To facilitate analysis, the implementation process can be subdivided into four tasks: (1) setting up the basic distributive structure, (2) recruiting and retaining the personnel necessary to effectuate the policy, (3) specifying the detailed form the benefit is to take, and (4) securing the funding to make the program operational.

A. Setting Up the Basic Distributive Structure

Movements for public education began early in America, even before the advent of legislatures as we know them. By the end of the seventeenth century, most colonial and local legislative bodies in New England had come to accept certain ideas about public education: (1) that legislative bodies had the power to set up and administer public schools, (2) that local communities could even be required to do as much, (3) that public revenues could be raised and used for this purpose, and (4) that parents could be required to educate their children, though not necessarily in public schools.

These ideas concerning public education were not much emphasized, however, until after the American Revolution. At that point, the conviction began to grow that if individuals were going to govern themselves and realize their potential as individuals, then they must be educated. If one nation were to be formed, then common values, a common language, and a common literature had to be taught. If religious liberty were to be a reality in a country divided in religion, then public education had to be available free of religious domination. Influenced by these ideas, state and local legislative bodies began the task of building public educational systems. The Congress played almost no role at all.

The ex-colonists did not immediately set up free public schools on a permanent basis. The New York state legislature, for example, experimented with the establishment of free schools to instruct children in "English language, . . . English grammar, arithmetic, mathematics, and such other branches of knowledge as are most useful and necessary to complete a good English education," but the law lasted only five years. Thereafter, the legislature continued to endorse the principle but, until 1867, allowed local schools to charge tuition. Nor was schooling generally compulsory until after the Civil War. According to M. Yudof, D. Kirp, T. van Geel & B. Levin, Kirp & Yudof's Educational Policy and the Law 12 (2d ed. 1982):

> Massachusetts passed the first compulsory education law in 1852, requiring that all children between the ages of eight and fourteen attend school for at least twelve weeks a year; twenty-eight states passed similar legislation in the years following the Civil War. But compulsory education, although legally required, did not immediately become social fact. The resistance of some educators affords one explanation of this phenomenon. In Auburn, New York, School Superintendent B.B. Snow voiced a common sentiment: "The compulsory attendance of the element attempted to be reached by law would be detrimental to the well-being of any respectable school." In many school systems, there was insufficient space to accommodate this class of youngsters: in Illinois, for instance, school buildings could house only one-third of all eligible schoolchildren, while in New York City the average elementary school class enrolled seventy-five pupils. The insatiable demand for cheap labor continued to be satisfied by the hiring of school-age youngsters, and officials—many of whom believed that the education of workers' children was a waste of time—often ignored these violations of the law. An 1884 report drafted by Charles Peck, New York commissioner of statistics of labor, pronounced the compulsory education statute a "dead letter." In the South, compulsory attendance laws were not enforced until well into the twentieth century, and the educational needs of black children were given lowest priority.
>
> By the end of the nineteenth century, however, the principle of compulsory schooling was generally accepted . . . .

Every state now requires compulsory attendance. Almost every state constitution addresses the question of public education. Most state constitutions simply authorize the legislature to establish and maintain a system of free public education, but some, like New York's, actually require the legislature to create a network of public schools: "The legislature shall provide for the maintenance and support of a system of free common schools, wherein all the children of this state may be educated." N.Y. Const. art. XI, § 1.

The basic structure of early American education—local schools supported by local funds, with only limited supervision and financing by state legislatures, and even less federal involvement—has proven remarkably resilient over time. Time has brought with it, however, significant movement toward increased central control. The federal government has become involved in programs to aid the handicapped, the disadvantaged, and other targeted groups and to attack other problems, and federal aid now accounts for about 8 percent of school revenues. The states have also become more deeply involved in funding public education, so that state aid now makes up about 44 percent of school revenues. The remaining 48 percent comes from local sources.

The two readings that follow describe structures for the governance of public education. As you read, take note of who the relevant lawmakers are and what functions they perform. Does the power of parents and other local taxpayers to set standards in their schools depend on the policy issue in question? As you read, make a list of policy issues that schools face, and note the most significant lawmakers for each issue.

PROJECT, EDUCATION AND THE LAW: STATE INTERESTS AND INDIVIDUAL RIGHTS

74 Mich.L.Rev. 1373, 1375–81 (1976).*

The several states have plenary power in the sphere of education so long as they do not violate provisions of the United States Constitution. In delegating considerable educational policy-making authority to local agencies, states have "not surrendered their prerogatives, but have merely determined the machinery by which the state function shall be performed."

Only rarely have legislatures taken a broad interest in formulating and controlling educational policy. Most states have left such matters to administrative agencies and various elected bodies at the state and local levels. At the summit of the administrative hierarchy is a board that has been established in all the states. The powers of the various state boards differ. In some, the board may control all aspects of the state's educational program; in others, wide delegation to local agencies may limit the board to a very narrow range of activities. While the boards are responsible for implementing legislation and also possess policy-making discretion, out of deference to local institutions this policy-making power is rarely exercised.

All states also have a superintendent of schools who typically performs such functions as the enforcement of laws, adoption of regulations, distribution of funds and financial accounting. In recent years, the state superintendents have been given greater responsibility for research and development and for general supervision of the schools. An institution at the state level, usually referred to as the "department of education," consists of supporting personnel who assist the superintendent in his administrative duties.

Many of the functions performed at the state level, such as the distribution of research data and the publication of journals, merely aid the schools in their daily operations. These have little direct impact on the student and thus rarely lead to conflicts among the various interests within the educational community. Other, typically regulatory, state functions are designed, however, to serve collectivist interests in educa-

* Reprinted with permission from 74 Michigan Law Review (June 1976).

tion. Most important are the controls on citizens that devolve from the legislature. Thus, socialization of all children is assured by compulsory education requirements, while the particular values and standards of achievement sought through socialization are defined by state curriculum requirements. Moreover, states have other, less direct means of defining the community norms that the educational system is designed to further. For example, all states require teachers to be certified. Licensing requirements narrow the class of individuals that will be allowed to teach to those who possess traits considered worthy of being nurtured in students. Thus, successful applicants must have a good, moral character, though what activities or traits satisfy this requirement is often uncertain. In addition, minimum education requirements for teacher's certification are typically prescribed by a state administrative agency. Such standards are intended to guarantee that teachers possess a minimum level of competence. They exemplify the state's interest in ensuring that students in *all* localities achieve a certain level of academic prowess through their exposure to teachers with adequate credentials. States also prescribe certain standards for such facilities as buildings, libraries, and equipment. This exercise of control over the quality of the student's environment is perfectly consistent with the state's interest in academic achievement. Yet the state may actually go further and impose requirements, such as the displaying of an American flag in each school, that advance the state's interest in inculcating patriotism in the young.

Despite these examples of control at the state level, the management of the educational system for the most part occurs at the local level. In recent years, state concern has been largely focused on increasing financial support for programs managed by the local communities. Great differences in wealth and resources exist among communities and some districts are unable to support an adequate system of public schools without state aid. Thus, much of the state effort in education in the past few years has been directed at these problems, but enormous discrepancies in expenditures per pupil remain.

Historically, Americans have considered schools to be an extension of the local community. Thus, although state legislatures possess plenary power over the educational system, local initiative with respect to education is so highly regarded that most states have delegated extensive authority over the actual administration of the schools to local institutions. States have divided their territory into "school districts" that perform the sole function of establishing and maintaining the public schools. Boards of education, commonly referred to as school boards, have been created as the governing body of the school district and are typically responsible for the day-to-day operation of the public schools.

Although the diversity of state statutory schemes makes it difficult to generalize about school board composition and authority, it is clear that the school board is intended to be the instrument for the public's expression of educational policy. That educational decision-making is regarded as requiring closer ties to the public than other governmental functions is demonstrated by the unique status accorded most boards. For example, school districts are usually distinct from their corresponding political units—village, city, or county—even though the boundaries may be identical. In states in which the school board is elected directly by a district's voters, the contests are held separately from those for municipal government offices and are almost always conducted on a nonpartisan basis. The severing of education from general local politics caused by these distinctions is generally respected by municipal officials, who avoid direct involvement in educational matters.

———

PETERSON, THE POLITICS OF AMERICAN EDUCATION

2 Rev.Research Educ. 348, 351–54 (1974).*

School Board Autonomy

The conduct of school affairs in most localities in the United States is legally distinct from the conduct of other municipal activities. Although school boards, like all other municipal entities, are constitutionally creatures of the state, those responsible for school affairs at the local level have considerably more legal independence from municipal authorities than do most city departments, and a good deal of freedom from state interference. Of course, the degree of legal independence varies widely from place to place. In many areas, the school board's jurisdictional boundaries do not coincide with city, township, village, or any other political lines; however, in the South they tend to coincide with county lines. The overwhelming majority of board members are elected, but a minority are appointed by another public official, who in most cases is the mayor of the municipality. Even where board members are appointed, they usually serve for fixed terms rather than "at the pleasure of the mayor," as is the case with most department heads. And at least in some of the largest cities, even the mayor's original appointment of board members is constrained so that he must reappoint members who do not wish to retire and select board members from a short list prepared by a nominating commission outside his sphere of control. Most school boards are fiscally independent as well. Although they may receive substantial aid from the state and federal governments, they have the independent authority to tax property within their jurisdictions. Other school boards, however, are dependent upon other local governments for the amount of money they receive from local sources.

The legal separateness of school boards as decision-making bodies is only the departure point for most analyses of school autonomy, however. Other formal and informal mechanisms reinforce the legal distinctness of school policy formation. In the first place, elected board members are usually chosen in nonpartisan, at-large elections held at times differing from those for other state and local elections. As a result, board members generally do not have close affiliations with political parties, seldom claim to represent any group or segment of the community, and are elected by only a small percentage of the eligible voters. As a consequence, board members are not beholden to groups or factions in the community but feel they can exercise their own good judgment in determining school policy. They thus discuss controversial questions in private sessions, present a facade of unanimity in sessions attended by the public, and hold their meetings in small rooms at times that are announced as unobtrusively as possible.

The Professionals

Even so, school boards are not necessarily the critical center of power in the educational decision-making system. They are unpaid lay citizens with other occupational and domestic concerns. They are easily ensnared by trivial details and leave major policy questions in the hands of administrators. As a result, the board comes to accept the fundamental role of expertness in managing the affairs of the school. In the end, the board becomes the agent of legitimation that provides a facade of public control, while power is really being exercised by administrators.

If boards have generally been dependent upon their administrative staff, this has not meant that teachers as a group exercised much influence over educational policy. As compared to most professions, a relatively larger number of teachers have been women, have only short-term or intermittent professional careers, have been opposed to engaging in political activities, and have been reluctant to challenge the authority of superiors. Their organization, the National Education Association (NEA), was traditionally dominated by administrators who were more concerned about broad educational policies than teacher welfare issues. They accepted an ideology which insisted that teachers were white-collar professionals for whom union tactics, such as the strike, were inappropriate. State laws against strikes by public employees reinforced whatever other inhibitions teachers had against closing the schools. Of course, teachers shaped the educational processes within their individual classrooms, and the NEA is believed to be an important lobby at federal and state levels. As a force influencing local district policies, however, the impact of teachers has traditionally been quite limited.

The growing militancy of teachers is beginning to change power relations at the local level. In recent years the NEA has been increasingly challenged by the more militant, more teacher-welfare-oriented American Federation of Teachers (AFT), an affiliate of the American Federation of Labor–Congress of Industrial Organizations (AFL-CIO). The AFT's success has been greatest in large cities, where the union movement as a whole has been particularly strong. . . .

The Laity

The greater influence of teacher organizations may have altered power relations within the educational profession, but the shift of power to lay groups is apparently much more difficult. Citizens' organizations, civil rights groups, and Parent-Teacher Associations (PTA's) have failed to win continuing influence over important school policies. PTA's tend to be supportive rather than demand-articulating organizations, and their activ-ities are carefully guided by local principals. They raise money for special activities in local schools, hold special events in honor of teachers, and often become the shock troops in bond and tax referendum cam-paigns. PTA's, moreover, tend to concentrate their attention on the problems of specific schools rather than attempt to influence overall school policies. . . .

The extent to which school policy-making is isolated from external political forces varies with the issue under discussion, of course. The professionals have the greatest control over curriculum policies, internal administrative organization of the schools, recruitment of staff, the bulk of the budgetary process, and the allocation of supplies among schools within the district. The location of new schools and the physical condi-tion of existing buildings are matters more frequently influenced, at least to some degree, by lay groups and even the voting public. This may be due to the visibility of the physical plant and the impact of land-use policies on property values. The overall size of the school budget is also influenced by institutions and political forces external to the school world. Since school financing typically needs to be approved by a state legislature or municipal government or the voters in a referendum, this becomes one of the most severe external constraints on school professionals, probably a major reason why finance is such an issue to educators.

———

Not until the mid-1960s did the basic structure of American public education become controversial. Criticism focused on tendencies toward coercion and conformity allegedly fostered by government's strong role in primary and secondary education. Some critics suggested dismantling the public-school system, in Ivan Illich's term, "deschooling" America. Illich even proposed a new article in the Bill of Rights that would read: "The State shall make no law with respect to the establishment of education." I. Illich, Deschooling Society (1971).

More recently, others have attacked the monopolistic tendencies of the current system, without going so far as to suggest its abolition. These writers focus particularly on the requirement that families who seek alternatives to the public schools must pay both school taxes and the cost of private schooling, with no tax breaks to ease this double burden. This means of ordering the distribution of educational benefits, critics argue, ensures that those who cannot afford the extra cost of private education have no freedom of choice. In Roger A. Freeman's words:

> Is it proper for government to force parents to send their children to a school which they would not choose if they had an option? Why should an option be available only to affluent parents? Is it good public policy and is it educationally productive to make alternative schools—whose spirit is more conducive to learning— inaccessible to most children? If millions of parents prefer the discipline enforced in nonpublic schools, why should they not have an opportunity to send their children there even if their economic circumstances do not allow them to pay high tuition charges?

Freeman, Educational Tax Credits, in The Public School Monopoly 471, 487 (R. Everhart ed. 1982).

Another advocate of reform has described the current system as biased against religion: "True government neutrality and genuine observance of the Constitution demand that government subsidize various types of schools, religious as well as secularist." McGarry, The Unconstitutionality of Exclusive Governmental Support of Entirely Secularistic Education, 28 Cath.Law. 1, 33 (1983). And critic James Coleman uses the language of free trade to argue for deregulating the schools: "[T]he matter can be usefully examined by viewing private school tuition as a protective tariff relative to tax support for free public schools." Coleman, Private Schools, Public Schools, and the Public Interest, 64 Pub.Interest 19, 28 (1981).

Were this challenge to the favored treatment of the public schools to result in state and federal legislation (tuition tax credits or school voucher plans, for example) and were this legislation to be held constitutional, the shape of public education as we now know it could change significantly. The proportion of children enrolled in public schools, currently about 90 percent of the total school-age population, would certainly drop. The size of the decline would depend on how much the new government subsidies cut into the costs of sending children to private schools.

After reading the following two excerpts, evaluate the arguments for and against abandoning the traditional approach to benefit conferral in education.

———

J. COONS & S. SUGARMAN, EDUCATION BY CHOICE
10–14, 45, 47, 52–53, 60–61 (1978).*

There is no easy way to tell if the needs and wants of most families are served by the local public school. The widespread criticism of American education in the 1960s and 1970s suggests they are not. Rather it seems likely that the preferences and phobias of many go undiscovered and unsatisfied. In place of compulsory assignment, many children and their families might prefer programs emphasizing science, the classics, McGuffey's reader, music, the Baltimore Catechism, or the sayings of Chairman Mao. Some might want an outdoor school, a school in a living room, a school that starts at 7:00 and ends at noon, a school with the long vacation in the fall, or a school whose teachers are artisans or otherwise employed part-time outside the school. Likewise, many teachers might wish they were free to enlist children in the enterprise of learning by offering the bait of their special abilities in dance, botany, French, Chinese culture, or the teachings of Muhammed. What we do know is that—even given a harmony of objectives among school, teacher, parent, and student—many families find it extremely difficult today to get the child and the preferred experience together except by happy accident. . . .

Why has the state adopted this policy? Is it the fear that some parents will choose inadequate education or none at all? This is a prudent concern. On grounds of simple fairness children should be guaranteed reasonable access to education whatever their parents' views. There are also the social benefits that are supposed to flow from education. These individual and social considerations together suggest the state should strictly enforce the parent's legal duty to educate. Would that not suffice? The humane response is that the right to education should not be limited by parental resources; parental duty means nothing to the child if the family cannot afford to educate him. Therefore, additional collective action is necessary, and unless the child is to be taken from his parents, this requires a subsidy of the parents by the state. Only in that way can the child's hope for education be delivered from the economic limitations of his family.

Perhaps the poor could simply be given money. But in a cash grant plan, education would compete with other wants of the child and with wants of other family members—including adults. Were the legal duty to educate one's child easily enforced, this might not be a serious problem. However, earmarking the subvention for spending on education would far more easily assure that parents did not make alternate allocations, either to themselves or their children.

But these observations carry us only a short distance toward a justification of the status quo in which tuition-free public education is made available to all. They leave unanswered two substantial questions: Why is the education subvention provided to those who are not poor? And, more importantly, why is it provided in kind? We will address these questions in order.

Many families today can afford to pay for the education of their children without state assistance. Others could provide for the education of their children if the state had not already appropriated a substantial portion of the family's resources through education taxes. And the number that could finance their own children's schooling would increase dramatically were parents able to borrow the money through government-guaranteed loans which they could repay over a long period. In short, ought not the state rest content with providing education grants to the children of the poor and loans to the middle class?

The answer is probably no. There are several plausible justifications for making tuition-free education available to children in all income groups. Eliminating income tests helps to avoid stigmatizing the poor in the manner they now experience in public hospital wards and in welfare. Alternatively, education subventions for all families could be seen as a benefit for large families, regardless of income—a fiscal cousin of the tax deduction for dependent children. Or maybe subventions to the middle and upper classes should be seen as a crude system of coercive loans for educational purposes; the school tax system in effect forces parents to borrow for their children's education and to repay over their lifetime. Finally, perhaps children themselves should be viewed as the borrowers who return the cost of their education through the taxes they pay as adults. Taken together or perhaps separately, these are reasonable justifications for the subsidy to nonpoor families, especially if the middle and upper classes bear a fair share of the taxes supporting the system (a matter outside our present concern). In no way, however, do they advance our understanding of the state's decision to provide the subsidy only in kind through publicly owned and administered schools. We now turn to that important question.

A family's poverty threatens more than its children's education; without money it cannot afford food, clothing, or shelter—for parents or children—any more than it can pay tuition. During this century, our society has increasingly taken collective responsibility to assure the poor, particularly those with children, their basic needs. In doing so, government has discovered several approaches in addition to in-kind distribution; outside of education, a variety of techniques has been tried. Housing exemplifies the full range of political instruments. Sometimes housing for lower income families has been provided directly through the construction of government-owned apartments with subsidized or free rent; this is the nearest analogue to our public education system, and has been the least successful effort to improve housing through government. Under other programs, however, private landlords have been encouraged with a variety of tax benefits and subsidies to provide low-income housing that meets certain specifications. A third technique provides poor families with housing coupons to be used toward payment of their rent in a dwelling of their selection; experimentation with this approach is now going on. Finally, and today most frequently, the poor are simply given cash to help them bargain in the private rental market.

The bulk of our "welfare" programs now are of this last type. Instead of government potatoes, poor families today are usually given money for the purchase of soup, soap, or stockings. In general this seems wise; not everybody likes potatoes or is nourished by them. Of course, some will decide to nourish themselves on booze, and this is a problem, especially where children suffer as a consequence. Thus the government sometimes earmarks the transfers to narrow the range of choice; for example, under the food stamp and Medicaid programs the government provides stamps or cards that can be used only to satisfy needs for food or for health care. Even with their restrictions, such programs are very different from those that simply give the recipients government soup and government doctors. Stamps and cards allow their holders to choose among foods and physicians.

Why not distribute school dollars in this way and permit the family to choose among educators? Just as some children may be allergic to the government's potato, some may be allergic to its schools or teachers. Yet the state has chosen not only to operate its own schools but, in practical economic effect, has required most children to attend them. The decision to leave the average family powerless regarding education, while permitting its choice of material goods, seems eccentric. Many families might be content with a relatively uniform and choiceless style of health maintenance or even an imposed diet, if it were adequate. Concerning the training of minds, a wider variety of opinions seems to obtain. One would suppose choice to be more, rather than less, significant to the family with respect to education than other human needs.

Of course, the stronger interest in choice might be seen as the very problem. Defenders of the status quo remind us that a certain level of education is essential in a democratic society, and that if families were given money to purchase education where they pleased, some would select the scholastic equivalent of booze. This fear is justified if the only alternative to herding the nonrich into public schools is outright parentocracy. But such a policy dilemma is hard to credit, at least on its face. The public and private schools created under any politically viable system of family choice would be required by law to meet a fair minimum standard. The child of the wayward parent would not face the dubious exchange of one educational autocrat (the state) for another (the parent); instead, he would be party to a balanced regime. The state would mandate that all children receive whatever elements of education command a public consensus. This could probably assure no more than exposure to the agreed minimum, but note that this is equally true of the existing scheme. Indeed, one argument for more voluntarism is that it will increase the rate at which children actually achieve the minimum. And beyond those politically determined essentials, families would be assured the economic capacity to pursue their educational preferences. . . .

The beginning of wisdom here is getting the question straight. We think the question for the state is whom it shall empower to decide what is best. Societal benevolence should move the state to locate power in those who seem most likely to serve the individual child. What the state needs is a theory of delegation whose object is the child's interest. It needs relevant criteria for deciding which unit or units smaller than society will best exercise the authority to decide for the individual child when society itself is blind to his interest. . . .

Viewed as a system of decision location, the present educational structure can be described largely as a regime of local government employees and elected officials who have been empowered to decide what form of education is in the best interest of the children resident within their district. These agents—school board members, administrators, and teachers—are moderately constrained by higher government authorities and by the attitudes of local residents, which together set political limits on the range of tolerable educational practices. Children themselves rarely have anything to say about their school assignment except as it may influence the location of family residence. Once residence is decided, individual public school families have little formal voice in determining the education their child receives, though the sophisticated parent with spare time may employ harassment and persuasion to secure a preferred assignment.

If we were to attribute to this present "decentralized" scheme a primary concern for the best interest of individual children, its rationale would have to be that—apart from those families able to pay for private schools or a change of residence—local government agents make better school assignments for individual children they have never met than would the family, even were the family to be supported by professional counseling. The underlying argument would be that, by imposing on individual children the decisions made for them by professional and elected local decision makers, the public system gives them advantages unattainable by any other form of assignment. He receives the benefits of educational expertise while eluding the risks of mistakes, negligence, and exploitation by those amateurs who are his family. Power is placed in the hands of disinterested elders and experts who are outside the family yet are subject to public scrutiny. . . .

We come, then, to an evaluation of the family as decider. We will argue that, above the societally agreed minimum, as long as it has ready access to information and professional counseling, the family's claim to special competence is strong; that in its unique opportunity to listen and to know and in its special personal concern for the child, the family is his most promising champion and a fit senior partner of the decision-making team. The family's capacities for voice, knowledge, and caring are inextricable one from the other; indeed, to separate their description here would be excessively analytical. Each is a complementary aspect of the intimate and continuing domestic environment; each is a facet of the family members' relation to one another and particularly to the younger child. And that relation holds even for families whose members are not particularly fond of one another but who gladly or grudgingly accept responsibility. . . .

The best protection against permanent misassignment is to give the power of reconsideration to those who must bear the consequences of error over an extended period. The family is not likely to ignore for long its child's annoying complaint before taking steps to understand and, together with the child and his counselors, to seek to correct the problem. The family is not likely to tolerate for long the assignment of the child to a special program that yields nothing but frustration and stigma. Its intervention on occasion may make matters temporarily worse, but at least that intervention can initiate an intelligible search for alternative solutions; and the family will be around to seek them long after the child's teacher and counselor have moved on to new children, new problems, and new schools.

LEVIN, EDUCATIONAL VOUCHERS AND SOCIAL POLICY

in Care and Education of Young Children in America 106, 116–20
(R. Haskins & J. Gallagher eds. 1979).*

Perhaps the greatest social dilemma raised by vouchers is the potential divergence between private choices and the social benefits of education. Presumably, so many of our social resources are devoted to education because the reproduction of our social, economic, and political systems depends heavily on preparing the young to understand and participate in these systems. . . .

This concern has at least two major dimensions: First, the schools are expected to provide students with an understanding of the role and functioning of our democratic system of government as well as to prepare them for participating in such a system. Second, the schools are expected to create and sustain a system of social mobility in which a child's eventual income and occupational status are not linked inextricably to those of his parents. The schools are expected to more nearly equalize adult opportunities among youngsters born into different racial, social, and economic circumstances. In this section, we shall explore the probable impact of the voucher mechanism on these two social goals of the schools.

Vouchers and Preparation for Democracy

A major function of the public schools is the transmission of a common language, heritage, set of values, and knowledge necessary for appropriate political functioning in our democratic society. To a large degree, the schools attempt to reproduce these traits through a common curriculum and heterogeneous enrollments. That is, we presume that exposure to a variety of students from different backgrounds and to a common curriculum of social studies and civic content will prepare students adequately to participate in democratic institutions.

In almost every respect, the voucher approach would violate these premises by encouraging separation and stratification of students according to parental commitments and orientations and by tailoring curricula to appeal to and reinforce these parental concerns. Neighborhood residential patterns in the United States prevent complete heterogeneity in student attendance patterns; even within most neighborhoods different religions, political viewpoints, ethnic backgrounds, and ideologies are represented. Further, there is some degree of racial heterogeneity in a large number of public schools, even though the overall picture on racial integration is not a happy one. The voucher approach would systematize the allocation of youngsters to schools according to family background and identity to an incomparably greater extent than even the more segregated of our current neighborhood-based schools.

Indeed, the great appeal of vouchers is that parents can choose the type of education they desire for their children by simply selecting a school that addresses those needs. True, parents might wish to choose schools that emphasize to a greater degree the arts or sciences or sports or basic skills or humanistic objectives than the present schools, but these differences can be sought and attained through a variety of arrangements in the current public school system. What makes the voucher approach unique is that parents will be able to send their children to schools that will reinforce in the most restrictive fashion the political, ideological, and religious views of the family. School will be treated as a strict extension of the home, with little opportunity for students to experience the diversity of backgrounds and viewpoints that contributes to the democratic process.

The importance of being exposed to conflicting positions in forming democratic values cannot be overstated. This fact is illustrated by a recent study of attitudes toward dissent among West German youth. The central finding of this study was that young people who showed high tolerance for viewpoints different from the majority ones on specific subjects had been more exposed to controversy or conflict than those who had little tolerance for dissenting views. Even more to the point, the greater the reported frequency with which controversial topics had been entertained in classrooms, the higher the tolerance of students toward dissenting viewpoints.

But if we consider that under a voucher approach, parents will tend to select schools that reinforce their own views, the opportunities for exposure to constructive conflict and controversy will be significantly narrowed for their children. It is highly dubious that Catholic schools will or even should promote discussions about the pros and cons of birth control and abortion; that Ku Klux Klan schools will provide anything but the most negative stereotypes of Blacks, while Black Panther schools will treat whites similarly. John Birch schools are not likely to expose students to a debate on the virtues of Medicare and public assistance under monopoly capitalism; Maoist schools are not likely to find any virtues in the political institutions of America. This situation is hardly likely to have salubrious consequences for a democracy in which disputed issues must be addressed and resolved continually.

Vouchers and Equality

. . . Even though there will be differences from plan to plan, vouchers will tend to create greater transmission of inequalities from generation to generation than the present public schools. This problem tends to assert itself because parents seem to pursue child-rearing patterns that are consistent and reinforce their own values and class position in the society. This can best be understood by considering what these values are and how they might affect the choice of school.

Let us assume parents wish to select that school which they believe will have the most chance of making their child a success in life. Clearly, the rules for success differ according to where parents are situated in the productive and occupational hierarchy. Kohn has shown that working-class families seem to emphasize conformity in their children (obedience to rules), whereas parents in relatively higher occupational positions stress independence and ability to choose among available alternatives. The research of Hess and Shipman on maternal-child interactions also tends to substantiate these differences, with lower-class mothers stressing a "do as I tell you" approach in teaching their children and middle-class mothers seemingly using a more heuristic approach. Obviously, conformity and "do as I tell you" are ingredients for success in working-class occupations. Such occupations require workers to report to work on time, follow orders of superiors, carry out repetitive tasks, and obey all the rules and regulations of the firm in order to succeed. Individuals in these occupations who do not conform are not rewarded with steady work and job promotions. Thus, the research on behavior of working-class parents suggests that they will select for their children highly structured schools that emphasize a high degree of discipline, concentration on basic skills, and following orders.

In contrast, the occupational experience of the upper middle-class parent suggests that independence and mastery of principles or concepts breed success. Managerial and professional roles require the ability to consider alternative production techniques, products, marketing strategies, and personnel, to create the rules and regulations which define the work organization, to maintain relatively great flexibility in personal work schedules depending on individual needs, and to have the ability to give orders even more than to take orders. Parents with a background in such occupational positions are more likely to stress a great deal of freedom in the school environments of their children with a heavy emphasis on student choice, flexible scheduling, few significant rules, and light enforcement of rules that exist. These parents will expect the school to place a great deal of responsibility on the student in choosing and undertaking his educational experiences. The attainment of basic skills will be taken for granted, and the curriculum will pay much greater attention to written and verbal communication skills.

If parents choose those school environments they believe will maximize the probability of success as defined within the context of their experience, the working-class child will get schooling that reinforces working-class orientations, and upper-class children will attend schools that orient them toward the upper echelons of the occupational hierarchy. . . .

Further, to the degree that social class stratification increased, it would become easier to identify individuals for particular positions in the social class hierarchy by the schools they attend. Each school would connote a different breeding or charter that would have a certification value in preparing individuals for further educational opportunities or positions in the labor market. Even without identifying the actual proficiencies of students as individuals, the information connoted by the class orientation of schooling would tend to serve a stratification role.

The voucher approach to education represents a paradox. It seems reasonable to believe that greater choice among consumers and increased institutional responsiveness will enhance the welfare of society. At a rhetorical level, we would be improving the ability of families to obtain the education they want for their children. But as I have demonstrated, the expansion of choices and market responsiveness will be much greater for upper-income groups than for lower-income and minority citizens, and the element of choice will lead insidiously to an even greater degree of class stratification and socialization than exists now. That these latter effects will be based upon individual "choices" and "preferences" means that the exacerbation of social-class differences in the fortunes of children will be considered the responsibility of parents who chose the schools rather than the responsibility of the class-oriented society that predetermined the parents' values leading to the choices.

———

Comments and Questions

1. How do the two previous selections differ in the assumptions they make about the behavior of education consumers and providers under a more market-oriented system of public education? Do these writers differ in the policy goals they regard as most significant in the delivery of educational benefits?

2. What authorized lawmakers in the current system would stand to lose the most power if a voucher system were implemented? Do you think such a shift in the balance of power would be advantageous on the whole?

3. Review the Constitution in Appendix A at the back of this book. Does it discuss education, in the language of either rights or duties? Does it require that any particular educational programs be implemented? How might an opponent of vouchers frame an argument that they represent an unconstitutional means of distributing educational benefits?

4. How should the issue of vouchers versus traditional distribution of educational benefits be resolved? Should courts play a major role?

B. Recruiting and Retaining the Personnel

Staffing any benefit-conferral program that delivers an array of ongoing services to a broad public on a day-to-day basis is a complex, sometimes daunting task. Much legal ordering is required. The problems are particularly difficult in public education, where the quality of the personnel is so important to the effectiveness of the distributive program.

Many factors affect the availability of good personnel, including salaries and working conditions. By what law and by what legal means are salaries and working conditions determined? Collective bargaining is one approach. The next two selections survey the issues of legal ordering that arise when public-sector employees like schoolteachers use collective bargaining to negotiate the terms of their employment.

C. SUMMERS, PUBLIC SECTOR BARGAINING: PROBLEMS OF GOVERNMENTAL DECISIONMAKING

44 U.Cin.L.Rev. 669, 669–70, 674–75 (1975).*

There is nothing unique about the work which public employees perform. The private sector has school teachers, nurses and social workers, as well as secretaries, bookkeepers, janitors, maintenance employees, construction workers, and rubbish collectors. There are private police, private detectives, private armed guards, and even private firefighters. Nor is the work necessarily any more critical because it is performed by public employees. Strikes by parochial school teachers create substantially the same inconvenience as strikes by public school teachers. A strike by janitors in public buildings may create fewer problems than a strike by janitors in private apartment buildings. A disruption in garbage collection may be less serious than a disruption in electric power or telephone service.

The uniqueness of public employment is not in the employees nor in the work performed; the uniqueness is in the special character of the employer. The employer is government; the ones who act on behalf of the employer are public officials; and the ones to whom those officials are answerable are citizens and voters. We have developed a whole structure of constitutional and statutory principles, and a whole culture of political practices and attitudes as to how government is to be conducted, what powers public officials are to exercise, and how they are to be made answerable for their actions. Collective bargaining by public employers must fit within the governmental structure and must function consistently with our governmental processes; the problems of the public employer accommodating its collective bargaining function to government structures and processes is what makes public sector bargaining unique.

. . .

Collective bargaining creates a special process for making decisions concerning terms and conditions of employment. That process significantly increases the effectiveness of the public employees' voice in those decisions in several ways. First, the principle of exclusive representation gives public employees a unified and authoritative voice. The majority union becomes the sole spokesman for the employees, and an agreement with it settles the terms and conditions for all employees in the unit. The ability to speak with a single voice and to provide a binding settlement gives added force and political weight to that voice in the public forum.

Second, the bargaining process gives public employees special access to the political process. They are not limited to speeches at public meetings, petitions, circulars or personal presentations, as other interest groups are. The union, representing all employees in bargaining, can compel responsible officials to sit down at the bargaining table, confront them face to face, engage in discussion, respond to arguments, state positions, provide reasons and supply information. The process of interchange continues through countless meetings of interminable hours until either agreement is reached or all possibilities are exhausted. This direct and intensive access to responsible officials, with its structured process of persuasion, gives the union an especially effective voice in the decisionmaking.

Third, because bargaining normally comes before the budget is adopted, public employees may obtain prior consideration of their interests, with collective agreements worked out before other sets of decisions are made. Once the agreement is made, the ability to consider other interests becomes limited. Even tentative agreements made at the bargaining table by negotiators who do not have the power to bind cannot be rejected without political costs. The agreement carries a political force of its own, giving it a measure of priority over competing claims.

Fourth, if bargaining is conducted behind closed doors, as is customary in the private sector, the union's voice gains added effectiveness. The public official is confronted with the union's demands and arguments without direct exposure to the competing demands and arguments. The pressures of hard bargaining through extended sessions push toward acceptance of the union's demands at the expense of other interests which are unable to make their weight felt because they do not know what is being decided at the bargaining table. Once an agreement, even a merely tentative one, is reached at the bargaining table, the opposing interests are placed at a substantial political disadvantage. The issue becomes whether the agreement should be repudiated, rather than what agreement should be made in the first place.

Fifth, the union by obtaining bargaining rights can build an organizational structure and develop resources to be used in political forums other than bargaining. Practically, though not legally, it becomes the voice of the employees on all political issues. More importantly, it may provide the organizational base, if not the financial means, for electing those who support their bargaining demands and defeating those who oppose them.

I would emphasize that the political effectiveness of public employees and their organizations does not necessarily depend upon collective bargaining. Organizations of policemen and firemen were politically powerful in many cities long before they obtained bargaining rights. Teachers' organizations were able to obtain salary increases, reduced classes, and many other benefits even when they shunned the words "bargaining" and "negotiations." These organizations were able to bring effective pressure to bear through the ordinary political channels available to other interest groups.

Collective bargaining, however, does provide a special process available only to public employees, and equally available to all classes of public employees. It significantly increases the political effectiveness of public employees in determining their terms and conditions of employment, particularly relative to other competing political interest groups. This does not mean that collective bargaining gives public employees dominant political power or enables them to obtain more than their fair share. Arrayed against public employees are the massive interest groups of taxpayers and the users of public services. Nearly every voter is threatened in one or even both capacities by union demands which must increase either the size of the budget or the share allocated to labor costs or both. Those interest groups are not only massive, but are capable of effective political organization, as anyone who has confronted taxpayers' leagues, parents' organizations, property owners' associations, or chambers of commerce well knows. In my view, one of the principal justifications for public employee bargaining is that most public employees need this special process to give them an ability to counteract the overriding political strength of other voters who constantly press for lower taxes and increased services.

R. SUMMERS, COLLECTIVE BARGAINING AND PUBLIC BENEFIT CONFERRAL: A JURISPRUDENTIAL CRITIQUE
1–2, 4–6, 9 (1976).*

Unduly narrow concepts of law plague us. It is time to recognize that there are forms of law besides statutes and other "commands of the sovereign" and that there are ways of creating law besides the formal procedures of legislatures. Public employee collective bargaining is a lawmaking process to which a public employer is a party. By this process the parties adopt (and administer) *laws* and legally *authorized policies* that shape public benefit conferral. A collective bargaining agreement is law for the parties, for affected public beneficiaries, and for taxpayers. Our democratic ways call for laws to be made by democratic means. In a society more fully committed to democratic ways than any large society in all history, the threshold inquiry must therefore be: Is public employee collective bargaining democratic? Or does it conflict with democracy? . . .

In my analysis, the word "democracy" has two primary meanings. It is sometimes used to refer to those *procedures* of political communities that provide for public employing bodies which generally exercise exclusive decision-making powers on behalf of the public, and which consist of officials (or their appointees) elected by a citizenry with wide suffrage to whom the officials are regularly accountable. The word is also sometimes used to refer to certain "process values" served *by such procedures* (as distinguished from the values served by *outcomes* of the procedures), for example, participation, and the dignity and equality of citizens jointly engaged in self-governance. It is often unnoticed that process values are prizable whether or not the actual outcomes of democratic procedures are good. Appropriate participation, for example, is a process value because it is prizable even when specific outcomes are not good. Indeed, our democratic processes are not, as such, guarantees of good outcomes. No one should claim that because our public officials are elected or otherwise accountable to the public, they always make good decisions. School boards, for example, have made their share of bad ones. (Democratic processes are *more* efficacious as safeguards against *bad* outcomes.) But democratic processes can serve important process values, and this *alone* may justify resort to them.

And while democratic procedures do not guarantee good outcomes— good decisions—in any given time period, continued resort to democratic procedures often leads to correction and improvement. Thus, (as a colleague has put it) society may "range in" on a good or at least second-best solution over time even though some "single period" outcomes are bad or third-best. Democratic societies must be ever mindful of this possibility, lest their impatience with short-run outcomes lead them to "restructure" decisional processes in ways that diminish democracy not only for the decisions at hand but others, too. . . .

Under collective bargaining laws, public employing bodies and unions jointly make laws and authoritative policies for the community, all as part of shaping public benefit conferral. It may be thought that any resulting diminution of democracy is insignificant or inconsequential because the statutes calling for joint law and policy making apply only to "terms and conditions of public employment" and do not affect the powers of public employing bodies to determine the kind and character of public benefits to be provided—the only powers obviously appropriate for democratic decision making.

This view is oversimple. There are important respects in which most public employers are irreducibly different from private ones. In private business, it *is* often possible to draw a clear line between issues concerning "terms and conditions of employment" subject to bargaining and issues concerning "product character," which are "management prerogative" and not subject to bargaining. Most public employing bodies do not, however, make "products." Instead they carry on *activities* of providing public benefits. Commonly, as in public education, the nature of the personnel carrying on these activities is a prime determinant of the character of the activities—the "product." Yet, the nature of public employees recruited and retained is substantially affected by "terms and conditions of employment," especially economic ones, and under the statutes these are *not* the exclusive province of the electorate and public employers through democratic processes (as formerly), but are codetermined with unions through collective bargaining.

The character of the benefit (as affected merely by bargaining over economic issues) and the resulting tax levels (as so affected) are matters on which citizens and taxpayers ought to have a voice either directly or through their representatives *unaffected by* collective bargaining. Thus, even if, as in much private employment, a sharp line could be drawn between "terms and conditions of public employment" and the "character of the resulting public product," with bargaining confined to the former, it still would not follow that the public voice in the former should be diminished in the name of collective bargaining. At least tax levels would always be potentially affected. Budgetary priorities would be potentially affected, too: different unions will compete for their "shares" of the budget, and their views of the total share of the entire budget appropriately allocable to wages, salaries, and fringes and their views on what part of that total share should belong to particular competing unions may not coincide at all with the priorities of the relevant public authority.

Of course, as defined and interpreted, "terms and conditions of employment" extend beyond economic issues. Indeed, in some states legislators expanded the scope of bargaining to include noneconomic issues to give the parties more to "trade about" and thus enable bargaining to "work better." There, the intrinsic demands of bargaining take priority over democratic methods. In public education, for example, collective bargaining in many states extends to curriculum, methods of pupil discipline, class size, the timing of the beginning or ending of the school year or school day, the length of school day, and so on. Bargaining over such issues as these intimately affects the character of the benefit provided. With respect to issues of this nature, bargaining actually diminishes democratic control and accountability. . . .

The erosion of democratic control and accountability attributable to bargaining is not confined to the *creation* of the law embodied in collective agreements or arbitration awards that, among other things, define and shape benefit conferral activities. It also extends to the *administrative interpretation* of this law. Unions jointly participate in this administration, and some forms of "grievance" arbitration delegate important issues of administrative interpretation to other than elected officials. . . .

The great wave of public employee bargaining laws that swept the country over the last fifteen years probably reflected disillusionment with democracy (and its bureaucracy) on the part of interested pressure groups and some legislators. Rather than try to improve their lot and achieve desired influence over substance within democratic frameworks, public employee lobbies seem to have teamed up with private sector unions to influence legislatures to "restructure" the processes involved. This restructuring necessarily modified democratic processes by requiring a "sharing" of decisional power—power that had theretofore been exclusively the province of the public and its designates.

No one would deny that a proposed new statute requiring a school board to share power to select books with a private publishing house would be objectionable at least on the ground that it would *inherently* diminish democracy. No one would deny that this would give the publishing house far more leverage than before. Yet, in the relevant respect, the duty (imposed by bargaining statutes) of a school board to make and administer laws and authoritative policies shaping education *only in conjunction with unions* is no different. Both procedures would require a sharing of decisional power regarding a public governmental function with a private entity.

Nor would anyone deny that a proposed new federal statute requiring state legislatures to pass all laws affecting education *only* via a process of collective bargaining with a statewide teachers' union would be objectionable at least on the ground that it would inherently diminish democracy. Yet, in the relevant respect, the duty (imposed by bargaining statutes) that calls for a school board to make and administer law and authoritative policies shaping education *only in conjunction with unions* is no different. Both procedures would require a sharing of decisional power regarding a public governmental function with a private entity.

––––––––

Comments and Questions

1. The two authors you just read share the same last name but not the same perspective on public-sector bargaining. On what points do they differ?

2. The present estimate is that approximately 80 percent of America's public schoolteachers are organized into some form of collective-bargaining unit. What kind of impacts on the delivery of public education can we expect from the trend toward stronger teachers' unions and collective bargaining? The excerpt that follows, which is based on fieldwork probing the impact of collective bargaining in a sample of fifteen school districts, provides some evidence on impacts to date.

––––––––

L. McDONNELL & A. PASCAL, ORGANIZED TEACHERS IN AMERICAN SCHOOLS
75–76, 78–82 (1979).*

Clearly the major district-level effect of teacher collective bargaining has been to limit the flexibility of school boards in making budgetary decisions. Teacher salaries in unionized districts are proportionately higher and thus represent a larger share of these districts' budgets. Contractually mandated class-size limits, preparation periods, and minimum numbers of specialists consume a good deal of the remaining budget so that school boards have less discretionary budget power than in the past.

The other major constraint which bargaining imposes on school boards and district administrators stems from the pressure to count seniority as the single or primary criterion for transfer and reduction-in-force decisions. Sole or primary reliance on seniority has some or all of the following consequences for local districts:

- districts find it harder to meet federally imposed faculty desegregation mandates

- as enrollment declines, it is more difficult to match particular school needs with the most appropriate and competent faculty

- reduction-in-force provisions based on seniority not only interfere with the retention of younger and perhaps more competent teachers, but also raise the salary costs of the more senior teaching force which results

Collective bargaining, then, has narrowed district authority mainly in the areas of budgetary decisions and teacher transfer policies. However, in only one of the fifteen districts we visited did organized teachers have an effective *veto* over any aspect of district policy. . . .

In most districts, implementation of the contract is highly routinized. The administration usually works with school principals, briefing them on any new provisions, and preparing them to implement the contract at the building level. The teacher organization uses its building representatives as the vehicle for explaining the contract to rank-and-file teachers. Even though it is centrally negotiated, the contract is basically a mechanism for managing relations at the school level and it is there that it has its greatest effect (as we shall see below).

Both labor and management seem generally inclined to settle grievances as quickly and at as low a level as possible. Often grievances are settled at the building level, sometimes even before formal filing. But as in other aspects of collective bargaining we have discussed, the tenor of the grievance process is dependent on the quality of the relationship between the school district and the teacher organization. A mutually distrustful relationship means grievances are more apt to go to arbitration and to be settled by a third-party neutral. . . .

In general, our research indicates that collective bargaining has its greatest nonbudgetary effect at the school site. In fact, for many of the noncompensation items we examined during the contract analysis (e.g., teacher evaluation, assignment, discipline, and grading practices, etc.) the clearest effects are within individual school buildings. Consequences at the district level seem negligible.

Teachers and administrators alike reported that improved staff morale is the strongest effect of collective bargaining for teachers. Protected from arbitrary action by administrators, teachers now feel more secure about what they do in their own classrooms. Principals, on the other hand, reported that teacher assignment is the greatest constraint imposed by collective bargaining. Principals now have less freedom in selecting which teachers will work in their schools and what duties each will perform there. . . .

The majority of contracts in our fieldwork sample include (in addition to limits on the school year and day) all or most of the following provisions, influencing school-level operations:

- guaranteed teacher preparation periods and a limit on the number of different classes a teacher must prepare
- assignments restricted to the teacher's area of certification and made on the basis of seniority
- a limit on the nonteaching duties (e.g., clerical work and playground supervision) a teacher must perform
- class-size maximums which can be violated only if the district shows just cause
- a detailed evaluation procedure which specifies the number of evaluations a teacher is subject to, the length and format of classroom observations, teacher response to evaluations, and finally, advance warning from principals when they plan to evaluate teachers

While these provisions constrain school management, they basically deal with working conditions, rather than teacher influence over educational policy. In fact, several of the teacher organizations in our sample are taking a "bread and butter" orientation and thus concentrate on improving the strength of these provisions, rather than on expanding their contracts into areas of educational policy. . . .

While it is clear that collective bargaining has constrained management latitude, it is not so obvious that it has significantly affected classroom operations and the services delivered to students. The vast majority of teachers we interviewed responded that collective bargaining had little effect on what they do in their own classrooms. Most claimed their morale had improved, but few reported changes in teaching methods and relations with students. Some observers argue that collective bargaining, by limiting class hours, has meant that students have less time to learn. Conversely, others maintain that guaranteed preparation time and higher morale raise the quality of teaching. Since we collected neither achievement nor classroom observation data, we are not in the position to resolve this argument. However, we did observe that collective bargaining sometimes provides greater autonomy to teachers. In several districts we noted specific contractual provisions which fostered this feeling. For example, in two districts rules governing curriculum development funds for teachers were established as a result of the collective bargaining agreement. Grants were awarded competitively and were used by teachers to develop new curricula or instructional projects. In two other districts, the contracts stipulated that materials and discretionary resources should be allocated equally among schools and teachers. Teachers were also assured of some discretionary funding for use in their own classrooms. These examples involve relatively little money but they seem to encourage greater professionalism among teachers.

In conclusion, our examination of the school-level effects of collective bargaining suggests that management latitude has been reduced. . . .

The noneconomic effects of collective bargaining are more perceptible at the school level than the district level. Because of contractual provisions regulating teacher working conditions, principals have less latitude in managing their own buildings. However, collective bargaining does not seem to have affected significantly either classroom operations or the quality of educational services delivered to students.

———

C. Specifying the Detailed Form of the Benefit

Think for a moment about the range of decisions necessary to make a school system operate. The problems of structure and staffing discussed so far are fundamental, but they are by no means the only important issues that must be confronted if the public schools are to operate. Somehow decisions must be reached about what courses will be offered and what they will cover, what after-school activities will be sponsored or allowed space for meetings, how discipline is to be handled, what support services will be available and for whom, what lab equipment, library books, and computers will be purchased, how large classes will be, where and when they will meet, and so on.

A variety of lawmakers collaborate to deal with these concerns. Take curriculum, for example. Teachers and teachers' organizations are the source of many ideas about curriculum, but they seldom act alone. Principals and other supervisory personnel are commonly involved, and in most states the local school board has the power (granted by the legislature) to veto or pass upon changes in courses offered. State legislatures also commonly delegate authority over curricular innovation to the state education department and other central agencies or boards. These agencies advise the legislature on education-related issues; they make curricular law by laying down regulations on matters such as the required course of study; and they adjudicate disputes about course content pursued by parents and others. An example follows.

———

IN RE THE APPEAL OF DONNA PERCOSKY AND OTHERS FROM ACTION OF THE BOARD OF EDUCATION, CENTRAL SCHOOL DISTRICT NO. 3

6 N.Y.Educ.Dep't Rep. 46 (1966).

ALLEN, JR., COMMISSIONER.—The appellants complain that the "Initial Teaching Alphabet Program" is being given in only one of three first grade classes and should be given in at least two. The voters of the district do not have the legal power to establish the courses of study in the schools of the district. This is a matter which is vested by law in the board of education subject to the curriculum requirements and general supervisory powers established by the statute and by the State Education

Department.   There is nothing in the record before me to indicate that the respondent has acted illegally or in an arbitrary or capricious manner.

The appeal is dismissed.

––––––––

The voters in a school district, as this case indicates, do not generally have any direct power over curriculum.   Nor do parents or other residents.   Voters can exert some indirect influence by voting out the local board or rejecting the proposed district budget, but these are blunt tools for shaping local school policy.   Voters can expect to have even less influence over curricular policies set by central officials.   The state legislature, potentially a more responsive agency of government, does not usually concern itself with course offerings.

When the legislature does become involved, the only limits upon its discretion are the state and federal constitutions that restrict all legislative action.   Constitutional guarantees can, however, impose real limits on the power of legislators and other authorized lawmakers to mold course content.   The Arkansas legislature, for example, was blocked in its effort to revamp the teaching of high-school biology to provide equal time for the biblical theory of creation.   In a recent decision, United States District Judge William R. Overton declared the state's "Balanced Treatment for Creation-Science and Evolution-Science Act" an unconstitutional attempt to establish religion.   McLean v. Arkansas Board of Education, 529 F.Supp. 1255 (E.D.Ark.1982).

As the Arkansas case indicates, judges, too, can become involved in the task of curricular lawmaking.   Their operational method, however, is limited: they can veto decisions about curriculum, scheduling, and other matters relating to the delivery of educational services under some circumstances, but they are not ordinarily policy innovators.   In the case that follows, the plurality and the dissenters differ in the scope they would give judges to veto school-board decisions about educational policy—in this instance, the content of the school library.   As you read the case, decide which side has the more persuasive argument.

––––––––

BOARD OF EDUCATION, ISLAND TREES UNION FREE SCHOOL DISTRICT NO. 26 v. PICO

Supreme Court of the United States, 1982.
457 U.S. 853, 102 S.Ct. 2799.

JUSTICE BRENNAN announced the judgment of the Court and delivered an opinion, in which JUSTICE MARSHALL and JUSTICE STEVENS joined, and in which JUSTICE BLACKMUN joined except for Part II-A-(1).

The principal question presented is whether the First Amendment imposes limitations upon the exercise by a local school board of its discretion to remove library books from high school and junior high school libraries.

I

Petitioners are the Board of Education of the Island Trees Union Free School District No. 26, in New York, and Richard Ahrens, Frank Martin, Christina Fasulo, Patrick Hughes, Richard Melchers, Richard Michaels, and Louis Nessim. When this suit was brought, Ahrens was the President of the Board, Martin was the Vice President, and the remaining petitioners were Board members. The Board is a state agency charged with responsibility for the operation and administration of the public schools within the Island Trees School District, including the Island Trees High School and Island Trees Memorial Junior High School. Respondents are Steven Pico, Jacqueline Gold, Glenn Yarris, Russell Rieger, and Paul Sochinski. When this suit was brought, Pico, Gold, Yarris, and Rieger were students at the High School, and Sochinski was a student at the Junior High School.

In September 1975, petitioners Ahrens, Martin, and Hughes attended a conference sponsored by Parents of New York United (PONYU), a politically conservative organization of parents concerned about education legislation in the State of New York. At the conference these petitioners obtained lists of books described by Ahrens as "objectionable" and by Martin as "improper fare for school students." It was later determined that the High School library contained [ten] of the listed books, and that another listed book was in the Junior High School library. In February 1976, at a meeting with the Superintendent of Schools and the Principals of the High School and Junior High School, the Board gave an "unofficial direction" that the listed books be removed from the library shelves and delivered to the Board's offices, so that Board members could read them. When this directive was carried out, it became publicized, and the Board issued a press release justifying its action. It characterized the removed books as "anti-American, anti-Christian, anti-Sem[i]tic, and just plain filthy," and concluded that "[i]t is our duty, our moral obligation, to protect the children in our schools from this moral danger as surely as from physical and medical dangers." 474 F.Supp. 387, 390 (EDNY 1979).

A short time later, the Board appointed a "Book Review Committee," consisting of four Island Trees parents and four members of the Island Trees schools staff, to read the listed books and to recommend to the Board whether the books should be retained, taking into account the books' "educational suitability," "good taste," "relevance," and "appropriateness to age and grade level." In July, the Committee made its final report to the Board, recommending that five of the listed books be retained and that two others be removed from the school libraries. As for the remaining four books, the Committee could not agree on two, took no position on one, and recommended that the last book be made available to students only with parental approval. The Board substantially rejected the Committee's report later that month, deciding that only one book should be returned to the High School library without restriction, that another should be made available subject to parental approval, but that the remaining nine books should "be removed from elementary and secondary libraries and [from] use in the curriculum." The Board gave no reasons for rejecting the recommendations of the Committee that it had appointed.

Respondents reacted to the Board's decision by bringing the present action under 42 U.S.C. § 1983 in the United States District Court for the Eastern District of New York. They alleged that petitioners had

> ordered the removal of the books from school libraries and proscribed their use in the curriculum because particular passages in the books offended their social, political and moral tastes and not because the books, taken as a whole, were lacking in educational value.

Respondents claimed that the Board's actions denied them their rights under the First Amendment. They asked the court for a declaration that the Board's actions were unconstitutional, and for preliminary and permanent injunctive relief ordering the Board to return the nine books to the school libraries and to refrain from interfering with the use of those books in the schools' curricula.

The District Court granted summary judgment in favor of petitioners. . . .

A three-judge panel of the United States Court of Appeals for the Second Circuit reversed the judgment of the District Court, and remanded the action for a trial on respondents' allegations. 638 F.2d 404 (1980). . . . We granted certiorari.

II

We emphasize at the outset the limited nature of the substantive question presented by the case before us. Our precedents have long recognized certain constitutional limits upon the power of the State to control even the curriculum and classroom. For example, Meyer v. Nebraska, 262 U.S. 390, 43 S.Ct. 625 (1923), struck down a state law that forbade the teaching of modern foreign languages in public and private schools, and Epperson v. Arkansas, 393 U.S. 97, 89 S.Ct. 266 (1968), declared unconstitutional a state law that prohibited the teaching of the Darwinian theory of evolution in any state-supported school. But the current action does not require us to re-enter this difficult terrain, which *Meyer* and *Epperson* traversed without apparent misgiving. For as this case is presented to us, it does not involve textbooks, or indeed any books that Island Trees students would be required to read. Respondents do not seek in this Court to impose limitations upon their school Board's discretion to prescribe the curricula of the Island Trees schools. On the contrary, the only books at issue in this case are *library* books, books that by their nature are optional rather than required reading. Our adjudication of the present case thus does not intrude into the classroom, or into the compulsory courses taught there. Furthermore, even as to library books, the action before us does not involve the *acquisition* of books. Respondents have not sought to compel their school Board to add to the school library shelves any books that students desire to read. Rather, the only action challenged in this case is the *removal* from school libraries of books originally placed there by the school authorities, or without objection from them.

The substantive question before us is still further constrained by the procedural posture of this case. Petitioners were granted summary judgment by the District Court. The Court of Appeals reversed that judgment, and remanded the action for a trial on the merits of respondents' claims. We can reverse the judgment of the Court of Appeals, and grant petitioners' request for reinstatement of the summary judgment in their favor, only if we determine that "there is no genuine issue as to any material fact," and that petitioners are "entitled to a judgment as a matter of law." Fed.Rule Civ.Proc. 56(c). In making our determination, any doubt as to the existence of a genuine issue of material fact must be resolved against petitioners as the moving party. Adickes v. S.H. Kress & Co., 398 U.S. 144, 157–159, 90 S.Ct. 1598, 1608–1609 (1970). Furthermore, "[o]n summary judgment the inferences to be drawn from the underlying facts contained in [the affidavits, attached exhibits, and depositions submitted below] must be viewed in the light most favorable to the party opposing the motion." United States v. Diebold, Inc., 369 U.S. 654, 655, 82 S.Ct. 993, 994 (1962).

In sum, the issue before us in this case is a narrow one, both substantively and procedurally. It may best be restated as two distinct questions. First, does the First Amendment impose *any* limitations upon the discretion of petitioners to remove library books from the Island Trees High School and Junior High School? Second, if so, do the affidavits and other evidentiary materials before the District Court, construed most favorably to respondents, raise a genuine issue of fact whether petitioners might have exceeded those limitations? If we answer either of these questions in the negative, then we must reverse the judgment of the Court of Appeals and reinstate the District Court's summary judgment for petitioners. If we answer both questions in the affirmative, then we must affirm the judgment below. We examine these questions in turn.

A

(1)

The Court has long recognized that local school boards have broad discretion in the management of school affairs. See, e.g., Meyer v. Nebraska, supra, at 402, 43 S.Ct., at 627; Pierce v. Society of Sisters, 268 U.S. 510, 543, 45 S.Ct. 571, 573 (1925). Epperson v. Arkansas, supra, 393 U.S., at 104, 89 S.Ct., at 270, reaffirmed that, by and large, "public education in our Nation is committed to the control of state and local authorities," and that federal courts should not ordinarily "intervene in the resolution of conflicts which arise in the daily operation of school systems." . . .

At the same time, however, we have necessarily recognized that the discretion of the States and local school boards in matters of education must be exercised in a manner that comports with the transcendent imperatives of the First Amendment. . . .

Of course, courts should not "intervene in the resolution of conflicts which arise in the daily operation of school systems" unless "basic constitutional values" are "directly and sharply implicate[d]" in those conflicts. Epperson v. Arkansas, 393 U.S., at 104, 89 S.Ct., at 270. But we think that the First Amendment rights of students may be directly and sharply implicated by the removal of books from the shelves of a school library. Our precedents have focused "not only on the role of the First Amendment in fostering individual self-expression but also on its role in affording the public access to discussion, debate, and the dissemination of information and ideas." First National Bank of Boston v. Bellotti, 435 U.S. 765, 783, 98 S.Ct. 1407, 1419 (1978). And we have recognized that "the State may not, consistently with the spirit of the First Amendment, contract the spectrum of available knowledge." Griswold v. Connecticut, 381 U.S. 479, 482, 85 S.Ct. 1678, 1680 (1965). In keeping with this principle, we have held that in a variety of contexts "the Constitution protects the right to receive information and ideas." Stanley v. Georgia, 394 U.S. 557, 564, 89 S.Ct. 1243, 1247 (1969); see Kleindienst v. Mandel, 408 U.S. 753, 762–763, 92 S.Ct. 2576, 2581 (1972) (citing cases). This right is an inherent corollary of the rights of free speech and press that are explicitly guaranteed by the Constitution, in two senses. First, the right to receive ideas follows ineluctably from the *sender's* First Amendment right to send them: "The right of freedom of speech and press . . . embraces the right to distribute literature, and necessarily protects the right to receive it." Martin v. Struthers, 319 U.S. 141, 143, 63 S.Ct. 862, 863 (1943) . . . .

More importantly, the right to receive ideas is a necessary predicate to the *recipient's* meaningful exercise of his own rights of speech, press, and political freedom. . . . As we recognized in Tinker [v. Des Moines Independent Community School District, 393 U.S. 503, 89 S.Ct. 733 (1969)], students too are beneficiaries of this principle:

> In our system, students may not be regarded as closed-circuit recipients of only that which the State chooses to communicate. . . . [S]chool officials cannot suppress "expressions of feeling with which they do not wish to contend." (393 U.S., at 511, 89 S.Ct., at 739 (quoting Burnside v. Byars, 363 F.2d 744, 749 (CA5 1966)).)

In sum, just as access to ideas makes it possible for citizens generally to exercise their rights of free speech and press in a meaningful manner, such access prepares students for active and effective participation in the pluralistic, often contentious society in which they will soon be adult members. Of course all First Amendment rights accorded to students must be construed "in light of the special characteristics of the school environment." Tinker v. Des Moines School Dist., 393 U.S., at 506, 89 S.Ct., at 736. But the special characteristics of the school *library* make that environment especially appropriate for the recognition of the First Amendment rights of students.

. . . Petitioners emphasize the inculcative function of secondary education, and argue that they must be allowed *unfettered* discretion to "transmit community values" through the Island Trees schools. But that sweeping claim overlooks the unique role of the school library. It appears from the record that use of the Island Trees school libraries is completely voluntary on the part of students. Their selection of books from these libraries is entirely a matter of free choice; the libraries afford them an opportunity at self-education and individual enrichment that is wholly optional. Petitioners might well defend their claim of absolute discretion in matters of *curriculum* by reliance upon their duty to inculcate community values. But we think that petitioners' reliance upon that duty is misplaced where, as here, they attempt to extend their claim of absolute discretion beyond the compulsory environment of the classroom, into the school library and the regime of voluntary inquiry that there holds sway.

(2)

In rejecting petitioners' claim of absolute discretion to remove books from their school libraries, we do not deny that local school boards have a substantial legitimate role to play in the determination of school library content. We thus must turn to the question of the extent to which the First Amendment places limitations upon the discretion of petitioners to remove books from their libraries. In this inquiry we enjoy the guidance of several precedents. *West Virginia Board of Education* v. *Barnette* stated:

> If there is any fixed star in our constitutional constellation, it is that no official, high or petty, can prescribe what shall be orthodox in politics, nationalism, religion, or other matters of opinion . . . . If there are any circumstances which permit an exception, they do not now occur to us. (319 U.S. [624, 642, 63 S.Ct. 1178, 1187 (1943)].)

This doctrine has been reaffirmed in later cases involving education. . . .

With respect to the present case, the message of these precedents is clear. Petitioners rightly possess significant discretion to determine the content of their school libraries. But that discretion may not be exercised in a narrowly partisan or political manner. If a Democratic school board, motivated by party affiliation, ordered the removal of all books written by or in favor of Republicans, few would doubt that the order violated the constitutional rights of the students denied access to those books. The same conclusion would surely apply if an all-white school board, motivated by racial animus, decided to remove all books authored by blacks or advocating racial equality and integration. Our Constitution does not permit the official suppression of *ideas.* Thus whether petitioners' removal of books from their school libraries denied respondents their First Amendment rights depends upon the motivation behind petitioners' actions. If petitioners *intended* by their removal decision to deny respondents access to ideas with which petitioners disagreed, and if this intent was the decisive factor in petitioners' decision, then petitioners have exercised their discretion in violation of the Constitution. To permit such intentions to control official actions would be to encourage the precise sort of officially prescribed orthodoxy unequivocally condemned in *Barnette.* On the other hand, respondents implicitly concede that an unconstitutional motivation would *not* be demonstrated if it were shown that petitioners had decided to remove the books at issue because those books were pervasively vulgar. Tr. of Oral Arg. 36. And again, respondents concede that if it were demonstrated that the removal decision was based solely upon the "educational suitability" of the books in question, then their removal would be "perfectly permissible." Id., at 53. In other words, in respondents' view such motivations, if decisive of petitioners' actions, would not carry the danger of an official suppression of ideas, and thus would not violate respondents' First Amendment rights.

As noted earlier, nothing in our decision today affects in any way the discretion of a local school board to choose books to *add* to the libraries of their schools. Because we are concerned in this case with the suppression of ideas, our holding today affects only the discretion to *remove* books. In brief, we hold that local school boards may not remove books from school library shelves simply because they dislike the ideas contained in those books and seek by their removal to "prescribe what shall be orthodox in politics, nationalism, religion, or other matters of opinion." . . .

B

We now turn to the remaining question presented by this case: Do the evidentiary materials that were before the District Court, when construed most favorably to respondents, raise a genuine issue of material fact whether petitioners exceeded constitutional limitations in exercising their discretion to remove the books from the school libraries? We conclude that the materials do raise such a question, which forecloses summary judgment in favor of petitioners. . . .

. . . . This would be a very different case if the record demonstrated that petitioners had employed established, regular, and facially unbiased procedures for the review of controversial materials. But the actual record in the case before us suggests the exact opposite. Petitioners' removal procedures were vigorously challenged below by respondents, and the evidence on this issue sheds further light on the issue of petitioners' motivations. Respondents alleged that in making their removal decision petitioners ignored "the advice of literary experts," the views of "librarians and teachers within the Island Trees School system," the advice of the Superintendent of Schools, and the guidance of publications that rate books for junior and senior high school students. Respondents also claimed that petitioners' decision was based solely on the fact that the books were named on the PONYU list received by petitioners Ahrens, Martin, and Hughes, and that petitioners "did not undertake an independent review of other books in the [school] libraries." Evidence before the District Court lends support to these claims. The record shows that immediately after petitioners first ordered the books removed from the library shelves, the Superintendent of Schools reminded them that "we already have a policy . . . designed expressly to handle such problems," and recommended that the removal decision be approached through this established channel. But the Board disregarded the Superintendent's advice, and instead resorted to the extraordinary procedure of appointing a Book Review Committee—the advice of which was later rejected without explanation. In sum, respondents' allegations and some of the evidentiary materials presented below do not rule out the possibility that petitioners' removal procedures were highly irregular and ad hoc—the antithesis of those procedures that might tend to allay suspicions regarding petitioners' motivations.

Construing these claims, affidavit statements, and other evidentiary materials in a manner favorable to respondents, we cannot conclude that petitioners were "entitled to a judgment as a matter of law." The evidence plainly does not foreclose the possibility that petitioners' decision to remove the books rested decisively upon disagreement with constitutionally protected ideas in those books, or upon a desire on petitioners' part to impose upon the students of the Island Trees High School and Junior High School a political orthodoxy to which petitioners and their constituents adhered. Of course, some of the evidence before the District Court might lead a finder of fact to accept petitioners' claim that their removal decision was based upon constitutionally valid concerns. But that evidence at most creates a genuine issue of material fact on the critical question of the credibility of petitioners' justifications for their decision: On that issue, it simply cannot be said that there is no genuine issue as to any material fact. .   .   .

Affirmed.

[Concurring opinions by Justices Blackmun and White are omitted. Justice Blackmun agreed with most of Justice Brennan's opinion. However, Justice White concurred in the affirmance on the sole ground that an unresolved factual issue—the reasons underlying the board's removal of the books—precluded summary judgment; his refusal to reach the First Amendment issue meant that there was no Supreme Court majority position on that point.]

CHIEF JUSTICE BURGER, with whom JUSTICE POWELL, JUSTICE REHNQUIST, and JUSTICE O'CONNOR join, dissenting.

The First Amendment, as with other parts of the Constitution, must deal with new problems in a changing world. In an attempt to deal with a problem in an area traditionally left to the states, a plurality of the Court, in a lavish expansion going beyond any prior holding under the First Amendment, expresses its view that a school board's decision concerning what books are to be in the school library is subject to federal-court review. Were this to become the law, this Court would come perilously close to becoming a "super censor" of school board library decisions. Stripped to its essentials, the issue comes down to two important propositions: *first,* whether local schools are to be administered by elected school boards, or by federal judges and teenage pupils; and *second,* whether the values of morality, good taste, and relevance to education are valid reasons for school board decisions concerning the contents of a school library. In an attempt to place this case within the protection of the First Amendment, the plurality suggests a new "right" that, when shorn of the plurality's rhetoric, allows this Court to impose its own views about what books must be made available to students.

I agree with the fundamental proposition that "students do not 'shed their constitutional rights to freedom of speech or expression at the schoolhouse gate.'" For example, the Court has held that a school board cannot compel a student to participate in a flag salute ceremony, West Virginia Bd. of Education v. Barnette, 319 U.S. 624, 63 S.Ct. 1178 (1943), or *prohibit* a student from expressing certain views, so long as that expression does not disrupt the educational process. Tinker v. Des Moines School Dist., 393 U.S. 503, 89 S.Ct. 733 (1969). Here, however, no restraints of any kind are placed on the students. They are free to read the books in question, which are available at public libraries and bookstores; they are free to discuss them in the classroom or elsewhere. Despite this absence of any direct external control on the students' ability to express themselves, the plurality suggests that there is a new First Amendment "entitlement" to have access to particular books in a school library.

The plurality cites Meyer v. Nebraska, 262 U.S. 390, 43 S.Ct. 625 (1923), which struck down a state law that restricted the teaching of modern foreign languages in public and private schools, and Epperson v. Arkansas, 393 U.S. 97, 89 S.Ct. 266 (1968), which declared unconstitutional under the Establishment Clause a law banning the teaching of Darwinian evolution, to establish the validity of federal-court interference with the functioning of schools. The plurality finds it unnecessary "to re-enter this difficult terrain," yet in the next breath relies on these very cases and others to establish the previously unheard of "right" of access to particular books in the public school library. The apparent underlying basis of the plurality's view seems to be that students have an enforceable "right" to receive the information and ideas that are contained in junior and senior high school library books. This "right" purportedly follows "ineluctably" from the sender's First Amendment right to freedom of speech and as a "necessary predicate" to the recipient's meaningful exercise of his own rights of speech, press, and political freedom. No such right, however, has previously been recognized.

It is true that where there is a willing distributor of materials, the government may not impose unreasonable obstacles to dissemination by the third party. And where the speaker desires to express certain ideas, the government may not impose unreasonable restraints. It does not follow, however, that a school board must affirmatively aid the speaker in his communication with the recipient. In short the plurality suggests today that if a writer has something to say, the government through its schools must be the courier. None of the cases cited by the plurality establish this broad-based proposition.

First, the plurality argues that the right to receive ideas is derived in part from the sender's First Amendment rights to send them. Yet we have previously held that a sender's rights are not absolute. Rowan v. Post Office Dept., 397 U.S. 728, 90 S.Ct. 1484 (1970). Never before today has the Court indicated that the government has an *obligation* to aid a speaker or author in reaching an audience.

Second, the plurality concludes that "the right to receive ideas is a necessary predicate to the *recipient's* meaningful exercise of his own rights of speech, press, and political freedom." However, the "right to receive information and ideas," Stanley v. Georgia, 394 U.S. 557, 564, 89 S.Ct. 1243, 1247 (1969), does not carry with it the concomitant right to have those ideas affirmatively provided at a particular place by the government. . . . Indeed, if the need to have an informed citizenry creates a "right," why is the government not also required to provide ready access to a variety of information? This same need would support a constitutional "right" of the people to have public libraries as part of a new constitutional "right" to continuing adult education. . . .

Whatever role the government might play as a conduit of information, schools in particular ought not be made a slavish courier of the material of third parties. The plurality pays homage to the ancient verity that in the administration of the public schools " 'there is a legitimate and substantial community interest in promoting respect for authority and traditional values be they social, moral, or political.' " If, as we have held, schools may legitimately be used as vehicles for "inculcating fundamental values necessary to the maintenance of a democratic political system," Ambach v. Norwick, 441 U.S. 68, 77, 99 S.Ct. 1589, 1594 (1979), school authorities must have broad discretion to fulfill that obligation. Presumably all activity within a primary or secondary school involves the conveyance of information and at least an implied approval of the worth of that information. How are "fundamental values" to be inculcated except by having school boards make content-based decisions about the appropriateness of retaining materials in the school library and curriculum. In order to fulfill its function, an elected school board *must* express its views on the subjects which are taught to its students. In doing so those elected officials express the views of their community; they may err, of course, and the voters may remove them. It is a startling erosion of the very idea of democratic government to have this Court arrogate to itself the power the plurality asserts today. . . .

What the plurality views as valid reasons for removing a book at their core involve partisan judgments. Ultimately the federal courts will be the judge of whether the motivation for book removal was "valid" or "reasonable." Undoubtedly the validity of many book removals will ultimately turn on a judge's evaluation of the books. Discretion must be used, and the appropriate body to exercise that discretion is the local elected school board, not judges.

We can all agree that as a matter of *educational policy* students should have wide access to information and ideas. But the people elect school boards, who in turn select administrators, who select the teachers, and these are the individuals best able to determine the substance of that policy. The plurality fails to recognize the fact that local control of education involves democracy in a microcosm. In most public schools in the United States the *parents* have a large voice in running the school. Through participation in the election of school board members, the parents influence, if not control, the direction of their children's education. A school board is not a giant bureaucracy far removed from accountability for its actions; it is truly "of the people and by the people." A school board reflects its constituency in a very real sense and thus could not long exercise unchecked discretion in its choice to acquire or remove books. If the parents disagree with the educational decisions of the school board, they can take steps to remove the board members from office. Finally, even if parents and students cannot convince the school board that book removal is inappropriate, they have alternative sources to the same end.

Books may be acquired from bookstores, public libraries, or other alternative sources unconnected with the unique environment of the local public schools.

No amount of "limiting" language could rein in the sweeping "right" the plurality would create. The plurality distinguishes library books from textbooks because library books "by their nature are optional rather than required reading." It is not clear, however, why this distinction requires *greater* scrutiny before "optional" reading materials may be removed. It would appear that required reading and textbooks have a greater likelihood of imposing a " 'pall of orthodoxy' " over the educational process than do optional reading. In essence, the plurality's view transforms the availability of this "optional" reading into a "right" to have this "optional" reading maintained at the demand of teenagers.

The plurality also limits the new right by finding it applicable only to the *removal* of books once acquired. Yet if the First Amendment commands that certain books cannot be *removed,* does it not equally require that the same books be *acquired?* Why does the coincidence of timing become the basis of a constitutional holding? According to the plurality, the evil to be avoided is the "official suppression of ideas." It does not follow that the decision to *remove* a book is less "official suppression" than the decision not to acquire a book desired by someone. Similarly, a decision to eliminate certain material from the curriculum, history for example, would carry an equal—probably greater—prospect of "official suppression." Would the decision be subject to our review?

. . . I categorically reject this notion that the Constitution dictates that judges, rather than parents, teachers, and local school boards, must determine how the standards of morality and vulgarity are to be treated in the classroom.

JUSTICE POWELL, dissenting.

The plurality opinion today rejects a basic concept of public school education in our country: that the States and locally elected school boards should have the responsibility for determining the educational policy of the public schools. After today's decision any junior high school student, by instituting a suit against a school board or teacher, may invite a judge to overrule an educational decision by the official body designated by the people to operate the schools.

School boards are uniquely local and democratic institutions. Unlike the governing bodies of cities and counties, school boards have only one responsibility: the education of the youth of our country during their most formative and impressionable years. Apart from health, no subject is closer to the hearts of parents than their children's education during those years. For these reasons, the governance of elementary and secondary education traditionally has been placed in the hands of a local board, responsible locally to the parents and citizens of school districts. Through parent-teacher associations (PTA's), and even less formal arrangements that vary with schools, parents are informed and often may influence decisions of the board. Frequently, parents know the teachers and visit classes. It is fair to say that no single agency of government at any level is closer to the people whom it serves than the typical school board.

I therefore view today's decision with genuine dismay. Whatever the final outcome of this suit and suits like it, the resolution of educational policy decisions through litigation, and the exposure of school board members to liability for such decisions, can be expected to corrode the school board's authority and effectiveness. As is evident from the generality of the plurality's "standard" for judicial review, the decision as to the educational worth of a book is a highly subjective one. Judges rarely are as competent as school authorities to make this decision; nor are judges responsive to the parents and people of the school district. . . .

In different contexts and in different times, the destruction of written materials has been the symbol of despotism and intolerance. But the removal of nine vulgar or racist books from a high school library by a concerned local school board does not raise this specter. For me, today's decision symbolizes a debilitating encroachment upon the institutions of a free people.

Attached as an Appendix hereto is [Circuit] Judge Mansfield's summary of excerpts from the books at issue in this case.

APPENDIX TO OPINION OF POWELL, J., DISSENTING

The excerpts which led the Board to look into the educational suitability of the books in question are set out (with minor corrections after comparison with the text of the books themselves) below. . . .

1) Soul On Ice by Eldridge Cleaver 157–158 ". . . There are white men who will pay you to fuck their wives. They approach you and say, 'How would you like to fuck a white woman?' 'What is this?' you ask. 'On the up-and-up,' he assures you. 'It's all right. She's my wife. She needs black rod, is all. She has to have it. It's like a medicine or drug to her. She has to have it. I'll pay you. It's all on the level, no trick involved. Interested?' You go with him and he drives you to their home. The three of you go into the bedroom. There is a certain type who will leave you and his wife alone and tell you to pile her real good. After it is all over, he will pay you and drive you to wherever you want to go. Then there are some who like to peep at you through a keyhole and watch you have his woman, or peep at you through a window, or lie under the bed and listen to the creaking of the bed as you work out. There is another type who likes to masturbate while he stands beside the bed and watches you pile her. There is the type who likes to eat his woman up after you get through piling her. And there is the type who only wants you to pile her for a little while, just long enough to thaw her out and kick her motor over and arouse her to heat, then he wants you to jump off real quick and he will jump onto her and together they can make it from there by themselves."

2) A Hero Ain't Nothing But A Sandwich by Alice Childress . . .

3) The Fixer by Bernard Malamud . . .

4) Go Ask Alice by Anonymous . . .

5) Slaughterhouse Five by Kurt Vonnegut, Jr. . . .

6) The Best Short Stories By Negro Writers Ed. by Langston Hughes . . .

7) Black Boy by Richard Wright . . .

8) Laughing Boy by Oliver LaFarge . . .

9) The Naked Ape by Desmond Morris . . .

10) Reader For Writers [Ed. by Jerome Archer] . . .

[The eleventh book was Down These Mean Streets by Piri Thomas. The board had removed all but books 8 and 7.

[Other dissenting opinions by Justices Rehnquist and O'Connor are omitted.]

Comments and Questions

1. Justice Powell claims, in his separate dissent, that the plurality unfairly hamstrings local school boards. Is Justice Powell correct in suggesting that this case has made it impossible for school boards to review and remove certain books from the school library? Assume that you are an attorney for a school board. Can you think of any way the board could proceed without offending the First Amendment?

2. Can the school board constitutionally become involved in decisions about after-school use of school facilities? In decisions about what numbers will be performed in the school variety show? In decisions about what will appear in the school newspaper?

3. The materials in this subsection suggest a limited role for parents in specifying the detailed form in which educational benefits will be distributed. Should parents be more directly involved in the process of designing and implementing school programs? Why or why not?

4. The state legislature has ultimate power over curriculum and many other matters relating to the delivery of educational services, but rarely exercises it. Central state officials, local school boards, and local teachers and administrators dominate most of these decisions. Is this state of affairs defensible? Might the proper role of the legislature vary with the particular benefit to be conferred? What types of public benefits call for detailed legislative oversight?

D. Securing the Necessary Funding

Public education is an expensive public benefit, second only to national defense in the costs it imposes upon taxpayers. The cost of supporting a large military establishment is borne through federal taxation and managed centrally: Congress votes upon appropriations, and military and civilian officials employed by the federal government are charged with spending that money intelligently. A large proportion of the costs of educating the young, on the other hand, is borne locally: local property taxes currently pay almost half of the cost of public education in most states; local school boards determine how much is needed each year and how that money will be spent.

This arrangement has had important consequences for the distribution of educational benefits in the United States, for districts differ significantly in their taxable resources and in the enthusiasm with which they finance public education. The upshot is that educational spending varies greatly from place to place within any given state. In 1984, for example, one wealthy district in Texas spent $10,602 per pupil annually, while one of the poorest districts in Texas spent $1,725. State and federal educational spending tends to mitigate, but not eliminate, these differences. The federal contribution is too small to make much of a difference in local budgets, and the states have not yet committed themselves to wiping out interdistrict inequalities in per-pupil spending. Indeed, little agreement exists among the states as to just how they should support public education; individual states vary considerably both in the amount they devote to public education and in the formulae they use to distribute these funds.

As education has grown more expensive in the past two decades, the differences between districts have grown larger, and calls to reform the traditional system have become more urgent. Reformers have brought their arguments for equalizing school-tax burdens and equalizing educational spending to the state legislatures and to the courts. Both have responded, but not always in the ways that advocates of change would prefer. The selections that follow describe the traditional system for financing public education and efforts to change it. The first outlines the property tax system and the difficulties involved in coming up with a more equitable alternative, and the second discusses the success of the reform movement in court.

M. YUDOF, D. KIRP, T. VAN GEEL & B. LEVIN, KIRP & YUDOF'S EDUCATIONAL POLICY AND THE LAW

567–71, 574–77 (2d ed. 1982).*

Revenues are generated primarily from a property tax, a tax on the ownership of wealth in the form of real property. The first step in raising revenue from a property tax is to assess the value of the property to be taxed. Assessment of property poses an extremely difficult problem for technical reasons—it is often difficult to establish the market value of such different kinds of property as residences, farmland, factories, utilities, golf courses—and for political reasons; that is, there is often great pressure to hold down assessments, particularly assessments on residential relative to commercial property. Once the total assessed value of property within a district is determined, the local government (school board) must adopt its budget. The projected expenditures of the governmental unit minus its income from other sources is the amount to be raised by local property taxes. This amount divided by the assessed valuation of the property within the jurisdiction of the government gives the tax rate to be applied to the property. The tax rate is usually expressed in mills (one-tenth of one cent or one-thousandth of a dollar). To compare the ability of school districts to raise revenues, a standardized unit is used. It is obtained by dividing the total value of the district's assessed property by the number of pupils in the district. Since the tax rate is the unit used to determine the district's "willingness" or "effort" to support its schools, a combined measure of ability and effort is derived by multiplying the district's tax rate by its assessed valuation per pupil. This figure is the amount of local revenue per pupil. For a more detailed discussion of property taxes, see W.I. Garms, J.W. Guthrie, and L.C. Pierce, School Finance 132–39 (1978).

. . . [V]ariations among districts in expenditures primarily result from differences in the amount each raises from its own resources. Although the principal reason for these inequalities is the inequalities in the amount of property wealth per pupil, the desire or lack of it of the school board and/or voters to support education also plays an important role in determining variations in the levels of expenditures. The wealth of the residents as measured by their income rather than in terms of property values must also be counted an important determinant of expenditures. For example, residents who are property rich but income poor will not be inclined to impose tax rates (even low tax rates) which produce yields that represent high proportions of their incomes. Moreover, some jurisdictions might be supporting a substantial number of other municipal services through the property tax, reducing the amount of money available for schools. The proportion of the property that is in industrial or commercial use also influences the amount of money raised; if voters determine that the major impact of the property tax is to fall on commercial enterprises that in turn shift the cost to customers located outside the district, there is a greater inclination to impose a higher tax rate in order to raise more money for the schools.

A school district's taxing policy can itself influence the value of property in the district. The higher the tax rate, the less incentive there is for business to move into or remain within the jurisdiction. Also, the higher the tax rate, the lower the property values are likely to be in the long run—property subjected to high taxes is less desirable and people will pay less for such property; similarly, the lower the tax rate, in the long term, the more desirable the property and the more people might be willing to pay for the property. Hence, it is not simply the case that property values determine tax rates and yields; tax rates and yields also affect property values. See R.D. Reischauer and R.W. Hartman, Reforming School Finance 67–71 (1973).

Although the bulk of the money expended on elementary and secondary education is raised locally, in 1975–76, on a nationwide basis, the states contributed an average of 43.7 percent and the federal government 8 percent of the total education dollar. The federal government's contribution was largely in the form of categorical grants, most importantly Title I of The Elementary and Secondary Education Act . . . . State aid has traditionally taken a variety of forms. Most states provide a basic or "flat grant"—a fixed number of dollars per school child to all school districts, rich and poor. The use of the flat grant has rested on two assumptions: that differences in local fiscal capacity are small and that the state's responsibility is limited to aiding local districts in providing a basic or minimum level of education, leaving the local community—or the individual parents—to provide for an education in excess of this minimum if so desired. Connecticut was the last state to fund education solely through the flat grant program.

The "foundation program" represents another aid scheme in wide use. The theory is that any school district, even a property-poor district, should be assured a certain minimum level of revenue per pupil, provided the district makes a minimum effort of its own by imposing a stipulated minimum property tax rate.

A district's aid entitlement is the difference (if greater than zero) between the foundation level of spending per pupil and the amount per pupil that the district raises locally at the specified minimum rate. Algebraically,

$$S = F - r_o V,$$

where

S = the amount of state aid per pupil,

F = the foundation amount per pupil established by the state,

r_o = the minimum tax rate specified by the state, and

V = taxable property per pupil, the local tax base.

Barro, "Alternative Post-*Serrano* Systems and Their Expenditure Implications," in J. Pincus, ed., School Finance in Transition 36 (1974).

The other traditional method of distributing state aid is a formula called "percentage equalizing." In contrast to the flat grant and the foundation program, under percentage equalizing, the state assists the district, depending upon its "ability," to attain the amount of education the district determines is appropriate.

Under percentage equalizing plans, the district determines the size of its budget, and the state provides a share of that budget determined by the district's "aid ratio." This aid ratio is defined by means of a formula usually written in the form

$$\left(1 - f\, \frac{y_i}{y}\right)$$

where y_i is the assessed valuation per pupil of the district,

y is the assessed valuation per student of the state as a whole, and

f is a scaling factor that is usually set somewhere between 0 and 1.

For example, if assessed valuation per pupil of the district were $10,000 and that of the state $40,000, and the scaling factor were .5, the aid ratio for the district would be

$$\left(1 - .5 \times \frac{10,000}{40,000}\right) = .875$$

This means that the state would provide 87.5 percent of the budget of the district, with the district expected to raise the remaining 12.5 percent from local taxes.

W.I. Garms, J.W. Guthrie, and L.C. Pierce, School Finance 193 (1978).

Each of these formulas, even the flat grant, can be demonstrated to have an equalizing effect; that is, it reduces the differences among districts in the amount of money spent per pupil and in the capacity to raise money. See Barro, supra, and Garms, et al., supra. But the equalizing effect is often not strong, even when these formulas are not encumbered by special provisions added for political reasons. Typically, however, legislatures have added "save harmless" provisions to their formulas that, for example, guarantee districts the same amount of aid they received the prior year even though a straight application of the formula would indicate a lowering of state aid for that district in the coming year. In short, the formulas in practice have the effect of maintaining the disparities among districts in the amount of money spent per pupil.

Defining Equal Educational Opportunity

When, as a moral, policy, or constitutional matter, should one conclude that inequalities among districts in the amount of money spent per pupil are wrong or impermissible? A variety of standards for assessing whether a school financing system provides students with an equal educational opportunity is available. Some of these standards measure equal educational opportunity in terms of "inputs,"—that is, dollars per pupil or the educational resources those dollars purchase (books per pupil, square feet per pupil, or number of pupils per qualified teacher). Inputs are to be distinguished from the "outcomes" of the educational process, such as reading achievement, attitudes, motivation, and so forth.

Input standards can be negative, the generalized formulation of such a standard being as follows: The pattern of distribution of inputs (whether it be expenditures per pupil, books per pupil, pupil-teacher ratios) within a state must not be a function of (be determined by, caused by, correlated with) _____. The blank could be filled in with such phrases as: the per-pupil property wealth of the school district in which the students reside; the median family income of the district in which the students reside; the "taste" for education of the voters in the district in which the students reside; the wealth of the pupils' own families; and the race, religion, or ethnic origin of the pupil. It is important to note that the negative-input standard does not require equality in the allocation of resources; it only demands that if there are inequalities, they must not be caused by or determined by a particular variable that is deemed a morally irrelevant basis for allocating resources.

There are also negative-outcome standards. Such a standard could state that academic achievement must not be a function of the social-class background of the students. This standard implies that to the extent students from lower socioeconomic backgrounds have lower achievement levels than other students, extra efforts must be made by schools to change this pattern. The correlation between social class background and school achievement must be broken; that is, it should no longer be possible to state with any degree of certainty that because a given student is black and from a poor family that he or she will do less well on standardized achievement tests than the national average. Stated differently, school achievement must be the result of individual talent only. Coleman, "The Concept of Equality of Educational Opportunity," 38 Harv. Educ.Rev. 7 (1968).

There are also positive-input and positive-outcome standards. An example of a positive-input standard is one that requires resources to be allocated among pupils within the state on the basis of complete equality. A variation of this standard is one that requires equal resources for a basic education, permitting local leeway for an "enriched" program. See Seattle School Dist. No. 1 v. Washington, 90 Wash.2d 476, 585 P.2d 71 (1978). Another positive-input standard is one specifying that variations in the allocation of resources may not exceed certain limits, for example, the variation in expenditures per pupil may not exceed one hundred dollars. See Serrano v. Priest, Civ. No. 938, 254 (Los Angeles Co. Super. Ct., Cal., April 10, 1974). Professor Richards, in a moral argument based on John Rawls' A Theory of Justice (1971), argues that justice requires the adoption of both negative and positive standards: " 'Each child, equal resources,' and 'the quality of public education is not to be a function of wealth other than the total wealth of the state.' " Richards, "Equal Opportunity and School Financing: Towards a Moral Theory of Constitutional Adjudication," 41 U.Chi.L.Rev. 32, 59 (1973).

Full-fledged positive-outcome standards are perhaps the most appealing but also the most demanding standards. These directly address what most people are concerned about—educational outcomes. They are truly *educational* standards, whereas the negative-input standard is concerned simply with general fairness or equity. But outcome standards, while appealing, are hard to attain given the present state of knowledge as to what it is that promotes learning. These problems aside, examples of positive-output standards include the following: All children of normal or above normal ability shall learn to read at a seventh grade reading level as measured by a standardized test; or all normal children shall at least achieve functional literacy. A different kind of positive-output standard might require that every child be equipped "for his role as a citizen, and as a competitor in the labor market." Robinson v. Cahill, 62 N.J. 473, 515, 303 A.2d 273, 295 (1973).

Standards that speak in terms of pupil needs are hard to classify—they speak in terms of inputs, but the level of educational resources each pupil or type of pupil requires has to be related to outcomes. For example, a student with a learning disability might require more educational resources to achieve a certain reading level than a nonhandicapped child. An educationally or economically disadvantaged student might require some form of compensatory education to enable him or her to achieve at grade level. The ultimate standard of this kind requires that each student be given the resources necessary to develop his or her talents to their fullest.

There is yet a different category of standards that is neither input nor output related but can be most properly described as one of taxpayer equity. For example, one such standard requires equal tax incidence according to the ability to pay. Application of this standard usually results in the imposition of a progressive or proportional tax system. Another standard is that equal effort (equal tax rates) produce an equal yield. In the case of school districts, this means freeing the tie between "capacity"—the district's per pupil property value—and "effort"—the district's tax rate. This standard is a variation of the negative-input standard which requires that the amount of money spent per child shall not be a function of property wealth per pupil other than that of the state as a whole. See *Serrano* v. *Priest, (Serrano I)*, contra Robinson v. Cahill, 62 N.J. 473, 502–3, 303 A.2d 273, 288 (1973).

Choosing among these and other similar standards is no easy task. The input standards are simple to use and administer but might be educationally irrelevant. Moreover, does it make a difference in the educational opportunity a child is afforded if the amount of money spent by the public school on his or her education is not a function of the property wealth of the school district but continues to be a function of the taste of the district's voters for education? The outcome standards are more truly "educational" standards, but they may be difficult to achieve for a variety of political, economic, and scientific reasons. See generally Yudof, "Equal Educational Opportunity and the Courts," 51 Tex.L.Rev. 411 (1973).

Finally, on what basis can the judiciary impose some of these standards? The judiciary may not have the constitutional warrant, the institutional capacity, or the political support to impose a particular standard. See Kurland, "Equal Educational Opportunity: The Limits of Constitutional Jurisprudence Undefined," 35 U.Chi.L.Rev. 583 (1968).

A concern with equity and fairness as a simple matter of justice is one thing, but as a practical matter, does it make an educational difference to pupils if their school district spends less money on them than another district spends on its pupils? The relationship between resources and outcomes is problematic. . . .

Interdistrict Inequalities

. . . [T]here exists in all states (except perhaps Hawaii which constitutes a single school district) a wide range of per-pupil expenditures among local school districts. Whether this difference constitutes a "problem" depends upon the standard one chooses for assessing the system. One of the first efforts to define the problem and seek a solution through the courts is represented in the decision in McInnis v. Shapiro, 293 F.Supp. 327 (N.D.Ill.1968), aff'd sub nom., McInnis v. Ogilvie, 394 U.S. 322 (1969). The data in the case showed that per-pupil expenditures among school districts varied between $480 and $1000 despite some effort on the part of the state through its state aid formula to equalize differences. The plaintiffs in the case argued that these differences were unconstitutional but seemed to suggest different and conflicting reasons for this conclusion. On the one hand, the plaintiffs argued that only a financing scheme that apportioned funds according to the needs of the students would satisfy the Fourteenth Amendment. However, they also suggested that a system that allocated funds on the basis of flat dollar equality or assured that equal tax rates yielded equal dollars would be constitutionally permissible. The district court did not dwell on this confusion but denied relief on a variety of grounds: a lack of judicially manageable standards, the rationality of the system insofar as it promoted local control, the fact that the allocation of public revenues was a basic policy decision more appropriately handled by a legislature than a court, and the fact that the Constitution did not require either allocation on the basis of need or on the basis of equal dollars per pupil. A "scarcely distinguishable" case, Burruss v. Wilkerson, 310 F.Supp. 572 (W.D.Va.1969), aff'd mem., 397 U.S. 44 (1970), received similarly curt judicial treatment.

Although the *McInnis* case was a setback to those seeking to reform educational finance, it did not signal the end of attempts to use the courts for that purpose. The reform effort was set in motion again with the publication of two books: A. Wise, Rich Schools, Poor Schools: The Promise of Equal Educational Opportunity (1968) and J. Coons, W. Clune, and S. Sugarman, Private Wealth and Public Education (1970).

Coons and his colleagues argued that Supreme Court precedent could be read to support the following proposition: The quality of public education may not be a function of wealth other than the total wealth of the state. Coons, Clune, and Sugarman, supra at 304. They called this proposition the principle of fiscal neutrality, in that it is designed to sever the correlation between local district property wealth per pupil and the amount of money spent per pupil. Fully implemented, the proposition would achieve the result that equal tax rates produced equal yields. It would not require that districts choose the same tax rates, however, thus preserving local control over how much money was to be raised locally. Inequalities in expenditures could persist under this standard, but they would not be caused by inequalities in property wealth per pupil. An important assumption was that the principle of fiscal neutrality would achieve not just taxpayer equity but also educational equity, because equal fiscal capacity—it was hoped and predicted—would mean that educational offerings would be equalized among districts. As just noted, however, the equalization of educational offerings is not a necessary result of the application of the fiscal neutrality principle.

Private wealth and public education fastened on the principle of fiscal neutrality for a number of legal, tactical, and policy reasons. First, they believed that the Supreme Court's own precedents seemed to be moving toward the notion that government may not discriminate on the basis of wealth. For example, in Griffin v. Illinois, 351 U.S. 12 (1956), and Douglas v. California, 372 U.S. 353 (1963), the Supreme Court ordered that a state must provide indigent criminal defendants appealing their convictions with a free trial transcript and a lawyer, respectively. These cases, it was argued, established the proposition that the "poor" constituted a "suspect" class entitled to special judicial protection and that governmental differences in treatment between rich and poor could only be sustained under the Fourteenth Amendment's equal protection clause if the government had a compelling interest and the differences in treatment were necessary to the achievement of that interest. It was thus an easy step to say that it was discrimination on the basis of wealth when the amount of money spent on a child (the quality of a child's education) differed depending upon the property wealth of the district in which the child resided. This was discrimination on the basis of school district wealth, equally as obnoxious as the discrimination on the basis of personal wealth that occurred in the cases of *Griffin* and *Douglas*.

Second, it was argued that education was a "fundamental interest," as that term was understood by the Supreme Court in the context of the equal protection clause; hence, since the finance system affected a fundamental interest, the courts had to examine the system in light of the strict scrutiny standard of review. Coons and his colleagues contended that the finance system could not survive strict scrutiny; that is, it did not serve a compelling state interest, and that even if local control were a compelling interest, the existing system was not "necessary" to the achievement of local control. Other finance systems (discussed below) would serve the interest of local control and yet not make the quality of a child's education a function of local district wealth.

Third, Coons and his coauthors also believed that the fiscal neutrality principle would be acceptable to the courts because it was judicially manageable and did not involve the courts in usurping the prerogative of the state legislatures to design their own system of school finance. The principle could be complied with in a number of different ways, and the choice among these ways was to be left to the legislature. A description of some of the options follows.

a. Full State Funding of Elementary and Secondary Education. Under this approach, all education revenues would be raised through a statewide property tax or some other state tax. These revenues could be distributed (a) on an equal per-pupil basis to school districts, or (b) according to some measure of educational need developed by the state, and/or (c) according to a formula taking account of the varying costs—based on such factors as cost-of-living differentials—of providing schooling within a given district. A fourth alternative would provide education vouchers directly to all children. See generally J. Berke, et al., Report of the New York State Commission on the Quality, Cost, and Financing of Elementary and Secondary Education (1972); President's Commission on School Finance, Schools, People and Money (1972).

b. State-Local Funding. The alternatives summarized above would take from school districts all authority to raise educational revenues. "District power equalizing" (DPE), by contrast, would preserve this authority but would guarantee to each district a given revenue yield for any tax rate a district chose to impose on itself. If two districts, whatever their relative wealth and tax base, set identical property tax rates, the per-pupil revenue in the two districts will be equal. This approach, first developed by Coons, Clune, and Sugarman, is better understood with an illustration:

How District Power Equalizing Might Work

District	Tax Rate Selected	Guaranteed Yield		Actual Yield		Difference Between Actual and Guaranteed Yield	
		.1%	3%	.1%	3%	Plan 1	Plan 2
		3% (plan 1)	3% (plan 2)				
Rich	3%	$30	$900	$750	$35 $1050	+$150	+$300
Poor	3%	$30	$900	$750	$15 $450	−$450	−$300

Under either power-equalizing plan (1 or 2), the rich district owes its "surplus" revenues—that is, revenues that exceed the guaranteed level for

3 percent—to the state, while the poor district is entitled to receive the difference between what it has collected and the guaranteed rate. When a district owes its "surplus" to the state, the DPE scheme is said to have a recapture provision. Plan 1 assumes a uniform tax rate/revenue guarantee ratio, that is, thirty dollars for each .1 percent (one mill), while under plan 2 the ratio is not uniform; a tax increment above a certain point (say 2 percent) would yield less than thirty dollars for each additional mill. Plan 2 permits the state to induce districts to limit their tax rates. As long as a given tax effort produces the same revenue, the effort-revenue ratio may vary in a district power-equalizing scheme.

A similar plan, called "family power equalizing," gives the family, not the school district, the power to set its own tax rate; the state would reward a given level of tax effort with a guaranteed amount of dollars, distributed to the family in the form of an education voucher. See Coons and Sugarman, "Family Choice in Education: A Model State System for Vouchers," 59 Calif.L.Rev. 321 (1971); cf. Center for the Study of Public Policy, Education Vouchers (1971).

c. *Mixed Models.* It is, of course, possible to combine several of these schemes. For example, the state could provide school districts with six-hundred-dollar grants for each child, as well as supplemental grants for particular categories of "child need" (for example, educationally disadvantaged or mentally retarded) or "district need" (for example, cost of living differentials); in addition, the state could permit, for example, the district to "power equalize" up to an additional two hundred dollars per child.

d. *Other Remedies.* While district power equalizing and full state funding are the most frequently cited remedies suggested to comply with the requirement of fiscal neutrality, other solutions are available. District boundaries could be redrawn so as to equalize the amount of property wealth per pupil in school districts. Limiting the school property tax to residential property and excluding commercial property from the local district tax rolls might have a similar equalizing effect. A state could mandate a certain expenditure level (and no more) at a given tax rate (or lower) and then guarantee that this tax rate would yield this minimum or foundation level in all districts. The richer districts would not have to use the state's mandated tax rate to raise their money; the poor districts would but would get state aid to assure they reached the mandated expenditure level. (Whether this scheme fully complies with fiscal neutrality is not certain.) See W.I. Garms, J.W. Guthrie, and L.C. Pierce, School Finance, chap. 9 (1978).

THOMAS, EQUALIZING EDUCATIONAL OPPORTUNITY THROUGH SCHOOL FINANCE REFORM: A REVIEW ASSESSMENT

48 U.Cin.L.Rev. 255, 278–80, 286–88, 318 (1979).*

The initial legal test of the fiscal neutrality principle brought the reformers their first major victory. In Serrano v. Priest [1971], the

California Supreme Court ruled that the state's school finance system violated the equal protection clauses of the state and federal constitutions because it made educational expenditures a function of community wealth. The court embraced the principle of fiscal neutrality, holding that education was a fundamental right, that school district wealth was a suspect classification and that the California school financing system based on local wealth was not necessary to the accomplishment of a compelling interest. In remanding the case to the trial court, the court stated that the "funding scheme invidiously discriminates against the poor because it makes the quality of a child's education a function of the wealth of his parents and neighbors." The court did not, however, rule out use of the property tax for educational financing, mandate the adoption of any specific remedy or require full equalization of per-pupil expenditures. It limited the effect of its ruling to breaking the link between district wealth and school expenditures. Development of a remedy was left to the discretion of the state legislature within the parameters of the opinion.

Initial reaction to *Serrano* was widespread and generally favorable. Its egalitarian implications gave encouragement to proponents of school finance reform. After the initial euphoria of reform had passed, scholarly commentary was considerably more restrained and less optimistic regarding the future of school finance reform. The most positive commentators applauded the California Supreme Court's acceptance of the principle of fiscal neutrality as providing an environment that would be congenial to major reforms but refrained from making outright predictions of such developments. Critics of *Serrano* ranged from the polemical, to the skeptical, to thoughtful analyses by those favorably and unfavorably disposed toward the result. . . .

Serrano sparked national interest in school finance, which was moving ahead on several fronts: increasing litigation challenging the constitutionality of school aid legislation in several states, major studies of school finance and the willingness of President Nixon to explore the possibility of relief through an expanded federal role in school finance.

The litigation which followed *Serrano* involved both federal and state courts. In *Van Dusartz* v. *Hatfield,* a United States district court held that Minnesota's school finance system, which made per-pupil spending a function of school district wealth, violated equal protection. The court applied the *Serrano* test of fiscal neutrality and ruled that education was a fundamental right; however, it left the formulation of the remedy to the state legislature. In doing so, it noted that the state was free "to adopt one of many optional school funding systems" and that "absolute uniformity of school expenditures" was not required. Six weeks later, in *Rodriguez* v. *San Antonio Independent School District,* another district court relied on *Serrano* and *Van Dusartz* in holding that the Texas school finance system, which involved local property taxes and a state-funded foundation program, violated the equal protection guarantee of the fourteenth amendment. It treated education as a fundamental right and refused to uphold the school finance system, which was based upon the suspect classification of wealth, in the absence of a showing of a compelling state interest. The Texas Board of Education appealed directly to the United States Supreme Court. The future of school finance reform through litigation based on the fourteenth amendment's equal protection clause was in limbo pending the Court's disposition of the *Rodriguez* case.

Meanwhile, state court decisions in Kansas, Michigan, New Jersey and Arizona invalidated school finance systems on the basis of state and federal constitutional provisions. Perhaps in response to the federal and state litigation, the states of California, Colorado, Florida, Illinois, Kansas, Maine, Michigan, Montana, North Dakota, Utah and Wisconsin enacted school finance reform legislation during 1972–73. . . .

The second and current phase of the school finance reform movement began on March 21, 1973, when the United States Supreme Court handed down its long-awaited ruling in *Rodriguez*. In a 5–4 decision, the Court reversed the district court's decision invalidating the Texas school finance system. The Supreme Court's opinion, written by Justice Powell, rested on two key findings: (1) that the Texas law did not "operate to the disadvantage of any clearly identifiable suspect class" (i.e., the poor) and (2) that education is not a fundamental right guaranteed by the Constitution. In consequence of its rejection of wealth as a suspect classification and its determination that education was not a fundamental right, the Court utilized the rational basis test rather than the more demanding standard of strict scrutiny to determine whether the Texas school finance scheme violated equal protection. The Court found the Texas school finance plan to be a reasonable means of accomplishing and protecting the state's interest in local control of and participation in educational decisions and in providing a minimum educational program in all districts.

Justice Powell emphasized the Court's reluctance to intervene in such a politically sensitive area and noted that traditional limitations on the judicial function require that ultimate solutions to social and economic problems be fashioned by legislatures responding to "democratic pressures." There was one note of encouragement for the reform movement, however, when the Court remarked that its action should not "be viewed as placing its judicial imprimatur on the status quo. The need is apparent for reform in tax systems which may well have relied too long and too heavily on the local property tax."

In the major dissent, Justice Marshall criticized the majority opinion as an abrupt departure from recent federal and state decisions invalidating state school finance systems dependent on taxable wealth and as a retreat from the Court's "historic commitment to equality of educational opportunity." Accepting the rationale of the district court and *Serrano*, Marshall concluded that education was indeed a fundamental right because it was intimately related to the exercise of first amendment freedoms and to the right to participate in the political process. Marshall believed that the Court should have applied the strict scrutiny test in judging the validity of the Texas school finance system, which, in his judgment, failed even to meet the more lenient rational basis test. It made little sense to Marshall to return the problem to "the vagaries of the political process" which has created it and proven singularly unable to remedy it.

Reaction to the *Rodriguez* decision varied widely. Some saw it as the death knell for school finance reform, and others called it a rejection of equal educational opportunity. Comment ranged from strong endorsement of Marshall's dissent, to cautious approval of the Court's position, to praise for the Court's recognition of the "limits to its own power to affect social change." Most immediate commentators expressed the opinion that the Court's refusal to invalidate the Texas school finance program did not lessen the need for reform. They were divided, however, in the degree of their optimism over the prospects for state legislative initiatives in the area.

Rodriguez removed the uncertainty over the fate of school finance reform in the federal courts. In doing so, it provided a breathing spell for states facing legal challenges on equal protection grounds, and it removed pressures for any immediate federal action to help states achieve equalization within their boundaries. The decision did not prevent state courts from hearing challenges on state constitutional grounds, which left state judges and legislators very much at liberty to implement reforms based on fiscal neutrality and the *Serrano* principle. *Rodriguez* left open the question how the Supreme Court would approach future cases involving other aspects of education, such as school desegregation. . . .

School finance reform is a complex issue that embodies a continuing dynamic tension between the core values of equity, equality and liberty. The strong upward surge of equality . . . carried through 1972 but was blunted by the *Rodriguez* decision. Since then, liberty and supportive values, such as efficiency, quality and localism, have grown in strength. Consequently, the radical restructuring of public school financing in the United States and accompanying changes in the overall pattern of public finance which appeared imminent in the early 1970's are no longer in prospect. Yet, the thrust toward reform, motivated by a desire to equalize educational opportunity in terms of per-pupil expenditures, the quest for greater equity for taxpayers as well as pupils and the attempt to make educational support more commensurate with educational needs, continue. Much has been accomplished through state courts and reform legislation in the states, and equalization remains a major concern of educational policymakers at all governmental levels.

––––––––

Equal Protection Analysis

References in the preceding discussion to terms like "fundamental right," "suspect classification," and "strict scrutiny" may be confusing. A brief introduction to these concepts is in order because they figure importantly in litigation involving public schools. These terms arise in public-school litigation involving claims based on the equal protection clause of the Constitution, which promises that government will not "deny to any person within its jurisdiction the equal protection of the laws." (The Fourteenth Amendment is reprinted in full in Appendix A at the end of this book.)

The courts have developed a more or less consistent approach for analyzing equal protection claims. The first step is to inquire: (1) Is a fundamental right that is protected by the Constitution, like the right to vote, implicated by the law or procedure in question? and (2) Is a distinction made on the basis of a constitutionally suspect classification, like race or national origin? If the answer to either of these questions is yes, the court will subject the rule in question to strict scrutiny, a tough standard of review. To pass constitutional muster under this standard, the rule must serve a compelling governmental interest and must be necessary to achieve that end. This was the standard the California Supreme Court applied in *Serrano* v. *Priest* and the federal district court applied in *Rodriguez* v. *San Antonio Independent School District*. The United States Supreme Court, as Professor Thomas noted, reversed the latter on the grounds that education is not a fundamental right guaranteed by the Constitution and that distinctions between poor and wealthy school districts involve no suspect classification.

Rules that do not involve fundamental rights or suspect classifications receive less exacting judicial review. In many instances, it is enough that a rational basis exists for any distinctions among students or other affected individuals, so that the rule represents a reasonable means to a legitimate end. Only rarely does a rule fail this constitutional test. In the *San Antonio* case, for example, the Supreme Court applied the rational-basis test to uphold the financing law that the plaintiffs challenged. The stark contrast between the strict-scrutiny and rational-basis tests of constitutionality has encouraged the courts to experiment with middle-level standards of review for interests that are basic to citizens but do not receive explicit consideration in the Constitution, and for classifications by sex and other "quasi-suspect" categories.

Comments and Questions

1. How would you summarize the principal arguments for and against allowing local revenues to provide the primary support for public education? Should communities be able to tax themselves heavily for education if they so choose and not have to pay back "excess" revenues to the state? But if we allow communities the freedom to tax themselves and to enjoy the benefits of their superior revenue-raising efforts without interference from the state, can we expect the state to "make up the difference" to districts less willing or able to raise local taxes?

2. If the states are to take a greater role in financing public education, which aid formula is most equitable, as judged from the public-school student's perspective? From the taxpayer's perspective? Do you have some difficulty determining just what the taxpayer's perspective is? Does your answer depend on the personal circumstances of the taxpayer? What circumstances?

3. Have the materials in this subsection on educational finance made you more or less enthusiastic about using a voucher system supported by state taxes to distribute educational benefits? Is the source of this state tax money (e.g., state income tax, state sales tax, federal revenue sharing) an important consideration?

4. Did the Supreme Court do the right thing when it found constitutional the school funding disparities in *San Antonio Independent School District* v. *Rodriguez*? If you think the Court should have found such interdistrict disparities unconstitutional, would you draw a distinction between education and other

locally variable public benefits supported primarily by local taxes, such as fire protection or highway expenditures?

Section Five. Necessity for and Nature of Coercive Power

As we noted earlier, public-benefit conferral is concerned primarily with distribution, not coercion. Still, on occasion the threat of force is necessary to effectuate distributive policies. We can anticipate that coercion will be necessary, for example, to get some people to pay taxes, license fees, or other assessments used to finance benefit programs. And the knowledge that sanctions can be imposed will be necessary to prevent some people from using fraud or other tactics to acquire benefits to which they are not entitled. Under some circumstances, we even use coercion to deal with the refusal to accept benefits, as in our response to youngsters who skip school or disrupt classes. Also, coercion is sometimes necessary if we are to prevent and control official misbehavior and overstepping.

Fines, jail terms, and other criminal sanctions can be used to induce cooperation with burden-imposing and benefit-conferring rules. Simply by threatening to cut off benefits, officials can see to it that beneficiaries stay in line. Recall, for example, the *Grove City College* case presented earlier in this chapter, where the federal government threatened to stop awarding student loan money unless the college complied with federal rules against sex discrimination. Termination of employment, demotions, and transfers to less desirable work sites are available tools for combating official misfeasance or nonfeasance. The grievance-remedial mode may be available to those harmed by official misbehavior, and it may also be possible to use the courts prophylactically to require proper performance of official duties.

The necessity for coercive rules and processes in distributive programs gives rise to a number of interesting and difficult questions, some of which concern the procedures that government uses to compel behavior from its own officials and from beneficiaries. Other questions concern the distribution of benefits per se. Many of the procedural questions occur whenever government administers programs, whether regulatory or distributive: What procedural protections should a government employee enjoy before sanctions are applied? To what extent should these protections depend on the severity of the sanction? Under what conditions should sanctions be used to maintain the chain of command? How intrusive can government be in ascertaining what the beneficiaries or the regulated are actually doing? Other questions, both procedural and substantive, are peculiar to benefit conferral: Under what circumstances should beneficiaries have the right to force benefits from government officials? What protections should beneficiaries enjoy before money or services are cut off? To what extent can people be forced to give up rights to privacy and free speech when they become beneficiaries of distributive programs?

Much legal ordering is required if government is to respond adequately to these questions. Still more legal ordering is required if government is to take seriously a fundamental tenet in all distributive programs: that goods and services should be distributed fairly among all eligible beneficiaries. Unfairness is always objectionable, but maldistribution of governmental benefits gives rise to special concern in countries that embrace the norm of equality under law. The offense has a double aspect: it is not simply that some are not getting their proportionate share of the government pie, but that the figurative pie is itself a public product composed of compulsory contributions from a taxpaying public who expects equity from government.

The judicial system is one locus for the coercive power necessary to make public-benefit conferral work equitably. The famous case that follows, *Brown* v. *Board of Education,* illustrates the necessity for occasional judicial intervention in benefit conferral. The case also illustrates some of the problems of legal ordering such intervention raises. In reading this decision, note how the Court justified its decision to intervene, and compare these reasons with those the Court gave for *not* intervening in *San Antonio Independent School District* v. *Rodriguez.* Note also the Court's unwillingness to discuss the question of specific relief in the same opinion that found a constitutional violation in the delivery of educational benefits. Would the Court have been as reluctant to discuss relief if the decision had outlawed segregation in the army?

BROWN v. BOARD OF EDUCATION

Supreme Court of the United States, 1954.
347 U.S. 483, 74 S.Ct. 686.

Mr. Chief Justice Warren delivered the opinion of the Court.

These cases come to us from the States of Kansas, South Carolina, Virginia, and Delaware. They are premised on different facts and different local conditions, but a common legal question justifies their consideration together in this consolidated opinion.

In each of the cases, minors of the Negro race, through their legal representatives, seek the aid of the courts in obtaining admission to the public schools of their community on a nonsegregated basis. In each instance, they have been denied admission to schools attended by white children under laws requiring or permitting segregation according to race. This segregation was alleged to deprive the plaintiffs of the equal protection of the laws under the Fourteenth Amendment. . . .

The plaintiffs contend that segregated public schools are not "equal" and cannot be made "equal," and that hence they are deprived of the equal protection of the laws. Because of the obvious importance of the question presented, the Court took jurisdiction. Argument was heard in the 1952 Term, and reargument was heard this Term on certain questions propounded by the Court.

Reargument was largely devoted to the circumstances surrounding the adoption of the Fourteenth Amendment in 1868. It covered exhaustively consideration of the Amendment in Congress, ratification by the states, then existing practices in racial segregation, and the views of proponents and opponents of the Amendment. This discussion and our own investigation convince us that, although these sources cast some light, it is not enough to resolve the problem with which we are faced. At best, they are inconclusive. The most avid proponents of the post-War Amendments undoubtedly intended them to remove all legal distinctions among "all persons born or naturalized in the United States." Their opponents, just as certainly, were antagonistic to both the letter and the spirit of the Amendments and wished them to have the most limited effect. What others in Congress and the state legislatures had in mind cannot be determined with any degree of certainty.

An additional reason for the inconclusive nature of the Amendment's history, with respect to segregated schools, is the status of public education at that time. In the South, the movement toward free common schools, supported by general taxation, had not yet taken hold. Education of white children was largely in the hands of private groups. Education of Negroes was almost nonexistent, and practically all of the race were illiterate. In fact, any education of Negroes was forbidden by law in some states. Today, in contrast, many Negroes have achieved outstanding success in the arts and sciences as well as in the business and professional world. It is true that public school education at the time of the Amendment had advanced further in the North, but the effect of the Amendment on Northern States was generally ignored in the congressional debates. . . . .

In the first cases in this Court construing the Fourteenth Amendment, decided shortly after its adoption, the Court interpreted it as proscribing all state-imposed discriminations against the Negro race. The doctrine of "separate but equal" did not make its appearance in this Court until 1896 in the case of Plessy v. Ferguson, [163 U.S. 537, 16 S.Ct. 1138], involving not education but transportation. American courts have since labored with the doctrine for over half a century. In this Court, there have been six cases involving the "separate but equal" doctrine in the field of public education. In Cumming v. Board of Education of Richmond County, 175 U.S. 528, 20 S.Ct. 197, and Gong Lum v. Rice, 275 U.S. 78, 48 S.Ct. 91, the validity of the doctrine itself was not challenged. In more recent cases, all on the graduate school level, inequality was found in that specific benefits enjoyed by white students were denied to Negro students of the same educational qualifications. In none of these cases was it necessary to re-examine the doctrine to grant relief to the Negro plaintiff. And in Sweatt v. Painter, [339 U.S. 629, 70 S.Ct. 848 (1950)], the Court expressly reserved decision on the question whether *Plessy* v. *Ferguson* should be held inapplicable to public education.

In the instant cases, that question is directly presented. Here, unlike *Sweatt* v. *Painter*, there are findings below that the Negro and white schools involved have been equalized, or are being equalized, with respect to buildings, curricula, qualifications and salaries of teachers, and other "tangible" factors. Our decision, therefore, cannot turn on merely a comparison of these tangible factors in the Negro and white schools involved in each of the cases. We must look instead to the effect of segregation itself on public education.

In approaching this problem, we cannot turn the clock back to 1868 when the Amendment was adopted, or even to 1896 when *Plessy* v.

Ferguson was written. We must consider public education in the light of its full development and its present place in American life throughout the Nation. Only in this way can it be determined if segregation in public schools deprives these plaintiffs of the equal protection of the laws.

Today, education is perhaps the most important function of state and local governments. Compulsory school attendance laws and the great expenditures for education both demonstrate our recognition of the importance of education to our democratic society. It is required in the performance of our most basic public responsibilities, even service in the armed forces. It is the very foundation of good citizenship. Today it is a principal instrument in awakening the child to cultural values, in preparing him for later professional training, and in helping him to adjust normally to his environment. In these days, it is doubtful that any child may reasonably be expected to succeed in life if he is denied the opportunity of an education. Such an opportunity, where the state has undertaken to provide it, is a right which must be made available to all on equal terms.

We come then to the question presented: Does segregation of children in public schools solely on the basis of race, even though the physical facilities and other "tangible" factors may be equal, deprive the children of the minority group of equal educational opportunities? We believe that it does.

In Sweatt v. Painter, supra, in finding that a segregated law school for Negroes could not provide them equal educational opportunities, this Court relied in large part on "those qualities which are incapable of objective measurement but which make for greatness in a law school." In McLaurin v. Oklahoma State Regents, [339 U.S. 637, 70 S.Ct. 853 (1950)], the Court, in requiring that a Negro admitted to a white graduate school be treated like all other students, again resorted to intangible considerations: ". . . his ability to study, to engage in discussions and exchange views with other students, and, in general, to learn his profession." Such considerations apply with added force to children in grade and high schools. To separate them from others of similar age and qualifications solely because of their race generates a feeling of inferiority as to their status in the community that may affect their hearts and minds in a way unlikely ever to be undone. The effect of this separation on their educational opportunities was well stated by a finding in the Kansas case by a court which nevertheless felt compelled to rule against the Negro plaintiffs:

> Segregation of white and colored children in public schools has a detrimental effect upon the colored children. The impact is greater when it has the sanction of the law; for the policy of separating the races is usually interpreted as denoting the inferiority of the Negro group. A sense of inferiority affects the motivation of a child to learn. Segregation with the sanction of law, therefore, has a tendency to [retard] the educational and mental development of Negro children and to deprive them of some of the benefits they would receive in a racial[ly] integrated school system.

Whatever may have been the extent of psychological knowledge at the time of *Plessy* v. *Ferguson*, this finding is amply supported by modern authority.[11] Any language in *Plessy* v. *Ferguson* contrary to this finding is rejected.

We conclude that in the field of public education the doctrine of "separate but equal" has no place. Separate educational facilities are inherently unequal. Therefore, we hold that the plaintiffs and others similarly situated for whom the actions have been brought are, by reason of the segregation complained of, deprived of the equal protection of the laws guaranteed by the Fourteenth Amendment. . . .

Because these are class actions, because of the wide applicability of this decision, and because of the great variety of local conditions, the formulation of decrees in these cases presents problems of considerable complexity. On reargument, the consideration of appropriate relief was necessarily subordinated to the primary question—the constitutionality of segregation in public education. We have now announced that such segregation is a denial of the equal protection of the laws. In order that we may have the full assistance of the parties in formulating decrees, the cases will be restored to the docket, and the parties are requested to present further argument on Questions 4 and 5 previously propounded by the Court for the reargument this Term.[13] The Attorney General of the United States is again invited to participate. The Attorneys General of the states requiring or permitting segregation in public education will also be permitted to appear as *amici curiae* upon request to do so by September 15, 1954, and submission of briefs by October 1, 1954.

It is so ordered.

---

11. K.B. Clark, Effect of Prejudice and Discrimination on Personality Development (Midcentury White House Conference on Children and Youth, 1950); Witmer and Kotinsky, Personality in the Making (1952), c. VI; Deutscher and Chein, The Psychological Effects of Enforced Segregation: A Survey of Social Science Opinion, 26 J.Psychol. 259 (1948); Chein, What are the Psychological Effects of Segregation Under Conditions of Equal Facilities?, 3 Int.J.Opinion and Attitude Res. 229 (1949); Brameld, Educational Costs, in Discrimination and National Welfare (MacIver, ed., 1949), 44–48; Frazier, The Negro in the United States (1949), 674–681. And see generally Myrdal, An American Dilemma (1944).

13. "4. Assuming it is decided that segregation in public schools violates the Fourteenth Amendment

"(a) would a decree necessarily follow providing that, within the limits set by normal geographic school districting, Negro children should forthwith be admitted to schools of their choice, or

"(b) may this Court, in the exercise of its equity powers, permit an effective gradual adjustment to be brought about from existing segregated systems to a system not based on color distinctions?

"5. On the assumption on which questions 4(a) and (b) are based, and assuming further that this Court will exercise its equity powers to the end described in question 4(b),

"(a) should this Court formulate detailed decrees in these cases;

"(b) if so, what specific issues should the decrees reach;

"(c) should this Court appoint a special master to hear evidence with a view to recommending specific terms for such decrees;

"(d) should this Court remand to the courts of first instance with directions to frame decrees in these cases, and if so what general directions should the decrees of this Court include and what procedures should the courts of first instance follow in arriving at the specific terms of more detailed decrees?"

Comments and Questions

1. Supreme Court intervention in the name of educational equity prior to *Brown* had always been premised on differences between black and white schools in educational resources, such as teachers and library books. Did the school systems challenged in this litigation offer decidedly fewer material resources to black students than to whites? If not, what was the Court's basis for finding a violation of the constitutional guarantee of equal protection of the law? Does the Court's reasoning suggest that the appropriate remedy for this violation is desegregation, or integration?

2. The elimination of state statutes mandating school segregation has not eliminated racial isolation in American schools, and schools that are segregated in fact, although not directly by law, continue to spawn lawsuits. In the following excerpt, David Kirp outlines the development of desegregation doctrine since *Brown*.

D. KIRP, JUST SCHOOLS: THE IDEA OF RACIAL EQUALITY IN AMERICAN EDUCATION
7, 284–86 (1982).*

What once seemed right and inevitable—a great declaration of law, morality, and politics—has been remade and in some sense diminished by subsequent history. Details that were thought trivial now dominate discussion. What is the meaning of "intentional discrimination" in desegregation cases? Just how should the benefits of desegregation—changes in student attitude and achievement, for example—be measured? What happens when the intended beneficiaries of racial equality resist the practical consequences of desegregation? In contrast with the lofty themes of *Brown*, these seem mere cavils, but they have come to occupy a central place in working out the meaning of equality. . . .

For nearly two decades following the *Brown* decision, the Supreme Court decided only Southern school desegregation cases. The cause of racial separation in those cases seemed, plainly enough, the officially maintained dual school system, whose effects lingered after its formal abolition. The justices did not belabor this point, but instead stipulated what remedies were constitutionally necessary to undo the continuing effect of segregation.

By 1971, however, when *Swann* v. *Charlotte-Mecklenburg Board of Education* was decided, the nexus between pre-1954 segregation and the present racial composition of the schools, so long presumed, had become attenuated. The Charlotte-Mecklenburg school district had some years earlier abandoned the evasions of *Brown*, which predictably produced dual schools. Other considerations contributed to racial identifiability in the schools, notably an increase in residential segregation coupled with the maintenance of neighborhood schools. In this respect, Charlotte-Mecklenburg did not seem so very different from Northern districts that, although untainted by a history of mandated dual schools, nonetheless operated substantially segregated school systems in which school attendance was largely determined by place of residence. *Swann* emphasizes the persisting consequences of the pre-1954 regime, but that portion of the opinion is factually unconvincing. Its very unpersuasiveness prompted speculation that the Supreme Court might abandon entirely the premise that only deliberate segregation was unconstitutional, treating desegregation as an affirmative constitutional right regardless of the cause of racial separation.

In *Keyes* v. *School District Number 1, Denver* the Court refused to adopt such an approach. In a community with no history of Jim Crow laws, the majority maintained, deliberate intent to segregate had to be shown before a court would grant relief; the mere fact of racial isolation was constitutionally irrelevant. Proof of intentional segregation affecting a substantial portion of a district presumptively demonstrated that deliberate segregation had a district-wide effect, and for that reason district-wide desegregation, including busing if necessary, was appropriate. The Court has been largely preoccupied since *Keyes* with elaborating the meaning of intent and refining the connection between wrong and remedy. Both are confusing enterprises.

Because Northern school districts had not been formally authorized in modern times to separate students on racial grounds, intentional segregation had to be inferred from the actions of the school board, its decisions concerning attendance boundaries, construction of new schools, teacher assignment, and the like. But how was this inference to be drawn? Was it sufficient to prove that school policy had the predictable effect of segregating students, or did intent carry a stronger meaning, implying some additional element of culpable conduct? Opinions after *Keyes* first contracted and later expanded the possibility of proving intentional segregation. The Court's determinations were similarly accordionlike with respect to the fit between wrong and remedy, increasing and diminishing plaintiffs' legal burdens.

The Supreme Court's vagueness and vacillation, the latter plainly visible in the Court's two very different decisions in the Dayton school case, has caused considerable trouble. Lower courts, unsure of what standard to apply, have reached varying decisions without being able clearly to communicate an explanation for the differences: Why should Pontiac and Kalamazoo, but not Grand Rapids, have to bus students? Policymakers have been baffled and infuriated by these turnabouts. *Brown* v. *Board of Education* was premised on values understandable and persuasive to the intelligent layman. *Keyes* and its progeny, by contrast, float in a sea of murky technicality, barely comprehensible to anyone, not obviously anchored to principles of fairness.

The constitutional standard propounded in *Keyes* is the chief culprit. Requiring proof of intentional segregation before calling for any remedy is a defensible reading of the Fourteenth Amendment—the language of equal protection is sufficiently capacious to tolerate a range of understandings—but not the most sensible reading. The injury that children suffer from racial separation has nothing to do with its cause. Does a black fourth grader know that her school is 95 percent black only because officials gerrymandered the attendance zone? Does it matter? The emphasis on intent also ignores the obvious point that segregation always results from official action—assigning children to particular schools. Intent is peculiarly susceptible to a host of different interpretations, in a policy universe where uniformity with respect to the bedrock of constitutional obligation seems an essential element of fair policy. Most important, because intentional segregation as the judges have defined the concept is neither a consistent nor a readily understandable basis for judicial intervention, the very legitimacy of the Court's effort is jeopardized. Why should people obey a decision whose rationale they cannot grasp and whose authoritativeness they doubt?

Comments and Questions

1. Kirp goes on to suggest that the Court would do better to "recognize the irrelevance of fault-finding with respect to most aspects of segregation" and mandate "uniform minimum integration." Id. at 286. This standard would be met if school administrators took steps to (a) integrate faculties and administration, (b) make facilities and instruction equal, (c) draw attendance zones to promote integration, and (d) locate new schools and make other changes with this objective in mind.

2. Do you agree with Kirp that past fault should not have to be demonstrated before courts can order school systems to work toward integration?

Section Six.   Roles of Private Citizens and Their Lawyers

Private citizens and their lawyers play important and varied roles in public-benefit conferral. Citizens elect the legislators who debate and pass upon taxation and spending bills; the electorate also elects the chief executives who bear final responsibility for the implementation of benefit-conferral legislation. Political campaigns to which citizens devote their time or money are part of the processes we have devised for selecting candidates and choosing among them. Campaigns and elections are characteristic of every level of government, from local school boards to the presidency, serving as they do to legitimate and limit the exercise of state power. So much is obvious to anyone schooled in the basics of American government.

Most of us are aware, too, of the citizens' power to contact legislators and policymaking boards to press for new programs or for new benefits under existing programs. Some citizens make these contacts directly, and a few even stay in regular communication with their representatives. Or individuals may join (or create) a group of like-minded people and try to influence lawmakers that way. Communication may be through direct political action, as through street demonstrations, or through more orderly processes involving letter writing, paid lobbyists, and the like. Interest groups, particularly those organized to provide long-term benefits to their members, are so common and so important in our form of government that some theorists see in pressure-group politics the essence of the American political system.

The kind of politicking that occurs between legislators and citizens seems to depend on the policy in question. The key variables, according to political scientist James Q. Wilson, lie in the perceived distribution of benefits and burdens embedded in the policy. J. Wilson, American Government: Institutions and Policies 419–23 (2d ed. 1983). Where both the benefits and the burdens to support the policy are widely distributed, as in social security or national defense, the attitudes of popular majorities play an important role in determining what legislators will do, and debate tends to be broad-based and open. When benefits are concentrated on a few, but burdens are widely shared and therefore not particularly onerous for any given individual, "client" politics is the rule, and ordinary citizens seldom play an active role; examples are price supports for farmers and public-works projects. The same is true when both benefits and burdens are concentrated, as when Congress enacts a tariff that hurts one industry but benefits another; in such situations, those organizations directly affected attempt to influence policy.

When benefits are distributed broadly, but burdens are concentrated on a few, one might anticipate that legislators would not act at all. Those who stand to benefit from the distributive policy do not benefit enough individually to induce them to act, and those who would be burdened have good reason to fight any impositions. Yet, government does selectively impose substantial burdens, even on powerful corporations, in part because policy "entrepreneurs" like Ralph Nader and organizations that claim to represent the public interest can mobilize citizen opinion in favor of such legislation. The following diagram illustrates this pattern:

	If perceived burdens are:	
	Distributed	Concentrated
Distributed	Majoritarian politics	Entrepreneurial politics

If perceived benefits are:

Concentrated	Client politics	Interest group politics

Discussion so far has emphasized the role of citizens and their lawyers in directly influencing the political process. The influence of the citizenry is broader, however. Public opinion helps set the policy agenda, and thus defines the needs to which governmental bodies respond and the means appropriate to the task. Consider, for example, contemporary interest in environmental protection, sexual and racial equality, and product safety— concerns that might have been, but were not, salient to an earlier generation. Just how societies arrive at their policy agendas and how they reach consensus on the tools of government appropriate to the task is not at all obvious.

We know more about how citizens and their lawyers influence the implementation, or carrying out, of programs already adopted. Sometimes citizen participation is mandated by law. A recent survey revealed that 155 federal grant programs have citizen participation requirements, and that these grant programs accounted for over 80 percent of the grant expenditures in 1977. M. Kweit & R. Kweit, Implementing Citizen Participation in a Bureaucratic Society: A Contingency Approach 6 (1981). These statutes vary in the means they employ to solicit citizen opinion. The Economic Opportunity Act of 1964, 42 U.S.C. § 2701, for example, mandated "maximum feasible participation" from the poor, a provision that proved highly controversial among local officials whose authority was displaced by this new requirement. Requirements that administrators hold public hearings and take views expressed there into account are less controversial and apparently less effective.[c]

The Education of the Handicapped Act takes another route toward ensuring that those affected by a benefit program will have a voice in running it. This statute gives parents important rights to consult and to challenge school administrators as they arrive at an "individualized educational program" for each handicapped child. The goal is to provide these students with a "free appropriate public education," though just what "appropriate" means Congress did not say. In *Board of Education* v. *Rowley,* the Supreme Court grappled with the question of what standard to apply when statutory procedures fail to produce consensus between parents and educators on how to educate a handicapped child.

BOARD OF EDUCATION v. ROWLEY

Supreme Court of the United States, 1982.
458 U.S. 176, 102 S.Ct. 3034.

JUSTICE REHNQUIST delivered the opinion of the Court.

This case presents a question of statutory interpretation. Petitioners contend that the Court of Appeals and the District Court misconstrued the requirements imposed by Congress upon States which receive federal funds under the Education of the Handicapped Act. We agree and reverse the judgment of the Court of Appeals.

I

The Education of the Handicapped Act (Act), 84 Stat. 175, as amended, 20 U.S.C. § 1401 et seq., provides federal money to assist state and local agencies in educating handicapped children, and conditions such funding upon a State's compliance with extensive goals and procedures. The Act represents an ambitious federal effort to promote the education of handicapped children, and was passed in response to Congress' perception that a majority of handicapped children in the United States "were either totally excluded from schools or [were] sitting idly in regular classrooms awaiting the time when they were old enough to 'drop out.'" [Citing House Report.] . . .

In order to qualify for federal financial assistance under the Act, a State must demonstrate that it "has in effect a policy that assures all handicapped children the right to a free appropriate public education." 20 U.S.C. § 1412(1). That policy must be reflected in a state plan

---

c. See Cole & Caputo, The Public Hearing as an Effective Citizen Participation Mechanism, 78 Am.Pol.Sci.Rev. 404 (1984). The authors studied the impact of hearings conducted under the General Revenue Sharing Program and found them "inconsequential."

submitted to and approved by the Secretary of Education, § 1413, which describes in detail the goals, programs, and timetables under which the State intends to educate handicapped children within its borders. §§ 1412, 1413. States receiving money under the Act must provide education to the handicapped by priority, first "to handicapped children who are not receiving an education" and second "to handicapped children . . . with the most severe handicaps who are receiving an inadequate education," § 1412(3), and "to the maximum extent appropriate" must educate handicapped children "with children who are not handicapped." § 1412(5). The Act broadly defines "handicapped children" to include "mentally retarded, hard of hearing, deaf, speech impaired, visually handicapped, seriously emotionally disturbed, orthopedically impaired, [and] other health impaired children, [and] children with specific learning disabilities." § 1401(1).

The "free appropriate public education" required by the Act is tailored to the unique needs of the handicapped child by means of an "individualized educational program" (IEP). § 1401(18). The IEP, which is prepared at a meeting between a qualified representative of the local educational agency, the child's teacher, the child's parents or guardian, and, where appropriate, the child, consists of a written document containing

> (A) a statement of the present levels of educational performance of such child, (B) a statement of annual goals, including short-term instructional objectives, (C) a statement of the specific educational services to be provided to such child, and the extent to which such child will be able to participate in regular educational programs, (D) the projected date for initiation and anticipated duration of such services, and (E) appropriate objective criteria and evaluation procedures and schedules for determining, on at least an annual basis, whether instructional objectives are being achieved. (§ 1401(19).)

Local or regional educational agencies must review, and where appropriate revise, each child's IEP at least annually. § 1414(a)(5).

In addition to the state plan and the IEP already described, the Act imposes extensive procedural requirements upon States receiving federal funds under its provisions. Parents or guardians of handicapped children must be notified of any proposed change in "the identification, evaluation, or educational placement of the child or the provision of a free appropriate public education to such child," and must be permitted to bring a complaint about "any matter relating to" such evaluation and education. §§ 1415(b)(1)(D) and (E). Complaints brought by parents or guardians must be resolved at "an impartial due process hearing," and appeal to the state educational agency must be provided if the initial hearing is held at the local or regional level. §§ 1415(b)(2) and (c). Thereafter, "[a]ny party aggrieved by the findings and decision" of the state administrative hearing has "the right to bring a civil action with respect to the complaint . . . in any State court of competent jurisdiction or in a district court of the United States without regard to the amount in controversy." § 1415(e)(2).

Thus, although the Act leaves to the States the primary responsibility for developing and executing educational programs for handicapped children, it imposes significant requirements to be followed in the discharge of that responsibility. Compliance is assured by provisions permitting the withholding of federal funds upon determination that a participating state or local agency has failed to satisfy the requirements of the Act, §§ 1414(b)(2)(A), 1416, and by the provision for judicial review. At present, all States except New Mexico receive federal funds under the portions of the Act at issue today.

II

This case arose in connection with the education of Amy Rowley, a deaf student at the Furnace Woods School in the Hendrick Hudson Central School District, Peekskill, N.Y. Amy has minimal residual hearing and is an excellent lipreader. During the year before she began attending Furnace Woods, a meeting between her parents and school administrators resulted in a decision to place her in a regular kindergarten class in order to determine what supplemental services would be necessary to her education. Several members of the school administration prepared for Amy's arrival by attending a course in sign-language interpretation, and a teletype machine was installed in the principal's office to facilitate communication with her parents who are also deaf. At the end of the trial period it was determined that Amy should remain in the kindergarten class, but that she should be provided with an FM hearing aid which would amplify words spoken into a wireless receiver by the teacher or fellow students during certain classroom activities. Amy successfully completed her kindergarten year.

As required by the Act, an IEP was prepared for Amy during the fall of her first-grade year. The IEP provided that Amy should be educated in a regular classroom at Furnace Woods, should continue to use the FM hearing aid, and should receive instruction from a tutor for the deaf for one hour each day and from a speech therapist for three hours each week. The Rowleys agreed with parts of the IEP, but insisted that Amy also be provided a qualified sign-language interpreter in all her academic classes in lieu of the assistance proposed in other parts of the IEP. Such an interpreter had been placed in Amy's kindergarten class for a 2-week experimental period, but the interpreter had reported that Amy did not need his services at that time. The school administrators likewise concluded that Amy did not need such an interpreter in her first-grade classroom. They reached this conclusion after consulting the school district's Committee on the Handicapped, which had received expert evidence from Amy's parents on the importance of a sign-language interpreter, received testimony from Amy's teacher and other persons familiar with her academic and social progress, and visited a class for the deaf.

When their request for an interpreter was denied, the Rowleys demanded and received a hearing before an independent examiner. After receiving evidence from both sides, the examiner agreed with the administrators' determination that an interpreter was not necessary because "Amy was achieving educationally, academically, and socially" without such assistance. The examiner's decision was affirmed on appeal by the New York Commissioner of Education on the basis of substantial evidence in the record. Pursuant to the Act's provision for judicial review, the Rowleys then brought an action in the United States District Court for the Southern District of New York, claiming that the administrators' denial of the sign-language interpreter constituted a denial of the "free appropriate public education" guaranteed by the Act.

The District Court found that Amy "is a remarkably well-adjusted child" who interacts and communicates well with her classmates and has "developed an extraordinary rapport" with her teachers. 483 F.Supp. 528, 531 (1980). It also found that "she performs better than the average child in her class and is advancing easily from grade to grade," but "that she understands considerably less of what goes on in class than she could if she were not deaf" and thus "is not learning as much, or performing as well academically, as she would without her handicap." This disparity between Amy's achievement and her potential led the court to decide that she was not receiving a "free appropriate public education," which the court defined as "an opportunity to achieve [her] full potential commensurate with the opportunity provided to other children." According to the District Court, such a standard "requires that the potential of the handicapped child be measured and compared to his or her performance, and that the resulting differential or 'shortfall' be compared to the shortfall experienced by nonhandicapped children." The District Court's definition arose from its assumption that the responsibility for "giv[ing] content to the requirement of an 'appropriate education' " had "been left entirely to the [federal] courts and the hearing officers."

A divided panel of the United States Court of Appeals for the Second Circuit affirmed. . . . 632 F.2d 945 (1980).

We granted certiorari to review the lower courts' interpretation of the Act. 454 U.S. 961, 102 S.Ct. 500 (1981). Such review requires us to consider two questions: What is meant by the Act's requirement of a "free appropriate public education"? And what is the role of state and federal courts in exercising the review granted by 20 U.S.C. § 1415? We consider these questions separately.

III

. . . . [C]ontrary to the conclusions of the courts below, the Act does expressly define "free appropriate public education":

> The term "free appropriate public education" means *special education* and *related services* which (A) have been provided at public expense, under public supervision and direction, and without charge, (B) meet the standards of the State educational agency, (C) include an appropriate preschool, elementary, or secondary school education in the State involved, and (D) are provided in conformity with the individualized education program required under section 1414(a)(5) of this title. (§ 1401(18) (emphasis added).)

"Special education," as referred to in this definition, means "specially designed instruction, at no cost to parents or guardians, to meet the unique needs of a handicapped child, including classroom instruction, instruction in physical education, home instruction, and instruction in hospitals and institutions." § 1401(16). "Related services" are defined as "transportation, and such developmental, corrective, and other supportive services . . . as may be required to assist a handicapped child to benefit from special education." § 1401(17).

Like many statutory definitions, this one tends toward the cryptic rather than the comprehensive, but that is scarcely a reason for abandoning the quest for legislative intent. . . .

According to the definitions contained in the Act, a "free appropriate public education" consists of educational instruction specially designed to meet the unique needs of the handicapped child, supported by such services as are necessary to permit the child "to benefit" from the instruction. Almost as a checklist for adequacy under the Act, the definition also requires that such instruction and services be provided at public expense and under public supervision, meet the State's educational standards, approximate the grade levels used in the State's regular education, and comport with the child's IEP. Thus, if personalized instruction is being provided with sufficient supportive services to permit the child to benefit from the instruction, and the other items on the definitional checklist are satisfied, the child is receiving a "free appropriate public education" as defined by the Act.

Other portions of the statute also shed light upon congressional intent. Congress found that of the roughly eight million handicapped children in the United States at the time of enactment, one million were "excluded entirely from the public school system" and more than half were receiving an inappropriate education. In addition, . . . the Act requires States to extend educational services first to those children who are receiving no education and second to those children who are receiving an "inadequate education." § 1412(3). When these express statutory findings and priorities are read together with the Act's extensive procedural requirements and its definition of "free appropriate public education," the face of the statute evinces a congressional intent to bring previously excluded handicapped children into the public education systems of the States and to require the States to adopt *procedures* which would result in individualized consideration of and instruction for each child.

Noticeably absent from the language of the statute is any substantive standard prescribing the level of education to be accorded handicapped children. Certainly the language of the statute contains no requirement like the one imposed by the lower courts—that States maximize the potential of handicapped children "commensurate with the opportunity provided to other children." That standard was expounded by the District Court without reference to the statutory definitions or even to the legislative history of the Act. Although we find the statutory definition of "free appropriate public education" to be helpful in our interpretation of the Act, there remains the question of whether the legislative history indicates a congressional intent that such education meet some additional substantive standard. For an answer, we turn to that history. . . .

That the Act imposes no clear obligation upon recipient States beyond the requirement that handicapped children receive some form of specialized education is perhaps best demonstrated by the fact that Congress, in explaining the need for the Act, equated an "appropriate education" to the receipt of some specialized educational services. The Senate Report states: "[T]he most recent statistics provided by the Bureau of Education for the Handicapped estimate that of the more than 8 million children . . . with handicapping conditions requiring special education and related services, only 3.9 million such children are receiving an appropriate education." This statement, which reveals Congress' view that 3.9 million handicapped children were "receiving an appropriate education" in 1975, is followed immediately in the Senate Report by a table showing that 3.9 million handicapped children were "served" in 1975 and a slightly larger number were "unserved." A similar statement and table appear in the House Report.

It is evident from the legislative history that the characterization of handicapped children as "served" referred to children who were receiving some form of specialized educational services from the States, and that the characterization of children as "unserved" referred to those who were receiving no specialized educational services. For example, a letter sent to the United States Commissioner of Education by the House Committee on Education and Labor, signed by two key sponsors of the Act in the House, asked the Commissioner to identify the number of handicapped "children served" in each State. The letter asked for statistics on the number of children "being served" in various types of "special education program[s]" and the number of children who were not "receiving educational services." . . .

Respondents contend that "the goal of the Act is to provide each handicapped child with an equal educational opportunity." We think, however, that the requirement that a State provide specialized educational services to handicapped children generates no additional requirement that the services so provided be sufficient to maximize each child's potential "commensurate with the opportunity provided other children." Respondents and the United States correctly note that Congress sought "to provide assistance to the States in carrying out their responsibilities under . . . the Constitution of the United States to provide equal protection of the laws." But we do not think that such statements imply a congressional intent to achieve strict equality of opportunity or services.

The educational opportunities provided by our public school systems undoubtedly differ from student to student, depending upon a myriad of factors that might affect a particular student's ability to assimilate information presented in the classroom. The requirement that States provide "equal" educational opportunities would thus seem to present an entirely unworkable standard requiring impossible measurements and comparisons. Similarly, furnishing handicapped children with only such services as are available to nonhandicapped children would in all probability fall short of the statutory requirement of "free appropriate public education"; to require, on the other hand, the furnishing of every special service necessary to maximize each handicapped child's potential is, we think, further than Congress intended to go. Thus to speak in terms of "equal" services in one instance gives less than what is required by the Act and in another instance more. The theme of the Act is "free appropriate public education," a phrase which is too complex to be captured by the word "equal" whether one is speaking of opportunities or services. . . .

The District Court and the Court of Appeals thus erred when they held that the Act requires New York to maximize the potential of each handicapped child commensurate with the opportunity provided non-handicapped children. Desirable though that goal might be, it is not the standard that Congress imposed upon States which receive funding under the Act. Rather, Congress sought primarily to identify and evaluate handicapped children, and to provide them with access to a free public education.

Implicit in the congressional purpose of providing access to a "free appropriate public education" is the requirement that the education to which access is provided be sufficient to confer some educational benefit upon the handicapped child. It would do little good for Congress to spend millions of dollars in providing access to a public education only to have the handicapped child receive no benefit from that education. The statutory definition of "free appropriate public education," in addition to requiring that States provide each child with "specially designed instruc-tion," expressly requires the provision of "such . . . supportive services . . . as may be required to assist a handicapped child *to benefit* from special education." § 1401(17) (emphasis added). We therefore conclude that the "basic floor of opportunity" provided by the Act consists of access to specialized instruction and related services which are individually designed to provide educational benefit to the handicapped child.

The determination of when handicapped children are receiving suffi-cient educational benefits to satisfy the requirements of the Act presents a more difficult problem. The Act requires participating States to educate a wide spectrum of handicapped children, from the marginally hearing-impaired to the profoundly retarded and palsied. It is clear that the benefits obtainable by children at one end of the spectrum will differ dramatically from those obtainable by children at the other end, with infinite variations in between. One child may have little difficulty competing successfully in an academic setting with nonhandicapped chil-dren while another child may encounter great difficulty in acquiring even the most basic of self-maintenance skills. We do not attempt today to establish any one test for determining the adequacy of educational bene-fits conferred upon all children covered by the Act. Because in this case we are presented with a handicapped child who is receiving substantial specialized instruction and related services, and who is performing above average in the regular classrooms of a public school system, we confine our analysis to that situation.

The Act requires participating States to educate handicapped children with nonhandicapped children whenever possible. When that "main-streaming" preference of the Act has been met and a child is being educated in the regular classrooms of a public school system, the system itself monitors the educational progress of the child. Regular examina-tions are administered, grades are awarded, and yearly advancement to higher grade levels is permitted for those children who attain an adequate knowledge of the course material. The grading and advancement system thus constitutes an important factor in determining educational benefit. Children who graduate from our public school systems are considered by our society to have been "educated" at least to the grade level they have completed, and access to an "education" for handicapped children is precisely what Congress sought to provide in the Act.

When the language of the Act and its legislative history are considered together, the requirements imposed by Congress become tolerably clear. Insofar as a State is required to provide a handicapped child with a "free appropriate public education," we hold that it satisfies this requirement by providing personalized instruction with sufficient support services to permit the child to benefit educationally from that instruction. Such instruction and services must be provided at public expense, must meet the State's educational standards, must approximate the grade levels used in the State's regular education, and must comport with the child's IEP. In addition, the IEP, and therefore the personalized instruction, should be formulated in accordance with the requirements of the Act and, if the child is being educated in the regular classrooms of the public education system, should be reasonably calculated to enable the child to achieve passing marks and advance from grade to grade.

IV

. . . [A] court's inquiry in suits brought under § 1415(e)(2) is two-fold. First, has the State complied with the procedures set forth in the Act? And second, is the individualized educational program developed through the Act's procedures reasonably calculated to enable the child to receive educational benefits? If these requirements are met, the State has complied with the obligations imposed by Congress and the courts can require no more.

In assuring that the requirements of the Act have been met, courts must be careful to avoid imposing their view of preferable educational methods upon the States. The primary responsibility for formulating the education to be accorded a handicapped child, and for choosing the educational method most suitable to the child's needs, was left by the Act to state and local educational agencies in cooperation with the parents or guardian of the child. The Act expressly charges States with the responsibility of "acquiring and disseminating to teachers and administrators of programs for handicapped children significant information derived from educational research, demonstration, and similar projects, and [of] adopting, where appropriate, promising educational practices and materials." § 1413(a)(3). In the face of such a clear statutory directive, it seems highly unlikely that Congress intended courts to overturn a State's choice of appropriate educational theories in a proceeding conducted pursuant to § 1415(e)(2). . . .

V

Entrusting a child's education to state and local agencies does not leave the child without protection. Congress sought to protect individual children by providing for parental involvement in the development of state plans and policies, and in the formulation of the child's individual educational program. . . .

VI

Applying these principles to the facts of this case, we conclude that the Court of Appeals erred in affirming the decision of the District Court. Neither the District Court nor the Court of Appeals found that petitioners had failed to comply with the procedures of the Act, and the findings of neither court would support a conclusion that Amy's educational program failed to comply with the substantive requirements of the Act. On the contrary, the District Court found that the "evidence firmly establishes that Amy is receiving an 'adequate' education, since she performs better than the average child in her class and is advancing easily from grade to grade." In light of this finding, and of the fact that Amy was receiving personalized instruction and related services calculated by the Furnace Woods school administrators to meet her educational needs, the lower courts should not have concluded that the Act requires the provision of a sign-language interpreter. Accordingly, the decision of the Court of Appeals is reversed, and the case is remanded for further proceedings consistent with this opinion.

So ordered.

JUSTICE BLACKMUN, concurring in the judgment.

Although I reach the same result as the Court does today, I read the legislative history and goals of the Education of the Handicapped Act differently. Congress unambiguously stated that it intended to "take a more active role under its responsibility for equal protection of the laws to guarantee that handicapped children are provided *equal educational opportunity.*" [Citing Senate Report and adding emphasis.]

As I have observed before, "[i]t seems plain to me that Congress, in enacting [this statute], intended to do more than merely set out politically self-serving but essentially meaningless language about what the [handicapped] deserve at the hands of state . . . authorities." Pennhurst State School v. Halderman, 451 U.S. 1, 32, 101 S.Ct. 1531, 1547 (1981) (opinion concurring in part and concurring in the judgment). The clarity of the legislative intent convinces me that the relevant question here is not, as the Court says, whether Amy Rowley's individualized education program was "reasonably calculated to enable [her] to receive educational benefits," measured in part by whether or not she "achieve[s] passing marks and advance[s] from grade to grade." Rather, the question is whether Amy's program, *viewed as a whole,* offered her an opportunity to understand and participate in the classroom that was substantially equal to that given her nonhandicapped classmates. This is a standard predicated on equal educational opportunity and equal access to the educational process, rather than upon Amy's achievement of any particular educational outcome.

In answering this question, I believe that the District Court and the Court of Appeals should have given greater deference than they did to the findings of the School District's impartial hearing officer and the State's

Commissioner of Education, both of whom sustained petitioners' refusal to add a sign-language interpreter to Amy's individualized education program. I would suggest further that those courts focused too narrowly on the presence or absence of a particular service—a sign-language interpreter—rather than on the total package of services furnished to Amy by the School Board.

As the Court demonstrates, petitioner Board has provided Amy Rowley considerably more than "a teacher with a loud voice." By concentrating on whether Amy was "learning as much, or performing as well academically, as she would without her handicap," 483 F.Supp. 528, 532 (S.D.N.Y. 1980), the District Court and the Court of Appeals paid too little attention to whether, on the entire record, respondent's individualized education program offered her an educational opportunity substantially equal to that provided her nonhandicapped classmates. Because I believe that standard has been satisfied here, I agree that the judgment of the Court of Appeals should be reversed.

JUSTICE WHITE, with whom JUSTICE BRENNAN and JUSTICE MARSHALL join, dissenting.

In order to reach its result in this case, the majority opinion contradicts itself, the language of the statute, and the legislative history. Both the majority's standard for a "free appropriate education" and its standard for judicial review disregard congressional intent. . . .

I agree that the language of the Act does not contain a substantive standard beyond requiring that the education offered must be "appropriate." However, if there are limits not evident from the face of the statute on what may be considered an "appropriate education," they must be found in the purpose of the statute or its legislative history. The Act itself announces it will provide a "*full* educational opportunity to all handicapped children." 20 U.S.C. § 1412(2)(A) (emphasis added). This goal is repeated throughout the legislative history, in statements too frequent to be " 'passing references and isolated phrases.' " . . .

The majority opinion announces a different substantive standard, that "Congress did not impose upon the States any greater substantive educational standard than would be necessary to make such access meaningful." While "meaningful" is no more enlightening than "appropriate," the Court purports to clarify itself. Because Amy was provided with *some* specialized instruction from which she obtained *some* benefit and because she passed from grade to grade, she was receiving a meaningful and therefore appropriate education.

This falls far short of what the Act intended. The Act details as specifically as possible the kind of specialized education each handicapped child must receive. It would apparently satisfy the Court's standard of "access to specialized instruction and related services which are individually designed to provide educational benefit to the handicapped child" for a deaf child such as Amy to be given a teacher with a loud voice, for she would benefit from that service. The Act requires more. It defines "special education" to mean "specifically designed instruction, at no cost to parents or guardians, to *meet the unique needs* of a handicapped child . . . . " § 1401(16) (emphasis added). Providing a teacher with a loud voice would not meet Amy's needs and would not satisfy the Act. The basic floor of opportunity is instead, as the courts below recognized, intended to eliminate the effects of the handicap, at least to the extent that the child will be given an equal opportunity to learn if that is reasonably possible. Amy Rowley, without a sign-language interpreter, comprehends less than half of what is said in the classroom—less than half of what normal children comprehend. This is hardly an equal opportunity to learn, even if Amy makes passing grades.

Despite its reliance on the use of "appropriate" in the definition of the Act, the majority opinion speculates that "Congress used the word as much to describe the settings in which handicapped children should be educated as to prescribe the substantive content or supportive services of their education." Of course, the word "appropriate" can be applied in many ways; at times in the Act, Congress used it to recommend mainstreaming handicapped children; at other points, it used the word to refer to the content of the individualized education. The issue before us is what standard the word "appropriate" incorporates when it is used to modify "education." The answer given by the Court is not a satisfactory one.

The Court's discussion of the standard for judicial review is as flawed as its discussion of a "free appropriate public education." According to the Court, a court can ask only whether the State has "complied with the procedures set forth in the Act" and whether the individualized education program is "reasonably calculated to enable the child to receive educational benefits." Both the language of the Act and the legislative history, however, demonstrate that Congress intended the courts to conduct a far more searching inquiry. . . .

The legislative history shows that judicial review is not limited to procedural matters and that the state educational agencies are given first, but not final, responsibility for the content of a handicapped child's education. The Conference Committee directs courts to make an "independent decision." S.Conf.Rep. No. 94-455, p. 50 (1975). The deliberate change in the review provision is an unusually clear indication that Congress intended courts to undertake substantive review instead of relying on the conclusions of the state agency.

. . . The legislative history reveals that the courts are to consider, de novo, the same issues. Senator Williams explicitly stated that the civil action permitted under the Act encompasses all matters related to the original complaint.

Thus, the Court's limitations on judicial review have no support in either the language of the Act or the legislative history. Congress did not envision that inquiry would end if a showing is made that the child is receiving passing marks and is advancing from grade to grade. Instead, it intended to permit a full and searching inquiry into any aspect of a handicapped child's education. The Court's standard, for example, would not permit a challenge to part of the IEP; the legislative history demonstrates beyond doubt that Congress intended such challenges to be possible, even if the plan as developed is reasonably calculated to give the child some benefits.

Parents can challenge the IEP for failing to supply the special education and related services needed by the individual handicapped child.

That is what the Rowleys did. As the Government observes, "courts called upon to review the content of an IEP, in accordance with 20 U.S.C. [§] 1415(e) inevitably are required to make a judgment, on the basis of the evidence presented, concerning whether the educational methods proposed by the local school district are 'appropriate' for the handicapped child involved." Brief for United States as *Amicus Curiae* 13. The courts below, as they were required by the Act, did precisely that.

Under the judicial review provisions of the Act, neither the District Court nor the Court of Appeals was bound by the State's construction of what an "appropriate" education means in general or by what the state authorities considered to be an appropriate education for Amy Rowley. Because the standard of the courts below seems to me to reflect the congressional purpose and because their factual findings are not clearly erroneous, I respectfully dissent.

Comments and Questions

1. A lawyer with expertise in the field of special education accuses the majority of "blatant disregard of Congressional intent" in the *Rowley* case, induced by "its unspoken fear that a contrary result would have opened the floodgates by allowing every seriously handicapped child in the nation to receive full-time individualized educational assistance where needed." Tucker, *Board of Education of the Hendrick Hudson Central School District* v. *Rowley*: Utter Chaos, 12 J.L. & Educ. 235, 235 (1983). Would the floodgates have opened if the majority had adopted the dissent's interpretation of the statute?

2. Should a school be required to reimburse parents who decide, against the recommendation of school authorities, to place a child in a state-approved private school, if a court later deems the private placement appropriate? See Burlington School Committee v. Department of Education, 105 S.Ct. 1996 (1985).

3. What if there were no Education of the Handicapped Act? Could the parents of handicapped children like Amy Rowley use *Brown* and other successful equal-protection-clause cases to force their public schools to provide them special services? What do you think the standard for judicial intervention in such situations might be?

The educational policy cases we examined in earlier sections made no provision for citizen participation. The success of some of these plaintiffs is a reminder that citizens can enlist the power of courts to influence the implementation of public policy, even without being invited to participate. And even when those that challenge distributive policies do not ultimately prevail, they can have an impact on policy implementation, for administrators often respond to pressures generated by the publicity associated with litigation. The threat of litigation, or even of adverse publicity, can also change policy implementation. Consider, for example, the probable impact of citizen complaints about "suggestive" books in the school library on the acquisition policies of the school library staff.

The important point to remember in considering the role of citizens at this stage in the policy process is that distributive policies are not self-actualizing. In the words of Frances Zemans:

Although what one gets is most certainly *related* to governmental allocative decisions, to a substantial degree what citizens *receive* from the government is dependent upon the demands they make for their entitlements and upon participation in the policy-implementation as well as the policy-making process. In particular, what the populace actually receives from government is to a large extent dependent upon their willingness and ability to assert and use the law on their own behalf.

Zemans, Legal Mobilization: The Neglected Role of the Law in the Political System, 77 Am.Pol.Sci.Rev. 690, 694 (1983).

When citizens mobilize to challenge distributive programs, it is usually to overturn legal requirements or administrative practices that cut them out of policy benefits or to avoid the imposition of tax or other burdens. The cases we have examined so far all involved citizens seeking to broaden the distribution of benefits. On occasion, though, citizens want out of a benefit-conferral program. Exiting from a program, as the case that follows demonstrates, can be surprisingly difficult. This case suggests that the state has the right to prevent citizens from trying to provide some kinds of benefits for themselves, without government assistance or oversight.

HANSON v. CUSHMAN

United States District Court, Western District of Michigan, 1980.
490 F.Supp. 109.

Benjamin F. Gibson, District Judge.

This is an action brought pursuant to 42 U.S.C. § 1983 alleging the deprivation under color of state law of rights secured by the Constitution of the United States. Plaintiffs, Lowell and Carol Hanson, seek a declaratory judgment declaring the Michigan Compulsory Attendance Law, Mich. Comp.Laws § 380.1561, unconstitutional as applied, "in that it denies parents the right to educate their children in their own home where the parents can give the children superior or comparable education as the public schools." . . .

. . . The Hansons are the parents of four children between six and sixteen years of age, and legal guardians of a fifth child, age thirteen. Another adult, Charlotte O'Brien, is living in the Hansons' home. Defendants [are various education officials and a police officer.]

During August of 1979 the Hansons and Ms. O'Brien decided to teach the above-mentioned children in the Hanson home. In pursuit of that objective the children were enrolled in the home study program of Clonlara School in Ann Arbor, Michigan, from September 4 to September 21, 1979. On or about September 21, defendant Christensen went to the Hanson home to determine why the children were not in Greenville School District schools. He was informed that the children had been enrolled in Clonlara. Christensen returned a day or so later to inform the plaintiffs that the children should be in school or the plaintiffs would be put in jail. On or about September 26, 1979 Christensen delivered a letter threatening court action against the plaintiffs if the children were not in school on the following day. . . .

On October 8, 1979, plaintiffs informed the state officials that they, along with Charlotte O'Brien and Pat Montgomery, Director of Clonlara School, were beginning a home study program which, they allege, "would provide their children with a comparable or better education than the public schools," and requested approval of their program, or an administrative review of it. Mrs. Hanson was informed that the State would recommend legal action against her by the local boards.

On October 9, 1979, Mrs. Hanson asked of defendant Cushman that plaintiffs be allowed to purchase textbooks that the Greenville School District was using so that her children would be able to study the same texts as other children in the area. Her request was turned down and she was again informed that she was subject to arrest if the children were not returned to public school. On the same day plaintiffs received a letter from defendant Sieter stating that the continued absence of the children from the Greenville public schools would result in a court action against them "for refusal or neglect to send your children to school." . . .

On November 6, 1979, defendant Coady filed a petition in the Montcalm County Juvenile Court alleging that the plaintiffs had neglected their children by failing to provide adequate education for their minor children. According to representations of counsel to this Court at its hearing of January 28, 1980, the result of the Montcalm County Juvenile Court proceeding was that the Hansons have agreed to hire a certified teacher to tutor their children in their home pending the outcome of this Court's proceedings. . . .

This Court need not decide whether parents have a right to educate their children at home, the state concedes that parents have that right so long as state laws are complied with. Rather the issue is the much narrower one of whether parents have the right to educate their children at home without complying with a state law requiring state certification of all persons who give instruction to children within the state.

Plaintiffs claim that the parental right to control the education that their children receive is protected by the penumbra of the first nine amendments and the Fourteenth Amendment to the United States Constitution. The case stands or falls on their argument that this claimed right rises to the level of a "fundamental" constitutional right. This argument is crucial because where governmental regulation impinges upon a fundamental constitutional right, the normal presumption of constitutionality accorded to governmental action is inverted. Instead of asking the usual question whether the regulation has any conceivable rational basis, the Court will insist that the governmental action be justified as necessary to achieve an interest of the state that is compelling.

Plaintiffs have cited no cases to the Court that have held that parents have a fundamental constitutional right to educate their children at home, nor has the Court's own research uncovered any. Rather, plaintiffs seek to establish this right through reliance upon dicta from several United States Supreme Court decisions. . . .

The plaintiffs' claimed right to educate their children through a program of home study free from the requirement of compliance with state education laws involving teacher certification does not rise above a personal or philosophical choice, and therefore is not within the bounds of constitutional protection. See Wisconsin v. Yoder, 406 U.S. 205, 92 S.Ct. 1526 (1972); Pierce v. Society of Sisters, 268 U.S. 510, 45 S.Ct. 571 (1925); Meyer v. Nebraska, 262 U.S. 390, 43 S.Ct. 625 (1923); Scoma v. Chicago Board of Education, 391 F.Supp. 452 (N.D.Ill.1974). Plaintiffs have established no fundamental right that has been abridged by Michigan's compulsory attendance statute, Mich.Comp.Laws § 380.1561, or by its requirement of teacher certification, Mich.Comp.Laws § 388.553. Thus the state need not demonstrate a "compelling interest" but only that it acted "reasonably" in requiring children to attend school and that children be taught only by certified teachers.

Although there is no allegation in the complaint, plaintiffs at oral argument raised the issue of equal protection as another challenge to the state's requirements. They argue that the position of the state treats those who wish to educate their children at home differently depending on whether or not they are certified teachers. Plaintiffs do not assert, nor does it appear, that this distinction has any adverse impact peculiar to members of a constitutionally protected suspect class, and, as discussed above, no "fundamental" right is involved. The Court, therefore, will apply the traditional standard of review which "requires only that the State's system be shown to bear some rational relationship to legitimate state purposes." San Antonio Independent School District v. Rodriguez, 411 U.S. 1, 40, 93 S.Ct. 1278, 1300 (1973). . . .

The state advances its interest in insuring the minimum competence of those entrusted to teach as justification for requiring certification of teachers. The distinction in treatment by the state between parents whose children are taught by state certified teachers, whether in a public or private educational institution or at home, and those parents who seek to educate their children at home without certified teachers, directly relates to the difficulty that the state would surely face in examining and supervising, at considerable expense, a host of facilities and individuals, widely scattered, who might undertake to instruct their children at home without certification; as compared with the less difficult and expensive mechanism of requiring certification as a standard for competency. This clearly satisfies the state's burden of acting rationally and reasonably.

It is therefore the opinion of this Court that the Michigan statutes and practices in question are constitutional. Plaintiffs have failed to set forth sufficient facts upon which either legal or equitable relief can be granted. Defendants' motions to dismiss the complaint for failure to state a claim is therefore granted, and the case is hereby dismissed.

Section Seven. Process Values

Process values, earlier chapters suggest, are fundamental to any conception of government under law. The significance of process values is most clear when government tells people what they cannot do or punishes them for violating established standards. Citizens would regard such government activities as sheer despotism if government did not, ordinarily at least, move in accordance with what are perceived to be fair procedures. Process values are no less important when government distributes goods to some and burdens to others. We have considered some process issues already, in the context of other sections in this chapter, but their significance merits a sharper focus.

Three clusters of process values are particularly important in benefit conferral: those associated with ensuring a representative government; those guiding duly elected representatives in policymaking; and those involved in the implementation of benefit-conferral legislation. These process values generate legal standards in all three areas, which are outlined in our state and federal constitutions, statutes, and administrative rules. Process values generate additional standards embodied in public opinion and political tradition. Just what these nonlegal standards entail becomes manifest only indirectly, through polls, elections, political contributions, editorials, and other social indicators.

Process values associated with the electoral system reveal themselves primarily through laws protecting the system against fraud, bribery, and the like, and through laws ensuring that the system does not disfranchise any group or region. "No taxation without representation" was a rallying cry of the American Revolution and remains an important value in our society. Our standards have grown more stringent with time. Consider, for example, how much broader the franchise has become since the nation's founding. And note the extent to which we now regulate campaign contributions, political advertising, and patronage. We have even attempted to reduce the advantage that candidates with wealth or a big campaign chest enjoy by extending federal financing to some electoral contests. Note also that the apportionment of legislative bodies, once virtually free of any judicial oversight, has become a significant issue in the courts and elsewhere. Ironically, as we have developed fairer standards for the conduct of elections and extended the franchise, the percentage of those eligible who vote has declined. See Abramson & Aldrich, The Decline of Electoral Participation in America, 76 Am.Pol.Sci.Rev. 502 (1982).

The process values involved in policymaking center on maintaining a healthy balance of power between the branches of government as they grow and change in character. Periodically, contests over the distribution of powers erupt, some of which are mediated by the courts in their role as interpreters of the Constitution. An example is the recent Supreme Court decision outlawing the one-house veto, a device Congress relied on to keep tabs on the exercise of administrative agency discretion. Sometimes the executive and the legislature negotiate their own disputes over how policy should be made, as when Congress resolved a crisis over presidential impoundment of funds by setting out procedures to be followed when the president seeks to avoid spending appropriated funds.

The implementation of distributive policies raises a different set of process issues. At this stage in the policymaking process, we want procedures that will, at a minimum, allow the allocation of benefits and burdens to occur in an orderly way, provide the government employees involved with certain protections against arbitrary dismissal or punishment, and protect those who receive benefits from arbitrary termination. The courts have wrestled with this last concern frequently in recent years, sometimes finding in the constitutional guarantee of due process the basis for their decisions. The two cases that follow explore the process issues raised by the termination of a public benefit that should be familiar to you by now: public education.

GOSS v. LOPEZ

Supreme Court of the United States, 1975.
419 U.S. 565, 95 S.Ct. 729.

MR. JUSTICE WHITE delivered the opinion of the Court.

This appeal by various administrators of the Columbus, Ohio, Public School System (CPSS) challenges the judgment of a three-judge federal court, declaring that appellees—various high school students in the CPSS—were denied due process of law contrary to the command of the Fourteenth Amendment in that they were temporarily suspended from their high schools without a hearing either prior to suspension or within a reasonable time thereafter, and enjoining the administrators to remove all references to such suspensions from the students' records.

I

Ohio law, Rev.Code Ann. § 3313.64 (1972), provides for free education to all children between the ages of five and 21. Section 3313.66 of the Code empowers the principal of an Ohio public school to suspend a pupil for misconduct for up to 10 days or to expel him. In either case, he must notify the student's parents within 24 hours and state the reasons for his action. A pupil who is expelled, or his parents, may appeal the decision to the Board of Education and in connection therewith shall be permitted to be heard at the board meeting. The Board may reinstate the pupil following the hearing. No similar procedure is provided in § 3313.66 or any other provision of state law for a suspended student. Aside from a regulation tracking the statute, at the time of the imposition of the suspensions in this case the CPSS itself had not issued any written procedure applicable to suspensions. Nor, so far as the record reflects, had any of the individual high schools involved in this case. Each, however, had formally or informally described the conduct for which suspension could be imposed.

The nine named appellees, each of whom alleged that he or she had been suspended from public high school in Columbus for up to 10 days without a hearing pursuant to § 3313.66, filed an action under 42 U.S.C. § 1983 against the Columbus Board of Education and various administrators of the CPSS. The complaint sought a declaration that § 3313.66 was unconstitutional in that it permitted public school administrators to deprive plaintiffs of their rights to an education without a hearing of any kind, in violation of the procedural due process component of the Fourteenth Amendment. It also sought to enjoin the public school officials from issuing future suspensions pursuant to § 3313.66 and to require them to remove references to the past suspensions from the records of the students in question.

The proof below established that the suspensions arose out of a period of widespread student unrest in the CPSS during February and March 1971. Six of the named plaintiffs, Rudolph Sutton, Tyrone Washington, Susan Cooper, Deborah Fox, Clarence Byars, and Bruce Harris, were students at the Marion-Franklin High School and were each suspended for 10 days on account of disruptive or disobedient conduct committed in the presence of the school administrator who ordered the suspension. One of these, Tyrone Washington, was among a group of students demonstrating in the school auditorium while a class was being conducted there. He was ordered by the school principal to leave, refused to do so, and was suspended. Rudolph Sutton, in the presence of the principal, physically attacked a police officer who was attempting to remove Tyrone Washington from the auditorium. He was immediately suspended. The other four Marion-Franklin students were suspended for similar conduct. None was given a hearing to determine the operative facts underlying the suspension, but each, together with his or her parents, was offered the opportunity to attend a conference, subsequent to the effective date of the suspension, to discuss the student's future.

Two named plaintiffs, Dwight Lopez and Betty Crome, were students at the Central High School and McGuffey Junior High School, respectively. The former was suspended in connection with a disturbance in the lunchroom which involved some physical damage to school property. Lopez testified that at least 75 other students were suspended from his school on the same day. He also testified below that he was not a party to the destructive conduct but was instead an innocent bystander. Because no one from the school testified with regard to this incident, there is no evidence in the record indicating the official basis for concluding otherwise. Lopez never had a hearing.

Betty Crome was present at a demonstration at a high school other than the one she was attending. There she was arrested together with others, taken to the police station, and released without being formally charged. Before she went to school on the following day, she was notified that she had been suspended for a 10-day period. Because no one from the school testified with respect to this incident, the record does not disclose how the McGuffey Junior High School principal went about making the decision to suspend Crome, nor does it disclose on what information the decision was based. It is clear from the record that no hearing was ever held.

There was no testimony with respect to the suspension of the ninth named plaintiff, Carl Smith. The school files were also silent as to his suspension, although as to some, but not all, of the other named plaintiffs the files contained either direct references to their suspensions or copies of letters sent to their parents advising them of the suspension. . . .

II

At the outset, appellants contend that because there is no constitutional right to an education at public expense, the Due Process Clause does not protect against expulsions from the public school system. This position misconceives the nature of the issue and is refuted by prior decisions. The Fourteenth Amendment forbids the State to deprive any person of life, liberty, or property without due process of law. Protected interests in property are normally "not created by the Constitution. Rather, they are created and their dimensions are defined" by an independent source such as state statutes or rules entitling the citizen to certain benefits. Board of Regents v. Roth, 408 U.S. 564, 577, 92 S.Ct. 2701, 2709 (1972). . . .

Here, on the basis of state law, appellees plainly had legitimate claims of entitlement to a public education. Ohio Rev.Code Ann. §§ 3313.48 and 3313.64 direct local authorities to provide a free education to all residents between five and 21 years of age, and a compulsory-attendance law requires attendance for a school year of not less than 32 weeks. Ohio Rev. Code Ann. § 3321.04. It is true that § 3313.66 of the Code permits school principals to suspend students for up to 10 days; but suspensions may not be imposed without any grounds whatsoever. All of the schools had their own rules specifying the grounds for expulsion or suspension. Having chosen to extend the right to an education to people of appellees' class generally, Ohio may not withdraw that right on grounds of misconduct, absent fundamentally fair procedures to determine whether the misconduct has occurred.

Although Ohio may not be constitutionally obligated to establish and maintain a public school system, it has nevertheless done so and has required its children to attend. Those young people do not "shed their constitutional rights" at the schoolhouse door. Tinker v. Des Moines Independent Community School Dist., 393 U.S. 503, 506, 89 S.Ct. 733, 736 (1969). . . . Among other things, the State is constrained to recognize a student's legitimate entitlement to a public education as a property interest which is protected by the Due Process Clause and which may not be taken away for misconduct without adherence to the minimum procedures required by that Clause.

The Due Process Clause also forbids arbitrary deprivations of liberty. "Where a person's good name, reputation, honor, or integrity is at stake because of what the government is doing to him," the minimal requirements of the Clause must be satisfied. Wisconsin v. Constantineau, 400 U.S. 433, 437, 91 S.Ct. 507, 510 (1971). . . .

Appellants proceed to argue that even if there is a right to a public education protected by the Due Process Clause generally, the Clause comes into play only when the State subjects a student to a "severe detriment or grievous loss." The loss of 10 days, it is said, is neither severe nor grievous and the Due Process Clause is therefore of no relevance. . . .

A short suspension is, of course, a far milder deprivation than expulsion. But, "education is perhaps the most important function of state and local governments," Brown v. Board of Education, 347 U.S. 483, 493, 74 S.Ct. 686, 691 (1954), and the total exclusion from the educational process for more than a trivial period, and certainly if the suspension is for 10 days, is a serious event in the life of the suspended child. Neither the property interest in educational benefits temporarily denied nor the liberty interest in reputation, which is also implicated, is so insubstantial that suspensions may constitutionally be imposed by any procedure the school chooses, no matter how arbitrary.

III

"Once it is determined that due process applies, the question remains what process is due." Morrissey v. Brewer, 408 U.S. [471, 481, 92 S.Ct. 2593, 2600 (1972)]. We turn to that question, fully realizing as our cases regularly do that the interpretation and application of the Due Process Clause are intensely practical matters and that "[t]he very nature of due process negates any concept of inflexible procedures universally applicable to every imaginable situation." Cafeteria Workers v. McElroy, 367 U.S. 886, 895, 81 S.Ct. 1743, 1748 (1961). . . .

There are certain bench marks to guide us, however. Mullane v. Central Hanover Trust Co., 339 U.S. 306, 70 S.Ct. 652 (1950), a case often invoked by later opinions, said that "[m]any controversies have raged about the crytic and abstract words of the Due Process Clause but there can be no doubt that at a minimum they require that deprivation of life, liberty or property by adjudication be preceded by notice and opportunity for hearing appropriate to the nature of the case." . . . At the very minimum, therefore, students facing suspension and the consequent inter-ference with a protected property interest must be given *some* kind of notice and afforded *some* kind of hearing. "Parties whose rights are to be affected are entitled to be heard; and in order that they may enjoy that right they must first be notified." Baldwin v. Hale, 1 Wall. 223, 233 (1864).

It also appears from our cases that the timing and content of the notice and the nature of the hearing will depend on appropriate accommodation of the competing interests involved. . . .

The difficulty is that our schools are vast and complex. Some modi-cum of discipline and order is essential if the educational function is to be performed. Events calling for discipline are frequent occurrences and sometimes require immediate, effective action. Suspension is considered not only to be a necessary tool to maintain order but a valuable education-al device. The prospect of imposing elaborate hearing requirements in every suspension case is viewed with great concern, and many school authorities may well prefer the untrammeled power to act unilaterally, unhampered by rules about notice and hearing. But it would be a strange disciplinary system in an educational institution if no communication was sought by the disciplinarian with the student in an effort to inform him of his dereliction and to let him tell his side of the story in order to make sure that an injustice is not done. . . .

We do not believe that school authorities must be totally free from notice and hearing requirements if their schools are to operate with acceptable efficiency. Students facing temporary suspension have inter-ests qualifying for protection of the Due Process Clause, and due process requires, in connection with a suspension of 10 days or less, that the student be given oral or written notice of the charges against him and, if he denies them, an explanation of the evidence the authorities have and an opportunity to present his side of the story. The Clause requires at least these rudimentary precautions against unfair or mistaken findings of misconduct and arbitrary exclusion from school.

There need be no delay between the time "notice" is given and the time of the hearing. In the great majority of cases the disciplinarian may informally discuss the alleged misconduct with the student minutes after it has occurred. We hold only that, in being given an opportunity to explain his version of the facts at this discussion, the student first be told what he is accused of doing and what the basis of the accusation is. . . . Since the hearing may occur almost immediately following the misconduct, it follows that as a general rule notice and hearing should precede removal of the student from school. We agree with the District Court, however, that there are recurring situations in which prior notice and hearing cannot be insisted upon. Students whose presence poses a continuing danger to persons or property or an ongoing threat of disrupting the academic process may be immediately removed from school. In such cases, the necessary notice and rudimentary hearing should follow as soon as practicable, as the District Court indicated.

In holding as we do, we do not believe that we have imposed procedures on school disciplinarians which are inappropriate in a classroom setting. Instead we have imposed requirements which are, if anything, less than a fair-minded school principal would impose upon himself in order to avoid unfair suspensions. . . .

We stop short of construing the Due Process Clause to require, countrywide, that hearings in connection with short suspensions must afford the student the opportunity to secure counsel, to confront and cross-examine witnesses supporting the charge, or to call his own witnesses to verify his version of the incident. Brief disciplinary suspensions are almost countless. To impose in each such case even truncated trial-type procedures might well overwhelm administrative facilities in many places and, by diverting resources, cost more than it would save in educational effectiveness. Moreover, further formalizing the suspension process and escalating its formality and adversary nature may not only make it too costly as a regular disciplinary tool but also destroy its effectiveness as part of the teaching process. . . .

We should also make it clear that we have addressed ourselves solely to the short suspension, not exceeding 10 days. Longer suspensions or expulsions for the remainder of the school term, or permanently, may require more formal procedures. Nor do we put aside the possibility that in unusual situations, although involving only a short suspension, something more than the rudimentary procedures will be required. . . .

Affirmed.

MR. JUSTICE POWELL, with whom THE CHIEF JUSTICE, MR. JUSTICE BLACKMUN, and MR. JUSTICE REHNQUIST join, dissenting.

The Court today invalidates an Ohio statute that permits student suspensions from school without a hearing "for not more than ten days." The decision unnecessarily opens avenues for judicial intervention in the operation of our public schools that may affect adversely the quality of education. The Court holds for the first time that the federal courts, rather than educational officials and state legislatures, have the authority to determine the rules applicable to routine classroom discipline of children and teenagers in the public schools. It justifies this unprecedented intrusion into the process of elementary and secondary education by identifying a new constitutional right: the right of a student not to be suspended for as much as a single day without notice and a due process hearing either before or promptly following the suspension.

The Court's decision rests on the premise that, under Ohio law, education is a property interest protected by the Fourteenth Amendment's Due Process Clause and therefore that any suspension requires notice and a hearing. In my view, a student's interest in education is not infringed by a suspension within the limited period prescribed by Ohio law. Moreover, to the extent that there may be some arguable infringement, it is too speculative, transitory, and insubstantial to justify imposition of a *constitutional* rule. . . .

In identifying property interests subject to due process protections, the Court's past opinions make clear that these interests "are created and their *dimensions are defined* by existing rules or understandings that stem from an independent source such as state law." Board of Regents v. Roth, 408 U.S. [564, 577, 92 S.Ct. 2701, 2709 (1972)] (emphasis supplied). The Ohio statute that creates the right to a "free" education also explicitly authorizes a principal to suspend a student for as much as 10 days. Ohio Rev.Code Ann. §§ 3313.48, 3313.64, 3313.66. Thus the very legislation which "defines" the "dimension" of the student's entitlement, while providing a right to education generally, does not establish this right free of discipline imposed in accord with Ohio law. Rather, the right is encompassed in the entire package of statutory provisions governing education in Ohio—of which the power to suspend is one.

The Court thus disregards the basic structure of Ohio law in posturing this case as if Ohio had conferred an unqualified right to education, thereby compelling the school authorities to conform to due process procedures in imposing the most routine discipline.

But however one may define the entitlement to education provided by Ohio law, I would conclude that a deprivation of not more than 10 days' suspension from school, imposed as a routine disciplinary measure, does not assume constitutional dimensions. . . .

In prior decisions, this Court has explicitly recognized that school authorities must have broad discretionary authority in the daily operation of public schools. This includes wide latitude with respect to maintaining discipline and good order. . . .

The Court today turns its back on these precedents. . . .

Moreover, the Court ignores the experience of mankind, as well as the long history of our law, recognizing that there *are* differences which must be accommodated in determining the rights and duties of children as compared with those of adults. Examples of this distinction abound in our law: in contracts, in torts, in criminal law and procedure, in criminal sanctions and rehabilitation, and in the right to vote and to hold office. Until today, and except in the special context of the First Amendment issue in *Tinker,* the educational rights of children and teenagers in the elementary and secondary schools have not been analogized to the rights of adults or to those accorded college students. Even with respect to the First Amendment, the rights of children have not been regarded as "coextensive with those of adults." *Tinker,* supra, 393 U.S., at 515, 89 S.Ct., at 741 (Stewart, J., concurring). . . .

The State's interest, broadly put, is in the proper functioning of its public school system for the benefit of *all* pupils and the public generally. Few rulings would interfere more extensively in the daily functioning of schools than subjecting routine discipline to the formalities and judicial oversight of due process. Suspensions are one of the traditional means— ranging from keeping a student after class to permanent expulsion—used to maintain discipline in the schools. It is common knowledge that maintaining order and reasonable decorum in school buildings and classrooms is a major educational problem, and one which has increased significantly in magnitude in recent years. Often the teacher, in protecting the rights of other children to an education (if not his or their safety), is compelled to rely on the power to suspend. . . .

The State's generalized interest in maintaining an orderly school system is not incompatible with the individual interest of the student. Education in any meaningful sense includes the inculcation of an understanding in each pupil of the necessity of rules and obedience thereto. This understanding is no less important than learning to read and write. One who does not comprehend the meaning and necessity of discipline is handicapped not merely in his education but throughout his subsequent life. In an age when the home and church play a diminishing role in shaping the character and value judgments of the young, a heavier responsibility falls upon the schools. When an immature student merits censure for his conduct, he is rendered a disservice if appropriate sanctions are not applied or if procedures for their application are so formalized as to invite a challenge to the teacher's authority—an invitation which rebellious or even merely spirited teenagers are likely to accept. . . .

One of the more disturbing aspects of today's decision is its indiscriminate reliance upon the judiciary, and the adversary process, as the means of resolving many of the most routine problems arising in the classroom. In mandating due process procedures the Court misapprehends the reality of the normal teacher-pupil relationship. There is an ongoing relationship, one in which the teacher must occupy many roles—educator, adviser, friend, and, at times, parent-substitute. It is rarely adversary in nature except with respect to the chronically disruptive or insubordinate pupil whom the teacher must be free to discipline without frustrating formalities.

The Ohio statute, providing as it does for due notice both to parents and the Board, is compatible with the teacher-pupil relationship and the informal resolution of mistaken disciplinary action. . . .

In my view, the constitutionalizing of routine classroom decisions not only represents a significant and unwise extension of the Due Process Clause, but it also was quite unnecessary in view of the safeguards prescribed by the Ohio statute. This is demonstrable from a comparison of what the Court mandates as required by due process with the protective procedures it finds constitutionally insufficient.

The Ohio statute, limiting suspensions to not more than eight school days, requires *written* notice including the "reasons therefor" to the student's parents and to the Board of Education within 24 hours of any suspension. The Court only requires oral *or* written notice to the pupil, with no notice being required to the parents or the Board of Education. The mere fact of the statutory requirement is a deterrent against arbitrary action by the principal. The Board, usually elected by the people and sensitive to constituent relations, may be expected to identify a principal whose record of suspensions merits inquiry. In any event, parents placed on written notice may exercise their rights as constituents by going directly to the Board or a member thereof if dissatisfied with the principal's decision. . . .

Not so long ago, state deprivations of the most significant forms of state largesse were not thought to require due process protection on the ground that the deprivation resulted only in the loss of a state-provided "benefit." In recent years the Court, wisely in my view, has rejected the "wooden distinction between 'rights' and 'privileges,' " Board of Regents v. Roth, 408 U.S., at 571, 92 S.Ct., at 2706, and looked instead to the significance of the state-created or state-enforced right and to the substantiality of the alleged deprivation. Today's opinion appears to abandon this reasonable approach by holding in effect that government infringement of any interest to which a person is entitled, no matter what the interest or how inconsequential the infringement, requires *constitutional* protection. As it is difficult to think of any less consequential infringement than suspension of a junior high school student for a single day, it is equally difficult to perceive any principled limit to the new reach of procedural due process.

ROSE v. NASHUA BOARD OF EDUCATION

United States Court of Appeals, First Circuit, 1982.
679 F.2d 279.

Before CAMPBELL, BOWNES and BREYER, CIRCUIT JUDGES.
BREYER, CIRCUIT JUDGE.

This case raises the question of the extent to which the Fourteenth Amendment imposes "due process" obligations upon a school board seeking to suspend school bus trips briefly for disciplinary purposes. After examining the facts of this case, we have concluded that the school authorities complied with whatever obligations the Constitution might impose.

The law of the State of New Hampshire requires school districts to provide free school bus transportation to most pupils under the age of 14. N.H.Rev.Stat.Ann. §§ 189:6–8. Several years ago, bus drivers began to complain about vandalism and disruptive conduct on certain bus routes in Nashua. Students were apparently throwing things about inside the buses and at passing cars; they were slashing seats; they were excessively noisy and disrespectful to the drivers. Because the drivers had to watch the road, they could not tell which specific students were responsible. The private company supplying the bus service complained to the Nashua Board of Education. After hearings and consideration of alternatives, the Board adopted a suspension policy.

The policy applied to instances of serious disruption, significant vandalism, or danger. In such cases, when other methods of dealing with the disciplinary problem failed, a school official would board the bus and tell the students that the route would be suspended if the guilty students did not come forward. If this did not work, the Board's "transportation director" would write to the parents telling them that the bus route would be suspended unless the troublemakers were identified. As a last resort, the Board could suspend the route for up to five days.

When several parents objected to this policy, the Board held hearings. It considered several alternatives, such as seat assignments, ID cards, even special police ("monitors") to ride the bus. But, believing that these alternatives were either too expensive, or not always effective, it retained its rule allowing temporary (five day) suspensions after advance notice to affected students and parents.

According to the Board, the policy has been successful. During the first year of the policy's operation there were only 12 suspensions. Since there are 150 school bus routes and each bus makes two trips per day for 180 school days, the total number of bus trips lost could not have amounted to more than 120 out of 54,000. And, judging from the fact that the Board wishes to keep the policy, it believes that the threat of suspension has a salutary effect on discipline. Its belief is supported by the fact that only 3 or 4 routes were suspended in the policy's second year of operation.

The objecting parents, however, claim that their children are not the ones who cause the trouble. They attack the policy as unfair, for it makes their children suffer for the sins of others, and they claim it violates both state and federal law. The district court, 506 F.Supp. 1366, rejected their legal claims, as do we. . . .

Appellants' main argument is that New Hampshire law, as so interpreted, is unconstitutional. They claim that the Fourteenth Amendment, in forbidding deprivation of "property . . . without due process of law," requires a prior hearing to determine likely guilt or innocence before the Board can deprive a pupil of bus transportation—even for five days. We do not agree.

As an initial matter, we have serious doubts about whether the pupils or their parents have asserted a property interest sufficiently weighty for the Due Process Clause to apply. No one here complains about any deprivation of education, or educational opportunity. Compare Goss v. Lopez, 419 U.S. 565, 576, 95 S.Ct. 729, 737 (1975). . . .

The fact that New Hampshire law guarantees free bus transportation does not seem sufficient to create a constitutionally protected interest in the *suspension-free* service that appellants seek. In deciding whether an interest in a government benefit rises to the level of protected property, the Supreme Court has us look to the reasonable expectations of those who receive the benefit. . . .

Even if there were constitutionally protected "property" at stake, however, the appellants received the "process" they are "due." In determining whether "due process" requires a particular procedural safeguard (say, a hearing prior to deprivation), we are to take at least three factors into account: 1) the value or importance of the property interest at stake; 2) the probability of an erroneous deprivation if the safeguard is not provided; and 3) the cost of, or the burden imposed by, the safeguard.

In this case, as already pointed out, the importance of the property interest is small. The likelihood of an erroneous deprivation without a prior hearing, however, is significant. The Board's policy deprives students of bus transportation who took no part in any trouble-making activities. A prior hearing might prevent this, but at substantial cost— namely, the cost of abandoning the suspension program altogether. The program was instituted because the Board could not identify the trouble-makers in advance. To require an individual hearing is to require identification before suspension—the very thing the Board is unable to do.

The issue then comes down to the reasonableness of the suspension program itself. Appellants, citing Thompson v. Louisville, 362 U.S. 199, 80 S.Ct. 624 (1960), claim that the program is inherently unreasonable, for it punishes the "innocent" along with the "guilty." We are not dealing here, however, with criminal punishments or with sending someone to prison without evidence. At issue is discipline on school buses, quite another matter, and one where the lessons drawn from criminal trials may not be totally appropriate. On the one hand, the notion of penalizing a whole class (by, say, keeping them after school or cancelling "recess") because of trouble caused by a few is (or at least used to be) fairly common in the world of school discipline. The serious risks and dangers associated with throwing objects in and outside of moving buses, on the other hand, are obvious, and warrant serious measures aimed at avoiding them. Moreover, the Board here has held full hearings on its policy, it has considered alternatives, and it has decided that its policy offers the most promising avenue to avoid vandalism, disruption, and driving hazards on school buses. We cannot find that judgment unreasonable, particularly when the Supreme Court "has repeatedly emphasized the need for affirming the comprehensive authority of the States and . . . school officials, consistent with fundamental constitutional safeguards, to prescribe control of conduct in the schools." Tinker v. Des Moines School District, 393 U.S. 503, 507, 89 S.Ct. 733, 736 (1969).

From a constitutional perspective, then, we find no interests here at stake either sufficiently great in amount or fundamental in nature to require greater procedural protection than the Board has offered—particularly when increased protection would merely prevent the implementation of a reasonable disciplinary policy aimed at securing the safety of the children riding school buses.

For these reasons, the decision of the district court is
Affirmed.

Comments and Questions

1. Can you deduce from these two cases what process the Constitution demands for the welfare recipient threatened with a cutoff of support? The contractor who loses a bid to build a new submarine? The winner of a government lottery? Are you satisfied that the court of appeals got the balance right in *Rose*?

2. The dissenters in *Goss* at one point claimed that "[n]o one can foresee the ultimate frontiers of the new 'thicket' the Court now enters." Justice Powell and his fellow dissenters were concerned that failing grades, failure to be promoted to the next grade, exclusion from interscholastic athletics or other extracurricular activities, transfers to new schools, and tracking decisions would be challenged in the courts. Does the Constitution require the schools to provide notice, a hearing, and other protections before they take such actions?

3. What competing values are at stake in these two cases? Can you state the dissent's position in *Goss* in terms of process values?

Section Eight.   Improving the Public-Benefit Instrument

Public-benefit conferral, as we have seen, depends heavily on legislative and administrative processes and executive leadership. There is no shortage of ideas on how any of these could be improved. Every election year, for example, political analysts speculate about the defects of our electoral system, and some of these speculations have led to reform legislation. Occasionally the courts even become involved in the reform process, as in Baker v. Carr, 369 U.S. 186, 82 S.Ct. 691 (1962), the historic Supreme Court decision mandating one person-one vote. The legislative process, with its delays, frustrations, and vulnerability to the pressure of special interests, is also the object of constant critical attention from scholars, journalists, and others. Here, too, reforms are often suggested and occasionally adopted. Other observers analyze the implementation of social-welfare law and make suggestions. The debate over school vouchers discussed earlier in this chapter is an example.

We shall limit our consideration here to the difficult problem of maintaining some measure of popular control over the bureaucracy that distributes public benefits. The two excerpts that follow differ in their analysis of the route to improved distribution. How fundamental are these differences?

T. LOWI, THE END OF LIBERALISM

298–303, 305, 307–10 (2d ed. 1979).*

[A] new public philosophy does not come out of a package. It will emerge from a kind of political discourse in which few of us have engaged during the false consensus of our generation. As a contribution to this discourse, I offer *juridical democracy*.

In our everyday lives we speak of civility and propriety without defining them, because we have some reasonable expectation we will be understood. The need to define juridical democracy is to me a measure of the decline of law and of legitimate government in the United States. Juridical democracy is rule of law operating in institutions. . . .

. . . Much of the deceit we now associate with American politicians and officials—all the way up to the White House—is attributable to the impossible expectations policies-without-law impose upon them. The juridical principle puts the burden upon the law itself; and the law, when clear, would displace vague public expectation as the criterion by which the performance of governments and government officials would be judged. According to the juridical principle, a bad program is worse than no program at all. And when the rule of law is clear and the program nevertheless fails, we would then have a basis for changing the law rather than vilifying the responsible individuals as though they were guilty of malfeasance and bad faith. Moreover, the juridical principle would provide a basis for collective responsibility; the president or a specific agency would no longer be alone but would share responsibility with all those who supported the program from start to finish. . . .

. . . The Court's rule must once again become one of declaring invalid and unconstitutional any delegation of power to an administrative agency or to the president that is not accompanied by clear standards of implementation. . . .

. . . Under present conditions, when Congress delegates without a shred of guidance, the courts usually end up rewriting many of the statutes in the course of construction. Since the Court's present procedure is always to find an acceptable meaning of a statute in order to avoid invalidating it, the Court is constantly legislating. . . .

. . . Granted, rule of law requirements are likely to make far more difficult the framing and passage of some policies. But why indeed should any program be acceptable if the partisans cannot fairly clearly state its purpose and means? . . .

. . . Ignorance of changing social conditions is important, although it is much overused as an alibi for malfeasance in legislative drafting. Social pressure for some kind of quick action also interferes with drafting of a proper rule, even though this too is a much overused alibi. Nevertheless, even if it would often be impossible for Congress to live by the juridical principle despite sincere efforts to do so, there are at least two ways to compensate for that slippage and to bring these necessarily vague legislative formulations back to a much closer approximation of the juridical principle. The first of these is administrative formality. The second . . . is codification.

Administrative formality would simply be a requirement for early and frequent administrative rule-making. When an agency formulates a general rule it is without any question committing a legislative act. But in so doing, the agency is simply carrying out the responsibility delegated to it by Congress in the enabling statute for that agency, and is also carrying out the general intent of Congress as spelled out in the Administrative Procedure Act. This power to promulgate general rules has been validated by the Supreme Court. But the trouble is, few agencies do this, and even fewer like to do it. Most of the administrative rhetoric in recent years espouses the interest-group ideal of administration by favoring the norms of flexibility and decision by bargaining. Pluralism applied to administration usually takes the practical form of an attempt to deal with each case on its merits. But the ideal of case-by-case administration is in most instances a myth. Few persons affected by a decision have an opportunity to be heard. And each agency, regulatory or not, disposes of the largest proportion of its cases without any procedure at all, least of all by formal adversary processes. In practice, agencies end up with the worst of case-by-case adjudication *and* of rule-making. They try to work without rules in order to live with the loose legislative mandate, and then they try to treat their cases and practices as though they were operating under a rule. . . .

The second approach to the problem of Congress's inherent inability to live by the juridical principle, codification, is highly consistent with and complementary to the first. Even if Congress is unable to provide good legislative guidelines at the time of the passage of the original organic act, there is no reason why Congress has to remain permanently incapable. The answer here is codification. Let us consider it in light of the modest proposition that Congress ought to be able to learn from its own experience.

Codification is nothing more than the effort to systematize, digest, and simplify all of the provisions of law relating to a particular subject. The most famous and successful effort at codification was probably that of the French law in 1804 (eventually called Code Napoleon to honor the emperor), which was sought because there were so many sources of law in France: Roman law in the south, customary law in the north, canon law over marriage and family, case law and government edict in an increasing number of areas by the time of the Revolution. Voltaire is said to have observed that travelers in France changed law as often as they changed horses. . . .

If Congress got regularly and routinely into the business of serious revision of its laws in light of administrative experience, it would then be perfectly possible for Congress to live according to the juridical principle and yet delegate broad powers to administrators. Everyone would be aware of the fact that the first enactment is only the beginning. Every administrator would be making decisions with an eye toward review for consistency, and every agency would have incentive to influence this process by promulgation of the early rules proposed [above]. Every regulated corporation and individual would be pushing the regulatory agency toward general rulings and away from individual decisions because of the knowledge that these are likely to become legislation eventually. Finally, when these rulings are brought back to Congress and put through the regular legislative mill, they will not only be elevated in stature as law but very probably would go through further change and further clarification on their way back to the administrative agency. The regulator would then be participating in the legislative process in a way that is consonant with the Constitution and the juridical principle. This should definitely elevate the status of the regulator and at the same time would be far more honest and open from the standpoint of the regulated corporation and individual.

None of this conflicts in any way with existing congressional procedures. However, a commitment to serious legislative revision which attempted to fuse administrative experience would supplement and could eventually displace much of the futile oversight process. . . .

Legislative oversight tends to have two frustrating results. Either it has a marginal influence on substantial problems or a significant influence on marginal problems. It is a myth that programs and administrative agencies are given thorough evaluation at least once a year through normal appropriations processes that extend through the Executive Office of the President to the two Appropriations Committees of Congress and their specialized subcommittees. These yearly evaluations get only at the marginal and incremental aspects of most programs. Substantive questions are most often treated as off limits, while individual members of Congress often ask substantive questions, they are likely to be disregarded or ruled out of order. The very cost-consciousness and care for detail that makes appropriations review functionally rational is also the source of its weakness as a means of achieving any substantive accountability. . . .

The juridical principle may be suffering most from the immortality of administrative agencies. Enabling legislation is as indefinite on agency duration as on substantive guidelines. Once an agency is established, its resources favor its own survival, and the longer agencies survive, the more likely they are to continue to survive. The only direct antidote to immortality would appear to be an attack upon the Frankenstein legislation creating each monster, and in that spirit the final reform proposal is for a general statute setting a Jeffersonian limit of from five to ten years on the life of every enabling act. . . .

Indeed, most agencies will survive the renewal process, and most will probably be able to avoid any serious alterations in the way they conduct their business. But each agency will be a different one if in the process its true nature has been exposed. My own hypothesis is that few agencies can withstand public scrutiny. And it is not a hypothesis but a certainty that the public will gain immensely from any effort, even when unsuccessful, to codify past rulings and to enact them as a code to guide future conduct—until the next sunset.

———

J. PRESSMAN & A. WILDAVSKY, IMPLEMENTATION
168–72, 175–76 (3d ed. 1984).*

We begin by observing that the essential constituents of any policy are objectives and resources. In most policies of interest, objectives are characteristically multiple (because we want many things, not just one), conflicting (because we want different things), and vague (because that is how we can agree to proceed without having to agree also on exactly what to do). So if the objectives are not uniquely determined, neither are the modes of implementation for them.

Because of cognitive limitations and the dynamic quality of our environment, moreover, there is no way for us to understand at first all the relevant constraints on resources. We can discover and then incorporate them into our plans only as the implementation process unfolds. As long as we cannot determine what is feasible, we cannot carry out any well-defined policy univocally; all we can do is carry along a cluster of potential policies. Implementation begins neither with words nor deeds, but with multiple dispositions to act or to treat certain situations in certain ways. . . .

Policies grow out of ideas, and ideas are inexhaustible. What can be done with them depends as much on their intrinsic richness as on the quality of the minds and the nature of their environment. As problems are truly understood only after they have been solved, so the full implications of an idea can often be seen only from hindsight, only after the idea has been used and adapted to a variety of circumstances. . . .

. . . Policies are continuously transformed by implementing actions that simultaneously alter resources and objectives. Varying the amount of resources need not require doing more or less of the same thing: one might do quite different things with $1 million than if one had $10 million. Altering objectives may change the significance of behaviors that are seemingly the same. Suppose the actual purpose of a system of effluent charges gradually shifts from pollution control to raising general revenue. The fiscal and administrative mechanisms may remain the same, but the policy would change significantly. When social security changes from insurance to income redistribution, the same name covers very different realities.

Which objectives are to be implemented, in what order, with what proportion of available resources? Constraints are also objectives. There is no such thing as "the objective"—reducing poverty or improving health. There are always constraints as to time allowed, money permitted, procedures allowable, liberties held inviolable, and so on. That we focus our attention on a particular one, singling it out as our objective, does not mean there are not others within which we must also operate or, at least, find ways to relax or overcome. Knowing only the avowed programmatic objective without being aware of other constraints is insufficient for predicting or controlling outcomes. When we are able to confront the multiplicity of objectives and constraints—so little inflation versus so much unemployment—or to observe the juggling acts of ill-fated commissions on national goals, in which the early objectives are likely to catch the worm of scarce resources, then the necessity to continuously readjust the means and ends becomes evident.

The goal of the British National Health Service Act of 1946 was the "improvement in the physical and mental health of the people of England and Wales, and the prevention, diagnosis, and treatment of illness." "The services so provided," the Act continues, "shall be free of charge, except where provision of this act expressly provides for the making and recovery of charges." But how is the government to provide, at no cost to users, services whose demand elasticity is on the average quite high, and whose costs keep rapidly rising?　No independent economist or government adviser seems to have raised this question at the time the National Health Service was created.　Instead, the advocates of the new system relied on three implicit assumptions: (1) that health needs could be determined on the basis of purely medical criteria; (2) that it was possible to meet those needs without placing too heavy a burden on the national resources; and (3) that by reducing ill health, the Service would contribute to increased production, and would in fact become "a wealth-producing as well as health-producing Service."

Experience has shown that the first two assumptions were incorrect, and the third one is still highly doubtful.　The costs of the Service soon proved much higher than initial estimates.　It became necessary to introduce charges for drug prescriptions, dentures, spectacles, replacement of surgical appliances and equipment, and for hospital treatment following road accidents.　Because the prevailing ideology has prevented the development of a coherent system for rationing medical services, unplanned rationing took place, resulting in congestion, and, in the opinion of many observers, a decrease in quality of services.　Since available resources were not even sufficient to meet current demands, very little investment in new facilities was possible, and the goal of prevention kept receding into the distant future.　In sum, the goals of the National Health Service had to be adjusted and readjusted as the impossibility of efficiently providing "free" services with high elasticity of demand became increasingly clear.

Conversely, the discovery that some constraints are no longer binding can suggest to implementers possibilities that the original planners did not envisage or desire.　Significant developments in social security in the United States since 1935 (in particular, the repeated extensions of coverage to new groups) appear to be due not only to political pressures, but even more to organizational breakthroughs in data collection and information handling.

How well policies respond to opportunities, how well they facilitate adaptation and error correction, are qualities insufficiently discussed. For our purposes, however, it is more important to observe that keeping things going rather than getting things started is the ordinary condition of administration.　It is not policy design but redesign that occurs most of the time.　Who is to say, then, whether implementation consists of altering objectives to correspond with available resources (as social welfare spending decreases, inflation increases), or of mobilizing new resources to accomplish old objectives (as the United States buys foreign currencies to defend the dollar)?　Indeed, old patterns of behavior are often retrospectively rationalized to fit new notions about appropriate objectives.　We do not always decide what to do and succeed or fail at it; rather, we observe what we have done and try to make it consistent in retrospect.　If Head Start finds it difficult to demonstrate lasting improvement in children's reading abilities, it may stress its clear capacity for increasing parents' involvement, which in turn may lead to educational improvement in their children.　We choose after the act as well as before.

. . .

. . . [I]mplementation is the continuation of politics by other means. According to the planning model, implementation is an extension of organizational design. To say that implementation should be part of design is to suggest that policy theory be formulated with a view toward its execution. This may mean at least two things: policy relevance—the variables in the theory should be manipulable by those with authority; and the specification of a variety of conditions that might occur, with instructions as to what to do under different circumstances. In view of our limited knowledge, this list would be relatively short and inevitably insufficient. Although it is usual to speak of making authority commensurate with responsibility, it is rare for an official to coerce all others, both because the political system divides authority and because it is costly to use up persuasiveness for this purpose. Additional authority therefore must be acquired along the way without necessarily being able to anticipate objections from all interested actors.

Since administrative discretion can be used as a cover for arbitrary behavior that is unrelated to policy intentions, some authors feel that the problem of administration is, purely and simply, one of controlling discretion. Controlling it how? Unless one is willing to assume that policies spring fully armed from the forehead of an omniscient policymaker, discretion is both inevitable and necessary. Unless administration is programmed—a robot comes to mind—discretion can be controlled only by indirect means. Again, we must rely on learning and invention rather than on instruction and command. In punishing his generals for failing to execute his orders faithfully even when their disobedience brought him victory, Frederick the Great of Prussia was at least consistent. We require the impossible when we expect our bureaucrats to be at the same time literal executors and successful implementers of policy mandates. Something has to be left to chance. In a world of uncertainty, success is only loosely correlated with effort, and chance can never be ruled out as the main cause of either success or failure. To the extent that success *is* related to effort, it depends more on "knowing how" than on "knowing that," on the ability to select appropriate types of behavior and rules of conduct, more than on abstract knowledge of decision rules or on blind obedience to directives. . . .

How effectively can implementation bring out one rather than another range of results? The more general an idea and the more adaptable it is to a range of circumstances, the more likely it is to be realized in some form, but the less likely it is to emerge as intended in practice. The more restricted the idea, and the more it is constrained, the more likely it is to emerge as predicted, but the less likely it is to have a significant impact. At one extreme we have the ideal type of the perfectly preformed policy idea; it only requires execution, and the only problems it raises are those of control. At the other extreme, the policy idea is only an expression of basic principles and aspirations, a matter for philosophical reflection and political debate. In between, where we live, is a set of more or less developed potentialities embedded in pieces of legislation, court decisions, and bureaucratic plans.

Comments and Questions

1. What are the chances that Congress and the president will see things Professor Lowi's way and move forcefully to establish juridical democracy? Consider how Lester Salamon, whose ideas we discussed in Section 2, might respond to this question.

2. Is juridical democracy, which focuses on the problem of legislative delegation of authority, the key to improving public-benefit conferral? One of Lowi's critics claims that the problems in the American welfare state lie elsewhere, and that Lowi's proposals "would do little to strengthen political parties, lessen the tendency of disgruntled citizens to direct their energies into single-issue interest groups, and enable Congress to provide independent policy leadership. Nor will they increase citizen trust and confidence in government, expand direct individual participation in politics, or produce effective executive leadership." Thomas, Book Review, 74 Am.Pol.Sci.Rev. 206, 207 (1980) (reviewing T. Lowi, The End of Liberalism (2d ed. 1979)). Do you agree?

3. How would the authors of the selection from Implementation respond to the concept of juridical democracy? What, in their view, is the key to designing and implementing effective distributive policies?

Section Nine. Limitations of Law as a Public-Benefit Instrument

The aims of public-benefit programs tend to be expansive (and expensive). Consider, for example, the myriad of statutes and regulations addressed to providing adequate medical care, the education of youth, efficient transportation, and the national defense. And the trend is toward a broader role for government in providing security and benefits to individuals and organizations, despite the current mood favoring some dismantling of government regulation.

The tendency toward an ever-expanding governmental role is obvious when one considers just how recent much important social-welfare legislation is. Old-age assistance, disaster relief, tuition benefits for college students, aid to dependent children, company bailouts, Medicare, government-subsidized mass transit, the space shuttle—all of these government activities are less than a century old, and many are much younger.

Considering the problems government takes on in the distributive mode, it should come as no surprise that its effectiveness is limited. Public-education policy is a useful case in point, for public education is, relatively speaking, a successful policy. The primary aim of our policy of providing free schooling through high school is to educate those who attend. Yet, an education is not a thing one acquires; it is a process in which one participates. And not everyone can or will participate. We make primary and secondary education compulsory, but that is no solution to this problem. "Compulsory education," in a real sense, is a contradiction in terms.

Another important aim of public education is to redress inequalities of opportunity. But how far can education go to equalize the opportunities of rich and poor children, and of children who differ in talent and motivation? Can we even specify with clarity what we mean by "equality" in the context of public education? The cases we have read on the subject and the debate on the organization and financing of public education suggest that "equality" is an elusive goal. David Kirp, an expert on education law, suggests why:

> The specifics bespeak a larger truth: equality does not assume a single, simple, unitary, and invariant form. It is at root ambiguous, and this very ambiguity gives the concept much of its power to motivate, incite, and disappoint. Equality seems at once luminous and elusive, or perhaps luminous *because* elusive, evolving as a consequence of altered social circumstance and moral perception. It is not just that as a society we attend to smaller and smaller degrees of differentness, but also that the differences we find offensive change over time. In this sense, loyalty to equality resides not in allying oneself with a firmly settled principle but rather in the very process of pursuing the elusive, for it is the pursuit itself that counts. As Tocqueville observed: "Democratic institutions awaken and flatter the passion for equality without ever being able to satisfy it entirely. Thus complete equality is always slipping through the people's fingers at the moment when they think to grasp it." Progress entails capturing the meaning of equality in a specific setting and translating that meaning into official action, not securing a single coherent, timeless understanding.

D. Kirp, Just Schools 9 (1982).

Some goals of public education conflict, such as maintaining a neighborhood focus for schools and promoting racial and ethnic integration. Other goals, such as fostering citizenship and democratic values in young people, can never be fully realized in a school setting. Some children will be turned off by efforts to teach them patriotism and civic values, and there are limits on the extent to which even receptive children will internalize the social norms their schools promote.

Educational goals are limited, too, by financial considerations, and by the capacities of teaching and administrative personnel. Teachers, like the other "street-level bureaucrats" discussed in Section 3, can become exhausted by the strain of dealing face-to-face with a demanding and sometimes unruly clientele. Lack of knowledge in the community leadership that sets some educational policies, and in those who administer educational programs, also limits the extent to which educational policies will be effective.

The obvious constraints within which public education and every other benefit-conferral program must proceed sometimes provoke calls for reducing or even eliminating distributive programs. The argument that government cannot efficiently do all that is asked of it, surprisingly, is not new. It predates even the dramatic expansion of social-welfare activities that occurred earlier in this century. Note that the author of the following remarks was a nineteenth-century social theorist.

———

H. SPENCER, OVER–LEGISLATION

in 3 Essays: Scientific, Political, and Speculative 229, 232–33, 235, 271 (1891).

Thus, while every day chronicles a failure, there every day reappears the belief that it needs but an Act of Parliament and a staff of officers, to effect any end desired. Nowhere is the perennial faith of mankind better seen. Ever since society existed Disappointment has been preaching— "Put not your trust in legislation"; and yet the trust in legislation seems scarcely diminished.

Did the State fulfil efficiently its unquestionable duties, there would be some excuse for this eagerness to assign it further duties. . . . [H]ad we, in short, proved its efficiency as judge and defender, instead of having found it treacherous, cruel, and anxiously to be shunned, there would be some encouragement to hope other benefits at its hands. . . .

Seriously, the case, while it may not, in some respects, warrant this parallel, is, in one respect, even stronger. For the new work is not of the same order as the old, but of a more difficult order. Ill as government discharges its true duties, any other duties committed to it are likely to be still worse discharged. To guard its subjects against aggression, either individual or national, is a straightforward and tolerably simple matter; to regulate, directly or indirectly, the personal actions of those subjects is an infinitely complicated matter. It is one thing to secure to each man the unhindered power to pursue his own good; it is a widely different thing to pursue the good for him. To do the first efficiently, the State has merely to look on while its citizens act; to forbid unfairness; to adjudicate when called on; and to enforce restitution for injuries. To do the last efficiently, it must become an ubiquitous worker—must know each man's needs better than he knows them himself—must, in short, possess super-human power and intelligence. . . .

. . . And if an institution undertakes, not two functions but a score— if a government, whose office it is to defend citizens against aggressors, foreign and domestic, engages also to disseminate Christianity, to administer charity, to teach children their lessons, to adjust prices of food, to inspect coal-mines, to regulate railways, to superintend house-building, to arrange cab-fares, to look into people's stink-traps, to vaccinate their children, to send out emigrants, to prescribe hours of labour, to examine lodging-houses, to test the knowledge of mercantile captains, to provide public libraries, to read and authorize dramas, to inspect passenger-ships, to see that small dwellings are supplied with water, to regulate endless things from a banker's issues down to the boat-fares on the Serpentine—is it not manifest that its primary duty must be ill discharged in proportion to the multiplicity of affairs it busies itself with? Must not its time and energies be frittered away in schemes, and inquiries, and amendments, in discussions, and divisions, to the neglect of its essential business?

———

Comments and Questions

1. What, according to Herbert Spencer, are the generic limitations of public-benefit conferral as a legal-governmental tool?

2. How would you describe the public philosophy that justifies current levels of public-benefit conferral?

Section Ten. Bibliography

1. *General.* C. Lindblom, Politics and Markets (1977); T. Lowi, The End of Liberalism (2d ed. 1979).

2. *Public-Benefit Techniques.* R. Dahl & C. Lindblom, Politics, Economics, and Welfare (1953); G. Hale & M. Palley, The Politics of Federal Grants (1981); P. Peterson, City Limits (1981).

3. *Authorized Makers of Public-Benefit Law and Their Appropriate Collaborative Roles.* R. Ripley & G. Franklin, Congress, the Bureaucracy, and Public Policy (1980); J. Sundquist, The Decline and Resurgence of Congress (1981); S. Wayne, The Legislative Presidency (1978); J. Wilson, Political Organizations (1973).

4. *Structures and Processes for Applying Public-Benefit Law and Techniques.* E. Levine & E. Wexler, PL 94: An Act of Congress (1981); F. Wirt & M. Kirst, Schools in Conflict (1982); M. Yudof, D. Kirp, T. van Geel & B. Levin, Kirp & Yudof's Educational Policy and the Law (2d ed. 1982).

5. *Necessity for and Nature of Coercive Power.* M. Rebell & A. Block, Educational Policy-Making and the Courts (1982); D. Rosenbloom, Public Administration and Law (1983); J. Vining, Legal Identity (1978).

6. *Roles of Private Citizens and Their Lawyers.* V. Key, The Responsible Electorate (1966); D. Ross, A Public Citizen's Action Manual (1973); P. Schuck, Suing Government: Citizen Remedies for Official Wrongs (1983).

7. *Process Values.* K. Davis, Discretionary Justice (1969); J. Mashaw, Bureaucratic Justice (1982).

8. *Improving the Public-Benefit Instrument.* S. Krislov & D. Rosenbloom, Representative Bureaucracy and the American Political System (1981); D. Mitchell, Shaping Legislative Decisions (1981); Why Policies Succeed or Fail (H. Ingram ed. 1980).

9. *Limitations of Law as a Public-Benefit Instrument.* D. Mazmanian & P. Sabatier, Implementation and Public Policy (1983); J. Pressman & A. Wildavsky, Implementation (3d ed. 1984).

CHAPTER FIVE

Law as an Instrument for Facilitating Private Arrangements

Legal rules defining the ways in which valid contracts or wills or marriages are made . . . provide individuals with facilities for realizing their wishes . . . within the coercive framework of the law. The power thus conferred . . . is one of the great contributions of law to social life . . . .

H.L.A. HART

Section One. Introduction
(Pedagogic Vehicles Drawn Mainly from Contracts Law)

Private arrangements facilitate many of the basic goals of our society. Through private arrangements, people achieve their desires without the intrusion of government. When you agree to mow your neighbor's lawn for fifteen dollars, when you incorporate your burgeoning gardening business, when you marry a gardening customer and have children, when you join a private gardening club, or when you write a will leaving your gardening fortune to your child, you exercise individual choice, determination, and judgment in ordering your own affairs. Private arrangements also help stimulate the economy through the efficient distribution of goods and services. Can you imagine a governmental agency attempting to provide for all of the food and clothing needs of the people of one of our big cities? Not surprising, therefore, is that many societies utilize law as an instrument to facilitate private arrangements.

The law facilitates private arrangements in three primary ways. First, the law grants private persons the legal power to create various private arrangements (e.g., you have the power to create an enforceable contract with your neighbor to mow his lawn for remuneration). Second, the law specifies the steps to be taken to create a legally recognized arrangement, such as the steps necessary to incorporate your gardening business. Third, the law specifies the legal consequences to be afforded the resultant arrangement, such as your right to enforce your contract with your neighbor through legal remedies. We shall examine each of these methods of facilitation in detail in this chapter.

The private-arrangement instrument is different from the other instruments studied in Chapters 1 through 4. Unlike the other instruments, the prime thrust of the private-arrangement instrument is to enable private citizens to achieve their goals by themselves. The instrument does not give things to people (public-benefit conferral); it is not primarily regulative (administrative-regulatory), nor primarily prohibitive (penal-corrective), nor primarily reparative (grievance-remedial).

Private parties determine the content of their arrangements, acting as private legislators. Substituting official for private judgment would destroy the essence of the private-arrangement instrument. If officials decided the proper fee for mowing your neighbor's lawn, for example, the resulting arrangement would not be essentially private. Private parties also generally administer their arrangements, in contrast to the other instruments in which officials typically perform substantial administrative roles.

Some arrangements are inherently private in Western culture, such as marriage and parenthood. Other arrangements are too cumbersome or costly in the hands of government administrators. Consider again the array of bureaucrats that would be required to administer to the food and clothing needs of the general populace. Still other activities could be either private or public. For example, the basic means of production are in part owned publicly in Britain, but they are in private hands in the United States. Whether there should be more or less private arranging in this country is one question underlying this chapter.

Section Two. Private-Arrangement Techniques

In this section we look more closely at the three primary methods or techniques of the law that facilitate private arrangements. First, we introduce many (but not all) of the kinds of private arrangements that people have the power to make. The parties have the power to make their own arrangements in the sense that their arrangements are recognized by the law and are not treated as nullities on the ground that they are illegal, unconscionable, or the like (see Section 7). These arrangements create a normative set of rights and duties and justify the parties' subsequent actions without the need for any formal enforcement mechanism (see Sections 3 and 6). Second, we offer some examples of rules of validation—rules that specify the steps to be taken to create a private arrangement. Third, we demonstrate the more formal legal consequences of private arrangements.

As you are introduced to various kinds of private arrangements, you should consider whether any of the four basic legal instrumentalities studied in the previous chapters could serve as a substitute for the private arrangement.

A. Types of Private Arrangements

i. Marriages

H. CLARK, THE LAW OF DOMESTIC RELATIONS IN THE UNITED STATES

34–35 (1968).[*]

In the American colonies marriage was regulated by the civil authorities, and informal marriages were recognized as valid, at least in the absence of statute requiring a ceremony. In fact the informal marriage was a more useful device on the American frontier than in England, since it enabled parties to contract valid marriages when no clergyman or civil officer was at hand to perform a ceremony.

The history of English marriage law also produced some rules for the validity of marriages which have largely affected American law. The English law recognized several impediments to the formation of valid marriages. Relationship between the parties, either by blood or marriage, was the one most commonly asserted as a cause for declaring the marriage invalid. At first the range of relationship which disqualified the parties to marry was extremely broad. It was narrowed somewhat in 1215, and then in the early sixteenth century, after the Reformation, it was limited to the Levitical degrees.

Infancy was likewise a disqualification for marriage, children below the age of seven being incapable of marrying. After that age they might marry, but the marriage was voidable until they became able to consummate it, which the law presumed to be at age fourteen for boys and twelve for girls. Beyond those ages the marriages were valid, even though the parties were under twenty-one and though they did not have their parents' consent. Later statutes imposed the requirement of parents' consent.

A distinction was made by some authorities between canonical disabilities which were said to make marriages only voidable, and civil disabilities making marriages void. The former, resulting from the ecclesiastical rules, included consanguinity, affinity, and impotence. The latter included prior marriage, infancy, fraud, duress, and insanity. Though this distinction is not universally accepted even as a statement of historical fact, it has retained enough vitality in American law to produce unnecessary confusion in the law of annulment. The ancient void-voidable distinction still plagues us.

American law largely adopted, either as part of the common-law heritage or expressly by statute, the principles by which English law determined the validity of marriage. . . .

Although historically in English law marriage was the exclusive concern of ecclesiastical courts and the canon law, and although we received a substantial amount of our marriage law from this source, in America marriage has always been regulated by the civil authorities. In many states statutes making this plain have been enacted, providing that marriage is a civil contract. Therefore, the various religious denominations, in spite of their continuing interest in the marital status and its obligations, are clearly subordinate to the law with respect to marriage. Their precepts may be enforced by appeals to conscience, or by other religious sanctions, but the ultimate power to regulate marriage rests with the state.

------

ii. Private Associations

2 A. DE TOCQUEVILLE, DEMOCRACY IN AMERICA
128–30 (1961) (1st Eng. ed. London 1840).

Americans of all ages, all conditions, and all dispositions, constantly form associations. They have not only commercial and manufacturing companies, in which all take part, but associations of a thousand other kinds,— religious, moral, serious, futile, extensive or restricted, enormous or diminutive. The Americans make associations to give entertainments, to found establishments for education, to build inns, to construct churches, to diffuse books, to send missionaries to the antipodes; and in this manner they found hospitals, prisons, and schools. If it be proposed to advance some truth, or to foster some feeling by the encouragement of a great example, they form a society. Wherever, at the head of some new undertaking, you see the Government in France, or a man of rank in England, in the United States you will be sure to find an association.
. . .

Aristocratic communities always contain, amongst a multitude of persons who by themselves are powerless, a small number of powerful and wealthy citizens, each of whom can achieve great undertakings single-handed. In aristocratic societies men do not need to combine in order to act, because they are strongly held together. Every wealthy and powerful citizen constitutes the head of a permanent and compulsory association, composed of all those who are dependent upon him, or whom he makes subservient to the execution of his designs.

Amongst democratic nations, on the contrary, all the citizens are independent and feeble; they can do hardly anything by themselves, and none of them can oblige his fellowmen to lend him their assistance. They all, therefore, fall into a state of incapacity, if they do not learn voluntarily to help each other. If men living in democratic countries had no right and no inclination to associate for political purposes, their independence would be in great jeopardy; but they might long preserve their wealth and their cultivation: whereas if they never acquired the habit of forming associations in ordinary life, civilization itself would be endangered. A people amongst which individuals should lose the power of achieving great things single-handed, without acquiring the means of producing them by united exertions, would soon relapse into barbarism.

DEVELOPMENTS IN THE LAW—JUDICIAL CONTROL OF ACTIONS OF PRIVATE ASSOCIATIONS

76 Harv.L.Rev. 983, 987–89 (1963).*

[I]t may be helpful to set out the advantages thought to accrue to society from the presence of many diverse private associations. Such groups are formed when individuals, having become aware of a common interest, mutually assist one another over a period of time to promote that interest. They organize and distribute tasks so as to achieve a common end which otherwise would be less easily attainable. The ability to organize and participate in collective action thus increases the range of alternatives from which an individual may choose his social, intellectual, religious, economic and political activities. In addition, voluntary associations relieve the feeling of isolation which tends to plague modern society. They provide opportunity for creativity and responsibility. Because of their presence a person is not forced to choose between conformity with the majority and complete isolation: he has numerous choices and can indulge his idiosyncrasies with others of similar inclination. Voluntary associations help stabilize the political system. The more numerous and diversified organized groups become, the more individuals will tend to develop loyalties to associations which have conflicting interests. Such overlapping loyalties decrease the danger that any particular group of individuals will find all its basic interests opposed to those of the rest of society and react by rejecting the norms which underpin the political system, thus frustrating the possibility of resolving conflict by compromise. One reason why the American labor movement developed with less violence, less fragmentation of society and less appeal to radical doctrine than did its European counterparts was the fact that unionists had loyalties to church, ethnic communities and other associations not organized along economic class lines. Private voluntary groups serve also as a buffer between the individual and the large modern government. The protest of an organized group is more likely to be an effective deterrent against arbitrary governmental activity. Moreover, the very fact that citizens can form private groups with relative ease acts to restrain the activities of both the government and other private groups which have power. Finally, voluntary associations are able to perform many tasks beneficial to society that it would be impossible or less desirable to leave to public or semipublic groups. They offer numerous alternative methods of approaching a problem; they are likely to experiment; they are often more free to criticize public bodies and each other than are public groups; frequently they are more flexible in approach because they do not have to comply with the statutory standards imposed in enabling acts; and often private organizations can offer higher compensation than can the government. Even when problems require some governmental action, delegation of power to a private group may be desirable where the private body has more skill and knowledge in the area; the rules made by such a group also are more likely to find ready acceptance among those to whom they apply than if the same rules had been imposed by a governmental agency.

NOTE, JUDICIAL INTERVENTION IN THE CONDUCT OF PRIVATE ASSOCIATIONS: BASES FOR THE EMERGING TREND OF JUDICIAL ACTIVISM

4 N.Y.U.Rev.L. & Soc.Change 61, 61–62 (1974).*

The last century has seen a dramatic increase in the size and number of voluntary associations in the United States. These associations now encompass such diverse groups as bankers and bar owners, farmers and cemetary managers, doctors and athletes, to name only a few. Understandably, the expanding presence of such voluntary groups has had its concomitant effect, in their detrimental impact upon the lives of members and nonmembers alike.

Although it is impossible to catalogue exhaustively the private interests which may be adversely affected by the actions of these groups, one can include an individual's mental [3] or physical well-being,[4] social relations,[5] reputation,[6] intellectual development, religious activities, access to forums for the expression of beliefs,[9] property interests, ability to earn a living and political advocacy.[12] In addition, a private association may also have a serious impact upon public interests, when, for example, it controls the discharge of a public office, forbids members to join the armed forces, to testify against the group's interests, or to advocate the enactment of legislation which the group opposes.

---

iii.　Contracts

R. POUND, AN INTRODUCTION TO THE PHILOSOPHY OF LAW

133–34 (rev. ed. 1954).

Wealth, in a commercial age, is made up largely of promises. An important part of everyone's substance consists of advantages which others have promised to provide for or to render to him; of demands to

---

* Copyright © 1974 by New York University. Reprinted by permission.

3. See, e.g., Carter v. Papineau, 222 Mass. 464, 111 N.E. 358 (1916) (mental anguish caused by refusal of priest to administer Communion to parishioner).

4. See, e.g., State v. Williams, 75 N.C. 121 (1876) (member of local benevolent association suffered injuries while suspended from wall by a cord).

5. See, e.g., Yoder v. Helmuth (Ohio C.P. 1947), noted in L. Green and others, Cases on Injuries to Relations 47 (1959) (church member ostracized by an entire community for using an automobile).

6. See, e.g., Anthony v. Syracuse University, 130 Misc. 249, 223 N.Y.S. 796 (Sup.Ct.1927), rev'd, 224 App.Div. 487, 231 N.Y.S. 435 (4th Dep't 1928) (expulsion from university without explanation).

9. See, e.g., Madden v. Atkins, 4 N.Y.2d 283, 174 N.Y.S.2d 633, 151 N.E.2d 73 (1958) (expulsion from union for organizing against union leadership).

12. See, e.g., Smith v. Allwright, 321 U.S. 649 (1944) (candidate barred from primary).

have the advantages promised, which he may assert not against the world at large but against particular individuals. Thus the individual claims to have performance of advantageous promises secured to him. He claims the satisfaction of expectations created by promises and agreements. If this claim is not secured friction and waste obviously result, and unless some countervailing interest must come into account which would be sacrificed in the process, it would seem that the individual interest in promised advantages should be secured to the full extent of what has been assured to him by the deliberate promise of another. . . . Hence in a commercial and industrial society, a claim or want or demand of society that promises be kept and that undertakings be carried out in good faith, a social interest in the stability of promises as a social and economic institution, becomes of the first importance.

JONES, THE JURISPRUDENCE OF CONTRACTS
44 U.Cin.L.Rev. 43, 47–49 (1975).*

In a society like ours, people live not by birds in the hand but by promises: for example, anyone's job is an exchange of promises, by him to work and by his employer to pay agreed or understood wages. Investments are essentially promises by corporate powerholders to manage a business in proper ways and to pay dividends as earned. A bank account is a promise to hold and return money deposited; even money is a promise, though rather less reliable than in earlier days, by government to pay something on due presentation. A few years ago, there was a lively musical comedy called "Promises, Promises!", and that is largely what our material society amounts to. John Kenneth Galbraith may or may not have been right to characterize our national community as The Affluent Society; he would have said something unquestionably true, and perhaps of even greater economic significance, if he had called us the *promissory* society. A promissory society, by definition, is one energized and bound together by the institution of contract. That may seem a very remote consideration when you are reading an ordinary contract case, but it is a perspective not to be forgotten altogether when you are trying to arrange the details of contract law into a form that makes practical working sense.

The philosophers and historians of law have not, perhaps, spoken in quite these terms, but they have certainly not been unaware of what we are calling today "the *jurisprudence* of contracts." Thus Jeremy Bentham, when he set out to formulate the ends or values of a legal order, put "security of expectations" in the very first place.[9] Law and government exist, said Bentham, to insure the security, that is, the practical realization, of the reasonable expectations of the men and women who constitute a given civil society. An enforceable bill of rights, considered in Benthamite terms, insures my *expectation* that my freedoms of movement and expression will not be interfered with arbitrarily and without suffi-

* Copyright © 1975 by University of Cincinnati Law Review. Also printed in Jus Et Societas: Essays in tribute to Wolfgang Friedman. Copyright © 1979 by Martinus Nijhoff Publishers. Reprinted by permission.
9. J. Bentham, Theory of Legislation 126 (C. Atkinson ed. 1913).

cient cause. The criminal law, when effective, serves to secure my expectation that my liberty to go about my own business will not be impaired by the violence or overreaching of nongovernmental wrongdoers. The law of property secures my expectation that I may continue to enjoy what is mine unless I have freely parted with it. The law of contract . . . has as its ultimate purpose the security of those reasonable expectations that arise from agreement between seller and buyer, borrower and depositor, stockholder and corporation, employer and organized employees. This is essentially Bentham's analysis and it has never been improved on.

The best known statement of this thesis is, I suppose, the conclusion expressed by Sir Henry Maine, late in the 19th century, in his renowned study, Ancient Law. After surveying most of what was then known about the primitive and early legal systems of the Eastern and Western worlds, Maine recorded this judgment: "The movement of the progressive societies has hitherto been a movement *from status to contract.*" [10] What Maine is saying here is that in primitive communities and others that have kept the character of "static" societies, what a man or woman is or does depends above all on his status, that is, on the fixed legal and social condition into which he was born or into which he, willy-nilly, has been moved. Thus to know what X's legal rights and duties are, the important question to ask is whether X be wife, child, slave, serf, feudal retainer, Brahmin, untouchable, master, servant or whatever. In "progressive" societies, as Maine characterizes them, one's legal rights and duties depend far less on caste or fixed social condition and far more on expectations created and obligations assumed by his own contracts.

Maine's aphorism that historical progress has been a movement from status to contract reflects, of course, the great social value attributed to freedom of contract in the 19th century liberal tradition of the English Whigs and their American counterparts. But freedom of contract is far from an absolute value . . . . We have learned since Maine . . . that outer limits have to be put on freedom of contract in a less individualistic, more highly industrialized society like our own, and there are countless legal interventions into freedom of contract even in "capitalist" countries: minimum wage acts, workmen's compensation, required social security contributions, prescribed contract forms for insurance policies, to name only a few. Looking at Maine's aphorism another way, the legal rights and duties that exist between today's industrial worker and his employer are created not by private contract between them but by a collective bargain negotiated between the employer and the union to which the employee belongs. X's take-home pay from General Motors and his other working conditions depend not on a contract between X and General Motors but on X's *status* as a union member and General Motors employee. Indeed, the development toward collective and standardized bargains has gone so far in our day that many analysts of our society see Maine's movement as cyclical, that is, a movement, particularly in the "progressive" societies, from status to contract and now *back* to status.

---

10. H. Maine, Ancient Law 141 (New Universal Library ed. 1905) (emphasis in original).

LLEWELLYN, WHAT PRICE CONTRACT?—AN ESSAY IN PERSPECTIVE

40 Yale L.J. 704, 717, 736–37 (1931).*

Bargain is then the social and legal machinery appropriate to arranging affairs in any specialized economy which relies on exchange rather than tradition (the manor) or authority (the army, the U.S.S.R.) for apportionment of productive energy and of product. It is a machinery which like status, but in contrast to tort, makes it easy to insist on positive, affirmative action. *Contract* in the strict sense is the specifically legal machinery appropriate when such an economy moves into the phase of credit—meaning or connoting thereby future dealings in general; in which aspect the mutual reliance of two dealers on their respective promises comes of course into major importance. This machinery of contract applies in general to the market for land, goods, services, credit, or for any combination of these. . . .

To sum up, the major importance of legal contract is to provide a frame-work for well-nigh every type of group organization and for well-nigh every type of passing or permanent relation between individuals and groups, up to and including states—a frame-work highly adjustable, a frame-work which almost never accurately indicates real working relations, but which affords a rough indication around which such relations vary, an occasional guide in cases of doubt, and a norm of ultimate appeal when the relations cease in fact to work. The trend toward standardization, despite its values where power is balanced, raises doubts as to policy where its effects are lop-sided, because the norm of ultimate appeal is then so tremendously deflected to the one side. The direct legal sanctions are not the major measure of importance. Their effect as a threat is uncertain. In the credit field, they break down in the case of greatest need, unless strengthened by security. And indirect sanctions—at least in the case of "inducing breach"—or indirect effects by way of ideology and marginal operation, may lie close to the heart of the protection sought.

———

Division of Labor and the Origins of Exchange

A productive unit in a modern economy specializes in making one type or a few types of goods. It does not make enough types to satisfy all of its needs and must look elsewhere for that purpose. To resume our gardening business example, you may own a plant that manufactures lawn mowers. Because the plant does not supply you with food, clothing, shelter, or other material goods, you must look elsewhere for these—hence, the necessity for exchange.

What leads to specialization in the first place? Because people and organizations have different capacities and abilities, matching those capacities and abilities with productive tasks is efficient. Similarly, regions differ in material resources and climate, and it is efficient for people to

* Reprinted by permission of The Yale Law Journal Company and Fred B. Rothman & Company from *The Yale Law Journal*, Vol. 40, pp. 717, 736, 737.

engage in productive activities best suited to the particular conditions. In addition, consider this famous excerpt from A. Smith, The Wealth of Nations 7–9 (1937) (1st ed. London 1776):

First, the improvement of the dexterity of the workman necessarily increases the quantity of the work he can perform; and the division of labour, by reducing every man's business to some one simple operation, and by making this operation the sole employment of his life, necessarily increases very much the dexterity of the workman. A common smith, who, though accustomed to handle the hammer, has never been used to make nails, if upon some particular occasion he is obliged to attempt it, will scarce, I am assured, be able to make above two or three hundred nails in a day, and those too very bad ones. A smith who has been accustomed to make nails, but whose sole or principal business has not been that of a nailer, can seldom with his utmost diligence make more than eight hundred or a thousand nails in a day. I have seen several boys under twenty years of age who had never exercised any other trade but that of making nails, and who, when they exerted themselves, could make, each of them, upwards of two thousand three hundred nails in a day. The making of a nail, however, is by no means one of the simplest operations. The same person blows the bellows, stirs or mends the fire as there is occasion, heats the iron, and forges every part of the nail: In forging the head too he is obliged to change his tools. The different operations into which the making of a pin, or of a metal button, is subdivided, are all of them much more simple, and the dexterity of the person, of whose life it has been the sole business to perform them, is usually much greater. The rapidity with which some of the operations of those manufactures are performed, exceeds what the human hand could, by those who had never seen them, be supposed capable of acquiring.

Secondly, the advantage which is gained by saving the time commonly lost in passing from one sort of work to another, is much greater than we should at first view be apt to imagine it. It is impossible to pass very quickly from one kind of work to another, that is carried on in a different place, and with quite different tools. A country weaver, who cultivates a small farm, must lose a good deal of time in passing from his loom to the field, and from the field to his loom. When the two trades can be carried on in the same workhouse, the loss of time is no doubt much less. It is even in this case, however, very considerable. A man commonly saunters a little in turning his hand from one sort of employment to another. When he first begins the new work he is seldom very keen and hearty; his mind, as they say, does not go to it, and for some time he rather trifles than applies to good purpose. The habit of sauntering and of indolent careless application, which is naturally, or rather necessarily acquired by every country workman who is obliged to change his work and his tools every half hour, and to apply his hand in twenty different ways almost every day of his life;

renders him almost always slothful and lazy, and incapable of any vigorous application even on the most pressing occasions. Independent, therefore, of his deficiency in point of dexterity, this cause alone must always reduce considerably the quantity of work which he is capable of performing.

Thirdly, and lastly, everybody must be sensible how much labour is facilitated and abridged by the application of proper machinery. It is unnecessary to give any example. I shall only observe, therefore, that the invention of all those machines by which labour is so much facilitated and abridged, seems to have been originally owing to the division of labour. Men are much more likely to discover easier and readier methods of attaining any object, when the whole attention of their minds is directed towards that single object, than when it is dissipated among a great variety of things.

Comments and Questions

1. What are some of the negative effects of specialization?
2. On balance, is modern specialization desirable?

---

iv. Corporations

C. STONE, WHERE THE LAW ENDS
19–20 (1975).

To obtain a charter, early corporations had had to apply to the Crown (and, later, Parliament, or in the United States, a state house). This procedure of incorporation by special charter had at least one strong virtue. It gave the issuer of the charter a chance to consider each particular application on its merit, and to tailor the company-to-be's powers and privileges, and even its size and debt structure, to the limits appropriate to its particular undertaking. . . .

Unfortunately, this system was simply not feasible in the face of the flood of applications for new charters. In addition, the special charter procedure was becoming increasingly unpopular, not merely because of its earlier association with monopoly favors, but because, especially in the United States, of its taint of legislative corruption. As a result, general incorporation laws gradually grew up to compete with the practice of applying for special charters. Under these laws, anyone who filled out the proper form, paid the fees, and met certain other requirements could operate as a corporation without applying specially to the legislature. By the end of the nineteenth century, the practice of general incorporation, begun in North Carolina in 1795, was not only a competing mode of incorporation, it had displaced special charters entirely.

A. CONARD, R. KRAUSS & S. SIEGEL, CORPORATIONS
37 (2d ed. 1982).

What is it that makes corporate organization so desirable?

Probably the primal consideration has been to establish a fund of property which is distinct from the property of any of the members, and therefore free from the hazards of the members' debts, and from the uncertainties of descent and distribution on the members' deaths. The reverse of this coin is the maintenance of the members' individual property separate from that of the corporation, and presumptively free from claims of the corporation's creditors. Going along with these attributes is the capacity of the organization to sue or be sued collectively without regard to the citizenship or residence or presence within the jurisdiction of the members. These characteristics, which might be described as "separateness" from the individual members, have been conceptualized as "entity" or "personality," and whole books have been written about them—rather more in Europe than in the United States.

EPSTEIN, SOCIETAL, MANAGERIAL, AND LEGAL PERSPECTIVES ON CORPORATE SOCIAL RESPONSIBILITY—PRODUCT AND PROCESS
30 Hastings L.J. 1287, 1288–89 (1979).

Like such intellectual constructs as the economist's mythical "firm" or the social and behavioral scientist's "organization," the term "corporation" is a broad conceptual category encompassing highly diverse entities with widely differing societal roles. The City of Berkeley (a municipality), the United Way of the Bay Area (a nonprofit association), the University of California (a public body), Barrister, Solicitor and Advocate, P.C. (a professional grouping), Mom-and-Pop Corner Store, Co. (a neighborhood business), and the Standard Oil Company of California (a multinational energy producer) are all corporations incorporated under the laws of the State of California. Although all of these entities are engaged in the production and distribution of socially useful goods and services, each performs a very different social task, has different constituencies, affects widely divergent sectors of the public, has different human and capital resources, and poses substantially different issues of corporate power and accountability.

v. Wills

T. ATKINSON, HANDBOOK OF THE LAW OF WILLS
2–3 (2d ed. 1953).*

The celebrated nineteenth century English writer Jarman says: "A will is an instrument by which a person makes a disposition of his

---

* Reprinted with permission from Thomas E. Atkinson's Handbook of the Law of Wills, Copyright © 1953 By West Publishing Co.

property to take effect after his decease, and which is in its nature ambulatory and revocable during his lifetime." This definition properly calls attention to the two principal characteristics of wills, that they are revocable and ambulatory. Ambulatory is sometimes used to denote the quality of being inoperative until death. At other times it is employed to indicate the feature of being capable of dealing with the situation at the time of the maker's death, e.g. by passing property then owned though not acquired until after the will was made. The modern will is ambulatory in both respects, and is revocable as well.

However, Jarman's definition is inadequate in certain other respects. A will is not always a written instrument; there may be oral wills which are valid under some circumstances. In addition, while wills usually dispose of property, this is not necessarily true; for example a duly executed instrument which merely appoints a person to have charge of the property after the death is a will, although it contain no direction as to whom the decedent's property passes. Again a will may simply appoint a guardian for the maker's children, or merely revoke former wills. Instruments which have been intended to have testamentary effect have been considered to be wills though they make no effective disposition of property.

FRIEDMAN, THE LAW OF THE LIVING, THE LAW OF THE DEAD: PROPERTY, SUCCESSION, AND SOCIETY

1966 Wis.L.Rev. 340, 354–55.

Despite the formality of the document, the general rule is said to be that the testator (that is, the man who executes a will) may make any disposition of his property he pleases within the will; he has freedom of testation. There are limitations (most notably in favor of the widow), but he may, for example, totally exclude his children from any share in the estate.

Freedom of testation is thus a powerful principle of law. It continues after death the market rights of an owner. Just as property during an owner's lifetime is not "bound," but may be dealt with by him as he pleases, so too at death. The power of disposition is felt psychologically to constitute an essential element of power over property. The intestacy laws can even be analyzed as an extension of the principle of free disposition of property at death. These laws can be looked upon as empirical recognition of the fact that most people choose close relatives as heirs; the man who dies without a will may be voluntarily adopting the statutory plan and saving himself trouble and legal fees.

M. RHEINSTEIN & M. GLENDON, THE LAW OF DECEDENTS' ESTATES

2, 3–4, 5, 8 (1971).*

Insofar as ownership in a given society is organized along individual lines, some fixed rules for the reallotment of property left behind by a dead member of the community are an absolute necessity for the preservation of peace and order among the remaining members. But in societies where property is regarded as being owned, not by mortal individuals, but by such groups as families, clans, tribes, corporations, or the state, no law of succession is necessary respecting such property, although rules are necessary for redistribution of property left by a group, for instance a family, which has become extinct. Whether there has ever existed anywhere a society where *all* property is owned collectively can neither be proved nor disproved. Anthropological data seems to indicate that some objects such as weapons, jewelry, utensils for personal use, and clothing are owned individually even in those societies where land, cattle, or other wealth is owned collectively. In a modern industrial society in particular, it appears impossible to eliminate individual ownership completely. In those industrialized countries where collective ownership is regarded as the very basis of the social order, collective ownership is limited to the means of production, while ownership in the goods of use and consumption is organized on individual lines. . . .

Apart from its principal social function of transferring wealth from generation to generation in an orderly fashion, the law of succession has served and has been made to serve diverse other functions. It has been said to be necessary to guarantee the continuity of enterprise, without which long-range economic activity could not flourish in an economy where property is individually owned. This argument has lost much of its force in an economic system in which large-scale enterprise has come to be carried on in corporate form, and to be directed not by owners but by specialists in management succeeding each other in the manner of office-holders. For the same reason there is also less force in the argument that without the incentive of handing on the fruits of one's work, competition and consequently the growth of the total economy would be hampered.

While inheritance is essential at least for the proper functioning and the continued existence of any system of individual ownership, it also serves to determine or reinforce, accentuate or perpetuate, the patterns of distribution of wealth, and consequently of power and status in any given society. The political implications of the law of inheritance are considerable. Its tendency to produce inequality of wealth and power has been attacked by some [e.g., Aristotle] and exploited by others [e.g., Napoleon]. It has been attacked on moral as well as economic grounds by those who object to the acquisition of wealth without work.

The criticism of inheritance as such based upon the ground that it tends to increase inequalities of weath has lost much of its significance not only because it has been found possible to counteract that effect by taxation, but also because of the general development of modern society. In contrast to the conservative and stratified society of 19th century Europe, newer countries like the United States offered opportunities not only for the active individual to acquire wealth on his own but also for the less capable individual to lose quickly what he might have inherited. Above all, the spread of general education has tended to diminish the advantage which the child of the wealthy would have over that of the poor, and the general suffrage, partly as a result of these developments, has further tended to broaden the sphere of sharing the wealth. Thus the attention of those concerned with income distribution has shifted away from inheritance toward those factors which enable or inhibit an individual in his attempts to produce income through his own efforts. . . .

In addition to its effect on wealth distribution, there is reason to believe that the system of inheritance in any society, being deeply rooted in and reflecting the family structure, in turn reinforces existing patterns of family organization, and provides security within these patterns. Thus change in the system of inheritance has been seen to accompany, or to have been accompanied by, far-reaching social changes. . . .

. . . [A] society may solve the problem of determining to whom property shall pass after the death of its owner by giving the property owner himself the power to designate the recipient or recipients.

In our society, where property owners are endowed with this "power of testation", its existence is easily taken for granted. However, when we start to think about it, it is by no means self-evident that a man should have the power of disposing of his property beyond his grave. This world belongs to the living. Why should the dead be permitted to control its riches and their recipients? The question has often been asked and the responses have not always favored freedom of testation. As a matter of fact, in history freedom of testation has rather been the exception than the rule.

A great variety of arguments has been adduced in favor of freedom of testation. It has been said to be a necessary complement of the immortality of the soul, a stimulus to increased productive or acquisitive activity, a means of maintaining family discipline, and a postulate necessarily flowing from the democratic principle of freedom. Freedom of testation, as an alternative to the fixed, unbending rules of intestacy, permits a property owner flexibility in considering and weighing the individual needs and deserts of the various members of his family as well as of other persons and institutions that may be dependent upon him.

B. Rules of Validation

Now that we have introduced various types of private arrangements, it is important to consider the rules that must be followed to create such arrangements. Such rules can be court-made or statutory. We shall focus on rules of validation in the areas of contracts, which are predominantly court-made rules, and corporations, which are rules predominantly enacted by legislatures.

i. Contracts

LUCY v. ZEHMER

Supreme Court of Appeals of Virginia, 1954.
196 Va. 493, 84 S.E.2d 516.

BUCHANAN, JUSTICE.

This suit was instituted by W.O. Lucy and J.C. Lucy, complainants, against A.H. Zehmer and Ida S. Zehmer, his wife, defendants, to have specific performance of a contract by which it was alleged the Zehmers had sold to W.O. Lucy a tract of land owned by A.H. Zehmer in Dinwiddie county containing 471.6 acres, more or less, known as the Ferguson farm, for $50,000. J.C. Lucy, the other complainant, is a brother of W.O. Lucy, to whom W.O. Lucy transferred a half interest in his alleged purchase.

The instrument sought to be enforced was written by A.H. Zehmer on December 20, 1952, in these words: "We hereby agree to sell to W.O. Lucy the Ferguson Farm complete for $50,000.00, title satisfactory to buyer," and signed by the defendants, A.H. Zehmer and Ida S. Zehmer.

The answer of A.H. Zehmer admitted that at the time mentioned W.O. Lucy offered him $50,000 cash for the farm, but that he, Zehmer, considered that the offer was made in jest; that so thinking, and both he and Lucy having had several drinks, he wrote out "the memorandum" quoted above and induced his wife to sign it; that he did not deliver the memorandum to Lucy, but that Lucy picked it up, read it, put it in his pocket, attempted to offer Zehmer $5 to bind the bargain, which Zehmer refused to accept, and realizing for the first time that Lucy was serious, Zehmer assured him that he had no intention of selling the farm and that the whole matter was a joke. Lucy left the premises insisting that he had purchased the farm.

Depositions were taken and the decree appealed from was entered holding that the complainants had failed to establish their right to specific performance, and dismissing their bill. The assignment of error is to this action of the court.

W.O. Lucy, a lumberman and farmer, thus testified in substance: He had known Zehmer for fifteen or twenty years and had been familiar with the Ferguson farm for ten years. Seven or eight years ago he had offered Zehmer $20,000 for the farm which Zehmer had accepted, but the agreement was verbal and Zehmer backed out. On the night of December 20, 1952, around eight o'clock, he took an employee to McKenney, where Zehmer lived and operated a restaurant, filling station and motor court. While there he decided to see Zehmer and again try to buy the Ferguson farm. He entered the restaurant and talked to Mrs. Zehmer until Zehmer came in. He asked Zehmer if he had sold the Ferguson farm. Zehmer replied that he had not. Lucy said, "I bet you wouldn't take $50,000.00 for that place." Zehmer replied, "Yes, I would too; you wouldn't give fifty." Lucy said he would and told Zehmer to write up an agreement to that effect. Zehmer took a restaurant check and wrote on the back of it, "I do hereby agree to sell to W.O. Lucy the Ferguson Farm for $50,000 complete." Lucy told him he had better change it to "We" because Mrs. Zehmer would have to sign it too. Zehmer then tore up what he had written, wrote the agreement quoted above and asked Mrs. Zehmer, who was at the other end of the counter ten or twelve feet away, to sign it. Mrs. Zehmer said she would for $50,000 and signed it. Zehmer brought it back and gave it to Lucy, who offered him $5 which Zehmer refused, saying, "You don't need to give me any money, you got the agreement there signed by both of us."

The discussion leading to the signing of the agreement, said Lucy, lasted thirty or forty minutes, during which Zehmer seemed to doubt that

Lucy could raise $50,000. Lucy suggested the provision for having the title examined and Zehmer made the suggestion that he would sell it "complete, everything there," and stated that all he had on the farm was three heifers.

Lucy took a partly filled bottle of whiskey into the restaurant with him for the purpose of giving Zehmer a drink if he wanted it. Zehmer did, and he and Lucy had one or two drinks together. Lucy said that while he felt the drinks he took he was not intoxicated, and from the way Zehmer handled the transaction he did not think he was either.

December 20 was on Saturday. Next day Lucy telephoned to J.C. Lucy and arranged with the latter to take a half interest in the purchase and pay half of the consideration. On Monday he engaged an attorney to examine the title. The attorney reported favorably on December 31 and on January 2 Lucy wrote Zehmer stating that the title was satisfactory, that he was ready to pay the purchase price in cash and asking when Zehmer would be ready to close the deal. Zehmer replied by letter, mailed on January 13, asserting that he had never agreed or intended to sell.

Mr. and Mrs. Zehmer were called by the complainants as adverse witnesses. Zehmer testified in substance as follows:

He bought this farm more than ten years ago for $11,000. He had had twenty-five offers, more or less, to buy it, including several from Lucy, who had never offered any specific sum of money. He had given them all the same answer, that he was not interested in selling it. On this Saturday night before Christmas it looked like everybody and his brother came by there to have a drink. He took a good many drinks during the afternoon and had a pint of his own. When he entered the restaurant around eight-thirty Lucy was there and he could see that he was "pretty high." He said to Lucy, "Boy, you got some good liquor, drinking, ain't you?" Lucy then offered him a drink. "I was already high as a Georgia pine, and didn't have any more better sense than to pour another great big slug out and gulp it down, and he took one too."

After they had talked a while Lucy asked whether he still had the Ferguson farm. He replied that he had not sold it and Lucy said, "I bet you wouldn't take $50,000.00 for it." Zehmer asked him if he would give $50,000 and Lucy said yes. Zehmer replied, "You haven't got $50,000.00 in cash." Lucy said he did and Zehmer replied that he did not believe it. They argued "pro and con for a long time," mainly about "whether he had $50,000 in cash that he could put up right then and buy that farm."

Finally, said Zehmer, Lucy told him if he didn't believe he had $50,000, "you sign that piece of paper here and say you will take $50,000.00 for the farm." He, Zehmer, "just grabbed the back off of a guest check there" and wrote on the back of it. At that point in his testimony Zehmer asked to see what he had written to "see if I recognize my own handwriting." He examined the paper and exclaimed, "Great balls of fire, I got 'Firgerson' for Ferguson. I have got satisfactory spelled wrong. I don't recognize that writing if I would see it, wouldn't know it was mine."

After Zehmer had, as he described it, "scribbled this thing off," Lucy said, "Get your wife to sign it." Zehmer walked over to where she was and she at first refused to sign but did so after he told her that he "was just needling him [Lucy], and didn't mean a thing in the world, that I was not selling the farm." Zehmer then "took it back over there . . . and I was still looking at the dern thing. I had the drink right there by my hand, and I reached over to get a drink, and he said, 'Let me see it.' He reached and picked it up, and when I looked back again he had it in his pocket and he dropped a five dollar bill over there, and he said, 'Here is five dollars payment on it.' . . . . I said, 'Hell no, that is beer and liquor talking. I am not going to sell you the farm. I have told you that too many times before.' " . . .

On examination by her own counsel [Mrs. Zehmer testified] that her husband laid this piece of paper down after it was signed; that Lucy said to let him see it, took it, folded it and put it in his wallet, then said to Zehmer, "Let me give you $5.00," but Zehmer said, "No, this is liquor talking. I don't want to sell the farm, I have told you that I want my son to have it. This is all a joke." Lucy then said at least twice, "Zehmer, you have sold your farm," wheeled around and started for the door. He paused at the door and said, "I will bring you $50,000.00 to-morrow. . . . No, tomorrow is Sunday. I will bring it to you Monday." She said you could tell definitely that he was drinking and she said to her husband, "You should have taken him home," but he said, "Well, I am just about as bad off as he is." . . .

The defendants insist that the evidence was ample to support their contention that the writing sought to be enforced was prepared as a bluff or dare to force Lucy to admit that he did not have $50,000; that the whole matter was a joke; that the writing was not delivered to Lucy and no binding contract was ever made between the parties.

It is an unusual, if not bizarre, defense. When made to the writing admittedly prepared by one of the defendants and signed by both, clear evidence is required to sustain it.

In his testimony Zehmer claimed that he "was high as a Georgia pine," and that the transaction "was just a bunch of two doggoned drunks bluffing to see who could talk the biggest and say the most." That claim is inconsistent with his attempt to testify in great detail as to what was said and what was done. It is contradicted by other evidence as to the condition of both parties, and rendered of no weight by the testimony of his wife that when Lucy left the restaurant she suggested that Zehmer drive him home. The record is convincing that Zehmer was not intoxicated to the extent of being unable to comprehend the nature and consequences of the instrument he executed, and hence that instrument is not to be invalidated on that ground. It was in fact conceded by defendants' counsel in oral argument that under the evidence Zehmer was not too drunk to make a valid contract.

The evidence is convincing also that Zehmer wrote two agreements, the first one beginning "I hereby agree to sell." Zehmer first said he could not remember about that, then that "I don't think I wrote but one out." Mrs. Zehmer said that what he wrote was "I hereby agree," but that the "I" was changed to "We" after that night. The agreement that was written and signed is in the record and indicates no such change. Neither are the mistakes in spelling that Zehmer sought to point out readily apparent.

The appearance of the contract, the fact that it was under discussion for forty minutes or more before it was signed; Lucy's objection to the first draft because it was written in the singular, and he wanted Mrs. Zehmer to sign it also; the rewriting to meet that objection and the signing by Mrs. Zehmer; the discussion of what was to be included in the sale, the provision for the examination of the title, the completeness of the instrument that was executed, the taking possession of it by Lucy with no request or suggestion by either of the defendants that he give it back, are facts which furnish persuasive evidence that the execution of the contract was a serious business transaction rather than a casual, jesting matter as defendants now contend. . . .

If it be assumed, contrary to what we think the evidence shows, that Zehmer was jesting about selling his farm to Lucy and that the transaction was intended by him to be a joke, nevertheless the evidence shows that Lucy did not so understand it but considered it to be a serious business transaction and the contract to be binding on the Zehmers as well as on himself. The very next day he arranged with his brother to put up half the money and take a half interest in the land. The day after that he employed an attorney to examine the title. The next night, Tuesday, he was back at Zehmer's place and there Zehmer told him for the first time, Lucy said, that he wasn't going to sell and he told Zehmer, "You know you sold that place fair and square." After receiving the report from his attorney that the title was good he wrote to Zehmer that he was ready to close the deal.

Not only did Lucy actually believe, but the evidence shows he was warranted in believing, that the contract represented a serious business transaction and a good faith sale and purchase of the farm.

In the field of contracts, as generally elsewhere, "We must look to the outward expression of a person as manifesting his intention rather than to his secret and unexpressed intention. 'The law imputes to a person an intention corresponding to the reasonable meaning of his words and acts.' " First Nat. Exchange Bank of Roanoke v. Roanoke Oil Co., 169 Va. 99, 114, 192 S.E. 764, 770.

At no time prior to the execution of the contract had Zehmer indicated to Lucy by word or act that he was not in earnest about selling the farm. They had argued about it and discussed its terms, as Zehmer admitted, for a long time. Lucy testified that if there was any jesting it was about paying $50,000 that night. The contract and the evidence show that he was not expected to pay the money that night. Zehmer said that after the writing was signed he laid it down on the counter in front of Lucy. Lucy said Zehmer handed it to him. In any event there had been what appeared to be a good faith offer and a good faith acceptance, followed by the execution and apparent delivery of a written contract. Both said that Lucy put the writing in his pocket and then offered Zehmer $5 to seal the bargain. Not until then, even under the defendants' evidence, was anything said or done to indicate that the matter was a joke. Both of the Zehmers testified that when Zehmer asked his wife to sign he whispered that it was a joke so Lucy wouldn't hear and that it was not intended that he should hear.

The mental assent of the parties is not requisite for the formation of a contract. If the words or other acts of one of the parties have but one reasonable meaning, his undisclosed intention is immaterial except when an unreasonable meaning which he attaches to his manifestations is known to the other party. Restatement of the Law of Contracts, Vol. I, § 71, p. 74. . . .

An agreement or mutual assent is of course essential to a valid contract but the law imputes to a person an intention corresponding to the reasonable meaning of his words and acts. If his words and acts, judged by a reasonable standard, manifest an intention to agree, it is immaterial what may be the real but unexpressed state of his mind. 17 C.J.S., Contracts, § 32, p. 361; 12 Am.Jur., Contracts, § 19, p. 515.

So a person cannot set up that he was merely jesting when his conduct and words would warrant a reasonable person in believing that he intended a real agreement.

Whether the writing signed by the defendants and now sought to be enforced by the complainants was the result of a serious offer by Lucy and a serious acceptance by the defendants, or was a serious offer by Lucy and an acceptance in secret jest by the defendants, in either event it constituted a binding contract of sale between the parties. . . .

The complainants are entitled to have specific performance of the contract sued on. The decree appealed from is therefore reversed and the cause is remanded for the entry of a proper decree requiring the defendants to perform the contract in accordance with the prayer of the bill.

Reversed and remanded.

LEFKOWITZ v. GREAT MINNEAPOLIS SURPLUS STORE, INC.

Supreme Court of Minnesota, 1957.
251 Minn. 188, 86 N.W.2d 689.

MURPHY, JUSTICE.

This is an appeal from an order of the Municipal Court of Minneapolis denying the motion of the defendant for amended findings of fact, or, in the alternative, for a new trial. The order for judgment awarded the plaintiff the sum of $138.50 as damages for breach of contract.

This case grows out of the alleged refusal of the defendant to sell to the plaintiff a certain fur piece which it had offered for sale in a newspaper advertisement. It appears from the record that on April 6, 1956, the defendant published the following advertisement in a Minneapolis newspaper:

Saturday 9 A.M. Sharp
3 Brand New
Fur Coats
Worth to $100.00
First Come
First Served
$1
Each

On April 13, the defendant again published an advertisement in the same newspaper as follows:

Saturday 9 A.M.
2 Brand New Pastel
Mink 3-Skin Scarfs
Selling for $89.50
Out they go
Saturday, Each $1.00
1 Black Lapin Stole
Beautiful,
worth $139.50 . . . . $1.00
First Come
First Served

The record supports the findings of the court that on each of the Saturdays following the publication of the above-described ads the plaintiff was the first to present himself at the appropriate counter in the defendant's store and on each occasion demanded the coat and the stole so advertised and indicated his readiness to pay the sale price of $1. On both occasions, the defendant refused to sell the merchandise to the plaintiff, stating on the first occasion that by a "house rule" the offer was intended for women only and sales would not be made to men, and on the second visit that plaintiff knew defendant's house rules.

The trial court properly disallowed plaintiff's claim for the value of the fur coats since the value of these articles was speculative and uncertain. The only evidence of value was the advertisement itself to the effect that the coats were "Worth to $100.00," how much less being speculative especially in view of the price for which they were offered for sale. With reference to the offer of the defendant on April 13, 1956, to sell the "1 Black Lapin Stole . . . worth $139.50 . . . " the trial court held that the value of this article was established and granted judgment in favor of the plaintiff for that amount less the $1 quoted purchase price.

. . . [The defendant] relies upon authorities which hold that, where an advertiser publishes in a newspaper that he has a certain quantity or quality of goods which he wants to dispose of at certain prices and on certain terms, such advertisements are not offers which become contracts as soon as any person to whose notice they may come signifies his acceptance by notifying the other that he will take a certain quantity of them. Such advertisements have been construed as an invitation for an offer of sale on the terms stated, which offer, when received, may be accepted or rejected and which therefore does not become a contract of sale until accepted by the seller; and until a contract has been so made, the seller may modify or revoke such prices or terms.

. . . On the facts before us we are concerned with whether the advertisement constituted an offer, and, if so, whether the plaintiff's conduct constituted an acceptance.

There are numerous authorities which hold that a particular advertisement in a newspaper or circular letter relating to a sale of articles may be construed by the court as constituting an offer, acceptance of which would complete a contract.

The test of whether a binding obligation may originate in advertisements addressed to the general public is "whether the facts show that some performance was promised in positive terms in return for something requested." 1 Williston, Contracts (Rev. ed.) § 27.

The authorities above cited emphasize that, where the offer is clear, definite, and explicit, and leaves nothing open for negotiation, it constitutes an offer, acceptance of which will complete the contract. The most recent case on the subject is Johnson v. Capital City Ford Co., La.App., 85 So.2d 75, in which the court pointed out that a newspaper advertisement relating to the purchase and sale of automobiles may constitute an offer, acceptance of which will consummate a contract and create an obligation in the offeror to perform according to the terms of the published offer.

Whether in any individual instance a newspaper advertisement is an offer rather than an invitation to make an offer depends on the legal intention of the parties and the surrounding circumstances. We are of the view on the facts before us that the offer by the defendant of the sale of the Lapin fur was clear, definite, and explicit, and left nothing open for negotiation. The plaintiff having successfully managed to be the first one to appear at the seller's place of business to be served, as requested by the advertisement, and having offered the stated purchase price of the article, he was entitled to performance on the part of the defendant. We think the trial court was correct in holding that there was in the conduct of the parties a sufficient mutuality of obligation to constitute a contract of sale.

The defendant contends that the offer was modified by a "house rule" to the effect that only women were qualified to receive the bargains advertised. The advertisement contained no such restriction. This objection may be disposed of briefly by stating that, while an advertiser has the right at any time before acceptance to modify his offer, he does not have the right, after acceptance, to impose new or arbitrary conditions not contained in the published offer.

Affirmed.

HAMER v. SIDWAY

Court of Appeals of New York, 1891.
124 N.Y. 538, 27 N.E. 256.

Appeal from an order of the general term of the supreme court in the fourth judicial department, reversing a judgment entered on the decision of the court at special term in the county clerk's office of Chemung county on the 1st day of October, 1889. The plaintiff presented a claim to the executor of William E. Story, Sr., for $5,000 and interest from the 6th day of February, 1875. She acquired it through several mesne assignments from William E. Story, 2d. The claim being rejected by the executor, this action was brought. It appears that William E. Story, Sr., was the uncle of William E. Story, 2d; that at the celebration of the golden wedding of Samuel Story and wife, father and mother of William E. Story, Sr., on the

20th day of March, 1869, in the presence of the family and invited guests, he promised his nephew that if he would refrain from drinking, using tobacco, swearing, and playing cards or billiards for money until he became 21 years of age, he would pay him the sum of $5,000. The nephew assented thereto, and fully performed the conditions inducing the promise. When the nephew arrived at the age of 21 years, and on the 31st day of January, 1875, he wrote to his uncle, informing him that he had performed his part of the agreement, and had thereby become entitled to the sum of $5,000. The uncle received the letter, and a few days later, and on the 6th day of February, he wrote and mailed to his nephew the following letter: "Buffalo, Feb. 6, 1875. W.E. Story, Jr.—Dear Nephew: Your letter of the 31st ult. came to hand all right, saying that you had lived up to the promise made to me several years ago. I have no doubt but you have, for which you shall have five thousand dollars, as I promised you. I had the money in the bank the day you was twenty-one years old that I intend for you, and you shall have the money certain. Now, Willie, I do not intend to interfere with this money in any way till I think you are capable of taking care of it, and the sooner that time comes the better it will please me. I would hate very much to have you start out in some adventure that you thought all right and lose this money in one year. The first five thousand dollars that I got together cost me a heap of hard work. You would hardly believe me when I tell you that to obtain this I shoved a jack-plane many a day, butchered three or four years, then came to this city, and, after three months' perseverance, I obtained a situation in a grocery store. I opened this store early, closed late, slept in the fourth story of the building in a room 30 by 40 feet, and not a human being in the building but myself. All this I done to live as cheap as I could to save something. I don't want you to take up with this kind of fare. . . . Willie, you are twenty-one, and you have many a thing to learn yet. This money you have earned much easier than I did, besides acquiring good habits at the same time, and you are quite welcome to the money. Hope you will make good use of it. I was ten long years getting this together after I was your age. . . . Truly yours, W.E. Story. P.S. You can consider this money on interest." The nephew received the letter, and thereafter consented that the money should remain with his uncle in accordance with the terms and conditions of the letter. The uncle died on the 29th day of January, 1887, without having paid over to his nephew any portion of the said $5,000 and interest.

PARKER, J. . . . The defendant contends that the contract was without consideration to support it, and therefore invalid. He asserts that the promisee, by refraining from the use of liquor and tobacco, was not harmed, but benefited; that that which he did was best for him to do, independently of his uncle's promise,—and insists that it follows that, unless the promisor was benefited, the contract was without consideration,—a contention which, if well founded, would seem to leave open for controversy in many cases whether that which the promisee did or omitted to do was in fact of such benefit to him as to leave no consideration to support the enforcement of the promisor's agreement. Such a rule could not be tolerated, and is without foundation in the law. The exchequer chamber in 1875 defined "consideration" as follows: "A valuable consideration, in the sense of the law, may consist either in some right, interest, profit, or benefit accruing to the one party, or some forbearance, detriment, loss, or responsibility given, suffered, or undertaken by the other." Courts "will not ask whether the thing which forms the consideration does in fact benefit the promisee or a third party, or is of any substantial value to any one. It is enough that something is promised, done, forborne, or suffered by the party to whom the promise is made as consideration for the promise made to him." Anson, Cont. 63. . . . Pollock in his work on Contracts, (page 166,) after citing the definition given by the exchequer chamber, already quoted, says: "The second branch of this judicial description is really the most important one. 'Consideration' means not so much that one party is profiting as that the other abandons some legal right in the present, or limits his legal freedom of action in the future, as an inducement for the promise of the first." Now, applying this rule to the facts before us, the promisee used tobacco, occasionally drank liquor, and he had a legal right to do so. That right he abandoned for a period of years upon the strength of the promise of the testator that for such forbearance he would give him $5,000. We need not speculate on the effort which may have been required to give up the use of those stimulants. It is sufficient that he restricted his lawful freedom of action within certain prescribed limits upon the faith of his uncle's agreement, and now, having fully performed the conditions imposed, it is of no moment whether such performance actually proved a benefit to the promisor, and the court will not inquire into it; but, were it a proper subject of inquiry, we see nothing in this record that would permit a determination that the uncle was not benefited in a legal sense. Few cases have been found which may be said to be precisely in point, but such as have been, support the position we have taken. . . .

   . . . The order appealed from should be reversed, and the judgment of the special term affirmed, with costs payable out of the estate. All concur.

---

1 S. WILLISTON, A TREATISE ON THE LAW OF CONTRACTS

§ 112, at 445–46 (3d ed. 1957).*

If a benevolent man says to a tramp,—"if you go around the corner to the clothing shop there, you may purchase an overcoat on my credit," no reasonable person would understand that the short walk was requested as the consideration for the promise, but that in the event of the tramp going to the shop the promisor would make him a gift. Yet the walk to the shop is in its nature capable of being consideration. It is a legal detriment to the tramp to take the walk, and the only reason why the walk is not consideration is because on a reasonable interpretation, it must be held that the walk was not requested as the price of the promise, but was merely a condition of a gratuitous promise.

It is often difficult to decide whether words of condition in a promise indicate a request for consideration or state a mere condition in a gratuitous promise. An aid, though not a conclusive test in determining which interpretation of the promise is more reasonable, is an inquiry whether the happening of the condition will be a benefit to the promisor. If so, it is a fair inference that the happening was requested as a consideration. On the other hand, if, as in the case of the tramp stated above, the happening of the condition will be not only of no benefit to the promisor but is obviously merely for the purpose of enabling the promisee to receive a gift, the happening of the event on which the promise is conditional, though brought about by the promisee in reliance on the promise, will not be interpreted as consideration.

————

FULLER, CONSIDERATION AND FORM

41 Colum.L.Rev. 799, 799–800, 806–07, 813–14 (1941).

That consideration may have both a "formal" and a "substantive" aspect is apparent when we reflect on the reasons which have been advanced why promises without consideration are not enforced. It has been said that consideration is "for the sake of evidence" and is intended to remove the hazards of mistaken or perjured testimony which would attend the enforcement of promises for which nothing is given in exchange. Again, it is said that enforcement is denied gratuitous promises because such promises are often made impulsively and without proper deliberation. In both these cases the objection relates, not to the content and effect of the promise, but to the manner in which it is made. Objections of this sort, which touch the form rather than the content of the agreement, will be removed if the making of the promise is attended by some formality or ceremony, as by being under seal. On the other hand, it has been said that the enforcement of gratuitous promises is not an object of sufficient importance to our social and economic order to justify the expenditure of the time and energy necessary to accomplish it. Here the objection is one of "substance" since it touches the significance of the promise made and not merely the circumstances surrounding the making of it. . . .

. . . Among the basic conceptions of contract law the most pervasive and indispensable is the principle of private autonomy. This principle simply means that the law views private individuals as possessing a power to effect, within certain limits, changes in their legal relations. The man who conveys property to another is exercising this power; so is the man who enters a contract. When a court enforces a promise it is merely arming with legal sanction a rule or lex previously established by the party himself. This power of the individual to effect changes in his legal relations with others is comparable to the power of a legislature. It is, in fact, only a kind of political prejudice which causes us to use the word "law" in one case and not in the other, a prejudice which did not deter the Romans from applying the word lex to the norms established by private agreement. . . .

. . . Form has an obvious relationship to the principle of private autonomy. Where men make laws for themselves it is desirable that they should do so under conditions guaranteeing the desiderata described in our analysis of the functions of form. Furthermore, the greater the assurance that these desiderata are satisfied, the larger the scope we may be willing to ascribe to private autonomy.

Gratuitous Promises

Some promises are enforceable without consideration. We now turn to the subject of the enforcement of such gratuitous promises.

JAMES BAIRD CO. v. GIMBEL BROS.

United States Circuit Court of Appeals, Second Circuit, 1933.
64 F.2d 344, 346 (L. Hand, J.).

Offers are ordinarily made in exchange for a consideration, either a counter-promise or some other act which the promisor wishes to secure. In such cases they propose bargains; they presuppose that each promise or performance is an inducement to the other. But a man may make a promise without expecting an equivalent; a donative promise, conditional or absolute. The common law provided for such by sealed instruments, and it is unfortunate that these are no longer generally available. The doctrine of "promissory estoppel" is to avoid the harsh results of allowing the promisor in such a case to repudiate, when the promisee has acted in reliance upon the promise.

SHATTUCK, GRATUITOUS PROMISES—A NEW WRIT?

35 Mich.L.Rev. 908, 943 (1937).

Experience has proved that [promisees] all too frequently rely to their injury on gratuitous promises. It is useless to argue that they should not rely where there is no consideration for the promise. The uncontrovertible fact is that they do rely. Not infrequently the law steps in to protect people from their own credulity. Many courts, voicing, we believe, a sound and current ethical opinion, have chosen to put the risk of such reliance on the promisor. He is bound to make no promises which are calculated to induce injurious reliance, on pain of responsibility for the consequences.

BOYER, PROMISSORY ESTOPPEL: REQUIREMENTS AND LIMITATIONS OF THE DOCTRINE

98 U.Pa.L.Rev. 459, 497 (1950).

The doctrine of promissory estoppel does not purport to enforce *all* gratuitous promises. Only those promises which are likely to and have induced reliance of a substantial character are within the scope of the present doctrine, and then only when the need to avoid injustice demands their inclusion. When the limitations and requirements of the doctrine, as discussed herein, are recognized, it is clear that it stands midway between those promises which have been bought and paid for with a price and those which are purely gratuitous. Purely gratuitous promises are not now enforced in the Anglo-American legal system.

RICKETTS v. SCOTHORN

Supreme Court of Nebraska, 1898.
57 Neb. 51, 77 N.W. 365.

SULLIVAN, J.

In the District Court of Lancaster county, the plaintiff, Katie Scothorn, recovered judgment against the defendant, Andrew D. Ricketts, as executor, of the last will and testament of John C. Ricketts, deceased. The action was based upon a promissory note, of which the following is a copy: "May the first, 1891. I promise to pay to Katie Scothorn on demand, $2,000, to be at 6 per cent. per annum. J.C. Ricketts." In the petition the plaintiff alleges that the consideration for the execution of the note was that she should surrender her employment as bookkeeper for Mayer Bros., and cease to work for a living. She also alleges that the note was given to induce her to abandon her occupation, and that, relying on it, and on the annual interest, as a means of support, she gave up the employment in which she was then engaged. These allegations of the petition are denied by the administrator.

The material facts are undisputed. They are as follows: John C. Ricketts, the maker of the note, was the grandfather of the plaintiff. Early in May—presumably on the day the note bears date—he called on her at the store where she was working. What transpired between them is thus described by Mr. Flodene, one of the plaintiff's witnesses: "A. Well, the old gentleman came in there one morning about nine o'clock, probably a little before or a little after, but early in the morning, and he unbuttoned his vest, and took out a piece of paper in the shape of a note; that is the way it looked to me; and he says to Miss Scothorn, 'I have fixed out something that you have not got to work any more.' He says, none of my grandchildren work, and you don't have to. Q. Where was she? A. She took the piece of paper and kissed him, and kissed the old gentleman, and commenced to cry." It seems Miss Scothorn immediately notified her employer of her intention to quit work, and that she did soon after abandon her occupation. The mother of the plaintiff was a witness, and testified that she had a conversation with her father, Mr. Ricketts, shortly after the note was executed, in which he informed her that he had given the note to the plaintiff to enable her to quit work; that none of his grandchildren worked, and he did not think she ought to. For something more than a year the plaintiff was without an occupation, but in September, 1892, with the consent of her grandfather, and by his assistance, she secured a position as bookkeeper with Messrs. Funke & Ogden. On June

8, 1894, Mr. Ricketts died. He had paid one year's interest on the note, and a short time before his death expressed regret that he had not been able to pay the balance. In the summer or fall of 1892 he stated to his daughter, Mrs. Scothorn, that if he could sell his farm in Ohio he would pay the note out of the proceeds. He at no time repudiated the obligation.

We quite agree with counsel for the defendant that upon this evidence there was nothing to submit to the jury, and that a verdict should have been directed peremptorily for one of the parties. The testimony of Flodene and Mrs. Scothorn, taken together, conclusively establishes the fact that the note was not given in consideration of the plaintiff pursuing, or agreeing to pursue, any particular line of conduct. There was no promise on the part of the plaintiff to do, or refrain from doing, anything. Her right to the money promised in the note was not made to depend upon an abandonment of her employment with Mayer Bros., and future abstention from like service. Mr. Ricketts made no condition, requirement, or request. He exacted no quid pro quo. He gave the note as a gratuity, and looked for nothing in return. So far as the evidence discloses, it was his purpose to place the plaintiff in a position of independence, where she could work or remain idle, as she might choose. The abandonment of Miss Scothorn of her position as bookkeeper was altogether voluntary. It was not an act done in fulfillment of any contract obligation assumed when she accepted the note.

The instrument in suit, being given without any valuable consideration, was nothing more than a promise to make a gift in the future of the sum of money therein named. Ordinarily, such promises are not enforceable, even when put in the form of a promissory note. But it has often been held that an action on a note given to a church, college, or other like institution, upon the faith of which money has been expended or obligations incurred, could not be successfully defended on the ground of a want of consideration. In this class of cases the note in suit is nearly always spoken of as a gift or donation, but the decision is generally put on the ground that the expenditure of money or assumption of liability by the donee on the faith of the promise constitutes a valuable and sufficient consideration. It seems to us that the true reason is the preclusion of the defendant, under the doctrine of estoppel, to deny the consideration. . . .

Under the circumstances of this case, is there an equitable estoppel which ought to preclude the defendant from alleging that the note in controversy is lacking in one of the essential elements of a valid contract? We think there is. An [equitable] estoppel . . . is defined to be "a right arising from acts, admissions, or conduct which have induced a change of position in accordance with the real or apparent intention of the party against whom they are alleged." . . . According to the undisputed proof, as shown by the record before us, the plaintiff was a working girl, holding a position in which she earned a salary of $10 per week. Her grandfather, desiring to put her in a position of independence, gave her the note, accompanying it with the remark that his other grandchildren did not work, and that she would not be obliged to work any longer. In effect, he suggested that she might abandon her employment, and rely in the future upon the bounty which he promised. He doubtless desired that she should give up her occupation, but, whether he did or not, it is entirely certain that he contemplated such action on her part as a reasonable and probable consequence of his gift. Having intentionally influenced the plaintiff to alter her position for the worse on the faith of the note being paid when due, it would be grossly inequitable to permit the maker, or his executor, to resist payment on the ground that the promise was given without consideration. The petition charges the elements of an equitable estoppel, and the evidence conclusively establishes them. If errors intervened at the trial, they could not have been prejudicial. A verdict for the defendant would be unwarranted. The judgment is right, and is

Affirmed.

————

The Proliferation of Promissory Estoppel

Although the theory of promissory estoppel was originally viewed as pertaining only to gratuitous promises, today the doctrine is applied much more expansively. For example, promises have been held enforceable on the basis of promissory estoppel in the context of precontract bargaining and when a contract is unenforceable for lack of sufficient certainty. Is the proliferation of promissory estoppel advisable? What arguments can you think of, pro and con?

————

ii. Corporations

OREGON REVISED STATUTES

61.305 Incorporators. One or more natural persons of the age of 18 years or more, a domestic or foreign corporation, a partnership or an association may incorporate a nonprofit corporation by signing and verifying articles of incorporation and delivering one original and one true copy of the articles to the Corporation Commissioner.

61.311 Articles of incorporation. (1) The articles of incorporation shall set forth:

(a) The name of the corporation.

(b) The period of duration, which may be perpetual.

(c) The purpose or purposes for which the corporation is organized. It shall be sufficient to state, either alone or with other purposes, that the purpose of the corporation is to engage in any lawful activity for which corporations may be organized under this chapter, and by such statement, all lawful activities shall be within the purposes of the corporation, except for express limitations, if any.

(d) Any provisions, not inconsistent with law, which the incorporators elect to set forth in the articles of incorporation for the regulation of the internal affairs of the corporation, including any provision for distribution of assets on dissolution or final liquidation.

(e) The address, including street and number, if any, of its initial registered office, and the name of its initial registered agent at such address.

(f) The number of directors constituting the initial board of directors, and the names and addresses, including street and number, if any, of the persons who are to serve as the initial directors.

(g) The name and address, including street and number, if any, of each incorporator.

(2) Duration shall be perpetual unless the articles of incorporation expressly limit the period of duration. . . .

61.315 Filing articles of incorporation. (1) One original, and one true copy of the articles of incorporation shall be delivered to the Corporation Commissioner. . . .

61.321 Effect of issuance of certificate of incorporation. Upon the issuance of the certificate of incorporation, the corporate existence shall begin . . . .

61.325 Organizational meeting of directors. After the issuance of the certificate of incorporation an organization meeting of the board of directors named in the articles of incorporation shall be held, either within or without this state, at the call of a majority of the incorporators, for the purpose of adopting bylaws, electing officers and transacting of such other business as may come before the meeting. The incorporators calling the meeting shall give at least three days' notice thereof by mail to each director so named, which notice shall state the time and place of the meeting.

NORTH DAKOTA CENTURY CODE

10–19–55. Effect of issuance of certificate of incorporation.— Upon the issuance of the certificate of incorporation, the corporate existence shall begin, and such certificate of incorporation shall be conclusive evidence that all conditions precedent required to be performed by the incorporators have been complied with and that the corporation has been incorporated under chapter 10–19, except as against this state in a proceeding to cancel or revoke the certificate of incorporation or for involuntary dissolution of the corporation.

WEISS v. ANDERSON
Supreme Court of North Dakota, 1983.
341 N.W.2d 367, 371 (Erickstad, C.J.).

A corporation cannot exist without the consent or grant of the sovereign. Under North Dakota statutory law, the corporate existence begins upon the issuance of the certificate of incorporation by the Secretary of State, and the certificate of incorporation is conclusive evidence that all conditions precedent have been performed. § 10–19–55, N.D.C.C. Section 10–19–23, N.D.C.C., states that "all persons who assume to act as a corporation without authority so to do shall be jointly and severally liable for debts and liabilities incurred or arising as a result thereof."

———

C. Legal Consequences

We shall again focus on contracts and corporations in studying the legal consequences of private arrangements. By way of introduction, however, it is useful to consider generally the variant forms of legal consequences that may be accorded to private arrangements.

Some private arrangements are legally enforceable when made; others are not. For example, a contract becomes immediately binding on both parties, but some wills and trusts are unilaterally revocable. Some private arrangements impose quasi-official duties on others, such as the appointment of an executor of a will. Others, like the typical contract between private parties, do not. A private arrangement may confer a particular status on the participants, such as marriage, ownership of property, or membership in an organization. Such status affords the participants certain privileges, such as the right to income from property, limited liability of corporate stockholders, and procedural rights of union members in disciplinary proceedings. A private arrangement may provide various remedies for its breach, such as claims to money damages for contract breach. But not all disputes involving private arrangements ultimately lead to legal intervention, as the next excerpt points out.

———

NOTE, JUDICIAL INTERVENTION IN THE CONDUCT OF PRIVATE ASSOCIATIONS: BASES FOR THE EMERGING TREND OF JUDICIAL ACTIVISM
4 N.Y.U.Rev.L. & Soc.Change 61, 62–64 (1974).*

A body of common law developments that may be termed collectively the "doctrine of private associations" partially insulates the conduct of private associations from judicial review. In justifying the development of this doctrine certain scholars have argued that because individuals have innumerable and often conflicting likes and dislikes it is impossible to generate a workable notion of what is the common good. Consequently they felt that the state should give maximum freedom not only to individuals but also to groups, and should intervene to settle conflicts only where it can clearly be demonstrated that private resolution of the conflict will harm interests which traditionally have been thought important enough to warrant legal protection. The state was conceived of as being but one of many groups to which individuals might owe allegiance; private associations were thus viewed as sovereignties, each competing with the state and other groups for individual loyalties, and each was therefore entitled to immunity from interference in its affairs by the state.

Likewise courts have traditionally been reluctant to interfere with the internal affairs of such associations in the belief that they require a certain degree of freedom from external intervention in order to achieve their purposes. Nonetheless, in particular situations where the considerations of public policy and justice are sufficiently compelling, the courts have been ready to grant relief—for the most part in cases involving improper expulsions from pre-existing membership which required mandamus for reinstatement or other suitable relief.

In granting limited judicial review to complaints of expulsion from membership, courts have generally founded their jurisdiction on either of two grounds—the plaintiff's property rights or the contract theory. The former basis is present where the complainant's expulsion has deprived him of some vested interest in the assets of the association. Examples of property rights, the denial of which is sufficient to authorize judicial review, are an individual's right to use his association's physical property and a member's right to a pro rata share of the association's assets in the event of dissolution. On rare occasions, even a denial of a personal interest has been held sufficient.

The contract theory rests on the assumption that the laws of an organization constitute a contract between the member and the organization. Under this approach, the courts will determine whether an association has acted in accordance with its rules, and whether those rules violate public policy. Consequently, on either of these jurisdictional bases, courts would intervene solely on behalf of aggrieved members; individuals who had been wrongfully denied membership could not expect judicial action on their behalf.

---

i. **Contracts**

COOPER v. CLUTE

Supreme Court of North Carolina, 1917.
174 N.C. 366, 93 S.E. 915.

BROWN, J.

[The plaintiff appealed an adverse judgment.]

. . . The findings of the jury establish that the defendant entered into a contract with plaintiff to deliver to him at the Hilton compress, near Wilmington, 1,430 bales of cotton not compressed at the price of 10⅞ cents per pound, delivery to be made on February 26, 1916; that plaintiff was ready, able, and willing to take and pay for the cotton according to contract; that defendant failed to deliver the cotton; and that its market value at time and place of delivery was 10⅞ cents per pound.

The measure of damage to be recovered for breach of an executory contract of this character is well settled to be the difference between the contract price and the actual or market value of the property at the time and place of the breach of the contract. Under this rule, if the market value is the same as the contract price when the contract is breached, only nominal damages can be recovered. . . .

Plaintiff contends that the court should have rendered judgment for plaintiff for the difference between $10^7/_8$ cents, the contract price, and 11.03 cents, which plaintiff claims the defendant received from Sprunt for the cotton. The plaintiff tendered no such issue, and there is no finding of fact that defendant received 11.03 for the cotton. But that is immaterial. The written contract shows that the defendant did not sell to plaintiff any particular cotton. Defendant could have performed the contract by purchasing similar cotton on the market and making the delivery.

.   .   . The evidence is conflicting as to the value of similar cotton at place of delivery on February 26, 1916, but the jury have fixed it at $10^7/_8$, which is the contract price. It therefore follows that the plaintiff has sustained no actual damage.

No error.

HADLEY v. BAXENDALE

Exechequer, 1854.
156 Eng.Rep. 145.

At the trial before Crompton, J., at the last Gloucester Assizes, it appeared that the plaintiffs carried on an extensive business as millers at Gloucester; and that, on the 11th of May, their mill was stopped by a breakage of the crank shaft by which the mill was worked. The steam-engine was manufactured by Messrs. Joyce & Co., the engineers, at Greenwich, and it became necessary to send the shaft as a pattern for a new one to Greenwich. The fracture was discovered on the 12th, and on the 13th the plaintiffs sent one of their servants to the office of the defendants, who are the well-known carriers trading under the name of Pickford & Co., for the purpose of having the shaft carried to Greenwich. The plaintiffs' servant told the clerk that the mill was stopped, and that the shaft must be sent immediately; and in answer to the inquiry when the shaft would be taken, the answer was, that if it was sent up by twelve o'clock any day, it would be delivered at Greenwich on the following day. On the following day the shaft was taken by the defendants before noon, for the purpose of being conveyed to Greenwich, and the sum of £ 2, 4s. was paid for its carriage for the whole distance; at the same time the defendants' clerk was told that a special entry, if required, should be made to hasten its delivery. The delivery of the shaft at Greenwich was delayed by some neglect; and the consequence was, that the plaintiffs did not receive the new shaft for several days after they would otherwise have done, and the working of their mill was thereby delayed, and they thereby lost the profits they would otherwise have received.

On the part of the defendants, it was objected that these damages were too remote, and that the defendants were not liable with respect to them. The learned Judge left the case generally to the jury, who found a verdict with [£ 50] damages .   .   .   .

[The defendants moved] for a new trial, on the ground of misdirection.
.   .   .

The judgment of the Court was now delivered by ALDERSON, B. We think that there ought to be a new trial in this case; but, in so doing, we deem it to be expedient and necessary to state explicitly the rule which the Judge, at the next trial, ought, in our opinion, to direct the jury to be governed by when they estimate the damages.

It is, indeed, of the last importance that we should do this; for, if the jury are left without any definite rule to guide them, it will, in such cases as these, manifestly lead to the greatest injustice. The Courts have done this on several occasions; and, in Blake v. Midland Railway Company, 18 Q.B. 93, the Court granted a new trial on this very ground, that the rule had not been definitely laid down to the jury by the learned judge at Nisi Prius.

"There are certain established rules," this Court says, in Alder v. Keighley, 15 M. & W. 117, "according to which the jury ought to find." And the Court, in that case, adds: "and here there is a clear rule, that the amount which would have been received if the contract had been kept, is the measure of damages if the contract is broken."

Now we think the proper rule in such a case as the present is this:— Where two parties have made a contract which one of them has broken, the damages which the other party ought to receive in respect of such breach of contract should be such as may fairly and reasonably be considered either arising naturally, i.e., according to the usual course of things, from such breach of contract itself, or such as may reasonably be supposed to have been in the contemplation of both parties, at the time they made the contract, as the probable result of the breach of it. Now, if the special circumstances under which the contract was actually made were communicated by the plaintiffs to the defendants, and thus known to both parties, the damages resulting from the breach of such a contract, which they would reasonably contemplate, would be the amount of injury which would ordinarily follow from a breach of contract under these special circumstances so known and communicated. But, on the other hand, if these special circumstances were wholly unknown to the party breaking the contract, he, at the most, could only be supposed to have had in his contemplation the amount of injury which would arise generally, and in the great multitude of cases not affected by any special circumstances, from such a breach of contract. For, had the special circumstances been known, the parties might have specially provided for the breach of contract by special terms as to the damages in that case; and of this advantage it would be very unjust to deprive them. . . . Now, in the present case, if we are to apply the principles above laid down, we find that the only circumstances here communicated by the plaintiffs to the defendants at the time the contract was made, were, that the article to be carried was the broken shaft of a mill, and that the plaintiffs were the millers of that mill. But how do these circumstances shew reasonably that the profits of the mill must be stopped by an unreasonable delay in the delivery of the broken shaft by the carrier to the third person? Suppose the plaintiffs had another shaft in their possession put up or putting up at the time, and that they only wished to send back the broken shaft to the engineer who made it; it is clear that this would be quite consistent with the above circumstances, and yet the unreasonable delay in the delivery would have no effect upon the intermediate profits of the mill. Or, again, suppose that, at the time of delivery to the carrier, the machinery of the mill had been in other respects defective, then, also, the same results would follow. Here it is true that the shaft was actually sent back to serve as a model for a new one, and that the want of a new one was the only cause of the stoppage of the mill, and that the loss of profits really arose from not sending down the new shaft in proper time, and that this arose from the delay in delivering the broken one to serve as a model. But it is obvious that, in the great multitude of cases of millers sending off broken shafts to third persons by a carrier under ordinary circumstances, such consequences would not, in all probability, have occurred; and these special circumstances were here never communicated by the plaintiffs to the defendants. It follows, therefore, that the loss of profits here cannot reasonably be considered such a consequence of the breach of contract as could have been fairly and reasonably contemplated by both the parties when they made this contract. For such loss would neither have flowed naturally from the breach of this contract in the great multitude of such cases occurring under ordinary circumstances, nor were the special circumstances, which, perhaps, would have made it a reasonable and natural consequence of such breach of contract, communicated to or known by the defendants. The Judge ought, therefore, to have told the jury, that, upon the facts then before them, they ought not to take the loss of profits into consideration at all in estimating the damages. There must therefore be a new trial in this case.

—————

Specific Performance

Consider again the case of *Lucy* v. *Zehmer*, set forth previously. There the court remanded the case for the entry of a decree requiring the Zehmers to perform the contract. How is this remedy different from the remedy studied in *Cooper* v. *Clute* and *Hadley* v. *Baxendale*?

Because land is "assumed to have a peculiar value," Kitchen v. Herring, 42 N.C. 190, 193 (1851), specific performance is generally available to purchasers of land. In other types of agreements, as we shall see, specific performance is granted only when money damages are inadequate. Even in such cases, a court may decline to grant specific performance. One reason is the difficulty of enforcing the decree, such as in complex construction contract settings where supervision of a recalcitrant contractor would be impractical.

Courts are also hesitant to grant specific performance in personal service contract cases. Can you think of reasons why? If the contract contains a promise by the employee not to work for others and the employee's skills are "unique," however, courts typically will order the employee not to work for others. Will this have the same effect as a decree of specific performance?

Decrees of specific performance are enforced through the court's contempt power. This is discussed in Section 5 of this chapter.

—————

PIERCE–ODOM, INC. v. EVENSON

Court of Appeals of Arkansas, 1982.
632 S.W.2d 247.

CORBIN, JUDGE.

Appellant, Pierce-Odom, Inc., appeals from a judgment granting appellees' petition for specific performance of a contract for the sale of a mobile home to appellees, Melvin Evenson and his wife, Sybil. We reverse and remand.

The testimony at trial indicated that the litigation arose out of the following transactions. On October 16, 1980, appellees went to appellant's mobile lot in Conway, Arkansas, to look for a new mobile home. Gene DeHart, who was employed by appellant, told appellees that he was the sales manager for the business and he showed the appellees several different models of mobile homes on the lot. Appellees told DeHart that they could not buy a mobile home until they sold some property they owned in Hamilton Hills subdivision in Fairfield Bay. Appellees testified that there was some discussion about appellees' property and the selling price. Appellees left the lot without entering into an agreement with DeHart. DeHart called the appellees on October 20 to inquire if they had sold their property and the appellees told him that they had not. According to appellees, DeHart then stated that his boss, Jerry Odom, had told him that Pierce-Odom would take their lot in on a trade for a new mobile home. DeHart told them that Pierce-Odom was not interested in the mobile home they were presently living in and appellees told him that they had a buyer for their mobile home. Appellees returned to the mobile home lot on October 21 and met again with DeHart. They inquired as to the whereabouts of Mr. Odom and were told by DeHart that he was out-of-town that day.

Appellees signed a contract prepared by DeHart for the sale of a mobile home. The contract set forth the terms of the sale including the trade-in of the appellees' property at Fairfield Bay as partial payment for the new mobile home. However, no representative of Pierce-Odom signed the contract. Appellees paid $100.00 as a down-payment and told DeHart that they would call back and arrange for delivery of the new mobile home after talking with the purchaser of their old mobile home. The appellees later called Mr. DeHart and he reported that the mobile home could be delivered on Friday of that week.

Prior to the time that the mobile home was to be delivered, the appellees cashed a certificate of deposit and had a deed prepared to transfer the real property in preparation for carrying out the contract. They also sold their old mobile home and had it removed from their lot in preparation for the delivery of the new mobile home. On the day before the mobile home was to be delivered, Jerry Odom, owner of the mobile home lot, called the appellees and asked for directions to their lot in Hamilton Hills subdivision which the appellees provided. Later that evening, DeHart called the appellees and told them that Jerry Odom had changed his mind on the agreement because he did not want the lot after seeing it. Appellees then brought this action for specific performance asking the court to order Pierce-Odom, Inc., to deliver the particular mobile home they had selected and also asking the court to require Pierce-Odom, Inc., to take the lot at Fairfield Bay. The Court granted the petition for specific performance and this appeal resulted. . . .

. . . [W]e do not believe this was a proper case for specific performance of a contract for the sale of a mobile home based on either prior case law or § 85–2–716 of the Uniform Commercial Code.

The cases prior to the adoption of the Uniform Commercial Code in Arkansas held that courts of equity would generally not order the specific performance of a contract for the sale of a chattel. See McCallister v. Patton, 214 Ark. 293, 215 S.W.2d 701 (1948), and cases cited therein. There was an exception to this general rule where the goods or chattels had a peculiar, unique, or sentimental value to the buyer not measurable in money damages. See Morris v. Sparrow, 225 Ark. 1019, 287 S.W.2d 583 (1956).

Arkansas cases have recognized that a mobile home is goods and therefore covered by the provisions of the Uniform Commercial Code. The Uniform Commercial Code [Ark.Stat.Ann. § 85–2–716 (Add.1961)] provides that "[s]pecific performance may be decreed where the goods are unique or in other proper circumstances." . . .

There were no allegations or proof by appellees that this particular mobile home in question had a unique or peculiar value or that there were any circumstances requiring specific performance of the contract. Therefore, specific performance was not a proper remedy for the breach of this contract; but appellees are entitled to damages for its breach.

We hold that appellee should retain ownership to their lot at Fairfield Bay and we reverse and remand this case for the chancellor to determine appellees' damages for breach of the contract.

Reversed and remanded.

---

3 R. POUND, JURISPRUDENCE

§ 88 (1959).

In a developed economic order the claim to promised advantages is one of the most important of the individual interests that press for recognition. If it is a task of the legal order to secure reasonable individual expectations so far as they may be harmonized with the least friction and waste, in an economic order those arising from promises have a chief place. Credit is a principal form of wealth. It is a presupposition of the whole economic order that promises will be kept. Indeed, the matter goes deeper. The social order rests upon stability and predictability of conduct, of which keeping promises is a large item.

Comments and Questions

1. In light of the Pound view, why are courts, such as the Court of Appeals of Arkansas, reluctant to grant specific performance?

2. Do you agree with those reasons?

ADLER, BARISH, DANIELS, LEVIN & CRESKOFF
v. EPSTEIN

Supreme Court of Pennsylvania, 1978.
482 Pa. 416, 393 A.2d 1175.

ROBERTS, JUSTICE.

Appellant, the law firm of Adler, Barish, Daniels, Levin and Creskoff, filed a Complaint in Equity in the Court of Common Pleas of Philadelphia. It sought to enjoin appellees, former associates of Adler Barish, from interfering with existing contractual relationships between Adler Barish and its clients. The court of common pleas entered a final decree granting the requested relief, but a divided Superior Court dissolved the injunction and dismissed Adler Barish's complaint. We granted allowance of appeal. We now reverse and direct reinstatement of the decree of the court of common pleas.

From the formation of Adler Barish in February, 1976, through March of the next year, appellees were salaried associates of Adler Barish.[3] Appellees were under the supervision of Adler Barish partners, who directed appellees' work on cases which clients brought to the firm.

While still working for Adler Barish, appellees decided to form their own law firm and took several steps toward achieving their goal. They retained counsel to advise them concerning their business venture, sought and found office space, and early in March, 1977, signed a lease.

Shortly before leaving Adler Barish, appellees procured a line of $150,000 from First Pennsylvania Bank. As security, appellees furnished bank officials with a list of eighty-eight cases and their anticipated legal fees, several of which were higher than $25,000, and together exceeded $500,000. No case on the list, however, was appellees'. Rather, each case was an Adler Barish case on which appellees were working.

Appellee Alan Epstein's employment relationship with Adler Barish terminated on March 10, 1977. At his request, Epstein continued to use offices of Adler Barish until March 19. During this time, and through April 4, when Adler Barish filed its complaint, Epstein was engaged in an active campaign to procure business for his new law firm. He initiated contacts, by phone and in person, with clients of Adler Barish with open cases on which he had worked while a salaried employee. Epstein advised the Adler Barish clients that he was leaving the firm and that they could choose to be represented by him, Adler Barish, or any other firm or attorney.

Epstein's attempt to procure business on behalf of the firm did not stop with these contacts. He mailed to the clients form letters which could be used to discharge Adler Barish as counsel, name Epstein the client's new

---

3. In establishing Adler Barish, its partners brought with them approximately 1300 cases from their old law firm, Freedman, Borowsky and Lorry, in which they shared approximately half the profits, losses, and assets. The two firms later signed a writing whose terms gave Adler Barish custody and control over the 1300 files transferred, and preserved the financial interest partners of Adler Barish had before leaving the Freedman firm. Clients whose files were transferred became clients of Adler Barish. From March, 1976 to April, 1977, Adler Barish opened over six hundred new case files.

Appellees were salaried employees of the Freedman firm at the time Adler Barish was formed. Appellees left Freedman and went to work for Adler Barish.

counsel and create a contingent fee agreement. Epstein also provided clients with a stamped envelope addressed to Epstein. Appellees Richard Weisbord, Arnold Wolf, and Sanford Jablon, who left Adler Barish on April 1, 1977, were aware of Epstein's efforts to procure this business on behalf of their new firm and did not attempt to curtail them. Indeed, Weisbord and Wolf, upon leaving Adler Barish, also immediately began to seek business, as did Epstein, for the new firm. They too informed clients of Adler Barish of their plans and that the clients were free to discharge Adler Barish and retain Weisbord and Wolf in its stead. Their efforts continued until Adler Barish filed its complaint.

Thus, clients of Adler Barish served a dual purpose in appellees' effort to start their own law firm. First, while appellees still worked for Adler Barish, Adler Barish cases formed the basis for appellees' obtaining bank credit. Then, appellees, as they left Adler Barish, made a concentrated attempt to procure the cases which had been used to obtain credit.

On April 4, the court of common pleas granted Adler Barish preliminary relief, enjoining appellees' campaign to obtain the business of Adler Barish clients. One month later, on May 5, the court entered its final decree, which provided:

> [T]he defendants, ALAN B. EPSTEIN, RICHARD A. WEISBORD, ARNOLD J. WOLF and SANFORD I. JABLON, and all persons acting in concert with them or otherwise participating with them or acting in their aid or behalf, are permanently enjoined and restrained from contacting and/ or communicating with those persons who up to and including April 1, 1977, had active legal matters pending with and were represented by the law firm of ADLER, BARISH, DANIELS, LEVIN and CRESKOFF, except that:
>
> 1. Nothing in this Final Decree shall be construed to preclude the defendants from announcing the formation of their new professional relationship . . . .
>
> 2. Nothing in this Final Decree shall preclude those persons who, up to and including April 1, 1977, had active legal matters pending with and had been represented by the law firm of ADLER, BARISH, DANIELS, LEVIN and CRESKOFF from voluntarily discharging their present attorney and selecting any of the defendants, or any other attorney, to represent them.

The court concluded that appellees "engaged in illegal solicitation in complete and total disregard for the Code of Professional Responsibility" and thereby "tortiously interfered with the contractual and business relations that exist between Adler Barish and its clients." It found equitable relief appropriate in view of appellees' "avowed intentions . . . to continue their illegal solicitation."

Appellees appealed to the Superior Court, which reversed. In addition to granting Adler Barish's petition for allowance of appeal, we granted a stay and expedited argument.

[The court first concluded that appellees' conduct was not protected free speech under the First and Fourteenth amendments to the United States Constitution. The court reasoned that speech simply proposing a commercial transaction is protected, so that appellees could inform the general public, including Adler Barish clients, of their availability to perform legal services. Nevertheless, appellees could not attempt to induce Adler Barish clients to change law firms while their cases were active, at least not where appellees' "immediate personally created financial interest in the clients' decisions" posed a great risk that the clients could not make a "careful, informed decision."]

. . . [W]e turn to whether the court of common pleas properly concluded that Adler Barish is entitled to relief. In Birl v. Philadelphia Electric Co., 402 Pa. 297, 167 A.2d 472 (1961), this Court adopted Section 766 of Restatement of Torts and its definition of the right of action for intentional interference with existing contractual relations. There, we stated:

> At least since Lumley v. Gye (1853), 2 Ell. & Bl. 216, 1 Eng.Rul.Cas. 706, the common law has recognized an action in tort for an intentional, unprivileged interference with contractual relations. It is generally recognized that one has the right to pursue his business relations or employment free from interference on the part of other persons except where such interference is justified or constitutes an exercise of an absolute right: Restatement, Torts, § 766. The Special Note to comment m. in § 766 points out: "There are frequent expressions in judicial opinions that 'malice' is requisite for liability in the cases treated in this Section. But the context and course of decision make it clear that what is meant is not malice in the sense of ill will but merely purposeful interference without justification." Our cases are in accord . . . .

In its continuing effort to provide the judicial system orderly and accurate restatements of the common law, the American Law Institute has reviewed each section of the Restatement of Torts, including Section 766. Section 766 of the Restatement (Second) of Torts (Tent. Draft No. 23, 1977), states the Institute's present view of what constitutes the elements of the cause of action before us:

Intentional Interference with Performance of Contract by Third Person

> One who intentionally and improperly interferes with the performance of a contract (except a contract to marry) between another and a third person by inducing or otherwise causing the third person not to perform the contract, is subject to liability to the other for the pecuniary loss resulting to the other from the third person's failure to perform the contract.

This Court constantly seeks to harmonize common law rules, principles, and doctrines with modern perceptions of societal needs and responsibilities. Accordingly, we believe it appropriate to analyze this case in light of the approach fashioned by Restatement (Second).

An examination of this case in light of Restatement (Second) of Torts, § 766, reveals that the sole dispute is whether appellees' conduct is "improper." There is no doubt that appellees intentionally sought to interfere with performance of the contractual relations between Adler

Barish and its clients. While still at Adler Barish, appellees' behavior, particularly their use of expected fees from Adler Barish clients' cases, indicates appellees' desire to gain a segment of the firm's business. This pattern of conduct continued until the court of common pleas enjoined it. Indeed, appellees' intentional efforts to obtain a share of Adler Barish's business were successful. The record reveals that several clients signed the forms Epstein prepared on behalf of appellees notifying Adler Barish that the clients no longer wished the services of Adler Barish. Likewise, the record reveals that Adler Barish and its clients were parties to valid, existing contracts.

In assessing whether appellees' conduct is "improper," we bear in mind what this Court stated in Glenn v. Point Park College, [441 Pa. 474, 482, 272 A.2d 895, 899 (1971)], where we analyzed "privileges" in conjunction with the closely related right of action for intentional interference with prospective contract relations:

> The absence of privilege or justification in the tort under discussion is closely related to the element of intent. As stated by Harper & James, The Law of Torts, § 6.11, at 513–14: ". . . where, as in most cases, the defendant acts at least in part for the purpose of protecting some legitimate interest which conflicts with that of the plaintiff, a line must be drawn and the interests evaluated. This process results in according or denying a privilege which, in turn, determines liability." What is or is not privileged conduct in a given situation is not susceptible of precise definition. Harper & James refer in general to interferences which "are sanctioned by the 'rules of the game' which society has adopted," and to "the area of socially acceptable conduct which the law regards as privileged," id. at 510, 511, and treat the subject in detail in §§ 6.12 and 6.13. . . .

We find nothing in the " 'rules of the game' which society has adopted" which sanctions appellees' conduct. . . .

Appellees' conduct adversely affected more than the informed and reliable decisionmaking of Adler Barish clients with active cases. Their conduct also had an immediate impact upon Adler Barish. Adler Barish was prepared to continue to perform services for its clients and therefore could anticipate receiving compensation for the value of its efforts. Moreover, as we concluded in Richette v. Pennsylvania Railroad, 410 Pa. 6, 187 A.2d 910 (1963), Adler Barish's fee agreements with clients were a source of anticipated revenue protected from outside interference.

It is true that, upon termination of their employment relationship with Adler Barish, appellees were free to engage in their own business venture. But appellees' right to pursue their own business interests is not absolute. "[U]nless otherwise agreed, after the termination of the agency, the agent . . . has a duty to the principal not to take advantage of a still subsisting confidential relation created during the prior agency relation." Restatement (Second) of Agency, . . . § 396(d).

Appellees' contacts were possible because Adler Barish partners trusted appellees with the high responsibility of developing its clients' cases. From this position of trust and responsibility, appellees were able to gain knowledge of the details, and status, of each case to which appellees had been assigned. In the atmosphere surrounding appellees' departure, appellees' contacts unduly suggested a course of action for Adler Barish clients and unfairly prejudiced Adler Barish. No public interest is served in condoning use of confidential information which has these effects. Clients too easily may suffer in the end. . . .

Order of the Superior Court reversed and court of common pleas directed to reinstate its final decree. Each party pay own costs.

APPENDIX

Epstein sent the following cover letter:

> 404 South Camac Street
> Philadelphia, Pennsylvania 19147
> March 25, 1977

Re:

Dear

In confirmation of our recent conversation, I have terminated my association with the offices of Adler, Barish, Daniels, Levin and Creskoff and will be continuing in the practice of law in center city Philadelphia. As I explained, you have the right to determine who shall represent your interests and handle the above-captioned matter in the future. You may elect to be represented by my former office, me or any other attorney permitted to practice in this jurisdiction.

During our conversation, you expressed a desire to have me continue as your legal representative, and in recognition of your choice in this regard, I have enclosed two documents which must be signed and returned to me in the enclosed stamped, addressed envelope to effect this end. Copies of these documents are also enclosed for your records.

If you have any questions regarding these materials or any other matter, feel free to call me at KI 6–5223.

> Sincerely,
> Alan B. Epstein

ABE/ete
Enclosure

The Form discharging Adler Barish provides:

Messrs. Adler, Barish, Daniels,
   Levin & Creskoff
2nd Floor, Rohm & Haas Building
Sixth & Market Streets
Philadelphia, PA 19106

Re:

Gentlemen:

I have been advised that Alan B. Epstein, Esquire has terminated his association with your firm of attorneys and it has been carefully explained to me that I have the right to determine who shall represent me and handle the above-captioned matter.

This correspondence is to serve notice I hereby discharge the office of Adler, Barish, Daniels, Levin & Creskoff from any further representation of me whatsoever and request that the members of your firm and/or your employees or agents refrain from acting against my wishes in this regard or my interests in any way whatsoever.

This letter is to also serve as my notice and request that I want Alan B. Epstein to be my attorney in this matter, to keep or secure my file and all allied papers, and to handle this matter and represent me.

I further direct you to deliver immediately to my attorney, Alan B. Epstein, my entire file and all allied papers and to refrain further from any actions contrary to my attorney's wishes or directions in connection with this matter.

Very truly yours,

The following fee agreement was also sent to Adler Barish clients:

CONTINGENT FEE AGREEMENT

_____

Date

I (we) hereby constitute and appoint ALAN EPSTEIN as my (our) attorney to prosecute a claim for me (us) for _____ against all responsible parties, including, but not limited to _____. The claimant (deceased) is _____, and the cause of action arose on _____.

I (we) hereby agree that the compensation of my (our) attorney for services shall be determined as follows:

_____
_____
_____

I (we) hereby acknowledge receipt of a duplicate copy of this Contingent Fee Agreement.

_____   _____

Name   Name

_____   _____

Address   Address

[The dissenting opinion of Justice Manderino is omitted.]

———

Comments and Questions

1. How does _Adler, Barish_ demonstrate the legal consequences of contracts?
2. Is this different from the other cases in this subsection?

———

ii. Corporations

CRANSON v. IBM

Court of Appeals of Maryland, 1964.
234 Md. 477, 200 A.2d 33.

HORNEY, JUDGE.

On the theory that the Real Estate Service Bureau was neither a de jure nor a de facto corporation and that Albion C. Cranson, Jr., was a partner in the business conducted by the Bureau and as such was personally liable for debts, the International Business Machines Corporation brought this action against Cranson for the balance due on electric typewriters purchased by the Bureau. At the same time it moved for summary judgment and supported the motion by affidavit. In due course, Cranson filed a general issue plea and an affidavit in opposition to summary judgment in which he asserted in effect that the Bureau was a de facto corporation and that he was not personally liable for its debts.

The agreed statement of facts shows that in April 1961, Cranson was asked to invest in a new business corporation which was about to be created. Towards this purpose he met with other interested individuals and an attorney and agreed to purchase stock and become an officer and director. Thereafter, upon being advised by the attorney that the corporation had been formed under the laws of Maryland, he paid for and received a stock certificate evidencing ownership of shares in the corporation, and was shown the corporate seal and minute book. The business of the new venture was conducted as if it were a corporation, through corporate bank accounts, with auditors maintaining corporate books and records, and under a lease entered into by the corporation for the office from which it operated its business. Cranson was elected president and all transactions conducted by him for the corporation, including the dealings with I.B.M., were made as an officer of the corporation. At no time did he assume any personal obligation or pledge his individual credit to I.B.M. Due to an oversight on the part of the attorney, of which Cranson was not aware, the certificate of incorporation, which had been signed and acknowledged prior to May 1, 1961, was not filed until November 24, 1961. Between May 17 and November 8, the Bureau purchased eight typewriters from I.B.M., on account of which partial payments were made, leaving a balance due of $4,333.40, for which this suit was brought.

Although a question is raised as to the propriety of making use of a motion for summary judgment as the means of determining the issues presented by the pleadings, we think the motion was appropriate. Since there was no genuine dispute as to the material facts, the only question was whether I.B.M. was entitled to judgment as a matter of law. The trial court found that it was, but we disagree.

The fundamental question presented by the appeal is whether an officer of a defectively incorporated association may be subjected to personal liability under the circumstances of this case. We think not.

Traditionally, two doctrines have been used by the courts to clothe an officer of a defectively incorporated association with the corporate attribute of limited liability. The first, often referred to as the doctrine of de facto corporations, has been applied in those cases where there are elements showing: (1) the existence of law authorizing incorporation; (2) an effort in good faith to incorporate under the existing law; and (3) actual use or exercise of corporate powers. Ballantine, Private Corporations, § 23; 8 Fletcher, Cyclopedia of the Law of Private Corporations, § 3777; 13 Am.Jur., Corporations, §§ 49–56; 18 C.J.S. Corporations § 99. The second, the doctrine of estoppel to deny the corporate existence, is generally employed where the person seeking to hold the officer personally liable has contracted or otherwise dealt with the association in such a manner as to recognize and in effect admit its existence as a corporate body. Ballantine, op. cit., § 29; Machen, Modern Law of Corporations, §§ 278–282; 18 C.J.S. op. cit. § 109.

It is not at all clear what Maryland has done with respect to the two doctrines. There have been no recent cases in this State on the subject and some of the seemingly irreconcilable earlier cases offer little to clarify the problem. . . .

. . . There is, as we see it, a wide difference between creating a corporation by means of the de facto doctrine and estopping a party, due to his conduct in a particular case, from setting up the claim of no incorporation. Although some cases tend to assimilate the doctrines of incorporation de facto and by estoppel each is a distinct theory and they are not dependent on one another in their application. See 8 Fletcher, op. cit., § 3763; France on Corporations (2nd ed.), § 29; 18 C.J.S. op. cit. § 111h. Where there is a concurrence of the three elements necessary for the application of the de facto corporation doctrine, there exists an entity which is a corporation de jure against all persons but the state. On the other hand, the estoppel theory is applied only to the facts of each particular case and may be invoked even where there is no corporation de facto. Accordingly, even though one or more of the requisites of a de facto corporation are absent, we think that this factor does not preclude the application of the estoppel doctrine in a proper case, such as the one at bar.

I.B.M. contends that the failure of the Bureau to file its certificate of incorporation debarred *all* corporate existence. But, in spite of the fact that the omission might have prevented the Bureau from being either a corporation de jure or de facto, we think that I.B.M. having dealt with the Bureau as if it were a corporation and relied on its credit rather than that of Cranson, is estopped to assert that the Bureau was not incorporated at the time the typewriters were purchased. In 1 Clark and Marshall, Private Corporations, § 89, it is stated:

> The doctrine in relation to estoppel is based upon the ground that it would generally be inequitable to permit the corporate existence of an association to be denied by persons who have represented it to be a corporation, or held it out as a corporation, or by any persons who have recognized it as a corporation by dealing with it as such; and by the overwhelming weight of authority, therefore, a person may be estopped to deny the legal incorporation of an association which is not even a corporation de facto.

In cases similar to the one at bar, involving a failure to file articles of incorporation, the courts of other jurisdictions have held that where one has recognized the corporate existence of an association, he is estopped to assert the contrary with respect to a claim arising out of such dealings.

Since I.B.M. is estopped to deny the corporate existence of the Bureau, we hold that Cranson was not liable for the balance due on account of the typewriters.

Judgment reversed; the appellee to pay the costs.

A. CONARD, CORPORATIONS IN PERSPECTIVE
147–48 (1976).*

The principal behavioral difference between corporate and noncorporate enterprise is that the former have filed papers in a governmental office declaring themselves to be corporations, while the latter have not. From this follow important legal differences which the state attaches to this minor ceremony. The best known, and probably the most nearly universal, relates to the liability of the owners' individual assets—those which are not employed by or appropriated to the enterprise—for enterprise debts. Even this difference is not invariable. As Dodd's study shows, shareholders of corporations in the first years of the United States were frequently liable without limit for the enterprise debts. In most states, bank shareholders retained individual liability up to an amount equal to the par value of their shares until the 1930's. In New York and Michigan, shareholders remained liable for labor debts into the 1930's; some of them still do.

Another prevalent difference which follows from the paper-filing is a different regime of taxation. In the United States, corporations normally pay property tax on their properties and income tax on their profits, while their shareholders pay property taxes on their interests in the corporation and income taxes on their dividends from it; there is a "double taxation." In sole proprietorships and partnerships, only the owners are taxed; there is no separate tax on the enterprise. But this difference is extremely variable. Enterprises which are partnerships for purposes of private law may be treated as corporations under tax law. Moreover, the U.S. tax laws have occasionally permitted corporations to be taxed under the partnership regime, and partnerships to be taxed under the corporation regime, by their own choice.

In other attributes, the difference between corporate and noncorporate enterprise have shrunk to almost nothing. Since Roman times, it has been said that corporations exist only by act of the state. But the state now does nothing except require the filing of papers. This change is recognized in the terminology of the Delaware and New York statutes which provide that the "certificate of incorporation" is not issued by the state; it is composed and subscribed by the founders, and the state merely marks it "filed." This is hardly more than the business name which must be filed in many states by all partnerships, and by sole proprietors who adopt a business name differing from their personal name.

For years it was said that partnerships could not sue or be sued in their business name, as a corporation must be. But statutes in most states now permit them to litigate under firm names just like corporations.

Secondary Techniques for Facilitating Private Arrangements

The preceding materials in this section examined the primary techniques of law as an instrument of private arrangements. The law also facilitates private arrangements in less direct or in secondary ways. For example, the law assists private parties in obtaining information necessary to enter private arrangements. Governmental market and weather reports, requirements of full disclosure in certain dealings, and land registries are illustrative. Laws that provide for and protect a uniform monetary system or a system of weights and measures are additional examples of secondary facilitation.

Private arrangements also depend on the other legal instrumentalities studied in this book for secondary support. Public-benefit conferral, such as the creation of highway, communication, and educational systems, obviously facilitates private arrangements. Administrative rules such as those regulating interstate commerce and anticompetitive behavior are facilitative also. In addition, the grievance-remedial and penal-corrective modes ensure that people can be secure in person and property.

Section Three.   Authorized Makers of Private-Arrangement Law and Their Appropriate Collaborative Roles

In this section, we shall consider the roles of private persons (sometimes lawyers, sometimes not), legislatures, and courts—and the relationships among them—in making private-arrangement law.

A. Private Persons

Most private arrangements are made by individuals, either with the aid of lawyers or without them, and are completed without the intervention of courts or others. For example, if you agree to mow your neighbor's lawn each Thursday during July and August for fifteen dollars per week, chances are that your agreement will be carried out without dispute. Even when a dispute does arise, you and your customer may be expected to refer to your agreement as a basis for your respective positions ("we agreed on Thursdays, not Wednesdays") and to settle the dispute voluntarily without resort to court action. The "law" of your private arrangement is thus found in your agreement (or in your will, articles of incorporation, club bylaws, or whatever). For this reason, we say that private persons make their own private arrangements.

Let us now closely examine a group of persons making private arrangements. First you should review the Oregon Revised Statutes set forth supra p. 561.

ARTICLES OF INCORPORATION

The University of Oregon Portland Alumni, Incorporated

We, D. DONALD LONIE, JR., CORLAND P. MOBLEY, and WALTER E. HOLMAN, JR., whose names are hereunto subscribed, desiring to form a corporation under and by virtue of Chapter 61, Title 7, Oregon Revised Statutes, which provides for the creation of nonprofit corporations, do hereby make and execute the following articles of incorporation, to wit:

Article I

The name assumed by this corporation and by which it shall be known is The University of Oregon Portland Alumni, Incorporated, and its duration shall be perpetual.

Article II

The purposes for which this corporation is organized are as follows:

To sponsor activities designed to provide funds for the University of Oregon Development Fund and other projects or programs benefiting the University of Oregon and its alumni;

To sponsor programs designed to improve the quality and number of students attending the University of Oregon;

To sponsor athletic events in Portland, Oregon, including an indoor track and field meet;

To sponsor social events for the benefit of the University of Oregon alumni;

To sponsor any other programs or projects designed to promote the interests and increase the usefulness of the University of Oregon and its alumni.

(No part of the income derived from the above-described activities and events shall be distributable to the members, directors, or officers of this corporation.)

Article III

The members of this corporation shall consist of one class and shall be the members of the University of Oregon Alumni Association, residing in the Portland metropolitan area, each of whom shall be entitled to one vote in electing directors of the corporation. Members of this corporation shall have no other voting rights or privileges. No certificates evidencing membership shall be issued by this corporation. Notice of annual or special meetings of the members shall be given to the members by including such notice in an issue of Old Oregon (a bimonthly publication of the University of Oregon Alumni Association), mailed not less than seven nor more than fifty days before the meeting date.

Article IV

The estimated value of the property and money possessed by this corporation at the time of executing these articles of incorporation is four hundred dollars ($400), and its revenue shall be derived from sponsorship of educational, social, and athletic activities in Portland, Oregon.

Article V

The names and the post-office addresses of the persons executing these articles are:

D. Donald Lonie, Jr.	4365 S.W. Fraser Avenue Portland, Oregon
Corland P. Mobley	12437 S.W. 62nd Avenue Portland 19, Oregon
Walter E. Holman, Jr.	595 S.E. Andover Place Portland 2, Oregon

The governing body of this corporation shall be the board of directors, which shall consist of nine elected members and two ex officio nonvoting members. One ex officio member shall be the University of Oregon alumni secretary, and the other ex officio member shall be the president of the Oregon Duck Club, and these officers and their successors in office shall serve on the board of directors of this corporation during the terms of their respective offices.

The initial board of directors shall consist of the following present members of the board of directors of that association known as the Portland Alumni Association of the University of Oregon (together with the above-named ex officio members) and their terms shall expire on the dates of the annual membership meetings held in the years set forth below. . . .

Article VI

Upon any dissolution of this corporation, all liabilities and obligations of the corporation shall be paid, satisfied, and discharged, or adequate provision shall be made therefor, and all remaining assets, if any, shall be transferred or conveyed to the University of Oregon Development Fund, or if such fund is not then in existence, then to the University of Oregon.

Article VII

The address of the registered office of this corporation shall be:

The University of Oregon Portland Alumni, Incorporated
1200 American Bank Building
621 S.W. Morrison Street
Portland 5, Oregon

The address of the registered agent of the corporation shall be:

Mr. Robert S. Summers
1200 American Bank Building
621 S.W. Morrison Street
Portland 5, Oregon

IN WITNESS WHEREOF, we have hereunto set our hands, this 5th day of August, 1960.

D. Donald Lonie, Jr.

Corland P. Mobley

Walter E. Holman, Jr.
Incorporators

BYLAWS

The University of Oregon Portland Alumni, Incorporated

Article I: Membership

§ 1. Eligibility of members. The members of this corporation shall consist of one class and shall be the members of the University of Oregon Alumni Association residing in the Portland metropolitan area. No certificates evidencing membership shall be issued by this corporation.

§ 2. Voting rights of members. Each member shall be entitled to one vote in electing directors of the corporation. Members of this corporation shall have no other voting rights or privileges. . . .

Article III: Powers and action of the board of directors

§ 1. Powers. The governing body of this corporation shall be the board of directors. The board of directors, by resolution adopted by a majority of the directors in office, may designate and appoint one or more committees, each of whom shall consist of two or more directors, which committees, to the extent provided in such resolution, shall have and exercise the authority of the board of directors in the management of any or all the affairs of the corporation.

§ 2. Quorum. Directors present at a meeting of the board of directors shall constitute a quorum; but in no event shall a quorum consist of less than one-third of the number of elected directors. The action of a majority of the directors present at a meeting at which a quorum is present shall constitute action of the board of directors.

§ 3. Action by directors without a meeting. Any action which may be taken at a meeting of the directors may be taken without a meeting if a consent in writing setting forth the action so taken shall be signed by all the directors. Such consent shall have the same force and effect as a unanimous vote. . . .

MINUTES OF ORGANIZATION MEETING
Board of Directors
The University of Oregon Portland Alumni, Incorporated

The organization meeting of the board of directors of The University of Oregon Portland Alumni, Incorporated, was held August 10, 1960, at 2:00 p.m., at the Congress Hotel, Portland, Oregon, pursuant to call of the incorporators and pursuant to waiver of notice and consent of all the directors.

There were present the following directors of the corporation:

D. Donald Lonie, Jr.
C.P. Mobley
Mrs. Robert J. Koch
Mrs. Edward T. Parry
Mrs. Joseph D. Montag
Walter E. Holman, Jr.
Robert S. Summers
James W. Frost
Charles N. Covey

The following directors were absent:

Albert R. Bullier, Jr.
Marvin D. Butterfield

James W. Frost was selected chairman, and Mrs. Robert J. Koch was selected secretary of the meeting.

The chairman declared the next order of business to be the adoption of bylaws of the corporation. Upon motion duly made and seconded, the following resolution was unanimously adopted:

RESOLVED that the following bylaws be and the same hereby are adopted as the bylaws of this corporation. . . .

The chairman declared the next order of business to be the election of officers of the corporation to serve until the first annual meeting of the members and until their successors are elected. Thereupon, the following persons were elected to the offices set opposite their respective names:

D. Donald Lonie, Jr.	President
C.P. Mobley	Vice-president
Mrs. Robert J. Koch	Secretary
Albert R. Bullier, Jr.	Treasurer.

. . . .

The chairman then declared that the board of directors should resolve to assume sponsorship of those activities and functions heretofore sponsored by that organization known as the Portland Alumni Association of the University of Oregon. Upon motion duly made and seconded, the following resolution was unanimously adopted:

RESOLVED that this corporation assume sponsorship of those activities and functions heretofore sponsored by that organization known as the "Portland Alumni Association of the University of Oregon."

The chairman proposed that the board of directors consider sponsorship of an indoor track and field meet at the Memorial Coliseum in Portland, Oregon, on January 14, 1961. After a discussion of the proposal and upon motion duly made and seconded, the following resolutions were unanimously adopted:

RESOLVED that this corporation sponsor an indoor track and field meet at the Memorial Coliseum in Portland, Oregon, on January 14, 1961.

RESOLVED FURTHER that D. Donald Lonie, Jr., C.P. Mobley, and Robert S. Summers be empowered to commence negotiations with the general manager of the Memorial Coliseum for a contract, the same to be presented to the board of directors for discussion and approval prior to the signing thereof.

RESOLVED FURTHER that the president appoint a committee of directors to negotiate for the purchase of an indoor track and other necessary facilities.

RESOLVED FURTHER that the president appoint a committee of directors to secure necessary financial support for the purchase of said track and facilities. . . .

The chairman then proposed that the board consider adoption of a resolution providing for the retention of an attorney as counsel for the corporation. After discussion and upon motion duly made and seconded, the following resolutions were adopted:

RESOLVED that Robert S. Summers be retained as attorney for this corporation upon the basis that, if the track and field meet to be sponsored annually by this corporation is financially successful, this corporation shall pay said Robert S. Summers the usual fees for legal services performed by him for this corporation, but that, if said meet is not financially successful, this corporation shall pay said Robert S. Summers only a nominal fee for said legal services.

The chairman then opened for discussion the question whether the corporation should retain someone to promote the track and field meet and to supervise the budget therefor. Without arriving at a decision on this question, and upon motion duly made and seconded, the meeting was adjourned.

_____

Secretary

_____

Mr. Donald Jewell
General Manager
Memorial Coliseum
Portland, Oregon

> Subject: Lease of Memorial Coliseum for sponsorship of track and field meet January 14, 1961 by The University of Oregon Portland Alumni, Incorporated

Dear Mr. Jewell:

You have requested that the following terms and conditions of the subject lease be provided for in letter form. Please signify agreement hereto by appropriate signature as provided for on the final page hereof.

THIS AGREEMENT, IN ADDITION TO AND IN MODIFICATION OF a lease agreement made and entered into this _____ by and between the EXPOSITION–RECREATION COMMISSION of the City of Portland, acting by its General Manager, (hereinafter referred to as Coliseum), and the University of Oregon Portland Alumni, Incorporated, an Oregon nonprofit corporation, (hereinafter referred to as Lessee), Coliseum and Lessee FURTHER AGREE AS FOLLOWS:

I

That the entire agreement for the lease of the Memorial Coliseum (hereinafter referred to as the premises) is embodied in two documents: this letter and the lease form entitled LEASE to which this letter is attached (hereinafter referred to as Lease Form), and that insofar as any provisions of these two documents may be construed to be in conflict the provisions embodied in this letter shall be controlling;

II

That Lessee shall have the right at its option to lease the premises annually during the months of January, February, and March for the purpose of conducting track and field meets therein; that Lessee shall notify Coliseum by letter of its intention to exercise said right not later than three months prior to January 1 of each year during which Lessee intends to conduct said meets; that if Lessee notifies Coliseum of its intention to exercise said right, Coliseum agrees to make available to Lessee dates during the months of January or February or March for the conducting of said meets which are reasonably suitable to Lessee; Lessee shall designate dates for said meets no later than two months prior to January 1 of each year in which Lessee intends to conduct a meet or meets; and, Coliseum shall not, without Lessee's consent, lease its premises to any other party for the purpose of conducting a track and field meet therein or a track meet therein on any date within sixty days prior and within sixty days subsequent to any date selected by Lessee for the conducting of a track and field meet in that year; . . .

V

January 14, 1961 Meet:

1. That, notwithstanding any part of provisions 3, 4, 9, and 14 of Lease Form which may be construed to the contrary, Lessee assumes no responsibility whatsoever for the acts or conduct of any person or persons on the premises who is acting pursuant to the supervision and control of the Coliseum, whether or not said person or persons are on the premises with the consent of Lessee and whether or not said person or persons are acting for or on behalf of Lessee, and whether or not said person or persons ultimately receive salaries or wages from Lessee for work performed on the premises;

2. That Lessee shall pay $1125.00 or 10% gross proceeds, (less federal taxes), whichever is greater, for rental of the Memorial Coliseum, necessary heating and lighting thereof, loudspeaker equipment, the services of one watchman, and cleanup of said building; . . . .

IN WITNESS WHEREOF, EXPOSITION–RECREATION COMMISSION of the City of Portland has caused these presents to be signed by its General Manager, and the LESSEE has signed the same in duplicate the day and year first hereinabove written.

EXPOSITION–RECREATION   THE UNIVERSITY OF OREGON
COMMISSION   PORTLAND ALUMNI,
                                     INCORPORATED

By: _____   _____
      General Manager   President

                        _____

AGREEMENT FOR CONSTRUCTION AND PURCHASE
OF TRACK

THIS AGREEMENT, made and entered into this _____ day of _____ 1960, by and between THE UNIVERSITY OF OREGON PORTLAND ALUMNI, INCORPORATED, (hereinafter referred to as "Purchaser"), and Ralph Parr, Morven C. Thomas, Gerald S. Moshofsky, Jack S. Thomas, and Joyce A. Dion consisting of a general partnership doing business by the name and style of WOOD COMPONENTS COMPANY, of Eugene, Oregon,

WITNESSETH:

That whereas Purchaser is a non-profit corporation which has contracted with the EXPOSITION–RECREATION COMMISSION of the City of Portland, Oregon to conduct an indoor track and field meet on January 14, 1961 in the Memorial Coliseum located in said city,

That whereas Purchaser desires to have constructed and to buy an oval type indoor running track, an indoor dash track, a pole vault runway and pit, and a broad jump runway and pit, and

Whereas Builder is willing and able to build said tracks and said other facilities,

NOW THEREFORE, it is agreed by and between the parties as follows:

I

That Builder shall procure necessary materials and construct said tracks and said other facilities,

II

That Builder shall substantially complete construction of said oval type running track not later than December 1, 1960, and that Builder shall complete construction of said dash track and said other facilities not later than December 24, 1960,

III

That Builder shall construct said tracks and said other facilities in accordance with (1) a drawing prepared by John E. Stafford, architect, a copy of which is attached hereto, marked exhibit A, and by this reference specifically made a part hereof, and (2) further specifications as follows: Builder shall, if required by Purchaser, place coatings of rubber and asphalt on said pole vault and broad jump runways, and shall provide necessary materials therefor,

Provided However, that if either John E. Stafford or William J. Bowerman determines that either of said tracks or any of said other facilities is unsuitable though the same conform to the aforesaid specifications, Builder shall be required to reconstruct the same in such manner as to be suitable to the aforesaid John E. Stafford and William J. Bowerman, and to the extent that the costs of such reconstruction are significant Purchaser shall reimburse Builder for such costs, . . .

VII

That Purchaser shall pay Builder $9,100.00 for the aforesaid tracks suitably completed, and

That Purchaser shall pay Builder $1,729.44 for the aforesaid other facilities when suitably completed, provided however, that if Builder is required to place coatings of rubber and asphalt on the surface of the pole vault and broad jump runways Purchaser shall pay Builder an additional $300.00 therefor, ...

IN WITNESS WHEREOF, Purchaser has caused these presents to be signed by its President, and Builder has caused the same to be signed by its duly authorized agent the day and year first hereinabove written:

THE UNIVERSITY OF OREGON   WOOD COMPONENTS
PORTLAND ALUMNI,   COMPANY
INCORPORATED

By: _____   _____
     D. Donald Lonie, Jr., President

THE KIWI AND KID

Sports Illustrated, Jan. 23, 1961, at 9.

Inspired by the completion of the Portland Memorial Coliseum, a glass-and-concrete-and-steel arena with 9,000 theater-type cushion seats, a group of University of Oregon alumni raised $21,000 and last Saturday night put on the first indoor track meet in the Northwest in 21 years. The group—called the Nervous Nine when only $8,000 in advance sales came in—had the foresight to enlist Oregon's Bill Bowerman, one of America's outstanding track coaches, as meet director.

"We figured we had to have at least three really outstanding events," Bowerman said, "so we tried for six." He got all six, and the meet was a success—financially, because more than 7,000 spectators poured in on Saturday night to cover the expenses, and artistically, because a calm, thin Olympic champion named Murray Halberg flew 7,000 miles from his native New Zealand to run a two-mile race indoors in 8:34.3—faster, by nearly 12 seconds, than anyone had ever run it indoors before.

B. Legislatures

Consider once again the Oregon Revised Statutes set forth previously. These rules, adopted by the state legislature of Oregon, dictate the manner in which the corporate arrangement may be accomplished (rules of validation). Legislatures may also specify remedies for departures from private arrangements and adopt rules prohibiting certain kinds of agreements. Uniform Commercial Code § 2–716, set forth earlier in *Pierce-Odom, Inc.* v. *Evenson,* is an example of the former, and the Sherman Antitrust Act, 15 U.S.C. §§ 1–7, prohibiting certain contracts in restraint of trade, is an example of the latter. Legislatures may also enact rules of disclosure, such as consumer protection legislation requiring disclosure of rates of interest, and rules attaching certain legal consequences to an arrangement, such as the support duties of a spouse.

Legislatures influence private-arrangement law in less direct ways as well, as suggested by J. Mashaw & R. Merrill, An Introduction to the American Public Law System 936 (1975):

> [W]ith the proliferation of public regulatory legislation in this century it would be surprising if judges had not increasingly looked to statutes, and to the legal principles they were perceived as embodying, in the course of resolving essentially private disputes. The introduction of public regulation is, after all, premised on the notion that private transactions, and the supportive structure of tort, contract, and property law that makes them possible, are inadequate to accomplish desired social goals. A regulatory statute may therefore be viewed by courts as altering the social presuppositions upon which the private law has developed, although the statute makes no explicit change in the private legal order or that part of it directly relevant to decision of a particular case.

C. Courts

Through case decisions, the judiciary promulgates rules of validation and rules specifying the legal consequences of private arrangements. We have seen, for example, that the rules of offer and acceptance and of consideration in making a contract are judge-made. We have also seen that the rules of general and consequential damages for breach of contract are pronounced in judicial decisions.

Two additional functions of the courts in making private-arrangement law are interpreting legislation and interpreting the language of parties' private arrangements.

————

RIGGS v. PALMER

Court of Appeals of New York, 1889.
115 N.Y. 506, 22 N.E. 188.

EARL, J. On the 13th day of August, 1880, Francis B. Palmer made his last will and testament, in which he gave small legacies to his two daughters, Mrs. Riggs and Mrs. Preston, the plaintiffs in this action, and the remainder of his estate to his grandson, the defendant Elmer E. Palmer, subject to the support of Susan Palmer, his mother, with a gift over to the two daughters, subject to the support of Mrs. Palmer, in case Elmer should survive him and die under age, unmarried, and without any issue. The testator, at the date of his will, owned a farm, and considerable personal property. He was a widower, and thereafter, in March, 1882, he was married to Mrs. Bresee, with whom, before his marriage, he entered into an antenuptial contract, in which it was agreed that in lieu of dower and all other claims upon his estate in case she survived him she should have her support upon his farm during her life, and such support was expressly charged upon the farm. At the date of the will, and subsequently to the death of the testator, Elmer lived with him as a member of his family, and at his death was 16 years old. He knew of the provisions made in his favor in the will, and, that he might prevent his grandfather from revoking such provisions, which he had manifested some intention to do, and to obtain the speedy enjoyment and immediate possession of his property, he willfully murdered him by poisoning him. He now claims the property, and the sole question for our determination is, can he have it? . . .

What could be more unreasonable than to suppose that it was the legislative intention in the general laws passed for the orderly, peaceable, and just devolution of property that they should have operation in favor of one who murdered his ancestor that he might speedily come into the possession of his estate? Such an intention is inconceivable. We need not, therefore, be much troubled by the general language contained in the laws. Besides, all laws, as well as all contracts, may be controlled in their operation and effect by general, fundamental maxims of the common law. No one shall be permitted to profit by his own fraud, or to take advantage of his own wrong, or to found any claim upon his own iniquity, or to acquire property by his own crime. These maxims are dictated by public policy, have their foundation in universal law administered in all civilized countries, and have nowhere been superseded by statutes. . . .

. . . It was evidently supposed that the maxims of the common law were sufficient to regulate such a case, and that a specific enactment for the purpose was not needed. For the same reasons the defendant Palmer cannot take any of this property as heir. Just before the murder he was not an heir, and it was not certain that he ever would be. He might have died before his grandfather, or might have been disinherited by him. He made himself an heir by the murder, and he seeks to take property as the fruit of his crime. What has before been said as to him as legatee applies to him with equal force as an heir. He cannot vest himself with title by crime. My view of this case does not inflict upon Elmer any greater or other punishment for his crime than the law specifies. It takes from him no property, but simply holds that he shall not acquire property by his crime, and thus be rewarded for its commission.

[Elmer Palmer was enjoined from using any of the property left by Francis Palmer to Elmer, the will was declared ineffective to pass title to him, and he was deprived of any interest in the estate.]

GRAY, J., (dissenting). . . . [I]f I believed that the decision of the question could be affected by considerations of an equitable nature, I should not hesitate to assent to views which commend themselves to the conscience. But the matter does not lie within the domain of conscience. We are bound by the rigid rules of law, which have been established by the legislature, and within the limits of which the determination of this question is confined. The question we are dealing with is whether a testamentary disposition can be altered, or a will revoked, after the testator's death, through an appeal to the courts, when the legislature has by its enactments prescribed exactly when and how wills may be made, altered, and revoked, and apparently, as it seems to me, when they have been fully complied with, has left no room for the exercise of an equitable jurisdiction by courts over such matters. . . .

The statutes of this state have prescribed various ways in which a will may be altered or revoked; but the very provision defining the modes of alteration and revocation implies a prohibition of alteration or revocation in any other way. The words of the section of the statute are: "No will in writing, except in the cases hereinafter mentioned, nor any part thereof, shall be revoked or altered otherwise," etc. Where, therefore, none of the cases mentioned are met by the facts, and the revocation is not in the way described in the section, the will of the testator is unalterable. . . .

I cannot find any support for the argument that [Elmer's] succession to the property should be avoided because of his criminal act, when the laws are silent. Public policy does not demand it; for the demands of public policy are satisfied by the proper execution of the laws and the punishment of the crime. . . . The appellants' argument practically amounts to this: that, as the legatee has been guilty of a crime, by the commission of which he is placed in a position to sooner receive the benefits of the testamentary provision, his rights to the property should be forfeited, and he should be divested of his estate. To allow their argument to prevail would involve the diversion by the court of the testator's estate into the hands of persons whom, possibly enough, for all we know, the testator might not have chosen or desired as its recipients. Practically the court is asked to make another will for the testator. . . .

DANFORTH, J., concurs [in dissent].

––––––––––

A century after *Riggs* v. *Palmer*, a husband shot and killed his wife and from prison claimed $25,000 from his wife's estate and life insurance policy. The husband had been convicted of second-degree manslaughter. The New York Times, Apr. 29, 1984, § 1, at 42, col. 1, reported that the surrogate "ruled that the policy set in the *Palmer* case was still applicable. Even though second-degree manslaughter is a lesser offence [involving recklessness rather than intent], it is still punishable by 15 years in prison—and, therefore, it is 'within the category of such iniquity that its perpetrator should be precluded from profiting from his course of conduct.'"

ERMOLIEFF v. RKO RADIO PICTURES, INC.

Supreme Court of California, 1942.
19 Cal.2d 543, 122 P.2d 3.

CARTER, JUSTICE.

Plaintiff and defendant are producers and distributors in the motion picture industry. Plaintiff was the owner and producer of a foreign language motion picture entitled "Michael Strogoff," based on a novel by Jules Verne, which prior to July 6, 1936, he had produced in the German and French languages. On that date the parties entered into a contract in which plaintiff granted to defendant the exclusive right to produce and distribute an English version of that picture in only those "countries or territories of the world" listed on an exhibit annexed to the contract. On the exhibit is listed among other places "The United Kingdom." Plaintiff reserved the rights in the picture in both foreign and English languages in all countries or territories not listed in the exhibit. The contract was modified in December, 1936, and September, 1937, to add other countries or territories to the list. Plaintiff commenced the instant action on May 8, 1940, pleading the contract and its modifications and alleging that defendant had produced an English version of the picture under the title "Soldier and a Lady" in the United States and elsewhere; and that a controversy had arisen between the parties as to the countries and territories granted to defendant and those reserved by plaintiff under the contract and its modifications. Those allegations were admitted by defendant and it alleges that the only controversy between the parties is with respect to the area referred to as "The United Kingdom"; that the only dispute is whether "The United Kingdom," in which the contract grants rights to defendant, includes Eire or the Irish Free State; and that there is a custom and usage in the motion picture industry that that term does include Eire and that such usage is a part of the contract. Both the complaint and the answer pray for declaratory relief, namely, a declaration of their rights with respect to those areas embraced in the contract which are in dispute.

It was stipulated that the sole issue with respect to the territory embraced in the contract was whether defendant or plaintiff held the rights in the picture in Eire, which in turn depended upon whether The United Kingdom included Eire; that defendant did distribute the picture in Eire, and that The United Kingdom, from a political and legal viewpoint, did not include Eire, the latter being independent from it. . . .

Defendant asserts, however, that the judgment must be reversed because of the granting of plaintiff's motion to strike defendant's evidence that according to the custom and usage of the moving picture industry Eire is included in The United Kingdom. With that contention we agree. Both plaintiff and defendant are engaged in the business of producing and distributing moving pictures and rights in connection therewith. Defendant's evidence consisted of the testimony of several witnesses familiar with the distribution of motion pictures to the effect that in contracts covering the rights to produce pictures the general custom and usage was that the term "The United Kingdom" included Eire, the Irish Free State. Plaintiff's motion to strike out all of that evidence on the ground that it was incompetent, irrelevant and immaterial was granted. Plaintiff, reserving his objection to defendant's evidence, offered contrary evidence concerning such custom and usage.

The correct rule with reference to the admissibility of evidence as to trade usage under the circumstances here presented is that while words in a contract are ordinarily to be construed according to their plain, ordinary, popular or legal meaning, as the case may be, yet if in reference to the subject matter of the contract, particular expressions have by trade usage acquired a different meaning, and both parties are engaged in that trade, the parties to the contract are deemed to have used them according to their different and peculiar sense as shown by such trade usage. Parol evidence is admissible to establish the trade usage, and that is true even though the words are in their ordinary or legal meaning entirely unambiguous, inasmuch as by reason of the usage the words are used by the parties in a different sense. The basis of this rule is that to accomplish a purpose of paramount importance in interpretation of documents, namely, to ascertain the true intent of the parties, it may well be said that the usage evidence does not alter the contract of the parties, but on the contrary gives the effect to the words there used as intended by the parties. The usage becomes a part of the contract in aid of its correct interpretation. . . .

The judgment is reversed.

————

H. JONES, E. FARNSWORTH & W. YOUNG, CASES AND MATERIALS ON CONTRACTS
260 (1965).*

To what extent are the rules and techniques for the interpretation of other kinds of legal writings applicable to contracts? Consider contracts, statutes and wills. In each case an "intention" is sought—that of the parties in the case of a contract, that of the legislature in the case of a statute, and that of the testator in the case of a will. Is it significant that there are two contracting parties but only one legislature and only one testator? Does the existence of a bicameral legislature pose the same kinds of problems as to intention that the existence of two contracting parties poses? Is it significant that when a dispute over interpretation arises parties to the contract are usually available to testify as to their intention, whereas testators are not? Is there a difference in the care ordinarily used in the drafting of contracts, statutes and wills? If so, should this affect their interpretation? Compare an oral contract with the Uniform Commercial Code; compare an oil concession agreement between a large American company and a foreign government with a state statute for the protection of fur-bearing animals. Are there important differences in the numbers of people affected by interpretation? Compare a contract for the sale of a private home with the Internal Revenue Code; compare a standard insurance policy with a private bill to compensate an injured person for damages caused by a state employee. How probable is it that an interpretation in one case will be followed in like future cases involving the same language contained in a contract? a statute? a will? If the court's interpretation did not, in fact, accord with the appropriate intention, how easy a matter is it to make appropriate changes to govern future disputes in the case of contracts? statutes? wills?

PENNYRILE TOURS, INC. v. COUNTRY INNS, USA, INC.

United States District Court, Eastern District of Tennessee, 1982.
559 F.Supp. 15.

ROBERT L. TAYLOR, CHIEF JUDGE.

This is an action for refund of cash deposits paid for room reservations during the 1982 World's Fair. The Court has listened carefully to each witness who has testified during the trial. The Court has examined each of the exhibits which have been filed and now makes and adopts the following findings of fact and conclusions of law:

In December 1981 the defendant, Country Inns, USA, Inc., mailed a brochure to the plaintiff, Pennyrile Tours, Inc., advertising that defendant was accepting reservations at its modern facilities at three locations in Sevier County, Tennessee. The brochure was not in any way solicited by the plaintiff.

Subsequent to receipt of the brochure, plaintiff orally contracted for various group room reservations with the defendant by telephone and was required to pay advance deposits totalling $10,720.00. Defendant represented that its facilities would be completed well before May 1982, the opening day of the 1982 World's Fair. At this time there was no discussion between the parties of a cancellation policy. Plaintiff's first reservations were for May 16 and May 17, 1982.

Subsequent to the telephone conversation between the parties, plaintiff received written confirmation of room reservations on the dates requested at each of defendant's three locations. Subsequent to the receipt of confirmation of room reservations, the plaintiff mailed checks at various times which totalled $10,720.00 to the defendant as deposits for room reservations.

The Court is convinced from the testimony of Mr. Rick Etherson that there is an industry-wide custom and standard used in the motel business for a refund of reservation deposits. A refund is made if reservations are cancelled at least 30 days prior to the reserved dates.

On or about March 27, 1982, representatives of plaintiff inspected the facilities advertised by the defendant. The facilities were not near completion as of that date, as the defendant had previously represented they would be. This caused plaintiff's representatives to seriously doubt whether the facilities could be completed by the date of plaintiff's first reservations.

On or about April 16, 1982, plaintiff's representatives returned to Knoxville to again inspect defendant's facilities. The facilities remained far from completion and serious doubts were raised as to whether the facilities would ever be completed. Facility Number 2, set out in defendant's brochure, was, in fact, never built.

Plaintiff's representatives were unable to determine if the uncompleted facilities would meet the standards and qualifications expected and demanded by plaintiff's customers. Because of defendant's representations about the number of facilities and the date of completion, the plaintiff, by letter dated April 18, 1982, cancelled its reservations with the defendant and demanded full refund of all deposits.

By letter dated April 23, 1982, the defendant refused to refund any deposits made by the plaintiff because of company policy. Mrs. Miller, representative of plaintiff, testified that she never received the company policy until she cancelled the reservations. She says that the letter of April 23, 1982, was the first knowledge that she had of any cancellation policy contrary to the industry-wide standard. The Court is of the opinion that Mrs. Miller is a truthful person and that although the policy letter may have been sent, it was not received by her.

By letter dated and effective May 14, 1982, the defendant cancelled plaintiff's group reservation for May 16–17, August 12–13, and October 22–25, due to non receipt of deposits in the amount of $3,345.00. The plaintiff has not received any refund of the deposits in the amount of $10,720.00 from the defendant.

The parties agree that they had a valid oral contract. Defendant promised to provide motel accommodations in exchange for plaintiff's promise to pay for the accommodations. The Court has found that the parties did not discuss the terms for cancellation of the contract and that there was no written provision relating to refunds of deposits. We must therefore look to the intention of the parties for the fair and reasonable construction under the circumstances. "Also we must look to the situation involving the parties, the nature of the business in which they are engaged and the subject matter to which the contract relates." Stovall [v. Dattel, 619 S.W.2d 125, 127 (Tenn.Ct.App.1981)]. Specific contract terms, not expressly agreed on, may be implied. Hoskins v. United States, 299 F.Supp. 1229 (E.D.Tenn.1969), aff'd, 425 F.2d 1301 (6th Cir.1970).

Since the instant contract is not for the sale of goods, this is not a case controlled by the Tennessee version of the Uniform Commercial Code. Tenn.Code Ann., § 47–2–102. See Fuller v. Orkin Exterminating Co., 545

S.W.2d 103 (Tenn.App.1975). We can look to the Code, however, for guidance in the interpretation of the contract. Under the Code, usages of trade may be considered in determining the intentions of the parties. Tenn.Code Ann. § 47–1–205. A usage of trade is defined as:

> any practice or method of dealing having such regularity of observance in a place, vocation or trade as to justify an expectation that it will be observed with respect to the transaction in question.

The practice of refunding deposits if reservations are cancelled thirty days prior to the scheduled arrival date is a regular method of dealing in the tourist business. Exceptions to the usual practice are made known during initial negotiations between the parties. Plaintiff relied on defendant's silence and the customary practice in this case. We have considered the nature of the tour and motel business, the subject matter of the contract, and the dealings of the parties. In the opinion of the Court, plaintiff is entitled to a full refund of its $10,720.00 deposit, pursuant to the implied terms of the contract.

Accordingly, it is ORDERED that judgment be entered in favor of plaintiff in the amount of $10,720.00.

Section Four. Structures and Processes for Applying Private-Arrangement Law and Techniques

In the absence of a dispute, private-arrangement law applies when people seek to enter arrangements or when they seek to determine their rights under arrangements. If a person asks how to make a will or set up a trust or enter a contract, or whether to change a will in light of a divorce, or whether to perform at a particular time under a contract, lawyers serving as counselors must interpret and apply private-arrangement law to answer the question. None of these common questions presupposes that a dispute has arisen. The track meet arranged by the University of Oregon Portland Alumni demonstrates the application of private-arrangement law in the absence of a dispute.

In Section 3 of this chapter, we observed that when a dispute arises, it is usually settled short of a formal proceeding. When a dispute does lead to formal resolution, the forum may be a court or a less traditional forum such as an arbitration proceeding.

How does a private-arrangement dispute lead to a less traditional forum for resolution? First, the arrangement may provide a regularized means of resolving disputes in a less traditional forum. An agreement between a professional athlete and his or her team owner typically includes a provision calling for arbitration or mediation of disputes. Collective bargaining agreements between unions and employers generally provide internal grievance procedures. Trade associations also frequently provide for arbitration of disputes between members. Simple commercial contracts may also call for arbitration, as in the following sample provision:

ARBITRATION

A. All questions subject to arbitration under this Contract shall be submitted to arbitration at the choice of either party to the dispute.

B. The parties may agree upon one arbitrator. In all other cases there shall be three arbitrators. One arbitrator shall be named by each party to this Contract; each party shall notify the other party and the Engineer of such choice in writing. The third arbitrator shall be chosen by the two arbitrators named by the parties. If the two arbitrators fail to select a third within fifteen days, the third arbitrator shall be chosen by the presiding officer of the bar association nearest to the location of the work. Should the party demanding arbitration fail to name an arbitrator within ten days of his demand, his right to arbitration shall lapse. Should the other party fail to choose an arbitrator within the said ten days, the presiding officer of the bar association nearest to the location of work shall appoint such arbitrator. Should either party refuse or neglect to supply the arbitrators with any papers or information demanded in writing, the arbitrators are empowered by both parties to proceed ex parte.

C. If there be one arbitrator, his decision shall be binding; if there are three, the decision of any two shall be binding. Such decision shall be a condition precedent to any right of legal action, and wherever permitted by law it may be judicially enforced.

Second, a dispute may be resolved by arbitration or the like because the parties simply agree to that approach after a dispute has arisen.

Why would parties seek dispute resolution other than in courts? Consider arbitration as an alternative. It is often less expensive and less time-consuming than litigation. Formalities of proof such as the hearsay rule and rules for authentication of documents are often ignored. In addition, as you can see from the prior provision, the parties are often entitled to select their own arbitrators.

When informal and formal dispute resolution other than judicial resolution fail or are not utilized, the parties may resort to a court to settle their differences. In some instances, however, it may be too late to expect much help from the court except to ratify what has already been done, as indicated in Fudickar v. Guardian Mutual Life Insurance Co., 62 N.Y. 392, 399–400 (1875):

The arbitrator is a judge appointed by the parties; he is by their consent invested with judicial functions in the particular case; he is to determine the right as between the parties in respect to the matter submitted, and all questions of fact or law upon which the right depends are, under a general submission, deemed to be referred to him for decision. The court possesses no general supervisory power over awards, and if arbitrators keep within their jurisdiction their award will not be set aside because they have erred in judgment either upon the facts or the law. If courts should assume to rejudge the decision of arbitrators upon the merits, the value of this method of settling controversies would be destroyed, and an award instead of being a final determination of a controversy would become but one of the steps in its progress. The courts in this State have adhered with great steadiness to the general rule that awards will not be opened for errors of law or fact on the part of the arbitrator.

In Chapter 1 and in this chapter, we examined how courts resolve disputes arising out of private arrangements. You should not assume, however, that all judicial processes must inevitably follow the traditional adversarial pattern.

ADLER, CHILD ABUSE VICTIMS: ARE THEY ALSO VICTIMS OF AN ADVERSARIAL AND HIERARCHIAL COURT SYSTEM?

5 Pepperdine L.Rev. 717, 732 (1978).

Adversary systems have intrinsic vulnerabilities. In Judge Delaney's words, "[S]uspicion supplants trust; tactics and strategy replace openness; competition supplants cooperativeness." [47] A judicial environment of competing attorneys and tactical operations is not unlike the behavior of abusive families who characteristically use non-cooperation and denial as a defense against detection. In this sense the adversary court environment cannot serve as a corrective model for families.

DYSON & DYSON, FAMILY COURTS IN THE UNITED STATES

8 J.Fam.L. 505, 507–08, 517 (1968).[*]

The decline of the American family is a popular theme today. Critics warn that the family is losing its grip as an agency of social control. Statistics are advanced to buttress this view: one out of every four American marriages ends in divorce, broken homes cause juvenile delinquency, juvenile delinquency is on the rise.

. . . . [T]he view appears to be widespread that divorce and delinquency presage the decline of the family and that "unless something is done—and done quickly—we are going to be faced with a social problem in this country, which conceivably could cause a collapse of our society."

The validity of such beliefs is not a primary concern of this study. But such views—mythical or real—have generated considerable pressure for altering the legal institutions that affect family life. Some suggested reforms involve changes in substantive aspects of family law. Most of them fall short of overhauling the court system itself. But the most ambitious suggestion has been to establish a court that is solely concerned with the family and its legal manifestations of disharmony. Instead of

---

47. J. Delaney, New Concepts of the Family Court, in Child Abuse and Neglect: The Family and the Community 335, 357 (1976).

processing family problems by archaic methods and scattering them in a wide variety of unrelated courts, reformers have urged that all family cases be brought before one court, with a specialized judge, and with all the social services that the legal system offers under the same institutional roof. They would dignify this agency by the name of Family Court. . . .

Underlying this conceptual structure is a philosophy similar to that of the juvenile court. Just as the best interest of the child is the guiding standard of the juvenile court, the family's best interest is the family court's guide. If psychological tests are necessary to assess a family's needs, these may be supplied by the court's trained staff. If counseling or therapy are considered desirable, these too should be available in court. The judge of one well-known family court put it thusly:

> Why can we not apply that same logic, same philosophy, same diagnostic and therapeutic approach to the family . . . [as we apply to the juvenile court?] Why can we not ask what is best for this family, diagnose the case, find out what caused the rift, and then apply all the skills of all the professions we can bring to bear on the problem? [3]

Besides creating a unitary framework for applying social casework methods to family conflicts, certain administrative benefits are claimed for family courts. Proponents assert that properly established family courts will lead to more efficiency by unifying practices and procedures, eliminating conflicting decisions, promoting better services through continuity in treatment, reducing administrative costs, eliminating duplication of services, and improving supervision, training and recruitment of staff.

Section Five. Necessity for and Nature of Coercive Power

The law does not require a citizen to marry, to make a will or a contract, or to form and join organizations. Moreover, if a citizen attempts some of these things and fails to comply with legal formalities, the law does not impose any sanction. The only consequence is that the arrangement is a nullity. For example, if a person fails to have enough witnesses for a will, the only result is that the will is unenforceable.

Nonetheless, as we have seen, the legal significance of many arrangements depends on the ultimate capacity of one party to bring the coercive power of the state to bear in at least some situations. Thus, the remedy of money damages for breach of contract would be worthless if unenforceable against an unwilling party. An order requiring restitution of money paid to another pursuant to a transaction entered by mistake, an order directing an executor of a will to make payment to named beneficiaries, or a decree of divorce awarding custody of children to the mother would also be worthless if unenforceable.

---

3. Alexander, The Therapeutic Approach, University of Chicago Law School Conference Series, No. 9, 51–54 (1952).

WILSON v. SANDSTROM

Supreme Court of Florida, 1975.
317 So.2d 732.

ADKINS, CHIEF JUSTICE:

This is an original proceeding in habeas corpus wherein 18 owners of racing greyhounds seek relief from incarceration resulting from violation of an injunctive order of the circuit court entered July 8, 1975. A return to the petition has been filed. . . .

For clarity, West Flagler Associates, Ltd., the owner and operator of the race track is hereinafter referred to as Flagler; the owners of the greyhounds used at the race track are referred to as the kennel owners.

Flagler instituted suit against the kennel owners and a kennel owners' association seeking a temporary and permanent mandatory injunction requiring the defendants to comply with contracts for furnishing greyhounds to the race track commencing July 3, 1975. The State of Florida and Metropolitan Dade County were allowed to intervene as parties-plaintiff.

Flagler alleged that under the contract it granted exclusive right to the named kennel owners to race their dogs and agreed to furnish purses, and that Flagler has complied with the contract. . . .

Under the contracts the kennel owners agreed not to take any action which would be detrimental to the race track and greyhound racing. It was specifically provided that the kennel owners would not do any act which would bring about a temporary or permanent cessation or suspension of racing during the period of time covered by the contract.

It was alleged that under the rules of the Department of Business Regulation the kennel owners were required to present their dogs for schooling in June for the race meet commencing July 3, 1975. On June 10, 1975, the kennel owners [notified Flagler that pursuant to state rules and regulations they desired to renegotiate provisions of their agreement with Flagler and implicitly threatened not to furnish any greyhounds without a new agreement]. As a result, Flagler alleges it would be unable to conduct its race meet; that the kennel owners are required to supply "chattel of unusual and unique character; namely racing greyhounds which are not readily obtainable in the ready market". Flagler alleges that it will not be able to get the owners to supply greyhounds and suffers irreparable damage for each day it is not open. It was also alleged that, if notice were given the dog owners, the dogs may be removed from the jurisdiction. . . .

. . . . [The state court entered an ex parte order on July 3, 1975, granting a] temporary mandatory injunction. This order recited that the State of Florida was suffering a loss of tax revenue of $64,000 per day, and that Flagler was suffering irreparable damage because of the kennel owners' refusal to supply dogs. The court ordered immediate compliance with the contracts by the filing of entries not later than July 4, 1975, at 10:00 a.m.; that upon refusal of the kennel owners to file entries that Perrine Palmer take custody and control of the dogs for the purpose of running them.

The kennel owners refused to submit their entry and Palmer attempted to take control of the dogs. Because of the number of dogs and inability to get adequate help, a hearing was held at the request of the receiver [Palmer] on July 5, 1975. Custody of the dogs was thereupon returned to the kennel owners, who were informed that a contempt hearing would be held on Monday, July 7, 1975. . . .

At the hearing on July 7, 1975, each kennel owner was called to the stand and interrogated concerning his knowledge of the order and whether he had willfully and deliberately refused to comply with the order of July 3, 1975. On July 8, 1975, the kennel owners were adjudged guilty of contempt and 18 of them were incarcerated in the Dade County penal facilities. These are the petitioners in the habeas corpus proceeding. . . .

A mandatory temporary injunction may be issued requiring specific performance of a contract. Bowling v. National Convoy and Trucking Co., 101 Fla. 634, 135 So. 541 (1931). . . .

The record clearly demonstrates that the kennel owners willfully and deliberately violated the injunctive order of the court. The courts and judges have inherent power by due course of law to punish by appropriate fine or imprisonment or otherwise any conduct that in law constitutes an offense against the authority and dignity of a court or a judicial officer in the performance of judicial functions. State ex rel. Buckner v. Culbreath, 147 Fla. 560, 3 So.2d 380 (1941). The sole reason for the incarceration of the kennel owners was their willful failure to comply with the temporary injunctive order of the court. Just as in any other contempt proceedings, the kennel owners carry the keys of their prison in their own pocket. Demetree v. State, 89 So.2d 498 (Fla.1956).

. . . Misunderstandings among parties should be adjusted where possible without litigation, for a fair settlement is preferable to a good law suit. On the other hand, the judicial process is always available in the event the fair settlement is not reached. When the judicial process is involved, all parties are bound by the orders and judgments of the court having jurisdiction until such orders or judgments are reversed or modified by an appellate court. Although the kennel owners may feel justified in their complaints, their course of action in depriving the State and the counties of needed revenue certainly warrants the actions of the trial court. Their business is profitable only by virtue of a State statutory permission to operate dog tracks guided by regulatory measures adopted by the State. It might be said they are "biting the hand that feeds them".

In summary, we hold that . . . the orders entered by the trial court were proper under the circumstances and without error. The writ of habeas corpus is discharged and the petitioners therein are remanded to the custody of respondent, such incarceration to begin on Tuesday, July 22, 1975, at 5:00 p.m. . . .

It is so ordered.

ROBERTS, OVERTON and ENGLAND, JJ., concur.

BOYD, J., concurs in part and dissents in part with opinion. . . .

———

Although the coercive power of the state is essential, it is not commonly exercised. Most private arrangements achieve fruition without it. But coercion may play a role other than supporting a remedy and providing a deterrent.

HALE, COERCION AND DISTRIBUTION IN A SUPPOSEDLY NON–COERCIVE STATE

38 Pol.Sci.Q. 470, 471–73 (1923).*

The government, [an individualist might say], should exercise sufficient constraint to prevent destruction and deception, to standardize measures, qualities and coins, to enforce contracts, to conduct certain enterprises (like lighthouses) which cannot well be carried on otherwise, to regulate monopoly prices and to control the feeble-minded and the otherwise incompetent in their own interest. It should not coerce people to work, nor should it, with rare exceptions, undertake to direct the channels into which industry should flow. It should, however, prevent any private person or group from exercising any compulsion. The government must also impose taxes; it should restrict immigration and furnish educational opportunities. Such a scheme has the appearance of exposing individuals to but little coercion at the hands of the government and to none at all at the hands of other individuals or groups. Yet it does in fact expose them to coercion at the hands of both, or at least to a kind of influence indistinguishable in its effects from coercion. This will shortly appear more clearly, it is hoped. Meanwhile, let it be kept in mind that to call an act coercive is not by any means to condemn it. It is because the word "coercion" frequently seems to carry with it the stigma of impropriety, that the coercive character of many innocent acts is so frequently denied.

What is the government doing when it "protects a property right"? Passively, it is abstaining from interference with the owner when he deals with the thing owned; actively, it is forcing the non-owner to desist from handling it, unless the owner consents. Yet [the individualist] would have it that the government is merely preventing the non-owner from using force against the owner. This explanation is obviously at variance with the facts—for the non-owner is forbidden to handle the owner's property even where his handling of it involves no violence or force whatever. Any lawyer could have told him that the right of property is much more extensive than the mere right to protection against forcible dispossession. In protecting property the government is doing something quite apart from merely keeping the peace. It is exerting coercion wherever that is necessary to protect each owner, not merely from violence, but also from peaceful infringement of his sole right to enjoy the thing owned.

That, however, is not the most significant aspect of present-day coercion in connection with property. The owner can remove the legal duty under which the non-owner labors with respect to the owner's property. He can remove it, or keep it in force, at his discretion. To keep it in force

* Reprinted with permission from *Political Science Quarterly* 38 (September 1923): 471–73.

may or may not have unpleasant consequences to the non-owner—consequences which spring from the law's creation of legal duty. To avoid these consequences, the non-owner may be willing to obey the will of the owner, provided that the obedience is not in itself more unpleasant than the consequences to be avoided. Such obedience may take the trivial form of paying five cents for legal permission to eat a particular bag of peanuts, or it may take the more significant form of working for the owner at disagreeable toil for a slight wage. In either case the conduct is motivated, not by any desire to do the act in question, but by a desire to escape a more disagreeable alternative. In the peanut case, the consequence of abstaining from a particular bag of peanuts would be, either to go without such nutriment altogether for the time being, or to conform to the terms of some other owner. Presumably at least one of these consequences would be as bad as the loss of the five cents, or the purchaser would not buy; but one of them, at least, would be no worse, or the owner would be able to compel payment of more. In the case of the labor, what would be the consequence of refusal to comply with the owner's terms? It would be either absence of wages, or obedience to the terms of some other employer. If the worker has no money of his own, the threat of any particular employer to withhold any particular amount of money would be effective in securing the worker's obedience in proportion to the difficulty with which other employers can be induced to furnish a "job". If the non-owner works for anyone, it is for the purpose of warding off the threat of at least one owner of money to withhold that money from him (with the help of the law). Suppose, now, the worker were to refuse to yield to the coercion of any employer, but were to choose instead to remain under the legal duty to abstain from the use of any of the money which anyone owns. He must eat. While there is no law against eating in the abstract, there is a law which forbids him to eat any of the food which actually exists in the community—and that law is the law of property. It can be lifted as to any specific food at the discretion of its owner, but if the owners unanimously refuse to lift the prohibition, the non-owner will starve unless he can himself produce food. And there is every likelihood that the owners will be unanimous in refusing, if he has no money. There is no law to compel them to part with their food for nothing. Unless, then, the non-owner can produce his own food, the law compels him to starve if he has no wages, and compels him to go without wages unless he obeys the behests of some employer. It is the law that coerces him into wage-work under penalty of starvation—unless he can produce food. Can he? Here again there is no law to prevent the production of food in the abstract; but in every settled country there is a law which forbids him to cultivate any particular piece of ground unless he happens to be an owner. This again is the law of property. And this again will not be likely to be lifted unless he already has money. That way of escape from the law-made dilemma of starvation or obedience is closed to him. It may seem that one way of escape has been overlooked—the acquisition of money in other ways than by wage-work. Can he not "make money" by selling goods? But here again, things cannot be produced in quantities sufficient to keep him alive, except with the use of elaborate mechanical equipment.

To use any such equipment is unlawful, except on the owner's terms. Those terms usually include an implied abandonment of any claim of title to the products. In short, if he be not a property owner, the law which forbids him to produce with any of the existing equipment, and the law which forbids him to eat any of the existing food, will be lifted *only* in case he works for an employer. It is the law of property which coerces people into working for factory owners—though, . . . the workers can as a rule exert sufficient counter-coercion to limit materially the governing power of the owners.

Not only does the law of property secure for the owners of factories their labor; it also secures for them the revenue derived from the customers. The law compels people to desist from consuming the products of the owner's plant, except with his consent; and he will not consent unless they pay him money. They can escape, of course, by going without the product. But that does not prevent the payment being compulsory, any more than it prevents the payment of the government tax on tobacco from being compulsory. The penalty for failure to pay, in each case, may be light, but it is sufficient to compel obedience in all those cases where the consumer buys rather than go without.

Section Six.   Roles of Private Citizens and Their Lawyers

Private citizens and their lawyers create the underlying arrangement and define its content. They also determine whether to contest any performance or nonperformance of the arrangement. In Section 3 we saw how private parties set up the track meet in Portland, Oregon. Here we see the creation of another arrangement with additional focus on the roles of the lawyer and the client.

The following episode is also based on actual facts. The Whites wished to buy residential property next to the Benkowskis, but water for the property came from a well on the Benkowskis' property. The Whites negotiated with the Benkowskis concerning the Benkowskis' supplying water to the Whites. The parties reached an agreement, but instead of consulting a lawyer, they had the Benkowskis' real estate agent draw up the deal. The agreement follows.

————

AGREEMENT AS TO SUPPLY OF WATER

This agreement, made this 28 day of November, 1962, between Paul Benkowski Jr., and Ruth Benkowski, his wife (first parties), and Virgil A. White and Gwynneth A. White, his wife (second parties),

WITNESSETH

WHEREAS, first parties are the owners of the following described real estate situated in the City of Oak Creek, Milwaukee County, Wisconsin, to-wit:

[The legal description of real estate is omitted.]

AND, WHEREAS, second parties are the owners of the following described real estate situated in the City of Oak Creek, Milwaukee County, Wisconsin, to-wit:

[The legal description of real estate is omitted.]

* This agreement shall become null and void whenever water is supplied by any municipal system or if the existing well should go dry or become inadequate to supply said 2 homes or if second parties would drill their own well.

AND, WHEREAS, there is now situated on the above real estate of first parties, one certain water well operated by an electric submercible system motor,

AND, WHEREAS, the parties hereto desire that the source of water from the well upon parties of the first part's property be supplied unto the parties of the second part's home through the system of piping now there existing, it is hereby mutually agreed:

1. That first parties will furnish water for the use of the occupants of the house located on the lands of the second parties for a period of ten (10) years from _____ November, 1962.

2. That the second parties will pay for said water supply service the sum of Three ($3.00) Dollars per month, commencing with 1 December, 1962, payable on the first day of each and every month, in advance, and that in addition, second parties shall contribute to first parties, one-half (½) of the cost of any repairs or maintenance expense to said water system; also including replacements of motor, tank or accessories; (* above)

3. It is further hereby agreed between the parties hereto that at the end of the ten year period referred to in Paragraph One above, parties of the second part shall have the option to renew this agreement.

This agreement shall be binding upon and shall extend unto the respective grantees, successors, heirs, executors, administrators and assigns of each of the respective parties hereto.

IN WITNESS WHEREOF, the parties hereto have hereunto set their hands and seals of the day and year first above written.

WITNESSES TO FOUR
SIGNATURES:

Adrian Legendre

Shaine Schaefer

Paul Benkowski Jr. ____ (SEAL)
Paul Benkowski Jr.

Ruth Benkowski (SEAL)
Ruth Benkowski

Virgil A. White (SEAL)
Virgil A. White

Gwynneth A. White (SEAL)
Gwynneth A. White

The Whites and Benkowskis enjoyed a harmonious relationship until the fall of 1963, when, according to Mrs. White, the Whites' daughter picked an apple in the Benkowskis' yard and Mrs. Benkowski called the child an "S.O.B." Later, Mrs. Benkowski called Mrs. White "a redheaded bitch." Mr. White claimed that Mr. Benkowski complained to Mr. White's superior officer (White was a police officer) that White tried to run over the Benkowskis' child and had wild parties at home. The district attorney absolved Mr. White of any such wrongdoing.

The Benkowskis then claimed that the Whites were using too much water and on several occasions in early 1964 turned off the water supply to the Whites. The parties were unable to resolve their differences, and the Whites brought a lawsuit against the Benkowskis. We now present the final resolution of the case before considering how the parties might have utilized lawyers to reach a better agreement.

———

WHITE v. BENKOWSKI

Supreme Court of Wisconsin, 1967.
37 Wis.2d 285, 155 N.W.2d 74.

This case involves a neighborhood squabble between two adjacent property owners.

Prior to November 28, 1962, Virgil and Gwynneth White, the plaintiffs, were desirous of purchasing a home in Oak Creek. Unfortunately, the particular home that the Whites were interested in was without a water supply. Despite this fact, the Whites purchased the home.

The adjacent home was owned and occupied by Paul and Ruth Benkowski, the defendants. The Benkowskis had a well in their yard which had piping that connected with the Whites' home.

On November 28, 1962, the Whites and Benkowskis entered into a written agreement wherein the Benkowskis promised to supply water to the White home for ten years or until an earlier date when either water was supplied by the municipality, the well became inadequate, or the Whites drilled their own well. The Whites promised to pay $3 a month for the water and one-half the cost of any future repairs or maintenance that the Benkowskis well might require. As part of the transaction, but not included in the written agreement, the Whites gave the Benkowskis $400 which was used to purchase and install a new pump and an additional tank that would increase the capacity of the well.

Initially, the relationship between the new neighbors was friendly. With the passing of time, however, their relationship deteriorated and the neighbors actually became hostile. In 1964, the water supply, which was controlled by the Benkowskis, was intermittently shut off. Mrs. White kept a record of the dates and durations that her water supply was not operative. Her record showed that the water was shut off on the following occasions:

    (1) March 5, 1964, from 7:10 p.m. to 7:25 p.m.
    (2) March 9, 1964, from 3:40 p.m. to 4:00 p.m.
    (3) March 11, 1964, from 6:00 p.m. to 6:15 p.m.
    (4) June 10, 1964, from 6:20 p.m. to 7:03 p.m.

The record also discloses that the water was shut off completely or partially for varying lengths of time on July 1, 6, 7, and 17, 1964, and on November 25, 1964.

Mr. Benkowski claimed that the water was shut off either to allow accumulated sand in the pipes to settle or to remind the Whites that their use of the water was excessive. Mr. White claimed that the Benkowskis breached their contract by shutting off the water.

Following the date which the water was last shut off (November 25, 1964), the Whites commenced an action to recover compensatory and punitive damages for an alleged violation of the agreement to supply water. A jury trial was held. Apparently it was agreed by counsel that for purposes of the trial "plaintiffs' case was based upon an alleged deliberate violation of the contract consisting of turning off the water at the times specified in the plaintiffs' complaint." [The reporter then set forth the special verdict submitted to the jury.]

Before the case was submitted to the jury, the defendants moved to strike the verdict's punitive-damage question. The court reserved its ruling on the motion. The jury returned a verdict which found the Benkowskis maliciously shut off the Whites' water supply for harassment purposes. Compensatory damages were set at $10 and punitive damages at $2,000. On motions after verdict, the court reduced the compensatory award to $1 and granted defendants' motion to strike the punitive-damage question and answer.

Judgment for plaintiffs of $1 was entered and they appeal.

WILKIE, J.

Two issues are raised on this appeal.

1. Was the trial court correct in reducing the award of compensatory damages from $10 to $1?

2. Are punitive damages available in actions for breach of contract?

REDUCTION OF JURY AWARD

The evidence of damage adduced during the trial here was that the water supply had been shut off during several short periods. Three incidents of inconvenience resulting from these shut-offs were detailed by the plaintiffs. Mrs. White testified that the lack of water in the bathroom on one occasion caused an odor and that on two other occasions she was forced to take her children to a neighbor's home to bathe them. Based on this evidence, the court instructed the jury that: [the court here set forth the portion of the jury charge indicating that the Whites could recover only nominal damages for their harm suffered from the breach].

Plaintiffs did not object to this instruction. In the trial court's decisions on motions after verdict it states that the court so instructed the jury because, based on the fact that the plaintiffs paid for services they did not receive, their loss in proportion to the contract rate was approximately 25 cents. This rationale indicates that the court disregarded or overlooked Mrs. White's testimony of inconvenience. In viewing the evidence most favorable to the plaintiffs, there was some injury. The plaintiffs are not required to ascertain their damages with mathematical precision, but rather the trier of fact must set damages at a reasonable amount. Notwithstanding this instruction, the jury set the plaintiffs' damages at $10. The court was in error in reducing that amount to $1.

The jury finding of $10 in actual damages, though small, takes it out of the mere nominal status. The award is predicated on an actual injury. This was not the situation present in *Sunderman* v. *Warnken*.[2] Sunderman was a wrongful-entry action by a tenant against his landlord. No actual injury could be shown by the mere fact that the landlord entered the tenant's apartment, therefore damages were nominal and no punitory award could be made. Here there was credible evidence which showed inconvenience and thus actual injury, and the jury's finding as to compensatory damages should be reinstated.

PUNITIVE DAMAGES

If a man shall steal an ox, or a sheep, and kill it, or sell it; he shall restore five oxen for an ox, and four sheep for a sheep.[3]

Over one hundred years ago this court held that, under proper circumstances, a plaintiff was entitled to recover exemplary or punitive damages.[4]

Kink v. *Combs*[5] is the most recent case in this state which deals with the practice of permitting punitive damages. In *Kink* the court relied on *Fuchs* v. *Kupper*[6] and reaffirmed its adherence to the rule of punitive damages.

In Wisconsin compensatory damages are given to make whole the damage or injury suffered by the injured party. On the other hand, punitive damages are given

. . . on the basis of punishment to the injured party not because he has been injured, which injury has been compensated with compensatory damages, but to punish the wrongdoer for this malice and to deter others from like conduct.[8]

Thus we reach the question of whether the plaintiffs are entitled to punitive damages for a breach of the water agreement.

The overwhelming weight of the authority supports the proposition that punitive damages are not recoverable in actions for breach of contract. In Chitty on Contracts, the author states that the right to receive punitive damages for breach of contract is now confined to the single case of damages for breach of a promise to marry.

Simpson states:

Although damages in excess of compensation for loss are in some instances permitted in tort actions by way of punishment . . . in contract actions the damages recoverable are limited to compensation for pecuniary loss sustained by the breach.[11]

2. (1947), 251 Wis. 471, 29 N.W.2d 496.
3. Exodus 22:1.
4. McWilliams v. Bragg (1854), 3 Wis. 377.
5. (1965), 28 Wis.2d 65, 135 N.W.2d 789.
6. (1963), 22 Wis.2d 107, 125 N.W.2d 360.
8. Malco, Inc. v. Midwest Aluminum Sales (1961), 14 Wis.2d 57, 66, 109 N.W.2d 516, 521.
11. Simpson, Contracts, (2d ed. hornbook series), p. 394, sec. 195.

Corbin states that as a general rule punitive damages are not recoverable for breach of contract.[12] . . .

Persuasive authority from other jurisdictions supports the proposition (without exception) that punitive damages are not available in breach of contract actions. This is true even if the breach, as in the instant case, is wilful.

Although it is well recognized that breach of a contractual duty may be a tort, in such situations the contract creates the relation out of which grows the duty to use care in the performance of a responsibility prescribed by the contract. Not so here. No tort was pleaded or proved.

Reversed in part by reinstating the jury verdict relating to compensatory damages and otherwise affirmed. Costs to appellants.

———————

Now consider what might have occurred had the Whites consulted a lawyer before entering the agreement with the Benkowskis. Generally, the lawyer's roles would have included the following:

1. Planning the basic agreement

The lawyer must assist the client in avoiding disputes and unexpected consequences of an arrangement. The client is sometimes experienced and knowledgeable, sometimes not. Especially in the latter case, the lawyer must ascertain the client's goals and attempt to plan an arrangement that will satisfy those goals. Often helpful is asking directly, "What do you wish to achieve by making this agreement?"

The lawyer must plan for flexibility in the arrangement because the client's needs may change over time. For example, a buyer of goods may need different quantities over time, so that a fixed quantity contract may be inapposite. One way to cope with such a quantity problem is for the lawyer to draft a *requirements contract,* in which the seller agrees to supply all of the buyer's needs and the buyer agrees to buy only from the seller.

2. Planning for compliance with the law

The lawyer must also plan for compliance with the law. For example, contracting parties today do not enjoy complete freedom of contract. The lawyer must plan in light of regulatory law that may supersede a contrary contract clause. Again referring to the requirements contract as an example, the lawyer must consider Uniform Commercial Code § 2–306(1):

> A term which measures the quantity by the output of the seller or the requirements of the buyer means such actual output or requirements as may occur in good faith, except that no quantity unreasonably disproportionate to any stated estimate or in the absence of a stated estimate to any normal or otherwise comparable prior output or requirements may be tendered or demanded.

3. Planning for risks

The lawyer must also plan for risks by attempting to foresee and to allocate them. If the seller in our requirements contract experiences a shortage of raw materials, is the buyer entitled to performance? What if the buyer's need for the goods evaporates because of an explosion that

---

12. 5 Corbin, Contracts, p. 438, sec. 1077.

destroys the buyer's business? Lawyers often include a *force majeure clause* to allocate such risks, as in the following example:

(a) The term "Force Majeure" as used herein shall mean and include: . . . lack of labor or means of transportation of labor or material; Acts of God; insurrection; flood; strike.

(b) If by reason of Force Majeure as herein defined, lessee is prevented from or delayed in drilling, completing or producing any wells for oil, gas or other mineral on the leased premises, then while so prevented or during the period of such delay lessee shall be relieved from all obligations, whether express or implied, imposed on lessee under this lease, to drill, complete or produce such well or wells on the leased premises, and lessee shall not be liable in damages and this lease shall not be subject to cancellation for failure of lessee to drill, complete or produce such well or wells during the time lessee is relieved from all obligations to do so.

Of course, lawyers are not omniscient. Sometimes contingencies that were totally unforeseeable at the time of contracting, and therefore unallocated, arise during performance of the contract. For example, who could have foreseen the Arab oil boycott of the early 1970s that caused such inflation in the price of oil?

4. Negotiating the terms

Parties do not always agree on the terms of a prospective arrangement. The lawyer may be called on to negotiate with the other side over various terms.

H. EDWARDS & J. WHITE, THE LAWYER AS A NEGOTIATOR
112–13 (1977).*

[I]t is perhaps useful to state three propositions, truisms really, that hold true for almost every negotiation and that define the negotiator's role to a considerable degree. In every negotiation a principal responsibility of the negotiator is to find his opponent's settling point. In almost every negotiation in which there is at least a moderately well-defined controversy the opponent will have or will develop some point at which he will settle. With a union in a bargaining session this may be the number of cents per hour it must have in order not to strike; for the plaintiff's lawyer, the number of dollars he must receive in settlement in order not to go to trial; for the landlord this is the minimum number of dollars and cents per square foot at which he will lease.

In any negotiation, and particularly in lawsuit settlement negotiation, the opposing negotiators may have widely different views of the same case. Commonly, one will assign a lower value to an opponent's case than the opponent will assign to it. Because of that fact and because one assumes that the opponent regards his case as stronger than it looks from across the table, negotiators frequently assume the opponent's settling point is higher than it really is. One should always keep the possibility in mind—notwithstanding the statements of the opposing negotiator—that his opponent has evaluated his own case as weaker than you evaluate it. If somehow one can determine that settling point, he can settle the case for that amount not for some higher amount which he has placed on the case himself.

The logical corollary to the foregoing principle is that one should not reveal his own settling point. Much of the material that follows on nonverbal communication is designed to assist the negotiator in reading his opponent. Conversely the negotiator should be aware that he is transmitting not only verbal but also nonverbal signals. Particularly if his settling point is some distance from the point at which he is bargaining, one should use care not to reveal that settling point. Presumably in the optimal negotiation, one will determine his opponent's settling point without revealing his own. Doubtless such absolute knowledge on one side coupled with absolute ignorance on the other seldom occurs in practice.

The third truism with respect to most negotiations deals with the negotiator's responsibility to change his opponent's position. In some cases it will be enough simply to know the opponent's settling point and to agree to settle at that point. More commonly it will be the job of the negotiator not only to determine the settling point but also to convince the opponent that his case has a lower value than he has put upon it.

Comments and Questions

1. If lawyers for both sides of a negotiation have read the previous excerpt advising that "one should not reveal his own settling point," will the negotiation ever lead to agreement?

2. Consider again the plight of the Whites and the Benkowskis. If the Whites had consulted a lawyer, a letter like the one that follows might have been prepared. Evaluate the letter in terms of the lawyer's roles.

Virgil & Gwynneth White
3837 East Garden Place
Oak Creek, Wisconsin

Dear Mr. & Mrs. White:

You have asked me to draft an agreement with Paul and Ruth Benkowski to supply you with water from their well through existing pipes connected to your new home. You have told me that you have already agreed to a monthly service charge of $3.00 to be paid in advance on the first day of each month, that you have agreed to pay $400 for a new pump and an additional tank, and that you have agreed to pay one-half of the cost of additional repairs, maintenance or replacement expenses. The agreement is to last for ten years with an option to renew, but will terminate when water is supplied by a municipal system or the Benkowskis' well goes dry or is inadequate to supply the two homes, or if you drill your own well.

Before I draft the agreement there are certain additional issues that we should clear up with the Benkowskis. Concerning the duration of the agreement, if you exercise the renewal option is the renewal period for ten years? May you renew the agreement more than once? You certainly should have that right since you do not want to be without a water supply after one renewal period. Are you *required* to be connected to the municipal system if it becomes available or may you continue to receive water from the Benkowskis' well (it may be cheaper from the Benkowskis)? When does the Benkowskis' well "become inadequate" to supply both homes? For example, will merely one or a few periods of low water pressure be sufficient? We need to discuss this further with the Benkowskis and see if we can nail down some agreement on precisely when the well "becomes inadequate."

Concerning the price to you of the water service, does the $3.00-per-month charge continue under all circumstances during the period of the agreement? For example, suppose the value of water increases dramatically because of a drought or pollution or the like? We need to include a provision specifically indicating that such events do not trigger a right of the Benkowskis to raise the price (or to get out of the agreement). In addition, you agree to pay one-half of repairs, maintenance and replacement costs to the system. We should make it clear that only such repairs, maintenance and replacement costs that are necessary to continue the supply of water to both homes are included, not repairs, etc., that are solely beneficial to the Benkowskis.

Payment is to be on the first day of each month. We should include a provision enabling you to pay "on or about" the first day of each month in case you are slightly late in a particular month.

Are there to be any limits on your usage of water? I assume that the Benkowskis' attorney (if they retain one) will raise this issue. If the issue is not raised, we need to decide whether to raise it ourselves by seeking a provision specifically ensuring that you can use all of the water you desire. Offering such a provision may prod the Benkowskis into seeking a price scheme based on the amount of water-usage. I assume that we can agree on a mutually agreeable scale. If we remain silent on this issue, I can foresee disagreements about water usage later on, so perhaps we should consider the issue now.

We also need to consider whether there should be any adjustment of the $3.00-per-month fee in case of an inadvertent interruption of the water supply, for example, because of equipment failure. In addition, are the Benkowskis going to warrant the quality of the water? We should include such a promise if possible. We could require that the water meet the potability standards of the local department of health.

Finally, while I know you people are on good terms now, unfortunately we lawyers have seen too many deals go sour. So it is appropriate to think of remedies that you desire if the Benkowskis breach their agreement; for example, by turning off the water on you. We should try to get an agreement as to how much the Benkowskis will have to pay you for each hour that the water is purposefully turned off to discourage such behavior, should your relationship with the Benkowskis not remain cordial. Such an amount must necessarily reflect the damages to you or it will not be legally enforceable.

We need to have a meeting first on these matters, and then later with the Benkowskis. Of course we will need to compromise on many of them, but the important thing is to have your agreement clearly deal with these issues so as to avoid trouble in the future.

Sincerely yours,

Jean L. Smith

Jean L. Smith

Comments and Questions

1. Why did the parties rely on a real estate agent to draft their agreement? Many property lawyers have complained that such activity by real estate agents is a great source of litigation. But can everyone afford a lawyer? Even if some people can afford lawyers, can you think of additional reasons why they might want to avoid them?

2. Rollie Massimino, head coach of Villanova's basketball team, is reported to have said in explaining why he turned down the coaching job with the New Jersey Nets: "The Nets were very professional in all their dealings with me. We had some 20 telephone conversations and about five face-to-face meetings. Everything was agreed on verbally and then the lawyers took over with their legalese and there were snags." Ithaca Journal, June 26, 1985, at 16, col. 3.

Section Seven. Process Values

There is no unitary "private-arrangement process." Like the grievance-remedial instrument, the private-arrangement instrument breaks down into many processes, including the negotiating process, performance process, private dispute-settling process, adjudicative process, and others.

The following readings focus on the negotiating and performance processes. Evaluate how the law polices against parties taking advantage of these processes. Does the law go too far in protecting weak parties and thereby threaten the efficacy of the private-arrangement instrument? Or is the mix of policing and private freedom about right?

KESSLER, CONTRACTS OF ADHESION—SOME THOUGHTS ABOUT FREEDOM OF CONTRACT

43 Colum.L.Rev. 629, 640–41 (1943).

With the decline of the free enterprise system due to the innate trend of competitive capitalism towards monopoly, the meaning of contract has changed radically. Society, when granting freedom of contract, does not guarantee that all members of the community will be able to make use of it to the same extent. On the contrary, the law, by protecting the unequal distribution of property, does nothing to prevent freedom of contract from becoming a one-sided privilege. Society, by proclaiming freedom of contract, guarantees that it will not interfere with the exercise of power by contract. Freedom of contract enables enterprises to legislate by contract and, what is even more important, to legislate in a substantially authoritarian manner without using the appearance of authoritarian forms. Standard contracts in particular could thus become effective instruments in the hands of powerful industrial and commercial overlords enabling them to impose a new feudal order of their own making upon a vast host of vassals. This spectacle is all the more fascinating since not more than a hundred years ago contract ideology had been successfully used to break down the last vestiges of a patriarchal and benevolent feudal order in the field of master and servant (*Priestley* v. *Fowler*). Thus the return back from contract to status which we experience today was greatly facilitated by the fact that the belief in freedom of contract has remained one of the firmest axioms in the whole fabric of the social philosophy of our culture.

UNIFORM COMMERCIAL CODE

§ 2–302. Unconscionable Contract or Clause.

(1) If the court as a matter of law finds the contract or any clause of the contract to have been unconscionable at the time it was made the court may refuse to enforce the contract, or it may enforce the remainder of the contract without the unconscionable clause, or it may so limit the application of any unconscionable clause as to avoid any unconscionable result.

(2) When it is claimed or appears to the court that the contract or any clause thereof may be unconscionable the parties shall be afforded a reasonable opportunity to present evidence as to its commercial setting, purpose and effect to aid the court in making the determination.

WILLIAMS v. WALKER–THOMAS FURNITURE CO.

United States Court of Appeals, District of Columbia Circuit, 1965.
350 F.2d 445.

Before Bazelon, Chief Judge, and Danaher and Wright, Circuit Judges.

J. Skelly Wright, Circuit Judge:

Appellee, Walker-Thomas Furniture Company, operates a retail furniture store in the District of Columbia. During the period from 1957 to 1962 each appellant in these cases purchased a number of household items from Walker-Thomas, for which payment was to be made in installments. The terms of each purchase were contained in a printed form contract which set forth the value of the purchased item and purported to lease the item to appellant for a stipulated monthly rent payment. The contract then provided, in substance, that title would remain in Walker-Thomas until the total of all the monthly payments made equaled the stated value of the item, at which time appellants could take title. In the event of a default in the payment of any monthly installment, Walker-Thomas could repossess the item.

The contract further provided that "the amount of each periodical installment payment to be made by [purchaser] to the Company under this present lease shall be inclusive of and not in addition to the amount of each installment payment to be made by [purchaser] under such prior leases, bills or accounts; *and all payments now and hereafter made by [purchaser] shall be credited pro rata on all outstanding leases, bills and accounts* due the Company by [purchaser] at the time each such payment is made." (Emphasis added.) The effect of this rather obscure provision was to keep a balance due on every item purchased until the balance due on all items, whenever purchased, was liquidated. As a result, the debt incurred at the time of purchase of each item was secured by the right to repossess all the items previously purchased by the same purchaser, and each new item purchased automatically became subject to a security interest arising out of the previous dealings.

On May 12, 1962, appellant Thorne purchased an item described as a Daveno, three tables, and two lamps, having total stated value of $391.10. Shortly thereafter, he defaulted on his monthly payments and appellee sought to replevy all the items purchased since the first transaction in 1958. Similarly, on April 17, 1962, appellant Williams bought a stereo set of stated value of $514.95. She too defaulted shortly thereafter, and appellee sought to replevy all the items purchased since December, 1957. The Court of General Sessions granted judgment for appellee. The District of Columbia Court of Appeals affirmed, and we granted appellants' motion for leave to appeal to this court.

Appellants' principal contention, rejected by both the trial and the appellate courts below, is that these contracts, or at least some of them, are unconscionable and, hence, not enforceable. In its opinion in Williams v. Walker-Thomas Furniture Company, 198 A.2d 914, 916 (1964), the District of Columbia Court of Appeals explained its rejection of this contention as follows:

> Appellant's second argument presents a more serious question. The record reveals that prior to the last purchase appellant had reduced the balance in her account to $164. The last purchase, a stereo set, raised the balance due to $678. Significantly, at the time of this and the preceding purchases, appellee was aware of appellant's financial position. The reverse side of the stero contract listed the name of appellant's social worker and her $218 monthly stipend from the government. Nevertheless, with full knowledge that appellant had to feed, clothe and support both herself and seven children on this amount, appellee sold her a $514 stereo set.
>
> We cannot condemn too strongly appellee's conduct. It raises serious questions of sharp practice and irresponsible business dealings. A review of the legislation in the District of Columbia affecting retail sales and the pertinent decisions of the highest court in this jurisdiction disclose, however, no ground upon which

this court can declare the contracts in question contrary to public policy. We note that were the Maryland Retail Installment Sales Act, Art. 83 §§ 128–153, or its equivalent, in force in the District of Columbia, we could grant appellant appropriate relief. We think Congress should consider corrective legislation to protect the public from such exploitive contracts as were utilized in the case at bar.

We do not agree that the court lacked the power to refuse enforcement to contracts found to be unconscionable. In other jurisdictions, it has been held as a matter of common law that unconscionable contracts are not enforceable. While no decision of this court so holding has been found, the notion that an unconscionable bargain should not be given full enforcement is by no means novel. In Scott v. United States, 79 U.S. (12 Wall.) 443, 445 (1870), the Supreme Court stated:

> . . . If a contract be unreasonable and unconscionable, but not void for fraud, a court of law will give to the party who sues for its breach damages, not according to its letter, but only such as he is equitably entitled to. . . .

Since we have never adopted or rejected such a rule, the question here presented is actually one of first impression.

Congress has recently enacted [for application in the District of Columbia] the Uniform Commercial Code, which specifically provides that the court may refuse to enforce a contract which it finds to be unconscionable at the time it was made. 28 D.C.Code § 2–302 (Supp. IV 1965). The enactment of this section, which occurred subsequent to the contracts here in suit, does not mean that the common law of the District of Columbia was otherwise at the time of enactment, nor does it preclude the court from adopting a similar rule in the exercise of its powers to develop the common law for the District of Columbia. In fact, in view of the absence of prior authority on the point, we consider the congressional adoption of § 2–302 persuasive authority for following the rationale of the cases from which the section is explicitly derived. Accordingly, we hold that where the element of unconscionability is present at the time a contract is made, the contract should not be enforced.

Unconscionability has generally been recognized to include an absence of meaningful choice on the part of one of the parties together with contract terms which are unreasonably favorable to the other party. Whether a meaningful choice is present in a particular case can only be determined by consideration of all the circumstances surrounding the transaction. In many cases the meaningfulness of the choice is negated by a gross inequality of bargaining power. The manner in which the contract was entered is also relevant to this consideration. Did each party to the contract, considering his obvious education or lack of it, have a reasonable opportunity to understand the terms of the contract, or were the important terms hidden in a maze of fine print and minimized by deceptive sales practices? Ordinarily, one who signs an agreement without full knowledge of its terms might be held to assume the risk that he has entered a one-sided bargain. But when a party of little bargaining power, and hence little real choice, signs a commercially unreasonable contract with little or no knowledge of its terms, it is hardly likely that his consent, or even an objective manifestation of his consent, was ever given to all the terms. In such a case the usual rule that the terms of the agreement are not to be questioned should be abandoned and the court should consider whether the terms of the contract are so unfair that enforcement should be withheld.

In determining reasonableness or fairness, the primary concern must be with the terms of the contract considered in light of the circumstances existing when the contract was made. The test is not simple, nor can it be mechanically applied. The terms are to be considered "in the light of the general commercial background and the commercial needs of the particular trade or case." Corbin suggests the test as being whether the terms are "so extreme as to appear unconscionable according to the mores and business practices of the time and place." We think this formulation correctly states the test to be applied in those cases where no meaningful choice was exercised upon entering the contract.

Because the trial court and the appellate court did not feel that enforcement could be refused, no findings were made on the possible unconscionability of the contracts in these cases. Since the record is not sufficient for our deciding the issue as a matter of law, the cases must be remanded to the trial court for further proceedings.

So ordered.

DANAHER, CIRCUIT JUDGE (dissenting):

The District of Columbia Court of Appeals obviously was as unhappy about the situation here presented as any of us can possibly be. Its opinion in the *Williams* case, quoted in the majority text, concludes: "We think Congress should consider corrective legislation to protect the public from such exploitive contracts as were utilized in the case at bar."

My view is thus summed up by an able court which made no finding that there had actually been sharp practice. Rather the appellant seems to have known precisely where she stood.

There are many aspects of public policy here involved. What is a luxury to some may seem an outright necessity to others. Is public oversight to be required of the expenditures of relief funds? A washing machine, e.g., in the hands of a relief client might become a fruitful source of income. Many relief clients may well need credit, and certain business establishments will take long chances on the sale of items, expecting their pricing policies will afford a degree of protection commensurate with the risk. Perhaps a remedy when necessary will be found within the provisions of the "Loan Shark" law, D.C.Code §§ 26–601 et seq. (1961).

I mention such matters only to emphasize the desirability of a cautious approach to any such problem, particularly since the law for so long has allowed parties such great latitude in making their own contracts. I dare say there must annually be thousands upon thousands of installment credit transactions in this jurisdiction, and one can only speculate as to the effect the decision in these cases will have.

I join the District of Columbia Court of Appeals in its disposition of the issues.

Comments and Questions

1.   What is the dissent's specific quarrel with the majority decision in *Williams* v. *Walker-Thomas Furniture Co.?*

2.   Consider again the material presented in Section 3 of this chapter concerning the roles of legislatures and courts, and also the following excerpt.

HILLMAN, DEBUNKING SOME MYTHS ABOUT UNCONSCIONABILITY: A NEW FRAMEWORK FOR U.C.C. SECTION 2–302

67 Cornell L.Rev. 1, 27–29 (1982).*

Broad legislative standards that delegate to courts the responsibility of "legislating" are often criticized on the theory that courts are ill-equipped to evaluate social policy issues. Judges, it is said, do not have sufficient resources or time to evaluate the effects of their decisions on society, while vast resources are available to legislators to investigate such matters. At best, courts can compare the conduct of similar commercial parties to determine whether particular behavior fits a community standard; but this approach to fairness questions ensures adherence to the "predominant morals of the marketplace" and precludes serious consideration of more desirable alternatives.

Even if the judiciary is equipped to explore issues of social policy and the effects of alternative approaches on society, the argument goes, the common law process may be an inferior method of achieving the social policy goals that are ultimately identified. For example, Professor Leff contended that after cases such as *Williams* v. *Walker-Thomas Furniture Co.*, sellers affected by unconscionability findings simply will alter their forms slightly to avoid repetition of the findings and that these alterations will not cure the fundamental ills of the sellers' practices. Nor will the decisions curb similar abuses that are not addressed specifically by the cases. Leff maintained that common law development is costly, time-consuming, and possibly ineffective: "One cannot think of a more expensive and frustrating course than to seek to regulate goods or 'contract' quality through repeated lawsuits against inventive 'wrongdoers.'"

These arguments in favor of legislative control over social policy issues have been challenged. For example, Professor Posner has suggested that judge-created rules are more "efficiency-promoting" than legislative rules. Appellate judges, he asserts, view the parties as representing activities and make their decisions based on which activity is more valuable economically. Legislators, on the other hand, are subject to interest group pressure and depend on the electoral process; therefore, they "sell" legislation to those parties that can enhance their prospects of reelection. One may question Posner's premise that judges adhere to a model of economic efficiency and that efficiency is the appropriate basis upon which to make policy. Nevertheless, his theory does point out that, at least to the extent that judges are insulated from lobbying groups and politics, judicial decisions can be more objective than decisions made by their legislative counterparts.

The argument that the common law process is an inferior method of achieving favorable reform may also be overdrawn. The general threat of an unconscionability finding may have an *in terrorem* effect that alone deters sellers from including suspect terms in commercial agreements. In addition, legislators cannot successfully draft legislation to encompass unforeseen circumstances. New approaches are needed to deal with unforeseen problems constantly disclosed through litigation; many of these problems occur with sufficient frequency so that it would be unfair and inefficient to await legislative enactment. For this reason, legislative regulation of contract terms generally has been confined to distinct segments of business such as the insurance industry, where issues are already well-defined and narrowed.

The availability of judicial intervention ensures that fairness in particular controversies is achieved. As suggested earlier, some consumers are entitled to protection from egregious contract terms because, despite the clarity of disclosure of the offending terms, they are incapable of comprehending the significance of the agreement. Courts can evaluate the facts of a particular case to determine whether the consumer was capable of understanding the subject of disclosure. Legislatures, on the other hand, can only establish broad classifications of those consumers who should not be presumed to have assented.

All of the arguments about the proper forum for effectuating social change probably have some merit. Because of the inconclusiveness of the debate, and because of the pervasiveness of judicial activism, judicial administration of fairness principles in commercial cases should not be precluded.

ALASKA PACKERS' ASS'N v. DOMENICO

United States Circuit Court of Appeals, Ninth Circuit, 1902.
117 F. 99.

Before GILBERT AND ROSS, CIRCUIT JUDGES, and HAWLEY, DISTRICT JUDGE.
ROSS, CIRCUIT JUDGE.

The libel [or complaint] in this case was based upon a contract alleged to have been entered into between the libelants and the appellant corporation on the 22d day of May, 1900, at Pyramid Harbor, Alaska, by which it is claimed the appellant promised to pay each of the libelants, among other things, the sum of $100 for services rendered and to be rendered. In its answer the respondent denied the execution, on its part, of the contract sued upon, averred that it was without consideration, and for a third defense alleged that the work performed by the libelants for it was performed under other and different contracts than that sued on, and that, prior to the filing of the libel, each of the libelants was paid by the respondent the full amount due him thereunder, in consideration of which each of them executed a full release of all his claims and demands against the respondent.

The evidence shows without conflict that on March 26, 1900, at the city and county of San Francisco, the libelants entered into a written contract with the appellant, whereby they agreed to go from San Francisco to Pyramid Harbor, Alaska, and return, on board such vessel as might be designated by the appellant, and to work for the appellant during the fishing season of 1900, at Pyramid Harbor, as sailors and fishermen, agreeing to do "regular ship's duty, both up and down, discharging and loading; and to do any other work whatsoever when requested to do so by the captain or agent of the Alaska Packers' Association." By the terms of this agreement, the appellant was to pay each of the libelants $50 for the season, and two cents for each red salmon in the catching of which he took part.

On the 15th day of April, 1900, 21 of the libelants signed shipping articles by which they shipped as seamen on the Two Brothers, a vessel chartered by the appellant for the voyage between San Francisco and Pyramid Harbor, and also bound themselves to perform the same work for the appellant provided for by the previous contract of March 26th; the appellant agreeing to pay them therefor the sum of $60 for the season, and two cents each for each red salmon in the catching of which they should respectively take part. Under these contracts, the libelants sailed on board the Two Brothers for Pyramid Harbor, where the appellant had about $150,000 invested in a salmon cannery. The libelants arrived there early in April of the year mentioned, and began to unload the vessel and fit up the cannery. A few days thereafter, to wit, May 19th, they stopped work in a body, and demanded of the company's superintendent there in charge $100 for services in operating the vessel to and from Pyramid Harbor, instead of the sums stipulated for in and by the contracts; stating that unless they were paid this additional wage they would stop work entirely, and return to San Francisco. The evidence showed, and the court below found, that it was impossible for the appellant to get other men to take the places of the libelants, the place being remote, the season short and just opening; so that, after endeavoring for several days without success to induce the libelants to proceed with their work in accordance with their contracts, the company's superintendent, on the 22d day of May, so far yielded to their demands as to instruct his clerk to copy the contracts executed in San Francisco, including the words "Alaska Packers' Association" at the end, substituting, for the $50 and $60 payments, respectively, of those contracts, the sum of $100, which document, so prepared, was signed by the libelants before a shipping commissioner whom they had requested to be brought from Northeast Point; the superintendent, however, testifying that he at the time told the libelants that he was without authority to enter into any such contract, or to in any way alter the contracts made between them and the company in San Francisco. Upon the return of the libelants to San Francisco at the close of the fishing season, they demanded pay in accordance with the terms of the alleged contract of May 22d, when the company denied its validity, and refused to pay other than as provided for by the contracts of March 26th and April 15th, respectively. Some of the libelants, at least, consulted counsel, and, after receiving his advice, those of them who had signed the shipping articles before the shipping commissioner at San Francisco went before that officer, and received the amount due them thereunder, executing in consideration thereof a release in full, and the others being paid at the office of the company, also receipting in full for their demands.

On the trial in the court below, the libelants undertook to show that the fishing nets provided by the respondent were defective, and that it was on that account that they demanded increased wages. On that point, the evidence was substantially conflicting, and the finding of the court was against the libelants . . . .

The evidence being sharply conflicting in respect to these facts, the conclusions of the court, who heard and saw the witnesses, will not be disturbed.

The real questions in the case as brought here are questions of law, and, in the view that we take of the case, it will be necessary to consider but one of those. Assuming that the appellant's superintendent at Pyramid Harbor was authorized to make the alleged contract of May 22d, and that he executed it on behalf of the appellant, was it supported by a sufficient consideration? From the foregoing statement of the case, it will have been seen that the libelants agreed in writing, for certain stated compensation, to render their services to the appellant in remote waters where the season for conducting fishing operations is extremely short, and in which enterprise the appellant had a large amount of money invested; and, after having entered upon the discharge of their contract, and at a time when it was impossible for the appellant to secure other men in their places, the libelants, without any valid cause, absolutely refused to continue the services they were under contract to perform unless the appellant would consent to pay them more money. Consent to such a demand, under such circumstances, if given, was, in our opinion, without consideration, for the reason that it was based solely upon the libelants' agreement to render the exact services, and none other, that they were already under contract to render. The case shows that they willfully and arbitrarily broke that obligation. As a matter of course, they were liable to the appellant in damages, and it is quite probable, as suggested by the court below in its opinion, that they may have been unable to respond in damages. But we are unable to agree with the conclusions there drawn, from these facts, in these words:

> Under such circumstances, it would be strange, indeed, if the law would not permit the defendant to waive the damages caused by the libelants' breach, and enter into the contract sued upon,—a contract mutually beneficial to all the parties thereto, in that it gave to the libelants reasonable compensation for their labor, and enabled the defendant to employ to advantage the large capital it had invested in its canning and fishing plant.

Certainly, it cannot be justly held, upon the record in this case, that there was any voluntary waiver on the part of the appellant of the breach of the original contract. The company itself knew nothing of such breach until the expedition returned to San Francisco, and the testimony is uncontradicted that its superintendent at Pyramid Harbor, who, it is claimed, made on its behalf the contract sued on, distinctly informed the libelants that he had no power to alter the original or to make a new contract; and it would, of course, follow that, if he had no power to change the original, he would have no authority to waive any rights thereunder. The circumstances of the present case bring it, we think, directly within the sound and just observations of the supreme court of Minnesota in the case of King v. Railway Co., 61 Minn. 482, 63 N.W. 1105:

> No astute reasoning can change the plain fact that the party who refuses to perform, and thereby coerces a promise from the other party to the contract to pay him an increased compensation for doing that which he is legally bound to do, takes an unjustifiable advantage of the necessities of the other party. Surely it would be a travesty on justice to hold that the party so making the promise for extra pay was estopped from asserting that the promise was without consideration. A party cannot lay the foundation of an estoppel by his own wrong, where the promise is simply a repetition of a subsisting legal promise. There can be no consideration for the promise of the other party, and there is no warrant for inferring that the parties have voluntarily rescinded or modified their contract. The promise cannot be legally enforced, although the other party has completed his contract in reliance upon it. . . .

[Judgment reversed.]

WEINTRAUB v. KROBATSCH

Supreme Court of New Jersey, 1974.
64 N.J. 445, 317 A.2d 68.

JACOBS, J.

The judgment entered in the Law Division, as modified in an unreported opinion of the Appellate Division, directed that the appellants Donald P. Krobatsch and Estella Krobatsch, his wife, pay the sum of $4,250 to the plaintiff Natalie Weintraub and the sum of $2,550 to the defendant The Serafin Agency, Inc. We granted certification on the application of the appellants. 63 N.J. 498, 308 A.2d 663 (1973). . . .

Mrs. Weintraub owned and occupied a six-year-old Englishtown home which she placed in the hands of a real estate broker (The Serafin Agency, Inc.) for sale. The Krobatsches were interested in purchasing the home, examined it while it was illuminated and found it suitable. On June 30, 1971 Mrs. Weintraub, as seller, and the Krobatsches, as purchasers, entered into a contract for the sale of the property for $42,500. The contract provided that the purchasers had inspected the property and were fully satisfied with its physical condition, that no representations had been made and that no responsibility was assumed by the seller as to the present or future condition of the premises. A deposit of $4,250 was sent by the purchasers to the broker to be held in escrow pending the closing of the transaction. The purchasers requested that the seller have the house fumigated and that was done. A fire after the signing of the contract caused damage but the purchasers indicated readiness that there be adjustment at closing.

During the evening of August 25, 1971, prior to closing, the purchasers entered the house, then unoccupied, and as they turned the lights on they were, as described in their petition for certification, "astonished to see roaches literally running in all directions, up the walls, drapes, etc." On the following day their attorney wrote a letter to Mrs. Weintraub, care of her New York law firm, advising that on the previous day "it was discovered that the house is infested with vermin despite the fact that an exterminator has only recently serviced the house" and asserting that "the presence of vermin in such great quantities, particularly after the exterminator was done, rendered the house as unfit for human habitation at this time and therefore, the contract is rescinded." On September 2, 1971 an exterminator wrote to Mr. Krobatsch advising that he had examined the premises and that "cockroaches were found to have infested the entire house." He said he could eliminate them for a relatively modest charge by two treatments with a twenty-one day interval but that it would be necessary to remove the carpeting "to properly treat all the infested areas." . . .

Before us the purchasers contend that they were entitled to a trial on the issue of whether there was fraudulent concealment or nondisclosure entitling them to rescind; if there was, then clearly they were under no liability to either the seller or the broker and would be entitled to the return of their deposit held by the broker in escrow. See Keen v. James, 39 N.J.Eq. 527, 540 (E. & A.1885) where Justice Dixon, speaking for the then Court of last resort, pointed out that "silence may be fraudulent" and that relief may be granted to one contractual party where the other suppresses facts which he, " 'under the circumstances, is bound in conscience and duty to disclose to the other party, and in respect to which he cannot, innocently, be silent.' "

Mrs. Weintraub asserts that she was unaware of the infestation and the Krobatsches acknowledge that, if that was so, then there was no fraudulent concealment or nondisclosure on her part and their claim must fall. But the purchasers allege that she was in fact aware of the infestation and at this stage of the proceedings we must assume that to be true. She contends, however, that even if she were fully aware she would have been under no duty to speak and that consequently no complaint by the purchasers may legally be grounded on her silence. She relies primarily on cases such as Swinton v. Whitinsville Sav. Bank, 311 Mass. 677, 42 N.E.2d 808 (1942) . . . . *Swinton* is pertinent but, as Dean Prosser has noted, it is one of a line of "singularly unappetizing cases" which are surely out of tune with our times.

In *Swinton* the plaintiff purchased a house from the defendant and after he occupied it he found it to be infested with termites. The defendant had made no verbal or written representations but the plaintiff, asserting that the defendant knew of the termites and was under a duty to speak, filed a complaint for damages grounded on fraudulent concealment. The Supreme Judicial Court of Massachusetts sustained a demurrer to the complaint and entered judgment for the defendant. In the course of its opinion the court acknowledged that "the plaintiff possesses a certain appeal to the moral sense" but concluded that the law has not "reached the point of imposing upon the frailties of human nature a standard so idealistic as this." That was written several decades ago and we are far from certain that it represents views held by the current members of the Massachusetts court. See Kannavos v. Annino, 356 Mass. 42, 247 N.E.2d 708, 711 (1969). In any event we are certain that it does not represent our sense of justice or fair dealing and it has understandably been rejected in persuasive opinions elsewhere.

In Obde v. Schlemeyer, . . . 56 Wash.2d 449, 353 P.2d 672 [(1960)], the defendants sold an apartment house to the plaintiff. The house was termite infested but that fact was not disclosed by the sellers to the purchasers who later sued for damages alleging fraudulent concealment. The sellers contended that they were under no obligation whatever to speak out that they relied heavily on the decision of the Massachusetts court in *Swinton*. The Supreme Court of Washington flatly rejected their contention, holding that though the parties had dealt at arms length the sellers were under "a duty to inform the plaintiffs of the termite condition" of which they were fully aware. In the course of its opinion the court quoted approvingly from Dean Keeton's article . . . in 15 Tex.L. Rev. 1. There the author first expressed his thought that when Lord Cairns suggested in Peek v. Gurney, L.R. 6 H.L. 377 (1873), that there was no duty to disclose facts, no matter how "morally censurable," he was expressing nineteenth century law as shaped by an individualistic philosophy based on freedom of contracts and unconcerned with morals. He then made the following comments which fairly embody a currently acceptable principle on which the holding in *Obde* may be said to be grounded:

> In the present stage of the law, the decisions show a drawing away from this idea, and there can be seen an attempt by many courts to reach a just result in so far as possible, but yet maintaining the degree of certainty which the law must have. The statement may often be found that if either party to a contract of sale conceals or suppresses a material fact which he is in good faith bound to disclose then his silence is fraudulent.

> The attitude of the courts toward nondisclosure is undergoing a change and contrary to Lord Cairns' famous remark it would seem that the object of the law in these cases should be to impose on parties to the transaction a duty to speak whenever justice, equity, and fair dealing demand it. This statement is made only with reference to instances where the party to be charged is an actor in the transaction. This duty to speak does not result from an implied representation by silence, but exists because a refusal to speak constitutes unfair conduct. 15 Tex.L.Rev. at 31. . . .

In Simmons v. Evans, [185 Tenn. 282, 206 S.W.2d 295 (1947)], the defendants owned a home which was serviced by a local water company. The company supplied water during the daytime but not at night. The defendants sold their home to the plaintiffs but made no mention of the limitation on the water service. The plaintiffs filed an action to rescind their purchase but the lower court dismissed it on the ground that the defendants had not made any written or verbal representations and the plaintiffs had "inspected the property, knew the source of the water supply, and could have made specific inquiry of these defendants or ascertained from other sources the true situation and, therefore, are estopped." The dismissal was reversed on appeal in an opinion which took note of the general rule that " 'one may be guilty of fraud by his silence, as where it is expressly incumbent upon him to speak concerning material matters that are entirely within his own knowledge.' " With respect to the plaintiffs' failure to ascertain the water situation before their purchase the court stated that the plaintiffs were surely not required "to make a night inspection in order to ascertain whether the water situation with reference to this residence was different from what it was during the day." . . .

. . . [T]he purchasers here were entitled to withstand the seller's motion for summary judgment. They should have been permitted to proceed with their efforts to establish by testimony that they were equitably entitled to rescind because the house was extensively infested in the manner described by them, the seller was well aware of the infestation, and the seller deliberately concealed or failed to disclose the condition because of the likelihood that it would defeat the transaction. The seller may of course defend factually as well as legally and since the matter is primarily equitable in nature the factual as well as legal disputes will be for the trial judge alone.

If the trial judge finds such deliberate concealment or nondisclosure of the latent infestation not observable by the purchasers on their inspection, he will still be called upon to determine whether, in the light of the full presentation before him, the concealment or nondisclosure was of such significant nature as to justify rescission. Minor conditions which ordinary sellers and purchasers would reasonably disregard as of little or no materiality in the transaction would clearly not call for judicial intervention. While the described condition may not have been quite as major as in the termite cases which were concerned with structural impairments, to the purchasers here it apparently was of such magnitude and was so repulsive as to cause them to rescind immediately though they had earlier indicated readiness that there be adjustment at closing for damage resulting from a fire which occurred after the contract was signed. We are not prepared at this time to say that on their showing they acted either unreasonably or without equitable justification. . . .

Reversed and remanded.

———

ESTATE OF BAKER

Court of Appeal of California, 1982.
131 Cal.App.3d 471, 182 Cal.Rptr. 550.

LILLIE, ACTING PRESIDING JUSTICE.

This is an appeal from a judgment entered on a special verdict in a will contest and an action to set aside a deed which were consolidated for trial.

Dorothy Mae Baker died February 15, 1978, at the age of 81, leaving an estate valued at $73,131. Her will (executed Jan. 6, 1977) included bequests of $4,500 to her brother Clarence Baker Coleman, $4,500 to Coleman's wife, $100 to each of his two daughters, $1,000 to Dorothy's "godson" David N. Lee and $5,000 to Richard Whitaker, grandson of Dorothy's friend Alta Clifford Potter; Alta was given a tea and coffee service, Dorothy's residence and the residue of the estate;[1] the will named Alta as executrix and Elmer Bromley as attorney for the estate and the executrix. Alta petitioned for probate of the will. Clarence Coleman, as Dorothy's sole blood heir, filed a contest and opposition to probate of those provisions of the will relating to Alta (both bequests and devise to her and her nomination as executrix), Richard Whitaker and Elmer Bromley.[2] The contest alleged: When Dorothy executed the will she was not of sound and disposing mind and was acting under undue influence and fraud on the part of Alta, who stood in a confidential relationship with Dorothy; Alta told Dorothy that she (Alta) was in direct communication with deceased relatives of Dorothy and that she had received messages from them directing Dorothy to make and execute the will in question. David Lee contested the will on the same grounds, alleging that his grandmother was the blood sister of Mary Baker, who had adopted Dorothy.

After filing his contest to the will, Clarence Coleman commenced a separate action (No. C 250700) against Alta to set aside a grant deed executed by Dorothy conveying to Alta a joint tenancy interest in a condominium, and to recover money and securities given to Alta by Dorothy. The complaint alleged that such inter vivos conveyance and gifts were made as the result of Alta's undue influence and fraud practiced in the manner set forth in the will contest. By leave of court, David Lee intervened as a plaintiff. On Coleman's motion, and over objection by Alta and Whitaker, the action was ordered consolidated with the will contest for trial only.

A jury trial resulted in a special verdict which determined: Dorothy was of sound and disposing mind in including in her will the provisions challenged by the contestants; each of such provisions was obtained through undue influence exerted, and fraud perpetrated, by Alta upon Dorothy; during Dorothy's lifetime Alta obtained from her, through the exercise of undue influence and fraud, checks totaling $55,027.37 and shares of stock in Holofile, Inc. and Beehive, Inc.; Alta obtained her joint tenancy interest in the condominium by undue influence and fraud practiced upon Dorothy. . . .

Alta and Whitaker appeal from the judgment contending that the evidence does not support the special verdict of undue influence and fraud in the procurement of parts of the will. . . .

Dorothy never married. She had been adopted by Mary Baker and lived with Mary and Mary's son Arthur ("Bake"), a paraplegic, at 1412

---

1. The will also included bequests totaling $12,000 to religious and charitable institutions and a bequest of $1,000 to Dorothy's goddaughter.

2. "A will or *part of a will* procured to be made by duress, menace, fraud or undue influence, may be denied probate . . . . " (Prob.Code § 22; emphasis added. See also Estate of Molera (1972) 23 Cal.App.3d 993, 1001, 100 Cal.Rptr. 696.)

North Alta Vista in Los Angeles. Mary died in 1964, and Arthur in 1971. Dorothy had a blood brother, Clarence, who was reared by foster parents named Coleman. Clarence and his wife stayed at the Baker house for four months in 1965. Dorothy often spoke of Clarence, stating that she was proud of him and loved him. David Lee's grandmother was the sister of Mary Baker, Dorothy's adoptive mother. Lee therefore was Dorothy's cousin by adoption, and she called him her favorite cousin. When Lee's family lived in California (1951–1965) they visited constantly with the Baker family. After the Lees moved to Texas, the Bakers visited them there; following the death of "Bake," Dorothy continued the visits. Until 1976 David Lee saw Dorothy every year; theirs was a warm, close association.

In 1969 Dorothy executed a will leaving $100 to her brother Clarence and the residue of her estate to Mary Baker and "Bake." After their deaths Dorothy said that she intended to divide her estate among Clarence, David Lee and Wallace Baker, another cousin. She told David Lee many times that family heirlooms which had come into her possession would be returned to him upon her death; she promised her cousin Amy Bice that she would leave Amy an antique silver-plated tea service which always had been in the Baker family.

Alta first met Dorothy in 1938 and thereafter continued to see her on a casual basis. Alta also was acquainted with Dorothy's adoptive mother and brother, Mary Baker and "Bake," and knew of their deaths. In 1960 Alta was licensed as a security broker, and occasionally advised Dorothy on investments. Dorothy met Alta's grandson, Richard Whitaker, when he was 3 or 4 years old but did not see him again until he was 32. In 1976 and 1977 Dorothy, at Whitaker's invitation, spent Christmas Eve with him and his family at their home.

Lawrence Gelbmann worked 3 or 4 days a week in the Baker home from 1952 until Dorothy's death in 1978; thus, he was in close contact with Dorothy over a period of 26 years. Gelbmann testified: He first heard of Alta in 1971 when she came to the Baker house to pick up an envelope Dorothy had left for her; before that, he had neither seen Alta nor heard her name mentioned. After his initial meeting with Alta, Gelbmann next saw her in October 1975 when she came to the Baker house and said she had three "visitations" from "Bake" and messages from him for Dorothy. Thereafter, and continuing through January 1978, Alta relayed to Dorothy messages which she (Alta) said she had received from the spirits of Mary Baker and "Bake." These messages included the following: Dorothy should go out more, enjoy life and spend money; she should dispose of her 34 cats so that she would be free to travel; she should get rid of "false friends"; she should sell her house and use the money for travel and to have fun; she should rent an apartment and leave behind the work of managing a house; she should borrow money in order to "live better"; she should sell her unproductive securities and thereafter let Alta manage her securities; she should not go to the home of David Lee for Christmas in 1977, but should spend Christmas with Alta and the Whitakers; she should give $1,000 to Alta's nephew, Steven, for his education. The messages sometimes were accompanied by pleas from

"Bake" and mother that unless Dorothy did as they suggested, they would be earthbound and could not go on to a higher plane. The spirits (speaking through Alta) also warned Dorothy occasionally that if she did not do as they advised, they would leave her and she would be on her own. With the exception of selling her house and renting an apartment, Dorothy did exactly as Alta had told her the spirits of mother and "Bake" advised.

David Lee and several of Dorothy's friends testified that Dorothy told them she had met a real psychic (Alta) who gave her messages from "Bake" and mother. Dorothy truly believed in the messages and believed that they came from "Bake" and mother.

The final message from the spirits through Alta was that Dorothy should take a trip to Peru. Dorothy was 81 years old and weighed 78 pounds; she had suffered heart attacks in 1975 and 1976, and also suffered from emphysema; her doctor warned her against high altitudes. Therefore, she was reluctant to go and worried about going to Peru but felt that she must because Alta had told her mother and "Bake" wanted her to take the trip and "Bake" said she would be all right. She had to go and was afraid not to go because if she did not "Bake" and mother would be earthbound and could not move to a higher plane, and Alta told her she might be unable to communicate with the spirits again. Alta knew that Dorothy had been hospitalized in 1976 with a heart attack and that she could have another heart attack on the trip. In January 1978, Dorothy and Alta went to South America, including Peru. There, Dorothy visited Cuzco and Machu Picchu; several days later in Ecuador, she was hospitalized for a coronary for one day. Dorothy returned to Los Angeles in a wheelchair and again was hospitalized; on February 15, 1978, she died as a result of cardiorespiratory arrest.

In the fall of 1976, Dorothy asked Alta to recommend an attorney to draw a will. Alta supplied the name of Elmer Bromley, whom she had known for over 30 years. At Dorothy's request, Alta made an appointment for Dorothy with Bromley and drove her to his office to keep the appointment. After they arrived Dorothy said that she was going to discuss the terms of her will. Alta said, "Well, this doesn't concern me so I am going to leave," then left Bromley's office. Dorothy told Bromley that she did not want the will to be contested and was thinking of leaving her brother Clarence a small sum of money. Bromley suggested that if she left him "a little more," perhaps he would not contest the will. Dorothy then decided to leave Clarence and his wife $4,500 each. On January 6, 1977, Dorothy executed her will in Bromley's office. Present on that occasion were Bromley, his secretary and Robert Ross, an attorney; the secretary and Ross acted as witnesses.

Between December 17, 1976 and December 22, 1977, Bateman, Eichler, Hill Richards issued to Dorothy checks totaling $181,678.60, representing proceeds from sales of her securities. Dorothy deposited these checks in her checking account and wrote on that account checks payable to Alta totaling $50,348.95 which Alta deposited in her account. Dorothy also wrote checks payable to Alta totaling $9,809.50 which Alta did not deposit, but cashed instead.

Alta testified: In December 1976 she and Dorothy arranged for the purchase of a condominium and the purchase of shares of Holofile and Beehive stock; under this arrangement Alta was to acquire a half interest in the condominium by paying for the shares of stock which were to be issued in the names of Alta and Dorothy; however, Dorothy actually supplied Alta with all of the funds for the purchase of both the Holofile and the Beehive shares (total purchase price of $12,437); the purchase price of the condominium was $64,000; Dorothy made the down payment of $26,577 and signed a promissory note for the balance; she made payments of $413 per month on the note until her death; Alta moved into the condominium and paid Dorothy no rent for it; Dorothy originally took title to the condominium in her name alone by grant deed recorded March 31, 1977; she subsequently executed a deed, recorded May 24, 1977, conveying to Alta a joint tenancy interest in the condominium; Alta gave Dorothy no valuable consideration in exchange for such interest; Dorothy had trust and confidence in Alta in December 1976 and January 1977. Gelbmann testified: Dorothy told him that she trusted Alta because Alta was a "woman of the world," knew real estate, was an investment counselor and broker, and knew about "buying and selling and the money market."

Undue influence consists of conduct which subjugates the will of the testator to the will of another and causes the testator to make a disposition of his property contrary to and different from that which he would have done had he been permitted to follow his own inclination or judgment. (Estate of Franco (1975) 50 Cal.App.3d 374, 382, 123 Cal.Rptr. 458.) A presumption of undue influence arises when there is a concurrence of the following elements: (1) the existence of a confidential or fiduciary relationship between the testator and the person alleged to have exerted undue influence; (2) active participation by such person in the preparation or execution of the will; and (3) an undue benefit to such person or another person under the will thus procured. The evidence establishes the existence of the first element, for Alta herself testified that Dorothy had trust and confidence in her. "Confidential and fiduciary relations are, in law, synonymous, and may be said to exist whenever trust and confidence is reposed by one person in the integrity and fidelity of another." (Estate of Cover (1922) 188 Cal. 133, 143, 204 P. 583.) Nor can it be denied that Alta (and her grandson Whitaker) unduly profited under Dorothy's will. The question whether the proponent unduly profited by the will is resolved by the terms of the will itself. (Estate of Bucher (1941) 48 Cal.App.2d 465, 473, 120 P.2d 44.) Under the will in question Alta was given the bulk of the estate and Whitaker was given $5,000, a sum greater than any of the bequests to members of Dorothy's family. . . .

Activity on the part of the proponent in procuring execution of the will may be established by inference, that is, by circumstantial evidence. . . . In determining whether undue influence was exerted by the proponent upon the testator in the execution of his will, the jury is not limited to the actual time the will was executed, but may consider facts bearing upon undue influence both before and after execution so long as they tend to show such influence when the will was executed. (See Estate of Larendon (1963) 216 Cal.App.2d 14, 19, 30 Cal.Rptr. 697.) Nor need the one using the undue influence be present in person at the time of the execution of the document if the influence is present to constrain the party from exercising his free will. The evidence of the use of undue influence need not be direct but may be circumstantial. (Estate of Greuner (1939) 31 Cal.App.2d 161, 162, 87 P.2d 872.) " 'That the alleged wrongdoer had power or ability to control the testamentary act may be established by a variety of circumstances,—such as control over the decedent's business affairs, dependency of the decedent upon the beneficiary for care and attention, or domination on the part of the beneficiary and subserviency on the part of the deceased. Unless explained, a transfer of property by the decedent to the alleged wrongdoer has a tendency to establish the charge of undue influence. . . . ' " (Estate of Washington (1953) 116 Cal.App.2d 139, 145–146, 253 P.2d 60.)

The evidence establishes: After the death of mother and "Bake," Alta, who had been only a casual acquaintence, represented herself to Dorothy as a medium or psychic able to communicate with the spirits of the dead; beginning in 1975 and continuing to the time of Dorothy's death in 1978, Alta relayed to Dorothy "messages" from her mother and brother "Bake" instructing her to do or not to do certain things; Dorothy believed Alta to be a true psychic and medium, and believed in the messages and, with but two exceptions, did as they instructed; Alta thus obtained total control of Dorothy's mind; her mind was under Alta's domination, and Dorothy's conduct was guided by the messages to the extent that Alta was able to and did direct her in financial matters, succeeded in alienating Dorothy from her relatives and friends, prevailed upon her to kill her pet cats and persuaded her to terminate her relationship with her stockbroker and turn over to her her stocks; during the year in which Dorothy executed her will, she was induced by Alta through her "messages" from dead relatives to and did give to Alta over $60,500 in checks, free trips and other benefits, and paid for stocks and a condominium in which Alta was given a joint tenancy interest, all without any consideration having been furnished by Alta in return. Then within a year of the execution of her will, and knowing Dorothy had had several heart attacks and could have another in high altitudes, Alta prevailed upon Dorothy to take a trip to Peru by representing to her that mother and "Bake" wanted her to go and would remain earthbound and be unable to rise to a higher plane if she did not; Dorothy was thus persuaded by Alta to make the trip even though she knew she could suffer another heart attack and it would hasten her death. From this evidence the jury reasonably could infer that Alta procured the will through the same means (acting as a medium with messages from the dead) whereby she obtained from Dorothy gifts of money and interests in the stocks and condominium. Such inference is particularly compelling in light of the evidence that Alta had the same control over Dorothy's mind after execution of the will that she had prior thereto even to the point of persuading her by messages from her dead relatives to take a trip she knew could endanger her life. The record demonstrates that Alta's control over Dorothy's mind and her influence so pervaded Dorothy's thought processes that they completely subverted her

will to the wishes and domination of Alta, and that this imposition
continued from the moment Dorothy was convinced Alta was a true
psychic and medium to immediately before her death.

Alta's procurement of the will, coupled with the remaining two facts
(confidential relations and undue profiting), gave rise to a presumption of
undue influence; the burden then was cast upon appellants to show that
the will was not the result of undue influence. Alta produced evidence
that she was not present at the execution of the will; but that fact alone
does not, as a matter of law, overcome the inference of undue influence in
procuring the will which may be drawn from other evidence. It is for the
trier of fact to determine whether the presumption of undue influence has
been rebutted. The question of whether or not this burden was met was
for the jury. On this record we must sustain the jury's implied finding
that appellants did not meet the burden of overcoming the presumption of
undue influence which arises under the circumstances in this case.[5]

. . .

The judgment is affirmed.

L. THAXTON HANSON and DALSIMER, JJ., concur.

Section Eight.   Improving the Private-Arrangement Instrument

From the preceding materials in this chapter, you have probably formed
some opinions on how private arrangements could better be facilitated by
a legal system. See what you can add to the discussion that follows about
improving the private-arrangement mode.

In terms of the grant of power to private parties to enter their own
arrangements, *Williams* v. *Walker-Thomas Furniture Co.* suggests
bounds—those with a powerful bargaining advantage should not be permitted to dictate the terms of private arrangements, at least not when the
resultant terms are unconscionably one-sided. At the same time, power to
effect private arrangements should not be granted too sparingly. For
example, judges should not too often substitute their own judgments for
those of the parties as to what is a fair bargain.

Private parties should receive as much pertinent information as feasible prior to their entering an arrangement. For example, rules of
disclosure should be strengthened (*Weintraub* v. *Krobatsch*), and secondary techniques of facilitation such as governmental weather and market
reports should be improved. Relatedly, protection of the deliberative
process from undue influence (*Estate of Baker*) and duress (*Alaska Packers' Ass'n* v. *Domenico*) should be ensured.

Sufficient legal forms or devices such as contracts, wills, and corporations should be available to facilitate private planning. But this is not
enough. The rules of validation must be sufficiently clear and simple to
encourage, or at least not discourage, the exercise of private powers. For
example, we have introduced briefly the benefits of private contracting; it

---

5. Undue influence and fraud are separate and distinct grounds for setting aside a will.
(Prob.Code, § 22; Estate of Newhall (1923) 190 Cal. 709, 718, 214 P. 731.) However, the
evidence herein likewise supports the special finding of fraud in the procurement of the
challenged portions of the will.

logically follows that the rules of offer and acceptance should facilitate contract formation rather than impede it (*Lefkowitz* v. *Great Minneapolis Surplus Store, Inc.*). At the same time, complete evisceration of rules of validation must be avoided because they provide evidence of the parties' intentions and caution the parties about the ramifications of their conduct.

The methods for determining the meaning and significance of private arrangements, such as the rules of interpretation and gap filling of contracts, should be clear, logical, consistent, and fair. Consider again *Pennyrile Tours, Inc.* v. *Country Inns, USA, Inc.* Do the rules of gap filling offered in that case contribute to clarity and consistency?

Private-arrangement law should also offer clear, logical, consistent, and fair remedies for breach. At the same time, the law should support private dispute resolution to aid the parties in keeping their deal together and to avoid clogging the courts. Nonadversarial proceedings, such as those suggested for family dispute settling, should be available when such proceedings would best facilitate private arrangements. Government should also provide, through courts and other bodies, administrative supervision such as the administration of wills and trusts.

Finally, individuals trained in the law should be accessible to all private persons who require advice and aid either in setting up a private arrangement or in administering it. The *White* v. *Benkowski* episode portrayed in Section 6 was not merely propaganda for the legal industry! The costs involved in retaining a lawyer for a simple transaction can, however, sometimes outweigh the benefits of the services. Private-arrangement law must therefore facilitate such nonlawyer-assisted deals by promoting the use of plain language and avoiding technical interpretations.

Most Western legal systems strive for all of the foregoing elements. Many, if not all, of them fall short in various ways. There is always room for improvement—more in some legal systems than in others. In Anglo-American legal systems, relevant proposals for reform have been legion.

Section Nine. Limitations of Law as a Private-Arrangement Instrument

What are the law's limits in facilitating private arrangements? One obvious limitation can be seen from the discussion in Section 8. Much of the discussion suggests the need for finding the proper balance between conflicting approaches. For example, the law must deny those with powerful bargaining advantages the right to dictate unconscionable terms, but at the same time judges must not substitute their judgment for the parties' as to what is a fair bargain. Rules of validation must be simple to facilitate the exercise of private powers, but they must also be somewhat onerous to preserve their formalistic functions. Can the law successfully draw such lines? Consider the guidance offered on the bargaining power problem by the official comment to Uniform Commercial Code § 2–302: "The principle is one of the prevention of oppression and unfair surprise . . . . and not of disturbance of allocation of risks because of superior bargaining power." Is this any guidance at all?

Another limitation of law is that it cannot ensure that the ultimate aims of private parties in entering an arrangement will be fulfilled. This is so largely because of the varied and personal nature of these aims. Through marriage, parties seek love and happiness. In drafting a will, the testator may hope to make a particular beneficiary independent. Contracting parties may want financial satisfaction or something else— recall *Hamer* v. *Sidway*. The goals of people in setting up corporations, joining churches, and becoming members of social clubs or other organizations are also numerous and varied.

What are the sources of law's limits in helping to effectuate aims of the foregoing kinds? First, people often do not know their own minds. Even if the law were perfectly adapted to effectuate an arrangement, the participants might still not realize the benefits that they anticipated. For example, consider the high divorce rate in this country. Second, even if individuals know what they want, they may choose an inappropriate arrangement to secure it. This, too, is not uncommon. A bequest of certain property to one son, and of other property to the other, may make both unhappy. Third, even if people know what they want and decide upon the right private arrangement to achieve that end, the kinds of legal consequences afforded such arrangements can hardly substitute for the private working of the arrangement itself. Law cannot make marriage partners love each other. Indeed, many types of contract performances cannot be coerced, or at least performance is not likely to be the same if an opera star, a painter, or a musician performs under a court decree. Moreover, even if specific performance would result in satisfactory performance, the law cannot force performance without violating precious freedoms.

Section Ten.   Bibliography

1. *General.* H.M. Hart & A. Sacks, The Legal Process 207–365 (tent. ed. 1958); M. Phillips, The Dilemmas of Individualism 69–119 (1983).

2. *Private-Arrangement Techniques.* A. Conard, Corporations in Perspective 1–74 (1976); C. Fried, Contract as Promise (1981); L. Friedman, Contract Law in America (1965); G. Gilmore, The Death of Contract (1974); Weitzman, Legal Regulation of Marriage: Tradition and Change, 62 Calif.L.Rev. 1169 (1974).

3. *Authorized Makers of Private-Arrangement Law and Their Appropriate Collaborative Roles.* Cavers, Legal Education and Lawyer-made Law, 54 W.Va.L. Rev. 177 (1952); Jaffe, Law Making by Private Groups, 51 Harv.L.Rev. 201 (1937); Kennedy, Form and Substance in Private Law Adjudication, 89 Harv.L.Rev. 1685 (1976); Patterson, The Codification of Commercial Law in the Light of Jurisprudence, Report of the New York Law Revision Commission for 1955, 1 Study of the Uniform Commercial Code 41 (1955).

4. *Structures and Processes for Applying Private-Arrangement Law and Techniques.* Arbitration in Practice (A. Zack ed. 1984); Eisenberg, Private Ordering Through Negotiation: Dispute Settlement and Rulemaking, 89 Harv.L.Rev. 637 (1976).

5. *Necessity for and Nature of Coercive Power.* D. Dobbs, Handbook on the Law of Remedies 93–104 (1973); H.L.A. Hart, The Concept of Law 91, 193–94 (1961); Hale, Force and the State: A Comparison of "Political" and "Economic" Compulsion, 35 Colum.L.Rev. 149 (1935).

6. *Roles of Private Citizens and Their Lawyers.* Q. Johnstone & D. Hopson, Lawyers and Their Work (1967); Brown, Planning with Your Client—Two Steps in Advance, 39 Cal.St.B.J. 478 (1964); Macneil, A Primer of Contract Planning, 48 S.Cal.L.Rev. 627 (1975).

7. *Process Values.* Ellinghaus, In Defense of Unconscionability, 78 Yale L.J. 757 (1969); Kessler & Fine, Culpa in Contrahendo, Bargaining in Good Faith, and Freedom of Contract: A Comparative Study, 77 Harv.L.Rev. 401 (1964); Kronman, Contract Law and Distributive Justice, 89 Yale L.J. 472 (1980); Perr, Wills, Testamentary Capacity, and Undue Influence, 9 Bull.Am.Acad.Psychiatry & L. 15 (1981).

8. *Improving the Private-Arrangement Instrument.* Farnsworth, Disputes over Omissions in Contracts, 68 Colum.L.Rev. 860 (1968); Gordon, The Family Court: When Properly Defined, It Is Both Desirable and Attainable, 14 J.Fam.L. 1 (1975); Kronman, Mistake, Disclosure, and the Law of Contract, 7 J.Legal Stud. 1 (1978).

9. *Limitations of Law as a Private-Arrangement Instrument.* R. Neely, Why Courts Don't Work (1983); Kraakman, Corporate Liability Strategies and the Costs of Legal Controls, 93 Yale L.J. 857 (1984); Leff, Unconscionability and the Code, 115 U.Pa.L.Rev. 485 (1967).

Part Two

THE ENDS OF LAW

Chapter Six

LAW CAN HELP PROMOTE SAFETY

Chapter Seven

LAW CAN HELP PROMOTE EQUALITY

Each of the foregoing chapters contains an introduction, five sections that respectively apply the five legal instruments to the social end, and a bibliography.

PREFATORY NOTE TO PART TWO

In Part 1 we treated the nature of law principally by considering the range and limits of law's methodology. The central question was *how* law does what it does. Chapters 1 through 5 compared and differentiated the five basic instruments of law, which constitute the means at law's disposal.

Thus far, however, we have slighted part of law's nature: we have not considered many of the social functions to which people commonly assign law. Part 2, then, elaborates on *what* law does. What can law do and not do? That is, what are the range and limits of the ends of law? Four themes predominate.

First, modern societies assign a variety of tasks to law. The variety is wide, the end uses may be good or bad, and different societies discharge different functions in different degrees by different techniques. We employ illustration to suggest this variety. In this part, we look at how law can help promote safety and equality in American society. Chapter 6 considers safety, an old and tangible concern rooted in tort and private law. Chapter 7 considers equality, a newer and more intangible effort emerging from constitutional and public law. Comparisons and contrasts between these two chapters should lead students to a deeper understanding of the ends of law.

Second, observe that the foregoing formulation of the illustrative tasks contains the words "can help promote." This formulation acknowledges that law does not always achieve society's aims. But those words express more than that. A common, as well as a professional, fallacy about law is that what law does achieve, it achieves all alone. Morality, however, assists the penal-corrective mode, does it not? For another example, self-interest makes the job of safety regulation vastly easier. Thus, law receives large assists from nonlegal techniques—a second theme we develop through Part 2.

Third, law typically does not rely on just one of its basic instruments to address a given social problem. It may apply a variant of a basic instrument. It may invent a combination mode that draws ideas from several of the basic instruments. Most likely, law brings a number of the five instruments to bear simultaneously, and in their characteristically different ways, on the social task. Consider again the example of slaughter on the highways. Here, remedies are available that allow the injured or bereaved to exact monetary compensation (the grievance-remedial instrument); punishment is imposed for reckless or drunken driving (the penal-corrective instrument); licenses are required of drivers (the administrative-regulatory instrument); safe highways can be constructed and maintained (the public-benefit instrument); and insurers protect the injured against crippling losses (the private-arrangement instrument). In this part, the two chapters each center on five sections that explore how the five basic instruments can all contribute to promoting safety and equality.

Fourth, Part 2 develops the theme that law may be fruitfully viewed from the vantage point of an imaginary social engineer or manager who has power over the law's resources and has responsibility for their rational allocation to given tasks. Total rationality is impossible, because the manager does not know enough and cannot anticipate all consequences of action. And many social phenomena are not readily subject to conscious alteration, but instead change through some poorly understood and slow evolutionary process. Nevertheless, the managerial viewpoint, when combined with the conception of law as five distinct instruments, has value as a critical apparatus in several ways.

Along a first dimension, we may criticize the appropriateness of the selection among the legal instruments. The manager might simply choose an *inapt* instrument for the job. For example, if the end were to ensure a minimal living standard for all members of the society, we would then expect less reliance on grievance-remedial methods and more on public-benefit conferral. Or the manager's choice of an instrument might be otherwise *unwise,* being impractical or somehow detrimental. For example, use of the private-arrangement instrument to achieve a minimal living standard for everyone may be unwise. Or the manager's resort to a particular instrument might under the circumstances be *unnecessary* and hence wasteful or even counterproductive. For example, given that drug manufacturers are already subject to civil remedies for most injuries they inflict, and given that the administrative-regulatory mode already supervises the manufacturing process, invoking the penal-corrective instrument by imposing criminal liability for producing unsafe drugs may be unnecessary. Or the manager might employ an *insufficient* number of instruments. For example, we have already indicated how all five basic instruments prove useful in combating the problem of slaughter on the highways.

A second dimension of criticism looks not at the selection among instruments but at the effectiveness of their use. Even if a particular instrument is appropriate for a given task, the manager might not be using it in its most effective form. The manager may have framed an ineffective remedy for the grievance, an unduly stringent penalty for the crime, an unrealistic regulatory standard to meet, and so on.

A third dimension of criticism opens up. In Part 1 we examined the distinctive conditions for maximal effectiveness of each of the law's instruments. This led us to consider their correlative limitations. When this kind of critical evaluation is applied to all five instruments in relation to a given social problem, we can ascertain whether law as a whole is likely to be less effective in dealing with the problem than in dealing with others, or whether law stands much of a chance of success at all. That is, Part 2 not only will refine your idea of the nature of law by stressing its functions but also will heighten your consciousness of the limits of law as a whole.

GENERAL BIBLIOGRAPHY FOR PART TWO

1. *General Criteria for Evaluating the Uses of Law.* J. Bentham, An Introduction to the Principles of Morals and Legislation (rev. ed. London 1823) (1st ed. London 1789); D. Braybrooke, Three Tests for Democracy (1968); L. Fuller, The Morality of Law (rev. ed. 1969); H.L.A. Hart, The Concept of Law (1961); R. Pound, An Introduction to the Philosophy of Law (rev. ed. 1954); V. Rosenblum, Law as a Political Instrument (1955); Cohen, The Interests Served by the Law and the Methods of Their Evaluation, 14 J.Phil.Psychology & Sci.Methods 189 (1917); Laswell, The Interplay of Economic, Political, and Social Criteria in Legal Policy, 14 Vand.L.Rev. 451 (1961).

2. *Managerial Perspective on the Use of Law's Instruments.* R. Pound, Social Control Through Law (1942); Chroust, The Managerial Function of Law, 34 B.U.L. Rev. 261 (1954); Rhees, Social Engineering, 56 Mind (n.s.) 317 (1947); Simpson & Field, Social Engineering Through Law: The Need for a School of Applied Jurisprudence, 22 N.Y.U.L.Q.Rev. 145 (1947).

CHAPTER SIX

Law Can Help Promote Safety

[I]t is the right of the people . . . to institute new government, laying its foundation on such principles, and organizing its powers in such form, as to them shall seem most likely to effect their safety and happiness.

DECLARATION OF INDEPENDENCE

Section One. Introduction

(Pedagogic Vehicles Drawn Mainly from Product Safety Law)

This chapter concerns how the law functions to promote safety. We shall focus on the problem of product safety, and you will be exposed to much law dealing with the problem. Our goal, however, is not to teach product safety law. Instead, we use that law to illustrate how each of the law's five basic instrumentalities presented in the first five chapters of this book can help achieve an important social goal.

Hardly surprising is that law is utilized to deal with the problem of product safety. Today, consumers may choose from a host of products, and they are barraged with propaganda from producers extolling the virtues of their products. As product usage increases and as modern technology increases the complexity of products and their danger, the ranks of injured consumers have swollen. Injuries may result from design defects, defects in manufacturing, or failure to warn about proper usage.[a] Consider the power lawn mower. Although in the late 1940s, injuries caused by such mowers were unusual, the number of such injuries mushroomed dramatically as technology increased their power and sophistication and as consumers increasingly used such mowers.[b]

Although injuries from defective products are increasing and although the public may clamor for legal relief, it is not self-evident what form the

---

a. In this chapter, the term *defective* encompasses all of these problems. "Defective" condition is defined in the Restatement (Second) of Torts § 402A comment g (1965) as "a condition not contemplated by the ultimate consumer, which will be unreasonably dangerous to him."

b. 1 L. Frumer & M. Friedman, Products Liability § 1, at 4–5 (1984) (reporting that a twenty-four-inch blade of a power lawn mower can pick up an object and hurl it at a speed of 225–240 MPH).

relief should take or, for that matter, whether there should be any relief at all, at least for some injuries from some defects. As you consider the materials in this chapter, remember that the most fundamental question is whether the law should step in at all. The two excerpts at the end of this introduction deal with this question.

Assuming that law should be utilized to deal with product safety, as you read this chapter you should also evaluate the appropriateness of each legal instrumentality in achieving the goal of product safety. For example, should criminal liability be imposed on companies that produce unreasonably dangerous products? To answer this question, one must focus on the particular characteristics of the penal-corrective mode, but the problem is also a comparative one. Are other instrumentalities better suited to achieve the goal of protecting people from dangerous products? If manufacturers are civilly liable for negligent manufacture and for breach of contract, for example, are criminal sanctions or administrative regulations necessary? One may conclude that a combination of instrumentalities best serves the particular goal. Or one may conclude that none of the law's instrumentalities alone or in concert with others can achieve the goal. This chapter is about the law's limits as well as its functions.

Even assuming the appropriateness of a particular legal instrumentality, another issue is whether the instrumentality is utilized effectively. For example, some argue that punitive damages should not be recoverable for injuries resulting from product defects because, among other reasons, companies will simply raise the prices of their products to finance their punitive liability or insure against such liability. Even if this criticism is correct, however, other forms of civil relief may be effective to compel companies to manufacture safer products, and lawmakers must consider such alternatives. As you read this chapter, consider whether any appropriate instrumentality of the law is misused and what changes in application you would propose.

R. EPSTEIN, MODERN PRODUCTS LIABILITY LAW

5-7 (1980).*

It is useful to trace products liability law through three main stages in its development. The first stage, from *Winterbottom* v. *Wright*[4] in 1842 until *MacPherson* v. *Buick Motor Co.*[5] in 1916, had as its major premise the belief that the grave administrative complications and adverse social consequences of products liability suits were so manifest that strenuous efforts were needed to fashion "fixed and definite" rules to prevent the economic ruin of product suppliers. In most cases, but not all, the result of this attitude was to place upon product users and consumers the burden of ferreting out and correcting all manner of product weaknesses and deficiencies. The privity rule—riddled with exceptions before it toppled—

---

* Copyright © 1980 by Richard Epstein. Reprinted by permission.
4. 10 M. & W. 109, 152 Eng.Rep. 402 (Exch.1842).
5. 217 N.Y. 382, 111 N.E. 1050 (1916).

was a major tool, but by no means the only one, used to achieve that end. The need to prove the defendant's negligence helped insulate manufacturers from liability for defective products they placed upon the marketplace. The narrow conception of causal connection spared them liability whenever the negligence of other parties farther down the chain of distribution and use substantially contributed to the occurrence of injury. Strong affirmative defenses, whether of contributory negligence or assumption of risk, placed still further obstacles in the way of recovery, and rigorous requirements of proof everywhere blocked the plaintiff. The law was altogether too restrictive, as many of the barriers to recovery could not be justified either as a matter of substantive principle or administrative necessity.

The second stage of the development began with the epic decision in *MacPherson* v. *Buick* and continued until, roughly speaking, shortly after the publication in 1965 of the Restatement (Second) of Torts. In this period products liability law achieved what in retrospect appears to be the best balance between the dual constraints of substantive justice and administrative need. The manufacturer was required to supply the individual consumer with the product that had been promised or take the consequences if that product proved dangerous because it deviated from the manufacturer's own formula, design, or performance standards. The individual consumer or user was bound, as a condition of recovery, to treat that product with the respect that it deserved, to use it in the proper way and for its appropriate ends. The legal rules functioned like an elaborate set of implied contracts that carefully distributed losses from product-related accidents in accordance with the shared expectations of manufacturer and user. The privity limitation upon recovery was everywhere rejected; the negligence requirements were first eroded and then eliminated; the defect requirement in products liability actions was sensibly applied, if not always fully defined; and a workable set of affirmative defenses tied the fortunes of the injured party to his own conduct. While by no means perfect, the system evenly distributed the burdens of loss between manufacturers and consumers.

The third stage of development, which began sometime between 1968 and 1970, starts from totally different philosophical premises. Administrative necessities, which loomed all too large in the nineteenth century, are taken all too lightly by modern judges. In the surge toward ever greater public control, courts have radically redefined the relative obligations of manufacturers and consumers. The plaintiff must still show some defect in the defendant's product, but the defect concept has been expanded far beyond its traditional confines. No longer can a product escape legal scrutiny because it was supplied in the very condition in which the defendant represented it to be, for now in many jurisdictions a jury may treat that product as defective if it thinks that some alternative design or plan on balance is preferable. As a common law matter, the entire system cares much less for contractual models for setting liability and much more for public law models of regulation—judicial regulation to be sure, but regulation nonetheless.

The redefinition of the manufacturer's obligation has brought with it a correlative shift in the obligations of the product consumer. Whereas the consumer was once regarded as an essential and responsible link in the chain of product use, today he is often viewed more as an object of legal protection and less as a bearer of independent responsibilities. Instead of being held accountable for the consequences of his own misconduct, the consumer is all too often insulated from his own recklessness, foolishness, and neglect. In years past, a drunken driver could never dream of recovery against the manufacturer of his own automobile; today such recoveries can, and do, take place.

————

M. SHAPO, A NATION OF GUINEA PIGS

xi, xiv–xv, 90, 253–56 (1979).*

The march of science has proved a boon for most, but it also has brought tragedy to a few.

The media deluge us with stories about beneficial products of scientific progress that cause or threaten harm to those in no position to make meaningful choices. The case of oral contraceptives is a benchmark in the history of medical progress. Though the Pill has freed millions from sexual constraints, it has proved, over a decade of marketing, to have serious side effects for a relatively small number of users, and the returns on its long-term consequences are not in yet. The seemingly miraculous versatility of the sex hormones used to prevent conception has been utilized in other ways to preserve it, and in the fullness of the cycle of the life they control, to promote growth. Thus, the hormone diethylstilbestrol (DES) has been employed to prevent miscarriages, and also to improve the rate of weight gain in livestock. Yet in the former instance there is evidence that it has caused cancers in the very children whose conception it fostered. And in the latter case, controversy has arisen about the possible cancer-causing properties of the tiny residues of the chemical in marketed meat. . . .

. . . [A] major thesis of this book is that over a period of about forty years a consensus has developed among the American people and their representatives about the risks that attend the benefits of scientific and technological progress. This consensus holds in effect that when concern and suspicion about these potential hazards find their way into the public eye, Americans adopt a generally risk-averse perspective on being exposed to dangers that are cumulative, unseen, and uncertain over the long term. A large part of this concern, articulated as well as implicit in several safety-focused statutes, is based in motives of self-protection against the uncertain danger. Part of it is founded in a sense that we should make strong efforts to limit the exposure of random groups of the population to the risks of serious physical injury or even death from dangers that are unpredictable and unknowable and may strike without warning. This view may be especially strong when the traumatic connotations of dangers that "strike" cannot adequately describe a process that may take months or even years in the human body. Further, when public anxiety about such hazards finds its way into legislation, judges tend to credit this risk-averse tendency, motivated interstitially by the factors described above as well as responding to the specific public concern embodied in safety statutes.

Americans have generally been a self-reliant, confident, and optimistic people. At the same time, a frontier heritage has given them a certain philosophical approach to the risks of living. Moreover, their principal choice of economic mechanisms, even well into a century that has seen increasing collectivization and regulation, has involved reliance on the market. It is therefore especially noteworthy when law, in the form of both legislation and judicial decision, manifests on their behalf a view of risk that is relatively defensive and regulatory.

The explanation for this, I think, lies in part in the relatively unknowable and insidious character of the risks discussed here. It also lies in the manmade origin of these dangers, as compared with the stark, natural character of the hazards that were the lot of our forebears. In addition, the hidden nature of these risks presents sharp contrasts with the glossy picture of the good life, achievable through new possessions and processes, painted by the mass media. When the heightened expectations thus created are disappointed by injury and disease, frustration and even anger set in. This has contributed to an increasing belief that regulation of technical progress must respond to the fact that progress often brings savage disappointment to some.

It is against this background that the view has developed that those who market new goods or create external consequences from processes that are novel or not thoroughly tested owe the community a scientific affirmation of safety at particular levels of use, or at least an abundance of warnings and opportunities to make a choice. It is for these reasons that legislatures, abetted by courts, have chosen to impose more caution on the development and marketing of new forms of products and processes. . . .

. . . The premise, significant in the background of public regulation, is that [physical harm caused by trauma or disease] cannot easily be quantified in dollars in the way that consumers assign values when they conventionally trade off one form of economic goods for another. Implicit in social judgments in this realm is a notion that there is a qualitative feature of pain and death, particularly the kinds of pain and death caused by the sort of products discussed in this book, that our humanity refuses to balance nicely against marginal gains in welfare. Associated with this is the perception that it is unfair to impose these special costs on unsuspecting individuals—or even on those who cannot adequately take precautions although information about risk is generally public—in order to benefit others. A related set of considerations concerns information deficiencies—both the dearth of raw facts about the effects of goods, and ignorance resulting from the inability to assess data. These factors are indivisibly entwined with issues of fairness. We should not fail to ask what individuals want and what is efficient; and government intervention often represents an effort to compensate for market inefficiencies related to information costs. But public regulation also embraces questions of what society desires in the way of justice. . . .

It bears emphasis that the reasons for regulating scientific activity that creates uncertain, long-term risks derive in large part from the arcane nature of those risks. The fact that the public often has no idea of their existence and no understanding of their character provides an important rationale for regulation. A related component of the problem is the inability of individuals to take precautions that will avoid personal injury. Another important factor, not often expressed, is the relative inefficacy of post injury remedies as deterrents to conduct that may cause widespread suffering only after long periods. Thus, for example, the long-range action of carcinogens makes the prospect of punishment rather unimposing as a check on officials of technology-based firms who choose to take cancer-causing risks. Even disregarding statutes of limitations for personal injury actions, many such decisionmakers will have completed their working lives before harm becomes apparent. This time problem exacerbates difficulties of proof in addition to bringing into play the tendency to forgive and forget long past conduct. Moreover, it is rather difficult both under public regulation and at common law to fix personal financial, much less criminal, liability on corporate officials for such decisions. . . .

I have dealt principally thus far with the external consequences of risky innovation as they provide rationales for regulation. By contrast, it is well to mention a number of problems associated with the encroachment of regulation on untrammeled inquiry and production. Of particular concern is the tendency of increased regulation to produce disincentives to creative investigation. This is why before one advocates government intervention, it is necessary to show some reason to believe that new lines of inquiry or new production techniques or designs are hazardous. This is a principal reason that we require expert identification of risk. . . .

Still another consideration, which may be called the time-discount factor, further complicates analysis of hazards whose uncertain potential extends over the long term. Everyone is willing to trade a certain amount of future disadvantage for some present gains. The immediate utility of an activity may be so great that we will choose the benefit now and take our chances with the future, especially knowing that there are many other fatal events that may intervene. Culture does limit our inclination to act this way, and indeed a predominant strain of thought through most of our national history has checked this tendency, emphasizing present self-denial for future gain. Without drawing normative conclusions about this approach to life, one must note that many of the problems discussed here involve the reaping of present benefits, traded off against the risk of future harms. Because this is so, we may not concentrate solely on requiring the proponents of novelties to prove their safety; we must consider the advantages these innovations presently confer.

Comments and Questions

1. What accounts for the increase in the use of law to deal with product safety?

2. What are the benefits and drawbacks of such a trend? Why not simply let the consumer decide whether to buy or not?

Section Two. Product Safety and the Private-Arrangement Instrument

Chapter 5 focused on how private individuals arrange their affairs and how law is utilized to facilitate those arrangements. Enforcing private contracts is one method of dealing with the problem of product safety. A seller may promise that his goods are free from defects in order to make a sale. A seller who makes such a promise is liable for its breach. Such potential liability will presumably encourage the seller to exercise care in manufacturing and distributing the product. Still, private contracting may not ensure product safety. First, some sellers may be able to raise prices to cover potential liability for defects. Second, buyers who suffer injuries from defective products are not ensured a recovery on breach of contract grounds. Many issues must be resolved in favor of the buyer. For example, what was the content of the seller's promise (i.e., what representations concerning the product's quality—called warranties— were made) and what representations were inaccurate? In addition, who is entitled to sue and who can be sued for a product defect? Can a nonbuyer user of a defective product bring a breach of warranty action for injuries suffered while using the product? May the injured person sue the remote manufacturer of a product instead of the immediate seller? The potential for a defendant's victory in litigation on any of these issues creates a disincentive to provide product quality in the first place.

Although we cannot hope to resolve all of the previous questions (and others) in this chapter, what follows is a brief overview of warranty law. Much of warranty law is statutory. The Uniform Commercial Code (U.C.C. or Code), drafted by practicing lawyers, judges, and law teachers to govern commercial transactions and subsequently enacted, at least in part, by all of our fifty state legislatures, contains rules pertaining to warranty law in Article 2, which deals with the sale of goods.

Article 2 treats four warranties, among which are the express warranty and the implied warranty of merchantability. An express warranty may be made by affirmation, promise, description, sample, or model, but it must be more than the salesperson's opinion, sometimes called puffing. Generally, the more specific and verifiable an assertion, the greater the likelihood that the assertion will create an express warranty. Thus, a salesperson's assertion that a television is "A–1" probably does not create an express warranty. An affirmation or the like must also be the "basis of the bargain" to constitute a warranty. Generally, the test of "basis of the bargain" appears to focus on whether it would be reasonable for a purchaser to rely on the affirmation. Although express warranties seemingly provide some protection to consumers of defective products, such warranties may be disclaimed by the seller in the contract of sale.

According to the U.C.C., when a seller is a merchant dealing in goods of the kind sold, a warranty of merchantability is implied in the contract of sale, unless such a warranty is expressly excluded by the seller. A contract of sale silent on the quality of goods, then, would require a seller to deliver merchantable goods. Merchantability requires that the goods are "fit for the ordinary purpose for which such goods are used." U.C.C. § 2–314(2)(c). Is this definition clear and easily applied? Consider whether cigarettes are merchantable.

Under Article 2, the remedies for breach of warranty include damages for "injury to person . . . proximately resulting from the breach." U.C.C. § 2–715(2). Nevertheless, the parties to a contract of sale are free to shape the remedies for breach of warranty. Unfortunately, this typically results in sellers' severely limiting available remedies for breach, for example, limiting them to repair of a defective product (with the cost of labor sometimes allocated to the consumer!). If a given remedy "fails of its essential purpose," such as when the remedy is repair of a defective part but the repair is never successful, or if the remedy limitation is unconscionable, then the purchaser is free to pursue other remedies. U.C.C. § 2–719(2) to (3). Limitation of damages for personal injury is "prima facie unconscionable," meaning that the seller has the burden of proving that such a limitation is *not* unconscionable in the particular context. U.C.C. § 2–719(3).

Early contract law permitted only those in "privity of contract" (i.e., those parties who signed a contract) to sue each other for breach. According to the privity requirement, then, only the buyer could sue for a product defect, not other people who were injured by the product, and only the immediate seller could be sued, not others in the distributive chain. The drafters of the U.C.C., reflecting more modern cases that diluted or ignored the privity requirement, presented the states with three alternative approaches to the question of who can sue for a product defect, ranging from people in the family or household and guests in the home to all people "who may reasonably be expected to . . . be affected by the goods." U.C.C. § 2–318. The alternatives also differ concerning the type of injury that is actionable; nonbuyer plaintiffs under two of the alternatives, for example, can recover only if injured in person. Different states therefore have different approaches to the problem of who can sue for what. Although the Code is silent on whether a remote manufacturer can be sued for defects and so leaves existing law unchanged, the Code includes an invitation to the courts to expand the potential defendants (and plaintiffs) through case-law development. U.C.C. § 2–318 comment 3; U.C.C. § 2–313 comment 2. Many courts have done just that.

Comments and Questions

1. In light of the principle of freedom of contract and the concomitant right of manufacturers and sellers to disclaim liability for both express and implied warranties, and to limit remedies, is the private-arrangement mode appropriate for protecting people from shoddy products? If so, is the private-arrangement mode currently utilized effectively to achieve this goal?

2. Can consumers effectively bargain for warranty protection? What would happen if you told your local car dealer that you will not purchase a car unless the dealer deletes all of the warranty disclaimers from the contract?

3. Consumers in the aggregate enjoy bargaining leverage in many settings. In a free-market system, sellers often must consider general consumer demand if they want to remain competitive.

Magnuson-Moss Warranty Act

In 1975, the United States Congress enacted warranty legislation known as the Magnuson-Moss Warranty–Federal Trade Commission Improvement Act, 15 U.S.C. §§ 2301–2312. Magnuson-Moss supplements the Uniform Commercial Code and protects buyers of consumer goods. A principal purpose of the act is to require greater clarity and disclosure concerning the protection afforded buyers of defective products.

The act does not *require* a seller to make a warranty, but any warranty made must be clear and conspicuous. The warranty must be labeled either "full" or "limited." The maker of a full warranty must satisfy certain standards, such as remedying defects quickly and without a labor charge. The hope was that competitive pressures would cause most warrantors to make full warranties, but such warranties appear to be the exception. If any warranty is made, disclaimer of implied warranties is foreclosed, and the warrantor must identify to whom the warranty is extended, describe the product, and explain what will be done in the event of breach and how the consumer should go about obtaining relief. A seller who violates Magnuson-Moss is subject to sanctions applied by the Federal Trade Commission and is subject to a private right of action by a consumer.

PRIEST, A THEORY OF THE CONSUMER PRODUCT WARRANTY

90 Yale L.J. 1297, 1297–98 (1981).*

Consumer product warranties are our most common of written contracts, but little is known about what determines their content or how they relate to the reliability and the durability of goods. Since the first appearance of standardized warranties early in this century, two theories have been proposed to explain their role in sales transactions. The first emphasizes the absence of bargaining over warranty provisions. It views warranties as devices of manufacturers to exploit consumers by unilaterally limiting legal obligations. The second and more recent theory focuses on the difficulty consumers face at the time of purchase in estimating the risk of product defects. This theory regards express warranties as messages signaling the mechanical attributes of goods.

Both theories have influenced substantially judicial and legislative responses to product warranties. The view of the warranty as an exploitative device has provided crucial support to the policy of enterprise liability and the replacement of contract principles with tort principles in

* Reprinted by permission of The Yale Law Journal Company and Fred B. Rothman & Company from *The Yale Law Journal*, Vol. 90, pp. 1297–98.

product defect cases. In addition, the exploitation theory is the intellectual basis for the modern judicial treatment of consumer warranty issues, in particular for the expansive interpretation of warranties implied by law, for the elimination of the requirement of privity of contract, and for the restriction of the manufacturer's authority to limit available remedies or to disclaim general obligations. More recently, the signal theory has informed the design of the federal Magnuson-Moss Warranty Act, which directly regulates both the form and content of consumer product warranties.

Neither the exploitation nor the signal theory, however, has contributed to the understanding of warranty practices. The exploitation theory derives from the presupposition of overwhelming manufacturer market power, but the connection remains vague between the extent of market power and the specific definition of warranty coverage. Similarly, the signal theory derives from the assumption of consumer misperception of product risks. However, plausible this assumption as a general matter, consumer perceptions are very difficult to identify or to measure. As a consequence, hypotheses concerning the relationship between perceptions and specific warranty provisions are highly speculative and essentially nonfalsifiable.

This article proposes a new theory of the standardized warranty and of the determinants of the content of the warranties of individual products. . . . A warranty is viewed as a contract that optimizes the productive services of goods by allocating responsibility between a manufacturer and consumer for investments to prolong the useful life of a product and to insure against product losses. According to the theory, the terms of warranty contracts are determined solely by the relative costs to the parties of these investments. An insurance function of warranty coverage, of course, is well-known. The novelty of the theory is its emphasis on the variety of allocative investments that consumers may make to extend productive capacity and its consideration of the difficulties of drafting warranty contracts to encourage such investments.

Section Three. Product Safety and the Grievance-Remedial Instrument

The grievance-remedial instrument defines grievances, specifies remedies, and provides for enforcement of awards, as we learned in Chapter 1. This instrument can be employed in the field of product safety. A cause of action in negligence can be asserted against a seller or manufacturer when a product defect causes personal injury or injury to property. The injured party is unaffected by any warranty disclaimers but must demonstrate a lack of reasonable care on the part of the defendant and must contend with disputes about contributory negligence. Because of dissatisfaction with both warranty and negligence theories to protect consumers adequately from defective goods, the theory of strict tort liability evolved.

GREENMAN v. YUBA POWER PRODUCTS, INC.

Supreme Court of California, 1963.
59 Cal.2d 57, 377 P.2d 897, 27 Cal.Rptr. 697.

TRAYNOR, JUSTICE.

Plaintiff brought this action for damages against the retailer and the manufacturer of a Shopsmith, a combination power tool that could be used as a saw, drill, and wood lathe. He saw a Shopsmith demonstrated by the retailer and studied a brochure prepared by the manufacturer. He decided he wanted a Shopsmith for his home workshop, and his wife bought and gave him one for Christmas in 1955. In 1957 he bought the necessary attachments to use the Shopsmith as a lathe for turning a large piece of wood he wished to make into a chalice. After he had worked on the piece of wood several times without difficulty, it suddenly flew out of the machine and struck him on the forehead, inflicting serious injuries. About ten and a half months later, he gave the retailer and the manufacturer written notice of claimed breaches of warranties and filed a complaint against them alleging such breaches and negligence.

After a trial before a jury, the court ruled that there was no evidence that the retailer was negligent or had breached any express warranty and that the manufacturer was not liable for the breach of any implied warranty. Accordingly, it submitted to the jury only the cause of action alleging breach of implied warranties against the retailer and the causes of action alleging negligence and breach of express warranties against the manufacturer. The jury returned a verdict for the retailer against plaintiff and for plaintiff against the manufacturer in the amount of $65,000. The trial court denied the manufacturer's motion for a new trial and entered judgment on the verdict. The manufacturer and plaintiff appeal. Plaintiff seeks a reversal of the part of the judgment in favor of the retailer, however, only in the event that the part of the judgment against the manufacturer is reversed.

Plaintiff introduced substantial evidence that his injuries were caused by defective design and construction of the Shopsmith. His expert witnesses testified that inadequate set screws were used to hold parts of the machine together so that normal vibration caused the tailstock of the lathe to move away from the piece of wood being turned permitting it to fly out of the lathe. They also testified that there were other more positive ways of fastening the parts of the machine together, the use of which would have prevented the accident. The jury could therefore reasonably have concluded that the manufacturer negligently constructed the Shopsmith. The jury could also reasonably have concluded that statements in the manufacturer's brochure were untrue, that they constituted express warranties,[1] and that plaintiff's injuries were caused by their breach. . . .

1. In this respect the trial court limited the jury to a consideration of two statements in the manufacturer's brochure. (1) "WHEN SHOPSMITH IS IN HORIZONTAL POSITION—Rugged construction of frame provides rigid support from end to end. Heavy centerless-ground steel tubing insures perfect alignment of components." (2) "SHOPSMITH maintains its accuracy because every component has positive locks that hold adjustments through rough or precision work."

. . . [T]o impose strict liability on the manufacturer under the circumstances of this case, it was not necessary for plaintiff to establish an express warranty [or negligence] . . . . A manufacturer is strictly liable in tort when an article he places on the market, knowing that it is to be used without inspection for defects, proves to have a defect that causes injury to a human being. Recognized first in the case of unwholesome food products, such liability has now been extended to a variety of other products that create as great or greater hazards if defective.

Although in these cases strict liability has usually been based on the theory of an express or implied warranty running from the manufacturer to the plaintiff, the abandonment of the requirement of a contract between them, the recognition that the liability is not assumed by agreement but imposed by law, and the refusal to permit the manufacturer to define the scope of its own responsibility for defective products make clear that the liability is not one governed by the law of contract warranties but by the law of strict liability in tort. Accordingly, rules defining and governing warranties that were developed to meet the needs of commercial transactions cannot properly be invoked to govern the manufacturer's liability to those injured by their defective products unless those rules also serve the purposes for which such liability is imposed.

. . . The purpose of [strict tort] liability is to insure that the costs of injuries resulting from defective products are borne by the manufacturers that put such products on the market rather than by the injured persons who are powerless to protect themselves. Sales warranties serve this purpose fitfully at best. (See Prosser, Strict Liability to the Consumer, 69 Yale L.J. 1099, 1124–1134.) In the present case, for example, plaintiff was able to plead and prove an express warranty only because he read and relied on the representations of the Shopsmith's ruggedness contained in the manufacturer's brochure. Implicit in the machine's presence on the market, however, was a representation that it would safely do the jobs for which it was built. Under these circumstances, it should not be controlling whether plaintiff selected the machine because of the statements in the brochure, or because of the machine's own appearance of excellence that belied the defect lurking beneath the surface, or because he merely assumed that it would safely do the jobs it was built to do. It should not be controlling whether the details of the sales from manufacturer to retailer and from retailer to plaintiff's wife were such that one or more of the implied warranties of the sales act arose. "The remedies of injured consumers ought not to be made to depend upon the intricacies of the law of sales." (Ketterer v. Armour & Co., D.C., 200 F. 322, 323.) To establish the manufacturer's liability it was sufficient that plaintiff proved that he was injured while using the Shopsmith in a way it was intended to be used as a result of a defect in design and manufacture of which plaintiff was not aware that made the Shopsmith unsafe for its intended use . . . .

The judgment is affirmed.

———

T. DALRYMPLE, BRIEF OPPOSING STRICT LIABILITY IN TORT

16 (Defense Research Institute, Inc. 1966).*

Policy Considerations Reveal The Undesirability Of Strict Liability In Tort As A Rule Of Law

There is a moral element to a move from liability for fault to liability without fault. Liability for fault is within the realm of normal expectation of right in our society. Liability without fault is a strange creation which arouses the antagonism of a wrong.

As industrialization, mechanization and communication have progressed in this country, safety has become increasingly a matter of general concern. Substantial and expensive programs are pursued to impress the significance of safety upon the public consciousness. Improvements for safety are constantly sought. The doctrine of strict liability in tort runs counter to this significant public policy; manufacturers and sellers are no longer economically encouraged to exercise due care in order to prevent liabilities under this doctrine.

The doctrine of strict liability in tort has another aspect which deserves attention. This rule is a vehicle of subtle socialization. While the proponents of strict liability proclaim that it is but a means of imposing the economic impact upon manufacturers and sellers, who can bear this burden, rather than upon users and consumers, in truth the manufacturers and sellers are but collectors of funds from the ultimate users and consumers of products. Strict liability can only raise prices; so ultimately each consumer and user must underwrite the ability of others to impose liability without fault.

Pronouncement of the doctrine of strict liability in tort involves a sweeping change of the law in the form of a new public policy. This type of development is traditionally legislative, not judicial. In Lombardi v. California Packing Sales Co., 83 R.I. 51, 112 A.2d 701 (1955), the court denied recovery for breach of implied warranty in the absence of privity, saying at page 704:

> . . . But it seems to us that ordinarily the declaration of such a public policy is a function of the legislature and not of the court. . . . we ought not to resort to judicial legislation, at least where no emergency or extreme conditions exist.

The same court has subsequently ascribed legislative approval to continued inaction of the legislature in the area of strict liability in Henry v. John W. Eshelman & Sons, 209 A.2d 46 (R.I.Sup.Ct., 1965), when, in denying recovery for breach of implied warranty in the absence of privity, it said:

> . . . A decade has passed since we declared in *Lombardi* that if any change in the law was to be made from consideration of public policy

the legislature should make it. During that period the legislature has met in annual sessions and has not seen fit to alter in any way the policy of the law underlying that decision notwithstanding its attention was again called to the continuing criticism of such policy . . . .

Such long acquiescence in decisional law by the legislature, especially after its attention has been called to repeated litigious criticism of its underlying policy, is persuasive proof of at least implied legislative approval of the decisions. . . . [P. 48.]

PROSSER, THE ASSAULT UPON THE CITADEL (STRICT LIABILITY TO THE CONSUMER)

69 Yale L.J. 1099, 1122–24 (1960).*

[T]he arguments which have proved convincing to the courts which have accepted the strict liability are three:

1. The public interest in human life, health and safety demands the maximum possible protection that the law can give against dangerous defects in products which consumers must buy, and against which they are helpless to protect themselves; and it justifies the imposition, upon all suppliers of such products, of full responsibility for the harm they cause, even though the supplier has not been negligent.[149] This argument, which in the last analysis rests upon public sentiment, has had its greatest force in the cases of food, where there was once popular outcry against an evil industry, and injuries and actions have multiplied, and public feeling is most obvious. It is now being advanced as to other products for bodily use, such as cosmetics. It suggests that as to still other products, distinctions may yet be drawn according to the probable danger, the frequency of injury, and what the public reasonably and rightfully expects.

2. The supplier, by placing the goods upon the market, represents to the public that they are suitable and safe for use; and by packaging, advertising or otherwise, he does everything that he can to induce that belief. He intends and expects that the product will be purchased and used in reliance upon this assurance of safety; and it is in fact so purchased and used. The middleman is no more than conduit, a mere mechanical device, through whom the thing sold is to reach the ultimate

* Reprinted by permission of The Yale Law Journal Company and Fred B. Rothman & Company from *The Yale Law Journal*, Vol. 69, pp. 1099, 1122–24.

149. It is a well-known fact that articles of food are manufactured and placed in the channels of commerce, with the intention that they shall pass from hand to hand until they are finally used by some remote consumer. It is usually impracticable, if not impossible, for the ultimate consumer to analyze the food and ascertain whether or not it is suitable for human consumption. Since it has been packed and placed on the market as a food for human consumption, and marked as such, the purchaser usually eats it or causes it to be served to his family without the precaution of having it analyzed by a technician to ascertain whether or not it is suitable for human consumption. In fact, in most instances the only satisfactory examination that could be made would be only at the time and place of the processing of the food. It seems to be the rule that where food products sold for human consumption are unfit for that purpose, there is such an utter failure of the purpose for which the food is sold, and the consequences of eating unsound food are so disastrous to human health or life, that the law imposes a warranty of purity in favor of the ultimate consumer as a matter of public policy.

Jacob E. Decker & Sons v. Capps, 139 Tex. 609, 612, 164 S.W.2d 828, 829 (1942).

user. The supplier has invited and solicited the use; and when it leads to disaster, he should not be permitted to avoid the responsibility by saying that he has made no contract with the consumer.[150]

3. It is already possible to enforce strict liability by resort to a series of actions, in which the retailer is first held liable on a warranty to his purchaser, and indemnity on a warranty is then sought successively from other suppliers, until the manufacturer finally pays the damages, with the added costs of repeated litigation. This is an expensive, time-consuming, and wasteful process, and it may be interrupted by insolvency, lack of jurisdiction, disclaimers, or the statute of limitations, anywhere along the line. What is needed is a blanket rule which makes any supplier in the chain liable directly to the ultimate user, and so short-circuits the whole unwieldy process. This is in the interest, not only of the consumer, but of the courts, and even on occasion of the suppliers themselves.

R. HILLMAN, J. McDONNELL & S. NICKLES, COMMON LAW AND EQUITY UNDER THE UCC

8–59 to –63 (1985).*

Strict Tort and Code Warranties: A Comparison

The primary expression of the doctrine of strict tort liability is contained in section 402A of the Restatement (Second) of Torts:

> (1) One who sells any product in a defective condition unreasonably dangerous to the user or consumer or to his property is subject to

150. A party who processes a product and gives it the appearance of being suitable for human consumption, and places it in the channels of commerce, expects some one to consume the food in reliance upon its appearance that it is suitable for human consumption. He expects the appearance of suitableness to continue with the product until some one is induced to consume it as food. But a modern manufacturer or vendor does even more than this under modern practices. He not only processes the food and dresses it up so as to make it appear appetizing, but he uses the newspapers, magazines, billboards, and the radio to build up the psychology to buy and consume his products. The invitation extended by him is not only to the house wife to buy and serve his product, but to the members of the family and guests to eat it. In fact, the manufacturer's interest in the product is not terminated when he has sold it to the wholesaler. He must get it off the wholesaler's shelves before the wholesaler will buy a new supply. The same is not only true of the retailer, but of the house wife, for the house wife will not buy more until the family has consumed that which she has in her pantry. Thus the manufacturer or other vendor intends that this appearance of suitability of the article for human consumption should continue and be effective until some one is induced thereby to consume the goods. It would be but to acknowledge a weakness in the law to say that he could thus create a demand for his products by inducing a belief that they are suitable for human consumption, when, as a matter of fact, they are not, and reap the benefits of the public confidence thus created, and then avoid liability for the injuries caused thereby merely because there was no privity of contract between him and the one whom he induced to consume the food.

Id. at 619, 164 S.W.2d at 832–33.

liability for physical harm thereby caused to the ultimate user or consumer, or to his property, if

(a) the seller is engaged in the business of selling such a product, and

(b) it is expected to and does reach the user or consumer without substantial change in the condition in which it is sold.

(2) The rule stated in Subsection (1) applies although

(a) the seller has exercised all possible care in the preparation and sale of his product, and

(b) the user or consumer has not bought the product from or entered into any contractual relation with the seller.

Generally, under section 402A, a manufacturer, distributor, wholesaler, or retail dealer who sells a defective product is liable for the physical harm to person or property of a user or consumer of the product. Such "sellers" must be in the business of selling such products, but no privity of contract is required, nor must negligence of the seller be shown.

A comparison of strict tort and warranty liability must focus primarily on the nature of the product defect and the nature of the loss caused by the defect.

[a] The Nature of the Defect

A seller is liable under section 402A of the Restatement if the product sold is "defective" and "unreasonably dangerous." The Code provisions concerning defective products are less demanding. Breach of the implied warranty of merchantability standard of Section 2–314, for example, requires only that a product be "unfit for the ordinary purposes for which such goods are used." An implied warranty of merchantability might be breached, for instance, when the roof of a mobile home leaks. Unlike the implied warranty of merchantability, strict tort, it can be seen, emphasizes product safety. Beyond this distinction, however, the strict tort and merchantability standards are very similar because goods that are "unsafe" necessarily are also "unfit." [375]

Strict tort also diverges from the express warranty standard under Section 2–313. Under that Section, a seller who makes quality claims exposes itself to liability beyond the levels of merchantability and strict tort. Indeed, an express warranty may be breached where there is no defect at all if the product does not live up to the seller's representations of quality.

[b] The Nature of the Loss

The scope of strict tort and warranty liability differs significantly depending upon the type of loss incurred. Traditionally, protection under tort law has been limited to physical injury to person or property. On the other hand, recovery for economic loss such as loss of bargain and consequential damages typically has been afforded warranty claimants (at least those in privity with the defendant). In *Santor* v. *A & M Karagheu-*

---

375. As stated by one court, "the negative implication of the warranty requirement that goods be 'fit for the ordinary purpose for which such goods are used' is that the goods not be unreasonably dangerous." Foster v. Ford Motor Co., 621 F.2d 715, 719 (5th Cir.1980).

sian, Inc.,[379] however, the New Jersey Supreme Court rejected this distinction and permitted a recovery of the difference between the contract price and the actual market value of the defective goods against a manufacturer based upon strict tort theory. . . .

Although some courts have followed the *Santor* approach of permitting a loss of bargain recovery in strict tort, awarding damages in strict tort for other than personal injury and property damage is disfavored in most jurisdictions. In *Seely* v. *White Motor Co.,*[382] for example, the California Supreme Court refused to extend strict tort liability to economic loss, directly refuting the *Santor* claim that the physical injury-economic loss distinction was arbitrary.[383] The court reasoned that the manufacturer fairly could insure against strict liability for personal injury, which liability was based on the potential for "overwhelming misfortune" to the consumer. Imposing strict liability for economic loss, on the other hand, would expose manufacturers to liability of "unknown and unlimited scope." This risk, the court believed, could fairly be borne by the consumer. In addition, such manufacturer liability would result in increased costs of products to all consumers.[384]

Most recent decisions support the conclusion that the risk of economic loss is best allocated contractually. Tort law seeks to protect against hazardous products that cause injury, the argument goes; other losses are better governed by the parties' own risk allocation. In supporting the *Seely* position, some authorities also emphasize the comprehensiveness of the Code warranty approach. Such a detailed framework as exists in the Code suggests that Code warranties displace tort liability at least with respect to economic loss from defective products.

Perhaps the physical injury-economic loss distinction is the best approach to harmonizing the roles of strict tort and warranty in products defect cases. Code requirements for recovery, such as privity, notice, and absence of disclaimers, seem better suited to economic loss claims. Such barriers to recovery are inconsistent with the notion that one who puts a dangerous product on the market should be liable for the harm caused by the product. A better approach, of course, would be to combine tort and contract actions in the product liability area into one uniform approach that takes the best from each system. It is doubtful that such an idea will soon be reality.

———————

WILLIAMS, MASS TORT CLASS ACTIONS: GOING, GOING, GONE?

22 Judges' J., Spring 1983, at 8, 9–10.*

State and federal trial judges are being inundated with mass filings of lawsuits by individual plaintiffs—an event unprecedented in legal history.

---

379. 44 N.J. 52, 207 A.2d 305 (1965).

382. 63 Cal.2d 9, 403 P.2d 145, 45 Cal.Rptr. 17 (1965).

383. Id. at 17–18, 403 P.2d at 151, 45 Cal.Rptr. at 23. The court did award consequential damages for lost profit, however, on the basis of breach of warranty.

384. Id. at 16–18, 403 P.2d at 150–151, 45 Cal.Rptr. at 22–23.

Each plaintiff seeks compensation and a share of large punitive damage awards based on a single catastrophe or a defective product. These "big cases" are widely publicized. They involve asbestos, "Agent Orange," Dalkon Shield, DES, Rely tampons, PCBs, and countless others. Virtually thousands of courts in this country are ensnared in costly and repetitive litigation, threatening to last well into the next century.

These cases are but a harbinger of the judiciary's role in an increasingly complex society, where huge multinational corporations peddle their mass-produced consumer goods and drugs by instantaneous satellite communication. In such a society, it is not an overly pessimistic prediction that, absent some legislative or judicial solution, our attempt to try these virtually identical lawsuits, one-by-one, will bankrupt both the state and federal court systems. In one year, between 1980 and 1981, there was a 17 percent increase in the filing of product liability cases in federal district courts alone; this represents approximately 15 new product cases per year for each federal judge.

The questions confronting the nation on mass product liability actions are many and varied, and transcend more mundane concerns of calendar management and court congestion:

• To what extent, if any, must the litigation preferences of each of the thousands of plaintiffs in a "big case" yield to a more socially optimal, cost-efficient form of representative adjudication?

• Is our traditional model, pitting one plaintiff's gladiator against one defendant's gladiator, an outmoded and overly expensive means to redress similar injuries inflicted by the same misconduct upon multiple plaintiffs?

• Must there be a dollar-by-dollar liability accumulated by society's producers until the business, or even an entire industry, is forced into bankruptcy, or is it more sensible to have a forum in which all potential ramifications upon workers, owners, and the future course of product development are aired in court?

• Must a single defendant be subjected to numerous and conflicting punitive damage awards, even when such awards threaten, as a legal or practical matter, to deprive future litigants of such recovery, or any recovery at all?

• Is it fair that a third of any recovery received in early litigation go to the early plaintiffs' attorneys, when injured later plaintiffs may be left without any practical means of redress?

• Is it effective or efficient use of limited juridical resources to subject a judge to the tedious and frustrating task of presiding over identical lawsuits, or even to distribute these cases throughout the court system to occupy calendars in many courts?

• Is this one-by-one adjudication the fastest, most equitable way to permit all the injured to recover?

These questions are easy to pose, but solutions are more difficult to formulate. Perhaps we need a major reinterpretation of some procedural aspects of our traditional adversary system, but this would be a long-term endeavor. Perhaps legislative solutions to this problem will provide the easiest and best answers to these questions, but Congress may not address these issues. It could by enacting comprehensive federal products liability law for application in new administrative courts, or make serious adjustments to the bankruptcy and reorganization provisions as applied to manufacturers faced with numerous products liability claims. But until it does, the inequities and shortcomings of the present system require that we judges work in an innovative fashion, adapting aspects of the current system to address these challenging problems.

It is my belief that for those inevitable cases involving hundreds or thousands of persons injured in similar ways by a single occurrence, the class action device holds the most promise.[c] It can be an effective tool to accommodate competing interests—each plaintiff clamoring for his slice of a large, but finite, damage pie; a defendant seeking a binding final determination of its liability for a product run amok; and a judicial system searching for the most equitable and efficient solution for all the interests involved.

Comments and Questions

1. The potential liability is massive when thousands (or more) seek compensation for catastrophic injuries suffered as the result of using a defective product or coming into contact with a harmful substance such as asbestos. Judge Williams's excerpt presents many of the issues involved in resolving claims arising from such "mass torts."

2. In May of 1985, the manufacturers of Agent Orange agreed to pay $180 million to settle a class action by veterans of the Vietnam conflict. Besides driving some companies out of business, might potential liability of this magnitude have a chilling effect on some companies' willingness to put new products on the market, thereby depriving us of the best that science has to offer?

3. One major defect of the present tort compensation system may be the amount of money that goes to lawyers who represent victims of the mass tort. The New York Times, Mar. 10, 1985, § 3, at 9, col. 3, reported that "[i]n 1983 the Rand Corporation estimated that 63 cents of every dollar spent on asbestos litigation went to the opposing attorneys and for legal costs."

Section Four.   Product Safety and the Administrative-Regulatory Instrument

In Chapter 3 we learned that the administrative-regulatory instrument of the law operates to prevent grievances before they arise. Administrators take steps to ensure that parties, engaging in primarily beneficial activity, comply with regulations designed to avoid grievances. This basic technique can be employed to regulate the production of goods to promote their safety.

---

c. Class actions are a "judicial mechanism to try similar individual actions either entirely together, or jointly on a piecemeal basis for common issues." They involve numerous parties whose "claims share at least one common question of law or fact." Williams, Mass Tort Class Actions: Going, Going, Gone?, 22 Judges' J., Spring 1983, at 8, 10.

HENDERSON, JUDICIAL REVIEW OF MANUFACTURERS' CONSCIOUS DESIGN CHOICES: THE LIMITS OF ADJUDICATION

73 Colum.L.Rev. 1531, 1573–76 (1973).*

[B]y and large, the courts have refrained from attempting to establish product safety standards; the question is whether they will continue to do so. In cases involving manufacturing flaws and inadvertent design errors, one can safely predict that they will continue to refrain. For some time, social policies favoring the expansion of manufacturers' liability have been mounting to pressure courts in these cases to adopt strict liability responses that avoid the necessity of establishing independent product safety standards. Because the solutions adopted by a growing majority of courts in cases involving manufacturing flaws and inadvertent design errors represent a happy coincidence of what is demanded by social policy and what is feasible in light of institutional limitations, there is no reason whatsoever to expect that courts will deviate substantially from their present course of development.

Cases involving manufacturers' conscious design choices, however, present a more difficult problem. Here, pressures favoring governmental intervention in the form of an expansion of manufacturers' liability are pushing the courts toward, rather than away from, the necessity of establishing independent standards. Up until now, the courts for the most part have reacted with the proper degree of restraint. While they have occasionally intervened in unusual cases, they have not yielded to the pressures so frequently as to threaten the integrity of the adjudicative process. But what of the future? Even if the courts are inherently unsuited to perform the standard-setting function, will not the pressures favoring expansion of manufacturers' liability be too strong to resist in the years ahead? Are not the recent examples of judicial standard-setting to be viewed, after all, as the first indications of what will soon develop into a sweeping wave of reform?

I think not. Several factors combine to assure that the pressures favoring independent judicial review of manufacturers' conscious design choices will never become too strong for courts generally to resist. Perhaps the most significant factor is the likelihood, approaching certainty, that legislative action will operate to reduce these pressures, for the legislature is, even more than the courts, also subjected to the demands for adequate product safety levels. To be sure, as law reform advocates have long been aware, the legislative process tends to respond slowly to pressures for change, but the adjudicative process tends no less stubbornly to resist efforts to force it to exceed its proper limits. Therefore, one may reasonably expect that when the pressures favoring independent judicial review of manufacturers' conscious design choices in a given product area build to the point that courts can no longer resist them, these same pressures will move legislatures to devise more appropriate solutions to the difficulties.

This expectation of legislative action is based upon more than mere speculation. In the two product categories most frequently encountered in recent manufacturers' design choice cases, automobiles and heavy industrial machinery, Congress has already responded, establishing specialized administrative agencies and procedures for handling problems, including the establishment and enforcement of standards relating to product design. As these programs become increasingly active, and the administrative agencies begin vigorously to address the broad spectrum of issues involved in the design of automobiles and heavy industrial machinery, pressures upon the courts to engage in standard-setting should correspondingly diminish.

Moreover, recent enactment of the Federal Consumer Product Safety Act, creating a new administrative agency empowered to establish safety standards for a wide range of consumer products, strongly suggests that the trend toward legislative and administrative standard-setting will continue. The report of the National Commission on Product Safety, upon whose recommendations the Product Safety Act is largely based, clearly indicates that the priorities of the new agency will correspond almost exactly to those product areas exerting the greatest pressures upon the courts. Included in the Act is a provision authorizing suits for damages to be brought in the federal courts by persons injured by reason of knowing violations of any consumer product safety rule. Since the role of applying administratively established standards is one for which the courts are very well suited, this provision will surely be given full effect in actions against manufacturers by injured plaintiffs. While the Act also provides that compliance with such product safety rules shall not relieve any person of liability at common law, the inherent limits of adjudication should prevent courts from making extensive use of this latter provision to establish independent design standards.

Consumer Product Safety Act

There is much federal regulation of potentially dangerous products, such as food, drugs, and automobiles. The Consumer Product Safety Act, 15 U.S.C. §§ 2051–2083, mentioned in the Henderson excerpt, was promulgated in 1972. The history of the act is briefly described in Wahba v. H & N Prescription Center, Inc., 539 F.Supp. 352, 354 (E.D.N.Y.1982):

> The Consumer Product Safety Act was the fruit of years of work by the legislature and others who recognized that modern technology and merchandising methods posed increasing threats to the nation's consumers. Prior to 1972, Congress had enacted a number of laws designed to combat dangers posed by specific categories of consumer products. See, e.g., Flammable Fabrics Act of 1953, 15 U.S.C. §§ 1191–1204; Federal Hazardous Substances Act, 15 U.S.C. §§ 1261– 1274; Child Protection Act of 1966 and Child Protection and Toy Safety Act of 1969, 15 U.S.C. §§ 1261–1265, 1273, 1274; Refrigerator Safety Act, 15 U.S.C. §§ 1211–1214; Poison Prevention Packaging Act of 1970, 15 U.S.C. §§ 1261, 1471–1476; Federal Caustic Poison Act, 15 U.S.C. §§ 401–411 (repealed); Radiation Control for Health and Safety Act of 1968, 42 U.S.C. §§ 263b–263n; National Traffic & Motor

Vehicle Safety Act of 1966, 15 U.S.C. §§ 1391–1409, 1421–1426, 1431. This categorical approach "resulted in a patchwork pattern of laws which, in combination, extend[ed] to only a small portion of the multitude of products produced for consumers." Consumer Product Safety Act of 1972, House Commerce Committee, H.R.Rep. No. 1153, 92d Cong., 2d Sess. 22 (1972), reprinted in The Consumer Product Safety Act, Text, Analysis, Legislative History (BNA), Appendix 211, 212–13 (1973). Accord, Consumer Safety Act of 1972, Senate Commerce Committee, S.Rep. No. 749, 92d Cong., 2d Sess. 1–3 (1972), reprinted in The Consumer Product Safety Act, Text, Analysis, Legislative History (BNA), Appendix 61, 61–63 (1973).

In 1967 Congress established the National Commission on Product Safety to examine methods of protecting consumers against unreasonable risks of injury from household products and to propose remedies for existing legal inadequacies. Act of Nov. 20, 1967, Pub.L. No. 90-146, 81 Stat. 466. After more than two years of study, the Commission submitted its final report to Congress in June, 1970. In 1972 the Act established the Consumer Products Safety Commission, an independent federal regulatory agency vested with broad authority to protect against hazardous consumer products. Pub.L. No. 92-573, 86 Stat. 1207 (1972), 15 U.S.C. §§ 2052–2082. See generally P. Sherman, Products Liability for the General Practitioner, §§ 4.04–4.06 (1981).

One of the Act's primary purposes, and one of the Commission's principal means of fulfilling its mission, has been the promulgation of uniform national safety standards for consumer products. 15 U.S.C. § 2051(b)(3). The statute contains a comprehensive enforcement scheme including such measures as civil and criminal penalties, injunctive remedies and seizure. Id. §§ 2069–2071, 2073 (1976 & Supp. II 1978).

In addition the Act expressly affords a private right of action to any person who sustains injury by reason of any knowing violation of a consumer product safety rule.

The Consumer Product Safety Commission may also bar hazardous products or compel the repair, modification, or replacement of a defective product or compel a seller to refund the purchase price. See M. Greenfield, Consumer Transactions 292 (1983). Manufacturers, distributors, and retailers all come within the purview of the legislation.

SOUTHLAND MOWER CO. v. CONSUMER PRODUCT SAFETY COMMISSION

United States Court of Appeals, Fifth Circuit, 1980.
619 F.2d 499.

GEE, CIRCUIT JUDGE:

Approximately 77,000 people are injured each year in the United States by contacting the blades of walk-behind power mowers.[1] Of these

---

1. 44 Fed.Reg. 9990, 10030 (1979). The estimates are based on 1977 data.

injuries, an estimated 9,900 involve the amputation of at least one finger or toe, 11,400 involve fractures, 2,400 involve avulsions (the tearing of flesh or a body part), 2,300 involve contusions, and 51,400 involve lacerations. The annual economic cost inflicted by the 77,000 yearly blade-contact injuries has been estimated to be about $253 million. This figure does not include monetary compensation for pain and suffering or for the lost use of amputated fingers and toes.[2]

To reduce these blade-contact injuries, the Consumer Product Safety Commission ("CPSC" or "the Commission") promulgated [3] a Safety Standard for Walk-Behind Power Lawn Mowers, 16 C.F.R. Part 1205 (1979), 44 Fed.Reg. 9990–10031 (Feb. 15, 1979), pursuant to section 7 of the Consumer Product Safety Act ("CPSA" or "the Act"), 15 U.S.C. § 2056 (1976).[4] In

---

2. Id.

3. The gestation period for the safety standard was long and complex. The administrative process was initiated on August 15, 1973, when, pursuant to § 10 of the CPSA, 15 U.S.C. § 2059, the Outdoor Power Equipment Institute, Inc. (OPEI) petitioned the CPSC to begin a proceeding to develop a consumer product safety standard addressing the hazards of power lawn mowers and asked the Commission to adopt a voluntary standard, ANSI B71.1–1972, "Safety Specifications for Power Lawn Mowers, Lawn & Garden Tractors, & Lawn Tractors," approved by the American National Standards Institute, Inc. as the proposed consumer product safety standard. On November 16, 1973, the Commission, after considering information about injuries associated with power lawn mowers, granted that portion of OPEI's petition that requested a proceeding to develop the power lawn mower safety standard. The Commission denied OPEI's request to publish ANSI B71.1–1972, with amendments, as a proposed consumer product safety standard however.

Instead, the Commission solicited offers to develop a standard pursuant to § 7(b) of the CPSA, 15 U.S.C. § 2056(b). Subsequently, the Commission selected Consumers Union of United States, Inc. (CU) to develop the safety standard. See 39 Fed.Reg. 37803 (1974). As the offeror, CU gave representatives of industry, consumers, and other interests the opportunity to participate in developing the standard. It submitted the resulting proposal to the Commission on July 17, 1975. The recommended standard comprehensively addressed all types of lawn mowers and lawn mower injuries and contained requirements relating to blade-contact and thrown-object injuries, as well as injuries resulting from lawn mowers' slipping, rolling, overturning, or failing to steer or brake, injuries caused by burns from direct contact with exposed heated surfaces of mowers or from fires ignited by lawn mower ignition fluids, and injuries caused by electric shock from electrically powered lawn mowers or electric ignition systems.

After analyzing the recommended CU standard, on May 5, 1977, the Commission published a proposed comprehensive power lawn mower safety standard for public comment. 42 Fed.Reg. 23052 (1977). The proposal elicited more than 100 initial comments, and the Commission solicited and received further comments on these already submitted comments. 42 Fed.Reg. 34892 (1977). On June 7, 1978, the Commission published a notice that it would issue requirements addressing injuries from blade contact with walk-behind power mowers before issuing separate standards dealing with injuries associated with thrown objects, fuel and electrical hazards, and riding mowers. 43 Fed.Reg. 24697 (1978). In November 1978, the Commission requested additional comments on the safety and reliability of brake-clutch mechanisms. 43 Fed.Reg. 51638 (1978). On February 26, 1979, Part 1205—Safety Standard for Walk-Behind Power Lawn Mowers, applying only to blade-contact injuries from walk-behind power lawn mowers, was issued, to become effective December 31, 1981.

4. 15 U.S.C. § 2056(a) (1976) provides:

(a) The Commission may by rule, in accordance with this section and section 2058 of this title, promulgate consumer product safety standards. A consumer product safety standard shall consist of one or more of any of the following types of requirements:

(1) Requirements as to performance, composition, contents, design, construction, finish, or packaging of a consumer product.

(2) Requirements that a consumer product be marked with or accompanied by clear and adequate warnings or instructions, or requirements respecting the form of warnings or instructions.

Any requirement of such a standard shall be reasonably necessary to prevent or reduce an unreasonable risk of injury associated with such product. The requirements of such a standard (other than requirements relating to labeling, warnings, or

the present case we consider petitions by the Outdoor Power Equipment Institute ("OPEI"), manufacturers of power lawn mowers,[5] and an interested consumer to review[6] the Safety Standard for Walk-Behind Power Lawn Mowers.

The standard consists of three principal provisions: a requirement that rotary walk-behind power mowers pass a foot-probe test, 16 C.F.R. § 1205.4, 44 Fed.Reg. 10025–26, a requirement that rotary machines have a blade-control system that will stop the mower blade within three seconds after the operator's hands leave their normal operating position, 16 C.F.R. § 1205.5(a), 44 Fed.Reg. 10029, and a requirement, applicable to both rotary and reel-type mowers, that the product have a label of specified design to warn of the danger of blade contact, 16 C.F.R. § 1205.6, 44 Fed.Reg. 10029–30. The standards also contain additional directives that are intended to increase the effectiveness of the primary regulations. Thus, because the foot-probe provision can be satisfied by shielding the blade area, the standard mandates tests to assure that shields have a certain minimum strength, 16 C.F.R. § 1205.4(a)(2), 44 Fed.Reg. 10026–28, and that a shielded mower can traverse obstructions. 16 C.F.R. § 1205.4(a)(3), 44 Fed.Reg. 10028–29. The standard also stipulates that shields that move to permit attachment of auxiliary equipment must either automatically return to their normal position when the supplemental equipment is not attached or prevent blade operation unless the shield is manually returned to its normal position when the added equipment is not used. 16 C.F.R. § 1205.4(c). Similarly, the three-second blade-stop requirement is supported by ancillary instructions that mowers employing engine cutoff to halt the blade have power restart mechanisms, 16 C.F.R. § 1205.5(a)(iv), and that all mowers have a control that must be activated before the blade can resume operation in order to prevent the blade from accidentally restarting. 16 C.F.R. § 1205.5(a)(2).

. . . OPEI . . . argues that substantial evidence on the record as a whole does not support the Commission's determination that the foot-probe and shielding requirements "are reasonably necessary to reduce or eliminate an unreasonable risk of injury"[8] associated with walk-behind power lawn mowers. . . .

FOOT–PROBE AND SHIELDING REQUIREMENTS

The standard mandates that walk-behind power rotary mowers pass a foot-probe test designed to assure that the machine guards the operator's

instructions) shall, whenever feasible, be expressed in terms of performance requirements.

5. For convenience, we shall refer to the lawn mower industry petitioners collectively as OPEI.

6. Review of a safety standard by this court is authorized by § 11 of the CPSA, 15 U.S.C. § 2060 (1976).

8. 15 U.S.C. § 2058(c)(2)(A) directs that:

The Commission shall not promulgate a consumer product safety rule unless it finds (and includes such finding in the rule)—

(A) that the rule (including its effective date) is reasonably necessary to eliminate or reduce an unreasonable risk of injury associated with such product. . . .

Every part of the standard must meet the "reasonably necessary" criterion. *Aqua Slide 'N' Dive Corp. v. Consumer Product Safety Commission*, 569 F.2d 831, 838 (5th Cir.1978) (hereinafter *Aqua Slide*).

feet against injuries caused by contact with the moving blade. The test requires that a probe simulating a human foot be inserted along the rear 120 degrees of the mower and at the discharge chute without coming into contact with the blade when inserted. 16 C.F.R. § 1205.4, 44 Fed.Reg. 10025–26. See also Fed.Reg. 10001–10002. Mowers meet the foot-probe test by having shields that prevent the probe from entering the blade's path. 16 C.F.R. § 1205(a)(1), 44 Fed.Reg. 10025.

OPEI does not deny that a foot-probe test for the rear area of the mower is reasonably necessary to reduce injuries.[16] Rather, it asserts that application of the test to the discharge chute is not supported by substantial record evidence. It alleges that the injury data does not show that foot injuries occur at that location and that it would be theoretically impossible for an operator to suffer a foot injury at the discharge chute while holding the "deadman's" blade-control[17] switch on the mower handle.[18]

The Act requires that safety standards be supported by "substantial evidence on the record as a whole." 15 U.S.C. § 2060(c). The foot-probe provision can be sustained only if the record contains " 'such relevant evidence as a reasonable mind might accept as adequate to support a conclusion' " that an unreasonable risk of foot injury exists from blade-contact at the discharge chute, that the foot-probe test will ameliorate it, and that the benefits of this proposed reform make it reasonable in light of the burdens it imposes on product manufacturers and consumers. Aqua Slide 'N' Dive v. Consumer Product Safety Commission, 569 F.2d 831, 838–40 (5th Cir.1978) [hereinafter cited as *Aqua Slide*] (quoting Consolidated Edison Co. v. NLRB, 305 U.S. 197, 229, 59 S.Ct. 206, 216 (1938)).

The determination of whether an unreasonable risk of discharge-chute injury exists involves "a balancing test like that familiar in tort law: The regulation may issue if the severity of the injury that may result from the product, factored by the likelihood of the injury, offsets the harm the regulation imposes upon manufacturers and consumers." *Aqua Slide*, 569 F.2d at 839 (quoting Forester v. Consumer Product Safety Commission, 559 F.2d 774, 789 (D.C.Cir.1977) (defining "unreasonable risk" in case brought under the Federal Hazardous Substances Act, 15 U.S.C. §§ 1261–74 (1976), and referring to "similar language" and legislative history of CPSA for support)).[20] See H.R.Rep. No. 1153, 92d Cong., 2d Sess. 33

16. Both OPEI and the Commission agree that the evidence establishes that the great majority of operator foot injuries occur at the rear of the mower.

17. A deadman control refers to a device on the mower handle that requires continuous pressure to sustain rotation of the mower blades. Only if the operator can reach the discharge chute with his foot while holding the mower handle can he suffer blade-contact injuries at the discharge chute by mowers meeting the blade-stop requirement. Discharge-chute foot injuries suffered after the operator has released the mower handle and deadman's controls are addressed in the standard's blade-stop provision.

18. The rear 120 degrees of the mower and the discharge chute were selected for the foot-probe test because the Commission found that they are "areas where foot contact injuries are known to occur while the operator is holding the [mower] handle. Foot contact injuries that occur while the operator is not holding the handle will be addressed by the blade control . . . . " 44 Fed.Reg. 9993.

20. The Federal Hazardous Substances Act provides in part that "[a]n article may be determined to present a mechanical hazard if, in normal use or when subjected to reasonably

(1972).[21] Thus, under the unreasonable risk balancing test, even a very remote possibility that a product would inflict an extremely severe injury could pose an "unreasonable risk of injury" if the proposed safety standard promised to reduce the risk effectively without unduly increasing the product's price or decreasing its availability or usefulness. *Aqua Slide*, 569 F.2d at 839–40.[22] Conversely, if the potential injury is less severe, its occurrence must be proven more likely in order to render the risk unreasonable and the safety standard warranted.

In the present case, the discharge-chute probe is intended to reduce the risk of such injuries as amputation of toes, fractures of bones in the feet or toes, avulsions, deep lacerations, and contusions. While the seriousness of these injuries cannot be gainsaid, it does not rise to the level of gravity that would render almost any risk, however remote, unreasonable if the risk could be reduced effectively by the proposed regulation. Substantial evidence that such injury is significantly likely to occur is therefore necessary to sustain this portion of the lawn mower safety standard.

Our examination of the record has failed to reveal substantial evidence that injury at the discharge chute was sufficiently probable that it made the risk addressed by the foot probe of this area unreasonable. In a study of 36 blade-contact foot injuries conducted for the CPSC by the National Electronic Injury Surveillance System (NEISS),[24] one injury occurred when the operator inserted his foot into the blade path at the discharge chute while holding the mower handle. This injury represented almost

foreseeable damage or abuse, its design or manufacture presents an *unreasonable risk of personal injury or illness . . . .*" 15 U.S.C. § 1261(s) (1976) (emphasis added).

21. The House Committee Report on the CPSA stressed that:
[T]he Commission's authority to promulgate standards under this bill is limited to instances where the hazard associated with a consumer product presents an unreasonable risk of death, injury, or serious or frequent illness. . . .
[I]t is generally expected that the determination of unreasonable hazard will involve the Commission in balancing the probability that risk will result in harm and the gravity of such harm against the effect on the product's utility, cost and availability to the consumer. An unreasonable hazard is clearly one which can be prevented or reduced without affecting the product's utility, cost or availability; or one which the effect on the product's utility, cost or availability is outweighed by the need to protect the public from the hazard associated with the product.

22. For example, in *Aqua Slide* this court ruled that the severity of paraplegic injury from swimming pool slides was so great that a one in ten million risk of such injury, which is less than the risk that an average person will be killed by lightning, would be an "unreasonable risk" if the proposed safety standard "actually promised to reduce the risk without unduly hampering the availability of the slides or decreasing their utility . . . . " 569 F.2d at 840. The court found, however, that the necessary showing of the standard's effectiveness had not been made and that the burdens the regulation would impose had not been adequately evaluated. Id. at 840–44.

24. NEISS collects data from selected hospitals and reports them to the CPSC. The system, which has been operational since July 1, 1972, was designed to develop statistically valid, rationally representative product-related injury data. It employs a computer-based network of 119 statistically selected hospital emergency rooms located throughout the country. 15 U.S.C. §§ 2054, 2055. See "Draft Hazard Analysis of Power Mower Related Injuries & Analysis of Proposed Power Mower Standard," U.S. CPSC, Bureau of Epidemiology (March 1977), at pp. 3–5. The Commission also obtains injury information from in-depth investigations (IDI's) of particular accidents reported through the NEISS network. IDI's conducted by the Commission, unlike basic NEISS accident data, are not statistically representative of all injuries in a particular product category. IDI's do, however, provide details concerning the sequence of events involved in the injury not available from NEISS surveillance information. Id. at 5. To overcome this deficiency, the Commission weighted IDI cases involving specified types of injuries to derive an adjusted IDI sample that conforms to NEISS data.

three percent of the blade-contact foot injuries in the sample. However, the study did not involve a random sample, and it is not possible to extrapolate the percentage of total blade-contact injuries represented by discharge-chute incidents involving the operator's feet from the limited information furnished in the record. In any event, trustworthy statistical inferences cannot be drawn from a single incident of discharge-chute injury. Without reliable evidence of the likely number of injuries that would be addressed by application of the foot-probe test to the discharge chute, we are unable to agree that this provision is reasonably necessary to reduce or prevent an unreasonable risk of injury. See D.D. Bean & Sons Co. v. Consumer Product Safety Commission, 574 F.2d 643, 650–51 (1st Cir.1978) (hereinafter *D.D. Bean*) (holding that absence of relevant injury data associated with particular hazards renders requirements of safety standard addressed to them invalid and observing that "a single injury . . . is not substantial evidence of an 'unreasonable risk of injury.'"). It must be remembered that "[t]he statutory term 'unreasonable risk' presupposes that a real, and not a speculative, risk be found to exist and that the Commission bear the burden of demonstrating the existence of such a risk before proceeding to regulate." Id. at 651.

Our conclusion that substantial evidence fails to justify this provision is not altered by the fact that the industry's voluntary standard, ANSI B71.1-1972 § 1968, and ANSI 71.1b-1977 § 11.8, requires probing of the discharge chute. See 44 Fed.Reg. at 10003. A private industry safety standard cannot, by itself, provide sufficient support for a Commission regulation. " 'While such private standards may tend to show the reasonableness of similar Commission standards, they do not prove the *need* for such provisions.' " *Aqua Slide*, 569 F.2d at 844 (quoting Forester v. Consumer Product Safety Commission, 559 F.2d at 793 (emphasis in original)). We therefore vacate that part of the standard requiring the discharge-chute area of power lawn mowers to pass a foot-probe test.

OPEI also attacks certain aspects of the shielding requirements that supplement the foot-probe test as devoid of substantial evidentiary support. The standard directs that shielding must pass a shield-strength test in order to assure that shields maintain their structural integrity and remain attached under conditions of use and provide the intended protection. 16 C.F.R. § 1205.4(a)(2).[25] Similarly, the standard requires that shielded mowers undergo an obstruction test, 16 C.F.R. § 1205.4(b)(2), which simulates surface irregularities that the mower may encounter in normal use.[26] The test is designed to ascertain that the shielding will not interfere with mower performance by catching on obstructions and stopping the mower. It is also intended to prevent the shields themselves from contributing to lawn mower hazards, either by lifting the mower excessively when it meets an obstruction and thus exposing the blade or

25. This provision mandates that any shield in the areas to be foot probed shall not permanently separate, crack, or deform when subjected for 10 seconds to a 50-pound static tensile force uniformly distributed over not less than half the shield's length.

26. The obstruction test consists of moving the mower back and forth at a set speed over a test surface that has specified depressions and raised obstacles. The mower may not stop as a result of contacting a raised obstacle nor may more than one wheel at a time lift from the surface. In addition, the shield may not enter the path of the blade.

by suddenly halting the mower and causing it to lift and/or the operator to stumble on it.

The Commission estimates that the foot-probe/shielding requirements, including the supporting strength and obstruction tests, will reduce blade-contact foot injuries by 13,000 incidents each year. It did not apportion this injury reduction among the respective foot-probe shielding requirements on the ground that this was impossible because they are interrelated. The Commission estimates that the shield provisions will cost about $4 per mower, primarily for redesigning shields. Little expense is believed to result from the shield-strength test, since it is similar to a requirement in the existing voluntary industry standard, ASNI B71.1-1972 §§ 11.5, 11.15; ANSI B71.1b-1977 §§ 11.5, 13.2.1, which receives almost universal compliance.

OPEI readily admits that shielding is necessary to protect operators against blade-contact foot injuries at the rear of the mower. It contends, however, that the shield-strength test is invalid because few injuries have been shown to be caused by inadequately strong shields. OPEI also argues that the possibility that users might remove the protective shielding if it interfered with mower utility by catching on surface irregularities cannot justify the obstruction test and asserts that the test has not been proven necessary to guard against injuries caused by the mower's sudden stopping when it catches on obstacles.

We find that OPEI's approach to the shield-strength test is misconceived. It is true that were this requirement viewed in isolation as intended to address a risk of injury from mower shields falling off or cracking and exposing the operator's foot to the blade, independent of the standard's requirement that mowers be equipped with foot-probe shields, the record would not contain sufficient evidence that such injuries are so numerous that they support the regulation.[28] But the shield-strength test is mandated as an ancillary feature of the foot-probe and shielding requirements that in turn are concededly necessary to reduce an unreasonable risk of operator blade-contact foot injuries. The shield-strength provision is not to be understood as a discrete measure addressing a distinct type of operator foot injury but as part of the Commission's effort to make the shielding remedy itself effective and safe. Since an unreasonable risk of operator foot injury from blade contact has been established, the shields are reasonably necessary to prevent access to the blade, and the "curative effect" of the shield-strength requirement in preventing blade exposure from inadequate shielding is "*patent*," we "do not think that the Commission had to cite empirical data in support of its finding that the particular [shield strength] requirement [was] likely to reduce the risk of injury." *D.D. Bean*, 574 F.2d at 649. . . .

. . . [T]he shield-strength test is a particularly appropriate exercise of Commission authority to implement remedies for unreasonable risks because the hazards that will accompany structurally unsound shielding will not become widely manifest until shielding is generally required for

---

28. The record contains an in-depth CPSC investigation of 102 blade-contact injuries that revealed only two incidents in which the operator's foot was hurt by the blade at the rear of a mower that had a broken or missing shield. It also contains a few letters from consumers complaining of shields that did not remain attached to their mowers.

consumer power lawn mowers by the standard. When part of a standard is directed at making sure that required safety measures provide their intended level of protection, and it is clear that if they do not " 'it seems conceptually clear that an injury will occur, it is primitive to wait until a number of people have lost their lives, or sacrificed their limbs before we attempt to prevent those accidents.' . . . [N]o precise statistical showing is required." Forester v. Consumer Product Safety Commission, 559 F.2d 774, 789 (D.C.Cir.1977) (quoting 1969 Senate Report to the Federal Hazardous Substances Act, S.Rep. No. 71,237, 71st Cong., 1st Sess. 2–3 (1969)). We therefore uphold the shield-strength test provision of the standard.

For similar reasons we reject OPEI's challenge to the obstruction test requirement and find that it is reasonably necessary to guard against intentional consumer defeat of the shielding safety device and to prevent shielding from interfering with mower utility. Although OPEI does not dispute the likelihood that consumers will remove shields if they interfere with mower performance[30] or contest the feasibility of the obstruction test, it does contend that the possibility that consumers may remove protective shielding if it hampers mower utility by catching on surface obstructions does not present the kind of unreasonable risk of injury that the Commission has authority to regulate. In essence, OPEI argues that the risk of injury from consumer defeat of safety shielding is not "unreasonable" because consumers would have chosen to incur the risk, and their judgment must be respected.

However, Congress intended for injuries resulting from foreseeable misuse of a product to be counted in assessing risk. *Aqua Slide,* 569 F.2d at 841. See S.Rep. No. 92–749, 92d Cong., 2d Sess. 14, 92 Cong.Rec. 36198 (1972) (remarks of Sen. Moss) (risk of injury "associated with" consumer products, 15 U.S.C. § 2052(a)(3), to be regulated by CPSC includes risks of injury resulting from "exposure to or reasonably foreseeable misuse of a consumer product"); Kimber, Federal Consumer Product Safety Act § 94 at 109 (1975). Cf. Pacific Legal Foundation v. Department of Transportation, 593 F.2d 1338, 1345 (D.C.Cir.1979) (Secretary of Transportation required to consider probable public reaction to passive automobile restraints, including possibility of attempts to deactivate them, in promulgating safety standard under National Traffic & Motor Vehicle Safety Act of 1966, 15 U.S.C. §§ 1381 et seq. (1976)). This principle, and not the tort liability concept of "assumption of risk," governs the Commission's authority to treat consumers' foreseeable action of removing safety shields as creating an unreasonable risk of injury and to issue rules addressing that danger. See United States v. General Motors Corp., 518 F.2d 420, 434–35 (D.C.Cir.1975) ("[d]eterminations of fault or liability relevant to the award of damages . . . are not controlling on the interpretation of the" meaning of product "defect" in prophylactic defect notification legislation

---

30. The experience of massive consumer resistance to ignition lock-seat belt systems is instructive as to the possibility that consumers will defeat safety devices they find inconvenient to use despite the loss of safety benefits such avoidance entails. See Pacific Legal Foundation v. Department of Transportation, 593 F.2d 1338, 1340–42 (D.C.Cir.1979); "Safety Belt Interlock System Usage Survey" (August 1976) (reporting high percentage of drivers defeated seat belt system).

of National Traffic & Motor Vehicle Act of 1966). Of course, a fully informed choice on the part of consumers to employ a dangerous product may provide information that is relevant to the Commission's assessment of the reasonableness of a risk of injury. For example, consumers' decisions to use sharp knives may pose a *reasonable* risk of injury because duller knives, while safe, would be useless for cutting purposes, and the Commission could reasonably find that consumers have accurate information of the severity and likelihood of injury posed by sharp knives. See *Aqua Slide*, 569 F.2d at 839; S.Rep. No. 92–749, supra at 6–7. In the present case, however, there is no evidence that consumers accurately appreciate the nature of the risk of blade-contact injuries and that their presumed willingness to defeat protective measures is reasonable.

The record contains substantial evidence, in the form of comment letters from both consumers and consulting engineers, that shields on some mowers interfered with the machine's mobility and consequently were removed by their owners, thus eliminating any safety benefits they were intended to provide. Since a risk of blade-contact injury is clearly created by removing the protective shields and the risk can be effectively reduced by eliminating the annoyance imposed by shields that interfere with mower movement, it was proper for the standard to include an obstruction test to reduce the risk of this foreseeable misuse of lawn mowers.

The obstruction test is valid also as a measure designed to assure that shielding is feasible as a method of reducing the risk, see *Aqua Slide*, 569 F.2d at 839; Forester v. Consumer Product Safety Commission, 559 F.2d at 789 n. 21, and does not inordinately interfere with mower utility. In promulgating a safety standard, the Commission must consider the "probable effect of such rule upon the *utility* . . . of such products . . . . ." 15 U.S.C. § 2058(c)(1)(C) (emphasis added). See *Aqua Slide*, 569 F.2d at 839; H.R.Rep. No. 1153, 92d Cong., 2d Sess. 33 (1972). In order to fulfill its statutory responsibility to determine that the requirements of a safety standard will not unreasonably reduce product usefulness, the Commission must have authority to establish performance criteria for its chosen remedies. Therefore, the obstruction test, as a component of the foot-probe/shielding requirements, is reasonably necessary to ensure that mowers satisfy the standard in ways that do not decrease the product's utility. Accordingly, we uphold the obstruction-test provision. . . .

FINDING OF REASONABLE NECESSITY AND PUBLIC INTEREST

In the preceding discussion, we have examined the petitioners' challenges to specific provisions of the standard and have found several of the complaints unfounded. However, OPEI also contends that the standard as a whole is not supported by substantial record evidence. It claims that the Commission based its determination that the standard was "reasonably necessary" and would produce a net benefit to society upon a document, "Economic Impact of Blade Contact Requirements for Power Mowers" ("the economic report"), which was unreliable because its methodology was fatally flawed, and its findings had never been exposed to public scrutiny in the administrative rulemaking process. Petitioner Hayward also criticizes the Commission's evaluation of the standard's net social benefit. He argues that the CPSC undervalued the safety benefits of the standard by erroneously failing to place a monetary value on the pain and suffering inflicted by the injuries that the rule was expected to reduce.

The Commission seeks to counter OPEI's broad attack on the standard by defending the final economic report's data and methodology and by asserting that the report was, in essence, merely a revision of earlier cost-benefit analyses of shielding and blade-stop requirements in light of additional evidence introduced into the record by OPEI. The Commission further contends that it adequately considered pain and suffering in evaluating the standard's benefits and that it was not required to quantify these aspects of the cost of lawn mower accidents.

We have carefully scrutinized the record and find the substantial evidence supports the conclusion that the safety benefits expected from the standard bear a reasonable relationship to its costs and make the standard reasonably necessary and in the public interest. The cost-benefit analysis contained in the final economic report and adopted by the standard, 44 Fed.Reg. at 10020–21, 10030, is not methodologically flawed. The Commission estimated that the regulations would raise the retail price of a complying lawn mower $35, costing the consumer $4.40 per year over the projected eight-year life of the mower. Total yearly compliance costs were believed to be $189 million for 5.4 million mower units (1978 production estimate). Blade-contact injuries were calculated to cost $253 million annually, exclusive of pain and suffering. Since, as we have noted, there are approximately 77,000 blade-contact injuries from walk-behind power mowers each year, each injury costs about $3,300, without counting the cost of pain and suffering. Currently there are some 40 million mowers in use by consumers, so that a consumer has about one chance in 500 ($1/520$) of incurring an injury costing $3,300, exclusive of pain and suffering. The standard's injury cost associated with each mower without the safety features is thus $6.35 per year. The Commission anticipated that implementation of the standard would reduce this injury cost by 83 percent, for an annual savings of $5.30 per mower, exclusive of the savings of pain and suffering costs. Because the standard would result in a net benefit of $.90, a mower meeting the standard's safety requirements would represent a worthwhile investment for the consumer, and the standard's implementation is in the best interests of society.

. . .

OPEI asserts that the figures from the final economic report lack the indicia of reliability because they differ from estimates of annual injury costs in a previous economic report and because the final economic report was completed after the period for public comment had closed and therefore was not exposed to such public scrutiny as would bolster confidence in its accuracy. The petitioner thus seeks to bring the present case within the holding of *Aqua Slide*. There we decided that when the *only* record evidence pertaining to the economic impact of a safety standard was a Commission report that was never exposed to public comment and was allegedly unreliable, it did not provide substantial evidence that the standard was reasonably necessary and in the public interest.   569 F.2d at 842–43.

As proof of the final economic report's unreliability, OPEI points to alleged discrepancies between the economic data in the final report and in previous cost-benefit studies.   OPEI claims that in a February 1977 economic analysis entitled "Preliminary Assessment of the Possible Economic Effects of the Draft Safety Standard for Power Lawn Mowers," the annual injury costs of all power mower accidents was reported to be $93 million, exclusive of pain and suffering, while in the 1979 final economic report the yearly cost associated with walk-behind mower blade-contact injuries alone was $253 million.   We have searched the 35,000-page record, guided by the index approved by all parties in the case, and have been unable to locate the alleged earlier inconsistent estimate of lawn mower injury costs.

In any event, our examination of the final economic report and the Stanford Research Institute (SRI) study [49] upon which it purports to place primary reliance for its cost estimates convinces us that the standard's economic findings, derived from the final economic report, do have the requisite "indicia of reliability" and have not been impermissibly shielded from public scrutiny.   We do not base our holding that the standard's economic analysis is reliable on a weighing of diverse technical data, for such an evaluation is beyond the function and capacity of this or any other court.   See *Aqua Slide*, 569 F.2d at 838.   Rather, our decision is founded on the judgment that the "Commission 'carried out [its] essentially legislative task in a manner reasonable under the state of the record before [it].'"   Id. (quoting Florida Peach Growers Association v. United States Department of Labor, 489 F.2d 120, 129 (5th Cir.1974)).

In making its economic findings, the Commission estimated that there were approximately 77,000 blade-contact power mower injuries each year. It obtained this figure from 1977 National Electronic Injury Surveillance System data, which is public information.   The Commission's analysis of the NEISS data, establishing its understanding of the number of annual injuries caused by blade contact, was placed on the record and made available to public critique in a preliminary staff report that was eventually incorporated into the final economic report.   See W.D. Barr, CPSC Memorandum, "Estimates of Power Blade Contact Injuries & Proposed Blade Contact Effectiveness" (Oct. 6, 1978).   Thus, the petitioners and the public had an opportunity to present their views on the threshold finding of the number of annual injuries addressed by the standard, and this finding therefore enjoys the presumption of reliability afforded by public examination.   *Aqua Slide*, 569 F.2d at 842;   see BASF Wyandotte v. Costle, 598 F.2d 637, 642 (1st Cir.1979);   South Terminal Corp. v. EPA, 504 F.2d 646, 658–59 (1st Cir.1974).

In addition, the Commission explained in its final economic report that it had modified its earlier calculations of the yearly costs attributable to blade-contact injuries because it agreed with criticism of its previous

---

49. The SRI study was commissioned and submitted into the administrative record by OPEI.

injury-costing approaches presented in the Stanford Research Institute (SRI) report. SRI had observed that the injury-costing methods suggested by the National Safety Council and the National Highway Traffic Safety Administration and evidently used initially by the CPSC understated injury costs by failing to account for such factors as the victims' ages, the rate of hospitalization from lawn mower injuries, and the severity of the injuries. Accordingly, the Commission raised its estimates of injury costs to accommodate these considerations. That the Commission learned from the comments on its proposals and adjusted its conclusions accordingly increases, rather than undermines, our confidence in the reliability of the economic analysis justifying the standard. The changes made by the Commission in response to submissions from the public do "not automatically generate a new opportunity for comment." International Harvester Co. v. Ruckelshaus, 478 F.2d 615, 632 (D.C.Cir.1973). "A contrary rule would lead to the absurdity that in rule-making . . . the agency can learn from the comments on its proposals only at the peril of starting a new procedural round of commentary." Id. at 632 n.51. See also South Terminal Corp. v. EPA, 504 F.2d at 659.

The Commission also explained in the final economic report that it had revised upward earlier projections of the costs of injuries and the savings offered by the standard's safety measures because consumer prices for medical care had risen 8.3 percent from April 1977 to April 1978. It therefore adjusted SRI's injury cost figures to accommodate this price increase. Thus, the Commission not only carefully explained the rationale for its evaluation of the standard's costs and benefits and submitted much of the material used in the final economic report to public scrutiny in its preliminary form, but it also significantly based its final assessment of the cost effectiveness of the safety requirements on data from interested parties, most notably OPEI. These attributes of the standard's cost-benefit analysis cloak it in a sufficient mantle of reliability for us to find that substantial record evidence supports the Commission's finding that the rule is in the public interest. . . .

Affirmed in part, vacated in part.

Comments and Questions

1. Consider the history of the promulgation of the safety standard for power mowers described in footnote 3 of the *Southland Mower* case. Is this appropriate utilization of the administrative-regulatory instrument?

2. Why is there a need for the Consumer Product Safety Act and other similar legislation? Why is the potential liability of manufacturers and suppliers for breach of warranty, negligence, and strict tort liability insufficient to compel manufacturers and suppliers to take greater precautions to ensure the safety of their products? According to one view, even all of this potential liability together does not prevent unsafe products from entering the market, because increased costs of insurance or payment of judgments and settlements can simply be passed on to the public by increasing the price of goods. Some manufacturers, in addition, are unable to incorporate all of the technological advances in safety design into their products. Empirical evidence also suggests that private remedies

are insufficient, as injuries from defective products increase year after year. 1 L. Frumer & M. Friedman, Products Liability § 1A.01, at 2–3 (1984).

3. Is the promulgation of safety standards an effective utilization of the administrative-regulatory instrument? Consider the following statement of a Consumer Product Safety Commissioner:

> Considering product safety standards cost-ineffective, the Consumer Product Safety Commission is switching towards a more "imaginative" use of its enforcement powers . . . .
>
> Speaking before the American Trial Lawyers Association's Seventh Circuit Meeting April 11, [Commissioner] Statler said the commission's regulatory record and its limited impact on the safety of consumer products in the marketplace have been largely determined by its size and budget. In fact, he suggested that judging the commission by the number of standards it has promulgated since 1973 is "meaningless."
>
> Statler told his audience that, after some "soul searching," the commission has decided to embark on a "more vigorous and imaginative" use of [its enforcement powers]. Under the [act], manufacturers must report a potential safety hazard in their product, and, either voluntarily or pursuant to an order, offer measures to remedy the safety problem.
>
> Under this approach, he said, the commission might declare a product "de facto dangerous," and instead of developing a standard for it, commence an enforcement proceeding to get the product modified or off the market. For example, Statler explained, to eliminate a safety hazard posed by chain saws' kickback, the commission, instead of promulgating a safety [standard], could declare chain saws without a nose guard substantially hazardous and enforce a recall and modification. This procedure, he said, "is for the CPSC the most cost-effective," and given the size of its budget, the most appropriate.

Prod.Safety & Liab.Rep. (BNA) No. 8, at 281 (Apr. 18, 1980).[d]

4. Section 2074(a) of the Consumer Product Safety Act, dealing with private remedies, states:

> Compliance with consumer product safety rules or other rules or orders under this chapter shall not relieve any person from liability at common law or under state statutory law to any other person. . . .

In Gryc v. Dayton-Hudson Corp., 297 N.W.2d 727, 737 (Minn.), cert. denied, 449 U.S. 921, 101 S.Ct. 320 (1980), the court stated that § 2074(a) "makes it clear that . . . there is no preemption of private remedies." But what if a product that satisfies a safety standard promulgated by a federal agency nevertheless causes injury? Consider the next case.

WILSON v. PIPER AIRCRAFT CORP.

Supreme Court of Oregon, 1978.
282 Or. 61, 577 P.2d 1322.

HOLMAN, JUSTICE.

These two products liability cases, consolidated for trial and appeal, are wrongful-death actions brought by the personal representatives of two passengers who died after the crash of a small airplane. The only defendant is Piper Aircraft Corporation, the manufacturer of the aircraft.

d. Reprinted by permission from *Product Safety & Liability Reporter,* copyright 1980 by The Bureau of National Affairs, Inc., Washington, D.C.

The airplane, a Piper Cherokee manufactured in 1966, took off from the Eugene airport on January 22, 1971, with a licensed student pilot at the controls and a qualified instructor in the copilot's seat. Plaintiffs' decedents, Douglas Wilson and Arbie MacDonald, were passengers in the two rear seats. The airplane crashed in the Cascade Mountains southeast of Oakridge, after entering a cloud. All four occupants of the plane survived the crash itself, but plaintiffs' decedents and the student pilot died at the crash site before rescuers arrived. The only survivor was the instructor, Terry Liittschwager, who, at the time of trial, had no memory of the events immediately prior to the crash.

Plaintiffs' theory was that the crash was caused by engine failure resulting from carburetor icing, and that the deaths of Douglas Wilson and Arbie MacDonald were caused in part by injuries resulting from certain design features in the rear passenger compartment. There was evidence to support both of these contentions. The jury returned substantial verdicts for both plaintiffs, and defendant appeals.

Plaintiffs alleged the defendant furnished an airplane which was dangerously defective in various particulars having to do with both the engine's susceptibility to icing and the crashworthiness of the rear passenger compartment. The assignments of error require us to consider both aspects of the case.

In support of their theory that the airplane was dangerously defective because of its susceptibility to icing, plaintiffs alleged the following design defects: (1) the aircraft was not equipped with an injection type fuel system; (2) the carburetor was not so designed and equipped that it would provide a proper fuel-air mixture under icing conditions; (3) the aircraft was not supplied with an adequate carburetor heating system; and (4) the aircraft was not equipped with a carburetor heat gauge. Defendant contends first that these allegations, regardless of the state of the evidence, do not present a jury question; and second that the evidence was insufficient to justify submitting them to the jury.

In support of its first contention, defendant points out that it is undisputed that the design of this model of airplane was specifically approved by the Federal Aviation Administration (FAA) under its statutory authority to set safety standards for aircraft, and that this particular airplane had been issued an FAA certificate of airworthiness. It is defendant's position that the airplane's design could not be dangerously defective since it met the applicable FAA safety standards, and that FAA approval of the design has foreclosed any further inquiry into its adequacy from a safety standpoint.

We have found no support for this position. Neither the applicable statutes themselves, 49 U.S.C. §§ 1421(a)(1) and 1423(a) and (c), nor the legislative history (see 1958 U.S.Code Cong. & Admin.News, p. 3741) indicates any Congressional intent to provide that FAA approval of either the general model design or the airworthiness of the particular craft is a complete defense to the claim of civil liability for faulty design. Indeed, 49 U.S.C. § 1421(a)(1) provides that the FAA design standards are minimum standards only.

We have, in other contexts, refused to hold compliance with statutory or administrative safety standards to be conclusive on the question of tort liability where there is no evidence of a legislative intent that the standards are to be applied for that purpose. Other courts have treated compliance with the FAA safety standards as appropriate for consideration by the trier of fact in products liability cases involving aircraft. We have found no cases holding that compliance is a complete defense. We hold that it is not. . . .

[Reversed on other grounds.]

LINDE, JUSTICE, concurring.

While I join in the court's decision, the relationship between the allegedly defective design of the aircraft and the FAA's certification of that design perhaps deserves additional discussion.

Defendant contends that the approval of the design by a federal agency charged with responsibility for aircraft safety "preempts" any state law that would predicate liability on the production and sale of this aircraft type for use within the conditions for which it is certified. The contention blends two arguments: an argument based on federal supremacy, particularly with respect to equipment used in transportation across state lines, and another argument that the lawmaker has assigned the decision on the acceptable safety of the design to someone other than common-law courts and juries.

The question of federal preemption is essentially one of statutory interpretation or, if one prefers, of Congressional "intent." If Oregon undertook to declare that an aircraft type certificated by the Federal Aviation Administration is not safe enough to fly in Oregon and therefore prohibited such flights, this would present a serious issue of federal preemption. But Oregon interposes no such prohibition against the operation of FAA-approved aircraft; it only imposes a certain measure of civil liability for injuries caused thereby. It might seem that exposure to potential civil liability of millions of dollars, under state rules which might even be closer to absolute liability than Oregon's, is a greater state-created obstacle to the federally approved operation than, for instance, a moderate fine would be, and we do not suppose that Congress could not also preempt such state rules of civil liability if it chose. But there is no reason to believe that it did so. In the rare case when Congress has considered the question, e.g., in the Consumer Product Safety Act, it adopted a policy against preempting state laws on civil liability,[2] and we have been offered no evidence that it intended a different policy under the Federal Aviation Act and its 1938 predecessor.

The second argument concerns the reexamination in a common-law trial of a determination first assigned to an expert agency, either by Congress or by the state legislature. This problem arises not from any federal or legislative "preemption" but from the particular nature and elements of the test for the aircraft manufacturer's civil liability for alleged design defects. In a state where common law or legislation imposed absolute liability on a producer for certain kinds of harm in fact caused by his product, the fact that it had been thoroughly tested and approved for safety would be immaterial. But when liability is predicated on finding a design "dangerously defective," not "duly safe," or short of

2. 15 U.S.C. § 2074 (1976). . . .

some similarly phrased standard of safety, then a careful comparison of that standard and the one attested to by the certificate becomes important. Under such a test for civil liability, as well as under government regulation, the question, at least within the limits of the state of the art, is "how much safety is enough." But the factors that enter into the answer may or may not be the same.

It is true that compliance with government safety standards will generally not be held to negate a claim of "dangerously defective" design, but it would equally be an oversimplification to say that it can never do so. The role of such compliance should logically depend on whether the goal to be achieved by the particular government standards, the balance struck between safety and its costs, has been set higher or lower than that set by the rules governing the producer's civil liability. It may well be that when government intervenes in the product market to set safety standards, it often confines itself to demanding only minimum safeguards against the most flagrant hazards, well below the contemporary standards for civil liability. But that was not necessarily the case when the first safety standards were legislated, and it is not necessarily so for all products today.

In the design of aircraft, government regulation obviously places a much greater weight on the side of safety than it does for most products. The FAA not only sets detailed performance standards for the operational aspects of the design, it also requires that the design be tested for compliance with these standards by the producer and ultimately by the agency itself before a certificate is issued. This does not mean that an aircraft design, to be certified, must be the safest that could be built at any cost in money, speed, or carrying capacity. No doubt the FAA does not demand for small, single-engined recreational aircraft the redundant circuits and fail-safe systems expected in commercial airliners, not to mention the space program. It does mean, however, that FAA certification of a design represents a more deliberate, technically intensive program to set and control a given level of safety in priority to competing considerations than is true of many run-of-the-mill safety regulations.

The question remains how this policy assigned to the FAA compares with Oregon's standards of products liability for design defects. In two decisions in 1974, this court quoted a series of factors suggested by Professor Wade as posing the preliminary issue for a court whether a claim of "defect" crosses the legal threshold for submission to the jury. The difficulty in the present case springs from the fact that most of these factors—briefly summarized, the safety risks, the availability of safer design, the financial and other costs of the safer alternative, and the user's awareness of and ability to avoid the risks—are at least very similar to the factors that are presumably meant to enter into the FAA's judgment whether an aircraft design is safe enough.[5]

---

5. A final factor listed by Wade, but of no apparent concern to the FAA, is the producer's ability to spread the risk of injury from his product through its price, with or without liability insurance. As stated previously, if a state predicates a producer's civil liability on a theory of loss-spreading or "enterprise liability," then of course compliance even with the most demanding government safety standards will not relieve the producer of liability. But this court has in the past downplayed the loss-spreading capacity of an enterprise as a premise for tort liability.

It must be kept in mind that this aircraft is alleged to be defective not because it fell short of the safety standards set for its type, but on the ground that these standards provide insufficient safety for the whole series. But once the common-law premise of liability is expressed as a balance of social utility so closely the same as the judgment made in administering safety legislation, it becomes very problematic to assume that one or a sequence of law courts and juries are to repeat that underlying social judgment de novo as each sees fit. Rather, when the design of a product is subject not only to prescribed performance standards but to government supervised testing and specific approval or disapproval on safety grounds, no further balance whether the product design is "unreasonably dangerous" for its intended or foreseeable use under the conditions for which it is approved needs to be struck by a court or a jury *unless* one of two things can be shown: either that the standards of safety and utility assigned to the regulatory scheme are less inclusive or demanding than the premises of the law of products liability, or that the regulatory agency did not address the allegedly defective element of the design or in some way fell short of its assigned task.[7]

It is these two questions, rather than a de novo evaluation of the safety of a design and the technological feasibility and costs of an even safer alternative, that properly become the issues for preliminary determination by a trial court in deciding whether a "design defect" claim against a product specifically tested and approved under government safety regulations should nevertheless go to a jury. In other words, it should be defendant's burden to show that a governmental agency has undertaken the responsibility of making substantially the same judgment that the court would otherwise be called on to make; and if so, it should then be plaintiff's burden to show that the responsible agency has not in fact made that judgment with respect to the particular "defect" at issue. When the product has been tested and approved by a federal agency, these issues can normally be decided simply by examining the statutory assignment of the agency (including relevant legislative history), the further standards adopted by the agency itself, and the records and reports underlying its approval of the product. In the case of a state agency, the documentation may be less extensive but other evidence of the actual process may be more accessible to a state court.

With respect to the present case, the cited sources seem likely to show that the FAA's goals and standards match this court's criteria for a "duly safe" design, at least as far as an aircraft's airworthiness is concerned. It is not inconceivable that the answers might prove to come out one way with respect to FAA criteria and tests for aircraft engines and differently with respect to seat belts, or instrument knobs, or entry and exit steps, or other features whose risks are less central to airworthiness. Of course we do not know all that the parties might be able to show in this regard.

---

7. According to one study, this may have been the court's judgment in a case rejecting an FAA standard, Berkebile v. Brantly Helicopter Corp., 219 Pa.Super. 479, 281 A.2d 707 (1971), and in similar decisions rejecting reliance on compliance with the Federal Flammable Fabrics Act. See IV Interagency Task Force on Product Liability, Product Liability: Final Report of the Legal Study 134–136 (1977). . . .

I repeat that this need to examine the precise standards and findings of the governing safety program results not from legislative preemption of common-law standards of liability, absent indications to that effect, but rather from these standards themselves when they are identical with those underlying the regulatory scheme. It may be that the tension between the policies embodied in intensive safety regulation and licensing and in case-by-case civil liability premised on "dangerously defective" design cannot remain unresolved, especially with respect to goods federally approved for a national market. A choice may have to be made between a theory of recovery premised on the need to compensate victims of product-caused injuries and one premised on liability for "faulty" products, no matter how attenuated the "fault" has become. Since 1976 this question has been one part of a larger study of product liability conducted by an interagency task force under the direction of the United States Department of Commerce, which also encompasses questions of liability insurance, improved preventive measures, and alternatives to present modes of compensating the victims of product-caused injuries. The final report of the task force, which contains suggestions for possible legislative action, became available early this year.[8] Meanwhile, given our present premises for "design defect" liability, I believe we must deal with cases involving products that have been tested and certified for safety according to the principles here stated.

Comments and Questions

1. The effectiveness of the administrative-regulatory instrument depends on good-faith enforcement of regulations by administrators. Is such enforcement guaranteed?

2. In Ford Motor Co. v. Stubblefield, 171 Ga.App. 331, 319 S.E.2d 470 (1984), the parents of a fifteen-year-old girl, who was killed in a Ford Mustang that was engulfed in flames when hit from behind by another car, brought a wrongful-death action against Ford. They claimed that Ford had negligently designed and placed the fuel system of the car. One issue was the admissibility of a transcript of a taped conversation between then President Richard Nixon, Lee Iacocca, who was then president of Ford, and Henry Ford II. The court found that the transcript was admissible, stating during the course of its discussion:

> Nor was [the transcript] inadmissible on grounds of irrelevance or prejudice. While there was no specific discussion among the participants as to fuel system integrity, the meeting took place just one day after the decision of Ford's management to defer the adoption of protective devices for the fuel tanks until required by law, and the gist of the taped conversation concerned the necessity for the Department of Transportation to "cool it" as to safety requirements and how the government might make those standards more responsive to the auto makers' cost effectiveness.

8. Interagency Task Force on Product Liability, Final Report ch. VII (1978); I Interagency Task Force on Product Liability, supra note 7. . . .

Section Five. Product Safety and the Penal-Corrective Instrument

On August 10, 1978, a Chevrolet van struck the back of a Ford Pinto car carrying three teenage girls. All three girls were killed when, upon impact, the Pinto went up in flames. The car had been designed to withstand a rear-end collision by a vehicle like the van traveling at 20 MPH. Contending that Ford should have designed the Pinto to withstand a rear-end impact in the range of 30–40 MPH and that the van hit the Pinto with an impact of less than 40 MPH, the state of Indiana brought criminal charges against Ford for recklessly designing and manufacturing the car and failing to recall it.[e] The prosecution's view was that Ford knew that some people would die in fires caused by rear-end collisions and, despite possessing the appropriate technology, Ford failed to remedy the problem because of a decision that it would be too costly.

Why bring a criminal charge against a corporation such as Ford? Are criminal charges necessary in light of the other instrumentalities of the law that have been applied to achieve product safety? Will the penal-corrective instrumentality itself be appropriate? These are fundamental questions that you should consider while reading this section.

DEVELOPMENTS IN THE LAW—CORPORATE CRIME: REGULATING CORPORATE BEHAVIOR THROUGH CRIMINAL SANCTIONS

92 Harv.L.Rev. 1227, 1229–30, 1241–43, 1365–68 (1979).*

The twentieth century has witnessed a tremendous explosion in the number and size of corporations, to the point that virtually all economic and much social and political activity is greatly influenced by corporate behavior. During this same period, and partly as a response, there has been a dramatic increase in the efforts of the federal government to regulate that activity through the creation of multitudinous administrative agencies and volume upon volume of regulatory laws.

While many of the early attempts at regulating corporate behavior included criminal sanctions for enforcing compliance, criminal prosecution was generally employed only as a supplement to the general pattern of civil regulations, a last resort to punish particularly recalcitrant or egregious corporate behavior. During the last decade, however, in areas ranging from tax, securities, and antitrust to the newer fields of environ-

e. State v. Ford Motor Co., No. 5,324 (Ind.Super.Ct. indictment Sept. 13, 1978). These facts are based on Maakestad, *State* v. *Ford Motor Co.*: Constitutional, Utilitarian, and Moral Perspectives, 27 St. Louis U.L.J. 857 (1983); Wheeler, Manufacturers' Criminal Liability, in 1 L. Fruman & M. Friedman, Products Liability § 1B, at 3, § 1B.04, at 42 (1984); Note, Corporate Homicide: A New Assault on Corporate Decision-making, 54 Notre Dame Law. 911 (1979).

Because the Pinto was designed and manufactured prior to and during 1973, and because two provisions of the Indiana Criminal Code under which the prosecution proceeded became effective in 1977 and 1978, the focus of the case for the prosecution was on proving Ford's recklessness in failing to recall the Pinto.

* Copyright © (1979) by the Harvard Law Review Association. Reprinted by permission.

mental control, safety regulation, and the prevention of "corrupt practices," the federal government has come to rely more and more on the deterrent effect of criminal punishment to shape corporate action. . . .

Two themes emerge in the Parts that follow. First are the problems engendered by the use of criminal sanctions in the regulatory field. Foremost among these is that the choice made between criminal and civil sanctions often accords neither with the rationales that have traditionally characterized the criminal law, nor with the specific aims of the regulatory provisions themselves. For example, corporate criminal sanctions sometimes deviate greatly from the general mens rea model of the criminal law, purportedly in the name of increased deterrence. Yet the resulting invocation of the procedural protections afforded criminal defendants renders enforcement more difficult, undermining any deterrent effect. On top of this, the crazy quilt pattern of overlapping, duplicative, and even contradictory civil and criminal regulations diminishes the coherence of regulatory efforts and impedes the achievement of government objectives.

Second, the very involvement of a collective corporate entity in criminal cases is problematic. The difficulty of dealing with this entity as a "person" is particularly acute in the area of criminal law. The artificial and inanimate nature of the corporation renders uncertain the range of constitutional protections which a corporation may invoke when prosecuted. It also opens to question the necessity and utility of employing criminal sanctions directly against corporations themselves in order to regulate their behavior. The inability to imprison a corporation and the questionable effect of a criminal stigma on such an entity often leads to the prosecution of individuals within the corporation, both for their own acts and the acts of others. This focus upon individual defendants, however, serves to heighten the concern engendered by the use of criminal laws which deviate from the traditional mens rea model. Any fair and rational approach to the problem of corporate crime requires that decisions regarding which individuals within a corporation should be punished be made at least partly contingent upon the nature of the sanction and the elements of the crime. . . .

Corporate Moral Blameworthiness

There is no single, broadly accepted theory of corporate blameworthiness which justifies the imposition of criminal penalties on corporations. For an individual defendant, the mental state with which he committed the illegal act determines his moral culpability. But mental state has no meaning when applied to a corporate defendant, since an organization possesses no mental state. Three different theories of corporate blameworthiness are reflected in the various systems of corporate criminal liability.

The first theory of corporate blameworthiness considers the corporation morally responsible for the acts and intent of each of its agents. This theory treats a corporation as a principal responsible for the acts of every one of its agents, imputing to the corporation through the theory of agency the mental state of any employee. Under this theory, a corporation is blameworthy even when a single agent commits a crime for the benefit of the corporation. Yet, it is unfair to impute to the corporation the intent of a lone agent without also considering whether conscientious efforts were made by other agents to prevent the crime.

The second moral theory identifies the corporation only with its policymaking officials, and so holds the corporation morally responsible only for their acts and intent, but not for those of lower-level employees. This theory distinguishes top officials from other employees on the ground that stockholders, through their elected representatives on the board of directors, have the power to appoint and the opportunity to supervise only high-level executives. Recognizing that criminal sanctions against the corporation often harm stockholders, this theory attempts to implement the just deserts principle that individuals should not be punished for acts they had no power to control. However, in any but small, closely held corporations, the average stockholder wields no actual influence over the decisions of even the highest-placed executives. If this interpretation of the just deserts principle were applied in practice, so that corporate liability was imposed only when stockholders could bring pressures to bear to prevent the crime, corporations would be virtually immune from liability. . . .

The third theory proposes that a corporation is blameworthy only when its procedures and practices unreasonably fail to prevent corporate criminal violations. More than the two preceding theories, this theory recognizes that generally the criminal acts of a modern corporation result not from the isolated activity of a single agent, but from the complex interactions of many agents in a bureaucratic setting. Illegal conduct by a corporation is the consequence of corporate processes such as standard operating procedures and hierarchical decisionmaking. Therefore, just as an individual's moral blameworthiness depends on his mental processes, corporate moral fault may be said to depend on its internal processes. Thus, under the third theory, a corporation is blameworthy when its practices and procedures are inadequate to protect the public from corporate crimes. Corporate blameworthiness therefore depends not solely on the commission of a crime but on the overall reasonableness of corporate practices and procedures designed to avert injurious regulatory offenses. . . .

The Effectiveness of Criminal Sanctions in Deterring Corporate Crime

In order to deter certain undesirable conduct, the criminal law has traditionally employed such sanctions as imprisonment, fines, and the stigma of criminality. While the effectiveness of these sanctions in criminal law generally has been debated, it has been persuasively argued that they can effectively deter corporate crime. Since corporations are primarily profit-seeking institutions, they choose to violate the law only if it appears profitable. Profit-maximizing decisions are carefully based upon the probability and amount of potential profit, so a corporate decision to violate the criminal law would generally include a calculation of the likelihood of prosecution and the probable severity of any punishment. Making these costs sufficiently high should eliminate the potential benefit of illegal corporate activity and hence any incentive to undertake such activity.

Improper corporate conduct could be deterred by applying criminal sanctions either to the corporation itself or to its officers and employees. A corporation cannot, of course, be imprisoned. It may also be argued that the stigma of a criminal label is of little significance to an inanimate business organization. Such stigma could influence corporate behavior if it led to diminished profits, but it is questionable whether the mere stigma of a criminal conviction would in fact produce this result. Furthermore, in most cases there is little likelihood that any stigma of criminality will filter down to particular individuals in the corporate structure, especially in a large corporation. A system of fines imposed on corporations, however, should adequately deter illegal corporate activity as long as the fines are large enough to force the corporation to disgorge all benefit gained from illicit conduct.

While the preceding analysis may be theoretically sound, commentators disagree about the effectiveness of criminal sanctions as presently administered. Some argue that vigorous prosecution will indeed prevent corporate crime, but others believe that the criminal sanctions now applied to corporations and individuals are ineffective deterrents. The latter view is based primarily upon the present administration of criminal penalties; small fixed fines levied on corporations are viewed as little more than fees for licenses to engage in illegal activities. As one commentator has noted, the "possible profits so outweigh the possible penalties that widespread noncompliance is inevitable." Since the stigma of a criminal fine alone will not affect corporate behavior, some commentators have concluded that sanctions applied to corporations must be financial, and that present penalties are too small to achieve a significant level of deterrence.

It might still be possible to deter corporate misbehavior by applying criminal sanctions to individuals in the organization. Since businessmen fear the stigma of criminality for both personal and economic reasons, such penalties might be thought to be effective deterrents. Indeed, the fear of criminal indictment or investigation, even in the absence of conviction, may effectively deter corporate officials. But this approach has not been effective. Prosecutions directed against corporations and individuals often result in no more than small corporate fines; holding the corporation liable for crimes committed by its officers or directors has long been a favorite device of juries who apparently wish to force the business to disgorge at least some of its ill-gained profits, but who are unwilling to impose the criminal label and stigma upon individuals who have committed no ostensibly immoral act. Moreover, it is often difficult, especially in large corporations, to determine which individuals are responsible for the illegal activity. The unwillingness of juries to convict individual defendants of corporate criminal violations and the difficulty in pinpointing responsible persons in the corporate structure lessens the likelihood that a businessman will in fact be convicted of criminal activity. Thus corporate crime may not be adequately deterred by criminal sanctions designed for individuals.

In order to alleviate these problems in the present administration of corporate criminal statutes, commentators have proposed a variety of solutions, ranging from more vigorous enforcement to tougher sanctions, such as fines based upon a proportion of the income of a convicted corporation. Vigorous enforcement alone is unlikely to solve the problems: corporations will not be deterred by threat of prosecution as long as corporate fines remain small and the difficulties of convicting individual defendants are substantial. And perhaps the juries unwilling to convict defendants are right, since vigorous application of strict criminal sanctions raises questions of fairness where the individual has done nothing or little that is morally blameworthy. Tougher sanctions against corporations themselves might increase deterrence, but since such sanctions would take the form of fines, one must wonder whether the same or a higher level of deterrence could be better achieved through civil penalties.

WHEELER, MANUFACTURERS' CRIMINAL LIABILITY

in 1 L. Frumer & M. Friedman, Products Liability § 1B.02[1], at 12–14 (1984).*

The manufacturer of a particular product might be criminally prosecuted under either or both of two types of statutes for having produced and marketed a product with a design defect, a manufacturing defect, or inadequate warnings. One type is the criminal regulatory statute—one specifying design, performance, or warning requirements for a class of products that includes the manufacturer's product. Such a statute might be, for example, a law requiring automobiles to have seatbelts (design requirement), a law requiring automobiles to withstand collisions of a specified magnitude without leaking fuel (performance requirement), or a law requiring that fabrics of specified flammability contain a label stating that fact (warning requirement). The second type is the general criminal statute—one prohibiting conduct not necessarily linked to the manufacture and sale of a particular class of products, or even to the manufacture and sale of products generally. General criminal statutes include, for example, murder, assault, and fraud statutes.[1]

Criminal regulatory statutes reflect a legislature's judgment regarding the specific instances in which manufacturers of specific products should be held criminally responsible. The legislature often expresses such judgments indirectly, through regulations promulgated by an administrative agency created by the legislature and authorized to promulgate standards the violation of which is punishable as a crime. The statutes in this category can be as numerous and as varied as the number of products appearing in commerce.[2] As a general rule, a product manufacturer can readily determine whether its product violates such a statute, because the

---

1. Of course, product manufacturers can be prosecuted under many other criminal statutes, such as those regulating anticompetitive conduct, occupational health and safety, pollution of the environment, and securities transactions. Generally, however, those statutes are not aimed at regulating product safety and therefore are not pertinent to this chapter.

2. See, e.g., Federal Food, Drug, and Cosmetic Act § 301, 21 USC § 333(a) (1976).

statute specifies requirements aimed at a particular type of product, articulates specific design features, performance standards, or warnings, and does not require the manufacturer to speculate as to whether a jury in a criminal prosecution is likely to find something about the product sufficiently dangerous to constitute a negligent, reckless, or knowing creation of danger rising to the level of criminality.

General criminal statutes, on the other hand, present product manufacturers with greater uncertainty. It is far from clear, for example, what product design or what product warning suffices to permit a jury to find a product manufacturer guilty of a general crime such as "recklessly endangering another person," defined as follows:

> A person commits a misdemeanor if he recklessly engages in conduct which places or may place another person in danger of death or serious bodily injury.[3]

. . . [T]he prosecution of Ford Motor Company for reckless homicide in 1980 apparently is the only instance in which a product manufacturer has been prosecuted under a general criminal statute for having produced and sold a product with a manufacturing defect, a design defect, or an insufficient warning. Nevertheless, the broad language of several criminal statutes and of the judicial decisions interpreting those statutes, together with the increasing use of criminal sanctions to regulate the conduct of corporations generally,[4] suggests the likelihood of future attempts to prosecute product manufacturers, under general criminal statutes, for the production and sale of defective products.

———

Comments and Questions

1. Note that the discussion in the Developments excerpt focuses on deterrence as the purpose of applying criminal sanctions to corporations. What of other purposes of such sanctions, such as removal of criminals from society, retribution, and rehabilitation? Can corporations effectively be removed from society? If a corporation's charter were revoked, couldn't management and shareholders set up another corporation? What about retribution and rehabilitation? See Chapter 2. Most analysts agree that deterrence is the proper goal here.

2. Is the penal-corrective instrument suited to achieve the goal of product safety? What are the problems with the use of criminal sanctions against corporations?

3. Review the theories of corporate liability set forth in the Developments excerpt. Which, if any, are persuasive?

4. The Ford Pinto case was prosecuted under Indiana Code § 35–42–1–5. That section and other pertinent sections of the Indiana Code in force at the time of the case follow:

> § 35–42–1–5. . . . A person who recklessly kills another human being commits reckless homicide . . . .
>
> § 35–41–1–2. . . . "Person" means a human being, corporation, partnership, unincorporated association, or governmental entity.

3. Model Penal Code § 211.2 (1962).

4. There is little doubt that the use of criminal sanctions to regulate corporate conduct has increased in recent years. . . .

§ 35–41–2–3. . . . . A corporation . . . may be prosecuted for any offense; it may be convicted of an offense only if it is proved that the offense was committed by its agent acting within the scope of his authority. . . .

5. One of the reasons for Ford's criminal prosecution may have been the lack of satisfactory civil sanctions. Because the victims were killed, the parents' recourse was a wrongful-death action. But, under the governing Indiana statute, the parents' recovery would have been meager. The statute measured the recovery in terms of the value of the child's services from the time of death until the age of majority, less support and maintenance, Indiana Code § 34–1–1–2; but the victims had reached or were soon to reach eighteen, the age of majority. In addition, according to Indiana common law, damages for pain and suffering of the victims, mental anguish of the survivors, and punitive damages were *not* recoverable against Ford. See Maakestad, *State* v. *Ford Motor Co.*: Constitutional, Utilitarian, and Moral Perspectives, 27 St. Louis U.L.J. 857, 870–71 (1983).

6. Ford was acquitted in March 1980, after a jury trial in the Indiana criminal proceeding. Various grounds for the acquittal were possible. The jury could have believed, for example, that the van that hit the Pinto was traveling at a speed over 40 MPH, as was contended by Ford. For another example, one article reports that a postverdict poll of the jurors showed that most jurors thought Ford was reckless in its design and manufacture of the Pinto but not in its failure to recall. Id. at 860 n.14. Because no judicial opinion was issued, we have no view from the judge who tried the case of the general merits of bringing criminal charges in such cases. The following excerpt was written by one of Ford's attorneys in the case. This is followed by two excerpts that take a decidedly different view.

WHEELER, MANUFACTURERS' CRIMINAL LIABILITY

in 1 L. Frumer & M. Friedman, Products Liability § 1B.06,
at 54–61, 73–76, 78–81 (1984).*

The theory of deterrence assumes that a person contemplating the commission of a particular act will commit that act only if the benefits he expects to reap outweigh the anticipated costs he expects to incur, with anticipated costs being a function of both the possible costs and the probability that those possible costs will be incurred.[3] Thus, to increase deterrence, one can increase either the costs the actor might incur by engaging in the conduct or the probability that the actor will in fact incur those costs.

Even absent the threat of criminal sanctions, manufacturers, in deciding whether to implement any modification affecting product safety, must consider several costs they might incur by producing and selling products that could be made safer. These potential costs include amounts awarded in civil lawsuits for compensatory damages, where compensatory damages may include lost income, medical expenses, property damage and intangibles such as pain and suffering, loss of consortium and mental distress to family members. In any one lawsuit these can total several millions of dollars.

3. See generally Becker, Crime and Punishment: An Economic Approach, 76 J.Pol.Econ. 1969 (1968).

Other potential costs to be considered are civil lawsuits for punitive damages—where awards can be several million dollars in any one lawsuit—and civil lawsuits for fraud, breach of contract, or breach of warranty. These may even include class actions in which purchasers who have not suffered physical injury seek equitable relief or damages.

In addition, administrative or judicial proceedings by regulatory agencies to require recalls, warnings, or other remedial conduct may cost the manufacturer several million dollars. Critical publicized evaluations of the product by government agencies or by private testing entities, such as Consumers' Union, may cause consumers to eschew the particular product and, perhaps, other products made by the manufacturer. Adverse publicity about injuries suffered by the product's users, about lawsuits brought against the manufacturer, or about proceedings instituted by regulatory agencies may cause additional consumers to shun the manufacturer's products. Finally, a manufacturer must consider the costs of defending lawsuits and other proceedings, even where no adverse judgment or settlement ever occurs.

Such a broad array of non-criminal deterrent costs attends few other activities engaged in by members of our society. Moreover, the probability that at least some of these costs will be incurred by a manufacturer that makes and sells a product which could have been made safer and which injures someone appears to be substantial and growing. In 1974, 1,579 product liability cases were filed in federal courts, while 7,775 such cases were filed in federal courts in the year ending June 30, 1980. The magnitude of jury awards has risen so substantially that million-dollar verdicts are now common.

This increase in the likelihood that manufacturers will incur substantial costs for selling defective products has been spurred by the steady stream of doctrinal developments in tort law that favor plaintiffs, both in liability and in damages issues. Since the turn of the century we have seen, for example, the demise of the privity requirement; the adoption of strict liability as generally defined in section 402A of the Restatement (Second) of Torts; the occasional shifting to the defendant of the burden of proof on causation issues; . . . rejection of the section 402A "unreasonably dangerous" limitation on strict liability; the shifting of the burden of proof to the defendant in strict liability cases, once the plaintiff has established that his injury was caused by the design of the manufacturer's product, to prove that the product is not defective; . . . and inflation-adjusted damage awards, to name but a few.

Despite the impressive array of potential costs that tend to deter manufacturers from producing and selling products that courts, regulators, testing entities, or consumers are likely to consider defective, and despite the apparently substantial probability that some of those costs will be incurred by any manufacturer who markets such products, it is theoretically possible that even more deterrence is socially desirable and that the additional deterrence could be efficiently achieved by the use of criminal sanctions. The threat of such sanctions would increase the magnitude of the possible costs of marketing "defective" products, because the possible costs would include the cost of defending the criminal case, a fine, and lost sales attributable to public antipathy for convicted criminals. The threat of criminal sanctions also increases the probability that other costs will be incurred, because more public resources will be devoted to detecting and prosecuting the conduct in issue, which in turn will bring the manufacturer's conduct to the attention of more persons who can impose the various noncriminal costs discussed above.

Recognition that more deterrence *may* be desirable, however, does not ineluctably mean that more deterrence *is* desirable. Before deciding whether more deterrence is needed or can efficiently be obtained through the use of criminal sanctions, one must identify what it is that one wishes to deter.

The events surrounding the reckless-homicide prosecution of Ford Motor Company by the State of Indiana in 1980 suggest one form of product-manufacturer conduct that many persons believe should be deterred: the use of cost-benefit analysis in which human safety is treated as just one of several factors to be weighed, when choosing among alternative product designs. Thus, for example, the prosecutor accused Ford of having "consciously decided to sacrifice human life for private profit." Others who supported the criminal prosecution denounced the company for having used "cost-benefit analysis . . . over the cost of human life." These statements indicate that advocates of the use of criminal sanctions to regulate product designs and warnings base their argument in large part on a deep-seated antipathy for any managerial or engineering analysis that, under any circumstances, would permit non-safety considerations to dictate the adoption of a product design that is less safe than an available alternative design. Accordingly, those advocates appear to believe that criminal sanctions are necessary and desirable to deter the use of such cost-benefit analysis.

That belief, however, is both illogical and clearly contrary to the consuming public's best interests. It rests on reasoning that is inherently self-contradictory, on erroneous factual premises, on a misunderstanding of the meaning of cost-benefit analysis, and on a misperception of the public interest.

First, as noted above, the very essence of deterrence theory *requires* that an actor weigh the costs and benefits of contemplated conduct in deciding whether to engage in that conduct. It would be self-contradictory, therefore, to assert that society should deter the use of cost-benefit analysis by relying upon a theory that necessarily recognizes and encourages cost-benefit analysis.

Second, it is literally impossible to prevent any person from using cost-benefit analysis (except by preventing the person from acting altogether) because the very act of choosing one form of conduct over other forms of conduct necessarily entails a cost-benefit analysis. The person who goes to work decides that the anticipated benefits of work outweigh the risk of injury that necessarily attends the trip to the place of employment; the person who plays golf decides that the anticipated pleasure of that exercise outweighs the risk of being hit by a ball or of pulling a muscle; the person who smokes, drinks, skis, swims, or rides a motorcycle decides that those pleasures are worth the attendant risks. Similar decisions are made where actors' conduct implicates the safety of other persons; for example, the parents who leave their baby unattended in bed for one hour have decided that the pleasure of turning their attention elsewhere justifies the risk that their unattended infant will injure itself in the next room.

The examples are infinite in number, because *some* danger inheres in every human action and omission; and *some* amount of safety is sacrificed by every action and omission. The variables in every instance are the probability of harm and the possible scope of the harm.

Product manufacturers—large or small, sole proprietor or large corporation, simplistic or mathematically sophisticated—are no different. Consider, for example, a manufacturer who makes automobiles for sale to the public. That manufacturer knows that a prospective car owner will want some combination of safety, durability, reliability, speed, acceleration, comfort, passenger space, luggage space, handling, ease of repair, low cost of repair, aesthetics, low price, low cost of operation, and other factors. The manufacturer also knows that it is literally impossible to maximize all of those desires; for example, more passenger space and luggage space require larger overall size, which is inconsistent with better handling, better acceleration, better mileage and lower price.

Further, even within any of the many areas, balancing is required. A thoroughly rigid rear structure in an automobile will protect the fuel tank from being damaged by a rear impact, but that same rigidity will cause the occupants to suffer injury or death from whiplash and from being thrown against parts of the vehicle's interior during the impact. Similarly, lighter weight yields better handling and, therefore, better accident avoidance, but the same absence of structure increases the likelihood of injury if the car does crash.

To strike a balance among the numerous variables, the manufacturer must decide what balance the public would strike if given the chance to make a fully informed choice among available alternative designs. In a basically free-market system, the manufacturer whose product most closely approximates the public's desired balance will sell the most units. If the public values safety features over low price and fuel economy, manufacturers of safer, more expensive, less efficient cars will succeed, and the public's wishes will be satisfied. Ascertaining the public's hypothetical fully informed desires, however, is no mean task. The manufacturer may try to ascertain the public's desire through public opinion polls, dealer information, consumer letters, sales volumes, sales trends for available alternatives, market studies, or analyses of external factors. Such external factors may include population growth, family size, oil supplies, state of the national economy, weather trends, and air quality. . . .

Just as cost-benefit analysis is a logical necessity, it in turn necessarily entails the use of some common measuring device to compare the values of entirely disparate factors; and the only readily available such device is dollars. Therefore, however arbitrary and crude the valuation process might be, the decision-maker must assign some dollar value to human life, injury, and suffering, as well as to comfort, convenience, aesthetics, and other factors. The valuation process can be intuitive, as it is in most of our personal, minute-by-minute decisions, or it can be a sophisticated, quantitative, computerized analysis. Thus, when a highway safety engineer for the government decides whether to put a stoplight, a stopsign, a traffic officer or no traffic-control device at an intersection, he cannot rationally decide which choice to make unless he first decides how much of the public's money should be spent to prevent one injury or one death; and he cannot make that decision without first putting some value on human life and limb.

The same problem faces a legislature trying to decide whether to impose a 65-mile-per-hour speed limit, a 55-mile-per-hour speed limit, a 25-mile-per-hour speed limit or a ban on all automobile traffic. Each more restrictive law will prevent more highway deaths, but each has a greater cost in terms of convenience, pleasure, and the delivery of goods and services, including health services. A rational decision requires using a common valuation tool: dollars.

Out of ignorance or for political purposes, one can argue that it is immoral to put a dollar value on human life. The inevitable effect of such a position, however, is that cost-benefit analyses will still be made by every decision-maker, but they will be made in a cruder, less informed, less open manner that is less susceptible to rational review by the public and by the courts. . . .

Alternatively, . . . one might contend that criminal sanctions are needed to deter manufacturers from marketing any product that could be made safer by using current technology, irrespective of the cost consumers might have to pay for the added safety. Costs of additional safety might include higher price, lower reliability, shorter useful life, reduced efficiency, higher maintenance and service costs, and many others.

This contention, however, ignores the indisputable fact that the public does not want all technologically feasible safety at any cost. Rather, individual citizens constantly choose to risk their own personal safety and the safety of others, including their loved ones, for a variety of reasons, including price, function, convenience, aesthetics, vanity and pleasure. For example, women wear high-heeled shoes despite the obvious risk of tripping or damaging their Achilles tendons; men undergo hair transplants despite the well-known risk of infection and other injury; men and women undergo face-lifts and other cosmetic surgery, smoke cigarettes, take drugs, drink liquor, drive over the speed limit, play contact sports, shoot guns and engage in innumerable other activities that risk their own safety and the safety of others.

Thus, if criminal sanctions were to be applied to product manufacturers for marketing products that are somewhat less safe, but somewhat cheaper, more reliable, more durable or better in some other respect, criminal sanctions should be applied with equal vigor to Congress for not lowering the speed limit below 55 miles-per-hour; to state and federal agencies responsible for the construction of highways that have curves, go over hills and have only two lanes (since all such highways are known to result in more highway deaths than straight, multi-lane highways); to drivers who drive at the maximum allowable speed rather than at a lower allowable speed; to parents who do not strap seatbelts onto their children in automobiles; to parents who give their children motorcycles and toys that (like all toys) can injure; to retail stores that sell liquor; to homeowners who burn leaves or use fireplaces; and so forth. Obviously, no sensible person wishes to apply criminal sanctions in that manner.

Alternatively, therefore, the criminal-sanctions proponent might contend that such sanctions are needed to deter manufacturers from marketing any product without giving the public the opportunity to exercise an informed choice—that is, without informing the public of every respect in which the product could be made safer, the costs of making each available safety modification and the extent to which safety would be increased by each such modification.

The absurdity of that contention can be seen by considering the implications for almost any product. For example, an automobile has approximately 14,000 parts, each of which can be made safer in at least one way, such as by using higher-grade materials or narrower manufacturing tolerances. To inform the public of each such available modification, of the effects on price, comfort, durability, fuel economy and other factors, and of the effect of each modification on the overall safety risk would require a multi-volume buyers' guide that would cost thousands of dollars and go unread by the public.

Alternatively, therefore, the criminal-sanctions proponent might contend that such sanctions are needed to deter manufacturers from marketing products that are less safe than the public wants them to be, all factors considered. This seems to be the proper basis on which to try to justify the application of criminal sanctions under a deterrence theory. Application of the deterrence theory on this basis would be consistent with the present application of criminal sanctions to deter recklessness in other forms of conduct. It would be consistent, for example, with imposing criminal sanctions against drivers who drive 60 miles-per-hour in a 55-mile-per-hour zone, but not against drivers who drive 55-miles-per-hour, even though both activities create a risk to the driver, his passengers, pedestrians and occupants of other vehicles. It would be consistent with imposing criminal sanctions against persons who fire their guns in urban areas, but not against persons who fire their guns on skeet ranges or in authorized hunting areas, even though each of these activities creates a risk to human safety. In short, the use of criminal sanctions based on a deterrence theory may be desirable where—because manufacturers have inadequate information, because of high transaction costs in negotiations between buyers and sellers and bystanders, because of a low probability that manufacturers will pay the social costs of marketing products that are less safe than the public wants when all factors are considered, or because of any other circumstance—a manufacturer is not sufficiently likely to calculate and to internalize accurately the full social costs of manufacturing a particular product.

That, however, serves only to state a theoretical justification for using criminal sanctions to regulate product safety. Several additional questions must be answered before it can sensibly be concluded that such a use of the criminal law is desirable.

First, one must explain why, in the face of dramatic increases in recent years in government regulation of product safety, in the number of product-liability lawsuits and in the size of plaintiffs' monetary recoveries in product-liability lawsuits, it suddenly is socially desirable to add the further threat of criminal sanctions to achieve the proper balance of safety and all other factors that make up a product. It might be argued, for example, that communications, transportation and other developments of the past few decades have caused an increasing number of products to be marketed on a national or international basis and that when a manufacturer sells a product that causes serious physical injury, many consumers will be harmed before the product can be withdrawn from the market and before consumers can be warned. It might further be argued that more products are now being made that can cause injuries in more ways that the average consumer is unlikely to foresee. It might further be argued that, with so many more persons being injured in so many ways in so many locations, manufacturers are more likely to underestimate the social costs of marketing any particular product, are more likely to think that a greater percentage of the injured persons will fail to sue or are for some other reason more likely to fail to internalize all of the social costs of their manufacturing decisions. But this chain of propositions merely states a theoretical possibility, not a proven fact.

Similarly, one must produce evidence proving that the public in fact wishes to pay higher prices or to have less reliable, less durable, less efficient, less comfortable, less serviceable, uglier, or otherwise more undesirable products in return for some marginal increase in overall product safety. . . .

. . . [E]ven a decision that more deterrence is needed does not mean that *any* additional amount, no matter how large, is needed or desirable. As an extreme example, if it were made a capital crime to market any automobile the usage of which may result in injury, it is likely that no one would manufacture an automobile—presumably, an undesirable amount of deterrence.

The deterrent effect of applying general criminal recklessness or criminal negligence laws to product manufacturers is a complete unknown. This is so because the deterring costs depend so greatly upon factors external to the criminal proceedings: the amount of publicity, the accuracy of the reporting, the variety of products sold by the defendant, the public's knowledge of what company manufactures those products and the elasticity of demand for the product in issue, to name a few.

Applying criminal sanctions may therefore result in much more deterrence than is socially desirable. Again, to paint an extreme picture, the result may be that manufacturers will produce ugly, fuel-guzzling, expensive, uncomfortable, slow, cumbersome, inconvenient, short-lived automobiles that are difficult to service, but that are marginally safer than today's models.

The public's recent mass move to small, fuel-efficient, more dangerous cars designed to deal better with the world oil situation dramatically demonstrates that maximum safety is not the foremost consideration in product purchases. If any legislative body tries to force manufacturers to produce more safety at costs that the public does not wish to pay, that body is performing a paternalistic disservice to the public welfare.

. . . [I]t is [also] far from clear that it is socially desirable to devote already scarce police, prosecutorial and judicial resources to the criminal prosecution of product manufacturers. Such resources would have to be diverted from the policing and prosecuting of other crimes, or more of the public's resources would have to be used to hire police officers, prosecutors, judges and supporting personnel.

In addition, as the Pinto prosecution showed, such enforcement agencies would have to hire scientists, engineers, statisticians and other personnel to analyze, advise and testify about products ranging from automobiles to chemical products. . . .

In addition, several practical considerations should be weighed before a decision to use criminal sanctions to regulate product safety is made. For example, given that the shareholders of any corporation are likely to change between the time when a product is designed or manufactured and the time when a prosecution alleging a defect commences, several questions can be raised:

- Is it desirable to punish shareholders who not only did not benefit from previous wrongful conduct, but who may have paid a higher price for their stock than they would have paid had the conduct been publicly known?

- Is it desirable to stigmatize all of the officers, directors and employees of a large corporation for the conduct of, for example, one engineer who—in contravention of clear corporate policy—ignored a safety problem?

- Is it desirable to employ criminal sanctions to deter when, as previously explained, there is no way to assure any semblance of proportionality between the crime and the punishment?

- If individual employees are to be prosecuted, will the threat of such prosecutions evoke a spate of self-serving, self-protective internal memoranda by fearful employees?

- Will intra-company communications offering creative but unproven ideas cease being written?

- Will an inordinate amount of employee effort be diverted to minuscule risk-reductions and away from other areas of concern, such as avoidance of environmental pollution, quality control, durability, efficient use of scarce resources, and productivity?

- Will engineers and managers become unwilling to approve new design concepts? . . .

In sum, use of general criminal laws to regulate product safety would constitute a major development in American law and in the American economy. That use has been too readily espoused by advocates who have shown no sign that they have considered the far-reaching effects that might result. It may be that more product safety is needed and that the use of criminal sanctions is the only way to achieve it. But the limitations of the criminal sanction should be remembered, and it should be clearly understood that the price to be paid will include the likes of lower productivity, less innovation and growth in non-safety matters, increases in prosecutorial and judicial expenditures, higher product prices, fewer exports to countries with less-stringent safety standards, and products that are less durable, less efficient, less convenient, less attractive, less serviceable and less reliable.

NOTE, CORPORATE HOMICIDE: A NEW ASSAULT ON CORPORATE DECISION–MAKING

54 Notre Dame Law. 911, 922–24 (1979).*

[I]t should be noted that *State* v. *Ford Motor Co.* presents issues which transcend those of existing precedents. Prior indictments of corporations for homicide resulted from acts of corporate agents performed within the scope of employment. The engineer recklessly operating the train or a repairman recklessly installing a gas pipe, are examples of the norm. The prosecution of Ford, however, occurs in a completely different setting. Ford's alleged illegal conduct is comprised of three acts: (1) defectively designing the vehicle, (2) defectively manufacturing the vehicle, and (3) allowing the vehicle to remain on the public highways.[91] Each of these acts is the product of a complex business decision. Both the design and manufacture of automobiles are subject to extensive federal regulation.[92] Rigorous testing precedes marketing. Defects discovered after sale to the public may involve recalls, either voluntary or compulsory.[93] Therefore, the Pinto which exploded on August 10, 1978, was the product of many substantial business decisions occurring at various levels of the corporate hierarchy. The deterrent effect of corporate liability for criminal homicide, therefore, must be assessed by the effect of conviction on this decision-making process.

The maximum penalty which can be imposed on a corporation convicted under the Indiana reckless homicide statute is a $10,000 fine.[94] The effectiveness of this sanction as a deterrent to a large, profitable corporation is questionable. The imposition of a $10,000 fine in itself is a nominal burden. Opponents of corporate criminal liability for homicide might contend that companies such as Ford are not likely to alter internal policies for fear of such sanctions. Thus, superficially, such indictments appear as futile attempts to impede corporate recklessness when deterrence is the standard of evaluation and "small" fines are the sanction.

The inherent flaw in this analysis is the assumption that the $10,000 fine is the only consequence of conviction. The negative publicity of a criminal conviction is the consequence most likely to deter reckless corporate conduct. A guilty verdict could threaten the fate of a corporation's entire product line by inspiring public mistrust and thereby jeopardizing future revenues. Short-term cost reductions due to relaxed concern for safety would have to be discounted by the potential impact on sales revenue. Therefore, the imposition of corporate criminal penalties should deter the instigation of corporate policies that produce incidents such as

---

  91.   State v. Ford Motor Co., No. 5324 (Indictment at 1).
  92.   See, e.g., National Traffic and Motor Vehicle Safety Act of 1966, 15 U.S.C. §§ 1381–1431 (1976).
  93.   See 15 U.S.C. §§ 1411–1420 (1976).
  94.   Ind.Code § 35–50–2–6 (Supp.1978).

the Pinto explosion of August 10, 1978, by stimulating greater managerial scrutiny of the design and manufacture of products.

The Pinto case, regardless of its outcome, will also heighten corporate concern regarding recalls. A product designed and manufactured with proper care but subsequently found to be defective may be the basis of a homicide indictment. Thus, a new variable enters decisions concerning the recall of defective products. Simple cost analysis will no longer suffice because the company must account for potential public animosity in the event of criminal indictment. The net result is increased concern for product safety and consumer protection.

Arguably, a products liability suit might provide the necessary deterrence offered by criminal liability. The monetary concern is potentially much greater and the victim is compensated more directly. Also, the impact on corporate sales has the potential of being equally devastating. Although this argument has its merits, it fails to note that criminal liability is generally reserved for egregious deviations from the standard of care required of corporations. Furthermore, civil remedies might not be available in all cases,[95] thus leaving criminal prosecution as the only sanction. The social and moral condemnation associated with a homicide conviction also provides an added variable of immense proportions that is not offered by civil litigation. Media coverage of such events generates national exposure. The result should be much stronger deterrence of reckless disregard for product safety.

Absent potential criminal responsibility for marketing a defective product, the value of human life is reduced to mere cost analysis. Probability distributions estimating potential consumer deaths and resulting civil liabilities pitted against the cost of adequate safety precautions threatens to become the standard of corporate decision-making. Thus, potential criminal liability provides a prophylactic variable likely to weigh heavily in contemporary decision-making models, thereby enhancing corporate responsibility to consumers.

MAAKESTAD, *STATE* v. *FORD MOTOR CO.*: CONSTITUTIONAL, UTILITARIAN, AND MORAL PERSPECTIVES

27 St. Louis U.L.J. 857, 872–78 (1983).*

A majority of states are in accordance with Indiana's nineteenth century method of computing and limiting compensatory damages in cases involving the wrongful death of a dependent child. More important in terms of the potential role of the criminal law, however, is the fact that as many as *thirty-one states do not allow recovery of punitive damages in any wrongful death cases,* notwithstanding that the defendant's reckless, malicious, or willful and wanton state of mind can be proven. Furthermore,

---

95. This is the case in Indiana. Indiana law does not provide a civil remedy to the families of the deceased girls. State's Memorandum in Rebuttal to Motion to Dismiss (filed Dec. 20, 1978).

although the issue is far from finally settled, the clear majority of courts that have decided the issue have held that general insuring language in business liability policies *includes coverage of punitive damages*; since the effect of such indemnification agreements is to shift the punishment to a third party, it also shifts the retributive effect and at least partially loses the deterrent function. The end result is that civil remedies in a majority of states do not sufficiently address the culpability of a corporation for doing business in such a way as to recklessly endanger the health and safety of the public. Indiana's prosecution of corporate homicide may have served to provide a striking example of one state's response to the conflict created by the law's desire to achieve its reductive goal and the existing civil process' inability to carry it out.

At the federal level, it is still not a crime for a corporation's officers to knowingly market an unsafe product, conceal a workplace hazard, or fail to report life threatening dangers of a product or business practice. Although bills were introduced during both the 96th and 97th Congress in the House and the Senate that would have provided stiff criminal penalties for such activities, none of them were enacted into the law due to intensive lobbying efforts launched by business groups. If reckless business decisions that endanger lives are going to be deterred in a comprehensive manner, it can realistically be done only through federal legislation. Although the threat of more state prosecutions like the Pinto case might help narrow the "deterrent gap," it has its obvious limitations; mainly, the disparity in legal and financial resources available to a state or county prosecutor vis-à-vis a large corporation. This leaves us solely with administrative regulations, which might: (1) provide for no criminal sanctions for reckless endangerment by corporations (e.g., the National Highway Traffic Motor Vehicle Safety Act provides for civil penalties only); (2) receive reduced funding by Congress or less attention in terms of enforcement by the presidentially appointed and politically sensitive agency heads (e.g., under the Reagan administration, Food and Drug Administration enforcement efforts against unsafe products have dropped by sixty-five percent from 1980 levels); and (3) subordinate interests of the public to those of the regulated industry, following the not uncommon political phenomenon of role reversal between the regulator and the regulated (e.g., the now defunct Atomic Energy Commission's promotional rather than regulatory efforts concerning the nuclear power industry). . . .

. . . Although most scholarly discussion of criminal sanctions against corporations is strictly utilitarian (i.e., will such sanctions effectively deter corporate wrongdoing), perhaps such concerns, while important, are secondary to the moral implications in the context of the Pinto prosecution. . . .

The Elkhart, Indiana community's immediate reaction to the fiery accident on U.S. Highway 33 was the kind of shock and profound sense of loss that can follow only a local tragedy which takes the lives of young people. Certain irregularities discovered during the state police's investigation that implicated Ford were discovered, however, and grief turned to outrage as many in the community began to tie together the information they were receiving locally with the legacy of Pinto deaths and injuries nationwide, which had received extensive publicity on television and in newspapers and magazines. As public and private debate intensified, the question that emerged most frequently was, "What legal response can, and should, be made?" Preliminary legal research revealed the severe limitations of civil remedies . . . ; moreover, a civil remedy would do little to give fruition to the community's sentiments. If a meaningful legal response was to be forthcoming, it would have to take the form of a criminal prosecution against either a particular Ford executive, or executives, or the corporation itself. Elkhart County Prosecutor Michael A. Cosentino, who had carefully directed the investigation of the accident from the beginning, weighed the alternatives, realizing that taking any criminal action against Ford would mean an extensive commitment of time, effort, and money. Following informative conversations with attorneys who had successfully sued Ford in civil court and were therefore familiar with available documentary evidence relevant to the Pinto's development, a decision was made: an indictment by grand jury would be sought against Ford Motor Company, a corporation, for three counts of reckless homicide.[74]

We thus return to our original query: was the prosecution primarily concerned with utilitarian values or moral values? Although the law professors and their students who soon became an integral part of the volunteer prosecutorial staff may have viewed the case as an opportunity to establish a precedent and create a new means by which to fight corporate crime, the local prosecutor's initial and primary concern was to respond to the outrage which followed the local family's tragedy. What was actually being conceived in Indiana, then, was not a proposed panacea for the corporate crime problem but a new moral boundary of permissible corporate conduct. It should be recalled that prior to this case, Ford's conduct surrounding the Pinto had already triggered nearly every legal response possible other than criminal prosecution: civil cases involving compensatory damages, civil cases involving both compensatory and punitive damages, and federal administrative agency actions. . . . Although a jury chosen from a different community, following a change of venue, ultimately rendered a verdict of acquittal, the real significance of the prosecution was undiminished: local people who had considered their *moral boundaries* transgressed had risen up and expressed their outrage by requiring a corporation, like any other person, to stand judgment before a criminal jury. . . .

Clearly, the attempt to place criminal responsibility upon Ford for reckless homicide, an offense carrying a maximum penalty of only $30,000 ($10,000 per count) under Indiana law, holds much greater import as a symbolic declaration of public morality than it does as an instrument by which to combat corporate crime effectively in the future.

As one of Ford's defense attorneys observed after the trial, the prosecution of a serious offense against an individual is admittedly different than

---

74. The choice between prosecuting the corporation or corporate officers is a dilemma frequently encountered in cases of corporate crime. Although most legal commentators agree that sanctions directed at corporate actors are more effective as a deterrent in most instances, it is extremely difficult to pinpoint individual responsibility for a policy or even a single decision in the labyrinthian structure of modern corporations.

the prosecution of a corporation, where adverse publicity may affect the company's employees and their families, the company's suppliers and shareholders, and the consuming public. Nonetheless, if corporations are to be personified in terms of maintaining a separate legal identity cloaked with most of the protections afforded by The Bill of Rights, it should not be considered unrealistic to require that they occasionally abide by the same moral duties and submit to the same legal mechanisms through which all other persons in our society are judged.

Comments and Questions

1. Summarize the three preceding excerpts. With whom do you agree?
2. If you were a prosecutor considering criminal charges against Ford under facts similar to *State* v. *Ford Motor Co.*, what would you have done?

Epilogue

What has been the aftermath of the Pinto case? The National Law Journal, Mar. 31, 1980, at 3, col. 3, reported that prosecutors predicted more such prosecutions because a "psychological barrier" had been broken. But corporate executives thought that the attempt to "pound away at the corporations in court had peaked." As of 1986, the latter prediction seems more accurate, at least with respect to prosecutions under general criminal statutes.

PROD. SAFETY & LIAB. REP. (BNA)
No. 8, at 297–98 (Apr. 25, 1980).*

CONSUMER GROUP SEEKS NEW HOMICIDE PROSECUTION OF FORD MOTOR COMPANY

A Washington, D.C.-based consumer group asked Wisconsin authorities April 17 to bring criminal charges against Ford Motor Company for a transmission defect the group blames for the death of an 18-month-old boy.

In a letter to Wisconsin Attorney General Bronson C. LaFollette, the Center for Auto Safety requested that Ford and certain unnamed Ford executives be prosecuted "for homicide by reckless conduct" in the April 15 death of Michael Cannon of Hartland, Wisc.

According to the letter, the boy was drowned when the idling 1977 Thunderbird in which he was sitting while his mother opened the garage door, jumped, by itself, from "park" into "reverse" gear and backed into a

---

* Reprinted by permission from *Product Safety & Liability Reporter,* copyright 1980 by The Bureau of National Affairs, Inc., Washington, D.C.

20-foot deep pond across the street from his home. The letter noted that the child was strapped into a child restraint seat at the time.

"The Center believes that Michael's death was caused by a defective automatic transmission that Ford has known about for at least 10 years," the group told LaFollette. Only two days before the fatality, the center told reporters at a Washington, D.C., press conference that automatic transmissions in as many as 26 million Fords can jump from "park" into "reverse" while the engine is idling, and threatened to sue the National Highway Traffic Safety Administration to force a recall of the involved vehicles (Current Report, April 18, 1980, p. 286).

PROD. SAFETY & LIAB. REP. (BNA)
No. 8, at 356 (May 23, 1980).*

ACTING ON RESULTS OF INQUIRY, WISCONSIN WILL NOT PROSECUTE FORD

The Wisconsin attorney general's office decided not to bring criminal charges against Ford Motor Company for the death of a 15-month-old child, following a coroner's jury determination that not enough facts were presented to establish criminal negligence.

Calls for criminal prosecution of Ford came from the Center for Auto Safety, a Washington, D.C.-based consumer group, which claimed that a defect in the transmission of a Ford car was responsible for the death of a 15-month-old Hartland, Wisc. boy. . . .

Not Enough Evidence

A six-member jury, impanelled by the Waukesha County, Wisc. coroner, however, concluded after two days of hearings . . . [in their verdict:] "We do not find the negligence of Ford Motor Company to fulfill our understanding of the legal definition of criminal negligence, because that definition calls for the establishment of an existing high probability of death or serious injury to another; and we can not establish what we determine to be a high probability of incidence (sic) on the basis of evidence presented to us."

But Design Found Faulty

But the jury did determine that Ford "has been aware of an existent problem in design and function of their FMX and C6 transmissions which has caused involuntary shifting from the indicated park position to reverse causing involuntary movement of the vehicle which has in some cases resulted in death, personel (sic) injury, and/or property damage."

In addition, the jury said, "It is our determination that the major perpetrating cause of the accident resulting in the death of Michael

---

Cannon was this faulty design and function and the Ford Motor Company's omission of its correction."

Specific Criminal Statutes

Criminal prosecution under specific criminal statutes rather than general criminal statutes has been more common and more successful. For example, the Chicago Tribune, Jan. 6, 1985, § 4, at 1, col. 4, reported that SmithKline Beckman Corporation, the manufacturer of Selacryn, a drug used for hypertension, and its doctors in charge of reporting information to the Food and Drug Administration pleaded guilty to criminal misdemeanor charges.

The defendants violated FDA regulations requiring timely reports to the FDA of information acquired by SmithKline on liver damage and deaths caused by the drug, as well as regulations involving accurate labeling. Among information withheld by SmithKline beyond the FDA's fifteen-day timely notification requirement was information that the French company that had sold SmithKline the license to manufacture Selacryn in the United States had linked the drug to liver damage and information from doctors "across the country" that their patients were "developing hepatitis, falling into . . . coma[s] and dying." In addition, SmithKline had labeled the drug inaccurately with a statement that no "cause and effect relationship" existed between Selacryn and liver disease.

Violations of these regulations are misdemeanors. SmithKline and its doctors pleaded guilty to thirty-four counts, each punishable by a $1,000 fine and one year of prison. Thus, the maximum fine against SmithKline was $34,000. The company's 1983 profits, according to the article, were $490 million. Selacryn was linked to 36 deaths and 500 serious injuries while it was on the market.

Section Six. Product Safety and the Public-Benefit Instrument

We learned in Chapter 4 that another basic legal instrument involves conferring on individuals various substantive governmental benefits, such as education, health programs, and welfare payments. Our government also allocates vast amounts of resources to protect people from dangerous products. For example, the Consumer Product Safety Commission not only issues safety standards, brings actions, and so forth, but also provides the public with information through the National Injury Information Clearinghouse. According to the 1983 Annual Report of the commission, the commission responded in that year to about 12,000 requests for information. The commission also issued reports of almost 4,000 "product-related incidents" to manufacturers.[f] In addition, the commission issued safety alerts to the public about unsafe products.

The 1984 Catalog of Federal Domestic Assistance, which lists federal programs that provide assistance or benefits to groups and individuals, lists the following additional instance of public-benefit conferral:

f. 1983 U.S. Consumer Prod. Safety Comm'n Ann.Rep. pt. I, at 12.

87.001 VOLUNTARY STANDARDS ASSISTANCE

FEDERAL AGENCY: CONSUMER PRODUCT SAFETY COMMISSION

AUTHORIZATION: Consumer Product Safety Act, Public Law 92–573, 15 U.S.C. 205, et seq., as amended by the Consumer Product Safety Amendment of 1981, Public Law 97–35.

OBJECTIVES: To assist voluntary standards groups in developing and revising commercial voluntary product safety standards to prevent or reduce hazards.

TYPES OF ASSISTANCE: Advisory Services and Counseling.

USES AND USE RESTRICTIONS: Use is restricted to safety concerns of the Consumer Product Safety Commission. These concerns include product hazards identified by the Commission or external parties. When hazards are identified, voluntary standard remedies are developed.

ELIGIBILITY REQUIREMENTS:

Applicant Eligibility: Specialized groups.

Beneficiary Eligibility: General public.

Credentials/Documentation: None.

APPLICATION AND AWARD PROCESS:

Preapplication Coordination: None.

Application Procedure: Petition or request is made to the CPSC.

Award Procedure: Not applicable.

Deadlines: Not applicable.

Range of Approval/Disapproval Time: Not applicable.

Appeals: Not applicable.

Renewals: Not applicable.

ASSISTANCE CONSIDERATIONS:

Formula and Matching Requirements: None.

Length and Time Phasing of Assistance: Limited to the time required to complete development of standard.

POST ASSISTANCE REQUIREMENTS:

Reports: Not applicable.

Audits: Not applicable.

Records: Not applicable.

FINANCIAL INFORMATION:

Account Identification: 61–0100–0–1–554.

Obligations: (Salaries expenses) FY 83 $1,100,000; FY 84 est $1,250,000; and FY 85 est $1,400,000.

Range and Average of Financial Assistance: Not applicable.

PROGRAM ACCOMPLISHMENTS: Not applicable.

REGULATIONS, GUIDELINES, AND LITERATURE: CPSC Voluntary Standards Semi-Annual Reports and CPSC Policy Statements on Voluntary Standards, Office of the Secretary, Consumer Product Safety Commission, Washington, DC 20207.

INFORMATION CONTACTS:

Regional or Local Office: None.

Headquarters Office: Iris R. Liskey, Office of Program Management, Rm. 426–WTB, Consumer Product Safety Commission, Washington, D.C. 20207. Telephone: (301) 492–6554.

RELATED PROGRAMS: None.

EXAMPLES OF FUNDED PROJECTS: Assisted in development of engineering data; provided hazard analyses and direct advisory assistance in the development and revision of voluntary standards on space heaters, upholstered furniture, log splitters, clothes dryers, baby walkers, cribs, and hot tubs/spas.

CRITERIA FOR SELECTING PROPOSALS: Not applicable.

———

PRECLINICAL AND CLINICAL TESTING BY THE PHARMACEUTICAL INDUSTRY, 1977

Hearings Before the Subcomm. on Health and Scientific Research of the Senate
Comm. on Human Resources and the Subcomm. on Administrative Practice
and Procedure of the Senate Comm. on the Judiciary, 95th Cong.,
1st Sess. 28, 29–32 (March 10, 1977) (statement of Sherwin
Gardner, Acting Commissioner, FDA).

Mr. Chairman and Members of the Subcommittees:

We have been invited to appear here today to provide the Subcommittees with a status report on the Food and Drug Administration's (FDA) Bio-Research Monitoring Program.

As you know, this program began in July of 1976, following approval by Congress and the Administration of the necessary resources. Although funding for the program was not finally approved until last July, we began planning for it some months before in order to begin implementation as soon as possible. We are especially grateful to these Subcommittees and to you, Mr. Chairman, for your efforts in this area.

ORIGIN OF PROGRAM

During testimony before these Subcommittees on July 19, 1976, we discussed events which led to the establishment of the program and provided our first progress report on its implementation. We noted then that the program was established as the result of serious concern on the part of the Administration and Congress over findings of certain FDA inspections of research laboratories.

Under the laws which FDA administers, manufacturers are responsible for performing tests and submitting data to ensure the safety of drugs and other products which FDA must approve. The FDA requires that extensive animal and other types of human clinical testing be carried out in accordance with certain provisions of these laws.

For some time, the Agency has been concerned about the absence of industrywide standards for the conduct of bio-research studies. Until our inspection in 1975 and 1976, however, we had no reason to believe that the quality of research in some firms was disturbingly poor and that this circumstance might conceivably be common. We had proceeded on the assumption that the evidence submitted to support an application reflected high quality professional science. Based on this assumption, our practice had been to examine the results of scientific studies, as well as the adequacy of the procedures and methods described in written reports of those studies. With rare exceptions, where cause was demonstrated, we did not examine work in progress.

I should add that the deficiencies we uncovered in quality assurance were not confined to substances under FDA jurisdiction. As you know, we found there was a general problem shared by other agencies responsible for evaluating or regulating chemicals. This fact was confirmed by representatives from the Environmental Protection Agency (EPA) and the National Cancer Institute (NCI) at the hearing last July before these Subcommittees.

In the spring of last year, when it became evident that the needed additional resources might be approved, we began initial planning for a comprehensive bio-research monitoring program, which would embrace the full range of research areas relating to FDA. We also wanted a program which would be compatible with—but would not unnecessarily duplicate—programs of other Federal agencies receiving similar types of research data. We determined that the program should cover the following major research areas:

1. *Preclinical laboratory testing*—These are approximately 450 to 500 toxicology laboratories maintained either by sponsors or by independent contractors, which test drugs, biologics, food additives and other chemicals on animals.

2. *Investigators and sponsors of clinical investigations*—There are several thousand investigators who conduct human drug and other trials for firms and other sponsors of testing. We will monitor both the investigator and the sponsor who usually work closely together in preparing reports on the results of test for submission to FDA or other agencies.

3. *Institutional review committees or boards*—These are the committees which review protocols, test procedures and results of human drug, device and biologic trials performed in institutional settings. The committees must be composed of persons with varying backgrounds, such as lawyers, clergymen and laymen, as well as scientists. They are appointed by the institution in which the study is done.

4. *Food additive research*—This activity will include both inspections or laboratories which have conducted studies in support of food additive petitions, as well as an additive review program to reevaluate the safety of food additives in accordance with modern scientific criteria.

STATUS REPORT ON THE BIO–RESEARCH MONITORING PROGRAM

With the approval of the 1977 budget amendment, which provided 606 positions and $16.4 million for the first year of this program, former Commissioner Schmidt created a Steering Committee to oversee the development of a comprehensive Agency program. The Committee consists of the Agency's top management staff and is chaired by the Associate Commissioner for Compliance. In addition, task groups were established to develop a basic monitoring strategy for the four major areas of bioresearch which I just mentioned. The authority and objectives of the Steering Committee and task groups were outlined in a June 11, 1976 memo from the Commissioner to the Policy Board members. I will submit a copy of that memo for the record.

Comments and Questions

1. Reread the introduction in Section 1 of this chapter. Rethink the questions raised there. Should the law be utilized to deal with product safety?

2. Which instrumentalities of the law (if any) are most appropriate in this area? Least appropriate? Why?

Section Seven. Bibliography

G. Eads & P. Reuter, Designing Safer Products: Corporate Responses to Product Liability Law and Regulation (1983); A. Weinstein, A. Twerski, H. Piehler & W. Donaher, Products Liability and the Reasonably Safe Product: A Guide for Management, Design, and Marketing (1978); J. White & R. Summers, Handbook of the Law Under the Uniform Commercial Code 325–485 (2d ed. 1980); Cook, The Use of Criminal Statutes to Regulate Safety: Comment on Wheeler, 13 J.Legal Stud. 619 (1984); Klayman, Standard Setting Under the Consumer Product Safety Amendments of 1981—A Shift in Regulatory Philosophy, 51 Geo.Wash.L.Rev. 96 (1982); Larsen, Strict Products Liability and the Risk-Utility Test for Design Defect: An Economic Analysis, 84 Colum.L.Rev. 2045 (1984); Metzger, Corporate Criminal Liability for Defective Products: Policies, Problems, and Prospects, 73 Geo.L.J. 1 (1984); Owen, Rethinking the Policies of Strict Products Liability, 33 Vand.L.Rev. 681 (1982); Pearsall, Risks, Decisions, and Product Safety, 5 J.Prod. Liab. 219 (1982); Pierce, Encouraging Safety: The Limits of Tort Law and Government Regulation, 33 Vand.L.Rev. 1281 (1980); Schwartz, The Consumer Product Safety Commission: A Flawed Product of the Consumer Decade, 51 Geo. Wash.L.Rev. 32 (1982); Schwartz & Means, The Need for Federal Product Liability and Toxic Tort Legislation: A Current Assessment, 28 Vill.L.Rev. 1088 (1983); Special Project, Article Two Warranties in Commercial Transactions, 64 Cornell L.Rev. 30 (1978).

CHAPTER SEVEN

Law Can Help Promote Equality

But, with such inequality as ours, a perfect civilization is impossible.

MATTHEW ARNOLD

Equality is thus the beginning, not the end . . . .

SIR ERNEST BARKER

Section One. Introduction
(Pedagogic Vehicles Drawn Mainly from Racial Equality Law)

This chapter concerns how the law functions to promote equality. Just as the goal of the last chapter was not to teach product safety law but to provide an example of how each of the five instrumentalities of law can help achieve a specific, concrete societal objective, the goal of this chapter is not to teach the law of the Fourteenth Amendment or the civil rights statutes. Instead, this chapter aims to illustrate the use of the various instrumentalities to further the other kind of societal objective: a broad, abstract principle.

We shall focus on the objective of racial equality for two reasons: first, because the struggle for racial equality in this country has been long and hard; second, because that struggle has provided the model for those seeking to eliminate other kinds of inequality, such as discrimination based on gender, age, or sexual preference. The materials in this chapter therefore address when law should be used to promote racial equality, which instrumentality of the law should be used, and how that instrumentality should be used. You will learn the most from this chapter, however, if you pause after each selection to consider the extent to which the constitutional principles and statutory policies that evolved to promote racial equality should be used to promote equality between men and women, between the old and the young, and between heterosexuals and homosexuals.

In the United States, law furthers equality by acting as both a shield and a sword. The Fourteenth Amendment to our Constitution provides that "[n]o state shall . . . deny to any person within its jurisdiction the equal protection of the laws." As you probably know, this amendment was adopted after the Civil War primarily to protect the rights of former slaves. Notice that the amendment does not assure blacks (or anyone else) that they will be treated equally by private persons; by its terms, the amendment applies only to actions taken by a state. Although the Supreme Court has interpreted the Fifth Amendment's due process clause, which applies to actions taken by the federal government, to embody a guarantee of equal protection of the laws analogous to that contained in the Fourteenth Amendment, no provision of the Constitution has been interpreted to mandate equal treatment by private citizens. The Constitution thus shields the individual from governmental actions that discriminate unfairly between people of different races. The state and federal governments may pursue a wide variety of goals other than racial equality, but the constitutional provisions concerning race limit the means by which these goals may be pursued.

Law also furthers equality aggressively, as a sword. Statutes are passed and regulations are promulgated with the goal of increasing racial equality. These statutes and regulations may attempt to prevent private persons from discriminating on the basis of race, or they may seek to eliminate the effects of past discrimination. Just as the constitutional provisions concerning equality limit the government's pursuit of other societal objectives, statutes and regulations aimed at increasing equality interfere with individuals' pursuit of their personal objectives. Both kinds of law will therefore reflect a balancing of racial equality with other competing values as well as a judgment of how effective various measures are in achieving racial equality.

The remaining sections of this chapter concern how each of the five instrumentalities of law promotes or fails to promote racial equality. For each instrumentality, we shall first consider the extent to which the constitutional provisions concerning racial equality limit the pursuit of other societal goals through that instrumentality. We shall then consider some examples of how that instrumentality has been or could be used to promote the goal of racial equality.

Section Two.   Racial Equality and the Penal-Corrective Instrument

A.   Racial Equality as a Limit on the Penal-Corrective Mode

Early in this country's history, a crime sometimes depended upon the defendant's race. Some actions were illegal only if taken by a black or Native American. In this century, few statutes have singled out one race as the object of criminal prohibitions. Miscegenation statutes were one notable exception, and the Supreme Court eventually struck them down as unconstitutional. The other prominent exception involved the drastic restrictions placed on the freedom of Japanese Americans during World War II, which were upheld in the following case.

KOREMATSU v. UNITED STATES

Supreme Court of the United States, 1944.
323 U.S. 214, 65 S.Ct. 193.

MR. JUSTICE BLACK delivered the opinion of the Court.

The petitioner, an American citizen of Japanese descent, was convicted in a federal district court for remaining in San Leandro, California, a "Military Area", contrary to Civilian Exclusion Order No. 34 of the Commanding General of the Western Command, U.S. Army, which directed that after May 9, 1942, all persons of Japanese ancestry should be excluded from that area. No question was raised as to petitioner's loyalty to the United States. The Circuit Court of Appeals affirmed, and the importance of the constitutional question involved caused us to grant certiorari.

It should be noted, to begin with, that all legal restrictions which curtail the civil rights of a single racial group are immediately suspect. That is not to say that all such restrictions are unconstitutional. It is to say that courts must subject them to the most rigid scrutiny. Pressing public necessity may sometimes justify the existence of such restrictions; racial antagonism never can.

In the instant case prosecution of the petitioner was begun by information charging violation of an Act of Congress, of March 21, 1942, 56 Stat. 173, 18 U.S.C. § 97a, which provides that

> . . . whoever shall enter, remain in, leave, or commit any act in any military area or military zone prescribed, under the authority of an Executive order of the President, by the Secretary of War, or by any military commander designated by the Secretary of War, contrary to the restrictions applicable to any such area or zone or contrary to the order of the Secretary of War or any such military commander, shall, if it appears that he knew or should have known of the existence and extent of the restrictions or order and that his act was in violation thereof, be guilty of a misdemeanor and upon conviction shall be liable to a fine of not to exceed $5,000 or to imprisonment for not more than one year, or both, for each offense.

Exclusion Order No. 34, which the petitioner knowingly and admittedly violated was one of a number of military orders and proclamations, all of which were substantially based upon Executive Order No. 9066, 7 Fed. Reg. 1407. That order, issued after we were at war with Japan, declared that "the successful prosecution of the war requires every possible protection against espionage and against sabotage to national-defense material, national-defense premises, and national-defense utilities. . . ."

One of the series of orders and proclamations, a curfew order, which like the exclusion order here was promulgated pursuant to Executive Order 9066, subjected all persons of Japanese ancestry in prescribed West Coast military areas to remain in their residences from 8 p.m. to 6 a.m. As is the case with the exclusion order here, that prior curfew order was designed as a "protection against espionage and against sabotage." In Kiyoshi Hirabayashi v. United States, 320 U.S. 81, 63 S.Ct. 1375, we sustained a conviction obtained for violation of the curfew order. . . .

Like curfew, exclusion of those of Japanese origin was deemed necessary because of the presence of an unascertained number of disloyal members of the group, most of whom we have no doubt were loyal to this country. It was because we could not reject the finding of the military authorities that it was impossible to bring about an immediate segregation of the disloyal from the loyal that we sustained the validity of the curfew order as applying to the whole group. In the instant case, temporary exclusion of the entire group was rested by the military on the same ground. The judgment that exclusion of the whole group was for the same reason a military imperative answers the contention that the exclusion was in the nature of group punishment based on antagonism to those of Japanese origin. That there were members of the group who retained loyalties to Japan has been confirmed by investigations made subsequent to the exclusion. Approximately five thousand American citizens of Japanese ancestry refused to swear unqualified allegiance to the United States and to renounce allegiance to the Japanese Emperor, and several thousand evacuees requested repatriation to Japan.

We uphold the exclusion order as of the time it was made and when the petitioner violated it. Cf. Chastleton Corporation v. Sinclair, 264 U.S. 543, 547, 44 S.Ct. 405, 406; Block v. Hirsh, 256 U.S. 135, 154, 155, 41 S.Ct. 458, 459. In doing so, we are not unmindful of the hardships imposed by it upon a large group of American citizens. Cf. Ex parte Kumezo Kawato, 317 U.S. 69, 73, 63 S.Ct. 115, 117. But hardships are part of war, and war is an aggregation of hardships. All citizens alike, both in and out of uniform, feel the impact of war in greater or lesser measure. Citizenship has its responsibilities as well as its privileges, and in time of war the burden is always heavier. Compulsory exclusion of large groups of citizens from their homes, except under circumstances of direst emergency and peril, is inconsistent with our basic governmental institutions. But when under conditions of modern warfare our shores are threatened by hostile forces, the power to protect must be commensurate with the threatened danger. . . . .

It is said that we are dealing here with the case of imprisonment of a citizen in a concentration camp solely because of his ancestry, without evidence or inquiry concerning his loyalty and good disposition towards the United States. Our task would be simple, our duty clear, were this a case involving the imprisonment of a loyal citizen in a concentration camp because of racial prejudice. Regardless of the true nature of the assembly and relocation centers—and we deem it unjustifiable to call them concentration camps with all the ugly connotations that term implies—we are dealing specifically with nothing but an exclusion order. To cast this case into outlines of racial prejudice, without reference to the real military dangers which were presented, merely confuses the issue. Korematsu was not excluded from the Military Area because of hostility to him or his race. He was excluded because we are at war with the Japanese Empire, because the properly constituted military authorities feared an invasion of our West Coast and felt constrained to take proper security measures, because they decided that the military urgency of the situation demanded that all citizens of Japanese ancestry be segregated from the West Coast temporarily, and finally, because Congress, reposing its confidence in this time of war in our military leaders—as inevitably it must—determined that they should have the power to do just this. There was evidence of disloyalty on the part of some, the military authorities considered that the need for action was great, and time was short. We cannot—by availing ourselves of the calm perspective of hindsight—now say that at that time these actions were unjustified.

Affirmed.

[A concurring opinion by Justice Frankfurter and a dissenting opinion by Justice Roberts are omitted.]

MR. JUSTICE MURPHY, dissenting.

This exclusion of "all persons of Japanese ancestry, both alien and non-alien," from the Pacific Coast area on a plea of military necessity in the absence of martial law ought not to be approved. Such exclusion goes over "the very brink of constitutional power" and falls into the ugly abyss of racism. . . .

It must be conceded that the military and naval situation in the spring of 1942 was such as to generate a very real fear of invasion of the Pacific Coast, accompanied by fears of sabotage and espionage in that area. The military command was therefore justified in adopting all reasonable means necessary to combat these dangers. In adjudging the military action taken in light of the then apparent dangers, we must not erect too high or too meticulous standards; it is necessary only that the action have some reasonable relation to the removal of the dangers of invasion, sabotage and espionage. But the exclusion, either temporarily or permanently, of all persons with Japanese blood in their veins has no such reasonable relation. And that relation is lacking because the exclusion order necessarily must rely for its reasonableness upon the assumption that *all* persons of Japanese ancestry may have a dangerous tendency to commit sabotage and espionage and to aid our Japanese enemy in other ways. It is difficult to believe that reason, logic or experience could be marshalled in support of such an assumption. . . .

The military necessity which is essential to the validity of the evacuation order thus resolves itself into a few intimations that certain individuals actively aided the enemy, from which it is inferred that the entire group of Japanese Americans could not be trusted to be or remain loyal to the United States. No one denies, of course, that there were some disloyal persons of Japanese descent on the Pacific Coast who did all in their power to aid their ancestral land. Similar disloyal activities have been engaged in by many persons of German, Italian and even more pioneer stock in our country. But to infer that examples of individual disloyalty prove group disloyalty and justify discriminatory action against the entire group is to deny that under our system of law individual guilt is the sole basis for deprivation of rights. Moreover, this inference, which is at the very heart of the evacuation orders, has been used in support of the abhorrent and despicable treatment of minority groups by the dictatorial tyrannies which this nation is now pledged to destroy. To give constitutional sanction to that inference in this case, however well-intentioned may have been the military command on the Pacific Coast, is to adopt one of the cruelest of the rationales used by our enemies to destroy the dignity of the individual and to encourage and open the door to discriminatory actions against other minority groups in the passions of tomorrow.

No adequate reason is given for the failure to treat these Japanese Americans on an individual basis by holding investigations and hearings to separate the loyal from the disloyal, as was done in the case of persons of German and Italian ancestry. . . .

I dissent, therefore, from this legalization of racism. Racial discrimination in any form and in any degree has no justifiable part whatever in our democratic way of life. It is unattractive in any setting but it is utterly revolting among a free people who have embraced the principles set forth in the Constitution of the United States. All residents of this nation are kin in some way by blood or culture to a foreign land. Yet they are primarily and necessarily a part of the new and distinct civilization of the United States. They must accordingly be treated at all times as the heirs of the American experiment and as entitled to all the rights and freedoms guaranteed by the Constitution.

MR. JUSTICE JACKSON, dissenting.

. . . Had Korematsu been one of four—the others being, say, a German alien enemy, an Italian alien enemy, and a citizen of American-born ancestors, convicted of treason but out on parole—only Korematsu's presence would have violated the order. The difference between their innocence and his crime would result, not from anything he did, said, or thought, different than they, but only in that he was born of different racial stock. . . .

Much is said of the danger to liberty from the Army program for deporting and detaining these citizens of Japanese extraction. But a judicial construction of the due process clause that will sustain this order is a far more subtle blow to liberty than the promulgation of the order itself. A military order, however unconstitutional, is not apt to last longer than the military emergency. Even during that period a succeeding commander may revoke it all. But once a judicial opinion rationalizes such an order to show that it conforms to the Constitution, or rather rationalizes the Constitution to show that the Constitution sanctions such an order, the Court for all time has validated the principle of racial discrimination in criminal procedure and of transplanting American citizens. The principle then lies about like a loaded weapon ready for the hand of any authority that can bring forward a plausible claim of an urgent need. Every repetition imbeds that principle more deeply in our law and thinking and expands it to new purposes. All who observe the work of courts are familiar with what Judge Cardozo described as "the tendency of a principle to expand itself to the limit of its logic." A military commander may overstep the bounds of constitutionality, and it is an incident. But if we review and approve, that passing incident becomes the doctrine of the Constitution. There it has a generative power of its own, and all that it creates will be in its own image. Nothing better illustrates this danger than does that Court's opinion in this case. . . .

Comments and Questions

1. *Korematsu* upholds the use of a racial classification in a criminal statute. What is the standard by which the Court tested the constitutionality of that statute? More recent cases have continued to describe the standard of review for racial classifications as "strict scrutiny" but have phrased the test as requiring that the racial classification be a "necessary means" to further a "compelling governmental [or state] interest." Would the result in *Korematsu* be different under this formulation? Do you think that racial classifications in criminal statutes should be absolutely prohibited? More broadly, why should racial classifications be permitted in any kind of statute?

2. Assuming that the standard of review selected by the Court was the appropriate one for testing the validity of a racial classification, did the Court properly apply the standard? What is the significance of the failure to place Americans of Italian or German descent in concentration camps? Did the extensive prior discrimination against Japanese Americans justify an inference that they were more likely to be disloyal? Eventually, Japanese Americans did serve in the United States armed forces—and were repeatedly decorated for heroism. What does that suggest about inferring loyalty from heredity?

3. Nearly forty years after *Korematsu* was decided by the Supreme Court, a federal district court vacated Mr. Korematsu's conviction based upon new evidence not available at the time of his appeal. Korematsu v. United States, 584 F.Supp. 1406 (N.D.Cal.1984). Mr. Korematsu's lawyers presented proof that the government had fabricated some of its evidence concerning the danger of sabotage by Japanese Americans. Should the Court have been alert to the possibility of fabrication? Assuming that reliance on the honesty of government officials was entirely reasonable at the time that *Korematsu* was originally decided, if a similar situation were to arise now, would more skepticism be warranted?

B. Racial Equality as the Goal of the Penal-Corrective Mode

The penal-corrective mode has often been needed to protect the most basic rights of racial minorities. Sometimes ordinary criminal statutes, such as those prohibiting assault and murder, function to promote racial equality. At times when these have failed to provide racial minorities with even the minimal right to physical safety, specialized criminal statutes such as the Ku Klux Klan Act have been enacted. The effectiveness of these statutes has varied widely.

In addition, comprehensive civil and voting rights legislation has utilized criminal penalties as well as civil remedies for enforcement of the rights they confer. Generally, opposition to the use of the penal-corrective mode in such statutes has been limited to those who disagree with the underlying goal of racial equality. The following case presents a more controversial use of the penal-corrective mode to further racial equality.

BEAUHARNAIS v. ILLINOIS
Supreme Court of the United States, 1952.
343 U.S. 250, 72 S.Ct. 725.

Mr. Justice Frankfurter delivered the opinion of the Court.

The petitioner was convicted upon information in the Municipal Court of Chicago of violating § 224a of Division 1 of the Illinois Criminal Code, Ill.Rev.Stat.1949, c. 38, § 471. He was fined $200. The section provides:

> It shall be unlawful for any person, firm or corporation to manufacture, sell, or offer for sale, advertise or publish, present or exhibit in any public place in this state any lithograph, moving picture, play, drama or sketch, which publication or exhibition portrays depravity, criminality, unchastity, or lack of virtue of a class of citizens, of any race, color, creed or religion which said publication or exhibition exposes the citizens of any race, color, creed or religion to contempt, derision, or obloquy or which is productive of breach of the peace or riots. . . .

Beauharnais challenged the statute as violating the liberty of speech and of the press guaranteed as against the States by the Due Process Clause of the Fourteenth Amendment, and as too vague, under the restrictions implicit in the same Clause, to support conviction for crime. The Illinois courts rejected these contentions and sustained defendant's conviction. 408 Ill. 512, 97 N.E.2d 343. We granted certiorari in view of the serious questions raised concerning the limitations imposed by the Fourteenth Amendment on the power of a State to punish utterances promoting friction among racial and religious groups. 342 U.S. 809, 72 S.Ct. 39.

The information, cast generally in the terms of the statute, charged that Beauharnais "did unlawfully . . . exhibit in public places lithographs, which publications portray depravity, criminality, unchastity or lack of virtue of citizens of Negro race and color and which exposes [*sic*] citizens of Illinois of the Negro race and color to contempt, derision, or obloquy . . . . " The lithograph complained of was a leaflet setting forth a petition calling on the Mayor and City Council of Chicago "to halt the further encroachment, harassment and invasion of white people, their property, neighborhoods and persons, by the Negro . . . . " Below was a call for "One million self respecting white people in Chicago to unite . . . . " with the statement added that "If persuasion and the need to prevent the white race from becoming mongrelized by the negro will not unite us, then the aggressions . . . rapes, robberies, knives, guns and marijuana of the negro, surely will." This, with more language, similar if not so violent, concluded with an attached application for membership in the White Circle League of America, Inc. . . .

Libel of an individual was a common-law crime, and thus criminal in the colonies. Indeed, at common law, truth or good motives was no defense. In the first decades after the adoption of the Constitution, this was changed by judicial decision, statute or constitution in most States, but nowhere was there any suggestion that the crime of libel be abolished. Today, every American jurisdiction—the forty-eight States, the District of Columbia, Alaska, Hawaii and Puerto Rico—punish libels directed at individuals. "There are certain well-defined and narrowly limited classes of speech, the prevention and punishment of which has never been thought to raise any Constitutional problem. These include the lewd and obscene, the profane, the libelous, and the insulting or 'fighting' words—those which by their very utterance inflict injury or tend to incite an immediate breach of the peace. It has been well observed that such utterances are no essential part of any exposition of ideas, and are of such slight social value as a step to truth that any benefit that may be derived from them is clearly outweighed by the social interest in order and morality. 'Resort to epithets or personal abuse is not in any proper sense communication of information or opinion safeguarded by the Constitution, and its punishment as a criminal act would raise no question under that instrument.' Cantwell v. State of Connecticut, 310 U.S. 296, 309, 310, 60 S.Ct. 900, 906." Such were the views of a unanimous Court in Chaplinsky v. State of New Hampshire, [315 U.S. 568, 571–72, 62 S.Ct. 766, 769 (1942)].

No one will gainsay that it is libelous falsely to charge another with being a rapist, robber, carrier of knives and guns, and user of marijuana. The precise question before us, then, is whether the protection of "liberty" in the Due Process Clause of the Fourteenth Amendment prevents a State from punishing such libels—as criminal libel has been defined, limited and constitutionally recognized time out of mind—directed at designated collectivities and flagrantly disseminated. There is even authority, however dubious, that such utterances were also crimes at common law. It is certainly clear that some American jurisdictions have sanctioned their punishment under ordinary criminal libel statutes. We cannot say, however, that the question is concluded by history and practice. But if an utterance directed at an individual may be the object of criminal sanctions, we cannot deny to a State power to punish the same utterance directed at a defined group, unless we can say that this a wilful and purposeless restriction unrelated to the peace and well-being of the State.

Illinois did not have to look beyond her own borders or await the tragic experience of the last three decades to conclude that wilful purveyors of falsehood concerning racial and religious groups promote strife and tend powerfully to obstruct the manifold adjustments required for free, ordered life in a metropolitan, polyglot community. From the murder of the abolitionist Lovejoy in 1837 to the Cicero riots of 1951, Illinois has been the scene of exacerbated tension between races, often flaring into violence and destruction. In many of these outbreaks, utterances of the character here in question, so the Illinois legislature could conclude, played a significant part. . . .

In the face of this history and its frequent obligato of extreme racial and religious propaganda, we would deny experience to say that the Illinois legislature was without reason in seeking ways to curb false or malicious defamation of racial and religious groups, made in public places and by means calculated to have a powerful emotional impact on those to whom it was presented. "There are limits to the exercise of these liberties [of speech and of the press]. The danger in these times from the coercive activities of those who in the delusion of racial or religious conceit would incite violence and breaches of the peace in order to deprive others of their equal right to the exercise of their liberties, is emphasized by events familiar to all. These and other transgressions of those limits the states appropriately may punish." This was the conclusion, again of a unanimous Court, in 1940. Cantwell v. State of Connecticut, supra, 310 U.S. at page 310, 60 S.Ct. at page 906. . . .

We find no warrant in the Constitution for denying to Illinois the power to pass the law here under attack. But it bears repeating—although it should not—that our finding that the law is not constitutionally objectionable carries no implication of approval of the wisdom of the legislation or of its efficacy. These questions may raise doubts in our minds as well as in others. It is not for us, however, to make the legislative judgment. We are not at liberty to erect those doubts into fundamental law.

Affirmed.   .   .   .

MR. JUSTICE DOUGLAS, dissenting.

Hitler and his Nazis showed how evil a conspiracy could be which was aimed at destroying a race by exposing it to contempt, derision, and obloquy. I would be willing to concede that such conduct directed at a race or group in this country could be made an indictable offense. For such a project would be more than the exercise of free speech. Like picketing, it would be free speech plus.

I would also be willing to concede that even without the element of conspiracy there might be times and occasions when the legislative or executive branch might call a halt to inflammatory talk, such as the shouting of "fire" in a school or a theatre.

My view is that if in any case other public interests are to override the plain command of the First Amendment, the peril of speech must be clear and present, leaving no room for argument, raising no doubts as to the necessity of curbing speech in order to prevent disaster.   .   .   .

The Court in this and in other cases places speech under an expanding legislative control. Today a white man stands convicted for protesting in unseemly language against our decisions invalidating restrictive covenants. Tomorrow a negro will be hailed before a court for denouncing lynch law in heated terms. Farm laborers in the west who compete with field hands drifting up from Mexico; whites who feel the pressure of orientals; a minority which finds employment going to members of the dominant religious group—all of these are caught in the mesh of today's decision. Debate and argument even in the courtroom are not always calm and dispassionate. Emotions sway speakers and audiences alike. Intemperate speech is a distinctive characteristic of man. Hot-heads blow off and release destructive energy in the process. They shout and rave, exaggerating weaknesses, magnifying error, viewing with alarm. So it has been from the beginning; and so it will be throughout time. The Framers of the Constitution knew human nature as well as we do. They too had lived in dangerous days; they too knew the suffocating influence of orthodoxy and standardized thought. They weighed the compulsions for retrained speech and thought against the abuses of liberty. They chose liberty. That should be our choice today no matter how distasteful to us the pamphlet of Beauharnais may be. It is true that this is only one decision which may later be distinguished or confined to narrow limits. But it represents a philosophy at war with the First Amendment—a constitutional interpretation which puts free speech under the legislative thumb. It reflects an influence moving ever deeper into our society. It is notice to the legislatures that they have the power to control unpopular blocs. It is a warning to every minority that when the Constitution guarantees free speech it does not mean what it says.

[The dissenting opinions of Justices Black, Reed, and Jackson are omitted.]

Comments and Questions

1. As noted in the introductory section, this chapter examines how racial equality may limit the government's pursuit of other goals. Notice that the defendant in this case was arguing that the First Amendment's guarantee of freedom of speech limits the government's pursuit of racial equality. Turn to the Constitution at the back of this book. Can you see how other constitutional provisions might limit the government's pursuit of racial equality?

2. Although *Beauharnais* has never been overruled or expressly limited by the Supreme Court, lower courts and commentators have questioned whether *Beauharnais* is still "good law" in light of new developments in First Amendment doctrine. Turn back to the *Skokie* case found at the beginning of this book. Can the decision in that case be reconciled with *Beauharnais*? Do you think that the *Skokie* decision reflects a weakening commitment to racial equality?

3. If you think that *Beauharnais* was wrongly decided, do you think the only flaw in the statute was the use of the penal-corrective instrument? Or would you also oppose the use of other instruments of law to discourage group libel?

Section Three. Racial Equality and the Grievance-Remedial Instrument

A. Racial Equality as a Limit on the Grievance-Remedial Mode

Unlike the criminal law, substantive tort law never made many distinctions based upon race. This does not mean that issues of racial equality as a limit on the grievance-remedial mode have never been litigated. Prior to the Civil War, slaves—but not all blacks—were generally unable to seek redress of grievances from the state courts. Moreover, in the infamous *Dred Scott* decision, the Supreme Court held that blacks were not citizens of the United States, thus sharply limiting the right of blacks—slave or free—to seek redress of their grievances in the federal courts. Dred Scott v. Sandford, 60 U.S. (19 How.) 393 (1857).

The Thirteenth and Fourteenth amendments ended slavery and granted equal citizenship rights to all races, thus eliminating these inequalities. Nevertheless, the question of whether the grievance-remedial instrument is equally applied to litigants of all races remains. Recall the discussion in Chapter 1 concerning the role of the jury in resolving factual issues. We noted there that there is no way of knowing whether the jury decided on the basis of some irrelevancy. One such irrelevancy might be the race of the litigants. How can law protect minority race litigants from unfair application of the grievance-remedial instrument? The power of trial court judges to set aside an unreasonable verdict and the power of appellate courts to review the trial judge's decision constitute one check on prejudiced fact-finding, but it will provide no remedy in reasonably close cases.

One other way to check prejudiced verdicts is to control the composition of the jury. Would it be most fair to make the jury half black and half white when one litigant is black and one is white? The Supreme Court has rejected the argument that a litigant has the right to any particular composition of his or her jury. This does not mean that a state may deliberately rig the system so that all juries exclude persons of one race. In Strauder v. West Virginia, 100 U.S. 303 (1880), the Court overturned a black criminal defendant's conviction, ruling that the West Virginia statute excluding blacks from jury service was unconstitutional. In Thiel v. Southern Pacific Co., 328 U.S. 217, 66 S.Ct. 984 (1946), a personal injury case, the Court made it clear that racial groups could not be excluded from civil juries either.

Suppose that persons of all races are included in the jury rolls but that only white jurors happen to be called for a particular case involving a minority race plaintiff and a white defendant. Is the plaintiff out of luck? The following case discusses another means of controlling prejudice in the jury box.

BLAKE v. CICH

United States District Court, District of Minnesota, 1978.
79 F.R.D. 398.

MacLaughlin, District Judge.

This matter comes before the Court on plaintiffs' motion for a new trial. Plaintiffs, who are Native Americans, brought this action under 42 U.S.C. §§ 1983, 1985, with pendent common-law tort claims of assault and battery, charging defendant police officers with beating them in the course of their arrest and delivery to jail. Plaintiffs also sued the City of Minneapolis, alleging that the city was liable for the actions of defendant officers under the doctrine of respondeat superior and for negligence. At the close of plaintiffs' case, the Court directed a verdict for the city. The jury returned a verdict in favor of defendant officers.

This lawsuit arises out of incidents which occurred on October 17, 1974. That afternoon, Officers Michael Cich and Michael Sundstrom were on duty in their capacity as police officers for the City of Minneapolis. At approximately 2 p.m., in answer to a radio call, the officers investigated a complaint of vandalism at a church at the intersection of Chicago Avenue and 31st Street in Minneapolis. Officer Sundstrom went inside the church to discover the cause of the complaint, while Officer Cich remained in the squad car. A passing motorist directed Officer Cich's attention across Chicago Avenue to a house from which two young men were taking a stereo to a nearby car. Officer Cich crossed the street to investigate and encountered plaintiffs on their way back to the house. He asked them to stop and provide identification. Plaintiffs indicated that their identification was in the house. At this point, the testimony of the plaintiffs and defendants diverged. Plaintiffs testified that Officer

Cich grabbed and then began to strike Stephen Blake. They testified that Cich did not relent when Stephen's brother Michael summoned their father from the house, but instead continued to strike both Blake brothers and sprayed Mace on all three Blakes. Officer Cich testified that both plaintiffs attacked him and that such force as he used was necessary to defend himself. Officer Sundstrom emerged from the church during the struggle and came to the aid of his partner. Michael and Stephen Blake were arrested and placed in the squad car.

The testimony of the parties concerning the delivery of plaintiffs to jail also materially differed. In arriving at the courthouse, the officers drove through a tunnel into a basement delivery area. There, plaintiffs testified, both officers resumed the beating begun at the scene of the arrest, using gloves, boots, a flashlight, and a cigarette to inflict pain. The officers admitted that some force was used but testified that it was necessary to remove the uncooperative prisoners from the squad car and to defend themselves from attack. Each denied any sadistic attack upon plaintiffs.

Testimony commenced on January 24, 1978, and lasted four days. The jury deliberated for three days, twice reporting to the Court that they were deadlocked. Upon the second report, the parties stipulated to accept the verdict of five jurors as the verdict of the six-person jury. See Fed.R. Civ.P. 48. The jury returned a short time later with a verdict for defendant officers. Plaintiffs advance several grounds for a new trial, including jury selection, juror misconduct, evidentiary error, dismissal of the city, and that the verdict was against the weight of the evidence.

. . . .

One of the grounds plaintiffs advance as a basis for their motion for a new trial is alleged inadequacies in jury selection. Plaintiffs argue, first, that the jury panel was not representative of the community, second, that the Court failed to inquire sufficiently as to racial bias, and, third, that the Court abused its discretion in excusing a juror during trial.

In their memorandum in support of the motion, plaintiffs raise for the first time the contention that the jury panel "appeared to be skewed against minorities and youths." The Court finds this bare conclusory allegation both substantively inadequate, see 28 U.S.C. § 1867(d) (requiring a sworn statement of facts), and untimely, id. § 1867(c).

A trial court has broad discretion in determining the proper scope of voir dire. Labbee v. Roadway Express, Inc., 469 F.2d 169, 172 (8th Cir. 1972); cf. United States v. Kershman, 555 F.2d 198, 202 (8th Cir.1977), cert. denied, 434 U.S. 892, 98 S.Ct. 268 (1977). The breadth of this discretion is circumscribed where voir dire interrogation introduces prejudicial matter before prospective jurors, Wichmann v. United Disposal, Inc., 553 F.2d 1104, 1108–09 (8th Cir.1977) (inquiry as to abstract feelings about insurance coverage), or is of too limited scope to reveal possible biases among the veniremen, cf. United States v. Bowles, 574 F.2d 970 (8th Cir.1978) (failure to inquire about racial prejudice where criminal defendant is black).

In the instant case, the Court conducted the voir dire and asked the following question of the jury panel:

Plaintiffs in this case are Native Americans. All individuals bringing or defending lawsuits stand equal in a court of law, no matter their race, heritage, or position in society. Have any of you had any dealings or experiences with Indian individuals or Native Americans that might make it difficult for you to make an impartial judgment about this case?

There was no affirmative response from any members of the jury panel. After questioning the jury panel, the Court called counsel to the bench and asked for requests for supplementary inquiries. See Fed.R.Civ.P. 47(a). Plaintiff's counsel did not request further interrogation of the jury panel or individual veniremen as to racial bias. The Court finds that in the circumstances of this case, the question it asked adequately explored possible racial prejudice among members of the jury panel.

[The court turned to the other arguments made by the plaintiffs.]

The Court having considered and rejected for the reasons advanced above each ground plaintiffs have advanced for a new trial, it is hereby ordered that plaintiffs' motion for a new trial is denied.

Comments and Questions

1. Should the outcome of this case depend upon whether or not the defendant's attorney requested further questions on racial prejudice?

2. Do you think that those who are prejudiced would respond affirmatively to the trial judge's questions? Can you think of other questions that would be more fruitful? Suppose that a person is subconsciously biased against people of another race. Is it impossible to discover this by questioning? Does the likelihood of fair application of the grievance-remedial instrumentality—or any instrumentality—then depend upon the number of people who are racially prejudiced?

3. If you suspect that voir dire will not be successful in screening out biased jurors, what other procedures might be adopted to ensure fair application of the grievance-remedial mode? Do you think an explicit instruction to disregard the race of the litigants would be useful? Should it be required?

B. Racial Equality as the Goal of the Grievance-Remedial Mode

Following the Civil War, the Reconstruction Congress attempted to use the grievance-remedial instrumentality to block efforts to force blacks into a condition of de facto slavery. The Civil Rights Act of 1866 provided that all citizens would have the same right as a white person to make and enforce contracts and to own or lease property. The Civil Rights Act of 1870 extended federal protection to black voting rights, and the Civil Rights Act of 1871 provided civil remedies and criminal penalties for violations of constitutional rights. Finally, the Civil Rights Act of 1875 prohibited racial discrimination in public accommodations. But these statutes were of little practical significance, in part because of Supreme Court decisions striking down key provisions and in part because in 1894

Congress repealed the most effective provisions—those protecting voting rights.

Not until the second half of the twentieth century did the grievance-remedial instrumentality begin to play an important role in promoting racial equality. A number of new civil rights statutes, combined with Supreme Court decisions resurrecting some of the older statutes, resulted in a reasonably comprehensive—and correspondingly controversial—package of protections. The Civil Rights Acts of 1957 and 1960 improved remedies against racial discrimination in voting; the Civil Rights Act of 1964 added remedies for discrimination in private employment, public accommodations, and federally assisted programs; and the Civil Rights Act of 1968 outlawed most private discrimination in housing. Some of the key provisions of the last two statutes follow. The first three sections are from what is known as Title VII of the Civil Rights Act of 1964, and the other sections are part of the 1968 act.

UNITED STATES CODE, TITLE 42

§ 2000e. Definitions

For the purposes of this subchapter [42 USC §§ 2000e et seq.]—

(a) The term "person" includes one or more individuals, governments, governmental agencies, political subdivisions, labor unions, partnerships, associations, corporations, legal representatives, mutual companies, joint-stock companies, trusts, unincorporated organizations, trustees, trustees [in bankruptcy], or receivers.

(b) The term "employer" means a person engaged in an industry affecting commerce who has fifteen or more employees for each working day in each of twenty or more calendar weeks in the current or preceding calendar year, and any agent of such a person, but such term does not include (1) the United States, a corporation wholly owned by the Government of the United States, an Indian tribe, or any department or agency of the District of Columbia subject by statute to procedures of the competitive service (as defined in section 2102 of title 5 of the United States Code), or (2) a bona fide private membership club (other than a labor organization) which is exempt from taxation under section 501(c) of the Internal Revenue Code of 1954, except that during the first year after the date of enactment of the Equal Employment Opportunity Act of 1972, persons having fewer than twenty-five employees (and their agents) shall not be considered employers. . . .

§ 2000e–1. Exemption

This subchapter shall not apply to an employer with respect to the employment of aliens outside any State, or to a religious corporation, association, educational institution, or society with respect to the employment of individuals of a particular religion to perform work connected with the carrying on by such corporation, association, educational institution, or society of its activities.

§ 2000e–2. Discrimination because of race, color, religion, sex, or national origin

(a) Employers. It shall be an unlawful employment practice for an employer—

(1) to fail or refuse to hire or to discharge any individual, or otherwise to discriminate against any individual with respect to his compensation, terms, conditions, or privileges of employment, because of such individual's race, color, religion, sex, or national origin; or

(2) to limit, segregate, or classify his employees or applicants for employment in any way which would deprive or tend to deprive any individual of employment opportunities or otherwise adversely affect his status as an employee, because of such individual's race, color, religion, sex, or national origin.

[Subsections (b) and (c) impose similar prohibitions upon employment agencies and labor organizations.]

(d) Training programs. It shall be an unlawful employment practice for any employer, labor organization, or joint labor-management committee controlling apprenticeship or other training or retraining, including on-the-job training programs to discriminate against any individual because of his race, color, religion, sex, or national origin in admission to, or employment in, any program established to provide apprenticeship or other training.

(e) Religion, sex, or national origin as bona fide occupational qualification; educational institutions with employees of particular religions. Notwithstanding any other provision of this subchapter, (1) it shall not be an unlawful employment practice for an employer to hire and employ employees, for an employment agency to classify, or refer for employment any individual, for a labor organization to classify its membership or to classify or refer for employment any individual, or for an employer, labor organization, or joint labor-management committee controlling apprenticeship or other training or retraining programs to admit or employ any individual in any such program, on the basis of his religion, sex, or national origin in those certain instances where religion, sex, or national origin is a bona fide occupational qualification reasonably necessary to the normal operation of that particular business or enterprise, and (2) it shall not be an unlawful employment practice for a school, college, university, or other educational institution or institution of learning to hire and employ employees of a particular religion if such school, college, university, or other educational institution or institution of learning is, in whole or in substantial part, owned, supported, controlled, or managed by a particular religion or by a particular religious corporation, association, or society, or if the curriculum of such school, college, university, or other educational institution or institution of learning is directed toward the propagation of a particular religion. . . .

§ 3601. Declaration of policy

It is the policy of the United States to provide, within constitutional limitations, for fair housing throughout the United States. . . .

§ 3603. Effective dates of certain prohibitions

(a) Application to certain described dwellings. . . .

(2) After December 31, 1968, to all dwellings covered by paragraph (1) and to all other dwellings except as exempted by subsection (b).

(b) Exemptions. Nothing in [42 USC § 3604] (other than subsection (c)) shall apply to—

(1) any single-family house sold or rented by an owner: Provided, That such private individual owner does not own more than three such single-family houses at any one time: Provided further, That in the case of the sale of any such single-family house by a private individual owner not residing in such house at the time of such sale or who was not the most recent resident of such house prior to such sale, the exemption granted by this subsection shall apply only with respect to one such sale within any twenty-four month period: Provided further, That such bona fide private individual owner does not own any interest in, nor is there owned or reserved on his behalf, under any express or voluntary agreement, title to or any right to all or a portion of the proceeds from the sale or rental of, more than three such single-family houses at any one time: Provided further, That after December 31, 1969, the sale or rental of any such single-family house shall be excepted from the application of this title only if such house is sold or rented (A) without the use in any manner of the sales or rental facilities or the sales or rental services of any real estate broker, agent, or salesman, or of such facilities or services of any person in the business of selling or renting dwellings, or of any employee or agent of any such broker, agent, salesman, or person and (B) without the publication, posting or mailing, after notice, of any advertisement or written notice in violation of [42 USC § 3604(c)]; but nothing in this proviso shall prohibit the use of attorneys, escrow agents, abstractors, title companies, and other such professional assistance as necessary to perfect or transfer the title, or

(2) rooms or units in dwellings containing living quarters occupied or intended to be occupied by no more than four families living independently of each other, if the owner actually maintains and occupies one of such living quarters as his residence. . . .

§ 3604. Discrimination in the sale or rental of housing

As made applicable by [42 USC § 3603] and except as exempted by [42 USC §§ 3603(b), 3607], it shall be unlawful—

(a) To refuse to sell or rent after the making of a bona fide offer, or to refuse to negotiate for the sale or rental of, or otherwise make unavailable or deny, a dwelling to any person because of race, color, religion, sex, or national origin.

(b) To discriminate against any person in the terms, conditions, or privileges of sale or rental of a dwelling, or in the provision of services or facilities in connection therewith, because of race, color, religion, sex, or national origin.

(c) To make, print, or publish, or cause to be made, printed, or published any notice, statement, or advertisement, with respect to the sale or rental of a dwelling that indicates any preference, limitation, or discrimination based on race, color, religion, sex, or national origin, or an intention to make any such preference, limitation, or discrimination.

(d) To represent to any person because of race, color, religion, sex, or national origin that any dwelling is not available for inspection, sale, or rental when such dwelling is in fact so available.

(e) For profit, to induce or attempt to induce any person to sell or rent any dwelling by representations regarding the entry or prospective entry into the neighborhood of a person or persons of a particular race, color, religion, sex, or national origin.

[Sections 3605 and 3606 prohibit discrimination in the financing of housing and the provision of brokerage services.]

§ 3607. Religious organization or private club exemption

Nothing in this title shall prohibit a religious organization, association, or society, or any nonprofit institution or organization operated, supervised or controlled by or in conjunction with a religious organization, association, or society, from limiting the sale, rental or occupancy of dwellings which it owns or operates for other than a commercial purpose to persons of the same religion, or from giving preference to such persons, unless membership in such religion is restricted on account of race, color, or national origin. Nor shall anything in this title prohibit a private club not in fact open to the public, which as an incident to its primary purpose or purposes provides lodgings which it owns or operates for other than a commercial purpose, from limiting the rental or occupancy of such lodgings to its members or from giving preference to its members.

Comments and Questions

1. Suppose that Ms. Jones does not like Democrats. If she is the president of a large company or the owner of an apartment complex, may she lawfully refuse to hire a Democrat or rent to one? Why does federal law prohibit employment and housing discrimination based upon race but not upon political affiliation?

2. Suppose that Mr. King lives in an area where a large number of Asian Americans also reside. If he refuses to rent to anyone with black hair—with the purpose of avoiding renting to any Asian Americans—would an Asian American have a cause of action against him? Would a black-haired Italian American?

3. Look at the exceptions written into the definition and exemption sections of the two statutes. Do you think that the exceptions reflect legitimate balancing of other values or expedient political compromise?

Pornography as Discrimination

In the 1980s, feminists and moralists in several cities proposed ordinances that would make the production and distribution of pornography a violation of women's civil rights enforceable under civil rights ordinances. For example, consider the following excerpts from the ordinance proposed in

Minneapolis, which was passed by the city council but vetoed by the mayor:

139.10　Findings, declaration of policy and purpose

.　　.　　.　　.　　.　　.　　.　　.　　.　　.

(1) Special findings on pornography: The council finds that pornography is central in creating and maintaining the civil inequality of the sexes. Pornography is a systematic practice of exploitation and subordination based on sex which differentially harms women. The bigotry and contempt it promotes, with the acts of aggression it fosters, harm women's opportunities for equality of rights in employment, education, property rights, public accommodations and public services; create public harassment and private denigration; promote injury and degradation such as rape, battery and prostitution and inhibit just enforcement of laws against these acts; contribute significantly to restricting women from full exercise of citizenship and participation in public life, including in neighborhoods; damage relations between the sexes; and undermine women's equal exercise of rights to speech and action guaranteed to all citizens under the Constitutions and laws of the United States and the State of Minnesota. . . .

139.20　Definitions

.　　.　　.　　.　　.　　.　　.　　.　　.　　.

(gg) Pornography. Pornography is a form of discrimination on the basis of sex.

(1) Pornography is the sexually explicit subordination of women, graphically depicted, whether in pictures or in words, that also includes one or more of the following:

(i) women are presented dehumanized as sexual objects, things or commodities; or

(ii) women are presented as sexual objects who enjoy pain or humiliation; or

(iii) women are presented as sexual objects who experience sexual pleasure in being raped; or

(iv) women are presented as sexual objects tied up or cut up or mutilated or bruised or physically hurt; or

(v) women are presented in postures of sexual submission; or

(vi) women's body parts—including but not limited to vaginas, breasts, and buttocks—are exhibited, such that women are reduced to those parts; or

(vii) women are presented as whores by nature; or

(viii) women are presented being penetrated by objects or animals; or

(ix) women are presented in scenarios of degradation, injury, abasement, torture, shown as filthy or inferior, bleeding, bruised, or hurt in a context that makes these conditions sexual.

.　　.　　.　　.

139.40 Acts of discrimination specified

. . . .

(*l*) Discrimination by trafficking in pornography. The production, sale, exhibition, or distribution of pornography is discrimination against women by means of trafficking in pornography:

(1) City, state, and federally funded public libraries or private and public university and college libraries in which pornography is available for study, including on open shelves, shall not be construed to be trafficking in pornography but special display presentations of pornography in said places is sex discrimination.

(2) The formation of private clubs or associations for purposes of trafficking in pornography is illegal and shall be considered a conspiracy to violate the civil rights of women.

(3) Any woman has a cause of action hereunder as a woman acting against the subordination of women. Any man or transsexual who alleges injury by pornography in the way women are injured by it shall also have a cause of action.

(m) Coercion into pornographic performances. Any person, including transsexual, who is coerced, intimidated, or fraudulently induced (hereafter "coerced") into performing for pornography shall have a cause of action against the maker(s), seller(s), exhibitor(s) or distributor(s) of said pornography for damages and for the elimination of the products of the performance(s) from the public view.

(1) Limitation of action. This claim shall not expire before five years have elapsed from the date of the coerced performance(s) or from the last appearance or sale of any product of the performance(s), whichever date is later;

(2) Proof of one or more of the following facts or conditions shall not, without more, negate a finding of coercion;

(i) that the person is a woman; or

(ii) that the person is or has been a prostitute; or

(iii) that the person has attained the age of majority; or

(iv) that the person is connected by blood or marriage to anyone involved in or related to the making of the pornography; or

(v) that the person has previously had, or been thought to have had, sexual relations with anyone, including anyone involved in or related to the making of the pornography; or

(vi) that the person has previously posed for sexually explicit pictures for or with anyone, including anyone involved in or related to the making of the pornography at issue; or

(vii) that anyone else, including a spouse or other relative, has given permission on the person's behalf; or

(viii) that the person actually consented to a use of the performance that is changed into pornography; or

(ix) that the person knew that the purpose of the acts or events in question was to make pornography; or

(x) that the person showed no resistance or appeared to cooperate actively in the pornographic sessions or in the sexual events that produced the pornography; or

(xi) that the person signed a contract, or made statements affirming a willingness to cooperate in the production of pornography; or

(xii) that no physical force, threats, or weapons were used in the making of the pornography; or

(xiii) that the person was paid or otherwise compensated.

(n) Forcing pornography on a person. Any woman, man, child, or transsexual who has pornography forced on him/her in any place of employment, in education, in a home, or in any public place has a cause of action against the perpetrator and/or institution.

(o) Assault or physical attack due to pornography. Any woman, man, child, or transsexual who is assaulted, physically attacked or injured in a way that is directly caused by specific pornography has a claim for damages against the perpetrator, the maker(s), distributor(s), seller(s), and/or exhibitor(s), and for an injunction against the specific pornography's further exhibition, distribution, or sale. No damages shall be assessed (A) against maker(s) for pornography made, (B) against distributor(s) for pornography distributed, (C) against seller(s) for pornography sold, or (D) against exhibitors for pornography exhibited prior to the enforcement date of this act.

(p) Defenses. Where the materials which are the subject matter of a cause of action under subsections (l), (m), (n), or (o) of this section are pornography, it shall not be a defense that the defendant did not know or intend that the materials were pornography or sex discrimination.

(q) Severability. Should any part(s) of this ordinance be found legally invalid, the remaining part(s) remain valid. . . .

Comments and Questions

1. Would such an ordinance further gender equality in a way similar to the way in which federal civil rights statutes further racial equality? If not, what aspect of equality is being furthered? Could you design an analogous statute aimed at racial equality? What kinds of materials would be prohibited?

2. Is this proposed ordinance more or less objectionable than the group libel law at issue in *Beauharnais*? Does the use of the grievance-remedial mode rather than the penal-corrective mode eliminate freedom of speech concerns? Are there other instrumentalities through which egalitarian attitudes might be promoted without posing freedom of speech concerns?

Section Four.   Racial Equality and the Private-Arrangement Instrument

A.   Racial Equality as a Limit on the Private-Arrangement Mode

As explained in the introduction to this chapter, the constitutional provisions concerning racial equality do not speak to individuals but to the government. A natural assumption, therefore, would be that these provisions do not limit the private-arrangement mode. This assumption, however, would be erroneous. This mode facilitates private arrangements by legitimizing and enforcing them, but it can also shape these arrangements by disapproving or refusing to enforce certain variations. The first case in this subsection clearly involves racially discriminatory governmental action favoring some private arrangements; here the issue is whether the discrimination can be justified under the strict-scrutiny standard. The second case is different; the issue is whether the government's role in enforcing a discriminatory private arrangement is significant enough to require application of the strict-scrutiny standard.

PALMORE v. SIDOTI

Supreme Court of the United States, 1984.
466 U.S. 429, 104 S.Ct. 1879.

CHIEF JUSTICE BURGER delivered the opinion of the Court.

We granted certiorari to review a judgment of a state court divesting a natural mother of the custody of her infant child because of her remarriage to a person of a different race.

I

When petitioner Linda Sidoti Palmore and respondent Anthony J. Sidoti, both Caucasians, were divorced in May 1980 in Florida, the mother was awarded custody of their three-year-old daughter.

In September 1981 the father sought custody of the child by filing a petition to modify the prior judgment because of changed conditions. The change was that the child's mother was then cohabiting with a Negro, Clarence Palmore, Jr., whom she married two months later. Additionally, the father made several allegations of instances in which the mother had not properly cared for the child.

After hearing testimony from both parties and considering a court counselor's investigative report, the court noted that the father had made allegations about the child's care, but the court made no findings with respect to these allegations. On the contrary, the court made a finding that "there is no issue as to either party's devotion to the child, adequacy of housing facilities, or respect[a]bility of the new spouse of either parent."

The court then addressed the recommendations of the court counselor, who had made an earlier report "in [another] case coming out of this circuit also involving the social consequences of an interracial marriage. Niles v. Niles, 299 So.2d 162." From this vague reference to that earlier case, the court turned to the present case and noted the counselor's recommendation for a change in custody because "[t]he wife [petitioner] has chosen for herself and for her child, a life-style unacceptable to her father *and to society*. . . . The child . . . is, or at school age will be, subject to environmental pressures not of choice." (emphasis added)

The court then concluded that the best interests of the child would be served by awarding custody to the father. The court's rationale is contained in the following:

> The father's evident resentment of the mother's choice of a black partner is not sufficient to wrest custody from the mother. It is of some significance, however, that the mother did see fit to bring a man into her home and carry on a sexual relationship with him without being married to him. Such action tended to place gratification of her own desires ahead of her concern for the child's future welfare. *This Court feels that despite the strides that have been made in bettering relations between the races in this country, it is inevitable that Melanie will, if allowed to remain in her present situation and attains school age and thus more vulnerable to peer pressures, suffer from the social stigmatization that is sure to come.* (emphasis added)

[The decision was affirmed in the state court system, and certiorari was granted.]

II

The judgment of a state court determining or reviewing a child custody decision is not ordinarily a likely candidate for review by this Court. However, the court's opinion, after stating that the "father's evident resentment of the mother's choice of a black partner is not sufficient" to deprive her of custody, then turns to what it regarded as the damaging impact on the child from remaining in a racially-mixed household. This raises important federal concerns arising from the Constitution's commitment to eradicating discrimination based on race. . . .

The court correctly stated that the child's welfare was the controlling factor. But that court was entirely candid and made no effort to place its holding on any ground other than race. Taking the court's findings and rationale at face value, it is clear that the outcome would have been different had petitioner married a Caucasian male of similar respectability.

A core purpose of the Fourteenth Amendment was to do away with all governmentally-imposed discrimination based on race. See Strauder v. West Virginia, 100 U.S. 303, 307–308, 310 (1880). Classifying persons according to their race is more likely to reflect racial prejudice than legitimate public concerns; the race, not the person, dictates the category. See Personnel Administrator v. Feeney, 442 U.S. 256, 272, 99 S.Ct. 2282, 2292 (1979). Such classifications are subject to the most exacting scrutiny; to pass constitutional muster, they must be justified by a compelling governmental interest and must be "necessary . . . to the accomplishment" of its legitimate purpose, McLaughlin v. Florida, 379 U.S. 184, 196, 85 S.Ct. 283, 290 (1964). See Loving v. Virginia, 388 U.S. 1, 11, 87 S.Ct. 1817, 1823 (1967).

The State, of course, has a duty of the highest order to protect the interests of minor children, particularly those of tender years. In common with most states, Florida law mandates that custody determinations be made in the best interests of the children involved. Fla.Stat. § 61.13(2) (b)(1) (1983). The goal of granting custody based on the best interests of the child is indisputably a substantial governmental interest for purposes of the Equal Protection Clause.

It would ignore reality to suggest that racial and ethnic prejudices do not exist or that all manifestations of those prejudices have been eliminated. There is a risk that a child living with a step-parent of a different race may be subject to a variety of pressures and stresses not present if the child were living with parents of the same racial or ethnic origin.

The question, however, is whether the reality of private biases and the possible injury they might inflict are permissible considerations for removal of an infant child from the custody of its natural mother. We have little difficulty concluding that they are not. The Constitution cannot control such prejudices but neither can it tolerate them. Private biases may be outside the reach of the law, but the law cannot, directly or indirectly, give them effect. "Public officials sworn to uphold the Constitution may not avoid a constitutional duty by bowing to the hypothetical effects of private racial prejudice that they assume to be both widely and deeply held." Palmer v. Thompson, 403 U.S. 217, 260–261, 91 S.Ct. 1940, 1962–1963 (1971) (White, J., dissenting).

This is by no means the first time that acknowledged racial prejudice has been invoked to justify racial classifications. In Buchanan v. Warley, 245 U.S. 60, 38 S.Ct. 16 (1917), for example, this Court invalidated a Kentucky law forbidding Negroes from buying homes in white neighborhoods.

> It is urged that this proposed segregation will promote the public peace by preventing race conflicts. Desirable as this is, and important as is the preservation of the public peace, this aim cannot be accomplished by laws or ordinances which deny rights created or protected by the Federal Constitution. (Id., at 81, 38 S.Ct., at 20.)

Whatever problems racially-mixed households may pose for children in 1984 can no more support a denial of constitutional rights than could the stresses that residential integration was thought to entail in 1917. The effects of racial prejudice, however real, cannot justify a racial classification removing an infant child from the custody of its natural mother found to be an appropriate person to have such custody.[3]

The judgment of the District Court of Appeal is reversed.

It is so ordered.

---

3. This conclusion finds support in other cases as well. For instance, in Watson v. City of Memphis, 373 U.S. 526, 83 S.Ct. 1314 (1963), city officials claimed that desegregation of city parks had to proceed slowly to "prevent interracial disturbances, violence, riots, and community confusion and turmoil." Id., at 535, 83 S.Ct., at 1319. The Court found such predictions no more than "personal speculations or vague disquietudes," id., at 536, 83 S.Ct., at 1320, and held that "constitutional rights may not be denied simply because of hostility to their assertion or exercise," id., at 535, 83 S.Ct., at 1319–1320. In Wright v. Georgia, 373 U.S. 284, 83 S.Ct. 1240 (1963), the Court reversed a Negro defendant's breach-of-peace conviction, holding that "the possibility of disorder by others cannot justify exclusion of persons from a place if they otherwise have a constitutional right (founded upon the Equal Protection Clause) to be present." Id., at 293, 83 S.Ct., at 1246.

Comments and Questions

1. The opinion says that the existence of private bias can never justify racially discriminatory public actions. Is this true? In Lee v. Washington, 390 U.S. 333, 88 S.Ct. 994 (1968), the Court issued a per curiam affirmance of a federal court order holding Alabama's segregated prison system unconstitutional. The opinion noted Alabama's argument that the lower-court order had made no allowance for the necessities of prison security and discipline, commenting that "we do not so read" the order. In a separate concurring paragraph, three justices explained: "[W]e wish to make explicit [that] prison authorities have the right, acting in good faith and in particularized circumstances, to take into account racial tensions in maintaining security, discipline, and good order in jails." Can this be reconciled with *Palmore* v. *Sidoti*? If not, is there another explanation for the result in *Palmore*?

2. Following the reasoning of the *Palmore* case, would you infer that a state family services agency may not take race into account when it places children for adoption? There is currently a severe shortage of white infants available for adoption. Suppose that a black couple and a white couple applied to adopt an available black infant. Could the state agency give preference to the black couple on the ground that the child would be the victim of social prejudice if placed in the white home? On any other ground? Suppose that there is no black couple seeking to adopt the child. Should the state be allowed to keep the child in a foster home rather than place her with a white couple?

3. Do you think social psychologists' findings should be consulted by the courts before they make these kinds of decisions? The early studies comparing interracial and intraracial adoption show that the adopted children are equally happy and well adjusted. Does this suggest a better rationale for the Court's decision in *Palmore*?

SHELLEY v. KRAEMER

Supreme Court of the United States, 1948.
334 U.S. 1, 68 S.Ct. 836.

MR. CHIEF JUSTICE VINSON delivered the opinion of the Court.

These cases present for our consideration questions relating to the validity of court enforcement of private agreements, generally described as restrictive covenants, which have as their purpose the exclusion of persons of designated race or color from the ownership or occupancy of real property. Basic constitutional issues of obvious importance have been raised.

The first of these cases comes to this Court on certiorari to the Supreme Court of Missouri. On February 16, 1911, thirty out of a total of thirty-nine owners of property fronting both sides of Labadie Avenue between Taylor Avenue and Cora Avenue in the city of St. Louis, signed an agreement, which was subsequently recorded, providing in part:

> . . . the said property is hereby restricted to the use and occupancy for the term of Fifty (50) years from this date, so that it shall be a condition all the time and whether recited and referred to as [*sic*] not in subsequent conveyances and shall attach to the land, as a condition precedent to the sale of the same, that hereafter no part of said

property or any portion thereof shall be, for said term of Fifty-years, occupied by any person not of the Caucasian race, it being intended hereby to restrict the use of said property for said period of time against the occupancy as owners or tenants of any portion of said property for resident or other purpose by people of the Negro or Mongolian Race.

The entire district described in the agreement included fifty-seven parcels of land. The thirty owners who signed the agreement held title to forty-seven parcels, including the particular parcel involved in this case. At the time the agreement was signed, five of the parcels in the district were owned by Negroes. One of those had been occupied by Negro families since 1882, nearly thirty years before the restrictive agreement was executed. The trial court found that owners of seven out of nine homes on the south side of Labadie Avenue, within the restricted district and "in the immediate vicinity" of the premises in question, had failed to sign the restrictive agreement in 1911. At the time this action was brought, four of the premises were occupied by Negroes, and had been so occupied for periods ranging from twenty-three to sixty-three years. A fifth parcel had been occupied by Negroes until a year before this suit was instituted.

On August 11, 1945, pursuant to a contract of sale, petitioners Shelley, who are Negroes, for valuable consideration received from one Fitzgerald a warranty deed to the parcel in question. The trial court found that petitioners had no actual knowledge of the restrictive agreement at the time of the purchase.

On October 9, 1945, respondents, as owners of other property subject to the terms of the restrictive covenant, brought suit in the Circuit Court of the city of St. Louis praying that petitioners Shelley be restrained from taking possession of the property and that judgment be entered divesting title out of petitioners Shelley and revesting title in the immediate grantor or in such other person as the court should direct. The trial court denied the requested relief on the ground that the restrictive agreement, upon which respondents based their action, had never become final and complete because it was the intention of the parties to that agreement that it was not to become effective until signed by all property owners in the district, and signatures of all the owners had never been obtained.

The Supreme Court of Missouri sitting en banc reversed and directed the trial court to grant the relief for which respondents had prayed. That court held the agreement effective and concluded that enforcement of its provisions violated no rights guaranteed to petitioners by the Federal Constitution. At the time the court rendered its decision, petitioners were occupying the property in question.

The second of the cases under consideration comes to this Court from the Supreme Court of Michigan. The circumstances presented do not differ materially from the Missouri case. . . .

Whether the equal protection clause of the Fourteenth Amendment inhibits judicial enforcement by state courts of restrictive covenants based on race or color is a question which this Court has not heretofore been called upon to consider. . . .

Since the decision of this Court in the Civil Rights Cases, 1883, 109 U.S. 3, 3 S.Ct. 18, the principle has become firmly embedded in our constitutional law, that the action inhibited by the first section of the Fourteenth Amendment is only such action as may fairly be said to be that of the States. That Amendment erects no shield against merely private conduct, however discriminatory or wrongful.

We conclude, therefore, that the restrictive agreements standing alone cannot be regarded as a violation of any rights guaranteed to petitioners by the Fourteenth Amendment. So long as the purposes of those agreements are effectuated by voluntary adherence to their terms, it would appear clear that there has been no action by the State and the provisions of the Amendment have not been violated.

But here there was more. These are cases in which the purposes of the agreements were secured only by judicial enforcement by state courts of the restrictive terms of the agreements. The respondents urge that judicial enforcement of private agreements does not amount to state action; or, in any event, the participation of the State is so attenuated in character as not to amount to state action within the meaning of the Fourteenth Amendment. Finally, it is suggested, even if the States in these cases may be deemed to have acted in the constitutional sense, their action did not deprive petitioners of rights guaranteed by the Fourteenth Amendment. We move to a consideration of these matters.

That the action of state courts and of judicial officers in their official capacities is to be regarded as action of the State within the meaning of the Fourteenth Amendment, is a proposition which has long been established by decisions of this Court. That principle was given expression in the earliest cases involving the construction of the terms of the Fourteenth Amendment. Thus, in Commonwealth of Virginia v. Rives, 1880, 100 U.S. 313, 318, this Court stated: "It is doubtless true that a State may act through different agencies,—either by its legislative, its executive, or its judicial authorities; and the prohibitions of the amendment extend to all action of the State denying equal protection of the laws, whether it be action by one of these agencies or by another." . . .

We have no doubt that there has been state action in these cases in the full and complete sense of the phrase. The undisputed facts disclose that petitioners were willing purchasers of properties upon which they desired to establish homes. The owners of the properties were willing sellers; and contracts of sale were accordingly consummated. It is clear that but for the active intervention of the state courts, supported by the full panoply of state power, petitioners would have been free to occupy the properties in question without restraint.

These are not cases, as has been suggested, in which the States have merely abstained from action, leaving private individuals free to impose such discriminations as they see fit. Rather, these are cases in which the States have made available to such individuals the full coercive power of government to deny to petitioners, on the grounds of race or color, the enjoyment of property rights in premises which petitioners are willing and financially able to acquire and which the grantors are willing to sell. The difference between judicial enforcement and nonenforcement of the restrictive covenants is the difference to petitioners between being denied rights of property available to other members of the community and being accorded full enjoyment of those rights on an equal footing.

The enforcement of the restrictive agreements by the state courts in these cases was directed pursuant to the common-law policy of the States as formulated by those courts in earlier decisions. In the Missouri case, enforcement of the covenant was directed in the first instance by the highest court of the State after the trial court had determined the agreement to be invalid for want of the requisite number of signatures. In the Michigan case, the order of enforcement by the trial court was affirmed by the highest state court. The judicial action in each case bears the clear and unmistakable imprimatur of the State. We have noted that previous decisions of this Court have established the proposition that judicial action is not immunized from the operation of the Fourteenth Amendment simply because it is taken pursuant to the state's common-law policy. Nor is the Amendment ineffective simply because the particular pattern of discrimination, which the State has enforced, was defined initially by the terms of a private agreement. State action, as that phrase is understood for the purposes of the Fourteenth Amendment, refers to exertions of state power in all forms. And when the effect of that action is to deny rights subject to the protection of the Fourteenth Amendment, it is the obligation of this Court to enforce the constitutional commands.

We hold that in granting judicial enforcement of the restrictive agreements in these cases, the States have denied petitioners the equal protection of the laws and that, therefore, the action of the state courts cannot stand. . . .

For the reasons stated, the judgment of the Supreme Court of Missouri and the judgment of the Supreme Court of Michigan must be reversed.

Reversed.

MR. JUSTICE REED, MR. JUSTICE JACKSON, and MR. JUSTICE RUTLEDGE took no part in the consideration or decision of these cases.

———

Comments and Questions

1. Suppose that your great-aunt leaves a will providing that you shall receive $10,000 a year unless and until you marry a person of the white race, at which time the money will be donated to her favorite charity. Should a court enforce that will?

2. If you think that it should, how would the court's action differ from the action condemned in *Shelley* v. *Kraemer*? If the judicial involvement is the same in both cases, what would justify differing results?

———

B. Racial Equality as the Goal of the Private-Arrangement Mode

The law does not attempt to coerce racial equality in the most intimate of private arrangements. Why are there no laws prohibiting discrimination on the basis of race in decisions concerning marriage or adoption? Is it merely because enforcement would be impossible?

On the other hand, private arrangements that do not involve family matters are sometimes regulated to promote racial equality. Here enforcement is feasible, and the only question is the desirability of intruding upon private choices.

RUNYON v. McCRARY

Supreme Court of the United States, 1976.
427 U.S. 160, 96 S.Ct. 2586.

Mr. Justice Stewart delivered the opinion of the Court.

The principal issue presented by these consolidated cases is whether a federal law, namely, 42 U.S.C. § 1981, prohibits private schools from excluding qualified children solely because they are Negroes.

I

The respondents in No. 75-62, Michael McCrary and Colin Gonzales, are Negro children. By their parents, they filed a class action against the petitioners in No. 75-62, Russell and Katheryne Runyon, who are the proprietors of Bobbe's School in Arlington, Va. Their complaint alleged that they had been prevented from attending the school because of the petitioners' policy of denying admission to Negroes, in violation of 42 U.S.C. § 1981 and Title II of the Civil Rights Act of 1964, 78 Stat. 243, 42 U.S.C. § 2000a et seq. They sought declaratory and injunctive relief and damages. On the same day Colin Gonzales, the respondent in No. 75-66, filed a similar complaint by his parents against the petitioner in No. 75-66, Fairfax-Brewster School, Inc., located in Fairfax County, Va. The petitioner in No. 75-278, the Southern Independent School Association, sought and was granted permission to intervene as a party defendant in the suit against the Runyons. That organization is a nonprofit association composed of six state private school associations, and represents 395 private schools. It is stipulated that many of these schools deny admission to Negroes.

[The respondents prevailed in the federal courts below.]

II

It is worth noting at the outset some of the questions that these cases do not present. They do not present any question of the right of a private social organization to limit its membership on racial or any other grounds. They do not present any question of the right of a private school to limit its student body to boys, to girls, or to adherents of a particular religious faith, since 42 U.S.C. § 1981 is in no way addressed to such categories of selectivity. They do not even present the application of § 1981 to private sectarian schools that practice *racial* exclusion on religious grounds. Rather, these cases present only two basic questions: whether § 1981 prohibits private, commercially operated, nonsectarian schools from denying admission to prospective students because they are Negroes, and, if so, whether that federal law is constitutional as so applied.

A.   Applicability of § 1981

It is now well established that § 1 of the Civil Rights Act of 1866, 14 Stat. 27, 42 U.S.C. § 1981, prohibits racial discrimination in the making and enforcement of private contracts. See Johnson v. Railway Express Agency, 421 U.S. 454, 459–460, 95 S.Ct. 1716, 1719–1720; Tillman v. Wheaton-Haven Recreation Assn., 410 U.S. 431, 439–440, 93 S.Ct. 1090, 1094–1095. Cf. Jones v. Alfred H. Mayer Co., 392 U.S. 409, 441–443, n. 78, 88 S.Ct. 2186, 2204–2205. . . .

. . . The statutory holding in *Jones* was that the "[1866] Act was designed to do just what its terms suggest: to prohibit all racial discrimination, whether or not under color of law, with respect to the rights enumerated therein—including the right to purchase or lease property," 392 U.S., at 436, 88 S.Ct., at 2201. One of the "rights enumerated" in § 1 is "the same right . . . to make and enforce contracts . . . as is enjoyed by white citizens . . . ." 14 Stat. 27. Just as in *Jones* a Negro's § 1 right to purchase property on equal terms with whites was violated when a private person refused to sell to the prospective purchaser solely because he was a Negro, so also a Negro's § 1 right to "make and enforce contracts" is violated if a private offeror refuses to extend to a Negro, solely because he is a Negro, the same opportunity to enter into contracts as he extends to white offerees. . . .

It is apparent that the racial exclusion practiced by the Fairfax-Brewster School and Bobbe's Private School amounts to a classic violation of § 1981. The parents of Colin Gonzales and Michael McCrary sought to enter into contractual relationships with Bobbe's School for educational services. Colin Gonzales' parents sought to enter into a similar relationship with the Fairfax-Brewster School. Under those contractual relationships, the schools would have received payments for services rendered, and the prospective students would have received instruction in return for those payments. The educational services of Bobbe's School and the Fairfax-Brewster School were advertised and offered to members of the general public. But neither school offered services on an equal basis to white and nonwhite students. As the Court of Appeals held, "there is ample evidence in the record to support the trial judge's factual determinations . . . [that] Colin [Gonzales] and Michael [McCrary] were denied admission to the schools because of their race." The Court of Appeals' conclusion that § 1981 was thereby violated follows inexorably from the language of the statute, as construed in *Jones, Tillman,* and *Johnson.*

The petitioning schools and school association argue principally that § 1981 does not reach private acts of racial discrimination. That view is wholly inconsistent with *Jones'* interpretation of the legislative history of § 1 of the Civil Rights Act of 1866, and interpretation that was reaffirmed in Sullivan v. Little Hunting Park, Inc., 396 U.S. 229, 90 S.Ct. 400, and again in Tillman v. Wheaton-Haven Recreation Assn., supra. And this consistent interpretation of the law necessarily requires the conclusion that § 1981 . . . reaches private conduct. See Tillman v. Wheaton-

Haven Recreation Assn., 410 U.S., at 439–440, 93 S.Ct., at 1094–1095; Johnson v. Railway Express Agency, 421 U.S., at 459–460, 95 S.Ct., at 1719–1720.

It is noteworthy that Congress in enacting the Equal Employment Opportunity Act of 1972, 86 Stat. 103, as amended, 42 U.S.C. § 2000e et seq. (1970 ed. Supp. IV), specifically considered and rejected an amendment that would have repealed the Civil Rights Act of 1866, as interpreted by this Court in *Jones,* insofar as it affords private-sector employees a right of action based on racial discrimination in employment. See Johnson v. Railway Express Agency, supra, at 459, 95 S.Ct., at 1719. There could hardly be a clearer indication of congressional agreement with the view that § 1981 *does* reach private acts of racial discrimination. In these circumstances there is no basis for deviating from the well-settled principles of *stare decisis* applicable to this Court's construction of federal statutes. See Edelman v. Jordan, 415 U.S. 651, 671 n. 14, 94 S.Ct. 1347, 1359.

B. Constitutionality of § 1981 as Applied

The question remains whether § 1981, as applied, violates constitutionally protected rights of free association and privacy, or a parent's right to direct the education of his children.

1. *Freedom of Association.* In NAACP v. Alabama, 357 U.S. 449, 78 S.Ct. 1163, and similar decisions, the Court has recognized a First Amendment right "to engage in association for the advancement of beliefs and ideas . . . ." Id., at 460, 78 S.Ct., at 1171. That right is protected because it promotes and may well be essential to the "[e]ffective advocacy of both public and private points of view, particularly controversial ones" that the First Amendment is designed to foster. Ibid. See Buckley v. Valeo, 424 U.S. 1, 15, 96 S.Ct. 612, 632–633; NAACP v. Button, 371 U.S. 415, 83 S.Ct. 328.

From this principle it may be assumed that parents have a First Amendment right to send their children to educational institutions that promote the belief that racial segregation is desirable, and that the children have an equal right to attend such institutions. But it does not follow that the *practice* of excluding racial minorities from such institutions is also protected by the same principle. As the Court stated in Norwood v. Harrison, 413 U.S. 455, 93 S.Ct. 2804, "the Constitution . . . places no value on discrimination," id., at 469, 93 S.Ct., at 2813, and while "[i]nvidious private discrimination may be characterized as a form of exercising freedom of association protected by the First Amendment . . . it has never been accorded affirmative constitutional protections. And even some private discrimination is subject to special remedial legislation in certain circumstances under § 2 of the Thirteenth Amendment; Congress has made such discrimination unlawful in other significant contexts." Id., at 470, 93 S.Ct., at 2813. In any event, as the Court of Appeals noted, "there is no showing that discontinuance of [the] discriminatory admission practices would inhibit in any way the teaching in these schools of any ideas or dogma."

2. *Parental Rights.* In Meyer v. Nebraska, 262 U.S. 390, 43 S.Ct. 625, the Court held that the liberty protected by the Due Process Clause of the Fourteenth Amendment includes the right "to acquire useful knowledge, to marry, establish a home and bring up children," id., at 399, 43 S.Ct., at 626, and, concomitantly, the right to send one's children to a private school that offers specialized training—in that case, instruction in the German language. In Pierce v. Society of Sisters, 268 U.S. 510, 45 S.Ct. 571, the Court applied "the doctrine of *Meyer* v. *Nebraska*," id., at 534, 45 S.Ct., at 573, to hold unconstitutional an Oregon law requiring the parent, guardian, or other person having custody of a child between 8 and 16 years of age to send that child to public school on pain of criminal liability. The Court thought it "entirely plain that the [statute] unreasonably interferes with the liberty of parents and guardians to direct the upbringing and education of children under their control." Id., at 534–535, 45 S.Ct., at 573. In Wisconsin v. Yoder, 406 U.S. 205, 92 S.Ct. 1526, the Court stressed the limited scope of *Pierce,* pointing out that it lent "no support to the contention that parents may replace state educational requirements with their own idiosyncratic views of what knowledge a child needs to be a productive and happy member of society" but rather "held simply that while a State may posit [educational] standards, it may not pre-empt the educational process by requiring children to attend public schools." Id., at 239, 92 S.Ct., at 1545 (White, J., concurring). And in Norwood v. Harrison, 413 U.S. 455, 93 S.Ct. 2804, the Court once again stressed the "limited scope of *Pierce*," id., at 461, 93 S.Ct., at 2809, which simply "affirmed the right of private schools to exist and to operate . . . ." Id., at 462, 93 S.Ct., at 2809.

It is clear that the present application of § 1981 infringes no parental right recognized in *Meyer, Pierce, Yoder,* or *Norwood.* No challenge is made to the petitioner schools' right to operate or the right of parents to send their children to a particular private school rather than a public school. Nor do these cases involve a challenge to the subject matter which is taught at any private school. Thus, the Fairfax-Brewster School and Bobbe's School and members of the intervenor association remain presumptively free to inculcate whatever values and standards they deem desirable. *Meyer* and its progeny entitle them to no more.

3. *The Right of Privacy.* The Court has held that in some situations the Constitution confers a right of privacy. See Roe v. Wade, 410 U.S. 113, 152–153, 93 S.Ct. 705, 726–727; Eisenstadt v. Baird, 405 U.S. 438, 453, 92 S.Ct. 1029, 1038; Stanley v. Georgia, 394 U.S. 557, 564–565, 89 S.Ct. 1243, 1247–1248; Griswold v. Connecticut, 381 U.S. 479, 484–485, 85 S.Ct. 1678, 1681–1682. See also Loving v. Virginia, 388 U.S. 1, 12, 87 S.Ct. 1817, 1824; Skinner v. Oklahoma ex rel. Williamson, 316 U.S. 535, 541, 62 S.Ct. 1110, 1113.

While the application of § 1981 to the conduct at issue here—a private school's adherence to a racially discriminatory admissions policy—does not represent governmental intrusion into the privacy of the home or a similarly intimate setting, it does implicate parental interests. These interests are related to the procreative rights protected in Roe v. Wade, supra, and Griswold v. Connecticut, supra. A person's decision whether to bear a child and a parent's decision concerning the manner in which his child is to be educated may fairly be characterized as exercises of familial rights and responsibilities. But it does not follow that because government is largely or even entirely precluded from regulating the child-bearing decision, it is similarly restricted by the Constitution from regulating the implementation of parental decisions concerning a child's education.

The Court has repeatedly stressed that while parents have a constitutional right to send their children to private schools and a constitutional right to select private schools that offer specialized instruction, they have no constitutional right to provide their children with private school education unfettered by reasonable government regulation. See Wisconsin v. Yoder, supra, 406 U.S., at 213, 92 S.Ct., at 1532; Pierce v. Society of Sisters, supra, 268 U.S., at 534, 45 S.Ct., at 573; Meyer v. Nebraska, 262 U.S., at 402, 43 S.Ct., at 627. Indeed, the Court in *Pierce* expressly acknowledged "the power of the State reasonably to regulate all schools, to inspect, supervise and examine them, their teachers and pupils . . . ." 268 U.S., at 534, 45 S.Ct., at 573. See also Prince v. Massachusetts, 321 U.S. 158, 166, 64 S.Ct. 438, 442.

Section 1981, as applied to the conduct at issue here, constitutes an exercise of federal legislative power under § 2 of the Thirteenth Amendment fully consistent with *Meyer, Pierce,* and the cases that followed in their wake. As the Court held in Jones v. Alfred H. Mayer Co., supra: "It has never been doubted . . . 'that the power vested in Congress to enforce [the Thirteenth Amendment] by appropriate legislation' . . . includes the power to enact laws 'direct and primary, operating upon the acts of individuals, whether sanctioned by State legislation or not.' " 392 U.S., at 438, 88 S.Ct., at 2202 (citation omitted). The prohibition of racial discrimination that interferes with the making and enforcement of contracts for private educational services furthers goals closely analogous to those served by § 1981's elimination of racial discrimination in the making of private employment contracts . . . .

For the reasons stated in this opinion, the judgment of the Court of Appeals is in all respects affirmed.

It is so ordered.

Mr. Justice Powell, concurring.

If the slate were clean I might well be inclined to agree with Mr. Justice White that § 1981 was not intended to restrict private contractual choices. Much of the review of the history and purpose of this statute set forth in his dissenting opinion is quite persuasive. It seems to me, however, that it comes too late.

The applicability of § 1981 to private contracts has been considered maturely and recently, and I do not feel free to disregard these precedents. . . .

Although the range of consequences suggested by the dissenting opinion go far beyond what we hold today, I am concerned that our decision not be construed more broadly than would be justified.

By its terms § 1981 necessarily imposes some restrictions on those who would refuse to extend to Negroes "the same right . . . . to make and enforce contracts . . . as is enjoyed by white citizens." But our holding that this restriction extends to certain actions by private individuals does not imply the intrusive investigation into the motives of every refusal to contract by a private citizen that is suggested by the dissent. As the Court of Appeals suggested, some contracts are so personal "as to have a discernible rule of exclusivity which is inoffensive to § 1981."

In Sullivan v. Little Hunting Park, supra, we were faced with an association in which "[t]here was no plan or purpose of exclusiveness." Participation was "open to every white person within the geographic area, there being no selective element other than race." 396 U.S., at 236, 90 S.Ct., at 404. See also Tillman v. Wheaton-Haven Recreation Assn., supra, 410 U.S., at 438, 93 S.Ct., at 1094. In certain personal contractual relationships, however, such as those where the offeror selects those with whom he desires to bargain on an individualized basis, or where the contract is the foundation of a close association (such as, for example, that between an employer and a private tutor, babysitter, or housekeeper), there is reason to assume that, although the choice made by the offeror is selective, it reflects "a purpose of exclusiveness" other than the desire to bar members of the Negro race. Such a purpose, certainly in most cases, would invoke associational rights long respected.

The case presented on the record before us does not involve this type of personal contractual relationship. As the Court of Appeals said, the petitioning "schools are private only in the sense that they are managed by private persons and they are not direct recipients of public funds. Their actual and potential constituency, however, is more public than private." The schools extended a public offer open, on its face, to any child meeting certain minimum qualifications who chose to accept. They advertised in the "Yellow Pages" of the telephone directories and engaged extensively in general mail solicitations to attract students. The schools are operated strictly on a commercial basis, and one fairly could construe their open-end invitations as offers that matured into binding contracts when accepted by those who met the academic, financial, and other racially neutral specified conditions as to qualifications for entrance. There is no reason to assume that the schools had any special reason for exercising an option of personal choice among those who responded to their public offers. A small kindergarten or music class, operated on the basis of personal invitations extended to a limited number of preidentified students, for example, would present a far different case.

I do not suggest that a "bright line" can be drawn that easily separates the type of contract offer within the reach of § 1981 from the type without. The case before us is clearly on one side of the line, however defined, and the kindergarten and music school examples are clearly on the other side. Close questions undoubtedly will arise in the gray area that necessarily exists in between. But some of the applicable principles and considerations, for the most part identified by the Court's opinion, are clear: § 1981, as interpreted by our prior decisions, does reach certain acts of racial discrimination that are "private" in the sense that they involve no *state* action. But choices, including those involved in entering into a contract, that are "private" in the sense that they are not part of a commercial relationship offered generally or widely, and that reflect the selectivity exercised by an individual entering into a personal relationship, certainly were never intended to be restricted by the 19th century Civil Rights Acts. The open offer to the public generally involved in the cases before us is simply not a "private" contract in this sense. Accordingly, I join the opinion of the Court.

[The concurring opinion of Justice Stevens is omitted.]

Mr. Justice White, with whom Mr. Justice Rehnquist joins, dissenting.

We are urged here to extend the meaning and reach of 42 U.S.C. § 1981 so as to establish a general prohibition against a private individual's or institution's refusing to enter into a contract with another person because of that person's race. Section 1981 has been on the books since 1870 and to so hold for the first time would be contrary to the language of the section, to its legislative history, and to the clear dictum of this Court in the Civil Rights Cases, 109 U.S. 3, 16–17, 3 S.Ct. 18, 25–26 (1883), almost contemporaneously with the passage of the statute, that the section reaches only discriminations imposed by state law. The majority's belated discovery of a congressional purpose which escaped this Court only a decade after the statute was passed and which escaped all other federal courts for almost 100 years is singularly unpersuasive. I therefore respectfully dissent.

. . . On its face the statute gives "[a]ll persons" (plainly including Negroes) the *same right . . . to make . . . contracts . . .* as is enjoyed by white citizens." (Emphasis added.) The words "right . . . enjoyed by white citizens" clearly refer to rights existing apart from this statute. Whites had at the time when § 1981 was first enacted, and have (with a few exceptions mentioned below), no right to make a contract with an unwilling private person, no matter what that person's motivation for refusing to contract. Indeed it is and always has been central to the very concept of a "contract" that there be "assent by the parties who form the contract to the terms thereof," Restatement of Contracts § 19(b) (1932); see also 1 S. Williston, Law of Contracts § 18(3) (3 ed., 1957). The right to make contracts, enjoyed by white citizens, was therefore always a right to enter into binding agreements only with willing second parties. Since the statute only gives Negroes the "same rights" to contract as is enjoyed by whites, the language of the statute confers no right on Negroes to enter into a contract with an unwilling person no matter what that person's motivation for refusing to contract. What is conferred by 42 U.S.C. § 1981 is the *right*—which was enjoyed by whites—"to make contracts" with other willing parties and to "enforce" those contracts in court. Section 1981 would thus invalidate any state statute or court-made rule of law which would have the effect of disabling Negroes or any other class of persons from making contracts or enforcing contractual obligations or otherwise giving less weight to their obligations than is given to contractual obligations running to whites. The statute by its terms does not require any private individual or institution to enter into a contract or perform any other act under any circumstances; and it consequently fails to supply a cause of action by respondent students against petitioner schools based on the latter's racially motivated decision not to contract with them. . . .

. . . [A]s a matter of common sense, it would seem extremely unlikely that Congress would have intended . . . to pass a statute prohibiting every racially motivated refusal to contract by a private individual. It is doubtful that all such refusals could be considered badges or incidents of slavery within Congress' proscriptive power under the Thirteenth Amendment. A racially motivated refusal to hire a Negro or a white babysitter or to admit a Negro or a white to a private association cannot be called a badge of slavery—and yet the construction given by the majority to the Thirteenth Amendment statute attributes to Congress an intent to proscribe them.

The Court holds in McDonald v. Santa Fe Trail Transp. Co., 427 U.S. 273, 96 S.Ct. 2574, that § 1981 gives to whites the same cause of action it gives to blacks. Thus under the majority's construction of § 1981 in this case a former slaveowner was given a cause of action against his former slave if the former slave refused to work for him on the ground that he was a white man. It is inconceivable that Congress ever intended such a result.

The majority's holding that 42 U.S.C. § 1981 prohibits all racially motivated contractual decisions—particularly coupled with the Court's decision in *McDonald*, supra, that whites have a cause of action against others including blacks for racially motivated refusals to contract—threatens to embark the Judiciary on a treacherous course. Whether such conduct should be condoned or not, whites and blacks will undoubtedly choose to form a variety of associational relationships pursuant to contracts which exclude members of the other race. Social clubs, black and white, and associations designed to further the interests of blacks or whites are but two examples. Lawsuits by members of the other race attempting to gain admittance to such an association are not pleasant to contemplate. As the associational or contractual relationships become more private, the pressures to hold § 1981 inapplicable to them will increase. Imaginative judicial construction of the word "contract" is foreseeable; Thirteenth Amendment limitations on Congress' power to ban "badges and incidents of slavery" may be discovered; the doctrine of the right to association may be bent to cover a given situation. In any event, courts will be called upon to balance sensitive policy considerations against each other—considerations which have never been addressed by any Congress—all under the guise of "construing" a statute. This is a task appropriate for the Legislature, not for the Judiciary.

Such balancing of considerations as has been done by Congress in the area of racially motivated decisions not to contract with a member of the other race has led it to ban private racial discrimination in most of the job market and most of the housing market and to go no further. The Judiciary should not undertake the political task of trying to decide what other areas are appropriate ones for a similar rule. . . .

Accordingly, I would reverse.

Comments and Questions

1. Why would a member of a minority race want to go to an institution that taught white supremacy? How is racial equality promoted by creating a right to enroll regardless of race? By providing all people with the equal opportunity to go to a good school? By showing how strong public disapproval of segregation is? By eventually forcing such schools to close? Would this kind of legislation be desirable absent a history of pervasive segregation? Should the prohibition against racial discrimination extend to private minority race schools?

2. Should the law prohibit a club from discriminating on the basis of race? Would you distinguish between purely social clubs and those designed in part to promote business connections? Between small selective clubs and those open to almost all people of one race? A Minnesota statute prohibiting sex discrimination in "places of public accommodation" had been applied to the Jaycees, a civic organization that restricted voting membership to men between the ages of eighteen and thirty-five. The Jaycees argued that this statute interfered with their members' free association rights. In Roberts v. United States Jaycees, 104 S.Ct. 3244 (1984), the Supreme Court upheld application of the statute to the Jaycees. The Court reasoned that the core of the right of free association was marriage and family relationships, and if it extended to other relationships, they would have to be relatively small, selective, and secluded from others. Because the Jaycees had none of these traits, their constitutional rights had not been violated. Do you accept the distinction between intimate and more public associations? Would you support the enactment of such a statute in your state? Would you distinguish between discrimination on the basis of race and discrimination on the basis of gender? Age? Sexual preference?

NOTE, THE EXPANDING SCOPE OF SECTION 1981: ASSAULT ON PRIVATE DISCRIMINATION AND A CLOUD ON AFFIRMATIVE ACTION

90 Harv.L.Rev. 412, 424–27 (1976).*

The question then becomes whether clear and principled distinctions can be formulated which restrict the application of section 1981 to cases in which its policies are in fact implicated. The operative language of the statute, construed in light of contract principles, can provide guidance. Section 1981 guarantees to all persons the *same right* to make and enforce contracts *as is enjoyed by white citizens.* As *Jones* and *Runyon* make clear, the "right" of white citizens to contract cannot be interpreted as referring to contract rights in the technical sense—to those rights enforceable in a court of law. Thus, it must be recognized that the right protected is not a legally enforceable contractual right but the *opportunity* to deal in the contractual sphere on equal footing with whites. Under such an interpretation of the statute's language, the critical question is not what contractual rights white citizens enjoy, but what opportunities they have to enter into or be considered for contractual relationships.

While such an inquiry necessarily results in the abrogation of traditional contract law, it is not wholly inconsistent with, and indeed may be

---

informed by, the policies underlying the contract law doctrine against forcing unwilling parties to enter into contracts. Essentially, this doctrine reflects the concerns for individual autonomy and choice which would be implicated whenever a court of law orders an unwilling individual to contract. Certainly, individual autonomy and personal choice are not absolute values in our system of contract law; despite the putative commitment to enforcing "the will of the parties," there are numerous instances in which contract law cannot be justified in these terms but rather serves broader social interests. Nonetheless, in cases involving contractual refusals which may now be actionable under section 1981, the infringement on these values has been considered sufficient to lead courts acting only on the basis of contract law to refuse to force a party into the given contract. These values underlying contract law are not involved, however, to the same degree in all potential section 1981 cases. Nonetheless contract principles should require the presence of a strong countervailing interest in advancing the policies underlying civil rights legislation where the values of individual choice and personal autonomy are most severely implicated.

Three factual situations may be considered to shed light on the application of these considerations of language, civil rights policy, and contract principles. In the first, suggested by Justice White, an individual of one race has made an offer to a member of another race. The offeree in no way invited or solicited the offer. In this situation, there seems little basis for allowing the offeror to bring suit under section 1981. The concerns for personal autonomy and choice embodied in traditional contractual principles are in this case most compelling, since the potential 1981 defendant has been completely passive. Moreover, the policies of section 1981 are here least compelling: because no person of any race in practice enjoys any opportunity to force acceptance of an unsolicited offer, the goal of equal opportunity does not require that a black be given such an opportunity. Finally, since the offeree has remained passive, he has in no way overtly manifested racist motivations.

A different situation arises when a seller of goods or services, an employer, an educational institution or the like invites the public at large, or a subgroup thereof meeting certain qualifications, to make offers. This is the situation presented in *Jones, Runyon* and the typical employment discrimination case arising under section 1981. Here, the potential section 1981 defendant has initiated the contracting process by soliciting offers. While contract law permits an inviter to reject such solicited offers for any reason, *Runyon*'s construction of section 1981 requires that the rejection not be based on the race of the offeror. This result seems justified, for were it not so, a black meeting whatever qualifications are required would not enjoy the same contractual opportunities as are enjoyed by similarly situated or qualified whites. In practice the inviter is prepared to sell to or accept the offer of any white person meeting whatever nonracial qualifications or conditions that the inviter has imposed on the invitation. Thus, to insure equality of opportunity, section 1981 should permit rejection of solicited offers for racially neutral reasons, but must be construed to prohibit denial of the opportunity to contract to an otherwise qualified applicant because of the applicant's race.

Additionally, the interest of the potential section 1981 defendant in personal choice in this case is insubstantial. By extending an invitation to a non-individualized group, the inviter has indicated a lack of concern for personal choice and intimacy. Moreover, the harms from the public manifestation of racially motivated contractual refusals are substantial. Invitations which are extended to whites only, or those extended to the public but which are followed by a rejection of non-whites on the basis of race, are public announcements of racial discrimination which inflict psychological harms on members of excluded races by suggesting notions of racial inferiority.

A third situation obtains when an invitation to contract is extended only to one specified individual or a preselected group of individuals. Here the interests of personal choice appear more compelling than those underlying section 1981. As a practical matter, no individual outside the group of specified invitees enjoys the opportunity to deal with the inviter. Since the opportunity is not available to individuals of any race generally, section 1981 need not be applied to give an excluded member of another race equality of opportunity. Thus, if those seeking personal services of the variety described by Justice Powell make their offers or invitations only to specific individuals of the race with whom they desire to deal, section 1981 need not be construed to aid an excluded member of any other race.

This construction derives largely from the language of section 1981, is consistent with the *Runyon* Court's emphasis on the private schools' advertisements addressed to the public, and seems compatible with the goals of the statute. First, if some persons genuinely desire to deal with members of their own race in certain contractual relationships in which they deem close personal association to be important, they may do so by taking the trouble personally to preselect their offerees. By so doing, they manifest the importance of personal choice which they attach to the relationship. Those extending open invitations to a non-individualized segment of the public, on the other hand, can be said to have indicated that they attach little real importance to personal selectivity. Moreover, whatever racial considerations motivate those who preselect their offerees remain unarticulated and thus the stigmatizing effect of publicly or overtly announced racial bias is avoided.

Second, the application of section 1981 to invitations made to non-individualized groups will render racial discrimination impractically expensive and burdensome in commercial transactions where its harms are great and where the importance of personal intimacy is generally nonexistent. Thus, the statute would bar discrimination in the vast majority of contracts for important social benefits—education, employment, health care, recreational facilities, insurance and credit—areas where the right to contract is most vital to social opportunity and personal fulfillment.

Section Five. Racial Equality and the Administrative-Regulatory Instrument

A. Racial Equality as a Limit on the Administrative-Regulatory Mode

It is easy to see why the constitutional limits on racial discrimination must apply to the administrative-regulatory instrumentality. If they did not, legislatures would be free to pass laws that were facially fair and then delegate their application to biased agencies. For this reason, early Supreme Court opinions made it clear that racial discrimination by administrative-regulatory agencies was subject to the strict-scrutiny standard. Nevertheless, controversy concerning racial equality constraints frequently arises in the administrative-regulatory instrumentality. At least in part, this results from the increasing significance of the administrative-regulatory mode.

YICK WO v. HOPKINS

Supreme Court of the United States, 1886.
118 U.S. 356, 6 S.Ct. 1064.

. . . .

The plaintiff in error, Yick Wo, on August 24, 1885, petitioned the supreme court of California for the writ of habeas corpus, alleging that he was illegally deprived of his personal liberty by the defendant as sheriff of the city and county of San Francisco. The sheriff made return to the writ that he held the petitioner in custody by virtue of a sentence of the police judge's court No. 2 of the city and county of San Francisco, whereby he was found guilty of a violation of certain ordinances of the board of supervisors of that county, and adjudged to pay a fine of $10, and, in default of payment, be imprisoned in the county jail at the rate of one day for each dollar of fine until said fine should be satisfied; and a commitment in consequence of non-payment of said fine.

The ordinances for the violation of which he had been found guilty are set out as follows:

Order No. 1,569, passed May 26, 1880, prescribing the kind of buildings in which laundries may be located.

"The people of the city and county of San Francisco do ordain as follows:

"Section 1. It shall be unlawful, from and after the passage of this order, for any person or persons to establish, maintain, or carry on a laundry, within the corporate limits of the city and county of San Francisco, without having first obtained the consent of the board of supervisors, except the same be located in a building constructed either of brick or stone.

"Sec. 2. It shall be unlawful for any person to erect, build, or maintain, or cause to be erected, built, or maintained, over or upon the roof of any building now erected, or which may hereafter be erected, within the limits of said city and county, any scaffolding, without first obtaining the written permission of the board of supervisors, which permit shall state fully for what purpose said scaffolding is to be erected and used, and such scaffolding shall not be used for any other purpose than that designated in such permit.

"Sec. 3. Any person who shall violate any of the provisions of this order shall be deemed guilty of a misdemeanor, and upon conviction thereof shall be punished by a fine of not more than one thousand dollars, or by imprisonment in the county jail not more than six months, or by both such fine and imprisonment."

Order No. 1,587, passed July 28, 1880, the following section:

"Sec. 68. It shall be unlawful, from and after the passage of this order, for any person or persons to establish, maintain, or carry on a laundry within the corporate limits of the city and county of San Francisco without having first obtained the consent of the board of supervisors, except the same be located in a building constructed either of brick or stone."

The following facts are also admitted on the record: That petitioner is a native of China, and came to California in 1861, and is still a subject of the emperor of China; that he has been engaged in the laundry business in the same premises and building for 22 years last past; that he had a license from the board of fire-wardens, dated March 3, 1884, from which it appeared "that the above-described premises have been inspected by the board of fire-wardens, and upon such inspection said board found all proper arrangements for carrying on the business; that the stoves, washing and drying apparatus, and the appliances for heating smoothing-irons, are in good condition, and that their use is not dangerous to the surrounding property from fire, and that all proper precautions have been taken to comply with the provisions of order No. 1,617, defining 'the fire limits of the city and county of San Francisco, and making regulations concerning the erection and use of buildings in said city and county,' and of order No. 1,670, 'prohibiting the kindling, maintenance, and use of open fires in houses;' that he had a certificate from the health officer that the same premises had been inspected by him, and that he found that they were properly and sufficiently drained, and that all proper arrangements for carrying on the business of a laundry, without injury to the sanitary condition of the neighborhood, had been complied with; that the city license of the petitioner was in force, and expired October 1, 1885; and that the petitioner applied to the board of supervisors, June 1, 1885, for consent of said board to maintain and carry on his laundry, but that said board, on July 1, 1885, refused said consent." It is also admitted to be true, as alleged in the petition, that on February 24, 1880, "there were about 320 laundries in the city and county of San Francisco, of which about 240 were owned and conducted by subjects of China, and of the whole number, viz., 320, about 310 were constructed of wood, the same material that constitutes nine-tenths of the houses in the city of San Francisco. The capital thus invested by the subjects of China was not less than two hundred thousand dollars, and they paid annually for rent, license, taxes, gas, and water about one hundred and eighty thousand dollars." It is alleged in the petition that "your petitioner, and more than one hundred and fifty of his countrymen, have been arrested upon the charge of carrying on business without having such special consent, while those who are not subjects of China, and who are conducting eighty odd laundries under similar conditions, are left unmolested, and free to enjoy the enhanced trade and profits arising from this hurtful and unfair discrimination. The business of your petitioner, and of those of his countrymen similarly situated, is greatly impaired, and in many cases practically ruined, by this system of oppression to one kind of men, and favoritism to all others."

The statement therein contained as to the arrest, etc., is admitted to be true, with the qualification only that the 80-odd laundries referred to are in wooden buildings without scaffolds on the roofs. It is also admitted "that petitioner and 200 of his countrymen similarly situated petitioned the board of supervisors for permission to continue their business in the various houses which they had been occupying and using for laundries for more than twenty years, and such petitions were denied, and all the petitions of those who were not Chinese, with one exception of Mrs. Mary Meagles, were granted." . . .

MATTHEWS, J. . . .

In the present cases, we are not obliged to reason from the probable to the actual, and pass upon the validity of the ordinances complained of, as tried merely by the opportunities which their terms afford, of unequal and unjust discrimination in their administration; for the cases present the ordinances in actual operation, and the facts shown establish an administration directed so exclusively against a particular class of persons as to warrant and require the conclusion that, whatever may have been the intent of the ordinances as adopted, they are applied by the public authorities charged with their administration, and thus representing the state itself, with a mind so unequal and oppressive as to amount to a practical denial by the state of that equal protection of the laws which is secured to the petitioners, as to all other persons, by the broad and benign provisions of the fourteenth amendment to the constitution of the United States. Though the law itself be fair on its face, and impartial in appliance, yet, if it is applied and administered by public authority with an evil eye and an unequal hand, so as practically to make unjust and illegal discriminations between persons in similar circumstances, material to their rights, the denial of equal justice is still within the prohibition of the constitution. This principle of interpretation has been sanctioned by this court in Henderson v. Mayor of New York, 92 U.S. 259; Chy Luny v. Freeman, 92 U.S. 275; Ex parte Virginia, 100 U.S. 339; Neal v. Delaware, 103 U.S. 370; and Soon Hing v. Crowley, 113 U.S. 703; S.C. 5 Sup.Ct.Rep. 730.

The present cases, as shown by the facts disclosed in the record, are within this class. It appears that both petitioners have complied with every requisite deemed by the law, or by the public officers charged with its administration, necessary for the protection of neighboring property from fire, or as a precaution against injury to the public health. No reason whatever, except the will of the supervisors, is assigned why they should not be permitted to carry on, in the accustomed manner, their harmless and useful occupation, on which they depend for a livelihood; and while this consent of the supervisors is withheld from them, and from 200 others who have also petitioned, all of whom happen to be Chinese subjects, 80 others, not Chinese subjects, are permitted to carry on the same business under similar conditions. The fact of this discrimination is admitted. No reason for it is shown, and the conclusion cannot be resisted that no reason for it exists except hostility to the race and nationality to which the petitioners belong, and which, in the eye of the law, is not justified. The discrimination is therefore illegal, and the public administration which enforces it is a denial of the equal protection of the laws, and a violation of the fourteenth amendment of the constitution. The imprisonment of the petitioners is therefore illegal, and they must be discharged. To this end the judgment of the supreme court of California in the *Case of Yick Wo,* and that of the circuit court of the United States for the district of California in the *Case of Wo Lee,* are severally reversed, and the cases remanded, each to the proper court, with directions to discharge the petitioners from custody and imprisonment.

Comments and Questions

1. In *Yick Wo,* the administrative board followed a blatant course of discrimination and did not deny that it had done so. Presumably most modern agencies would attempt to hide discriminatory actions. How can a person who believes that racial discrimination is taking place prove it? Should it be enough to show that a greater percentage of whites were granted permits, received favorable rulings, or benefited from the adopted regulations? The Supreme Court has held that such a showing, called disproportionate impact, is not enough to warrant application of the strict-scrutiny standard. Instead, discriminatory purpose, or the *intent* to discriminate on the basis of race, must be shown before the agency is called upon to justify its actions. In Arlington Heights v. Metropolitan Housing Development Corp., 429 U.S. 252, 97 S.Ct. 555 (1977), the Court explained that a variety of factors could be used to show discriminatory purpose, including disproportionate impact, the historical background of the decision, the specific sequence of events leading up to the decision, procedural irregularities, unexpected or unusual decisions, and explanatory statements by members of the decision-making body.

2. Since *Arlington Heights,* few litigants have cleared the hurdle of showing discriminatory purpose. Do you think that is because the number of racially motivated administrative-regulatory decisions is very small?

MOOSE LODGE NO. 107 v. IRVIS

Supreme Court of the United States, 1972.
407 U.S. 163, 92 S.Ct. 1965.

Mr. Justice Rehnquist delivered the opinion of the Court.

Appellee Irvis, a Negro (hereafter appellee), was refused service by appellant Moose Lodge, a local branch of the national fraternal organization located in Harrisburg, Pennsylvania. Appellee then brought this action under 42 U.S.C. § 1983 for injunctive relief in the United States

District Court for the Middle District of Pennsylvania. He claimed that because the Pennsylvania liquor board had issued appellant Moose Lodge a private club license that authorized the sale of alcoholic beverages on its premises, the refusal of service to him was "state action" for the purposes of the Equal Protection Clause of the Fourteenth Amendment. He named both Moose Lodge and the Pennsylvania Liquor Authority as defendants, seeking injunctive relief that would have required the defendant liquor board to revoke Moose Lodge's license so long as it continued its discriminatory practices. Appellee sought no damages. . . .

Moose Lodge is a private club in the ordinary meaning of that term. It is a local chapter of a national fraternal organization having well-defined requirements for membership. It conducts all of its activities in a building that is owned by it. It is not publicly funded. Only members and guests are permitted in any lodge of the order; one may become a guest only by invitation of a member or upon invitation of the house committee.

Appellee, while conceding the right of private clubs to choose members upon a discriminatory basis, asserts that the licensing of Moose Lodge to serve liquor by the Pennsylvania Liquor Control Board amounts to such state involvement with the club's activities as to make its discriminatory practices forbidden by the Equal Protection Clause of the Fourteenth Amendment. The relief sought and obtained by appellee in the District Court was an injunction forbidding the licensing by the liquor authority of Moose Lodge until it ceased its discriminatory practices. We conclude that Moose Lodge's refusal to serve food and beverages to a guest by reason of the fact that he was a Negro does not, under the circumstances here presented, violate the Fourteenth Amendment.

In 1883, this Court in The Civil Rights Cases, 109 U.S. 3, 3 S.Ct. 18, set forth the essential dichotomy between discriminatory action by the State, which is prohibited by the Equal Protection Clause, and private conduct, "however discriminatory or wrongful," against which that clause "erects no shield," Shelley v. Kraemer, 334 U.S. 1, 13, 68 S.Ct. 836, 842 (1948). That dichotomy has been subsequently reaffirmed in Shelley v. Kraemer, supra, and in Burton v. Wilmington Parking Authority, 365 U.S. 715, 81 S.Ct. 856 (1961).

While the principle is easily stated, the question of whether particular discriminatory conduct is private, on the one hand, or amounts to "state action," on the other hand, frequently admits of no easy answer. "Only by sifting facts and weighing circumstances can the nonobvious involvement of the State in private conduct be attributed its true significance." Burton v. Wilmington Parking Authority, supra, at 722, 81 S.Ct., at 860.

Our cases make clear that the impetus for the forbidden discrimination need not originate with the State if it is state action that enforces privately originated discrimination. Shelley v. Kraemer, supra. The Court held in Burton v. Wilmington Parking Authority, supra, that a private restaurant owner who refused service because of a customer's race violated the Fourteenth Amendment, where the restaurant was located in a building owned by a state-created parking authority and leased from the authority. The Court, after a comprehensive review of the relationship between the lessee and the parking authority concluded that the latter had "so far insinuated itself into a position of interdependence with Eagle [the restaurant owner] that it must be recognized as a joint participant in the challenged activity, which, on that account, cannot be considered to have been so 'purely private' as to fall without the scope of the Fourteenth Amendment." 365 U.S., at 725, 81 S.Ct., at 862.

The Court has never held, of course, that discrimination by an otherwise private entity would be violative of the Equal Protection Clause if the private entity receives any sort of benefit or service at all from the State, or if it is subject to state regulation in any degree whatever. Since state-furnished services include such necessities of life as electricity, water, and police and fire protection, such a holding would utterly emasculate the distinction between private as distinguished from state conduct set forth in The Civil Rights Cases, supra, and adhered to in subsequent decisions. Our holdings indicate that where the impetus for the discrimination is private, the State must have "significantly involved itself with invidious discriminations," Reitman v. Mulkey, 387 U.S. 369, 380, 87 S.Ct. 1627, 1634 (1967), in order for the discriminatory action to fall within the ambit of the constitutional prohibition.

Our prior decisions dealing with discriminatory refusal of service in public eating places are significantly different factually from the case now before us. Peterson v. City of Greenville, 373 U.S. 244, 83 S.Ct. 1119 (1963), dealt with the trespass prosecution of persons who "sat in" at a restaurant to protest its refusal of service to Negroes. There the Court held that although the ostensible initiative for the trespass prosecution came from the proprietor, the existence of a local ordinance requiring segregation of races in such places was tantamount to the State having "commanded a particular result," 373 U.S., at 248, 83 S.Ct., at 1121. With one exception, which is discussed infra, there is no suggestion in this record that the Pennsylvania statutes and regulations governing the sale of liquor are intended either overtly or covertly to encourage discrimination. . . .

Here there is nothing approaching the symbiotic relationship between lessor and lessee that was present in *Burton*, where the private lessee obtained the benefit of locating in a building owned by the state-created parking authority, and the parking authority was enabled to carry out its primary public purpose of furnishing parking space by advantageously leasing portions of the building constructed for that purpose to commercial lessees such as the owner of the Eagle Restaurant. Unlike *Burton*, the Moose Lodge building is located on land owned by it, not by any public authority. Far from apparently holding itself out as a place of public accommodation, Moose Lodge quite ostentatiously proclaims the fact that it is not open to the public at large. Nor is it located and operated in such surroundings that although private in name, it discharges a function or performs a service that would otherwise in all likelihood be performed by the State. In short, while Eagle was a public restaurant in a public building, Moose Lodge is a private social club in a private building.

With the exception hereafter noted, the Pennsylvania Liquor Control Board plays absolutely no part in establishing or enforcing the membership or guest policies of the club that it licenses to serve liquor. There is no suggestion in this record that Pennsylvania law, either as written or as applied, discriminates against minority groups either in their right to apply for club licenses themselves or in their right to purchase and be served liquor in places of public accommodation. The only effect that the state licensing of Moose Lodge to serve liquor can be said to have on the right of any other Pennsylvanian to buy or be served liquor on premises other than those of Moose Lodge is that for some purposes club licenses are counted in the maximum number of licenses that may be issued in a given municipality. Basically each municipality has a quota of one retail license for each 1,500 inhabitants. Licenses issued to hotels, municipal golf courses, and airport restaurants are not counted in this quota, nor are club licenses until the maximum number of retail licenses is reached. Beyond that point, neither additional retail licenses nor additional club licenses may be issued so long as the number of issued and outstanding retail licenses remains at or above the statutory maximum.

The District Court was at pains to point out in its opinion what it considered to be the "pervasive" nature of the regulation of private clubs by the Pennsylvania Liquor Control Board. As that court noted, an applicant for a club license must make such physical alterations in its premises as the board may require, must file a list of the names and addresses of its members and employees, and must keep extensive financial records. The board is granted the right to inspect the licensed premises at any time when patrons, guests, or members are present.

However detailed this type of regulation may be in some particulars, it cannot be said to in any way foster or encourage racial discrimination. Nor can it be said to make the State in any realistic sense a partner or even a joint venturer in the club's enterprise. The limited effect of the prohibition against obtaining additional club licenses when the maximum number of retail licenses allotted to a municipality has been issued, when considered together with the availability of liquor from hotel, restaurant, and retail licensees, falls far short of conferring upon club licensees a monopoly in the dispensing of liquor in any given municipality or in the State as a whole. We therefore hold that, with the exception hereafter noted, the operation of the regulatory scheme enforced by the Pennsylvania Liquor Control Board does not sufficiently implicate the State in the discriminatory guest policies of Moose Lodge to make the latter "state action" within the ambit of the Equal Protection Clause of the Fourteenth Amendment.

The District Court found that the regulations of the Liquor Control Board adopted pursuant to statute affirmatively require that "[e]very club licensee shall adhere to all of the provisions of its Constitution and By-Laws." Appellant argues that the purpose of this provision "is purely and simply and plainly the prevention of subterfuge," pointing out that the bona fides of a private club, as opposed to a place of public accommodation masquerading as a private club, is a matter with which the State Liquor Control Board may legitimately concern itself. Appellee concedes this to be the case, and expresses disagreement with the District Court on this point. There can be no doubt that the label "private club" can be and has been used to evade both regulations of state and local liquor authorities, and statutes requiring places of public accommodation to serve all persons without regard to race, color, religion, or national origin. This Court in Daniel v. Paul, 395 U.S. 298, 89 S.Ct. 1697 (1969), had occasion to address this issue in connection with the application of Title II of the Civil Rights Act of 1964, 78 Stat. 243, 42 U.S.C. § 2000a et seq. . . .

Even though the Liquor Control Board regulation in question is neutral in its terms, the result of its application in a case where the constitution and bylaws of a club required racial discrimination would be to invoke the sanctions of the State to enforce a concededly discriminatory private rule. State action, for purposes of the Equal Protection Clause, may emanate from rulings of administrative and regulatory agencies as well as from legislative or judicial action. Robinson v. Florida, 378 U.S. 153, 156, 84 S.Ct. 1693, 1695 (1964). Shelley v. Kraemer, 334 U.S. 1, 68 S.Ct. 836 (1948), makes it clear that the application of state sanctions to enforce such a rule would violate the Fourteenth Amendment. Although the record before us is not as clear as one would like, appellant has not persuaded us that the District Court should have denied any and all relief.

Appellee was entitled to a decree enjoining the enforcement of § 113.09 of the regulations promulgated by the Pennsylvania Liquor Control Board insofar as that regulation requires compliance by Moose Lodge with provisions of its constitution and bylaws containing racially discriminatory provisions. He was entitled to no more. The judgment of the District Court is reversed, and the cause remanded with instructions to enter a decree in conformity with this opinion.

Reversed and remanded.

MR. JUSTICE DOUGLAS, with whom MR. JUSTICE MARSHALL joins, dissenting.

My view of the First Amendment and the related guarantees of the Bill of Rights is that they create a zone of privacy which precludes government from interfering with private clubs or groups. The associational rights which our system honors permit all white, all black, all brown, and all yellow clubs to be formed. They also permit all Catholic, all Jewish, or all agnostic clubs to be established. Government may not tell a man or woman who his or her associates must be. The individual can be as selective as he desires. So the fact that the Moose Lodge allows only Caucasians to join or come as guests is constitutionally irrelevant, as is the decision of the Black Muslims to admit to their services only members of their race.

The problem is different, however, where the public domain is concerned. I have indicated in Garner v. Louisiana, 368 U.S. 157, 82 S.Ct. 248, and Lombard v. Louisiana, 373 U.S. 267, 83 S.Ct. 1122, that where restaurants or other facilities serving the public are concerned and licenses are obtained from the State for operating the business, the "public" may not be defined by the proprietor to include only people of his choice; nor may a state or municipal service be granted only to some. Evans v. Newton, 382 U.S. 296, 298–299, 86 S.Ct. 486, 487–488.

Those cases are not precisely apposite, however, for a private club, by definition, is not in the public domain. And the fact that a private club gets some kind of permit from the State or municipality does not make it ipso facto a public enterprise or undertaking, any more than the grant to a householder of a permit to operate an incinerator puts the householder in the public domain. We must, therefore, examine whether there are special circumstances involved in the Pennsylvania scheme which differentiate the liquor license possessed by Moose Lodge from the incinerator permit.

Pennsylvania has a state store system of alcohol distribution. Resale is permitted by hotels, restaurants, and private clubs which all must obtain licenses from the Liquor Control Board. The scheme of regulation is complete and pervasive; and the state courts have sustained many restrictions on the licensees. See Tahiti Bar Inc. Liquor License Case, 395 Pa. 355, 150 A.2d 112. Once a license is issued the licensee must comply with many detailed requirements or risk suspension or revocation of the license. Among these requirements is Regulation § 113.09 which says: "Every club licensee shall adhere to all of the provisions of its Constitution and By-laws." This regulation means, as applied to Moose Lodge, that it must adhere to the racially discriminatory provision of the Constitution of its Supreme Lodge that "[t]he membership of lodges shall be composed of male persons of the Caucasian or White race above the age of twenty-one years, and not married to someone of any other than the Caucasian or White race, who are of good moral character, physically and mentally normal, who shall profess a belief in a Supreme Being."

It is argued that this regulation only aims at the prevention of subterfuge and at enforcing Pennsylvania's differentiation between places of public accommodation and bona fide private clubs. It is also argued that the regulation only gives effect to the constitutionally protected rights of privacy and of association. But I cannot so read the regulation. While those other purposes are embraced in it, so is the restrictive membership clause. And we have held that "a State is responsible for the discriminatory act of a private party when the State, by its law, has compelled the act." Adickes v. S.H. Kress & Co., 398 U.S. 144, 170, 90 S.Ct. 1598, 1615. See Peterson v. City of Greenville, 373 U.S. 244, 248, 83 S.Ct. 1119, 1121. It is irrelevant whether the law is statutory, or an administrative regulation. Robinson v. Florida, 378 U.S. 153, 156, 84 S.Ct. 1693, 1695. And it is irrelevant whether the discriminatory act was instigated by the regulation, or was independent of it. Peterson v. City of Greenville, supra. The result, as I see it, is the same as though Pennsylvania had put into its liquor licenses a provision that the license may not be used to dispense liquor to blacks, browns, yellows—or atheists or agnostics. Regulation § 113.09 is thus an invidious form of state action.

Were this regulation the only infirmity in Pennsylvania's licensing scheme, I would perhaps agree with the majority that the appropriate relief would be a decree enjoining its enforcement. But there is another flaw in the scheme not so easily cured. Liquor licenses in Pennsylvania, unlike driver's licenses, or marriage licenses, are not freely available to those who meet racially neutral qualifications. There is a complex quota system, which the majority accurately describes. What the majority neglects to say is that the quota for Harrisburg, where Moose Lodge No.

107 is located, has been full for many years. No more club licenses may be issued in that city.

This state-enforced scarcity of licenses restricts the ability of blacks to obtain liquor, for liquor is commercially available *only* at private clubs for a significant portion of each week. Access by blacks to places that serve liquor is further limited by the fact that the state quota is filled. A group desiring to form a nondiscriminatory club which would serve blacks must purchase a license held by an existing club, which can exact a monopoly price for the transfer. The availability of such a license is speculative at best, however, for, as Moose Lodge itself concedes, without a liquor license a fraternal organization would be hard pressed to survive.

Thus, the State of Pennsylvania is putting the weight of its liquor license, concededly a valued and important adjunct to a private club, behind racial discrimination. . . .

I would affirm the judgment below.

[Justice Brennan, joined by Justice Marshall, also filed a dissenting opinion.]

Comments and Questions

1. If an administrative body could issue only one license—perhaps to decide what company should operate a natural monopoly such as a public utility—would a decision to issue the license to a racially discriminatory company be constitutional? If it could issue two licenses, and chose to issue one to a discriminatory company, would that be permissible? How can the line drawn by the Court—or any line other than that of scarce versus infinite—be defended?

2. If the dissent's view had prevailed, what other constitutional limitations would have applied to Moose Lodge? The Fourteenth Amendment also provides that no state shall "deprive any person of life, liberty, or property, without due process of law." If the dissent's view had prevailed, would this apply to Moose Lodge, too, and mean that Moose Lodge would have to hold hearings before fining its members? Can you justify one meaning for state action under the due process clause and a different meaning under the equal protection clause?

B. Racial Equality as the Goal of the Administrative-Regulatory Mode

In Chapter 3, we saw that the administrative-regulatory instrument operates to prevent grievances from arising and to resolve disputes before they reach a court.

Most of the examples of the administrative-regulatory mode we have thus far examined involve the setting of regulatory standards or the enforcement of those standards through administrative hearings. Although these techniques of the administrative-regulatory mode are often used to promote racial equality (for example, by the Equal Employment Opportunity Commission), we shall not consider them here.

You may recall that the administrative-regulatory instrument also has less overtly coercive techniques, including the power to investigate, the power to publicize unfavorable findings, and the power to encourage self-regulation. The Civil Rights Commission exemplifies the use of these techniques because it has no power to adjudicate or take any action that will affect an individual's rights. Established in 1957, the commission was designed to terminate two years later upon the submission of a final report, but amendments have repeatedly extended its life. Consider the current enabling legislation in title 42 of the United States Code:

§ 1975. Commission on Civil Rights

(a) **Establishment.** There is established a Commission on Civil Rights (hereafter in this Act referred to as the "Commission").

(b) **Membership.** (1) The Commission shall be composed of eight members. Not more than four of the members shall at any one time be of the same political party. Members of the Commission shall be appointed as follows:

(A) four members of the Commission shall be appointed by the President;

(B) two members of the Commission shall be appointed by the President pro tempore of the Senate, upon the recommendations of the Majority Leader and the Minority Leader, and of the members appointed not more than one shall be appointed from the same political party; and

(C) two members of the Commission shall be appointed by the Speaker of the House of Representatives upon the recommendations of the Majority Leader and the Minority Leader, and of the members appointed not more than one shall be appointed from the same political party.

(2) The term of office of each member of the Commission shall be six years; except that (A) members first taking office shall serve as designated by the President, subject to the provisions of paragraph (3), for terms of three years, and (B) any member appointed to fill a vacancy shall serve for the remainder of the term for which his predecessor was appointed.

(3) The President shall designate terms of members first appointed under paragraph (2) so that two members appointed under clauses (B) and (C) of paragraph (1) and two members appointed under clause (A) of paragraph (1) are designated for terms of three years and two members appointed under clauses (B) and (C) of paragraph (1) and two members appointed under clause (A) of paragraph (1) are designated for terms of six years. No more than two persons of the same political party shall be designated for three year terms.

(c) **Chairman and Vice Chairman.** The President shall designate a Chairman and a Vice Chairman from among the Commission's members with the concurrence of a majority of the Commission's members. The Vice Chairman shall act in the place and stead of the Chairman in the absence of the Chairman.

(d) **Removal.** The President may remove a member of the Commission only for neglect of duty or malfeasance in office.

(e) **Vacancies.** Any vacancy in the Commission shall not affect its powers and shall be filled in the same manner, and subject to the same limitation with respect to party affiliation as the original appointment was made.

(f) Quorum. Five members of the Commission shall constitute a quorum.

[Section 1975a sets out the rules of procedure for commission hearings, and § 1975b provides for compensation of commission members.]

§ 1975c.   Duties of the Commission

(a) The Commission shall—

(1) investigate allegations in writing under oath or affirmation that certain citizens of the United States are being deprived of their right to vote and have that vote counted by reason of their color, race, religion, sex, age, handicap, or national origin; which writing, under oath or affirmation, shall set forth the facts upon which such belief or beliefs are based;

(2) study and collect information concerning legal developments constituting discrimination or a denial of equal protection of the laws under the Constitution because of race, color, religion, sex, age, handicap, or national origin or in the administration of justice;

(3) appraise the laws and policies of the Federal Government with respect to discrimination or denials of equal protection of the laws under the Constitution because of race, color, religion, sex, age, handicap, or national origin or the administration of justice;

(4) serve as national clearinghouse for information in respect to discrimination or denials of equal protection of the laws because of race, color, religion, sex, age, handicap, or national origin, including but not limited to the fields of voting, education, housing, employment, the use of public facilities, and transportation, or in the administration of justice; and

(5) investigate allegations, made in writing and under oath or affirmation, that citizens of the United States are unlawfully being accorded or denied the right to vote, or to have their votes properly counted, in any election of the Presidential electors, Members of the United States Senate, or the House of Representatives, as a result of any patterns or practice of fraud or discrimination in the conduct of such election.

(b) Nothing in this or any other Act shall be construed as authorizing the Commission, its Advisory Committees, or any person under its supervision or control to inquire into or investigate any membership practices or internal operations of any fraternal organization, any college or university fraternity or sorority, any private club or any religious organization.

(c) The Commission shall submit reports to the Congress and the President at such times as the Commission, the Congress or the President shall deem desirable.   .   .   .

(f) The Commission shall appraise the laws and policies of the Federal Government with respect to denials of equal protection of the laws under the Constitution involving Americans who are members of eastern- and southern-European ethinc groups and shall report its findings to the Congress. Such reports shall include an analysis of the adverse consequences of affirmative action programs encouraged by the Federal Government upon the equal opportunity rights of these Americans.

§ 1975d. Powers of the Commission

(a) **Staff director and other personnel.** (1) There shall be a full-time staff director for the Commission who shall be appointed by the President with the concurrence of a majority of the Commission.

(2)(A) Effective November 29, 1983, or on the date of enactment of this Act [enacted Nov. 30, 1983], whichever occurs first, all employees (other than the staff director and the members of the Commission) of the Commission on Civil Rights are transferred to the Commission established by [42 USC § 1975(a)].

(B) Upon application of any individual (other than the staff director or a member of the Commission) who was an employee of the Commission on Civil Rights established by the Civil Rights Act of 1957 on September 30, 1983, the Commission shall appoint such individual to a position the duties and responsibilities of which and the rate of pay for which, are the same as the duties, responsibilities and rate of pay of the position held by such employee on September 30, 1983.

(C)(i) Notwithstanding any other provision of law, employees transferred to the Commission under subparagraph (A) shall retain all rights and benefits to which they were entitled or for which they were eligible immediately prior to their transfer to the Commission.

(ii) Notwithstanding any other provision of law, the Commission shall be bound by those provisions of title 5, United States Code [5 USC §§ 101 et seq.], to which the Commission on Civil Rights, established by the Civil Rights Act of 1957, was bound.

(3) Within the limitation of its appropriations, the Commission may appoint such other personnel as it deems advisable, in accordance with the civil service and classification laws, and may procure services as authorized by section 3109 of title 5, United States Code, but at rates for individuals not in excess of the daily equivalent paid for positions at the maximum rate for GS–15 of the General Schedule under section 5332 of title 5, United States Code.

(b) **Services of voluntary or uncompensated personnel.** The Commission shall not accept or utilize services of voluntary or uncompensated personnel, and the term "whoever" as used in [42 USC § 1975a(g)] shall be construed to mean a person whose services are compensated by the United States.

(c) **Advisory committees.** The Commission may constitute such advisory committees within States as it deems advisable, but the

Commission shall constitute at least one advisory committee within each State composed of citizens of that State. The Commission may consult with governors, attorneys general, and other representatives of State and local governments and private organizations, as it deems advisable. . . .

(e) Cooperation with Federal agencies. All Federal agencies shall cooperate fully with the Commission to the end that it may effectively carry out its functions and duties.

(f) Hearings; issuance of subpena. The Commission, or on the authorization of the Commission any subcommittee of two or more members, at least one of whom shall be of each major political party, may, for the purpose of carrying out the provisions of this resolution, hold such hearings and act at such times and places as the Commission or such authorized subcommittee may deem advisable. Subpenas for the attendance and testimony of witnesses or the production of written or other matter may be issued in accordance with the rules of the Commission as contained in [42 USC § 1975a(j), (k)], over the signature of the Chairman of the Commission or of such subcommittee, and may be served by any person designated by such Chairman. The holding of hearings by the Commission, or the appointment of a subcommittee to hold hearings pursuant to this subparagraph, must be approved by a majority of the Commission, or by a majority of the members present at a meeting at which at least a quorum of five members is present.

(g) Order requiring appearance. In case of contumacy or refusal to obey a subpena, any district court of the United States or the United States court of any territory or possession, or the District Court of the United States for the District of Columbia, within the jurisdiction of which the inquiry is carried on or within the jurisdiction of which said person guilty of contumacy or refusal to obey is found or resides or is domiciled or transacts business, or has appointed an agent for receipt of service of process, upon application by the Attorney General of the United States shall have jurisdiction to issue to such person an order requiring such person to appear before the Commission or a subcommittee thereof, there to produce pertinent, relevant and nonprivileged evidence if so ordered, or there to give testimony touching the matter under investigation; and any failure to obey such order of the court may be punished by said court as a contempt thereof.

(h) Oaths and affirmations. Without limiting the application of any other provision of this Act, each member of the Commission shall have the power and authority to administer oaths or take statements of witnesses under affirmation.

(i) Rules and regulations. (1) The Commission shall have the power to make such rules and regulations as are necessary to carry out the purposes of this Act.

(2) To the extent not inconsistent with the provisions of this Act, the Commission established by [42 USC § 1975(a)] shall be bound by all rules issued by the Civil Rights Commission established by

the Civil Rights Act of 1957 which were in effect on September 30, 1983, until modified by the Commission in accordance with applicable law.

(3) The Commission shall make arrangements for the transfer of all files, records, and balances of appropriations of the Commission on Civil Rights as established by the Civil Rights Act of 1957 to the Commission established by this Act.

[Section 1975e appropriates funds for the operation of the commission, and § 1975f provides for the termination of the act on November 30, 1989.]

The Civil Rights Commission has been a highly visible and sometimes controversial advocate of minorities' and women's rights. During the Reagan administration, however, new appointments altered the traditionally liberal bent of the commission, causing first consternation and then condemnation from traditional allies of the commission. New appointees were known to oppose mandatory busing and to be critical of affirmative action programs.

In February of 1985, Chairman Clarence M. Pendleton, Jr. (a black California Republican), and Vice Chairman Morris B. Abram called on civil rights leaders "to acknowledge the difference between discriminatory affirmative action of racial preference, whether called a quota or a goal, and nondiscriminatory affirmative action such as that indorsed by the Commission." The two holdover members from the Carter administration, Blandina Cardenas Ramirez and Mary Frances Berry, issued a public response, asserting that civil rights laws were not passed to give protection to all Americans but "out of a recognition that some Americans already had protection because they belong to a favored group, and others, including blacks, Hispanics and women of all races, did not because they belonged to disfavored groups." The commission conducted a hearing on affirmative action in March, but all of the major civil rights groups that had been scheduled to testify, including the NAACP Legal Defense Fund, the National Urban League, NOW, and the Mexican American Legal Defense and Educational Fund, boycotted the proceedings. Citing Pendleton and Abram's statement to President Reagan that "affirmative action is dead," spokespersons from the civil rights groups explained the boycott as a protest against what they claimed were closed minds and open mouths.

The feud between Pendleton and civil rights activists has been acrimonious and has received quite a bit of publicity. Civil rights activists have accused Pendleton of being a "lackey" for the Reagan administration, and he has accused them of behaving like "new racists." Pendleton has stated that the only criticism he has heard came from other blacks, has called himself more a victim of intraracial racism than interracial racism, and has voiced his support for eliminating the commission after the public has debated what he calls the "central issue of preferential treatment." Civil rights activists have countered that debate over preferential treatment is a smoke screen designed to divide the civil rights community and distract attention from the Reagan administration's retreat on civil rights enforcement and cutbacks on social programs to aid minorities.

In May of 1985, a new controversy ignited when it was reported that the commission had reorganized its state advisory committees, which monitor and report on developments in their states. Three hundred thirteen of 500 state committee members were replaced, and the acting staff director of the commission explained that many of the new members would be in sympathy with the new conservative majority on the commission. Thirty-six of the new chairpersons were white, nine were black, three were Hispanic, and two were Native American, as compared with fifteen white, twenty-one black, seven Hispanic, six Native American, and two Asian-American chairpersons of the old panels. Moreover, of the fifty new chairpersons, only four were women, although women chaired twenty of the old panels. Commission member Mary Frances Berry voiced her objection: "When the chairmen all meet at once, I suppose what you wind up with is an old-boy network discussing the problems white males have in civil rights." Defending the appointments, Linda Chavez, deputy assistant to President Reagan for public liaison and former staff director of the Civil Rights Commission, stated that many of the new appointees were prominent in civil rights and should not be judged on race and sex alone.

Comments and Questions

1. Should appointments to the Civil Rights Commission and state advisory committees be based in part upon race?

2. Should appointments to the Civil Rights Commission be political? Have they always been?

3. Is it appropriate to select a Civil Rights Commission whose focus is the enforcement of the civil rights of white males? Does the answer to this question depend upon one's view of the prevalence of current discrimination against women and racial minorities as opposed to white men?

4. Is it time to disband the Civil Rights Commission? Consider the following view:

> When a man has emerged from slavery, and by the aid of beneficent legislation has shaken off the inseparable concomitants of that state, there must be some stage in the progress of his elevation when he takes the rank of a mere citizen, and ceases to be the special favorite of the laws . . . .

This statement appears in The Civil Rights Cases, 109 U.S. 3, 25, 3 S.Ct. 18, 31 (1883). Certainly it was a ludicrous description of the times in which it was written. Do you find it an apt or a naive characterization of the 1980s?

Section Six. Racial Equality and the Public-Benefit Instrument

A. Racial Equality as a Limit on the Public-Benefit Mode

You do not have to take a course about law to know that a state could not decide to provide education only for white students—or even provide separate education systems for white and black students. Virtually all Americans are aware of the Supreme Court's decision in *Brown* v. *Board of Education*, which you read in Chapter 4 and which outlawed segregated schools. By now you can guess that restricting other public benefits, such as social security, job programs, or police services, to whites would also be unconstitutional. The thorny question is whether racial equality as a limit on the public-benefit mode prohibits reserving some benefits for minorities in order to further the goal of racial equality.

———

FULLILOVE v. KLUTZNICK

Supreme Court of the United States, 1980.
448 U.S. 448, 100 S.Ct. 2758.

MR. CHIEF JUSTICE BURGER announced the judgment of the Court and delivered an opinion, in which MR. JUSTICE WHITE and MR. JUSTICE POWELL joined.

We granted certiorari to consider a facial constitutional challenge to a requirement in a congressional spending program that, absent an administrative waiver, 10% of the federal funds granted for local public works projects must be used by the state or local grantee to procure services or supplies from businesses owned and controlled by members of statutorily identified minority groups.

In May 1977, Congress enacted the Public Works Employment Act of 1977, Pub.L. 95-28, 91 Stat. 116, which amended the Local Public Works Capital Development and Investment Act of 1976, Pub.L. 94-369, 90 Stat. 999, 42 U.S.C. § 6701 et seq. The 1977 amendments authorized an additional $4 billion appropriation for federal grants to be made by the Secretary of Commerce, acting through the Economic Development Administration (EDA), to state and local governmental entities for use in local public works projects. Among the changes made was the addition of the provision that has become the focus of this litigation. Section 103(f)(2) of the 1977 Act, referred to as the "minority business enterprise" or "MBE" provision, requires that:

> Except to the extent that the Secretary determines otherwise, no grant shall be made under this Act for any local public works project unless the applicant gives satisfactory assurance to the Secretary that at least 10 per centum of the amount of each grant shall be expended for minority business enterprises. For purposes of this paragraph, the term "minority business enterprise" means a business at least 50 per centum of which is owned by minority group members or, in case of a publicly owned business, at least 51 per centum of the stock of which is owned by minority group members. For the purposes of the preceding sentence minority group members are citizens of the United States who are Negroes, Spanish-speaking, Orientals, Indians, Eskimos, and Aleuts.

In late May 1977, the Secretary promulgated regulations governing administration of the grant program . . . .

On November 30, 1977, petitioners filed a complaint in the United States District Court for the Southern District of New York seeking declaratory and injunctive relief to enjoin enforcement of the MBE provision. Named as defendants were the Secretary of Commerce, as the program administrator, and the State and City of New York, as actual and potential project grantees. Petitioners are several associations of construction contractors and subcontractors, and a firm engaged in heating, ventilation, and air conditioning work. Their complaint alleged that they had sustained economic injury due to enforcement of the 10% MBE requirement and that the MBE provision on its face violated the Equal Protection Clause of the Fourteenth Amendment, the equal protection component of the Due Process Clause of the Fifth Amendment, and various statutory antidiscrimination provisions.

After a hearing held the day the complaint was filed, the District Court denied a requested temporary restraining order and scheduled the matter for an expedited hearing on the merits. On December 19, 1977, the District Court issued a memorandum opinion upholding the validity of the MBE program and denying the injunctive relief sought.

The United States Court of Appeals for the Second Circuit affirmed

. . . . .

The MBE provision was enacted as part of the Public Works Employment Act of 1977, which made various amendments to Title I of the Local Public Works Capital Development and Investment Act of 1976. The 1976 Act was intended as a short-term measure to alleviate the problem of national unemployment and to stimulate the national economy by assisting state and local governments to build needed public facilities . . . .

The device of a 10% MBE participation requirement, subject to administrative waiver, was thought to be required to assure minority business participation; otherwise it was thought that repetition of the prior experience could be expected, with participation by minority business accounting for an inordinately small percentage of government contracting. The causes of this disparity were perceived as involving the longstanding existence and maintenance of barriers impairing access by minority enterprises to public contracting opportunities, or sometimes as involving more direct discrimination, but not as relating to lack—as Senator Brooke put it—"of capable and qualified minority enterprises who are ready and willing to work." In the words of its sponsor, the MBE provision was "designed to begin to redress this grievance that has been extant for so long." . . .

Our analysis proceeds in two steps. At the outset, we must inquire whether the *objectives* of this legislation are within the power of Congress. If so, we must go on to decide whether the limited use of racial and ethnic criteria, in the context presented, is a constitutionally permissible *means* for achieving the congressional objectives and does not violate the equal protection component of the Due Process Clause of the Fifth Amendment.

[Chief Justice Burger determined that the objectives of the legislation were within the spending power of Congress.]

We now turn to the question whether, as a *means* to accomplish these plainly constitutional objectives, Congress may use racial and ethnic criteria, in this limited way, as a condition attached to a federal grant. We are mindful that "[i]n no matter should we pay more deference to the opinion of Congress than in its choice of instrumentalities to perform a function that is within its power," National Mutual Insurance Co. v. Tidewater Transfer Co., 337 U.S. 582, 603, 69 S.Ct. 1173, 1183 (1949) (opinion of Jackson, J.). However, Congress may employ racial or ethnic classifications in exercising its Spending or other legislative powers only if those classifications do not violate the equal protection component of the Due Process Clause of the Fifth Amendment. We recognize the need for careful judicial evaluation to assure that any congressional program that employs racial or ethnic criteria to accomplish the objective of remedying the present effects of past discrimination is narrowly tailored to the achievement of that goal.

Again, we stress the limited scope of our inquiry. Here we are not dealing with a remedial decree of a court but with the legislative authority of Congress. Furthermore, petitioners have challenged the constitutionality of the MBE provision on its face; they have not sought damages or other specific relief for injury allegedly flowing from specific applications of the program; nor have they attempted to show that as applied in identified situations the MBE provision violated the constitutional or statutory rights of any party to this case. In these circumstances, given a reasonable construction and in light of its projected administration, if we find the MBE program on its face to be free of constitutional defects, it must be upheld as within congressional power.

Our review of the regulations and guidelines governing administration of the MBE provision reveals that Congress enacted the program as a strictly remedial measure; moreover, it is a remedy that functions prospectively, in the manner of an injunctive decree. Pursuant to the administrative program, grantees and their prime contractors are required to seek out all available, qualified, bona fide MBE's; they are required to provide technical assistance as needed, to lower or waive bonding requirements where feasible, to solicit the aid of the Office of Minority Business Enterprise, the SBA, or other sources for assisting MBE's to obtain required working capital, and to give guidance through the intricacies of the bidding process. The program assumes that grantees who undertake these efforts in good faith will obtain at least 10% participation by minority business enterprises. It is recognized that, to achieve this target, contracts will be awarded to available, qualified, bona fide MBE's even though they are not the lowest competitive bidders, so long as their higher bids, when challenged, are found to reflect merely attempts to cover costs inflated by the present effects of prior disadvantage and discrimination. There is available to the grantee a provision authorized by Congress for administrative waiver on a case-by-case basis should there be a demonstration that, despite affirmative efforts, this level of participation cannot be achieved without departing from the objectives of the program. There is also an administrative mechanism, including a complaint procedure, to ensure that only bona fide MBE's are encompassed by the remedial program, and to prevent unjust participation in the program by those minority firms whose access to public contracting opportunities is not impaired by the effects of prior discrimination.

(1)

As a threshold matter, we reject the contention that in the remedial context the Congress must act in a wholly "color-blind" fashion. In

Swann v. Charlotte-Mecklenburg Board of Education, 402 U.S. 1, 18–21, 91 S.Ct. 1267, 1277–1278 (1971), we rejected this argument in considering a court-formulated school desegregation remedy on the basis that examination of the racial composition of student bodies was an unavoidable starting point and that racially based attendance assignments were permissible so long as no absolute racial balance of each school was required. . . .

. . . In another setting, we have held that a state may employ racial criteria that are reasonably necessary to assure compliance with federal voting rights legislation, even though the state action does not entail the remedy of a constitutional violation. United Jewish Organizations of Williamsburgh, Inc. v. Carey, 430 U.S. 144, 147–165, 97 S.Ct. 996, 1000–1009 (1977) (opinion of White, J., joined by Brennan, Blackmun, and Stevens, JJ.); id., at 180–187, 97 S.Ct., at 1017–1020 (Burger, C.J., dissenting on other grounds).

When we have discussed the remedial powers of a federal court, we have been alert to the limitation that "[t]he power of the federal courts to restructure the operation of local and state governmental entities 'is not plenary. . . .' [A] federal court is required to tailor 'the scope of the remedy' to fit the nature and extent of the . . . violation." Dayton Board of Education v. Brinkman, 433 U.S. 406, 419–420, 97 S.Ct. 2766, 2775 (1977) (quoting Milliken v. Bradley, 418 U.S. 717, 738, 94 S.Ct. 3112, 3124 (1974), and Swann v. Charlotte-Mecklenburg Board of Education, supra, at 16, 91 S.Ct., at 1276).

Here we deal, as we noted earlier, not with the limited remedial powers of a federal court, for example, but with the broad remedial powers of Congress. It is fundamental that in no organ of government, state or federal, does there repose a more comprehensive remedial power than in the Congress, expressly charged by the Constitution with competence and authority to enforce equal protection guarantees. Congress not only may induce voluntary action to assure compliance with existing federal statutory or constitutional antidiscrimination provisions, but also, where Congress has authority to declare certain conduct unlawful, it may, as here, authorize and induce state action to avoid such conduct.

(2)

A more specific challenge to the MBE program is the charge that it impermissibly deprives nonminority businesses of access to at least some portion of the government contracting opportunities generated by the Act. It must be conceded that by its objective of remedying the historical impairment of access, the MBE provision can have the effect of awarding some contracts to MBE's which otherwise might be awarded to other businesses, who may themselves be innocent of any prior discriminatory actions. Failure of nonminority firms to receive certain contracts is, of course, an incidental consequence of the program, not part of its objective; similarly, past impairment of minority-firm access to public contracting opportunities may have been an incidental consequence of "business as usual" by public contracting agencies and among prime contractors.

It is not a constitutional defect in this program that it may disappoint the expectations of nonminority firms. When effectuating a limited and properly tailored remedy to cure the effects of prior discrimination, such "a sharing of the burden" by innocent parties is not impermissible. The actual "burden" shouldered by nonminority firms is relatively light in this connection when we consider the scope of this public works program as compared with overall construction contracting opportunities. Moreover, although we may assume that the complaining parties are innocent of any discriminatory conduct, it was within congressional power to act on the assumption that in the past some nonminority businesses may have reaped competitive benefit over the years from the virtual exclusion of minority firms from these contracting opportunities.

(3)

Another challenge to the validity of the MBE program is the assertion that it is underinclusive—that it limits its benefit to specified minority groups rather than extending its remedial objectives to all businesses whose access to government contracting is impaired by the effects of disadvantage or discrimination. Such an extension would, of course, be appropriate for Congress to provide; it is not a function for the courts.

Even in this context, the well-established concept that a legislature may take one step at a time to remedy only part of a broader problem is not without relevance. See Dandridge v. Williams, 397 U.S. 471, 90 S.Ct. 1153 (1970); Williamson v. Lee Optical Co., 348 U.S. 483, 75 S.Ct. 461 (1955). We are not reviewing a federal program that seeks to confer a preferred status upon a nondisadvantaged minority or to give special assistance to only one of several groups established to be similarly disadvantaged minorities. Even in such a setting, the Congress is not without a certain authority.

The Congress has not sought to give select minority groups a preferred standing in the construction industry, but has embarked on a remedial program to place them on a more equitable footing with respect to public contracting opportunities. There has been no showing in this case that Congress has inadvertently effected an invidious discrimination by excluding from coverage an identifiable minority group that has been the victim of a degree of disadvantage and discrimination equal to or greater than that suffered by the groups encompassed by the MBE program. It is not inconceivable that on very special facts a case might be made to challenge the congressional decision to limit MBE eligibility to the particular minority groups identified in the Act. But on this record we find no basis to hold that Congress is without authority to undertake the kind of limited remedial effort represented by the MBE program. Congress, not the courts, has the heavy burden of dealing with a host of intractable economic and social problems.

(4)

It is also contended that the MBE program is overinclusive—that it bestows a benefit on businesses identified by racial or ethnic criteria which cannot be justified on the basis of competitive criteria or as a remedy for the present effects of identified prior discrimination. It is conceivable that a particular application of the program may have this effect; however, the peculiarities of specific applications are not before us in this case. We are not presented here with a challenge involving a specific award of a construction contract or the denial of a waiver request; such questions of specific application must await future cases. . . .

Congress, after due consideration, perceived a pressing need to move forward with new approaches in the continuing effort to achieve the goal of equality of economic opportunity. In this effort, Congress has necessary latitude to try new techniques such as the limited use of racial and ethnic criteria to accomplish remedial objectives; this is especially so in programs where voluntary cooperation with remedial measures is induced by placing conditions on federal expenditures. That the program may press the outer limits of congressional authority affords no basis for striking it down. . . .

Affirmed. . . .

[Justice Powell concurred, filing a separate opinion. Justice Marshall, joined by Justices Brennan and Blackmun, concurred in the judgment, filing an opinion that argued that remedial legislation should not be subject to strict scrutiny but should be tested by a lesser standard, which would be satisfied by the MBE program.]

MR. JUSTICE STEWART, with whom MR. JUSTICE REHNQUIST joins, dissenting.

"Our Constitution is color-blind, and neither knows nor tolerates classes among citizens. . . . The law regards man as man, and takes no account of his surroundings or of his color . . . . " Those words were written by a Member of this Court 84 years ago. Plessy v. Ferguson, 163 U.S. 537, 559, 16 S.Ct. 1138, 1146 (Harlan, J., dissenting). His colleagues disagreed with him, and held that a statute that required the separation of people on the basis of their race was constitutionally valid because it was a "reasonable" exercise of legislative power and had been "enacted in good faith for the promotion [of] the public good . . . . " Id., at 550, 16 S.Ct., at 1143. Today, the Court upholds a statute that accords a preference to citizens who are "Negroes, Spanish-speaking, Orientals, Indians, Eskimos, and Aleuts," for much the same reasons. I think today's decision is wrong for the same reason that *Plessy* v. *Ferguson* was wrong, and I respectfully dissent. . . .

. . . Under our Constitution, the government may never act to the detriment of a person solely because of that person's race. The color of a person's skin and the country of his origin are immutable facts that bear no relation to ability, disadvantage, moral culpability, or any other characteristics of constitutionally permissible interest to government. "Distinctions between citizens solely because of their ancestry are by their very nature odious to a free people whose institutions are founded upon the doctrine of equality." Hirabayashi v. United States, 320 U.S. 81, 100, 63 S.Ct. 1375, 1385. In short, racial discrimination is by definition invidious discrimination.

The rule cannot be any different when the persons injured by a racially biased law are not members of a racial minority. The guarantee of equal protection is "universal in [its] application, to all persons . . . without regard to any differences of race, of color, or of nationality." Yick Wo v. Hopkins, 118 U.S. 356, 369, 6 S.Ct. 1064, 1070. The command of the equal protection guarantee is simple but unequivocal: In the words of the Fourteenth Amendment: "No State shall . . . deny to *any* person . . . the equal protection of the laws." Nothing in this language singles out some "persons" for more "equal" treatment than others. Rather, as the Court made clear in Shelley v. Kraemer, 334 U.S. 1, 22, 68 S.Ct. 836, 846, the benefits afforded by the Equal Protection Clause "are, by its terms, guaranteed to the individual. [They] are personal rights." From the perspective of a person detrimentally affected by a racially discriminatory law, the arbitrariness and unfairness is entirely the same, whatever his skin color and whatever the law's purpose, be it purportedly "for the promotion of the public good" or otherwise. . . .

The Fourteenth Amendment was adopted to ensure that every person must be treated equally by each State regardless of the color of his skin. The Amendment promised to carry to its necessary conclusion a fundamental principle upon which this Nation had been founded—that the law would honor no preference based on lineage. Tragically, the promise of 1868 was not immediately fulfilled, and decades passed before the States and the Federal Government were finally directed to eliminate detrimental classifications based on race. Today, the Court derails this achievement and places its imprimatur on the creation once again by government of privileges based on birth.

The Court, moreover, takes this drastic step without, in my opinion, seriously considering the ramifications of its decision. Laws that operate on the basis of race require definitions of race. Because of the Court's decision today, our statute books will once again have to contain laws that reflect the odious practice of delineating the qualities that make one person a Negro and make another white. Moreover, racial discrimination, even "good faith" racial discrimination, is inevitably a two-edged sword. "[P]referential programs may only reinforce common stereotypes holding that certain groups are unable to achieve success without special protection based on a factor having no relationship to individual worth." University of California Regents v. Bakke, [438 U.S. 265, 298, 98 S.Ct. 2733, 2753 (1978)] (opinion of Powell, J.). Most importantly, by making race a relevant criterion once again in its own affairs, the Government implicitly teaches the public that the apportionment of rewards and penalties can legitimately be made according to race—rather than according to merit or ability—and that people can, and perhaps should, view themselves and others in terms of their racial characteristics. Notions of "racial entitlement" will be fostered, and private discrimination will necessarily be encouraged. See Hughes v. Superior Court, 339 U.S. 460, 463–464, 70 S.Ct. 718, 720; T. Eastland & W. Bennett, Counting by Race 139–170 (1979); Van Alstyne, Rites of Passage: Race, the Supreme Court, and the Constitution, 46 U.Chi.L.Rev. 775 (1979).

There are those who think that we need a new Constitution, and their views may someday prevail. But under the Constitution we have, one practice in which government may never engage is the practice of racism—not even "temporarily" and not even as an "experiment."

For these reasons, I would reverse the judgment of the Court of Appeals.

MR. JUSTICE STEVENS, dissenting.

The 10% set-aside contained in the Public Works Employment Act of 1977 (Act), 91 Stat. 116, creates monopoly privileges in a $400 million market for a class of investors defined solely by racial characteristics. The direct beneficiaries of these monopoly privileges are the relatively small number of persons within the racial classification who represent the entrepreneurial subclass—those who have, or can borrow, working capital.
. . .

Racial characteristics may serve to define a group of persons who have suffered a special wrong and who, therefore, are entitled to special reparations. Congress has recognized, for example, that the United States has treated some Indian tribes unjustly and has created procedures for allowing members of the injured classes to obtain classwide relief. See, e.g., Delaware Tribal Business Committee v. Weeks, 430 U.S. 73, 97 S.Ct. 911. But as I have formerly suggested, if Congress is to authorize a recovery for a class of similarly situated victims of a past wrong, it has an obligation to distribute that recovery among the members of the injured class in an evenhanded way. See id., at 97–98, 97 S.Ct., at 925 (Stevens, J., dissenting). Moreover, in such a case the amount of the award should bear some rational relationship to the extent of the harm it is intended to cure.

In his eloquent separate opinion in University of California Regents v. Bakke, 438 U.S. 265, 387, 98 S.Ct. 2733, 2798, Mr. Justice Marshall recounted the tragic class-based discrimination against Negroes that is an indelible part of America's history. I assume that the wrong committed against the Negro class is both so serious and so pervasive that it would constitutionally justify an appropriate classwide recovery measured by a sum certain for every member of the injured class. Whether our resources are adequate to support a fair remedy of that character is a policy question I have neither the authority nor the wisdom to address. But that serious classwide wrong cannot in itself justify the particular classification Congress has made in this Act. Racial classifications are simply too pernicious to permit any but the most exact connection between justification and classification. Quite obviously, the history of discrimination against black citizens in America cannot justify a grant of privileges to Eskimos or Indians. . . .

At best, the statutory preference is a somewhat perverse form of reparation for the members of the injured classes. For those who are the most disadvantaged within each class are the least likely to receive any benefit from the special privilege even though they are the persons most likely still to be suffering the consequences of the past wrong. A random distribution to a favored few is a poor form of compensation for an injury shared by many.

My principal objection to the reparation justification for this legislation, however, cuts more deeply than my concern about its inequitable character. We can never either erase or ignore the history that Mr. Justice Marshall has recounted. But if that history can justify such a random distribution of benefits on racial lines as that embodied in this statutory scheme it will serve not merely as a basis for remedial legislation, but rather as a permanent source of justification for grants of special privileges. For if there is no duty to attempt either to measure the recovery by the wrong or to distribute that recovery within the injured class in an evenhanded way, our history will adequately support a legislative preference for almost any ethnic, religious, or racial group with the political strength to negotiate "a piece of the action" for its members.

Although I do not dispute the validity of the assumption that each of the subclasses identified in the Act has suffered a severe wrong at some time in the past, I cannot accept this slapdash statute as a legitimate method of providing classwide relief. . . .

Comments and Questions

1. Given the history of racial discrimination, how can blacks (or Hispanics or Native Americans) ever catch up with whites without some kind of compensatory programs? Some writers have drawn an analogy to a foot race: if certain runners are forced to carry heavy weights for the first half of the race, removing those weights in the middle of the race does not equalize the chances of all the runners. Notice that this problem is much more serious with respect to racial equality than with respect to gender or sexual preference equality. If we could end all discrimination, the problem of gender inequality would disappear within one generation; women now in the work force might never "catch up," but those entering the work force after gender discrimination had been eliminated would suffer no handicap. Racial inequality is more resistant to change because wealth and opportunity in this country are in large part dependent upon the family into which a child is born; the effects of the discrimination against a black person are passed on to his children. Should the law ignore this situation?

2. Japanese Americans were partially compensated for the property they lost because of the World War II evacuation from the West Coast. Justice Stevens says that monetary compensation to all blacks for prior discrimination would probably be constitutionally valid. Apparently he would agree that Native Americans could also be compensated for past injustices. Why have there been no proposals to offer lump-sum compensation to minorities other than the Japanese Americans? Justice Stevens's alternative would probably be more just than any affirmative action program, but is it disingenuous to argue that affirmative action programs should therefore be scrapped?

3. Some opponents of the MBE set-aside program and other racial quotas argue that they are counterproductive in that they sanction thinking in racial terms, while some proponents argue that the public can and should grasp the idea of redress of past injustices. Would an empirical investigation of white reactions to reverse discrimination be helpful to the courts? To the legislature? Do you think a public opinion poll would provide the information needed?

B.   Racial Equality as the Goal of the Public-Benefit Mode

The public-benefit instrumentality often indirectly promotes racial equality. Provision of public school education, for example, may benefit the poor more than the rich even when more educational dollars are spent on children from wealthy families than on children from poor families. This is because many wealthy parents would otherwise send their children to private schools, which poor parents could not afford to do. Because racial minorities are disproportionately poor, the public schools probably promote racial equality. Other governmental benefits programs, such as Aid to Families with Dependent Children, undoubtedly provide disproportionate benefits to poor racial minorities, thus increasing racial equality. This indirect promotion of racial equality is partly intentional and partly inadvertent; the motivation of individual legislators may vary widely.

The public-benefit mode can also be used more directly to promote racial equality. Affirmative action programs are one example of direct promotion of equality, and the statutory prohibition against racial discrimination in federally assisted programs is another. A third example is discussed in the following case.

––––––––

BOB JONES UNIVERSITY v. UNITED STATES

Supreme Court of the United States, 1983.
461 U.S. 574, 103 S.Ct. 2017.

Chief Justice Burger delivered the opinion of the Court.

We granted certiorari to decide whether petitioners, nonprofit private schools that prescribe and enforce racially discriminatory admissions standards on the basis of religious doctrine, qualify as tax-exempt organizations under § 501(c)(3) of the Internal Revenue Code of 1954.

Until 1970, the Internal Revenue Service granted tax-exempt status to private schools, without regard to their racial admissions policies, under § 501(c)(3) of the Internal Revenue Code, 26 U.S.C. § 501(c)(3), and granted charitable deductions for contributions to such schools under § 170 of the Code, 26 U.S.C. § 170.

On January 12, 1970, a three-judge District Court for the District of Columbia issued a preliminary injunction prohibiting the IRS from according tax-exempt status to private schools in Mississippi that discriminated as to admissions on the basis of race. Green v. Kennedy, 309 F.Supp. 1127 (D.D.C.), app. dismissed sub nom. Cannon v. Green, 398 U.S. 956, 90 S.Ct. 2169 (1970). Thereafter, in July 1970, the IRS concluded that it could "no longer legally justify allowing tax-exempt status [under § 501(c)(3)] to private schools which practice racial discrimination." IRS News Release (7/10/70). At the same time, the IRS announced that it could not "treat gifts to such schools as charitable deductions for income tax purposes [under § 170]." By letter dated November 30, 1970, the IRS formally notified private schools, including those involved in this case, of this change in policy, "applicable to all private schools in the United States at all levels of education."

On June 30, 1971, the three-judge District Court issued its opinion on the merits of the Mississippi challenge. Green v. Connally, 330 F.Supp. 1150 (D.D.C.), aff'd sub nom. Coit v. Green, 404 U.S. 997, 92 S.Ct. 564 (1971) (per curiam). That court approved the IRS' amended construction of the Tax Code. The court also held that racially discriminatory private schools were not entitled to exemption under § 501(c)(3) and that donors were not entitled to deductions for contributions to such schools under § 170. The court permanently enjoined the Commissioner of Internal Revenue from approving tax-exempt status for any school in Mississippi that did not publicly maintain a policy of nondiscrimination.

The revised policy on discrimination was formalized in Revenue Ruling 71-447, 1971-2 Cum.Bull. 230:

> Both the courts and the Internal Revenue Service have long recognized that the statutory requirement of being "organized and operated exclusively for religious, charitable, . . . or educational purposes" was intended to express the basic common law concept [of "charity"]. . . . All charitable trusts, educational or otherwise, are subject to the requirement that the purpose of the trust may not be illegal or contrary to public policy. (Id., at 230.)

Based on the "national policy to discourage racial discrimination in education," the IRS ruled that "a private school not having a racially nondiscriminatory policy as to students is not 'charitable' within the common law concepts reflected in sections 170 and 501(c)(3) of the Code." Id., at 231.

The application of the IRS construction of these provisions to petitioners, two private schools with racially discriminatory admissions policies, is now before us.

No. 81–3, *Bob Jones University* v. *United States*

Bob Jones University is a nonprofit corporation located in Greenville, South Carolina. Its purpose is "to conduct an institution of learning . . . , giving special emphasis to the Christian religion and the ethics revealed in the Holy Scriptures." Certificate of Incorporation, Bob Jones University, Inc., of Greenville, S.C. The corporation operates a school with an enrollment of approximately 5,000 students, from kindergarten through college and graduate school. Bob Jones University is not affiliated with any religious denomination, but is dedicated to the teaching and propagation of its fundamentalist Christian religious beliefs. It is both a religious and educational institution. Its teachers are required to be devout Christians, and all courses at the University are taught according to the Bible. Entering students are screened as to their religious beliefs, and their public and private conduct is strictly regulated by standards promulgated by University authorities.

The sponsors of the University genuinely believe that the Bible forbids interracial dating and marriage. To effectuate these views, Negroes were completely excluded until 1971. From 1971 to May 1975, the University accepted no applications from unmarried Negroes, but did accept applications from Negroes married within their race.

Following the decision of the United States Court of Appeals for the Fourth Circuit in McCrary v. Runyon, 515 F.2d 1082 (CA4 1975), aff'd 427 U.S. 160, 96 S.Ct. 2586 (1976), prohibiting racial exclusion from private schools, the University revised its policy. Since May 29, 1975, the University has permitted unmarried Negroes to enroll; but a disciplinary rule prohibits interracial dating and marriage. That rule reads:

There is to be no interracial dating

    1. Students who are partners in an interracial marriage will be expelled.

    2. Students who are members of or affiliated with any group or organization which holds as one of its goals or advocates interracial marriage will be expelled.

    3. Students who date outside their own race will be expelled.

    4. Students who espouse, promote, or encourage others to violate the University's dating rules and regulations will be expelled.

The University continues to deny admission to applicants engaged in an interracial marriage or known to advocate interracial marriage or dating.

    Until 1970, the IRS extended tax-exempt status to Bob Jones University under § 501(c)(3). By the letter of November 30, 1970, that followed the injunction issued in Green v. Kennedy, supra, the IRS formally notified the University of the change in IRS policy, and announced its intention to challenge the tax-exempt status of private schools practicing racial discrimination in their admissions policies. . . .

No. 81–1, *Goldsboro Christian Schools, Inc.* v. *United States*

    Goldsboro Christian Schools is a nonprofit corporation located in Goldsboro, North Carolina. Like Bob Jones University, it was established "to conduct an institution of learning . . . , giving special emphasis to the Christian religion and the ethics revealed in the Holy scriptures." Articles of Incorporation, ¶ 3(a). The school offers classes from kindergarten through high school, and since at least 1969 has satisfied the State of North Carolina's requirements for secular education in private schools. The school requires its high school students to take Bible-related courses, and begins each class with prayer.

    Since its incorporation in 1963, Goldsboro Christian Schools has maintained a racially discriminatory admissions policy based upon its interpretation of the Bible. Goldsboro has for the most part accepted only Caucasians. On occasion, however, the school has accepted children from racially mixed marriages in which one of the parents is Caucasian.

    Goldsboro never received a determination by the IRS that it was an organization entitled to tax exemption under § 501(c)(3). Upon audit of Goldsboro's records for the years 1969 through 1972, the IRS determined that Goldsboro was not an organization described in § 501(c)(3), and therefore was required to pay taxes under the Federal Insurance Contribution Act and the Federal Unemployment Tax Act. . . .

    [The government prevailed in the courts below.]

    In Revenue Ruling 71-447, the IRS formalized the policy first announced in 1970, that § 170 and § 501(c)(3) embrace the common law "charity" concept. Under that view, to qualify for a tax exemption pursuant to § 501(c)(3), an institution must show, first, that it falls within one of the eight categories expressly set forth in that section, and second, that its activity is not contrary to settled public policy.

Section 501(c)(3) provides that "[c]orporations . . . organized and operated exclusively for religious, charitable . . . or educational purposes" are entitled to tax exemption. Petitioners argue that the plain language of the statute guarantees them tax-exempt status. They emphasize the absence of any language in the statute expressly requiring all exempt organizations to be "charitable" in the common law sense, and they contend that the disjunctive "or" separating the categories in § 501(c)(3) precludes such a reading. Instead, they argue that if an institution falls within one or more of the specified categories it is automatically entitled to exemption, without regard to whether it also qualifies as "charitable." The Court of Appeals rejected that contention and concluded that petitioners' interpretation of the statute "tears section 501(c)(3) from its roots."

It is a well-established canon of statutory construction that a court should go beyond the literal language of a statute if reliance on that language would defeat the plain purpose of the statute:

> The general words used in the clause . . . , taken by themselves, and literally construed, without regard to the object in view, would seem to sanction the claim of the plaintiff. But this mode of expounding a statute has never been adopted by any enlightened tribunal—because it is evident that in many cases it would defeat the object which the Legislature intended to accomplish. And it is well settled that, in interpreting a statute, the court will not look merely to a particular clause in which general words may be used, *but will take in connection with it the whole statute . . . and the objects and policy of the law . . . .* (Brown v. Duchesne, 19 How. 183, 194 (1857) (emphasis added).)

Section 501(c)(3) therefore must be analyzed and construed within the framework of the Internal Revenue Code and against the background of the Congressional purposes. Such an examination reveals unmistakable evidence that, underlying all relevant parts of the Code, is the intent that entitlement to tax exemption depends on meeting certain common law standards of charity—namely, that an institution seeking tax-exempt status must serve a public purpose and not be contrary to established public policy. . . .

When the Government grants exemptions or allows deductions all taxpayers are affected; the very fact of the exemption or deduction for the donor means that other taxpayers can be said to be indirect and vicarious "donors." Charitable exemptions are justified on the basis that the exempt entity confers a public benefit—a benefit which the society or the community may not itself choose or be able to provide, or which supplements and advances the work of public institutions already supported by tax revenues. History buttresses logic to make clear that, to warrant exemption under § 501(c)(3), an institution must fall within a category specified in that section and must demonstrably serve and be in harmony with the public interest. The institution's purpose must not be so at odds with the common community conscience as to undermine any public benefit that might otherwise be conferred.

We are bound to approach these questions with full awareness that determinations of public benefit and public policy are sensitive matters with serious implications for the institutions affected; a declaration that a given institution is not "charitable" should be made only where there can be no doubt that the activity involved is contrary to a fundamental public policy. But there can no longer be any doubt that racial discrimination in education violates deeply and widely accepted views of elementary justice. Prior to 1954, public education in many places still was conducted under the pall of Plessy v. Ferguson, 163 U.S. 537, 16 S.Ct. 1138 (1896); racial segregation in primary and secondary education prevailed in many parts of the country. See, e.g., Segregation and the Fourteenth Amendment in the States (B. Reams & P. Wilson, eds. 1975). This Court's decision in Brown v. Board of Education, 347 U.S. 483, 74 S.Ct. 686 (1954), signalled an end to that era. Over the past quarter of a century, every pronouncement of this Court and myriad Acts of Congress and Executive Orders attest a firm national policy to prohibit racial segregation and discrimination in public education. . . .

Few social or political issues in our history have been more vigorously debated and more extensively ventilated than the issue of racial discrimination, particularly in education. Given the stress and anguish of the history of efforts to escape from the shackles of the "separate but equal" doctrine of Plessy v. Ferguson, supra, it cannot be said that educational institutions that, for whatever reasons, practice racial discrimination, are institutions exercising "beneficial and stabilizing influences in community life," Walz v. Tax Comm'n, 397 U.S. 664, 673, 90 S.Ct. 1409, 1413 (1970), or should be encouraged by having all taxpayers share in their support by way of special tax status.

There can thus be no question that the interpretation of § 170 and § 501(c)(3) announced by the IRS in 1970 was correct. That it may be seen as belated does not undermine its soundness. . . . Whatever may be the rationale for such private schools' policies, and however sincere the rationale may be, racial discrimination in education is contrary to public policy. Racially discriminatory educational institutions cannot be viewed as conferring a public benefit within the "charitable" concept discussed earlier, or within the Congressional intent underlying § 170 and § 501(c)(3). . . .

Petitioners contend that, even if the Commissioner's policy is valid as to nonreligious private schools, that policy cannot constitutionally be applied to schools that engage in racial discrimination on the basis of sincerely held religious beliefs. As to such schools, it is argued that the IRS construction of § 170 and § 501(c)(3) violates their free exercise rights under the Religion Clauses of the First Amendment. This contention presents claims not heretofore considered by this Court in precisely this context.

This Court has long held the Free Exercise Clause of the First Amendment an absolute prohibition against governmental regulation of religious beliefs, Wisconsin v. Yoder, 406 U.S. 205, 219, 92 S.Ct. 1526, 1535 (1972); Sherbert v. Verner, 374 U.S. 398, 402, 83 S.Ct. 1790, 1793 (1963); Cantwell v. Connecticut, 310 U.S. 296, 303, 60 S.Ct. 900, 903 (1940). As interpreted by this Court, moreover, the Free Exercise Clause provides substantial protection for lawful conduct grounded in religious belief, see Wisconsin v. Yoder, supra, 406 U.S., at 220, 92 S.Ct., at 1535; Thomas v. Review Board of the Indiana Emp. Security Div., 450 U.S. 707, 101 S.Ct. 1425 (1981); Sherbert v. Verner, supra, 374 U.S., at 402–403, 83 S.Ct., at 1793. However, "[n]ot all burdens on religion are unconstitutional. . . . The state may justify a limitation on religious liberty by showing that it is essential to accomplish an overriding governmental interest." United States v. Lee, 455 U.S. 252, 257–258, 102 S.Ct. 1051, 1055 (1982) (citations omitted). See, e.g., McDaniel v. Paty, 435 U.S. 618, 628, 98 S.Ct. 1322, 1328 and n. 8 (1978); Wisconsin v. Yoder, supra, 406 U.S., at 215, 92 S.Ct., at 1533; Gillette v. United States, 401 U.S. 437, 91 S.Ct. 828 (1971).

On occasion this Court has found certain governmental interests so compelling as to allow even regulations prohibiting religiously based conduct. In Prince v. Massachusetts, 321 U.S. 158, 64 S.Ct. 438 (1944), for example, the Court held that neutrally cast child labor laws prohibiting sale of printed materials on public streets could be applied to prohibit children from dispensing religious literature. The Court found no constitutional infirmity in "excluding [Jehovah's Witness children] from doing there what no other children may do." Id., at 170, 64 S.Ct., at 444. See also Reynolds v. United States, 98 U.S. 145 (1878); United States v. Lee, supra; Gillette v. United States, supra. Denial of tax benefits will inevitably have a substantial impact on the operation of private religious schools, but will not prevent those schools from observing their religious tenets.

The governmental interest at stake here is compelling. . . . [T]he Government has a fundamental, overriding interest in eradicating racial discrimination in education—discrimination that prevailed, with official approval, for the first 165 years of this Nation's history. That governmental interest substantially outweighs whatever burden denial of tax benefits places on petitioners' exercise of their religious beliefs. The interests asserted by petitioners cannot be accommodated with that compelling governmental interest, see United States v. Lee, supra, 455 U.S., at 259–260, 102 S.Ct., at 1056; and no "less restrictive means," see Thomas v. Review Board, supra, 450 U.S., at 718, 101 S.Ct., at 1432, are available to achieve the governmental interest.

The remaining issue is whether the IRS properly applied its policy to these petitioners. Petitioner Goldsboro Christian Schools admits that it "maintain[s] racially discriminatory policies," Brief of Petitioner, Goldsboro Christian Schools, No. 81-1, at 10, but seeks to justify those policies on grounds we have fully discussed. The IRS properly denied tax-exempt status to Goldsboro Christian Schools.

Petitioner Bob Jones University, however, contends that it is not racially discriminatory. It emphasizes that it now allows all races to enroll, subject only to its restrictions on the conduct of all students, including its prohibitions of association between men and women of different races, and of interracial marriage. Although a ban on intermarriage or interracial dating applies to all races, decisions of this Court firmly establish that discrimination on the basis of racial affiliation and association is a form of racial discrimination, see, e.g., Loving v. Virginia, 388 U.S. 1, 87 S.Ct. 1817 (1967); McLaughlin v. Florida, 379 U.S. 184, 85 S.Ct. 283 (1964); Tillman v. Wheaton-Haven Recreation Ass'n, 410 U.S. 431, 93 S.Ct. 1090 (1973). We therefore find that the IRS properly applied Revenue Ruling 71-447 to Bob Jones University.

The judgments of the Court of Appeals are, accordingly,

Affirmed.

[Justice Powell, in a separate opinion, concurred in the judgment.]

JUSTICE REHNQUIST, dissenting.

The Court points out that there is a strong national policy in this country against racial discrimination. To the extent that the Court states that Congress in furtherance of this policy could deny tax-exempt status to educational institutions that promote racial discrimination, I readily agree. But, unlike the Court, I am convinced that Congress simply has failed to take this action and, as this Court has said over and over again, regardless of our view on the propriety of Congress' failure to legislate we are not constitutionally empowered to act for them.

In approaching this statutory construction question the Court quite adeptly avoids the statute it is construing. This I am sure is no accident, for there is nothing in the language of § 501(c)(3) that supports the result obtained by the Court. Section 501(c)(3) provides tax-exempt status for:

> Corporations, and any community chest, fund, or foundation, organized and operated exclusively for religious, charitable, scientific, testing for public safety, literary, or educational purposes, or to foster national or international amateur sports competition (but only if no part of its activities involve the provision of athletic facilities or equipment), or for the prevention of cruelty to children or animals, no part of the net earnings of which inures to the benefit of any private shareholder or individual, no substantial part of the activities of which is carrying on propaganda, or otherwise attempting, to influence legislation (except as otherwise provided in subsection (h)), and which does not participate in, or intervene in (including the publishing or distributing of statements), any political campaign on behalf of any candidate for public office.

With undeniable clarity, Congress has explicitly defined the requirements for § 501(c)(3) status. An entity must be (1) a corporation, or community chest, fund, or foundation, (2) organized for one of the eight enumerated purposes, (3) operated on a nonprofit basis, and (4) free from involvement in lobbying activities and political campaigns. Nowhere is there to be found some additional, undefined public policy requirement. . . .

Comments and Questions

1. Religious tolerance is certainly an important and long-standing goal of our society, as is witnessed by the establishment and free exercise clauses of the First

Amendment. Nevertheless, it seems unlikely that tax-exempt status would be denied to a college that prohibited interfaith marriages. Would it be wise to extend the holding of *Bob Jones* to promote other kinds of equality? Why?

2. Is there something unique about racial discrimination?

Section Seven. Bibliography

D. Bell, Race, Racism, and American Law (2d ed. 1980); T. Eisenberg, Civil Rights Legislation (1981); G. Gunther, Constitutional Law (11th ed. 1985); W. Lockhart, Y. Kamisar & J. Choper, Constitutional Law: Cases—Comments—Questions (5th ed. 1980); Brest, The Supreme Court, 1975 Term—Foreword: In Defense of the Antidiscrimination Principle, 90 Harv.L.Rev. 1 (1976); Ely, The Constitutionality of Reverse Racial Discrimination, 41 U.Chi.L.Rev. 723 (1974); Fiss, School Desegregation: The Uncertain Path of the Law, 4 Phil. & Pub.Aff. 3 (1974); Kaplan, Equal Justice in an Unequal World: Equality for the Negro—The Problem of Special Treatment, 61 Nw.U.L.Rev. 363 (1966); Perry, The Disproportionate Impact Theory of Racial Discrimination, 125 U.Pa.L.Rev. 540 (1977); Rostow, The Japanese American Case—A Disaster, 54 Yale L.J. 489 (1945).

The Constitution of the United States of America

We the people of the United States, in order to form a more perfect Union, establish Justice, insure domestic Tranquility, provide for the common defense, promote the general Welfare, and secure the Blessing of Liberty to ourselves and our Posterity, do ordain and establish this constitution for the United States of America.

ARTICLE I

Section 1. All legislative Powers herein granted shall be vested in a Congress of the United States, which shall consist of a Senate and House of Representatives.

Section 2. The House of Representatives shall be composed of Members chosen every second Year by the People of the several States, and the Electors in each State shall have the Qualifications requisite for Electors of the most numerous Branch of the State Legislature.

No Person shall be a Representative who shall not have attained to the Age of twenty-five Years, and been seven Years a Citizen of the United States, and who shall not, when elected, be an Inhabitant of that State in which he shall be chosen.

Representatives and direct Taxes shall be apportioned among the several States which may be included within this Union, according to their respective Numbers, which shall be determined by adding to the whole Number of free Persons, including those bound to Service for a Term of Years, and excluding Indians not taxed, three fifths of all other persons.[a] The actual Enumeration shall be made within three Years after the first Meeting of the Congress of the United States, and within every subsequent Term of ten Years, in such Manner as they shall by Law direct. The Number of Representatives shall not exceed one for every thirty thousand, but each State shall have at Least one Representative; and until such enumeration shall be made, the State of New Hampshire shall be entitled to chuse three, Massachusetts eight, Rhode Island and Providence Plantations one, Connecticut five, New York six, New Jersey four, Pennsylvania eight, Delaware one, Maryland six, Virginia ten, North Carolina five, South Carolina five, and Georgia three.

a. This provision was modified by the Sixteenth Amendment. The three-fifths reference to slaves was rendered obsolete by the Thirteenth and Fourteenth Amendments.

When vacancies happen in the Representation from any State, the Executive Authority thereof shall issue Writs of Election to fill such Vacancies.

The House of Representatives shall chuse their Speaker and other Officers; and shall have the sole Power of Impeachment.

Section 3. The Senate of the United States shall be composed of two Senators from each State, chosen by the Legislature thereof,[b] for six Years; and each Senator shall have one Vote.

Immediately after they shall be assembled in Consequence of the first Election, they shall be divided as equally as may be into three Classes. The Seats of the Senators of the first Class shall be vacated at the Expiration of the second Year, of the second Class at the Expiration of the fourth Year, and of the third Class at the Expiration of the sixth Year, so that one-third may be chosen every second Year; and if Vacancies happen by Resignation, or otherwise, during the Recess of the Legislature of any State, the Executive thereof may make temporary Appointments until the next Meeting of the Legislature, which shall then fill such Vacancies.

No Person shall be a Senator who shall not have attained to the Age of thirty Years, and been nine Years a Citizen of the United States, and who shall not, when elected, be an Inhabitant of that State for which he shall be chosen.

The Vice-President of the United States shall be President of the Senate, but shall have no Vote, unless they be equally divided.

The Senate shall chuse their other Officers, and also a President pro tempore, in the absence of the Vice-President, or when he shall exercise the Office of President of the United States.

The Senate shall have the sole Power to try all Impeachments. When sitting for that Purpose, they shall be on Oath or Affirmation. When the President of the United States is tried, the Chief Justice shall preside; And no Person shall be convicted without the Concurrence of two thirds of the Members present.

Judgment in Cases of Impeachment shall not extend further than to removal from Office, and disqualification to hold and enjoy any Office of honor, Trust or Profit under the United States; but the Party convicted shall nevertheless be liable and subject to Indictment, Trial, Judgment and Punishment, according to Law.

Section 4. The Times, Places and Manner of holding Elections for Senators and Representatives, shall be prescribed in each State by the Legislature thereof; but the Congress may at any time by Law make or alter such Regulations, except as to the Places of chusing Senators.

The Congress shall assemble at least once in every Year, and such Meeting shall be on the first Monday in December, unless they shall by Law appoint a different Day.[c]

Section 5. Each House shall be the Judge of the Elections, Returns and Qualifications of its own Members, and a Majority of each shall constitute a Quorum to do Business; but a smaller Number may adjourn from day to day, and may be authorized to compel the Attendance of

b. See the Seventeenth Amendment.
c. See the Twentieth Amendment.

absent Members, in such Manner, and under such Penalties as each House may provide.

Each House may determine the Rules of its Proceedings, punish its Members for disorderly Behavior, and, with the Concurrence of two thirds, expel a Member.

Each House shall keep a Journal of its Proceedings and from time to time publish the same, excepting such Parts as may in their Judgment require Secrecy; and the Yeas and Nays of the Members of either House on any question shall, at the Desire of one fifth of those Present, be entered on the Journal.

Neither House, during the Session of Congress, shall without the Consent of the other, adjourn for more than three days, nor to any other Place than that in which the two Houses shall be sitting.

Section 6. The Senators and Representatives shall receive a Compensation for their Services, to be ascertained by Law, and paid out of the Treasury of the United States. They shall in all Cases, except Treason, Felony, and Breach of the peace, be privileged from Arrest during their Attendance at the Session of their respective Houses, and in going to and returning from the same; and for any Speech or Debate in either House, they shall not be questioned in any other Place.

No Senator or Representative shall, during the Time for which he was elected, be appointed to any civil Office under the Authority of the United States, which shall have been created, or the Emoluments whereof shall have been encreased during such time; and no Person holding any Office under the United States, shall be a Member of either House during his Continuance in Office.

Section 7. All Bills for raising Revenue shall originate in the House of Representatives; but the Senate may propose or concur with Amendments as on other Bills.

Every Bill which shall have passed the House of Representatives and the Senate, shall, before it becomes a Law, be presented to the President of the United States; If he approve he shall sign it, but if not he shall return it, with his Objections to that House in which it shall have originated, who shall enter the Objections at large on their Journal, and proceed to reconsider it. If after such Reconsideration two thirds of that House shall agree to pass the Bill it shall be sent, together with the Objections, to the other House, by which it shall likewise be reconsidered, and if approved by two thirds of that House, it shall become a Law. But in all such Cases the Votes of both Houses shall be determined by Yeas and Nays, and the Names of the Persons voting for and against the Bill shall be entered on the Journal of each House respectively. If any Bill shall not be returned by the President within ten Days (Sundays excepted) after it shall have been presented to him, the Same shall be a Law, in like Manner as if he had signed it, unless the Congress by their Adjournment prevent its Return, in which Case it shall not be a Law.

Every Order, Resolution, or Vote to which the Concurrence of the Senate and House of Representatives may be necessary (except on a question of Adjournment) shall be presented to the President of the United States: and before the Same shall take Effect, shall be approved by him, or being disapproved by him, shall be repassed by two thirds of the Senate and House of Representatives, according to the Rules and Limitations prescribed in the Case of a Bill.

Section 8. The Congress shall have Power To lay and collect Taxes, Duties, Imposts and Excises, to pay the Debts and provide for the common Defence and general Welfare of the United States; but all Duties, Imposts and Excises shall be uniform throughout the United States;

To borrow money on the Credit of the United States;

To regulate Commerce with foreign Nations, and among the several States, and with the Indian Tribes;

To establish an uniform Rule of Naturalization, and uniform Laws on the subject of Bankruptcies throughout the United States;

To coin Money, regulate the Value thereof, and of foreign Coin, and fix the Standard of Weights and Measures;

To provide for the Punishment of counterfeiting the Securities and current Coin of the United States;

To establish Post Officers and post Roads;

To promote the Progress of Science and useful arts, by securing for limited Times to Authors and Inventors the exclusive Right to their respective Writings and Discoveries;

To constitute Tribunals inferior to the supreme Court;

To define and punish Piracies and Felonies committed on the high Seas, and Offenses against the Law of Nations;

To declare War, grant Letters of Marque and Reprisal, and make Rules concerning Captures on Land and Water;

To raise and support Armies, but no Appropriation of Money to that Use shall be for a longer Term than two Years;

To provide and maintain a Navy;

To make Rules for the Government and Regulation of the land and naval Forces;

To provide for calling forth the Militia to execute the Laws of the Union, suppress Insurrections and repel Invasions;

To provide for organizing, arming, and disciplining the Militia, and for governing such Part of them as may be employed in the Service of the United States, reserving to the States respectively, the Appointment of the Officers, and the Authority of training the Militia according to the discipline prescribed by Congress;

To exercise exclusive Legislation in all Cases whatsoever, over such District (not exceeding ten Miles square) as may, by Cession of particular States, and the acceptance of Congress, become the Seat of the Government of the United States, and to exercise like Authority over all Places purchased by the Consent of the Legislature of the State in which the Same shall be, for the Erection of Forts, Magazines, Arsenals, dock-Yards, and other needful Buildings;—And

To make all Laws which shall be necessary and proper for carrying into Execution the foregoing Powers, and all other Powers vested by this Constitution in the Government of the United States, or in any Department or Officer thereof.

Section 9. The Migration or Importation of such Persons as any of the States now existing shall think proper to admit, shall not be prohibited by the Congress prior to the Year one thousand eight hundred and eight, but a tax or duty may be imposed on such Importation, not exceeding ten dollars for each Person.

The privilege of the Writ of Habeas Corpus shall not be suspended, unless when in Cases of Rebellion or Invasion the public Safety may require it.

No Bill of Attainder or ex post facto Law shall be passed.

No capitation, or other direct Tax shall be laid, unless in Proportion to the Census or Enumeration herein before directed to be taken.[d]

No Tax or Duty shall be laid on Articles exported from any State.

No Preference shall be given by any Regulation of Commerce or Revenue to the Ports of one State over those of another: nor shall Vessels bound to, or from one State, be obliged to enter, clear, or pay Duties in another.

No Money shall be drawn from the Treasury, but in Consequence of Appropriations made by Law; and a regular Statement and Account of the Receipts and Expenditures of all public Money shall be published from time to time.

No Title of Nobility shall be granted by the United States: And no Person holding any Office of Profit or Trust under them, shall, without the Consent of the Congress, accept of any present, Emolument, Office, or Title, of any kind whatever, from any King, Prince, or foreign State.

Section 10. No State shall enter into any Treaty, Alliance, or Confederation; grant Letters of Marque and Reprisal; coin Money; emit Bills of Credit; make any Thing but gold and silver Coin a Tender in Payment of Debts; pass any Bill of Attainder, ex post facto Law, or Law impairing the Obligation of Contracts, or grant any Title of Nobility.

No State shall, without the Consent of the Congress, lay any Imposts or Duties on Imports or Exports, except what may be absolutely necessary for executing its inspection Laws: and the net Produce of all Duties and Imposts, laid by any State on Imports or Exports, shall be for the Use of the Treasury of the United States and all such Laws shall be subject to the Revision and Control of the Congress.

No State shall, without the Consent of Congress, lay any duty of Tonnage, keep Troops, or Ships of War in time of Peace, enter into any Agreement or Compact with another State, or with a foreign Power, or engage in War, unless actually invaded, or in such imminent Danger as will not admit of delay.

ARTICLE II

Section 1. The executive Power shall be vested in a President of the United States of America. He shall hold his Office during the Term of four Years, and, together with the Vice-President, chosen for the same Term, be elected, as follows.

Each State shall appoint, in such Manner as the Legislature thereof may direct, a Number of Electors, equal to the whole number of Senators

d. See the Sixteenth Amendment.

and Representatives to which the State may be entitled in the Congress; but no Senator or Representative, or Person holding an Office of Trust or Profit under the United States, shall be appointed an Elector.

The Electors shall meet in their respective States, and vote by Ballot for two persons, of whom one at least shall not be an Inhabitant of the same State with themselves. And they shall make a List of all the Persons voted for, and of the Number of Votes for each; which List they shall sign and certify, and transmit sealed to the Seat of the Government of the United States, directed to the President of the Senate. The President of the Senate shall, in the Presence of the Senate and House of Representatives, open all the Certificates, and the Votes shall then be counted. The Person having the greatest Number of Votes shall be the President, if such Number be a Majority of the whole Number of Electors appointed; and if there be more than one who have such Majority, and have an Equal Number of Votes, then the House of Representatives shall immediately chuse by Ballot one of them for President; and if no Person have a Majority, then from the five highest on the List the said House shall in like Manner chuse the President, but in chusing the President, the Votes shall be taken by States, the Representation from each State having one Vote; A quorum for this Purpose shall consist of a Member or Members from two-thirds of the States, and a Majority of all the States shall be necessary to a Choice. In every Case, after the Choice of the President, the Person having the greatest Number of Votes of the Electors shall be the Vice-President. But if there should remain two or more who have equal Votes, the Senate shall chuse from them by Ballot the Vice-President.[e]

The Congress may determine the Time of chusing the Electors, and the Day on which they shall give their Vote; which Day shall be the same throughout the United States.

No person except a natural born Citizen, or a Citizen of the United States, at the time of the Adoption of this Constitution, shall be eligible to the Office of President; neither shall any Person be eligible to that Office who shall not have attained to the Age of thirty-five Years, and been fourteen Years a Resident within the United States.

In Case of the Removal of the President from Office, or of his Death, Resignation, or Inability to discharge the Powers and Duties of the said office, the same devolve on the Vice-President,[f] and the Congress may by Law provide for the Case of Removal, Death, Resignation or Inability, both of the President and Vice-President, declaring what Officer shall then act as President, and such Officer shall act accordingly, until the Disability be removed, or a President shall be elected.

The President shall, at stated Times, receive for his Services, a Compensation, which shall neither be encreased nor diminished during the Period for which he shall have been elected, and he shall not receive within that Period any other Emolument from the United States, or any of them.

e. This paragraph was superseded by the Twelfth Amendment.
f. See the Twenty-fifth Amendment.

Before he enter on the Execution of his Office, he shall take the following Oath or Affirmation:—"I do solemnly swear (or affirm) that I will faithfully execute the Office of President of the United States, and will to the best of my Ability, preserve, protect and defend the Constitution of the United States."

Section 2. The President shall be Commander in Chief of the Army and Navy of the United States, and of the Militia of the several States, when called into the actual Service of the United States; he may require the Opinion in writing, of the principal Officer in each of the executive Departments, upon any subject relating to the Duties of their respective Offices, and he shall have Power to Grant Reprieves and Pardons for Offenses against the United States, except in Cases of Impeachment.

He shall have Power, by and with the Advice and Consent of the Senate, to make Treaties, provided two-thirds of the Senators present concur; and he shall nominate, and by and with the Advice and Consent of the Senate, shall appoint Ambassadors, other public Ministers and Consuls, Judges of the supreme Court, and all other Officers of the United States, whose Appointments are not herein otherwise provided for, and which shall be established by Law: but the Congress may by Law vest the Appointment of such inferior Officers, as they think proper, in the President alone, in the Courts of Law, or in the Heads of Departments.

The President shall have Power to fill up all Vacancies that may happen during the Recess of the Senate by granting Commissions which shall expire at the End of their next Session.

Section 3. He shall from time to time give to the Congress Information of the State of the Union, and recommend to their Consideration such Measures as he shall judge necessary and expedient; he may, on extraordinary Occasions, convene both Houses, or either of them, and in Cases of Disagreement between them, with Respect to the Time of Adjournment, he may adjourn them to such Time as he shall think proper; he shall receive Ambassadors and other public Ministers; he shall take Care that the Laws be faithfully executed, and shall Commission all the Officers of the United States.

Section 4. The President, Vice-President and all civil Officers of the United States, shall be removed from Office on Impeachment for, and conviction of, Treason, Bribery, or other high Crimes and Misdemeanors.

ARTICLE III

Section 1. The judicial Power of the United States shall be vested in one supreme Court, and in such inferior Courts as the Congress may from time to time ordain and establish. The Judges, both of the supreme and inferior Courts, shall hold their offices during good Behaviour, and shall, at stated Times, receive for their Services a Compensation which shall not be diminished during their Continuance in Office.

Section 2. The judicial Power shall extend to all Cases, in Law and Equity, arising under this Constitution, the Laws of the United States and Treaties made, or which shall be made, under their Authority;—to all Cases affecting Ambassadors, other public Ministers and Consuls;—to all Cases of admiralty and maritime Jurisdiction;—to Controversies to which the United States shall be a Party;—to Controversies between two or more States;—between a State and Citizens of another State;—Between Citizens of different States;—between Citizens of the same State claiming Lands under Grants of different States, and between a State, or the Citizens thereof, and foreign States, Citizens or Subjects.[g]

In all Cases affecting Ambassadors, other public Ministers and Consuls, and those in which a State shall be Party, the supreme Court shall have original Jurisdiction. In all the other Cases before mentioned, the supreme Court shall have appellate Jurisdiction, both as to Law and Fact, with such Exceptions, and under such Regulations as the Congress shall make.

The trial of all Crimes, except in Cases of Impeachment, shall be by Jury, and such Trial shall be held in the State where the said Crimes shall have been committed; but when not committed within any State, the Trial shall be at such Place or Places as the Congress may by Law have directed.

Section 3. Treason against the United States, shall consist only in levying War against them, or in adhering to their Enemies, giving them Aid and Comfort. No Person shall be convicted of Treason unless on the Testimony of two Witnesses to the same overt Act, or on Confession in open Court.

The Congress shall have power to declare the Punishment of Treason, but no Attainder of Treason shall work Corruption of Blood, or Forfeiture except during the Life of the Person attainted.

ARTICLE IV

Section 1. Full Faith and Credit shall be given in each State to the public acts, Records, and judicial Proceedings of every other State. And the Congress may by general Laws prescribe the Manner in which such Acts, Records and Proceedings shall be proved, and the Effect thereof.

Section 2. The Citizens of each State shall be entitled to all Privileges and Immunities of Citizens in the several States.

A Person charged in any State with Treason, Felony, or other Crime, who shall flee from Justice, and be found in another State, shall on demand of the executive Authority of the State from which he fled, be delivered up, to be removed to the State having Jurisdiction of the Crime.

No Person held to Service or Labour in one State, under the Laws thereof, escaping into another, shall in Consequence of any Law or Regulation therein, be discharged from such Service or Labour, but shall be delivered up on Claim of the Party to whom such Service or Labour may be due.[h]

Section 3. New States may be admitted by the Congress into this Union; but no new States shall be formed or erected within the Jurisdiction of any other State; nor any State be formed by the Junction of two or more States, or parts of States, without the Consent of the Legislatures of the States concerned as well as of the Congress.

g. See the Eleventh Amendment.
h. This provision was rendered obsolete by the Thirteenth Amendment.

The Congress shall have Power to dispose of and make all needful Rules and Regulations respecting the Territory or other Property belonging to the United States; and nothing in this Constitution shall be so constructed as to Prejudice any Claims of the United States, or of any particular State.

Section 4. The United States shall guarantee to every State in this Union a Republican Form of Government, and shall protect each of them against Invasion; and on Application of the Legislature, or of the Executive (when the Legislature cannot be convened) against domestic Violence.

ARTICLE V

The Congress whenever two-thirds of both Houses shall deem it necessary, shall propose Amendments to this Constitution, or, on the Application of the Legislatures of two-thirds of the several States, shall call a Convention for proposing Amendments, which, in either Case, shall be valid to all Intents and Purposes, as part of this Constitution, when ratified by the Legislatures of three-fourths of the several States, or by Conventions in three-fourths thereof, as the one or the other Mode of Ratification may be proposed by the Congress; Provided that no Amendment which may be made prior to the Year One thousand eight hundred and eight shall in any Manner affect the first and fourth Clauses in the Ninth Section of the first Article; and that no State, without its Consent, shall be deprived of its equal Suffrage in the Senate.

ARTICLE VI

All Debts contracted and Engagements entered into, before the Adoption of this Constitution, shall be as valid against the United States under this Constitution, as under the Confederation.

This Constitution, and the Laws of the United States which shall be made in Pursuance thereof; and all Treaties made, or which shall be made, under the Authority of the United States, shall be the supreme Law of the Land; and the Judges in every State shall be bound thereby, any Thing in the Constitution or Laws of any State to the Contrary notwithstanding.

The Senators and Representatives before mentioned, and the Members of the several State Legislatures, and all executive and judicial Officers, both of the United States and of the several States, shall be bound by Oath or Affirmation, to support this Constitution; but no religious Test shall ever be required as a Qualification to any Office or public Trust under the United States.

ARTICLE VII

The Ratification of the Conventions of nine States shall be sufficient for the Establishment of this Constitution between the States so ratifying the Same.

Done in Convention by the Unanimous Consent of the States Present the Seventeenth Day of September in the Year of our Lord one thousand seven hundred and Eighty seven and of the Independence of the United

States of America the Twelfth. In Witness whereof We have hereunto subscribed our Names.

Go. WASHINGTON
Presid't and deputy from Virginia

Delaware

Geo: Read
John Dickinson
Jaco: Broom
Gunning Bedford jun
Richard Bassett

Maryland

James McHenry
Danl Carroll
Dan: of St. Thos Jenifer

South Carolina

J. Rutledge
Charles Pinckney
Charles Cotesworth Pinckney
Pierce Butler

Georgia

William Few
Abr Baldwin

New York

Alexander Hamilton

New Jersey

Wil: Livingston
David Brearley
Wm. Patterson
Jona: Dayton

New Hampshire

John Langdon
Nicholas Gilman

Massachusetts

Nathaniel Gorham
Rufus King

Connecticut

Wm Saml Johnson
Roger Sherman

Virginia

John Blair
James Madison, Jr.

North Carolina

Wm Blount
Hu Williamson
Richd Dobbs Spaight

Pennsylvania

B. Franklin
Robt. Morris
Thos. Fitzsimons
James Wilson
Thomas Mifflin
Geo. Clymer
Jared Ingersoll
Gouv Morris

Attest:

WILLIAM JACKSON, Secretary.

AMENDMENTS [i]

AMENDMENT I

Congress shall make no law respecting an establishment of religion, or prohibiting the free exercise thereof; or abridging the freedom of speech, or of the press; or the right of the people peaceably to assemble, and to petition the Government for a redress of grievances.

AMENDMENT II

A well regulated Militia, being necessary to the security of a free State, the right of the people to keep and bear Arms, shall not be infringed.

AMENDMENT III

No Soldier shall, in time of peace be quartered in any house, without the consent of the Owner, nor in time of war, but in a manner to be prescribed by law.

AMENDMENT IV

The right of the people to be secure in their persons, houses, papers, and effects, against unreasonable searches and seizures, shall not be violated, and no Warrants shall issue, but upon probable cause, supported by Oath or affirmation, and particularly describing the place to be searched, and the persons or things to be seized.

AMENDMENT V

No person shall be held to answer for a capital, or otherwise infamous crime, unless on a presentment or indictment of a Grand Jury, except in cases arising in the land or naval forces, or in the Militia, when in actual service in time of War or public danger; nor shall any person be subject for the same offense to be twice put in jeopardy of life or limb, nor shall be compelled in any criminal case to be a witness against himself, nor be deprived of life, liberty, or property, without due process of law; nor shall private property be taken for public use, without just compensation.

AMENDMENT VI

In all criminal prosecutions, the accused shall enjoy the right to a speedy and public trial, by an impartial jury of the State and district wherein the crime shall have been committed, which district shall have been previously ascertained by law, and to be informed of the nature and cause of the accusation; to be confronted with the witnesses against him; to have the compulsory process for obtaining witnesses in his favor, and to have the Assistance of Counsel for his defence.

i. The first 10 Amendments were adopted in 1791, as the Bill of Rights.

AMENDMENT VII

In suits at common law, where the value in controversy shall exceed twenty dollars, the right of trial by jury shall be preserved, and no fact tried by a jury, shall be otherwise reexamined in any Court of the United States, than according to the rules of the common law.

AMENDMENT VIII

Excessive bail shall not be required, nor excessive fines imposed, nor cruel and unusual punishments inflicted.

AMENDMENT IX

The enumeration in the Constitution, of certain rights shall not be construed to deny or disparage others retained by the people.

AMENDMENT X

The powers not delegated to the United States by the Constitution, nor prohibited by it to the States, are reserved to the States respectively, or to the people.

AMENDMENT XI [j]

The Judicial power of the United States shall not be construed to extend to any suit in law or equity, commenced or prosecuted against one of the United States by Citizens of another State, or by Citizens or Subjects of any Foreign States.

AMENDMENT XII [k]

The Electors shall meet in their respective states and vote by ballot for President and Vice-President, one of whom, at least, shall not be an inhabitant of the same state with themselves; they shall name in their ballots the person voted for as President and in distinct ballots the person voted for as Vice-President, and they shall make distinct lists of all persons voted for as President, and of all persons voted for as Vice-Presidents, and of the number of votes for each, which lists they shall sign and certify, and transmit sealed to the seat of the government of the United States, directed to the President of the Senate;—The President of the Senate shall, in the presence of the Senate and House of Representatives, open all the certificates and the votes shall then be counted;—The person having the greatest number of votes for President, shall be the President, if such number be a majority of the whole number of Electors appointed; and if no person have such majority, then from the persons having the highest numbers not exceeding three on the list of those voted for as President, the House of Representatives shall choose immediately, by ballot, the President. But in choosing the President, the votes shall be

j. Adopted in 1798.
k. Adopted in 1804.

taken by states, the representation from each state having one vote; a quorum for this purpose shall consist of a member or members from two-thirds of the states, and a majority of all the states shall be necessary to a choice. And if the House of Representatives shall not choose a President whenever the right of choice shall devolve upon them, before the fourth day of March next following, then the Vice-President shall act as President, as in the case of the death or other constitutional disability of the President.—The person having the greatest number of votes as Vice-President, shall be the Vice-President, if such number be a majority of the whole number of Electors appointed, and if no person have a majority, then from the two highest numbers on the list, the Senate shall choose the Vice-President; a quorum for the purpose shall consist of two-thirds of the whole number of Senators, and a majority of the whole number shall be necessary to a choice. But no person constitutionally ineligible to the office of President shall be eligible to that of Vice-President of the United States.

AMENDMENT XIII [l]

Section 1. Neither slavery nor involuntary servitude, except as a punishment for crime whereof the party shall have been duly convicted, shall exist within the United States, or any place subject to their jurisdiction.

Section 2. Congress shall have power to enforce this article by appropriate legislation.

AMENDMENT XIV [m]

Section 1. All persons born or naturalized in the United States, and subject to the jurisdiction thereof, are citizens of the United States and of the State wherein they reside. No State shall make or enforce any law which shall abridge the privileges or immunities of citizens of the United States; nor shall any State deprive any person of life, liberty, or property, without due process of law; nor deny to any person within its jurisdiction the equal protection of the laws.

Section 2. Representatives shall be apportioned among the several States according to their respective numbers, counting the whole number of persons in each State, excluding Indians not taxed. But when the right to vote at any election for the choice of electors for President and Vice President of the United States, Representatives in Congress, the Executive and Judicial Officers of a State, or the members of the Legislature thereof, is denied to any of the male inhabitants of such State, being twenty-one years of age, and citizens of the United States, or in any way abridged, except for participation in rebellion, or other crime, the basis of representation therein shall be reduced in the proportion which the number of such male citizens shall bear to the whole number of male citizens twenty-one years of age in such State.

l. Adopted in 1865.
m. Adopted in 1868.

Section 3. No person shall be a Senator or Representative in Congress, or elector of President and Vice President, or hold any office, civil or military, under the United States, or under any State, who, having previously taken an oath, as a member of Congress, or as an officer of the United States, or as a member of any State legislature, or as an executive or judicial officer of any State, to support the Constitution of the United States, shall have engaged in insurrection or rebellion against the same, or given aid or comfort to the enemies thereof. But Congress may by a vote of two-thirds of each House, remove such disability.

Section 4. The validity of the public debt of the United States, authorized by law, including debts incurred for payment of pensions and bounties for services in suppressing insurrection or rebellion, shall not be questioned. But neither the United States nor any State shall assume or pay any debt or obligation incurred in aid of insurrection or rebellion against the United States, or any claim for the loss or emancipation of any slave; but all such debts, obligations and claims shall be held illegal and void.

Section 5. The Congress shall have power to enforce, by appropriate legislation, the provisions of this article.

AMENDMENT XV [n]

Section 1. The right of citizens of the United States to vote shall not be denied or abridged by the United States or by any State on account of race, color, or previous condition of servitude.

Section 2. The Congress shall have power to enforce this article by appropriate legislation.

AMENDMENT XVI [o]

The Congress shall have power to lay and collect taxes on incomes, from whatever source derived, without apportionment among the several States, and without regard to any census or enumeration.

AMENDMENT XVII [p]

The Senate of the United States shall be composed of two Senators from each State, elected by the people thereof, for six years, and each Senator shall have one vote. The electors in each State shall have the qualifications requisite for electors of the most numerous branch of the State legislatures.

When vacancies happen in the representation of any State in the Senate, the executive authority of such State shall issue writs of election to fill such vacancies: Provided, That the legislature of any State may empower the executive thereof to make temporary appointments until the people fill the vacancies by election as the legislature may direct.

n. Adopted in 1870.
o. Adopted in 1913.
p. Adopted in 1913.

This amendment shall not be so construed as to affect the election or term of any Senator chosen before it becomes valid as part of the Constitution.

AMENDMENT XVIII [q]

Section 1. After one year from the ratification of this article the manufacture, sale, or transportation of intoxicating liquors within, the importation thereof into, or the exportation thereof from the United States and all territory subject to the jurisdiction thereof for beverage purposes is hereby prohibited.

Section 2. The Congress and the several States shall have concurrent power to enforce this article by appropriate legislation.

Section 3. This article shall be inoperative unless it shall have been ratified as an amendment to the Constitution by the legislatures of the several States, as provided in the Constitution, within seven years from the date of the submission hereof to the States by the Congress.

AMENDMENT XIX [r]

The right of citizens of the United States to vote shall not be denied or abridged by the United States or by any State on account of sex.

Congress shall have power to enforce this article by appropriate legislation.

AMENDMENT XX [s]

Section 1. The terms of the President and Vice President shall end at noon on the 20th day of January, and the terms of Senators and Representatives at noon on the 3d day of January, of the years in which such terms would have ended if this article had not been ratified; and the terms of their successors shall then begin.

Section 2. The Congress shall assemble at least once in every year, and such meeting shall begin at noon on the 3rd day of January, unless they shall by law appoint a different day.

Section 3. If, at the time fixed for the beginning of the term of the President, the President elect shall have died, the Vice President elect shall become President. If a President shall not have been chosen before the time fixed for the beginning of his term, or if the President elect shall have failed to qualify, then the Vice President elect shall act as President until a President shall have qualified; and the Congress may by law provide for the case wherein neither a President elect nor a Vice President elect shall have qualified, declaring who shall then act as President, or the manner in which one who is to act shall be selected, and such person shall act accordingly until a President or Vice President shall have qualified.

Section 4. The Congress may by law provide for the case of the death of any of the persons from whom the House of Representatives may

q. Adopted in 1919. Repealed by the Twenty-first Amendment.
r. Adopted in 1920.
s. Adopted in 1933.

choose a President whenever the right of choice shall have devolved upon them, and for the case of the death of any of the persons from whom the Senate may choose a Vice President whenever the right of choice shall have devolved upon them.

Section 5. Sections 1 and 2 shall take effect on the 15th day of October following the ratification of this article.

Section 6. This article shall be inoperative unless it shall have been ratified as an amendment to the Constitution by the legislatures of three-fourths of the several States within seven years from the date of its submission.

AMENDMENT XXI [t]

Section 1. The eighteenth article of amendment to the Constitution of the United States is hereby repealed.

Section 2. The transportation or importation into any State, Territory, or possession of the United States for delivery or use therein of intoxicating liquors, in violation of the laws thereof, is hereby prohibited.

Section 3. This article shall be inoperative unless it shall have been ratified as an amendment to the Constitution by conventions in the several States, as provided in the Constitution, within seven years from the date of the submission hereof to the States by the Congress.

AMENDMENT XXII [u]

Section 1. No person shall be elected to the office of the President more than twice, and no person who has held the office of President, or acted as President, for more than two years of a term to which some other person was elected President shall be elected to the office of the President more than once. But this article shall not apply to any person holding the office of President when this article was proposed by the Congress, and shall not prevent any person who may be holding the office of President, or acting as President, during the term within which this article becomes operative from holding the office of President or acting as President during the remainder of such term.

Section 2. This article shall be inoperative unless it shall have been ratified as an amendment to the Constitution by the legislatures of three-fourths of the several States within seven years from the date of its submission to the States by the Congress.

AMENDMENT XXIII [v]

Section 1. The District constituting the seat of Government of the United States shall appoint in such manner as the Congress may direct:

A number of electors of President and Vice President equal to the whole number of Senators and Representatives in Congress to which the District would be entitled if it were a State, but in no event more than the least populous State; they shall be in addition to those appointed by the

t. Adopted in 1933.
u. Adopted in 1951.
v. Adopted in 1961.

States, but they shall be considered, for the purposes of the election of President and Vice President, to be electors appointed by a State; and they shall meet in the District and perform such duties as provided by the twelfth article of amendment.

Section 2. The Congress shall have power to enforce this article by appropriate legislation.

AMENDMENT XXIV ^w

Section 1. The right of citizens of the United States to vote in any primary or other election for President or Vice President, for electors for President or Vice President, or for Senator or Representative in Congress, shall not be denied or abridged by the United States or any State by reason of failure to pay any poll tax or other tax.

Section 2. The Congress shall have power to enforce this article by appropriate legislation.

AMENDMENT XXV ^x

Section 1. In case of the removal of the President from office or of his death or resignation, the Vice President shall become President.

Section 2. Whenever there is a vacancy in the office of the Vice President, the President shall nominate a Vice President who shall take office upon confirmation by a majority vote of both Houses of Congress.

Section 3. Whenever the President transmits to the President pro tempore of the Senate and the Speaker of the House of Representatives his written declaration that he is unable to discharge the powers and duties of his office, and until he transmits to them a written declaration to the contrary, such powers and duties shall be discharged by the Vice President as Acting President.

Section 4. Whenever the Vice President and a majority of either the principal officers of the executive departments or of such other body as Congress may by law provide, transmit to the President pro tempore of the Senate and the Speaker of the House of Representatives their written declaration that the President is unable to discharge the powers and duties of his office, the Vice President shall immediately assume the powers and duties of the office as Acting President.

Thereafter, when the President transmits to the President pro tempore of the Senate and the Speaker of the House of Representatives his written declaration that no inability exists, he shall resume the powers and duties of his office unless the Vice President and a majority of either the principal officers of the executive department or of such other body as Congress may by law provide, transmit within four days to the President pro tempore of the Senate and the Speaker of the House of Representatives their written declaration that the President is unable to discharge the powers and duties of his office. Thereupon Congress shall decide the issue, assembling within forty-eight hours for that purpose if not in session. If the Congress, within twenty-one days after receipt of the latter

---

w. Adopted in 1964.
x. Adopted in 1967.

written declaration, or, if Congress is not in session, within twenty-one days after Congress is required to assemble, determines by two-thirds vote of both Houses that the President is unable to discharge the powers and duties of his office, the Vice President shall continue to discharge the same as Acting President; otherwise, the President shall resume the powers and duties of his office.

AMENDMENT XXVI [y]

Section 1. The right of citizens of the United States, who are eighteen years of age or older, to vote shall not be denied or abridged by the United States or by any State on account of age.

Section 2. The Congress shall have power to enforce this article by appropriate legislation.

y. Adopted in 1971.

Bibliography on Law and Literature

1. *General.* B. Cardozo, Law and Literature and Other Essays and Addresses (1931); R. Ferguson, Law and Letters in American Culture (1984); J. Gest, The Lawyer in Literature (1913); The Law as Literature (L. Blom-Cooper ed. 1961); Law in Action: An Anthology of the Law in Literature (E. Fuller ed. 1947); C. Smith, J. McWilliams & M. Bloomfield, Law and American Literature (1983); Voices in Court (W. Davenport ed. 1958); J. White, The Legal Imagination (1973); F. Windolph, Reflections of the Law in Literature (2d ed. 1970); The World of Law (E. London ed. 1960); Almand, Law, Language, and Literature, 14 Mercer L.Rev. 372 (1963); Cushing & Roberts, Law and Literature: The Contemporary Image of the Lawyer, 6 Vill.L.Rev. 451 (1961); Domnarski, Law-Literature Criticism: Charting a Desirable Course with Billy Budd, 34 J.Legal Educ. 702 (1984); Hitchler, The Reading of Lawyers, 33 Dick.L.Rev. 1 (1928); Hopkins, The Development of Realism in Law and Literature During the Period 1883–1933: The Cultural Resemblance, 4 Pace L.Rev. 29 (1983); Loesch, Is Acquaintance with Legal Novels Essential to a Lawyer?, 21 Ill. L.Rev. 109 (1926); Phelps, The Criminal as Hero in American Fiction, 1983 Wis.L.Rev. 1427; Re, Legal Writing as Good Literature, 59 St. John's L.Rev. 211 (1985); Symposium: Law and Literature, 32 Rut.L.Rev. 603 (1979); Symposium: Law and Literature, 60 Tex.L.Rev. 373 (1982).

2. *Law and the Litterateur.* C. Davis, The Law in Shakespeare (1884); G. Keeton, Shakespeare's Legal and Political Background (1967); Braithwaite, Poetry and the Criminal Law: The Idea of Punishment in Shakespeare's Measure for Measure, 13 Loy.U.Chi.L.J. 791 (1982); Coles, Charles Dickens and the Law, 59 Va.Q.Rev. 564 (1983); Domnarski, A Novelist's Knowing Look at the Law: Short Stories by John William Corrington, 69 A.B.A.J. 1706 (1983); Gutteridge, The Law and Lawyers of Jorrocks, 8 Cambridge L.J. 161 (1943); Holdsworth, The Case of Bardell v. Pickwick as an Historical Document, 13 Iowa L.Rev. 61 (1927); Watkin, Hamlet and the Law of Homicide, 100 L.Q.Rev. 282 (1984); Comment, Mark Twain: Doctoring the Laws, 48 Mo.L.Rev. 681 (1983).

3. *Novels, Short Stories, and Plays.* L. Auchincloss, The Great World and Timothy Colt (1956); H. Cecil, Brothers in Law (1955); W. Clark, The Ox-Bow Incident (1940); J. Cozzens, The Just and the Unjust (1942); C. Dickens, Bleak House (1853); F. Dostoevski, The Brothers Karamozov (1880); F. Kafka, The Trial (1937); J. Lawrence & R. Lee, Inherit the

Wind (1955); H. Lee, To Kill a Mockingbird (1960); M. Levin, Compulsion (1956); H. Melville, Billy Budd (1891); A. Miller, The Crucible (1953); J. Mortimer, Rumpole of the Bailey (1978); R. Rose, Twelve Angry Men, in Six Television Plays 111 (1956); W. Shakespeare, The Merchant of Venice (1596–1597); Sophocles, Antigone (442–441 B.C.); A. Train, Tutt and Mr. Tutt (1920); R. Traver, Anatomy of a Murder (1958); A. Trollope, Orley Farm (1862); M. Twain, Pudd'nhead Wilson (1894).

4. *Famous Cases as Literature.* J. Bichler, DES Daughter (1981); A. Lewis, Gideon's Trumpet (1964); G. Stern, The Buffalo Creek Disaster (1976).

5. *Biography and Autobiography.* T. Arnold, Fair Fights and Foul: A Dissenting Lawyer's Life (1965); A. Beveridge, The Life of John Marshall (1916–1919); Boswell for the Defense (K. Wimsatt & F. Pottle eds. 1959); B. Botein, Trial Judge: The Candid, Behind-the-Bench Story of Justice Bernard Botein (1952); C. Bowen, The Lion and the Throne: The Life and Times of Sir Edward Coke (1957); G. Dunne, Hugo Black and the Judicial Revolution (1977); G. Dunne, Justice Joseph Story and the Rise of the Supreme Court (1970); Felix Frankfurter Reminisces (H. Phillips ed. 1960); W. Harbaugh, Lawyer's Lawyer: The Life of John W. Davis (1973); Holmes-Pollock Letters (M. Howe 2d ed. 1961); A. Mason, Brandeis: A Free Man's Life (1946); A. Mason, Harlan Fiske Stone: Pillar of the Law (1956); The Mind and Faith of Justice Holmes (M. Lerner ed. 1943); Mr. Justice (A. Dunham & P. Kurland eds. 1956); L. Nizer, My Life in Court (1961); The Remarkable Hands (M. Nelson ed. 1983); H. Schwartz, Lawyering (1976); W. Seagle, Men of Law from Hammurabi to Holmes (1947); B. Shientag, Moulders of Legal Thought (1943); I. Stone, Clarence Darrow for the Defense (1941); C. Swisher, Roger B. Taney (1935); D. Walker-Smith, Lord Reading and His Cases (1934); G. White, Earl Warren: A Public Life (1982).

6. *Bibliographical.* J. Breen, Novel Verdicts: A Guide to Courtroom Fiction (1984); J. Marke & E. Bander, Deans' List of Recommended Reading for Prelaw and Law Students (2d ed. 1984); Chafee & Maguire, A List of Books for Prospective Law Students Now in Service Prepared by a Committee of the Faculty of Harvard Law School, 58 Harv.L.Rev. 589 (1945); Papke, Law and Literature: A Comment and Bibliography of Secondary Works, 73 L.Libr.J. 421 (1980); Suretsky, Search for a Theory: An Annotated Bibliography of Writings on the Relation of Law to Literature and the Humanities, 32 Rut.L.Rev. 727 (1979); Weisberg, Wigmore's "Legal Novels" Revisited: New Resources for the Expansive Lawyer, 71 Nw.U.L.Rev. 17 (1976); Wigmore, A List of One Hundred Legal Novels, 17 Ill.L.Rev. 26 (1922).

Index

ADMINISTRATIVE ADJUDICATION
Compared to,
  Administrative rulemaking, 336–342.
  Judicial adjudication, 342–344.
Consent decrees, 311.
Ex parte contacts and, 388–389.
Formal, 310–312, 358, 361, 389.
Informal, 310–311, 358, 361, 389.
Judicial review of, 344–352, 376.
Licensing, 304, 306–308, 313.
Policy making by, 322–323, 336–342, 349.
Private intervention in, 312–320, 382–386.
Public interest groups and, 382–386.
Requirements,
  Hearing, 309, 311, 318.
  Record, 389–390.
Standing, 316–318.
Stare decisis and, 349.

ADMINISTRATIVE AGENCIES
"Capture" by regulated interests, 319–320, 383–384, 392.
Compared to courts, 342–344.
Control by other branches,
  Executive, 390–392.
  Judiciary, 344–345, 362, 376, 377–378, 390.
  Legislature, 320–323, 326–329.
Delegation of power to, 320–323, 326–329, 374.
Ex parte contacts with, 388–389.
Federal Communications Commission, 311–404.
Improvement of, 390–392.
Independent agencies, 390–392.
Interstate Commerce Commission, 303.
Investigative powers, see Investigative Powers of Administrative Agencies.
Reasons for creating, 300–305, 320–322.
  Complexity of problems, 321–322.
  Market failures, 301–302.
Securities Exchange Commission, 303.

ADMINISTRATIVE ENFORCEMENT
Generally, 312, 378–382.
Cease and desist orders, 311.
Consent decrees, 311.
Formal proceedings, 353–356, 361.
Informal settlement, 310–311, 353, 356–357, 361.
Judicial review of, 362.
Means of, 310, 312, 353–356, 361–362, 382.
Publicity as, 309–310.
Role of courts in, 312, 362.
Role of private citizens in, 382.
Self-executing orders, 311.

ADMINISTRATIVE FACT–FINDING
Adjudicative and legislative facts, 49–50, 378, 388.
Compared to judicial fact-finding, 343–344.
Compulsory means of, 308–309, 377.
Effect on legal rules of, 377–378.
Investigative powers, 308–309.
Judicial review of, 377–378.
Reporting requirements, 308–309.

ADMINISTRATIVE OFFENSES
Compared to criminal offenses, 379–382.
Objectives of, 381–382.
Role of intent in, 379–382.

ADMINISTRATIVE PROCEDURE
Administrative Procedure Act, 344, 386–390.
Process values and, 386.

ADMINISTRATIVE RULEMAKING
Ad hoc rulemaking through adjudication, 322–323, 336–342, 349.
  Compared to judicial lawmaking, 342–344.
  Stare decisis and, 349.
Compared to administrative adjudication, 336–342.
Ex parte contacts and, 388–389.
Ex post facto application, 374.
Formal, 386, 389–390.
Informal, 386–390.
Judicial review of, 390.
Private suits and, 382–383.
Procedural elements of, 386–388.
Public interest groups and, 383–386.
Publication of standards, 306.
Requirements,
  Hearing, 306, 387–388, 390.
  Notice, 387–388, 390.
  Record, 389–390.

ADVERSARY SYSTEM
Generally, 71–72, 108, 112, 123.
Abandonment of, 160–169.
Criticism of, 142–144.
Rationale of, 139–141.

AFFIRMATIVE ACTION
Constitutionality of, 758–767.
Controversy concerning, 756–757.

APPEAL
Generally, 10–11, 117–119.
Administrative law, 344–345, 362, 376, 377–378, 390.

APPEAL—Cont'd
Appellate courts, 46, 76, 127.
Briefs, 119–123.
Criminal, see Criminal Procedure.
Final judgment rule, 118.
Procedure, 118–119.
Purposes of, 117.
Standard of review, see Standards.

ARBITRATION
Generally, 596–597.

BROADCAST REGULATION
Generally, 305–404.

CAPITAL PUNISHMENT
Constitutional constraints, 225.
Justifications for, 224–230.

CENSORSHIP
See also Freedom of Speech.
Prior restraints, 13.
Schools, 461–473.

CIVIL PROCEDURE
Generally, 108–112.
Affirmative defense, 83.
Answer, 83.
Appeal, see Appeal.
Burdens,
    Allegation, 84.
    Proof, 58, 84.
Cause of action, 75.
Class actions, 150, 657.
Complaint, 76–81.
Continuance, 84–85.
Default, 81.
Demurrer, 81–82.
Denial, 82–83.
Discovery, 85–88.
    Deposition, 85–87.
    Inspection, 87.
Dismissal for failure to prosecute, 131–138.
Economic analysis, 158–159.
"Exception," 101.
Fact and law, 75, 127–128.
German model, 161–165.
Judge, see Judge.
Judgment, 92, 116–117, 138–139.
Jury, see Jury.
Memoranda of law, 82.
Motions, 10, 92.
Pleadings, 77, 84–85.
    Amendment, 84–85, 101–102.
Pretrial conference, 89–91, 136.
"Procedural justice," 112.
Recusal, 149–156.
Reply, 83–84.
Summary judgment, 88–89, 467–468.
Summons, 76–77.
Trial, see Trial.

CIVIL RIGHTS LAWS
Generally, 716–717.
Attorneys' fees, 152.
Commission, see Commission on Civil Rights.
Contracts, 731–741.

CIVIL RIGHTS LAWS—Cont'd
Discrimination, see Discrimination.
Employment, 717–718.
Housing, 718–720.
Title IX, 426–433.
Title VII, 717–718.

COLLECTIVE BARGAINING
Public-sector employees, 442, 452–460.

COMMISSION ON CIVIL RIGHTS
Generally, 751–756.
Recent controversy concerning, 756–757.

COMMON LAW
Generally, 34–35, 38–39.
English courts, 34, 37, 46, 179.
Reception statutes, 39.

COMPARATIVE LAW
England, see Common Law.
Germany, 158, 161–165, 208.

COMPARATIVE NEGLIGENCE
See Negligence.

CONFESSIONS
Due process considerations, 244–253.

CONSIDERATION
Generally, 554–558.
Form, 557–558.
Gratuitous promises, see Promissory Estoppel.

CONSTITUTION
Complete text, 775–792.

CONTEMPT
Generally, 10, 599–601.
Fine, 600.
Imprisonment, 600.

CONTRACTS
Consideration, 554–558.
Construction agreement, 586–587.
Damages, 564–567, 606–608.
Disclosure, 621–624.
Duress, 618–621.
Expectations, 539.
Force majeure, 608–609.
Fraud, 624.
Freedom of, 612–613.
Implied terms, 593–595.
Interference, 570–575.
Interpretation, 591–593.
Lease, 585–586.
Negotiating, 609–610.
Offer and acceptance, 552–554.
Planning, 608–612.
Promises, 538–539, 556–557.
    Gratuitous, see Promissory Estoppel.
Racial discrimination and, 731–741.
Specific performance, 567–569.
Standard contracts, 612–613.
Status to contract, 540.
Unconscionability, 613–618.

CONTRIBUTORY NEGLIGENCE
See Negligence.

CORPORATIONS
Articles of incorporation, 561–562, 580–582.
Bylaws, 582–583.
Certificate of incorporation, 562–563.
Criminal law and, 678–698.
De facto, 576–578.
De jure, 576–578.
Entity, 544.
Estoppel, 576–578.
Incorporation, 543, 561–562.
Liability, 576–578.
Minutes, 583–584.
Organization, 561–562, 583–584.
Taxation, 578.

COST–BENEFIT ANALYSIS
Generally, 684–689.

COURTS
Delay in, 156–160.
Legislature versus, 49–51, 55–57, 168.

CRIMINAL LAW
Generally, 180–298.
Civil sanctions compared, 678–679, 693–694.
Corporations and, 678–698.
Fines, 680–682.
Manufacturers' liability, 682–698.
Racial equality and, 704–713.
Recklessness, 678.
Regulatory and general statutes, 682–683, 698.
Sanctions, 678–698.

CRIMINAL PROCEDURE
Generally, 209–211.
Breakdown of, 260–280.
Confessions, 244–253.
Defense counsel's role, 230–244.
Discretion, 212–224.
Guilty pleas, 253–260.
Judge's role, 217–224.
Jury's role, 216–217.
Police officer's role, 212–215.
Prosecutor's role, 215–216.
Public defender's role, 260–280.

DAMAGES
See Remedies.

DEATH PENALTY
See Capital Punishment.

DELEGATION OF LEGISLATIVE POWER
Generally, 320–329, 374, 417.
Administrative standards and, 323.
Federal Communications Commission and, 323–327, 374.
Implementation of delegated authority, 525–528.
Legislative oversight, 522–525.
Nondelegation doctrine, 327–329, 374.
Reasons for, 321–322, 326.
Statutory vagueness and, 322–323, 326, 391.
Substitute for legislation, 320–329.

DEREGULATION
Generally, 393–404.
Federal Communications Commission and, 393–404.
Limits of regulation and, 393.
Self-regulation, 306, 356, 361.

DETERRENCE
Generally, 180.
Capital punishment, 225.

DISCRIMINATION
See also Equal Protection.
Basis,
    Handicap, 496–507.
    Race, see Racial Discrimination.
    Sex, see Sex Discrimination.
School finance, 477–485.

DIVISION OF LABOR
Generally, 541–543.

DUE PROCESS
Generally, 244, 511–512, 513–515.
Confessions, 244–253.
Constitutional text, 785, 787.
Guilty pleas, 253–260.
Notice and hearing requirement, 81, 148, 201–208, 515–516, 521.
School discipline, 512–521.

DURESS
See Excuses.

ECONOMIC ANALYSIS
Civil procedure, 158–159.
Cost-benefit, 684–689.
Distributive applications, 409.
Negligence, 69–71.

EDUCATION
See Public Education.

EQUAL PROTECTION
See also Discrimination.
Generally, 485–486, 488–490, 703–704.
Compelling state interest, 480–481, 482–485.
Constitutional text, 787.
Doctrine of fiscal neutrality, 480–481, 482–483.
Educational spending, 477–485.
Fundamental right, 481, 482–486, 509–510.
Rational-basis test, 486.
Separate but equal doctrine, 489–491.
Strict-scrutiny test, 481, 484, 485–486, 709.
Suspect classification, 480, 482–486.

ESTOPPEL
See Promissory Estoppel.

ETHICS
See Lawyers.

EXCUSES
Generally, 185–186.
Duress, 189, 618–621.
Insanity, 190–201.
Mistake of fact, 201.
Mistake of law,
    Counsel's advice causing, 242–244.
    Ignorance causing, 201.
Necessity, 186–190.

EXECUTIVE
Control of agencies, 390–392.

FAIRNESS DOCTRINE
See Federal Communications Commission.

FAMILY COURT
Generally, 597–598.

**FEDERAL COMMUNICATIONS COMMIS-
SION**
Generally, 311–404.
Delegation and, 323–327, 374.
Equal time doctrine, 329, 334.
Fairness doctrine, 320, 329–404.
Criticism of, 394–404.
Deregulation and, 394–404.
Evolution of, 330–336, 340–342.
Justification for, 403–404.
Newspapers, magazines, and, 374–375.
Regulations under, 341–342.
Federal Communications Act, 323–326, 344, 353–356.

FEDERAL COURTS
Generally, 9.
Diversity of citizenship jurisdiction, example of, 131–137.
Federal question jurisdiction, example of, 149–155.
Federal Rules of Civil Procedure, 72, 81, 132.

FIRST AMENDMENT
See also Freedom of Speech.
Constitutional text, 785.
Public-school curriculum, 460–473.
Religion, 461.
Rights of children, 517–519.
Sex discrimination and, 426–433.

FOURTEENTH AMENDMENT
See also Due Process; Equal Protection.
Constitutional text, 787–788.
History of adoption, 488–490.

FREEDOM OF SPEECH
Basic doctrine, 12–14, 15–16.
Board of Education case, 461–473.
Censorship, see Censorship.
Group libel, 709–713.
Obscenity, 13.
Pornography, 16–17, 720–723.
Red Lion controversy, 356–377.
Skokie conflict, 1–17.

GOVERNMENT CORPORATIONS
Generally, 414.
Post office, 408.

GOVERNMENT EMPLOYMENT
Generally, 410.
Extent of, 410, 434–435.
Public education, 435, 437, 457–460.

GOVERNMENTAL ACTION
See State Action.

GOVERNMENTAL BENEFITS
Generally, 698–702.

GUILTY PLEAS
Due process considerations, 253–260.

HUMANISM
Law and, 17–24.

INCAPACITATION
Generally, 180–181.
Capital punishment, 225.

**INDEPENDENT REGULATORY COMMIS-
SIONS**
Generally, 390–392.

INJUNCTIONS
See Remedies.

INSANITY
See Excuses.

**INVESTIGATIVE POWERS OF ADMINISTRA-
TIVE AGENCIES**
Generally, 308–309, 343–344.
Compared to courts, 343–344.
Disclosure obligations and, 308–309.
Power to compel disclosure, 308–309, 377.

JUDGE
Discretion, 217–224.
Impartiality, 108, 149–156.
Review of, 117–118.

**JUDICIAL REVIEW OF ADMINISTRATIVE
ACTION**
Generally, 342–352.
Administrative adjudication and, 344–352, 376.
Administrative enforcement and, 362.
Administrative fact-finding and, 377–378.
Administrative rulemaking and, 390.
Arbitrary and capricious standard, 344–345, 349, 352.
Function of, 344, 349, 377.
Scope of, 344, 377.
Substantial evidence standard, 377–378.

JURIDICAL DEMOCRACY
Defined, 522–525.

JURY
Generally, 115–116.
Compromise verdict, 32–33.
Discretion, 216–217.
Jury trial scenario, 91–92.
Origins, 32, 113–115.
Racial discrimination and, 713–716.
Verdict, 92.
General, 115.
Special, 43, 115.
Voir dire, 714–716.

LAWYERS
Generally, 73–74.
Fees, 74.

LAWYERS—Cont'd
Professional responsibility,
  Adverse fact and law, 146–147.
  Defense counsel, 230–244.
  Incompetence, 141–142.
  Model Rules, 147, 231–232.
  Zealousness, 75, 142–146.
Role of,
  Adviser, 242–244.
  Advocate, 139–147.
  Negotiator, 91, 609–610.
  Planner, 608–609.

LEGAL SERVICES CORPORATION
Authorizing legislation, 418–425.

LEGISLATIVE PROCESS
Authorization and appropriation, 417.
Citizen roles, 494–496, 507–508, 511.
Delegation, see Delegation of Legislative
  Power.
One-house veto, 433, 511.

LEGISLATURES
Courts versus, 49–51, 55–57, 168.
Interpretation of statutes, 57, 592–593.

LIBERAL ARTS
Law and, 1, 17–24, 25–26.

LICENSING BY ADMINISTRATIVE AGEN-
  CIES
Generally, 304, 306–308, 313.

LITERATURE
Law and, 793–794.

LOCAL GOVERNMENT
  See also Public Education.
Spending, 411–412.

MARKET FAILURE
  Generally, 300–302.
Administrative remedy for, 303–305.

MARKET INCENTIVES
Containing health care costs, 408.

MARRIAGES
Generally, 535–536.

MISTAKE
See Excuses.

NECESSITY
See Excuses.

NEGLIGENCE
Burden of proof, 58.
Comparative negligence, 49–71.
  Pure versus modified, 65–66.
Contributory negligence, 33–35, 46–49.
Duty to rescue, 82, 171–173.
Economic analysis, 69–71.
Elements of cause of action, 33, 104–105.
Evolution of doctrine, 33–49.
Illustrative case, 71–129.
Last clear chance, 35–38, 48–49, 57, 141.

NEGLIGENCE—Cont'd
More blameworthy rule, 46, 51, 58–59.
No-fault insurance, 167–169.
Reform of doctrine, 49–71.
Self-created incapacity, 43–46, 48.
Strict tort liability, compared to, 648–655.
Wrongful-birth suits, 173–178.
Wrongful-death acts, 52.

OFFER
Advertisement, 552–554.

POLITICS
Government spending and, 407.
Law and, 28, 69.

PORNOGRAPHY
  See also Freedom of Speech.
Indianapolis case, 16–17.
Minneapolis ordinance, 720–723.

PRESIDENT
Control of agencies, 390–392.

PRETRIAL
See Civil Procedure.

PRIVATE ASSOCIATIONS
Generally, 536–538, 563–564.

PROCEDURE
Administrative, see Administrative Proce-
  dure.
Civil, see Civil Procedure.
Criminal, see Criminal Procedure.

PRODUCT LIABILITY LAW
Generally, 640-642.

PRODUCT SAFETY
  Generally, 639–640.
Administrative agencies, 659.
Class actions, 657.
Compliance with standards, 660–677.
Consumer Product Safety Act, 659–672.
Consumer Product Safety Commission, 660–
  672.
Contracts, 645.
Courts, 658–659.
Criminal law, 678–698.
Negligence, 648.
Product liability law, 640–642.
Risks, 642–644.
Standards, 660–677.
Strict tort liability, 649–655.
Warranties, 645–648.

PROFESSIONAL RESPONSIBILITY
See Lawyers.

PROMISSORY ESTOPPEL
Equitable estoppel, 560–561.
Gratuitous promise, 558.
Proliferation, 561.
Reliance, 558–561.

PUBLIC ASSISTANCE
See also Taxation.
Citizens' role in, 494–496, 507–508.
Forms of, 411–414.
Welfare, 406–407.

PUBLIC DEFENDERS
Generally, 260–280.

PUBLIC EDUCATION
Costs, 437, 473–485.
Curriculum, 460–473.
Discipline, 511–522.
Federal role in, 437–439.
Handicapped students, 496–507.
History, 437–439, 488–490.
Individualized educational program (IEP), 496–497.
Licensing requirements, 440, 508–510.
Numbers of students, 437–438.
Segregation by race, 488–494, 529–530.
Special education, 499–500, 505–507.
State and local controls, 437–443.
Teachers' unions, 442, 452–460.
Voucher system, 443–452.

PUBLIC INTEREST GROUPS
Awards of legal expenses to, 384–386.
Public financial assistance to, 384–386.
Role of, in administrative proceedings, 382–384.

PUBLIC WORKS
Contemporary art, 415–417.
Costs, 409.
Design and performance standards, 413–414.
Government action to promote, 406–407.

PUNISHMENT
Capital, see Capital Punishment.
Purposes of, 180–185.

PUNITIVE DAMAGES
See Remedies.

RACIAL DISCRIMINATION
See also Civil Rights Laws.
Generally, 488–494, 703–704.
Criminal statutes, 704–709.
Custody and adoption, 724–727.
Group libel as, 709–713.
Juries and, 713–716.
Public-school segregation, 488–494, 529–530.
Restrictive covenants, 727–730.
Tax-exempt organizations, 767–774.
Wartime, 705–709.

REASONS
Reason-giving,
Administrator, 389–390.
Appellate court, 128.
Jury, 115–116.
Trial judge, 390.
Types of, 13–15.

REHABILITATION
Generally, 180.
Capital punishment, 225.

REMEDIES
Damages, 9, 31–33, 564–567, 606–608.
Actual, 606–607.
Punitive, 607–608, 693–694.
Injunctions, 9–10, 33, 600.
Limits on, 170–171, 173–178.
Specific performance, 567–569.

RETRIBUTION
Generally, 180–185.
Capital punishment, 225.
Marxist critique of, 183–185.

SEGREGATION
See Racial Discrimination.

SELF–REGULATION
Generally, 306, 356, 361.

SETTLEMENT
Generally, 31, 72, 76, 85, 91, 128.

SEX DISCRIMINATION
Generally, 426–433.
Pornography as, 16–17, 720–723.

STANDARDS
Proof, of,
Beyond a reasonable doubt, 211.
Clear and convincing evidence, 199.
Fair possibility, 156.
Preponderance of the evidence, 104, 108.
Review, of,
Abuse of discretion, 137–138.
Arbitrary and capricious, 344–345, 349, 352.
Clear error, 10, 118.
De novo, 10, 118.
Substantial evidence, 377–378.

STANDING
Generally, 316–318.

STARE DECISIS
Generally, 39–43.

STATE ACTION
Generally, 12–13, 703–704.
Judicial enforcement of private arrangements, 727–730.
Licensing of private parties who discriminate, 745–751.
Unequal administration of neutral laws, 742–745.

STATE COURTS
Generally, 9.

STATUTORY INTERPRETATION
Generally, 57, 592–593.

STREET–LEVEL BUREAUCRATS
Defined, 434–436.

STRICT TORT LIABILITY
Generally, 649–655.
Negligence, compared to, 648.
Warranties, compared to, 653–655.

TAXATION
Generally, 406–407.
Credits, 408, 412.
Public schools, 473–485.
Voucher system, 443–444.

TORTS
Generally, 30–31, 176–177.
Negligence, see Negligence.

TRIAL
Battle, by, 115, 166.
Closing argument, 92.
Criminal, see Criminal Procedure.
Cross-examination, 142–144.
Evidence, 92.
Illustrative trial, 92–107.
Instructions, 34, 92, 104–107.
Judge, see Judge.
Jury, see Jury.
Motions,
    Directed verdict, 92, 103.
    Involuntary nonsuit, 92, 101.
    Judgment n.o.v., 92, 107, 108.
    New trial, 34, 92.
Opening statement, 92.
Ordeal, by, 113–114.
Standard of proof, see Standards.
Trial courts, 34, 76.
Wager of law, 114–115.

UNDUE INFLUENCE
Generally, 624–630.
Confidential relations, 629–630.

VICTIMLESS CRIME
Generally, 280–284.
Consensual sodomy, 284–291.
Costs of enforcement, 291–297.

WARRANTIES
Generally, 645–648.
Express, 645.
Implied, 645–646.
Magnuson-Moss Warranty Act, 647.
Merchantability, 645–646.
Privity, 646.
Puffing, 645.
Remedies, 646.
Strict tort liability, compared to, 653–655.

WELFARE
See Public Assistance.

WELFARE STATE
U.S. as, 406, 529–530.

WILLS
Freedom of testation, 544–547.
Interpretation, 592–593.
Ownership, 545–546.
Succession, 545–547, 589–591.
Undue influence, 624–630.